Praise for *The Companion*

"Only someone who knows and loves Princeton as much as Bob Durkee could have written this book. *The New Princeton Companion* is rich in history and chock full of little nuggets that will surprise and delight you. Anyone interested in Princeton should own a copy. The book answers thousands of questions and offers unexpected pleasures."
—Bill Bradley '65, Basketball Legend, Former United States Senator and Princeton Trustee, and Managing Director of Allen & Company

"*The New Princeton Companion* is an invaluable contribution to the university community. With his unique insight into Princeton, Bob Durkee has collected an intimate history of the university and the people who made this institution what it is today. Anyone seeking to understand Princeton will find what they're looking for in this skillfully composed and comprehensive volume."
—Marcia Brown '19, Former Editor-in-Chief of the *Daily Princetonian* and Correspondent for *The Capitol Forum*

"I can't think of a better person to update and expand such a massive compendium of material than Bob Durkee. From his days as a *Prince* reporter through his forty-seven-year career in Nassau Hall, he has seen (or fact-checked) it all. His keen eye for editing has resulted in an endearing and useful reference that is a delightful sampling of all things Princeton. As an emeritus trustee, I especially recommend this book to all current and future trustees, as it provides invaluable context for many of the board's deliberations, and lots of fun facts to share with others!"
—Brent Henry '69, Health Care Lawyer, Former Vice Chair of the Princeton Board of Trustees, and Former President of the Alumni Association

"In a feat of graceful compression, Bob Durkee locates in one place all the information that anyone interested in Princeton might want to consult. A labor of love, *The New Princeton Companion* is a careful, serious endeavor in which scholars can have confidence."
—Randy Kennedy '77, Harvard Law School Professor and Former Princeton Trustee

"Everything you ever wanted to know about Princeton University is at your fingertips from the man who monitored the pulse of the university for nearly half a century. *The New Princeton Companion* is an alphabetical reference text of entries from 'a cappella' to 'Wu Hall,' and also a highly readable series of stories from beginning to end. A must for any Princeton aficionado!"

—Nancy Newman '78, Emory University Professor and Director of Neuro-Ophthalmology, Former Chair of the Princeton Trustee Committee on Alumni Affairs, and Former President of the Princeton Alumni Association

"*The New Princeton Companion* is an extraordinary treasure trove of insight and information—past, present, and even future—that will satisfy the curiosity of both the casual reader and the serious scholar with interests in the 'Best Old Place of All.' It has been beautifully compiled by Bob Durkee '69, and it includes important new additions on topics such as the history of the physical campus, the modifications to the informal motto, and the reconsideration of the legacy of Woodrow Wilson."

—Shirley Tilghman, Nineteenth President of Princeton University and Emeritus Professor of Molecular Biology and Public Affairs

THE NEW PRINCETON COMPANION

THE NEW PRINCETON COMPANION

Robert K. Durkee

Princeton University Press
Princeton and Oxford

Copyright © 2022 by Princeton University Press

Princeton University Press is committed to the protection of copyright and the intellectual property our authors entrust to us. Copyright promotes the progress and integrity of knowledge. Thank you for supporting free speech and the global exchange of ideas by purchasing an authorized edition of this book. If you wish to reproduce or distribute any part of it in any form, please obtain permission.

Requests for permission to reproduce material from this work should be sent to permissions@press.princeton.edu

Published by Princeton University Press
41 William Street, Princeton, New Jersey 08540
99 Banbury Road, Oxford OX2 6JX

press.princeton.edu

All Rights Reserved

Library of Congress Cataloging-in-Publication Data

Names: Durkee, Robert K.
Title: The new Princeton companion / Robert K. Durkee.
Description: Princeton, New Jersey : Princeton University Press, [2022] | Includes index.
Identifiers: LCCN 2021026523 (print) | LCCN 2021026524 (ebook) | ISBN 9780691198743 (hardback) | ISBN 9780691210445 (ebook)
Subjects: LCSH: Princeton University.
Classification: LCC LD4608 .N48 2022 (print) | LCC LD4608 (ebook) | DDC 378.749/65—dc23
LC record available at https://lccn.loc.gov/2021026523
LC ebook record available at https://lccn.loc.gov/2021026524

British Library Cataloging-in-Publication Data is available

Editorial: Peter Dougherty, Alena Chekanov
Production Editorial: Terri O'Prey
Text Design: Wanda España
Cover Design: Kimberly Castaneda
Production: Erin Suydam
Publicity: Julia Haav, Kate Farquhar-Thomson

This book has been composed in Baskerville Display

Printed on acid-free paper. ∞

Printed in the United States of America

10 9 8 7 6 5 4 3 2 1

CONTENTS

Preface vii
Acknowledgments ix
Alphabetical List of Entries xiii

History of the University	1
Evolution of the Physical Campus	17
In the Nation's Service and the Service of Humanity	26
Entries	33
Reference Lists	505
Illustration Credits	527
Index	529

This Day in Princeton History Calendar follows page 503

PREFACE
A New *Princeton Companion*

In 1978, Princeton University Press published a book titled *A Princeton Companion*. In more than 400 articles over more than 550 pages, the *Companion* offered a compendium of information, observation, and anecdote, arranged alphabetically, and indexed so readers could look up subjects ranging from the University's history and traditions to its departments and programs, its teams and organizations, its personalities and presidents, its defining features and idiosyncrasies. For me, as a long-time denizen of Nassau Hall, it was a constant companion, and I turned to it often to check a recollection, answer a question, or simply learn something new about some aspect of Princeton.

The *Companion* was compiled by Alexander Leitch 1924, then Secretary of the University, Emeritus, who had retired 12 years earlier after serving for 42 years in various capacities under three presidents, John Grier Hibben 1882 *1893, Harold Dodds *1914, and Robert Goheen '40 *48. Leitch served as both author and editor, with articles written by some 70 faculty members and alumni in addition to himself. I was one of his authors.

As I approached emeritus status in 2019, after 47 years serving five presidents—Goheen, William Bowen *58, Harold Shapiro *64, Shirley Tilghman, and Christopher Eisgruber '83—the Press suggested I compile a new, updated *Princeton Companion*, building on the foundation created by my predecessor twice removed. This edition contains 289 entries from the first edition, although not one of them is carried over unchanged. Many had to be updated to incorporate developments since the 1970s; some had to be revised to reflect new discoveries and understandings about Princeton's history; and some were trimmed to make room for the 115 entries in this edition that are entirely new.

The new entries generally fall into three categories. Some describe new departments, programs, athletic teams, student organizations, buildings, and initiatives. Some are devoted to individuals who have played significant roles in shaping the evolution of the University over the past 50 years. The third category includes entries that respond to the call in a 2016 trustee report on the legacy of Woodrow Wilson to be more honest and transparent about aspects of the University that have often been "forgotten, overlooked, subordinated, or suppressed."

This third category includes entries on coeducation, on women, and on people of color. They include entries on the history of African American, Asian American and Asian, Hispanic/Latinx, Jewish, LGBTQIA, and Native American and Indigenous students at Princeton. They also include entries on the Civil War, the Princeton and Slavery Project, the Princeton Prize in Race Relations, Protest Activity, and the diversification of campus art, iconography, and portraiture.

In some respects, the *New Companion*, like its predecessor, is a narrative; in other respects, it is a reference work. Some of the 404 entries—on winners of Nobel and other major prizes, members of faculty honor societies, Pulitzer Prize winners, governors, members of Congress, and Princeton deans and vice presidents—provide lists that in large measure do not exist elsewhere. The book also includes a separate section with another dozen lists ranging from Baccalaureate speakers, Behrman Award winners, and honorary degree recipients to Olympians, Pyne Prize recipients, Jacobus fellows, Guggenheim fellows, valedictorians, salutatorians, and winners of the James Madison Medal and the Woodrow Wilson Award.

There are two other features that are new to this edition. One is a set of three thematic essays that are designed to introduce readers to the overall arc of the history of the University, the development of the physical campus (with maps), and the derivation and manifestations of its commitment to the nation's service and the service of humanity. The essays are intended to provide a broad overview, which may be especially helpful for readers who are unacquainted or newly acquainted with Princeton and can benefit from a more global introduction before getting into the details. Every development mentioned in the essay on Princeton's history, and many of the structures and initiatives cited in the other two essays, can be explored in more depth in the entries that follow.

The other new feature of this edition is a calendar that recalls something that happened in Princeton's history on all 366 days of the year. The calendar includes developments of great historical significance, but it also includes entries that help illustrate how much Princeton has changed over the years, and some entries that are just for fun.

There are many challenges in compiling a book of this kind. One is the challenge of what and whom to include. Just as the Princeton admission office could compose an excellent class with students fully qualified for admission who had to be turned down because there just was not enough room, so could one make a compelling case for topics that had to be set aside here for the same reason. With a few exceptions, this edition does not include entries on alumni unless they were part of the founding of the country or contributed in some special way to Princeton's evolution into the University it is today. Another challenge is deciding what to include in each entry. Many of the topics could be the subjects of senior theses, dissertations, or entire books; in fact, theses, dissertations, and books have been written about some of them.

Every effort has been made to be timely and accurate as of January 1, 2021, and it was possible to update some entries and lists later that year. As in any volume of this kind, errors of both commission and omission are bound to occur, and for those we apologize.

It may be worth saying a few words about two conventions that are followed in the book. When alumni status is known, a graduate's class numerals are cited. Undergraduate alumni who graduated prior to 1930 are designated by the four numerals of their class year, while graduate alumni from prior to 1930 are designated by an asterisk (*) followed by the four digits. Undergraduate alumni from 1930 on are designated by an apostrophe (') followed by the last two numerals of the year, and graduate alumni are designated by the asterisk and two numerals. For example, Princeton's 14th president, John Grier Hibben, has numerals 1882 and *1893 to indicate he received his undergraduate degree in 1882 and his graduate degree in 1893. Princeton's 16th president, Robert Goheen, is '40 and *48.

Since the entries on the alumni who have served as president indicate their alumni status, their numerals are omitted in other entries if they are cited in their role as president. When they are cited in their role as alumni, their numerals are included.

At Princeton's 250th anniversary celebration in 1996, Princeton faculty member and Nobel Laureate Toni Morrison delivered a keynote address on "the place of the idea and the idea of the place." The *New Companion* aims to shed light on both the place that is Princeton and the idea that is Princeton. My fondest hope is that readers will find the book useful; they will learn from it; they will enjoy it; and it will become a companion to which they return again and again.

Robert K. Durkee

ACKNOWLEDGMENTS

Conceptual work on the *New Princeton Companion* began in the spring of 2019. On June 30, 2019, I turned to the project full-time when I retired from the University after serving six years (1972–78) as assistant to the president, 30 years (1978–2018) as vice president for public affairs, and 15 years (2004–19) as vice president and secretary. For all 47 years my office was in Nassau Hall.

Upon retirement I moved into a carrel in Firestone Library, expecting to remain there for the duration of the project while making active use of the library's resources and those of the archives. Within nine month the archives were closed to permit a thorough renovation of their building and the library was closed because of the COVID-19 pandemic.

My first thanks go to the members of the library staff who supported me when I was there and arranged for me to retrieve materials after the shutdown, and to Joseph DeLucia in the office of information technology who helped me set up an office at home, install a new computer, and occasionally get the better of a recalcitrant printer and a mischievous keyboard. There would be no book without Joe.

There also would be no book without the remarkable team at Princeton University Press who worked with me from start to finish in conceptualizing the book, obtaining necessary assistance, and providing invaluable guidance and support. My principal contact was Peter Dougherty, director of the Press from 2005 to 2018 and now editor at large for higher education. Peter was unfailingly responsive to my needs and questions, and our periodic conversations always sparked ideas to improve the book. The current director, Christie Henry, was engaged and supportive from day one; Terri O'Prey and Alena Chekanov kept everything on schedule; Dimitri Karetnikov worked his magic in figuring out how to prepare hand-drawn maps for publication; and along with book designer Wanda Espana developed a format for the day-in-history calendar—an idea that arose well after work on the book had begun.

The Press engaged an outside firm, MTM Publishing, to assist in project management. MTM's president Valerie Tomaselli participated in all the critical planning meetings, but my day-to-day contact was with the indefatigable Zach Gajewski. For much of the project we were in touch almost every day and his timely queries and patient oversight provided welcome guidance and support. The Press engaged the cultural historian Jim Ashton as copyeditor for the project, and I benefited greatly from his careful review of both language and substance.

Early in the project, following its usual practice, the Press asked outside reviewers to make suggestions about the book's goals and overall design and about drafts of some of the entries. The responses of the reviewers were exceedingly helpful, and their suggestions shaped and improved the book in numerous ways.

While I was the principal author of most of the entries and the final editor of all of them, in many cases I built on the foundation established by Alexander Leitch 1924, editor of the original *Princeton Companion*, and the 70 faculty members and alumni who prepared entries for him.

For this edition I was exceedingly fortunate to be able to call upon gifted writers to provide some of the initial drafts. All of the entries on the humanities departments were initially prepared by Kathy Taylor '74, a longtime colleague in the office of alumni affairs and drafter of many an eloquent alumni service citation and alumni trustee biography. Kathy and another longtime colleague in alumni affairs, Margaret Miller '80, reviewed the entries related to alumni engagement, and Kathy made valuable editorial suggestions on a number of other entries as well.

Wendy Plump, whom I first knew as a local newspaper reporter and who now oversees communications for the Chemistry department, drafted the entries for the natural sciences departments, and Thomas Garlinghouse, a science writer in the dean for research and communications offices before relocating to California, drafted the entries on the departments in the school of Engineering and Applied Science. Carol Gould, a longtime member of the University community, helped draft some of the social science entries. In each case they worked closely with members of the faculty in the departments about which they were writing and incorporated their suggestions in their drafts.

Professors Angela Creager and William Jordan *73 drafted the entry on the History department and Janet Currie *88 drafted the one on Economics. Shirley Tilghman and Tom Shenk reviewed the entry on Molecular Biology and Elisabeth Donohue reviewed the one on the school of Public and International Affairs. Steve Schultz, director of communications for the Engineering school, reviewed the entries on the school and the Engineering Quadrangle.

Abby Klionsky '14, whose senior thesis traced the development of Jewish student life at Princeton and who as a member of the University staff led a project developing (In)Visible Princeton walking tours on African American life, Women, Princeton Firsts, and Princeton traditions, drafted the entries on African American, Asian American and Asian, Hispanic/Latinx, Jewish, LGBTQIA, and Native American and Indigenous students at Princeton, consulting in each case with members of those communities.

Brett Tomlinson, managing editor of the *Princeton Alumni Weekly*, and Mark Bernstein '83, *PAW*'s senior writer, drafted the entries on the University's varsity athletic teams. Mark also drafted the entries on Epidemics and the Ivy League.

The essay on the evolution of the physical campus and the hand-drawn maps that illustrate it were prepared by University Architect, Emeritus, Jon Hlafter '61 *63, who retired in 2008 after 40 years overseeing the development of the campus. The entry on Computing was drafted by vice president for information technology and chief information officer Jay Dominick, and the entries on Residential Colleges and the Senior Thesis were based on earlier drafts by Nancy Weiss Malkiel.

University Archivist Dan Linke drafted the entry on the Library. Dan also reviewed several other entries (including the Civil War, the Princeton and Slavery Project, and entries related to the library) and was the final set of eyes on the this-day-in-Princeton-history calendar before it went to press. The calendar came about largely through the resourcefulness and persistence of Helene van Rossum, a former member of the archives staff who shared my determination that we were going to find an entry for every day of the year. The calendar and many other entries also owe a debt of gratitude to the archives' Mudd Manuscript Library Blog, "This Week in Princeton History," a carefully and creatively researched weekly posting under the auspices of special collections assistant April Armstrong *14.

The calendar was a massive undertaking and it benefited enormously from the painstaking fact-checking of Jean Hendry *80. Jean also applied her research skills to the herculean task of compiling lists of winners of the Nobel and other major prizes, members of faculty honor societies, and winners of Pulitzer Prizes and Guggenheim Fellowships. Her patience and passion for accuracy were truly inspiring. Jean also helpfully reviewed the entries on Coeducation and Women.

In deciding which prizes and societies to include, I was guided by an early conversation with former dean of the faculty David Dobkin, and in making a number of other choices and drafting several entries related to the University's faculty and its academic program I benefited from the guidance of dean of the faculty Sanjeev Kulkarni and members of his staff, including, importantly, Jessica Mathewson '00. Similarly, dean of the college Jill Dolan and members of her staff were exceedingly helpful in reviewing many of the entries in the book that relate to programs overseen by her office.

Art museum director James Steward reviewed the entries on the Art Museum, Campus Art, and the Portrait Collection; Princeton University Investment Company president Andrew Golden did the same for entries on the Endowment, Divestment, and Princo; and Aly Kassam-Remtula, associate provost for international affairs and operations, reviewed the entries on International Initiatives, the Mpala Research Centre, the Princeton-Ins, and the Princeton Institute for International and Regional Studies.

Jerry Price, senior communications adviser and historian for the department of athletics, reviewed the entry on Athletics and provided the list of Princeton Olympians; Catherine Zandonella and her colleagues in the office of the dean for research reviewed the entries on the University Research Board and Entrepreneurship; Janet Finnie '84 reviewed the entry on University Health Services and, along with Karen Fuchs, reviewed the entry on McCosh Infirmary; Alison Boden reviewed the entries on the Chapel and Religious Life; and Kristin Appelget, the University's director of community and regional affairs, reviewed the entries on the Dinky and the Municipality of Princeton. Curt Emmich reviewed the entries on Princeton Forrestal Campus and Princeton Forrestal Center.

Claire Elson, a longtime colleague in the department of human resources, helped ensure the accuracy of the entry on University vice presidents, and Steve Runk and his colleagues did the same for the Lewis Center for the Arts. Chris Burkmar '00 provided helpful background information on ROTC, and Henry von Kohorn '66, a former chair of the Alumni Council and founder of the Princeton Prize in Race Relations, shared information on the history of the Alumni Association. Jennifer Rexford '91 provided helpful insights on Alan Turing *38.

The list of others who reviewed individual entries is long, but in each case their assistance was much appreciated. Those entries include A cappella (Tom Dunne and Jessica Bailey '19), Admission (Karen Richardson '93), African American Studies (Eddie Glaude Jr. *97), Andlinger Center for Energy and the Environment (Lynn Loo *01 and Molly Seltzer), *Alumni Weekly* (Marilyn Marks *86), Annual Giving (Bill Hardt '63), Anthropology (Carolyn Rouse), Bendheim Center for Finance (Yacine Ait-Sahalia), Council of the Humanities (Min Pullan, Kathy Crown, and Eric Gregory), Council on Science and Technology (Naomi Leonard '85), Natalie Davis (Angela Creager), Endowed Professorships (Kevin Heaney and colleagues), the Fields Center (Tennille Haynes), Financial Aid (Robin Moscato), Fundraising (Tracey Storey), General Counsel (Ramona Romero), Graduate School (Cole Crittenden *05), High Meadows Environmental Institute (Morgan Kelly and colleagues), Institute for Advanced Study (Elizabeth Wood), and Lewis-Sigler Institute for Integrative Genomics (Shirley Tilghman).

Other entries include McCarter Theatre Center (Bill Lockwood '59), University Orchestra (Michael Pratt), Pace Center for Civic Engagement (Kimberly de los Santos), Politics (Brandice Canes-Wrone '93), *Daily Princetonian* (Marcia Brown '19), Princeton Neuroscience Institute (Jonathan Cohen), Princeton Plasma Physics Laboratory (David McComas), Princeton Theological Seminary (Anne Stewart), Princeton University Press (Christie Henry and Peter Dougherty), Princeton University Store (Jim Sykes), Rhodes and Other Scholarships (Deirdre Moloney), Sustainability (Shana Weber), Triangle Club (Michelle McGorty '95), University Center for Human Values (Julie Clack and Melissa Lane), and University League/U-Now (Nancy Lin '77, who also reviewed the entry on Asian American and Asian Students, Martha Otis, and Carolyn Jones).

Two longtime colleagues and friends who tracked down various materials for me were the ever helpful and efficient Cristin Volz and Dan Day. Dan and two other colleagues in the communications office, Laurel Cantor and Iris Rubinstein, spent countless hours locating, obtaining, and assembling most of the photos in the book, and Iris compiled the information for the photo credits. Another colleague in that office, Mahlon Lovett, saved me many hours of research when he managed to unearth files from the 1990s in which some of the entries from the original *Companion* had been updated.

During Princeton's 250th anniversary celebration, I served as executive editor of *Princeton University: The First 250 Years*, beautifully written by Don Oberdorfer '52 and just as beautifully illustrated by J.T. Miller '70. That book was a helpful resource for me, as was James Axtell's *The Making of Princeton University*, Thomas Jefferson Wertenbaker's *Princeton 1746–1896*; V. Lansing Collins 1892's *Princeton Past and Present*; and Bill McCleery's *Conversations on the Character of Princeton*. I need to make special mention of Robert Spencer Barnett's *Princeton University and Neighboring Institutions*, which chronicles the history of Princeton's buildings, pathways, and landscapes. Barnett writes as a perceptive architect, but also as a wise observer of the University's history and culture.

Finally, I want to acknowledge the account of the University's "prank traditions" that Elizabeth Greenberg '02 compiled in her thesis "Barely Remembered," whose title evokes the late-twentieth-century tradition of the nude olympics; the work of the Alumni Council's Princetoniana committee and those responsible for the University's Princetoniana website; the archives of the *Alumni Weekly* and especially the "Rally 'Round the Cannon" columns of longtime P-rade emcee Gregg Lange '70; and the digitized Larry Dupraz archives of the *Daily Princetonian*.

I close with thanks to my daughters and many of my former colleagues for their interest and support throughout the project, and to Patti Swartz; because she was in Denver for much of the time, more than two dozen of the *Companion's* entries were drafted during my visits there, often with our dog Theo happily napping to the sound of keystrokes on my laptop.

ALPHABETICAL LIST OF ENTRIES

A cappella
Academic Program
Admission
Advisory Councils
African American Students at Princeton
African American Studies, The Department of
Alexander, Stephen
Alexander Hall
Alumni Affinity Conferences
Alumni Council
Alumni Day
Alumni Education Programs
Alumni Weekly, Princeton (PAW)
Andlinger Center for Energy and the Environment
Andlinger Center for the Humanities
Anniversary Celebrations
Annual Giving
Anthropology, The Department of
Architecture, The School of
Art and Archaeology, The Department of
Art Museum, Princeton University
Asian American and Asian Students at Princeton
Astrophysical Sciences, The Department of
Athletics
Auditing Program
Baccalaureate Address
Baker Memorial Rink
Band, University
Baseball
Basketball
Bayard, Samuel

Beer/Class/Senior Jackets
Behrman, Howard T., Awards
Belcher, Jonathan
Bendheim Center for Finance
Blair Hall
Bowen, William Gordon
Brackenridge, Hugh Henry
Brackett, Cyrus Fogg
Bridge Year Program, Novogratz
Brown, J. Douglas
Brown Hall
Bunn, B[enjamin] Franklin
Burr, Aaron, Jr.
Burr, Aaron, Sr.
Burr, Aaron, Hall
Butler, Howard Crosby
Cabinet Officers
Caldwell Field House
Campbell Hall
Campus
Campus Art
Campus Club
Cannons
Carnahan, James
Carnegie Lake
Carril, Peter J. "Pete"
Centers and Institutes
Chancellor Green
Chapel, The University
Charter, The
Chemical and Biological Engineering, The Department of
Chemistry, The Department of
Christian Student, The
Civil and Environmental Engineering, The Department of
Civil War
Classics, The Department of
Cleveland, Grover

Clio Hall
Coeducation
College and University Founders
College of New Jersey
Colors
Commencement
Comparative Literature, The Department of
Compton Brothers
Computer Science, The Department of
Computing
Concerned Alumni of Princeton
Constitutional Convention of 1787
Continental Congress
Co-ops
Corwin, Edward S.
Corwin Hall
Council of the Humanities
Council of the Princeton University Community (CPUC, U-Council)
Council on Science and Technology
Cowell, David
Cross-Country
Davies, Samuel
Davis, Natalie Zemon
Dean, The Office of
Dean of Admission
Dean of the College
Dean of the Departments of Science
Dean for Diversity and Inclusion
Dean of the Faculty
Dean of Freshmen
Dean of the Graduate School
Dean of Religious Life and of the Chapel

xiii

Dean for Research
Dean of the School of
    Architecture
Dean of the School of
    Engineering and Applied
    Science
Dean of the School of Public and
    International Affairs
Dean of Student Life
Dean of Undergraduate
    Students
Dean's Date
Dickinson, Jonathan
Dillon Gymnasium
Dinky, The
Divestment
Dod Hall
Dodds, Harold Willis
East Asian Studies, The
    Department of
East College
East Pyne
Eating Clubs
Ecology and Evolutionary
    Biology, The Department of
Economics, The Department of
Edwards, Jonathan
Edwards Hall
Einstein, Albert
Eisenhart, Luther Pfahler
Eisgruber, Christopher Ludwig
Electrical and Computer
    Engineering, The
    Department of
Ellsworth, Oliver
Endowed Professorships
Endowment
Engineering and Applied
    Science, The School of
Engineering Quadrangle
English, The Department of
Enrollment
Entrepreneurship/Innovation
Epidemics
Evelyn College for Women
Faculty
Faculty Honor Societies
Farrand, Beatrix
Fencing
Field Hockey
Fields, Carl A.

Fields Center for Equality and
    Cultural Understanding,
    Carl A.
Financial Aid
Fine, Henry Burchard
Fine Hall
Finley, Samuel
Fires
Fitzgerald, Francis Scott Key
FitzRandolph Gateway
Football
Forrestal Campus, Princeton
Forrestal Center, Princeton
Founding of Princeton, The
Fox, Frederic E.
Frank, Sally
Fraternities and Sororities
French and Italian, The
    Department of
Freneau, Philip Morin
Freshman Scholars Institute
Freshman Seminars
Frick Chemistry Laboratory
Frist Campus Center
Fundraising
Garrett, Robert
Gauss, Christian
General Counsel, Office of
Geosciences, The Department of
German, The Department of
Gildersleeve, Basil Lanneau
Glee Club, Princeton University
Goheen, Robert Francis
Golf
Governors
Graduate College
Graduate School
Green, Ashbel
Green, John Cleve
Green Hall
Guyot, Arnold Henri
Guyot Hall
Hall, Walter Phelps "Buzzer"
Health Services, University
Helm, Harold H.
Henry, Bayard
Henry, Joseph
Henry, Joseph, House
Hibben, John Grier
High Meadows Environmental
    Institute (HMEI)

Hispanic/Latinx Students at
    Princeton
History, The Department of
Hoaxes and Pranks
Holder Hall
Honor System
Honorary Degrees
Hooding Ceremony
Hosack, David
House of Representatives
Ice Hockey
Institute for Advanced Study
International Initiatives
Ivy League
Jacobus Fellows
Jadwin Gymnasium
Jefferson, Thomas, The Papers
    of
Jewish Students at Princeton
Johnson, James Collins
Jones Hall
Keller, Suzanne
Kelley, Stanley, Jr.
Kennedy, John Fitzgerald
Kopp, Wendy
Lacrosse
Lake Campus
Law School
Lee, Henry
Lefschetz, Solomon
Lewis, Sir Arthur
Lewis Center for the Arts
Lewis Library
Lewis-Sigler Institute for
    Integrative Genomics
LGBTQIA Students at Princeton
Library, Princeton University
Lincoln, Abraham
Little, Stafford, Hall
Lowrie, Walter, House
Maclean, John, Jr.
Maclean, John, Sr.
Maclean, John, House
Madison, James, Jr.
Madison, James, Medal
Madison Hall
Magie, William Francis
Malkiel, Nancy Weiss
Marquand, Allan
Mathematics, The Department
    of

Mather Sun Dial
Mathey, Dean
McCarter Theatre Center
McClenahan, Howard
McCormick Hall
McCosh, James
McCosh Hall
McCosh Infirmary
McGraw Center for Teaching and Learning
McMillan, Charles
McPhee, John
Mechanical and Aerospace Engineering, The Department of
Medieval Art, Index of
Molecular Biology, The Department of
Morrison, Toni
Morrison Hall
Movement for a New Congress
Mpala Research Centre
Murray, James Ormsbee
Murray-Dodge Hall
Music, The Department of
Nader, Ralph
Nash, John Forbes, Jr.
Nassau Hall
Native American and Indigenous Students at Princeton
Near Eastern Studies, The Department of
New South
Nobel and Other Major Prizes
Nude Olympics
Oates, Whitney Jennings
Obama, Michelle LaVaughn Robinson
"Old Nassau"
Olympians
Operations Research and Financial Engineering, The Department of
Orange Key Guide Service
Orchestra, University
Pace Center for Civic Engagement
Palmer Hall
Palmer House
Paterson, William
Patton, Francis Landey

Pell, Claiborne de Borda
Philosophy, The Department of
Physics, The Department of
Poe Brothers
Poler's Recess
Politics, The Department of
Portrait Collection
Postage Stamps
Pre-rade
President of the University
Presidents of the United States
Press Club, University
Princeton, Municipality of
Princeton in Asia, Africa, and Latin America
Princeton-Blairstown Center
Princeton Club of New York
Princeton Institute for International and Regional Studies (PIIRS)
Princeton Investment Company (Princo)
Princeton in the Movies and on Television
Princeton Neuroscience Institute
Princeton Plasma Physics Laboratory (PPPL)
Princeton Prize in Race Relations
Princeton and Slavery Project
Princeton in Space
Princeton Theological Seminary
Princeton University Preparatory Program
Princeton University Press
Princeton University Store
Princetonian, Daily
Prospect
Protest Activity
Provost
Psychology, The Department of
Public and International Affairs, The Princeton School of
Pulitzer Prizes
Pyne, Moses Taylor
Pyne Hall
Pyne Honor Prize
Reeve, Tapping
Religion, The Department of
Religious Life

Reserve Officers Training Corps (ROTC)
Residential Colleges
Residential Life
Reunion Hall
Reunions
Rhodes and Other Scholarships
Rittenhouse Orrery
Rivers, Robert J., Jr.
Root, Robert Kilburn
Roper Lane
Rowing
Rudenstine. Neil L.
Rugby
Rush, Benjamin
Russell, Henry Norris
Salutatory Oration
Sayre, Daniel Clemens
Scheide, William H.
Seal of Princeton University
Secretary of the University
Senate of the United States
Senior Thesis
Service of Remembrance
Seventy-Nine Hall
Shapiro, Harold Tafler
Sherrerd Hall
Simmons, Ruth
Slavic Languages and Literatures, The Department of
Smith, Samuel Stanhope
Smith, Tracy K.
Soccer
Sociology, The Department of
Softball
Sotomayor, Sonia
Spanish and Portuguese, The Department of
Spelman Halls
Spitzer, Lyman, Jr.
Sprint (Lightweight) Football
Squash
Stanhope Hall
Stevenson Hall
Stockton, Betsey
Stockton, Richard
Student Government
Student Publications
Supreme Court of the United States
Sustainability

Swimming and Diving
Taylor, Hugh Stott
Teacher Preparation
Tennis
Theatre Intime
Thomas, Norman Mattoon
Thompson, Henry Burling
Thompson Gateway
Tilghman, Shirley Marie
Track and Field
Triangle Club, Princeton
Trustees of Princeton University
Turing, Alan M.
University Center for Human Values (UCHV)
University League/UNOW
University Research Board (URB)
Upper and Lower Pyne
Valedictory Oration
Veblen, Oswald
Veterans of Future Wars
Vice President
Vice Presidents of the United States
Volleyball
von Neumann, John
Washington, George
Water Polo
West, Andrew Fleming
West, Cornel R.
Whig-Cliosophic Society, American
Whig Hall
Wilson, Thomas Woodrow
Wilson, Woodrow, Award
Wilson, Woodrow, National Fellowship Foundation
Wilson, Woodrow, The Papers of
Witherspoon, John
Witherspoon Hall
Women
WPRB
Wrestling
Wu Hall

Reference Lists

Baccalaureate Speakers: 1973–2021
Behrman Award Winners
Guggenheim Fellowships Since 1970
Honorary Degree Recipients Since 1970
Interdisciplinary/Interdepartmental Certificate Programs
Jacobus Fellows
Madison Medal Recipients
Princeton All-Time Olympians
Pyne Prize Recipients
Salutatorians Since 1970
Valedictorians Since 1970
Wilson Award Recipients

HISTORY OF THE UNIVERSITY

Like the country it helped create, Princeton University was founded on noble ideals and aspirations. Over more than 275 years it has expanded its ambitions, deepened its impact, and more fully embraced its commitment to "the nation's service and the service of humanity." It has developed academic programs of great distinction; created exceptional libraries, laboratories, performance spaces, and one of the world's leading university art museums; attracted faculty who are leaders in their fields; and educated students who have gone on to be leaders in theirs.

For most of those 275 years, it has celebrated this history in words, rituals, and the adornments of a physical space that was the first in the world to be called a "campus." There is no other university quite like Princeton, and there is much to extol. But there are aspects of its history that until recently have rarely been acknowledged, including acts of inhumanity and exclusion that are antithetical to the values the University espouses today.

A 2016 trustee report was unsparing in citing the University's "failure to acknowledge the pain and sense of exclusion that many people of color have experienced, and in some cases continue to experience . . . partly because of the narrow lens through which the University presents its history." The report called upon the University to be more honest and transparent about its history, and especially about aspects that have been "forgotten, overlooked, subordinated, or suppressed."

There are entries in this *Companion* that speak to these aspects of Princeton's history, along with entries that speak to its academic accomplishments; its athletic, artistic, cultural, and scientific achievements; and its impact on the world. There is no way to distill all this history into a single essay, but what follows attempts to provide a broad overview of the evolution of an all-male, all-white, colonial undergraduate college with a narrow classical curriculum into a coeducational, multiracial, multinational research university with a curriculum that spans the frontiers of knowledge in the arts and humanities, social sciences, natural sciences, and engineering.

Mission Statement

In September 2015, the trustees adopted the following as the University's mission statement:

> Princeton University advances learning through scholarship, research, and teaching of unsurpassed quality, with an emphasis on undergraduate and doctoral education that is distinctive among the world's great universities, and with a pervasive commitment to serve the nation and the world.

The trustees also identified 11 "defining characteristics and aspirations" (see page 2). It is striking how few of them pertained at the time of Princeton's founding. The early college certainly had a human scale. Its founders did establish a liberal arts college rather than a seminary. And they did aspire to prepare students to serve the state as well as the church.

But the curriculum was narrow and focused solely on undergraduate teaching; the residential experience was more confining than liberating; and to the extent that there were diverse perspectives, they derived largely from the fact that Princeton was unique among the early colleges in drawing its students from throughout the colonies. There were important early benefactors, but it would be more than a century before alumni began to become "intensely engaged and generously supportive."

The College of New Jersey, 1746-1768: Two Decades, Five Presidents

The College of New Jersey was founded by three lay Presbyterians and four ministers whose moderate religious views were considered radical if not heretical by the elders of the church. Six of the seven founders graduated from Yale, while one of the ministers

> ### Princeton University's Defining Characteristics and Aspirations
>
> The University's defining characteristics and aspirations include:
>
> - a focus on the arts and humanities, the social sciences, the natural sciences, and engineering, with world-class excellence across all of its departments.
> - a commitment to innovation, free inquiry, and the discovery of new knowledge and new ideas, coupled with a commitment to preserve and transmit the intellectual, artistic, and cultural heritage of the past.
> - a faculty of world-class scholars who are engaged with and accessible to students and devoted to the thorough integration of teaching and research.
> - a focus on undergraduate education that is unique for a major research university, with a program of liberal arts that simultaneously prepares students for meaningful lives and careers, broadens their outlooks, and helps form their characters and values.
> - a graduate school that is unusual in its emphasis on doctoral education, while also offering high quality masters programs in selected areas.
> - a human scale that nurtures a strong sense of community, invites high levels of engagement, and fosters personal communication.
> - exceptional student aid programs at the undergraduate and graduate level that ensure Princeton is affordable to all.
> - a commitment to welcome, support, and engage students, faculty, and staff with a broad range of backgrounds and experiences, and to encourage all members of the University community to learn from the robust expression of diverse perspectives.
> - a vibrant and immersive residential experience on a campus with a distinctive sense of place that promotes interaction, reflection, and lifelong attachment.
> - a commitment to prepare students for lives of service, civic engagement, and ethical leadership.
> - an intensely engaged and generously supportive alumni community.
>
> *Adopted by the Board of Trustees, September 26, 2015*

graduated from Harvard. The leader of the group, a pastor in Elizabethtown, New Jersey, was Jonathan Dickinson, who would become the College's first president.

With no college between Yale in Connecticut and William & Mary in Virginia, the founders felt it was urgent to establish one in the middle colonies. Their charter broke new ground in welcoming students "of every religious denomination" and assuring them "free and equal liberty . . . notwithstanding any different sentiments in religion." The College's location in a thinly populated province required it to look elsewhere for students. By drawing its students from 12 of the 13 colonies, the College was poised to become a national institution as soon as there was a nation.

The seven founders were granted a charter on October 22, 1746. They selected five additional trustees and, on April 27, 1747, elected Dickinson as president. The College held its first classes in his parsonage a month later. When Dickinson died in October, the College moved to the Newark parsonage of one of its other founders, Aaron Burr Sr., who was elected its second president. When the legitimacy of the initial charter was challenged because it had been granted by an acting governor, a new charter was issued on September 14, 1748, by the duly installed royal governor, Jonathan Belcher.

This charter increased the number of trustees to 23. At the time, even in the northern colonies, many landowners, merchants, and ministers owned slaves, and in one of its many findings about the connections between the College and slavery, the Princeton and Slavery Project found that 16 of these 23 early trustees had "bought, sold, traded, or inherited slaves." This was also true for its first nine presidents.

Eight weeks after the new charter was granted, on November 9, the College held its first Commencement, conferring six bachelor's degrees and its first honorary degree. The honorary degree was presented to Belcher, an important early benefactor who gave the College his library of 474 volumes, 10 framed portraits of kings and queens of England (its first art collection), and a portrait of himself.

As the College began outgrowing its quarters in Newark, the trustees looked for a location "more sequestered from the various temptations attending a promiscuous converse with the world" and nearer to the center of the province. In the winter of 1752–53 they chose the agrarian village of Princeton over the town of New Brunswick, after Princeton more than met the stipulations of the trustees to provide £1,000, 10 acres of cleared land, and 200 acres of woodland for fuel.

The citizens of Princeton primarily responsible for this were all slaveholding landowners. Principal among them was Nathaniel FitzRandolph who, with his wife Rebeckah, gave the four and a half acres that became the initial campus. The town of Princeton had been settled in the late seventeenth century on the historic homeland of the Lenni Lenape Native Americans; the FitzRandolphs' land was along the south edge of a Lenape trail that had connected the Raritan and Delaware rivers. Today, FitzRandolph's gift is commemorated by a ceremonial front campus gate that was long kept closed except during reunions and Commencement until the Class of 1970, at its graduation, called for it to be opened permanently "as a symbol of the University's openness to the local and worldwide community."

The trustees constructed the largest academic building in the colonies, which they proposed naming for Belcher. He persuaded them to name it Nassau Hall in honor of King William the Third of the royal house of Nassau—a king regarded as a champion of religious freedom and political liberty.

The trustees also constructed a home for the president, which is now named Maclean House in honor of Princeton's 10th president, John Maclean Jr. 1816, the first president who never owned slaves. Today the names of 16 enslaved African American men, women, and children who lived and worked there between 1756 and 1822 are commemorated on a plaque in front of the house. In 1766, six of them were sold at an estate sale on the front lawn following the death of President Samuel Finley. One of the other enslaved women, Betsey Stockton, became a missionary in Hawaii and, later, a beloved teacher in the town of Princeton; she is memorialized in a garden between Firestone Library and Nassau Street that the University named for her in 2018.

Nassau Hall opened its doors in 1756. Shortly thereafter the trustees bought land to its east, south, and west, widening its frontage on the town's main street and adding a back campus that reached what later generations came to know as McCosh Walk. Today the University's 600-acre main campus is part of the 1,000 acres it owns in Princeton. In the 1920s the University began to acquire lands in neighboring West Windsor, where it now owns more than 520 acres, and in the 1950s it purchased more than 835 acres in nearby Plainsboro. The Plainsboro lands include the home of the Princeton Plasma Physics Laboratory, the world's leading center for fusion energy research.

Nassau Hall, a national historic landmark since 1960, was designed to house the entire college: it contained rooms for students, tutors, and classes, in addition to a kitchen and dining room, a library, and a prayer hall. The first state legislature of New Jersey held its inaugural meeting there in 1776. Nassau Hall was a major flashpoint in the Battle of Princeton that helped turn the tide of the Revolutionary War in favor of the Americans, and, when the town of Princeton briefly became the new country's provisional capital in the summer of 1783, Nassau Hall served as its capitol building—the Confederation Congress met in its second floor library. The building would later be severely damaged by fire in 1802 and again in 1855.

The fledgling college attracted many students who played leading roles in the founding of the country. Around 1765 two debating societies, the Plain Dealing Club and the Well-Meaning Club, were established; they were succeeded in 1769 and 1770 by the American Whig Society and the Cliosophic Society. In their early days, the societies provided an arena in which future leaders of the republic, including James Madison 1771 (Whig) and Aaron Burr Jr. 1772 (Clio), honed their skills of disputation and persuasion. Today, Whig Clio remains the country's oldest college literary and debating society.

Over its first 20 years the College had five presidents, all of whom died in office, including Dickinson within a year of becoming president and Jonathan Edwards after only six weeks. In 1768 John Witherspoon arrived from Scotland as Princeton's sixth president, and his presidency of 26 years was longer than all his predecessors combined.

The "Seedbed" of the Revolution

Witherspoon accepted the presidency largely because of the persuasiveness of Benjamin Rush 1760. Rush would become the colonies' first professor of chemistry (at the College of Philadelphia, later the University of Pennsylvania); the founder of the first antislavery society; a signer of the Declaration of Independence; an army doctor during the Revolutionary War; the founder of a medical dispensary for the poor and a school for young women (both in Philadelphia); and the author of the first textbook on psychiatry in America.

During Witherspoon's presidency, the College became known as the "seedbed" of the Revolution. Witherspoon was the only college president and the only clergyman to sign the Declaration of Independence and for six years was a leading member of the Continental Congress. Madison stayed on after graduation to study with him, making Madison Princeton's first graduate student.

After leaving Princeton Madison went on to play a central role in drafting and securing adoption of the Constitution. He served as secretary of state from 1801–09 in the administration of Thomas Jefferson and was then elected the nation's fourth president. (He also became the first president of Princeton's alumni association when it was formed in 1826.) In addition to Madison (president) and Burr (vice president), Witherspoon taught nine cabinet officers, 21 senators, 39 members of Congress, three justices of the Supreme Court, and 12 governors. Five of the nine Princeton graduates among the 55 members of the Constitutional Convention had been his students.

Witherspoon added books to the library and acquired "philosophical apparatus," including the famous Rittenhouse Orrery (still in Peyton Hall), to teach science. He coined the term "campus," Latin for field, to describe the lawn that separated Nassau Hall from Nassau Street, a departure from the conventional practice in the colonies and Europe of placing academic buildings close to the street. Witherspoon's eminence and his travels through the south to preach and raise funds resulted in a disproportionate number of southern families sending their sons to Princeton.

Like other early Princeton presidents, Witherspoon had a complex relationship to slavery. As a minister in Scotland, he baptized an enslaved man and in the early 1770s he privately tutored two free Black men. In 1792 John Chavis, a free Black man from Virginia, began private lessons with him. The Princeton and Slavery project found that his teachings gave a generation of students "a language for challenging slavery." But Witherspoon also owned slaves, and in 1790 he chaired a committee that recommended that the state take no action to abolish slavery in New Jersey.

An Era of Decline, 1794-1868

The American Revolution wreaked havoc with the College's finances and its enrollment; when Witherspoon died in 1794, there were just over 75 students. This number almost doubled by 1820, but it then plummeted to 87 in 1829 before rebounding to 228 a decade later.

Witherspoon's immediate successor was Samuel Stanhope Smith 1769, the first graduate of the College to serve as president. The high point of his presidency came after the Nassau Hall fire of 1802 when he raised funds to reconstruct that building and add two new buildings on the front campus: Geological (later Stanhope) Hall, and its twin, Philosophical Hall, later razed to construct Princeton's first library building, Chancellor Green. The low point occurred when a student riot in 1807 led to the suspension of 125 students (three-fourths of the student body). In 1812 the trustees gave Smith no choice but to resign, and a decade later the same fate befell his successor, Ashbel Green 1783.

One of Smith's ideas, to resettle freed slaves in the west, was transformed by two of his students into a plan to relocate freed slaves to a colony in West Africa. This led in 1816 to the founding of the American Colonization Society (ACS), whose adherents believed emancipation would be disruptive to the country unless Blacks were separated from white society; by 1867 ACS had sent more than 13,000 people to Liberia. Prominent supporters of the ACS included many graduates of the College, including John Maclean Jr., President James Carnahan, and Madison, who in 1833 became its president.

The first half of the nineteenth century was a low point in Princeton's history, but a few developments had lasting impact. Early in the century the College appointed John Maclean Sr. as its first professor of chemistry, and in 1832 two of the leading scientists of the time arrived on campus: physics professor Joseph Henry, later the founding secretary of the Smithsonian Institution, and the astronomer Stephen Alexander. In 1855 the Swiss geographer Arnold Guyot was appointed professor of geology and two years later he founded a museum of natural history. Their legacy endures today in Princeton's eminence among the leading universities in the world in the natural sciences, including their fields of chemistry, physics, astrophysics, and the geosciences.

A second development was the growing presence of students from the south. From 1820 to 1860, 12 classes enrolled more southern than northern students, and in the Class of 1851 southern enrollment reached 63 percent. As early as 1835 southern students were expressing strong anti-abolitionist sentiments and defenders of slavery frequently won the Whig Clio debates on the subject. On the morning of April 13, 1861, following the Confederacy's first attack on Fort Sumter, southern students protested on the front lawn after northern students raised the stars and stripes over Nassau Hall.

With the onset of the Civil War about a third of the students left, dropping enrollment from 314 in 1861 to 221 in 1862. More than 600 Princeton students and alumni fought in the war and 86 died, 39 fighting for the north and 47 for the south. After the war, alumni classes and the University worked hard to achieve reconciliation; when it engraved the names of its Civil War dead in the memorial atrium in Nassau Hall, Princeton made the singular decision to list them without indicating the side for which they died.

A third development was the founding in 1826 of the Alumni Association of Nassau Hall. Its first secretary was the College's vice president, John Maclean Jr., and its first president was James Madison. Creating the alumni association was one of many ways in which Maclean kept the College afloat during Carnahan's lengthy (31 year) and undistinguished presidency. In 1854 Maclean succeeded to the presidency, and after his retirement in 1868 he became president of the alumni association, serving until his death.

Alumni had long returned to campus for Commencement—the centennial Commencement of 1847 drew 700 alumni for a formal dinner—but individual class reunions did not begin until 1859, with the idea of class gifts following about a decade later. The first regional alumni association (New York) was formed in 1866 and others soon followed.

A fourth development of the first half of the nineteenth century revolved around food and fellowship. In 1843 students for the first time were permitted to take their meals off campus, typically at boarding houses in town, although some students established what they called "select associations" to provide their meals. By 1856 all students were required to make their own arrangements off-campus, and by 1864 these associations were being called eating clubs. In 1853 the trustees banned Greek letter fraternities (the first had been founded in 1843 and soon there were a dozen), which had the effect of driving social life as well as culinary life to the clubs. In 1879 the first permanent club (Ivy) was formed and by the early 1990s there were seven; by the 1920s there would be 18 and 75 percent of all juniors and seniors would be members.

On campus, students began to engage in athletic contests and form student organizations in addition to Whig and Clio. As early as 1844 the green behind Nassau Hall (now Cannon Green) was the scene of spirited football games. The fall of 1857 brought a cricket club and two baseball clubs. The first baseball game against an outside opponent took place in 1860 (it ended in a 42–42 tie), and Princeton's first intercollegiate game was a 27–16 win over Williams in 1864. The first student publications appeared in the 1830s: the *Nassau Lit* was founded in 1842 and the *Nassau Herald* in 1864. Princeton's anthem, "Old Nassau," was composed in 1859, with words written by a freshman, Harlan Page Peck 1862, and music composed by Karl Langlotz, an instructor in German who also directed a choral group and taught fencing. In 1987 the words would be changed to make them gender neutral.

The "Electric Shock" of James McCosh

In the aftermath of the Civil War, Princeton again installed a transformative president from Scotland, James McCosh, who took office in 1868, exactly 100 years after Witherspoon. Andrew Fleming West 1874, who entered as a freshman in 1870 and would later become the first dean of Princeton's graduate school, compared the new president's influence to "an electric shock . . . paralyzing to the opposition and stimulating to all who were not paralyzed."

When McCosh arrived, the College had 20 faculty members (only 10 full-time) and fewer than 300 students. When he retired in 1888, the number of students had more than doubled and the size of the faculty had more than tripled. When he arrived almost none of the faculty had a PhD, but when he left a quarter of them did.

McCosh recruited distinguished faculty; modernized the undergraduate plan of study and developed elective courses; and instituted graduate work leading to master's and doctoral degrees—by 1877 there were 42 candidates for advanced degrees and in 1879 Princeton awarded its first PhDs. He founded a school of Science, Princeton's first engineering department (Civil Engineering), a department of Art and Archaeology, and an art museum. In 1873 Chancellor Green was constructed as the University's first library. McCosh considered the library essential for Princeton to become a respected academic institution, and he insisted the building open onto Nassau Street to reinforce his conviction that the University should face out into the world rather than in on itself.

Despite protests from some white students, McCosh admitted African American seminarians into his classes and lectures. During his presidency Hikoichi Orita 1876 became the first Asian student to graduate from Princeton and 12 years later Pedro Rioseco 1888 became the first Hispanic/Latino student to graduate. These were milestone moments, but a century would pass before the University would enroll significant numbers of minority and international students.

The graduations of Orita and Rioseco followed those of Princeton's first Native American alumni, which had occurred in the 1840s. Native students had enrolled in the nineteenth century, beginning with Jacob Woolley, a Lenape, in 1759, but the first to earn a degree was John McDonald Ross 1841. He attended Princeton with two other nephews of the principal chief of the Cherokee Nation: William Potter Ross 1842, who succeeded his uncle as chief in 1861, and Robert Daniel Ross 1843 *1846, who became one of the country's first Native physicians.

McCosh took an active interest in campus landscaping and student life. While he was president, the Glee Club, the Banjo and Mandolin clubs, the Princeton College Dramatic Association (precursor to the Triangle Club), the *Princetonian*, and other student organizations were formed; Princeton played in the first intercollegiate football game (1869); and three dormitories (Reunion, Witherspoon, and Edwards halls) were built so more students—including some with lesser means—could live on campus.

McCosh believed strongly in the value to the College of lifelong engagement by its alumni, so beginning early in his presidency he started traveling around the country to encourage the development of local and regional associations. By time he left office there were 17 of them.

McCosh prepared the way for the college he inherited from his predecessors to become the university he bequeathed to his successors. In 1885 he proposed changing the institution's name to Princeton University, but the trustees turned him down. The change in name would come 11 years later, as part of the University's sesquicentennial in 1896.

Princeton University, 1896–1910: Introducing a Graduate School and "Preceptors"

The sesquicentennial was a watershed moment for Princeton. The University changed its name and shortly thereafter enrolled advanced degree candidates in a graduate school (1901) and housed them in a graduate college (1913). Professor Woodrow Wilson 1879 gave an address that provided Princeton with its first informal motto, "Princeton in the Nation's Service," and helped propel him to its presidency. Professor Andrew Fleming West displayed the organizational talents that led to his appointment as the first dean of the graduate school. Scholars from abroad who attended the ceremonies helped Princeton expand the scope and stature of its scholarly pursuits, and both during and after Wilson's presidency the University created a distinctive undergraduate program that endures today.

During the post-McCosh presidency of Francis Patton, the size of the student body more than doubled (from slightly over 600 to more than 1,300) as did the size of the faculty. In 1893 the faculty approved a student-administered honor system for in-class exams, and in 1898 the University established an international service initiative that is now called Princeton in Asia. Princeton's first two Collegiate Gothic dormitories were constructed (Blair Hall in 1897 and Little Hall in 1899) and the *Princeton Alumni Weekly* began publication in 1900. The publication of the *Alumni Weekly* led to the founding of the Princeton University Press, which would publish its first book in 1912 (today the Press publishes approximately 250 new books each year). In a major departure from previous practice and in recognition of the growing influence of alumni, the governing board added five new positions for trustees who would be elected by the alumni (that number is now 13).

Even though the University was taking major steps forward, the trustees considered Patton a "wonderfully poor" administrator, and like Smith and Green before him he was asked to step down. At a trustee meeting on June 9, 1902, Patton resigned, and Wilson was elected immediately to succeed him as Princeton's first president who had not been a member of the clergy. That fall, Patton would become the first president of the neighboring Princeton Theological Seminary. Once when asked by a visitor to the seminary if he had any connection to the University, he said, "Yes, indeed, I am president of Princeton University—once removed."

Like McCosh's, Wilson's presidency was like an electric shock to the campus. He established an undergraduate curriculum of general studies with distribution requirements in the first two years followed by concentrated study during the junior and senior years. He created new deanships for the departments of science and the college. He shifted the power to make faculty appointments from the trustees to the president and the faculty. In 1904 he imposed an organizational structure by creating 11 academic departments,[1] and in 1905 he increased the size of the faculty by about 50 percent when he hired 49 assistant professors called "preceptors" to engage with undergraduates through guided reading and small group discussion.

One newspaper credited Wilson's changes in the curriculum and the faculty with transforming Princeton from a "country club . . . into an institution of learning." Long-time history professor Joseph Strayer 1925 later observed that while "McCosh cleared the ground and laid the foundation for the university," it was Wilson who "completed the structure" of a distinctive research university uniquely focused on undergraduate education, in which even its most eminent faculty would teach, and students would become active participants in the learning process.

As president, Wilson lost two major battles. His "quad plan" aimed to replace the socially exclusive eating clubs with residential colleges where undergraduates would live and take their meals with resident faculty, and he sought to locate the graduate college in the center of campus. He lost the first battle to stiff alumni opposition and the second to West, who outmaneuvered him to construct the graduate college in his preferred location overlooking the golf course. While Wilson hired Princeton's first Jewish and Catholic faculty members, he stood firm against any enrollment of Black students. In 1909, when a Black student inquired about attending, Wilson said, "it is altogether inadvisable for a colored man to enter Princeton."

When Wilson stepped down in 1910, he was elected governor of New Jersey, and in 1912 he won the first of two terms as president of the United States, joining another Virginian, James Madison, as the only Princeton alumni to serve in that office. Following Wilson, three alumni would gain their party's nomination to run for president: Adlai Stevenson 1922, the Democratic Party candidate against Dwight Eisenhower in 1952 and 1956; Norman Thomas 1905, the Socialist Party candidate in six elections from 1928 through 1948; and Ralph Nader '55, Green Party candidate in 1996 and 2000 and an independent candidate in the next two elections. In 2008, almost 100 years after Wilson's first inauguration, another Princetonian, Michelle Obama '85, would move into the White House as first lady.

The Aftermath of World War I: Academic Stature Grows, Policies of Exclusion Persist

Wilson's successor, John Grier Hibben 1882 *1893 (the first of five consecutive presidents with Princeton graduate degrees), steered Princeton through an east coast polio outbreak in 1916; an international influenza pandemic in 1918; the dislocations of World War I (by September 1918 there were only 60 undergraduates who were not in the military); and the onset of the Great Depression. Schools of Architecture (1919), Engineering (1921), and Public and International Affairs (1930) were established, as was a department of Oriental Languages and Literatures (1927).[2] An array of iconic campus buildings were constructed during Hibben's presidency, including

---

[1] Art and Archaeology; Biology; Chemistry; Classics; English; Geology; History, Politics, and Economics; Mathematics; Modern Languages; Philosophy; and Physics. Departments of Civil and Electrical Engineering already existed, and Astronomy became a department a few years later.

[2] In 1969 the department then called Oriental Studies split into East Asian Studies and Near Eastern Studies, joining a long list of departments that merged, split, or changed names. History, Politics, and Economics became separate departments; Economics spawned Sociology, which in turn gave rise to Anthropology; Modern Languages split several times—its descendants are French and Italian, German, Spanish and Portuguese, Slavic Languages and Literatures, and Comparative Literature; Biology became Molecular Biology and Ecology and Evolutionary Biology (and for a time there was a department of Biochemistry); Psychology emerged out of Philosophy; Statistics existed for a time after emerging out of Mathematics; Music began under the auspices of Art and Archaeology; and Geosciences changed its name several times. In engineering, Mechanical and Aerospace Engineering merged; for a time the department of Civil Engineering became Civil and Geological Engineering, then Civil Engineering and Operations Research, and then Civil and Environmental Engineering after Operations Research and Financial Engineering became a separate department; Electrical Engineering became Electrical Engineering and Computer Science before Computer Science became a separate department and later became Electrical and Computer Engineering; and Chemical Engineering became Chemical and Biological Engineering.

Palmer Stadium (football), Baker Rink (ice hockey), the second McCosh Infirmary, McCarter Theater, and the University Chapel.

In 1923 the University adopted an "upperclass plan of study" known as the "four-course plan" that had been conceived by mathematics professor and later dean of the faculty Luther Eisenhart. The plan reduced the number of courses for juniors and seniors from five to four; replaced the fifth course with independent thinking, research, and writing; and required a comprehensive senior-year examination in the student's field of concentration. While the plan did not mention a thesis, several departments soon expected one of all their seniors and by 1930 a senior thesis was required of practically all Princeton undergraduates. The four-course plan applied to all juniors and seniors, not just those who elected an "honors program." A century later, this all-honors program remains a distinctive characteristic of Princeton; every senior is still required to submit a thesis or comparable independent project, and many students regard the thesis as the capstone of their undergraduate experience. The University archives contain all theses from 1924 to the present, with all since 2013 in digital format.

Eisenhart was one of several young mathematicians (Oswald Veblen was another) who were brought to Princeton by dean of the faculty Henry Fine 1880. Fine and Eisenhart established Princeton as one of the world's leading centers for mathematical research, and as the first professor at the Institute for Advanced Study when it was founded in 1930, Veblen recruited to its faculty some of the best mathematicians and physicists in the world, including Albert Einstein. With the rise of fascism and anti-Semitism in Europe, Veblen's initiative and determination made the institute into a lifeline in the migration of European scholars to Princeton, and it remains today a magnet for some of the world's leading scholars, now spanning the fields of historical studies, natural sciences, and social sciences, in addition to mathematics.

While Princeton's academic stature grew, the size of its graduate school remained capped (initially at 200, then at 250) and the fundamental composition of the undergraduate student body remained largely unchanged. In 1922, as the number of undergraduates grew to more than 1,700, the trustees adopted a policy of selective admission and appointed English instructor Radcliffe Heermance *1909 to the newly created role of dean of admission, a position he held until 1950.

For its first century and a half, Princeton accepted almost all students who applied, including students with deficiencies in preparation who were admitted "with conditions." (In 1904, only about a quarter of the class was admitted unconditionally, and when asked early in his presidency how many students there were at Princeton, Wilson's answer was "about 10 percent.") In the College's earliest years, admission required knowledge of Latin, Greek, and "vulgar arithmetick," and even into the early twentieth century these subjects were part of entrance exams; in 1918 Princeton removed Greek as a Bachelor of Arts requirement, and in 1930 it did the same for Latin.

In colonial times some financial aid was available—as an undergraduate, James Leslie 1759 received assistance from a "fund for pious youth," and when he died in 1792, he gave Princeton its first endowed scholarship—but for most of the eighteenth and nineteenth centuries financial aid remained very limited. By 1921 nearly 300 scholarships were available, and one of every five students had a job through a Bureau of Self Help that had been founded in 1911.

With applications increasing and academic standards rising, especially after the introduction of standardized tests, Heermance assured alumni that "average students" with good records still had an excellent chance of being admitted. He told them that Princeton's highest priority was not in admitting superior students, but in admitting the "all-around boy."

President Hibben had come to Princeton from a public high school in Illinois, and he pressed for modified entrance requirements for applicants from schools in the west that did not prepare their students for the College Boards. That and the growth of alumni associations around the country eager to send local students to Princeton led to a broadening of the geographical distribution of Princeton classes beyond the middle Atlantic and the south. Even so, in the 1930s Princeton had a more homogeneous student body than most of its peers and it stood alone in drawing more than 80 percent of its students from private schools.

While Heermance insisted publicly that Princeton "did not discriminate against any race, color, or creed," the fact was that Princeton was inaccessible to some, including African Americans, and inhospitable to others, including Jewish students. The only Black undergraduate admitted (inadvertently) in the first half of the twentieth century, Bruce Wright, was asked to leave when his race was discovered as he arrived in 1935 to register. (In 2001 the senior class made him an honorary member.)

In 1924 the University limited Jewish enrollment to under three percent: in 1935 when 85 percent of all applicants were admitted, all but five of 28 Jewish applicants were turned down. In 1940 there were only seven Jewish freshmen in a class of 508. One magazine editor reported that anti-Semitism was "more dominant at Princeton" than at any of 14 other universities he visited.

The Dodds Era: Harbingers of Change

In 1933 the trustees chose politics professor Harold Dodds *14 to succeed Hibben. An expert on local government, Dodds had chaired the committee that established the school of Public and International Affairs. Dodds would remain in office for 24 years, guiding the University through the Great Depression, World War II, the postwar period of readjustment, and the Korean War.

During World War II, some students accelerated their studies, while others left hoping to return and finish later. In a gesture much appreciated and long remembered, in 1943 Dodds contacted 1,300 Princetonians serving in the armed forces and offered them, at no cost, three books of their choosing—wherever they might be. Many members of the faculty contributed to the war effort, instructing soldiers, sailors, and marines on campus, teaching off-campus courses for industrial chemists, serving in senior government positions, and conducting research in fields ranging from sonar technology to atomic weapons.

During Dodds' tenure, the faculty grew from 327 to 582; the number of graduate students more than doubled from 293 to 636; and the number of undergraduates increased from 2,309 to 2,948, having bulged to more than 3,400 in 1946 as war veterans returned to campus in droves (cots were installed in Baker Rink to accommodate them). The University added a program in the Creative Arts in 1939, founded departments of Aeronautical Engineering (1941), Religion (1945), and Music (1946), and established a Special Program in the Humanities, followed by a Council of the Humanities in 1953. A graduate program was added to the school of Public and International Affairs, which in 1948 was officially named for Woodrow Wilson.

In 1948 Firestone Library opened as a "laboratory for the humanities and social sciences"; today it is one of the largest open-stack libraries in the world and it has more books per student than any other university library in the United States. In 1951 the University purchased 825 acres (now the Princeton Forrestal Campus) and 16 laboratory buildings from the Rockefeller Center for Medical Research to provide urgently needed space for engineering and the natural sciences; the precursor to the Princeton Plasma Physics Laboratory was founded there in a former rabbit hutch.

Alumni volunteers launched an Annual Giving program in 1940 that encouraged classmates to make unrestricted gifts. The program raised $80,000 in its first year. In 1957, the final year of Dodds' presidency, it raised $1.3 million from more than 70 percent of all undergraduate alumni. Between 1940 and 2020, Annual Giving raised a total of more than $1.5 billion; almost 90 percent of undergraduate alumni participated at least once; and many graduate alumni and parents contributed as well. No other university comes close to Princeton's levels of participation. In recent years Annual Giving dollars have provided nearly 10 percent of the University's overall budget for educational expenses, providing it with flexibility to meet unanticipated needs and take advantage of unforeseen opportunities.

In 1942, 23 women became the University's first female students when they enrolled in a government-sponsored course in photogrammetry (making maps from aerial photographs) taught by a Princeton faculty member. Three women on the library staff enrolled in a Russian language course in 1947. Spouses of returning veterans sat in on courses informally and two wives of members of the Class of 1943 became the first female reporters for the *Daily Princetonian*. In 1942 the Physics department appointed a woman, Chien-Shiung Wu, to its faculty, and beginning in 1943, women were hired as instructors and lecturers in language courses. In 1948 Helen Baker, associate director of the Industrial Relations Section, became the first woman at Princeton granted "faculty status with the rank of associate professor."

The war years called attention to widespread discrimination throughout American society, and in 1942 the *Daily Princetonian* editorialized in favor of admitting African American students in a three-part series entitled "White Supremacy at Princeton." In 1945 four Black students arrived on campus as part of the Navy's V-12 program, and one of them, John Howard '47, would become the first Black student to earn a Princeton undergraduate degree. Two of the other students, basketball team captain Arthur

Jewell Wilson and James Ward, would graduate in the Class of 1948.

In 1947 Princeton admitted a Black undergraduate from the town of Princeton, Joseph Ralph Moss '51; another early Black undergraduate, Robert J. Rivers Jr. '53, also from the town of Princeton, later would become the first African American elected by the board to serve as a Princeton trustee. He is recognized on campus today by a roadway named in his honor and a portrait in the University's increasingly diverse portrait collection. In 1955 the University hired its first Black faculty member, assistant professor of English Charles Davis.

In 1946 the Student Hebrew Association was founded, and in 1947 it held its first official service on campus with Albert Einstein as one of its speakers. By 1948, 6.5 percent of the freshman class was Jewish, the highest percentage in any class to that time.

Post-World War II: The Emergence of Today's Princeton

These modest steps toward inclusion were a harbinger of what was to come, although it would still take decades before Princeton became the coeducational, multinational, and multicultural institution it is today.

By 1948 Princeton had more than 5,000 applicants for 725 spaces, and the University was actively seeking students beyond New York, New Jersey, and Pennsylvania. The GI Bill helped veterans pay for college and Princeton expanded its own commitment to financial aid (basing aid solely on need); by the early 1960s almost 40 percent of undergraduates were receiving some form of assistance. By 1955 students from public high schools were filling half the entering class; by 1958 they were filling more than half; and a decade later only 35 percent of the Class of 1973 came from private schools. The University was still admitting 80 percent of alumni children who applied, but in the 1970s this would drop to about 40 percent, and it would later settle in the range of 30 percent.

In 1950 more than 600 sophomores in the Class of 1952 declared they would not join eating clubs unless every sophomore who applied ("bickered") was admitted to at least one club. The concept of "100 percent bicker" was largely sustained except for a major setback in the "dirty bicker" of 1958 when 23 students, more than half of whom were Jewish, were not chosen for any club.

After 20 years of short-lived attempts to create alternatives to the clubs, in 1957 students formed Woodrow Wilson Lodge, with social and dining space in Madison Hall. In 1961 they relocated to Wilcox Hall and the lodge was renamed the Woodrow Wilson Society; in 1968 the society was transformed into Princeton's first residential college. In 2020, after Wilson College was temporarily renamed First College, it was announced that a gift from Mellody Hobson '91 would allow the University, beginning in 2023, to replace First College with a new residential college, Hobson College, the first residential college at Princeton named for an African American woman.

In the late 1960s and early 1970s some of the eating clubs abandoned bicker in favor of sign-in policies and two former eating clubs were converted into the University-operated Stevenson Hall, which included a kosher kitchen; the kitchen remained until the opening of a Center for Jewish Life in 1993. The Princeton Inn was converted into the University's second residential college, and in 1977 the first dining co-op opened at 2 Dickinson Street.

In the 1950s and 1960s graduate school enrollments and Princeton's research capacity increased dramatically as Cold War tensions fueled increased federal investments in science, engineering, and foreign language and area studies and national fellowship programs supported advanced training in other fields. Outside support for sponsored research helped increase the University's budget from just under $9 million in 1950 to more than $74 million in 1970.

While many other universities concentrated their resources on selected departments, Princeton's approach was to be selective about the fields it offered, but then aim for distinction in every one of them. Today the University has world-class faculty in every department and every department is highly ranked.

The course that Princeton charted also differed from its peers in other respects:

- As it expanded its scholarly eminence, it sustained its unique commitment to undergraduate education, with all faculty members expected to teach and with students expected to play an active role in the learning process; as one admission dean said, "a first-rate education is not something that happens to you—rather it is something you yourself make happen."
- As the graduate school increasingly attracted many of the best students in the world, it remained relatively small; while it offers highly selective master's programs in several fields, its overwhelming

emphasis is on doctoral education, with 90 percent of Princeton's graduate students pursuing PhDs.
- Unlike most research universities, Princeton does not have professional schools, with separate faculties, in law, medicine, business, and education; it has a single faculty focused on the liberal arts and sciences, and engineering.
- While some of its peers downplayed engineering or chose not to offer it, Princeton pursued scholarly and professional distinction in engineering, but within the framework of a liberal arts university; its engineering programs actively collaborate with the University's other academic divisions: the arts and humanities, social sciences, and natural sciences. In 2019, three of the University's most popular undergraduate majors were engineering departments. The most popular major, Computer Science[3], is the only department at Princeton that offers both Bachelor of Arts and Bachelor of Science in Engineering degrees.

Another Transformational President

On December 7, 1956, the trustees promoted a young assistant professor of classics, Robert Goheen '40 *48, to full professor and elected him Princeton's 16th president. Like Witherspoon, McCosh, and Wilson, he would transform the University in almost every dimension.

Goheen led the University's first comprehensive capital campaign, which surpassed its goal of $53 million by raising $60.7 million. The funds supported undergraduate financial aid and graduate fellowships; expansion of the graduate program and a new home for the school of Public and International Affairs; a new state-of-the-art complex for Engineering (the E-Quad); new buildings for Architecture, Music, Mathematics, Physics, and Astrophysics; and a new gymnasium (Jadwin).

In the early 1960s, Goheen committed the University to recruit and enroll significant numbers of Black students. In 1963 Princeton had only 10 Black undergraduates; by 1971 there were more than 300. In 1964 he hired Carl Fields as the University's first Black administrator; when he was promoted in 1968, Fields became the first Black dean in the Ivy League. In 1969 Goheen created a program in African American Studies that in time would become a center (2006) and then a department (2015). In 1971 the University opened a Third World Center to address the needs and concerns of students of color (the center would later be named for Fields).

In 1961 Princeton for the first time admitted a woman as a degree candidate when Sabra Follett Meservey *64 *66 became a graduate student in the department of Oriental Studies. In 1962 eight more women were admitted, including T'sai-Ying Cheng *63 *64, who in 1963 became the first woman to earn a Princeton degree when she received her master's in Biochemical Sciences; in 1964 she became the first woman to receive a Princeton PhD. By 1968 there were 56 female graduate students and by 1976 there were 367.

In 1963 the University established a Critical Languages program under which students from other colleges, including women, became visiting undergraduates for a year or two to study such languages as Chinese, Japanese, Russian, and Arabic. By 1967 an initially skeptical Goheen was ready to ask the trustees to authorize a comprehensive study of the desirability and feasibility of undergraduate coeducation. The study recommended admitting 1,000–1,200 women in addition to the existing enrollment of 3,200 men. In January 1969 the trustees approved coeducation "in principle," and in April they voted to admit women undergraduates beginning that fall.

That September the University enrolled 101 female first-year students in the Class of 1973, in addition to 70 female transfer students. The transfer students included nine women who had studied the previous year in the Critical Languages program (five of them Asian or Asian American) and thus could qualify as seniors in the Class of 1970, making them Princeton's first undergraduate alumnae. Four years later there were 1,000 women undergraduates on campus. In 1974 the trustees adopted a policy of "equal access" that eliminated the guaranteed number of men; by 1976 the number of women had increased to 1,395. In 2019, 49.7 percent of undergraduates were women. The Class of 2023, with 50.9 percent women, was the first Princeton class with more women than men.

In 1968 Suzanne Keller (Sociology) became the first tenured woman faculty member. In 1971 Ellen Chances *70 *72 (Slavic Languages and Literatures) was the first woman with a Princeton graduate degree to be appointed to the faculty. In 1973 Sylvia Molloy (Romance Languages and Literatures) was the first

---
[3] In 2018 the most popular majors were Computer Science (313), Economics (269), Public and International Affairs (240), Politics (147), History (144), Operations Research and Financial Engineering (139), Mechanical and Aerospace Engineering (110), Ecology and Evolutionary Biology (109), and Music (85).

woman promoted to tenure from the assistant professor ranks. In 1979 S. Georgia Nugent '73 (Classics) became the first undergraduate alumna on the faculty.

The first woman dean of students (Adele Simmons) was appointed in 1972; she was joined in 1977 by the first women deans of the college (Joan Girgus) and the graduate school (Nina Garsoian). A Women*s Center was established in 1971 and a Women's Studies program (now Gender and Sexuality Studies) began in 1982. In 1991, following a protracted legal battle persistently waged by Sally Frank '80, the last of the eating clubs (Tiger Inn) finally became coeducational.

An Era of Activism, Expansion, and New Approaches to Residential Life

The late 1960s and early 1970s were a turbulent period of activism and unrest, on campus and throughout the country. On May 2, 1968, more than 1,000 students rallied in front of Nassau Hall to demand a greater role in University governance, severance of the University's ties to a think tank that conducted secret military research, divestment from companies doing business in South Africa, and removal of academic credit from ROTC courses.[4]

Goheen appointed a student-faculty committee chaired by politics professor Stanley Kelley Jr. that proposed creation of a broadly representative Council of the Princeton University Community (CPUC), with committees that would advise the University on its operating budget, investment policies, rules of campus conduct, and other topics. The Kelley committee also proposed electing a graduating senior each year to the board of trustees. (In 2019 the trustees designated a position on the board for a recent graduate of the graduate school.)

On April 30, 1970, following the announcement of American bombing in Cambodia, more than 2,500 students gathered in the chapel to protest this escalation of the Vietnam War. On May 4 more than 4,000 students, faculty, and staff met in Jadwin Gym and endorsed a resolution calling for a "strike against the war." Most students elected not to take exams and most seniors chose not to participate in reunions or wear caps and gowns for Commencement.

The May 4 meeting also voted to create an organization called the Movement for a New Congress, headquartered in Princeton's Palmer Hall, to encourage students nationwide to participate in that fall's Congressional campaigns. The next day the faculty endorsed a CPUC resolution creating a two-week fall break so students could return home prior to election day to canvass and vote. A one-week fall break remains part of Princeton's academic calendar, providing a welcome respite from classes and time to pursue research and community service projects.

As the draft became a less pressing concern and the war in Vietnam came to an end, campus activism continued, largely focused on issues related to diversity. Students and others called for increased recruitment of students of color, fair treatment of LGBTQIA students, support for students with disabilities, and the creation of programs in Latino Studies and Asian American Studies. Other concerns included issues related to sexual misconduct and divestment. While the initial calls for divestment targeted apartheid in South Africa, later issues focused on genocide in Darfur, fossil fuel companies, and private prisons.

In 1972 Goheen was succeeded by his provost, William Bowen *58. As provost Bowen had been deeply involved in the implementation of coeducation, efforts to increase the enrollment of minority students, the defense of open inquiry and free speech, and an expanded commitment to financial aid. As president these remained priorities, along with enhancing the University's academic strengths and improving the quality of undergraduate life.

Bowen recognized that to remain one of the world's great universities, Princeton had to be much better than it was in the life sciences. He set out simultaneously to create a new department of Molecular Biology, build it a state-of-the-art laboratory, and attract transformative faculty leaders. The department achieved the level of international distinction he sought and attracted many faculty members who were leaders in the field, including Shirley Tilghman, who would become Princeton's nineteenth president.

In 1978 Bowen appointed a committee to make recommendations regarding undergraduate social and dining facilities. The committee proposed creating a system of five residential colleges to house all freshmen and sophomores and a limited number of juniors and seniors. In 1982 the colleges opened to freshmen and a year later they were fully operational. The one new facility that was required was given by one of the University's most generous donors of the

---

[4] By 1972 ROTC had become a noncredit program and only the Army unit remained on campus; in 2014 a Princeton Navy ROTC unit was re-established.

modern era, Gordon Wu '58, who had been an international student from Hong Kong as an undergraduate and whose name is affixed to the dining hall in Chinese characters as well as in English letters.

When the trustees decided in 2000 to increase undergraduate enrollment by 10 percent (from 4,600 to 5,100), a sixth college (Whitman) was constructed, and three of the colleges, including Whitman, were converted to four-year colleges, housing juniors and seniors along with freshmen and sophomores. In 2016 the trustees approved a further 10 percent increase in the number of undergraduates; this time two new colleges were to be constructed, one to accommodate the additional 500 students, and one to provide swing space in the short run and capacity for a further increase in undergraduate enrollment in the future.

In 1996, during the presidency of Harold Shapiro *64, the University made the first change in its motto since Wilson's address a century earlier, expanding its commitment beyond "the nation's service" to the "service of all nations." This reflected the growing international reach of the University—during Shapiro's presidency the percentage of international students in the undergraduate student body doubled to 10 percent and the Mpala Research Centre opened in central Kenya. Shapiro himself had first come to Princeton as a graduate student from Canada, and when elected he was Princeton's first Jewish president.

The revised motto also expressed a renewed and expanded commitment to service. Since 2001 opportunities for service have been enhanced and coordinated through one of the legacies of Princeton's 250th anniversary celebration, the Pace Center for Civic Engagement.

The Pace Center is one of many programs, centers, and activities located in the Frist Campus Center. When it opened in 2000 it brought to fruition an aspiration that traces back to the 1920s. Shapiro described it as "the absolute epicenter of campus life" and a "milestone for Princeton's history." The Frist Center serves so many purposes and brings together so many members of the campus community that it is difficult now to imagine the campus without it.

In 1998 the University reduced loan requirements for middle-income students on financial aid and eliminated them entirely for lower-income students. In 2001 it went further by adopting a policy of meeting the full need of financial aid recipients with grants—with no loan requirement, students could graduate debt-free. The University also excluded the value of the home from its calculation of need and extended its need-blind admission policy to include all international students. These policies secured Princeton's position as the national leader in assuring access and affordability for all admitted students, regardless of financial need.

Princeton in the Twenty-First Century

On June 15, 2001, Shirley Tilghman took office as Princeton's first woman president. Like Shapiro, she was a native of Canada. She had been in office only three months when the terrorist attacks of September 11 occurred, just as first-year students were arriving on campus. The attacks claimed the lives of 14 Princeton alumni (more than any other university except one); in 2003 the University dedicated a garden to their memory just outside the west door of Chancellor Green.

Over the course of Tilghman's presidency the percentage of undergraduates on financial aid increased from just under 40 percent to nearly 60 percent and the University began a concerted effort to increase the number of students in each class who receive federal Pell grants, which are awarded to students from lower economic backgrounds. Princeton ranked toward the bottom of its peer group when only about 7 percent of the Class of 2008 qualified; 15 years later Princeton ranked at the top when 24 percent of the Class of 2023 received the grants.

Tilghman launched several initiatives to expand Princeton's global presence. The Princeton Institute for International and Regional Studies was formed in 2003, and in 2007 it began offering global summer seminars, which allow students to study with faculty in locations around the world. In 2009 the University introduced a novel Bridge Year program that allows a number of admitted students each year to engage in a nine-month tuition-free international service program before beginning their freshman year.

In 2006 the University created an office of sustainability and two years later it issued its first comprehensive sustainability plan, which included a commitment to reduce carbon dioxide emissions to 1990 levels by 2020 without the purchase of off-campus offsets. By 2019 the University was close to achieving this goal and other benchmarks related to natural resource conservation, sustainable dining, construction, and other University operations. That year the University adopted a target of net zero campus greenhouse gas emissions by 2046.

The University established its first interdisciplinary research program on energy and the environment in 1971. In 1994 it founded what is now the High Meadows Environmental Institute (HMEI) as an interdisciplinary center for environmental research, education, and outreach. In 2008, a $100 million gift from Gerhard Andlinger '52 established an interdisciplinary research and education center for Energy and the Environment in the school of Engineering and Applied Science. In the words of its second director, chemical and biological engineering professor Yueh-Lin (Lynn) Loo *01, the Andlinger Center's mission is to find "new and creative ways to fuel societies and economies while minimizing carbon pollution."

During the first decade of the twenty-first century, the University established a center for innovation in engineering education and elevated the program in African American Studies to the status of a center, moving it to a prominent location on the front campus. The sciences were strengthened by the founding of the Princeton Neuroscience Institute; the construction of a new building and the recruitment of a group of exceptional new faculty for the Chemistry department; and a new library for the sciences that was named for its donor, Peter Lewis '55, and designed by the celebrated architect Frank Gehry.

In 2006 Tilghman announced a $101 million gift from Lewis to support a major new initiative in the creative and performing arts. The goal of the Lewis Center for the Arts, Tilghman said, was "to ensure that the arts become a part of every Princeton student's experience and that they play a greater and more central role in the life of our campus and community."

The Lewis Center is the academic home for Princeton's programs in Creative Writing, Dance, Music Theater, Theater, and Visual Arts and an interdisciplinary Atelier founded in 1994 by Princeton faculty member and Nobel Laureate Toni Morrison. When the Lewis Arts complex opened in 2017 it included a building for the department of Music, a building for theater and dance, a six-story arts tower, outdoor sculptures, a new train station, and a restaurant and café in two former train station buildings.

In 2013 Tilghman was succeeded by her provost, Christopher Eisgruber '83. As president he led efforts to increase the representation of low-income and first-generation students, and to protect from deportation students and other immigrants who came to this country as children. With his provost, David Lee *99, he established a Princeton Entrepreneurship Council to steer and coordinate efforts to "do entrepreneurship the Princeton way" and in 2020 the University appointed its first vice dean for innovation.

In 2018 the faculty voted to replace Princeton's traditional calendar, which conducted fall term exams in January, with a calendar that moved fall exams into December (effective with academic year 2020–21). The faculty also established an optional two-week January "Wintersession" program during which students may participate in a wide range of non-credit-bearing activities both on and off campus.

In 2016 the trustees adopted a strategic planning framework that called for increasing the undergraduate student body from 5,200 to 5,700 and reinstating a transfer admission program (suspended since 1990) with a focus on military veterans and community college students. In 2017 the University issued a campus planning framework that proposed initial development of a "lake campus" on portions of the lands in West Windsor that it began acquiring in the 1920s. The lake campus is located just south of Carnegie Lake, which was constructed in 1906 to provide a home for the University's rowing teams and as an amenity for the campus and the community. The 2017 framework also proposed locations for the two new residential colleges and for new and improved facilities for teaching and research in engineering and environmental studies.

In 2015 the University received title to the Scheide library, an extraordinary collection of some 2,500 rare books and manuscripts valued in the range of $300 million, one of many gifts to the University by William Scheide '36. (The collection had been housed in Firestone Library since 1959.) In 2019 the University completed a 10-year renovation of Firestone Library, and in 2020 it announced plans to begin construction of a new art museum that would double its size.

In 2015, after a 32-hour protest by the Black Justice League and other students in Nassau Hall, the trustees launched an extensive assessment of Woodrow Wilson's legacy at Princeton. In the spring of 2016 they issued a report in which they announced that they had decided to retain Wilson's name on the school of Public and International Affairs and Wilson College, but in 2020 they reconsidered and voted to remove his name, concluding that his "racist thinking and policies make him an inappropriate namesake for a school or college whose scholars, students, and alumni must stand firmly against racism in all its forms."

In their 2016 report the trustees modified the University's informal motto to connect Wilson's phrase "Princeton in the Nation's Service" with the phrase "In the Service of Humanity" that had been suggested by Supreme Court Justice Sonia Sotomayor '76 when she received the 2014 Woodrow Wilson Award, the highest honor Princeton can bestow on undergraduate alumni.

The trustees encouraged initiatives to diversify campus art and iconography. A committee was created to recommend the naming of buildings and spaces to recognize individuals who would bring a more diverse presence to campus, and its first recommendations were to rename West College for Toni Morrison and the auditorium in Robertson Hall for Nobel Laureate Sir Arthur Lewis, Princeton's first Black full professor. The committee later recommended naming a garden for Betsey Stockton; a roadway for Robert Rivers; an archway in East Pyne for James Collins Johnson, a fugitive slave who was a snack vendor on campus for almost 60 years in the second half of the nineteenth century, and a courtyard for Beatrix Farrand, the University's first landscape architect, who over more than three decades established landscape design as a defining feature of the Princeton campus.

Portraits of Morrison, Lewis, Rivers, Sotomayor, and Fields were added to the University's portrait collection, which in 2018 also commissioned portraits of basketball legend and former senator Bill Bradley '65; federal judge Denny Chin '75; molecular geneticist Elaine Fuchs *77; Ruth Simmons, a former senior administrator and trustee at Princeton who served as president of Smith College, Brown University—the first Black president in the Ivy League—and Prairie View A&M University; and Alan Turing *38, widely recognized as the father of computer science, a central figure in the successful effort to break the German Enigma codes during the Second World War, and an icon in the history of lesbian, gay, bisexual, and transgender rights.

In 2021 the trustees adopted principles to guide decisions about when and under what circumstances the University might remove or contextualize the names and representations of individuals on the campus as part of a wide-ranging set of initiatives to address "America's record of structural inequality and racism as well as Princeton's place in that history."

In 2020 the University, along with the rest of the world, was forced to contend with the COVID-19 pandemic. In March it moved all classes online and it remained fully remote for undergraduates through the fall semester before inviting students back to campus in the spring of 2021. The 2020 reunions and Commencement were converted to virtual formats, as were the 2021 reunions. With University encouragement and support, the campus community mobilized to pursue research, teaching, and service initiatives related to the pandemic and the University provided funds to support community organizations, families, and local businesses most severely impacted by it.

Princeton Today

Between 2000 and 2021, 26 Nobel Prizes were awarded to Princeton graduates and members of its faculty and research staff. No other university can claim as many twenty-first century winners. Between 1904 and 2020, only Harvard and Yale had more American Rhodes Scholars than Princeton, and Princeton ranks first in Churchill Scholarships, with 43 recipients since the award was first offered in 1963. Princeton students and faculty regularly win many other prestigious awards, make breakthrough discoveries, and achieve distinction as scholars, artists, activists, innovators, and in many other ways. In 2020 Princeton became the first school to win 500 Ivy League team championships; its women's teams claimed more than 200 of those championships, nearly one-third of all the women's titles in the history of the league.

In 2020 construction was underway or about to begin on the two new residential colleges, new homes for engineering and environmental studies, a new art museum, and the initial development of the lake campus. Initiatives were underway to combat systemic racism and expand teaching and research in fields ranging from bioengineering to Indigenous Studies.

Princeton's undergraduate enrollment in 2019 was 5,328, with 50.3 percent men and 49.7 percent women.[5] The student body was 40.1 percent white, 22.2 percent Asian American, 10.6 percent Hispanic/Latino, 7.9 percent Black/African American, 5.3 percent multiracial, 0.3 percent Native American and Pacific Islander, and 12.2 percent international. More than 60 percent received financial aid. In most years more than 80 percent of the class graduates debt-free; for those who choose to borrow, average indebtedness at graduation is just over $9,000.

Graduate school enrollment in 2020 was 3,065, with 90 percent pursuing doctoral degrees. Some

---

[5] While 2020 data for the graduate school and the faculty were not skewed by the COVID-19 pandemic, undergraduate enrollment in 2020 is unrepresentative as many students chose to take leaves of absence when the University prohibited most undergraduates from being on campus that fall. The 2019 data for undergraduates presents a much more accurate picture.

41 percent of the students were women and 41 percent were international. Among the US citizens and permanent residents, 55 percent were white, 15 percent Asian, 12 percent Hispanic/Latino, 5 percent Black/African American, 5 percent multiracial, and 8 percent were listed as unknown. By division, 21 percent were in the humanities, 23 percent in engineering, 26 percent in the social sciences, and 29 percent in the natural sciences.

In the fall of 2020, the faculty totaled 1,295, including 520 professors, 123 associate professors, 181 assistant professors, 18 instructors, 330 lecturers, 27 senior lecturers, 7 lecturers with the rank of professor, and 89 visitors. Excluding visitors, 455 members of the faculty were women and 277 self-identified as members of minority groups (114 as underrepresented minorities). Of the full professors, 27 percent were women; with respect to ethnicity, 10 percent of the full professors were Asian, four percent Black, two percent Hispanic, 80 percent white, and four percent unknown.

The academic units authorized to be the primary academic home for tenured and tenure-track faculty included 33 departments, the schools of Architecture and Public and International Affairs, the Lewis Center for the Arts, the Lewis-Sigler Institute for Integrative Genomics, the Princeton Neuroscience Institute, the program in American Studies, the program in Gender and Sexuality Studies, the program in Linguistics in the Council of the Humanities, and the University Center for Human Values. The University also pursues teaching and research through a wide range of other programs, centers, and institutes.

In 2020, of the 23 officers of the University, 13 were women and seven (including five of the women) were people of color.

In their 2016 strategic framework the trustees acknowledged that the University's "financial strength results first and foremost from the longstanding generosity of its alumni and friends" and "wise stewardship of the University's endowment." The endowment undergirds the University's excellence and its affordability; it covers roughly 60 percent of the University's annual operating budget; helps fund its highest priority strategic initiatives; and enables it to weather unanticipated challenges. By 2020 the endowment totaled almost $27 billion, making it the fifth largest overall and the largest per student in the country.

2046

Aaron Lemonick *54, dean of the graduate school and then for 16 years dean of the faculty, liked to say that life is what happens when you are expecting something else. The COVID-19 pandemic was a stark reminder that Princeton will continue to have to overcome unforeseen challenges as it makes its way toward its 300th anniversary in 2046. But its history of resilience and its confidence in the vitality of its mission suggest that the University will overcome these challenges and continue to "advance learning through scholarship, research, and teaching of unsurpassed quality . . . with a pervasive commitment to serve the nation and the world."

Most of the students who will graduate in 2046 will have been born in the 2020s. Their Princeton will be larger and more diverse, and they will have access to more extensive academic and artistic offerings. Technologies available by midcentury almost certainly will expand the University's capacities to pursue scholarship, research, and teaching, and students will have access to facilities only now being designed, perhaps along with others not yet even contemplated. The lake campus probably will have grown beyond its initial footprint, and the development of the Springdale lands for educational purposes may have begun.

And yet, while much will change, there is every reason to believe that the University will retain its "distinctive sense of place" and its other defining features. The University's 2026 campus plan noted that "there is something about the look and feel of the campus that is immutable, powerful, and both comforting and uplifting . . . it has managed to retain its core characteristics while becoming much larger, much more multifaceted, and much more diverse." This is likely to continue to be so.

One of Princeton's alumni once said that the University's purpose "is to advance the cause of humanity through the leverage of uncommon individuals and important ideas." This, too, is likely to continue to be so.

In 1974 Princeton won an Academy Award for a short documentary, available on its website, titled *A Search for Answers*. This is likely to remain an apt description of what animates Princeton—a search for answers, along with a continuing commitment, in the words of its trustees, to "prepare students for lives of service, civic engagement, and ethical leadership."

EVOLUTION OF THE PHYSICAL CAMPUS

Princeton's campus is widely considered one of the most beautiful in the world. It sits on high ground, with its most historic buildings facing the main street of the town whose name it adopted in 1896. It was the first college in the world to be set back from the street, thereby creating an expanse of land between buildings and street that in 1774 became the first collegiate space to be described as a "campus."

Despite early plans that called for symmetry, over time the College became characterized by an appealing asymmetry. It exudes a sense of both timelessness and spaciousness, offering a pleasing blend of traditional and modern architectural styles; a balance among open and enclosed spaces; and an array of thoughtfully designed landscapes, archways, pathways, and vistas. The campus is known for its careful attention to the relationship between structure and landscape; in the words of University architect Ron McCoy *80, they "co-exist to create a powerful sense of identity and an authentic sense of place."

As the College outgrew its original site, it expanded first to the immediate south and then east and west along established ridgelines. In time, it expanded farther south through a series of downward-stepped terraces, leading inexorably toward the southern border of its Princeton lands, a lake created in 1906, a former barge canal, and a towpath. Thanks to trustee foresightedness in the early- to mid-twentieth century, the University owns about as many acres south of the lake in West Windsor as its campus lands north of the lake in Princeton, and today's campus plans anticipate that, at some point in the not-too-distant future, the lake is likely to be more in the middle of the campus than along its edge.

The writer Lewis Thomas '33 described Princeton as a place "deliberately designed for thinking and kept that way down all its years." After more than two and a half centuries, the campus remains simultaneously a site of historic significance and a constantly evolving home, workshop, and source of inspiration for students, faculty, staff, alumni, and friends who make the University what it is—a community dedicated to excellence in teaching, learning, scholarship, and research, in service to the nation, the world, and humanity.

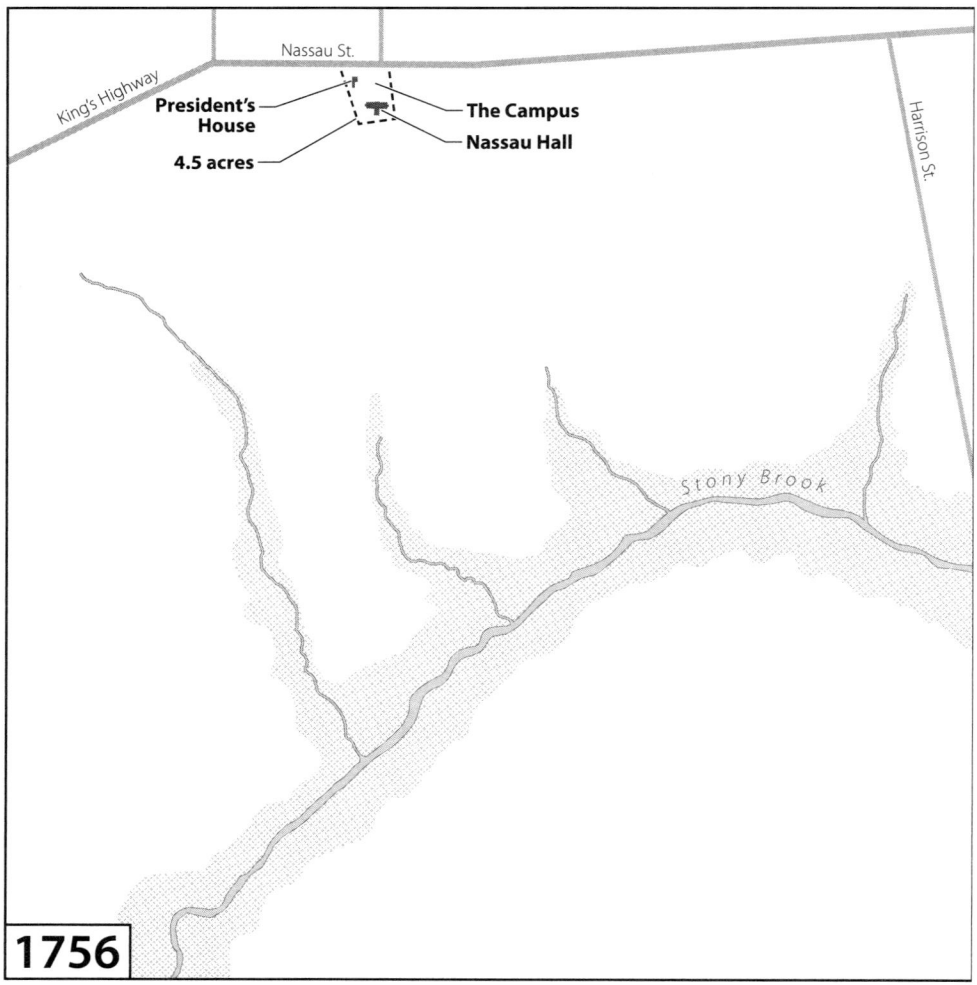

1756

The original Princeton campus was sited along a Lenni Lenape trail between the Raritan and Delaware rivers on land that separated the fields and stream valleys of south Jersey from the mountains and hills to the north. In the late 1600s the trail became the King's Highway (later Nassau Street) within the village of Prince-towne. By the mid-1700s, because it was located roughly halfway between New York and Philadelphia, the agrarian village became prosperous as a convenient overnight stop for travelers. It successfully competed against New Brunswick in persuading the College of New Jersey to relocate from Newark. Its first two buildings were constructed on a 4.5-acre site donated by Nathaniel FitzRandolph: Nassau Hall, the largest academic building in the colonies, and a nearby house where the president could keep close watch on his charges. The well-known carpenter/architect Robert Smith is reported to have consulted architectural pattern books to design Nassau Hall in a vernacular version of the Classical Georgian style. Although he intended that the walls be built of brick, it was constructed more frugally by a local carpenter using locally quarried stone. With its plaster still drying, the hall was occupied by Princeton's second president, Aaron Burr Sr., and his students in 1756. The vistas from its hilltop location, especially to the south, across meadows and woodlands to the Stony Brook, created a welcoming prospect that augured well for the future of the College.

Evolution of the Physical Campus 19

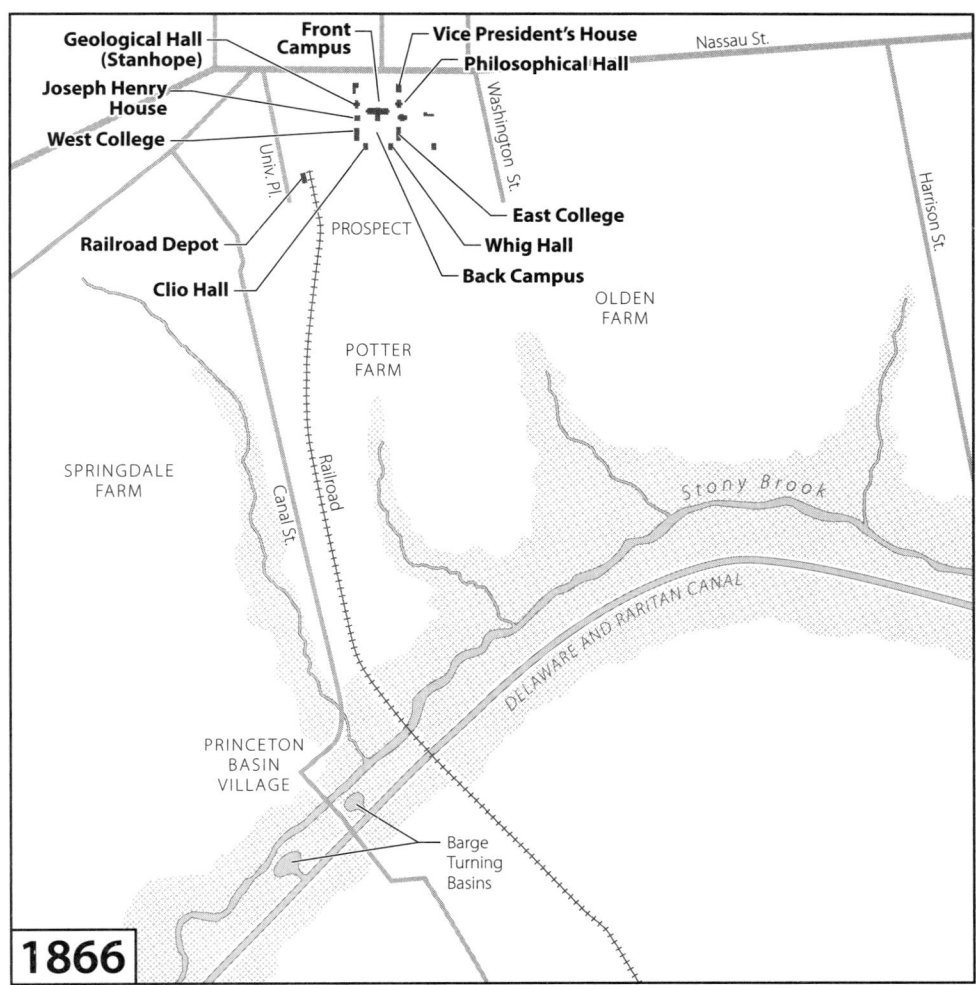

1866

The first expansion of the College occurred after an 1802 fire at Nassau Hall. When the reconstruction planned by Benjamin Latrobe (the first professionally trained architect in America) was completed under budget, he subsequently designed two flanking buildings: Geological Hall (now Stanhope), and its mirror image Philosophical Hall (demolished in 1871 to allow construction of Chancellor Green). That orderly grouping later grew into a formal quadrangle with compatible buildings symmetrically arranged around Nassau Hall at its center. They included a vice president's house, situated opposite the president's house on the front campus; two other houses, including one that was the home of physics professor Joseph Henry; and on the back campus two dormitories, East College (1833) and West College (1836), and two debating halls, Whig and Clio (1838). This formal arrangement followed a master plan drawn in 1832 by Henry, who left in 1846 to become the first director of the Smithsonian Institution. Often distracted by matters of student discipline and guided by a Calvinist frugality amidst a scarcity of resources, the College trustees gave little thought to campus beautification. By the end of the 1830's, connections to the enlarged campus and town included both the busy Delaware and Raritan Canal (on which students occasionally found time to row) and a rail link to the main line of what became the Pennsylvania Railroad. In 1865 a train depot was located just below what is now Blair Arch.

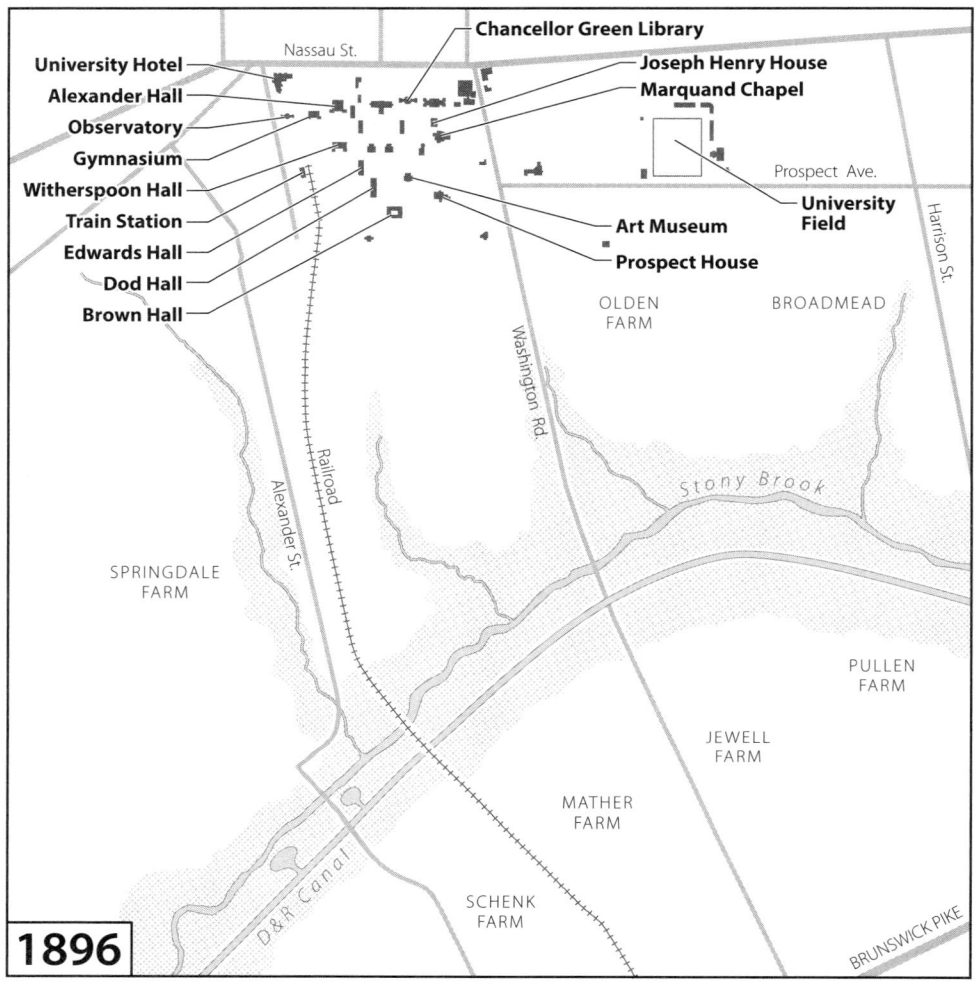

1896

No new buildings were constructed from the late 1840s to the end of the Civil War. Newly elected President James McCosh arrived from Scotland in the spring of 1868 with the goal of transforming the College into a university by enriching both its curriculum and its physical character. Having experienced the robust architecture of Queens College in Belfast and the picturesque estates of the English nobility, McCosh was disappointed by the College's spare buildings and sparse grounds. As early as 1869, he urged the hiring of a landscape gardener, and two years later he proposed the well-respected Donald Grant Mitchell "to furnish a plan for the improvement of the College." McCosh himself participated in the planting of trees and the laying out of paths to create an expanded park-like setting. He also commissioned outstanding architects of the day to create a rich showplace of architectural styles that would open the eyes of his students to a broader world beyond the campus. Beginning with Chancellor Green Library (1873) designed in the "Ruskinian Gothic" style by Alexander Potter, McCosh oversaw the construction of 13 buildings over his 20-year tenure, including three dormitories. Among the finest of his buildings was Witherspoon Hall (1877), designed by Potter in the image of a grand Victorian hotel and sited to impress travelers arriving by train. Many of the McCosh era buildings later fell victim to disastrous fires and changing architectural tastes.

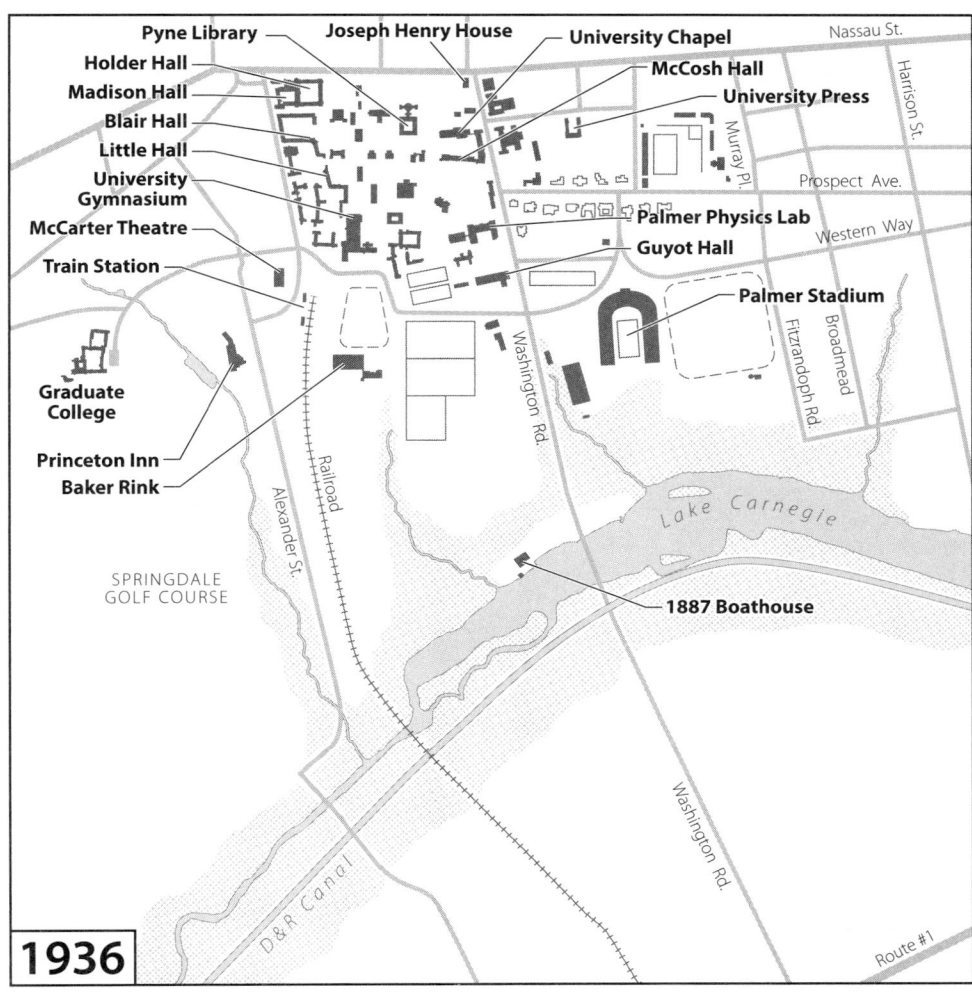

1936

When the College of New Jersey renamed itself Princeton University in 1896, many of its new leaders were former students of McCosh. Ironically, they immediately set out to change the campus McCosh had created. Trustee Moses Taylor Pyne 1877 and others, including soon-to-be president Woodrow Wilson 1879, were committed to the notion that a university should look like Oxford and Cambridge. They promptly commissioned architects to design new buildings in the appropriate Tudor Gothic style, beginning with Philadelphians Cope and Stewardson, who conceived Blair Hall (1897), Little Hall (1899), and University Gymnasium (1903) to form a "medieval wall" separating the campus from University Place and the railroad. After Bostonian Ralph Adams Cram was hired as supervising architect in 1906, his graduate college (1913) and University Chapel (1928) became masterpieces of the style. However, the symmetrical Beaux Arts formality of his 1911 master plan was never accepted by Princetonians who preferred more picturesque, asymmetrical vistas like the views to and from Blair that resulted from adjustments to Cram's plan by Charles Klauder, whose 15 buildings in the Collegiate Gothic style exceeded any other architect. Beginning with her landscaping of the graduate college, the unparalleled artistry of landscape gardener Beatrix Farrand enhanced both grounds and buildings for three decades.

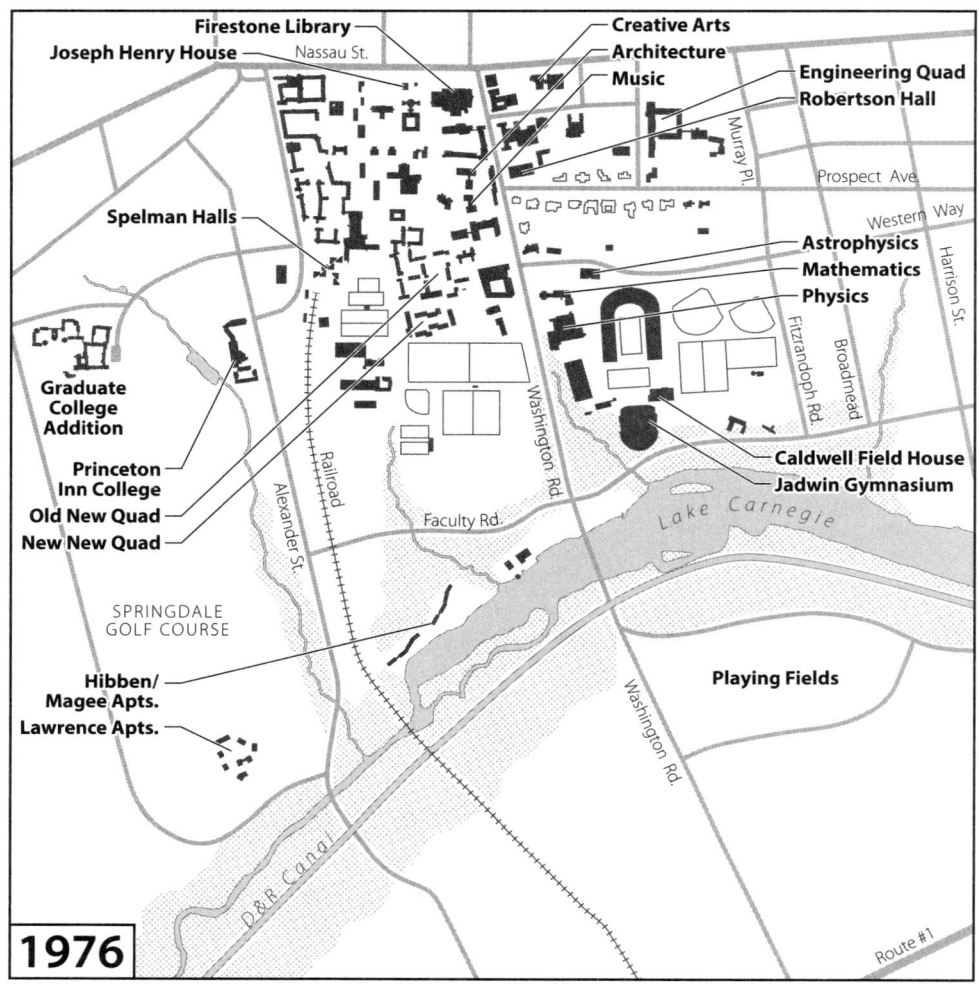

1976

Due to the Great Depression and World War II, there was no substantive change to the campus from the mid-1930s to 1960, except for the construction of Firestone Library (1948), which along with the reconstruction at Dillon Gymnasium was the last hurrah for twentieth-century Gothic. In the 1960s a tidal wave of "modern" buildings swept across tennis courts and playing fields to become the Old New Quad and the New New Quad—later Wilson College (renamed First College in 2020) and Butler College. East of Washington Road, new buildings were constructed for the school of Engineering and Applied Science, the school of Public and International Affairs, Astrophysics, Mathematics, and Physics. A decade of unprecedented construction ended with the completion of Jadwin Gymnasium (1969). Shortly thereafter, the 1969 decision to admit undergraduate women required additional growth: the repurposing and expansion of the Princeton Inn as a residential college (later Forbes), as well as the construction of apartments with kitchens at Spelman Halls (1971), which were designed by I. M. Pei. Landscape treatments during this period of rapid expansion were generally limited to modest, supplementary plantings in support of individual projects, although the unique precast structural system at Spelman did allow its careful placement within an existing stand of tall evergreen trees.

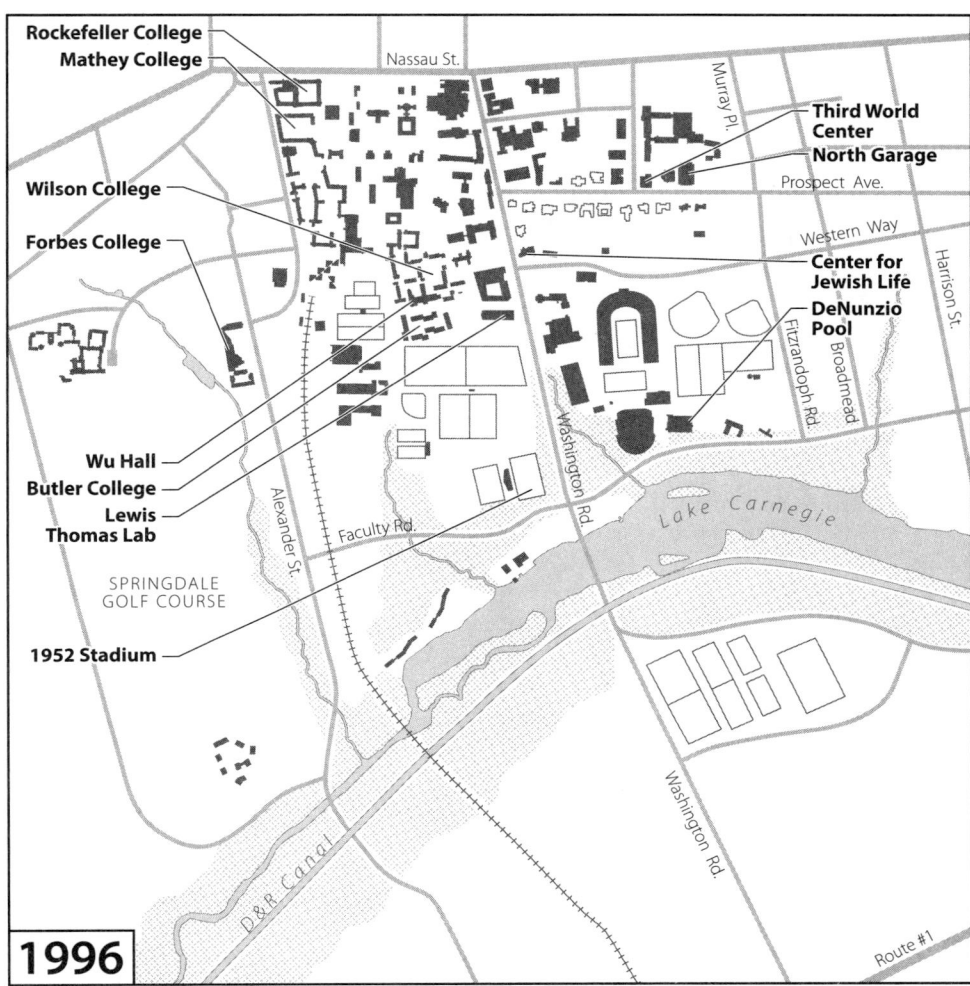

1996

Late twentieth-century planning focused on improvements within the existing campus. The Committee on Residential Life (CURL) concluded that freshmen and sophomores would be better served by living and eating in five residential colleges (Butler, Forbes, Mathey, Rockefeller, and Wilson). The 1982 plan relied heavily on the judicious use of existing facilities; the major new building was the dining hall for Butler College, Wu Hall (1983), designed by Robert Venturi '47, *50 and Denise Scott Brown in an idiosyncratic modern style that drew upon contextual and historical references for visual complexity. At nearby Lewis Thomas Laboratory (1986), Venturi and Scott Brown displayed their concept of a "decorated shed," using two-dimensional patterns to give visual interest to the façade of an otherwise simple building. Although Venturi disavowed the term, his several projects and those of other architects, like Robert Stern's Center for Jewish Life (CJL), marked an era of postmodernism in the campus's architecture. During this period, most growth consisted of "in-fill" buildings on restrictive sites or on portions of parking lots made available by the first campus parking structure, North Garage (1991), by the Boston firm of Machado Silvetti. Because such sites were intentionally of a limited size, the scope of appropriate landscaping was also limited.

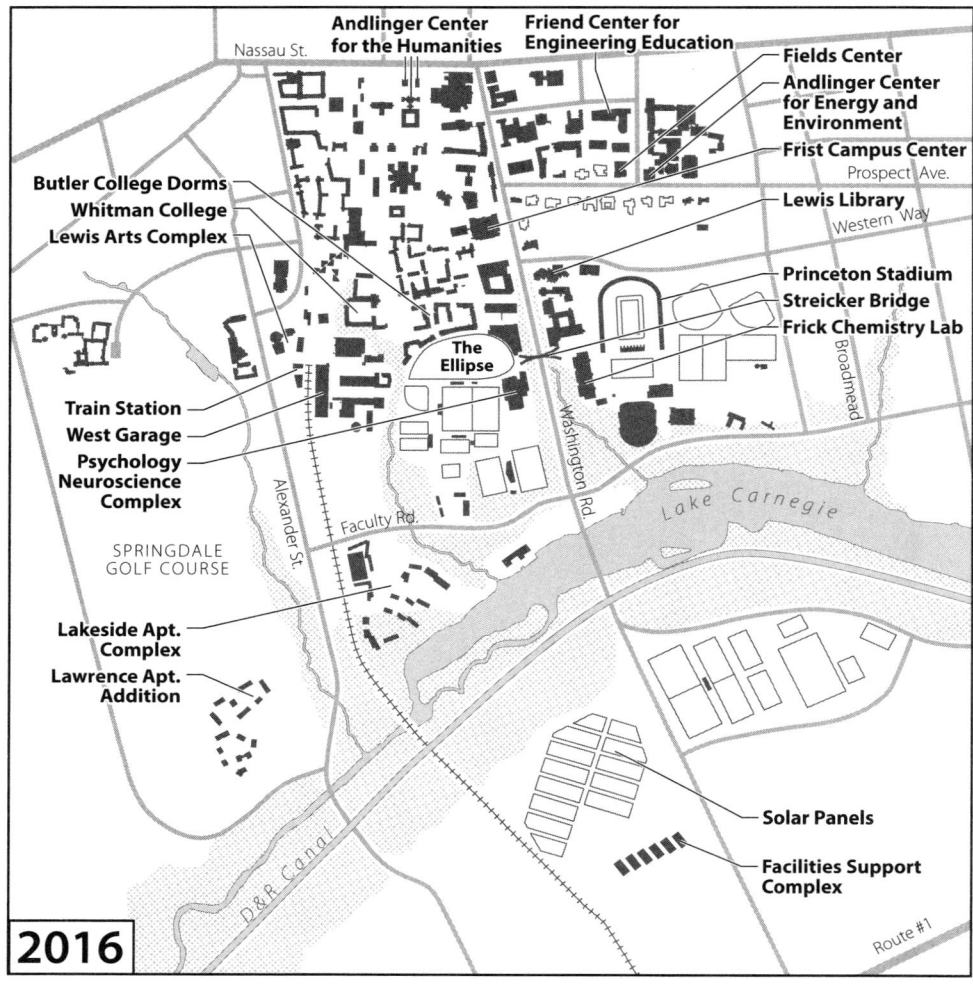

2016

The replacement of iconic but crumbling Palmer Stadium with Princeton Stadium (designed by Rafael Vinoly) in 1998, and Venturi's repurposing and expansion of venerable Palmer Hall two years later to become the Frist Campus Center highlighted campus development at the turn of the century. The Machado/Silvetti master plan calling for an architectural edge to the south campus was realized by the construction of two dormitories and a laboratory along a gently curving arc at "The Ellipse" (Poe/Pardee fields). Under President Shirley Tilghman, subsequent growth was characterized by a creative tension between tradition and innovation. On the west, Whitman College (2007), by Demetri Porphyrios *80, harkened back to the Collegiate Gothic style of Cope and Stewardson. Meanwhile, east of Washington Road, the sculptural, "deconstructivist" Lewis Science Library (2008), by "Starchitect" Frank Gehry, was realized as an entrée to the modern natural science neighborhood assembled since the 1960s. In between, replacement dorms for Butler College (2009) by Harry Cobb were constructed in moderating modern style. Elsewhere, the natural science neighborhood was extended with a new Frick Chemistry Laboratory (2010) by Sir Michael Hopkins and a Psychology/Neuroscience complex (2012) by Rafael Moneo. South of McCarter Theatre, the Lewis Arts complex took shape by the end of 2016. When Steven Holl's buildings were occupied a year later, their stark modern style echoed the earlier Bauhaus modernism of nearby New South and Spelman Halls. To soften the impact of big laboratories and other large building programs, robust landscape plans by Michael Van Valkenburgh were implemented, including the planting of heavily treed areas in the southern part of the campus.

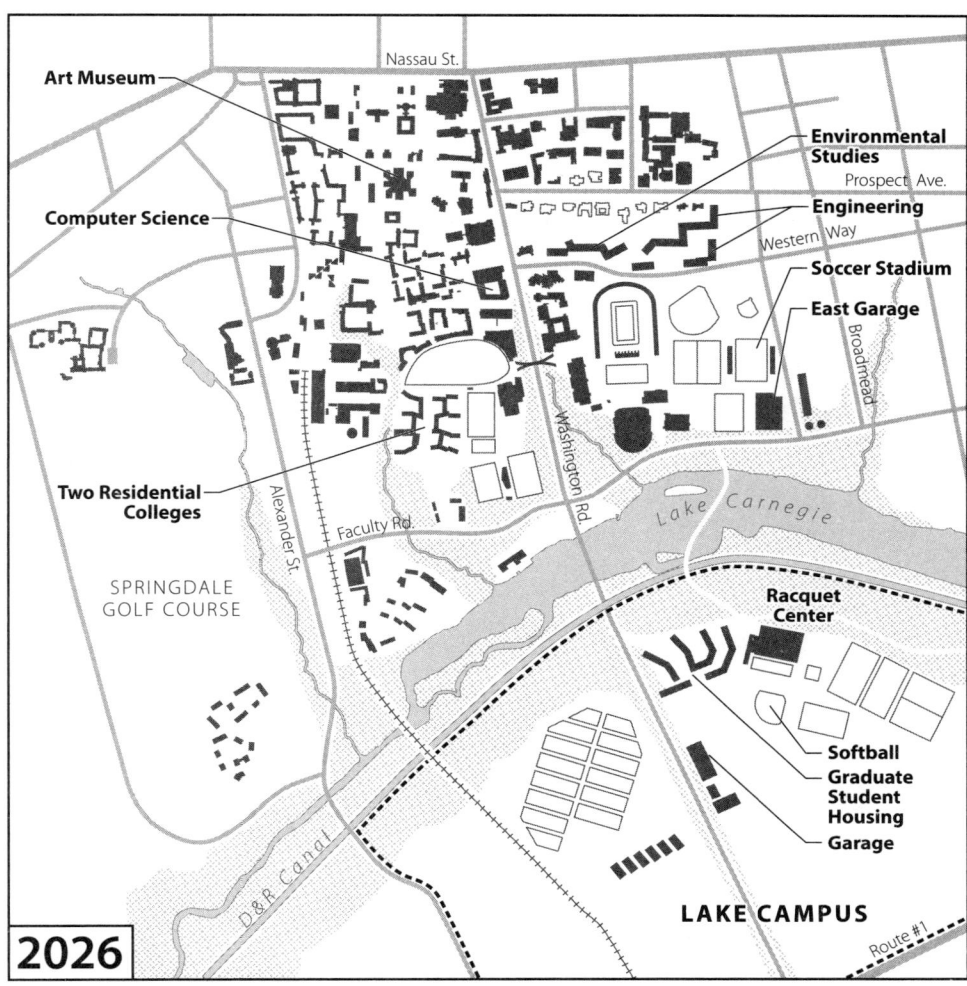

2026

The campus master plan for 2026 spoke not in terms of "neighborhoods" but of "campuses": a central campus, an east campus, and, across Lake Carnegie in West Windsor, a lake campus. A proposal to construct two new residential colleges to accommodate a 10 percent increase in the number of undergraduates received earliest attention. Designed by Deborah Berke, dean of architecture at Yale, the colleges were sited just south of Poe Field, displacing several athletic facilities, including softball, tennis, and soccer. A new softball field and a new racquet center were planned as part of the initial development of the lake campus, along with graduate student and post-doc housing, a new transit hub, employee parking, administrative space, and capacity to accommodate partners in the University's initiatives related to entrepreneurship and innovation. On the east campus, new construction for engineering and environmental studies was planned along Ivy Lane and Western Way. Although not addressed in the campus plan, an additional major project for the 2020s was a new and expanded art museum designed by David Adjaye, architect of the celebrated National Museum of African American History and Culture in Washington, DC. The campus plan identified the lands of the Springdale Golf Course as a site for future development, but not before the club's lease expired in 2036.

IN THE NATION'S SERVICE AND THE SERVICE OF HUMANITY

On September 26, 2015, the Princeton Board of Trustees approved a mission statement that reaffirmed the University's "pervasive commitment to serve the nation and the world." In a strategic planning document issued five months later, the trustees elaborated as follows on this core commitment to service:

> Service can take a variety of forms. Princetonians may hold leadership roles in the public or private sectors; they may involve themselves in local community organizations or international aid efforts; they may join the military or dedicate themselves to teaching. They may, as [Supreme Court] Justice [Sonia] Sotomayor ['76] pointed out, render quiet acts of kindness to friends or relatives who are in need. The commitment to service is not ultimately about what vocation or avocation one pursues, but about how one pursues it. Princeton should reinforce in its students an appreciation for the value of service as well as the skills and habits of mind needed to serve effectively.

This commitment to service is articulated in the University's informal motto—"In the Nation's Service and the Service of Humanity"—that is etched into a stone medallion where the walkways cross in front of Nassau Hall. The motto combines the phrase "Princeton in the Nation's Service" from an address given by Woodrow Wilson 1879, then a faculty member and later Princeton's 13th president, at the University's sesquicentennial in 1896, with the phrase "In the Service of Humanity" suggested by Justice Sotomayor when she received the Woodrow Wilson Award, the highest distinction the University can bestow on undergraduate alumni, in 2014.

In his address, Wilson argued that "When all is said and done, it is not learning but the spirit of service that will give a college place in the public annals of the nation." Princeton, he said, was founded "not to breed politicians, but to give young men such training as, it might be hoped, would fit them handsomely for

In 2016 the University modified its informal motto to connect the phrase "Princeton in the Nation's Service" from the 1896 sesquicentennial address of Woodrow Wilson 1879 with the phrase "In the Service of Humanity" that was suggested by Supreme Court Justice Sonia Sotomayor '76 when she received the 2014 Woodrow Wilson Award. The motto is engraved in this stone medallion on the front campus along with an expression of appreciation to alumni for "their devotion to the University and its mission of education, scholarship, and service."

the pulpit and for the grave duties of citizens and neighbors." In his inaugural address as Princeton president in 1902, he said, "We are not put into this world to sit still and know, we are put into it to act."

On its website today, the University says, "service and civic engagement are central to what it means to be a Princetonian... Various elements of the University's mission—educating students, discovering new knowledge, and developing students' character—have a common end goal, to improve the community and world around us... Students learn about how to contribute to society during their time on campus, faculty serve the public through their scholarship, and alumni go on to lives of leadership and engagement."

Ornaments of the State/Servants of All

This commitment to service was injected into the University's DNA from its earliest conception. One of the founders wrote: "Though our great intention was to erect a seminary for educating Ministers of the Gospel, yet we hope it will be useful in other learned professions—Ornaments of the State as well as the Church." In Princeton's first baccalaureate address, Princeton's fourth president, Samuel Davies, called upon the 11 members of the graduating class of 1760 to "serve your generation. Live not for yourself but the Publick. Be the Servants of the Church; the Servants of your Country; the Servants of all... Esteem yourselves... by how much the more useful you are. Let... your own private Interests yield to the common Good."

Princeton's early alumni included many "ornaments of the state" who helped create and shape the new nation. The Continental Congress (1774–1789) numbered among its members some 34 delegates who had attended Princeton, and other delegates included Princeton president John Witherspoon, the only college president and only clergyman to sign the Declaration of Independence, and Princeton trustee Elias Boudinot, who presided over the Congress and moved the nation's capital to Princeton in the summer of 1783.

The Constitutional Convention of 1787 was attended by more alumni of Princeton than of any other college or university and Princetonians were influential in formulating the three major proposals considered by the convention: the "large states" Virginia plan, drafted by James Madison 1771; the "small states" New Jersey plan presented by William Paterson 1763; and the ultimately successful Connecticut compromise proposed by Oliver Ellsworth 1766, later the only Princetonian to serve as chief justice of the US Supreme Court.

Madison is generally recognized as the central guiding hand in crafting the Constitution and advocating for its adoption through the Federalist papers. He went on to serve the country as a member of the House of Representatives, secretary of state, and president, and for the last decade of his life served Princeton as the first president of its alumni association.

Another early Princetonian, Benjamin Rush 1760, served Princeton by persuading John Witherspoon to leave Scotland to become its president and served the country as a delegate to the Continental Congress, a signer of the Declaration of Independence, and an army doctor during the Revolutionary War. But his service to humanity extended into many other fields. He helped organize the first antislavery society in America, the Pennsylvania Society for Promoting the Abolition of Slavery and the Relief of Free Negroes Unlawfully Held in Bondage (also called the Pennsylvania Abolition Society), and later became its president. He founded the Philadelphia Dispensary for the relief of the poor, the first of its kind in the United States. He founded Dickinson College, was a charter trustee of Franklin College (later Franklin and Marshall), and became an ardent incorporator of the Young Ladies Academy in Philadelphia to provide access to education for women. As a doctor, he introduced extensive reforms in the treatment of the mentally ill and published the first textbook on psychiatry in America. The American Psychiatric Association considers him the "Father of American Psychiatry."

The Nation's Service and the Service of All Nations

During Princeton's 250th anniversary in 1996, at the initiative of President Harold Shapiro, the phrase "in the service of all nations" was added to Wilson's hundred-year-old phrase "in the nation's service" to recognize the University's growing international reach. (This change was superseded in 2016 by the adoption of the current motto.) From the beginning, service to the nation, or to all nations, was never understood to apply solely to government or military service, but Princetonians have played leading roles in these forms of service from the founding of the country.

Two Princetonians, Madison and Wilson, served as president of the United States; two, Aaron Burr Jr. 1772 and George Mifflin Dallas 1810, served as vice president; and Michelle Obama '85 served as first lady.

More than three dozen alumni have served in the cabinet or in positions with cabinet rank, some in more than one position. (George Shultz '42, for example, was secretary of State, Treasury, and Labor, and James A. Baker III '52 was secretary of State and Treasury, as well as White House chief of staff.)

Some 86 alumni from 26 states have served in the United States Senate—there have been only 20 years since the founding of the country without a Princetonian in the Senate—and there has not been even one year since 1789 without a Princetonian in the House of Representatives. More than 225 Princetonians have served in the House, representing 29 states and territories.

Eleven Princeton graduates, including Ellsworth as chief justice, have served on the Supreme Court; when Elena Kagan '81 joined Samuel Alito '72 and Sonia Sotomayor '76 on the bench in 2010, it marked the first time since 1842 that three sitting justices had attended Princeton, and the first time ever that three graduates of Princeton had served at the same time.

Princetonians in other forms of government service have transformed everything from the nation's culture to its economy. One of the best-loved institutions in Washington, DC—the Smithsonian Institution—was led for its first 32 years by Princeton faculty member Joseph Henry as its founding secretary. Faculty member and alumnus James Billington '50 served for 28 years as the Librarian of Congress, while Paul Volcker '49 chaired the Federal Reserve, as did former faculty member Ben Bernanke and Jerome Powell '75. Longtime dean of the faculty J. Douglas Brown 1919 *1928 was one of the principal architects of the Social Security system. Several Princeton faculty members and alumni chaired the White House Council of Economic Advisers; in 2021 Cecilia Rouse, professor of economics and dean of the school of Public and International Affairs, became the first African American to chair the council as the position was elevated to cabinet rank.

Outside the Beltway

Princetonians have also been leaders in government positions outside of Washington. Fifty-one Princeton alumni have served as governors of 21 states (three of the governors, Adlai Stevenson 1922, Thomas Kean '57, and Mitchell Daniels Jr. '71, received the Woodrow Wilson Award). Countless others have served as mayors and other local officials, including William Hudnut III '54, four-term mayor of Indianapolis and also a Wilson Award recipient, and Eric Johnson *03, mayor of the Texas city named for one of the Princetonians who served as vice president, George Dallas. Other alumni have contributed to their communities on school boards, civic organizations, and service agencies; as religious leaders; and in countless other ways.

Princeton alumni have also held senior positions in Native American governments: Regis Pecos '77 as governor of Cochiti Pueblo; Helen Blue-Redner '85 as chair of the Upper Sioux tribe; Rex Lee Jim '86 as vice president of the Navajo Nation; and Doreen Hobson McPaul '95 as attorney general of the Navajo Nation. Kevin Gover '78 served as director of the National Museum of the American Indian after a career working with Native communities in legal affairs, academia, and the US government, including as secretary of Indian affairs, the highest-ranking Native American in the nation.

In addition to serving as governor of Illinois, Adlai Stevenson was the US ambassador to the United Nations, and many alumni have served as ambassadors to countries around the world. The first recipient of the Wilson Award, Norman Armour 1909, was posted to ambassadorships in Haiti, Canada, Chile, Argentina, Spain, Venezuela, and Guatemala. Other ambassadors who received the Wilson Award included Harlan Cleveland '38 (NATO), George Kennan 1925 (Soviet Union and Yugoslavia), and J. Stapleton Roy '56 (China).

Princeton alumni have also led other countries. Syngman Rhee *1910 was the first Korean student at Princeton and president of South Korea from 1948 to 1960; Paul van Zeeland *1921 was prime minister of Belgium from 1936 to 1937 and Chung Un-chan *78 filled that post in South Korea in 2009–10. Pedro Pablo Kucsynski *61 was president of Peru from 2016–18.

Princetonians have served in the military in all the nation's wars; the names of those who gave their lives are engraved in the memorial atrium in Nassau Hall. Students today continue to commit to military service through their participation in Army, Navy, and Air Force ROTC. Alumni have served in senior civilian positions as secretaries of war, defense, the Navy, the Army, and the Air Force. Navy Admiral William

Crowe *65 served as chair of the Joint Chiefs of Staff from 1985 to 1989 (and as a Princeton trustee from 1997 to 2000), and Army General Mark Milley '80 became chair in 2019. Army General Andrew Goodpaster *50 served as staff director of the joint chiefs in 1966–67 and as NATO supreme allied commander from 1969 to 1974.

One special form of service occurred at the end of World War II when art museum director Ernest DeWald *16 and other Princeton faculty and alumni were among the "Monuments Men" who were sent by the allied armies through Europe to preserve art and other cultural artifacts. Their recoveries received widespread recognition in 2014 with the release of a movie by that name; DeWald's diary describing his experiences is in Firestone Library.

Wilson Award Winners

The Wilson Award was established in 1956 as an "ever-living recognition of Woodrow Wilson's conviction that education is for 'use' and as a continuing confirmation . . . of the high aims expressed in his memorable phrase, 'Princeton in the Nation's Service.'" The award is presented each year at Alumni Day, and while it has recognized many alumni in government service, it also has recognized service in many other callings, including judges, writers, journalists, scientists, doctors, architects, humanitarians, heads of a broad range of organizations and institutions; a consumer advocate (Ralph Nader '55); and a queen (Queen Noor of Jordan, the former Lisa Halaby '73). Other winners have ranged from icons of the silver screen—James Stewart '32—to champions for diversity and inclusion (including John Rogers '80, Rajiv Vinnakota '93, Anthony Romero '87, and Mellody Hobson '91), and the influential pediatrician and author T. Berry Brazelton Jr. '40. (A list of Wilson award winners can be found on page 526, and a list of winners of the James Madison Medal, the comparable recognition for graduate alumni, can be found on page 519.)

The first woman to win the Wilson Award, Wendy Kopp '89, was honored for taking a concept she first developed in her senior thesis and turning it into a national organization, Teach For America, through which college graduates teach for at least two years in some of the nation's most under-resourced public schools. By the end of its third decade, Teach For America had trained and placed more than 60,000 teachers across America—in cities and in rural areas, and in both primary and secondary schools. More than 16,000 are still classroom teachers or principals, and Teach For America has spawned similar enterprises around the world.[1]

Many other senior theses over the years have led to lives of service. To cite just one example: the 1981 senior thesis of future trustee and part-time faculty member Martin Johnson '81 gave rise to Isles, Inc., a Trenton-based nonprofit community development and environmental organization whose mission is to foster self-reliant families and healthy, sustainable communities. In carrying out its mission, Isles frequently engages Princeton students in its work.

Many Forms of Service

While Princeton's commitment to service is certainly exemplified in all these ways, its scope is both broader and deeper. It encompasses contributions to the health, prosperity, and well-being of society that result from the research conducted by Princeton faculty, the innovations of Princeton entrepreneurs, and the contributions to culture of Princeton writers and artists of all kinds. The commitment is also expressed through the meaningful ways Princetonians live their lives; pursue their careers, avocations, and volunteer activities; and strengthen their families and communities.

Since the University is an educational institution, it is not surprising that its leaders and alumni have contributed to the expansion of educational opportunity in multiple ways. President John Maclean Jr. 1816 was one of the earliest advocates of public education in New Jersey and an architect of the state's public school system. In 1966 President Robert Goheen chaired the commission that proposed that New Jersey create a system of community colleges. Princeton alumni were the founders or first presidents, or played critical catalytic roles, in the creation and early development of almost 20 colleges and universities in the United States (including Lincoln University, the country's first historically Black college or university), and, in the case of the United Nations University, in Tokyo.

---

[1] While alumni for many years taught, counseled, and became headmasters at private secondary schools, not until the creation of the Teacher Preparation program in 1967 could Princeton students become certified to teach in public schools; Teach For America provided teaching opportunities for graduating students who had not participated in Teacher Preparation.

Beginning in 1962, Princeton faculty member David Hazen '48 *49 represented Princeton on a consortium that helped create the India Institute of Technology in Kanpur. Princeton faculty member and Nobel Laureate in Economics Sir Arthur Lewis, among many other forms of service, was the first West Indian-born principal and then vice chancellor of the University of the West Indies and served as chancellor of the University of Guyana. A group of alumni who created a program in China known as Princeton-in-Peking established the Princeton School of Public Affairs at Yenching University in Beijing in 1923.

Princeton-in-Peking—now Princeton in Asia, joined for the past two decades by Princeton in Africa and Princeton in Latin America—is one of several student-initiated service projects that trace their origins to an organization known as the Philadelphian Society, which held its first meeting on campus on February 4, 1825. According to the *Daily Princetonian*, the society was formed for the purpose of "associated action in doing good." The society had strong religious roots, and former dean of religious life Thomas Breidenthal described the aim of the society as promoting "personal holiness lived out in service to others."

Student Service

Despite its religious origins, the Philadelphia Society was ecumenical in its approach, and over time it established and nurtured not only Princeton in Asia but YMCAs in Princeton and Beijing, the latter in 1906. It also founded the Princeton-Blairstown Summer Camp (now the Princeton-Blairstown Center) in 1908, and the Student Volunteers Council (SVC) in the 1960s. Murray-Dodge Hall was originally built for use by the Philadelphian Society, with Dodge Hall named for one of the society's former presidents.

Today the SVC is a component of the John H. Pace Jr. '39 Center for Civic Engagement. The University proposed the Pace Center in connection with its 250th anniversary to "show that community service is . . . an essential part of a liberal education . . . not peripheral to the academy but rather directly connected to learning." The Pace Center opened in the new Frist Campus Center in 2001, and in 2007 it incorporated both the SVC and Community House. The SVC supports volunteering opportunities in fields ranging from health, education, and mentorship to the arts, special needs, and hunger and homelessness, while Community House, which began as a student-initiated off-campus drop-in center in 1969, engages Princeton students with families in the community to support students in preschool through high school.

Community Action, a program founded by students in 1987, provides opportunities during orientation for entering undergraduates to foster connections with local community organizations. Breakout Princeton offers students off-campus service-learning trips during fall and spring breaks. Pace offers a range of service-oriented summer internship and fellowship programs, including the John C. Bogle '51 Fellows in Civic Service, which gives first-year students an opportunity to design their own summer service internship experience, and the Princeton Internships in Civic Service program which has provided more than 1,500 undergraduates with internships and alumni mentoring since its founding in 1996.

The alumni-initiated organizations, Princeton AlumniCorps and ReachOut 56-81-06, offer public service-focused fellowships for graduating seniors and recent alumni, and other service-oriented fellowships are offered through the office of international programs. The Novogratz Bridge Year Program, established in 2009, provides opportunities for 40 newly admitted students in each class to defer admission for a year to engage in international service projects in five countries on three continents, with the hope that when these students enroll on campus they will inspire others to pursue their own international service experiences.

Athletic teams, religious groups, the residential colleges, and centers like the Carl A. Fields Center for Equality and Cultural Understanding and the Women*s Center offer a range of service opportunities. In recent years all the eating clubs have had community service chairs; in addition to organizing individual club initiatives, the chairs collaborate on an annual town-gown project to combat food insecurity in central New Jersey. Since 1971 Dillon Gym has partnered with the local Princeton Recreation Department to offer a recreational youth basketball league on Saturday mornings from January through March, through which Princeton students coach fourth-through-ninth graders from the community.

Some courses have hands-on components to engage students in service. Through the Program for

Community-Engaged Scholarship, students can enroll in courses to develop research projects, collect and analyze data, and share their results with local nonprofit organizations and other agencies that can use their findings. Students in the Keller Center's Tiger Challenge program work in small teams to address important social issues like affordable housing and adolescent mental health.

In 2018 the University launched a Service Focus program, led by the Pace Center, to bridge service and learning across the first two years of the undergraduate experience. Students participate from the spring of their first year to the spring of their sophomore year. The program includes a summer service internship following the first year, a service-related course in the second year, faculty mentorship, and a peer group with which the students can reflect on their experiences and engage with community partners.

Princeton alumni serve the University and their communities in countless ways, and many classes and regional associations have community service coordinators. Through the alumni-initiated Princeton Prize in Race Relations, alumni volunteers around the country recognize high school students who foster positive race relations in their schools and communities.

Meeting Special Needs

On a number of occasions, the University has launched service projects to respond to unanticipated challenges and needs. Following the terrorist attacks of September 11, 2001, a program called "Arts Alive" was developed with active student leadership to provide cultural experiences in New York in the spring of 2002 (primarily theater performances and museum visits) for schoolchildren in New York communities especially affected by the attacks, with Princeton students leading workshops in advance and then accompanying the schoolchildren to the events. Almost 200 Princeton students participated, as did more than 10,000 schoolchildren.[2]

Following Hurricane Katrina, which devastated New Orleans in August 2005, Princeton temporarily enrolled 24 visiting undergraduates and five visiting graduate students who had been displaced from their own colleges and universities, and partnered with Dillard University, a historically Black university in New Orleans, to help it restore its operations after the flooding. Students raised funds for relief organizations and school districts in the Gulf Coast, and five Princeton employees volunteered through the American Red Cross under a program that allowed employees to request up to two weeks of paid leave to participate in relief efforts.

In 2009, the University and the Princeton Fire Department launched a program that allowed University employees to volunteer as firefighters during their work shifts to augment the municipal department's ranks during critical daytime hours when other volunteers were not available. While University employees and students had long volunteered on their own with the department and the First Aid and Rescue Squad (which is heavily dependent on student participation), this formalized the partnership. In the first 10 years of the program, University employees responded to 1,950 fire and rescue calls.

In the spring of 2020, with the onset of COVID-19, Princetonians of all stripes—students, faculty, staff, and alumni—stepped forward to serve in front-line roles, address critical needs, conduct groundbreaking research, and help others. The University established a relief fund to support community organizations, families, and businesses in Princeton that were hit especially hard by the pandemic. This fund was in addition to providing direct support to organizations fighting food insecurity, donating personal protective equipment to state and local partners, hosting blood drives, and donating dorm refrigerators to local organizations and families.

While the pandemic kept most undergraduates and many faculty, staff, and alumni away from the campus, it did not diminish the University's commitment to the core tenets of its mission: scholarship, research, teaching, and service. And while the pandemic affected some of the ways in which service could be rendered, it reinforced the importance of contributing to those in need and to the common good, and of finding creative and meaningful ways to do so. It also reminded the University community of the importance of mobilizing the intellectual and scholarly resources of the University to increase understanding of the virus, develop

---

[2] Shortly after the September 11 attacks, when airports were locked down, alumni around the country posted online to invite alumni stranded in their communities to stay with them until the restrictions were lifted and they could return home.

tools and strategies to combat it, and find ways to predict, contain, and control other such pathogens in the future.

The heightened national focus on systemic racism and discrimination in the spring and summer of 2020 similarly inspired renewed commitments to service, fair treatment, and racial justice by the University, and by Princetonians on campus and around the world.

One early initiative was a grant program through the Pace Center that supported students working to address racial inequalities and injustices. Many other students, faculty, staff, and alumni found their own ways to contribute and to serve—on campus, in their home communities, in their places of work and civic engagement, and, in some cases, on a national or international level.

ENTRIES

A CAPPELLA singing groups, an iconic Princeton tradition, date back to 1941 when seven students who had broken away from the Glee Club first performed (at Yale) as the Nassoons. As of 2020, there were 17 such groups registered with the office of the dean of undergraduate students: four of them all male, three all female, and the rest coeducational (including one that identified itself as LGBT+ friendly). Among them were ensembles that specialized in rhythm and blues; soul; African, East Asian, and South Asian music; Jewish music; and Christian praise and worship music.

A cappella means "without instrumental accompaniment," and it relies on close harmony and blended voices. The groups are student run, and their officers arrange the music, organize arch sings (particularly in 1879, Blair, and East Pyne arches), plan tours, tend to alumni relations and fundraising, and set up recording sessions.

The Nassoons feature four-, five- and six-part harmonies; the first song they ever performed—the five-part harmony "Perfidia"—remains a highlight of every year's reunion luncheon honoring the Old Guard (alumni more than 65 years out of Princeton) just before the P-rade. The second all-male group, the Tigertones, was founded in 1946, and the third group, the Footnotes, began in 1959.

The first all-female group, the Tigerlilies, started in 1971 when eight women ran up the steps of 1879 arch and sang "How High the Moon." The other all-female groups are the Tigressions (1981) and the Wildcats (1986).

The Katzenjammers, founded in 1973 by a Nassoon and a Tigerlily, are the oldest coed a cappella group in the Ivy League. They were followed by Roaring 20 in 1983; Shere Khan in 1993; and Princeton Acapellago, a no-audition group, in 2013.

Groups with specialized repertoires include the LGBT+-friendly Fire Hazards, which has no gendered voice parts; the Christian group Kindred Spirit; the Jewish group Koleinu, which grew out of informal sing-alongs after Shabbat services at the Center for Jewish Life; Old NasSoul, the fourth all-male group, which specializes in R&B and soul; Tarana, which performs South Asian music; Umqombothi, which performs African music; and VTone, whose music comes from East Asia, including China, Korea, and Japan.

Many of the groups participate in arch sings, which are descended from the tradition of step sings that began as early as 1760 on the steps of Nassau Hall. The groups also perform off-campus, and some tour extensively throughout the country and around the world, including, on occasion, performing at the White House.

Of more recent vintage is a broad array of student dance groups. As of 2020, the following groups were actively registered with the office of the dean of undergraduate students and coordinated through a student-run Performing Arts Council: Aerial Arts Club, Black Arts Company, Blasé, BodyHype Dance Company, diSiac Dance Company, Dorobucci, eXpressions Dance Company (the oldest dance group, founded in 1979), Highsteppers, Irish Dance Company, KoKo Pops, Mas Flow, Naacho, Princeton Bhangra, Princeton TapCats, Princeton University Ballet, Raqs: Princeton Belly Dance Company, Six14 Christian Dance Company, Sympoh, and Triple 8.

ACADEMIC PROGRAM. In his history of Princeton from 1746 to 1896, Professor Thomas Jefferson Wertenbaker says the founders of the College of New Jersey "made their plans for a course of instruction so wide and comprehensive as to disarm in advance the criticisms of their enemies . . . There were to be courses in the classics, in divinity, in philosophy, and in science . . . this was not to be another advanced grammar school . . . but an institution of full collegiate grade."

In 1752 Princeton's second president, Aaron Burr Sr., wrote that the College intended to proceed "not so much in the method of a dogmatic institution, by prolix discourses on the different branches of the sciences, by burdening the memory and infusing heavy and disagreeable tasks; as in the Socratic way of free dialogue between teacher and pupil, or between the students themselves, under the inspection of their tutors."

As president from 1768 to 1794, John Witherspoon taught moral philosophy, divinity, rhetoric, history, and French; appointed a professor of mathematics and natural philosophy; introduced English grammar and composition to the curriculum; and added books for the library and "philosophical apparatus" (especially the famous Rittenhouse Orrery) for demonstrations in astronomy and other sciences.

Like Burr, Witherspoon believed in engaging his students in discussion and in exposing them to contrasting viewpoints. By the end of the eighteenth century, Wertenbaker said, "the Princeton undergraduate . . . had his regular allotment of the classics, philosophy, and science and had to do his share of memorizing, but more important for his future were the discussions with fellow students and instructors . . . his debates or his orations. It was this which gave him practice in exercising his creative ability. In after years . . . he could not only draw upon the experiences of other ages but could think the matter out for himself."

During the presidency of James McCosh, the College took major strides toward becoming a university. Electives were introduced for juniors and seniors: they ranged from logic, psychology, mechanics, physics, natural theology, physical geography, rhetoric, astronomy, chemistry, English literature, economics, and moral philosophy to mathematics, history, French, German, political science, and art. In the winter of 1885, McCosh debated President Charles Eliot of Harvard on the ideal college curriculum, espousing Princeton's model of obligatory core courses followed by a reasonable variety of electives, as opposed to a more unstructured Harvard model that, he argued, encouraged dilettantism.

McCosh also instituted graduate work leading to master's and doctoral degrees (Princeton awarded its first PhDs in 1879) and founded a school of Science. Throughout the eighteenth and most of the nineteenth century, all students had to read Latin and Greek authors during their first years of study, but in 1873 the requirement to study Greek was dropped for candidates for the Bachelor of Science degree, and in 1918 the Latin requirement was dropped as well; that same year, Greek was eliminated as a requirement for the Bachelor of Arts, and Latin as a requirement for that degree was eliminated in 1930.

Transformative changes in the academic program occurred during the eight-year presidency of Woodrow Wilson 1879. Wilson created academic departments, raised academic standards, revised the undergraduate curriculum, promoted the library and art museum as teaching instruments, and, in 1905, introduced a new model of teaching with his appointment of preceptors.

He replaced the free elective system with a unified curriculum of general studies with distribution requirements during the first two years, followed by concentrated study in one discipline and related fields during the junior and senior years. He made provision for an honors program for high-ranking seniors in some departments that included the preparation of independent papers that were read and discussed at weekly class meetings.

Wilson's preceptors—whose appointments increased the size of the faculty by about 50 percent—were to engage with undergraduates through guided reading and small group discussions; while he initially intended that they would stay for about five years, almost half of the preceptors remained until their retirement and many became leaders within the faculty and in their fields. Of the 49 preceptors appointed in 1905, 12 were already on the faculty, but the rest came from other campuses.

It was Wilson who proposed the term "preceptor," and he intended through "preceptorials" to "import into the great university the methods and personal contact between teacher and pupil which are characteristic of the small college, and so to gain the advantage of both." Under the initial concept, preceptors met only with juniors and seniors and most students had the same preceptor for all courses. Over time the concept evolved to refer to small discussion groups associated with lecture courses, with precepts for a particular course taught by the faculty member offering the course, other faculty in the department, and, in time, graduate students in the field. In the modern era, graduate students lead most precepts.

From 1913 to 1917, under Wilson's successor, John Grier Hibben 1882 *1893, an honors program was offered which allowed high-ranking students to substitute departmental independent work for a fifth course. This was followed in 1923 by adoption of the so-called four-course plan, largely developed and promulgated by professor (later dean) Luther Eisenhardt. The plan required all juniors and seniors seeking a Bachelor of Arts degree to do concentrated work in a single department, with two departmental courses and two electives each term, and with the substitution of junior and senior independent work for what had been a fifth course each semester. Students were required to pass departmental comprehensive examinations and the required senior independent work soon evolved into a required senior thesis. Princeton was unique in requiring independent work from all undergraduates, not just those electing an honors program.

With modifications over time, especially in the nature of the general education requirements that both Bachelor of Arts and engineering students must satisfy, this general approach to undergraduate education remains in place a century later. After World War II, departments were encouraged to develop broad introductory courses to acquaint entering students with their fields, and all students were required to take at least one course in each of four general areas: mathematics and the natural sciences, the social sciences, the humanities, and the related areas of history, philosophy, and religion. Today's general education requirements focus more on different ways of thinking and knowing than on distributions across departments.*

In the early 1980s, President William Bowen summarized Princeton's educational philosophy when he said the University hoped undergraduates would gain "a basic knowledge of the human condition, the societies human beings have created, and the physical world we inhabit—a knowledge that is historical as well as contemporary, that includes an appreciation for language and cultures other than one's own, that reflects some rigorous understanding of the principles and methods of modern science, and that encourages thoughtful consideration of ultimate values."

He said a liberal education should encourage the development of a "tough and disciplined mind," and help students become "compassionate and sensitive human beings" and develop "habits of thought which always ask why, which believe in evidence, which welcome new ideas, which seek to understand the perspectives of others, which accept complexity and grapple with it, which admit error, and which pursue truth, wherever it may lead, however uncomfortable it may be."

In addition to satisfying the general education requirements that pertain to them as Bachelor of Arts (AB) candidates or as candidates for the Bachelor of Science in Engineering (BSE), today's undergraduates must satisfy a writing requirement and complete a thesis or similar independent project in their senior year. AB candidates also have a foreign language requirement. In 1986 a freshman seminar program was introduced to give first-year students opportunities to interact directly with members of the faculty and a small group of students in a seminar setting.

Historically, the first degrees offered by medieval universities were Bachelor of Arts degrees, which were understood to be preliminary steps toward a more meaningful master's degree. Later, in England, the bachelor's degree became the important one, with a master's degree available several years after graduation merely by paying a few pounds. Princeton adopted this model, and until the end of the nineteenth century Princeton alumni could receive a master's degree three years after graduation simply by returning to campus to collect it.

In addition to the Bachelor of Arts degree, which it has awarded since its first Commencement in 1748, Princeton offered a Bachelor of Laws degree from 1847 to 1852 (it was earned by seven recipients); a Bachelor of Science degree from 1873 to 1930; and a Bachelor of Letters degree from 1904 to 1918. It has offered a Bachelor of Science in Engineering degree since 1921.

The Bachelor of Letters degree was introduced when it was found that some students were pursuing Bachelor of Science degrees solely to avoid the requirement to take Greek; it was, in effect, a Bachelor of Arts degree without Greek. When Greek was dropped as a Bachelor of Arts requirement in 1918, the Bachelor of Letters degree was discontinued. With Latin still a requirement for the Bachelor of Arts degree, students with interests in the humanities but seeking to avoid Latin would enroll for Bachelor of Science degrees; this was no longer necessary when the Latin requirement was dropped in 1930 and the Bachelor of Science degree was discontinued.

Graduate degrees were introduced at Princeton in the 1870s. At first there were two master's degrees (Master of Arts and Master of Science) and two doctoral degrees (Doctor of Philosophy and Doctor of Science; the degree of Doctor of Letters was awarded

---

* As of September 2020, Bachelor of Arts candidates were required to take at least one course in each of the following areas: culture and difference, epistemology and cognition, ethical thought and moral values, historical analysis, and quantitative and computational reasoning; two courses each in literature and the arts and social analysis; and two courses in science and engineering, including at least one with a laboratory.

twice in the 1890s). By 1905 the other degrees were discontinued, leaving only the Master of Arts and Doctor of Philosophy. Today, in addition to the Master of Arts, the University also offers master's degrees in Architecture, Engineering, Finance, Fine Arts, Near Eastern Studies, Public Affairs, Public Policy, and Science in Engineering.

In 1904, Wilson organized the University's academic program into 11 departments: Art and Archaeology; Biology; Chemistry; Classics; English; Geology; History, Politics, and Economics; Mathematics; Modern Languages; Philosophy; and Physics. (These departments joined existing departments in Civil Engineering and Electrical Engineering, with Astronomy added as a department a few years later.)

Over time, History, Politics, and Economics became separate departments; Economics spawned Sociology, which in turn gave rise to Anthropology, and Modern Languages split several times—its descendants are French and Italian, German, Spanish and Portuguese, Slavic Languages and Literatures, and Comparative Literature. A department of Oriental Studies was formed and then divided into East Asian and Near Eastern Studies. Biology evolved over time to become two departments: Molecular Biology and Ecology and Evolutionary Biology (for a time, there was a separate department of Biochemistry). Psychology emerged out of Philosophy; Statistics existed for a time after splitting off from Mathematics; Music began under the auspices of Art and Archaeology; and the department of Geosciences changed its name several times. The professional schools in both Architecture and Public and International Affairs function like departments, and the school of Engineering and Applied Sciences provides overall coordination for six engineering departments.

In 2020, undergraduates could concentrate in the departments listed below. They also could apply for an independent concentration of their own design, in cooperation with a supportive faculty member. A major in visual arts was offered through the "practice of art" program in the department of Art and Archaeology.

For the Bachelor of Arts Degree:

African American Studies
Anthropology
Architecture
Art and Archaeology
Astrophysical Sciences
Chemistry
Classics
Comparative Literature
Computer Science (students may elect either an AB or a BSE concentration)
East Asian Studies
Ecology and Evolutionary Biology
Economics
English
French and Italian
Geosciences
German
History
Mathematics
Molecular Biology
Music
Near Eastern Studies
Neuroscience (officially an institute, but with authority to grant degrees)
Philosophy
Physics
Politics
Psychology
Religion
Slavic Languages and Literatures
Sociology
Spanish and Portuguese
Public and International Affairs

For the Bachelor of Science in Engineering Degree:

Chemical and Biological Engineering
Civil and Environmental Engineering
Computer Science
Electrical and Computer Engineering
Mechanical and Aerospace Engineering
Operations Research and Financial Engineering

In 2018-19, the most popular majors were Computer Science (313), Economics (269), Public and International Affairs (240), Politics (147), History (144), Operations Research and Financial Engineering (139), Mechanical and Aerospace Engineering (115), Molecular Biology (110), Ecology and Evolutionary Biology (109), and Music (85).

The University grants doctoral degrees in the following departments and programs:

Anthropology
Applied and Computational Mathematics
Architecture
Art and Archaeology
Astrophysical Sciences

Atmospheric and Oceanic Sciences
Chemical and Biological Engineering
Chemistry
Civil and Environmental Engineering
Classics
Comparative Literature
Computer Science
East Asian Studies
Ecology and Evolutionary Biology
Economics
Electrical and Computer Engineering
English
French and Italian
Geosciences
German
History
History of Science
Mathematics
Mechanical and Aerospace Engineering
Molecular Biology
Music Composition
Musicology
Near Eastern Studies
Neuroscience
Operations Research and Financial Engineering
Philosophy
Plasma Physics
Politics
Population Studies
Psychology
Public and International Affairs
Quantitative and Computational Biology
Religion
Slavic Languages and Literatures
Sociology
Spanish and Portuguese

The following departments and programs offer Master's degrees:

Architecture
Chemical and Biological Engineering
Chemistry
Civil and Environmental Engineering
Computer Science
Electrical and Computer Engineering
Finance
Mechanical and Aerospace Engineering
Near Eastern Studies
Operations Research and Financial Engineering
Public and International Affairs

The graduate school offers joint degrees in Interdisciplinary Humanities, Materials Science, Neuroscience, and Social Policy, and two dual degree programs: an MD/PhD program through the department of Molecular Biology and an MPA/JD through the school of Public and International Affairs.

In addition to their areas of concentration, undergraduates may obtain certificates of proficiency in any of 55 interdisciplinary certificate programs. The certificate programs as of 2020 are listed on page 517. Also listed are interdisciplinary/interdepartmental programs in which PhD work may be concentrated or in which graduate-level certificates may be granted.

For most of its first century, Princeton's academic year ended in the fall. In 1844 the trustees advanced Commencement to June. In the mid-twentieth century, the University introduced "reading periods" prior to each semester's exams to allow students time to pursue independent study, complete papers, and prepare for finals.

Through 2019–20, Princeton retained its traditional fall semester calendar in which reading period and exams were held in January, but following an April 2018 faculty vote, the fall semester reading period and exams were moved into December, effective with academic year 2020–21; the faculty also voted to establish an optional two-week January "Wintersession" program during which students have opportunities between semesters to participate in a wide range of non-credit-bearing activities, both on and off campus. The revised calendar retained fall and spring semester reading periods, as well as the fall break that was first adopted in 1970, initially for the purpose of permitting students to participate in canvassing for that fall's Congressional elections.

ADMISSION to Princeton in its earliest years was based on knowledge of Latin and Greek, but by 1760 entering freshmen were required also to understand the principal rules of "vulgar arithmetick." The president of the College personally examined each applicant and determined whether he should be admitted.

Oral entrance examinations continued until well past the middle of the nineteenth century, when they began to be superseded by written examinations, first given only in Princeton, and after 1888 also at strategic points across the country. In the early twentieth century, the exams included English, Latin, mathematics, Greek, and French or German.

With the founding of the College Entrance Examination Board in 1900, Princeton honored the board's examinations as well as its own, and after 1915 it required them of all applicants, although it also relied on letters of recommendation ("testimonials of good moral character").

During its first century and a half Princeton accepted almost all who applied, including students who showed deficiencies in preparation but were admitted "with conditions." (In 1904, for example, only about a quarter of the class was admitted unconditionally.) Although some financial aid was available, it was limited: by 1900, about 110 scholarships were available for a student body of approximately 1,100. In 1911, a Bureau of Self Help was established to help needy students find jobs, and by 1923 one of every five students had a job.

Enrollment grew following World War I (there were 1,714 students in 1920, a significant increase from 1,053 at the beginning of the century), leading the trustees to adopt a policy of limited enrollment and selective admission in 1922. The University appointed English instructor Radcliffe Heermance *1909 to administer the policy through a newly created office of director of admission; Heermance served in this role from 1922 to 1950, while also serving as dean of freshmen from 1925 to 1942.

As admission director, Heermance served on the College Entrance Examination Board and chaired it from 1933 to 1936. Princeton psychology professor Carl Brigham was chiefly responsible for the development of the College Board's Scholastic Aptitude Test; the SAT verbal exam was first given in 1926, with the math exam following in 1930.

In the 1930s Princeton adopted a plan of admission without examination for students of exceptional achievement and promise in the far west and south, where school programs did not prepare them for College Board examinations. Thanks to this program and the nationwide efforts of alumni schools committee volunteers, the geographical distribution of Princeton's classes was substantially broadened beyond the states of the mid-Atlantic and the south that had previously been Princeton's principal sources of students. In 1940 the College Board replaced examinations based on a set curriculum with the SAT tests, and this change brought marked increases both in the number of applicants to Princeton and the number of schools from which they came.

With standards rising, Heermance assured alumni that "average students" with good records still had an excellent chance of being admitted. He also told them that Princeton's highest priority was not in admitting superior students, but in admitting the "all-around boy."

While the composition of Princeton classes was broadening in some respects, a combination of policy, practice, and culture made Princeton inaccessible to some students (including African American students) and inhospitable to others (including Jewish students). While Heermance insisted publicly that Princeton did "not discriminate against any race, color, or creed," the fact was that the only Black undergraduate admitted (inadvertently) in the first half of the twentieth century, Bruce Wright, was asked to leave when his race was discovered as he arrived in 1935 to register. (Sixty-six years later, the graduating class of 2001 made Wright an honorary member.)

During the Great Depression, Princeton had a more homogeneous student body than most of its peers and it stood alone in drawing more than 80 percent of its students from private preparatory schools. While admission standards were being relaxed to the point where some 85 percent of all applicants were being admitted, in 1935 only five of 28 Jewish applicants (18 percent) were admitted. In 1924 the University decided to limit Jewish enrollment to under three percent, and a year later only 11 Jews were admitted in a class of 641. The admission of Jewish students remained very low in 1940 with seven freshmen in a class of 508, but after World War II the numbers began to increase, with Jewish students comprising 6.5 percent of the freshman class in 1948.

The limitation on Jewish enrollment was accomplished in part through admission policies that introduced subjective assessments by headmasters and alumni interviewers of an applicant's overall character, promise, "manhood," leadership, participation in athletics, and social status. These assessments helped to weed out Jewish applicants and prevent them from being admitted.

After World War II, as returning veterans flocked to the nation's campuses with financial support from the GI Bill and New Jersey enacted antidiscrimination legislation, Princeton began to admit students from a broader range of socioeconomic as well as geographical and religious backgrounds. By 1948 there were more than 5,000 applicants for 725 spaces, and with the creation of a nationwide regional scholarship program, Princeton actively sought students beyond the states of New Jersey, New York, and Pennsylvania. There was an increase in the number of students from public high schools; by 1947 these students constituted 34 percent of the class, and by 1955 they filled half the class.

The formation of the Ivy League in 1954 and its adoption of a policy of financial aid provided solely on the basis of need accelerated these trends, although Princeton was assiduous in reassuring its alumni that their children would continue to receive favorable consideration in the admission process. In the mid-1950s, about 80 percent of alumni children who applied were admitted; this percentage dropped to about 40 percent in the 1970s and then declined into the 30 percent range. In the 1970s and 1980s alumni children constituted about 17 percent of each class, but by the 2000s their representation ranged between 10 and 15 percent.

In 1945, four Black students arrived on campus as part of the Navy's wartime V-12 program. One of them, John Howard '47, became the first Black student to earn a Princeton undergraduate degree when he graduated as a member of the Class of 1947; two of the other students, Arthur Jewell Wilson '48 and James Ward '48, graduated in the Class of 1948. (At least five Black students had previously received Master of Arts degrees: Abraham Parker Denny in 1891; James Monroe Berger in 1893; Irwin William Langston Roundtree in 1895; Leonard Zachariah Johnson in 1904; and George Shippen Stark in 1906.)

In 1947, Princeton admitted a Black undergraduate from the town of Princeton, Joseph Ralph Moss '51. Another early Black undergraduate from the town of Princeton, Robert J. Rivers Jr. '53, became the first African American elected by the trustees to a position on the board when he was named a term trustee in 1969. But it was not until the mid-1960s that Princeton, under the leadership of President Robert Goheen, began to make a concerted effort to identify and attract undergraduate students of color. In 1963 Princeton enrolled just 10 Black undergraduates, and even the last class of the decade, 1969, had only 16 Black students. By 1971, however, there were more than 300 Black undergraduates on campus.

In January 1969, the trustees voted "in principle" to admit undergraduate women, and in April they voted to begin admitting women that fall. That first year 70 female transfer students (including nine seniors who had been on campus as Critical Language students in their junior years) enrolled at Princeton, along with 101 women and 819 men as members of the Class of 1973. Initially there was a cap on the number of women, but in 1974 the trustees adopted a policy of equal access for men and women, allowing the number of men in the class to decrease as the number of women increased, but maintaining the total size of the class at roughly 1,100.

In the early years of coeducation, Princeton received about 10,000 applications for admission per year. By the mid-1980s that number (and the number of undergraduates) had grown modestly, but applications remained in the vicinity of about 15,000 for the next two decades. Beginning in 2007 the number of applicants began to rise dramatically, passing the 25,000 mark in 2011, and passing 30,000 in 2017. (In the pandemic year of 2020–21, applications spiked to more than 37,000.)

Meanwhile, in 2000 a trustee committee (named for its chair, Paul Wythes '55) recommended a 10 percent increase in the size of the undergraduate student body from 4,600 to 5,100, an expansion that began in 2007 following the construction of Whitman College. In 2016 the trustees authorized an additional 10 percent expansion, to begin as soon as additional residential college space was constructed.

Beginning in 1977, Princeton offered a non-binding early action program that allowed students to apply in November and receive a decision by mid-December; applicants admitted early did not have to decide whether to attend until after the regular admission process was completed in the spring. Princeton switched to a binding early decision program, under which students admitted early were required to enroll, in 1996.

In 2006 Princeton discontinued this program, and for the next five years it offered no early admission option. In 2011 it adopted a single-choice non-binding early action program that allowed students to apply early if they applied early only to Princeton, but then allowed admitted students until after the regular admission process to decide whether to attend. In 2020, in response to the challenges presented by the COVID-19 pandemic, the University suspended early admission for the 2020–21 admission cycle and also suspended its standardized testing requirement that year; while allowing applicants who took standardized ACT or SAT tests to submit their scores, the admission office emphasized that students who did not submit scores would not be at a disadvantage. In 2021 the admission office announced it would again suspend its standardized testing requirement in 2021–22.

Following World War II and into the second half of the twentieth century, academic expectations increased significantly; over recent decades, Princeton students have ranked among the very top nationally in standardized measures, and over time growing proportions of its classes have come to be filled by students with the highest academic ratings, who also bring impressive out-of-the-classroom accomplishments.

Princeton today seeks students who have the talent and motivation necessary to benefit from the demanding education the University offers, who will help one another grow and learn during their time on campus, and who will contribute in positive and meaningful ways to society and the world after they graduate. The admission office actively seeks students from many backgrounds from around the country and the world; it conducts a holistic process that evaluates each applicant's academic and extracurricular achievements on multiple dimensions, while seeking to enroll a class that brings to campus a range of backgrounds, viewpoints, and interests. Within this process it pays special attention to varsity-level athletes and artists; to racial, ethnic, and socioeconomic diversity; and to children of alumni, faculty, and staff. A major initiative that began in the mid-2000s sought to increase the percentage of the class that received federal Pell Grants, which are awarded to students from lower economic backgrounds. That percentage rose from about seven percent when the initiative began to 24 percent in the class admitted in 2019.

The 1,337 students who enrolled that year (the Class of 2023) included more women than men (50.9 percent women and 49.1 percent men); 49.7 percent students of color; 13.7 percent children of alumni; 16.8 percent recruited athletes; 16.1 percent who were the first in their family to attend college; 60.7 percent who attended public high schools; and 11.1 percent international students. Undergraduates come from all over the country, with the largest numbers from New Jersey, New York, California, Pennsylvania, and Texas, and at any one time on campus there typically are students from more than 100 countries. Some 61 percent of the class received financial aid, with an average award of almost $60,000.

In admitting the Class of 2024, the University accepted 5.5 percent of its 32,836 applicants. A year later, the University accepted 3.98 percent of a record-setting 37,601 applicants; 22 percent of those admitted were first-generation college students.

The Admission Office is assisted in its work by thousands of alumni volunteers (organized through alumni schools committees) who help identify promising candidates in their local schools, interview applicants, and encourage admitted students to attend. In most years alumni volunteers interview over 99 percent of all applicants, all over the world.

In 2018 Princeton reinstituted a transfer admission program that had been discontinued in 1990. This highly selective program allows a small number of undergraduates—primarily students from community colleges and military reservists and veterans—to transfer to Princeton.

While undergraduate admission, including transfer admission, is entirely overseen by one office, admission decisions at the graduate level are made separately by each degree-granting department and program, with administrative coordination by the office of the dean of the graduate school.

The six directors of undergraduate admission who followed Heermance were C. William Edwards '36, 1950–62; E. Alden Dunham III '53, 1962–66; John Osander '57, 1966–71; Timothy Callard '63, 1971–78; James W. Wickenden Jr. '61, 1978–83; and Anthony Cummings *80, 1983–88. In 1988 the title of the position was changed to dean of admission with the appointment first of Fred Hargadon, 1988–2003, and then his successors Janet Lavin Rapelye, 2003–18, and Karen Richardson '93, 2019–.

ADVISORY COUNCILS for the academic departments and some other academic units were first established in 1941. They play an important role in assessing the mission and effectiveness of the departments, supporting them, and advocating on their behalf. Advisory Councils consist of up to 20 members who serve three- or four-year terms, with membership rotated regularly. Appointments are made by the dean of the faculty upon the recommendation of the department, frequently following consultation with the advancement office, which provides administrative support for the selection process and helps to identify candidates who bring increased diversity to the councils' memberships.

Council members may include faculty at other institutions, experts and other leading figures in the field, graduates of the University, or friends of the department. Each council must include at least one alum, and it may include a trustee as an associate member if one wishes to serve in this capacity. Trustee associates often find that close contact with a department enables them to develop a deeper understanding of the University, which in turns helps them in exercising their overall responsibilities as trustees.

Typically, councils meet every two years in Princeton for the purpose of advising the departments or assisting them in other ways. They may canvass the opinions of students or junior faculty members, convey views or concerns to the central administration, or help raise funds and generate support for the departments and their various activities. Following their meetings, the councils submit reports to their departments, and these reports are then forwarded to the president through the dean of the faculty. The councils may make separate confidential reports to the president if they wish to do so, and on occasion the administration directs specific questions to a particular advisory council.

AFRICAN AMERICAN STUDENTS AT PRINCETON. African Americans have been a part of Princeton's history for as long as the University has existed. Princeton's first nine presidents were slaveholders at some point in their lives, and faculty members owned enslaved African Americans on or near campus well into the 1800s; by then, free Black laborers also were working on campus in a variety of roles. While a handful of African Americans earned graduate degrees in the late nineteenth and early twentieth centuries, Black undergraduates were not admitted to Princeton until after World War II.

Much of the funding that built Princeton into a world-class institution came from donors whose wealth derived from slavery or the slave trade, among them the donors of the land on which Nassau Hall stands. While the Princeton and Slavery Project did not find evidence that the College itself owned enslaved people, 16 enslaved African Americans, including children, lived and worked in Maclean House between 1756 and 1822, when it served as home to the College's presidents. The house was the site of a 1766 estate sale that included six enslaved people.

The large free Black community that lived north of Nassau Street played an important role on campus, before and after the Civil War. Members of the community worked in a variety of capacities, from janitors and cooks to messengers and research assistants. Some supplemented their incomes with entrepreneurial endeavors, like James Collins Johnson, an escaped former slave who became a janitor and snack vendor on campus and also owned an off-campus used clothing and furniture shop. Although alumni pooled money to purchase a headstone for Johnson in the Princeton Cemetery after his death, students also viewed him through the lens of racial stereotypes during his nearly six decades on campus.

Some free Black families, such as the Hillians, had many members who worked for Princeton. Tom Hillian was an orderly at McCosh Infirmary, while his sisters Mabel and Bessie were cooks at the infirmary for much of the twentieth century (their infirmary garden grew produce used at the health center for over a decade). In total, members of the Hillian family worked at Princeton for a combined total of 200 years.

In 1774 President John Witherspoon privately tutored two free African men, Bristol Yamma and John Quamine, and in 1792 John Chavis, a free Black man from Virginia, studied privately with him at his Tusculum home, though none received degrees. Later, African American men at the Princeton Theological Seminary attended classes at the College. In both 1868 and 1876, the presence of African American seminarians in lectures on campus prompted white students to protest, but President James McCosh affirmed their right to attend.

By the 1890s a few African American men, many of them alumni of Lincoln University, enrolled formally in graduate programs at Princeton. Early graduates included Abraham Parker Denny *1891, superintendent of Princeton's Witherspoon School for Colored Children, and Irwin William Langston Roundtree *1895, a pastor and civil rights advocate who had been born into slavery.

There were no Black undergraduates, and when one Black applicant, Bruce Wright, was inadvertently admitted in 1935, administrators asked him to leave when they discovered his race. In 1942 the *Daily Princetonian* editorialized unsuccessfully in favor of admitting African American students in a three-part series entitled "White Supremacy at Princeton."

It was not until the US Navy opened a V-12 training program on Princeton's campus during World War II that things began to change. Four African Americans participated in the program, and all of them accepted Princeton's invitation to enroll as full-time civilian students when the war ended. They held leadership positions in a variety of student activities, including managing the debating society and captaining the basketball team. Three of the four graduated, including John L. Howard '47, who, in February 1947, became the first African American student to receive an undergraduate degree from Princeton. Arthur Jewell Wilson '48 and James Ward '48 also graduated in 1947, although as members of the Class of 1948.

In the fall of 1947 Joseph Ralph Moss '51, a Princeton High School graduate, became the first African American to enroll at Princeton as a first-year student. His brother Simeon Moss *49 was simultaneously enrolled in the graduate school. Their father had worked as a servant for a Princeton professor.

In 1951 Ralph Bunche, winner of the Nobel Peace Prize, became the first African American to receive an honorary degree; he was followed eight years later by the singer Marian Anderson, the first African American woman to be recognized. It would take until 1996 for the first African American (Cornel West *80) to win the University's highest honor for graduate alumni, the James Madison Medal, and until 2008 for an African American (John Rogers '80) to win the comparable recognition for undergraduate alumni, the Woodrow Wilson Award.

Until the mid-1960s, the University made no effort to recruit Black students, so few applied—and even fewer attended. Finally, in 1963, President Robert Goheen committed the University to recruiting African American students. Whereas there were only three Black students in the Class of 1967, there were 11 in 1968, 16 in 1969, 18 in 1970, 16 in 1971, and 45 in 1972. By 1970 there were 120 Black students—including women—in the entering class and a total of almost 250 Black students on campus. For many, Carl Fields, the University's sole Black administrator when he came to Princeton in 1964, became a mentor and adviser. Many took advantage of the ties that Fields cultivated with the African American community in town.

Excluded from the existing social outlets on campus and contending with racism in their daily encounters, African American students created their own social settings and gathered in each other's rooms. They formed student groups, including the Association of Black Collegians (ABC), which was established in 1966 with Paul C. Williams '68 (now Paul X. Carryon '68) as its coordinator. With the help of Fields, ABC hosted conferences, organized social activities, planned protests, recruited Black applicants, and promoted Black culture on campus. The student groups offered respite from the overt and covert racism, prejudice, and exclusion many experienced on campus, while also helping them advocate for their needs as a community.

ABC's activism included a walkout from an on-campus speech by the segregationist former Alabama governor George Wallace, and multiple protests of Princeton's investment in apartheid South Africa, including a 1969 occupation of New South that garnered national attention. ABC's activism, in collaboration with other students of color, led to the creation in 1971 of a Third World Center (renamed the Carl A. Fields Center for Equality and Cultural Understanding in 2002). It became a community center for students of color and an umbrella organization for many student groups. The Fields Center, which moved into the former Elm Club on Prospect Avenue in 2009, coordinates each year's Pan-African graduation ceremony, and is also a home base for some of the student groups focusing on Black culture, history, and leadership on campus.

The ABC and others pressed for additional Black faculty members and courses on African and African American history and culture, and in 1969 a program in African American Studies was established. (In 2006 the program was elevated to a center, and in 2015 to departmental status.) New faculty included Cecelia Hodges Drewry in English and her husband Henry Drewry in History. (Henry Drewry also directed the Teacher Preparation program for 20 years.)

The Frederick Douglass Service award was created to recognize seniors for their work in deepening an understanding of the experiences of racial minorities, and in 1969 Robert Rivers Jr. '53 and Brent Henry '69 became the first African American members of the Board of Trustees. (Henry, one of the first young alumni trustees, later served as president of the Alumni Association, for two terms as a charter trustee, and as vice chair of the board.)

In the fall of 1969, the first undergraduate women arrived on campus, including Carla Wilson, Linda Blackburn, and Terrell Nash, members of the class of 1971 who became the first Black women to receive Princeton degrees. In 1970, Howard Bell '70 became the first Black student to receive the University's highest undergraduate honor, the Pyne Prize, and Jerome Davis '71, later Princeton's first Black Rhodes Scholar, became the first Black student body president. In 1983 Eugene Y. Lowe Jr. '71 became the first Black member of the president's cabinet when he was appointed dean of students.

The recruitment of African American students to the graduate school paralleled that of the college. Assistant dean Conrad Snowden began to pursue African American applicants in the 1960s. Snowden, a graduate of Howard University, also served as assistant provost, affirmative action coordinator, assistant dean of the faculty, and founding director of the Third World Center. Black enrollment in the graduate school reached 79 in 1973, and after recovering from a decline to a low of 28 later that decade, remained at roughly the 1973 level into the 2010s. Graduate students established the Black Graduate Caucus in 1983 to assist in recruitment efforts and to create a professional and social network. A decade later, Albert Raboteau, a professor of religion, became the first African American dean of the graduate school.

Although a scattered few individual African Americans worked in research and teaching roles as early as 1840, none were official members of the faculty until after World War II. In 1840, Sam Parker, a free Black man, became an assistant to physics professor Joseph Henry. For six years, Parker was indispensable to Henry's laboratory, carrying out routine tasks as well as more dangerous ones, like occasionally serving as a human test subject in electrical experiments. In the 1880s, Alexander Dumas Watkins, a self-taught biologist, came to Princeton as a laboratory assistant. For nearly 20 years until his death, Watkins not only prepared materials for Professor William Libbey's courses, he also conducted groundbreaking scientific research on mosquitos and malaria, tutored students, and delivered lectures in Libbey's absence.

After Watkins' death, more than half a century passed before Charles Davis, an African American scholar of poetry, was appointed to the faculty in 1955. Although African Americans served in multiple senior administrative posts by the early 1970s— including as assistant dean of the college and assistant provost—the number of Black faculty members remained low into the twenty-first century. The faculty included eight Black faculty members in 1985, a negligible increase over the previous decade, and by 2002 there were still fewer than 20 African American faculty members. Despite the small numbers, many of Princeton's African American scholars attained international recognition, and as public intellectuals reached broad audiences beyond campus. These included Princeton's first Black full professor, Nobel Laureate economist Sir Arthur Lewis, Nobel Laureate author Toni Morrison, Madison Medalist West, philosopher Kwame Anthony Appiah, historian Nell Painter, African American Studies department chair Eddie Glaude *97, and US Poet Laureate Tracy K. Smith.

Over the course of the 1970s and beyond, African American students performed with theater and dance groups and numerous athletics teams, successfully sought election to student government, filled leadership roles in student organizations, and continued to win awards like the Pyne Prize and be elected young alumni trustees. (By 2020 more than 30 percent of all young alumni trustees elected since 1969 had been African American.) In 1972 alumni established the Association of Black Princeton Alumni, which created a number of awards given annually to both students and alumni, many of which focus on service, and in 1977 it joined with the University in hosting the first conference for Black alumni, "Princeton Blacks: From the 60s into the 80s."

At the same time, students created spaces for Black culture on campus in places like the Princeton Inn (now Forbes College), where many Black students elected to live; in dining halls, (including Stevenson Hall), where Black tables were information hubs as well as places of camaraderie and support; in magazines and newspapers that published art, news, and essays by Black students; and in the dormitory suites and black boxes where they hosted late-night dancing and parties. During the mid- and late-1980s, students established campus chapters of Black sororities and fraternities, which emphasized community service and mentorship. Black students continued to establish new organizations during the 1990s and 2000s, including the Black Arts Company (BAC), the Black Student Union, pre-professional groups, and groups for Black men, women, and LGBTQIA students.

In her senior thesis, Michelle Robinson '85 (later Obama) examined the experiences of Black students at Princeton. Some of the issues she identified were still unresolved when vice provost Ruth Simmons, who later became the first Black president of an Ivy League institution (Brown), prepared a 1993 report on campus race relations that resulted in the appointment of an ombuds officer and the creation of a race relations working group. In 1996, Princeton's 250th anniversary celebration included screening of a documentary on the history of Black life and experiences at Princeton, produced by journalist Melvin McCray '74. McCray produced additional documentaries on this history for other major events, including alumni conferences and the 2017 Princeton and Slavery Project symposium.

In 2015 the Black Justice League coordinated a 32-hour sit-in at Nassau Hall protesting racial injustices on campus. The protest was a catalyst for creating cultural affinity rooms at the Fields Center and the establishment of a trustee committee to assess the legacy of Woodrow Wilson at the University. Five years later, the trustees voted to remove Wilson's name from the school of Public and International Affairs and one of the residential colleges.

When the University sponsored *Coming Back and Looking Forward*, a conference for Black alumni in 2006, it was carrying on a four-decade tradition of conferences for Black alumni that ABPA began hosting in the 1970s. In the fall of 2019 more than 1,200 alumni returned to campus—some for the first time since graduating—for the fourth such affinity conference for Black alumni. The following spring, the University named the first Black valedictorian in its history, Nicholas Johnson '20, an operations research and financial engineering major from Montreal.

Black alumni have been generous donors to the University, and two exceptional gifts were announced in the fall of 2020. First, Kwanza Jones '93, along with her husband José E. Feliciano '94, gave $20 million to name two adjoining dormitories in one of the two new residential colleges then being built, and then Mellody Hobson '91 donated funds to establish a new residential college on the site that since 1968 had been occupied by Wilson (later First) College. Scheduled to open in the fall of 2026, Hobson College would be the first residential college at Princeton named for a Black woman.

AFRICAN AMERICAN STUDIES, THE DEPARTMENT OF, grew from a fledgling program in 1969, to a center in 2006, to a department in 2015. Today it includes many of the world's most notable scholars of African American studies, and it provides an innovative model for teaching and research about African-descended people, with a central focus on their experiences in the United States. The curriculum reflects the complex interplay among the political, economic, and cultural forces that shape understanding of the historic achievements and struggles of African-descended people in this country and around the world.

The department offers a graduate certificate, an undergraduate concentration, and an undergraduate certificate for students majoring in other departments. The undergraduate program's three subfields are African American culture and life; race and public policy; and global race and ethnicity. The department's faculty, whether solely or jointly appointed, are established leaders or rising stars not only in African American studies, but in fields ranging from art and archaeology and comparative literature, to English, history, psychology, religion, and sociology.

In 1955, Princeton appointed its first African American faculty member, assistant professor of English Charles Davis. A conference in 1962 welcomed professors and novelists to present papers on the historical, political, psychological, and cultural aspects of Black life in America, and the participants discussed an agenda for two years' study of African American culture. A research center for Afro-American Studies existed for one year, between 1965 and 1966.

On the heels of a 1967 conference on the "Future of the Negro Undergraduate," a faculty steering committee recommended to President Robert Goheen the establishment of a program of research and teaching in African American culture, and in 1969 a program in African American Studies was founded with history professor and future provost Sheldon Hackney as chair. The teaching staff of seven was composed almost entirely of visiting lecturers and non-tenure-track faculty representing the program in African American Studies and the departments of English, History, Politics, and Psychology.

In the fall of 1969 the program offered two courses: a seminar on Black American writers and a course on African American history. In the spring the number of courses was increased by five, and enrollment in the seven courses amounted to more than 500 students. In its first year the program attracted almost 50 certificate students, but that number fell as the program struggled to find firm footing with four chairs in its first four years.

The program gained traction in 1973–74 when sociology professor Howard Taylor arrived from Syracuse University to chair the program, which he did with great success for 14 years. Faculty appointments during his tenure included John Jemott, Nobel Laureate Toni Morrison, Cornel West *80, and Nell Painter, making Princeton one of the leading centers of African American scholarship and teaching in the country.

A 1986 self-study recommended rigorous recruitment of more full-time faculty, an increase in library resources, the creation of an external advisory council, and the development of a regular series of lectures, conferences, and special events.

In 2005 President Shirley Tilghman convened an ad hoc committee on the future of African American studies at Princeton that was chaired by philosophy professor Kwame Anthony Appiah. The committee found that for more than 35 years the program had been recognized "as a center for the study of African American life and history, of race and ethnicity as social and cultural phenomena in both the domestic and global contexts, and of cutting-edge interdisciplinary cultural studies (involving) research and teaching."

Appiah said that "the idea behind the center is of spokes radiating out to make connections with students studying art, music, history, literature, philosophy, politics, religion, and other fields." He said Princeton recognized that "you can't do jazz studies . . . without taking on board the work of African American cultural studies, and you can't study politics or public policy, or even bioethics, without work that has been done in the areas of race."

The advisory committee noted that "because of the continuing and evolving centrality of race in American political, economic, social and cultural life, reflection on race and on the distinctive experience of Black people is an indispensable element in a preparation for life in this country."

The trustees approved the Appiah committee's recommendation that the program be elevated to a center for African American Studies, and English professor Valerie Smith was named its first director. The center moved from Dickinson Hall to a more prominent home in Stanhope Hall on the historic front campus. A strong core faculty emerged and sole appointments in African American Studies began. In 2009 religion professor Eddie Glaude Jr. *97 succeeded Smith as director.

In 2015 African American Studies was elevated to departmental status with Glaude as chair, and today the department includes many of the most prolific and notable African American studies scholars in the world. Members of its faculty who hold endowed chairs include Glaude; Wallace Best (jointly appointed with Religion), who was the first African American and first male to direct the program in Gender and Sexuality Studies; Tera Hunter (History); and Imani Perry, a scholar of law, literary and cultural studies, and an author of creative nonfiction.

Other tenured professors in the department include Wendy Belcher (Comparative Literature); Ruha Benjamin, who specializes in the study of science, medicine, and technology, race-ethnicity and gender, and knowledge and power; Joshua Guild (History); Naomi Murakawa, who specializes in crime policy and the carceral state; Kinohi Nishikawa (English); and Chika Okeke-Agulu (Art and Archaeology).

Departmental status means that undergraduates can major in African American Studies. The first cohort of 10 concentrators graduated in 2018; in that same year, 18 seniors from other departments received certificates. The graduate program in African American Studies provides an opportunity for students to complement doctoral studies in their home department with coordinated interdisciplinary training in African American studies, and in 2018 four PhD students completed their graduate certificates.

In 2020, the department graduated its third class of 10 concentrators and 19 seniors earned certificates. The department had five PhD students who earned graduate certificates.

Graduate student engagement with the department is open to any Princeton graduate student through the faculty-graduate student seminar. Recent seminar topics have included "Black Studies in the Digital Age," "Sexuality in African American Communities and Cultures," "Black Studies and Biopolitics," African/American Diasporic Literature," "The Politics of Black Families and Intimacies," and "How We Get Free: The Black Political Imagination."

The department and Princeton University Press jointly offer the annual Toni Morrison Lectures, which spotlight new and exciting work of scholars and writers from both academe and the broader world of letters. The lectures are published in book form by the Press, and celebrate the expansive literary imagination, intellectual adventurousness, and political insightfulness that characterized Toni Morrison's writing.

The department also offers podcasts, hosted by Glaude, which provide a platform for people outside the University to learn about the department's research and scholarship. The podcasts focus on the political, economic, and cultural forces that shape understandings of race in America in the twenty-first century.

In his 2019–20 annual report as chair, Glaude reflected on the department's strategies for coping with the COVID-19 pandemic and its response to the nation's struggle with racism. He wrote: "We have provided analyses, historical contexts, languages to talk about the problems we face, and moral provocations for a country on a knife's edge . . . we remain a national resource and the best department of African American Studies in the world."

He also noted that the department was preparing to move from Stanhope to a larger space in Morrison Hall, saying "While Stanhope Hall will be missed, we look forward to being housed in a building named after Toni Morrison, who helped build African American Studies at Princeton."

ALEXANDER, STEPHEN, who first developed astronomy as a separate discipline at Princeton, graduated with honors from Union College at the age of 18. A cousin and brother-in-law of Joseph Henry, he collaborated with Henry in his scientific investigations at Albany Academy and accompanied him to Princeton in 1832, when Henry became professor of natural philosophy. Appointed tutor in mathematics in 1833 and professor of astronomy in 1840, Alexander remained associated with the College for 50 years.

Alexander gave Princeton's first course in astronomy. The College's first astronomy building, the Halsted Observatory, which stood on University Place from 1869 to 1932, was built through his influence and from his plans; however, a telescope was not installed until after his retirement. Working with only his own small telescope, he carried on a steady program of research, published many papers, and studied comets, most notably the great comet of 1843, whose sudden appearance excited interest in astronomy throughout America.

He also studied the atmospheres of Venus, Mercury, and Jupiter; led expeditions for the Coast and Geodetic Survey and the National Academy of Sciences to observe solar eclipses; and, in collaboration with Henry, conducted experiments on the relative heat of sunspots. He was president of the American Association for the Advancement of Science in 1859 and was chosen as one of the original 50 members of the National Academy of Sciences in 1863.

The winter before he died, Alexander concluded his astronomical observations of more than half a century by observing the 1882 transit of Venus across the disk of the sun, a phenomenon that did not occur again until 2004.

ALEXANDER HALL was erected between 1892 and 1894 as a convocation venue that could seat the entire student body for commencement exercises and other large gatherings. It was given by Harriet Crocker Alexander in honor of her husband, Charles B. Alexander 1870; his father, Henry M. Alexander 1840; and his grandfather, Archibald Alexander, Princeton Theological Seminary's first professor, all of whom served as Princeton trustees.

During its early years, the building hosted the sesquicentennial (150th) anniversary celebration in 1896, Woodrow Wilson 1879's inauguration as Princeton president in 1902, and the Stafford Little Lectures given by former US President Grover Cleveland. For 30 years freshmen were welcomed and seniors graduated in Alexander, but by 1922 commencement exercises had outgrown the building and thereafter they were held in front of Nassau Hall.

After Marquand Chapel burned in 1920, Alexander Hall was used for Sunday services until the University Chapel was completed in 1928. An organ was installed in 1910 and was used for 40 years, but it is no longer functional. Into the 1960s, students made semiannual pilgrimages to Alexander Hall to learn their course grades, which were posted on the interior walls of the building for all to see.

Alexander Hall was the last High Victorian Gothic building constructed at Princeton. It was designed by William A. Potter, who also designed Chancellor Green Library and East Pyne Hall; Potter also participated in the design of Witherspoon Hall. The design of Alexander Hall is Richardsonian Romanesque, with rough-faced granite walls and brown sandstone trim, a steep gabled roof, tall dormers, and zig-zag detail under the eaves. Its unusual features have been described as conveying both monumentality and whimsy.

The building's arcaded ambulatory was originally open, creating seven entrances to the hall, but it was enclosed with glass windows in 1928. Carved above the window arches along the ambulatory on the east side of the building are the names of scientists and mathematicians; the names of writers and artists are engraved on the west side.

At the back of the stage is a rostrum with a large throne-like marble chair ("the President's seat"), surrounded by a semi-circle of seats for the faculty. Rising two stories behind this is a mosaic with scenes from Homer's *Iliad* and *Odyssey*. There is a carving of Henry Alexander set into the wall on the right side of the stage, with a Venetian choir loft above it. The balcony is reached by stairways in two towers on the north side of the structure; they, along with the taller southern towers, echo the towers of Witherspoon Hall.

The ornately carved southern exterior features a large Tiffany stained-glass rose window that portrays Genius, Knowledge, Study, and Fame. Under the window is a bas-relief sculpture of 36 figures in which Learning is balancing the Book of Knowledge on its knee, framed by Oratory, Theology, Law, History, Philosophy, and Ethics on the left, and Architecture, Sculpture, Painting, Poetry, Music, and Belles-Lettres on the right. There is a figure in an upper left panel representing Moses, and on the upper right sits Christ; they represent Law and Religion, as well as the words on Princeton's official seal, *Vet Nov Testamentum* (the Old and New Testaments).

Two Latin inscriptions appear on the southern exterior. The top message reads: *Harriet Crocker Alexander gave and dedicated this building to Princeton University in the glory of God and in the growth of knowledge the thirteenth of June 1894*. The lower inscription, translated from Lucretius, reads: *There is no greater joy than to hold high aloft the serene abodes well bulwarked by the learning of the wise.*

After deciding to locate Alexander Hall where he did, Potter sought—unsuccessfully—to persuade the University to demolish the church that stands between it and Nassau Street so that Chancellor Green, Nassau Hall, and Alexander Hall all would look out into the town from behind wide swaths of green.

In 1984–85 the interior of Alexander Hall was extensively renovated and renamed Richardson Auditorium following a gift from David A. Richardson '66 in memory of his father, David B. Richardson '33. Among other improvements, this project installed sound reflectors that converted the auditorium into an acoustically superior concert hall; it is often used for recording of chamber, orchestral, instrumental, and vocal music. While originally built as a 1,500-seat assembly hall with wooden benches, Alexander Hall now seats just under 900.

Alexander/Richardson have accommodated many different activities over the years—student mass meetings (including, memorably, one following the assassination of Dr. Martin Luther King Jr. in 1968), assemblies, ceremonies, lectures, dance and dramatic presentations, and speeches. It is home to the University Concert series, and it is the performance venue for the University Orchestra.

As one of the most historic and recognizable structures on the campus, Alexander Hall was selected by the US Postal Service to appear on a postcard commemorating Princeton's 250th anniversary in 1996. It features a painting of the south façade from the perspective of a quadrangle between Alexander Hall and Witherspoon Hall known colloquially as Alexander Beach. The first day of issue ceremony for the postcard, in September 1996, was held, fittingly, on the stage of Alexander Hall.

ALUMNI AFFINITY CONFERENCES. Alumni have been coming back to campus for class reunions since the middle of the nineteenth century, and for Alumni Day since 1915. They also come back on many other occasions, both formal and informal, and for conferences of many kinds. In 2005 the alumni office introduced a new concept: conferences organized in partnership with affiliated or affinity alumni groups. The conferences were open to all alumni, but they focused primarily on the experiences—as students and as alumni—of members of those groups.

The first two conferences took place in the fall of 2006. One, planned in collaboration with the Association of Black Princeton Alumni (ABPA), was the *Coming Back and Looking Forward Conference for Black Princeton Alumni*; the other, called *Kaleidoscope: An Alumni Conference on Race and Community*, was planned in consultation with Black, Latino, Asian-American, and Native American alumni.

The Black alumni conference, in particular, exceeded expectations in terms of attendance with some 500 participants; what was especially noteworthy was the number of attendees who had not been back on campus since their graduation. This and subsequent conferences sought to reach out to alumni who may not have felt fully validated as students or who later felt alienated, unconnected, or at least not ready to engage as alumni. The conferences were designed to demonstrate the University's interest in their participation, and the progress it had made and was continuing to make in becoming a more diverse, inclusive, and welcoming place.

In preparation for each conference, alumni council staff and volunteers conducted focus groups around the country, and sometimes around the world, with alumni from the affinity groups to plan the program in accordance with their principal interests. In most cases, hundreds of alumni were involved in the planning.

A second conference for Black alumni, *Coming Back, Moving Forward*, took place in October 2009 and attracted some 650 alumni, again including many who had not been on campus since graduation. This engagement by alumni returning for the first time characterized all the affinity conferences. Attendees especially appreciated that their peer group at the conferences was other members of their affinity group from different generations, including current

The University held affinity conferences for Black alumni in 2006, 2009, 2014, and 2019. This session from the 2019 *Thrive* conference filled McCosh 50.

At the 2017 *Adelante Tigres!* conference celebrating Latino alumni, Supreme Court Justice and former trustee Sonia Sotomayor '76 and then-trustee Margarita Rosa '74 discussed their experiences at and after Princeton.

Trustee Sheryl WuDunn *88 interviewed Gordon Wu '58 during the 2015 *We Flourish* conference celebrating Asian and Asian American alumni.

students, which shed light on both commonalities and differences over time. This differentiated the conferences from reunions, where one's peer group is one's class. The conferences attracted graduate alumni as well as undergraduate alumni, which further enriched the conversations and the networking that took place.

The subsequent conferences (with attendance in parentheses) were:

2011: *She Roars: Celebrating Women at Princeton* (1,300)
2013: *Every Voice: A Princeton University Conference for Lesbian, Gay, Bisexual, Transgender, and Ally Alumni* (550)
2013: *Many Minds, Many Stripes: A Princeton University Conference for Graduate Alumni* (1,000)
2014: *Coming Back: Reconnecting Princeton's Black Alumni* (750)
2015: *We Flourish: Celebrating Asian and Asian American Alumni at Princeton University* (700)
2016: *L'Chaim! To Life: Celebrating 100 Years of Jewish Life at Princeton* (900)
2017: *Adelante Tigres! Celebrating Latino Alumni at Princeton University* (750)
2018: *She Roars: Celebrating Women at Princeton* (3,000)
2019: *Thrive: Empowering and Celebrating Princeton's Black Alumni* (1,400)

ALUMNI COUNCIL, THE, is the governing body of the Princeton Alumni Association. All alumni are automatically members of the association and its president chairs the council. The purposes of the association are to "promote the interests, welfare, and educational aims of Princeton University and its alumni, establish and maintain a mutually beneficial relationship between Princeton University and its alumni, and encourage lifelong engagement of

Alumni Council   49

Rabbi Edward Feld, director of Princeton Hillel from 1973 to 1992, engaged in animated conversation with Sarah Klagsbrun '91 during the 2016 conference, *L'Chaim! To Life*, a celebration of 100 years of Jewish life at Princeton.

The 2013 conference *Many Minds, Many Stripes* brought 1,000 graduate alumni to campus. Participants included former president of the Association of Princeton Graduate Alumni Rose Li *92; behind her are Anne Sherrerd *87. the first graduate alum to chair the Alumni Council, and Margaret Clark *88.

These banners on the front campus welcomed alumni to the 2013 *Every Voice* conference for gay, bisexual, transgender, and ally alumni.

The first *She Roars* conference in 2011 attracted 1,300 alumnae; this photo is from the second conference which attracted more than 3,000 alumnae.

Princeton University's alumni with their fellow alumni and the University community."

The 300-plus members of the council include the presidents of all the alumni classes, regional associations, and the Princeton Club of New York; the members of the council's executive committee; the officers of the Association of Princeton Graduate Alumni (APGA); the presidents of the Asian American Alumni Association of Princeton, the Association of Black Princeton Alumni, the Association of Latino Princeton Alumni, the Fund for Reunion/Princeton Bisexual, Transgender, Gay and Lesbian Alumni, and the Princeton Prize in Race Relations; a representative of the Princeton Women's Network Advisory Council; up to 12 appointed term members; and, as "life members," all former chairs of the council, presidents emeriti of the University, and former directors of the council.

The council traces its ancestry to the Committee of Fifty, an alumni organization that was established by the trustees in 1904 to raise funds for "the immediate necessities and future development of the University." In 1909 the trustees transformed the committee into the Graduate Council of Princeton University, with a mandate that extended beyond fundraising into various areas of alumni engagement, including class activities and regional associations.

With its broader mandate, the Graduate Council superseded an entity known as the Alumni Association of Nassau Hall, which had been founded in 1826 "to promote the interests of the College and the friendly intercourse of its graduates." In its early years, the association held its annual meetings in the chapel at the time of Commencement, and they attracted coverage in the New York press. Its founding president was former US president James Madison 1771, and its first secretary was future College president John Maclean Jr. 1816; in 1868, upon his retirement from the Princeton presidency, Maclean became president of the association and served in that capacity until his death in 1886.

When James McCosh became president in 1868, he considered alumni to be an integral part of the institution and traveled around the country to encourage the development of local and regional associations. The first such association, in New York (now the Princeton Club of New York), had been formed in 1866, and others quickly followed: in Philadelphia in 1868; Washington, DC in 1872; Cincinnati and Western Pennsylvania in 1875; Chicago and St. Louis in 1876; Louisville, Omaha, and the Pacific Coast in 1884; Central Pennsylvania, Long Island, and Maryland in 1885; Trenton, Northeastern Pennsylvania, and the New Northwest (Minneapolis) in 1886; and Cleveland in 1887. By the time McCosh left office in 1888 there were 17 associations, and from 1893 to 1899 there was a Princeton National Alumni Association composed of delegates from the various clubs and associations.

On November 1, 1919, the Graduate Council and the clubs and associations were consolidated into a new entity called the National Alumni Association of Princeton University. In 1940 Annual Giving and other alumni-based fundraising activities were separated from the council, and in 1957 the council modified its name to become the Alumni Council. Its mission, as reiterated in 2002 by its executive committee and the trustee committee on alumni affairs, is "to engage as many alumni as possible in the ongoing life of the University in mutually beneficial ways and to support alumni initiatives that promote the goals of the University." In 1969 the National Alumni Association of Princeton University dropped the word "national" in recognition of its increasingly global reach.

Today there are more than 160 regional associations throughout the country and around the world; they engage undergraduate and graduate alumni, parents, and students, and their activities range from interviewing prospective applicants, conducting Annual Giving solicitations, and hosting speakers from the University to awarding the Princeton Prize in Race Relations, providing summer job and career counseling for local undergraduates, sponsoring educational programs, and organizing community service projects.

Princeton presidents regularly visit associations throughout the United States, and over recent decades they also have visited with alumni in Canada and throughout Europe, Asia, South America, and the Middle East. Classes conduct a broad range of programs and hold reunions every year, with classmates typically returning from all corners of the globe, especially for the major reunions every five years.

The Alumni Association officially meets once a year on Alumni Day, and the Alumni Council's annual meeting takes place on the Friday of reunions weekend. (In 2020 and 2021, due to the COVID-19 pandemic, the council held its annual meetings remotely on the appointed Friday, with more than 500 alumni registered to participate.)

The council's executive committee typically meets three times a year. The executive committee is composed of the officers of the council (including its director, who serves as secretary of the council and of the executive committee); the president and five other appointed members of the APGA; the chair and one other member of each standing committee and special committee; 10 appointed term members; the chairs of the Annual Giving committee, the Inter-Club Council, and the board of the *Princeton Alumni Weekly* (*PAW*); 10 regional association officers; eight class officers; two alumni serving on the Princeton faculty; the president of the senior class and one other undergraduate; a graduate student representative; the presidents of the affiliated groups who serve on the council; the four alumni members of the Council of the Princeton University Community (CPUC); the chair and vice chair of the Princeton Prize in Race Relations; and a representative of the Princeton Women's Network Advisory Council.

The council's standing committees include planning and review, communications and technology, class affairs, regional associations, Princeton schools, Princetoniana, and reunions. Its special committees include a committee to nominate alumni trustees that identifies candidates for each year's alumni trustee elections, a committee on nominations, a committee on awards for service to Princeton, and others as needed. The nominating committee proposes candidates for membership on the executive committee, and for the four alumni seats on the CPUC and the six elected alumni on the *PAW* board.

Through the schools committee thousands of volunteers each year work with the admission office to interview candidates for admission and encourage those admitted to attend. In recent years members of this committee have contacted more than 99 percent of all applicants. In addition to supporting the work of the committees, the professional staff of the office of alumni engagement offers a range of alumni education programs and sponsors TigerNet, an online alumni community first created in 1995 that provides a searchable directory, email accounts using the @alumni.princeton.edu email address, and discussion groups of many kinds.

The staff supports all the classes, with special assistance for the Old Guard classes who have passed their 65th reunion; it also supports the regional associations and the affinity groups, including the newest group, the Princeton Veterans Alumni Association, which includes alumni, students, faculty, and staff who have served, are serving, or are training to serve in the armed forces.

The staff also manages reunions, Alumni Day, the Service of Remembrance, affinity group conferences, and other on-campus programs.

In 1961, after a quarter of a century as secretary of the Graduate Council and then the Alumni Council, Donald Griffin '23 was appointed general secretary, serving until his retirement in 1964. Directors who have served as secretary of the council since 1970 have been David Rahr '60, Daniel White '65, M. Kathryn Taylor '74, Margaret Miller '80, and Alexandra Day '02.

Chairs of the council since 1970 have been: D. Bruce Merrifield '42, Mortimer Chute Jr. '56, Frederick Redpath '39, George Faunce III '47, Donald Dickson '49, Franklin Schaffer '45, Wesley Wright Jr. '51, Robert McCartney '56, W. Scott Magargee III '62, Richard Scribner '58, James "Poss" Parham Jr. '52, Dorothy Bedford '78, Elihu Inselbuch '59, Luther Munford '71, Brent Henry '69, Joseph Serafini '64, Diane deCordova '83, Clyde "Skip" Rankin III '72, Linda Francis Knights '77, David Siegfried '64, Anne Sherrerd *87, Henry Von Kohorn '66, Nancy Newman '78, Jeffrey Wieser '74, Jennifer Daniels '93, Richard Holland Jr. '96, and Mary Newburn '97.

ALUMNI DAY was first observed on Lincoln's birthday in 1915. According to the *Daily Princetonian*, it came about because "for some months past, the Graduate Council has had under consideration the suggested plan of holding an Alumni Day in Princeton at some time during the college year other than commencement." The council believed that many alumni would welcome an opportunity to visit Princeton "when they could combine many of the enjoyable features of an alumni reunion with an exceptional opportunity of seeing the University and its various departments under normal working conditions."

About a hundred alumni joined in what the *Alumni Weekly* called "an intellectual pilgrimage to their Alma Mater," highlighted by a meeting of the Alumni Association in the Faculty Room of Nassau Hall, during which alumni heard talks on such topics as the function of the university library, the physical care and development of students, and "standards of scholarship." After a luncheon at the graduate college, tours of the campus were offered, President John Grier Hibben and his wife hosted a reception at Prospect House, and the evening ended with what was described as a "smoker" at the Nassau Club.

The following day, the *Prince* reported that the meeting was "a revelation" to many of the alumni, who "had no idea what the college was doing in the scholastic line, and many had not even heard of the preceptorial system and the honors courses." The secretary of the Graduate Council declared the occasion a success and said, "there is little doubt but that it will be repeated on Washington's birthday next year."

In 1916 Alumni Day did take place on Washington's birthday (February 22), and that remained the case until 1955 when it was moved to the Saturday nearest February 22nd. The second Alumni Day featured more programming, including "a life-saving and swimming demonstration" in Brokaw tank. Further innovations in the years immediately following reflected the impact of a country at war; the 1920 program, for example, paid tribute to alumni who had died in the war and it featured a graduation ceremony for veterans who had not returned in time to participate in the June 1919 "victory commencement."

Gradually, attendance outgrew the Faculty Room, and since the late 1930s the Alumni Day luncheon has taken place at the old University Gymnasium, Baker Rink, Dillon Gym, and Jadwin Gym, preceded by a morning of lectures and discussions, and followed, since 1970, by the annual Service of Remembrance, which honors alumni, students, faculty, and staff whose deaths were recorded during the previous calendar year.

Alumni Day came to signify not only an occasion for alumni to re-engage in the academic and extracurricular life of the campus, but an opportunity for the University to recognize exceptional achievement. The Moses Taylor Pyne Honor Prize, the highest distinction the University can bestow on an undergraduate, was first awarded in 1922, and on Alumni Day 1957 the University presented the first Woodrow Wilson Award, the highest honor it can confer on undergraduate alumni. The highest honor for graduate alumni, the James Madison Medal, was awarded for the first time in 1973, and in recent years the graduate student winners of the prestigious Porter Ogden Jacobus Fellowships are also recognized during the Alumni Day ceremony.

The morning of Alumni Day offers faculty lectures and talks by the winners of the Madison Medal and Wilson Award. In addition to the awards presentations, the luncheon program includes remarks by the president of the Alumni Association and the chair of Annual Giving; announcement of the nominees for that year's alumni trustee elections; remarks by the president of the University; and the singing of "Old Nassau" by the roughly 1,000 alumni, parents, friends, and family typically in attendance.

ALUMNI EDUCATION PROGRAMS encompass a variety of learning opportunities on-campus, online, and around the world. Alumni Day was created in 1915 in part to acquaint alumni with the intellectual life of the campus, and as early as 1951 the Class of 1926 added academic content to the programming at reunions.

In 1970 the Alumni Council offered its first Alumni College, which it described as "an intensive period of study and dialogue for those whose curiosity and intellectual interest reach beyond their normal daily pursuits." The first college was a residential program held at the Princeton Inn during the week following reunions. It served as a model for what grew into a program of four or five colleges a year, organized and directed by members of the faculty in locations throughout the country and abroad. Each three- to 14-day college focused on a specific theme and typically included lectures, discussions, media presentations, and field trips. Most colleges were one-time events, but the college on geology and astronomy at the department of Geosciences' camp in Red Lodge, Montana, became a hardy perennial. The first international Alumni College was held in France in 1976.

An Alumni Studies program that was launched in 1996 as an outgrowth of an initiative by the Class of 1946 provided alumni with an introductory audio tape, written materials for home study, and on-campus lectures and precepts.

In 2004 the alumni affairs office launched an ambitious alumni travel-study program called Princeton Journeys that aims to offer between a dozen and 15 trips each year with unique educational and/or experiential components, typically involving one or more Princeton faculty members and sometimes in collaboration with other universities. The journeys are usually operated by outside vendors, but with active participation by University staff.

The alumni office also sends faculty speakers to regional associations around the country; sponsors lectures on Alumni Day and on mornings of selected home football games; and continues to offer academic programming at reunions through the Alumni-Faculty Forum program and in other ways. Many of the on-campus lectures, including those on Alumni Day, are made available online, and alumni also have access to Princeton Online, a program introduced in 2012 that makes not-for-credit courses by Princeton faculty available for free to anyone with an internet connection.

ALUMNI WEEKLY, THE PRINCETON, (PAW) has, for more than 120 years, kept Princeton alumni connected to each other and to the University. Its first editor, Jesse Lynch Williams 1892, described it as a kind of "long distance telephone . . . to keep a live connection between the University and its alumni . . . for their mutual enlightenment, benefit, and satisfaction." In the words of its current charter, its mission is "to arouse, foster, and maintain interest in, and disseminate information concerning, the University; . . . to convey as complete, fair, and accurate an understanding of the University and its alumni as possible; . . . to provide alumni with a continued sense of belonging to the University and with opportunities to communicate with each other; and to advance the long-term best interests of the University and the alumni."

The *PAW* was first published on April 7, 1900. It replaced the *Alumni Princetonian*, a weekly edition of the *Daily Princetonian* that its undergraduate editors started in 1894. The *Alumni Princetonian* was available to alumni by subscription, but fewer than 500 of the then-6,000 alumni subscribed.

The first issue of the *PAW* offered 16 pages of campus and alumni news and called for greater alumni involvement in the University. It also featured several pages of class notes and two obituaries. It was published by a company that had been founded just two months earlier at 2 Nassau Street. Seeking a more permanent arrangement, in 1906 alumni created Princeton University Press (its building at the corner of Charlton and William Streets opened in 1911) and the *PAW* became an administrative unit of the Press.

In 1915 the Press established a board of editorial direction for the *PAW* that included three members appointed by the alumni association and two members appointed by the Press. That same year the magazine's business manager devised a system by which undergraduate classes purchased subscriptions so that all their members would receive the 36 issues published each year.

During World War II frequency dropped to 32 issues a year, and by 1951 it was down to 30. With costs escalating, a publishing advisory group was formed in 1971 to provide advice on increasing advertising revenues and controlling production costs, and in 1977 the magazine dropped its frequency to 21 issues a year. By 1988 it was publishing 17 issues a year, and by the late 2010s it was publishing 14 times a year—still more than any other alumni magazine in the world. In 2020–21 the *PAW* announced it would publish 11 issues, monthly from September through July, while boosting coverage on its website and on social media.

In 1977 the *PAW*, the Press, and the University reached an agreement under which the University, in addition to continuing to pay for advertising and for subscriptions for faculty, staff, and the senior class, would contribute $35,000 a year toward a *PAW* budget of roughly $200,000 in return for access to 20 pages a year for messages to alumni (these later became the President's Page).

To help the *PAW* meet its voracious appetite for content, the University agreed to prepare articles that the *PAW* could publish prior to their compilation into a separate *University Magazine* that the University distributed to a different audience. This arrangement was discontinued in 1982; the resulting savings to the University were added to its base contribution, and the University agreed to increase its contribution each year thereafter at the same rate as the *PAW* budget.

In 1991 the *Alumni Weekly* moved out from under the umbrella of the Press and a new nonprofit corporation, Princeton Alumni Publications, Inc. (PAP), was formed to publish the magazine from office space that was secured on Nassau Street. All staff members of the new organization were designated University employees, but with no direct reporting relationship to University administrators.

In 2000, following extensive review by a committee composed of *PAW* board members, University trustees, alumni volunteers, and senior university officers, PAP was dissolved and the *PAW* was constituted as an office of the University associated with the Alumni Council, with the editor of the magazine reporting editorially to the board of the *PAW* and administratively to the director of the council.

At the same time the University more than doubled its financial contribution to the magazine to provide relief to the alumni classes, with an understanding that going forward the University and the classes would contribute equal amounts after accounting for advertising, other subscriptions, and other income, and with the goal that under this arrangement the classes and the University each would cover about one-third of the total budget. (Undergraduate classes would pay for subscriptions for all class members according to a graduated scale that charges lower rates to the younger and older classes.)

The 11-member *PAW* board includes alumni with professional experience in journalism and publishing who are elected to three-year terms by the Alumni Council, a member of the faculty, the council's vice chair and the chair of its committee on class affairs, the University's vice president for communications and public affairs, and the director of the council. There is also a non-voting representative from one of the recent alumni classes. The *PAW's* charter guarantees the magazine's editorial independence and gives the editor sole responsibility for its editorial content.

The *PAW* has a circulation of about 73,000, with all undergraduate alumni and all Association of Princeton Graduate Alumni (APGA) dues-payers receiving all issues; in recent years five of each year's issues have been sent to all graduate alumni, boosting the circulation for those issues to about 96,000. Princeton faculty and professional staff also receive the magazine.

The *PAW* has had an online presence since 1984, when then-editor Charles Creesy '65 created an "electronic paw," a kind of chat room that posted articles and news and even offered an "electronic precept." Today's *PAW Online* provides regular updates between print issues and additional online-only content and email alerts are sent to both undergraduate and graduate alumni when a new issue is posted online. There are also email alerts regarding books published by people with a Princeton connection and alumni in the news.

Williams, the *PAW's* first editor, was an undergraduate editor of the *Nassau Lit* and later a Pulitzer Prize-winning playwright. Edwin Mark Norris 1895, the second editor, devoted 21 years to the magazine. Subsequent editors and their years of service have been: W. Irving Harris 1920 (1925), Asa Bushnell 1921 (1925–1930), Edmund DeLong 1922 (1930–1931), Datus Smith 1929 (1931–1940), Douglas Stuart '35 (1940–1942), Frederick Osborne 1924 (1942–1946), Ernest Stewart '41 (1946–1951), Philip Quigg '43 (1951–1955), John Davies '41 (1955–1969), Landon Jones Jr. '66 (1969–1974); Charles Creesy '65 (1975–1987); Michelle Preston *86 (1987–1989); James Merritt '66 (1989–1999); Janice Harayda (1999); Jane Chapman Martin '89 (2000–2002); and Marilyn Marks *86 (2002–).

Over the years, many alumni have reported that when the *PAW* arrives, they turn first to the letters to the editor and class notes and memorials (although in the electronic age, younger alumni in particular may more likely keep up with their classmates through social media). From the beginning the magazine has included essays by students, and many alumni express appreciation for the magazine's reporting on campus news, its rich feature content, its strikingly designed covers, and the messages from the president of the University that appear in each issue.

In 2000 the magazine published a 518-page book entitled *The Best of PAW: 100 Years of the Princeton Alumni Weekly*, with selections made by former editors Jones, Creesy, and Merritt.

ANDLINGER CENTER FOR ENERGY AND THE ENVIRONMENT, THE, is an interdisciplinary research and education center that was established in 2008 with a gift of $100 million from international business leader and philanthropist Gerhard R. "Gerry" Andlinger '52. It began operation in 2010, and in 2016 it moved into a state-of-the-art building at the corner of Olden Street and Prospect Avenue adjacent to the Engineering Quadrangle and Bowen Hall. It is part of the school of Engineering and Applied Science; its founding director, mechanical and aerospace engineering professor Emily Carter, left that position to serve as dean of the school from 2016 to 2019.

The University's first interdisciplinary research program on energy and the environment, the Center for Energy and Environmental Studies (CEES), was founded in 1971 following the arrival of mechanical and aerospace engineering professor Robert Socolow. Senior research scientist Robert Williams founded CEES's energy systems analysis group (now part of the Andlinger center), and in 2000, Williams, Socolow, and ecology and evolutionary biology professor Stephen Pacala led a Princeton team that secured funding for a Carbon Mitigation Initiative that remains part of the High Meadows Environmental Institute.

The Andlinger Center was created to bring researchers from many disciplines and backgrounds together to develop new technologies and effective and sustainable solutions to problems related to energy and the environment. In the words of its second director, professor of chemical and biological engineering Yueh-Lin (Lynn) Loo *01, it seeks to find "new and creative ways to fuel societies and economies while limiting carbon pollution."

The center's interests include sustainable energy development, energy conservation, and environmental protection and remediation, with a focus not only on engineering, but on policy and human behavior as well. Its research areas include the built environment, transportation, and infrastructure; electricity production, transmission, and storage; fuels and chemicals; environmental sensing and remediation; decision and behavioral science, policy, and economics; and environmental and climate science.

The center is housed in a 129,000-square-foot complex of laboratories, offices, teaching spaces, courtyards, and gardens, designed by the architects Tod Williams '65 and Billie Tsien. It includes a 208-seat lecture hall (named for its donor, Paul Maeder '75), and presiding over the entrance to the center is a 19-foot-tall copper sculpture, *URODA*, by the artist Ursula von Rydingsvard.

The Andlinger Center collaborates with a broad range of engineering and natural science departments, the schools of Public and International Affairs and Architecture, and many other related entities and programs. It administers a corporate membership program, Princeton E-ffiliates Partnership, that promotes technology transfer between the University and corporate partners and enhances interactions between students and practitioners.

The Andlinger Center created an executive education program in partnership with the World Economic Forum to contextualize the complexities of the energy system and its impact on the environment for business and community leaders, as well as government officials, and to prepare them to think critically and creatively about the roles their organizations can play in addressing environmental and climate problems. Rapid Switch is a global research collaboration spearheaded by the center that investigates how to accelerate decarbonization efforts worldwide.

In 1948, as a teenager in Austria shortly after the end of World War II, Andlinger won an essay contest sponsored by the *New York Herald Tribune* that brought him to the United States and, ultimately, to Princeton. He made his gift, he said "out of a sense of responsibility that I feel that I can do something that not that many people can do." Andlinger chaired the center's advisory council from its founding until his death in December 2017.

ANDLINGER CENTER FOR THE HUMANITIES, THE, was formally established in 2004 to enhance the environment for the humanities at Princeton and reaffirm their central role in its educational mission. The center is named for Gerhard R. Andlinger '52, whose $25 million gift helped create a more visible, functional, and unified home for many of the University's humanities departments and programs.

The project began in 2000 with the renovation of the historic Joseph Henry House on the front campus. It also included renovations of two other historic buildings, Chancellor Green and East Pyne (the University's first and second library buildings and, before the renovation, home of its student center), and the construction of a new humanities building to the east of the Henry house which was named Scheide Caldwell House following a gift from William Scheide '36.

The Joseph Henry House is the home of the Council of the Humanities, the Society of Fellows in the Liberal Arts, and the Ferris, McGraw, and Robbins Seminars in Journalism, while the Scheide Caldwell House contains many interdisciplinary programs associated with the council. East Pyne houses the Classics department, Comparative Literature, and the language and literature departments; the Chancellor Green rotunda and the café provide space for study, discussion, relaxation, nourishment, and gatherings of many kinds.

The East Pyne/Chancellor Green renovations included construction of a 71-seat underground auditorium as well as a state-of-the-art language laboratory.

ANNIVERSARY CELEBRATIONS have been held to commemorate Princeton's 100th, 150th, 200th, and 250th anniversaries.

Centennial (100th)

The College celebrated its centennial at Commencement in 1847. Present besides the graduating seniors and their families were a large number of alumni, delegates from other colleges, the vice president of the United States (George Mifflin Dallas 1810), the governor and several ex-governors of New Jersey, a justice of the United States Supreme Court, the chief justice and chancellor of New Jersey and of Delaware, and other dignitaries.

The celebration lasted only two days—Tuesday and Wednesday, June 29 and 30—but much oratory was packed into that brief period. There were three sessions on Tuesday and two on Wednesday. All but the last were held in the First (now Nassau) Presbyterian Church.

At the first session, Chief Justice Henry W. Green 1820 (later Chancellor Green) gave an address formally opening a new law school, which ceased operations only a few years later. At the second session, James W. Alexander 1820, the historian for the centennial, spoke over two hours, "with such eloquence," the planning committee reported, "that the audience sat in rapt attention, missing not a single word."

On Tuesday evening eight representatives of the junior class delivered orations, including a student from Ireland on "The Faded Shamrock," and one from Mississippi on "Why Has America No National Literature?"

At the graduation exercises on Wednesday morning, 23 of the 62 seniors delivered orations.

In the afternoon a dinner was served to 700 people in a large tent in back of Nassau Hall. The toastmaster, trustee James S. Green (son of former president Ashbel Green) offered 13 formal toasts. To six of his toasts there were responses, by Vice President Dallas, former New Jersey governor William Pennington 1813, and others. The program concluded with nine impromptu toasts, some with responses, honoring President James Carnahan, physicist Joseph Henry, the oldest living graduate, Samuel Baldwin 1770, and others.

Sesquicentennial (150th)

The sesquicentennial took place from October 20 to 22, 1896, reaching a climax when the College of New Jersey formally announced its change of title to Princeton University. More than two years were spent in preparation for the celebration, which contemporary accounts described as the largest and best organized academic festival ever held in America. The previous winter and spring, President Francis Patton and Professor Andrew Fleming West 1874 had toured the country arousing alumni interest, while Professors Henry Fine 1880 and Allan Marquand 1874 had gone to Europe to invite eminent scholars to attend. That summer a trustee-faculty committee secured President Grover Cleveland's agreement to give the principal address.

During the week preceding the celebration, 18 lectures were given by six foreign scholars, and the American Mathematical Society held a special meeting in Princeton.

The first day of the celebration included a sermon by President Patton in the morning, a reception of delegates in the afternoon, and an orchestral concert that evening. At the convocation for the reception of delegates, Harvard's president, Charles W. Eliot, congratulated Princeton on the contributions it had made to public service, medicine, history, and science. Professor Joseph J. Thomson of Cambridge, speaking on behalf of European universities, extolled the achievements of three Princeton scientists: physicist Joseph Henry, geologist Arnold Guyot, and astronomer Charles Young.

The main events of the second day were a convocation in the morning, a football game in the afternoon, and a torchlight procession at night.

At the convocation, Professor Woodrow Wilson 1879 delivered an oration, "Princeton in the Nation's Service," which became the University's informal motto.

In the football game, Princeton defeated the University of Virginia, 48–0.

The torchlight procession, more than a mile long, began behind Nassau Hall and was led through the town by a hundred students wearing reproductions of the blue and buff uniforms of the Mercer Blues, a Princeton company that fought in the American Revolution. They were followed by a delegation of 25 Yale seniors, 800 Princeton undergraduates, and 2,000 alumni, representing classes back to 1839. Everyone carried an orange torch or lantern of some kind, and most of the alumni classes wore costumes. In front of Nassau Hall, where the procession ended, each class paused as it passed in review to cheer President and Mrs. Cleveland.

On the third morning, the historic City Troop of Philadelphia, whose forebears had served under Washington in the Battle of Princeton, led an academic procession from Marquand Chapel to Alexander Hall. President Patton announced that a special committee on endowment had raised more than $1.3 million for professorships, fellowships, a new library, and a new dormitory and proclaimed, "from this moment on, what heretofore for one hundred fifty years has been known as the College of New Jersey shall in all future time be known as Princeton University." Following the conferring of 58 honorary degrees, President Cleveland delivered the principal address, in which he made a plea for more earnest participation by educated men in the political affairs of the nation.

The sesquicentennial was a turning point in Princeton's history. Professor West demonstrated organizing talents that he later used as dean of the graduate school, and he developed friendships with alumni which proved invaluable in raising funds for the graduate college. President Cleveland, warmed by the reception he had received, came to live in Princeton the following spring; he was elected a trustee and served as first chair of its graduate school committee. Professor Fine's contacts with foreign scholars, especially with his house guest Professor Thomson, propelled his efforts to make Princeton a great center for mathematics and science. And Professor Wilson's celebrated address brought him to the fore as a potential leader of the University—and of the nation.

Bicentennial (200th)

The bicentennial of Princeton's founding on October 22, 1746, was celebrated in a year-long series of events in 1946–1947. The ceremonies began in September with a sermon in the chapel by the Archbishop of Canterbury and ended with an address by President Harry Truman in front of Nassau Hall at the concluding convocation in June. Intervening were three other convocations and 16 conferences whose proceedings were published.

President Harold Dodds made three major addresses at convocations in October, February, and June. During the year, he also conferred honorary degrees on some 100 eminent persons, including General Dwight Eisenhower and President Truman.

The chief designer of the bicentennial was dean of the faculty J. Douglas Brown 1919 *1928, who directed a series of conferences in the fall. Professor Whitney Oates 1925 *1931 directed a series in the winter and spring. Most of the conferences were led by Princeton professors and were concerned with broad topics in their fields of scholarship, such as "The Future of Nuclear Science," convened by Eugene Wigner; "The Humanistic Tradition in the Century Ahead," organized by Donald Stauffer; and "The University and Its World Responsibilities," led by Gordon Craig '36 *41 and Cyril Black.

The October convocation, commemorating Charter Day, began with an academic procession from Nassau Hall to the chapel; the undergraduate band, grouped about the cannon, played a hitherto unperformed march by Beethoven. At the exercises, the choir and the glee club sang an anthem, "Let Us Now Praise Famous Men," composed especially for the occasion by Professor Edward T. Cone '39 *42.

The February convocation was held in the chapel on Washington's Birthday, even more snowbound than usual in the late Princeton winter. At the luncheon that followed, alumni and guests heard Secretary of State George C. Marshall make his first address since taking office.

The bicentennial year reached its climax during the days from June 14 to 17. Saturday included the dedication of the new Dillon Gymnasium and a musical review of Princeton history narrated by José Ferrer '33. On Sunday there was a service of remembrance in the chapel and a concert by the Boston Symphony Orchestra. On Monday there was a service of dedication, the laying of the cornerstone of Firestone Library, a formal reception for visiting delegates, a garden party at the graduate college, and a dinner for 1,700 guests.

At the final convocation on Tuesday, an audience of 5,000 people seated in front of Nassau Hall watched an academic procession that included eminent figures like President Truman, former President Herbert Hoover, General Eisenhower, Field Marshall Viscount Alexander of Tunis (the Governor-General of Canada), Admiral Chester Nimitz, Chief Justice Fred Vinson, Judge Learned Hand, New Jersey Governor Alfred Driscoll, Albert Einstein, Eugene Cardinal Tisserant, T. S. Eliot, and Serge Koussevitsky.

The thousand-person procession also included delegates from universities and colleges in all parts of the United States and in 43 foreign countries. They walked in the order of the founding of their universities, beginning with twelfth-century Salamanca and thirteenth-century Paris, Oxford, Cambridge, and Toulouse, and ending with several American colleges established in the 1940s.

President Truman said the need for educated people in public life, which Grover Cleveland had stressed at the sesquicentennial 50 years before, was now greater than ever.

The guiding spirit in planning the bicentennial was Walter Hope 1901, chair of the trustee executive committee, and serving as chief marshal at the various convocations was Chauncey Belknap 1912, the clerk of the board. The chief organizer was Arthur Fox 1913, assistant to the president and secretary of the bicentennial executive committee.

Bicenquinquagenary (250th)

In 1992, the University began planning to celebrate its 250th anniversary four years later. Planning took place under the auspices of a committee chaired by economics professor Burton Malkiel *64; a former president of the Alumni Association, Dorothy Bedford '78, served as executive director.

The celebration officially began on February 23, 1996, the day before Alumni Day, with an address by former president Robert Goheen; remarks by President Harold Shapiro; the presentation of an anniversary banner that had flown into space with astronaut Daniel Barry *80; the premiere of a poem—"Taking the Air with James McCosh, Prospect Garden, February 1996"—written for the occasion by creative writing professor Paul Muldoon; and performance of a fanfare composed for the occasion by music professor Milton Babbitt *42 *92.

The previous fall the University had launched a 13-part lecture series examining many aspects of Princeton's history, beginning with a lecture by history professor Lawrence Stone on the place of Princeton in the history of higher education. The lectures were later compiled into a volume edited by history professors Anthony Grafton and John Murrin and published by Princeton University Press.

That fall the University mailed 1996 calendars filled with historical anecdotes and a schedule of celebratory events to all alumni and all members of the campus community. It earlier had commissioned a book, *Princeton University: The First 250 Years*, written by the renowned journalist Don Oberdorfer '52 and strikingly illustrated by J.T. Miller '70; an award-winning video, *Defining Moments;* and a feature-length film, *Princeton: Images of a University*—all for distribution during the anniversary year.

Later in the spring of 1996 the University hosted a conference on higher education co-chaired by Shapiro and former president William Bowen; McCarter Theater hosted a dance concert featuring prominent alumni choreographers; and the University held its first-ever international regional conference for alumni in Hong Kong. On the Saturday evening of reunions, there was a spectacular fireworks display that was originally intended to be replicated twice, on Charter Day in October and the following year at reunions, but proved so popular that it has become a fixture at reunions ever since.

Perpetuating a pattern of presidential visits during anniversary celebrations inaugurated by President Cleveland during the sesquicentennial and reprised by President Truman during the bicentennial, President Bill Clinton delivered the principal commencement address that spring. Later that June the Olympic torch passed through Princeton, carried part of the way by a Princeton student, in recognition of Princeton's pivotal role in the revival of the modern Olympics in 1896.

The fall of 1996 saw the issuance of a US Postal Service commemorative postcard featuring Alexander Hall; a special community program that included the dedication of a commemorative plaque in Palmer Square; and a joint ceremonial session of the New Jersey legislature in Nassau Hall to commemorate the 220th anniversary of the legislature's first session, which took place there.

The official Charter Day convocation took place on the front campus on the afternoon of Friday, October 25, and was taped along with other highlights of the day to be broadcast by satellite that evening to alumni around the world with trustee W. Hodding Carter III '57 as host.

The convocation included greetings from Harvard University president Neil Rudenstine '56 (former Princeton dean and provost), and Yale University president Richard Levin—Harvard as the country's oldest university and Yale because its alumni were instrumental in obtaining Princeton's initial charter.

President Shapiro unveiled an engraved stone at the intersection of the walkways in front of Nassau Hall that incorporated the University's revised motto—In the Nation's Service; In the Service of All Nations—with the following expression of appreciation to its alumni: *On the occasion of its 250th anniversary Princeton University here records its gratitude to its alumni for their devotion to the University and its mission of education, scholarship, and service.* President Shapiro also announced the creation of a Center for Community Service, later the Pace Center, to bring together all the University's service organizations.

The principal address, *The Place of the Idea, The Idea of the Place*, was delivered by Nobel Laureate and Princeton professor Toni Morrison. "The place of the idea," she said, "represents the value of tradition, of independence; the idea of the place is its insightful grasp of the future . . . Princeton's subtlety lies in its tradition of independence. Princeton's poise rests on its ability to revise itself."

The convocation was followed by a picnic that served more than 15,000 people, concerts, an illumination of Nassau Hall (a tradition dating from 1768), and the fireworks display.

The celebration continued into the spring of 1997 with distribution of a book, *Luminaries: Princeton Faculty Remembered*, a tribute to 48 former Princeton faculty members prepared by the Association of Princeton Graduate Alumni; completion of a video, *Oral*

History of African Americans at Princeton, by Melvin McCray '74 and Calvin Norman '77; an art museum exhibition; a concert by eight internationally prominent classical musicians plus faculty member Steve Mackey; an alumni regional conference in London; and a climb organized by Outdoor Action of Colorado's Mt. Princeton.

ANNUAL GIVING, the University's most important source of unrestricted operating income, began in 1940–41 under the leadership of founding chair Harold H. Helm '20. That first year, the results were modest: 3,371 alumni (18 percent of the alumni body) and a few friends contributed $80,000. The participants spanned some 75 years, with the oldest donor in the Class of 1865, and the underlying spirit of the enterprise was already evident: one donor gave the proceeds of a short story he had just published, another let his class agent cash in two Yale football tickets he couldn't use, and all 150 members of the Class of 1898 contributed, making them the first class to achieve 100 percent participation—a participation level they sustained for 25 years. President Harold Dodds told the class agents they had "started something which may well grow to be the most effective force for progress at Princeton."

At the end of that first campaign, Helm reported that gifts ranged from 10 cents to $1,000. Eighty years later, the largest gifts to Annual Giving reached the million dollar range, but gifts of all sizes have remained vitally important: in recent years, gifts of $100 or less have totaled $1.5 million each year, which is the equivalent of the annual earnings on $30 million of endowment.

In the second year's campaign, 25 percent of the alumni contributed a total of $102,000. (During World War II, foreign currency came in from alumni stationed in military theatres throughout the world; a Class of 1923 lieutenant colonel in Italy sent a 1,000 lira note in Allied Military currency, its modest value enhanced by Marlene Dietrich's autograph.)

Contributions grew steadily in the postwar period and in Annual Giving's 10th year, 1949–50, they passed the half-million-dollar mark. Non-alumni parents, in their second year of participation, contributed $60,000.

Six years later the million-dollar mark was passed, and alumni participation kept growing steadily; in 1958–59 it reached a staggering 72.2 percent. Contributing to these records were 2,000 volunteers around the world who followed up on the appeals of class agents with telephone calls and visits, in a program that started in 1947–1948 and continues with almost 3,000 volunteers today.

In the 1960s, total contributions increased dramatically. In the silver anniversary year of 1964–65, Annual Giving exceeded $2 million for the first time. Three years later, it reached $3 million.

One factor in the rapid rise in total contributions in the 1960s was the growing participation of graduate school alumni, which first began in 1957–58. Another factor was the support of corporations, who matched gifts of Princeton employees in a plan initiated in 1954–55 by General Electric and who, in some cases, made additional corporate contributions.

But the most important factor was the advent of a special focus on major reunion campaigns and rivalry among alumni classes vying for the honor of contributing the most to Princeton. The Class of 1922 was the first to top $100,000, just before its 42nd reunion in 1964. In 1966, the major reunion classes of 1926 and 1941 passed the $200,000 mark, and a year later, the Class of 1942 topped $300,000. In 1971 the 50th reunion Class of 1921 broke the $400,000 barrier, and three years later the 25th reunion Class of 1949 became Annual Giving's first half-million-dollar class.

In 1971–72 a special Annual Giving effort in honor of President Robert Goheen on the eve of his retirement brought in a record-breaking total of $3,805,872. The following year, another special effort in honor of newly elected President William Bowen produced another record: $3,955,842. These results, Bowen told the alumni, demonstrated once again their pride and confidence in Princeton. "We thank you for your trust," he said. "We shall strive to live up to it."

Following eight consecutive years in the $3 million range, contributions to Annual Giving in 1975–76 exceeded $4 million for the first time. In that same year two other major reunion records were set when the Class of 1951 became the first 25th reunion class to contribute as much as $700,000, and the 50th reunion Class of 1926 became the first class to pass the $2 million mark in accumulated contributions.

Beginning with the Class of 1916, seniors made 25-year pledges to class memorial funds whose accumulations they allocated at their 25th reunions—typically with some going to a class capital project like a scholarship fund and some to Annual Giving. In 1979 this was superseded by a program in which seniors encourage their classmates to make pledges to Annual

Giving for their first four alumni years, leading up to their fifth reunion.

In its early years, the Annual Giving campaign was officially launched in the fall, with solicitations concluded by Alumni Day and results announced in March or April, but in 1977 the deadline was moved to June 30. Some major reunion classes begin their planning a year or more in advance. This fuels a class's competitive spirit and helps ensure that campaign records will continually be broken.

Prior to the 2019–20 campaign, the dollar record for an Annual Giving campaign was the $74.9 million raised in 2016–17, a year in which 56.8 percent of undergraduate alumni contributed. In terms of all-time cumulative dollars, the Class of 1963 led with $45.9 million, while the Class of 1993 held the record for the largest total in a single year: $11.7 million in honor of its 25th reunion in 2017–18. In terms of cumulative participation, the leader among living classes was the Class of 2010 with 73.8 percent; the class had 80.6 percent participation for its fifth reunion. Giving by graduate alumni reached a then-record $2.3 million in 2017–18, with gifts from 2,667 donors, and giving by non-alumni parents reached a record $3.2 million in 2011–12, with gifts from more than 4,000 donors.

The 2019–20 campaign was suspended for nearly three months because of the COVID-19 pandemic, but it still raised some $66.3 million (the fourth-highest total ever), with gifts from more than 31,000 undergraduate alumni for a participation rate of 47.8 percent. The 25th-reunion Class of 1995 broke 1993's record for the largest total in a single year by raising $12.7 million.

Since 1940 Annual Giving has raised more than $1.5 billion, and almost 90 percent of undergraduate alumni have participated at some time. Gifts made through Annual Giving are flexible and immediately available; in recent years they have provided nearly 10 percent of the University's overall budget for educational expenses.

Credit for Annual Giving's perennial success belongs, in part, to its small professional staff, which has been headed by Edgar Gemmell '34, Edward Myers '38, George Cooke Jr. 1922, Arthur J. Horton '42, Joseph Bolster Jr. '52, William Hardt '63, and Sue Walsh. Credit also belongs to the legions of dedicated volunteers who work so effectively under the leadership of the Annual Giving chair and the national Annual Giving committee, a veritably indefatigable "army" that has a reputation for persistence, resourcefulness, and determination, right up to the closing weeks of each year's campaign when a remarkably high percentage of each year's gifts arrive with just days, hours, or even minutes to spare.

ANTHROPOLOGY, THE DEPARTMENT OF, was established in 1971, 25 years after Princeton's first course in cultural anthropology was offered by sociology professor Kingsley Davis. This introductory course was subsequently taught by sociology professor Melvin Tumin, and then at various times until 1965 by such distinguished visiting anthropologists as Lloyd Fallers and Paul Bohannan.

The course was first listed as part of the curriculum of the department of Economics and Social Institutions. When that department divided in 1960, a new department of Sociology and Anthropology was formed. In 1965 a separate program in Anthropology was launched, and in 1971 Anthropology became a full department with Martin Silverman as its first chair.

In 1970 Clifford Geertz, who developed the approach to anthropological knowledge production known as interpretivism, joined the newly established school of social science at the Institute for Advanced Study. While he had no direct connection to the University, his wife, Hildred Geertz, was appointed to a professorship at Princeton and served as the department's second chair. James Fernandez, its third chair, recruited legal anthropologist Lawrence Rosen in 1977. Rosen was among the first class of MacArthur Fellows in 1981.

In 1980 the Sri Lankan scholar Gananath Obeyesekere joined the faculty as a professor and his wife, Ranjini, joined as a lecturer; he later would twice chair the department. In 1982 Kay Warren joined the department as a tenured associate professor and became the first head of the Women's Studies program at Princeton (she also later chaired the department). Rena Lederman was recruited soon afterwards and eventually became one of the first women to be promoted to tenure by the University. In 1989 James Boon '68 joined the department; he had received his Princeton undergraduate degree in French language and literature and cultural anthropology.

In the 1990s medical anthropologist Emily Martin and Vincanne Adams joined the department, but then along with Kay Warren and John Kelly they were recruited away by other institutions. Their departures allowed Rosen, as chair, to recruit four new faculty members; two law and politics scholars, Carol

Greenhouse and John Bornemen; medical anthropologist Joao Biehl; and race and inequality scholar Carolyn Rouse. These new faculty members joined Isabelle Clark-Deces, Abdellah Hammoudi, Rosen, Boon, and Lederman to form a collegial and stable department for over a decade. During that time psychological anthropologist Elizabeth Davis and post-soviet scholar Serguei Oushakine also joined the department.

Early in its history, the faculty chose to dedicate the department to the field of socio-cultural anthropology rather than try to teach all four fields—archaeology, linguistics, biological anthropology, and socio-cultural anthropology. Within a few years of its founding the department developed a reputation as a place for specialized work in the theoretical problems of symbolism and cultural change, areas of research within cultural anthropology that were undergoing a good deal of ferment and development during the late 1960s and 1970s. The scholars were unified with respect to their methodological approach, namely ethnography and interpretivism, but the faculty have always held diverse perspectives and viewpoints with respect to theory.

While the department is dedicated to socio-cultural anthropology, the faculty have never lost sight of the importance of human evolution and human biology to the understanding of cultural systems. Physical anthropologists Alan Mann and Janet Monge taught for about two decades in the department, and biological anthropologist Agustin Fuentes joined the department in 2020 to expand course offerings at the intersections of socio-cultural anthropology and biological anthropology; he uses the Mpala Research Centre in Kenya as a classroom.

As a number of faculty began phased retirements and Isabelle Clark-Deces died tragically while leading a global seminar in India in 2017, the department entered a phase of rebuilding. It recruited legal anthropologist and religion scholar Lauren Coyle; political ecology and semiotics scholar Ryo Morimoto; race and policing scholar Laurence Ralph; environmental humanist Jerry Zee; and race, gender, and foodways scholar Hanna Garth.

Beyond teaching and curriculum development within the department, the faculty in Anthropology have helped found the Global Health Program (GHP), the Ethnographic Data Visualization Lab (VizE Lab), the Center for Transnational Policing (CTP), and the BrazilLab. Its faculty have led global seminars in Brazil, Greece, India, and Berlin, and have directed the program in Russian, East European, and Eurasian Studies; the program in Contemporary European Politics and Society; the program in South Asian Studies; and the program in African Studies. They have actively participated in the Princeton Institute for International and Regional Studies, the Law and Public Affairs program, and the Society of Fellows in the Humanities.

In its early years the department had only a handful of graduate students, but with the addition of new faculty members, the number grew. With that growth has come dissertation research in exciting and diverse subfields. The dissertations of PhD candidates have extended to such subjects as carceral systems, economic trade, neuroprosthetics, state infrastructures, global mental health, and drug courts.

From its earliest days, the department has had a reputation for hiring women and people of color; it has also had a reputation for excellence in teaching, and a number of its faculty have been honored with teaching awards. It also inaugurated and sponsors the annual Clifford Geertz Commemorative Lecture in honor of a colleague whose research and methods continue to inform the scholarship within the department.

ARCHITECTURE, THE SCHOOL OF. The study of architecture at Princeton began in 1832 with a course taught by the physicist Joseph Henry. Among Henry's hobbies was the study of construction, design, and landscaping. His drawings formed the basis of the first long-range building plan for the campus, and the quadrangle behind Nassau Hall remains much as he laid it out. Henry lectured on the history and appreciation of architecture until 1837, after which faculty members from various disciplines offered the course on a sporadic basis into the 1880s.

The formal study of architecture returned in 1882 when the department of Art and Archaeology was founded and its chair, Allan Marquand 1874, offered a course in the history of Christian architecture. He inspired many of his students to go on to be architects as well as art historians and archaeologists. Marquand's former student Howard Crosby Butler 1892 returned to campus in 1902 and regularly taught architectural courses as a faculty member in Art and Archaeology.

Professional design courses were added to the curriculum in 1915, and in that same year, at the urging of a group of Princeton alumni who had attended architecture schools, a committee was formed to investigate the formation of a school of Architecture at Princeton. Arrangements were made to open such a school in the fall of 1917, but World War I delayed its opening until 1919, with Butler as its first director. The first student to receive a professional degree in architecture from Princeton was Robert O'Connor *1920, who later succeeded Stephen Voorhees 1900 as the University's supervising architect.

Although the school of Architecture was separate from the department of Art and Archaeology, the two were closely allied and shared space and teaching staff. The school was the only architecture program in the country so closely integrated with an art history and archaeology program, and it was the only architecture program headed by a historian rather than a professional architect.

At its founding, the school's fundamental belief was that architects should have a well-rounded education in liberal studies; approach their profession primarily as an art; understand and appreciate the other arts in relation to architecture; and be taught the science of building construction as a part of their training in design rather than as an end in itself.

During the early years, the graduate curriculum was regularly reworked in response to rapid advances in the technology of the time. Student life was enriched by repeated visits from and teaching by many of the leading architects of the day, including Le Corbusier and Buckminster Fuller. In 1930, Frank Lloyd Wright gave his first lectures in the United States at Princeton. These lectures were later published as a monograph, *Modern Architecture*, Wright's first American book on his philosophy and his work.

In its formative years after Butler's death in 1922, the school was guided by some of the leading architectural educators of the times. One of them, the French architect and scholar Jean Labatut, was appointed resident design critic in 1928. Labatut founded both the Bureau of Urban Research (1941), which was managed by an interdepartmental committee to establish source material for urban studies, and the Princeton Architectural Laboratory, where, beginning in 1949, studies were conducted on the effects of climate and environment on building materials.

During Labatut's 39-year career at Princeton, students in the school won five Paris prizes and four Rome prizes in architecture. He himself was the first recipient of the award for distinction in education jointly sponsored by the American Institute of Architects and the Association of Collegiate Schools of Architecture.

As the school expanded, more space was required, and a new building was constructed adjacent to its former home in McCormick Hall and the art museum. The new building, dedicated in October 1963, housed drafting rooms, a freehand drawing room, a classroom, a seminar room, an exhibition gallery, faculty conference rooms, and offices with preceptorial areas. In addition, there was space for the offices of the center of Urban Research, a large sculpture studio, and an outdoor exhibition court for the Creative Arts program.

In 1965 noted architect Robert Geddes was appointed the first dean of the school of Architecture. The title of dean was chosen to reflect the school's expanding role within the University. Under Geddes' direction, the school continued its growth from a small program closely affiliated with the department of Art and Archaeology to a full-fledged professional school that coordinated with many departments within the University. This expansion helped the school attract a number of well-known architects to teach at Princeton, including Louis Kahn and Michael Graves.

Geddes also brought prominent visiting architects to Princeton and added sociologists and design theorists to the school's faculty. In 1967 the school established a master's degree program in urban planning, followed later by a PhD program, in cooperation with the school of Public and International Affairs, and for a time officially changed its name to Architecture and Urban Planning.

The noted British architect Robert Maxwell succeeded Geddes as dean in 1982 as the school firmly established itself as a principal center of design, research, history, and theory. Maxwell infused American pedagogy with a fresh point of view, relating modern architecture to similar themes in contemporary art, literature, and music.

Maxwell stepped down as dean in 1989 and was succeeded by Ralph Lerner. During the 1990s, the undergraduate curriculum was reorganized into a single path with more diverse options for individual students; classes in computing and imaging were added; courses in building science were restructured to reflect advances in that area; and selected areas of the architecture building were renovated.

In 2002, Stanley T. Allen *88, previously director of the advanced architectural design program at Columbia University, was appointed dean. During Allen's tenure, the school responded to the increasing complexity of architecture as a practice by developing interdisciplinary alliances in order to incorporate advanced computing capacities into the curriculum and to expand its focus on landscape, ecology, and the environment. A certificate program in Urban Studies was established, with a focus on the study of cities, metropolitan regions, and urban and suburban landscapes, as was a center for Architecture, Urbanism, and Infrastructure.

In 2007 the University completed construction of a three-story glass and steel pavilion, the first expansion of the building since it was constructed in 1962. The additional space made possible new facilities for program upgrades, including a model-making workshop and digital fabrication equipment.

In 2016 Monica Ponce de Leon became the first woman to be appointed dean of the school. A pioneering educator and award-winning architect, she was widely recognized as a leader in the application of robotic technology to building fabrication. In 2020 she was named one of 100 Latina leaders by Latina Leaders Magazine.

As she took office, the Princeton Architecture Laboratory (located between the Frick Chemistry Laboratory and Jadwin Gym) was renovated to become the home for the Embodied Computation Lab. This award-winning space is dedicated to architectural research, fabrication, and robotics. The lab offers students a unique opportunity to work one-on-one with cutting-edge technologies and helps transform innovative theoretical knowledge into practical applications. Its use of computation design, digital fabrication, sophisticated sensing activation, and control electronics make the lab a center for interdisciplinary work.

The lab also provides space for the construction of full-scale mock-ups to allow students to test actual models and study buildings systems and technologies. As a model for sustainability and low carbon emissions, the building itself serves as an example of the future of architectural production as well as a center for this type of research. It is the only building of its type among the leading architectural schools in America.

Although the school of Architecture has expanded its facilities, faculty, and student body over the years, it retains a small size that encourages close contact among faculty members, graduate students, and undergraduates. From the beginning, its curriculum has always responded to changes in the profession and in architectural education, providing students with courses that reflect contemporary and emerging issues in architecture.

Within this flexible academic framework, the school has remained committed to its original goals: providing undergraduates with a well-rounded liberal arts education and a strong basis for additional studies in architecture, and offering graduate students a comprehensive education in design, technology, and the history and theories of architecture. Undergraduates study architectural design, the history of architecture, architectural analysis, computing, and other topics. At the graduate level, the school offers both a professional degree (M. Arch.) and the PhD. The doctoral program has two tracks: one in history and theory and, since 2014, one in technology.

ART AND ARCHAEOLOGY, THE DEPARTMENT OF. Throughout history, the visual arts have encoded and displayed the ever-changing values of the world's diverse cultures. The academic origins of the study of the visual arts in America as a discipline can be traced back to 1882, when Allan Marquand 1874 began teaching art history at Princeton.

Before Marquand there were some rudimentary beginnings: in 1831 the catalogue mentioned the study of Roman antiquities, and in 1832 physicist Joseph Henry began giving a course of lectures on architecture. But it was Marquand, 50 years later, who became one of the first to see the cultural benefit to students of introducing the serious study of the history of art into American university life. Under his leadership, Princeton became the first college to offer consistent undergraduate and graduate work in classical and medieval art.

In the four decades before his death in 1924, Marquand built the department from three professors (including Howard Crosby Butler 1892, who taught graduate courses in early Christian and medieval architecture) to a group of scholars who brought Princeton national and international renown. By then the school of Architecture had been founded, with Butler as its first director, and the faculty had multiplied in size, with the addition of experts in both Italian and northern European painting and Renaissance sculpture.

Upon Marquand's death, Charles Rufus Morey, who had founded the Index of Christian Art at Princeton in 1917, became chair. Like Marquand, he nearly doubled the teaching staff, adding new faculty members who brought expertise in Byzantine and Far Eastern art as well as American art and architecture.

Morey was also a highly successful fundraiser, whose appeals brought gifts not only for a departmental endowment but also for the Marquand Library, which had been founded in 1908 and is still one of the great art libraries of the world. By the time Morey resigned from Princeton in 1945 to accept the first appointment as cultural attaché to the American Embassy in Rome, the department's undergraduate program was thriving and its graduate program was sending students of this relatively new discipline to teaching and administrative positions at academic institutions across the country.

The 1950s ushered in a new phase in the department's tradition of field archaeology. Onsite work began with Butler's expeditions in Syria in the early 1900s, and in Sardis in Turkey shortly before his death in 1922. The tradition was carried forward in a collaborative dig at Antioch, led by Princeton from 1932 to 1939. Later, Eric Sjöqvist, formerly the archeological secretary to King Gustav of Sweden, helped lead a 1955 excavation of the ancient Greek city of Morgantina in Sicily.

In 1956 George Forsyth 1923 of the University of Michigan invited the department's Kurt Weitzmann to join him on an exploratory trip to Mt. Sinai. From 1958 to 1965, the University of Michigan, Princeton University, and the University of Alexandria carried out four research expeditions to the remote monastery of Saint Catherine at Mount Sinai—the oldest continuously inhabited Orthodox Christian monastery in the world.

During the 1960s McCormick Hall, home of the department since 1922, was enlarged and its interior completely modernized at the same time that the adjoining art museum was being constructed. As its site expanded so too did the department's fields of study, as it added graduate programs and museum collections in oriental art. By the beginning of the 1970s the department had appointed Evelyn Harrison its first female full professor and had established new courses in twentieth-century art, Spanish art, Latin American art, the graphic arts, and the art of photography. Photography was taught by Peter Bunnell, then director of the art museum. In 1972 Bunnell was named the inaugural McAlpin Professor of the History of Photography and Modern Art, the nation's first endowed professorship of the history of photography.

The last quarter of the twentieth century was a time of transition in American academia, with traditional fields making room for new fields and new approaches, particularly in the humanities. These transitions were not always smooth, and as the department of Art and Archaeology went through its transitions it experienced periods of some disruption. In the 1980s, newer faculty members felt that the department remained too focused on a conservative "tripod": (1) the ancients (Greece and Rome), (2) East Asia, and (3) "everybody else." They pressed to expand the range of the department to other regions of the world. Their scholarship expanded from a focus on the aesthetic elements of art to consider how works of art expressed the socioeconomic climates of their times, and to apply different theoretical lenses, like Marxism and feminism.

At times, the tension between the old guard and the new spilled outside the campus into the public eye. In 1987 the department's denial of tenure for a junior faculty member made its way onto the front page of the *New York Times* Arts section. The story made clear that Princeton was not alone, as Yale and Harvard also made appearances in the article.

By the turn of the twenty-first century, the turmoil in the department had begun to subside as scholars with more progressive approaches joined the faculty. In 1999 Patricia Fortini Brown became the first woman to chair the department. She and later chairs worked to renovate and innovate, expanding both the fields of study and the diversity of the department's faculty with the appointment of more tenured women and people of color.

Today's department of Art and Archaeology is devoted to the study and criticism of the visual arts and the investigation of material artifacts from a wide range of cultures and historical periods. Studies are interdisciplinary and global in scope. Besides covering all periods of European art and architecture, faculty members teach in areas as varied as Chinese bronzes, pre-Columbian objects, Greek art, Japanese prints, African art, American art, the history of photography, and theory and criticism. They explore a diverse range of subjects like Roman city planning, Islamic archaeology, Chinese cinema, and contemporary painting.

The curriculum of an undergraduate major can include courses and independent work in any of these areas as well as in studio art taught by faculty in the program in Visual Arts. Students in the department learn techniques for analyzing visual materials and locating them within time and place. They also investigate the factors that influence the form and direction of stylistic change, such as religious beliefs, economic constraints, patronage demands, and technological change.

The graduate program prepares students for teaching and research at the university level, curatorial positions in museums, and other careers in the visual arts. Just as in the undergraduate program, interdisciplinary study is encouraged, and students take courses in related fields in the humanities, social sciences, and architecture. The program in Archaeology provides students with a foundation in the study of the material remains of the past and equips them to employ archaeological evidence in other fields of inquiry. While geopolitical tensions may limit field expeditions to some of the historic sites of the past, students still travel to participate in excavations and research trips in destinations such as Greece, Cyprus, Egypt, and China.

ART MUSEUM, THE PRINCETON UNIVERSITY, houses one of the oldest art collections in the United States. It is one of the most distinguished art museums in the country, encompassing over 110,000 works of art with a range of holdings that is rare among university art museums. Its central campus location allows it to be integrally connected to the University's programs of teaching and research, seeking to engage as many students as possible in what James Steward, director since 2009, describes as "the experience of great works of art in the original."

In Steward's words, "the goal that has been at the heart of the museum's mission from its earliest days" is "making Princeton University's art collections an instrument for bringing communities together." This means bringing art not only to students, but to the public; a decade into Steward's directorship, the museum was attracting over 200,000 visitors a year, and had opened a Nassau Street outpost in the colonial era Bainbridge House next to the Garden Theater to exhibit works by emerging contemporary artists and encourage local residents and tourists to visit the museum.

The museum's holdings range from antiquity to the present day and span the globe, with concentrations on the ancient Mediterranean, western Europe, Asia, the United States, Latin America, and Africa. Some of its collections, such as the indigenous arts of Central and South America, Chinese painting, and photography, are among the finest in the nation.

The museum's Greek and Roman antiquities include ceramics, marbles, bronzes, and Roman mosaics. Medieval Europe is represented by sculpture, metalwork, and stained glass. European paintings and sculpture range from the early Renaissance through the nineteenth century, while the collection of twentieth-century and contemporary art emphasizes undervalued artists of the late twentieth and early twenty-first centuries. The African collection spans 22 countries and 2,500 years, with particular depth in art from Nigeria.

The museum has an unusually robust acquisitions program that enables it to shape its collections in support of evolving teaching and research interests, including in recent years the arts of South Asia and both historical and contemporary works by women artists and artists of color. It also augments its collections with a number of long-term loans, as well as an impressive array of shorter-term exhibitions.

In the University's earliest days, its holdings were limited to a relative handful of items, including portraits of colonial New Jersey governor Jonathan Belcher and England's King George II, both destroyed during the Battle of Princeton in 1777, and some objects of natural history and ancient architectural fragments that were displayed in Nassau Hall. These early collections were built on Enlightenment principles, under which works of fine and applied arts, classical antiquity, and natural history were exhibited side by side, and learning from objects was an essential educational experience. Building on these origins, in 1856 a natural history museum was founded in the Faculty Room of Nassau Hall, and it remained there until it moved to the newly constructed Guyot Hall in 1909.

In 1868 President James McCosh arrived from Scotland with an interest in adding the study of art to the curriculum. As he later said to the alumni: "I believe that the Fine Arts should have a place, along with Literature, Philosophy, and Science, in every advanced College. If the students are required to know the literature of Greece, England, Germany, and France, why should they not have the means of becoming acquainted with their paintings, sculpture, and architecture, which have an equally refining and elevating character?"

In 1882 Allan Marquand 1874 began teaching art history, and over the next 40 years he built a department of Art and Archaeology, co-founded with a museum of historic art, that achieved national and international renown. Marquand felt strongly that students should be given access to original works of art and insisted that a museum be part of the department's program—a view influenced by the fact that his father was one of the founders of the Metropolitan Museum of Art in New York.

That same year McCosh charged William Cowper Prime 1843, also a founding trustee of the Metropolitan Museum of Art, and former Civil War general and New Jersey governor George McClellan with preparing a course of study in the history of art. They similarly envisioned a curriculum that would offer direct access to works of art in a museum, and Prime promised his collection of pottery and porcelain if the College constructed a fireproof building to safeguard it.

By 1887 the trustees had raised just over $40,000, not enough to build architect A. Page Brown's entire plan of a central section, two wings, and a lecture hall in the back, but sufficient to construct its core: a three-story Romanesque Revival building known as the museum of historic art that housed an art museum, the department of Art and Archaeology, a fine arts library, and the newly created school of Architecture. The brick building, measuring 75 by 25 feet, was completed in 1890 at a final cost of $49,061, and the Trumbull-Prime Collection, which also bore the name of Prime's wife, moved in.

During reunions in 1923, the University dedicated the newly constructed Venetian Gothic McCormick Hall, which was built as an addition to the west side of the museum to accommodate the department, the school, and the library, thus allowing the original space to be devoted solely to the museum.

Marquand held the position of director of the museum until his retirement in 1922. He expanded the museum's collections and, drawing largely on his own substantial resources, began to create an endowment to support acquisitions. His purchases included Cypriot pottery; Etruscan, Roman, and South Italian pottery; and objects from later periods. When Marquand retired, Frank Jewett Mather Jr., who had joined the faculty in 1910 to teach Renaissance art, became director of the museum. Mather collected in the fields of medieval and Renaissance art, but also added significant holdings of prints and drawings, as well as Classical and pre-Columbian antiquities, illuminated manuscripts, and works by American artists, including a collection of American drawings that became one of the finest in the country.

Mather also added a collection of antiquities unrivalled in the United States from excavations at Antioch-on-the-Orontes in modern-day Turkey in which Princeton played a leading role (the Antioch mosaics can be seen both in the museum and in Firestone Library), as well as the Dan Fellows Platt 1895 collection numbering thousands of objects. Other major gifts in the 1930s included Italian paintings, Chinese snuff bottles, Chinese and Japanese art, Ethiopian Christian art, and the museum's first works by a sub-Saharan African artist.

Both Marquand and Mather frequently added items that they purchased with their own very considerable funds. Among Marquand's gifts was one of the museum's treasures: Hieronymous Bosch's painting, "Christ before Pilate." Mather's collection of Italian drawings included many gems, among them a study by Carpaccio for one of his wall-paintings in Venice. Mather's connections in the art world made possible important exhibitions, including highlights from the Museum of Modern Art, whose founding director was a Princeton graduate, Alfred Barr Jr. 1922.

Between them, Marquand and Mather led the museum for more than half a century; a bronze plaque in the entrance court to the current museum recognizes their contribution: *By Scholarship, Vision, and Generosity, They Made Possible a Community of Students and Works of Art.*

Mather was succeeded in 1946 by Ernest DeWald *16, one of the "Monuments Men," who, along with a number of other Princeton faculty and alumni, served in the allied armies' Monuments, Fine Arts, and Archives program to preserve art and other cultural artifacts in Europe at the end of World War II. One of the rescued masterpieces was the Dutch painter Johannes Vermeer's most acclaimed work, *The Art of Painting*, which, in gratitude for Princeton's role in its rescue, the Austrian government loaned to the Princeton art museum in 1950 for an eight-day exhibition. The recoveries by the Monuments Men received wide recognition in 2014 with the release of a movie by that name; DeWald's diary describing his experiences is in Firestone Library.

As museum director, DeWald made a significant commitment to art conservation, reportedly cleaning paintings himself in his office. He oversaw refurbishing of the galleries for the University's bicentennial in 1946–47, and greatly expanded the museum's collections of Asian art under the guidance of Professor Wen Fong '51 *58, who went on to become the founding director of the Metropolitan Museum of Art's Asian department. DeWald enlarged the African collection, and in 1949 he obtained the museum's first photograph, Alfred Stieglitz's *The Steerage*. In 1950 he helped form the Friends of the Art Museum to support acquisitions and exhibitions.

Not long before retiring in 1960, DeWald was involved in planning a new home for the art museum that was made possible by the University's $53 million capital campaign. Another Monuments Man, Patrick Kelleher *47, succeeded DeWald as director, and oversaw the demolition of the museum of historic art in 1964 and the opening of the new art museum in 1966, designed in the International Style by the New York firm of Steinmann and Cain. A docent association was established to provide museum guides and staff the museum store, and the art of the ancient Americas became a new focus thanks to the leadership and benefactions of faculty curator Gillett Griffin.

In 1969 and 1970, the works of major twentieth-century sculptors were purchased through a fund given by an anonymous donor as a memorial to John B. Putnam Jr. '45, who left Princeton following his sophomore year to enlist in the Army Air Corps. He flew nine combat hours over Normandy Beach on D-Day in 1944 before being killed in a plane crash in England shortly afterward. The sculptures, known as the Putnam Collection and displayed outdoors throughout the campus, were selected by a committee of alumni who were current or former directors of art museums, including Kelleher and the Museum of Modern Art's Barr, Thomas Hoving '53 of the Metropolitan Museum of Art, and William Milliken 1911 of the Cleveland Museum of Art. The collection includes works by Alexander Calder, Henry Moore, Louise Nevelson, and Isamu Noguchi.

A new collection area was initiated in 1971 when David McAlpin 1920 gave about 500 photographs from one of the finest early collections of photography and established a fund for the purchase of additional examples of photography as an artistic medium. In 1972 Peter Bunnell came to Princeton to occupy the first endowed chair in the United States in the history of photography. Bunnell served as director of the museum from 1973 to 1978, leading Princeton to a preeminent role in the study of photography, with collections now numbering over 27,000 photographs, including the archives of photographers Clarence White, Minor White, and Ruth Bernhard, among others.

In 1980 Allen Rosenbaum was promoted from associate director to director. He built up holdings in Renaissance and Baroque painting, developed a major exhibition in Maya art and another drawing on the collections of alumni and other friends of Princeton in celebration of the University's 250th anniversary, and led a campaign that resulted in the renovation of the museum's interior and the 1989 addition of the 27,000-square-foot Mitchell Wolfson Jr. '63 wing. Rosenbaum's successor, Susan Taylor, arrived in 2000, and established the first endowed curator positions at the art museum, which advanced its professionalism and deepened its connections to the University's academic programs.

Steward's arrival in 2009 led to an expanded program of innovative exhibitions, publications, and educational activities and an increased commitment to diversity and inclusion in the art museum's acquisitions and programming. Acquisitions focused on such areas as works by women artists of the eighteenth to the late twentieth century, Indian art, African art, photojournalism, and African American artists from the 19th century to the present.

In 2018 over 5,000 objects in the drawings archive of architect and designer Michael Graves, a member of the Princeton faculty from 1962 to 2001, came to the museum by bequest. Just prior to that, in connection with the Princeton and Slavery project, the museum commissioned a work by Titus Kaphar and acquired his depiction of the 1766 sale of six enslaved African Americans on the grounds of Maclean House, then the president's house, in which they had worked. Steward also played leading roles in expanding and diversifying both the campus art collection and the University portrait collection.

In addition to the Bainbridge House outpost, which opened in 2019, and an off-site museum store also located in town, Steward's outreach initiatives included innovative programming inside the museum. A Nassau Street sampler event, begun in 2009, marks the beginning of each academic year with an open house that attracts thousands of students and community members to look at art, listen to music, and sample free food from restaurants in town. Steward and his staff teach or co-teach a number of courses in various departments, and in 2018–2019, 6,414 students, in courses spanning 51 departments and programs, visited the museum's study rooms and galleries as participants in nearly 600 individual classes and precepts.

Steward oversaw renovations within the building and made digitization of the museum's collections and archives one of his highest priorities so that digital access can be provided to users on campus and around the world.

In 2018 Sir David Adjaye, architect of the Smithsonian National Museum of African American History and Culture in Washington, DC, was selected to design a new and significantly larger museum building on the existing museum's site in the center of campus. The project aimed to retain important historical and intellectual relationships among the art museum, the department of Art and Archaeology, and Marquand library, while roughly doubling the museum's size and enhancing access. Adjaye's design, he said, aimed to create a building with "all fronts and no backs" that fit with both the architecture and the landscape to its north, south, east, and west.

When completed, the new building will provide dramatically enlarged space for the display and study of the museum's collections (in the previous museum only about two percent of its holdings could be displayed at any one time), as well as space for special exhibitions and art conservation, a lecture hall and performance space, additional classrooms and offices, and visitor amenities including a museum store and a café. Its outdoor terraces will be able to serve as performance and event spaces for up to 2,000 people.

Construction was scheduled to begin in June 2021, with a projected opening in fall 2024.

ASIAN AMERICAN AND ASIAN STUDENTS AT PRINCETON. Immigration limitations and exclusionary policies that lasted well into the twentieth century meant that, until the 1930s, all Asian students at Princeton were international students, primarily from East Asia.

Japanese men were the first Asian students at Princeton. Their arrival on campus in the 1870s coincided with the Meiji period in Japan, during which the country sent thousands of students to the United States. Preceded by three "special students" who did not receive degrees, Hikoichi Orita 1876 became the first Asian person known to graduate from Princeton. He and Habib Yusufji *1930, originally from India, were among the international students who converted to Christianity while in the US, perhaps as a way of fitting in with the dominant culture.

Among the first Chinese students at Princeton was Dong Seung 1905, originally from Canton (Guangzhou), who had attended an American high school. A few years after his graduation, support for the education of Chinese students under the Boxer Indemnity Scholarship program significantly increased their presence in the United States, including at Princeton. In addition to admitting a number of these students as undergraduates and graduate students, in 1911 Princeton hosted 150 Chinese students at the annual conference of the Chinese Students' Alliance of the Eastern States.

By 1913, the six Chinese students on campus formed the Princeton Chinese Students' Club, which planned social gatherings and discussions. Its president, Hsu Kun Kwong 1914, was also a member of the editorial board of the *Daily Princetonian*. For the next few years, members of the club served as contributors to and leaders of the *Chinese Students' Monthly*, a national magazine published by Chinese students in the United States.

The club and the magazine helped Chinese students adjust to life at a predominantly white American college. Many of these students returned to China and quickly achieved positions of responsibility in the government. By the time Chinese students began to enroll again in the 1970s and the first students admitted directly from China began to arrive in the early 1980s, Princeton's student body had grown to include considerably more Asians and Asian Americans, alongside increased racial diversity across the board.

By the 1930s, a generation of US-born children of Asian immigrants was old enough to attend college. That decade saw three first-generation Japanese Americans graduate from Princeton. Their experiences, and those of other Asian American students during the next couple of decades (still largely of East Asian origin), varied significantly, in part depending on their social class. For example, Masahiko Ralph Takami '34, born to an elite family of Japanese immigrants, attended the Lawrenceville School along with 58 of his future college classmates; his brother, Suyehiko Takami '40, joined Tiger Inn, one of the oldest eating clubs on campus. But Yeiichi "Kelly" Kuwayama '40—from a working-class Japanese immigrant family—was rejected when he tried to join a selective eating club, leaving him to focus more intently on academics.

During World War II, Japanese student Kentaro Ikeda '44, identified by the US government as an "enemy alien," was effectively under house arrest on Princeton's campus. A college administrator served as Ikeda's sponsor, allowing him to remain a student at Princeton, but his movement was restricted to campus, he was prohibited from communicating with his family, and he could not access his bank accounts. His closest friend was the one other Asian student on campus, Richard Eu '44, a native of Singapore. At the same time, while other colleges hosted Japanese American students who faced imprisonment in internment camps on the west coast, Princeton refused to do so.

The population of students from Asian backgrounds grew when women began to be admitted to Princeton in the 1960s. T'sai-Ying Cheng *63 *64, born in Taiwan, received her master's degree in biochemistry on June 18, 1963, becoming the first woman to earn a Princeton degree. A year later, she became the first woman to receive a doctorate.

The Class of 1970 included the first nine women to receive undergraduate degrees from Princeton; among them were five Asian and Asian American women. One of them, Sue-Jean Lee Suettinger '70, was the first woman cast in a Triangle Club show, and another, Lynn Nagasako '70, was the first woman to join an eating club.

Students of Asian backgrounds formed a number of identity and cultural organizations beginning in the 1970s. The Asian American Students Association (AASA), which was founded in the spring of 1971, joined Black and Latino students in calling for a Third World Center (now the Carl A. Fields Center), which opened that fall. In 1975 Stanley Kwong was appointed its first full-time director. Founding members of AASA, like activist and journalist Helen Zia '73, biologist and attorney Elaine Chan '73, architect Alfred Wen '72, and attorney Helen Doo '73, published a newsletter, organized lectures, and hosted social events. As Princeton's population began to include more students of South and Southeast Asian heritage in the 1980s, they formed identity groups of their own.

By the 2010s, there were more than 40 undergraduate and graduate student organizations focused on promoting Asian communities, cultures, and heritages through music, dance, martial arts, theater, and regional identity groups. Some of these groups hold events at the Fields Center, where there is an Asian American affinity room. There are also religious groups, some of which date back to the 1970s. Students lead some of the groups, with support from the Office of Religious Life. In 2008 Vineet Chander, who helped establish a popular annual Diwali at the Chapel celebration, became Princeton's (and the country's) first full-time Hindu chaplain.

Scholars from Asian backgrounds began to join the faculty in the 1940s, at first primarily as visiting scholars and then as full-time faculty members beginning in the 1950s. Many taught courses in subjects related to the cultures of their home countries. For example, a 1948 comparative religion course was among the first to teach Confucianism, Hinduism, and Buddhism in their own right, rather than through the lens of art. A few of the faculty members who came to Princeton during this period remained for decades and made lasting contributions to Princeton's curriculum and their fields. They included T. T. Chen (Chinese language and history), Wen Fong '51 *58 (Chinese art and archaeology), and Sau-Hai (Harvey) Lam *58 (fluid mechanics).

Another faculty member in the 1940s was Chien-Shiung Wu, a Chinese-born American physicist, who in 1942 became the first woman hired as a faculty member in Princeton's Physics department. In 1958 she became the first female recipient of a Princeton honorary doctorate in science. In 2021 the US Postal Service issued a "Forever" postage stamp in her honor.

Asian American students and alumni began to fill leadership positions in the 1980s. In 1984, Timothy Wu '84, who had been president of the senior class, was elected a young alumni trustee, and Eva Lerner-Lam '76, who had been the first female president of an eating club, was elected a term trustee. In 2001 P. J. Kim '01 was elected a young alumni trustee after serving as the first Asian American president of the Undergraduate Student Government (USG), and in 2015 Ella Cheng '16 became the first female Asian American USG president.

In 1986 Hisashi Kobayashi *67, a native of Japan, became dean of the school of Engineering and Applied Science; he was succeeded five years later by James Wei, who had come to the United States from China as a teenager. Since then, Asians and Asian Americans have served at the most senior levels of the administration, including as provost and other positions in the president's cabinet, and in leadership roles on the Board of Trustees.

In 2000 former trustee and former chancellor of the University of California-Berkeley Chang-Lin Tien *59 became the first Asian American to receive the James Madison Medal, the University's highest award for graduate alumni, and in 2009 and 2011 former trustee Rajiv Vinnakota '93 and future trustee Denny Chin '75 became the first Asian Americans to win the Woodrow Wilson Award, the highest distinction for undergraduate alumni. In 2014 Christopher Lu '88, White House Cabinet Secretary and then deputy Secretary of Labor during the presidency of Barack Obama, was the first Asian American baccalaureate speaker.

Course offerings grew from Orientalist-focused ones in the early 1900s (a department of Oriental

Languages and Literatures was established in 1927) to include Chinese and Japanese art and archaeology in the 1950s, followed by an independent East Asian Studies department (established in 1969) that offered courses in the languages, literatures, and histories of China and Japan. With a brief exception in the 1960s, courses in Korean language and culture did not have a permanent place in the curriculum until the end of the twentieth century, decades after the graduation of Syngman Rhee *1910, the first Korean student at Princeton and later president of South Korea. Southeast Asian languages joined the curriculum in 1998.

In the 2000s, the newly created Paul ('55) and Marcia Wythes Center for Contemporary China and the M.S. Chadna Center for Global India, as well as a program in South Asian Studies, began to sponsor lectures and research programs focusing on those areas.

Representation of Asian American studies in the curriculum took even longer. Student advocacy for such courses began in the 1970s. At first, students focused on creating student-initiated seminars, a few of which were offered during the 1980s. A cohort of Asian American students met with Harold Shapiro *64 shortly after he became Princeton's president in 1988 to request that Princeton create a formal Asian American Studies program. When a task force failed to yield the results they wanted, 17 students participated in a 35-hour sit-in in Nassau Hall in 1995 protesting the lack of courses in Asian American Studies and Latino Studies.

After decades of activism on the part of students, faculty, and alumni, Princeton created a certificate program in Asian American Studies in 2018, housed within the program of American Studies (AMS). Professor Anne Cheng '85, who had advocated for Asian American studies as a student and faculty member, was the director of AMS when the certificate was created. By that time, approximately 20 percent of undergraduates and eight percent of graduate students identified as Asian American, and 45 percent of all international students were from Asian countries.

More than 700 alumni returned to campus in 2015 for *We Flourish*, a conference for Asian and Asian American alumni. Many were members of the Asian American Alumni Association of Princeton (A4P), a group for all Asian and Asian American Princeton alumni first established in the late 1970s.

ASTROPHYSICAL SCIENCES, THE DEPARTMENT OF. Astronomy at Princeton was originally taught as part of natural philosophy, usually by professors who were primarily mathematicians. An early member of the faculty was Walter Minto, the author of a treatise on the newly discovered planet Uranus, who arrived from Scotland in 1787 as professor of mathematics and natural philosophy. The early college was proud of its Rittenhouse Orrery—a clock-like instrument devised to represent the motions of the planets around the sun—which it acquired in 1771, but it was unable to raise funds for an observatory. (The orrery can be seen today in the lobby of Peyton Hall.)

Astronomy began developing as a separate discipline under Stephen Alexander, who arrived at Princeton in 1833 and was appointed professor of astronomy in 1840. He gave the first course in the subject, made observations on a small telescope in his home, and through patience and persistence secured funds for the Halsted Observatory, completed in 1872. At that time, it had the world's fourth-largest telescope.

The observatory attracted Charles Young to Princeton as its first director. Seven years after his retirement in 1905, he was succeeded by Henry Norris Russell 1897 *1900, a theorist who earned his PhD under Young and remained on the faculty for 35 years. Young was the author of an authoritative work on the sun, while Russell laid much of the foundation of modern astrophysics by pioneering work in the use of atomic physics to study the sun and the stars. Russell analyzed the physical conditions and chemical compositions of stellar atmospheres and evaluated the relative abundance of elements, and was a leading authority on stellar evolution.

The next director of the observatory was Lyman Spitzer Jr. *38, who earned his doctorate at Princeton and went on to become one of the towering figures of twentieth-century astrophysical science. His contributions included seminal and fundamental advances in four fields: interstellar matter, stellar dynamics, plasma physics, and space astronomy.

In 1951 Spitzer initiated study of thermonuclear fusion at what became the Princeton Plasma Physics Laboratory, searching for an unlimited, safe, and affordable source of energy. Spitzer inspired the development of the National Aeronautics and Space Administration's orbiting astronomical observatory program, which led to the launching of the 32-inch Copernicus ultraviolet satellite in 1972 and, in 1990, the Hubble Space Telescope, which NASA called the most significant advance in astronomy since Galileo's telescope. Known for his unfailing civility, Spitzer served as department chair until 1979. He worked in Peyton Hall until the day he died in 1997.

Spitzer's closest colleague was Martin Schwarzschild, who joined the faculty the same year Spitzer was named director of the observatory. Schwarzschild was best known for his theoretical work on stellar evolution and his pioneering use of computers—including John von Neumann's computer at the Institute for Advanced Study—to model complex astrophysical systems. Spitzer and Schwarzschild together led a dramatic expansion in Princeton's role as a center of astronomical research; they died within 10 days of each other.

The modern department came into being in 1962 when its scope was broadened to include graduate programs in plasma physics and in atomic and molecular physics, as well as in astronomy and astrophysics. In 1966 its facilities were enhanced with the installation of a 36-inch reflecting telescope in the FitzRandolph Observatory, which had been built in 1934 to replace the Halstead Observatory, and by the completion of the department's current home, Peyton Hall, after its former home on Prospect Avenue was demolished to make way for Robertson Hall. Minoru Yamasaki designed both Peyton and Robertson halls.

By the end of the 1970s, the department was almost entirely theory-oriented. With the hiring of Edwin Turner in 1978, then the department's only primarily observational astrophysicist, the balance began to shift. It was an exciting time, as theories on cosmology and dark matter emerged, driven by two of the world's most accomplished astrophysicists: Jeremiah Ostriker in Astrophysics and James Peebles in Physics. Ostriker did pioneering work in computational astrophysics and chaired the department through 1995, when he became provost of the University; in 2019, Peebles was awarded the Nobel Prize in Physics for theoretical discoveries regarding the physical origins, evolution, and structure of the universe.

Dark matter was studied in earnest in the 1980s and 1990s, and it continues today as one of the department's—and the field's—most compelling challenges. In addition, gravitational lensing became a major tool of astronomy between 1980 and 2000. This is a kind of cosmic telescope for magnifying objects that are very far away; it is also one of the ways of "seeing" dark matter.

In the 1980s, Princeton investigators turned toward the study of the cosmic microwave background, a discovery that had its roots in the early 1960s and was eventually mapped by a satellite created by David Wilkinson as part of the Cosmic Background Explorer (COBE) project, launched in 1989. Later, under the leadership of theoretical astrophysicist David Spergel '83, the eponymous Wilkinson Microwave Anisotropy Probe (WMAP)—a successor satellite 45 times more sensitive—became one of the department's biggest projects. Launched in 2001, WMAP confirmed the inflationary model of the early universe and the nature of dark matter and dark energy. These projects were largely undertaken jointly with the department of Physics.

Spergel's first summary paper of this project in 2003, describing the implications for cosmology, is one of the most cited papers in the history of astronomy. Spergel chaired the department from 2005 to 2016.

Another breakthrough in the 1980s was Bohdan Paczynski's 1986 hypothesis that gamma-ray bursts lay at cosmological distances. He pursued this hypothesis to the point of its acceptance as an observationally confirmed fact.

One of the greatest achievements in the last 40 years of observational astrophysics is the Sloan Digital Sky Survey (SDSS), the brainchild of James Gunn. Gunn arrived from Caltech in 1980 and remained on the faculty until he transferred to emeritus status in 2011. Using a telescope loaded with the most complex camera ever built up to that point (it took six years to assemble in Peyton's basement), SDSS revolutionized the nature of ground-based astronomy.

By 2008, nearly 10 years after it began making observations, SDSS had created the most detailed 3D map of the cosmos in history and contributed fundamental insights into the distribution of matter in the universe. Many Princeton astronomers were involved in SDSS: they built the imaging camera, designed the telescope, and wrote much of the image-processing software. Gunn was awarded the Kyoto Prize in 2019.

As every recent denizen of Peyton Hall knows, another more modest project was completed in 2008: a 50-foot decorative "astronomical carpet" featuring a logarithmic scale map created by J. Richard Gott *73. A defining feature of the department, it takes visitors from Earth to the Big Bang in "17 easy strides."

A suite of projects grouped around the 8.2-meter Subaru Telescope on the summit of Mauna Kea in Hawaii mark continued collaborations with Japan's astronomical community that started 40 years ago.

Completed in the early 2000s, Subaru continues to support major research in both cosmology and the study of exoplanets. Eve Ostriker, daughter of Jeremiah, joined the faculty in 2012 and continued the department's research in the interstellar medium and the circumgalactic medium, and in computational astrophysics. Jo Dunkley joined the faculty in 2016 as a distinguished astrophysicist working on the early universe and interpretation of microwave background data.

As the department entered the 2020s, there were two driving questions of modern cosmology on which astrophysicists had made only limited progress: what are dark matter and dark energy? At the same time, as cosmologists wrestle with these puzzles, the search for exoplanets has exploded in the past 25 years and is the fastest-growing area in astronomy.

The department today has two divisions: astronomy and plasma physics, the latter a graduate program that continues the investigation into fusion as a source of clean, abundant energy at PPPL, with major funding from the US Department of Energy. The department continues to enjoy strong ties with the department of Physics, especially with the gravity group, as well as with Geosciences, Mechanical and Aerospace Engineering, Molecular Biology, Operations Research and Financial Engineering, and the neighboring Institute for Advanced Study.

ATHLETICS. In Princeton's earliest years, athletic activity was discouraged. In 1761, for example, the trustees decreed that students playing ball against the president's house would incur a fine of five shillings. Until the early nineteenth century outdoor exercise for Princeton students usually took the form of walking, horseback riding, canoeing down the Millstone River, and hunting small game in the nearby hills and fields. But by midcentury organized athletic contests—largely intramural at first, but soon intercollegiate—began to occur. Ever since, athletics have been a central feature of both campus life and alumni engagement.

The University is justly proud of its athletic success. In 2020 Princeton became the first Ivy League school to win 500 Ivy League team championships since the inception of Ivy competitions in 1956, a milestone it achieved by winning more than a quarter of all Ivy championships awarded. As of that year, Princeton had 14 teams that had won the most all-time Ivy titles in their sport, nine that ranked second, and four that ranked third. More than 200 of the championships had been won by Princeton's women's teams.

The University is also proud that it has achieved its success while sustaining a bedrock commitment to the primary goal of its athletics program, which it describes as "Education Through Athletics."

Although there were no intercollegiate football contests until 1869, as early as 1844 the green between East and West colleges was the scene of many spirited football games. Frequently the entire student body would turn out, divide themselves into teams, and endeavor to kick the ball until it touched the wall of either East or West college. The fall of 1857 brought a more organized form of athletics with the formation of a cricket club and two baseball clubs. The Nassau Baseball Club, founded in 1858, played its first game against an outside opponent two years later and its first intercollegiate contest, a 27–16 victory over Williams, in 1864.

In 1856 Karl Langlotz, a faculty member who composed the music for Princeton's anthem, "Old Nassau," began teaching fencing to a group of 50 students. Princeton's first crew race was in 1872 and the first track meet on campus was in 1873. Princeton lacrosse traces its roots to 1881, and Princeton students first participated in intercollegiate tennis in 1882 (the first official team match was in 1901). Recreational ice hockey began in the 1890s and Princeton joined in forming an intercollegiate league in 1899. Basketball played its first intercollegiate game in 1901; wrestling, a direct descendant of the on-campus tradition of cane spree, had its first match in 1905; and the first swim meet was in 1906.

During the early days, the teams had little organization or adult supervision; the best or most enterprising player was usually the leader. The first step toward a more formal mode of operation occurred when the players elected one of their members as captain, with sole charge and management of the games and players. The next step was the development of football, baseball, and later track, associations, whose student boards of directors were criticized for usurping the authority of the captains and were reduced in 1876 to two-man committees.

Alumni became involved in athletic management in 1885 when a graduate advisory committee of three was established by the baseball association. Before the year closed, the various student associations had agreed to give the graduate advisory committee general supervision over all athletics. In 1886 an executive committee composed of undergraduate representatives from all the associations was organized to take charge of the grounds and general athletic interests of the College.

The final step toward consolidation of athletics came with the adoption of an alumni proposal that each association turn over all surplus monies at year's end to a College fund managed by an elected officer eventually known as the general athletic treasurer. In 1890 the alumni and undergraduate committees joined to form an athletic association that was incorporated a year later under the laws of New Jersey. The general athletic treasurer became the first full-time officer to have administrative responsibility for all athletic programs.

At the same time, the faculty appointed a committee on outdoor sports to investigate and approve the academic standing of individual players and see that games and hours of training did not interfere with study. The faculty and alumni committees were amalgamated into a Board of Athletic Control in 1900, and this board provided general supervision for the organization of athletics at Princeton. A University Council on Athletics replaced the Board of Athletic Control in 1934, and in 1937 the athletic association was formally dissolved and reconstituted as an integral part of the University.

In 1939 R. Kenneth Fairman '34 was appointed graduate manager of athletics, a designation changed to director of athletics in 1941. As an undergraduate, Fairman had won eight varsity letters in basketball, football, and lacrosse, and had captained the basketball team his senior year. An integrated department of Physical Education and Athletics was established in 1947, bringing physical education and intramural programs under the same departmental purview as intercollegiate athletics. Major increases in Princeton's athletics plant took place during Fairman's leadership with the construction of Caldwell Field House and Jadwin Gymnasium.

Fairman retired in 1972 shortly after the formation of the first six women's varsity teams: basketball, crew, field hockey, squash, swimming, and tennis. (In 1970, before there was a tennis team, Margie Gengler '73 and Helena Novakova '72 represented Princeton in the Eastern Intercollegiate Championships for Women's Tennis, and when Gengler won the singles title and together they won the doubles, they brought the team trophy home to Princeton.) The women's lacrosse team began play in 1973, followed by volleyball in 1977, track and field and cross-country in 1978, and ice hockey in 1979; when women's rugby achieves varsity status in 2022–23, there will be 19 varsity women's teams and 19 varsity men's teams.

Fairman was succeeded by former football standout Royce Flippin Jr. '56. Shortly after his arrival, the department added "recreation" to its masthead in recognition of the growing interest in lifetime sports, recreational activities, and health fitness on the part of large numbers of the student body, faculty, and staff.

Former baseball captain Robert Myslik '61 succeeded Flippin in 1979, and in turn was succeeded by former star basketball point guard Gary Walters '67, who served from 1994 to 2014. During his tenure, Walters established a faculty academic-athletic fellows program, which, in partnership with the office of the dean of the college, identifies faculty and administrators who support the players and coaches of each of the varsity sports and reinforce the connections between athletics and the educational mission of the University. Walters also created the Princeton Varsity Club to provide financial and other forms of support for the intercollegiate teams.

In 1996 the University demolished the crumbling Palmer Stadium, which had been built in 1914 as a memorial to Stephen Palmer, the donor of Palmer Hall (originally Palmer Physical Laboratory). It was the second-oldest football stadium in the country and was the home of both football and track and field. In 1997, football moved into a new Rafael Vinoly-designed football stadium, named Princeton Stadium, which President Harold Shapiro described as "a work of art, of science, of intellect, of imagination, and of athletic grace." Track and field moved to its own dedicated stadium, also designed by Vinoly just south of Princeton Stadium, which was given by and named for William Weaver '34.

Walters' successor, Mollie Marcoux Samaan '91, was one of Princeton's top women student-athletes, winning four letters each in ice hockey and soccer. Like all her predecessors, she emphasized Princeton's commitment to education as well as to leadership and service, and she placed high priority on appointing coaches who reinforce this mission while also helping their teams to achieve exceptional competitive success. Her successor was former track and field captain John Mack '00.

Some 18 percent of Princeton undergraduates participate in 37 (soon to be 38) varsity men's and women's teams—the second highest number of varsity teams at any college or university, exceeded only by Harvard's 42. The department also sponsors

36 sport club teams, ranging from archery, badminton, climbing, cricket, cycling, equestrian, figure skating, and jiu-jitsu to powerlifting, men's and women's rugby, sailing, ski and snowboard, table tennis, taekwondo, and both men's and women's ultimate frisbee teams. Club teams play against other colleges, with an emphasis on participation, skill development, and student leadership.

Some of the sport club teams have long histories. When cricket made its first appearance at Princeton in 1857, the *Nassau Lit* predicted "the college authorities would stop it, as there was something wicket in it," but the Nassau Cricket Club went on to play several outside matches in the 1860s and 1870s. Bicycle racing began on campus in 1879 and a year later Princeton won the two-mile event during the first intercollegiate games; in the mid-twentieth century, Princeton won five consecutive national intercollegiate cycling championships between 1961 and 1966. While there is no gymnastics sport club team, there is a student-run gymnastics club that practices in Dillon Gym; gymnastics began as an organized sport at Princeton in 1870 upon the completion of the Bonner-Marquand gymnasium.

The athletics department oversees a broad range of intramural sports, including the popular annual dodgeball tournament that brings thousands of students and others into Dillon gym each spring for spirited competition, and an extensive program of fitness and informal recreation programs, including programs for faculty and staff as well as for undergraduates and graduate students.

AUDITING PROGRAM, THE, which began in 1999 under the auspices of the office of community and regional affairs, enables members of the community to attend undergraduate classes that permit auditing. Each semester about 150–175 classes are available, and approximately 700 area residents participate.

Auditors may register for up to three classes per semester. In registering for courses, priority is given to residents of the town of Princeton, alumni, and others who are affiliated with the University. Auditors attend lectures, but not precepts, seminars, field trips, language labs, or science labs; they do not take exams or participate in class unless requested to do so by the faculty member teaching the course. No credit or certification is given.

In addition, the program typically offers a small number of auditor-only courses each semester and an end-of-semester auditor lecture and reception.

The office of community and regional affairs also administers the University's continuing education program, founded in 1973, which admits qualified area residents, K–12 New Jersey teachers, and University employees, graduate students, and adult members of their families to undergraduate and graduate courses for credit. The credits do not count toward Princeton degrees.

There is also a community college faculty program that allows faculty members and administrators at participating community colleges in New Jersey to take up to two courses per semester with permission from their home institutions.

BACCALAUREATE ADDRESS, THE, is one of Princeton's oldest traditions. The earliest recorded address was delivered by President Samuel Davies in 1760 to the 11 members of the graduating class. Entitled "Religion and Public Spirit," it treated a topic that has been a frequently recurring theme. "Serve your Generation," he told his students.

> Live not for yourself but the Publick. Be the Servants of the Church; the Servants of your Country; the Servants of all . . . Esteem yourselves by so much the more happy, honourable and important, by how much the more useful you are. Let your own Ease, your own Pleasure, your own private Interests, yield to the common Good.

Davies delivered his address in the prayer hall of Nassau Hall. Today, Baccalaureate still takes place on the Sunday preceding Commencement, but as an interfaith service in the chapel that begins with an academic procession and includes music, blessings, and readings from a broad range of religious traditions.

Until 1972 the address was always delivered by the president, but since then it has been given by a different speaker each year. Speakers are chosen for their capacity to address topics related to ethical values and public service. Between 1973 and 2017, the speaker was invited by the president of the University, in later years after seeking the advice of the senior class. In 2017 a new selection process was instituted under which the trustee committee on honorary degrees (which also includes faculty, students, and staff) selects the speaker in consultation with the president and with the approval of the board.

Baccalaureate speakers between 1973 and 2021 are listed on page 505.

BAKER MEMORIAL RINK is dedicated to Hobart Amory Hare Baker 1914, one of Princeton's legendary athletes. He was an All-American halfback noted for catching punts on the run and hurtling downfield without a helmet, but his true greatness was in hockey. In his day he was regarded as the greatest amateur hockey player ever developed in North America. No other player had his uncanny ability to weave in and out of the opposing defense, constantly changing pace and direction. He led Princeton to national titles in his sophomore and senior years. When he continued his amateur career with the St. Nick's Club in New York, the sign "Hobey Baker Plays Tonight" would go up, and the line of limousines would stretch for blocks.

Baker is the only person in both the hockey hall of fame and the college football hall of fame. The most valuable player award for college men's hockey, first presented in 1981, is named for him.

A fighter squadron commander in World War I, Baker died testing a repaired plane with his orders to return home in his pocket. A $250,000 campaign was launched to construct an artificial-ice rink as his memorial. It was an intercollegiate effort, with 1,537 men from 39 colleges contributing, including 90 from Yale and 172 from Harvard. It remains the oldest continuously used collegiate rink in the country.

Baker Rink was opened in 1923. It was located just to the west of the University's early-twentieth-century playing fields. Its exterior, along with the exterior of the adjacent former boiler house (now known as 200 Elm Drive, the home of Public Safety), was designed to provide a Collegiate Gothic vista across the playing fields. The building has been renovated several times over the years, including a project in 1985 that added enclosed side aisles to the original building to facilitate spectator circulation and better control temperature and humidity within the rink, and a 2015 renovation that added theater-style seating.

With more than 2,000 seats, Baker is home to the University's men's and women's hockey teams and is a venue for club and intramural hockey, intramural broomball, figure skating, and recreational skating. Its trophy cases pay tribute to the history of Princeton hockey, with particular recognition of Baker and of Patty Kazmaier '86, a four-year letter-winner who helped lead Princeton's women's team to the Ivy League title in three consecutive seasons and was the League's most valuable player in her senior year.

At times in its history Baker Rink was pressed into service for purposes other than hockey. Following World War II, when the campus was flooded with returning veterans, Baker was covered with seas of cots to provide makeshift living quarters. Baker Rink also served for a time as the venue for Alumni Day, including the Alumni Day of 1947 that drew a then-record turnout of more than 3,500.

BAND, THE UNIVERSITY, also known as the Tiger Band, made its debut on October 9, 1920, when 20 undergraduates dressed in black sweaters and white flannel trousers appeared in Palmer Stadium and played Princeton songs during, and between halves of, the Princeton-Maryland football game. As the band is fond of saying, both the team (35–0) and the band won that day, and the band has remained undefeated ever since.

Thirty-five years later, the October 17, 1955, issue of *Sports Illustrated* pictured the band on its cover, attired in orange and black plaid blazers, gray flannel trousers, white shoes, and straw "boater" hats. Around that time, the band, whose numbers eventually topped 100, introduced satirical half-time shows, and began performing at home basketball and hockey games in addition to football.

The band also began to include nontraditional marching band instruments, such as accordions, a practice that later evolved to include a trash percussion section in which drum sticks were used on such items as stop signs, toilet seats, and plastic pink flamingos. When the band celebrated its 75th birthday in 1994, President Harold Shapiro performed in the halftime show playing a washboard.

More significantly, the band evolved into what is called a "scramble band," in which band members haphazardly scatter between formations. The band today remains one of only about a dozen scramble bands in the country. In 1976 the band introduced its "flasher routine" during which band members dressed in trench coats open them to reveal letters forming words on cue from the announcer reading a script.

In 1951 some of the marching band's more accomplished members formed a concert band, whose winter concerts in McCarter Theatre and spring concerts on the steps of Nassau Hall became Princeton traditions. The concert band existed alongside the marching band until 1981 and was a precursor to the Princeton wind ensemble. In 1954 the concert band joined Yale in a New York concert (described as not "half bad" by a *New York Times* music critic), and in May 1971 the band celebrated its 50th season in a joint performance with Harvard at Lincoln Center.

The band continues to play at football, basketball, hockey, lacrosse, and other sporting events, and on other occasions as well. It performs at the Pre-rade each fall and on Dean's Date each semester, and during reunions it conducts its annual Fred Fox '39 Memorial Concert on Cannon Green on Saturday morning and then participates in the P-rade.

Since 1952 the band has worn its distinctive orange and black plaid jacket (a design it replicates on its band van), but for indoor sports it wears orange and black rugby shirts. The drum major and student director wear white pants and long-tailed white dinner jackets.

Over time the band's halftime shows, which tend to traffic heavily in double entendre and innuendo as well as satire and irreverence, have provoked angry reactions from some administrators, alumni, and opposing schools. A notable prank occurred in 1967 when ABC televised a Princeton-Harvard football game. ABC had not planned to broadcast the band's halftime show, but when the band formed an "ABC" on the field, the cameras televised it, just as the band scrambled the "A" to form "NBC."

The band has its own "Princeton University Band March" with the following lyrics:

> Oh here we are,
> The Princeton Band,
> Playing songs of Old Nassau.
> That old refrain will sound again.
> And you will hear the tiger roar!
> The slide trombone,
> The saxophone,
> And the bass drum sounding grand!
> With a boom, boom, boom,
> And a zoom, zoom, zoom,
> Oh, when you hear the Princeton Band!

BASEBALL. Antecedents of what became known as the national pastime were played on campus shortly after the end of the American Revolution. On March 22, 1786, John Rhea Smith 1787 noted in his diary, "A fine day; played baste ball on the campus, but am beaten for I miss both catching and striking the Ball." The following year, the faculty banned the game as "low and unbecoming gentlemen & students."

Modern baseball, more or less as we now know it, arrived in 1858 when four freshmen from Brooklyn organized the Baseball Club of the Class of 1862 of Nassau Hall, which played intra-club matches every day except Sunday. The club's expenses in its first year amounted to $9.43, which were partially offset by fines, including ten cents for using profane language and five cents for arguing with an umpire or disobeying the team captain.

On October 22, 1860, Princeton met its first outside opponent, playing an Orange, New Jersey, team to a 42–42 tie in a long nine-inning game that was called on account of darkness. Four years later, on November 22, 1864, Princeton played its first intercollegiate game, defeating Williams 27–16.

Less than three years later, in a game at Yale on June 26, 1867, Princeton players wore orange and black for the first time. George Ward 1869 suggested orange in recognition of William the Third (also known as the Prince of Orange) of the House of Nassau, for whom Nassau Hall is named. Members of the Class of 1869 Base Ball Club wore badges of orange ribbon with "69 B.B.C." in black lettering to the game, which Princeton won in the ninth inning.

Three Princetonians made notable contributions to the development of baseball. William Gummere 1870 was the first player to use the hook-slide, stealing second successfully by throwing himself feet first under the second baseman's tag, in an exhibition game with the Philadelphia Athletics in the spring of 1870. (The modern code of collegiate amateurism did not develop until several decades later and Princeton occasionally played games against professional teams until the 1940s.)

Joseph McElroy Mann 1876 was the first college pitcher to control the curve ball and use it successfully in a game. His highly effective use of this novel delivery on May 29, 1875, in New Haven, Connecticut, enabled him to pitch the first no-hit game in the history of baseball, amateur or professional.

William Schenck 1880 was the first catcher to use a primitive kind of chest protector: copies of the *Princetonian* stuffed beneath his shirt. After the 1880 Harvard game, a Boston sporting goods manufacturer learned of this contrivance from Schenck, and within a year had developed a rudimentary form of the present pad.

In 1897, Bill Clarke, then a catcher for the Baltimore Orioles, came to Princeton to help coach the team. Known as "Boileryard" for his booming voice, Clarke coached in four stints: from 1897 to 1901, while he was still playing professionally; from 1909 to 1927; as an assistant in 1934 and 1935; and finally in a second turn as head coach from 1936 to 1944, before he finally retired at age 75. Clarke was Princeton's first paid coach, and he coached for more seasons (36) than anyone else in Princeton history. Clarke Field, the University's home diamond since 1961, is named in his honor.

Clarke's first team won the unofficial Big Three championship against Harvard and Yale in 1897, as did the teams of 1899, 1900, and 1901. A notable player of this era was catcher Frederick Kafer 1900, whose classmates later gave a trophy in his honor, awarded annually to the outstanding varsity player. Princeton continued to win the Big Three championships with near regularity, failing to take it in only two years from 1903 through 1912.

On May 17, 1939, Princeton took part in the first televised baseball game, the second half of a doubleheader against Columbia at Baker Field in New York City. NBC televised the game through its experimental station, W2XBS. A single camera mounted on a wooden platform just off home plate covered the action, but was directed only at the pitcher's mound and home plate; the announcer, Bill Stern, had to tell viewers whether a ball put into play was a hit or an out. The Tigers won the game 2–1 in ten innings when pitcher Dan Carmichael '41 scored on an infield single.

Another legendary coach, Eddie Donovan, arrived in 1952 and would lead the Tigers until 1975. Donovan's 1953 team was Eastern Intercollegiate as well as Big Three champion. Outstanding in later years were the 1960 and 1965 teams, both Big Three champions, and the 1971 team, which finished with a 22-7-1 record. In 1971, Donovan was voted District 2 Coach of the Year. Other longtime coaches include Tom McConnell (1982–97) and Scott Bradley (1998–present), a former major league catcher whose number of victories is now second only to Bill Clarke's 564.

From 1888 until 1966, Princeton hosted Yale in a baseball game on the Saturday before Princeton's Commencement. Beginning in 1897, alumni began to process to the game in order by graduation year; this was the beginning of what came to be known as the P-rade. The commencement game ended when Yale determined that it could no longer keep its team together for a post-season game. Until the late 1930s, if the teams had split their two regular season meetings, they would play a third game a week after Commencement, drawing thousands of spectators to games that were usually played at major league parks in New York.

From 1930 to 1992 Princeton played in the Eastern Intercollegiate Baseball League, which included the eight Ivy League schools plus Army and Navy. During that time, they won 10 EIBL championships. When the service academies joined the Patriot League for baseball after the 1992 season, the Ivy League began to sponsor baseball. Between 1993 and 2019, the Tigers won seven Ivy League titles and appeared in the NCAA tournament 11 times.

At least 30 Princeton players have gone on to play in the major leagues, most notably catcher Moe Berg 1923, who also served as a spy for the American Office of Strategic Service before and during World War II (a story recounted in the 2018 movie, *The Catcher Was a Spy*); pitcher Charlie Caldwell 1925, who went on to a highly successful career as Princeton's football coach; pitcher Chris Young '02, who won a World Series ring with the Kansas City Royals; and pitcher/first baseman Mike Ford '15, who in 2013 became the first Ivy League player to be named Player of the Year and Pitcher of the Year in the same season, and went on to play for the New York Yankees.

Young and Ford were two of seven Princeton players named All-Americans. The others were Ray Chirurgi '52, Arnie Holtberg '70, Jack Hittson '71, Dan Arendas '86, and Thomas Pauly '02.

BASKETBALL. Few sports at Princeton have produced as many memorable moments as basketball, from the men's team's 1965 Final Four appearance and the upset of defending national champion UCLA in the first round of the 1996 NCAA tournament, to the women's team's undefeated regular season in 2014–15.

Men's Basketball

Princeton men's basketball began in 1901, 10 years after James Naismith invented the game. The Tigers won the Eastern Intercollegiate Basketball League (EIBL) championship twice in the 1920s, in 1921–22 and 1924–25. All-American Ken Fairman '34 led Princeton to three consecutive winning seasons in the early 1930s, including an EIBL title in 1932.

In 1938, Franklin "Cappy" Cappon began 20 seasons as coach, which included five championships: EIBL titles in 1950, 1952, and 1955, and Ivy League titles in 1959 and 1960. Cappon's teams also made three appearances in the NCAA tournament. He coached the program's first five 1,000-point scorers—Bud Haabestad '55, Carl Belz '59, Jim Brangan '60, Pete Campbell '62, and Art Hyland '63.

Cappon died of a heart attack in November 1961, so he missed the opportunity to see the rise of Princeton's greatest player, Bill Bradley '65. That season,

Bradley made 57 straight free-throws for the freshman team (one more than the NBA record at the time), earning mention in *Sports Illustrated* as the "Princeton boy who beat the pros."

Bradley proved to be a relentlessly efficient scorer, averaging 30 points per game in his three varsity seasons (freshmen then could not play varsity), improving his field-goal percentage each year, and setting an Ivy single-game record with his 51 points against Harvard in 1964—all this before there was a shot clock or a three-point basket. But his brilliance went beyond the box score. John McPhee '53, writing for the *New Yorker*, described his first impressions of Bradley: "His play was integral. There was nothing missing. He not only worked hard on defense, for example, he worked hard on defense when the other team was hopelessly beaten. He did all kinds of things he didn't have to do simply because those were the dimensions of the game."

Princeton won three straight Ivy League championships with the All-American Bradley leading the way. In September 1964 he helped the United States win a gold medal at the Olympics. In March 1965 Princeton advanced all the way to the NCAA Final Four, where the Tigers lost to Michigan in the national semifinals. Bradley went on to score 58 points in the third-place game, breaking the NCAA tournament single-game scoring record as Princeton defeated Wichita State, 118–82. He finished his career with 2,503 points, and won the Sullivan Award as the nation's outstanding amateur athlete.

Bradley's success was guided by coach Willem "Butch" van Breda Kolff '45, the national coach of the year in 1964–65, who ran a fluid offense that stressed movement instead of set formations. Two starters from the Final Four team, Ed Hummer '67 and Gary Walters '67, led Princeton to a 21–2 regular-season record and another Ivy championship in 1966–67, followed by a trip to the NCAA tournament, where the Tigers fell in overtime to North Carolina in the second round. After that season, van Breda Kolff left to coach the Los Angeles Lakers and recommended one of his former players at Lafayette, Pete Carril, to succeed him at Princeton.

When Carril arrived, competition for the Ivy title was fierce. In his first season, Princeton finished 20–6 and tied for the crown but lost a playoff against Columbia. The 1968–69 Tigers, led by the frontcourt trio of Chris Thomforde '69, Geoff Petrie '70, and John Hummer '70, avoided a playoff by winning all 14 of their Ivy games—a feat not even the Bradley teams had managed. (Petrie and Hummer followed Bradley into professional basketball, with Petrie named NBA Rookie of the Year in 1971.)

Princeton followed with six winning seasons but failed to win the Ivy title as Penn won six straight championships. In that span, Brian Taylor '84 starred for the Tigers, averaging 24.3 points per game (second to Bradley on the program's all-time list). Taylor left for the pros in 1972 after his junior year (he was ABA Rookie of the Year in 1973) and completed his degree in 1984 after retiring from basketball.

Penn's championship run denied Princeton an opportunity to play in the NCAA tournament, but the Tigers earned bids to the National Invitation Tournament (NIT) twice, in 1972 and 1975. The 1975 team, led by Ivy Player of the Year Armond Hill '85 and Mickey Steuerer '76, closed out the regular season with nine straight wins and defeated Holy Cross and South Carolina handily in the NIT's first two rounds, setting up a semifinal game against Oregon in which Princeton's agile but undersized defense prevailed, 58–57. The Tigers faced Providence in the final, where Steuerer sparked a second-half run that secured an 80–69 win for the championship.

After the NIT-title season, Carril's teams won or shared the league title in 1976, 1977, 1980, 1981, 1983, and 1984. In 1980 and 1981, Princeton and Penn tied for the Ivy title and played for the league's tournament bid in a pair of neutral-site playoff games. Penn won the first and Princeton won the second, adding to a heated rivalry that defined Ivy men's basketball for five decades.

At the 1983 NCAA tournament, two-time Ivy Player of the Year Craig Robinson '83 and the Tigers won two games—in the preliminary round against North Carolina A&T and in the opening round against Oklahoma State—before bowing out to Boston College. The following year, Princeton won its NCAA tournament preliminary game against San Diego before falling to UNLV in the first round.

Princeton's next NCAA tournament bid came in 1989, when the Tigers drew a first-round matchup with top-seeded Georgetown and its towering center, Alonzo Mourning, the nation's leading shot-blocker. Carril's players masterfully controlled the pace, led at halftime, and were tied heading into the final minute before Mourning made a foul shot to put the Hoyas ahead, 50–49. Bob Scrabis '89 and Kit Mueller '91 each had shot attempts in the closing seconds, but Mourning blocked both, ending the upset bid. Scrabis was Ivy Player of the

Year in 1989; Mueller won the award in 1990 and 1991.

The early 1990s brought three more Ivy titles and three more close NCAA tournament losses. In 1995–96, the Tigers won 12 straight Ivy games, bookended by losses to Penn, and tied for the title. In a playoff held in Carril's hometown of Bethlehem, Pa., Princeton outlasted Penn, 63–56. Afterward, Carril announced his retirement.

The knowledge that the 1996 NCAA tournament would be Carril's last amplified the thrill that came a week later when Gabe Lewullis '99 made a backdoor cut for the winning layup against UCLA. The *Daily Princetonian*'s banner headline proclaimed the result as "David 43, Goliath 41." The five Princeton head coaches who would follow Carril each played a role in the win: Bill Carmody, John Thompson III '88, and Joe Scott '87 were assistant coaches, and Sydney Johnson '97 and Mitch Henderson '98 were key players. In a postgame interview, Carril said he was happy not to be known as "the guy who lost every close one."

Carmody took over as coach the following season and continued to build on the success of the "Princeton offense," a system that prizes cutting, passing, and quick decision-making. His Tigers won the next two Ivy titles without losing a single league game. In the 1997–98 regular season, Princeton was 26–1 (its only defeat came at North Carolina) and climbed as high as No. 7 in the national rankings. After dispatching UNLV in the 1998 NCAA tournament, the Tigers fell to Michigan State in the second round. Team captains won Ivy Player of the Year honors in three consecutive seasons: Johnson in 1997, Steve Goodrich '98 in 1998, and Brian Earl '99 in 1999. The 1998–99 squad finished second to Penn before making a successful NIT run.

Carmody left for Northwestern in 2000, and Thompson, his successor, won or shared the Ivy title three times (2001, 2002, and 2004) before leaving for Georgetown. Princeton returned to the NCAA tournament in 2011, with Johnson as coach, thanks to a buzzer-beating jump shot by Douglas Davis '12 in an Ivy playoff against Harvard. In the NCAA first round, Princeton fell to Kentucky by two points.

The men's team's most recent NCAA tournament appearance came under coach Henderson in 2017, following a season in which the Tigers won all 14 Ivy regular-season games and two contests in the inaugural Ivy postseason tournament. Squaring off against Notre Dame in the NCAA opening round, Princeton had a shot to win in the closing seconds but lost by two. By 2020 Henderson had become the third winningest coach in team history, behind only Carril and Cappon.

Two Princetonians have been enshrined in the Naismith Basketball Hall of Fame—Bradley in 1983 and Carril in 1997—and ten alumni have played professionally in the NBA or ABA. Ivy Players of the Year, in addition to those already cited, include Frank Sowinski '78, Sean Jackson '92, Ian Hummer '13, and Spencer Weisz '17.

Women's Basketball

Princeton women's basketball tipped off in February 1972 and won the first Ivy championship in 1974–75, sweeping all five of its league opponents in a two-day tournament. The Tigers won the next three Ivy tournament titles as well, paced by early stars Margaret Meier '78 and Claire Tomasiewicz '79. The 1975–76 team, coached by Pat Walsh, won the Eastern AIWA Small College tournament and advanced to the National Small College tournament.

Ivy women's teams began playing a double-round-robin schedule in 1982–83, and in 1985 coach Joan Kowalik led Princeton to its first share of the Ivy championship in the new format, tying Brown for the title. Kowalik also was at the helm for Princeton's first 20-win season, in 1987–88, and coached one of the program's most prolific scorers, Sandi Bittler '90, who finished her career with 1,683 points. (Her record was broken by Bella Alaire '20, who finished her Princeton career with 1,703 points—a total that would have been even higher if the COVID-19 pandemic had not caused cancellation of all post-season play her senior year.)

Since 1994 the Ivy champion has received an automatic berth in the NCAA tournament, but for more than a decade that honor eluded the Tigers. The 1995–96 team won 20 games and finished second in the Ivy standings, earning a spot in the National Women's Invitational tournament. The 1998–99 team tied for the league title but lost to Dartmouth in a playoff for the NCAA bid. The 2005–06 team, led by Becky Brown '06 and Meagan Cowher '08, finished in a three-way tie for the Ivy title and also lost in a playoff against Dartmouth.

Princeton's postseason hopes found new life under coach Courtney Banghart, a former Dartmouth star who arrived in 2007–08. She led the program to its first NCAA tournament in 2010, when freshman forward Niveen Rasheed '13 and the Tigers were 14–0 in Ivy games.

Rasheed, a dynamic scorer and dogged rebounder, would go on to score more than 1,600 points, win the Ivy Player of the Year award twice, and play a part in four straight Ivy championships. But those teams were far from a one-woman show: teammates Addie Micir '11, Devona Allgood '12, Lauren Edwards '12, Blake Dietrick '15, Michelle Miller '16, and Alex Wheatley '16 each scored more than 1,000 career points as well. Micir won Ivy Player of the Year honors in 2011, when Rasheed was sidelined with a knee injury.

During Banghart's 12 seasons, Penn emerged as Princeton's chief Ivy rival, halting the Tigers' championship streak in 2013–14. Princeton rebounded with the program's finest season in 2014–15. Captained by Ivy Player of the Year Dietrick, who led the team in scoring and set a program record with 157 assists, Princeton won all 30 of its regular-season games. The Tigers beat their opponents by an average of nearly 25 points per game and reached No. 13 in the national rankings. They also won their first NCAA tournament game, against Wisconsin–Green Bay (with President Barack Obama, uncle of freshman Leslie Robinson '18, in attendance), before losing to Maryland in the second round (this time with Supreme Court Justices Sonia Sotomayor '76 and Elena Kagan '81 in attendance). Dietrick later became the first alumna to play in the Women's National Basketball Association (WNBA), debuting with the Seattle Storm in 2016, and later playing for the San Antonio Stars and the Atlanta Dream.

Banghart was named the Naismith National Coach of the Year following the 2014–15 season and guided the Tigers to an at-large bid to the NCAA tournament in 2016, a WNIT bid in 2017, and Ivy championships in 2018 and 2019 before leaving for North Carolina in 2019. She was succeeded by Carla Berube, who, in her first year as coach, led the team to a 26–1 regular-season record, including a perfect 14–0 in the Ivy League, before the Ivy League and NCAA tournaments were canceled because of the COVID-19 pandemic.

Banghart's final two Ivy champions were built around the versatile 6-foot-4 forward/guard Bella Alarie, a three-time Ivy Player of the Year, who set a single-game Ivy record when she scored 45 points against Columbia in 2019. Alarie, who won 20 Ivy Player of the Week awards, was the first Ivy League women's basketball player named a two-time Associated Press All-American. She was drafted fifth overall in the 2020 WNBA draft by the Dallas Wings and made her professional debut that summer.

BAYARD, SAMUEL 1784, a Philadelphian, was valedictorian of his class at the age of 17. He served as clerk of the United States Supreme Court, prosecutor of United States claims before the British admiralty courts, and presiding judge of Westchester County. When he was 40, he returned to live in Princeton and became the first mayor of the borough. At different times he served the College as librarian, trustee, and treasurer, and he was a founder and a trustee of Princeton Theological Seminary. The street on which he lived was named Bayard Lane in his honor.

BEER/CLASS/SENIOR JACKETS, with distinctive designs imprinted on the back, have been worn by undergraduates in the spring of their senior year since early in the twentieth century. The practice was started by a small group in the Class of 1912 who, while quaffing beer and carving their initials on the tables of the old Nassau Inn, noticed that the foam from their steins sometimes spotted their clothes. To avoid dry-cleaning bills, they adopted a uniform of blue denim overalls and jackets.

The next year, with the first signs of spring, the whole Class of 1913 donned overalls and jackets, this time of white denim, and, although they were more a means of class identification than drinking uniforms, called them beer suits. Denim was quickly phased out and replaced with white canvas, which long remained the fabric of choice. Beer suits disappeared during World War I but were revived in 1919.

The Class of 1920 was the first to use a design; they wore black arm bands to mourn the imposition of prohibition. Other classes also acknowledged prohibition on the backs of their beer jackets; 1922 had a beer mug with wings. The Class of 1925 depicted a tiger crushed by four heavy tomes, in recognition of the burden imposed on them by the new four-course plan.

After World War II overalls were dispensed with, and since then only jackets have been worn. The tradition waned in the 1970s when a number of classes did not design jackets, but it revived in 1982 and has remained strong since then. In recent decades, the jackets have been officially renamed senior jackets, or class jackets, to eliminate the explicit reference to beer and to emphasize the role of the jacket in expressing the identity and unity of the class.

The jacket designs usually reflect on the University, current events, the numerals of the class, or the tiger; typically, they are chosen through a contest among class members. The design becomes the unofficial emblem of the class; the jacket serves as the class reunion costume, at least until its fifth reunion; and the seniors wear their jackets for Class Day. In recent years most jackets have been black, although the Class of 2012 celebrated the centennial of the jackets by reverting to white.

In 2018 the Association of Princeton Graduate Alumni, which had introduced a reunions blazer for all graduate alumni in 2003, created a graduate alumni beer jacket "styled after its undergraduate cousins in a unisex cut with many pockets both inside and out." The jacket is black with orange trim, and it is sold with a lapel pin to indicate the wearer's year of graduation.

BEHRMAN, HOWARD T., AWARDS, for distinguished achievement in the humanities, were established in 1975 by a gift from Howard T. Behrman, a dermatologist and book collector who had a home in Princeton. Recipients are chosen from among Princeton faculty members nominated by their colleagues; selections are made by an awards committee chaired by the dean of the faculty. The awards are conferred at a formal dinner in May.

Behrman served as vice chair of the council of the Friends of the Princeton University Library and as a member of the advisory councils of the departments of English and Art and Archaeology. Before his death in 1985, he created an endowment to support various aspects of scholarly endeavor in the humanities, including permanent support for the Behrman Awards and for his library of American literature, which he donated to the library.

Recipients of the Behrman Awards are listed on page 506.

BELCHER, JONATHAN, governor of the province of New Jersey from 1747 to 1757, granted Princeton its second charter and aided it in many other ways; the College, his fellow trustees declared in 1755, viewed him as "its founder, patron, and benefactor."

A native of Cambridge, Massachusetts, Belcher graduated from Harvard in 1699, second in a class of 12, and accumulated a fortune at an early age as a merchant in Boston. He held a succession of public offices: tithingman and town accountant of Boston, member of the Massachusetts Council, and governor of Massachusetts and New Hampshire. During the last decade of his life, to quote from his commission, which is preserved in the University Library, he was appointed "Captain General and Governor-in-Chief of the Province of New Jersey and territories thereupon depending in America, and Vice-Admiral of the same."

Belcher had a quick temper and a sharp tongue, which earned him many enemies in Massachusetts and New Hampshire, who brought about his dismissal in 1741. He was able to convince the English court that he had been maligned by his political enemies, and after living in England for several years he was appointed to the New Jersey governorship.

Soon after his arrival in New Jersey in 1747, Belcher, a Congregationalist, adopted the infant college of the dissenting Presbyterians as his own and sought to help it pursue its mission of "better enlightening the minds and polishing the manners of this and neighboring colonies." Finding the legality of the College's original charter under attack—it had been granted by acting governor John Hamilton, whose authority was questioned—Belcher granted a second charter on September 14, 1748. This charter provided for 23, rather than the original 12, trustees, thus permitting the governing board to broaden and strengthen its representation politically and religiously. (Of these additional trustees, at least seven were slaveholders, including Belcher himself.) Eight weeks after the second charter was granted, at the College's first Commencement, the trustees conferred on Belcher Princeton's first honorary degree.

Belcher encouraged the trustees to raise funds for a college building and a house for the president and, in the dispute as to where the College was to be settled, threw his influence in favor of Princeton—"as near the center of the Province as any and a fine situation."

Just before the College moved from Newark to Princeton, Belcher gave the trustees his library of 474 volumes, his full-length portrait, his carved and gilded coat-of-arms, a pair of terrestrial globes, and 10 framed portraits of kings and queens of England. In their address of thanks, the trustees asked his permission to name the first building, then being erected in Princeton, Belcher Hall. The governor declined this honor, persuading them instead to name it Nassau Hall for "the glorious King William the Third . . . of the illustrious House of Nassau," who was held in high regard by dissenters as a champion of religious freedom and political liberty.

Although only six of Belcher's books have survived, he is still recognized as the library's oldest benefactor: when Firestone Library was built in 1948, the governor's arms were carved in stone over the main entrance along with those of the University. His portrait and those of the 10 English monarchs were destroyed during the Revolution. The portrait of Belcher that now hangs in Nassau Hall was obtained from an English descendant of the governor and presented to the University in 1953.

BENDHEIM CENTER FOR FINANCE, THE, is an interdisciplinary center dedicated to fundamental research and education on how financial markets behave and how policies can shape these markets.

The center was established in 1997 at the initiative of Ben Bernanke, then chair of the department of Economics; Bernanke later chaired the White House Council of Economic Advisers, and then for two terms chaired the Federal Reserve. The center draws faculty from several departments, with the majority coming from Economics and Operations Research and Financial Engineering (ORFE), but with faculty also from Computer Science, the school of Public and International Affairs, History, and other departments. Its research forges links between economics and such fields as mathematics, computer science, engineering, operations research, psychology, politics, and history.

The center offers an undergraduate certificate in finance program that exposes students from many different majors to such concepts as asset pricing, portfolio management, financial engineering, banking, corporate finance and governance, and regulation. It also offers a master's degree in finance that equips students with technical expertise and a deep understanding of financial markets and instruments and the role of finance in society. The center provides advanced graduate students with opportunities to conduct research in finance as part of their PhD programs in Economics, ORFE, or the program in Applied and Computational Mathematics.

The founding director of the center, Professor Yacine Ait-Sahalia, who served in that role until 2014, described it as "a major venue where the world's leading experts in finance from academia, government, and the private sector can meet regularly to exchange views and information." Its corporate affiliates programs offers companies an opportunity to interact with faculty and engage students, and the center facilitates visits from leaders of major financial firms as well as influential individuals from the Federal Reserve and central banks around the world.

The center was established through a gift from the Leon Lowenstein Foundation and named for Robert Bendheim '37, a prominent business and civic leader and the president of the foundation. An additional gift in 1998 supported extensive renovation of the first home of the center, the former Dial Lodge, which was built in 1917 to house one of the University's eating clubs. The renovation preserved the Tudor Gothic stone exterior of the building while transforming its interior to support cutting-edge teaching and research.

In 2016 the center moved to the Julis Romo Rabinowitz building, which it shares with the Economics department. The building is strategically placed near many of the departments, including ORFE and the school of Public and International Affairs, with which the center most closely interacts.

BLAIR HALL, the University's first Collegiate Gothic dormitory, was a sesquicentennial gift from John Insley Blair, a trustee of Princeton from 1866 to 1899.

As a boy in Warren County, New Jersey, Blair left school at age 11 to work in a country store. At 18 he owned his own store, and at 27 he was operating a chain of five general stores and four large flour mills. He next acquired an interest in the iron mines at Oxford Furnace and helped found the Lackawanna Coal & Iron Company. He then helped organize the Delaware, Lackawanna & Western Railroad and, later, the Union Pacific Railroad. At one time he was president of 16 railroads and was reputed to own more miles of railroad right-of-way than any other man in the world.

In 1864 he endowed the professorship of geology then held by Arnold Guyot; it is Princeton's second oldest endowed chair. Asked for a few remarks after his installation as a trustee in 1866, he reminded the board that his own formal education was limited; he had spent most of his life learning addition and now, he said, "I have come to Princeton to learn subtraction." He gave the funds for Blair Hall in 1896; it was built in 1897. He was also a major donor to Blair Academy in Blairstown, New Jersey, and he made gifts of land and money toward the building of more than a hundred churches in towns across the country he had helped lay out along the route of the Union Pacific and other western railroads.

Blair Hall was designed by Cope and Stewardson, who were among the first to apply the Tudor Gothic style to American college dormitories. Blair Hall is considered their masterpiece.

In 1907 Blair's son, DeWitt Clinton Blair 1856, who was a trustee from 1900 to 1909, gave an extension of

Blair Hall that terminates in a gateway tower on University Place.

When first built, Blair, Little Hall, and a gymnasium on the site that now houses Dillon Gymnasium marked the western boundary of the campus. The Pennsylvania Railroad tracks came to the foot of the broad steps leading up to Blair Arch. In 1917 the railroad station was moved a quarter of a mile to the south and the intervening tracks were removed, making way for the post-World War I dormitory development (now known as the "junior slums") that Blair Tower still overlooks, and a landscaped pathway known as Blair Walk.

Following extensive renovation, in 2000 the portion of Blair Hall east and south of the arch was renamed Buyers Hall. Buyers serves as a dormitory for Rockefeller College, while Blair houses students in Mathey College. The room over Blair Arch, long a coveted dormitory space, is now a coveted seminar room. Because of its acoustics, the arch itself is a favorite site for a cappella groups. Blair's steps are home to step sings, for freshmen shortly after they arrive on campus and for seniors just before they graduate.

Bowen, William Gordon *58 was installed as Princeton's 17th president on June 30, 1972, in a simple ceremony in Nassau Hall's historic Faculty Room and began his presidency on the following day.

Born on October 6, 1933, in Cincinnati, Ohio, he was valedictorian and class president at Wyoming High School and then attended nearby Denison University, where he graduated with highest honors in economics. At Denison he was the leading scholar, the ranking member of the varsity tennis team (sweeping top honors for two years in both singles and doubles in the Ohio conference), and student body president, succeeding Richard Lugar, who later served as a US Senator from Ohio.

Bowen arrived in Princeton in 1955 as a graduate student in economics and the following year married Mary Ellen Maxwell of Cincinnati. In 1958, when he was not quite 25, he received his PhD and joined the faculty as an assistant professor of economics and a research associate in the Industrial Relations Section. He became director of graduate studies in the school of Public and International Affairs at 30, professor of economics and public affairs at 31, provost at 33, and president when he was 38 (one year older than his predecessor, Robert Goheen '40 *48, had been when he was elected).

Bowen was regarded as an outstanding teacher by his department and his students, and as president he continued to teach sections of the introductory course, Economics 101, both because he loved to teach and because it gave him opportunities each year to get to know a cross-section of students who had no agenda with him other than learning economics.

A tireless scholar and prolific writer, he authored numerous books and articles. He followed two studies on the wage-price issue and wage behavior in the postwar period with *The Federal Government and Princeton University; Economic Aspects of Education*, which included a skillful analysis of university financing in the United States and Great Britain; and, in 1968, *Economics of the Major Private Universities.*

In 1966 he and economics professor William Baumol published a book that examined the economic foundations of theater, opera, orchestra, and dance in the United States. *Performing Arts: The Economic Dilemma* was considered a landmark study of the economics of cultural organizations, pointing out, for example, the difficulty of achieving productivity gains when no matter what you do, it still takes four musicians to perform Beethoven's String Quartet No. 4 in C minor. In 1969 Bowen and T. A. Finegan of Vanderbilt University published *The Economics of Labor Force Participation*, which reviewers called the most authoritative work of its kind.

When Bowen was named provost in 1967, the position had existed for only one year. The provost was to be the general deputy of the president, and to signify its stature, the position was filled in its first year by J. Douglas Brown 1919 *1928, who had been dean of the faculty, previously the University's second-ranking position, since 1946. As provost, Bowen quickly became an active partner of the president, to the point where the campus press occasionally described Goheen and Bowen collectively as "Boheen."

While Goheen and Bowen had different skills and styles (Neil Rudenstine '56, who served Goheen as dean of students and Bowen as dean of the college and provost, once said that Goheen made decisions "more intuitively," while Bowen reached decisions "more analytically"), and while they occasionally held different views (Bowen was an early advocate of coeducation while Goheen had to overcome initial reservations) they effectively collaborated in leading the University through the tumultuous times of the late 1960s and early 1970s.

During his years as provost, Bowen was deeply involved in the University's adoption and implementation of coeducation, its efforts to increase the enrollment and engagement of minority students, its defense of open inquiry and free speech, and its efforts to strengthen its faculty and expand its commitment to financial aid while bringing its budget under control.

He was founding chair of the faculty-student-staff priorities committee of the newly formed Council of the Princeton University Community, which advises the president on each year's operating budget and makes recommendations regarding salary pools and tuition charges. He encouraged active participation by all members of the committee and used the committee's annual reports to inform the community not only of the committee's recommendations but the reasoning behind them. The priorities committee still functions much as Bowen structured it, and its level of campus-wide engagement and transparency remains unparalleled among research universities.

Although Bowen's expertise in the economics of education and his experience in the provost's office were significant factors in his election as president, the choice was further influenced by a general recognition of his enormous energy and broad intelligence, and, in the words of a faculty colleague, "his easy manner, his delightful sense of humor, his ability to get along with people and to listen and to understand their point of view, and his ability to take quick and decisive action once his mind was made up."

In his installation remarks he alluded to the contentiousness of the times. "Contention," he said, "is the lifeblood of any good university, for there has never been a single path to the truth and it is by testing ideas that we sharpen them and make them serviceable. But the spirit of our advocacy is as important as its quality. May all of us, and the many more whom we represent, continue to study and to think independently, to exercise our freedom, but always with mutual respect, with compassion as well as precision, with courage and good humor, and with the best interests of this University ever in mind."

As president, Bowen devoted his prodigious energies to enhancing the University's academic strengths—creating new departments and programs, dramatically increasing its investment in the arts and the life sciences, and attracting first-rate professors—while tripling the size of the endowment and creating the Princeton Investment Company to manage it.

In his book *Lessons Learned: Reflections of a University President*, Bowen recalls that by the early 1970s it was evident that "the intellectual breakthroughs in the life sciences were profound and that no university with high aspirations could be anything but very good in these fields" and that Princeton needed to be much better than it was. Deciding that "halfway measures . . . would not work," he set out simultaneously to create a new department of Molecular Biology, build a state-of-the-art laboratory (designed by Robert Venturi '47 *50 and Denise Scott Brown), and attract two transformative faculty leaders in Arnold Levine and Thomas Shenk. The department achieved the level of international distinction Bowen had sought and attracted many other faculty members who were leaders in the field, including Shirley Tilghman, who would become Princeton 19th president.

Other departments established during his tenure included Comparative Literature and Computer Science, and other programs included the Ancient World, Applied and Computational Mathematics, Population Studies, and Women's Studies. Programs in the creative and performing arts were strengthened (the program in Theater and Dance received separate status); the art museum and Firestone Library were renovated and expanded; and the acoustically superior Richardson Auditorium was installed in Alexander Hall.

In 1978 Bowen appointed a Committee on Undergraduate Residential Life to "study and make recommendations concerning the development of social and dining facilities that would have a direct bearing on the quality of undergraduate life." In its June 1979 report, the committee recommended creating a system of five residential colleges that would house all freshmen and sophomores and a limited number of juniors and seniors, and that fall the trustees agreed. Bowen set out to raise the necessary funds; by 1982 the colleges were open to freshmen and a year later they were fully operational.

The facilities to support molecular biology and the new system of residential colleges were among the beneficiaries of the five-year Campaign for Princeton that was launched on Alumni Day 1982 with a goal of $275 million. In January 1984, the campaign goal was increased to $330 million and when the campaign ended in 1986 more than $410 million had been raised.

In the early years of his presidency, Bowen persuaded the trustees in 1974 to adopt a policy of "equal access" that removed a cap on the number of women in each undergraduate class; pressed for the addition of women to the faculty and senior staff; and appointed the first woman dean of student affairs in 1972 and the first women deans of the college and the graduate school in 1977. He oversaw the return of Army ROTC to campus in 1972 after a year's absence, and he appointed a committee to consider whether Princeton should establish a law school. (The answer was no.)

Bowen defended freedom of speech, civility, and the right of student groups to invite speakers with controversial and even offensive views, and opposed the University taking political actions through boycotts or divestment except in exceptional circumstances following careful deliberation. He launched the University's development of Princeton Forrestal Center along Route 1 and sold its interest in downtown Palmer Square. He encouraged efforts to increase and support the diversity of the campus community, including development of a plan to construct a Center for Jewish Life at 70 Washington Road, the site of two former eating clubs.

To make the Baccalaureate service more welcoming to all students, he moved it from the morning to the afternoon and he added diversity by inviting outside speakers to deliver the principal address that previously had always been delivered by the University president. In 1978 an article he wrote for the *Princeton Alumni Weekly* was cited by Supreme Court Justice Lewis Powell in his Bakke decision upholding affirmative action. In his early years he also had to contend with a dissident alumni group called *Concerned Alumni of Princeton* that opposed many of the changes taking place on campus.

Known for his prodigious capacity for work, Bowen also was legendary for his attention to detail (making sure, for example, that the bricks for Molecular Biology's Lewis Thomas Laboratory were just the right color). He stayed abreast of all campus issues and was directly involved in every major decision; kept up a voluminous correspondence; traveled extensively; and still made time regularly to duck out of the office at noon to play tennis and squash.

When Princeton University Press compiled his writings as president in a volume titled *Ever the Teacher*, it recounted the process behind the drafting of his 1975 annual report. The report was written in large measure on the way to, from, and in the Los Angeles, Tokyo, and Hong Kong airports in connection with a visit to China as one of the earliest Americans to visit following the Cultural Revolution. He would write while flying to Los Angeles; mail back the handwritten draft from his hotel and then write more en route to Tokyo; mail back this new section from Tokyo while receiving a typed version of an earlier section that had been mailed to him there for editing; emerge from China to edit the section he had mailed from Los Angeles that was now awaiting him in Hong Kong; and so on.

His beloved summer home a block from the ocean in Avalon, NJ, was outfitted with everything he needed to put in five to six hours of work each day, even when he was on vacation.

Bowen published 15 annual reports, on topics ranging from liberal education, graduate education, and scholarship and research to coeducation, financial aid, the creative arts, and international studies. They were distributed on campus and to all alumni, but also to presidents of other colleges and universities, federal and state officials, and other educational leaders who welcomed his clear delineations of difficult topics and his thoughtful prescriptions for institutional and national policy.

After Bowen announced his intention to step down, the University awarded him an honorary degree at Commencement in 1987. The citation read:

> As a graduate student, faculty member, provost, and president, you have invigorated this community with your talents, your energies, and your vision for Princeton. You have led us, prodded us, befriended us, inspired us—teaching us always, in Adlai Stevenson's words, how much better to light a candle than to curse the darkness. Reaching well beyond this campus, whose beauty has moved you so deeply, you have been an eloquent and effective advocate for excellence, opportunity, and independence in this nation's institutions of learning. We salute your leadership and love of this University, and we send you on to new challenges with our appreciation, our affection, and your favorite injunction, "Onward."

After Bowen left office in 1988, he served for almost 20 years as president of the Andrew W. Mellon Foundation, where he created a program to study doctoral education, college admissions, independent research libraries, and charitable nonprofits. Under his leadership, the foundation sponsored the creation of JSTOR (short for Journal Storage), initially as an electronic archive of academic journals, and the ARTstor digital database of art works. In 2004 he cofounded ITHAKA, which provides digital services to the academic community.

Bowen was the author or co-author of some 20 books. With former Harvard president Derek Bok, he co-authored the groundbreaking work *The Shape of the River: Long-Term Consequences on Considering Race in College and University Admissions* in 1988, analyzing the use of race-sensitive admission policies and finding that they succeeded in educating minority students and creating diverse learning environments. Princeton's 20th president, Christopher Eisgruber, said *The Shape of the River* "may be the most important book ever written about the value of affirmative action in collegiate admissions."

Bowen's *Equity and Excellence in American Higher Education* in 2005 examined the importance of seeking diversity in building faculties and student bodies, and argued that, by neglecting low-income applicants, elite colleges and universities remained "bastions of privilege" rather than becoming "engines of opportunity." He also wrote about issues related to collegiate sports (*The Game of Life: College Sports and Educational Values*), university governance, and leadership in higher education. His *Lessons Learned* offered insights from his Princeton presidency and offered the following advice: "Plan carefully, then execute rapidly." He said it was important to listen with an open mind and then "formulate the question correctly. Assemble the evidence you need to make an informed choice, and then make the choice." It was also important, he said, to "do those things in that order."

With his successor as president of Princeton, Harold Shapiro *64, Bowen edited a volume of essays, *Universities and Their Leadership*, which were presented at a symposium held in March 1996 as part of the University's 250th anniversary and published by Princeton University Press in 1998. His 2013 book, *Higher Education in a Digital Age*, focused on how technology can address the economic challenges facing higher education. His 2016 book *Lesson Plan: An Agenda for Change in American Higher Education*, coauthored with Michael McPherson, was published only months before he died. In 2018 Princeton University Press published *Ever the Leader*, a compilation of his selected writings from 1995–2016.

In 1993 a new building for materials science and engineering research on Prospect Avenue near the Engineering Quadrangle was named for Bowen at the request of its donor, Gordon Wu '58, and in 1994 he was awarded the James Madison Medal, the highest distinction the University can bestow on alumni of the graduate school. In 2009 he participated in five oral history interviews with University archivist Daniel Linke that are available through the archives.

In 2013 Bowen was awarded the National Humanities Medal "for his contributions to the study of economics and his probing research on higher education in America," and for using his leadership "to put theories into practice and strive for new heights of academic excellence." In commenting on the award, Eisgruber said that Bowen's "legendary leadership" had "simultaneously elevated Princeton's stature and strengthened its core values," and that his scholarly work after stepping down from the presidency, emphatically supporting "the need to make college education accessible to all groups within our society," was continuing to have a "major impact on public policy debates and university leadership."

When Bowen died in 2016, the *New York Times* concluded its obituary by recounting an incident that demonstrated his "quick thinking." It occurred in the year he became Princeton's president. "While attending an academic meeting on Hilton Head Island, SC," the obituary said, "he saw a woman fall into a pond of alligators and raced to the rescue. As to who was more startled—the woman or the reptile on which she had suddenly landed—the question, he said, 'seemed something you didn't want to leave to the alligator.'"

BRACKENRIDGE, HUGH HENRY 1771 entered Princeton as a 20-year-old Scotsman. His classmates James Madison and Philip Freneau quickly recognized his impressive classical learning, oratorical skills, and wit. An avid Whig at Princeton and later a Jeffersonian democrat, Brackenridge joined Freneau, Madison, and others in forming the American Whig Society to counter the conservative Cliosophic Society. These activities led Freneau and Brackenridge to collaborate on *Father Bombo's Pilgrimage to Mecca in Arabia*, a satire on American manners that may have been the first work of prose fiction written in America. They also combined their talents in composing a patriotic poem of epic design, "The Rising Glory of America," which Brackenridge read at the 1771 commencement exercises at Nassau Hall.

After graduation Brackenridge completed his training for the ministry, taught for a while, and served successfully as headmaster of a Maryland academy. The Revolutionary War found him as an army chaplain preaching fiery patriotic sermons to the soldiers. Hoping for a wider sphere of influence, he started the *United States Magazine* in Philadelphia in 1778, but its lagging subscriptions convinced him to change his profession and location. He took a law degree and moved to the tiny village of Pittsburgh.

Soon a distinguished citizen of Pittsburgh and founder of the first western newspaper, *The Pittsburgh Gazette*, he was elected to the state assembly, where he fought for the adoption of the federal Constitution and obtained state endowments for the establishment of the Pittsburgh Academy (University of Pittsburgh).

While serving as a Pennsylvania Supreme Court judge, Brackenridge produced a steady flow of satires, narratives, and published sermons, while also devoting himself to his masterwork, *Modern Chivalry*, a long comic narrative in the tradition of *Don Quixote* and *Tom Jones*.

BRACKETT, CYRUS FOGG, founder of the Electrical Engineering department, was born on a farm in Parsonfield, Maine. He put himself through Bowdoin College by teaching in country schools, graduating in 1859 when he was 26. While continuing to teach, he studied medicine at Bowdoin and at Harvard and received his MD degree from the Medical School of Maine in 1863. For 10 years thereafter he held professorships of natural science, chemistry, zoology, geology, and physics at Bowdoin.

In 1873 Brackett was called to Princeton to occupy a new chair in physics founded in honor of Joseph Henry. He soon became an adviser to the trustees in their efforts to improve instruction in scientific subjects and was also influential with the faculty in the development of the curriculum in science. One of his first tasks was to build up the College's equipment, which, after Henry's departure in 1848, had been allowed to fall behind new developments in physics. He was mechanically skillful, and he constructed much of the apparatus needed for his ingenious lecture demonstrations himself.

Brackett's own interests were stimulated by the developments in electricity of the 1870s and 1880s. He was closely associated with Thomas Edison, who frequently sought his advice and counsel, and he developed a dynamometer to measure the power delivered by Edison's early generators. He was also acquainted with Alexander Graham Bell and testified in the litigation that established Bell's claims to the basic patents for the telephone.

Brackett's lecture room, according to tradition, was the first electrically lighted classroom in America. He constructed a dynamo and battery system for this purpose soon after Edison invented the incandescent lamp. He also rigged up the first telephone line in Princeton, which extended from his laboratory in the school of Science to Professor Charles Young's office in the observatory on Prospect Avenue.

In 1889 he undertook the development of a school of Electrical Engineering. The program of the new school was designed for college graduates with a strong background in mathematics, physics, and chemistry, and it emphasized the advanced study of general electrical science.

Brackett became a charter member of the American Physical Society when it was organized in 1899. He drew upon his early medical training as chair of the University's sanitary committee, originally in charge of the college infirmary, and as president of the Board of Health of New Jersey from 1888 to 1908.

Brackett's engaging personality inspired the gift of Palmer Physical Laboratory by Stephen Palmer, father of Edgar Palmer 1903, one of Brackett's students in electrical engineering, and its endowment by David B. Jones 1876 and Thomas D. Jones 1876, two of his early students in physics. Palmer Laboratory was completed in 1908, the year Brackett, then 75, retired. When the Engineering Quadrangle opened in 1962, one of its wings was named Brackett Hall in recognition of his role in bringing the study of engineering to Princeton.

BRIDGE YEAR PROGRAM, THE NOVOGRATZ, was established in 2009 to provide opportunities for 20 newly admitted students each year to engage in nine months of tuition-free, University-sponsored service in four international locations before beginning their first year of study at Princeton. In each location students would learn the local language, live with homestay families, participate in community service, and take part in a variety of cultural activities.

From the beginning the University hoped to increase the number of students and locations. The program expanded to 35 students in 2012 and then to 40 in 2019. That year a gift from Michael Novogratz '87 and Sukey Caceres Novogratz '89 provided funds to endow the program and support its expansion. The program's four initial sites were located in Ghana, India, Peru, and Serbia, but over time different locations were identified and their number was increased to five; by 2020 the program's sites were in Bolivia, China, India, Indonesia, and Senegal, although the 2020–21 program was canceled because of the COVID-19 pandemic.

Program participants actively contribute to the work of schools, environmental organizations, public health agencies, and other institutions that meet community needs.

The goals of the program were to provide participants with greater international perspective and intercultural skills, opportunities for personal growth, and a deeper appreciation of service in both a national and international context. It was hoped—and the hope was realized—that when the students returned to campus they would share their experiences and insights with other students and encourage them to find opportunities to study, serve, and live abroad. Program participants have been disproportionately represented in leadership roles on campus, and in such capacities as Pyne Prize winners and young alumni trustees.

BROWN, J. DOUGLAS 1919 *1928 was the University's longest-serving dean of the faculty, from 1946 to 1967, and during his final year as dean he also served as the University's first provost. He was "promoted" to that position when it was first established to signify its stature as the second-ranking officer of the University and general deputy to the president. He was an expert in the field of industrial relations, especially on Social Security and personnel and manpower issues, and one of the principal architects of the Social Security system.

Brown came to Princeton from a high school in Somerville, New Jersey, where he was a friend and academic rival of Princeton-born Paul Robeson, whose family had moved to Somerville; its schools, unlike Princeton's, were integrated. Unwelcome at Princeton University, Robeson went to Rutgers, where he was valedictorian and an All-American football player, and then to Columbia Law School before launching a career as an internationally prominent concert artist, actor, and activist.

Brown matriculated at Princeton in 1915 as a premed student, but with World War I raging in Europe, he left in 1917 to join the army and served in its medical corps in France until 1919. Returning to Princeton, he changed his focus to industrial relations and received his bachelor's degree in 1920, although he continued to affiliate with the Class of 1919. He received a master's degree from Princeton in 1921; taught economics there from 1921 to 1923; taught at New York University from 1923 to 1925; and then returned to Princeton and earned his PhD in 1928.

Brown was appointed an instructor in economics in 1926; a year later he became an assistant professor and in 1934 a full professor. In 1926 he was also named the second director of Princeton's Industrial Relations Section, which the Economics department had founded in 1922 to serve as a clearinghouse for information on employment policies and practices among American corporations, as analyzed from the perspectives of management, labor, and government. He served as director from 1926 to 1955 and remained affiliated with the section until his retirement in 1967.

His many years of service to the federal government began in 1930 when President Herbert Hoover appointed him to an Emergency Committee for Employment to help fight the depression. In 1934 he joined Franklin Roosevelt's administration as a member of a panel on economic security for the aged and played a leading role in creating Social Security, which Congress enacted in 1935. In 1937 he was asked to chair the first federal advisory council on Social Security, which made proposals to revise and extend the program. He served on four subsequent advisory councils (the last from 1969 to 1971). In 1939 he became a special adviser on Social Security to the Secretary of the Treasury. In the late 1940s, he served on the advisory council on Social Security for the Senate Finance Committee.

In 1940 Brown carried out a confidential study for Roosevelt on the manpower problems that would face the aircraft, machine tool, and steel industries if the United States entered World War II. In 1941 and 1942, he was chief of the priorities branch of the labor division of the Office of Production Management and the War Production Board, playing a key role in converting the American economy from civilian to wartime production. From 1942 to 1945 he was the principal consultant on manpower for the Secretary of War. He subsequently served as a consultant to the Social Security Administration, the Air Force, the Federal Advisory Council for Employment Security, the Department of Labor, the Department of Health, Education, and Welfare, and others.

During his career, Brown wrote 13 books, including six following retirement, including *The Liberal University: An Institutional Analysis*; *An American Philosophy on Social Security: Evolution and Issues*; *The Human Nature of Organizations*; *Essays on Social Security*; and *The Enjoyment of One's Older Years*.

In November 1969, he ordered that Princeton's flag, then normally flown only for Commencement or at half-staff upon the death of a faculty member, be raised atop Nassau Hall in honor of astronaut Charles "Pete" Conrad Jr. '53 bringing a Princeton flag to the surface of the moon, a feat that President Robert Goheen called "a noble summit for the Orange and Black."

As dean of the faculty at a time when most major administrative decisions were made by a triumvirate that included the president, the dean, and the financial vice president/treasurer, Brown played a central role in shaping the Princeton of the mid-twentieth century. Because of his particular responsibilities and his professional interests and inclinations, he took special interest in the development and well-being of the faculty.

He took pride in Princeton's commitment to teaching, which he described as demanding and multifaceted; a good teacher, he once said, "has regard for the mind *and* soul of the student, has integrity in that relationship, a mutuality of interests: 'You respect me, I respect you.'" He also took pride in Princeton's commitment to scholarship, including a liberal leave policy to give faculty time to do research and write. He said there was a "strong institutional interest in this: when a faculty member takes a leave and comes back with nothing, well, that suggests he's not a creative scholar. Those fellows wear out, like a carpet does; whereas the creative person is self-renewing, like a good lawn."

In 1973 the University presented Brown with an honorary degree, and as part of the Campaign for Princeton in the early 1980s it developed a fund named for him, the J. Douglas Brown Dean's Fund, to provide special one-time grants to faculty when unexpected opportunities, situations, or needs arise.

BROWN HALL was a gift of Susan Dod Brown in memory of her husband, David B. Brown. Mrs. Brown had previously donated funds for the construction of another dormitory in honor of her husband, but when the University decided to build the larger Brown Hall in 1892, she asked that the new dormitory be named for her husband and the earlier one be named for her brother, mathematics professor Albert B. Dod 1822.

Brown Hall was located on a site that then commanded an impressive view to the south. It was modeled after a Florentine palace, with the first two floors constructed of granite and the upper two floors of brick; a Florentine arch led to a large central courtyard which helped provide both light and ventilation to the rooms that look inward. In 2010 Brown was renovated to create a new portal through the south façade to provide a second means of egress and more open views through the building.

Brown is a dormitory for juniors and seniors. It includes a co-op, founded in 1994, for students (including students from outside Brown) who wish to prepare some of their own meals.

BUNN, B[ENJAMIN] FRANKLIN 1907 probably knew, and was known by, more people on campus and in the community than any other Princetonian in his time.

As manager of the University Store from 1908 to 1947, he was universally appreciated as the dispenser of the store's annual rebate checks, which he personally handed out to waiting queues several weeks before Christmas each year. For many years he served as a timer at football, basketball, track, and swimming contests. For half a century he was graduate treasurer of the Triangle Club and accompanied the club on its annual Christmas trip. For almost as long he was graduate treasurer of the *Daily Princetonian*, the *Princeton Tiger*, and a number of other student enterprises. For a score of years, he managed McCarter Theatre.

A farmer's son from Chester County, Pennsylvania, whose schooling had been interrupted by responsibilities at home, Bunn entered Phillips Exeter Academy when he was 25 and Princeton three years later at 28. He worked his way through Exeter by taking care of the headmaster's furnace, and through Princeton by working in a student-managed bookstore. Upon graduation in 1907 he became a clerk in the recently founded University Store, and in 1908 he became its manager.

In the Princeton community, Bunn was a founder and officer of the University Laundry and the Princeton Savings and Loan Association, and a director of the Princeton Water Company. He was mayor of Princeton Borough and later of Princeton Township, the only person ever to occupy both offices. For 30 years he was president of the trustees of the First Presbyterian Church and he helped select five of its pastors. He was a director of the United Fund, the Princeton Hospital, the Chamber of Commerce, and a trustee of Westminster Choir College.

Bunn chaired a citizens' committee that raised funds for the purchase of a ceremonial mace presented to the University in 1956 on the 200th anniversary of the opening of Nassau Hall—a symbol of the long and close relationship between the University and the Princeton community. A faculty "mace bearer" carries the mace each year at Opening Exercises, Baccalaureate, and Commencement.

In 1965 the Princeton YMCA established an award in Bunn's name, given annually for outstanding community service. His name is perpetuated at the University by a basketball award established in 1931 and by a prize for sophomores on the business staff of the *Daily Princetonian*, created by the senior business board in 1964. The recognition of which Bunn said he was most proud was the honorary degree the University bestowed on him during the bicentennial in 1947.

BURR, AARON, JR., 1772, third vice president of the United States, was considered by some to be one of the most brilliant students who graduated from Princeton in the eighteenth century. Woodrow Wilson 1879 said he had "genius enough to have made him immortal, and unschooled passion enough to have made him infamous." His father was Princeton's second president and his maternal grandfather, Jonathan Edwards, Princeton's third.

Burr was orphaned when he was two years old, his father, mother, and both maternal grandparents having died within a year, and his paternal grandparents having died before he was born. He did not respond well to the discipline of the austere uncle, Timothy Edwards, with whom he lived, and several times he ran away from home and attempted to go to sea. At the age of 13 he entered the sophomore class at Princeton, and he graduated with distinction at 16, a year after James Madison 1771 and Philip Freneau 1771. While they had been members of the American Whig Society, Burr affiliated with the Cliosophic Society.

Burr studied theology for a while and then law as one of the first students of his brother-in-law Tapping Reeve 1763. After serving as a field officer in the Revolutionary War, he took up the practice of law in New York City and entered politics, serving as a member of the New York state assembly, attorney general of New York, and United States senator. In the assembly, he supported laws for the manumission of slaves—even though he owned them—and he opposed ratification of the US Constitution.

In the presidential election of 1800 he received the same number of electoral votes as Thomas Jefferson. The tie was broken in the House of Representatives in Jefferson's favor and Burr became vice president. (That election led to the adoption of the 12th amendment to the constitution requiring separate ballots for president and vice president.) As vice president, he earned high marks for his role in presiding over the impeachment trial of Supreme Court Justice Samuel Chase.

On July 11, 1804, Burr mortally wounded his professional rival and political enemy, Alexander Hamilton, in a duel at Weehawken, New Jersey. He headed west to escape prosecution and engaged in a series of military and political adventures that led to his being tried for treason in 1807. After being acquitted he left for Europe, returning in 1812 to practice law in New York for the rest of his life.

In 1782 Burr married Theodosia Prevost, a widow, and they had four children, although only one lived past the age of three (also named Theodosia, she died at sea at the age of 30). He also had a number of children out of wedlock, including two with Mary Eugenie Beauharnais Emmons, a native of India who migrated to Haiti and then to the United States, and became part of Burr's household when he married Theodosia.

Burr's chief counsel at his trial for treason was Luther Martin 1766, one of the founders of the Cliosophic Society. A few years before Burr's death, the society invited him to preside at its commencement meeting, and its members took part in the procession at Burr's funeral in Princeton in 1836. President James Carnahan preached the funeral sermon in Nassau Hall (in which he decried the evils of dueling). Burr was buried with full military honors in the President's Lot at Princeton Cemetery, at the foot of his father's and grandfather's graves.

BURR, AARON, SR., was Princeton's second president, but because his predecessor, Jonathan Dickinson, died the year he took office, it was Burr who did most of the work making the College a reality. Burr's presidency was also cut short by death, but during his 10 years in office the curriculum was devised, the student body grew tenfold, substantial gifts were obtained, and the College moved to its permanent home in Princeton.

Burr was born in Fairfield, Connecticut, and graduated from Yale at the head of his class in 1735. After studying divinity, he became minister of the Presbyterian church in Newark, New Jersey, where he conducted a classical school similar to Dickinson's at Elizabethtown. He played a pivotal role, with Dickinson, in founding a college for the middle colonies, and he was the youngest clergyman among its original trustees. On Dickinson's death in October 1747 he was asked to take the embryonic college under his care, and he relocated it to his Newark parsonage. A year later, at age 32, he was formally elected as Princeton's youngest president.

Ezra Stiles, then tutor and afterwards president of Yale and an intimate acquaintance of Burr's, noted that Burr was a "small man as to body, but of great and well improved mind . . . A good classical scholar in the 3 learned Tongues [Hebrew, Greek, Latin] . . . well studied in Logic, Rhetoric, Natural and Moral Philosophy, the belles Lettres, History, Divinity, and Politics."

Burr applied his talents with diligence and devotion, beginning with his inauguration at the College's first Commencement on November 9, 1748, when he delivered, from memory, a 45-minute oration in Latin, reminding his graduating class of six of the "manifold Advantages of the liberal Arts and Sciences . . . rendering them useful Members of Church and State." He also conferred an honorary degree on the College's leading patron and benefactor, Governor Jonathan Belcher.

Burr instructed his students with the assistance of one tutor and later, as enrollment grew, of two. The students attended classes in the parsonage, and later in the courtrooms above the county jail, which was not far from the church.

Burr was a bachelor when he assumed the presidency. Some four years later, in 1752, he married Esther Edwards, third daughter of the celebrated divine, Jonathan Edwards, of Stockbridge, Massachusetts.

Burr served for three years without salary, filling both the offices of pastor and president until 1755 when, at the request of the trustees, he was relieved of his pastoral duties to devote full time to the College. He drew up the first entrance requirements, the first course of study, and the first set of rules and regulations; taught mathematics, languages, and surveying; handled administrative matters; and supervised the construction of Nassau Hall. In November 1756, he moved into his new office in Room 1—still the president's office—while his two tutors and 70 students moved into the rest of the building.

Burr, his family, his slave Caesar, and two other slaves resided in the College's one other building, now Maclean House. His slaves were the first three of at least 16 enslaved men, women, and children to live in the house. John Maclean Jr. 1816, who moved into the house in 1854, was the first president of the College who never owned slaves.

Soon after the move to Princeton, the illness of one of the tutors obliged Burr to perform his duties as well as his own. The growing needs of the College also required him to make frequent trips through the colonies in search of funds. On returning from one such arduous trip he learned of the death of his close friend and ally, Governor Belcher. Despite exhaustion and a high fever, he sat down at once to write the funeral sermon. Two days later he rode his horse to Elizabethtown, where he delivered the sermon, although "it was seen that he was fitter for his bed than the pulpit."

He returned to Princeton grievously ill and died several weeks later at the age of 41. He was buried in the Princeton Cemetery—the first to be interred in the President's Lot.

Esther Burr survived her husband by less than a year; she died of smallpox at the age of 26, leaving their two children, four-year-old Sarah and two-year-old Aaron Jr. Sarah married Tapping Reeve 1763, who founded one of America's earliest law schools in Litchfield, Connecticut, and later became the chief justice of that state's supreme court. Aaron Jr. graduated from Princeton in 1772 and became the third vice president of the United States.

In 1977, a building at the corner of Washington Road and Nassau Street, first built in 1891 as a chemical laboratory and now home to the department of Anthropology, was named for Aaron Burr Sr.

BURR, AARON, HALL, named in 1977 for Princeton's second president, occupies the southeast corner of Washington Road and Nassau Street. Built in 1891 as a chemical laboratory, it housed the department of Chemistry until 1929; then the department of Chemical Engineering until 1962 (during which time it was known as Green Annex, being adjacent to Green Hall); and then the department of Anthropology and other social science and humanities programs. It is one of only two buildings on campus (the other is Green Hall) to have housed, at one time or another, programs in all four of the University's academic divisions: humanities, social sciences, natural sciences, and engineering.

Burr Hall was the last legacy to Princeton of John Cleve Green's estate and the first academic building east of Washington Road. It was built in Renaissance Revival style, with top floors made of

Haverstraw brick in red mortar and its ground floor made of Trenton sandstone. Its flat roof features mock battlements. A 2005 addition increased the size of the building and created an entrance from Washington Road.

BUTLER, HOWARD CROSBY 1892, archaeologist and professor of the history of architecture, was the first master in residence of the graduate college and the first director of the school of Architecture. In his student days he played leading roles in the first productions of the newly founded Triangle Club and he helped organize the eating club, Tiger Inn, whose clubhouse he later designed. In his senior year, under the influence of Professor Allan Marquand 1874, he acquired a serious interest in the history of art, which he further developed in graduate study at Princeton, the Columbia School of Architecture, the American Academy in Rome, and the American School of Classical Study at Athens. He organized and led three archaeological expeditions into the Syrian Desert and two expeditions for the excavation of ancient Sardis, discovering there long-hidden artifacts that shed light on Lydian, Greek, Syrian, and Roman civilizations.

As master in residence, first at the experimental graduate hall "Merwick" and then at the graduate college itself, he influenced many of the graduate students of that era. His teaching inspired a group of alumni architects to initiate a movement that resulted in the establishment of the school of Architecture in 1919, with Butler as its first director.

A portrait of Butler hangs in Procter Hall in the graduate college and the following inscription, discovered on a tomb in northern Syria, appears on a stone in the vestibule: *I sojourned well; I journeyed well; and well I lie at rest. Pray for me.*

CABINET OFFICERS who attended Princeton and the presidents under whom they served are as follows:

Secretary of State

James Madison 1771 1801–09 (Jefferson)
Robert Smith 1781 1809–11 (Madison)
Edward Livingston 1781 1831–33 (Jackson)
John Forsyth 1799 1834–41 (Jackson and Van Buren)
Abel Upshur 1807 1843–44 (Tyler)
John Foster Dulles 1908 1953–59 (Eisenhower)
George Shultz '42 1982–89 (Reagan)
James A. Baker III '52 1989–92 (G.H.W. Bush)

Secretary of the Treasury

George Campbell 1794 1814 (Madison)
Richard Rush 1797 1825–28 (J. Q. Adams)
George Bibb 1792 1844–45 (Tyler)
George Shultz '42 1972–74 (Nixon)
W. Michael Blumenthal *53 *56 1977–79 (Carter)
James A. Baker III '52 1985–88 (Reagan)

Secretary of War

John Armstrong 1776 1813–14 (Madison)
George Crawford 1820 1849–50 (Taylor)
William Belknap 1848 1869–76 (Grant)
James Cameron 1852 1876–77 (Grant)

Secretary of the Navy

Robert Smith 1781 1801–05 (Jefferson)
Smith Thompson 1788 1818–23 (Monroe)
Samuel Southard 1804 1823–29 (Monroe and J. Q. Adams)
Mahlon Dickerson 1789 1834–38 (Jackson and Van Buren)
Abel Upshur 1807 1841–43 (Tyler)
George Robeson 1847 1869–77 (Grant)
James Forrestal 1915 1944–47 (F. D. Roosevelt and Truman)

Secretary of Defense

James Forrestal 1915 1947–49 (Truman)
Donald Rumsfeld '54 1975–76 (Ford) and 2001–06 (G. W. Bush)
Frank C. Carlucci III '52 1987–89 (Reagan)

Attorney General

William Bradford Jr. 1772 1794–95 (Washington)
Charles Lee 1775 1795–1801 (Washington and J. Adams)
Robert Smith 1781 1805 (Jefferson)
Richard Rush 1797 1814–17 (Madison)
John Berrien 1796 1829–31 (Jackson)
Benjamin Brewster 1834 1881–85 (Arthur)
Nicholas Katzenbach '43 1965–66 (L. Johnson)

Secretary of Commerce

Alexander Trowbridge '51 1967–68 (L. Johnson)

Secretary of Labor

George Shultz '42 1969–70 (Nixon)

Secretary of Housing and Urban Development

Robert Wood '44 1969 (L. Johnson)

When the national military establishment was reorganized under a Secretary of Defense in 1947, the office of Secretary of War was discontinued and the Secretary of Navy was no longer given cabinet rank, nor were the newly instituted Secretaries of the Army and the Air Force. Princetonians who served as Secretary of the Army included Frank Pace Jr. '33 (1950–53); Stephen Ailes '33 (1964–65); Martin Hoffman '54 (1975–76); and Norman Augustine '57 *59 (acting) 1975; serving as Secretary of the Air Force were James Douglas 1920 (1957–59) and Dudley Sharp 1927 (1959–61).

In recent decades, the White House chief of staff and the director of the Office of Management and Budget (OMB) have held cabinet rank. Alumni who have served as chief of staff include Donald Rumsfeld '54 (1974–75); James A. Baker III '52 (1981–85) and (1992–93); and Joshua Bolten '76 (2006–09). OMB directors have included George Shultz '42 (1970–72); Mitchell E. Daniels Jr. '71 (2001–03); Joshua Bolten '76 (2003–06); and Peter Orszag '91 (2009–10). In 2021 Eric Lander '78 joined the cabinet when he was appointed director of the Office of Science and Technology Policy as that position was elevated to cabinet rank.

CALDWELL FIELD HOUSE is a memorial to Charles W. Caldwell Jr. 1925, head coach of football from 1945 through 1956. It was built in 1963 with donations from his family and some 3,500 alumni and friends.

As an undergraduate, Caldwell played center and fullback on the 1922 "Team of Destiny" and was a star pitcher on the baseball team; he later had a tryout with the New York Yankees and played briefly in several games. He was assistant football coach at Princeton for three years and head coach at Williams for 17 before his appointment as Princeton's head coach in 1945. A keen student of the game, he developed a new kind of single wing football, adding to the traditional power plays of that formation elements of deception, which he borrowed from the T-formation.

Caldwell's teams of 1950 and 1951 were both Lambert Trophy winners as the best in the east. They won every game—the first time Princeton had two perfect seasons in succession since full-length schedules were introduced in 1878 (the teams of 1874 and 1875 also won all their games—two each year). Caldwell was voted Coach of the Year in 1950 and given the annual award of the Touchdown Club of New York in 1952. He was stricken with cancer early in the season of 1957 and died that fall.

Caldwell Field House was expanded in 1999. It contains locker rooms and training and sports medicine facilities for teams that use the neighboring athletic facilities, including the football stadium, Weaver Track, Jadwin Gymnasium, DeNunzio Pool, and other venues.

CAMPBELL HALL was a gift of the Class of 1877. The building was named for John A. Campbell 1877, a banker and leading citizen of Trenton who was president of the class all four years in college and for 50 years thereafter.

It took the class less than an hour to raise most of the funds for the dormitory—a unique instance in the long history of alumni generosity. The necessary pledges poured forth in a spontaneous outburst during a high-spirited dinner at the class's 30th reunion in 1907. Moses Taylor Pyne 1877, a trustee of the University, precipitated the outburst when, speaking of the University's need for more dormitories, he reminded his classmates that 1879 had given Seventy-Nine Hall and 10 other classes had each given an entry in Patton Hall. Someone asked how much an entire dormitory would cost; Campbell said he assumed at least $100,000. By the end of the evening they had raised more than $77,000; the class soon raised the balance; and Campbell Hall opened in the fall of 1909.

Campbell Hall was the only Princeton dormitory designed by Ralph Adams Cram, shortly after he was named the University's supervising architect. The building embodied his vision of Collegiate Gothic, and it joined with Blair Hall in framing a three-sided dormitory quadrangle that was completed in 1932 with the construction of Joline Hall. The entryways of all three buildings open onto the courtyard. There is an archway at the west end of the quadrangle that serves as an entrance to the campus from University Place; an archway on the north side of Campbell aligns with a facing archway on the south side of Holder Hall, extending a pathway from Nassau Street through Holder Tower and the Holder cloisters that passes through the Holder and Campbell arches on its way to Blair Arch.

CAMPUS. The use of the word *campus* (Latin for "field") to mean the grounds of a college originated at Princeton. Its earliest recorded use is found in a letter Charles Beatty 1775 wrote to his brother-in-law Enoch Green 1760 on January 31, 1774: "Last week to show our patriotism, we gathered all the steward's winter store of tea, and having made a fire in the Campus, we there burnt near a dozen pounds, tolled the bell and made many spirited resolves."

Previously *yard* was the word used at Princeton, as it was at Harvard (where it was first used in 1639) and other colleges. An example of this usage occurs in a letter James Madison 1771 wrote to his father on July 23, 1770. Referring to the interception by Princeton students of a letter from a group of New York merchants to merchants in Philadelphia, asking them to break the agreement not to import British goods, he said: "Their letter . . . was . . . burnt by the Students of this place in the college Yard, all of them appearing in their black Gowns and the bell Tolling."

In a monograph on the use of the word *campus* in the *Publications of the Colonial Society of Massachusetts*, etymologist Albert Matthews suggests that the word may have been introduced by President John Witherspoon, who came to Princeton from Scotland in 1768. Witherspoon, he said, was accustomed to the universities of Scotland, which were built along city streets, and must have been struck by the difference at Princeton, where the college grounds consisted of a flat field with no enclosures set back at a distance from the town. He would have been moved to apply to the grounds "a classical term which fitly described their character."

The word *yard* remained in use at Princeton after the introduction of *campus* and for some time the two terms were used interchangeably. Thus, while the faculty in 1787 spoke of "the back campus of the College," the trustees in 1802 referred to "the west side of the College yard," and then in 1807 to "the front Campus."

Gradually *campus* won out over *yard*. In 1833 it appeared in print for the first time in a book by an Englishman, James Finch, *Travels in the United States and Canada*, in which he writes of Princeton: "In front of the College is a fine campus ornamented with trees." In 1851, Benjamin Hall, in his *College Words and Customs*, noted that at Princeton "the college yard is denominated the *Campus*." After the Civil War the word spread to other colleges and was finally given lexicographical recognition by inclusion in the *Century Dictionary* of 1889. Samuel Eliot Morison, in *Three Centuries of Harvard* (1936), referring to Princeton's adoption of *campus* in 1774, wrote, "One by one every other American college has followed suit, until Harvard alone has kept her Yard."

The College possessed no grounds for the first six years after its founding in 1746. Classes were held at Elizabethtown in the parsonage of President Jonathan Dickinson and later at Newark in the parsonage of President Aaron Burr Sr. and, when numbers grew, in a room above the jail in the county courthouse. The trustees sought another location, "more sequestred [*sic*] from the various temptations attending a promiscuous converse with the world, that theatre of folly and dissipation"—and one nearer to the center of the province. In the winter of 1752–53, the agrarian village of Princeton won over the town of New Brunswick in securing the right to become the permanent home of the College when it more than met the stipulations of the trustees to provide £1,000 in proclamation money, 10 acres of cleared land, and 200 acres of woodland to provide fuel.

The citizens of Princeton primarily responsible for this were all large landowners: John Stockton, Thomas Leonard (a trustee), John Hornor, and Nathaniel FitzRandolph. All four contributed to what became a £1,700 fund and all four donated land.

Stockton's land holdings included Morven, a large plantation worked by slave labor, which later became the home of New Jersey's governor and is now a museum and historic site; in December 1752, he donated 40 acres of land to provide fuel for the College. That same month, Leonard, also a slave-owner who operated plantations and iron production facilities, gave 160 acres of woodland: his and Stockton's donated lands were a mile north of the village, about where Witherspoon Street now meets Route 206. Hornor, likely also a slaveholder, gave seven acres of cleared land near what is now the south end of Princeton Cemetery, and in 1754 the trustees purchased 10 additional acres from him surrounding the parcel he had donated. In the 1780s, when the College faced a serious financial crisis, the trustees sold much of the land they had obtained from Stockton, Leonard, and Hornor.

FitzRandolph was descended from one of the first white families to settle in Princeton, and he and at least some of his relatives owned slaves. At their winter meeting on January 24, 1753, the trustees voted to accept Princeton as the place of the College. The day after this meeting FitzRandolph and his wife Rebeckah gave the trustees a deed for "a certain plot of land bounded Northward by the King's Highway and containing about four acres and a half."

Before the arrival of white settlers, FitzRandolph's land had been part of the historic homeland of the Lenni Lenape. Now it became the site of Nassau Hall, the President's House, and what came to be called the front campus, to which President Burr and his pupils moved in 1756. At a sheriff's sale four years later the trustees bought land surrounding three sides of the College. These five or six acres widened the front campus and added what came to be known as the back campus, ending just behind what was to become the site of Whig and Clio halls, along what later generations knew as McCosh Walk.

The siting was fortuitous for the future evolution of the campus. FitzRandolph's four and a half acres were located on an elevation that looked north across a green into a town halfway between New York and Philadelphia, and south over fields and stream valleys. While the woodlands and fields on the stepped hillside below the original campus would permit growth over time, the College's first expansion was along the edges of the front campus, and on a back campus now known as Cannon Green.

Expanding the Campus

In its first 85 years the campus grew only modestly, its boundaries remaining largely unchanged. Then, over a period of about 30 years, it gradually increased in size to about 20 acres through small accretions by purchase and gift. In 1878, when Robert and Alexander Stuart of New York bought a house and 35-acre estate called Prospect, adjacent to the campus, they gave it to the College for use as the residence of President James McCosh, more than doubling the acreage of the campus.

In 1889 the grounds were quadrupled when the legatees of the estate of John C. Green (the most generous supporter of the college during McCosh's presidency) purchased and donated the Potter Farm, consisting of 155 acres of meadow and woodland extending from the campus to the Delaware and Raritan canal between Washington Road and the railroad. "This magnificent gift," said Moses Taylor Pyne 1877, chair of the trustee committee on grounds and buildings, "preserves forever our beautiful view, and leaves ample room for the growth of the University for many years to come." It made it possible to say, Pyne added, that Princeton now possessed "the finest Campus of any College in America."

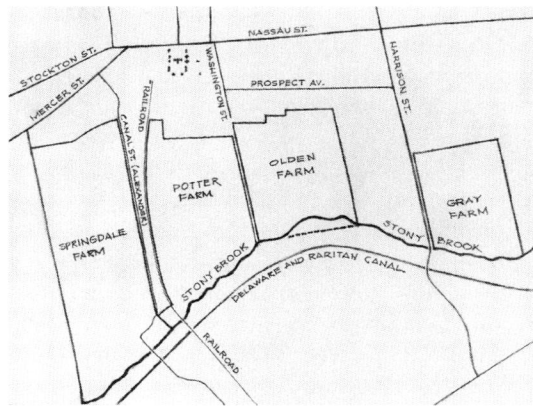

In the late nineteenth and early twentieth centuries the University dramatically expanded its landholdings in Princeton when it acquired the Springdale, Potter, Olden, and Gray farms.

About this time alumni began taking great interest in securing land for the University. The South East Club, a group who had lived in the south entry of East College in the 1870s, led the way. Their members included Howard Russell Butler, William Allen Butler, and Bayard Henry of the Class of 1876, and Pyne and Henry Thompson in the Class of 1877. For many years, the club met annually to discuss how best to meet the needs of the College.

Their efforts began to bring results in 1905. At the commencement meeting of the trustees that year, Pyne, as president of the Springfield Association, presented a deed to the University for a 230-acre tract lying between the Princeton Theological Seminary and Stony Brook, on which a golf course had recently been installed, and where the graduate college was soon to be built. That same day, James Laughlin Jr. 1868, president of the Olden Association, presented the University a deed for the 93-acre Olden Farm, extending from the ridge of Prospect Avenue to Stony Brook on the east side of Washington Road. This farm became the site of athletic facilities and playing fields, faculty housing, and a neighborhood for the natural sciences.

A year later, the creation of a lake, which Howard Russell Butler prevailed upon Andrew Carnegie to finance, resulted in the University's acquisition of some 400 acres—the lake itself and land fronting it for over a mile and a half. Acting as Carnegie's attorney in acquiring 33 parcels of land needed to construct the lake, Butler struck a snag in his negotiations for a small strip of land of about three acres just east of Harrison Street. The Gray family refused to sell unless their entire farm of 107 acres was purchased, and Carnegie was unwilling to buy more land than was needed to construct the proposed lake.

Butler's brother, William Allen Butler, organized a syndicate of South East Club members and others to purchase the farm, which they were able to do through a down payment, a bank loan, and a mortgage. After the loan was paid off, Butler induced his mother to satisfy the mortgage, enabling the syndicate in 1912 to present the deed for the property to the trustees. The major part of this gift, now the Butler Tract, became the W. B. Devereux Jr. (1904) Memorial Polo Field from 1927 until after World War II when it was used to accommodate barracks-style graduate student housing; a smaller part, retaining the name Gray Farm, was later developed for faculty housing.

In 1917 Bayard Henry obtained gifts from alumni and friends that permitted the University to negotiate, under his guidance, with the Pennsylvania Railroad to move the Princeton train station from the foot of Blair Tower to a more southerly location, thus releasing about seven acres of land which the University used to construct six dormitories south of Blair Hall along University Place.

At the spring meeting of the trustees in 1922, Henry informed the board that he and several other alumni would donate the Mather farm, extending south from Lake Carnegie along Washington Road, if the University would purchase the Schenck farm, adjoining it on the west, which had just come on the market. The board accepted the donation and made the additional purchase, thereby adding 216 acres to its holdings and giving the University ownership of all the land between Washington Road and Alexander Road. That same year Pyne bequeathed to the University 25 houses and lots and 27.5 undeveloped acres in the Broadmead area, east of the Olden Farm.

In 1945, and then again in 1948, the trustees purchased the two farms south of Lake Carnegie that were located to the east of Washington Road. With these acquisitions the University owned almost 400 acres in West Windsor between the lake and Route 1, and between Alexander Road and Harrison Street. In 2001 the University purchased approximately 90 acres from the Sarnoff Corporation along the northbound side of Route 1 just across from its other West Windsor lands.

Developing the Campus

In the College's early years, the campus had a rough symmetry and the Georgian style of Nassau Hall prevailed, with two minor but conspicuous exceptions. The Georgian style was followed in twin buildings, a library and a refectory (Geological, later Stanhope, Hall and Philosophical Hall) erected in the early 1800s on either side of Nassau Hall, and in twin dormitories, East College and West College, constructed in the 1830s on either side of the back campus. The two exceptions came in 1838 when Whig and Clio halls were built in the style of classical Greek temples.

After the Civil War, with the arrival of McCosh, the railroad, and aspirations to become a university, the rough symmetry of the historic campus gave way to a more informal and picturesque landscape, with expansion to the east and west along established ridgelines and to the south through a series of terraces. Georgian style gave way to Ruskinian Gothic buildings such as the Chancellor Green Library, which replaced Philosophical Hall, and Pyne Library which replaced East College. McCosh had an intense interest in landscaping (he hired the University's first gardener), and he took great pleasure in laying out the grounds, locating the buildings, and planning for the campus to take on a park-like appearance.

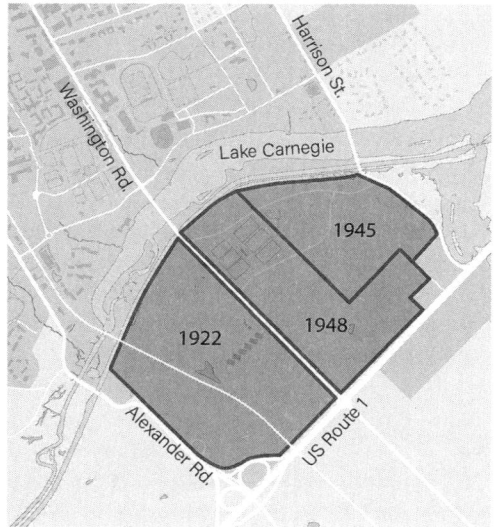

In the 1920s and 1940s the University acquired four farms in West Windsor Township between Lake Carnegie and Route 1.

The Ruskinian Gothic of the McCosh era was followed, after a few divergences such as Alexander Hall (Romanesque) and Brown and Dod dormitories (Italian Renaissance), by the Tudor Gothic of Oxford and Cambridge, adopted at the time of the sesquicentennial through the influence of Professor Andrew Fleming West 1874 and Pyne. From the completion of Pyne Library and Blair Hall in 1897 to the building of Firestone Library and Dillon Gym 50 years later, Collegiate Gothic was the prevailing architectural style at Princeton. It introduced enclosed and semi-enclosed courtyards, linked lawns, and what university architect Ron McCoy *80 has described as "a magical rhythm of episodic vistas and emerging spaces."

"The tradition of campus planning," McCoy has said, "is characterized by its ability to create an ideal form of community, where landscape and architecture co-exist to create a powerful sense of identity and an authentic sense of place."

The long-range development of the Princeton campus was facilitated by the creation of the office of supervising architect and the appointment of Ralph Adams Cram as its first incumbent in 1907. Henry Thompson, who succeeded his classmate Pyne as chair of the trustee committee on grounds and buildings, was instrumental in Cram's appointment, as he was in the appointment of Beatrix Farrand as the University's first consulting landscape architect in 1912. Farrand remained for 31 years; by the time she retired she had overseen the planting of trees and shrubs around some 75 buildings, beginning with the graduate college, and she had established landscape design as a defining feature of the Princeton campus.

Prominent architect Benjamin Latrobe designed the first expansion of the campus, following the Nassau Hall fire of 1802, while physics professor Joseph Henry drew the first master plan for the campus in 1832. The first formal master plan was developed by Cram, who attempted to express through his planning and his architecture the University's "lofty ideas of character, education, and scholarship."

Cram visualized two main axes, one extending south from the rear of Nassau Hall, and the other east and west from the gateway between Blair and Little along McCosh Walk to Washington Road. The north-south axis he conceived was never fully realized, but its northern terminus was accented in 1969 by the construction of a plaza and steps, guarded by male and female tigers, between Whig and Clio halls.

Cram served until 1929. One of his successors, Douglas Orr, devised a master plan in the late 1950s and early 1960s that added another east-west axis farther south, extending from what is now Whitman College to what is now Princeton Stadium. In 1995 the architectural firm of Machado and Silvetti was commissioned to develop a master plan that focused in particular on the southern precincts of the campus. This plan proposed a semicircle of buildings along the northern edge of Poe and Pardee fields, which eventually led to the construction of an academic building, Icahn Laboratory, for genomics, and two dormitories, Scully and Bloomberg halls. The two residential colleges constructed in the early 2020s border the southern edge of Poe Field.

The elliptical path along the northern edge of the fields, extending from the Lewis Arts complex to Streicker Bridge, is now named Tilghman Walk, in honor of Princeton's 19th president, Shirley Tilghman. (In addition to Tilghman and McCosh walks, two other east-west walks named for former presidents traverse the campus: Shapiro Walk, which extends from Washington Road to the Engineering Quadrangle, and Goheen Walk, which begins between Butler and Wilson colleges and then passes Lewis Thomas laboratory on its way to Washington Road.)

The Machado/Silvetti plan also proposed zoning the University's lands south of Lake Carnegie in West Windsor for future academic, residential, and athletic use.

The University's mid-twentieth century expansion south toward the lake and east of Washington

Beatrix Farrand, the University's first consulting landscape architect, served in that role from 1912–43. She played a leading role in creating the distinctive character of the Princeton campus.

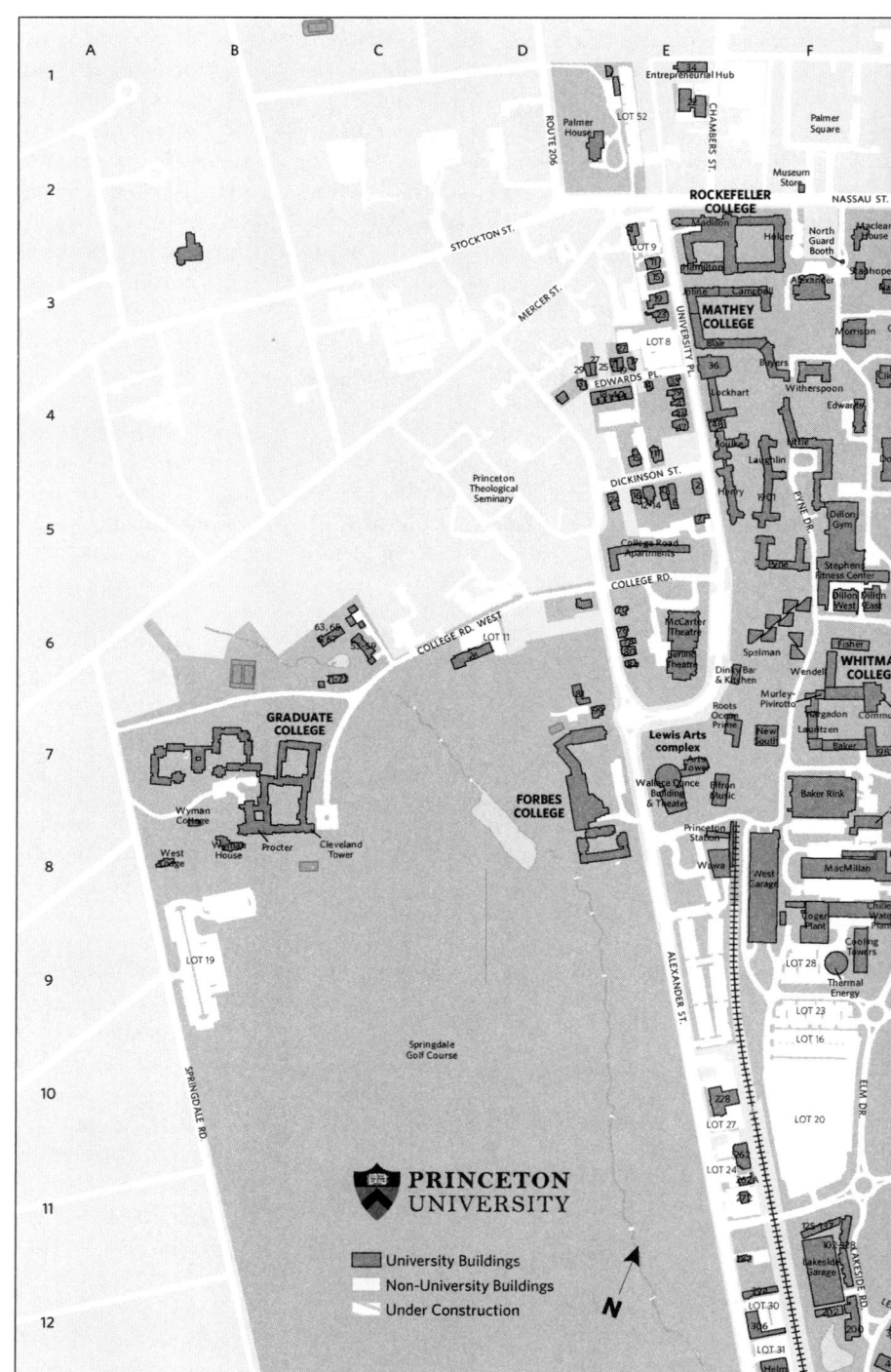

This map shows the Princeton campus in 2020, including the location for the two residential colleges then under construction.

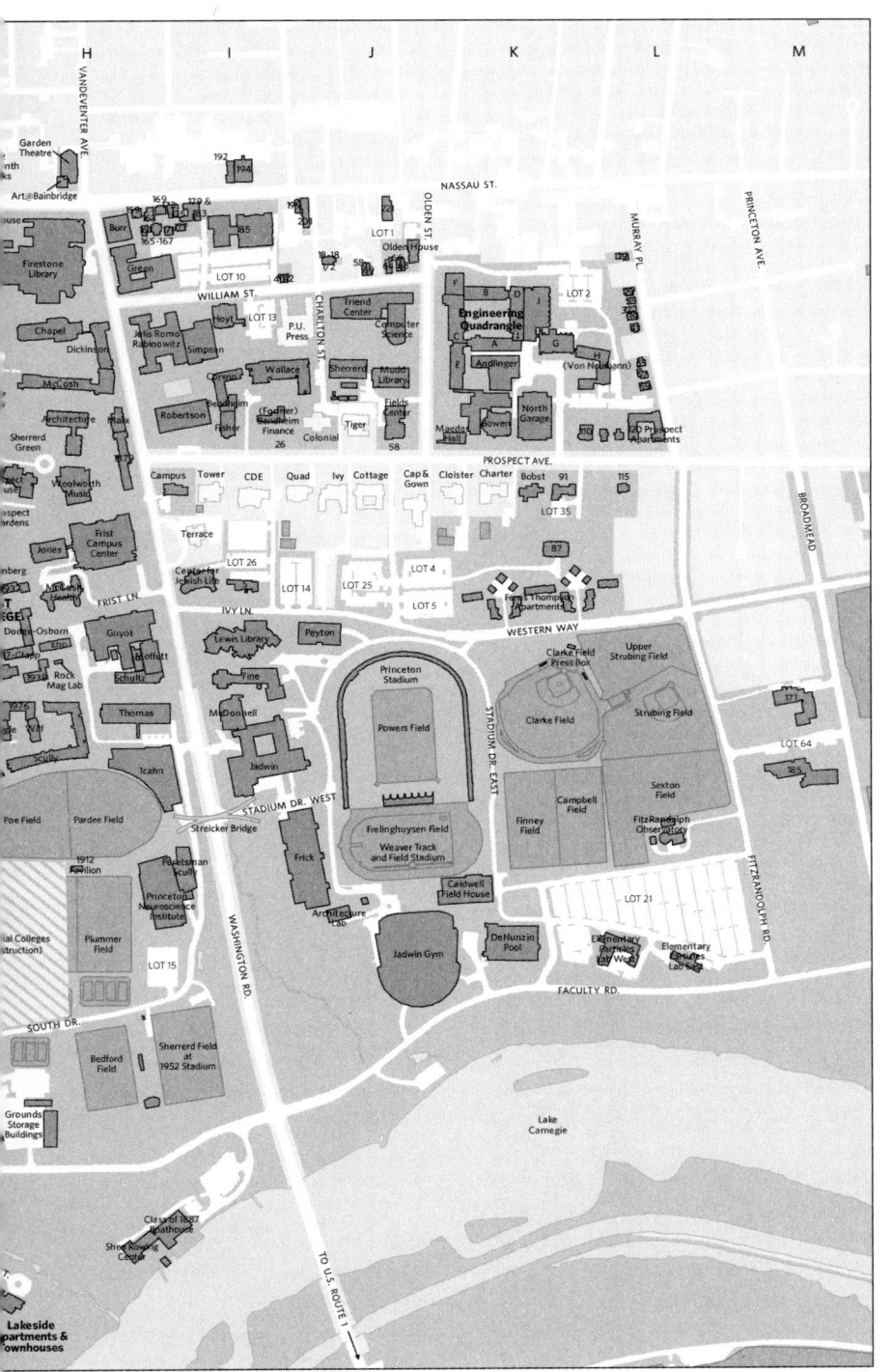

Road was so extensive that when the Frist Campus Center was created in 2000, its location in the former Palmer Hall was the geographical center of the campus. The expansion was needed to accommodate dramatically increased support for university-based sponsored research, especially in the sciences and engineering; increases in both the size and diversity of the student body, beginning with the introduction of undergraduate coeducation in 1969; and the decision in the early 1980s to create a system of residential colleges, initially for all freshmen and sophomores, and later for some juniors and seniors as well.

In the early 2000s, the campus remained distinctive, attractive, and beloved in many ways, but the University needed to prepare for an additional 10 percent increase in the number of undergraduates, increase its capacity to support the creative and performing arts and emerging fields in the sciences and engineering; meet sustainability goals; and accommodate new technologies.

In 2005 the University engaged the firm Beyer Blinder Belle to lead a campus planning process to guide campus development through 2016. The goals of the plan were to provide for significant academic expansion, maintain a pedestrian-oriented campus, preserve the campus's park-like character, and develop growth strategies that were sensitive to environmental impacts and helped the University achieve its commitments to sustainability. The plan proposed a campus of "neighborhoods," including, most significantly, an arts and transit neighborhood that would house the Lewis Center for the Arts, other arts buildings, and a multi-modal transit plaza with a new train station. The plan also proposed a natural sciences neighborhood that would link departments and programs on both sides of Washington Road with a pedestrian bridge and through the shared resource of the Lewis Science Library.

The legacy of the 2016 plan includes the Butler College dormitories, Frick Chemistry Laboratory, Sherrerd Hall (Operations Research and Financial Engineering), Peretsman Scully Hall (Psychology), the Princeton Neuroscience Institute, the Andlinger Center for Energy and the Environment, the Julis Romo Rabinowitz Building; the Louis A. Simpson International Building; Streicker Bridge; Roberts Stadium (soccer); Lakeside graduate student apartments; and the buildings and spaces of the Lewis Arts complex.

Construction begins on two new residential colleges south of Poe Field to accommodate a 10 percent increase in the number of undergraduates, beginning in 2022–23.

The 2016 plan explicitly deferred the question of when the University would begin to make fuller use of its lands to the south of Lake Carnegie. That question emerged as one of the central elements of a campus plan created with the assistance of the firm Urban Strategies, Inc., adopted in 2015, that provided a framework for continuing campus development through 2026 and beyond. By this time the University needed to plan for another 10 percent increase in the size of the undergraduate student body, further expansion of its programs in engineering and environmental studies, and growing interactions and academic partnerships with the corporate, government, and nonprofit sectors.

This plan proposed the sites along the southern border of Poe Field for the two new residential colleges, and to support teaching and research in engineering and environmental studies it proposed locations along Ivy Lane and Western Way east of Washington Road, along with other enhancements to what it called the University's East Campus. The plan also made recommendations regarding sustainability, land use, movement patterns through and around

Site Plan
ES+SEAS

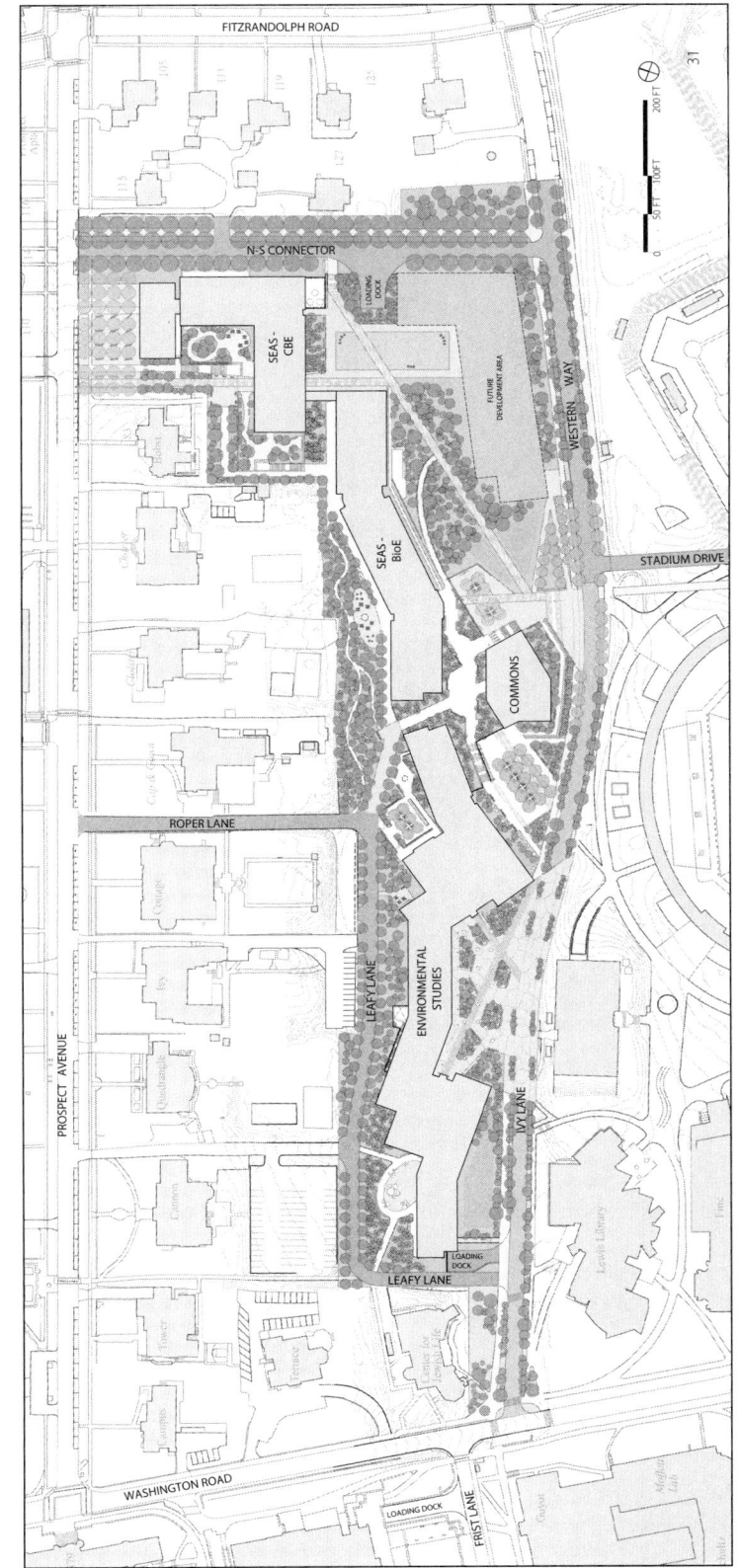

New spaces for engineering and environmental studies are planned between the eating clubs and the north side of Ivy Lane and Western Way.

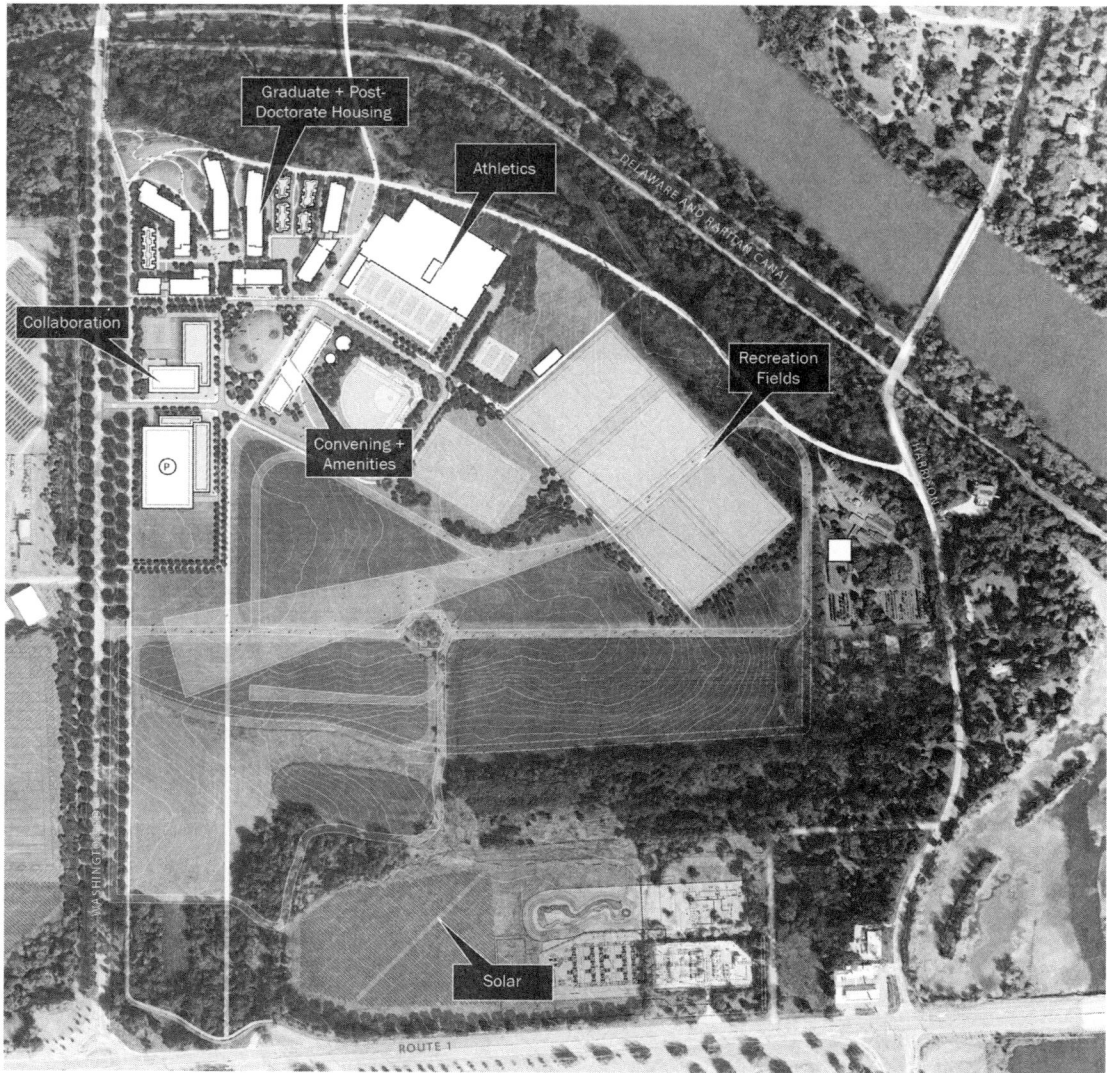

This diagram shows the proposed initial development of the Lake Campus, including new spaces for softball and racquet sports and for graduate student and postdoc housing.

campus, the University's utility infrastructure, and landscape.

Its most ground-breaking recommendation was that the University begin to develop a carefully planned and well-integrated Lake Campus on its West Windsor lands. It envisioned this campus as a "dynamic, mixed-use community in a gently sloping landscape that could accommodate athletic facilities; administrative and academic partnership space; housing for up to 500 graduate students and potentially for postdoctoral researchers; convening, retail, and amenity space; and a parking area and transit hub with shuttle, pedestrian, and bicycle connections to other parts of the campus and the community."

The plan for "development through 2026 and beyond" pointed out that Lake Carnegie, a welcome but peripheral addition to the campus and the town in 1906, would, over time, "evolve from a feature that defines the southern edge of the campus to a feature that is central to the campus, connecting campus lands to its north and its south."

CAMPUS ART. In its earliest days the Princeton campus was largely unadorned, either by landscape or by art. By the late nineteenth century, however, at the instigation of President James McCosh, the University began adding plantings to its grounds and constructing eye-catching and richly decorated buildings. These included Witherspoon Hall, Alexander Hall, a large number of Collegiate Gothic dormitories (beginning with Blair Hall), and other structures such as Chancellor Green and East Pyne. Many of its Gothic buildings included multiple design elements, including gargoyles and grotesques. East Pyne's exterior featured statues of John Witherspoon, James McCosh, James Madison 1771, and Oliver Ellsworth 1766, while Palmer Hall, constructed early in the twentieth century, had statuary honoring Benjamin Franklin and Joseph Henry.

In the late 1960s, largely as the result of an anonymous gift in honor of fighter pilot John B. Putnam Jr. '45 (Putnam flew 53 aerial missions in World War II and died in a plane crash in England in 1944 shortly after flying nine combat hours over the Normandy beaches on D-Day), the University was able to commission or acquire works by many of the most important twentieth-century sculptors and distribute them outdoors throughout the campus.

The initial sculptures in the Putnam Collection were selected by a committee of alumni who were directors or former directors of art museums: Alfred Barr Jr. 1921 (Museum of Modern Art), Thomas Hoving '53 (Metropolitan Museum of Art), P. Joseph Kelleher *47 (Princeton University Art Museum), and William Milliken 1911 (Cleveland Museum of Art).

The sculptors represented in the initial collection, their works, and the location of these works follow:

Reg Butler, *The Bride*, Hamilton courtyard
Alexander Calder, *Five Disks: One Empty*, Jadwin Hall plaza
Jacob Epstein, *Professor Albert Einstein*, Fine Hall library
Naum Gabo, *Spheric Theme*, Engineering Quadrangle courtyard
Michael Hall, *Mastodon VI*, MacMillan building
Gaston Lachaise, *Floating Figure*, Compton Quadrangle at the graduate college
Jacques Lipchitz, *Song of the Vowels*, between Firestone Library and the University Chapel
Clement Meadmore, *Upstart II*, at the entrance to the Engineering Quadrangle
Henry Moore, *Oval with Points*, between Morrison and Stanhope halls
Masayuki Nagare, *Stone Riddle*, Engineering Quadrangle courtyard
Louise Nevelson, *Atmosphere and Environment X*, between Firestone Library and Nassau Street
Isamu Noguchi, *White Sun*, in the lobby of Firestone Library
Eduardo Paolozzi, *Marok-Marok-Miosa*, Friend Center
Antoine Pevsner, *Construction in the Third and Fourth Dimension*, Jadwin Hall courtyard
Pablo Picasso, *Head of a Woman*, between Spelman Halls and New South
Arnaldo Pomodoro, *Sphere VI*, between Fine and McDonnell halls
George Rickey, *Two Planes Vertical Horizontal II*, between East Pyne and the University Chapel
David Smith, *Cubi XIII*, between McCormick and Whig halls
Tony Smith, *Moses*, on the front lawn of Prospect
Kenneth Snelson, *Northwood II*, in the east dormitory courtyard at the graduate college

Over time, the Putnam Fund helped bring additional outdoor sculptures to the campus, with a focus on contemporary master artists of their time, including George Segal's *Abraham and Isaac: In Memory of May 4, 1970, Kent State University*, along the walkway from Washington Road between the chapel and Firestone Library; and Doug and Mike Starn's *(Any) Body Oddly Propped*, outside the entrance to the art museum. Other important sculptures came to the campus as part of a revived commissioning program that began around 2008, including Ursula von Rydingsvard's *URODA*, near the main entrance to the Andlinger Center for Energy and the Environment, and Maya Lin's two-part project, *The Princeton Line* and *Einstein's Table*, adjacent to the Lewis Arts complex.

Lin, a 2016 recipient of the Presidential Medal of Freedom who designed the Vietnam Veterans Memorial in Washington, DC in 1982 while an undergraduate at Yale, was on campus in the fall of 2019 to dedicate her two works. *The Princeton Line* (named after the train known as the Dinky that connects the campus to New Jersey Transit's northeast corridor) is an undulating sculpted line of molded earth, while the granite water table called *Einstein's Table* is designed to suggest Earth's orbit, the Milky Way, and black holes as seen through gently moving water.

By 2020 there were some 50 objects in a variety of media in the University's campus art collection, adorning indoor public spaces as well as outdoor sites. Beyond the Putnam Collection and University commissions, other outdoor sculptures have been provided by gifts or loan. Among the works are Scott Burton's *Public Table*, between East Pyne and Murray Dodge; Michele Oka Donor's *Titan*, initially located outside Prospect House; a canvas by Friedel Dzubas, *Wende*, outside the Computer Science building; Richard Erdman's *Rhumba*, outside Mudd Library; Elisabeth Gordon's *James V. Forrestal, Class of 1915*, in the Engineering Quadrangle courtyard; Kate Graves, George Scherer, and David Robinson's *Stone Mancala Table*, outside the Friend Center; Rudolph Hoflehner's *Human Condition*, between McCormick and Clio halls; Walter Hood's *Double Sights*, in Scudder Plaza; Beverly Pepper's *Thetis Circle*, on the lawn north of Whitman College; Richard Serra's *The Hedgehog and the Fox*, between Lewis Library and Fine Hall; and Al Weiwei's *Circle of Animals/Zodiac Heads*, between New South and the Lewis Arts complex.

These join some older sculptures, such as James Fitzgerald's *Fountain of Freedom*, installed in Scudder Plaza in 1966, and Dimitri Hadzi's *Centaur* in Prospect garden and *Thermopylae* in the Engineering Quadrangle. Robert Tait McKenzie's statue of Andrew Fleming West 1874 has been at the graduate college since 1928, but newer additions to campus include Alexander Stoddart's *John Witherspoon, 1723–1794*, between East Pyne and the chapel, and Harry Weber's *Bill Bradley*, outside Jadwin Gym.

Alexander Proctor's *Pair of Tigers* have stood guard at Nassau Hall since 1911 when they replaced A. Schiffelman's *Pair of Lions*, which first moved to 1879 Hall and then, in 1998, to 1927-Clapp Hall. There are other tigers around the campus, including Bruce Moore's *Pair of Tigers* (one male, one female) between Whig and Clio halls, and Ruffin Hobbs' *Pair of Topiary Tigers*, just north of Princeton Stadium.

The growing number of campus art works commissioned for inside public spaces include Harry Bertoia's *The World*, in Robertson Hall; Kendall Buster's *Resonance*, at Frick Chemistry Laboratory; Frank Gehry's *Horse-Head Conference Room*, in Icahn Laboratory; Jim Iserman's *Untitled (ORFE/SEAS)*, in Sherrerd Hall; Win Knowlton's *Clouds Nine*, in the Andlinger Center for the Humanities; Sol Lewitt's *Wall Drawing #1134, Whirls & Twirls (Princeton)*, in the arch of Bloomberg Hall; Odili Donald Odita's *Up and Away*, in Butler College; Shahzia Sikander's *Ecstasy as Sublime, Heart as Vector*, in the Lewis A. Simpson International Building and *Quintuplet Effect*, in Julis Romo Rabinowitz; a contemporary tapestry, *Stardust*, by Bhakti Ziek in the Whitman College community hall; and Maria Berrio's *Augur*, in the third-floor reading room in Firestone Library.

CAMPUS CLUB was founded as an eating club in 1900 and moved into a three-story Collegiate Gothic building at the southeast corner of Prospect Avenue and Washington Road in 1910. When the club experienced financial difficulties and then closed in 2005, its membership voted to donate the building to the University as a gathering place for undergraduate and graduate students.

Anne Trevisan '86, chair of the club's graduate board, said at the time that "our donation of the club to the University ensures that the historic club building itself will continue to be cherished. Perhaps more importantly . . . Campus Club will have a dynamic and ongoing role at the center of the University campus, and will continue to enrich the lives of students and alumni for many years to come."

The building includes areas that can be reserved by student organizations for dinners, receptions, and musical and other cultural and social events. It also provides spaces and amenities for students to study, gather informally, or just enjoy some restorative time between or after classes. The ground floor of the club features a tap room with café seating and a lounge. The first floor includes a dining room that can seat 35–45 guests, a living room, a sun porch, a conference room, and the club director's office. The second floor provides a library and a den.

The club is open to all students. It defines its mission as promoting "social interaction that is community oriented, while fostering intellectual curiosity and the free exchange of ideas. . . . By bridging the social, cultural, and intellectual differences among students at Princeton, we are committed to making Campus Club a vibrant and inclusive community."

After spending its first year in temporary quarters, the Campus Club eating club moved in 1901 into the former residence of professor and newly appointed dean of the graduate school Andrew Fleming West 1874, which was located on the current site of the club. In 1909 the former West residence was moved to Nassau Street near Princeton Avenue, and was replaced by a Gothic structure designed by Raleigh Gildersleeve, who also designed McCosh Hall, Upper and Lower Pyne dormitories, and two other eating clubs: Elm and Cap and Gown.

Following the donation of the building to the University in 2006, an advisory committee of club and University representatives and a student advisory board composed of undergraduates and graduate students were consulted on the renovation and uses of the facility, which opened in 2009. As part of sustainability efforts, a new geothermal system for heating and cooling was added, along with 12 geothermal wells on the south side of the building.

Under the donation agreement, former eating club members and other alumni continue to have access to the building on certain occasions, such as after home football games and during Alumni Day and reunions.

CANNONS. The big cannon in the center of the quadrangle (Cannon Green) behind Nassau Hall and the little cannon between Whig and Clio halls were revolutionary war armaments abandoned by British troops following the Battle of Princeton in 1777.

After lying on the campus for years, the big cannon was taken to New Brunswick during the War of 1812 to defend that city from possible enemy attack. It remained there until a dark night in 1835 when the Princeton Blues, a volunteer military company of citizens in the town, loaded it on a wagon and headed back to Princeton. Their wagon broke down at the outskirts of town, and they abandoned the cannon at the side of the road. It lay there until another dark night a few years later when about a hundred students, led by Leonard Jerome 1839 (maternal grandfather of Winston Churchill), hoisted it onto a wagon, brought it to the campus, and dumped it in front of Nassau Hall. In 1840 it was moved and planted muzzle down in its present location.

Since the 1890s, the big cannon has been the focus of championship football bonfires. It inspired Joseph F. Hewitt 1907 and Arthur H. Osborne 1907 to compose "The Princeton Cannon Song" (*With cheers and songs we'll rally round The Cannon as of yore/And Nassau's walls will echo with the Princeton Tiger's roar*). In the late nineteenth century it was the starting point for cross-country races. For generations it has occupied a place of honor in the middle of the site that houses the graduating seniors' Class Day exercises, and more recently the graduate students' Hooding Ceremonies as well, on the day before Commencement.

For many years, the little cannon was used as a corner post at Nassau and Witherspoon streets; it was the marker from which the first formal survey of the town was made. It was moved to the campus and became the cause of a celebrated "Cannon War" with Rutgers in 1875 when it was taken to New Brunswick by Rutgers students under the mistaken impression that it belonged to that city. After a retaliatory raid by Princeton students and some sharp correspondence between the presidents of the two colleges, a joint committee was appointed by the respective faculties and the dispute was settled amicably, with Princeton students agreeing to return some muskets they had taken from New Brunswick and Rutgers students returning the cannon they had taken from Princeton.

In the fall of 1969, in honor of the centennial of the first intercollegiate football game, which was played by Princeton and Rutgers, the little cannon played a central role in the Princeton-Rutgers Centennial Hoax. A dozen Princeton students dug a hole next to the little cannon, piled the dirt on top of the cannon, and left a note suggesting the cannon had been carried away by Rutgers students. Early the next morning one of the Princeton students posed as an anonymous Rutgers student to notify WPRB, the campus radio station, that the cannon had been stolen, while another notified Princeton's Public Safety office, then headquartered about a hundred yards away in Stanhope Hall. The size of the hole and drag marks that had been made from the hole to the nearby street made the story seem credible, especially against a backdrop of Rutgers students previously having come to campus to paint the cannons red—as, on occasion, they still do.

The national press picked up the story, with the Associated Press reporting that "a band of Rutgers University students apparently staged a pre-dawn raid." When the students revealed the hoax, ABC television was on hand to watch as they scraped away the dirt to show that the cannon had remained safely in its resting place all the time, and the *Philadelphia Inquirer* headlined its story: "Princeton 'Outguns' Rutgers."

CARNAHAN, JAMES 1800 served 31 years as the ninth president of the College. He was the longest-serving president in Princeton's history, and one of the least distinguished.

Carnahan was born and raised in Pennsylvania, where his father farmed, first near Harrisburg, then near Pittsburgh. In 1798 he and his friend Jacob Lindly 1800 (later president of Ohio University) entered the junior class at Princeton after an arduous trip over the Allegheny Mountains. Having only one horse (Lindly's), they used a system called "ride and tie," under which each rode a number of miles every day and then, after tying up the horse so it could await his traveling companion, walked as many more.

After his graduation, Carnahan served as a tutor at Princeton, studied theology with President Samuel Stanhope Smith, and preached for six years before resigning because of a throat ailment that troubled him all his life. He then founded a classical seminary in Georgetown, DC. He had been there 11 years when the College notified him of his election to the presidency.

When Carnahan took office in 1823, he was a courtly schoolmaster who had not kept in touch with the College. He was thoroughly unprepared for the near anarchy and conflicting views of trustees, faculty, and students that he found when he got there. He thought of resigning at once, but a young professor, John Maclean Jr. 1816, persuaded him to stay. Enrollment dropped from 148 to 66 and he became so discouraged that he considered closing the institution, but Maclean proposed a plan to strengthen the faculty with the help of alumni.

In 1826 Maclean arranged for James Madison 1771 to become the first president of the alumni association, as Maclean became its secretary. Maclean became vice president of the College in 1829, and from that time on, as a trustee later observed, the College had an administration "in which two colleagues labored as one man." With funds raised by the alumni, Carnahan was able to strengthen the faculty and add modern languages as permanent features of the curriculum.

While president of the College, Carnahan also served as a director of the American Colonization Society of New Jersey, which promoted the relocation of free African Americans to a colony in Liberia. Carnahan himself had owned two slaves while living in Georgetown; in Princeton, the 1830 census recorded one male free colored person living in his household.

Reviewing his achievements upon his retirement in 1854, Carnahan was able to report a restoration of harmony between the trustees and faculty, the doubling of student enrollment, the tripling of the size of the faculty, and the construction of East and West colleges and Whig and Clio halls. As he then passed the torch to Maclean and became a trustee, Carnahan was modest about what he had done. What he hoped people would remember about him, he sometimes told his family, was that it was he who planted the trees on the front campus.

CARNEGIE LAKE was created in 1906 by the construction of a dam in the town of Kingston just northeast of Princeton that impounded the confluence of the Stony Brook and the Millstone River, producing a body of water three and a half miles long and 800 feet across at its widest point, covering 259 acres.

The lake was the gift of steel magnate Andrew Carnegie. He had built a number of lochs in Scotland and was easily persuaded to finance one for Princeton by Howard Russell Butler 1876 and his brother and classmate, William Allen Butler. (Howard Russell Butler met Carnegie when he was asked to paint his portrait.) The Butlers and some of their friends were determined that undergraduates should have a better place for rowing than the barge canal, which Princeton rowers had stopped using because it was too busy with commercial traffic.

The Butlers succeeded where James McCosh and Woodrow Wilson 1879 had failed. President McCosh had made repeated but unsuccessful efforts to interest his fellow Scot in his plans for the College. While the negotiations for the lake were in progress, President Wilson tried unsuccessfully to interest Carnegie in making a substantial contribution to the endowment of either the graduate school or the preceptorial system. Later when Wilson again asked for help and Carnegie answered, "I have already given you a lake," Wilson replied, "We needed bread and you gave us cake."

The student and community response to Carnegie's formal presentation of the lake on December 5, 1906, was enthusiastic. The creation of the lake did more than provide a place for undergraduate rowing, and for canoeing, sailing, fishing, and skating by students, faculty, staff, and residents of neighboring towns. There were significant aesthetic and environmental benefits that resulted from flooding a large marshy area and creating an attractive open space, and since Carnegie's gift included the purchase of hundreds of acres adjacent to the lake, it gave the University room for development it might not otherwise have been able to secure.

The lake was dredged in 1927 and again in the late 1930s. In the 1960s it became apparent that it was being threatened by the accumulation of sediment washed in by the Stony Brook from upstream communities and the deposition of sewage carried by the Millstone River from nearby towns where expansion of treatment facilities had not kept pace with rapid growth of population. In 1972, extensive dredging was undertaken to solve these problems; that dredging gave the lake a uniform depth of nine feet at a distance of 35 feet from the shoreline. The lake was dredged again in 2019 after the dam had been repaired four years earlier.

On the north shore of the lake near its western end is the Lakeside graduate student housing complex and the home of the Princeton crew teams, the C. Bernard Shea Rowing Center, which includes the Class of 1887 Boathouse. Olympic rowers have long used the lake as a training site, and the lake hosts numerous regattas each year. Community access to the lake is available at a boat launch near the Kingston dam. Swimming and gasoline powered boats are not permitted; skating is permitted in winters when the Princeton Recreation Department determines that the ice is safe. One of the most devoted users of the lake was Albert Einstein, who frequently roamed its waters in a small sailboat.

In 2017 the University released a campus plan that proposed development of a Lake Campus on University-owned lands south of the lake. According to the plan, "over time the Lake Carnegie landscape is expected to evolve from a feature that defines the southern edge of the campus to a feature that is central to the campus, connecting campus lands to its north and its south."

CARRIL, PETER J. "PETE," Princeton's legendary hall-of-fame basketball coach, led the Tigers to 514 wins over 29 seasons, including 13 Ivy League titles and 11 NCAA tournament appearances. In his final Princeton win he masterminded an upset of defending national champion UCLA in the first round of the 1996 NCAA tournament; his team scored the winning basket with 3.9 seconds to play on a signature backdoor play. The final score was immortalized in the *Daily Princetonian* headline: David 43, Goliath 41.

The upset was classic Carril: beating a higher ranked team by employing a patient, persistent, and unselfish offense, a stifling defense, meticulous preparation, and a generous application of brainpower. He often cited the lesson he learned at an early age from his father, a Spanish immigrant who worked in the steel mills of Bethlehem, Pennsylvania: the strong take from the weak, but the smart take from the strong.

Carril played basketball at Liberty High School in Bethlehem, where he was an all-state selection in 1947–48, and then at Lafayette College, where one of his head coaches was Willem "Butch" van Breda Kolff '45, who would become his predecessor at Princeton. After serving in the army, Carrill coached high school basketball in Easton and then Reading, Pennsylvania, and then became head coach at Lehigh University. (At Reading High he coached Gary Walters '67, who would serve from 1994 to 2014 as Princeton's director of athletics.)

Carril coached at Princeton from the 1967 through 1996, compiling a record of 514–263. In addition to the 11 NCAA tournaments, he also took his teams to two National Invitation tournaments (NITs), winning the NIT championship in 1975 in New York's Madison Square Garden with wins over Holy Cross, South Carolina, Oregon, and Providence. In 1989, his team almost became the first No. 16 seed ever to defeat a No. 1 seed in the first round of the NCAA tournament when it fell to Georgetown by one point, 50–49, after leading 29–21 at the half.

After leaving Princeton, Carril became an assistant coach and consultant for the National Basketball Association's Sacramento Kings. In 1997, he was inducted into the basketball hall of fame, and in 2009 the game floor of Jadwin Gym was named Carril Court in his honor.

Often characterized as "colorful," Carril was a gifted phrase-maker. Once, when Princeton won a game in the final seconds right after he called a timeout, reporters asked if he had called the winning play. Without missing a beat, he said the team had gone "with the third of the two options I gave them."

Carril's players often referred to him as a teacher. Walters described him as "inspirational both as a teacher in the classroom and as a teacher on the court." Another former player once said, "he wasn't just coaching basketball, he was coaching life."

In 2012, Princeton awarded Carril an honorary degree. His citation said:

More often than not, his players were shorter, slower, and less athletically gifted than their opponents, but he turned their limitations into strengths—teaching them that the greatest attributes were intelligence, discipline, selflessness, and commitment. His defense was tenacious, and his offense was legendary, where movement was paramount, the pass was as important as the shot, and the back door was often the portal to victory. David once again beat Goliath when he coached Princeton to one of the greatest upsets in NCAA history, but his greatest legacy was his teaching. He once wrote, "I think Princeton kept me because some of my players seemed better for the experience." So is college sport. So are we all.

CENTERS AND INSTITUTES. Prior to the twentieth century, Princeton had very little academic structure. This changed in 1904 when President Woodrow Wilson organized the academic programs of the University into departments. Over the following decades, the number of departments grew, some of them subdivided, and a number of interdisciplinary initiatives were launched, including, in the early 1930s, the school of Public and International Affairs and a special program in the humanities. Just prior to that, two special research units were established, the Industrial Relations Section in 1922 and the International Finance Section in 1928.

Today, interdisciplinary approaches to teaching and research are prevalent throughout the University, and special research units are plentiful. They bring together scientists, humanists, engineers, and social scientists in a variety of ways to enhance discovery and generate new ideas. Many of them also engage outside partners from industry, government, national laboratories, and other universities and research centers. A number of these centers and institutes are described elsewhere in the *Companion*, including the Andlinger Center for Energy and the Environment, the Lewis Center for the Arts, the Lewis-Sigler Institute for Integrative Genomics, the High Meadows Environmental Institute, the Princeton Institute for International and Regional Studies, the Princeton Neuroscience Institute, and the University Center for Human Values.

Other centers and institutes include:

The Center for Digital Humanities, an interdisciplinary research center that investigates how computational methods and digital technologies can foster better understanding of the human experience, past and present. It collaborates with faculty, students, and campus partners to create world-class humanities research using digital resources, offers training in cutting-edge scholarly methods, and develops open source software. The center produces innovative digital humanities projects and trains a new generation of digitally savvy humanities scholars.

The Center for Information Technology Policy, a nexus of expertise in technology, engineering, public policy, and the social sciences, addresses the impact and influence of digital technologies on society. Areas of interest include issues related to artificial intelligence, the internet of things, the availability and performance of internet connectivity across the United States and the world, privacy and security, censorship and filtering, cryptocurrencies, national security and surveillance, web transparency, internet governance, and electronic voting. The center offers an undergraduate certificate in cooperation with the Keller Center for Innovation in Engineering Education.

The Center for Statistics and Machine Learning, which seeks to foster and support scholars addressing the challenges of using data and algorithms to explore important scientific questions, the development of innovation methodologies for extracting from data across different domains, and the education of students in the foundations of modern data science. It harnesses insights from computation, machine learning, and statistics to advance both theoretical foundations and scientific discovery. The center offers two certificate programs, and co-sponsors seminars and workshops that expand and deepen the use and reach of data science on campus.

The Center for the Study of Religion, which encourages scholarship that examines religion or aspects of religion comparatively and in its diverse historical and contemporary manifestations through the lenses of humanities and social science disciplines. The center offers two interdisciplinary seminars, Religion and Culture and Religion and Public Life. It encourages students to develop a better understanding of the interactions among religions and their social contexts, and of the ethical, social, and cultural contributions and implications of religion.

The Princeton Center for Complex Materials, which was established in 1994 to explore the frontiers of complexity in materials science. Funded by the National Science Foundation, the center supports interdisciplinary research groups in areas such as quantum technologies and biology-inspired materials, and conducts educational and outreach programs for K–12 students and undergraduates that seek to cultivate an inclusive and diverse highly skilled workforce in science, technology, engineering, and mathematics (STEM).

The Princeton Institute for Computational Science and Engineering (PICSciE), an interdisciplinary institute that brings together faculty and researchers to address new and relevant computational problems. It provides state-of-the-art computing and visualization facilities in collaboration with the office of information technology's research computing unit. Created in 2002, it draws its members from the engineering, natural science, social science, and humanities departments, as well as from the Princeton Plasma Physics Laboratory and the Geophysical Fluid Dynamics Laboratory on the Forrestal campus.

The Princeton Institute for the Science and Technology of Materials (PRISM), a multidisciplinary research center driving advances in materials science and photonics. Its research combines expertise in "hard" materials such as conventional semiconductors and ceramics with knowledge of "soft" materials such as plastics, biological molecules, and fluids. Its six main areas of interest include quantum materials and structures, large-area materials and devices, optics and sensors, bio-nano interface, patterning and self-assembly, and computational materials science. At the center, new discoveries and properties emerge from new structures on the scale of atoms and nanometers, which are then tailored for devices and systems to address real world problems. Its research has led to breakthroughs in fields ranging from telecommunications and health to energy, biotechnology, and security. Critical to its work are two central research facilities: a micro/nano fabrication lab and an imaging and analysis center.

The Stanley J. Seeger Center for Hellenic Studies, an interdisciplinary community for the study of the Greek world from antiquity to the present. It was founded in 2011 to oversee and manage research on all aspects of Hellenic studies on campus and in Greece and the Hellenic Mediterranean. It is supported by a fund established in 1979 by Stanley Seeger Jr. '52 "to advance the understanding of the culture of ancient Greece and its influence . . . and to stimulate creative expression and thought in and about modern Greece." An integral part of the center is the program in Hellenic Studies that was founded in 1981. In 2016 the center founded the Princeton Athens Center for Research and Hellenic Studies to provide opportunities for on-site research and learning in the Stanley J. Seeger '52 House, a 1930s-era townhouse on a residential street in downtown Athens.

As of 2020, plans were being developed to elevate the *Program in American Studies* to the status of a center. The program already housed undergraduate certificate programs in American Studies, Asian American Studies, and Latino Studies, and its director, Anne Cheng '85, identified the creation of a certificate program in Native American/Indigenous Studies as one of the program's goals.

An interdepartmental program in American Studies (then American Civilization) was created in 1942 with faculty from 13 departments in the humanities and social sciences. During World War II it conducted weekend courses for British soldiers stationed in the United States, and in gratitude the British government later sent the University a stone from the bombed-out House of Commons which was embedded in the wall to the right of the main entrance to Firestone Library.

Today the program sponsors research, teaching, and public discussion about the history, literature, arts, politics, society, and culture of the United States "in all its diversities," examining questions of migration, colonization, race, borders, and diaspora; art, culture, and language; law and public policy; and gender and sexuality. "In short," it says, "we aim to understand America in the world as well as how the world lives in America."

CHANCELLOR GREEN was the College's first building designed to be a library, and its first building named out of deference to its donor. The building was given in 1873 by John Cleve Green, and at his request it was named for his brother, Henry Woodhull Green 1820, a trustee of the College and the chancellor of New Jersey's equity courts. Construction of a library was a high priority for President James McCosh, who wanted to elevate Princeton into the ranks of the world's leading academic institutions; McCosh insisted that the building's entrances face Nassau Street, to reinforce his view that the institution should face out into the world rather than in upon itself.

Victorian Gothic in design, the building is composed of three octagons on an east-west axis. The central octagon, known as the rotunda, is encircled by wooden bookcases on the main level and a balcony; the room features stained-glass in its windows and in a magnificent octagonal dome light. Two smaller reading rooms were constructed off the rotunda, and in 1913 the west room was converted into a trustee meeting room. Befitting its initial use as a library, the marble pillars that support the building's two north-entry porticos are topped by limestone carved to resemble stacks of books.

Chancellor Green was designed to hold 150,000 books, which at that time was three times the College's holdings. Within 15 years it reached capacity, prompting the construction of Pyne Library in 1897, with a physical connection to Chancellor Green known as the "hyphen." Chancellor Green served primarily as the library's reading room until both buildings could be repurposed when Firestone Library opened in 1948. The construction of Firestone resulted in the third relocation of Joseph Henry House, to a site that shielded Chancellor Green's north-facing entrances from Nassau Street.

In 1954 Chancellor Green was renovated along with Pyne Library (by then renamed East Pyne) to house a student center. When the New Jersey drinking age was lowered to 18 in 1973, a very popular pub was installed in the rotunda; when the drinking age was raised to 19 in 1980 and then to 21 in 1983, the pub was closed. In 2000 the student center was relocated to Frist Campus Center. In 2004 Chancellor Green was renovated to become part of the Andlinger Center for the Humanities, with an academic lounge and two seminar rooms on the main floor and a café in the former game room one level below.

Just outside the west door of Chancellor Green is a memorial garden that was dedicated in 2003 to commemorate the 14 Princeton alumni who died in the terrorist attacks of September 11, 2001. The garden includes star-shaped markers naming the alumni, as well as a bronze bell titled *Remembrance* that was created for the garden by Princeton's longtime visual arts professor, ceramist Toshiko Takaezu.

CHAPEL, THE UNIVERSITY, a majestic cathedral-like Collegiate Gothic structure between Firestone Library and McCosh Hall, is the site of the University's Opening Exercises each fall, its Service of Remembrance each winter, and its Baccalaureate service each spring. It is a year-round center of religious life on campus; an occasional venue of activism and protest; and a favored locale for weddings, memorial services, concerts, and other gatherings, including, since 2008, an annual celebration of the Hindu festival of Diwali. For many years it has hosted the graduations of Princeton Theological Seminary and the Westminster Choir College.

For the first 10 years of the University's existence, daily religious services were conducted in the studies of its first two presidents—Jonathan Dickinson in Elizabeth, New Jersey and Aaron Burr Sr. in Newark. After the nascent college moved to Princeton in 1756, a prayer hall in Nassau Hall (now the northern half of the Faculty Room) was used for services until 1847, when the first purpose-built chapel was constructed. This chapel was replaced in 1882 by the larger Marquand Chapel, a gift of Henry G. Marquand.

The first chapel, known as the "Old Chapel," was razed in 1896 to make way for Pyne Library. Its replacement, Marquand Chapel, was destroyed by fire in the spring of 1920. Services were then conducted in Alexander Hall until 1928. The cornerstone of the current University Chapel was laid in 1925, and the building was dedicated on Sunday, May 31, 1928.

President John Grier Hibben described the chapel as "the University's protest against the materialistic philosophy and drift of our age." It was designed by supervising architect Ralph Adams Cram, made of Pennsylvania sandstone and Indiana limestone, and built with impeccable craftsmanship in stone and wood at a cost of $2.5 million. With an official seating capacity of 1,233, it ranks among the largest collegiate chapels in the world, along with those at Cambridge University's King's College and the University of Chicago. It has been called the "finest Gothic interior in America" and the "finest ensemble [of stained glass] to be found in the western hemisphere."

Until 1928 the president of the University was directly responsible for supervision of the chapel programs. That year the office of dean of the chapel was created and Robert Russell Wicks was appointed as the first incumbent. On his retirement in 1947, Wicks was succeeded by Donald Aldrich, a charter trustee of the University. When Aldrich resigned in 1955 he was succeeded by Ernest Gordon, a former minister of Paisley Abbey in the same town in Scotland where John Witherspoon served as minister before his call to the Princeton presidency in 1768.

Gordon had decided on a career in the ministry while in a Japanese prison camp during World War II. He had marched with other prisoners through the Southeast Asian jungles to build a railroad over the River Kwai, and in a 1962 book, *Through the Valley of the Kwai*, he recounted the story behind the bridge and the spiritual awakening of those in the prison camp. He wrote his book partly to correct some aspects of the fictionalized account provided in the

Academy Award-winning 1957 film, *The Bridge on the River Kwai*.

Gordon served as dean through the upheavals on campus during the late 1960s and early 1970s. While he was dean, Dr. Martin Luther King Jr. spoke twice in the chapel (in 1960 and 1962), visits that are commemorated in a plaque installed on the interior south wall of the chapel at the initiative of Patricia Garcia Monet '92 during her tenure as president of the undergraduate student government.

In 1981, Gordon was succeeded as dean by Frederick Borsch '57, later a Princeton trustee, chair of the board's student life committee, and author of the 2011 book, *Keeping Faith at Princeton: A Brief History of Religious Pluralism at Princeton and Other Universities*. Borsch, in turn, was followed by Joseph Williamson in 1989, Thomas Breidenthal in 2001, and Alison Boden in 2007.

For 136 years after the College began, students were required to attend morning prayers (originally at 5 a.m.) and evening prayers daily, and morning and afternoon services on Sunday. These requirements were a source of student complaints and frequent pranks. Alumni recalled that on one occasion the seats of the Old Chapel were tarred; another time, the benches were literally buried in hay; and another time a cow was discovered near the pulpit before the morning service began.

By 1882, required attendance at daily vespers was abolished and in 1902 the required Sunday afternoon service was also discontinued. By 1905 attendance at morning prayers (then held at 7 a.m.) was required only twice a week, and in 1915 this requirement was abandoned entirely. Required attendance at Sunday chapel ended eventually: for juniors and seniors in 1935, for sophomores in 1960, and finally for freshmen in 1964.

Organ and choral music have always been an important part of the chapel program. Both have come a long way since Yale president Ezra Stiles visited in 1770 and declared the organ in Nassau Hall "an innovation of ill consequence" and future US president John Adams reported, after a visit in 1774, "The Scholars [*sic*] sing as badly as the Presbyterians at New York." When the chapel was dedicated in 1928, the University engaged Ralph Downes, the English organist and organ designer who went on to become professor of organ at the Royal College of Music, as the chapel's first organist and choirmaster. The chapel's magnificent Mander-Skinner organ, which in 1990 was shipped to London to be completely refurbished and restored, accompanies the 60-voice Chapel Choir and is played for many concerts and other events throughout the year; the organ has 109 stops and nearly 8,000 pipes.

The Chapel Choir has evolved over time from a male chorus that sang sacred music of the Renaissance and Baroque eras to a mixed choir, including undergraduates, graduate students, faculty, staff, and community members, whose repertoire extends from Gregorian chants to the music of Dave Brubeck. For the last 29 years, under director of chapel music Penna Rose, the choir has sung for Sunday morning services throughout the year and at Opening Exercises, the Service of Remembrance, and Baccalaureate and has given concerts in December and the spring. At the three University-wide convocations, students from the Chapel Choir fly colorful kites in the chapel that represent fire, earth, water, and air.

The chapel hosts a range of denominational services throughout the week and offers an ecumenical service every Sunday morning for a congregation that includes members of the campus community and residents from town. Student chapel deacons assist the dean and the associate or assistant deans in leading the weekly service.

Inside, the chapel is organized around the outline of a cross, with a 270-foot-long east-west axis. The height of the main section, or nave, is 76 feet. The pews are made from army surplus wood originally intended for Civil War gun carriages. Just before the chancel, where the short arm of the cross intersects the center aisle, the Marquand transept, an area used by the Aquinas Institute for Roman Catholic services and on other occasions for memorial services, baptisms, and other purposes, is to the left, and to the right is the Braman transept with a stairway to an outdoor pulpit. Above the west entry to the chapel (the narthex) is an upper gallery which seats about 90 people below the permanently installed fanfare trumpets that are used for ceremonial occasions.

The chancel at the front of the chapel is reached by a set of steps. To the left is a mid-sixteenth century pulpit from France and to the right is a lectern, also from France. The chancel itself is paneled in oak carved in England from trees that grew in Sherwood Forest. An altar stands at the far east end, and above it in the center of the chancel wall is the east window depicting love. The chancel is flanked by six bays with stained-glass windows, two representing the psalms of David and the other depicting Dante's *Divine Comedy*; Thomas Malory's *The Death of Arthur*;

John Milton's *Paradise Lost*; and John Bunyan's *Pilgrim's Progress*.

Other stained-glass windows throughout the chapel depict figures from Princeton's history and scenes from the bible, literature, history, and philosophy. The north, south, and west windows depict endurance, truth, and life. President John Witherspoon is incorporated into the south window, and Princeton luminaries in the chapel's other stained-glass windows include President Jonathan Edwards, physicist Joseph Henry, James Madison 1771, and Adlai Stevenson 1922.

In late morning on sunny days the light coming through the south-facing windows bathes the light-colored limestone columns inside the chapel in a breathtaking rainbow of colors. All told, the chapel contains over 10,000 square feet of stained glass in 27 windows.

The chapel also includes a number of *in memoriam* carvings along its walls and on its pews, six colorful 25-foot hanging silk banners painted by the artist Juanita Kauffman, and several flags, including one from the World War II–era USS *Princeton*.

Outside, over the west door of the chapel, is a carving of a seated Christ with the authors of the first four books of the New Testament: Matthew (angel), Mark (lion), Luke (ox), and John (eagle), along with words from the University shield: *Vet Nov Testamentum* (the Old and New Testaments) and *Dei sub numine viget* (under God's power she flourishes). On the south side of the chapel is the outdoor Bright Pulpit, with the carved quotation: "An instructed democracy is the surest foundation of government, and education and freedom are the only source of true greatness and happiness among any people."

To the east the chapel connects to Dickinson Hall by Rothschild Arch, and to the north are a garden named for President Hibben, a curved bench named for landscape architect Beatrix Farrand, and George Segal's sculpture, *Abraham and Isaac: In Memory of May 4, 1970, Kent State University*.

CHARTER, THE, which created the corporation originally known as The Trustees of the College of New Jersey, was granted in the name of King George II and "passed the Great Seal" of the Province of New Jersey on October 22, 1746.

The charter authorized the erection of a college "for the Education of Youth in the Learned Languages and in the Liberal Arts and Sciences;" designated seven men, with five others to be chosen by them, to be trustees of the college; and ordained that "the said Trustees and their Successors shall forever hereafter be, in Deed, Fact & Name a Body corporate & politick."

The charter granted the trustees and their successors full power and authority to acquire real and personal property; erect buildings; elect a president, tutors, professors, and other officers; grant degrees; and establish ordinances and laws "not repugnant" to the laws and statutes of Great Britain or New Jersey, and "not excluding any Person of any religious Denomination whatsoever from . . . any of the Liberties, Privileges, or immunities of the . . . College, on account of his . . . being of a Religious profession Different from the . . . Trustees of the College." This protection of religious freedom was unique among the colonial colleges.

John Hamilton, president of the Council of the Province of New Jersey and acting governor, issued the original charter. Because there was some question about his authority, the legal status of the College was attacked. To remove any uncertainty, in 1748 the newly appointed governor of the province, Jonathan Belcher, issued a second charter. For the most part it corresponded to the charter of 1746, but it increased the maximum number of trustees from 12 to 23, made the governor of New Jersey a trustee ex-officio, and stipulated that 12 trustees were to be inhabitants of New Jersey.

In 1780 the Council (i.e., Senate) and General Assembly of the State of New Jersey, on petition of the trustees, confirmed the royal charter of 1748 with minor changes, one being that each trustee would swear allegiance to the state in which he resided instead of to the king of Great Britain. A further legislative enactment, adopted in 1799, required each trustee also to affirm support for the constitution of the United States. Still another, adopted in 1866, added a third part to the oath, requiring each trustee to swear to perform the duties of the office faithfully and impartially; later the word justly was added, and the oath in this form is still used today, with appropriate modification for trustees who are not US citizens.

On February 13, 1896, the corporation adopted a resolution changing its name to The Trustees of Princeton University. President Francis Patton publicly proclaimed this change on October 22, 1896, the 150th anniversary of the granting of the first charter.

The maximum number of trustees was increased to 27 in 1868, 32 in 1901, and 35 in 1921. An amendment adopted in 1926 provided that thereafter there should be from 23 to 40 trustees, with the exact number to be fixed from time to time in the bylaws. The number who had to be residents of New Jersey was reduced to eight; in 1963 this number was reduced to one in addition to the governor and the president of the University; and in 1991 this requirement was eliminated, although the governor and the president remain ex officio members of the board.

Until 1939 the governor was the presiding officer of the board; since then the president has been the presiding officer. Prior to 2011 the highest-ranking trustee was the chair of the executive committee. Since 2011 the trustees have elected one of their members as chair of the board; the chair convenes board meetings while the president presides.

The current charter identifies the purposes of the corporation as:

- The conduct of a university not for profit, including colleges and schools . . . both graduate and undergraduate.
- The promotion, advancement, evaluation, and dissemination of learning by instruction, study, and research in the humanities, religion, social sciences, natural sciences, engineering and applied sciences.
- The awarding of certificates, diplomas, and degrees.
- Engagement and participation in projects of instruction, study, and research for the benefit of national, state, and local governments and for the general public welfare.

The charter vests all powers "necessary, convenient, or incident to its purposes and all powers given by law" in the trustees and stipulates that "the property and affairs of the Corporation shall be managed and conducted by a Board of Trustees." Enumerated powers include:

- Acquiring property and borrowing money.
- Providing for the selection of its students and for the "government and well-being" of its students, faculty, and staff.
- Appointing and employing such faculty, staff, officers, managers, agents, and employees as the purposes and powers of the corporation may require.
- Adopting bylaws.

The only officers of the University required by the charter are a president of the University, a clerk of the board, a secretary of the University, and a treasurer of the University. (The original charter required a president, "treasurer, clerk, usher, and steward.") The president serves as chief executive officer of the corporation, and according to the charter has "chief responsibility for the academic affairs of the University, the activities of the faculty . . . and the selection, education, government, and well-being of the students of the University."

The charter originally limited the value of real and personal property the trustees could acquire and use to an amount from which the yearly income would not exceed 2,000 pounds sterling. This limit was increased in 1780 to the value of 20,000 bushels of wheat; in 1799 to $20,000; in 1864 to $100,000; and in 1889 to $500,000. In 1903 the limitation was removed entirely.

The last complete revision of the charter was completed in 1963 when the Board of Trustees simplified and modernized its language to reflect the requirements and benefits of then-current law and corporate practice.

CHEMICAL AND BIOLOGICAL ENGINEERING, THE DEPARTMENT OF, originated at Princeton in 1922 as a special program in chemical engineering administered jointly by the department of Chemistry and the newly formed school of Engineering; the program drew on existing courses in both fields. The senior professor of physical chemistry, Hugh Stott Taylor, watched over the fledgling program and groomed one of his graduate students, Joseph Elgin *1929 (whose undergraduate work at the University of Virginia had been in chemical engineering), for its eventual leadership.

After receiving his PhD, Elgin was appointed Princeton's first instructor in the newly formed department of Chemical Engineering and was responsible for developing the new department's courses and facilities. After spending eight months visiting the chemical engineering department at the Massachusetts Institute of Technology, then regarded as one of the best in the country, he returned to Princeton and set up quarters in the old chemical laboratory (now Aaron Burr Hall), which housed the department until 1962 when it moved into the newly constructed Engineering Quadrangle.

One of Elgin's first students and the department's first graduate student, John Whitwell '31 *32, became his colleague in 1932. Two years later the department of Chemical Engineering officially separated from the department of Chemistry and Elgin and Whitwell were joined by Richard Wilhelm, who had just received his doctorate in chemical engineering at Columbia.

Along with Richard Toner, who came from New York University in 1942, and Ernest Johnson, who arrived in 1948 from the University of Pennsylvania, the initial faculty members built the department and created a curriculum. Undergraduate enrollment grew steadily and at one time was larger than any other engineering department in the University. In 1946 a PhD program was added to the original master's program, and in April 1948 a student in the department earned the first doctoral degree ever granted in the school of Engineering.

By 1954, when Elgin gave up his position as chair to become dean of the school of Engineering, the department had grown to an enrollment of 100 undergraduates and 25 graduate students, and a faculty of seven.

Further growth, particularly in graduate instruction and research, came under the leadership of the second chair, Wilhelm, with the assistance of new members of the department, including Leon Lapidus, William Schowalter, Robert Axtmann, and Bryce Maxwell. In 1966 a report by the American Council on Education cited the department as having the country's second most attractive chemical engineering graduate program. When Wilhelm died suddenly in 1968, the faculty was twice as large as when he took over; there were three times as many graduate students; the department had expanded into chemical reactor engineering, transport phenomena, and control and optimization theory; and it was one of the first departments in the country to make extensive use of computer technology.

Lapidus, who succeeded Wilhelm as chair, was widely known for the application of computer techniques in chemical engineering. Two additional areas of instruction and research that were developed during his tenure were the Polymer Science and Materials program, directed by Maxwell, and the Fusion Reactor Technology Program, closely integrated with the Princeton Plasma Physics Laboratory, which was directed by Johnson.

Under Lapidus, the department branched out into new areas of research such as biochemical engineering, energy conversion, and pollution control. The interest in pollution control was underscored in 1971 when the name of a professorship held by Axtmann was changed from Chemical Engineering for Nuclear Studies to Chemical Engineering for Environmental Studies. Axtmann was the first chair of the University's Council on Environmental Studies and of the Engineering school's program on Energy Conversion and Resources.

In 1975 the first two women students graduated with bachelor's degrees in chemical engineering. In 1977, Carol K. Hall became the first woman appointed to the department's faculty, and the following year Maria K. Burka became the first Princeton woman to earn a PhD in chemical engineering. She later became a program director at the National Science Foundation.

When Lapidus died suddenly in May 1977, Johnson chaired the department for a brief period and then Schowalter, who had been associate dean of the school of Engineering since 1972, served as chair from 1978 to 1987. He attained international status for his contributions to non-Newtonian fluid mechanics and later became dean of engineering at the University of Illinois.

The department continued to grow, adding faculty and acquiring new facilities in the Engineering Quadrangle, including the energy (G) wing and von Neumann Hall (H wing). Bowen Hall (opened in 1993) housed a materials laboratory where researchers pursued broad-based materials research. This research, especially the program in Polymer Science, led to greater national recognition.

As computational techniques became more sophisticated over the latter half of the twentieth century, the department expanded its traditional strength in this area by investigating such topics as molecular simulation, nonlinear dynamics, and protein folding.

A succession of chairs navigated the department through the succeeding years, each bringing a particular area of expertise while maintaining the department's commitment to broad-based research.

William Russel, chair of the department from 1987 to 1996, director of the Princeton Materials Institute from 1996 to 1998, and dean of the graduate school from 2002 to 2014, was an expert in the study of surface and colloid chemistry. Pablo Debenedetti, chair from 1996 to 2004, vice dean of the Engineering school from 2008 to 2013, and then dean for research, focused on thermodynamics, statistical mechanics, and computational simulations of liquids and glasses. T. Kyle Vanderlick, chair between 2004 and 2007, studied the properties of synthetic and biological membranes as well as the molecular engineering of structured surfaces and nanostructures. The chair from 2008 to 2016, Richard Register, investigated complex materials and processing to demonstrate how these materials may be applied in new and existing technologies.

The department today focuses on many areas of research that have immediate real-world applications, such as biomedical engineering. In 2010 the change of name to Chemical and Biological Engineering (CBE) recognized the increasing role of biotechnology in chemical engineering and acknowledged the importance of biology in understanding chemical processes. The department began requiring basic biology courses in its undergraduate curriculum, and as of 2020 half the department's faculty had projects that involved research in bio-related fields, such as cell biophysics and embryogenesis. CBE faculty member Celeste Nelson was directing an interdepartmental program in Engineering Biology designed for undergraduates interested in careers or graduate study in biotechnology or bioengineering.

Clifford Brangwynne, who received a MacArthur Fellowship in 2018, conducts innovative research into understanding physical processes by which living cells form specialized structures known as organelles, especially the process known as "liquid-liquid phase separation." His research has implications for a greater understanding of neurodegenerative diseases such as Alzheimer's and Huntington's. In 2020 Brangwynne was appointed the inaugural director of a new bioengineering initiative that was created to support and expand bioengineering at Princeton and pave the way for a bioengineering institute to catalyze research at the intersection of the life sciences and engineering.

Polymer and related materials research have been important areas of investigation in the department since the mid-1970s, and they remain so. Along with the Physics department, CBE has conducted extensive research into the properties of graphene, a new form of carbon that is used in high-performance composite materials. This research could dramatically boost energy efficient power transmission and could lead to a whole host of new technologies. The department also launched research programs in alternative energy generation and conversion technologies.

While traditional subjects such as thermodynamics and polymers continue to be taught, classes geared toward facing the challenges of the twenty-first century, such as "green and catalytic chemistry," "fundamentals of biofuels," and "ethics and technology: engineering in the real world," play an ever-increasing role in the curriculum. These courses are designed to equip students with the necessary tools and knowledge to confront many of the world's most urgent challenges.

The chair since 2016, Athanassios Panagiotopoulos, specializes in the application of theoretical and computer simulation techniques in the study of fluids and materials. He oversees a department whose core research areas include biomolecular engineering, cellular and tissue engineering, complex materials and processing, energy and environment, surface science and catalysis, and theory and simulation. Graduate students in the department may pursue certificates in bioengineering, statistics and machine learning, and computational and information science.

The department's faculty has been recognized through awards from the American Institute of Chemical Engineers, the American Chemical Society, the Society of Rheology, the American Ceramic Society, and the American Physical Society, as well as membership in the National Academy of Sciences and the National Academy of Engineering. One of its faculty members, Yueh-Lin (Lynn) Loo *01, served as director of the Andlinger Center for Energy and the Environment.

CHEMISTRY, THE DEPARTMENT OF. The history of chemistry at Princeton is bookended by the 1795 arrival on campus of John Maclean Sr., a medical doctor who was appointed professor of chemistry and set up the nation's first undergraduate chemistry laboratory (in Nassau Hall), and the construction of a new Frick Chemistry Laboratory in 2010 to house an expanding department of growing international stature. Princeton's is one of the oldest departments of chemistry in the country.

Because of its association with medicine, chemistry enjoyed a preeminence among the sciences throughout the nineteenth century and was a required subject for all Princeton students. Toward the end of the century, when exploration of the nation's mineral resources became important, the University added mineralogists to the faculty.

In 1914 a young Englishman, Hugh Stott Taylor, arrived on campus as a chemistry instructor. By age 32 he was a full professor; for 25 years, from 1926 to 1951, he chaired the department of Chemistry, and from 1945 until his retirement in 1958 he served as dean of the graduate school. An inspiring teacher, bold leader, and recipient of many honors for his pioneering work in catalysis, he set the pattern for research and teaching at Princeton for the next half century.

Taylor's research paved the way for other discoveries. In 1928, when the chain reaction theory of inhibition catalysis was elucidated at Princeton, it was illustrated with rows of falling dominoes decades before "domino theory" would become a political catchphrase.

During this period the home of the Chemistry department, Frick Laboratory, was renowned for research in photochemistry and the mechanisms of chemical reactions. When heavy water was discovered in 1931 and used as a tool in these areas, there was more heavy water in Frick than anywhere in the world—a test tube of it.

Notable scholars attracted to Princeton included N. Howell Furman, president of the American Chemical Society in 1950; the physical chemists Charles Smyth 1916 *1917 and Robert Pease, authorities in dipole moments and combustion kinetics; and two organic chemists, Eugene Pacsu in carbohydrates, and Everett Wallis, who made notable contributions in the areas of molecular rearrangements and especially in hormone research. Wallis conducted some of his research with visiting professor Edward Kendell, who arrived at Princeton in 1951 a year after winning the Nobel Prize for Physiology and Medicine. From 1931 to 1946, Henry Eyring was one of the department's bright stars, developing the theory of absolute reaction rates and applying it to chemical and biological processes, viscosity, diffusion, and ion transport.

During World War II, Taylor and Furman traveled daily to Columbia University, where Taylor was associate director of a branch of the Manhattan Project. Under the Government Engineering Science and Management Training Program, all members of the department traveled to Newark, Elizabeth, and Bound Brook, New Jersey, to conduct graduate courses for over 3,000 chemists in industry.

The postwar years brought radical changes to the department because the making and manipulation of molecules now required costly equipment. A new wing doubled the research space in Frick in 1964 and housed a biochemistry faculty that formed a separate department in 1970 before becoming fully absorbed into the department of Molecular Biology in 1990.

In the 1970s the department remained active in physical chemistry, but also added new strengths in organic and organometallic chemistry. Of the senior faculty, Jeffrey Schwartz and Martin Semmelhack were pioneers in the new area of organometallic chemistry while Kurt Mislow and Maitland Jones Jr. used physical organic chemistry to give deeper understanding of organic molecules. The physical chemists were investigating the nature and strength of chemical bonds, submicroscopic molecular arrangements, catalytic effects, electronic and photochemical processes, proteins, and nuclear transmutations. During the 1970s, women began pursuing graduate degrees in the physical sciences; in 1971, Joan Selverstone Valentine became the first woman to receive a Princeton PhD in chemistry.

In the 1980s, Edward C. Taylor, a distinguished heterocyclic chemist who made leading contributions to synthetic methodology, natural products synthesis, and medicinal chemistry, developed a chemical compound in his Princeton lab that showed potential to fight cancer cells. His discovery capped a journey that began decades earlier with curiosity about the properties of butterfly wing pigments. Princeton licensed the drug, named Alimta, to pharmaceutical company Eli Lilly, which worked with Taylor to develop it. Alimta became one of the world's best-selling cancer drugs, and Princeton's share of the royalties (in excess of $500 million) paid for the construction of a new Frick Chemistry Laboratory, which opened in 2010. Taylor retired in 1997 after 43 years on the faculty.

To mark Princeton's 250th anniversary in 1996, the department hosted a national symposium with addresses from six Nobel Laureates in chemistry. In 1999 the department succeeded in attracting Roberto Car, who developed the Car-Parrinello molecular dynamics method for studying chemical structures, and Annabella Selloni, who pioneered first-principles computational studies of surfaces and interfaces that made possible the interpretation of complex experiments. In general, however, the 1990s saw the department fall into a period of decline, with the size of its faculty dropping from 20 to about 13.

President Shirley Tilghman (herself trained as a chemist) recognized an urgent need to restore Princeton's eminence in chemistry, and in 2005 a committee was formed to map out a new future. Under chair Robert Cava, the committee identified four areas of concentration: catalysis and synthesis; new alternative energies; searching for new materials; and chemical biology. All emphasized applications to real-world challenges, and all attracted the interest of both students and donors.

The committee concluded that the existing Frick Laboratory had become an unsuitable home for a twenty-first century chemistry department and set the process in motion for a new building. The new Frick Laboratory was an immediate success both aesthetically—it is often referred to as a "cathedral" to chemistry—and as a draw for new faculty. The four-story, 265,000-square-foot open-lab structure with an open atrium and both a commons area and an auditorium named for Edward Taylor, breathed new life into the department.

Reorganization plans included the recruitment of exceptional young faculty. Among them was Abigail Doyle, who joined in 2008 as one of nine new professors sought and hired under the plan. Doyle's research focused on changing the way molecules are coupled together with implications for the way pharmaceuticals are made.

Also joining the faculty were Paul Chirik, one of the leading organometallic chemists in the world, who developed a new method for replacing platinum with less expensive iron metal; Haw Yang, an experimental physical chemist; Tom Muir, a leading chemist specializing in protein function in complex systems of biomedical interest; David MacMillan, whose research focused on chemical reactions that allow organic molecules to be built faster, more cheaply, more safely, and on the basis of completely new concepts; and Greg Scholes, whose group uses ultrafast lasers to probe how molecular systems in chemistry and biology interact with light.

MacMillan chaired the department from 2010 to 2015. In 2015 leadership passed to Muir. MacMillan also initiated the interdisciplinary and collaborative Princeton Catalysis Initiative.

As of 2021, Princeton counted six Nobel Laureates in chemistry among its faculty, staff, and alumni: David MacMillan (2021); Frances Arnold '79 (2018); former postdoctoral student Tomas Lindahl (2015); Edwin McMillan *33 (1951); former research staff member Osamu Shimomura (2008); and Richard Smalley *74 (1996). In addition, research conducted at Princeton in the 1930s by Arne Tiselius on a Rockefeller Foundation fellowship contributed to his 1948 Nobel in Chemistry, and research conducted in 1941 by Willard Libby on a Guggenheim fellowship contributed to his prize in 1960.

Moving into the 2020s, the department has been consistently ranked among the country's top 10 programs in chemistry. Its six main areas of research include catalysis/synthesis; chemical biology; inorganic chemistry; materials; spectroscopy/physical chemistry; and theoretical chemistry. The department enjoys broad collaborations with disciplines throughout campus, particularly molecular biology, physics, genomics, engineering, nanotechnology, and geosciences.

The department has a tradition of public lecture demonstrations that dates back to the days of Maclean. As early as 1795 the trustees allocated funds for his demonstrations, and alumni from the mid-to-late twentieth century will recall the last lecture of the year in freshman chemistry and the lectures at reunions by long-time faculty member Hubert Alyea '25 *28, including his pyrotechnic lecture on "Lucky Accidents, Great Discoveries, and the Prepared Mind." Alyea and his lectures were the inspiration for the 1961 Disney movie *The Absent-Minded Professor*. Similar demonstrations continue to this day.

CHRISTIAN STUDENT, THE, was the name undergraduates gave to a statue that stood on the lawn just south of Pyne Library, across from Murray-Dodge Hall, in the years immediately before and after World War I. The life-size bronze statue, depicting an undergraduate in football uniform, an academic gown slung over his shoulder, and a pile of books in his left arm, was given by Cleveland H. Dodge 1879 as a memorial to his brother W. Earl Dodge 1879, leader of a group of students who formed the Intercollegiate YMCA in 1876. Remembered by his classmates as captain of the championship football team, president of the student religious organization, and an honor student who graduated near the top of his class, Dodge died suddenly at the age of 25.

The statue was the work of Daniel Chester French, who also did the figures of Joseph Henry and Benjamin Franklin flanking the entrance to Palmer Hall (now Frist Campus Center), John Harvard in Harvard Yard, Alma Mater at Columbia, and Abraham Lincoln in the Lincoln Memorial.

Erected in 1913, the statue was twice torn down: in 1929 by some seniors during a spree the night of Commencement, and in 1930 during a riot that grew out of a football rally. The second time it was torn down, the statue was put in storage; it was later placed on permanent loan in the Daniel Chester French Museum in Stockbridge, Massachusetts, which was subsequently turned over to the National Trust for Historic Preservation.

In 1987 a group of alumni arranged to bring the statue, now known as The Princeton Student (French's original name for the statue), back to campus. It is on display in Jadwin Gymnasium as a tribute to long-time friend of Princeton football Harland "Pink" Baker 1922, a member of the legendary 1922 football Team of Destiny.

CIVIL AND ENVIRONMENTAL ENGINEERING, THE DEPARTMENT OF, began life as a department of Civil Engineering, so named to differentiate it from military engineering. It was first taught at Princeton in 1875 by Charles McMillan, the first engineering professor in the newly established John C. Green School of Science and founder of the department.

McMillan educated the earliest generation of Princeton civil engineers single-handedly, but as enrollment grew additional appointments were needed, and within 15 years he had been joined by three others who were to spend life-long careers in the department. Frederick Newton Willson, like McMillan a graduate of Rensselaer Polytechnic Institute, organized the department's work in graphics in 1880 and taught that subject for 43 years. As a hobby, Willson enjoyed inspecting new bridges; in 1935, on his 80th birthday, he crossed the catwalk atop one of the towers of the Golden Gate bridge in San Francisco, having previously traversed the catwalks of the Brooklyn and George Washington bridges in New York.

One of McMillan's first students, Herbert Stearns Squier Smith 1878 (known to generations of students as H_2S Smith), taught applied mechanics, water supply, and hydraulics for 40 years; he was secretary of the civil engineering faculty for most of his career and secretary of his class for 62 years. Another McMillan student, Walter Butler Harris 1886 (who, while still an undergraduate, designed and built the first jetty on the Atlantic coast), taught railroad engineering and surveying for 45 years and by the time of his retirement in 1934 had left his mark by laying out a part of the University campus and designing 25 faculty houses in the Broadmead area.

McMillan retired in 1914 and was succeeded as chair by Frank Constant, who served until 1937. The year of McMillan's retirement marked the arrival of George Beggs, who became internationally known for his pioneering work in the model analysis of bridges and other structures. Beggs followed Constant as chair, serving for two years until his death in 1939. He was succeeded by Philip Kissam until 1946 and Elmer Timby, who resigned in 1949 to enter private practice. (In 1942 Kissam taught a government-sponsored photogrammetry course that enrolled Princeton's first women students.) The chair from 1950 to 1961 was W. Mack Angas, who, as a vice-admiral in the United States Navy, had supervised the construction of 16 bases by naval construction battalions (the famed "seabees") in the Southwest Pacific during World War II.

An interdepartmental plan of study, the Basic Engineering program, was instituted in 1938 to meet the needs of students wishing to prepare for the administrative and economic aspects of an engineering career in industry or government. It eventually was renamed Engineering Management Systems, or EMS, and became part of the curriculum of Operations Research and Financial Engineering (ORFE) when that department separated from Civil Engineering in 1999. In 1966 Civil Engineering merged with the Geological Engineering department, which had been founded in 1922. The resulting department of Civil and Geological Engineering continued until 1974, when Geological Engineering became a program within the department of Civil Engineering.

Norman Sollenberger's 10 years as chair (1961–71) were marked by substantial expansion of the department's PhD program and the recruitment of new faculty, reinforcing Princeton's strong tradition in structural engineering while developing a new theoretical undergirding in mechanics. Two new faculty members, 2015 Princeton honorary degree recipient David Billington '50 (thin shell concrete structures) and Robert Mark (experimental stress analysis), also taught in the school of Architecture, thereby encouraging fruitful relations between humanistic and engineering teaching and research, involving, for example, structures of historical and cultural interest such as bridges and Gothic cathedrals.

Under Ahmet Cakmak, a specialist in the mechanics of materials who became chair in 1971, the department gave special attention to strengthening the program in Water Resources and the development of a new Transportation program. The Water Resources program later evolved into today's Environmental Engineering and Water Resources (EEWR) program, offered jointly with the department of Geosciences.

George Pinder, who had previously worked for the United States Geological Survey, was hired to lead the Water Resources program. He was widely acclaimed as an expert in hydrogeology (the study of the underground movement of water) and served as a professional witness during several famous environmental cases during the 1970s, including Love Canal and the Woburn groundwater contamination case. As chair from 1980 until 1989, he built up the Water Resources program significantly, focusing on solutions to "the increasingly acute water resources problem[s] attending world population growth."

The Transportation program was organized in 1972 as a multidisciplinary project involving faculty and students from the school of Engineering and Applied Science, the school of Architecture, and the school of Public and International Affairs. It offered a master's degree and was directed by Alain Kornhauser *71, who later taught in ORFE.

In the 1970s Civil Engineering experienced a significant increase in enrollment, which Cakmak attributed to the department's efforts to make its programs attractive to students interested "in applying their technical knowledge to actual problems of social concern." By the mid-1970s, Civil Engineering had become the fifth largest department in undergraduate concentrators, surpassed only by History, English, Economics, and Politics.

In 1986 Civil Engineering added operations research to its name, so the department for a time became Civil Engineering and Operations Research. This change occurred when the department of Statistics was discontinued, and several statistics faculty members moved to engineering. The change in name also recognized the increasing role financial analysis and statistics were playing in engineering.

The EEWR program continued to prosper during these years and became a major area of interest for the department. Today, the program focuses on problems related to the hydrological and biogeochemical cycles and their sensitivity to climate change and weather extremes, among other topics. Eric Wood, a member of the National Academy of Engineering with extensive background in hydrology and water issues, directed the program from 1982 to 1993.

In the 1990s the department hired Ignacio Rodriguez-Iturbe, who had played an important pioneering role in the field of hydrology and was internationally known for his work on river networks and their control of hydrologic processes. He is one of the founders of ecohydrology, a discipline that examines the roles of landscapes, plants, and soil in the water cycle. He also became acting director of what was then known as the Princeton Environmental Institute (PEI).

In 1999, while Erhan Cinlar was chair of the department, the operations research faculty formed the new Operations Research and Financial Engineering (ORFE) department, and the Civil Engineering department became the department of Civil and Environmental Engineering (CEE). Cinlar became the first chair of ORFE while Peter Jaffe assumed the chair of CEE.

CEE added strengths in materials science and what has been called "structural art." George Scherer, a renowned materials scientist who worked for many years in private industry, led research in the former field. He studied the chemical properties and potentialities of cement and created and applied sophisticated mathematical models to explain complex degradation phenomena, such as salt scaling (the progressive damage to concrete structures from saline). Billington built a program around "structural art," which is defined as a discipline that allows for aesthetic expression under the practical constraints of engineering. His classes, which routinely attracted between 200 and 300 students, were later taught by Maria Garlock, who also co-directs the department's program in Architecture and Engineering.

Michael Celia became department chair in 2005. His research interests included subsurface hydrology and ground-water contamination, with an emphasis on computational methods for complex contamination problems. During his tenure, the National Research Council ranked Civil Engineering's PhD program number one in the nation. Celia stepped down as chair in 2011 to direct the EEWR program and then became director of PEI.

From 2011 to 2017 James Smith headed the department, focusing on hydrology and meteorology, with an emphasis on extreme storms and flooding. He was succeeded as chair by Catherine Peters, who focuses on such topics as geologic sequestration of carbon dioxide, geothermal energy production, and hydrofracking for shale gas extraction. She also has been actively involved in efforts to recruit more women to be scientists and engineers.

Peters has said that civil and environmental engineers "are called upon to solve the world's most important and challenging problems . . . by devising clever technological advancements that balance human needs with earth's resources. It is civil and environmental engineers who design the cities of the future and ensure safe and resilient infrastructure . . . protect the earth's environment while providing humanity with fresh water resources [and] determine how humans will live on this planet as climate change increases the severity of natural hazards and threatens the livability of the built environment."

For undergraduates interested in professional accreditation, CEE offers programs in structural engineering, environmental engineering, geological engineering, and architecture and engineering with a focus on structures. For undergraduates with career interests in other professions it offers programs in engineering and the liberal arts and in architecture and engineering with a focus on architecture. The department offers graduate degree programs in mechanics, materials, and structures, and in environmental engineering and water resources; students may also earn a PhD in civil and environmental engineering and materials science that CEE offers jointly with the Princeton Institute for Science and Technology of Materials (PRISM).

Civil War. In the years leading up to the Civil War defenders of slavery frequently won the Whig-Clio debates on the subject, but in large measure both the students and the administration sought to mute discussion that could undermine intersectional harmony on a campus in which about 60 percent of the students came from the north and about 40 percent from the south.

In its earliest days, Princeton was unique among American colleges in enrolling students from throughout the colonies, in a sense becoming a national institution before there was a nation. President John Witherspoon traveled extensively through the south, successfully attracting both students and donors.

From 1820 to 1860, 12 classes enrolled more southern than northern students, and in the Class of 1851 southern enrollment reached 63 percent. As a result, the Princeton student body had strong ties to the slaveholding south, and in 1835 southern students attacked a visiting abolitionist; in 1846 two southern students instigated a brawl between southern and northern students when they attacked a local Black man.

In 1831 and 1838, a slaveholder named James McDowell 1817 gave the commencement addresses and called for the nation to leave the problem of slavery to the slaveholders. In 1850, US Representative from Texas David Kaufman 1833 spent most of his hour-and-a-half commencement address arguing that abolishing slavery would lead to anarchy and abolishment of the Bible.

In December 1859, southern students led a march on Nassau Street protesting John Brown's raid and other abolitionist activities. A student from Mississippi wrote home that "probably there will be some hot times here if an abolitionist is elected next president," and with the election of Abraham Lincoln in 1860 his prophecy was fulfilled. (New Jersey was the only northern state where Lincoln lost the popular vote, although he won four of its seven electoral votes.)

As southern states began seceding, students from the south began leaving the campus to return home to take up arms. Frequently the southerners were escorted to the train station by their northern friends, knowing if they met again it could well be on opposite sides of a battlefield. On the morning of April 13, 1861, following the first attack by the Confederacy on Fort Sumter, a group of northern students raised the stars and stripes over Nassau Hall. Southern students demonstrated on the front lawn and President John Maclean Jr. had the flag removed. He and his decision were widely condemned in the northern press, the flag was reinstated, and the southern students still on campus joined in a ceremony to salute it one last time before they, too, left to go home.

Later that year, a northern student expressed sympathy for secession and three other students from northern states dragged him from his bed and held him under the water pump behind Nassau Hall. The incident was widely publicized, and Maclean and the faculty suspended the three students. But the students were treated as heroes by the town and their fellow students, and all three later served in the Union army.

According to historian Thomas Jefferson Wertenbaker, of the 88 students in the Class of 1861 who began their senior year in the fall of 1860, only 45 remained on campus to take final exams in the spring. Twenty from the class served in the Union army and 21 in the Confederate army. While total enrollment in 1861 had been 314, in 1862 it was only 221. In all, more than 600 Princeton students and alumni fought in the Civil War and 86 died. Of those 86, 47 fought for the Confederacy and 39 for the Union. Princeton contributed at least eight generals to the Confederacy and four to the Union.

In an essay for the Princeton and Slavery Project, W. Barksdale Maynard '88 describes what happened at the end of the war:

> When Richmond fell in the first days of April 1865 . . . the African American troops who marched into the stunned city were commanded by . . . Colonel Lucius Warren 1860. Back on campus, the defeat of the rebel stronghold was celebrated with a torchlight parade and bonfire. After General Lee's surrender . . . Princeton students celebrated with bonfires at the Big Cannon. But soon after, college buildings were draped in black for the martyred Lincoln, and "WE MOURN OUR LOSS" was etched on a Nassau Hall windowpane. The president's family doctor, Robert King Stone 1842, had stood at his deathbed. A mournful student body marched to the new Princeton Junction station to see the funeral train roll by.

Shortly after the end of the war, alumni classes began taking steps toward reconciliation, and well into the twentieth century efforts were being made to repair any continuing divisions within the alumni body. In 1924 the University held the biennial convention of the Princeton Alumni Association in Atlanta, and a week later the association announced a donation of $1,000 toward the construction of a memorial at Stone Mountain near Atlanta depicting Confederate leaders, including Robert E. Lee, the son of Revolutionary War hero Henry "Light-Horse Harry" Lee III 1773.

On Alumni Day in 1920 the University dedicated the memorial atrium in Nassau Hall, with the names of alumni who died in World War I engraved in its marble walls. When the names of those who had been identified as its Civil War dead were added beginning in 1923, President John Grier Hibben rejected the idea of grouping them according to their Union and Confederate affiliations, and instead the names were placed alphabetically, making Princeton's memorial perhaps the only one in the nation to list the dead from both sides without indicating the cause for which they died. In the words of the Princeton and Slavery Project, "Well into the twentieth century, then, Princeton sought to remain a congenial home for northerners and southerners alike, emphasizing the sacrifice that drew its students together rather than the politics that pushed them apart."

Seventy names are listed in the atrium, and for years Orange Key guides told visitors that half died for the north and half for the south. Research by the University Archives and the Princeton and Slavery Project found that the correct number of war dead was 86, with more dying for the south (47) than for the north (39). Of the 86 Princetonians who died fighting in the war, 62 are included in the list on the wall, leaving 24 who are not listed; for eight of the names on the wall there is no conclusive proof that they fought (2) or died (6) during the war.

CLASSICS, THE DEPARTMENT OF. Princeton's Classics department investigates the history, language, literature, and thought of ancient Greece and Rome. It draws on the perspectives of multiple disciplines to understand and imagine the diversity of these civilizations over almost 2,000 years, as well as to reflect on what the classical past has meant to later ages, including our own.

Although Princeton's Classics department was not formally established until 1904, Latin and Greek were central to the earliest Princeton students' lives from the moment they considered matriculating. At the University's founding in 1746, the trustees based admission on students' knowledge of Latin and Greek. To know Latin and Greek meant knowing formal rhetoric, an essential element of speaking in public, and all students receiving degrees in Princeton's early years were expected to present model orations, in both Latin and Greek, on such themes as governance, vice, and virtue.

During the remainder of the eighteenth and throughout the nineteenth century, admission to the University continued to require prior study of Latin and Greek. Once enrolled, all students had to read Latin and Greek authors during their first years of study. Beginning in 1873, applicants for the newly introduced degree of Bachelor of Science could graduate without taking Greek. In 1919 Greek was dropped as a requirement for the Bachelor of Arts and applicants for the Bachelor of Science were also relieved of Latin. In 1930 the Latin requirement was abolished for Bachelor of Arts candidates.

In actuality, during Princeton's first 150 years applicants' knowledge of the ancient languages on arrival (and even upon leaving) was uneven, as were the skills of their teachers. Study of the two languages was little more than memorization, translation, and recitation.

Under President James McCosh, knowledge of the ancient world became an organized field of study, with its own library, seminar, course of study, and named professorships. Prominent classicists of his era included Samuel Winans, a future dean of the faculty, who became professor of Greek in 1883; Andrew Fleming West 1874, later the founding dean of the graduate school, who became professor of Latin in 1883 and professor of pedagogics in 1885; and John Westcott, later chair of the department, who became professor of Latin in 1885. The history of the modern department begins with these three.

Under their leadership, new faculty arrived on campus with advanced degrees. One was Allan Marquand 1874, who returned in 1881 with a PhD from Johns Hopkins to teach Latin and logic. In 1882 he helped to create the department of Art and Archaeology, thereby beginning a longstanding close collaboration between that discipline and Classics. At the time, serious students of the classics would often go on to study at American archaeological institutes in Rome or Athens after graduation. They might come back to the US for a brief stint of teaching, then revisit Europe to enroll in doctoral programs, often in Germany, before finally returning with PhDs in hand to teach at Princeton.

One such student was David Magie 1897, grandson of President McCosh. Magie returned with his PhD from Germany at a particularly auspicious moment in the life of the University. Student enrollment and the number of faculty had increased through the late 1890s. At the turn of the century the University moved toward founding a graduate school, and West was put in charge of establishing a research library for a new classics seminar to be housed in recently constructed East Pyne Hall. President Woodrow Wilson created 11 new departments in 1904, with Classics among them, and he introduced the new preceptorial system in 1905. Of the 49 newly hired preceptors, nearly one quarter were classicists, including Magie.

The new preceptors were credited with invigorating the teaching of classics and bringing the department national renown. However, even into midcentury, Wilson's call for the department to reform its course of study and address its "sequence and system" went unanswered. Instead, course offerings reflected the individual interests of the faculty and there was no clear program of classics as a subject of instruction and research.

After World War II a more coherent program emerged. The war, the GI bill, and the gradual arrival of a more diverse student body compelled many universities, including Princeton, to rethink old approaches. Whitney Oates 1925 *1931, chair of the department after 1945, instituted a program to attract veterans (and later women) to do graduate studies. With this move, Princeton became the incubator for what later grew into the national Woodrow Wilson Fellowship Program. (The program removed Wilson's name in 2020.) Oates also directed an interdisciplinary Special Program in the Humanities, the forerunner of the Humanities Council.

Princeton's 16th president, Robert Goheen, was one of the first new Woodrow Wilson graduate fellows when he returned to campus following his service in World War II. His dissertation was a model of new critical methods for the study of ancient literature and classical scholarship. His leadership during his presidency in bringing undergraduate coeducation to Princeton in 1969 ushered in a new academic climate that directly benefited the Classics department. Among the classicists of the early coeducational class of 1973 was S. Georgia Nugent, who returned to Princeton to teach after receiving her PhD from Cornell, becoming Princeton's first undergraduate alumna to hold a full-time faculty appointment at the University. In 1976 Janet Martin became the department's first tenured female faculty member, followed a year later by Froma Zeitlin, who was awarded a Princeton honorary degree in 2016.

By the 1980s the Classics department was the home of a wide range of research interests in addition to language study, including semiotics and French structuralism in the study of Greek literature, the practices of scholarship and education in antiquity, Greek historiography, and Roman law. By the 1990s and beyond, the transformation of the study of textual criticism and the spotlight on philology, as much as intellectual history, yoked the department with Comparative Literature. Computers came to be used in the classroom as well as in the digitalization of classical texts.

Today, the department concentrates on Greek and Latin languages and literatures and Greek and

Roman history. It has close ties to a number of programs and departments, including the program in the Ancient World, which links it to the departments of History, Religion, and Art and Archaeology; the program in Classical Philosophy, which links it to the department of Philosophy; the department of Comparative Literature; the Stanley J. Seeger Center for Hellenic Studies; the program in Linguistics; and several interdepartmental committees. Members of its faculty have strong interests in drama, epic and lyric poetry, the ancient novel, ancient critical theory, medicine, philosophy, historiography, linguistics, social history, and material culture.

Students engage with the cultures of ancient Greece and Rome to understand better how classical antiquity has shaped and continues to shape the present. They also build a wide range of intellectual and practical skills: how to make sense of and learn from foreign languages and distant cultures; how to analyze an argument, interrogate a long-standing assumption, and see the ancient roots of contemporary concepts; and how to develop, communicate, and defend their ideas. The department involves students in a millennia-long conversation about value, justice, beauty, power, and the human condition—what Socrates famously called the examined life.

CLEVELAND, GROVER, and his wife first visited Princeton in October 1896, when he addressed the sesquicentennial celebration. At that time Cleveland began his friendship with Andrew Fleming West 1874, the chief organizer of the celebration, who later became dean of the graduate school. The Clevelands liked Princeton so much they decided to live there at the close of his second term as president. With West's help, Cleveland arranged for the purchase of a colonial mansion surrounded by spacious grounds at 15 Hodge Road which he named "Westland."

The Clevelands moved into Westland in March 1897, and soon took a central place of honor in the community. During their visit at the sesquicentennial they had reviewed a torchlight procession of alumni and students from the steps of Nassau Hall; one of the signs the undergraduates carried read "Grover, send your boys to Princeton." This invitation was somewhat premature since the three Cleveland children were all girls. But the next fall, the Clevelands' first son, Richard Folsom, was born, and the undergraduates welcomed his arrival with an oracular announcement on the campus bulletin board that he would enter Princeton with the Class of 1919 and play center on a championship football team all four years.*

Westland became the destination for undergraduate processions after triumphs in athletics or debating or other times of student jubilation. Cleveland would come out on the porch and respond with a few pleasant words and sometimes even lead a locomotive cheer. The students paraded to his house every March 18 to cheer him on his birthday, and when he reached 70 they gave him a silver loving cup, which Professor John Grier Hibben 1882 *1893 presented on their behalf. "I feel young at 70," Cleveland told them, "because I have here breathed the atmosphere of vigorous youth."

The ex-president had many acquaintances and some close friends on the faculty. West was the closest and was a frequent caller at Westland. Hibben also went there often. Paul van Dyke 1881, the historian, was Cleveland's favorite hunting and fishing companion. Cleveland befriended John Finley when he came to Princeton as professor of politics and built a house for his use in a corner of his spacious grounds.

Cleveland presided at Princeton-Yale debates and other campus meetings, and at Commencement each year he walked at the head of the academic procession at the side of the president of the university. In 1899, Henry Stafford Little 1844 founded a public lectureship, stipulating that Cleveland should be its incumbent as long as he lived. Cleveland accepted and lectured once or twice each year before capacity audiences in Alexander Hall on such subjects as the Independence of the Executive, the Venezuelan Boundary Controversy, and Government in the Chicago Strike.

In the fall of 1901 Cleveland was elected a trustee and took an active part in University affairs until his death. He thought it "a serious thing to be a trustee of Princeton" and gave painstaking attention to all the details of the operation of the University that came before the board. He spoke for the trustees at Woodrow Wilson's inauguration in 1902 and at the dedication of the Faculty Room in Nassau Hall in 1906. In 1904 he was appointed chair of the trustee

---

* This prophecy was fulfilled in part. Richard Cleveland *did* enter, and did graduate, with the Class of 1919. But he played football only one year—he was fullback on his freshman team which beat the Yale freshmen—and thereafter concentrated on track. However, his son, Thomas Grover Cleveland '49, was a varsity guard for three years, in two of which the team beat Harvard and Yale.

committee on the graduate school and became a staunch advocate of the plan for its development; he wrote a fellow trustee that it was "laying the foundation of Princeton's largest element of future greatness." He sided with West in his dispute with Wilson about the location of the graduate college. Cleveland also opposed Wilson's quad plan, in part because he feared it would delay realization of the graduate college. He sought to influence Andrew Carnegie to contribute to the University's endowment, and it was during one of Carnegie's visits to Westland that the idea of creating a lake for Princeton was first broached.

Cleveland died at Westland on June 24, 1908. The simple funeral services at the house were attended by the family, President Theodore Roosevelt, others eminent in the government, and Princeton friends. He was buried in the Princeton Cemetery.

Cleveland's association with Princeton is commemorated by the Cleveland Tower of the graduate college, erected in 1913 by popular subscription: "a tower of strength and beauty," ex-President William Howard Taft said at its dedication, "and most expressive of his character."

CLIO HALL, originally the home of the Cliosophic Society, was built in 1893 at the same time as its identical neighbor to the east, Whig Hall. The Cliosophic Society had been established in 1770 as a successor to the short-lived Well-Meaning Club (founded in 1765). Housed at first in Nassau Hall, and then in what is now Stanhope Hall, the Cliosophic Society and its counterpart American Whig Society paid for the construction of two neoclassical halls made of wood, stucco, brick, and white paint along the south edge of Cannon Green, which they moved into in 1838.

The current marble halls were commissioned by the University in 1893 and were similarly designed in the Ionic style of a Greek temple, although they were larger, closer together, and much more fire-resistant than their predecessors. Inside, both buildings were designed to have libraries, reading rooms, gathering spaces, and third-floor senate chambers. When the original halls were first built, their main meeting rooms were the largest indoor spaces on campus outside of Nassau Hall.

After the Cliosophic Society merged with the American Whig Society in 1928 to form what became known as Whig-Clio and moved into Whig Hall, Clio Hall was used for a variety of purposes and became for a time the home of the department of Music. In 1963, upon the completion of the Woolworth Center for Musical Studies, Clio Hall's interior was renovated, and it was then used by personnel services (later human resources), career services, offices for student agencies and student employment, and other administrative offices. In 2005, Clio Hall was again renovated, this time to accommodate the administrative offices of the graduate school and a reception space for the office of admission (relocated in 2020 to 36 University Place), and to make the building accessible from McCosh Walk.

In October 1969, shortly after female undergraduates had arrived on campus for the first time, two bronze Bengal tiger sculptures, one male and one female, were installed on the plaza (Adams Mall) between Whig and Clio halls. The sculptures were designed by the artist Bruce Moore and funded by a gift from Hugh Trumbell Adams '35.

COEDUCATION. Princeton's first female students arrived on campus in 1942 when 23 women were admitted to a government-sponsored course during World War II on making maps for the military from aerial photographs.

In 1961 Sabra Follett Meservey *64 *66, a faculty member at Douglass College in New Brunswick who lived in Princeton, became the first woman to be admitted as a graduate student when she was accepted into the department of Oriental Studies. Two years later T'sai-Ying Cheng *63 *64 became the first woman to earn a Princeton degree when she received her master's in Biochemical Sciences, and in 1964 she became the first woman to receive a Princeton PhD.

After admitting Meservey in 1961, the University admitted eight women (including Cheng) as graduate students in 1962, although it took pains to explain that it was admitting "only women for whom it is particularly and peculiarly appropriate to do work at Princeton." By 1968, when a cap on the admission of women was lifted, there were 56 female graduate students; a year later 200 women were enrolled out of a total graduate student enrollment of about 1,500; and by 1976 there were 367 women.

In 1963 the University created a Critical Languages program that allowed students from other colleges, including women, to become visiting undergraduate students at Princeton for a year or two to study such languages as Chinese, Japanese, Russian, and Arabic. Five women were among the first Critical Language students (or, as the male students called them, "Critters"); they took regular courses on campus with men, but lived in a rooming house off campus.

By the mid-1960s there was serious discussion among the University's senior leadership about whether Princeton should admit women undergraduates. In a May 1967 interview with the *Daily Princetonian*, President Robert Goheen said that, in his view, it was "inevitable that, at some point in the future, Princeton is going to move into the education of women." The only questions, he said, were those of strategy, priority, and timing.

The questions of timing and strategy included whether to aim for 1,000–1,200 "ladies" in residence in five years (what he called a crash effort), or to expand much more slowly by taking over local boarding houses and gradually expanding over a 10-year period. Either way, he said, Princeton would go into coeducation without reducing the number of male students.

Goheen seemed to be leaning more toward "coordinate" education, a model under which a separate women's college (e.g., Sarah Lawrence) might be persuaded to relocate to the University's lands just across Lake Carnegie (along the lines of discussions that were taking place at Yale about a merger with Vassar), but he acknowledged that campus sentiment was moving toward full coeducation. (The coordinate model had a Princeton antecedent from 1887 to 1897, when Evelyn College for Women was located just east of the campus near the intersection of Nassau and Harrison Streets.)

In June 1967 Goheen obtained trustee approval for a comprehensive study of the desirability and feasibility of undergraduate coeducation. That study, under the leadership of economics professor Gardner Patterson, recommended 1,000–1,200 women on campus within the next decade. Goheen said the report offered evidence that "the presence of talented young women at Princeton would enhance the total educational experience and contribute to a better balanced social and intellectual life." It also would help "sustain Princeton's ability to attract outstanding students" (both men and women), and would provide a Princeton education for women who would be expected "to make worthy contributions to the national life."

The major constraint was housing for this number of additional students, a need first met by converting the University-owned Princeton Inn hotel into a residential college (now Forbes College) and through a gift from Laurance Rockefeller '32 that enabled the construction of Spelman Halls.

In January 1969 a special trustee committee chaired by Harold Helm 1920 recommended that the University undertake the education of women at the undergraduate level and the trustees agreed. By a vote of 24–8, they approved coeducation "in principle," but they adopted no specific plan and set no date. With women applying on the chance that Princeton would open its doors that fall, the Admission office prepared two sets of letters; one set conveying admission decisions, and the other explaining that Princeton would not be admitting women that year.

In April the trustees voted to admit women undergraduates beginning that fall, and the first set of admission letters was mailed. Following the decision, the *Daily Princetonian* congratulated the trustees on their "courage, foresight, and ability to change with the times," and the radio station WPRB concluded its broadcast of the news with the *Hallelujah Chorus*.

In fall 1969 the University enrolled 101 female first-year students and a total of 70 female transfer students, most of whom entered as sophomores and juniors. Nine of the transfer students were women who studied at Princeton in 1968–69 under the Critical Languages program; by staying on campus for their senior year they met the University's requirement that students had to be enrolled on campus for at least two years to receive a Princeton degree, and thus were able to graduate in the Class of 1970 as Princeton's first undergraduate alumnae.

Four years later there were 1,000 women undergraduates on campus. In 1974 the trustees adopted a policy of "equal access" that allowed men and women to compete for admission without guaranteeing a specific number of men, and by 1976 the undergraduate body numbered 1,395 women and 2,965 men. (In 2017, 50.5 percent of the students admitted to the Class of 2021 were women, the first time Princeton admitted more women than men.)

Among the alumnae in the Class of 1970 were five Asian and Asian-American women, including Sue-Jean Lee Suettinger '70, the first woman cast in a Triangle Club show, and Lynn Nagasako '70, the first woman to join an eating club. The Class of 1970 also included the first female member of the student government, Susan Craig '70, later a Princeton trustee. The Class of 1971 included the first Black women to graduate: Linda Blackburn '71, Terrell Nash '71, and Carla Wilson '71.

In 1973 Marsha Levy-Warren '73 became the first female Pyne Prize recipient and the first female young alumni trustee. The Pyne Prize recipient three years later, Sonia Sotomayor '76, became the first Hispanic woman on the US Supreme Court, and the young alumni trustee elected that year, Nancy Peretsman '76, went on to serve a total of 24 years on the board.

Other early milestones included the first Marshall Scholarship winner (Princeton's only winner that year), Annalyn Swan '73; the first woman Fulbright recipient, Dinah Seiver '73; the first women valedictorian and salutatorian, Cynthia Chase '75 and Lisa Siegman '75; the first woman Rhodes Scholar, Suzanne Perles '75 (one of the first 13 American women chosen when the Rhodes Scholar program became coeducational); the first woman president of Whig-Clio, Tina Ravitz '76; the first woman eating club president (Campus Club), Eva Lerner-Lam '76; the first Princeton female athlete to win 12 varsity letters, Emily Goodfellow '76; the first woman senior class president, Valerie Bell '77; the first woman to chair the *Daily Princetonian*, Anne Mackay-Smith '80; the first woman ROTC cadet commander, Kimberlee Thompson '81; the first woman Honor Committee chair, Barbara Barrow '81; the first woman student government (USG) president, Michelle Woods '84; the first woman to chair the Alumni Council, Dorothy Bedford '78; and the first woman to receive the Woodrow Wilson Award, Wendy Kopp '89.

During the first year of undergraduate coeducation (1969–70), all women students lived in one dormitory, Pyne Hall, which was outfitted with lounges, a kitchen, a laundry room, additional toilet facilities, and electronic locks. The administration spent $70,000 buying new furniture for the women, $10,000 changing plumbing, and $55,000 relighting half the campus. It expanded staffing for the programs in Teacher Preparation and the Creative Arts.

Halcyone "Halcy" Bohen, who joined the staff in 1969 and served for eight years as assistant dean of students with special responsibility for women, later recalled that when the University hired choreographer Ze'eva Cohen to teach dance, 60 students signed up for her first class and 50 of them were men. In 1970 Cecelia Hodges Drewry became an assistant dean of the college, one of only 18 Black administrators on campus.

Other early initiatives included the creation and expansion of extracurricular opportunities (the first female a cappella group, the Tigerlilies, began in 1971) and the establishment of support organizations, including the Women*s Center in 1971 and the Society of Women Engineers in 1973.

Women's athletic teams were formed (the first six to be awarded varsity status were basketball, crew, field hockey, squash, swimming, and tennis) and many had exceptional success. In 1970, Merrily Dean Baker arrived as the director of physical education for women (she also coached field hockey, and later gymnastics), and in 1973 she was named associate director of athletics for physical education and women's athletics. In 2014 one of Princeton's most accomplished women athletes, Mollie Marcoux Samaan '91, was named Princeton's first female director of athletics. By 2020 women's teams had won more than 200 Ivy League championships (nearly one-third of all women's titles), along with 22 individual and 33 team national championships.

In 1987, after the USG, led by its president, Cece Rey Hallisey '88 (later a young alumni trustee), passed a resolution endorsed by the Alumni Council, the University officially changed the male-specific verses in its alma mater, "Old Nassau."

The first woman dean of students, Adele Simmons, was appointed in 1972, and the first women deans of the college (Joan Stern Girgus) and of the graduate school (Nina Garsoian) were appointed in 1977. A program in Women's Studies (now the program in Gender and Sexuality Studies*) began in 1982, with anthropology professor Kay Warren *74 as its director. By the end of 1970, nine of the then-13 eating clubs were coeducational, but it took more than 20 years and a lawsuit by Sally Frank '80 for all the clubs to admit women.

By the mid-1980s, Princeton had evolved from an all-male institution that had gone co-ed to a coeducational institution that had once been all-male. There were still ample vestiges of its all-male history, but there were also growing numbers of students who applied and arrived on campus without knowing that history. By 2006 almost equal numbers of men and women were graduating, but, consistent with patterns at other colleges, women were underrepresented in the principal leadership roles in student organizations.

A committee on undergraduate women's leadership appointed in 2009 by President Shirley Tilghman

---

* The Women's Studies program was renamed Gender and Sexuality Studies (GSS) in 2011 to reflect the expanded reach of teaching and scholarship in the field. GSS offers undergraduate and graduate certificates to students interested in the complex articulation of gender and sexuality with race, ethnicity, class, disability, religion, nationality, and other intersections of identity, power, and politics. In 2020 professor of religion and African American studies Wallace Best was named the first African American and first male director of the program.

and chaired by Princeton professor and former Duke University president Nannerl Keohane found "an upward trajectory of women in highly visible leadership positions at Princeton in the 1970s, '80s and '90s, including Undergraduate Student Government president, student newspaper editor, Honor Committee chair and class president, with the numbers rising across the decades from six women in such positions to 18 to 22," but that in the 2000s the number had receded to 12. To cite just one example: of the 54 graduating seniors who have been elected young alumni trustees since the position was established with the Class of 1968, 21 have been women, but no women were elected between 1997 and 2007.

The leadership committee, composed of 18 students, faculty, and staff, made recommendations to reverse this trend. One measure of its success: of the 14 young alumni trustees elected between 2008 and 2021, eight were women. In 2018 nine of the then-11 eating clubs elected women as presidents.

For a fuller account of women at Princeton, please see the entry on that topic.

COLLEGE AND UNIVERSITY FOUNDERS. Princeton graduates were founders or first presidents of the following institutions*:

Austin College, Sherman, Texas

Daniel Baker 1815 was chiefly responsible for securing its charter in 1849 and was its president from 1853 to 1857. The trustees proposed naming the college for him, but he declined the honor.

Brown University, Providence, Rhode Island

James Manning 1762 was its first president. Nassau Hall was the model for its first building.

Dickinson College, Carlisle, Pennsylvania

Begun as a school in 1773, it was chartered as a college in 1783. Benjamin Rush 1760 was chiefly responsible for securing the charter, for naming the college after his fellow patriot, John Dickinson, and for bringing its first president from Scotland.

Hamilton College, Clinton, New York

Samuel Kirkland 1765, with the help of Alexander Hamilton, founded the Hamilton-Oneida Academy in 1793; in 1812 it was reorganized as Hamilton College.

Hampden-Sydney College, Hampden-Sydney, Virginia

In 1776 Samuel Stanhope Smith 1769 founded and became first rector of Hampden-Sydney Academy, which was chartered as a college in 1783. When Smith returned to Princeton as professor of moral philosophy in 1779 (later to serve as Princeton's president), his brother John Blair Smith 1773 succeeded him at Hampden-Sydney. Five of the original Hampden-Sydney trustees were Princeton graduates, among them James Madison 1771.

Hobart College, Geneva, New York

John Henry Hobart 1793, Protestant Episcopal Bishop of New York, led a movement in 1822 to reorganize Geneva Academy, begun in 1796, as Geneva College. In 1852 the college was renamed in his honor.

Keller School of Management, Downers Grove, Illinois

In 1973, Dennis Keller '63 and Ronald Taylor cofounded the Keller School of Management. In 1977 it became the first for-profit institution to be accredited by the North Central Association of Colleges and Schools. In 1987 it acquired the DeVry Institute of Technology and the two schools combined to form DeVry Inc. with Keller as chair of the board. The schools ultimately merged to form DeVry University and its Keller School of Management.

University of Medicine and Dentistry of New Jersey, Newark, New Jersey

Stanley Bergen Jr. '51 was the founding president of the University of Medicine and Dentistry of New Jersey (UMDNJ), serving in that role from 1971 to 1988. He was awarded a Princeton honorary degree in 1995.

University of North Carolina, Chapel Hill, North Carolina

In 1789, as a member of the state legislature, William Richardson Davie 1776 drafted and introduced a bill that established "the first state

---

* While John Miller Dickey, the founder and first president of the country's first degree-granting Historically Black College or University (HBCU)—established outside Philadelphia in 1854 as Ashmun Institute and renamed Lincoln University in 1866—was not a Princeton graduate, but rather a graduate of neighboring Princeton Theological Seminary, Lincoln was known for much of its first century as "the Black Princeton," partly because of the large number of Princeton graduates on its faculty, and partly because of an uninterrupted succession of Princeton alumni who served as its president from 1865 to 1945: Isaac Rendell 1852, John Rendell 1870, William Johnson 1888, and Walter Wright 1892.

university in the United States to open its doors to students." Later he was chiefly responsible for locating the university and providing for its future development. Joseph Caldwell 1791 was the first president.

Ohio University, Athens, Ohio

Ohio University was chartered in 1804 and opened in 1808. Jacob Lindly 1800 was the first member of its faculty and administered its affairs until 1822. Its first two buildings were erected under his direction; one of them, according to tradition, was patterned after Nassau Hall.

Transylvania College, Lexington, Kentucky

John Todd 1749 and Caleb Wallace 1770 were influential in securing a charter and endowment for Transylvania Seminary in 1783, and David Rice 1761 was the first chair of its board of trustees. It became Transylvania University in 1798; since 1915 it has been called a college.

Tusculum College, Greenville, Tennessee

Hezekiah Balch 1766 was the first president of Greenville College in 1794. Samuel Doak 1775 founded Tusculum Academy, later chartered as Tusculum College, in 1819. After the Civil War, the two colleges merged and came to be known as Tusculum College.

Union College, Schenectady, New York

Dirck Romeyn 1765 provided the leadership for founding Schenectady Academy in 1785 and for its reorganization as Union College in 1795. John Blair Smith 1773 was the first president of the college.

United Nations University, Tokyo, Japan

James Hester '46, who served as president of New York University from 1962 to 1975, became the first rector of the United Nations University at its founding in September 1975.

Washington and Jefferson College, Washington, Pennsylvania

John MacMillan 1772 and Thaddeus Dod 1773 founded Washington Academy, later chartered as Washington College, in 1787. John Watson 1797 was the first president of Jefferson College (1802). The two colleges merged in 1865.

Washington and Lee University, Lexington, Virginia

Washington and Lee University began in 1749 as Augusta Academy; it was renamed Liberty Hall in 1776, chartered as Liberty Hall Academy in 1782, renamed Washington Academy (following a gift from George Washington) in 1798, and then renamed Washington College in 1813 and Washington and Lee University (following Robert E. Lee's presidency) in 1871. William Graham 1773 was in charge of the institution from 1774 to 1796 and was its first president after its incorporation.

COLLEGE OF NEW JERSEY was Princeton's legal name during its first 150 years, although the College was usually referred to as Nassau or Nassau Hall or Princeton College after it moved to Princeton in 1756. In the 1860s the baseball team used the name "Nassau," and starting in 1870 all athletic teams were designated "Princeton."

On October 22, 1896, on the 150th anniversary of the signing of the College's first charter, President Francis Patton announced that "from this moment what heretofore for 150 years has been known as the College of New Jersey shall in all future time be known as Princeton University."

One hundred years later, the college then known as Trenton State College in nearby Ewing Township, New Jersey, adopted the name of the College of New Jersey (TCNJ). Founded in 1855 as the first teacher training school in New Jersey, TCNJ is today a highly regarded multi-purpose public institution; in 2018 Princeton presented an honorary degree to TCNJ's then-retiring president, R. Barbara Gitenstein. Her successor, Kathryn Foster, received her Princeton PhD in 1993.

COLORS. Princeton's use of orange and black began soon after the Civil War. On April 5, 1866, a freshman named George Ward 1869 observed at a class meeting that, unlike other colleges, Princeton had no distinctive colors. He suggested orange since King William the Third of the House of Nassau (after whom Nassau Hall was named) was also Prince of Orange. His classmates agreed, but the idea failed to win approval in the other classes.

Ward persisted, and on June 26, 1867, when his teammates in the Class of 1869 Base Ball Club assembled at Princeton Junction on their way to play Yale, he provided them with badges of orange ribbon with '69

B.B.C. printed in black ink. The team wore the badges on the train to New York and on a steamer to New Haven; came from behind in the ninth inning to win the game 19–18; and continued to wear the badges that evening when they had dinner with their opponents.

More general use came a year later on October 12, 1868, when, in response to a petition from all four undergraduate classes, the faculty voted to permit students "to adopt and wear as the College Badge an orange colored Ribbon bearing upon it the word 'Princeton.'" Two weeks later the badges were much in evidence at the inauguration of President James McCosh.

Ward had suggested orange, and the pairing with black came about only as a result of the color of the printer's ink. In the fall of 1873 black took on more official status when a freshman named William Libbey Jr. 1877 wore a necktie made of yellow and black silk that he had seen advertised in England as "the Duke of Nassau's colors."

The following spring, Libbey arranged through his father for a silk mill in Paterson, New Jersey, to manufacture a thousand yards of orange and black ribbon for use at a July 15, 1874, intercollegiate regatta in Saratoga, New York. The members of the freshman crew used the ribbon as hatbands and the remaining supply was sold at a local hotel as "Princeton's colors."

This set the stage for use of orange and black by Princeton's other athletic teams, and for a song, "The Orange and the Black," that was written by a junior and arranged by a senior in 1888—a song that remains a favorite today.

> Although Yale has always favored the violet's
>   dark blue,
> And the many sons of Harvard to the crimson
>   rose are true,
> We will own the lilies slender, nor honor shall
>   they lack,
> While the Tiger stands defender of the
>   Orange and the Black.

In 1896 the trustees adopted orange and black as the official colors for academic gowns despite a plea from Professor Allan Marquand 1874 that Princeton's colors should be changed to orange and blue, which were the true colors of the House of Nassau. Marquand made a strong pitch for his proposal on aesthetic as well as historical grounds, but by then the tradition of orange and black was too well established to be overturned.

COMMENCEMENT, the ceremony at which degrees are formally conferred, marks the end of the academic year and the beginning of life after Princeton for those graduating. As early as the fourteenth century, at Cambridge University, a student who had passed the requisite examinations was said to "commence Bachelor of Arts (or Master or Doctor)," and the occasion when the degree was presented was called commencement.

At Princeton's first Commencement, held in 1748 in the Newark "meeting-house" where President Aaron Burr Sr. was pastor, seven persons took degrees: Jonathan Belcher, the royal governor of the province of New Jersey, was awarded an honorary master's degree, and six students received bachelor's degrees.

These few "commencers" were the objects of much oratory. At the morning exercises (one of the trustees reported in a New York newspaper), the clerk of the board read the 3,700-word royal charter that Governor Belcher had granted the College. In the afternoon, President Burr delivered an "elegant Oration in the Latin Tongue" that lasted three quarters of an hour, and, after public disputations in Latin by the six candidates and the conferring of degrees, the student salutatorian spoke in Latin for half an hour, after which the president prayed in English and dismissed the assembly. These proceedings gave "universal Satisfaction, even the Unlearned being pleased with [their] Solemnity and Decorum."

After the College moved to Princeton in 1756, commencements were held in the prayer hall in Nassau Hall (now the Faculty Room) until 1764 when more adequate space became available in the First Presbyterian Church's new building. Latin continued to be the language of choice, but, according to contemporary newspaper accounts, the proceedings were enlivened by an occasional speech in English and by music. At the 1760 Commencement, Benjamin Rush "in a very sprightly and entertaining Manner delivered an ingenious English Harangue in Praise of Oratory," and the graduating seniors sang two compositions by President Samuel Davies.

Under President John Witherspoon commencements took on a revolutionary flavor. In 1770 the entire graduating class wore American-made clothes, and in 1771 (when James Madison graduated) Hugh Henry Brackenridge read a prophetic poem on "The Rising Glory of America," which his classmate Philip Freneau and he had written. The Commencement of 1783 was made memorable by the presence of George

Washington, the foreign ministers of France and Holland, seven signers of the Declaration of Independence, nine signers of the Articles of Confederation, 11 future signers of the Constitution, and many members of the Continental Congress, then meeting in Princeton.

For almost a century, commencements took place in the fall. Coming at the end of the harvest season, the occasion became a public holiday for the entire countryside, and speakers at the exercises in the church (as President John Maclean Jr. recalled) had to compete with the crowds on the street outside "drinking, fiddling and dancing, playing for pennies, and testing the speed of their horses." In 1844, on petition of the faculty, the trustees advanced the commencement ceremonies to June.

Exercises continued to be held in the First Church until 1892, when Alexander Hall was completed. Alexander was outgrown in turn, and since 1922 the June commencements have been held in front of Nassau Hall except when rain forced the ceremonies indoors or the COVID-19 pandemic necessitated other arrangements.

In February of 1920 there was a special graduation ceremony for returning veterans in the classes of 1918 and 1919, and during World War II there were a number of modifications: in 1943 there were four commencements (January, May, September, and October) to accommodate students who had accelerated their studies before leaving for military service; in 1944 there were seven ceremonies, including three for participants in the Navy V-12 program; and in 1945 there were three, including an October ceremony in President Harold Dodds' office.

The modern commencement season officially lasts almost a week; in addition, a number of campus-based affinity groups hold special ceremonies for their members in the days and weeks prior to Commencement. Alumni and seniors take part in reunion activities on the Thursday through Saturday of the week prior to Commencement, culminating in the alumni parade—the P-rade—on Saturday afternoon. Seniors march in their class jackets at the end of the P-rade, and as they gather in front of the reviewing stand, they are officially welcomed into the alumni ranks.

For undergraduates, Sunday is devoted to the Baccalaureate service in the afternoon and the senior prom at Jadwin Gym in the evening. Monday includes Class Day exercises, departmental receptions, and at night the senior step sing on the stairs of Blair Hall. Class Day dates back to 1856; in 1898 it was described as "a day over which the graduating class has full charge and which we run to suit ourselves."

Weather permitting, Class Day takes place on Cannon Green, immediately behind Nassau Hall; the program features student speakers, remarks by the president of the University, the conferring of awards, the presentation to the class of a symbolic key to the campus, the induction of honorary class members, and a talk by an outside speaker selected by the class. In recent years most speakers have come from the worlds of entertainment or public affairs.

On Monday afternoon, graduate students receiving masters and doctoral degrees attend a Hooding Ceremony on Cannon Green where they are presented with hoods that signify their degree and their discipline; they wear their hoods the next day at Commencement.

The Commencement ceremony begins with an academic procession that is led by a member of the faculty who serves as chief marshal. The procession consists of advanced degree candidates, graduating seniors, faculty, senior administrators, trustees, award-winners, and invited guests, including the president of the Alumni Association, the mayor of Princeton, and the heads of the Institute for Advanced Study and Princeton Theological Seminary. Participants in the procession wear caps, gowns, and hoods, brightened by the colors of Princeton and many other universities. Faculty marshals wear distinctive orange gowns and black sixteenth-century caps. A faculty member designated the "mace bearer" carries the ceremonial mace that was given to the University by the town of Princeton in 1956 to celebrate the 200th anniversary of the opening of Nassau Hall.

The ceremony itself is relatively brief. One graduating senior delivers a salutatory address in Latin (with students prompted when to laugh, groan, hiss, and applaud) and another delivers the valedictory address; bachelor's, master's and doctoral degrees are conferred in Latin by the president on behalf of the trustees; prizes are presented to four New Jersey secondary school teachers and to four Princeton faculty members who have been selected to receive the President's Distinguished Teaching award; honorary degree citations are read by a trustee selected to be University Orator and the degrees are conferred; the president makes remarks; and following a benediction the alma mater, "Old Nassau," is sung.

All told, the ceremonies usually last just over an hour, although abbreviated scenarios are followed in inclement weather. Jadwin Gym is the fallback if severe and dangerous weather forces the ceremonies indoors, but every effort is made to stay outside if at all possible; in the event of rain, a canopy is erected over the platform that is constructed each year in front of Nassau Hall for trustees, faculty, and other program participants; up to 10,000 ponchos are provided for all in attendance; and simulcast locations are available. The last indoor Commencement was in 1981.

Princeton does not have an outside speaker at Commencement except on the occasion of major anniversaries every 50 years when the President of the United States is invited to speak, as Grover Cleveland did in 1896, Harry Truman in 1946, and Bill Clinton in 1996.

Following Commencement, seniors receive their diplomas at their residential colleges and graduate students receive theirs on Cannon Green.

While the Commencement ceremony is steeped in tradition and carefully scripted, there are occasional unscripted moments. One occurred in 1999 when the salutatorian proposed marriage, in English, at the end of his Latin address (his proposal was accepted), and another occurred in 2018 when the valedictorian leaped off and then back on the stage during his address.

The 1970 Commencement departed from tradition in two respects: the eight women who graduated that day were the first to receive Princeton undergraduate degrees, and during the ceremony most members of the class wore "together for peace" armbands rather than caps and gowns. The 1970 Commencement is also remembered for the "high whining trill" of the 17-year cicadas, which was immortalized in the song "Day of the Locusts" by one of that year's honorary degree recipients, a later Nobel Laureate, Bob Dylan.

Fifty years later, the 2020 COVID-19 pandemic required the cancellation of Baccalaureate and Class Day, while the graduate student Hooding Ceremony took place virtually on Friday afternoon. On Sunday afternoon the University conducted a virtual Commencement which included many of the traditional elements of the ceremony: conferral of undergraduate and advanced degrees, the salutatory address (translated into English by on-screen captioning), the valedictory address (by Princeton's first Black valedictorian), the conferring of honorary degrees, remarks by the president, an invocation and benediction, and the singing of "Old Nassau."

Since that year's baccalaureate speaker, Maria Ressa '86, was unable to give her address in the chapel, she instead was invited to speak at Commencement. The ceremony concluded with a poem by Professor Tracy K. Smith, chair of the Lewis Center for the Arts and, from 2017–2019, Poet Laureate of the United States.

In 2020–21 graduate students remained on campus and undergraduates were invited to return for the spring semester. On May 16, 2021, a week earlier than usual because of the pandemic, the University conducted an in-person Commencement in Princeton Stadium with degree recipients, their guests (two each), and other participants masked and socially distanced. Portions of the ceremony were conducted virtually, including the introduction of honorary degree recipients, all of whom were New Jersey residents. The 2021 ROTC commissioning ceremony also took place in the stadium, while other commencement-related ceremonies, including Baccalaureate, Class Day, the Hooding Ceremony, and the cultural graduations for affinity groups, were conducted virtually.

COMPARATIVE LITERATURE, THE DEPARTMENT OF. When new departments encompassing Germanic Languages and Romance Languages (French, Italian, Spanish, and Russian) were created in 1958, the old department known as Modern Languages and Literatures, founded in 1904 under President Woodrow Wilson, existed no more. The study of modern European languages and literatures was now on the same footing as the study of Latin, Greek, and English literatures.

With students having the opportunity to take literature courses in multiple departments, an interdepartmental committee was created under the auspices of the Council of the Humanities in 1962. The first four faculty members of the committee included Victor Lange, chair of the new German Department; Edmund Keeley '48, a specialist in Hellenistic studies; Claudio Guillén, professor of Spanish and son of the famous Spanish poet Jorge Guillén; and Bartlett Giamatti, a scholar of English Renaissance literature who was at Princeton briefly before becoming, among other things, the president of Yale in 1978 and the commissioner of Major League Baseball in 1989.

Within a few years the committee recognized a great interest among graduate students in cross-disciplinary study, and in 1966 a program in

Comparative Literature was inaugurated with noted translator Robert Fagles of the department of English as its director. The program included faculty members already at Princeton, as well as two newly appointed professors of comparative literature, Ralph Freedman and Joseph Frank.

First open to graduate students only, the program expanded to include undergraduate courses in 1972. Responding to requests from students and faculty members who had been teaching comparative courses for several years, Fagles worked with Frank and Freeman to elevate the program to department status in 1975. Fagles was appointed the founding chair and served until 1994.

At the time of its founding, the department's mission was to provide a liberal, humanizing discipline for the study of language and literature as a whole. The strengths of the department included the history, theory, and practice of literary criticism; the study of literary forms, particularly narrative forms, the epic, and the novel; the classical tradition; and the main chronological periods of literature.

The linguistic range covered the major European languages, and the historical range stretched from antiquity to the modern period. As one of the early members of the department, English and Japanese specialist Earl Miner quickly extended its reach beyond the European literatures, introducing a strong East Asian component. The department initially had 13 full professors, and in 1976 it welcomed two new assistant professors with the support of the Mellon Foundation.

Through the latter years of the twentieth century, the department began to reach beyond traditional views and subjects. While not abandoning attention to the great works of Western literature, scholarship also turned to broader relationships, such as the outside influences of philosophy or anthropology on literatures. Interest grew in the literatures of Latin and South America, South Asia, and Africa, as well as in exploring voices not usually heard, such as Third World women. "Literature" could encompass media beyond print, including film and music.

By the turn of the twenty-first century Sandra Bermann, one of the "Mellon" assistant professors in 1976, was chair of the department as nationally the field of comparative literature was embarking on a time of transition. The core faculty of the department was expanded not only to bolster existing fields, but also to welcome new fields that both reached more cultures, such as Chinese, Hebrew, Arabic, and Egyptian, and addressed more sociological concerns, such as identity and gender studies. The department became global and even more interdisciplinary. The practice of translation was joined by translation theory and translation studies.

In 2007, comparative literature faculty member David Bellos became the first director of the program in Translation and Intercultural Communication, open to students in all departments and under the auspices of the Princeton Institute for International and Regional Studies. Princeton's department became a national leader in its vision.

Current core faculty members have a broad range of interests, not only in literatures ancient and modern from around the globe, but also in areas such as aesthetics, linguistics, Marxism, and postcolonial criticism. Many have joint appointments in other departments and programs, from language and literature departments to Art and Archaeology, African American Studies, Philosophy, and the History of Science. Associated faculty represent departments and programs across the campus, including East Asian Studies and Near Eastern Studies, Creative Writing, and Media and Modernity.

The department of Comparative Literature today invites undergraduate students both to read texts closely and to think about the nature, function, and value of literature within a broad context. Courses are not confined to a single national literature; they engage many different traditions, genres, and languages across the globe. They also juxtapose literature with art, film, philosophy, psychology, history, law, and other fields that provide context and comparison. While all undergraduates must have proficiency in one non-English language on entering the department and reading ability in a second one by graduation, students have considerable freedom to construct their own programs and to use courses from other disciplines as part of the major.

The department continues to offer the PhD in cooperation with the other departments of literature. The rigorous program of study enables students with exceptional training in languages and literatures to profit from the increased awareness and understanding that can be derived from the consideration of more than one literature and of the theoretical presuppositions behind literary study as a whole. While originally the graduate program served to train students for teaching careers, it now also prepares its PhD graduates to serve in a variety of roles in institutions of higher education, as well as for careers in global nonprofit and nongovernmental organizations where a deep knowledge of multiple languages and cultures is invaluable.

COMPTON BROTHERS, THE, were among the earliest alumni of the Princeton graduate school. All three graduated from the College of Wooster, where their father, a Presbyterian minister, was dean and professor of philosophy, and all three earned their PhDs at Princeton. Karl T. Compton, who received his PhD in 1912, was professor of physics and chair of the department at Princeton, and later president and chair of the corporation of Massachusetts Institute of Technology. Wilson M. Compton, who received his PhD in 1915, taught economics, worked in the lumber industry and then the federal government as a specialist in forest conservation and timber management, and became president of the State College of Washington, later Washington State University. Arthur H. Compton, who received his PhD in 1916, was a distinguished service professor at the University of Chicago, a Nobel Prize winner in physics (1927), played a leading role in the development of the atomic bomb, and was for a time chancellor of Washington University in St. Louis.

In 1963, when two quadrangles were added to the original graduate college, the trustees named one the Compton Quadrangle in their honor.

COMPUTER SCIENCE, THE DEPARTMENT OF. Although Princeton's Computer Science department was not created until 1985 when Electrical Engineering and Computer Science split into separate departments, it traces its origins to the 1930s. It was then that three Princeton-affiliated scholars, Alonzo Church 1924 *1927, Alan Turing *38, and John von Neumann, began innovative mathematical research that would have lasting consequences not only for Princeton and its Computer Science department, but for the development of the modern digital computer.

Church taught mathematics for nearly four decades at Princeton and was the inventor of *lambda calculus*, a system of formal mathematical logic and computation that is a precursor to today's modern programming languages. One of his students was Turing, who described a concept known as the Turing machine—an early form of today's computer—and collaborated with Church on what became known as the Church-Turing thesis, a computing hypothesis that provided the theoretical model for digital computers.

Von Neumann, one of the original members of the Institute for Advanced Study (IAS), was a Hungarian-born mathematician and physicist who worked on the Manhattan Project during World War II and was later a member of the Atomic Energy Commission. He both worked on and helped design some of the world's first computers—massive devices that occupied multiple rooms and weighed several tons.

For many years, computer science at Princeton was taught under the aegis of the Electrical Engineering department. In 1973 Bruce Arden became chair, and he and several of his colleagues, including John Hopcroft and Jeffrey Ullman *66, placed growing emphasis on the use of computers to solve many classic engineering problems. The department officially changed its name to Electrical Engineering and Computer Science (EECS), and as early as 1977 the faculty began considering a split.

By 1985, when the split occurred, the University had recognized that it needed to devote more resources and greater attention to computer science as an important field in its own right. The Computer Science department continued to emphasize theoretical computer science, a perspective fostered by the department's first chair, Robert Sedgewick, who held the position until 1994 and brought two future Turing Award winners, Robert Tarjan and Andrew Yao, to Princeton. (The Turing Award is the field's most prestigious award and is frequently cited as the Nobel Prize of computer science; it was also won by Hopcroft after he left Princeton and by another former faculty member, Patrick Hanrahan.) During his tenure, in addition to building and expanding the department's curriculum, Sedgewick oversaw construction of a four-story, 50,000-square-foot Computer Science building across Olden Street from the Engineering Quadrangle.

In 1989, Tarjan played a leading role in creating DIMACS (Center for Discrete Mathematics and Theoretical Computer Science), a research effort in theoretical computer science initiated jointly with Rutgers University, AT&T, and Bell Labs. This helped solidify Princeton's department as a national center of work in this area.

The department continued to grow during David Dobkin's tenure as chair, from 1994 until 2003, when he was appointed dean of the faculty. Several new faculty members were hired, putting the number of total faculty at 25, and the department broadened its research objectives to create a balance between theory and practice. The faculty began to focus on new areas of study, such as programming languages, computer graphics, and operating systems. Interdisciplinary work also began during this time, with collaborations between the Computer Science department and the Lewis-Sigler Institute for Integrative Genomics, the department of Music, and the school of Public and International Affairs.

This last collaboration resulted in the creation of the Center for Information Technology Policy, an interdisciplinary research center that specializes in the interface between computing and such topics as privacy, security, ethics, bias, and machine learning. Edward Felten, a recognized national expert in software security, internet security, electronic voting, cybersecurity policy, technology for government transparency, network neutrality, and internet policy, served as its founding director from July 2007 through June 2019, but the work of the center built on scholarship pursued as early as 1995 by Felten, Andrew Appel '81, and others.

Another major initiative during Dobkin's tenure was a display wall project led by Professor Kai Li through which a screen 18 feet by 8.5 feet was created in the department and run by a collection of CPUs and projectors to create a massive display. The project supported experimental efforts in the department as faculty and graduate students had to figure out how to make the display work, and it supported the department's efforts in graphics and sound.

Larry Peterson served as chair from 2003 to 2009. A leader in the field of computer networking, his research contributed to the development of the internet. In 2003 he headed PlanetLab, an experimental global network of computers on which many researchers worldwide could test algorithms for such things as faster downloads and more powerful search engines.

During Appel's tenure as chair, between 2009 and 2015, the department experienced dramatic growth. By 2017, computer science had become the University's most popular major and one of its courses, "Introduction to Programming," which had been developed over two decades by Sedgewick, was its most popular undergraduate class, taken by majors and nonmajors alike.

Jennifer Rexford '91 became chair in 2015 and continued her predecessor's hiring of additional faculty to accommodate growth. The department grew to 43 tenure-track and 13 teaching faculty, and approximately 155 undergraduate majors per graduating class. About 25 percent of undergraduates either concentrate or earn a certificate in the discipline and about 60 percent of undergraduates enroll in its introductory computer course. Overall, it has been estimated that Computer Science teaches some 70 percent of Princeton's undergraduates.

This growth created a need for a larger facility, which was met when Eric Schmidt '76 and his wife Wendy Schmidt made a gift in 2019 that allowed the University to substantially rebuild and expand Guyot Hall as the Computer Science department's new home, with move-in anticipated by 2026.

Rexford was the second Princeton graduate to chair the department (following Appel) and the first woman. The department's efforts to diversify date back to 1981 when Andrea LaPaugh joined the faculty; for a time, she was the only woman on the faculty of the school of Engineering, and subsequently the only tenured woman in the school.

In recent years Margaret Martonosi, Olga Troyanskaya, Mona Singh, Rexford, and numerous other women have played significant roles in the department and the field. In 2004, Rexford won the Association for Computing Machinery's Grace Murray Hopper Award for outstanding young computer professional of the year, and in 2020 assistant professor Olga Russakovsky received the Anita Borg Early Career Award that honors women who have made significant research contributions in computer science or engineering and have contributed to their profession, especially in outreach to women. Interest in the department by women undergraduates grew to the point where some 37 percent of its concentrators were women; at Commencement in 2018, the salutatorian was computer science major Katherine Lim '18.

Princeton's department of Computer Science ranks among the best in the world. The department lists its research areas as computational biology, computer architecture, economics/computation, graphics/vision/human-computer interaction, machine learning, natural language processing, policy, programming languages/compilers, security and privacy, systems, and theory. The department also continues its longstanding relationship with the Institute for Advanced Study; one recent example was a three-year program (2017–20) on foundational issues in theoretical machine learning led by Princeton PhD in computer science and IAS faculty member Avi Wigderson *83 and Princeton faculty member Sanjeev Arora.

Rexford has observed that "computer science is transforming nearly every human endeavor and every academic discipline." Because of the broad range of topics in computer science and the diverse interests of undergraduates, the department allows students to major through either the Bachelor of Arts or the Bachelor of Science in Engineering degree program (it is the only department that offers that option). Graduate students may pursue a Master of Science in Engineering degree or the PhD.

COMPUTING. Princeton was among the earliest and most influential pioneers in the development of modern computing. From the visionary work on numerical computing of Alan Turing *38 in the 1930s, through John von Neumann's essential contributions to the architecture of digital computing in the 1940s, to Robert Khan *64's fundamental work on the Internet Protocol, Princeton faculty, students, and alumni have played critical roles in nearly every important computing innovation.

Computing as a campus service was first established in 1962 under electrical engineering professor Edward McCluskey Jr. with the installation of an IBM 7090 in the Engineering Quadrangle. Initially serving primarily the science and engineering departments, the computer was subsequently enlarged, replaced, and enlarged again to accommodate growing demand for service. In 1969 the University built a computer center building at 87 Prospect Avenue and installed an IBM 360/91, one of the largest and fastest computers available at the time. In 1975 it acquired an IBM 370/158.

Computing capacity grew exponentially, demand mushroomed, and today computing is an indispensable component of research, teaching, administration, and campus life.

The University provides extensive computing resources for research. Every discipline uses computing to advance scholarship and enable discovery. Faculty employ a wide array of computing resources depending on the needs and type of their research. They all have modern personal computers that are connected through a sophisticated and powerful network to the remarkable digital resources of the University library, museum, and high-performance computing infrastructure. Resources beyond campus are accessible through connections to national research networks like Internet 2 and the United States Energy Department's ESNet at speeds in excess of 500 billion bits per second (Gbit/s).

In 2010, Princeton built a special purpose High Performance Computing Research Center (HPCRC) on the Forrestal Campus. The HPCRC was specifically designed as a home for some of the world's most powerful computers. This 40,000-square-foot facility has enough power and cooling to support the University's current computing needs and the capacity to provide space for growth.

Designed with energy efficiency in mind, the HPCRC achieved "LEED Gold" certification by the United States Green Building Council at its commissioning in 2011 and began full-scale operation shortly thereafter. Its four powerful computer clusters support the University and the Princeton Plasma Physics Laboratory. These computer clusters, in total, provide about 40 *billion* times more computing power than the University had when it installed its first IBM 7090 in 1962—at about the same inflation-adjusted cost.

Historically, computing capability on campus has doubled about every two years. It is likely that this rate will continue for the next 60 years as it has for the past 60.

With 40 billion times more capacity, researchers use computing for virtually every facet of their research. Faculty in the Andlinger Center for Energy and the Environment use computing to observe atoms at the smallest level with instruments like the Cryo Electron Microscope (CryoEM), while faculty in the department of Astrophysical Sciences use it to model and simulate black holes. The Princeton Institute for Computational Science (PICSciE) is the academic home for research computing and provides support for faculty and students in partnership with the office of information technology (OIT). Over 30 full-time staff are engaged in enabling the remarkable computing capacity available to Princeton faculty.

By far the largest change in research computing over the past decade has been the exponential growth in the production of data. Instruments like the CryoEm, Large Hadron Collider (LHC), and the Spitzer Space Telescope produce data at an almost unimaginable rate. That data has to be stored, processed, analyzed, and curated over time.

Princeton has a comprehensive data storage infrastructure that supports open science and the long-term preservation of published research data. Under the management of the Princeton University Library and with support from the dean for research and OIT, Princeton provides long term archiving for published research data to ensure the widest possible dissemination of scientific information.

In addition to the tools available for high intensity computational research, both undergraduate and graduate students at Princeton have access to a comprehensive set of online resources to help them achieve their academic goals. Electronic course materials are available in a campus-wide learning management system which includes digital reserve materials from the library. Classroom audio visual technology is available in every classroom on campus. The University also provides specialized software for students either through electronic download to their personal computers or through student computer clusters located around campus. Printing services are available at a number of locations around campus.

Princeton also provides a wide array of technologies that support the administrative operations of the University. Princeton is, in many ways, a small city with services that range from housing to parking to power generation. Information technology supports virtually every facet of this complex community. At the foundational level, Princeton has an extensive network that provides a pathway for data to travel on campus and to the Internet. That network supports over 340,000 unique devices per year for faculty, staff, students, and visitors. On any given day, over 50,000 devices of every conceivable variety are connected to its network. The volume of network traffic to and from campus grew from 1 million bits per second (bit/s) in 1985 to over 6 billion bit/s in 2020—a 6,000-fold increase in 25 years.

Students, faculty, and staff connect to the network primarily through more than 12,000 WiFi access points on campus. A robust wired network supports data-intensive research, secure computing, and extensive industrial control and life safety systems. A 24/7 help desk provided by OIT ensures that the technology resources are available at all times.

In addition to the network, Princeton has an extensive array of servers that run the software for the administrative departments on campus: finance systems, student record systems, payroll systems, and human resource systems are on an Oracle PeopleSoft software suite. Alongside the PeopleSoft system, OIT supports over 150 applications that enable the unique business processes that Princeton requires. The servers and data storage that support these applications are housed in two data centers, one in the HPCRC on the Forrestal Campus and the other in a data center in New South.

As the campus has become more dependent on technology, keeping the University's assets safe from hacking and intrusion has become paramount. Princeton utilizes advanced threat detection and evaluation technologies to prevent attacks. There is also an incident response protocol to remediate attacks when they do happen. Fundamental to the University's efforts to secure its resources is a training and awareness program led by the chief information security office.

While the technology of computing has evolved dramatically since the computer center first opened in 1962, what has not changed is that the effective use of the technology depends on capable and caring staff. Over the years, the computer center has evolved from a small group of staff located at the Engineering Quadrangle and at 87 Prospect into a staff of over 300 information technology professionals in six locations on campus. The staff members of OIT, along with IT colleagues across campus in departments large and small, are the key to bringing technology to life in ways that advance the mission of the University—even as technology change continues to accelerate in nearly unimaginable ways and even as unanticipated challenges, such as the COVID-19 pandemic, require significant modifications and expanded use of technology in how the University conducts its teaching, its research, and its day-to-day operations.

Princeton faculty were pioneers in the early days of the computing and networking era and they are now at the forefront of the next great leap in computing technology—quantum computing—with faculty in Electrical and Computer Engineering, Computer Science, Chemistry, and Physics playing leading roles in the National Quantum Initiative. These technologies are the first fundamental change to the principles of computing developed by John von Neumann during his time at Princeton, and when the quantum computing future finally does arrive, the University will be ready for it.

CONCERNED ALUMNI OF PRINCETON (CAP) was founded in 1972 by alumni who opposed many of the changes that were taking place on campus. In November it began publishing a magazine, *Prospect*, that was sent monthly to about 13,000 alumni. In a report endorsed by the Board of Trustees in October 1975, the board's committee on alumni affairs described CAP as "a persistently hostile and negative voice" that through its magazine and its mailings to alumni and parents "presented a distorted, narrow, and hostile view of the university," with a "tendency . . . to exaggerate the University's flaws, to trumpet its mistakes, and to judge it always from a narrow ideological perspective."

A predecessor organization, the Alumni Committee to Involve Ourselves Now (ACTION), had been founded in 1969, largely in opposition to the University's decision to admit women undergraduates, but also with concerns about the increased role of students in campus governance, the increased presence on campus of students of color, the status of ROTC, the liberal leanings of the faculty, and the lack of what it considered adequate disciplinary action against students engaged in protest activities.

CAP's founding co-chairs were Asa Bushnell 1921, a former editor of the *Princeton Alumni Weekly* and former commissioner of the Eastern Collegiate Athletic Conference, and Shelby Cullom Davis '30, then the United States ambassador to Switzerland and donor in 1964 of $5.3 million to support the department of History, which was used to establish its Shelby Cullom Davis Center for Historical Studies.

The group hired a young alumnus, T. Harding Jones '72, to serve as its executive director and publish its magazine. Jones had served as a summer intern at the White House in 1971 and as an undergraduate had founded a conservative group called Undergraduates for a Stable America (USA). In a 1974 column in the *Daily Princetonian*, Jones described the alumni in CAP as "concerned, upset, enraged, sickened, or doubtful about some or all of the following: admissions policy, coeducation, athletics, radicals on campus, the Gay Alliance of Princeton . . . the abolishment of almost all rules, the oneness of mind of the Board of Trustees . . . the *Alumni Weekly*, and the failure of the administration to take the leadership in the moral and spiritual development of undergraduates."

By the time the trustees issued their report, *Prospect* had published 34 issues and CAP had circulated at least 10 pamphlets on issues affecting the University and at least seven solicitations for funds. The report cited, in particular, an "irresponsible" 1974 mailing to the parents of first-year students about crime on campus that was so alarmist that the officers of the freshman class felt obliged to issue a statement clarifying the facts. The trustee report rejected a characterization of CAP as a "loyal opposition," saying that its opposition "has been carping, not constructive" and that its effect had been to sow "doubt, discontent, and disaffection."

One of the authors of the trustee report was the most recently elected young alumni trustee, William Frist '74, a role that attracted national attention in 2006 when Frist was serving as majority leader of the US Senate during the confirmation hearings on the nomination of Samuel Alito '72 to become a justice of the Supreme Court. Alito had listed membership in CAP in a 1985 application for a job at the Department of Justice and was questioned about his reasons for joining. (Alito said he was not an active member and did not recall joining; a former member of the Alumni Council, chair of its committee on careers, and P-rade marshal, Alito cited his continuing service to the University as a schools committee volunteer.)

According to an account of the hearings in the *Princeton Alumni Weekly*, one member of the Judiciary Committee, Delaware Senator Joe Biden, "jokingly informed Alito that 'I really didn't like Princeton,'" but the next day Biden appeared at the hearing "wearing a Princeton cap." (Seven years later another Princetonian on the Supreme Court, Sonia Sotomayor '76, administered the oath of office to Biden when he began his second term as vice president, and eight years after that, when Biden was inaugurated as president, he named a Princeton professor, Cecilia Rouse, and a Princeton graduate, Eric Lander '78, to his first cabinet.)

In the decade following the trustee report CAP experienced a steady decline in activity and impact. None of the several editors who succeeded Jones were Princeton graduates. The last editor, Laura Ingraham, published only one issue, in October 1985, before resigning in March 1986. In the fall of 1986 CAP closed the offices it had been renting at 20 Nassau Street.

CONSTITUTIONAL CONVENTION OF 1787, THE, was attended by more alumni of Princeton than of any other college or university. Nine men, who had studied at Princeton under Presidents Aaron Burr Sr., Samuel Finley, and John Witherspoon, represented six states at the convention:

Alexander Martin 1756 (North Carolina)
William Paterson 1763 (New Jersey)
Oliver Ellsworth 1766 (Connecticut)
Luther Martin 1766 (Maryland)
William C. Houston 1768 (New Jersey)

Gunning Bedford Jr. 1771 (Delaware)
James Madison 1771 (Virginia)
William R. Davie 1776 (North Carolina)
Jonathan Dayton 1776 (New Jersey)

Five of the alumni at the convention had attended William & Mary, five (including Ellsworth) Yale, three Harvard, three Columbia, two the University of Pennsylvania, one Oxford, one Glasgow, and one had studied at three universities in Scotland. (Twenty-five of the 55 members of the convention, including George Washington and Benjamin Franklin, had not attended college.) The large number of Princeton graduates, and the large number of states they represented, reflected the wide geographic distribution of its student body at a time when Princeton was unique in drawing students from all regions of the new country.

Two competing proposals at the convention presented very different ideas about the scope and basic elements of a new government. The Virginia Plan, generally favored by the large states and those laying claim to western land, sought a strong national government with two legislative houses elected on the basis of population. In contrast the New Jersey Plan, favored principally by the small states, called for equal representation of the states in a single legislative body. The Connecticut Compromise, which broke the deadlock, proposed a lower house elected in proportion to population, and an upper house in which each state, regardless of size, would have equal representation.

A Princetonian was influential in the formulation of both proposals and the compromise. The Virginia Plan was outlined in resolutions heavily crafted by James Madison, while the New Jersey Plan was presented and vigorously defended by William Paterson. And although each of the three delegates from Connecticut has been credited with bringing about the compromise, it was Oliver Ellsworth who made the motion that carried the day.

At the conclusion of the convention, Madison sent a copy of the Constitution to Thomas Jefferson in Paris. It was impossible, he wrote Jefferson, "to consider the degree of concord which ultimately prevailed as less than a miracle." Madison is generally recognized as the strongest guiding hand not only in drafting the Constitution and reaching this accord, but in advocating for its adoption through his critical contributions to the Federalist Papers.

Madison went on to serve and continue to shape the newly established federal government for 24 years as a member of the House of Representatives, secretary of state, and president. Although he once said that his labors at the convention had "almost killed" him, he outlived all the other delegates and spent his last years, in his 80s, at his home in Montpelier, receiving visitors, answering letters, serving as president of the Princeton alumni association, and still explaining and expounding the Constitution.

CONTINENTAL CONGRESS, THE (1774–89) numbered among its members some 34 delegates who had attended Princeton. They came from all the colonies except Massachusetts. Other delegates included John Witherspoon, the only college president and only clergyman to sign the Declaration of Independence, and Princeton trustee Elias Boudinot, who served as president of the Congress in 1782–83.

From July through October 1783, the Congress met in what was then the second-floor library of Nassau Hall, making Princeton the young nation's provisional capital. It was here that Congress received word that the Treaty of Paris, officially ending the war with Great Britain, had been signed; where it welcomed an ambassador from the Netherlands as the first foreign minister to be accredited to the United States; and where it officially thanked George Washington for his services as commander-in-chief during the American Revolution.

The decision to relocate from Philadelphia was made hastily to allow members of Congress to escape mutinous soldiers who were demanding long-overdue back pay. Given a choice between Trenton and Princeton, Boudinot chose his wife's hometown of Princeton, but the small village of no more than 300 people was given less than a week to prepare.

One of the Congressional delegates described what it was like to make his way through Nassau Hall to attend a meeting: "I passed by the chambers of the students, from whence in the sultry heat of the day issued warm streams from the beds, foul linens, and dirty lodgings of the boys." He also described some of the local cuisine: "I have the honor of breakfasting at my lodging, of eating stinking fish and heavy half-baked bread and drinking if I please abominable wine at a dirty tavern . . . Yesterday I had the honor of drinking water to wash down some ill-cooked victuals." But, he added, "we are honorable gentlemen and (at least) we are out of Philadelphia."

CO-OPS, or, more formally, dining cooperatives, are University-supported, student-led organizations that provide opportunities for interested juniors and seniors to take responsibility for food purchasing, meal planning, and meal preparation for themselves and the other members of their co-op. They appeal to students because of the "home-cooked" meals they provide, the sense of community they engender, and a cost that is dramatically lower than joining an eating club or purchasing a University dining contract.

The oldest and largest co-op, 2D, was founded in 1977–78. It is located in a house at 2 Dickinson Street, just across Alexander Street from many of the dormitories that house juniors and seniors. About half of its members live in the house. 2D is vegetarian, and its 50 members each cook once a week in groups of five or six. Dinner is served every night at 6:30 and there are brunches on Saturday and Sunday. In addition to ordering food and preparing meals, the members bake their own bread and keep the house clean.

The Brown Food Cooperative, founded in 1994, is located in 217 Brown Hall. It includes 34 members each semester, and each person cooks along with two or three others once a week. Members do not need to live in Brown Hall.

The International Food Cooperative, located in the 4th entry of Laughlin Hall, was founded in 2009 and has 20–30 members each semester. It describes itself as "international in cuisine, perspective, and community," and has traditions and events that celebrate the holidays of cultures across the globe. Members cook once a week with three others.

The Scully Co-Op began operations in 2017 in 319 Scully Hall. It has 40 members who each cook once a week in groups of four or five.

One of the residential colleges, Mathey College, sponsors a co-op in the Edwards Hall kitchen that allows its members to supplement their meal plans with food they select and prepare themselves.

CORWIN, EDWARD S., was considered one of the leading twentieth-century expositors of the intent and meaning of the Constitution.

Born on a farm near Plymouth, Michigan, Corwin first developed his interest in constitutional law at the University of Michigan, where he was Phi Beta Kappa and president of the Class of 1900, and at the University of Pennsylvania, where he completed his doctoral work in American history in 1905.

That fall, Corwin accepted a position at Princeton as one of Woodrow Wilson's original group of preceptors and began an association with Princeton that was to last almost 60 years. In 1918 he was appointed to the chair first occupied by Wilson, the McCormick Professorship of Jurisprudence, which he held until his retirement in 1946. When a separate department of Politics was formed in 1924, Corwin became its first chair, serving in that post until 1935.

Corwin's performance as a teacher led seniors repeatedly to vote his undergraduate course, Constitutional Interpretation, "most difficult" and "most valuable." Because of his erect posture and military bearing, he was affectionately known to generations of graduate students as "The General." According to his former student, Alpheus T. Mason *1923, who succeeded him as McCormick Professor, he had the special gift "of reaching within each person, of discovering something firm and worthwhile, of encouraging him to stand on it," and the ability, "rare among teachers . . . to judge young men, not by what they are, but by what they may yet become."

Corwin's influence eventually extended beyond the campus to the federal government, which he served in 1935 as an adviser to the Public Works Administration, and in 1936 and 1937 as a special assistant and consultant to the attorney general on constitutional issues.

Of the more than 20 books Corwin wrote, the best known and most influential were his studies of the Constitution and the presidency. His most successful book was written at the suggestion of his companions in the Snuff Club—a small cross-departmental group that included Corwin, E. G. Conklin (biology), Luther Eisenhart (mathematics), Christian Gauss (literature), and Duane Reed Stuart (classics)—who, after hearing several papers he read to the club, urged him to write an exposition of the Constitution for the general reader. *The Constitution and What It Means Today* was first published by Princeton University Press in 1920 and was reprinted in 13 revised editions and numerous translations.

On Constitution Day in 1961, when Corwin was cited for his "brilliant service to both institutions—the Constitution and Princeton University," one of his former students, Adlai E. Stevenson 1922, recalled how much Corwin had enriched his undergraduate days at Princeton with his "warmth, his wisdom, and his wit."

CORWIN HALL at one time stood on Washington Road near Prospect Avenue, where it was erected in 1951 to house the school of Public and International Affairs. To preserve a handsome old copper beech tree the architect sited the building farther from the corner than he otherwise would have done, and to keep out traffic noises he installed windows only on the north and east sides. On the west side, which faced

Washington Road and McCosh Walk, the long unbroken expanse of brick wall to the right of the main entrance was troubling to many. Soon after the building's completion there appeared on it in foot-high white letters these words from Shelley's *Ozymandias*: "Look on my work, ye mighty, and despair!"

The building was moved almost a hundred yards northeast to its present site on May 20, 1963. This engineering feat was accomplished by using hydraulic jacks to push the building along 12 steel tracks. The actual moving took only 12 hours, but two months were needed to prepare for it and another three months were required to secure the building to its new foundation.

When the new Public and International Affairs building (later named Robertson Hall) was completed in 1965, the relocated building was assigned to the department of Politics and the center of International Studies, and its name was changed from Woodrow Wilson Hall to Corwin Hall in honor of Edward S. Corwin, Wilson's successor as McCormick Professor of Jurisprudence and the first chair of the department of Politics.

COUNCIL OF THE HUMANITIES, THE, was established in 1953 to foster teaching and research in the humanities. Known informally as "the Humanities Council," its program was devised by a faculty committee headed by Professor Whitney Oates 1925 *1931, who served as the council's chair until his retirement from the faculty in 1970.

Six previously established programs came under the purview of the council at its founding: the Special Program in the Humanities, the Creative Arts program, the Christian Gauss Seminars in Criticism, and programs in American, European, and Near Eastern studies. Subsequently, the council helped develop interdepartmental programs in Linguistics, Medieval Studies, Classical Philosophy, Political Philosophy, the Ancient World, Film Studies, Renaissance Studies, and Comparative Literature, which became a department in 1975.

Today the council is academic home to more than a dozen interdisciplinary programs, committees, and initiatives. It continues to "nurture the humanities locally and globally, engage diverse perspectives past and present, and enrich public dialogue with humanistic approaches." It offers a year-long course for first- and second-year students on interdisciplinary approaches to western culture that it describes as "2 semesters, 12 professors, 2,500 years," along with newer interdisciplinary sequences on East Asian and Near Eastern humanities. The council has been an incubator for such initiatives as the freshman seminars in the residential colleges, the program in Gender and Sexuality Studies, the Center for Digital Humanities, and the programs now encompassed by the Lewis Center for the Arts.

The council oversees an undergraduate certificate program in Humanistic Studies and an interdisciplinary doctoral program in the humanities that allows graduate students to receive an extra fellowship year and receive a joint degree in the program and their home department. It oversees the Ferris seminars in journalism and the McGraw seminars in writing, and it supports certificate programs in American Studies, European Cultural Studies, Linguistics, and Medieval Studies; in 2018–19 it launched a new certificate program in Journalism. It also supports graduate-level initiatives in the ancient world, classical philosophy, and renaissance and early modern studies.

The council continues to house the Gauss Seminars, which were first established in 1949. It also houses the Eberhard L. Faber IV lectures (since 1963), the Belknap Visitor, the Stewart Seminars in Religion, and an annual humanities colloquium. It enjoys a close collaborative relationship with the Society of Fellows in the Liberal Arts, which brings 13 postdoctoral Cotsen fellows to Princeton for three-year terms to join with Princeton faculty fellows in exploring innovative interdisciplinary approaches to scholarship and teaching in the humanities and humanities-related social sciences.

The council brings distinguished scholars from around the world to spend time in residence at Princeton as visiting fellows. It appoints Princeton faculty in the humanities and humanistic social sciences as Old Dominion professors to provide them with a year of leave to engage in intensive research. It also supports the Behrman professors who teach for three years in the Humanistic Studies program, and it convenes the Old Dominion faculty fellows, who come together from all four academic divisions for monthly seminars, and the Behrman fellows, recently tenured professors who meet regularly for discussion.

The Edmund N. Carpenter II Class of 1943 chair in the humanities brings a senior scholar to Princeton on a permanent shared appointment between a department and the council.

The council's priorities encompass interdisciplinary teaching and research in a global context, with particular focus on digital humanities, including support for work in film and media studies; identity and diversity (the council was the incubator for the Princeton and Slavery project); environmental and medical humanities; urban humanities, in collaboration with the Princeton-Mellon Initiative on Architecture, Urbanism, and the Humanities; public humanities; and bridges between the creative arts and the humanities, in collaboration with the Lewis Center for the Arts.

The council provides funding for a wide array of faculty, graduate student, and undergraduate student projects related to humanistic inquiry. One major source of funding that it administers is the David A. Gardner '69 Magic Project, which provides grants to support global initiatives, innovation, and the development of team-taught interdisciplinary courses. The council also supports public humanities ventures such as collaborations with high schools, community colleges, prisons, and nonprofit and community organizations.

The council is located in Joseph Henry House and Scheide Caldwell House, as part of the Andlinger Center for the Humanities. Its members include 17 humanities departments and more than 35 interdisciplinary centers, programs, and committees.

COUNCIL OF THE PRINCETON UNIVERSITY COMMUNITY, THE (CPUC, U-Council), is primarily a deliberative and consultative body, with authority to "consider and investigate any question of University policy, any aspect of the governing of the University, and any general issue related to the welfare of the University; and to make recommendations regarding any such matters to the appropriate decision-making bodies . . . or to the appropriate officers of the University."

The Council also has authority to "make rules regarding the conduct of resident members of the University community," to oversee rule making by other bodies within the University community, and to oversee all applications of rules.

The Council normally does not consider matters primarily academic in nature.

A Special Committee on the Structure of the University chaired by Professor Stanley Kelley Jr. proposed the creation of the Council in May 1969. Sometimes referred to as "Kelley's Republic," the Council was designed as "a permanent conference of the representatives of all major groups of the University" where "they could each raise problems that concern them and . . . be exposed to each other's views."

The Council first met on October 27, 1969. Typically, it meets six times a year, with special meetings as needed.

Following a series of charter amendments, membership of the Council was set at 51, including six senior officers of the administration (including the president and provost), 15 faculty members, 12 undergraduates, seven graduate students, seven staff members, and four alumni. The president of the University is the presiding officer of the Council and the provost chairs its executive committee.

Much of the work of the Council is conducted through its standing committees, including the executive committee (sets CPUC agendas and appoints members of CPUC committees); committees on rights and rules, governance (helps select honorary degree recipients and baccalaureate speakers), priorities (advises on each year's operating budget, including the setting of tuition levels and salary pools), and resources (advises on issues related to divestment); and the judicial committee.

Special committees and task forces have been established from time to time, including in recent years a committee that advises the trustees on the naming of programs, positions, and spaces to bring a more diverse presence to the campus. In 2014 a special task force on diversity, equity, and inclusion was established; it issued a report and recommendations in May 2015 and provided an update to its report a year later.

COUNCIL ON SCIENCE AND TECHNOLOGY, THE, works to advance literacy in science, technology, engineering, and mathematics (STEM) across the University and beyond through course development, interdisciplinary programming, and research. The CST seeks to ensure that all members of the university community, regardless of their background, experience, or discipline, can engage with, appreciate, and apply science in their everyday lives, in their careers, and in society. It was founded on the belief that scientific and technological literacy are essential for responsible decision-making and innovation in the twenty-first century and that STEM literacy is a key component of a quality liberal arts education.

The CST designs, teaches, and promotes innovative, interdisciplinary courses in science and engineering for all students, including those concentrating in the humanities and social sciences. These courses frequently engender collaboration and integration between STEM and the arts, humanities, and social sciences. Course topics have ranged from the art of mapping and the design of musical instruments to transformative questions in biology and physics for future leaders. The CST also advises on, supports, and designates many other science and engineering courses that students take to fulfill their general education requirements.

The council provides funding for student organizations and student projects that align with its mission. It provides faculty with funding and technical support for innovative course and co-curricular program development. With students and faculty, it nurtures interdisciplinary networks of arts, engineering, sciences, and humanities practitioners in its StudioLab, a 2,500-square-foot creative technology space. Opportunities in the StudioLab include workshops, classes, collaborations, and hackathons, as well as experience with digital fabrication technologies and immersive media.

The CST sponsors visiting instructors, scholars, and artists who enhance STEM learning experiences across the disciplines, and it provides opportunities for research on STEM teaching and learning. It awards the Pope Prize for Science Writing and sponsors lectures and other public events that address STEM questions of interest to the wider university community and the general public.

COWELL, DAVID, a Presbyterian minister in Trenton, New Jersey, was named a trustee of the College in the charter of 1748. He served briefly as acting president in 1757–1758. Like Princeton's first nine presidents, he was a slaveholder.

Cowell promoted a lottery for the College and, since New Jersey refused to sanction it, persuaded a Harvard classmate who lived in Connecticut to manage the drawing in that state, where lotteries were permitted. He also conducted the negotiations that led to Samuel Davies' acceptance of the board's invitation to become fourth president of the College.

CROSS-COUNTRY. Princeton has been competing in cross-country races since the turn of the twentieth century, but the Tigers did not win an Ivy League team championship until 1975. Since then, the men's and women's teams have combined to win more Ivy titles than any other school, with 20 for the men and nine for the women.

Men's Cross-Country

Princeton students began competing in intramural cross-country races in the 1880s, and their talent for distance running was apparent when the Tigers ventured into intercollegiate competition. John Cregan 1899 won the inaugural Intercollegiate Cross-Country Meet at New York's Morris Park in 1899, seven years before Princeton's first varsity cross-country dual meet. The Tigers were title contenders in the early years of the Intercollegiate Association of Amateur Athletes of America (IC4A) championships, finishing second four times between 1914 and 1921.

Track star Bill Bonthron '34 excelled in cross-country, going undefeated in dual meets in his freshman, sophomore, and junior years. As a senior, he lost in a dramatic Harvard-Yale-Princeton meet when he led the field before collapsing 100 yards from the finish line. Two days later, coach Matty Geis told the *Daily Princetonian* that Bonthron was done with cross-country and would concentrate on shorter distances.

The Heptagonal cross-country championships began in 1939, and Princeton's 1949 team was the top Ivy League finisher at the meet, placing second behind champion Army. Rod Zwirner '59 became Princeton's first individual Heptagonal champion in 1956, but team success continued to elude the Tigers until the arrival of Larry Ellis as coach in 1970.

In 1971 Princeton qualified for the NCAA championships for the first time. In 1975 the Tigers broke through with their first Heptagonal title, beginning the most successful stretch in program history. From 1975 to 1983, Princeton won the Heptagonal meet eight times in nine years. The 1981 team may have been Ellis's best: the Tigers went 12–0 in dual meets and won the Heptagonal meet with six runners in the top 10, led by individual champion Matt Farmer '83.

Under coaches Fred Samara and Mike Brady, Princeton won four straight Ivy titles from 1996 to 1999. The 1997 team swept the top three individual spots in the Heptagonal meet, led by champion Tony Barroco '98. In 1999, Paul Morrison '02 won the Heptagonal meet and placed eighth at the NCAA championships, the best finish by an Ivy runner in more than a decade.

With Samara, Steve Dolan, and Jason Vigilante coaching them, the Tigers had another golden era from 2006 to 2014, winning seven Ivy titles in nine years. In 2010, Heptagonal champion Donn Cabral '12 ran Princeton's fastest time at Van Cortlandt Park in the Bronx (24:03.8). Two years later, Chris Bendtsen '13 won the Heptagonal meet with a school-best time on Princeton's home course on the West Windsor fields (23:41.8). The 2012 Tigers also had a program-best 11th-place finish at the NCAA championships.

Vigilante, the Tigers' coach since 2012, led Princeton to Ivy championships and NCAA Mid-Atlantic regional titles in 2017 and 2018. Princeton men have won the individual championship at Heptagonals eight times: Zwirner (1956); Farmer (1981); Bill Burke '91 (1990); Barroco (1997); Morrison (1999); Michael Maag '09 (2007); Cabral (2010); and Bendtsen (2012).

Women's Cross-Country

The women's cross-country team made its Ivy debut at the first women's Heptagonal meet in 1977, before the program was an official varsity sport. The Tigers finished second to Harvard. The following year, with new coach Peter Farrell and freshman star Lynn Jennings '83, Princeton won the Heptagonal crown, repeating as champions in 1979 and 1980.

Jennings, who won the individual Heptagonal title in 1979, was an accomplished distance runner and eventual Olympic medalist on the track. But she was truly in her element on the cross-country course. Dubbed "the queen of hill and dale" by *Sports Illustrated*, she won the USA Cross-Country championships nine times and the World Cross-Country championships three times, in 1990, 1991, and 1992.

Farrell's program experienced a resurgence in the 2000s, with remarkable team depth and a string of extraordinary individual champions. In 2003, Emily Kroshus '04 became the first Princeton woman in 16 years to win the Heptagonal meet. She followed that with an eighth-place finish at the NCAA championships. Cack Ferrell '06 succeeded Kroshus as the team's top runner, placing in the top 25 at the NCAA meet three times, including a 10th-place showing in 2005. And behind Ferrell came the most-decorated Ivy cross-country runner in Princeton history: Liz Costello '10, who won the Heptagonal meet in three consecutive years from 2007 to 2009. She set an Ivy record in 2009, running the five-kilometer Van Cortlandt Park course in 16:55.7. (Her record may never be broken now that the event has switched to a six-kilometer loop.)

Princeton won five consecutive Ivy championships from 2006 to 2010. In 2008, the team placed fifth in the NCAA meet, the best finish by an Ivy team in more than a decade. In 2009 the Tigers ran a perfect race at the Heptagonals, sweeping the first five individual spots for a team score of 15 points. Alex Banfich '12, the runner-up in 2009, would succeed Costello as the Heptagonal champion in 2010, and in 2011 she finished fifth at the NCAA championships. Princeton won its ninth and final Ivy title under Farrell in 2015, his final cross-country season. Brad Hunt took the helm in 2016.

Seven Princeton women have won the individual Heptagonal championship: Jennings (1979); Laura Cattivera '89 (1987); Kroshus (2003); Costello (2007, 2008, and 2009); Banfich (2010); Megan Curham '18 (2014); Lizzie Bird '17 (2015); and Gabi Forrest '19 (2017).

DAVIES, SAMUEL, fourth president of Princeton, was born the son of a farmer in New Castle County, Delaware. His parents could not afford to send him to college but were determined that he should be trained for the ministry. Davies studied at a school in Fagg's Manor, Pennsylvania, run by New Light minister and early College of New Jersey trustee Samuel Blair, and was licensed to preach by the presbytery of New Castle when he was just 22. A year later, Davies was ordained as an evangelist to Virginia, settling in Hanover on the colony's western frontier.

Although the Church of England was dominant in Virginia, Davies built up a strong Presbyterian following and became an advocate and defender of civil rights and religious freedom. He conducted services in seven houses of worship dispersed through five counties, riding horseback through fields and forests to minister to his scattered congregations. Suffering from tuberculosis, "he preached in the day and had his hectic fever by night." As a principal founder and first moderator of the presbytery of Hanover, which comprised all the Presbyterian ministers in Virginia and North Carolina, he was considered "the animating soul of the whole dissenting interests in these two colonies."

Davies had extensive contact with enslaved people during his decade in Virginia. He owned at least two slaves himself and ministered to the area's growing population of enslaved people. He pressed slaveholders to provide religious education to their slaves and teach them to read, and, through a relationship with the Society for Promoting Religious Knowledge Among the Poor in London, distributed books to enslaved people. He was credited with converting hundreds of slaves to Christianity and bringing his literacy campaign to more than a thousand enslaved men and women.

In 1753 Davies and Gilbert Tennant, another well-known Presbyterian minister and a Princeton trustee, were chosen by the trustees to go on a 14-month expedition to Great Britain and Ireland seeking donations for the College. They raised more than 10 times their goal of £300; the funds were used to build Nassau Hall and the president's house and establish a charitable fund "for the education of pious and indigent youth." During the trip, Davies preached some 60 times, burnishing his already well-established reputation as an orator.

In 1758 Davies was elected to succeed Jonathan Edwards as president of the College. He declined the position, partly because he was reluctant to quit his pastoral work in Virginia, and partly because he knew that while a majority of the trustees had voted for his election, a minority shared his belief that Samuel Finley, a member of the board, was better qualified for the office. The trustees eventually persuaded Davies to accept, and he took up his duties on July 26, 1759. (Trustee Jacob Green served as acting president between Edwards' death and Davies' installation.)

On January 1, 1761, Davies delivered his last published sermon, entitled "This Very Year You Shall Die." On February 4, at age 37 and only 18 months after becoming president, he did die, of pneumonia, a few weeks after having been bled for "a bad cold." He was succeeded as president by Finley.

During his brief tenure Davies raised the standards for admission and for the bachelor's degree, instituted monthly orations by members of the senior class (an important part of undergraduate education at Princeton for more than a century), composed odes to peace and to science which were sung at Commencement, and compiled a catalogue of the 1,281 volumes in the college library, then housed in Nassau Hall. "A large and well-sorted collection of books," he said, "is the most ornamental and useful furniture of a college."

Davies left his mark as scholar and patriot on his students, particularly the 11 members of the Class of 1760 whom he taught as seniors. In what appears to have been Princeton's first baccalaureate address, he told them, "Whatever be your Place, imbibe and cherish a public spirit. Serve your generation." This they did. Their class ranks would come to include a member of the Continental Congress, chaplains in the Continental Army, judges in Maine and Pennsylvania, the founder of a college in North Carolina, a member of the United States House of Representatives, and a signer of the Declaration of Independence.

Davies was renowned as one of the great pulpit orators of his generation. Patrick Henry, who as a boy frequently heard him preach, acknowledged Davies' influence on his own oratory. Davies' sermons were printed in some 20 editions in the United States and England, and for more than 50 years after his death they were among the most widely read of any in the English language. He also was one of the first American-born hymn writers and the author of a book of poetry.

DAVIS, NATALIE ZEMON, a trailblazing scholar with interests in areas of social and cultural history previously ignored by most scholars, and an important figure in the study of the history of women and gender, served as a senior member of the Princeton faculty from 1978 until her retirement in 1996. From 1990 to 1994, she directed the Shelby Cullom Davis Center for Historical Studies, succeeding its founding director, Lawrence Stone; the center conducts weekly seminars during the academic year that focus on broad themes and emphasize interdisciplinary approaches and subjects that span different geographical areas and periods.

Davis first lived in Princeton in 1957–58 with her husband, the mathematician Chandler Davis, when he was at the Institute for Advanced Study. At that point they were in the midst of what she describes as a "six-year saga" that began with the FBI investigating their political leanings and ended with her losing her passport (thereby foreclosing visits to European archives and forcing her to make innovative use of the sources she could access) and him being blacklisted by American universities and jailed for six months for defying the House Un-American Activities Committee. He moved to Canada and they had a long commuting marriage as she returned to Princeton in 1978, first at the institute's school of social sciences and then at the University.

In her study of the social and cultural history of sixteenth-century France and early modern Europe, and in her later work that extended into other parts of Europe, North Africa, North America, and the Caribbean, Davis focused on uncovering the lives and values of peasants, artisans, and women. Her work was widely read outside of academic circles, including especially *The Return of Martin Guerre* (1983), which grew out of her work as historical consultant on a 1982 movie of that name.

Her other books included *Society and Culture in Early Modern France* (1975), *Fiction in the Archives:*

Pardon Tales and Their Tellers in 16th-Century France (1987), *Women on the Margins: Three 16th-Century Lives* (1995), *The Gift in 16th-Century France* (2000), *Slaves on Screen: Film and Historical Vision* (2000), and *Trickster Travels: A 16th-Century Muslim Between Worlds* (2006).

In 1987, Davis became the second woman to serve as president of the American Historical Association (the first was in 1943). In 2010 she was awarded the Holberg Prize, a major international honor that recognizes outstanding scholarly work in the arts and humanities, social sciences, law, or theology. Her citation described her as "one of the most creative historians writing today" and cited her "cross-fertilization between disciplines."

Known for her intensive archival research and her gifted storytelling, she received the 2012 National Humanities Medal for her "insights into the study of history and her exacting eloquence in bringing the past into focus." In accepting the medal, she said, "I have tried my best to be not only a truth-teller about the past, but also to be a historian of hope."

At Princeton, Davis taught courses in history, anthropology, early modern Jewish social history, and history and film, and promoted opportunities and recognition for women scholars at Princeton and beyond. In 1983 she received a Howard T. Behrman award for distinguished achievement in the humanities. In 2003, the University awarded her an honorary degree, noting that "her scholarship extends across the full range of the human arts and sciences. Not content to write about women on the margins, she has guided them to the center of university life; and she has enriched the university by opening it up to talent and ideas beyond the confines of disciplines and conventions."

Following her retirement from Princeton in 1996, she moved to the University of Toronto where she became an adjunct professor of history and anthropology, a senior fellow in comparative literature, and a professor of medieval studies.

DEAN, THE OFFICE OF, came into being in 1883 with the creation of the position of dean of the faculty. Since then deans have been appointed in a total of 14 areas. Listed below are the current or most recent titles, along with the founding dates (and in some cases, ending dates) of the position.

Dean of the Faculty 1883
Dean of the Graduate School 1901
Dean of the Departments of Science 1909–28
Dean of the College 1909
Dean of the School of Engineering and Applied Science 1922
Dean of Freshmen 1925–43
Dean of Religious Life and of the Chapel 1928
Dean of Student Life 1954–99
Dean of the School of Public and International Affairs 1964
Dean of the School of Architecture 1965
Dean of Admission 1988
Dean of Undergraduate Students 1999
Dean for Research 2006
Dean for Diversity and Inclusion 2016

DEAN OF ADMISSION, THE, has administrative oversight of the office of admission, which oversees the recruitment and selection of each year's entering undergraduate class and the University's transfer admission program. The dean reports to the dean of the college. Prior to 1988, the head of the admission office carried the title of director.

Deans of admission have been:

Fred Hargadon 1988–2003
Janet Lavin Rapelye 2003–18
Karen Richardson '93 2019–

DEAN OF THE COLLEGE is an office that the trustees established in 1909 to assume the responsibility for undergraduate discipline that previously had been vested in the dean of the faculty. The position was intended to be called dean of discipline, but by the time the catalogue appeared that fall, the title had become dean of the college. In 1946 the dean of the college was made responsible for the enforcement of rules relating to undergraduate scholastic standing, and for oversight of the services and agencies designed to promote the academic development of undergraduates; in 1954 responsibility for undergraduate discipline and extracurricular activities (and in 1957 athletic activities) was assigned to a new position, the dean of students.

Today the dean of the college, reporting to the provost, has administrative oversight of undergraduate studies, admission to the undergraduate college, the curriculum of the college, the services and agencies designed to promote the academic development of undergraduates, the residential colleges, and the office of the registrar. The dean is also charged with the application and enforcement of the rules and standards relating to undergraduate scholarship, standing, and attendance at the University.

Deans of the college have been:

Edward Elliott (Politics) 1909–12
Howard McClenahan 1894 (Physics) 1912–25
Christian Gauss (Modern Languages) 1925–46
Francis Godolphin (Classics) 1946–55
Jeremiah Finch (English) 1955–61
J. Merrill Knapp (Music) 1961–66
Edward Sullivan (French) 1966–72
Neil Rudenstine '56 (English) 1972–77
Joan Girgus (Psychology) 1977–87
Nancy Weiss Malkiel (History) 1987–2011
Valerie Smith (English) 2011–15
Jill Dolan (English and Theater) 2015–

DEAN OF THE DEPARTMENTS OF SCIENCE was a title held by only one person, Henry B. Fine 1880. He was appointed to the post in 1909 and held it until his death in 1928. The position provided administrative oversight of the departments of Astronomy, Biology, Chemistry, Geology, Mathematics, and Physics. After Dean Fine's death, these duties were assigned to the dean of the faculty.

DEAN FOR DIVERSITY AND INCLUSION. The position of dean for diversity and inclusion was established in 2016 on the recommendation of a special task force on diversity, equity, and inclusion. The dean reports to the vice president for campus life. The first incumbent was LaTanya Buck.

DEAN OF THE FACULTY, the University's oldest and highest-ranking deanship, was established by the trustees in 1883 as a means of releasing President James McCosh, then 72 years old, from certain onerous duties, and thus persuading him to remain as president as well as professor of philosophy. The trustees charged the dean of the faculty "with oversight of whatever does not pertain directly to the work of instruction, such in particular as the discipline of the College, the assignment of rooms and the sanitary condition of the Institution." As thus defined, this continued to be the dean of the faculty's function until 1909 when, with the creation of the office of the dean of the college, these duties were assigned to the new dean, and the dean of the faculty took over from the president oversight of the application and enforcement of rules and standards of scholarship in the University; the dean of the faculty also chaired, ex-officio, the faculty committee on examinations and standing, and was responsible for discharging the general duties of the president in his absence or disability.

During the post-World War II years, as the dean of the college assumed increasing responsibility for the academic life of undergraduates, the dean of the faculty took on increasing responsibility for oversight of the departments of instruction and concern for the well-being of the faculty. In 1967 the newly created office of provost took over the responsibility of acting for the president in his or her absence or disability.

Today the dean of the faculty has administrative oversight of the academic departments, centers, and programs, and of all matters that pertain to the effectiveness and well-being of the faculty, and of the professional librarians, researchers, and specialists.

Deans of the faculty have been:

James Murray (English) 1883–99
Samuel Winans (Greek) 1899–1903
Henry Fine 1880 (Mathematics) 1903–12
William Magie 1879 (Physics) 1912–25
Luther Eisenhart (Mathematics) 1925–33
Robert Root (English) 1933–46
J. Douglas Brown 1919 *1928 (Economics) 1946–67
Robert Palmer (History) 1967–68
Richard Lester *36 (Economics) 1968–73
Aaron Lemonick *54 (Physics) 1973–89
Robert Gunning *55 (Mathematics) 1989–95
Amy Gutmann (Politics) 1995–97
Joseph Taylor (Physics) 1997–2003
David Dobkin (Computer Science) 2003–14
Deborah Prentice (Psychology) 2014–17
Sanjeev Kulkarni (Electrical Engineering) 2017–21
Gene Andrew Jarrett '97 (English) 2021–

DEAN OF FRESHMEN. From 1925 to 1942, this position was held by Radcliffe Heermance *1909, who was also director of admission. As dean of freshmen he was charged with administrative oversight of the academic work of the freshman class and direction of the board of advisors. Burnham N. Dell was dean of freshmen for one year, 1942–43; thereafter the position was eliminated and the dean of the college absorbed the duties of the office.

DEAN OF THE GRADUATE SCHOOL was established in 1901. The dean, reporting to the provost, has administrative oversight of graduate studies, the curriculum of the graduate school, graduate student affairs, and the graduate college.

Deans of the graduate school have been:

Andrew West 1874 (Latin) 1901–28
Augustus Trowbridge (Physics) 1928–33
Luther Eisenhart (Mathematics) 1933–45
Hugh Taylor (Chemistry) 1945–58
Donald Hamilton (Physics) 1958–65
Colin Pittendrigh (Biology) 1965–69
Aaron Lemonick *54 (Physics) 1969–73
Alvin Kernan (English) 1973–77
Nina Garsoian (Near Eastern Studies) 1977–79
Theodore Ziolkowski (German) 1979–92
Albert Raboteau (Religion) 1992–93
John Wilson (Religion) 1994–2002
William Russel (Chemical and Biological Engineering) 2002–14
Sanjeev Kulkarni (Electrical Engineering) 2014–17
Sarah-Jane Leslie *07 (Philosophy) 2018–21

Dean of Religious Life and of the Chapel, The, oversees religious activities on campus and provides leadership for the denominational and nondenominational chaplaincies and student religious organizations. The dean supports all religious traditions while also serving as liturgical leader of the University Chapel congregation. The dean is responsible for ecumenical worship in the chapel and for the University's three principal interfaith services: Opening Exercises, the Service of Remembrance, and Baccalaureate.

Deans of religious life and of the chapel have been:

Robert Wicks 1928–47
Donald Aldrich 1947–55
Ernest Gordon 1955–81
Frederick Borsch '57 1981–88
Joseph Williamson 1989–2001
Thomas Breidenthal 2001–07
Alison Boden 2007–

Dean for Research, The, reporting to the provost, has administrative oversight of organized research activities throughout the University, is responsible for dealing with questions of policy regarding the acceptance and administration of research grants and contracts, and has general supervision over the application of policy in this area. The dean also has administrative responsibility for programs designed to enlist financial support for the University from corporations and foundations, and for research translation and technology licensing.

Prior to the creation of this position, responsibility for oversight of organized research was vested in the faculty chair of the University Research Board (URB). The first dean for research was named to the deanship while chairing the URB.

Deans for research have been:

A.J. Stewart Smith *66 2006–13
Pablo Debenedetti 2013–

Dean of the School of Architecture was a title introduced in 1965; previously heads of the school carried the title of director. The dean has administrative oversight, under the provost, of the school of Architecture.

Deans of the school of Architecture have been:

Robert Geddes 1965–82
Robert Maxwell 1982–89
Ralph Lerner 1989–2002
Stanley Allen *88 2002–12
Alejandro Zaera-Polo 2012–14
Monica Ponce de Leon 2015–

Dean of the School of Engineering and Applied Science, The, has administrative oversight of the school of Engineering and Applied Science.

Deans of the school of Engineering and Applied Science have been:

Arthur M. Greene Jr. (Mechanical Engineering) 1922–40
Kenneth Condit 1913 (Mechanical Engineering) 1940–54
Joseph Elgin *1929 (Chemical Engineering) 1954–71
Robert Jahn '51 *55 (Aerospace and Mechanical Engineering) 1971–86
Hisashi Kobayashi (Electrical Engineering) 1986–91
James Wei (Chemical Engineering) 1991–2002
Maria Klawe (Computer Science) 2003–06
H. Vincent Poor *77 (Electrical Engineering) 2006–16
Emily Carter (Mechanical and Aerospace Engineering) 2016–19
Andrea Goldsmith (Electrical Engineering) 2020–

Dean of the School of Public and International Affairs, The, reporting to the provost, has administrative oversight of the school. The position of dean was created in 1964; previously the head of the school was the chair of the administrative committee (1930–33) and then the director of the school (1933–64).

Incumbents as dean have been:

Marver Bernstein 1964–69
John Lewis 1969–74
Donald Stokes '51 1974–92
Henry Bienen 1992–94
Michael Rothschild 1995–2002
Anne Marie Slaughter '80 2002–09
Christina Paxson 2009–12
Cecilia Rouse 2012–21
Amaney Jamal 2021–

DEAN OF STUDENT LIFE. The position of dean of student life was established in 1954 (originally titled dean of students, later dean of student affairs) to provide oversight of undergraduate social, extracurricular, and athletic activities, and to be responsible for matters relating to the conduct and discipline of undergraduates. In 1999 the position was superseded by the newly created position of vice president for campus life, and a separate position of dean of undergraduate students was established.

The deans of students, student affairs, and student life have been:

William Lippincott '41 1954–68
Neil Rudenstine '56 1968–72
Adele Simmons 1972–77
J. Anderson Brown Jr. '69 1977–82
Eugene Y. Lowe Jr. '71 1983–93
Janina Montero 1993–99

DEAN OF UNDERGRADUATE STUDENTS is a position that was created in 1999 when the position of dean of student life was transformed into the position of vice president for campus life. Kathleen Deignan, who had been serving as associate dean of student life, was named the first incumbent of the new deanship.

The dean of undergraduate students' office (ODUS) works to provide undergraduates with opportunities for personal, cultural, and social development that complements the academic life of the University. ODUS works with many partners in campus life, the office of the dean of the college, the residential colleges, and many student organizations. The dean chairs the faculty committee on discipline.

DEAN'S DATE is the last day of reading period at the end of each semester. With the exception of take-home exams, there is a 5 p.m. deadline that day for all written coursework, and as more and more courses moved from final exams to papers in the 1980s and 1990s, dean's date loomed larger and larger in the lives of students. There were occasional post-deadline parties in those years, and then in 1999 Rakesh Satyal '02 and a few friends set up a "reading period theater" in McCosh courtyard to applaud students as they raced to turn in their papers on time and to offer them last-minute supplies, like staplers and snacks. By Satyal's senior year, about 400 students were participating, with free Italian ice donated by the Undergraduate Student Government (USG).

By 2005 the hoopla of dean's date had expanded in scope under the co-sponsorship of the USG and the office of the dean of undergraduate students, and a pattern had been established that continues today. Each year's celebration is a bit different, but the common elements are free food and drinks, free giveaways, music by the University Band, entertainment, and in some years an evening concert or comedy show. There is also, of course, the shared commiseration and relief over the successful completion of a workload that, for some students, can entail the submission of 50 pages or more by the deadline.

The evening before dean's date the band marches through Firestone Library and Frist Campus Center and students in several residential colleges let off steam with the Holder Howl, the Whitman Wail, or the Wilson Whimper—tamer versions of the Poler's Recess, a noisy 10-minute pre-exam break that Princeton students observed from the turn of the late nineteenth century almost up to World War II.

DICKINSON, JONATHAN, Princeton's first president, died after only four and a half months in office and is chiefly remembered for having been the leader of the little group who, in his words, "first concocted the plan and foundation of the College." To him, "more than to any other man, the college . . . owes its origin," wrote William A. Packard in *The Princeton Book* (1879).

Born in Hatfield, Massachusetts, Dickinson was a member of the fifth class to graduate, in 1706, from the Collegiate School of Connecticut, which later changed its name to Yale. He studied theology, and in 1709, when he was 21, he was ordained minister of the church in Elizabethtown, New Jersey.

Dickinson served this church all his life, ministering as pastor, lawyer, physician, and, in later years, as an instructor of young men preparing for professional study. The church was originally Congregational, as was Dickinson, but because he felt a need for stronger ties with other churches in meeting the

Church of England's opposition to New Jersey dissenters, he persuaded his congregation in 1717 to change its form of government and place itself under the care of the presbytery of Philadelphia. Dickinson became a leader of this presbytery and also of the higher ecclesiastical body of which it was a member—the synod of Philadelphia, which twice elected him moderator.

As a former Congregationalist he exerted a moderating influence on the deliberations of his Presbyterian colleagues. In 1729, he opposed a proposal that every minister in the synod of Philadelphia should be required "to give his hearty assent" to the Westminster Confession of Faith, holding on principle that the imposition of any creed was an infringement of an individual's rights. He played an active role in defending Presbyterianism from external criticism, publishing frequent articles in this cause. These earned him a reputation second only to Jonathan Edwards as a champion of Calvinism in America.

Dickinson's best-known book, *Familiar Letters to a Gentleman, upon a Variety of Seasonable and Important Subjects in Religion*, was frequently reprinted both in the colonies and abroad.

Dickinson was one of the leaders of a movement to found a "seminary of learning" for the middle colonies. He was disappointed by Harvard's and Yale's opposition to the "New Lights" of the church and by Yale's harsh treatment of his young friend, David Brainerd, a student who was dismissed because of his outspoken opposition to the faculty's conservative religious views. He considered the only other college in the colonies, William & Mary, to be too far away and too Anglican. He was a member of a committee appointed in 1739 to plan a fund-raising expedition to Great Britain for such a college, but the plan had to be tabled when war broke out between England and Spain.

Meanwhile, the influence of the Great Awakening brought a division between the "New Sides" and the "Old Sides" in the Presbyterian Church. When the presbytery of New Brunswick was expelled from the synod of Philadelphia in 1741, and Dickinson, a moderate New Sider, and his associates were unable to bring about a reconciliation, they withdrew in 1745 to form, in association with the presbytery of New Brunswick, the synod of New York, and Dickinson was elected the first moderator.

Dickinson revived his earlier interest in a much-needed college for the middle colonies. With the help of three laymen from New York, he and three other pastors (including Aaron Burr Sr.), applied to Governor Lewis Morris for a charter; Morris refused, but following his death, they renewed their application to acting governor John Hamilton, who granted the charter on October 22, 1746.

The first trustees announced Dickinson's appointment as president in April 1747. Classes began the fourth week in May in Elizabethtown, with about 10 students. One of Dickinson's divinity students, Caleb Smith, served as tutor, and the parsonage served as the college—the only library available was Dickinson's. His parlor was probably the classroom, and his dining room the refectory. It is likely that Genny, an enslaved girl he purchased in 1733, worked beside him, his tutor, and his students.

The first months of the college's life were Dickinson's last. His sudden death from pleurisy on October 7, 1747, was reported in *The New York Weekly Post Boy* on October 10:

> On Wednesday morning last, about four o'clock, died here, of a pleuritic illness, that eminently learned and pious minister of the Gospel and President of the College of New Jersey, the Rev. Mr. Jonathan Dickinson, in the sixtieth year of his age, who had been Pastor of the First Presbyterian Church in this Town for nearly forty years, and was the Glory and Joy of it.... By his death our Infant College is deprived of the Benefit and Advantage of his superior Accomplishments.... Never any Person in these Parts died more lamented.

The portrait of Dickinson in the Faculty Room in Nassau Hall was copied from an engraving prefixed to the Glasgow edition of his *Familiar Letters* and was presented to the College by the artist, Edward Ludlow Mooney, in 1872. Dickinson Hall, the home of the department of History, is named for him; it was built in 1930 as an extension of McCosh Hall, replacing an earlier Dickinson Hall that burned down in 1920 after standing for 50 years on the site now occupied by Firestone Library.

DILLON GYMNASIUM was opened in 1947 on the site of a former gymnasium that was destroyed by fire. When the earlier structure, known as University Gymnasium, was built in 1903, it was the largest collegiate gym in the country, but Dillon was significantly larger. Named in honor of Herbert Lowell Dillon 1907, one-time football captain and a principal donor to the building, Dillon was one of Princeton's last Collegiate Gothic buildings, and the last to be extensively adorned with gargoyles.

Prior to the opening of Jadwin Gymnasium in 1969 and DeNunzio Pool in 1990, Dillon was home to almost all intercollegiate indoor sports. It was probably best known nationally as the home court of Bill Bradley '65 during his legendary Princeton basketball career.

Dillon is now used mainly as the headquarters for campus recreation and physical fitness programs. Its facilities include the Stephens Fitness Center; a six-lane pool; basketball, volleyball, badminton, and squash courts; a table tennis room; an indoor driving range; a martial arts room; a dance studio; instructional spaces; athletic training spaces; and some coaches' offices. At the intercollegiate level, it is the home venue for men's and women's varsity volleyball competitions and some varsity wrestling matches.

In 2005 Dillon began hosting a dodgeball tournament each spring in which thousands of students, representing residential colleges, eating clubs, student organizations of various kinds, and other groups, compete in pitched battles that often last well past midnight.

Since 1971 Dillon has partnered with the local Princeton Recreation Department to offer a recreational youth basketball league on Saturday mornings from January through March in which Princeton students instruct and coach as many as 300 fourth-through-ninth graders from the community.

DINKY, THE, known to earlier generations of Princetonians as the PJ&B (Princeton Junction and Back), is a two-car train that shuttles 2.7 miles between the Princeton campus and the New Jersey Transit Northeast Corridor station at Princeton Junction. It is the shortest passenger train route in the country; the run takes approximately five minutes along a single track.

In 1839 Princeton's first train station was constructed by the Camden and Amboy Rail Road and Transportation Company at the end of Canal Street (now Alexander Road) on the east bank of the newly completed Delaware and Raritan Canal. As passenger and freight travel grew, the railroad line from Trenton to New Brunswick was straightened, moving the depot to Princeton Junction and leading to the construction of a new line connecting Princeton to the Junction, which opened in May 1865. The Princeton train stopped just below what is now Blair Arch; in those days, the trip took 20 minutes. In 1871 the Pennsylvania Railroad began to operate the route.

Blair Hall was built in 1897, and while it offered arriving passengers a majestic entrance to town and campus, the students who lived there complained about the noise, soot, and smoke. In 1917 the University negotiated with Pennsylvania Railroad to move the station south. Two Collegiate Gothic buildings opened a year later at the location on University Place where they served as train stations for the next 95 years. The move gave the University seven acres of land on which it built dormitories, and the University's landscape architect, Beatrix Farrand, created a walkway from Blair Arch to the new location.

In 1933 the coal-burning steam locomotive was replaced with a gasoline-electric train, and in 1936 the train was fully electrified. From 1905 until 1956, there were two tracks to handle heavy train travel on football weekends and other occasions that brought many alumni to campus.

Penn Central took over operation of the Princeton branch in 1968, followed by Conrail, and in 1984 by the New Jersey Department of Transportation. Knowing that the future of the money-losing Dinky was imperiled, the University entered into a contract with New Jersey Transit to purchase the two station buildings, the land on which the Dinky operated, and other adjacent lands for just under $900,000, with the understanding, reinforced by discussions between New Jersey Transit and Princeton Borough Mayor Barbara Sigmund, that the purchase funds would be used to sustain operation of the Dinky. New Jersey Transit had an easement that allowed it to operate the Dinky on what were now campus lands.

As part of the 1984 contract, the University also committed to spend another $400,000 to improve the stations, the platform, and the surrounding area; agreed to provide and maintain 150 commuter parking spaces; and gained the "right to move the existing terminus of the rail line southward," which the University anticipated it might do if, in the future, it developed the lands around the station for educational or other purposes. If it did, it would provide New Jersey Transit with a new easement to operate the Dinky at the new site.

In 2006 the University issued a campus plan that proposed developing the area around the Dinky station as an "arts and transit neighborhood" that would house the Lewis Center for the Arts, other arts buildings, and a multi-modal transit plaza with a new train station. The proposal was controversial in part because it required moving the train's terminus about 460 feet to the south; because of the location of the dividing line between the two municipalities, which bisected Forbes College, the proposed relocation would move the station from Princeton Borough to Princeton Township. (In 2013 the borough and township consolidated into a single municipality.)

Following a lengthy and contentious approval process and several legal challenges, the project was approved in 2012 and in 2014 a new station opened with an outdoor canopy connection to a new and larger Wawa convenience store that replaced a fabled ramshackle structure that had been near but not adjacent to the former station buildings. Both the new station and the new store were designed by Rick Joy Architects. The station has a pitched roof rising to 42 feet and includes black walnut benches designed and created by the New Hope, Pennsylvania, studio of George and Mira Nakashima.

At the dedication ceremony the new station was described as "a civic space" that was inspiring, beautiful, comfortable, and functional, and that "announces clearly and compellingly to passengers and passersby that Princeton not only has a train station but is proud of its train station—and its train, which comes to visit many times a day." The station was designed to serve both town and gown; the town has a significant commuter population, and at the time more than half of all Dinky riders were associated with the University as students, faculty, staff, alumni, or visitors to the campus.

Joy also redesigned one of the former station buildings to become a bar (eventually named the Dinky Bar & Kitchen) and expanded the other to become a restaurant.

During the approval process, the Princeton community addressed, and opposed, a suggestion by New Jersey Transit that the Dinky be replaced with a dedicated bus rapid transit connection between Princeton and Princeton Junction. While the idea was withdrawn at the time, the University designed the project to permit adaptation to bus rapid transit in the future if necessary. In 2019 New Jersey Transit again began a study to evaluate potential alternatives to the Dinky line, including a possible light rail replacement for the train and a possible conversion of the existing Dinky tracks to a roadway to be used by rubber-wheeled trams or buses.

As part of the approval process, the University agreed to install several historical markers near the former station buildings. Some of them recount the history of the rail line, but one notes that Princeton's homecoming song, "Going Back to Nassau Hall," written by Kenneth Clark 1905 in his senior year, makes reference to the Dinky in the lyric, "We'll clear the track as we go back, going back to Nassau Hall." (A reference to the Dinky of more recent vintage occurred in the television program "Family Ties" when young Alex Keaton went for his on-campus admission interview.)

Another marker recalls the Great Dinky Robbery of May 3, 1963, when four Princeton students riding horses and wearing cowboy outfits ambushed the 6:14 train as it arrived on campus just prior to Houseparties weekend, abducted four women passengers, and carried them off on horseback to Prospect Avenue, home of the eating clubs.

A much more dangerous incident occurred in 1990 when B. J. Miller '93 climbed on top of the Dinky while it was parked at the Princeton station and touched its 11,000-volt power line. He was severely hurt, losing part of his left arm and both legs below the knee. Miller used the settlement from the case to cover his medical bills and attend medical school, eventually becoming a hospice and palliative-care physician at the Zen Hospice Project in San Francisco.

DIVESTMENT. On May 2, 1968, more than 1,000 students rallied in front of Nassau Hall to call for a greater role for students in University governance, demonstrate heightened opposition to the war in Vietnam, press the University to become coeducational and more diverse, and protest the investment of the University's endowment in companies doing business in South Africa because of that country's policies of racial segregation and suppression.

Earlier that spring six students had submitted a proposal to the trustees that recommended against any future University investments "in banks, companies, and other financial institutions which presently participate in the South African, Rhodesian, Angolan, and Mozambique economies." The students called for the University to remove existing investments from companies that participated in these economies and to "refuse to accept monies, bequests, and endowments which come . . . primarily from the profits made in southern Africa."

An Ad Hoc Committee on Princeton's Investment in Companies Operating in South Africa, composed of faculty, staff, and students and chaired by economics professor Burton Malkiel *64, was formed to consider whether the University should adopt a policy of divestment. The committee recommended—without the support of its student members—that the University should not divest, but that it should communicate its concerns directly to the management of these companies. In January 1969, the faculty adopted the committee's report after adding a resolution calling for the University not to hold "any securities in companies that do a primary amount of their economic activity in South Africa."

In March 1969 the trustees accepted the recommendations and the resolution. They announced that the University would not hold stock in companies that did a primary amount of their business in South Africa and that it would convey the University's abhorrence of apartheid to companies in which it continued to hold stock. Later that month 51 members of the Association of Black Collegians occupied New South for 11 hours to call for full divestment.

In announcing their decision the trustees noted that the resources committee of the Council of the Princeton University Community (CPUC) was being established to "consider questions of general policy concerning the procurement and management of the University's financial resources," and said that in the future they would look to this committee for advice on investor responsibility issues.

In its early years, the resources committee spent most of its time working with the trustees (largely through a policy and budget subcommittee of the trustee finance committee) to determine what actions the University should take on shareholder resolutions related to corporate activity in southern Africa. These resolutions often sought disclosure of information about employment practices, requested that companies curtail their operations in southern Africa, or required cessation of sales or loans to the governments.

In 1977 the Rev. Leon Sullivan, an African American minister in Philadelphia who served on the board of General Motors, developed a set of principles that called on companies in South Africa to provide fair and equal treatment of all employees regardless of race, increase the number of Blacks and other people of color in management and supervisory positions, and take steps to improve their quality of life outside work. Princeton joined with other colleges and universities in pressing the companies in its investment portfolio to adhere to the Sullivan Principles.

In response to continuing campus activism, the trustees issued a statement in February 1978 affirming that the "basic functions of the University are to transmit and expand knowledge through teaching and scholarship" and that "in carrying out these functions there is a strong presumption against the University as an institution taking a position or playing an active role with respect to external issues of a political, economic, social, moral, or legal character."

In May 1978 the trustees issued a statement on "University Investments and South Africa" in which they said they would be "extremely reluctant to override this presumption because to do so may threaten the essential independence of the University." At the same time, they recognized "that the racially defined and repressive policies of South Africa create a situation so compelling as to warrant special attention" and that the University did have a "responsibility as a shareholder to take positions on questions raised by shareholder resolutions."

The May 1978 statement opposed a policy of "general disinvestment" from companies that did business in South Africa and urged caution in considering any policy of "selective disinvestment" beyond the already adopted policy of not investing in companies that did a primary amount of their business in South Africa. Before coming to a decision to exclude a company from the Princeton portfolio, there would have to be a thorough assessment of the full range of a company's activities and its overall commitment "to pursue generally accepted canons of corporate responsibility" and an opportunity for a full exchange of views between the company and the University.

The trustee statement followed weeks of picketing outside Nassau Hall and several large rallies organized by a student group called the People's Front for the Liberation of Southern Africa. On April 14, 1978, 210 students began a 27-hour sit-in at Nassau Hall; when they left the next morning, more than 300 other students joined them in marching to Corwin Hall where the trustees were meeting. (As a result of the sit-in, 205 students were given warnings.) On March 16, 1980, more than 70 students staged a "study-in" in the economics and finance section of Firestone Library, and on May 23, 1985, 88 members of the University community, now organized by a successor group called the Coalition for Divestment, were arrested for blocking access to Nassau Hall. (The disciplinary action again consisted of warnings.)

In October 1985 the trustees approved a set of academic initiatives to bring South African students and scholars to Princeton and specified criteria to be used and a process to be followed "in considering the possible selective divestiture of securities in companies doing business in South Africa." Actions that could lead to divestiture included failure to sign the Sullivan Principles, to achieve satisfactory ratings under the Principles, or to engage in a satisfactory exchange of views with the University.

The trustees emphasized that selective divestiture should be considered only when such action was required to prevent the University from being associated, as a stockholder or in other ways, with a company whose behavior represented, "in substantial degree, a clear and serious conflict with central values of the University."

In November 1985, the faculty voted 114–96 to adopt a resolution calling for compete divestment from companies doing business in South Africa.

By January 1987, the University had dissociated from three companies, and it eventually dissociated from one more. The trustees issued a statement reiterating that "for Princeton, divestiture means disassociation," which meant that the University would not hold a company's stock, purchase its products, accept gifts or grants from it, allow it to recruit on campus, or do any other form of business with it. The statement also reiterated that "for Princeton, the purpose of selective divestiture is to separate the University from companies whose conduct contravenes the values of the University; the purpose is not to make political statements, to censure governments, or to pressure either companies or governments to adopt particular policies."

In 1992 the trustees and the resources committee codified "Guidelines for Resources Committee Consideration of Investment-Driven 'Social Responsibility' Issues." The guidelines called for considering, first, whether there is "considerable, thoughtful, and sustained campus interest in a particular issue." (While granting flexibility in determining "sustained campus interest," the guidelines suggested that the issue would need to be raised "over an extended period of time, say two academic years.") When such interest exists, the committee would then consider "the magnitude, scope, and representativeness of the expressions of campus opinion," whether central University values are at stake, and whether it is "possible for the University community to reach a consensus on how the University should respond."

In June 2006 the trustees approved a resources committee recommendation that the University dissociate from companies that directly or indirectly conducted operations in Darfur that supported acts of genocide, and that it prevent future investment in such companies. Although the University held no direct equity positions in any companies doing business in Sudan, the trustees directed the University to review the behavior of five companies where it might have indirect involvement through mutual funds or other commingled investments. The University determined it did have exposure to one company that had ceased doing business in Sudan, and it decided to liquidate its holdings in that company for unrelated reasons.

The fundamental goal of the University's investment strategy is to maximize the total long-term return on investments to support the University's core mission of teaching and research. The resources committee continues to provide a venue where investment-driven social responsibility issues can be considered within this context, and each year the chair of the committee meets with the trustee finance committee to discuss the resources committee's work. Over recent years the committee considered proposals to divest from companies doing business in Israel, gun manufacturers, and private prisons, without recommending additional divestments. After periodically considering proposals to divest from fossil fuel companies, in May 2021 the committee recommended that the University dissociate from "fossil fuel companies that deny climate change and/or spread climate disinformation" and from "the highest greenhouse gas-emitting sectors of the fossil fuel industry (e.g., thermal coal)."

In the late 1990s and early 2000s, the resources committee provided a forum for review of the University's policy and practices regarding labor issues, including fair labor standards, in the manufacture of products licensed by Princeton and bearing the University's name or logo. Beginning in 1998, campus activists expressed concerns about sweatshop conditions in factories producing such products. The committee received updates from the University as it became a founding member of the Fair Labor Association and later joined the Worker Rights Consortium, Washington, DC-based organizations that assist universities in holding licensees accountable for adhering to codes of conduct regarding the treatment of workers and working conditions in the factories where collegiate merchandise is made.

DOD HALL, named for Professor Albert Baldwin Dod 1822, was given to Princeton by his sister, Susan Dod Brown, who also donated Brown Hall in honor of her husband.

Albert Baldwin Dod entered the College when he was 15, graduated two years later, and was appointed professor of mathematics when he was 25. Dod also taught political economy and architecture. The Princeton and Slavery project found that he was the last Princeton faculty member recorded as owning a slave.

Dod Hall opened in 1890 at a time when dormitory room rates varied; its rent fell between pricey Witherspoon and the "poor man's dormitory," Edwards. The four-story Italianate Dod had three vertical entryways opening to the east, and its main, central door featured a distinctive Romanesque arch supported by marble pillars.

In a 1909 master plan, supervising architect Ralph Adams Cram proposed that Dod be relocated and reduced in height so as not to interfere with the sightlines south from Nassau Hall and the terrace between Whig and Clio halls. His proposal was not enacted and today Dod remains in its original location and at its original height, with its 80 rooms providing housing for juniors and seniors.

DODDS, HAROLD WILLIS *14 was the 15th president of Princeton. He was born in Utica, Pennsylvania, on June 28, 1889. His father, a Presbyterian minister, was a professor at Grove City College, and Harold spent most of his youth on or near the campus. He graduated from Grove City in 1909 and, after teaching public school for two years, did graduate work in politics at Princeton (MA 1914) and the University of Pennsylvania (PhD 1917). After completing his doctorate, he married Margaret Murray of Halifax, Canada, on Christmas Day, 1917.

During World War I he served in the US Food Administration, and then taught at Western Reserve University. He gained a reputation as an expert on problems of local government, and in 1920 he became secretary of the National Municipal League, a post he held until 1928.

The president of the league was the secretary of state, Charles Evans Hughes. Hughes formed a high opinion of his young executive officer and got him involved in the electoral problems of Latin America. As adviser to the president of Nicaragua, Dodds drafted the Nicaraguan electoral law of 1923 and helped supervise the elections of 1928. He also served as an adviser to the commission that vainly sought to arrange a plebiscite to end a long dispute between Chile and Peru over the provinces of Tacna and Arica.

During this period, Dodds gave lecture courses at various eastern colleges. In 1925, he joined the Princeton faculty as a professor of politics. He was promoted to full professor in 1927, and in 1930 he was asked to chair the committee overseeing the newly established school of Public and International Affairs. He had been a leader in forming the school, which was a cooperative enterprise of Politics, Economics, History, and, later, Sociology. He and his colleagues conducted an intensive survey of the government of New Jersey and made recommendations to achieve savings and improve the administration of the state. Some of their recommendations were put into effect—an unusual occurrence in the history of such reports.

When the trustees chose Dodds as president in 1933, they were selecting a scholar with wide experience in administration and in public and international affairs, and they also were selecting the youngest president of Princeton in over a century. He was not an obvious choice. As he himself said, "It was a surprise to me and quite a shock. The last thing in the world I wanted to be was a university president. But I felt I either had to accept the offer or leave town."

Dodds more than rose to the occasion. He remained in office until 1957, and during that time he steered the University through the Great Depression, World War II, the postwar period of readjustment, and the Korean War.

At the June 1940 Commencement, Dodds declared that "no matter what the future holds, the University pledges its full cooperation with our government in its program of national defense." Two days after Japan attacked Pearl Harbor on December 7, 1941, he sent a telegram to the White House placing the resources of the University at the country's disposal. While the University was adopting an accelerated program to give its students an opportunity to graduate before they entered the armed forces, the army and navy were sending hundreds of young men to the campus for general or specialized training, along with the first 23 women to take a course at Princeton, in photogrammetry.

The number of students on campus fluctuated widely from month to month, and a faculty depleted by enlistments or calls to government service had to teach unfamiliar subjects at breakneck speed. Among the students in the Navy's V-12 training program were four African Americans who were allowed to enroll as full-time civilian students when the war ended; three of them graduated, beginning with John Howard '47, who became the first Black student to receive an undergraduate degree from Princeton. The University had one Japanese undergraduate, Kentaro

Ikeda '44, on campus during the war. With an administrator serving as his sponsor, the government permitted him to stay, but he was effectively under house arrest; unlike some other colleges, Princeton did not agree to host Japanese American students who faced imprisonment in internment camps on the west coast.

During the war, Dodds made efforts to keep in touch with Princeton students throughout the world. In 1943 he contacted 1,300 Princetonians in the armed services and offered them three books of their choosing, wherever they might be—an offer that was deeply appreciated and long-remembered. At the end of the war he set up the Princeton program for servicemen, which made it easy for former students to resume their educations almost as soon as they were discharged, which many did.

Supported in many cases by the GI Bill, veterans returned to campus in unprecedented numbers to complete, and in some cases to begin, their studies. In 1946 the campus bulged with more than 3,400 undergraduates (some with wives and families), as compared to a pre-war peak of about 2,400, as cots were installed in Baker Rink and Brown Hall became married student housing.

Despite these challenges, the intellectual stature of the University and the breadth of its interests increased steadily during Dodds' presidency. He had a remarkable talent for recognizing excellence. Bright young men were quickly promoted; first-rate scholars were attracted from other institutions and abroad (especially from war-ravaged Europe); and new departments and programs were created. To cite just two examples: he helped lure Jacob Viner from the University of Chicago to strengthen the department of Economics, and he strongly supported the decision of the Classics department to promote a young instructor named Robert Goheen '40 *48.

The creative arts and a program in American Civilization (later American Studies) were added to the curriculum; the Office of Population Research was founded; the departments of Aeronautical Engineering (1941), Religion (1945), and Music (1946) were established; and a Council of the Humanities (1953) was formed. These initiatives, along with the postwar expansion of the school of Public and International Affairs and of sponsored research programs, vastly increased the size of the faculty and led to the creation of a professional research and library staff, which by 1956 numbered 237. Over the course of Dodds' presidency, between 1933 and 1956, the faculty grew from 327 to 582; the number of undergraduates grew from 2,309 to 2,948, and the number of graduate students more than doubled from 293 to 636.

As Princeton was adjusting to the return of students and faculty from the war, it welcomed the opportunity to celebrate the 200th anniversary of its founding. The year 1946–47 featured an almost continuous series of scholarly conferences and three major convocations. Over a thousand scholars and leaders from all parts of the world attended, including President Harry Truman, former President Herbert Hoover, and future President Dwight Eisenhower. Some 100 honorary degrees were conferred over the course of the year, and as a continuing memorial of the anniversary, bicentennial preceptorships were established to enable promising junior members of the faculty to spend a year in uninterrupted research.

In addressing the final bicentennial convocation, Dodds outlined his view of the future:

> Princeton enters her third century with certain convictions as to what she wants her future to be. We shall uphold the banner of the general as the only safe foundation for the particular. We shall strive for quality rather than quantity; we have no illusions of grandeur that bigness will satisfy. As a residential university, we shall emphasize the community of students and teachers, believing that the life of the campus is a potent supplement to formal study and instruction.

The growth that had taken place was expensive, including, especially, some badly needed additions to the physical plant. The open-stack Firestone Library was opened in 1948 as a "laboratory for the humanities and social sciences," 15 years after Dodds began working toward it. When the cornerstone was laid, he said: "Within the walls of this building the miracle will constantly occur that we take for granted . . . the miracle of the imagination kindled, prejudice thrown overboard, dogma rejected, conviction strengthened, perspective lengthened. This miracle is performed by teachers and students together through the instrumentality of books."

In 1947 Dillon Gymnasium opened on the site of the former gym, which had been destroyed by fire. The acquisition of the Forrestal campus (formerly part of the Rockefeller Center for Medical Research) in 1951 made urgently needed space available for engineering and the sciences. Woodrow Wilson Hall (now Corwin Hall) provided a home for the school of Public and International Affairs. And when a new dormitory, 1915 Hall, was constructed in 1949, it helped house the growing student population.

All this cost money. In 1940–41, with Dodds' encouragement, alumni volunteers launched an Annual Giving program that encouraged classmates to make unrestricted gifts; the program raised $80,000 in its first year, and by 1957 was raising $1.3 million. Annual Giving continues to be a critical source of revenue for the University, particularly because it is both spendable when received and unrestricted. In 1938 Dodds began an effort to increase the number of endowed professorships at Princeton, and by the end of his tenure 30 new ones had been established, almost doubling the number and more than doubling the income from this source.

As Princeton grew, both physically and in intellectual stature, and as demographic changes in the composition of the student body began slowly to take shape in the latter years of his presidency (in 1947 the Student Hebrew Association held its first official service on campus with Albert Einstein as one of its speakers), the external challenges continued: the Korean War impacted students in the early 1950s, as did the tensions of the Cold War. When Whig Clio invited Alger Hiss to speak on campus in 1956, Dodds diffused intense campus controversy when he expressed his personal disapproval but allowed the students to go ahead with their invitation.

At Dodds' final faculty meeting in the spring of 1957, the faculty noted that during his presidency, "Princeton has grown . . . in all the things which make a university—in intellectual eminence and in influence on our society. It is a better place for scholars to do their work than it was when you became president, and we are grateful for all that you have done to make it so."

At his final Commencement that June, he received an honorary degree; the citation described him as "a man of honor and courage, integrity and humor." In bidding farewell to the graduating seniors, he said: "My fondest wish for every member of the class is that each one of you will have an experience similar to mine; that you will find a work which you love above everything else under circumstances which spell fulfillment; and that you may have the good fortune to find it in a place which you love above all other places on earth."

One of the most prestigious undergraduate awards, the Harold Willis Dodds Achievement Prize, was established in 1957 by the trustees of the *Daily Princetonian*. It is presented each year at Class Day to a senior who best embodies qualities associated with Dodds, including "clear thinking, moral courage, a patient and judicious regard for the opinions of others, and a thorough devotion to the welfare of the University and to the life of the mind."

The graduate school confers honorific Harold Dodds fellowships, and Dodds Atrium in Robertson Hall serves as the entryway into the school of Public and International Affairs in recognition of his role as chair of the committee that initially directed the school, and his success as president in raising funds to support the school, create its graduate program, and construct its first free-standing home. There is also a street in Princeton, Dodds Lane, named in his honor.

EAST ASIAN STUDIES, THE DEPARTMENT OF. Although the department of East Asian Studies can trace its roots to the department of Oriental Languages and Literatures, founded in 1927, that department originally had no East Asian component. It was established to provide graduate work in Semitic and Indo-European philology, with no plan for an undergraduate program. Undergraduates could take courses in Far Eastern politics in the school of Public and International Affairs or in Chinese art in the department of Art and Archaeology, and after World War II they could take additional courses in the social sciences thanks to the appointment of William Lockwood in political economy and Marion Levy Jr. in sociology.

The real origin of today's department of East Asian Studies dates to the appointment in 1956 of historian Frederick W. "Fritz" Mote. During World War II, Mote served in China in the Office of Strategic Services, and after the war he returned to China as one of the first westerners to enroll as an undergraduate at the University of Nanjing (where he studied Chinese history). Mote received his PhD in Sinology in 1954 at the University of Washington-Seattle, and in 1954–55 he was a postdoctoral researcher at National Taiwan University.

Three years after arriving at Princeton, Mote was joined by Ta-Tuan Ch'en, and together they worked to establish a rigorous Chinese language program and to improve the facilities and expand the holdings of the Gest Collection (then known as the Gest Oriental Library), which had moved to Princeton from McGill University in 1937. Originally begun with the acquisition of many rare books, the Gest Collection now holds more than 600,000 volumes of Chinese, Japanese, and Korean books; it is a working collection that supports all types of research done in the department and program of East Asian Studies.

In 1959 Mote was joined by Marius Jansen '44, a specialist in Japanese history. Jansen was one of a small group of scholars who deepened American understanding of Japanese history and helped introduce Japan into college and university curricula. His students in turn fanned out to develop Japanese studies throughout the United States.

Mote and Jansen together were key figures in the growth of East Asian studies at Princeton in the 1960s. They secured financial support from the John D. Rockefeller and Ford foundations in 1961, the Carnegie Corporation in 1963, and the US Department of Education in 1965. That support enabled the University to acquire a wealth of new materials for the Gest Library; to establish a highly regarded Chinese linguistics program, which Mote directed from 1966 to 1974; and to add a number of new East Asian specialists to the faculty.

In 1961 an interdepartmental program in East Asian Studies was set up under the direction of Jansen, and in 1969 Oriental Studies was transitioned into two independent departments, Near Eastern Studies and East Asian Studies. In addition to directing the program in East Asian Studies, Jansen served as the first chair of the East Asian Studies department.

Mote and Jansen were instrumental in the growth of East Asian studies at colleges beyond Princeton. They worked with colleagues at other universities to establish inter-university centers in Tokyo and Taipei. In 1966, a summer school—initially in Chinese and, after 1970, also in Japanese—was established at Middlebury College with Princeton direction and cooperation. The inter-university programs (now in Yokohama and Beijing) and Middlebury summer schools continue to thrive.

Jansen taught at the University until his retirement in 1992. His long service and many contributions to the study of Japan and its culture were recognized by his appointment to the Japan Academy in the spring of 1999; later that year, Japan awarded him the Prize for Distinguished Cultural Merit (Bunka Korosho). Jansen was the first person not of Japanese descent to receive this award.

From the first, East Asian Studies focused on undergraduate mastery of the modern colloquial languages. Today, the Chinese, Japanese, and Korean language programs are renowned for their exceptional achievement. Princeton professor Chih-p'ing Chou's innovative 14-volume graduated Chinese language textbook series, published from 1992 to 2016, has been acknowledged as the best in the world, and has been adopted by academic institutions around the globe. In the expanding Korean language program, faculty have received grants to explore using advanced technology, such as virtual-reality video, to promote Korean language learning in virtual environments.

All language courses offer instruction from elementary to highly advanced levels and operate entirely in the primary language in terms of reading materials and assignments; classroom discussion is in the colloquial version of the language. The department encourages overseas study and runs intensive summer-language programs in Chinese and Japanese through Princeton in Beijing and Princeton in Ishikawa that attract students from around the country. Princeton students have access to departmental resources about other approved overseas summer programs in Chinese, Japanese, and Korean as well.

East Asian Studies faculty have offered summer Global Seminars in China, Japan, Korea, and Vietnam.

Along with its language training, the department offers undergraduate classes in the literature, history, anthropology, media, and cultural studies of China, Japan, and Korea. Classes explore the perspectives of each country and broader perspectives across East Asia. The program in East Asian Studies offers a certificate of proficiency to students in other departments and provides funding for undergraduates to study languages in East Asia. Along with the department of East Asian Studies, other cooperating departments in the program include Anthropology, Art and Archaeology, Comparative Literature, Economics, History, Music, Politics, Religion, Sociology, and the school of Public and International Affairs.

Princeton's PhD program in East Asian Studies has long been recognized as one of the leading graduate programs in its field. Doctoral students train in Chinese and Japanese history and literature, Korean cultural studies, anthropology of East Asia, and the transnational social and cultural study of contemporary East Asia.

East Asian Studies faculty members commonly hold joint appointments in other departments, such as History and Comparative Literature. Its associated faculty includes professors from the departments of Religion, Philosophy, Anthropology, and Art and Archaeology. The department regularly coordinates with the Princeton Institute for International and Regional Studies (PIIRS) to offer lectures and conferences on campus.

In today's world, East Asia is a center for culture, economics, science, and technology. By teaching both the contemporary languages and the history and cultures that underpin those languages, the department prepares students to be global citizens in an ever more globalized world.

East College, Princeton's first building used exclusively as a dormitory, was erected in 1833. It stood on the east side of Cannon Green, later facing its identical twin, West College (1836). With Nassau Hall on the north and Whig and Clio halls on the south, East and West colleges helped to form a symmetrical quadrangle. The razing of East College in 1896 to make way for Pyne Library was called by some alumni "the Crime of Ninety-Six."

In its day East College was the undergraduate home of a number of eminent Princetonians. A notable group lived on the fourth and fifth floors of the south entry in the 1870s: Charles Scribner in the Class of 1875; Howard Russell Butler, William Allen Butler, and Bayard Henry in the Class of 1876; Henry B. Thompson and Moses Taylor Pyne in the Class of 1877; Percy Pyne 1878; and Cleveland and Earl Dodge in the Class of 1879.

These nine called themselves the South East Club and for many years after graduation they met annually to talk about the University and its advancement. They were especially interested in enlarging the campus, and their combined lifetime efforts secured for the University nearly a square mile of additional property. As individuals they gave five buildings and made large gifts to the endowment. At one of their annual meetings they chipped in to endow a fellowship in the graduate school which they called the South East Club Fellowship in Social Science.

East College was designed to provide 32 double rooms on four floors; unlike Nassau Hall, where students' rooms faced north and south, the rooms in East College were sited to capture the prevailing westerly breezes.

East Pyne, originally Pyne Library, was built in 1897, a sesquicentennial gift of Albertina Shelton Pyne, mother of Moses Taylor Pyne 1877. Designed by William A. Potter (architect also of Chancellor Green Library and Alexander Hall) in Collegiate Gothic, it was used with Chancellor Green as the university's library until the completion of Firestone Library in 1948. Thereafter, as Pyne Administration Building, it housed various administrative offices until 1965, when, with the completion of New South Building, it assumed its current name and was renovated to accommodate offices and classrooms of various language and literature departments and programs and also to form the southern part of the Chancellor Green student center.

The opening of the Frist Campus Center in 2000 allowed for the removal of the student center from East Pyne, and in 2004 the building was renovated again. An underground addition provided a 71-seat auditorium, classrooms, and a language laboratory. The building became part of the Andlinger Center for the Humanities, housing departments of Classics, Comparative Literature, German, French and Italian, Slavic Languages and Literatures, and Spanish and Portuguese.

In niches above the western arch at the foot of the tower are statues of John Witherspoon and James McCosh, and, higher up, James Madison 1771 and Oliver Ellsworth 1766. On the south side of the tower is a sun dial. The court in the center of East Pyne is dedicated to Henry B. Thompson 1877, longtime chair of the trustee committee on grounds and buildings, who as an undergraduate lived in East College, which was razed to make way for Pyne Library.

The arches of East Pyne are popular sites for performances by a cappella groups. In 2018, the easternmost arch was named for James Collins Johnson, a fugitive slave who arrived on campus in 1839 and worked first as a janitor, and then for almost 60 years as the only licensed campus vendor, selling fruits, candies, lemonade, and other snacks to students from a wheelbarrow near the site of the arch. Collins Arch is the first arch freshman pass through after they leave Opening Exercises to make their formal entrance onto the campus during the Pre-rade, and it is the first arch seniors walk through when they leave the Baccalaureate service that begins three days of ceremonies culminating in Commencement.

Eating Clubs were first formed in the nineteenth century when the College was unable to provide adequate dining facilities for its growing student population. With the banning of Greek-letter fraternities in 1855, eating clubs became the dominant social scene for undergraduates.

From 1756 until 1803, students ate in Nassau Hall. In 1803 dining facilities moved to a refectory in a building later named Philosophical Hall, on the current site of Chancellor Green. From 1834 to 1846 the College also operated a cheaper refectory on William Street (charging $1.50 rather than $2 a week) that became known as the "poor house." Originally, all undergraduates were required to take their meals on campus, but by the 1840s student revulsion at the bare bones provisions had become so intense that, beginning in 1843, they were permitted to board with families in town, where the rate was higher but the offerings more palatable. In some cases, students established "select associations" to provide their meals, with charges that were lower than on campus.

In 1855 the College discontinued food service and in 1856 the refectory was permanently closed, requiring all students to take their meals in town. Many chose the "select associations," and by 1864 there were 12 of them, by then called eating clubs. The clubs grew in number—there were 25 in 1876—but since they served only the students who established them, they lasted only four years at most. They usually sported playful names like "Knights of the Round Table," "Old Bourbon," or "Hole in the Wall"; some had names that hungry students of earlier years would have appreciated, such as "Hollow Inn," "Nunquam Plenus [Never Full]," and "More." (Woodrow Wilson 1879 ate with the "Alligators.")

This expansion of the clubs occurred at a time when most extracurricular activities were prohibited and after the trustees had voted in 1853 to ban Greek-letter fraternities. (The first fraternity at Princeton had been founded in 1843, and within a few years 12 fraternities had Princeton chapters.) With the lack of campus dining options and the prohibition on extracurricular life and fraternities, student life increasingly focused on these off-campus dining arrangements.

In 1879 a group of students rented Ivy Hall on Mercer Street (originally the home of the College's short-lived law school), engaged their own steward, and began a more formal kind of eating club. Four years later they incorporated and built a simple frame house on Prospect Avenue, thus becoming the first self-perpetuating eating club.

Ivy was followed in 1886 by the University Cottage Club, which got its start in the "University cottage" on Railroad Avenue (now University Place), and in the early 1890s by Tiger Inn, Cap and Gown, Colonial, Cannon, and Elm. By the turn of the century, about a quarter of the juniors and seniors belonged to these seven clubs, while other students continued to take their meals in boardinghouses. As the size of the student body increased from 603 to 1,354 between 1888 and 1902, seven more clubs were added in the first decade of the twentieth century: Campus, Charter, Quadrangle, Tower, Terrace, Key and Seal, and Dial Lodge. By the end of the decade, two-thirds of juniors and seniors were eating in 14 clubs, and while the newer clubs were housed in modest frame buildings, the older ones now enjoyed handsome brick or stone clubhouses, some of them designed by architects of campus buildings.

Meanwhile, the College acquired the short-lived University Hotel at the corner of Nassau Street and University Place in the 1870s, converted it to University Hall, and began serving meals there in a "Commons." (At University Hall's inaugural dinner in 1892 students dined on consommé Italienne, filet of striped bass, filet of beef, spaghetti Napolitane, ribs of beef, Vermont turkey, mashed potatoes, green peas, mashed turnips, apple pie, and souffle of rice.) By 1906 all freshmen were eating there, and they were joined two years later by all sophomores. The undergraduate student government issued an edict abolishing the freshman and sophomore "waiting clubs" that had grown up as pipelines to the eating clubs.

When Wilson became president in 1902, he called the condition of the students left out of clubs "a little less than deplorable." His greatest concern, however, was that the clubs emphasized social rather than intellectual aspects of student life, with the result that the University was becoming for club members "only an artistic setting and background for life on Prospect Avenue." Wilson's proposed alternative to the eating clubs was the ill-fated Quad Plan he presented to the trustees in 1907. Under its terms, the clubs would either have been abolished or developed into smaller residential quads as part of the University.

The trustees rejected the plan, and after Wilson's departure new clubs continued to form—the short-lived Arch Club in 1911 (disbanded in 1917), Cloister Inn in 1912, and Gateway Club in 1913—and eight more new clubhouses replaced frame-house "incubators." Some students and alumni began to express opposition to the club system, and as early as 1907 the *Daily Princetonian* reported a "social crisis" on campus triggered by concerns about the growing selectivity of the clubs. By 1914 the election of new members was governed by a system of "bickering" that took place in February of sophomore year, with the term "bicker" meaning "any talk, argument, or discussion designed to induce any man to join any club."

In January 1917 five sophomores issued a manifesto in the *Princetonian* which declared that the club system operated against the best interests of the University. The spokesman for the group was Richard Cleveland 1919, the son of former US president and Princeton trustee Grover Cleveland. Some 90 sophomores (more than a quarter of the class) boycotted bicker and continued to eat at commons in the newly built Madison Hall. The *Prince* called for the University to acquire the club buildings and operate them as dining halls with no membership restrictions, but the reform movement was short-circuited later that spring when the United States declared war on Germany and normal college activities ceased for the duration of the war.

After the war Court Club opened in 1921 and Arbor Inn in 1923, bringing the total number of clubs to 18. The proportion of juniors and seniors who were club members rose to 75 percent. The administration and the clubs reached a "Gentlemen's Agreement" under which the clubs were largely permitted to police themselves, and house parties became an established custom each spring.

A Graduate Inter-Club Council, composed of the chairs of the clubs' graduate boards, was formed, as was an Undergraduate Inter-Club Association (later Inter-Club Council) composed of club presidents. They were charged with recommending improvements in bicker, and their suggestions (made but not enacted) included abolition of bicker week, establishment of a system of lot drawing for club selection, removal of dining facilities from the clubs, and the creation of a University-sponsored club on campus.

Arbor Inn and Gateway failed to survive the Great Depression, but the rest of the clubs remained the center of campus social activity, and by the end of the 1930s 90 percent of juniors and seniors were club members. Arbor Inn's building on Ivy Lane was converted to academic uses, and after Gateway closed in 1937 the University operated it for a few years as a nonselective club with a faculty member in residence. The clubhouse was then taken over by the new Prospect Club, which tried to operate it as a co-op from 1941 to 1943 and again after the war until it eventually closed in 1959 following the founding of Woodrow Wilson Lodge in 1957 as a different kind of alternative to the selective clubs.

When the clubs resumed operations after World War II on a campus brimming with returning veterans, they faced class sections nearly double their previous size and renewed criticism of the club selection process. The practice at that time was that sophomores would bicker all the clubs; during bicker week they would wait for delegations from the clubs to call on them in their rooms, and they could receive bids from more than one. In 1950, more than 600 sophomores in the Class of 1952 (75 percent) declared that they would not join clubs unless every sophomore who bickered received at least one bid. (In later years this guarantee of admission was achieved by a "hat bid" process, in which the names of any students with no bids at the end of bicker were put in a hat and drawn by each selective club in turn until everyone had a bid; one member of the Class of 1983 later recalled: "I know we had a hat bid procedure senior year because I held the hat.")

The concept of 100-percent-bicker was violated in the "dirty bicker" of 1958 when 23 students, more than half of whom were Jewish, were not chosen for any club. Dirty bicker attracted national attention and led to renewed calls for alternative dining and social facilities. In 1961 Wilson Lodge moved into Wilcox Hall as the renamed Woodrow Wilson Society, and in 1968 it became Princeton's first residential college. In 1969 the University created a lower-cost Madison Society in which juniors and seniors could have breakfast at Wilcox, lunch at Commons, and dinner in New South's top floor cafeteria. In 1970 Princeton Inn College (later Forbes) opened as Princeton's second residential college.

In 1966 President Robert Goheen expressed his dissatisfaction with the "brutal" bicker system and 10 student leaders published a report declaring that the system imposed "a false hierarchy on Princeton social life" and erected "artificial barriers among its students." The students suggested replacing bicker with a process that would have allowed sophomores to express preferences in a procedure that also had elements of random selection. The proposal was not adopted, but shortly thereafter several clubs, beginning with Terrace in 1967 and then Colonial, discontinued bicker and adopted sign-in policies. By the end of the 1970s, eight of the then-13 clubs admitted members on a sign-in basis.

Court Club closed in 1964 and Key and Seal in 1968. The University used both buildings to create Stevenson Hall as a dining and social facility open to all juniors and seniors; in 1972 membership was extended to sophomores and a kosher kitchen was added. (The kosher kitchen remained until the Center for Jewish Life opened in 1993 on the site of the former Gateway/Prospect Club.)

In 1968 only 70 percent of the sophomore class joined the clubs, and in 1971 the percentage dropped to fewer than half. The University provided funds to renovate Terrace Club and managed the club's operations from 1970 to 1972; Dial Lodge closed briefly in 1969 and then reopened; Elm and Campus joined forces for several years; Cloister closed in 1972 and reopened in 1977; and when Cannon closed in 1975 it became Notestein Hall, home of the Office of Population Research.

In 1988 the Cannon graduate board merged with Dial, and a year later the merger expanded to include Elm, creating an entity known as Dial, Elm, Cannon (DEC); it closed in 1998 and then reopened in the former Cannon building in 2011 after the club bought back the building from the University. (The University obtained the Dial Lodge building, which for a time became the Bendheim Center for Finance, and the Elm Club building, which became the Carl A. Fields Center for Equality and Cultural Understanding.)

In 1969 Colonial and Terrace became the first clubs to announce they would admit women undergraduates, followed a year later by seven other clubs. Cannon remained all-male until it closed in 1975. In 1979, Sally Frank '80 filed a lawsuit against the three remaining all-male clubs. In 1986 Cottage reached a settlement and admitted women, but Tiger Inn and Ivy held out until the New Jersey Supreme Court ruled in 1990 that they could not deny membership to women. Ivy complied immediately while Tiger waited to admit women until early 1991 after the US Supreme Court refused to entertain an appeal of the ruling.

In the 1980s four major developments helped reshape the social environment for Princeton students. One was the creation in 1982 of a residential college system for all freshmen and sophomores. Another was a change in the New Jersey drinking age from 18 to 19 in 1980 and then to 21 in 1983, which led to the closing of the campus pub. A third was the reintroduction of Greek-letter fraternities and then sororities, which by 1993 were enrolling about 15 percent of the student body and had become pipelines for freshmen and sophomores into the selective eating clubs. The fourth was a change in the bicker process so that sophomores could apply to only one club, resulting in single up-or-down decisions for all who bickered.

In 2000 the University opened the Frist Campus Center, which included extensive dining, social, and meeting spaces, and in 2007 it began implementing a revised residential college system that included three four-year colleges with spaces for juniors and seniors. It introduced shared-meal plans that allowed some juniors and seniors who were club members to live in the colleges and eat some of their meals there while also eating meals at their clubs. In 2005 Campus Club closed its doors and gave its building to the University, which re-opened it in 2009 as a student-programmed facility for undergraduates and graduate students. In 2006 the University changed its calculation of financial aid for all juniors and seniors to set the student's assumed dining cost for those two years at the level of an average eating-club dining contract.

In 2009 a student-faculty-staff-alumni task force on the relationships between the University and the eating clubs was asked to "examine whether there are steps that can and should be taken to strengthen those relationships for the mutual benefit of the clubs and the University, and for the benefit of Princeton students and the undergraduate experience." In May 2010, the task force issued a report that reaffirmed the important roles clubs played at Princeton, identifying their strengths as their relatively small size, the "familial ethos" they evoke, the responsibility students are given in managing and programming the clubs, and the lifelong connections to the clubs of many alumni.

The task force made recommendations to address several areas of concern, including lower participation in the clubs by students from lower-income and minority backgrounds; a "culture of alcohol" that characterized much of club life; a "hurtful" selection process; the pipeline relationships between the selective clubs and Greek-letter organizations; and the financial viability of the clubs, particularly the sign-in clubs. The task force believed it was "important to sustain both a critical mass of clubs and a significant number of spaces available on a sign-in basis" and suggested consideration of an alternative selection process that would match students based on rankings from students and the clubs. The clubs did eventually create an online admission system that allowed clubs and students to rank and match; they also reintroduced a multi-club bicker process in which students could bicker at more than one selective club.

In 2017–18 a subsequent task force composed of students, alumni, and staff made additional recommendations to ensure that the clubs "are inclusive, that they contribute in positive ways to the undergraduate experience, and that their memberships reflect the increasingly diverse student body." It made recommendations related to diversity and inclusion, student health and well-being, eating club costs, and new eating club–University partnerships.

In 2018, nine of the 11 eating clubs elected women as presidents.

In 2020, 11 clubs were operating; five (Charter, Cloister, Colonial, Quadrangle, and Terrace) were admitting students on a sign-in basis and six (Ivy, Cap and Gown, Cottage, Dial-Elm-Cannon, Tiger Inn, and Tower) still practiced bicker. (Charter had announced but deferred plans to reinstate bicker.) About two-thirds of juniors and seniors were members of clubs. The clubs continued to be managed by independent graduate boards, undergraduate officers, and professional staff; the graduate boards hired outside advisers to assist them and the club officers; and the officers met regularly with representatives of the University. (In 2020–21 the clubs suspended operations because of the COVID-19 pandemic.)

In addition to dining spaces, the clubs have game rooms, libraries, study spaces, and media rooms, and the University provides them with wireless connections to the University's network. Activities at the clubs include dinner discussions, dances, intramural sports, and community service projects. (The clubs cooperate each year in sponsoring a street fair on Prospect Avenue known as "Truckfest," with proceeds going to local charities that address issues of food insecurity.) Each club has a liaison to the University's SHARE office (Sexual Harassment/Assault Advising, Resources, and Education), which works with the clubs on matters related to sexual harassment and assault. Each fall and spring the clubs host "lawnparties," with programming at each club supplemented by a concert sponsored by the Undergraduate Student Government and open to all students.

In 1958 the graduate board of Tower Club examined ways to introduce educational programming at the clubs, and in 1961 the nonprofit Princeton Tower Foundation (later the Princeton Prospect Foundation) was formed; it allows tax-exempt fundraising to support educational pursuits (library facilities, computer clusters, faculty fellows) and public service activities at the clubs, and efforts to preserve and improve their historic and architecturally significant buildings. All the clubs except Cottage are members of the foundation.

To help sustain its exempt status, the foundation provides periodic public access to the clubs. In 2017 it engaged the author Clifford Zink to write a book, *The Princeton Eating Clubs*, about the origins, evolution, and historic significance of the clubs and their buildings.

The complete list of clubs follows:

Ivy Club 1879
University Cottage Club 1886
Tiger Inn 1890
Cap and Gown Club 1890
Colonial Club 1891
Cannon Club 1895–1975
Elm Club 1895–1973, 1978–89
Campus Club 1900–2005
Charter Club 1901
Quadrangle Club 1901
Tower Club 1902
Terrace Club 1904
Key and Seal Club 1904–68
Dial Lodge 1907–88
Arch Club 1911–17
Cloister Inn 1912–72, 1977
Gateway Club 1913–37
Court Club 1921–64
Arbor Inn 1923–39
Prospect Club 1941–59
Dial, Elm, Cannon 1989–98, 2011

ECOLOGY AND EVOLUTIONARY BIOLOGY, THE DEPARTMENT OF. Like many departments in the natural sciences, the department of Ecology and Evolutionary Biology (EEB) has its roots in several disciplines, including biology, biochemistry, and molecular biology. From 1965 until his premature death in 1972. Robert H. MacArthur, a member of the biology faculty, drove the foundation of theoretical ecology when most ecologists were still devotedly empirical. He laid the groundwork for Princeton's preeminence in the area by applying mathematical insights to his observations. Physicist-turned-theoretical ecologist Robert May, whose first work at Princeton overturned conventional wisdom regarding the relationship between the stability of ecosystems and diversity of species, followed in MacArthur's footsteps, and strengthened Princeton's position in the emerging field.

EEB faculty occupied seats in the departments of Biology, Biochemistry, and Molecular Biology as program and department boundaries shifted over time.

In 1988–89 Biology and Molecular Biology fused into one department, and a year later this "mega-department" subdivided into a department of Molecular Biology and a new department of Ecology and Evolutionary Biology. Daniel Rubenstein, back from a sabbatical in Kenya, took on the role of founding chair, holding the position from 1991 to 2014 while conducting leading research on how animal behavior adapts to changes in the natural environment, in particular through his population counts of the endangered Grevy's zebra.

Under Rubenstein, EEB housed its "muddy boots" faculty and theorists in Eno Hall and expanded its laboratory and experimentalist space in Guyot Hall. The department began with a faculty of six, but during Rubenstein's tenure its size more than doubled. One of the first faculty members hired was Simon Levin, who arrived at Princeton in 1992 and went on to make major contributions to the field. His research focused on how large-scale patterns are maintained by small-scale behavioral and evolutionary factors at the level of individual organisms. He used observational data and mathematical models to explore topics such as biological diversity, the evolution of structure and organization, and the management of public goods and shared resources.

Levin is credited with transforming ecology from a largely measurement-based and descriptive science into one that is conceptual. For this work, he was awarded a National Medal of Science. He published the landmark *Encyclopedia of Biodiversity* in 2000, and won the 2005 Kyoto Prize for Basic Sciences.

Other faculty nourished the field with research that tackled the world's expanding ecological concerns. Stephen Pacala, a leading plant ecologist, joined Levin in 1992. His research focuses on all aspects of the global carbon cycle as he develops, calibrates, and tests mathematical models to explain ecological structure and function.

Jeanne Altman, who arrived at Princeton in 1998, is one of the founders of primate behavioral ecology. Her contributions include a definitive guide to observational sampling methods and completion of the first detailed study of maternal behavior in a wild mammal. Her brainchild, the Amboseli Baboon Project, started in 1971 in East Africa. Today, it is one of the longest-running studies in the world of wild primates.

The husband-and-wife team of Rosemary Grant and Peter Grant tracked behavior, evolution, and genetic mutation among several Galapagos finch species, and in 2019 became the first couple to be awarded Princeton honorary degrees.

Population biologist Bryan Grenfell worked at the interface between theoretical models and empirical data. For example, he used mathematical modeling and data from the 2001 foot-and-mouth disease epidemic in the United Kingdom to examine how reactive vaccination could be effectively deployed in a complex, heterogeneous environment. The research marked a fourth dimension to EEB's areas of focus, introducing the study of disease to established department work in ecology, evolution, and behavior. Like many EEB faculty, Grenfell holds a joint appointment, in his case with the school of Public and International Affairs.

Andrea Graham studies the evolution of the mammalian immune system. She connects EEB to global health issues and scholarship as co-director of the program in Global Health and Health Policy.

Through the years, EEB has had the use of three field stations that have augmented undergraduate and graduate study along with faculty research. Stony Ford Research Station, originally overseen by the department of Biology, consists of 99 acres of former farmland about four and a half miles from campus that is used for ecological and behavioral studies of plants, animals, and environments.

The Mpala Research Centre in central Kenya opened in 1994. The University serves as its managing partner, with the other partners being the Kenya Wildlife Service, the National Museums of Kenya, and the Smithsonian Institution. Today, it is one of the world's leading field-based research centers for the study of ecology, evolution, conservation, public health, sustainable development, and climate change.

The Smithsonian Tropical Research Institute, based in Panama, enables the Princeton in Panama Field Semester, a 12-week course in which students conduct research in the Amazonian ecosystem.

Recently appointed members of the faculty conduct research that fundamentally advances understanding of biological invasions and species coexistence; provides a window into how genes dictate behavior and how they impact the desire for insects to fly towards human hosts rather than other mammals, with implications for the treatment of mosquito-borne illness; investigates how natural selection shapes genetic variation and reshapes the genomic architecture to produce adaptive phenotypes; studies the behavioral genetics and evolution of sociality by looking at bees that show solitary and social tendencies under different conditions; and explores social evolution by examining cooperative breeding birds who help others—mostly kin—while foregoing their own reproduction at least for a short time.

Heading into the 2020s, EEB ranks as one of the top whole-organism biology departments in the country. Its research falls into five areas: ecology and the environment; evolution and genomics; animal behavior and sensory biology; conservation and biodiversity; and infectious disease. All department projects have a field component and a computational component, which was infused into the curriculum early in EEB's life.

The department's research and teaching engage some of the most urgent ecological problems of the day, including how climate change is stressing ecosystems, the public's misunderstanding of evolution, the dynamics of disease in a world where people and pathogens move and evolve with unprecedented ease, and the effects of biodiversity loss on the ability of ecosystems to provide for the future. Construction of a new building along Ivy Lane to house the department is projected to begin in 2022.

ECONOMICS, THE DEPARTMENT OF. Although topics in political economy received attention in "moral philosophy" courses almost from Princeton's founding in 1746, there was no specific course in political economy until 1819, when the College initiated a one-term course that all students were required to take. This constituted the entire curriculum in economics until 1890, when Woodrow Wilson 1879 arrived as Princeton's first professor of jurisprudence and political economy. Wilson moved the required senior course in political economy to junior year and introduced an "advanced" course, the History of Political Economy, as a senior elective. In 1892 Wilson relinquished the teaching of political economy to Winthrop More Daniels 1888, who had been valedictorian of his class.

Daniels was the first faculty member to specialize in economics. He reputedly caused a panic among students by announcing that "economics would no longer be a snap," which was considered a bold break with tradition. In 1904 Daniels became the first chair of the newly created department of History, Politics, and Economics. By 1911, when he left Princeton to take an appointment (from then-Governor Wilson) as chair of the New Jersey Public Utility Commission, there were six faculty members in economics, five undergraduate courses (most extending over two terms), and some graduate seminars. Daniels was succeeded by Frank Fetter, who was recruited from Cornell University and was elected president of the American Economic Association in 1912. When Economics was split off from History and Politics to form a separate department of Economics and Social Institutions in 1913, Fetter became its first chair.

By 1929, the economics faculty had grown to 22 members, the undergraduate curriculum included 13 courses and a program for independent work, and Economics had become one of the largest departments for undergraduate majors in the University, a position it has maintained until the present day with 125 economics majors graduating in 2018 and many more students taking at least one economics course. In 2018, 35 percent of the department's majors were women. The department has 56 tenure track faculty members, many of whom are jointly appointed with the school of Public and International Affairs.

Graduate study in economics also rose markedly, although consistent with University policy at the time, the number of graduate students was small. The University awarded only five doctoral degrees in economics before 1920 and only 37 were awarded in the next two decades. Now the Economics department places 15–25 new PhDs each year in positions ranging from academic appointments, to international organizations, to consulting companies. As of 2019 there were 142 PhD students enrolled, including 25 women. There were 12 Latino students but no African American students, indicating that diversifying the graduate student body remains a work in progress.

Efforts to diversify the faculty proceeded slowly. After his appointment as a University Professor in 1959, W. Arthur Lewis remained the only person of color on the economics faculty until his retirement in 1983. Nine years then passed before the department hired its next minority faculty member—Cecilia Rouse. In addition to her distinguished career as a researcher and teacher, she served as an economic adviser in both the Clinton and Obama administrations. She served Princeton as dean of the school of Public and International Affairs from 2012 until 2021, when she was nominated by newly elected President Joe Biden to chair the Council of Economic Advisers and serve in his cabinet.

Efforts to achieve gender balance also proceeded slowly. Claudia Goldin, who was an assistant professor at Princeton from 1973–79 and later held an endowed professorship at Harvard, was the first woman hired in a tenure-track position. A decade later Rebecca Blank, who served as acting US Secretary of Commerce and went on to become Chancellor of the University of Wisconsin–Madison, was an assistant professor from 1983–89. Several other distinguished female economists such as Christina Romer and Penelope Goldberg (who held endowed chairs at Berkeley and Yale respectively) also served as assistant professors. (Goldberg also was chief economist at the World Bank.)

Christina Paxson was the first woman to achieve tenure in Princeton's Economics department (in 1994) and the first woman to chair the department. Paxson was later appointed dean of the school of Public and International Affairs, and then president of Brown University. She was followed in the tenure ranks by Anne Case and Cecilia Rouse, who were tenured in 1997 and 1998, respectively.

Today the Princeton faculty has nine women in tenure-track positions, six tenured and three untenured, out of a total of 56 tenure-track faculty. Six of these women were hired by Janet Currie *88, who was recruited by Christina Paxson in 2011 to head the school of Public and International Affair's Center for Health and Wellbeing, and went on to become the second female chair of the Economics department from 2014–18. Over the same period Currie hired five senior and 10 junior male faculty, so that 29 percent of new hires during her tenure were women. This fraction can be compared to the approximately one third of PhDs in economics that go to women.

Two research programs were established during the years between World Wars I and II: the Industrial Relations Section and the International Finance Section. The Industrial Relations Section (IRS) was inaugurated in 1922 at the suggestion of Clarence Hicks of the Standard Oil Company (New Jersey). Hicks was instrumental in securing an endowment from John D. Rockefeller Jr. His son, John D. Rockefeller III '29, provided additional funds, which were augmented by contributions from over 60 companies and six national unions. The IRS was first headed by Robert Foerster, who was recruited from Harvard for this purpose, and then by J. Douglas Brown 1919 *1928, who later became dean of the faculty and was one of the architects of the US Social Security system.

The International Finance Section (IFS), which has since become the International Economics Section, was established in 1929. Its first director, Edwin Kemmerer, had been chair of commissions to stabilize the finances of several countries and he was concerned about a scarcity of qualified specialists. The section was funded chiefly by a gift of $490,000 from Gerard Lambert 1908 and his family in memory of James Theodore Walker 1927, who died shortly after his graduation. In addition to supporting research and training, the IFS sponsored several historic series of conferences such as the "Joint Conference of Officials and Academics on International Monetary Reform," first convened in Bellagio, Italy, and widely known as the Bellagio Group, which met 18 times from 1964–77.

While these remain the largest and best endowed research programs in the department, other programs have followed. These include: the Econometric Research Program, first directed by Oskar Morgenstern and later by Gregory Chow; the Research Program in Economic Development, begun by W. Arthur Lewis and then headed by John P. Lewis; the Center for Financial Research, led by Burton Malkiel *64, which later merged with the Bendheim Center for Finance; the Lewis A. Simpson Center for the Study of Macroeconomics headed by Richard Rogerson; and the program in Public Finance which is run through the consensus of its members (as the IRS is now).

In January 2016, all members of the Economics department, who had been scattered across five different physical locations, were brought together in the beautifully renovated Julis Romo Rabinowitz Building (formerly the Frick Chemistry Laboratory).

The Princeton Economics department faculty is distinguished by any measure, but the number of Nobel Prize winners is one metric with special resonance. In 1979 W. Arthur Lewis was the first member of the faculty to receive the Nobel Prize in Economics; he was followed by John Nash *50 (1994); Daniel Kahneman (2002); Eric Maskin (2007); Paul Krugman (2008); Thomas Sargent (2011); Christopher Sims (2011); and Angus Deaton (2015). Laureates James Heckman *71 (2000), Lloyd Shapley *53 (2012), Oliver Hart *74 (2016), Joshua Angrist *89 (2021), and David Card *83 (2021) received PhDs from Princeton, while Gary Becker '51 (1992) and Michael Spence '66 (2001) received Princeton undergraduate degrees.

Election as president of the American Economic Association (AEA) is another metric that reflects one's standing within the American economics community. In addition to Fetter (1912), Kemmerer (1926), and Lewis (1983), other Princeton faculty members who have achieved that distinction include Fritz Machlup (1966); William Baumol (1981); Avinash Dixit (2008); Deaton (2009); Orley Ashenfelter *70 (2011); and Sims (2012). Several Princeton faculty members have been awarded the AEA's Clark medal for the best economist under 40 years of age. They include: Joseph Stiglitz (1979), Sanford Grossman (1987), Paul Krugman (1991), David Card (1995), Andrei Shleifer (1999), and Yuliy Sannikov (2016).

EDWARDS, JONATHAN, who served briefly in 1758 as Princeton's third president, was born in East Windsor, Connecticut, where his father was pastor. The only son in a family of 11 children, he entered Yale when he was 12 years old and graduated four years later at the head of his class. He studied theology, preached in a Presbyterian pulpit in New York, and in 1724 returned to Yale as a tutor for two years, the second year as senior tutor and de facto head of the college, the position of rector then being vacant.

In 1729, at age 26, he succeeded his maternal grandfather as pastor of the Congregational church in Northampton, Massachusetts, where his preaching inspired an outpouring of religious revivalism which paved the way for the Great Awakening, a zealous style of religion that was based more on inner experience than the doctrines of the church. His sermons, including the highly influential "Sinners in the Hands of an Angry God," were widely circulated.

The Princeton and Slavery project found that Edwards purchased his first slave in 1731 and, in time, owned one or two others. In 1741, when he was asked by a neighboring congregation to respond to church members who had denounced their minister for owning a slave, he defended his fellow cleric. On other occasions, however, he condemned the cruelty of the slave trade, and sought to convert slaves to Christianity. He admitted nine Africans to his Northampton congregation, including one of his slaves, and his church also admitted Native American members.

In 1748 he had a falling out with his congregation over his proposal to administer the sacrament of communion only to those who gave satisfactory evidence of being truly converted, and in 1750 he was dismissed. He moved west to the frontier settlement of Stockbridge, Massachusetts, where he ministered to a tiny congregation and served as missionary to Mahican and Mohawk Indians. There, having more time for study and writing, he completed his celebrated work, *The Freedom of the Will*.

Edwards was elected the third president of the College of New Jersey on September 29, 1757, five days after the death of his son-in-law, Aaron Burr Sr. He was a popular choice, for he was then the most eminent American philosopher-theologian of his time. Edwards shrank from taking on "such a new and great business in the decline of life," but he finally yielded when a group of ministers in the Stockbridge area persuaded him that it was his duty to accept.

Late in January 1758 he came to Princeton, where he preached in the chapel and gave questions in divinity to the senior class for each to study and write "what he thought proper" before coming together to discuss them—an eighteenth-century seminar. The seniors spoke enthusiastically of the "light and instruction which Mr. Edwards communicated."

He was installed on February 16, and a week later he had himself and members of his family inoculated against smallpox. Thirty-five days after his installation, on March 22, he died from the disease. He was buried in the President's Lot in Princeton Cemetery beside his son-in-law, Aaron Burr Sr.

Edwards and his wife, Sarah, had three sons and eight daughters. Their three sons graduated from Princeton; one of them, Jonathan Edwards Jr. 1765, became president of Union College. Three of their daughters married Yale graduates: one was Burr Sr.; another was Timothy Dwight, forebear of three Yale presidents.

In 1860 Edwards' great-grandsons had a copy made of Yale's eighteenth-century portrait of him and presented it to Princeton, where it hangs in the Faculty Room of Nassau Hall. He is also commemorated in Edwards Hall, which was constructed in 1880 as one of Princeton's first dormitories. In 1928 a wood statuette of Edwards was carved on the back of the altar in the newly constructed chapel.

EDWARDS HALL commemorates the College's third president, Jonathan Edwards. It was built in 1880 at the behest of President James McCosh to fill a need for a "new and plain dormitory to provide cheap rooms for . . . struggling students," and to reduce the number of freshmen compelled "to live beyond our walls and under no tutorial inspection." In those days room rates varied by room (a practice that continued until the middle of the 20th century), and McCosh was sensitive to reports "zealously propagated by the friends of rival institutions" that Princeton was becoming a rich man's college and was not "making provisions for a class of persons for whom the College was originally instituted." He was also persuaded that the student disturbances that had brought the College unfavorable attention in the newspapers in the late 1870s "were hatched in extra-collegiate rooms in town."

The construction of east-facing Edwards, known at the time as the "poor man's dormitory," followed the completion of north-facing Witherspoon Hall, which provided much more commodious rooms at relatively steep prices. As Robert Spencer Barnett points out in his excellent *Princeton University and Neighboring Institutions*, whereas Witherspoon was designed by an architect, Edwards was designed by the College's curator of buildings and grounds; while Witherspoon had suites, Edwards had only single rooms; and the cost to build Edwards was less than a third of that for Witherspoon because Edwards was one story smaller and made of more common materials, such as Trenton brownstone trimmed with sandstone.

A 1985 renovation added a fifth floor, introduced new design elements, and removed exterior fire escapes. In addition to coveted single rooms for students in Mathey College, Edwards today houses a "Real Food Co-op" where students prepare meals for each other, and the Edwards Collective where students who share a deep interest in the humanities and creative arts live near each other in a designated area of the dorm.

EINSTEIN, ALBERT, first visited Princeton in 1921—the year before he received the Nobel Prize—to deliver five lectures on the theory of relativity and accept an honorary degree. He returned again in 1933 as a life member of the newly founded Institute for Advanced Study and lived in Princeton for the remaining 22 years of his life.

Although his two-month visit to the United States in 1921 was made primarily to seek support for the creation of a Jewish state in Israel, Einstein accepted Princeton's invitation to deliver the tour's most extensive series of scientific lectures because he felt more had been done at Princeton in relation to his theory of relativity than anywhere else in the country. At ceremonies in Alexander Hall on the morning of May 9, President John Grier Hibben welcomed Einstein in German and conferred on him an honorary Doctor of Science degree, following the reading of a citation that saluted him as "the new Columbus of science, 'voyaging through strange seas of thought alone.'"

Later that day, scientists from all over the country packed McCosh 50 for the first of five lectures. Each lecture, delivered by Einstein in German, was followed by a resumé in English by Princeton physicist Edwin P. Adams. After being submitted to Einstein for revision and final approval, a transcript of the lectures was translated into English by Adams for publication in 1922 by Princeton University Press, which became the first United States publisher to produce a book by the world's most acclaimed living scientist. The book, *The Meaning of Relativity*, has remained in print ever since and has been translated into more than 50 languages.

After Einstein's acceptance of an appointment at the Institute for Advanced Study in 1933, the University renewed its earlier association with him. All four of his colleagues in the institute's School of Mathematics—its first branch—had previously been professors at the University, and until the institute erected its first building in 1939, their offices and Einstein's (Room 109) were located on the Princeton campus in the original Fine Hall (now Jones Hall). The building contained several decorative tributes to Einstein: his relativity equations were among the motifs in the leaded windows, and his famous remark, "God is subtle, but he is not malicious," was carved in the original German over the fireplace in the common room.

When the institute's Fuld Hall was completed in 1939, Einstein moved into an office there, customarily walking the mile-and-a half between his white frame house at 112 Mercer Street and the institute. He lived with his wife, Elsa (who died in 1936), and his secretary-housekeeper, Helen Dukas. His daughter, Margot, joined them in 1934, and later his sister, Maja, also lived there, along with a wirehaired terrier and a tomcat named Tiger. He found life at Princeton "indescribably enjoyable," and wrote his friend, the physicist Max Born, that he had "settled down splendidly . . . I hibernate like a bear in its cave, and really feel more at home than ever before in all my varied existence."

Einstein was a familiar and generally approachable figure in town, with a mass of unruly white hair, a pipe in hand, and often wearing sandals or shoes with no socks. His chief recreations in Princeton were playing the violin with friends, sailing in a secondhand sailboat on Lake Carnegie, and walking in the countryside near the institute. In 1947, when the newly formed Student Hebrew Association held its inaugural Friday Shabbat service in Murray-Dodge Hall, Einstein attended.

During his Princeton years, Einstein continued his studies in general relativity, his critical discussion of the interpretation of quantum theory, and his work on a unified field theory. He was also increasingly prominent on the world stage as an advocate for the control of atomic energy and for world peace.

On the occasion of Einstein's seventieth birthday, some 300 scientists gathered in Frick Laboratory for a symposium on his contributions to modern science, held under the joint auspices of the University and the institute. When Einstein died six years later in 1955, the *Daily Princetonian* devoted an entire issue to him, with tributes from friends and colleagues. Physics department chair Allen G. Shenstone, who was Einstein's neighbor on Mercer Street, said his character was "the most beautiful" he had ever known. Henry D. Smyth 1918 *1921, chair of the University Research Board and a former member of the Atomic Energy Commission, declared that physics at Princeton had "immeasurably benefited by his presence at the Institute for Advanced Study."

In the years following his death, Einstein's association with Princeton was commemorated in a number of ways. A United States postage stamp bearing his photograph was issued in Princeton in 1966 under the sponsorship of the University and the institute. Nine years later, a professorship was endowed in his name, and Robert H. Dicke '39, a former Physics department chair known for his studies in the field of gravity and for important experimental tests of Einstein's general theory of relativity, was named the first Albert Einstein Professor of Science. Princeton University Press began publishing Einstein's collected papers; by 2018 the Press had completed 15 of a projected almost 30 volumes.

In 1994 the actor Walter Matthau, portraying Einstein, spent the summer in Princeton filming the movie *I.Q.*, a romantic comedy in which Einstein played cupid for his fictional niece and her lovestruck suitor. In 2005, a larger-than-life bronze bust of Einstein was installed in Princeton at the corner of Stockton Street and Bayard Lane near what was then Borough Hall. The plaque quotes Einstein as saying "Imagination is more important than knowledge; knowledge is limited whereas imagination embraces the entire world."

On December 26, 2017, one of the "answers" on the Jeopardy TV show was: "Oddly, the only US museum devoted to this physicist is tucked inside a woolens' shop in Princeton, New Jersey." The reference was to Landau's, then a Nassau Street store across from the front campus, and the question, of course, was: Who is Albert Einstein?

EISENHART, LUTHER PFAHLER, contributed to Princeton's development as a mathematician, teacher, chair of his department, chair of the committee on scientific research, dean of the faculty, dean of the graduate school, and creator of the four-course plan.

Born in York, Pennsylvania, Eisenhart graduated in 1896 from Gettysburg College, where he excelled in baseball and mathematics. He completed all the mathematics courses the college offered by the end of his sophomore year and spent his last two years studying mathematical problems on his own under the general guidance of his professor. This experience, he said later, gave him the idea for the four-course plan. He went on to graduate study at Johns Hopkins University, where he found the emphasis on study and research and the low priority given to rules and restrictions congenial and stimulating.

After receiving his PhD in 1900, Eisenhart was called to Princeton by President Francis Patton as an instructor in mathematics. He soon earned a reputation as a stimulating teacher, and in 1905 was selected by President Woodrow Wilson to be one of the original preceptors. He was one of the elite group of promising young mathematicians nurtured by Dean Henry Fine 1880 and rose to the rank of full professor in 1909 when he was only 33.

In 1925, following Eisenhart's work on the early development of the four-course plan, President John Grier Hibben chose him as dean of the faculty. Four years later, after Fine's death, Eisenhart was also appointed chair of the committee on scientific research, named Dod Professor of Mathematics, and made chair of the department. Eisenhart's continuation of Fine's work brought Princeton to a preeminent place among the world's centers for mathematical study and prepared the way for the outstanding scientific contributions the University was able to make to the national effort in World War II. In 1933 newly installed President Harold Dodds named Eisenhart dean of the graduate school.

Eisenhart's opportunity to introduce the four-course plan came in the early 1920s when Hibben appointed a subcommittee of the course of study committee to consider the question of reinstating honors courses, which had been discontinued during World War I. These honors courses began soon after the adoption of the preceptorial method in 1905, but they never attracted many students and enrollment dropped steadily in the years before the war. Eisenhart persuaded the committee and then Hibben, who in turn convinced the faculty, to adopt a radical and more ambitious plan that "sought to elevate the plane of endeavor and attainment of the whole undergraduate body rather than to provide honors courses for a comparatively few students."

Under the new plan, every candidate for the Bachelor of Arts degree would take four courses, instead of five as formerly, each semester in the junior and senior year, with two of the four in the student's field of concentration. In the time made available by the reduction in the course load the student would engage in independent study and, in the senior year, write a major paper (later a thesis) on a subject of the student's own choosing. At the end of the senior year, the student would take a written comprehensive examination on selected topics in the field of concentration, and honors would be awarded on the basis of this examination and the thesis.

Eisenhart's four-course plan was ground-breaking at the time both for the emphasis it placed on independent study and for its support of the principle that honors at graduation should be open to all students and not just to a restricted group. This latter provision was the most controversial feature of the plan. It was also the one in which Eisenhart believed most strongly. He insisted that grades made in freshman and sophomore years did not constitute a reliable test of a student's ability to qualify for honors. Eisenhart would cite with relish the instances of students who, after receiving mediocre grades in the first two years, found their interest aroused by independent work and went on to graduate with honors.

Eisenhart had to contend with apathy and some opposition in the early days of the plan. Many faculty members lacked enthusiasm for it; some undergraduates felt that the plan was too specialized and even more thought it was too hard; and skeptical alumni questioned whether the plan was appropriate for undergraduates.

The alumni discussions came to a head in the fall of 1930 and resulted in the Alumni Council appointing a committee to study the matter. Eisenhart proposed that alumni who had experienced the plan be asked their opinion of its value. A letter sent to graduates from 1925 through 1930 brought back a favorable response and concrete evidence from graduates in many different occupations that the plan was accomplishing what Eisenhart had promised it would.

In his later years Eisenhart had the satisfaction of knowing not only that the four-course plan had won general acceptance, but that most Princetonians had come to regard the senior thesis, the capstone of independent study, as the most valuable element in their undergraduate education.

EISGRUBER, CHRISTOPHER LUDWIG '83 became the University's 20th president on July 1, 2013. Like many of his predecessors he came from the faculty, which he joined in 2001 as a professor in the school of Public and International Affairs and the University Center for Human Values and director of the program in Law and Public Affairs. He was the second Princeton provost, following William Bowen *58, to ascend to the presidency. He was the first Princeton president who attended the University when it was coeducational; the first to have been a Rhodes Scholar; and the first whose advanced degree was in law.

As president, Eisgruber led efforts to increase the representation of low-income and first-generation students and to protect from deportation students and other immigrants who came to the United States as children. He emphasized the importance of both free speech and inclusivity to Princeton's mission, led efforts to increase the diversity of campus iconography, and encouraged greater honesty and transparency in how the University presents its history. He championed the University's commitment to service and launched initiatives to fortify its connections to the innovation ecosystem in New Jersey and beyond.

Eisgruber was born in Lafayette, Indiana, where his parents met as graduate students at Purdue University. Although raised Catholic, Eisgruber was helping his then-fourth grade son with a school project when he discovered his mother, who had initially arrived in the United States as an eight-year-old refugee, was Jewish; "understanding myself as Jewish," he has said, "helps me understand who I am."

When Eisgruber was 12 his family moved to Oregon, where his mother worked on the staff of Oregon State University and his father served as dean of its school of agricultural sciences. At Corvallis High School he edited the school newspaper and during his senior year he captained a national championship chess team.

At Princeton Eisgruber majored in physics. He earned an MLitt in politics at Oxford University as a Rhodes Scholar and a law degree from the University of Chicago law school, where he served as editor-in-chief of the law review and met his wife, Lori Martin, later a securities litigator in the New York office of the law firm WilmerHale. After clerking for US Court of Appeals Judge Patrick Higginbotham and US Supreme Court Justice John Paul Stevens, Eisgruber taught at New York University law school for 11 years before joining the Princeton faculty.

A renowned constitutional scholar, Eisgruber published numerous articles on constitutional issues and testified multiple times before legislative bodies on the issue of religious freedom. His books include *Constitutional Self-Government* (2001); *Global Justice and the Bulwarks of Localism: Human Rights in Context* (edited with Andras Sajo, 2005); *Religious Freedom and the Constitution* (with Lawrence Sager, 2007); and *The Next Justice: Repairing the Supreme Court Appointments Process* (2007).

In 2004 President Shirley Tilghman appointed Eisgruber the University's 11th provost. He was an active partner in many of the key initiatives of her presidency and played a central role in navigating the University successfully through the severe economic downturn of 2008–09. When the trustees selected him as Tilghman's successor, board chair Kathryn Hall '80 said "Chris Eisgruber has all the qualities we were looking for in Princeton's next president. He has keen intelligence and excellent judgment; he cares passionately about teaching and research of the highest quality; he is deeply committed to principles of excellence, equity, and integrity; and he is devoted to Princeton."

Even before taking office he initiated a "Pre-read" program in which he sends a book each year to all incoming freshmen to introduce them to the intellectual life of the University. Members of the entering class read the book and then discuss it with classmates and others, including Eisgruber, over the course of the academic year. The first Pre-read selection, in 2013, was *The Honor Code: How Moral Revolutions Happen*, by Kwame Anthony Appiah, a professor in the department of Philosophy and the University Center for Human Values.

Early in his presidency, Eisgruber launched two major planning efforts, one to develop a framework for strategic planning and the other a framework for campus planning.

The trustees adopted the strategic planning framework in January 2016. It aimed to enhance the University's core commitments to teaching and research and to such fundamental principles as affordability, diversity, inclusivity, and service, while also strengthening its capacity to have "significant and lasting impact" at a time of transformative social and technological change. Incorporated into the framework was a mission statement that called upon the University to continue to advance learning "through scholarship, research, and teaching of unsurpassed quality, with an emphasis on undergraduate and doctoral education that is distinctive among the world's great universities, and with a pervasive commitment to serve the nation and the world."

Among other initiatives, the framework called for an increase of 125 undergraduates per class (increasing the undergraduate student body from 5,200 to 5,700); the construction of an additional (seventh) residential college with "the expectation of a further increase in the number of undergraduates in the future"; a concerted effort to identify and attract more students from low-income families and provide them with the support they need once they are on campus; reinstatement of a small transfer admission program (suspended since 1990) with a focus on military veterans and students from low-income backgrounds, including students from community colleges; expansion of the faculty in computer science and the fields of statistics and machine learning; and continued development and expansion of Princeton's distinctive approach to entrepreneurship.

In 2017 the University issued a campus planning framework that proposed locations for new residential colleges; new and improved facilities for teaching and research in engineering and environmental studies; and space to accommodate academic partnerships with the corporate, government, and nonprofit sectors. The framework paid particular attention to campus lands east of Washington Road where new facilities for engineering and environmental studies would be located, and it proposed that the University begin developing a new Lake Campus on lands south of Lake Carnegie that the University had purchased almost a century ago.

In a 2019 update to the strategic framework the trustees endorsed the planning under way to develop the Lake Campus as a site for research collaborations between the University and other entities, as well as for graduate student housing, athletic facilities, administrative offices, convening spaces, and other initiatives. The trustees also encouraged the administration to explore ways to increase connections between the University and the Princeton Plasma Physics Laboratory, the world's leading center for fusion energy research, which the University manages for the US Department of Energy.

By 2020 progress was being made toward many of the goals identified in the planning frameworks. The percentage of students who qualified for federal Pell Grants for lower-income students rose from 7.2 percent of the Class of 2008 to 24 percent of the Class of 2023. Gifts had been announced to construct two new residential colleges south of Poe Field, along with gifts from Kwanza Jones '93 and José E. Feliciano '94 to build adjoining dormitories in one of the new colleges, and a gift from Mellody Hobson '91 to create a new college on the site of the existing First College (originally Wilson College).

Wendy and Eric Schmidt '76 provided funds to expand and renovate Guyot Hall as a new home for the department of Computer Science, and progress toward goals in entrepreneurship had been made with the development of an Entrepreneurial Hub on Chambers Street in downtown Princeton, the opening of incubator space at Princeton Innovation Center BioLabs at Princeton Forrestal Center, and the establishment of new collaborations with Celgene, Google, Microsoft, and other partners. A gift from Judy and Carl Ferenbach III '64 enhanced the University's capacity for teaching and research on environmental issues, and construction of a new and expanded art museum was scheduled to begin in 2021.

In 2013, Eisgruber was faced with a campus health challenge when eight undergraduates and a visiting high school student were infected by meningitis B; the University received federal approval to use a vaccine that had been licensed in other countries but not yet in the United States, and a massive campus-wide inoculation effort vaccinated nearly 5,300 undergraduates and others with specific medical conditions in a program that continued through June 2015. In 2014 Eisgruber played a leading role in re-establishing a Naval ROTC unit at Princeton for the first time since 1971; in 2017 he received the Navy's Distinguished Public Service Award, the highest civilian honor given by the Secretary of the Navy.

In 2015, following a 32-hour protest by the Black Justice League and other students in the president's office in Nassau Hall, the trustees launched an extensive assessment of Woodrow Wilson's legacy at Princeton. In their 2016 report, the trustees retained Wilson's name on the school of Public and International Affairs and the residential college (Princeton's first) that had been named for him but called for the University to create a more multi-faceted understanding and representation of Wilson on campus and focus attention on "aspects of Princeton's history that have been forgotten, overlooked, subordinated, or suppressed."

The board called for greater efforts to encourage students from underrepresented groups to pursue graduate degrees; modified the University's informal motto to connect Wilson's phrase "Princeton in the Nation's Service" with the phrase "In the Service of Humanity" that had been suggested by Supreme Court Justice Sonia Sotomayor '76 when she received the 2014 Woodrow Wilson Award; and encouraged initiatives to diversify campus art and iconography. A "permanent marker" was installed outside the school of Public and International Affairs to depict "both the positive and negative dimensions of Wilson's legacy," And broadly representative committees were established to diversify campus iconography, the honorific naming of campus spaces, and the University's portrait collections.

In June 2020, on Eisgruber's recommendation, the trustees reconsidered their earlier decision and voted to remove Wilson's name from the school and college, concluding that his "racist thinking and policies make him an inappropriate namesake for a school or college whose scholars, students, and alumni must stand firmly against racism in all its forms."

That same month Eisgruber charged his cabinet with identifying actions that could be taken to "identify, understand, and combat systemic racism within and beyond the University" as part of a broader effort to ask how the University could "more effectively fight racism—through our teaching and research, through our operations, and through our interactions and partnerships with those around us." That fall a number of initiatives were announced, including "exploring the possibility of a new credit- or degree-granting program that would extend Princeton's teaching to a new range of students from communities disproportionately affected by systemic racism and related forms of disadvantage." On June 19, the University designated Juneteenth, the oldest nationally celebrated commemoration of the ending of slavery in the United State, as an official University holiday, and it later announced that the holiday would continue to be observed annually.

In 1916, Princeton's 14th president, John Grier Hibben 1882 *1893, confronted a polio outbreak along the east coast of the United States, and in 1918 he had to deal with a massive worldwide outbreak of influenza.

In 1957 an influenza epidemic affected a quarter of the undergraduates and 10 percent of the graduate students. But none of these earlier incidents compared with the COVID-19 pandemic that required the University in March 2020 to move all remaining classes for the rest of the spring semester online; convert Commencement and reunions to virtual formats; and make the undergraduate program fully remote for the fall semester before inviting undergraduates back to campus for the spring 2021 semester with most classes still taught virtually.

Eisgruber issued periodic updates to the campus community, in writing, by video, and online; presided over the virtual Commencement; participated in the virtual reunions; led efforts to provide support for research, teaching, and service initiatives related to the pandemic; authorized installation of a COVID-19 testing laboratory on campus; and encouraged a variety of initiatives to assist the local community, including a $1 million fund to support community organizations working to relieve economic distress and small businesses impacted by the pandemic.

One of the lighter moments of his presidency occurred in 2016 when Eisgruber, a long-suffering Chicago Cubs baseball fan, was able to celebrate the Cub's first World Series championship since 1908 by raising a flag celebrating the victory on the flagpole over the entrance to Nassau Hall.

ELECTRICAL AND COMPUTER ENGINEERING, THE DEPARTMENT OF. Originally, engineering was associated primarily with the construction of military fortifications and devices. Early in the nineteenth century the application of this rapidly developing body of knowledge for nonmilitary purposes was designated civil engineering. Civil engineering came to encompass all engineering practice until later in the century, when increasing knowledge and technological innovation led to specialization and division into various subfields. Electrical engineering was often the first specialty so identified in universities because of the burgeoning activity in electrical research, development, and innovation in the 1870s.

The stage was set at Princeton when Cyrus Fogg Brackett arrived in 1873 as professor of physics. Very much a Renaissance scholar, he was keenly interested in and knowledgeable about several fields of science, including natural science, chemistry, zoology, geology, and physics. He was a friend of Thomas Edison and often supplied the theoretical basis for the inventor's amazing practical intuition and insight. Brackett established a two-year graduate program, leading to the degree of electrical engineer, first announced in the College's 1889 catalogue.

One of Brackett's first tasks was to build up the department's equipment, which had been allowed to fall behind new developments in physics. Brackett was mechanically inclined, and he constructed much of the apparatus needed for his ingenious lecture demonstrations himself. Brackett's lecture room, according to tradition, was the first electrically lighted classroom in America. He constructed a dynamo and battery system for this purpose soon after Edison invented the incandescent lamp. He also rigged up the first telephone line in Princeton, which extended from his laboratory in the school of Science to Professor Charles Young's office in the observatory on Prospect Avenue.

Although engineering has changed dramatically over the past 130 years, one prerequisite has remained much the same: the statement in the 1889 catalogue that "Mathematics will be treated as a working instrument of which the student has already acquired control . . ." is consistent with the continuing emphasis on applied mathematics in electrical engineering today.

Brackett's role in establishing electrical engineering at Princeton was recognized in 1962 when the wing housing this department in the Engineering Quadrangle was named for him.

Brackett retired in 1908 as the department of Electrical Engineering was moving along with the Physics department into newly constructed Palmer Hall. Not long after, the technological demands of World War I accentuated the need for engineering education and special intensive programs were established by the University. When the school of Engineering was officially established in 1921, Electrical Engineering was one of five departments offering the Bachelor of Science in Engineering degree.

Brackett's successor, Malcolm MacLaren, a practicing electrical engineer from Westinghouse, retired in 1937 and was succeeded by Clodius Willis, an expert in power conversion. During World War II, the department became adept at making necessary adaptations because of the demands the war placed on developing sophisticated electronic devices, such as sonar and radar. Willis directed a graduate radar training program that was housed in a garage opposite the University Press on William Street.

In 1950, Willis was succeeded by Walter Johnson, who was instrumental in developing a post-World

War II curriculum that succeeded in modernizing many aspects of the department. Research was organized into three areas: communications and signal processing, digital systems (later computer science), and electronic devices. A PhD program had been introduced in 1946, and during Johnson's tenure doctoral education and the accompanying faculty and student research became increasingly important departmental activities. Johnson was especially known for his teaching ability—the Walter Johnson Prize for Excellence in Teaching was established in his honor—and he was the author of several textbooks.

In 1962 the department moved out of Palmer Hall into the newly constructed Engineering Quadrangle and in 1966 Mac Elwyn Van Valkenburg, a nationally known circuit theorist, came from the University of Illinois to chair the department. Under his direction, research and graduate education were further strengthened, and the undergraduate curriculum was revised to reflect changing directions in the field. Van Valkenburg initiated an annual Conference on Information Services and Systems, held during Princeton's spring break, that now draws attendees from around the country and abroad.

Van Valkenburg returned to the University of Illinois in 1973 and Bruce Arden arrived from the University of Michigan to become chair. Arden ushered in an emphasis on computing, which with the development of the electronic digital computer profoundly changed many of the classical engineering problem-solving techniques. This new emphasis stimulated a name change, and in 1973 the department became Electrical Engineering and Computer Science. As computers came to dominate many aspects of engineering, and with computing developing as a distinct discipline, it soon became clear that computer science should become its own department.

This was realized in 1985 when the department split into separate Electrical Engineering and Computer Science departments. Stuart Schwartz, who became Electrical Engineering chair when the departments split, actively encouraged the department to continue to conduct research using complex computer systems and to place an even greater emphasis on computing. He aggressively recruited new faculty—expanding the department from 13 to 24 faculty members by the time he left in 1994—and many of them, such as later chair Sharad Malik, had backgrounds in computing and computer systems.

Schwartz also directed departmental resources toward new research emphases, especially photonics (the use of light instead of electricity to carry information). He created the center for Photonics and Optoelectronic Materials (POEM), which later became the Princeton Institute for the Science and Technology of Materials (PRISM). Today it is a leading center for the integration of science and engineering, and it works closely with industry, governmental laboratories, and other academic institutions.

Bede Liu was chair from 1994 to 1997. He conducted pioneering research on signal processing, video coding, digital watermarking, and multimedia technology, and is recognized as one of the fathers of the technology of digital signal processing.

During the 1990s the Electrical Engineering department played a key role in the development of optics and optical research. Stephen Forrest, who chaired the department from 1997 to 2001, had earlier served as the director of POEM, where he oversaw its growth into a prominent center for innovative research. During his tenure as chair of the department he led research into devices based on conventional semiconductors, including photonic integrated circuits and photonic crystals as well as photovoltaic cells, lasers, organic light emitters and transistors, and new methods for growth and processing of organic thin films.

The 1990s also saw the department heavily invested in the development of computer chip technology, a research field that has continued to the present day. Efforts in this area include developing "next generation" computer chips—chip technology that will lead to improvements in speed, efficiency, and flexibility. Research in this area also involves designing the appropriate algorithms for designing these chips, an area of study in which Malik has played a leading role.

In 2001 Peter Ramadge was appointed chair of the department. Machine learning and data analysis became prominent research areas under his tenure, and he later became the director of the center for Statistics and Machine Learning.

Malik became chair in 2012. His area of expertise is designing future computer systems, with an emphasis on security. The department's associate chair, Claire Gmachl, a 2005 MacArthur fellow and a former vice-dean of the Engineering school, specializes in optics, photonics, and lasers.

The department's research areas include applied physics, biological and biomedical systems, computing and networking, data and information science, energy and environment, integrated circuits and systems, materials and devices, photonics, quantum engineering, robotics and cyberphysical systems, and security and privacy. For graduate students, the main themes of research span areas from applied physics, devices, advanced circuits, and high-performance computing to security, data and information science, and artificial intelligence.

For undergraduates, possible areas of concentration include data and information, security and privacy, computer systems, energy and environment, quantum computing, and applied physics. Faculty, graduate students, and undergraduates all typically engage in interdisciplinary research and certificate programs.

To convey its strengths and impacts more fully, in February 2021 the department changed its name to Electrical and Computer Engineering. The change recognized that roughly half of the department's research efforts and seven of its 10 undergraduate concentrations were investigating aspects of computing and information systems.

ELLSWORTH, OLIVER 1766, one of the nation's founders, received half of his undergraduate education at Yale and half at Princeton. In his junior year, he and others founded the Well-Meaning Club, which later became the Cliosophic Society.

Returning to his home in Windsor, Connecticut, he studied theology and then law, and was admitted to the bar in 1771. At first his law practice was so unprofitable that he had to support himself by farming and occasional wood-chopping, and on days when the court was sitting he was obliged to walk from his farm in Hartford and back, a round trip of 20 miles, since he was too poor to keep a horse.

In 1775 he moved to Hartford. There his rise at the bar was rapid, and before long there were few important cases in Connecticut in which Ellsworth did not represent one side or the other.

He was a delegate to the General Assembly of the state that met soon after the Battle of Lexington, and throughout the Revolutionary War he was a member of the Continental Congress. He was one of the delegates from Connecticut in the federal Constitutional Convention, one of the first two senators from Connecticut, and, on appointment of President George Washington, served as the third Chief Justice of the United States from 1796 to 1800.

At the Constitutional Convention, Ellsworth supported the Connecticut Compromise, which broke the deadlock between the large states, represented by James Madison 1771 of Virginia, and the small states, represented by Ellsworth's fellow Well-Meaner and Cliosophian, William Paterson 1763 of New Jersey.

Ellsworth made his greatest contribution while serving in the Senate by drafting the Judiciary Act of 1789; the court system it established has continued to the present with little change.

ENDOWED PROFESSORSHIPS first were established at Princeton in the middle of the nineteenth century. In 1827 the newly formed Alumni Association of Nassau Hall stressed the importance of raising funds for the endowment of professorships, but it was not until 1857 that Silas Holmes, a sea captain from New York City, gave Princeton's first endowed chair—in belles-lettres—which was named for him. Since its founding, 14 faculty members have held the Holmes professorship.

Other endowed professorships soon followed: in 1864 John Blair gave a professorship in geology that bears his name; in 1869 Samuel Dod 1857 gave one in mathematics in memory of his father, Professor Albert Dod 1822; in 1870 John Woodhull 1828. a local physician, founded a chair in modern languages; and in 1872 John C. Green gave a physics professorship in honor of Professor Joseph Henry.

With the growing prosperity of the country, gifts for new chairs increased steadily and by 1900 there were 16. By the end of President John Grier Hibben's administration in 1932 there were 35; by the end of Harold Dodds' presidency in 1957 there were 65; and when President Robert Goheen left office in 1972 there were 87.

Fifty years later there are more than 250 university, departmental, and general professorships supported by endowed and term funds. In addition, the University, along with Columbia University, Harvard University, and Yale University, benefits from a trust created in 1948 by a Columbia graduate (Eugene Higgins) that is used to support between 15 and 17 Princeton professorships in the sciences.

Professorships recognize both scholarly distinction and exceptional teaching. Almost half of Princeton's full professors hold named professorships.

The University also has several endowed visiting professorships for distinguished teaching, and 48 endowed "preceptorships" that are awarded to especially promising nontenured assistant professors. Ten such preceptorships were established following the University's 1946 bicentennial to encourage the development of teaching capacity and scholarship at the assistant professor level. There are now 16 bicentennial preceptorships, which provide assistant professors with a year of paid leave for scholarship and a research fund, along with another 32 university preceptorships that provide one semester of paid leave and a research fund.

ENDOWMENT. On March 25, 1745, 10 donors pledged a total of £185 "for the purpose of Erecting a Collegiate School in the province of New Jersey for the instructing of youth in the Learned Languages, Liberal Arts, and Sciences." The pledges were made a year and a half before the first charter establishing the College of New Jersey was granted. The document provided that only the interest earned on the principal could be expended for current purposes and that the principal was to be continuously reinvested to generate income for the future.

These modest pledges—insufficient even to cover the president's salary—marked the beginning of a Princeton endowment that by 2020 totaled almost $27 billion (the fifth largest in the country and the largest per student) and whose payout, along with other investment income, covered 60 percent of the University's operating budget of $2.3 billion. Earnings from the endowment also support high priority capital projects and strategic initiatives. Some earnings are reinvested so the endowment can sustain its real value through future generations, so that a fund that pays a faculty salary now is still capable of doing so a hundred years from now.

Princeton's first endowed scholarship was established in 1792 by James Leslie 1759, a schoolteacher in New York City, and its first endowed chair was given in 1857. In 1853 a permanent endowment fund was created, but the endowment grew slowly as the University focused more on spendable gifts to meet its expenses and to fund new buildings and other capital projects. The early twentieth century brought increased interest in obtaining endowment support to help meet the substantial ongoing expenses of the new preceptorial program and the University's growing commitment to scholarship and research. During the 20-year presidency (1912–32) of John Grier Hibben 1882 *1883, the endowment nearly quadrupled to more than $24 million, with expenditures allocated primarily to faculty salaries and the library.

In the mid-1920s, New York investment banker Dean Mathey 1912 became the de facto director of Princeton's endowment, even before he became a trustee in 1927. Prior to the stock market crash of 1929, he moved much of the endowment from stocks to bonds, and in early 1942 he reversed course long before most other investors. Under his stewardship, Princeton's endowment lost value in only one year during the Great Depression (in 1932, when its value fell 16 percent as the Dow dropped 71 percent); its value increased dramatically after the war as Mathey contravened conventional wisdom by investing as much as 80 percent of the portfolio in equities.

In 1949 Mathey officially became chair of the trustee finance committee, and by the time he stepped down in 1960 the value of the University's investments had doubled. One of the investments of the 1950s was a loan to Ray Kroc, the founder of McDonald's, with a provision that entitled Princeton to a share of the proceeds on every hamburger sold.

Until the late 1970s, policies for managing the endowment were set by an investment committee of three trustees who served as a subcommittee of the board's finance committee. For many years, the investment committee approved the purchase and sale of all securities in advance. In 1977, the committee adopted a new procedure under which it delegated responsibility for day-to-day selection of securities to four outside investment advisers. Since the University began hiring external managers, its endowment investments have earned a compound annualized return of 12.9 percent, which ranks in the top percentile of all institutional investors.

In 1987, when endowment assets were $2.2 billion, the University created the Princeton University Investment Co. (Princo) to manage investment of the endowment "subject to the general control of the board and the committee on finance." Princo is organizationally distinct from the University, but its staff members are University employees and its president reports to both the University president and the chair of what is now a 12-member Princo board of directors. The directors oversee the development of investment strategies and review the performance of outside managers who make investment decisions in designated asset categories. The Princo staff selects, monitors, and engages in active partnership with over 60 external investment firms that span the globe and the various asset categories.

The University's investment strategy is to achieve the highest possible long-term returns consistent with acceptable levels of risk; it also seeks to achieve a reasonable degree of stability and predictability in funds available for distribution from year to year. Meeting the University's current and future needs while preserving real value for future generations requires a return on investment that exceeds the sum of its annual rate of spending and its inflation. This means Princo must seek long-term returns (depending on inflation) close to 10 percent per year, which can be achieved only through an equity-based approach.

The University follows a spending policy that seeks a prudent trade-off between current needs and the preservation of long-term purchasing power. In 2020 the spending policy called for the University to aim for a "spending rate" each year in the range of 4 to 6.25 percent of the value of the endowment. The University's "payout inflator assumption" allows programs supported by endowment earnings to plan future expenditures; for 2020 it called for a 4 percent annual increase in payout per unit of endowment. The inflator can change—as it has on numerous occasions over recent decades—if an adjustment is necessary to return to the prescribed spending range.

The endowment consists of more than 4,000 separate funds. (The purpose supported by the largest number of funds is financial aid.) Most of the funds were donated as endowment (in these cases the principal must remain intact), and in many cases the donors restricted the purposes for which the earnings can be spent. The endowment also includes "funds functioning as endowment" (sometimes called "quasi-endowment") where the University has chosen to treat an invested fund as an endowment to support a particular purpose, but the fund is not legally restricted; unlike true endowment funds, the University could redirect the income to different purposes and the principal of these funds could be liquidated.

In their 2016 strategic framework, the trustees acknowledge that the University's "financial strength results first and foremost from the longstanding generosity of its alumni and friends" and that "wise stewardship of the University's endowment and other resources has multiplied the impact of those gifts and ensured that new generations of faculty and students continue to benefit from past philanthropy." They note that as late as the 1980s, tuition and fees were the largest source of general funds revenue to the University; in 1985 endowment payout provided only about 14 percent of the operating budget. Since then the University has transitioned from a tuition-driven financial model to one that is principally endowment-driven.

The trustees point out that there are enormous benefits in having such a sizeable endowment. It provides most of the funding for the University's best-in-class financial aid programs for undergraduates and graduate students, allows the University to pursue especially promising new initiatives, and enables it to weather unanticipated challenges—including, as it turned out, the 2020–21 COVID pandemic. But the trustees also caution that such heavy reliance on endowment earnings entails risks, which make it all the more important for the University to safeguard the capacity of the endowment to sustain its value not only for the immediate future, but in perpetuity.

ENGINEERING AND APPLIED SCIENCE, THE SCHOOL OF, traces its origin to the philanthropist John C. Green, who provided funding in 1873 for a school of Science that was named for him, and the pioneering efforts of two early professors in that school, Cyrus Fogg Brackett and Charles McMillan. McMillan, who was hired in 1875 to fill a civil engineering chair endowed by Green, was the first engineering professor in the school and the founder of the department of Civil Engineering. Brackett arrived in 1873 to fill a physics chair endowed by Green in honor of Joseph Henry; in 1889 he began developing a school of Electrical Engineering, in which he conducted Princeton's first graduate course in engineering. In 1908 the Electrical Engineering department moved with the Physics department into newly constructed Palmer Hall.

The civil engineers trained by McMillan and Brackett's electrical engineers were at first few in number, but by 1912 there were enough of them to organize the Princeton Engineering Association toward "the single end that the interests, influence, and efficiency of Princeton University be advanced through its Department of Engineering." Enthusiastic about the professional training Princeton had given them, they were eager to have the University broaden its curriculum to include other branches of engineering and to think of engineers as appliers "of science for the benefit of mankind."

Spurred on by this association, the University announced the formation of a school of Engineering in 1921. The following year Arthur Greene Jr. came from Rensselaer Polytechnic Institute to serve as its first dean and establish a department of Mechanical Engineering. In that same year, the school of Engineering and the department of Chemistry established a special program in Chemical Engineering that in 1934 became a separate department.

Greene proved to be, in the words of his successor, Kenneth Condit 1913, "a born teacher, an able administrator, and a dynamo of energy." Under his guidance, four-year undergraduate programs were offered in civil, chemical, electrical, mechanical, and mining (later geological) engineering. These fields also offered one-year graduate courses leading to master's degrees.

When the Green School of Science building burned down in 1928, the Engineering school moved across Washington Road into a new building, the Green engineering building (Green Hall), that had just been completed. In 1938 an interdepartmental Basic Engineering program was created to meet the needs of students wishing to study engineering in preparation for careers in business or government.

Between 1922 and 1940, when Greene retired, the number of engineering students grew from 84 to 379. Perhaps his most important contribution was the staunch support he gave to a Princeton concept of engineering education that combined instruction in science and fundamental engineering subjects with courses in the liberal arts to provide what he and President John Grier Hibben called "Engineering Plus."

In 1941, Condit invited Daniel Sayre to study the "possibility and desirability" of adding aeronautical engineering courses to the department of Mechanical Engineering, but instead a department of Aeronautical Engineering was created, initially with Sayre as its only professor. A pioneering interdisciplinary program in plastics was begun that evolved into Polymer Sciences and Materials. Two undergraduates founded *The Princeton Engineer* magazine, and the undergraduate curriculum introduced special programs which permitted students to work in two fields of engineering or to combine their study of one engineering field with additional concentration in a related field of science or mathematics.

Graduate training, previously limited to the one year required for the Master of Science in Engineering degree, was gradually extended to include work for the doctorate: PhD programs were introduced in Chemical Engineering and Electrical Engineering in 1946; Aeronautical Engineering in 1949; Civil Engineering in 1951; and Mechanical Engineering in 1952. In April 1948, a student in Chemical Engineering earned the school's first doctoral degree.

The growth of the school exceeded the capacity of the Green engineering building, which had been designed to accommodate 400 undergraduates. Chemical Engineering operated out of the old chemical laboratory building next door (now Aaron Burr Hall); Aeronautical Engineering moved to several buildings near the lake which had been built for the Physics department during World War II; and a wing was added to Green for Mechanical Engineering. In 1951 the acquisition of the Rockefeller Institute for Medical Research site just north of Princeton on Route 1 permitted development of the James Forrestal Campus, largely for the use of Aeronautical Engineering.

When Condit retired in 1954, the engineering faculty was three times as large as when he took office; the number of undergraduates had grown to 528 in that time, while the number of graduate students had increased from 11 to 87.

Joseph Elgin *1929 was the first faculty member to teach chemical engineering at Princeton and the department's first chair. In 1954 he became the third dean of the Engineering school, serving until 1971. During this time, the school placed increasing emphasis on engineering science, which, in his words, was concerned with "the principles upon which all technologies and engineering skills are ultimately based." In 1962 Princeton was one of five universities to receive grants of $1 million each from the Alfred P. Sloan Foundation in recognition of its scientific approach to engineering education.

New quarters for the school of Engineering was one of the highest priorities for the University's first major capital fundraising effort, the $53 Million Campaign. In the fall of 1962, the school moved into the new state-of-the-art Engineering Quadrangle, whose five connecting halls gave it four times the space it had in Green Hall and its satellites, and whose library capacity was seven times that of its former library. (In 1979 an additional wing for an Energy Research Laboratory was constructed with a connection to adjacent von Neumann Hall, and in 1993 another new wing was added.)

The increasing emphasis on engineering science was recognized by changing the school's name to Engineering and Applied Science. In 1963 the departments of Aeronautical Engineering and Mechanical Engineering merged to form a department of Aerospace and Mechanical Sciences (later Mechanical and Aerospace Engineering). In 1966 Civil Engineering merged with Geological Engineering, resulting in a department of Civil and Geological Engineering, which continued until 1974 when Geological Engineering became a program within Civil Engineering. The school fostered interdisciplinary research and instruction through the initiation of programs jointly offered by several engineering departments, sometimes in cooperation with nonengineering departments, in such fields as solid state and materials sciences, water resources, geophysical fluid dynamics, and environmental studies.

By the time Elgin retired as dean in 1971, the faculty had almost doubled to 97, the annual volume of sponsored research had more than tripled to $3.8 million, and the number of graduate students had almost tripled to 241. The most significant growth was in the number of engineering PhDs awarded, which had increased from seven in 1953–54 to 50 in 1970–71; in 1968 future trustee Wesley Harris *68 was the first Black student to earn a Princeton engineering PhD.

Elgin's successor, Robert Jahn '51 *55, did both his undergraduate work (in mechanical and aerospace engineering) and his graduate work (in physics) at Princeton. In an interview soon after he took office, Jahn outlined the distinctive role of the Princeton school of Engineering in this way:

> We cannot pretend that we are a major technological institute like MIT or Caltech. Nor can we replicate a large university complex, like Michigan or Minnesota. We have a small engineering school which must flourish in the framework of a small, liberal, excellent university. That I regard as an advantage, especially in an era which favors individually tailored, liberal engineering education for its students. We must respond . . . to the needs of society for solutions to some very pressing problems. What better place to do it than at a university which has well-developed programs in the humanities, social sciences, and natural sciences; and which has a heritage of engineering education that has always emphasized the development of the mind of the student more than the simple transfer of technical facts and techniques?

Four interdisciplinary topical programs were introduced in 1972: Bioengineering, Energy Conversion and Resources, Environmental Studies, and Transportation. Enrollment in the freshman class, which had dropped to 135 in the fall of 1971, increased sharply to 185 in 1972, and reached a then-all-time high of 250 in 1976. That same period also saw the first significant enrollment of women in the school. In 1973 women constituted 11 percent of the entering class, and by 1977 nearly 18 percent of the University's undergraduate engineering students were women—almost three times the national average.

Jahn stepped down as chair in 1986 and was succeeded by Hisashi Kobayashi (Electrical Engineering), 1986–91; James Wei (Chemical Engineering), 1991–2002; Maria Klawe (Computer Science), 2003–06; H. Vincent Poor *77 (Electrical Engineering), 2006–16; Emily Carter (Mechanical and Aerospace Engineering), 2016–19; and Andrea Goldsmith (Electrical Engineering), 2020– .

In 1973 the department of Electrical Engineering became Electrical Engineering and Computer Science, and in 1985 it split into separate Electrical Engineering and Computer Science departments. In 1986 Civil Engineering became the department of Civil Engineering and Operations Research; in 1999 a separate department of Operations Research and Financial Engineering (ORFE) was formed, and the Civil Engineering department became Civil and Environmental Engineering. In 2010 the name of the Chemical Engineering department was changed to Chemical and Biological Engineering. In 2021 the name of the Electrical Engineering department was changed to Electrical and Computer Engineering.

In 1989 Computer Science moved across Olden Street into a new building designed for it. In 2001 the engineering library also crossed the street when it relocated into the Friend Center—a building that also houses classrooms and computer clusters, a convocation space which includes portraits of all of Princeton's engineering deans, and a 250-seat auditorium. (In 2020 the engineering library moved to the Lewis Science Library.) ORFE crossed the street to Sherrerd Hall in 2008.

In 2020, the school of Engineering and Applied Science describes itself in words that echo Jahn's: it is

> unique in combining the strengths of a world-leading research institution with the qualities of an outstanding liberal arts college. In both its teaching and research, Princeton engineering pursues fundamental knowledge as well as multidisciplinary collaborations that make technology effective in solving complex societal problems. The school is committed to preparing all students—engineers as well as students from across the University—to become leaders in a technology-driven society.

In addition to its six departments (Chemical and Biological Engineering, Civil and Environmental Engineering, Computer Science, Electrical and Computer Engineering, Mechanical and Aerospace Engineering, and Operations Research and Financial Engineering), the school offers programs in Applications of Computing (for students who want to combine the study of computing with another academic concentration); Architecture and Engineering; Engineering and Management Systems (a direct descendant of the Basic Engineering program); Engineering Biology; Engineering Physics; Entrepreneurship; Geological Engineering; Materials Science and Engineering; Robotics and Intelligent Systems; Sustainable Energy; and Technology and Society. Graduate students may also earn certificates in Bioengineering, Computational and Information Science, and Statistics and Machine Learning.

The Engineering school houses several interdisciplinary research centers, including the Andlinger Center for Energy and the Environment, and the Center for Information Technology Policy (both of which the school helped create), as well as the Princeton Institute for the Science and Technology of Materials (PRISM). It also houses the Keller Center for Innovation in Engineering Education which was founded in 2005 to help students across campus achieve greater societal impact through entrepreneurship, design and design thinking, and innovative education. The center supports courses that cut across conventional discipline boundaries, special events, internships, and start-up incubator and accelerator programs.

In 2019–20, about a quarter (640) of Princeton's roughly 2,600 juniors and seniors were majoring in the school of Engineering and Applied Science, and 37 percent of them were women. Engineering degree recipients in the Class of 2020 included 26 students in Chemical and Biological Engineering; 17 in Civil and Environmental Engineering; 125 BSE recipients in Computer Science (there were also 33 AB recipients); 21 in Electrical Engineering; 52 in Mechanical and Aerospace Engineering; and 69 in Operations Research and Financial Engineering. As of June 2018, 676 graduate students, including 28 percent women, were pursuing advanced degrees in engineering.

In its 2016 strategic planning framework, the University said that Princeton's school of Engineering and Applied Science "which uniquely blends the qualities of a great engineering school and Princeton's commitment to the liberal arts, gives the University a special advantage in addressing technological change and its consequences for society. Princeton embraced engineering during a period when some Ivy League universities ignored the field. Princeton thereby made a wise choice . . . Princeton is fortunate to have a superb engineering faculty that is notable for its interdisciplinary character and its commitment to liberal arts education."

At the same time, the framework said, most of the school remained "housed in facilities that were constructed to a utilitarian standard more than a half-century ago and that are no longer adequate to the School's research and teaching. The University will need to invest aggressively to support both the School's existing programs and new initiatives in emerging fields. Fields related to information science—including computer science, statistics, and machine learning—will require special attention . . . Not surprisingly, they attract students in droves . . ."

The University's 2026 campus plan called for significant enhancement and expansion of space to support engineering. In 2020 the University began planning for the first new space, a 300,000-square-foot building along the north side of Ivy Lane and Western Way to house teaching and research laboratories, classrooms, and offices for the department of Chemical and Biological Engineering and a new initiative in bioengineering. The building would be connected to a new building to house the department of Geosciences, the department of Ecology and Evolutionary Biology, and the High Meadows Environmental Institute.

ENGINEERING QUADRANGLE, THE, was dedicated on October 13, 1962, an occasion that attracted national media attention because of the then state-of-the-art nature of its facilities. The quadrangle housed four engineering departments (Civil, Chemical, Electrical, and Mechanical and Aerospace), a library, and administrative space in six interconnecting halls surrounding a central court. It was located on land formerly a part of University Field, a large athletic venue that until 1961 was, among other uses, home of the baseball team and terminus of the reunions P-rade. Von Neumann Hall, an adjacent freestanding building, was constructed at the same time; later that decade it became a target of anti-Vietnam War protests as the rented home of the Institute for Defense Analyses, which conducted classified research for the US Department of Defense.

Five of the halls, now known more by their letters than by their names, commemorated faculty and alumni: (A) James Hayes 1895; (B) Cyrus Fogg Brackett, founder of the department of Electrical Engineering; (C) George Beggs, professor of civil engineering; (D) John Thomas Duffield, professor of mechanics and mathematics; and (E) John Maclean Sr., Princeton's first professor of chemistry. The sixth hall

(F) housed the library and the main entrance to the building.

The landscaped court at the center of the quadrangle, which includes a sculpture and a fountain, was named for one of the architects for the building, Stephen Voorhees 1900, a trustee and, from 1930 to 1949, the University's supervising architect. On the plaza outside the main entrance to the building is a soaring weathered-steel sculpture, Clement Meadmore's *Upstart II*.

In 1979 an Energy Research Laboratory (labeled on maps as G wing) was constructed with a connection to von Neumann Hall (H), and in 1993 a J wing was added that linked the D wing to the Energy Research Laboratory. In 1991 a parking garage opened on the E-Quad site, followed in 1993 by the adjacent Bowen Hall. In 2016 the 129,000-square-foot Andlinger Center for Energy and the Environment opened, with connections to Bowen Hall and the E-Quad's E wing.

In 1989 the department of Computer Science moved across Olden Street to a new Computer Science building, and in 2008 the department of Operations Research and Financial Engineering moved into Sherrerd Hall. In 2001 the engineering library moved across the street to the newly constructed Friend Center for Engineering Education, and some of its former space at the main entrance to the E-Quad was converted into a café, lounge, and study space. In 2020 the library moved again, from the Friend Center to the Lewis Science Library, and much of the former library space in the E-Quad was renovated to create a two-story laboratory space for robotics.

The University's 2026 campus plan calls for significant enhancement and expansion of space to support engineering teaching and research. It identifies the future of the E-Quad as a question still to be resolved, noting that "the E-Quad could be reused as is (e.g., for swing space), or renovated, or replaced, consistent with the zoning for that site, to serve academic or administrative purposes."

The zoning for the site reflects its proximity to private homes immediately to the east on Murray Place; in 1990 the Borough of Princeton adopted an ordinance that constrained net new development on the E-Quad site to an additional 200,000 square feet plus a 140,000 square foot garage, and in 2005 it adopted a revised ordinance that increased the permitted square footage by another 100,000 square feet, while also imposing constraints related to building design and use, parking and traffic circulation, landscaping and other buffering, and overall site design.

ENGLISH, THE DEPARTMENT OF. While lectures in English literature were delivered as early as 1838 and a lecturer on English literature was appointed in 1864, the surest indication that English literature was evolving into a legitimate discipline came in 1868 when the title of the University's first endowed professorship was changed from Holmes Professor of Belles-Lettres and Elocution to Holmes Professor of Belles-Lettres and English Language and Literature. In 1870 the first description of courses in English literature appeared in the catalogue.

By the beginning of the twentieth century, the study of English literature as a discipline was clearly established. Faculty at the rank of professor included Theodore Hunt, who had introduced the study of Anglo-Saxon and Middle English in 1878, and Henry van Dyke 1873, who was noted for his work in American literature. James Murray was a Shakespeare and Wordsworth scholar, and Bliss Perry taught the poetry of Scott and Emerson until he left to become editor of the *Atlantic Monthly*. In 1900 George McLean Harper, a Renaissance specialist and another pioneer in Wordsworth studies, gave up his professorship in modern languages to take on a professorship in English.

With its eminent faculty, English literature joined Greek literature, Roman literature, and philosophy as the first humanistic disciplines to offer a full roster of graduate as well as undergraduate courses when the graduate school was founded in 1901. It was also well situated three years later when President Woodrow Wilson created 11 departments, with English among them and Hunt as its first chair.

In 1904 Wilson also established what was to become the standard collegiate course: two years of general study, followed by two years of concentrated study in a major. The following year he further revolutionized Princeton's teaching by introducing the preceptorial system and hiring 49 assistant professors known as "preceptor guys." The English department was allotted seven immediately, and several more were added in the years soon after. Many of them, in fields ranging from *Beowulf* to Browning, and from Donne to Dickens, went on to have long and distinguished careers at the University.

In the decades just before World War II, the faculty was joined by a new generation of scholars who would become well-known names to students and the academic world through the rest of the century. Among them was Carlos Baker *40, who gained international recognition as the biographer of Hemingway. He arrived in 1937 to teach while completing his doctoral work. Lawrance Thompson arrived in 1939, the year he was appointed the official biographer of Robert Frost. The department played an integral role in the 1942 creation of the University's first interdepartmental plan of study, a program in American Civilization that is now the program in American Studies under the aegis of the Humanities Council.

Donald Stauffer 1923 *1924, who joined the department's faculty in 1928, and Richard Blackmur, who joined in 1940, were not only esteemed literary critics, but also poets. They were both instrumental in moving forward a Creative Writing program that had grown out of an advanced composition course first offered in 1915. By 1939 creative writing was formalized within a Creative Arts program, with Allen Tate as its first resident fellow until he was appointed Chair of Poetry at the Library of Congress. By 1971, increasing student interest led to Creative Writing becoming a separate program.

Appointments just after World War II included faculty whose work would change the face of twentieth-century scholarship. One was A. Walton Litz '51, who joined the faculty in 1956 and whose pioneering work on T. S. Eliot, James Joyce, Ezra Pound, and Wallace Stevens made him one of the most distinguished modernist scholars of his generation.

Another was medievalist D. W. Robertson Jr., who joined the faculty in 1946 and whose journal papers were already causing a stir among medievalists by the late 1950s. His major study *A Preface to Chaucer*, published in 1962, challenged the standard approaches to medieval studies. Robertson's approach and its supporters became known as the Robertsonian school of medieval criticism.

John Fleming *63 wrote his dissertation under the direction of Robertson, joined the faculty in 1965, and became a towering figure in medieval studies. A popular lecturer, he was widely recognized on campus, serving for 11 years as head of Wilson College and for almost 20 years as chief faculty marshal at Commencement. He wrote a weekly column for the *Daily Princetonian*, and in 2021 received a Princeton honorary degree.

Faculty appointments in the last quarter of the twentieth century put Princeton at the forefront of other emerging critical schools of thought. In 1970 Ann Wood, author of *The Feminization of American Culture*, was the department's first female professor. In the mid-1980s, two of the pillars of feminist literary criticism joined the faculty: Sandra Gilbert, co-author of *The Mad Woman in the Attic*, and Elaine Showalter. Showalter made Princeton her academic home until she retired in 2003; she is considered the founder of gynocritics, a school of feminist criticism.

In 1990 Arnold Rampersad joined the faculty, and in 1991 he was chosen as a MacArthur Fellow, with the foundation recognizing him for helping "to define the field of African-American literary biography." *Days of Grace: A Memoir*, which he co-authored with Arthur Ashe, and his two-volume Library of America edition of the works of Richard Wright both came out while he was teaching at Princeton.

Valerie Smith, noted scholar of African American literature and culture, was a member of the English department from 1980 to 1989 and returned to Princeton in 2001; a year later she was appointed director of Princeton's African American Studies program. She was then the founding director of the center for African American Studies when it was established in 2006; in 2011 she was appointed dean of the college, and in 2015 she was named president of Swarthmore College.

Students in the twenty-first-century department of English still read the texts studied in the early twentieth century. But concentrators also now read widely in literature written in English across the globe, including literatures of India and Africa, Australia, and the Caribbean. They study literature in relation to other media and to the broader category of culture. Study can include courses on Toni Morrison, William Shakespeare, Jacques Derrida, and Emily Dickinson. Special tracks within the major, from arts and media, to criticism and theory, to drama and performance studies, allow for a wide range of interdisciplinary study.

The department encourages and supports study abroad. Juniors can spend their spring term at University College London, the oldest and largest of the colleges of the University of London. In collaboration with Middlebury College's Bread Loaf School of English, the department offers a six-week summer program of study at Lincoln College, Oxford, for rising seniors.

A rigorous graduate program continues to produce field-transforming scholars, insightful and imaginative critics, and effective and creative teachers. Offerings include seminars in every major historical field of concentration as well as a wide range of theoretical specializations in fields such as feminist theory, gender and sexuality studies, psychoanalysis, Marxism, post-colonialism, environmental studies, political and social theory, and cultural studies.

Many faculty members of the department are affiliated with other departments and programs, including the department of African American Studies, the High Meadows Environmental Institute, the Center for Digital Humanities, and the Princeton-Mellon Initiative in Architecture, Urbanism, and the Humanities. As of 2020, the Creative Writing program, now part of the Lewis Center for the Arts, had one of the most outstanding faculties in the country, including Jhumpa Lahiri, YiYun Li, Aleksandar Hemon, John McPhee '53, Paul Muldoon, James Richardson '71, Susan Wheeler, and Tracy K. Smith, former US Poet Laureate, who chaired the center.

ENROLLMENT in the College of New Jersey probably numbered no more than 10 students when President Jonathan Dickinson began instruction in his Elizabethtown parsonage in 1747. During the College's first 21 years, the 338 students in attendance came from 12 of the 13 colonies. Although the majority lived in New Jersey, New York, and Pennsylvania, more than a quarter were from New England, and a fair number came from the south, thus preparing Princeton to become a national institution when the colonies became a nation.

After President John Witherspoon arrived in 1768, he attracted more students from the south, where early graduates were serving as ministers and teachers. While most students still came from the middle colonies, the representation from New England declined markedly as the enrollment from the southern colonies increased. Under Witherspoon, the College enjoyed something of a cosmopolitan flavor, with students "not only from almost every province," Philip Fithian 1771 wrote in his senior year, "but . . . also many from the West Indies & some few from Europe."

An enrollment of just over 75 students in 1794 had almost doubled to 142 by 1820, but it then plummeted in the early years of the presidency of James Carnahan 1800. Carnahan's vice president and successor, John Maclean Jr. 1816, reversed this troubling trend, increasing enrollment from 87 in 1829 to 228 a decade later.

By 1861 enrollment had reached 314, with heavy representation from the south. From 1820 to 1860, 12 classes enrolled more southern than northern students, and in the Class of 1851 southern enrollment reached 63 percent. With the onset of the Civil War, about a third of the students left, dropping enrollment in 1862 to 221. But by 1870, early in the administration of James McCosh, the size of the undergraduate student body had returned to pre-war levels (328 in 1870), and by the end of his administration it had doubled.

Until the 1870s Princeton's enrollment was entirely undergraduate except for occasional non-degree postgraduate students. By 1877, however, the number of candidates for advanced degrees was 42 and increasing. By the time the graduate school was formally established in 1900 there were 117 graduate students. After World War I enrollment in the graduate school was limited to 200 (soon increased to 250), but following World War II a policy of controlled expansion was adopted, allowing a marked rise in the number of graduate students enrolled.

Undergraduate enrollment continued its upward trend under Presidents Francis Patton (1,053 in 1900), Woodrow Wilson (1,253 in 1910), and John Grier Hibben (1,714 in 1920). The growth led the trustees in 1922 to adopt a policy of limited enrollment and selective admission. Enrollments from the midwest began to rise in the 1880s as alumni associations were formed throughout that region and the rest of the country; by the time McCosh left office in 1888 there were 17 of them. In the 1920s enrollments from the west coast grew as admission policies were modified to encourage greater geographical diversity. But other forms of diversity were actively discouraged as the University enrolled no Black and very few Asian or Hispanic students, and in 1924 limited Jewish enrollment to less than three percent.

Just prior to World War II, undergraduate enrollment was around 2,400 and there were fewer than 300 graduate students. After the war enrollments skyrocketed, and by 1950 there were almost 3,200 undergraduates and more than 600 graduate students. With the GI Bill and other financial aid programs, increasing admission of students from public high schools, a small number of African American students, and a considerable influx (especially at the graduate level) of students from other countries, Princeton began growing larger and more diverse. By 1976 approximately four percent of undergraduates and 22 percent of graduate students came from outside the United States; by 2020 roughly 12 percent of undergraduates and 41 percent of graduate students were international students.

In the 1950s and 1960s graduate school enrollments increased significantly as the Cold War fueled federal investments in science, engineering, and foreign language and area studies, and as national fellowship programs encouraged advanced training in other fields. In the early 1960s the University began to admit women graduate students and in 1969 began enrolling female undergraduates, with a goal of increasing the undergraduate population by about 1,000. A decade into coeducation, in 1980, the University was enrolling 4,400 undergraduates and 1,485 graduate students.

In 2000 a trustee committee named for its chair, Paul Wythes '55, recommended a 10 percent increase in undergraduate enrollment (from 4,600 to 5,100) as soon as an additional residential college could be constructed, and in 2016 the trustees authorized a further 10 percent expansion (from 5,200 to 5,700), again as soon as additional residential college space could be provided, with "the expectation of a further increase in the number of undergraduates in the future."

In 2019, undergraduate enrollment was 5,328, with 50.3 percent men and 49.7 percent women. The student body was 40.1 percent white, 22.2 percent Asian American, 10.6 percent Hispanic/Latino, 7.9 percent Black/African American, 5.3 percent multiracial, 0.3 percent Native American and Pacific Islander, and 12.2 percent international.

The size of the graduate school increased in the late twentieth century and early twenty-first century as the size of the faculty increased and as new academic programs were introduced. Between 2006 and 2007 the number of enrolled students jumped as a new status of "dissertation completion enrollment" was created to permit continued enrollment of PhD students who do not complete their dissertations within their department's normal enrollment period.

Of a total graduate school enrollment in 2020–21 of 3,065 students, 90 percent were pursuing doctoral degrees. Some 41 percent of the students were women and 41 percent were international. Among the US citizens and permanent residents, 55 percent were white, 15 percent Asian, 12 percent Hispanic/Latino, 5 percent Black/African American, 5 percent multiracial, and 8 percent were listed as unknown. By division, 21 percent were in the humanities, 23 percent in engineering, 26 percent in the social sciences, and 29 percent in the natural sciences.

ENTREPRENEURSHIP/INNOVATION. The University's Keller Center for Innovation in Engineering Education defines entrepreneurship as "identifying a problem and having the motivation or desire to solve it." The center's history course says entrepreneurship is "an ancient activity that first appeared 8,500 years ago," and its foundations of entrepreneurship course describes it as a process of taking risks to create value for the benefit of others. Entrepreneurship, the center says, "is about innovating, marshalling limited resources, inspiring teams, and persisting through challenges and uncertainty, often by trying, learning from what happens, and trying something better."

In a sense, Princeton's eighteenth-century founders were entrepreneurs, and the University's history is replete with both faculty members and alumni who applied their knowledge, creativity, and determination to serve and change society in multiple ways. Prominent entrepreneurs in the early stages of the information age included Jeff Bezos '86, the founder and CEO of Amazon; Eric Schmidt '76, CEO of Google and later executive chair of its parent company, Alphabet, Inc.; and Meg Whitman '77, CEO of eBay, Hewlett-Packard, and Quibi. The alumni body also includes a broad range of social entrepreneurs, including Wendy Kopp '89, founder of Teach For America.[*]

In 2014, with student, faculty, and alumni interest in entrepreneurship growing rapidly, Provost David Lee *99 created a Princeton Entrepreneurship Advisory Committee to consider how the University could best support entrepreneurs "in a way that is rooted in Princeton's strengths as a liberal arts institution and as a leading research university." In short, he said, he was asking the committee how the University could "do entrepreneurship the Princeton way."

The committee defined entrepreneurship broadly. In a statement following the release of the committee's report, Lee and President Christopher Eisgruber

---

[*] In 2011 Bezos and his wife MacKenzie Scott '92 donated $15 million to establish the Bezos Center for Neural Circuit Dynamics in the Princeton Neuroscience Institute and in 2012 Schmidt and his wife Wendy created a $25 million transformative technology fund for the invention, development, and utilization of cutting-edge technology that has the capacity to transform research in the natural sciences and engineering. Both gifts support the University's initiatives in innovation and entrepreneurship.

said, "Entrepreneurs can be engineers or humanists. They can work in the private sector or the public sphere, driving positive change in all kinds of industries and in organizations of all shapes and sizes. Entrepreneurs challenge themselves to ask hard questions, think critically, develop innovative solutions, and create organizations that effect meaningful change."

In response to the report's recommendations, the University established a Princeton Entrepreneurship Council (PEC) "to steer and coordinate entrepreneurship-related programs across campus," as well as an undergraduate certificate program in entrepreneurship. With support from alumni, an Alumni Entrepreneurs Fund was created to provide funding and mentorship to student entrepreneurs, and an alumni-supported Tiger Challenge program was established to "encourage Princeton students to . . . work in diverse teams to develop solutions to unanswered challenges."

The PEC focuses on building Princeton's entrepreneurial community by hosting events and conferences, providing mentorship, assisting new ventures in finding funding, and engaging with the regional innovation ecosystem. In 2020 it became part of the office of the dean for research, reporting to the University's first vice dean for innovation, professor of chemical and biological engineering Rodney Priestley, who himself was a co-founder of two startup companies based on inventions made in his laboratory at Princeton.

The PEC is located in the Princeton Entrepreneurial Hub on Chambers Street in downtown Princeton, a 10,000-square-foot space that the University opened in 2015 to offer support and co-working space for University-related startups. Operated by the Keller Center, the Hub also houses an eLab program that supports student teams seeking to start new ventures.

The Keller Center was started in 2005, and in 2007 it appointed the University's first "entrepreneur-in-residence," Greg Olsen, a pioneer in the sensors industry and in civilian space travel. In 2008 the center was named for educational innovator Dennis Keller '63 and his wife, Constance, when they gave $20 million to endow it. The center offers curricular and co-curricular programs organized around design, design-thinking, entrepreneurship, and innovative teaching, all at the intersection of technology and society. It sponsors an undergraduate certificate program in entrepreneurship; supports courses that focus on entrepreneurship and design-oriented thinking; and offers co-curricular opportunities such as internships and startup incubator and accelerator programs to undergraduates and graduate students.

The center's Innovation Forum is an annual competition and networking event that showcases research with the potential to be commercialized. While traditionally focused on innovations in the sciences and engineering, in 2020 the forum added a track focused on innovations in the humanities and social sciences.

In 2018 the University spearheaded the opening of a new incubator space at Princeton Forrestal Center. Princeton Innovation Center BioLabs provides co-working, lab, and office space for high-tech science- and engineering-based startup companies formed by University faculty, students, and alumni, as well as members of the wider New Jersey community. In 2019, when the trustees updated the University's strategic planning framework, they emphasized that one major goal of the Lake Campus to be developed south of Lake Carnegie was to "contribute to the regional innovation ecosystem by providing co-working spaces for projects that will bring together Princeton faculty, postdocs, or students with industry, government, nonprofits, or other research institutions."

In 2011 the University created an Intellectual Property Accelerator Fund in the office of the dean for research to help speed the development of innovative projects into real world applications. The fund supports proof-of-concept research, prototypes, or other steps to bring fundamental discoveries to the point where they can be developed; the six discoveries funded in 2020 ranged from new treatments for cancer, hepatitis B, and obesity to pain-free intravenous injections and low-cost water purification.

When Priestly was appointed vice dean in 2020 to provide academic leadership for innovation and entrepreneurship activities across campus, he created Princeton Innovation, a campus-wide initiative to encourage, facilitate, and promote innovation, entrepreneurship, and partnerships that enhance the quality and impact of research and teaching, with the goal of benefitting society.

At Engage, Princeton's fall 2020 innovation and entrepreneurship conference, Priestly announced three new programs to help faculty, postdocs, and graduate students develop entrepreneurial skills: an executive education program in collaboration with the Wharton School of the University of Pennsylvania that prepares faculty to take on advisory roles at companies formed around their innovations; Techstars, which offers "bootcamps" for graduate students and postdocs who want to lead startup companies; and Intelispark Consulting, which offers advice on how to seek federal small business research funding.

One speaker at the conference was Andrea Goldsmith, who arrived on campus in September 2020 as a professor of electrical engineering and dean of the school of Engineering and Applied Science. A cofounder of two successful wireless technology startups, Goldsmith said, "entrepreneurship is not just about starting companies; it is also about forging new paths and taking risks, not only in commercial companies but in social endeavors, and in any organization." Her goal for Princeton, she said, "is to foster a diverse and inclusive tech hub in the tri-state area."

Shortly after the conference the University announced it was joining Rutgers University and two New Jersey health care companies as tenants in an innovation and startup complex in New Brunswick, New Jersey, called The Hub (scheduled to open by 2024).

EPIDEMICS. Princeton, for the most part, has been spared major epidemics, but on several occasions disease has forced changes to the academic schedule, and in 2020–21 the global COVID-19 pandemic had wide-ranging impacts on the lives of students, faculty, staff, and alumni.

A cholera epidemic in August 1832, attributed to laborers digging the Delaware & Raritan Canal, forced President James Carnahan to close the College. "[B]y reason of the alarm occasioned by the threatened approach of Pestilence," the trustees' minutes state, "it became impossible to keep any of the College Classes together." Nevertheless, Commencement occurred on schedule in late September, although classes did not resume until mid-October, nearly a month late.

President James McCosh closed the College for three weeks in March 1871 after a student came down with smallpox, although there were no further incidents and the student recovered. Typhoid fever killed 10 students and sickened 30 others in 1880, an outbreak that again forced McCosh to close the College, as well as to cancel Class Day and shorten the commencement exercises to just the orations and awarding of degrees. The outbreak was later traced to the campus's primitive sewer system, which contaminated nearby water wells. By August 1880, the College had begun to build a new, cement-lined cesspool, disinfect the sewer pipes, and dig new wells.

Isabella McCosh, the president's wife, cared for many of the students who fell ill during this period. The daughter of a surgeon, she visited the proctor's office each morning to obtain a list of students needing care and then visited them in their rooms, bearing food and medicine. She also pushed her husband to raise funds for Princeton's first infirmary, which opened in 1892 and was named (over her objections) in her honor.

Polio first appeared on campus in the early twentieth century. Two Princeton students died of it within a month of each other in 1910, although neither contracted the disease locally. When a much bigger polio outbreak spread along the east coast in 1916, President John Grier Hibben postponed Opening Exercises for three weeks. Students agreed to avoid local movie theaters, restaurants, and shopping areas and refrain from going out of town until the risk had passed. Nevertheless, one student, an incoming freshman, died.

Princeton University was spared any deaths during a massive international outbreak of influenza in 1918 that eventually killed 50 million people worldwide, including 32 in the town of Princeton. Because the outbreak occurred during World War I, many normal University operations had already been suspended. Military officials overseeing army and navy training units instituted a strict quarantine restricting access to and from campus and meticulously cleaned the dormitories. In an order dated Oct. 10, 1918, for example, Col. John A. Pearson, who oversaw the Student Army Training Corps, ordered that Pyne Hall "be thoroughly cleaned with a carbolic acid solution . . . The bedding to be hung in the open air for 24 hours, the doors closed and the windows opened for 24 hours." Travel restrictions remained in effect until November 7, four days before the Armistice.

An influenza epidemic in the fall of 1957 affected one quarter of the undergraduates and 10 percent of the graduate students; it did not require a disruption of the academic schedule, but it did tax university facilities. The first case was reported in early October and by the middle of the month the number had spiked to 150. McCosh Infirmary placed extra beds in its hallways and all student activities for the upcoming football weekend were canceled. As the number of sick students continued to climb, the University converted Chancellor Green, including the cafeteria, the library, and the balcony, into an infirmary annex to handle the overflow.

A flu vaccine, which had been developed over the summer, reached campus in late October and 1,176 students were inoculated, at the cost of $1 apiece. By the second week of November 1957, the flu had largely run its course, leaving "several hundred wan undergraduates to dig themselves out from under weeks of neglected course assignments," the *Princeton Alumni Weekly* reported. Significant flu outbreaks again filled the infirmary beds in 1968, 1974, and 1978.

An outbreak of meningitis B, which infected eight undergraduates and a visiting high school student in 2013, led to a massive campus-wide inoculation effort. With federal approval to use a vaccine that had been licensed in other countries but not yet in the United States, the University offered free vaccines to all undergraduates, as well as some graduate students and members of the University community with specific medical conditions, promoted by a poster and video campaign. Nearly 5,300 people received the vaccinations when they were first offered in December 2013, and the University continued to offer free vaccines through June 2015.

In March 2020, the University closed the campus during a global pandemic as students and staff members began testing positive for the coronavirus COVID-19. Classes for the remainder of the spring semester were moved online, as were commencement exercises. Reunions and the Baccalaureate service were both canceled for the first time ever during peacetime, although virtual reunions took place and a virtual P-rade began at the traditional starting time of 2 p.m. on Saturday. Spring sports were canceled and campus tours were suspended. The University made special funds available to faculty for what it described as "rapid, novel, and actionable COVID-19 research projects" designed to address scientific and policy questions related to the pandemic. The University provided funds to help the local Princeton community cope with the crisis, and members of the local and worldwide Princeton University community—students, faculty, staff, and alumni—contributed in countless ways on the front lines as doctors, nurses, and emergency responders, as researchers and policy makers, and as volunteers serving their communities and others.

In August 2020, the University announced that the undergraduate program would be fully remote that fall, with accommodations on campus only for undergraduates whose situations made it extremely difficult or impossible to study from home and for a very limited number of students who needed to be on campus to participate in Army ROTC, or for senior thesis research or other work essential to their degree programs. Some 265 undergraduates were approved to live on campus, while 713 undergraduates, including 217 first-year students, deferred admission or took leaves of absence.

The University announced that tuition would be reduced by 10 percent and activities fees would not be charged; all graduate students would be permitted to stay in campus graduate housing; Ivy League sports would be canceled through the fall semester (they were later canceled through the spring semester as well); and students, faculty, and staff members on campus would have to be tested weekly for the coronavirus. The eating clubs remained closed for the academic year, and many student organizations and other activities suspended their operations or offered them only remotely.

In preparation for fully remote learning, the Mc-Graw Center for Teaching and Learning collaborated with faculty members to move courses from the classroom to the computer or to design new classes for virtual instruction. Faculty and staff also worked on other innovative strategies, like shipping laboratory kits to students around the world so they could conduct at-home experiments in science and engineering courses.

In November, the University announced that all undergraduates would be invited to return to campus for the spring semester, but that all who returned would need to participate in a stringent testing protocol (the University constructed its own COVID-19 testing facility) and follow strict public health guidelines, and almost all classes would remain virtual. Some 2,887 undergraduates elected to live on campus and another 670 lived off-campus but locally.

Since 2020–21 was the first year under the University's new academic calendar, the first optional January "Wintersession" program had to be conducted as a fully virtual experience; more than 2,200 students signed up. Alumni Day 2021 was canceled, although the annual Service of Remembrance took place online. The University announced that reunions would again be virtual in 2021, but that it would conduct an in-person outdoor Commencement, relocated from the traditional front-campus location to the more commodious Princeton Stadium.

EVELYN COLLEGE FOR WOMEN was founded in 1887 by a 72-year-old clergyman and former Princeton professor, Joshua Hall McIlvaine 1837, who named it after Sir John Evelyn, a seventeenth-century English writer and diarist. The college (pronounced EE-va-lin) was the first college for women in New Jersey, and its principals were McIlvaine's daughters, Alice and Elizabeth. It was housed in two buildings about a mile east of the center of town; one, the former home of Professor Allan Marquand 1874, was on what is now called Evelyn Place (now a private residence), and the other was on the southwest corner of Nassau and Harrison Streets.

Evelyn had no legal connection with Princeton and its students could not take Princeton classes, but Princeton's president, one of its deans, and three of its faculty members were on its board of trustees, and most of Princeton's senior professors lectured there. Evelyn's colors were orange and white, reminiscent of Princeton's orange and black.

One of Evelyn's faculty members was Helen Magill White, the first woman in the United States to receive a PhD. By 1889 Evelyn students had access to Princeton's library and museums and, informally, to labs and classrooms. Enrollment at Evelyn probably never exceeded 50 in one year, and it was composed largely of daughters of professors in the College and the seminary and sisters of Princeton undergraduates. In total, 15 women graduated from Evelyn during the 10 years it was open.

Not surprisingly, Princeton and Evelyn students took great interest in each other. When the newly formed Colonial Club rented the house next door to Evelyn College for its first clubhouse, it found its competitive position strengthened vis-à-vis the four older eating clubs. Princeton students were said to visit Evelyn frequently, chanting "Eva, Eva, l-y-n, Eva, Eva, let me in."

During the four-year depression that followed the Panic of 1893, hard times suppressed enrollment and diminished any chances of obtaining sizable gifts for endowment and buildings. Efforts were made to sustain the college, and in 1895 15 women joined what had previously been an all-male board of trustees. But after President McIlvaine died in 1897 the college could no longer afford to continue operating and it closed its doors for the last time.

FACULTY. At the core of any great university is its faculty. It is the faculty that teaches, advises, supervises independent work, works closely with graduate and postdoctoral students as they prepare for careers both inside and outside academia, and serves humanity through the new discoveries and insights that result from scholarship and research.

Princeton has long been distinctive among research universities by having a single, integrated faculty (as opposed to having separate faculties for the undergraduate college or for professional schools) and by insisting that all members of the faculty teach. On occasion, Princeton has parted company with distinguished scholars who preferred to be at institutions where they were not required to teach.

In its earliest days, Princeton's faculty consisted of the president of the University and one or two tutors. Over time, the faculty expanded in size and scope, and over recent decades it has become increasingly international and diverse. In 1905 the faculty grew by almost 50 percent with the appointment of 49 "preceptors"—assistant professors brought to Princeton by President Woodrow Wilson to engage with students through guided reading and small group discussions. In the late 1920s and 1930s, the University became a home for scholars and intellectuals from Europe who were escaping the pernicious spread of fascism and anti-Semitism.

The first African American faculty member, assistant professor of English Charles Davis, was appointed in 1955; the first woman to receive tenure at Princeton was Suzanne Keller, who was named a professor of sociology in 1968; and the first woman promoted to tenure from the assistant professor ranks was Sylvia Molloy in 1973, in what was then the department of Romance Languages and Literatures.

In the fall of 2020 the faculty (including visitors and part-time faculty) totaled 1,295, including 520 professors, 123 associate professors, 181 assistant professors, 18 instructors, 330 lecturers, 27 senior lecturers, 7 lecturers with the rank of professor, and 89 visitors. (In April 2020 the faculty created two new ranks, "Professor of the Practice" for faculty members who demonstrate eminence and sustained accomplishment in their area of practice, such as industry, entrepreneurship, government, journalism, or the creative or performing arts, and who teach subject matter that is not normally taught or represented by the tenured or tenure-track faculty; and "University Lecturer" for faculty members who demonstrate eminence and sustained accomplishment in traditional academic fields.)

As of that fall, 78 percent of the professorial faculty was tenured. Excluding visitors, 455 members of the faculty were women and 277 self-identified as members of minority groups (114 as underrepresented minorities). Of the full professors, 27 percent were women; with respect to ethnicity, 10 percent of the full professors were Asian, four percent Black, two percent Hispanic, 80 percent white, and four percent were of unknown ethnicity.

In addition to the faculty, the University's 2020–21 academic population included 1,027 professional researchers (including 705 postdocs), 195 professional specialists, 72 professional librarians, and 236 visitors.

Each faculty member has an official academic home, and some faculty are jointly appointed with other departments, institutes, or programs. The academic units that are authorized to be the primary academic home for tenured and tenure-track faculty are the 33 departments* and the professional schools of Architecture and Public and International Affairs, along with the Lewis Center for the Arts, the Lewis-Sigler Institute for Integrative Genomics, the Princeton Neuroscience Institute, the program in American Studies, the program in Gender and Sexuality Studies, the program in Linguistics in the Council of the Humanities, and the University Center for Human Values.

While meetings of the faculty are scheduled during most months of the academic year, and while these meetings occasionally attract sizeable attendance and robust discussion, as in the early 1970s when the faculty addressed concerns related to the war in Vietnam, or in the spring of 2018 when the faculty changed the academic calendar by moving fall-term exams from January into December, for the most part the work of the faculty is done through its elected faculty committees.

The Faculty Advisory Committee on Appointments and Advancements, first created during the presidency of John Grier Hibben 1882 *1893 and known colloquially as the "committee of three" because of its initial composition, consists of six full professors representing each of the four academic divisions[†] of the University. It is chaired by the president; the dean of the faculty serves as secretary; and the provost, the dean of the graduate school, and the dean of the college regularly meet with the committee. The committee advises the president on the appointment of professors; the appointment and promotion of associate professors; the reappointment and promotion of assistant professors; the salaries of these members of the faculty; and the awarding of preceptorships to assistant professors.

The Faculty Advisory Committee on Policy consists of the six tenured or tenure-track members of the faculty elected to represent it on the executive committee of the Council of the Princeton University Community. The president chairs the committee, the dean of the faculty serves as secretary, and the provost, while not a member of the committee, regularly attends its meetings. The dean of the graduate school and the dean of the college are invited to meet with the committee as needed. The committee may meet at the president's request, at the request of the faculty, or on its own motion to provide advisory consultation on matters of University-wide policy of concern to the faculty and not primarily within the jurisdiction of other established committees. This committee must approve any proposed changes to the *Rules and Procedures of the Faculty* before they can be brought to the faculty for a vote.

The Committee on Conference and Faculty Appeal may be called upon to act as a board of review in cases involving the dismissal or suspension of a member of the faculty, or any question of unfair treatment in relation to the appointment, reappointment, or academic duties or privileges of a member of the faculty.

A Faculty Advisory Committee on Diversity advises the president, provost, and dean of the faculty on issues and initiatives related to diversity and inclusion.

Other faculty committees include:

- The Committee on the Course of Study, which considers and recommends to the faculty appropriate action on all matters connected with the educational policy of the undergraduate program.

---

* The 33 departments are: African American Studies, Anthropology, Art and Archaeology, Astrophysical Sciences, Chemical and Biological Engineering, Chemistry, Civil and Environmental Engineering, Classics, Comparative Literature, Computer Science, East Asian Studies, Ecology and Evolutionary Biology, Economics, Electrical and Computer Engineering, English, French and Italian, Geosciences, German, History, Mathematics, Mechanical and Aerospace Engineering, Molecular Biology, Music, Near Eastern Studies, Operations Research and Financial Engineering, Philosophy, Physics, Politics, Psychology, Religion, Slavic Languages and Literatures, Sociology, and Spanish and Portuguese.

† The four academic divisions are (1) the humanities, including architecture; (2) the social sciences, including history and public and international affairs; (3) the natural sciences, including mathematics and psychology; and (4) engineering and applied science.

- The Committee on Discipline, which is responsible for the administration of rules and regulations governing student conduct and the adjudication of all alleged academic infractions not under the jurisdiction of the Undergraduate Honor Committee.
- The Committee on Examinations and Standing, which administers all regulations concerning the program of study and the scholastic standing of undergraduate students and recommends candidates for bachelor's degrees; this committee is also charged with reviewing the grading history of each department and program to ensure consistency with University policy regarding assessment and grading standards.
- The Committee on the Graduate School, which oversees all matters related to the Graduate School; the committee includes the directors of graduate studies of the departments and programs that offer graduate degrees and has subcommittees on policy, student life and discipline, fellowships, and curriculum.
- The Committee on Library and Computing.
- A Policy Committee on Athletics and Campus Recreation.
- The Committee on Public Lectures.
- The Committee on Classrooms and Schedules.
- The Committee on Undergraduate Admission and Financial Aid.
- A University Student Life Committee.
- The Council of College Heads (the heads of the residential colleges).
- The University Research Board, which advises the dean for research and the president on matters pertaining to research administration and policy.
- A Council on Teaching and Learning.

A September 2013 report by a trustee ad hoc committee on diversity called for a "sense of urgency" to make Princeton's faculty more inclusive. The office of the dean of the faculty works with all the academic departments to develop comprehensive diversity plans and provides a best practices guide for faculty searches. It also oversees a target of opportunity program that provides incentives to departments to diversify their ranks.

The dean of the faculty's office supports a presidential postdoctoral research fellows program that encourages early-career scholars from underrepresented groups to pursue careers in academia, and a presidential visiting scholars program that supports up to four visitors a year from academia or relevant professional fields who can contribute to the diversity of the campus.

FACULTY HONOR SOCIETIES. Princeton faculty are disproportionately represented in the major American honor societies, including the American Academy of Arts and Letters, the American Academy of Arts and Sciences, the American Philosophical Society, the National Academy of Engineering, the National Academy of Medicine, and the National Academy of Sciences.

American Academy of Arts and Letters

The American Academy of Arts and Letters was founded in 1898 as the National Institute of Arts and Letters and incorporated by Act of Congress in 1913 for the purpose of furthering literature and the fine arts in the United States. It admits members in the fields of architecture, art, literature, and music; its membership is limited to 250 at any one time.

Princeton faculty who have been members of the academy and the years of their election follow:

1898   Henry Van Dyke 1873
        Woodrow Wilson 1879
1906   Basil Gildersleeve 1849
1911   George Harper 1884
        Andrew Fleming West 1874
1912   John Grier Hibben 1882 *1893
1913   Frank Mather Jr.
1927   Paul Van Dyke 1881
1938   Roger Sessions
1946   Aymar Embury II 1900
1949   Allen Tate
1956   Richard P. Blackmur
1965   Milton Babbitt *42 *92
1978   Joyce Carol Oates
1981   Toni Morrison
1988   John McPhee '53
1991   Michael Graves
1996   Edmund White
1998   Russell Banks
        Robert Fagles
2008   Kwame Anthony Appiah
        Paul Muldoon
2012   Elizabeth Diller
        Jhumpa Lahiri
2016   Paul Lansky *73
2017   Julia Wolfe *12

2018 Jeffrey Eudenides
      Lynn Nottage
2019 Claudia Rankine
2020 Colson Whitehead

American Academy of Arts and Sciences

Chartered in Boston in 1780, the American Academy of Arts and Sciences is the second oldest learned society in the United States, exceeded in age only by the American Philosophical Society. The "end and design" of the academy, according to its charter, is "to cultivate every art and science which may tend to advance the interest, honor, dignity, and happiness of a free, independent, and virtuous people."

Princeton faculty who have been members of the academy and the years of their election follow:

1840 Joseph Henry
1841 John Torrey
1849 Arnold Guyot
1850 Stephen Alexander
1871 Charles Young
1874 James McCosh
1901 Henry Fairfield Osborn 1877
1911 Woodrow Wilson 1879
1912 William Berryman Scott 1877
1914 Edwin Grant Conklin
1917 Allan Marquand 1874
1918 Edward Capps
1921 Henry Norris Russell 1897 *1900
1923 Oswald Veblen
1929 Hermann Weyl
1931 Edward Armstrong
      Frank Mather
      Robert Root
1932 Morris Croll
1933 Carroll Pratt
1934 Edwin Kemmerer
      Theodore Leslie Shear
      Jacob Viner
1936 Frank Fetter
1943 Hugh Stott Taylor
1944 C. Rufus Morey
      John von Neumann
1948 Arthur Buddington
      E. Newton Harvey
1949 Julian Boyd
      Gilbert Chinard
1950 Eugene Wigner
1951 Edward Kendall
      Walter Stace

1952 Donald Hornig
1953 Lyman Spitzer Jr. *38
1954 Martin Schwarzschild
      Joseph Strayer 1925
      John Wheeler
1956 Henry D. Smyth 1918
1957 Emil Artin
      Carl Hempel
1958 Henry Eyring
      Colin Pittendrigh
1959 P. J. Conkwright
      Harold Dodds *1914
1960 J. Douglas Brown 1919 *1928
      Alonzo Church 1924 *1927
1961 Fritz Machlup
      John Milnor '51 *54
      Roger Sessions
1962 Gordon Craig '36 *41
      Robert Goheen '40 *48
      Roman Smoluchowski
      Oliver Strunk
1963 Walker Bleakney
      Robert Dicke '39
      Charles Gillispie
      E. H. Harbison 1928
      Walter Kauzmann
      Thomas Kuhn
      Alpheus Mason *1923
      Frank Notestein
      Arthur Pardee
      Erik Sjöqvist
      Ernest Wever
      Samuel Wilks
1964 Richard Blackmur
      Rensselaer Lee 1920 *1926
      John Tukey *39
      Richard Wilhelm
1965 Georges Florovsky
      Marvin Goldberger
      Wallace Hayes
1966 Val Fitch
      Joseph Kohn *56
      Marshall Rosenbluth
      Carl Schorske
      Arthur Wightman
      Sheldon Wolin
1967 James Cronin
      Donald Spencer
      Gregory Vlastos
1968 Valentine Bargmann
      Stuart Hampshire

Faculty Honor Societies 191

	Harry Hess		James Wei
	Lawrence Stone		Theodore Ziolkowski
1969	John Bonner	1983	Robert Keohane
	Joseph Frank		Martin Kruskal
	Noboru Sueoka		Bernard Lewis
1970	Marver Bernstein		David Lewis
	Ansley Coale '39 *47		Richard Rorty
	Harry Eckstein		Yakov Sinai
1971	William Baumol	1984	William Browder *58
1972	Charles Fefferman *69		David Wilkinson
	Arthur Link	1985	David Botstein
	Dana Scott		Robert Tarjan
	Irene Taeuber	1986	Joseph Smagorinsky
1973	William Bowen *58	1987	Curtis Callan *64
	Evelyn Harrison		Robert Gilpin
	Marius Jansen '44		Albert Tucker *32
	Arthur Mendel	1988	Toni Morrison
	Sam Treiman		Christopher Sims
1974	Stephen Adler	1989	Harold Furth
	Milton Babbitt *42 *92		Wu-chung Hsiang *63
	Victor Brombert	1990	Harold Shapiro *64
	Kurt Mislow		Shirley Tilghman
	William Moulton '35	1991	Alan Blinder '67
	Richard Ullman		Stanley Katz
1975	Gerald Bentley '52		Nannerl Koehane
	Cyril Black		Alexander Polyakov
	Edward Cone '39 *42		Joan Ruderman
	John Hopfield		Peter Sarnak
	Edward Nelson		William Schowalter
	Jeremiah Ostriker	1992	William Brinkman
	Robert Tucker		John Conway
1976	John Bahcall		Angus Deaton
	Jerome Blum		F. Duncan Haldane
	Fred Greenstein		Alison Jolly
	Oskar Morgenstern		Edmund Keeley '48
	Albert Rees		Paul Krugman
1977	Robert May		Harold Kuhn *50
	Walter Murphy		Simon Levin
	P. James Peebles *62		Elaine Pagels
	Norman Ryder		Margaret Dauler Wilson
	Donald Stokes '51	1993	Orley Ashenfelter *70
1978	Wesley Frank Craven		John Groves
	William Thurston		Samuel Hynes
	Kurt Weitzmann		Daniel Kahneman
	Charles Westoff		Stanley Kelley Jr.
1979	Peter Brown		John McPhee '53
	Arno Mayer		Albert Raboteau
1980	Donald McClure		Marta Tienda
1982	Edward Jones		Eric Wieschaus
	Elias Stein	1994	Hans Aarsleff
	Joseph Taylor Jr.		Leonard Barkan

Faculty Honor Societies

	Robert Fagles	2004	Bernard Chazelle
	Philip Holmes		Michael Cook
	Richard Jeffrey *57		Lyman Page Jr.
	Elliott Lieb		Gang Tian
	Alexander Nehamas *71		Bess Ward
	Richard Quandt '52		Yu Xie
	Michael Rothschild	2005	John Darley
1995	Christopher Achen		Susan Fiske
	Harry Frankfurt		Gilbert Harman
	William Happer *64		Robert Hollander '55
	Douglas Massey *78		Stephen Morris
	John Nash Jr. *50		H. Vincent Poor *77
	Harold Powers *59		Thomas Silhavy
	William Russel		Susan Stewart
	Anne Treisman		Mark Watson
1996	Jeanne Altmann	2006	Bryan Grenfell
	Russell Banks		Guust Nolet
	Sergiu Klainerman		Nai Phuan Ong
	Michael Levine	2007	Bonnie Bassler
1997	B. Rosemary Grant		Nell Irvin Painter
	Peter Grant		John Waterbury '61
	Gene Grossman		Bruce Western
	Amy Gutmann		Viviana Zelizer
	George Kateb	2008	Robert Austin
1998	Paul Benacerraf '52 *60		Charles Beitz '78
	David Billington '50		Emily Carter
	Alejandro Portes		Sun-Yung Alice Chang
1999	Gertrud Schupbach		Pablo Debenedetti
	Cornel West *80		Elizabeth Diller
	Edmund White		John Fleming *63
2000	Anthony Evans		Daniel Rodgers
	Helen Milner		Marlan Scully
	Paul Muldoon		Jeffrey Stout *76
	David Tank		Robert Wuthnow
	Daniel Tsui	2009	Paul DiMaggio
	C. K. Williams		William Jordan *73
	Andrew Yao		James McPherson
2001	Dilip Abreu *83		Guy Nordenson
	Ben Bernanke		Philip Pettit
	Demetrios Christodoulou *71	2010	Charles Boix
	John Cooper		Adam Burrows '75
	Michael Doyle		Peter Constantin
	Froma Zeitlin		Lynn Enquist
2002	R. Douglas Arnold		Hal Foster '77
	Anthony Grafton		David Huse
	Alan Krueger		Chung Law
	Thomas Shenk		James Marrow
	Anne-Marie Slaughter '80		Nolan McCarty
2003	Nicholas Katz *66		Wolfgang Pesendorfer
	Stephen Pacala	2011	Roland Benabou
	S. George Philander		Stanley Corngold
	Michael Wood		Edward Felten

Daniel Garber
W. Jason Morgan *64
Thomas Romer
Howard Stone
Shou-wu Zhang
2012 Athanassios Panagiotopoulos
Ignacio Rodriguez-Iturbe
Carol Greenhouse
John Burgess '69
Igor Klebanov *86
David Spergel '82
Keith Whittington
David MacMillan
2013 Jeffrey Eugenides
Robert Kaster
Naomi Leonard '85
Stephen Macedo *87
Jennifer Rexford '91
Yoshiaki Shimizu *75
Michael Smith
Leonard Wantchekon
2014 Neta Bahcall
Charles Cameron *88
Janet Currie '88
Christopher Eisgruber '83
David Gabai *80
Susan Naquin
Robert Socolow
2015 Sanjeev Arora
Martin Gilens
Ali Yazdani
2016 Brandice Canes-Wrone '93
Jill Dolan
Denis Feeney
Joanne Gowa '80
G. John Ikenberry
Janos Kollar
Kim Lane
Elke Weber
2017 Michael Aizenman
Manjul Bhargava *01
Anne Case *88
Dalton Conley
Yannis Kevrekidis
Eldar Shafir
Suzanne Staggs *93
2018 Simon Gikandi
Daniel Heller-Roazen
Tali Mendelberg
Jacqueline Stone
2019 Kathryn Edin
Brian Kernigham *69

Frances Lee
Sara McLanahan
Judith Weisenfeld *92
Virginia Zakian
2020 Ruben Gallo
M. Zahid Hasan
Amaney Jamal
Ruby Lee
Margaret Martonosi
Tom Muir
Eve Ostriker
Alexander Smits
James Stone
Leeat Yariv
Muhammad Qasim Zaman
2021 Mitchell Duneier
J. Nicole Shelton
Keith Wailoo
Nieng Yan
Deborah Yashar

American Philosophical Society

The American Philosophical Society is the oldest learned society in the United States. It was formed by Benjamin Franklin in 1743 and reorganized in its present form in 1769. It resulted from "A Proposal for Promoting Useful Knowledge Among the British Plantations in America," which Franklin circulated among a carefully selected number of "ingenious Men residing in the several colonies." The fields for selection of new members are: 1) mathematical and physical sciences; 2) geological and biological sciences; 3) social sciences; 4) humanities; and 5) administration, the fine arts, and public affairs. Membership is limited to 500 residents of the United States and 100 residents of foreign countries.

Princeton faculty who have been members of the society and the years of their election follow:

1769 John Witherspoon
1780 William Houston 1768
1785 Samuel Stanhope Smith 1769
1789 Ashbel Green 1783
     Walter Minto
1806 John Maclean Sr.
1831 Henry Vethake
1835 Joseph Henry
     John Torrey
1839 Stephen Alexander
1844 John Hart 1830
1856 George Matile
1867 Arnold Guyot

1871	James McCosh	1943	Julian Boyd
1874	Charles Young		Charles Osgood
1877	Cyrus Fogg Brackett	1944	Eugene Wigner
	Charles Shields 1844	1945	Frank Notestein
1886	William Berryman Scott 1877	1947	Henry D. Smyth 1918
1887	Henry Fairfield Osborn 1877	1948	Elmer Butler
1896	William Magie 1879		Samuel Wilks
1897	Edwin Conklin	1949	Glenn Jepsen 1927
	Henry Burchard Fine 1880	1951	Edward Kendall
	John Hatcher		John Wheeler
	William Libbey 1877	1952	Albert Friend Jr. *1917
	Leroy McCay 1878	1958	Wilbert Moore
	Charles McClure 1888	1959	Robert Palmer
	Arnold Ortmann		Lyman Spitzer Jr. *38
	Francis Landey Patton		Joseph Strayer 1925
	Woodrow Wilson 1879	1960	Harry Hess *32
1901	Dana Munro	1962	John Tukey *39
1908	Charles H. Smyth Jr.	1963	Ansley Coale '39 *47
1911	Augustus Trowbridge		Gordon Craig '36 *41
1912	John Grier Hibben 1882 *1893		Fritz Machlup
	Oswald Veblen	1964	Kurt Weitzmann
1913	Luther Eisenhart	1965	John Milnor '51 *54
	George Hulett 1892	1966	William Feller
	Henry Norris Russell 1897 *1900		Carl Hempel
1915	Edwin Adams		W. Arthur Lewis
1918	George Shull		Arthur Link
1919	Ulric Dahlgren 1894	1967	Donald Hornig
1920	Edward Capps	1969	Frederick Harbison '34 *40
1923	Karl Compton *1912	1970	Gerald Bentley
1928	James Alexander 1910 *1915		Lawrence Stone
	Hugh Stott Taylor	1971	George A. Miller
1929	E. Newton Harvey	1972	John Bonner
	Solomon Lefschetz		Charles Gillispie
1931	Arthur Buddington	1973	Bernard Lewis
	Raymond Dugan	1974	Thomas Kuhn
	Howard McClenahan 1894	1976	W. Frank Craven
1932	Gilbert Chinard	1977	William Baumol
	Edwin Kemmerer	1978	Robert Dicke '39
	Charles P. Smyth 1916 *1917	1979	Jerome Blum
1935	Harold Dodds *1914	1981	Martin Schwarzschild
	Frank Fetter	1984	Theodore Ziolkowski
	Hermann Weyl	1985	John Rupert Martin *47
1936	Edward Corwin	1986	Herbert Bailey '42
1938	C. Rufus Morey		Robert Goheen '40 *48
	John von Neumann	1987	Victor Brombert
1939	Theodore Leslie Shear		James Gunn
1940	Frank Mather	1988	Charles Fefferman *69
	Howard Robertson		John Hopfield
1941	Henry Eyring		Kenneth Levy *55
	Thomas Wertenbaker	1990	Harold Shapiro *64
1942	Jacob Viner		Robert Tarjan

1991 Philip Anderson
     Edward Cone '39 *42
     Peter Grant
     A. Walton Litz '51
     James McPherson
     Richard Quandt '52
1992 Gregory Chow
     Wen Fong '51 *58
     Joseph Taylor
1993 Anthony Grafton
1994 Hans Aarsleff
     Nannerl Keohane
     Toni Morrison
     Jeremiah Ostriker
1995 Peter Brown
     Val Fitch
     Charles Ryskamp
1996 Alan Blinder '67
     Lionel Gossman
     Stanley Katz
1997 Robert Fagles
     Peter Schafer
     Cornel West *80
1998 William Happer *64
     Barbara Oberg
     Paul Volcker '49
     Eric Wieschaus
1999 Sam Treiman
2000 William Jordan *73
     Frederick Mote
     Shirley Tilghman
2001 Michael Cook
     Burton Malkiel *64
2003 Peter Brooks
     Caryl Emerson
     Simon Levin
2004 Daniel Kahneman
     Saul Kripke
     Douglas Massey *78
     P. James Peebles *62
     Michael Wood
     Ying-shih Yu
2005 Leonard Barkan
     Jorge Durand
     Anne Treisman
2006 Philip Johnson-Laird
     John Nash Jr. *50
     John Wilmerding
2007 Robert Keohane
     Viviana Zelizer
2008 David Botstein

     Susan Naquin
     Peter Sarnak
2009 Alejandro Portes
2010 Avinash Dixit
     B. Rosemary Grant
2011 Natalie Zemon Davis
     Carol Greenhouse
     Paul Krugman
2012 Bonnie Bassler
     Brent Shaw
     Christopher Sims
2013 Robert Wuthnow
2014 Angus Deaton
     Susan Fiske
2015 John Fleming *63
     Martin Kern
     Thomas Eugene Shenk
2016 Paul DiMaggio
     Sara McLanahan
     Alexander Nehamas *71
     Joyce Carol Oates
2017 Orley Ashenfelter *70
     Anne Case *88
2019 David Cannadine
     Nancy Weiss Malkiel
2020 Jeanne Altmann
     Angela Creager

National Academy of Engineering

The National Academy of Engineering was established in 1964 "to honor distinguished engineers of the nation and to bring to bear an unusual depth and breadth of engineering knowledge on matters of national concern." From 1919 until 1964, engineering had been a separate section of the National Academy of Sciences.

Princeton faculty members have been elected to the academy in the following years:

1968 Richard Wilhelm
1969 Courtland Perkins
1973 Mac Van Valkenburg
1975 Wallace Hayes *47
1976 Leon Lapidus
1977 Seymour Bogdonoff *48
1978 James Wei
1982 William Schowalter
1985 Vern Weekman Jr.
1986 David Billington '50
1988 Robert Tarjan
1990 William Graessley

1993 William Russel
1996 Irvin Glassman
1997 George Scherer
2000 Pablo Debenedetti
2001 H. Vincent Poor *77
2002 Brian Kernighan *69
 Chang Law
 Bede Liu
2003 Stephen Forrest
 Dudley Saville
2004 Athanassios Panagiotopoulos
 Daniel Tsui
2005 J. Steward Hunter
2006 Sau-Hai Lam *58
2007 Stephen Chou
 Sergio Verdu
2009 Howard Stone
2010 Ilhan Aksay
 Larry Peterson
2011 Christodoulos Floudas
 Richard Miles
 Alexander Smits
2012 Kai Li
2013 Edward Felton
2014 Jennifer Rexford '91
 Robert E. Schapire
2015 Eric Wood
2016 Emily Carter
 Michael Celia *83
2017 Andrea Goldsmith
2018 William Gray *74
2020 Yannis Kevrekidis
2021 Margaret Martonosi

National Academy of Medicine

The National Academy of Medicine was founded in 1970 as the Institute of Medicine. Its members are elected based on their distinguished professional achievement in a field related to medicine and health.

Princeton faculty who have been members of the academy and the years of their election follow:

1972 Paul Ramsey
1979 Uwe Reinhardt
1983 Leon Rosenberg
1986 Charles Westoff
1987 Adel Mahmoud
1989 Harold Shapiro *64
1995 Shirley Tilghman
1996 Thomas Shenk
2005 Burton Singer
2007 Keith Wailoo
2013 Janet Currie *88
2016 Bonnie Bassler
2017 Anne Case *88

National Academy of Sciences

The National Academy of Sciences is a society of scholars "dedicated to the furtherance of science and its use for the general welfare." It was established in 1863 by an Act of Congress, which empowered it to create its own organization and by-laws and called upon it to serve as an official adviser to the federal government on any question of science or technology. Among the academy's 50 founding members were four scientists associated with Princeton: Stephen Alexander, Arnold Guyot, Joseph Henry, and John Torrey. Henry was the academy's second president, from 1866 to 1878.

Princeton faculty have been elected to the academy in the following years:

1863 Stephen Alexander
 Arnold Guyot
 Joseph Henry
 John Torrey
1872 Charles Young
1900 Henry Fairfield Osborn 1877
1906 William Berryman Scott 1877
1908 Edwin Conklin
1918 Henry Norris Russell 1897 *1900
1919 Augustus Trowbridge
 Oswald Veblen
1922 Luther Eisenhart
 George Hulett 1892
1924 Karl Compton *1912
1925 Solomon Lefschetz
1930 James Alexander 1910 *1915
1934 E. Newton Harvey
1937 John von Neumann
1940 Ernest Wever
 Hermann Weyl
1943 Arthur Buddington
1945 Henry Eyring
 Hassler Whitney
 Eugene Wigner
1950 Salomon Bochner
 Edward Kendall
1951 Howard Robertson
1952 Harry Hess *32
 Lyman Spitzer Jr. *38
 John Wheeler

1955 Charles P. Smyth 1916 *1917
1956 Martin Schwarzschild
     Norman Steenrod *36
1957 Walter Elsasser
     Donald Hornig
1959 Walker Bleakney
1960 William Feller
     Hollis Hedberg
1961 John Tukey *39
     Donald Spencer
1962 George Miller
1963 Marvin Goldberger
     John Milnor '51 *54
     Colin Pittendrigh
1964 Walter Kauzmann
1965 Vincent Dethier
1966 Val Fitch
1967 Philip Anderson
     Robert Dicke '39
1968 Arthur Pardee
1969 Robert MacArthur
     Marshall Rosenbluth
1970 James Cronin
     Arthur Wightman
1972 Kurt Mislow
     Sam Treiman
1973 John Bonner
     Ansley Coale '39 *47
     John Hopfield
1974 Jeremiah Ostriker
     Elias Stein
1975 Stephen Adler *64
1976 John Bahcall
     Harold Furth
1977 James Gunn
     Julian Wolpert
1979 Charles Fefferman *69
     Valentine Bargmann
1980 William Browder *58
     Martin Kruskal
1981 Joseph Taylor Jr.
1982 Donald McClure
1983 David Wilkinson
1984 William Brinkman
     Elliott Lieb
     Bohdan Paczynski
     Frank Stillinger
1985 Leon Rosenberg
1987 Robert Tarjan
     Daniel Tsui
     William Baumol

1988 Joseph Kohn *56
     John Mather *67
     P. James Peebles *62
1989 Curtis Callan *64
     Christopher Sims
1990 Syukuro Manabe
1994 Anne Treisman
     Eric Wieschaus
1996 William Happer *64
     John Nash *50
     Thomas Shenk
     Shirley Tilghman
1997 Michael Aizenman
     Neta Bahcall
     Edward Nelson
1998 Michael Levine
     Charles Gross
     Douglas Massey *78
     William Schowalter
     Paul Steinhardt
1999 Robert Austin
     Yakov Sinai
2000 Francis Dahlen
     Simon Levin
     Alejandro Portes
2001 Michael Bender
     Robert Cava
     Daniel Kahneman
     David Tank
2002 Peter Sarnak
2003 Jeanne Altmann
     Isaac Held *76
2004 Nicholas Katz *66
     George Philander
2005 Avinash Dixit
     Robert Keohane
     Sergiu Klainerman
     Janos Kollar
     Alexander Polyakov
     Gertrud Schupbach
     Thomas Silhavy
2006 Bonnie Bassler
     Lyman Page
2007 Bruce Draine
     Peter Grant
     Philip Johnson-Laird
     Stephen Pacala
     David Spergel '83
2008 B. Rosemary Grant
2009 Sun-Yung Alice Chang
     Francois Morel

Yu Xie
2011 David Gabai *80
Sara McLanahan
Loren Pfeiffer
H. Vincent Poor *77
2012 William Bialek
Pablo Debenedetti
John Groves
Nai Phuan Ong
2013 Manjul Bhargava *01
Susan Fiske
2014 Kathryn Edin
Howard Stone
2015 Adam Burrows '75
Angus Deaton
2016 Roberto Car
Igor Klebanov *86
2017 F. Duncan Haldane
David Huse
2018 Sanjeev Arora
Orley Ashenfelter *70
Dalton Conley
David MacMillan
Peter Ozsvath *94
Virginia Zakian
2019 Janet Currie *88
Helen Milner
Nieng Yan *05
Ali Yazdani
2020 Anne Case *88
Jennifer Rexford '91
Suzanne Staggs *93
Elke Weber

FARRAND, BEATRIX, the only woman among the founders of the American Society of Landscape Architects, served in that role at Princeton from 1912 through 1943 and played a leading role in creating the distinctive character of the Princeton campus. Her designs can be found at the graduate college (her first project), along McCosh and Blair walks, in Hamilton and Holder courtyards, at Prospect gardens, and in many other areas of the campus.

Her designs were known for simplicity and ease of maintenance; she favored native plants and trees that bloom in spring or fall when the University is in session. Her signature was the espalier—securing trees and shrubs against walls to bring life and color to courtyards while keeping them open and not shading the rooms. She was fond of wisteria, jasmine, sugar maples, sweet gums, beeches, yews, dogwoods, rhododendrons, and the tulip poplar and other magnolias.

A 2015 book, *Princeton University and Neighboring Institutions*, described as "an architectural tour of the campus," says Farrand's "work and the rules she established for Princeton's landscape design" are "as defining an element of the Princeton style as Collegiate Gothic . . . It is a tribute to Farrand's genius . . . that so much of her work survives and flourishes . . . Even after Farrand's relationship with Princeton ended, succeeding landscape architects and gardeners followed the design and planting principles she laid down."

As a child, Farrand was nurtured by her aunt, the novelist Edith Wharton (also an avid gardener), and other writers in her family's social circle, including Henry James. She served an apprenticeship with Charles Sprague Sargent, founder of Harvard University's Arnold Arboretum, where she learned how to fit a plan to the grounds rather than the other way around. At the age of 20 she started her own business from a room in her mother's New York City brownstone. A year after beginning her work at Princeton, she met her future husband, Max Farrand of the Princeton Class of 1892, who was then chair of the history department at Yale.

At the height of her career, Farrand had offices in New York, Connecticut (later California), and Maine. Her other projects included helping to transform the grounds of Yale; assisting with plantings at the White House; designing landscaping for the J. Pierpont Morgan Library in New York; and creating the gardens at Dumbarton Oaks in Washington, DC.

Several times each year Farrand would walk through the Princeton campus inspecting every tree and bush and giving instructions for pruning, planting, and cultivation. She once told the *Princeton Alumni Weekly*: "We all know that education is by no means a mere matter of books, and that the aesthetic environment contributes as much to growth as facts assembled from a printed page." On a curved bench installed in her honor next to the chapel, the inscription reads: "Her love of beauty and order is everywhere visible in what she planted for our delight."

In 2019 the University named the courtyard framed by Henry, Foulke, Laughlin, and 1901 halls—one of the landscapes she helped design—the Beatrix Farrand Courtyard in her honor. The plaque says:

This courtyard is named in honor of Beatrix Farrand, the only woman among the founders of the American Society of Landscape Architects, who served Princeton in that role from 1912 through 1943. She played a leading role in creating the distinctive character of the Princeton campus, with designs that included Blair Walk, the Graduate College, Prospect Gardens, Hamilton and Holder Courtyards, elements of this courtyard, and other areas of the campus. Her legacy endures not only through her beautiful, practical, and still flourishing designs, but through continuing application of guidelines she developed that have shaped Princeton's landscape through successive generations.

Fencing. In 1856, three years before he wrote the music to "Old Nassau," Karl Langlotz arrived at Princeton as a German instructor and began teaching fencing to a group of 50 students. Later in the century, informal fencing clubs fostered intramural competition. In 1905 a three-year spell of intercollegiate competition began when a devotee of the sport, Henry Breckinridge 1907 (later president of the Amateur Fencers League of America and Charles Lindbergh's lawyer during the Lindbergh kidnapping trial) organized a team that beat Yale in 1906 and 1907. Breckenridge later won a bronze medal in team foil at the 1920 Olympics.

A Fencing Association, organized in 1924, created such interest that fencing was recognized as a team sport. Intercollegiate competition began in 1926 with a 9–8 victory over Syracuse. An outstanding performer in the early years was Tracy Jaeckel 1928, who was Intercollegiate Fencing Association (IFA) champion in épée his senior year, and in 1932 was an Olympics bronze medalist.

F. G. McPherson, team coach in 1926, was succeeded a year later by Joseph De Vos, a Belgian native and former fencing instructor at the Dutch royal court. DeVos was succeeded in 1933 by Hubert Pirotte, who invented a mechanical fencing target while coaching at Rutgers and led Princeton's team until the outbreak of World War II. The 1935 captain, Todd Harris '35, secured critical alumni financial support and donated the Princeton Fencing Trophy, which is awarded annually to the fencer "who best exemplifies ability, good sportsmanship, and loyalty to the interest of the sport."

Stanley Sieja, who coached from 1946 to 1982, was one of the most influential figures in the program's history. His teams shared the Ivy crown in 1959, 1960, 1966, and 1969, and won it outright in 1975. Sieja's teams also finished third in the annual NCAA tournament in 1960 and 1965, second in 1961 (falling to Cornell), and captured the national championship in 1964, defeating NYU. Sieja was elected Coach of the Year by the National Fencing Coaches Association in 1964, 1968, and 1976, and was inducted into the Helms Foundation Hall of Fame in 1967. The fencing practice room in Dillon Gym was named in his honor.

Upon Sieja's retirement in 1982, Michel Sebastiani became the men's coach, and later became the coach of Princeton's women's team when women's fencing was granted varsity status in 1988. In 1994 and 1995, the women won the Mildred Stuyvesant-Fish Trophy as champions of the National Intercollegiate Women's Fencing Association, making Sebastiani the first coach to win that title at three institutions. (He had previously won at Cornell and NYU.) In 2000, the women won the Intercollegiate Fencing Association (IFA) championship. Sebastiani also won six men's Ivy League titles (1994, 1995, 1997, 1998, 2000, 2001) and three women's titles (1999, 2000, 2001).

His successor, Zoltan Dudas, likewise became coach of both the men's and women's teams in 2006. Dudas won men's titles in 2010, 2012, 2016, and 2017, and women's titles every year from 2010 through 2014 and in 2016 and 2017. Dudas was named Ivy women's Coach of the Year in 2015, 2016, and 2017.

Although the men's and women's teams continued to compete separately in the Ivy League, the NCAA championship meet became a combined men's and women's event beginning in 1990. In 2013, the Tigers won their only NCAA combined title, finishing with 182 points to 175 for Notre Dame. Princeton's teams have also won numerous individual and team titles at the IFA championships.

Over the last few decades, nearly two dozen Princeton fencers have won individual Ivy League and NCAA titles. Two men, Alexander Mills '12 (2011) and Michael Dudey '16 (2013), and two women, Ambika Singh '15 (2012) and Eliza Stone '13 (2013), were recognized as the Ivy League championship's most outstanding performer. Five Princetonians have been named NCAA Fencer of the Year: Chambless Johnson '51, Fleet Johnston '56, Frank Anger '61, Bill Hicks '64, and John Nonna '70. Maya Lawrence '02, Jacqueline Leahy '06, Eliza Stone '13, Susannah Scanlan '14, Gracie Stone '16, and Katharine Holmes '17 are all four-time All-Americans in the women's program, three in épée (Lawrence, Scanlan, Holmes), two in saber (E. Stone and G. Stone), and one in foil (Leahy).

In addition to Breckinridge and Jaeckel, who won bronze medals, 11 other Princeton fencers (six men and five women) have competed in the Olympics for the United States and for other countries. Jim Adams '61, an All-American as an undergraduate, joined a national seniors team in 1995 and became the only American to be national champion in all three weapons—foil, épée, and saber—which he did twice, in 2010 and 2019.

FIELD HOCKEY. One of six original women's sports at Princeton, field hockey has achieved a record of excellence that is nearly unmatched among the University's athletic teams. The program has won 26 Ivy League field hockey championships (no other Ivy school has won more than eight), advanced to the NCAA title game three times, and won the national championship in 2012, the only Ivy League squad to do so. In the 22-year period from 1994 to 2015, Princeton won or shared 21 Ivy titles.

Although undergraduate women were first admitted to Princeton in 1969, the University fielded no intercollegiate athletic teams for them until 1971, as facilities were built. The first women's intercollegiate teams at Princeton were field hockey, tennis, crew, basketball, squash, and swimming.

On October 1, 1971, Princeton's field hockey team played its first game, meeting Temple University on Poe Field. The game resulted in a 5–0 defeat, but the team rebounded to record its first victory, against a local club team, six days later. The *Princeton Alumni Weekly* took note, placing a field hockey player on its cover with the title, "*This* is Princeton's newest sport?"

Indeed, it was. The team finished its inaugural season with a 5-3-1 record, including a 3–2 victory over Yale in its first game against an Ivy League opponent. They were the only Princeton team to beat the Elis that day.

Merrily Dean Baker, the team's first coach, was hired in 1970 as the director of women's physical education and in 1973 was named associate director of athletics for physical education and women's athletics. She coached for three seasons but remained at Princeton for 12, and was integral in establishing the women's athletics program, serving also as president of the Association for Intercollegiate Athletics for Women. Baker later served as assistant executive director of the NCAA and director of athletics at Michigan State. Her successor as coach, Penny Hinkley, compiled a .750 winning percentage from 1974 to 1976; Hinkley also coached the team to its only undefeated season, in 1974.

Ivy League round robin play began in 1979. Princeton hosted the national field hockey championships that year, finishing sixth. Field hockey did not become an NCAA sport until 1981, the year in which the Tigers shared their first Ivy title. They won the title outright for the first time in 1982.

In 1988, Princeton hired Beth Bozman as head coach. A graduate of Trenton State (later the College of New Jersey), Bozman had already taken her alma mater to four NCAA championship games, winning twice, and led Hofstra to a national ranking. Bozman remained at Princeton for 15 seasons and is its all-time winningest field hockey coach, with a record of 188-73-6.

Under her leadership, the team began a dazzling run of success. After falling to Penn on the last day of the 1993 season, they did not lose another Ivy League match for five and a half years, compiling a 35-game winning streak. During that streak, on November 5, 1997, the Tigers shut out Columbia, 12–0, setting Ivy records both for the most goals scored in a game and largest margin of victory. Bozman was named the National Field Hockey Coaches Association Coach of the Year in 1996, the year the team advanced to its first NCAA final, losing to North Carolina. Two years later, in 1998, the Tigers returned to the final, losing to Old Dominion.

Bozman's successor, Kristen Holmes-Winn, arrived in 2003, and the team continued to reel off Ivy championships. On November 18, 2012, the Tigers finally reached the pinnacle, winning the NCAA national championship in a thrilling game against North Carolina. The team overcame a pair of one-goal deficits before Amanda Bird '14 scored the winner on a penalty stroke. Holmes-Winn was named NFHCA Coach of the Year while Katie Reinprecht '13, who starred with her sister, Julie Reinprecht '14, was named the national Player of the Year.

Over four decades, Princeton's field hockey program earned 24 of the Ivy League's 36 appearances in the NCAA tournament. The Tigers advanced to the NCAA Final Four nine times (1996, 1997, 1998, 2001, 2009, 2012, 2016, 2018, 2019), and the finals four times.

Princeton has produced 32 first team All-Americans, 18 Ivy Players of the Year, and 16 Ivy Rookies of the Year. Four Tigers have been named Ivy Player of the Year in consecutive seasons: Liz Fagan '95 (1993–94), Amy Macfarlane '97 (1996–97), Ilvy Friebe '03 (2001–02), and Katie Reinprecht (2008–09). Defensive standout Paige Schmidt '08 won the award in three consecutive years (2005–07), something no other Ivy field hockey player has accomplished. In 2019, Clara Roth '21 was named the NFHCA Mid-Atlantic Region Player of the Year, the first Princeton player to earn that distinction since Katie Reinprecht in 2012.

Kathleen Sharkey '13 holds the Ivy League records for most goals in a game (6, against Richmond in 2010), in a season (38, in 2012), and in a career (107). The team also holds a slew of Ivy records, including those for goals, assists, fewest goals allowed, games won, and shutouts in a season.

In 2012, the University completed 1,200-seat Bedford Field, a state-of-the-art facility dedicated solely to field hockey, adjacent to Class of 1952 Stadium where the lacrosse teams play (and where field hockey previously played). Prior to the 2016 season the playing surface was replaced with a revolutionary artificial turf field with a built-in, programmable, watering system. The field is lined with metric marks, which allows it to host international events at any level.

FIELDS, CARL A., was the first Black administrator at Princeton and the first African American dean in the Ivy League.

Fields was born in Columbus, Ohio, and grew up in Brooklyn, New York. He graduated from St. John's University in 1942 as the first African American member of its honor society and the first Black man to serve as captain of its track and field team. After army service in World War II (for which he received a Bronze Star), he earned a master's degree from New York University in 1950, and in 1967 he obtained his PhD in educational philosophy from Philathea College in Canada.

When Fields came to Princeton in 1964 as assistant director of student aid, he was the University's first Black administrator. He introduced a surrogate family hosting program that paired Black students with members of the community, helped develop the Association of Black Collegians (ABC) and other student groups, and with the ABC organized a conference in 1967 that brought together Black students from 41 predominantly white universities.

In 1968, when he was promoted to assistant dean of the college, he was the first African American dean at any Ivy League school. He helped establish the Frederick Douglass Service Award, which is given each year to a senior who has exhibited "courage, leadership, intellectual achievement, and a willingness to contribute unselfishly toward a deeper understanding of the experiences of racial minorities . . ." In 1983 the Association of Black Princeton Alumni (ABPA) commissioned a bust of Douglass, the first piece of art on the Princeton campus to depict an influential African American; when the department of African American Studies moved into Stanhope Hall in 2007, the bust was placed there as well.

Fields worked tirelessly to implement policies and practices to increase the enrollment, retention, and support of students of color. He was instrumental in establishing the Third World Center, renamed in 2002 as the Carl A. Fields Center for Equality and Cultural Understanding, which was conceived as a gathering place for students of color and a focal point for the activities of the University's minority groups. He also chaired the University's human relations committee and played an active role in the Princeton-Blairstown Center, which served disadvantaged youth.

When Fields left the University in 1971, he wrote "I left with full confidence that Blacks and other minority members had established themselves as a significant presence at Princeton." He served for three years as planning officer at the five-year-old University of Zambia, and from 1974–84 he was the principal partner and founder of the African Technical Educational Consultant Service which assisted organizations in the creation of programs to serve disadvantaged communities. In 1984 he became administrative officer of Riverside Church in New York City, and in 1988 he was named associate director of the Bishop Tutu Southern African Refugee Scholarship Fund.

In 1985 Fields received the ABPA University Service Award, which was subsequently renamed the Dr. Carl A. Fields Memorial University Service Award. In 1996 he received the Alumni Council Award for Service to Princeton. In 2019 his portrait was added to the University portrait collection; it hangs inside the south entrance to Morrison Hall, the building in which he worked as a Princeton administrator.

Fields died in 1998. In 2006 his book, *Black in Two Worlds: A Personal Perspective on Higher Education*, was published posthumously. The first half of the book recounts his decision to come to Princeton and his experiences on campus. He describes how determined he was not to be pigeonholed as an adviser only to Black students. In his foreword to the book, President Emeritus Robert Goheen writes that by the time Fields left, the University had "come a long way toward being an institution in which young men and women of whatever race or persuasion could move about freely and with confidence . . . being regarded and regarding each other as equals."

Fields' papers are housed in the University's Seeley G. Mudd manuscript library.

FIELDS CENTER FOR EQUALITY AND CULTURAL UNDERSTANDING, THE CARL A., originally named the Third World Center (TWC), was created in 1971 when the trustees approved the conversion of the 80-year-old Osborn Field House into a University facility designed to provide a social, cultural, and political environment to address the needs and concerns of students of color.

Creation of the center resulted from persistent student advocacy by students in the Association of Black Collegians. They called initially for a "Black house," and then for a "home base" for students of African, Asian, Latin, and Native American descent where "close examination can be given to the political, cultural, and social movements of the minority groups in the United States."

One pivotal moment occurred in the fall of 1970 when a delegation of Black undergraduates led by Marion Humphrey '72, Gregory Howard '74, and Thurman White '72 called upon President Robert Goheen at his home to propose such a space. Another occurred in March 1971 when 170 student members of the Third World Coalition staged a sit-in at Firestone Library. Key to the board's approval was the endorsement by Goheen and provost William Bowen *58 and the support of the chair of the trustee student life committee, John Doar '44.

The Third World Center officially opened on October 16, 1971. Although all students were welcome, the center was intended primarily to be a space for Blacks, Latinos, Chicanos, Asian Americans, Native Americans, and other students from minority or third-world backgrounds. It initially operated under an ad hoc committee composed of two representatives each from the Association of Black Collegians, the Unión Latinoamericana, and the Asian American Students Association, with Conrad Snowden—then an assistant dean of the graduate school, later an assistant provost—serving as its first administrative head.

In 1975 an annex, Liberation Hall, was added to the building and that year the first student-led governance board was elected. Among those who have served on the governing board are Supreme Court Justice Sonia Sotomayor '76 and First Lady of the United States Michelle Obama '85, who also served as coordinator of the center's after-school program. Under the leadership of its first full-time director, Stanley Kwong, TWC became a haven for Black and other students of color, a place where they could explore their respective cultures while acclimating to Princeton and forging connections with others.

The TWC was renamed in 2002 to reflect the center's evolving mission to include the broader community in a dialogue on race and to honor Carl A. Fields, who arrived at Princeton in 1964 as the University's first Black administrator and four years later became the Ivy League's first African American dean. In 2009 the center moved across Olden Street into a renovated building at 58 Prospect Avenue that formerly housed one of the eating clubs (Elm). As part of a further renovation in 2016, cultural affinity rooms were created for Black, Asian and Asian American, Latinx, and Arab and Middle Eastern students, with each room designed by students to give it a distinctive personality.

Through the center's programs, activities, gatherings, and events, diverse perspectives and experiences of race, class, gender, and intersections are supported, challenged, questioned, and affirmed. The center seeks to empower, engage, and educate individuals and institutions within the University community to develop, implement, and support systems of inclusion.

The center's primary programs and initiatives include the Fields Center Fellows, peer leaders who educate and advocate for diversity, inclusion, and social justice through peer-facilitated workshops, trainings, and dialogues, while also serving as informal support for students who experience discrimination and bias; the Princeton University Mentoring Program (PUMP), which assists first-year students of color in their academic, cultural, and social acclimation to Princeton; and heritage month programs, including Latinx, Native American, and Black History Month, as well as Asian Pacific Islander Desi American Heritage Month.

The center organizes cultural graduation celebration ceremonies for undergraduate and graduate students in connection with each year's Commencement. In 2018 the center launched the Brave Voices Project, a multimedia initiative to highlight the experiences of alumni of color who graduated between 1990 and 2018. The project expanded to include alumni who graduated after 2018, and in 2020 it announced a further expansion to focus on Native and Indigenous alumni.

FINANCIAL AID. When James Leslie 1759 attended the College of New Jersey, he was aided by a gift of £13 from a "Fund for Pious Youth." After graduation, he became a schoolteacher in New York City, and when he died, he left his frugally guarded savings to the College as a perpetual fund "for the education of poor and pious youth."

Over the years, as part of the University's endowment, the Leslie Fund has helped support an undergraduate financial aid program that today makes it possible for every student admitted to Princeton—whether from the United States or from around the world—not only to afford to attend, but to graduate debt-free because Princeton's aid program does not require students to take loans.

More than 60 percent of Princeton undergraduates receive financial aid. While amounts vary depending on a student's need, the average scholarship exceeds tuition. Grants for students from families with incomes below $65,000 typically cover tuition, fees, room, board, and other expenses, while grants to families with incomes up to $160,000 typically cover full tuition. For the Class of 2023, all families making up to $180,000 a year who applied for aid qualified, as did many families at higher income levels, including families with incomes above $250,000 (depending on their circumstances). In recent years more than 80 percent of each class graduated debt free, and for those who chose to borrow (including some students not receiving financial aid) the average indebtedness at graduation was just over $9,000.

The financial aid office regularly reviews its criteria for determining a family's ability to pay to be sure its assessment is as fair and generous as possible. Unlike many other colleges and universities, when Princeton calculates a family's financial assets it excludes the family's equity in its primary residence and its retirement savings; when it determines what the family can afford, it considers the family's other obligations, such as educational expenses for other children and medical bills for dependents. Costs covered by aid include tuition, room, board, fees, miscellaneous expenses, and travel. Aid packages are recalculated each year to offset increases in tuition and other costs and to account for changes in a family's financial circumstances.

All admission to Princeton is "need-blind," meaning that admission decisions are made without regard to a student's need for aid, and when students with need are offered admission, the University meets 100 percent of their need with grants. (Princeton is one of only a handful of universities that admit international students on a need-blind basis.)

The University places no limits on the number of aid applicants who can be admitted each year and it meets each applicant's full need with no preset budgetary limit, which means its financial aid budget functions as an entitlement, fluctuating as necessary to meet every student's full need. Endowment funds cover well over 80 percent of the aid budget, with other support coming from federal aid programs (including Pell Grants), other gifts and grants, and, as needed, University general funds.

After reducing its loan requirement for middle-income students and eliminating it entirely for lower-income students in 1998, in 2001 the University adopted its policy of no required loans and its practice of excluding home equity from its need calculation. At that time, 38 percent of the graduating class was receiving aid. Ten years later 54 percent of the class was on aid, and in recent years that percentage has exceeded 60 percent.

In 2006 the University modified its aid policy to increase the meal allowance it provides for juniors and seniors to help them cover the costs of joining eating clubs if they choose to do so. (Students who do not join a club may use the additional funds to meet other expenses.) In 2020 the University reduced to $3,500 the amount students on aid are expected to contribute each year from summer earnings, campus jobs, and other outside sources. (Under normal circumstances, each year more than 3,000 undergraduates work on campus.)

Despite the generosity of the University's aid program, only 7.2 percent of the Class of 2008 qualified for Pell Grants, a federal program that provides aid for low-income students, ranking Princeton toward the bottom in comparison with its principal competitors. Through determined efforts, the representation of Pell recipients in entering classes increased dramatically until in the Class of 2023 it reached 24 percent, ranking Princeton at the top among its peers.

At the graduate level, Princeton guarantees funding for all its regularly enrolled degree-seeking PhD candidates for all years of regular program enrollment and the majority of its master's programs are funded either partially or fully.

Princeton's tradition of financial aid dates to its earliest years, but the first major appeal for student aid funds was not launched until 1853 when President John Maclean Jr. set a goal of raising $100,000 to establish 100 scholarships. About 60 scholarships were created between 1853 and 1858, and by 1900 an additional 46 had been endowed, providing just over 110 endowed scholarships for a student body of 1,053. Beginning in 1885, the catalogue claimed that "no candidate for admission . . . will be refused admission because of inability to pay the charge for tuition."

During the presidency of Woodrow Wilson 1879, the endowment for scholarships nearly doubled and preference was given to students with need who had performed well academically (a policy not fully rescinded until 1958). Freshmen typically were given a "remission of tuition," essentially a no-interest loan to be repaid after graduation. In 1911 a Student Bureau of Self Help was established and by 1923 one of every five undergraduates had a job. In 1934 the University created an office to consolidate the administration of all aspects of undergraduate financial aid. During the bicentennial celebration in 1947, President Harold Dodds said, "We shall always see to it that our students represent a democratic cross-section of American youth, geographically and with respect to economic circumstance."

The post–World War II GI Bill provided substantial federal funding for veterans returning to campus and altered national expectations about educational opportunity. In his 1983 annual report on undergraduate financial aid at Princeton, President William Bowen noted that "throughout the 1950s, the University raised endowment funds for scholarships, increased self-help requirements for students, and continued to draw upon general funds—yet still fell short of the goal of meeting the full need of all admitted students."

By 1962, 39 percent of undergraduates were receiving some form of aid. During the 1960s and 1970s federal grant, loan, and work-study programs became important components of Princeton's aid program and, by the mid-1980s, 43 percent of Princeton's larger post-coeducation student body was receiving aid.

By then the University had solidified four principles that, with one modification, continue to govern its financial aid policies: (1) admission decisions are made without reference to an applicant's financial circumstances; (2) eligibility for financial aid is solely a function of "need"; (3) the demonstrated financial need of all offered admission is met; and (4) financial aid shall consist of a combination of work opportunities, loans, and grants. The modification, of course, is that financial aid now is provided without requiring loans.

In their 2016 strategic planning framework, the trustees noted, "in the years since 2001, Princeton has continued to improve its scholarship program with the goal of ensuring that students on aid are able not only to attend Princeton but also to share fully in the educational opportunities it offers." By then the aid budget exceeded $140 million per year (more than three times its size in 2001) and plans were being made to increase the size of the undergraduate student body by 10 percent. The trustees concluded: "We should expect the budget to continue growing as Princeton attracts a more socioeconomically diverse student body. The University must be ready to invest as needed to ensure that Princeton's aid program meets the needs of its students."

FINE, HENRY BURCHARD 1880 played a major role in transforming Princeton from a college into a university. He made Princeton a leading center for mathematics and fostered the growth of creative work in other branches of science as well. Nationally, in Oswald Veblen's words, Fine "carried American mathematics forward from a state of approximate nullity to one verging on parity with the European nations."

After Fine's father, a Presbyterian minister in Chambersburg, Pennsylvania, died when Fine was young, he and his three siblings were brought up by their mother. (Two of the other children also became educators: John B. Fine 1882, founder of the Princeton Preparatory School; and May Margaret Fine, founder of Miss Fine's School in Princeton. which later became part of Princeton Day School.) The family came to live in Princeton in 1875, and Henry entered the College the following year.

Fine played flute in the college orchestra, rowed on one of the crews, and served for three years as an editor of the *Princetonian*, where he began a life-long friendship with Woodrow Wilson 1879, whom he succeeded as managing editor. He led his class all four years and was Latin salutatorian at Commencement. Although he specialized in Latin and Greek, he adopted mathematics as a career toward the end of his time in college.

After a postgraduate year studying science and three years as a tutor in mathematics, Fine went to Leipzig to study with the eminent geometer Felix

Klein. Although he knew very little German and almost no mathematics, he developed so rapidly that he obtained his PhD in little more than a year.

In 1885 Fine returned to Princeton as an assistant professor. He was promoted to professor in 1889, appointed Dod Professor of Mathematics in 1898, and made chair of the department when departments were first organized in 1904.

After Wilson returned to Princeton as professor of jurisprudence in 1890, he and Fine resumed the close friendship they had begun in college. In 1903, shortly after he became president of the University, Wilson appointed Fine dean of the faculty, and the two worked closely together on improving the curriculum and strengthening the faculty. In the controversies over the quad plan and the graduate college, Fine supported Wilson completely. After Wilson resigned to run for governor of New Jersey in 1910, Fine carried the chief burden of the university administration for two years until the trustees elected John Grier Hibben 1882 *1893 as Wilson's successor. Fine, who many thought would be selected, pledged Hibben his wholehearted support.

After his election as president of the United States, Wilson urged Fine to accept appointment as ambassador to Germany and later as a member of the Federal Reserve Board, but Fine declined both appointments, saying quite simply that he preferred to remain at Princeton as a professor of mathematics. Fine also declined a call to the presidency of the Johns Hopkins University and several to the presidency of the Massachusetts Institute of Technology.

The introduction of the preceptorial system in 1905 required a considerable expansion of the faculty in the humanities and social sciences. Fine persuaded Wilson that a similar enlargement was desirable in the natural sciences and began to build a department of Mathematics of the first rank while at the same time helping his colleagues lay the foundations for strong departments in other fields.

For suggestions and advice, Fine turned first to his friend, Sir Joseph J. Thomson, the Cambridge physicist who had been his house guest at the University's sesquicentennial celebration in 1896. They discussed Fine's hopes for making Princeton a scientific center, and as a result James Jeans came to Princeton in 1905 as professor of mathematical physics and O. W. Richardson arrived the following year as professor of experimental physics. A survey of younger mathematicians in this country led to other promotions and appointments. Oswald Veblen recalled that Fine's department contained a considerable proportion of the best mathematicians in America at the time. "In every case," Veblen said, "these men were called in before they became well known, at the time when recognition meant the most to them. Though many of them stayed only a few years, their contact with Fine and his group was important both to them and in the continuing growth of this group as an organism."

In 1909, when the dean of the faculty's duties were lightened by the creation of the office of the dean of the college, Fine became in title what he had been in fact—dean of the departments of science. When Hibben became president in 1912, Fine resigned as dean of the faculty but continued as dean of the departments of science.

In his last years he was able to seize another opportunity for the advancement of science at Princeton. Largely because of the confidence he inspired, the General Education Board offered Princeton a grant of one million dollars for research in pure science on condition that the University raise two million for the same purpose. The fundraising was completed in 1928. The Henry B. Fine Professorship of Mathematics was established, and as a further memorial, Fine's close friend Thomas D. Jones 1876 and his niece gave a building for mathematics, named Fine Hall, which was built in 1930. When a larger building for mathematics was dedicated in 1970, it was named Fine Hall, and the former mathematics building, converted for use by other departments, was renamed Jones Hall in honor of the original donors.

Fine was one of the founders of the American Mathematical Society and its president in 1911 and 1912.

Dean Fine was a familiar figure on his bicycle, which he rode to and from classes and used for long rides in the country. While riding his bicycle on the way to visit his brother at the Princeton Preparatory School late one December afternoon, he was struck from behind by an automobile whose driver had failed to see him in the uncertain light of dusk. He died the next morning without having recovered consciousness, three months after his 70th birthday.

FINE HALL, home of the department of Mathematics and the program in Applied and Computational Mathematics, was dedicated in 1970 as a memorial to Henry Burchard Fine 1880, the central figure in the early development of an eminent mathematics faculty at the University. It was constructed to provide the department with more space than was available in its previous home, an older Fine Hall built 40 years earlier that was renamed Jones Hall.

The new Fine Hall was located very close to what was then the dividing line between Princeton Borough and Princeton Township (it was in the township), and because of its height was controversial when it was first proposed. At 170 feet, Fine Tower is a shade shorter than the 173-foot Cleveland Tower at the graduate college and taller than the 140-foot tower at Holder Hall. Approval was obtained when the local authorities agreed that, because of its downhill location, it would not seem to exceed the heights of the roof of the chapel or the cupola atop Nassau Hall.

Fine Hall and the neighboring Jadwin and McDonnell Halls form a center for the departments of Mathematics and Physics along the east side of Washington Road, in a natural sciences complex that also includes Frick Chemistry Laboratory, Peyton Hall (Astrophysical Sciences), and the Lewis Science Library, and is planned to house the departments of Geosciences and Ecology and Evolutionary Biology. Across Washington Road, linked by Streicker Bridge, are buildings for the other natural science departments and programs, including Molecular Biology, Genomics, Neuroscience, and Psychology.

Fine Hall is a 10-story vertical tower set on a three-story horizontal base. Twelve of the floors contain faculty offices and seminar rooms, while the entire top floor is devoted to a lounge whose large picture windows afford panoramic views of the campus and the surrounding countryside. On its second floor, Fine houses Taplin Auditorium, a 200-seat recital hall that provides performance space for the Music department and others.

FINLEY, SAMUEL, fifth president of Princeton, came to America from Ireland with his parents when he was 19. He attended William Tennent's Log College in Neshaminy, Pennsylvania, a school for ministers. His early career as an evangelical preacher was marked by an energetic, contentious, and sometimes acrimonious spirit that was not uncommon in the eighteenth-century religious revival known as the Great Awakening. As one of his students said, his sermons "were calculated to inform the ignorant, to alarm the careless and secure, and to edify and comfort the faithful."

For 17 years he was pastor of a church at Nottingham, Maryland, where he also conducted an academy renowned for its standards of scholarship. In recognition of this work he received an honorary degree from the University of Glasgow in 1763, making him the first Princeton president and only the second American cleric to receive an honorary degree abroad. One of the students at Finley's academy was his nephew Benjamin Rush 1760, a renowned physician, a signer of the Declaration of Independence, and the person most responsible for bringing John Witherspoon to Princeton as the College's sixth president.

Finley was one of the original trustees of the College of New Jersey. On May 31, 1761, he succeeded Samuel Davies as the College's fifth president. His presidency was marked by steady growth in enrollment, by his planting of shade trees—two sycamores that he planted in front of the President's House (now Maclean House) are still standing, and by his effective teaching of Hebrew, Latin, and Greek.

In 1766, at the age of 51, he died in Philadelphia, where he had gone for medical treatment; many students journeyed from Princeton to pay their last respects, and eight members of the senior class bore his body to the grave. At the time of his death, his estate included six enslaved people—"two Negro women, a negro man, and three Negro children"—who were sold at auction, along with furniture, livestock, and books, on the grounds of the President's House, and perhaps under the sycamores he had planted.

Midway through Finley's administration the trustees declared, "Our idea is to send into the World good Scholars and useful members of Society." Some of the 130 graduates Finley sent out during his five-year presidency more than fulfilled this modest purpose, notably James Manning 1762, founder and first president of Brown University; William Paterson 1763, governor of New Jersey; Samuel Kirkland 1765, founder and first president of Hamilton College; and Oliver Ellsworth 1766, chief justice of the United States Supreme Court.

Samuel F.B. Morse, developer of the telegraph, was Finley's great grandson; in 1870 he gave the portrait of Finley that hangs in the Faculty Room in Nassau Hall.

FIRES have completely or partially destroyed campus buildings on six occasions: Nassau Hall in 1802 and 1855; Marquand Chapel and Dickinson Hall in 1920; John C. Green School of Science in 1928; University Gymnasium in 1944; and Whig Hall in 1969.

Nassau Hall

The fire of 1802 started about one o'clock on the windy afternoon of Saturday, March 6, and after two hours only the blackened walls of Nassau Hall were left standing. President Samuel Stanhope Smith declared the fire the result of vice and irreligion. A trustee investigating committee thought it was begun intentionally. Then George Strawbridge 1802 (later a supreme court judge in Louisiana) made an independent investigation and concluded that no student was in any way guilty; he thought sooty chimneys were probably responsible. The trustees made a public appeal for funds to rebuild Nassau Hall and in less than a year it was again ready for use.

The 1855 fire also occurred on a windy Saturday in March (the 10th). It started about eight o'clock in the evening and by midnight only the walls were left standing. This time there was no suspicion of arson. Many students suffered large losses of clothing and furniture, but Latin professor George Giger, with the help of some tutors and students, rescued Peale's portrait of Washington and other valuable paintings from the portrait gallery. President John Maclean Jr. braved the smoke and flames to search for a student mistakenly reported trapped in an upper story room. "Johnny . . . got so nearly suffocated," Alfred Woodhull 1856 wrote his mother, "that a party of students scarcely saved him."

Nassau Hall was reopened to house students in August 1856, but the reconstruction was not completed until June 1860. Once again donations were obtained, and they helped pay for the cost not only of rebuilding, but of enlarging and improving the building; one donor was President Maclean himself, who contributed part of his salary.

Fires in the 1920s

On May 14, 1920, a fire broke out in the original Dickinson Hall, which stood on the southwest corner of the present site of Firestone Library, and spread southward to Marquand Chapel, just northeast of Murray-Dodge Hall. Dickinson and Marquand were completely destroyed, but the Joseph Henry House, which at that time stood between them, escaped with little damage. Volunteer fire fighters, helped by students in evening clothes—the eating clubs were holding their house parties and there was a freshman dance at the gymnasium—and by an engine company from Trenton, kept the fire from spreading. Marquand Chapel was replaced by the University Chapel in 1928 and the present Dickinson Hall was built in 1930.

The fire that demolished the John C. Green School of Science was discovered a little before midnight on November 16, 1928. The tower was already in flames when the fire fighters arrived; by 4 a.m. the last of the roof had caved in, and by daybreak the unlamented building was a total loss. The Joseph Henry House, which had been moved to a location just north of the School of Science to make way for the University Chapel, again escaped unscathed. This fire created a shortage of laboratories and classrooms which was not relieved until the completion of Frick Laboratory in 1929 and Dickinson Hall in 1930.

University Gymnasium

University Gymnasium, built in 1903, was destroyed by fire the morning of May 13, 1944. The fire was discovered, and an alarm was turned in at 2:47 a.m. by Naval watches in Little and Patton halls where members of the Navy V-12 unit were quartered. The building was completely gutted, and all its contents were lost, including scores of athletic trophies and relics; among the losses was a ball from the first Yale-Princeton football game of 1873. University Gymnasium was replaced by Dillon Gymnasium in 1947.

Whig Hall

The Whig Hall fire on November 9, 1969, was discovered by a public safety officer at 5:45 a.m. and was brought under control by 7:30 a.m. All but one of the exterior marble walls remained intact, but 80 percent of the wooden interior was destroyed, although most of the historic portraits in the building escaped damage. An award-winning renovation that dramatically redesigned the building's east wall was completed in 1972.

No loss of life resulted from any of these fires; the only serious injury was a broken leg incurred by a spectator at the Nassau Hall fire of 1855.

FITZGERALD, FRANCIS SCOTT KEY 1917, named after his distant relative Francis Scott Key (who penned the lyrics to "The Star Spangled Banner" during the War of 1812), was born in St. Paul, Minnesota, in 1896. He entered Princeton "on trial" in the fall of 1913 from the Newman School, a Catholic prep school in Hackensack, New Jersey, charming the admission committee and squeaking past his entrance examinations by the narrowest margin. At Princeton, after being quickly cut from the football team, he hurled himself into extracurricular activities with so much enthusiasm that he barely survived his first two years.

After three months as a junior, he withdrew because of ill health and poor grades. Following nine months of recuperation at home in St. Paul, he reentered as a beginning junior in the fall of 1916. He managed to complete that academic year and one month of his senior year before withdrawing again to join the army in October 1917.

The fact that he never graduated did nothing to dampen his memories of Princeton, Cottage Club, football, the Triangle Club, *The Nassau Lit*, and the *Tiger*, to say nothing of the look and feel of Prospect Avenue in all seasons, and the mossy spires and gargoyles of the campus. He was a legendary and prolific writer for Triangle, writing the song lyrics for three shows, beginning with the highly acclaimed "Fie! Fie! Fi-Fi!" in 1914.

Apart from Princeton, three great forces guided Fitzgerald's tragically abbreviated life. One was writing, which enthralled him in childhood, occupied many of his collegiate hours, supported him in maturity, and continued to engage his devotion until his dying day. A second was his romances, including those with Chicago socialite Ginevra King, the inspiration for several characters in his novels and stories (including Daisy in *The Great Gatsby*), and Zelda Sayre, a southern belle from Montgomery, Alabama, whom he coveted, courted, and at last married, sharing with her a tabloid life in America and Europe during the 1920s. The third was alcoholism, a disease that afflicted his father and with which Fitzgerald battled all his life.

This Side of Paradise, published by Scribner's in 1920 when Fitzgerald was just 23, draws heavily on his years at Princeton. In it, Amory Blaine, Fitzgerald's handsome and insouciant hero, invents his way through various love affairs and much bad poetry and indulges his awakening brain with highly intellectual bull sessions. Fitzgerald describes Princeton as "the pleasantest country club in America" (much to the annoyance of then-President John Grier Hibben), and his depiction of social life among Princeton's gothic towers and exclusive eating clubs etched stereotypes into the American consciousness that successive generations of Princetonians have sought to escape and overcome ever since.

However banal the novel may seem today, it was a huge commercial success at the time, and Fitzgerald became a regular contributor of short stories to *The Smart Set*, *The Saturday Evening Post*, and *Scribner's Magazine*. Selections from these appeared in *Flappers and Philosophers* and *Tales of the Jazz Age*, which helped to stamp Fitzgerald forever as the poster child for the roaring twenties. His second novel, *The Beautiful and the Damned*, accurately summarized in its title if not in its substance the course of his life with Zelda. There was also a satirical play, *The Vegetable: or From President to Postman*, published in 1923. Two further short-story collections, *All the Sad Young Men* and *Taps at Reveille*, appeared in 1926 and 1935.

The Great Gatsby (1925), generally regarded as his finest novel, eschewed the Princeton scene in favor of Long Island and New York City. *Tender Is the Night* (1934) borrowed its title from Keats and its locale and characters from Fitzgerald's experiences on the French Riviera in the mid-1920s. Behind the stories of Gatsby's longing for Daisy Buchanan and Dick Driver's for the beautiful Nicole, one can discern some of the tragic implications of Fitzgerald's love for the increasingly mentally ill Zelda.

From time to time Fitzgerald overcame his drinking and worked with some success as a screenwriter in Hollywood, where he gathered material for his final—though unfinished—novel, *The Last Tycoon*. This was published posthumously in 1941 under the editorship of Edmund Wilson 1916, with whom Fitzgerald had collaborated 25 years earlier on "The Evil Eye" for the 1915 Triangle show.

In an article in the *Nassau Lit* in 1942, Fitzgerald's daughter, Frances Scott "Scottie" Fitzgerald Lanahan, wrote that "My father belonged all his life to Princeton." "I believe," she said, "that Princeton played a bigger part in his life . . . than any other single factor." Although he sometimes uttered harsh words about his alma mater, his loyalty remained undimmed until the end. At the very moment of his death in Hollywood in 1940, at age 44, he was scribbling notes in the margin of his copy of the *Princeton Alumni Weekly* beside an article about the Princeton football team.

Firestone Library contains Fitzgerald's papers, which were given to the University by his daughter in 1950.

FITZRANDOLPH GATEWAY, THE, an imposing wrought-iron gate set among four limestone pillars, is the symbolic main entrance to the campus from Nassau Street. The shield of the University is centered over the main gate; the two central pillars are topped by stone-carved eagles; and the flanking pillars are topped by decorative urns that recall the caps of the original central pediment of Nassau Hall. Designed by McKim, Meade and White, the gateway was erected in 1905 following a bequest from Augustus van Winkle, a great-grandson of Nathaniel FitzRandolph, who, along with his wife, Rebeckah, gave the land on which Nassau Hall was built in 1756.

FitzRandolph was a son of one of the original 17th-century Quaker settlers of Princeton. More than anyone else, he was responsible for raising the money and securing the land that the trustees of the College of New Jersey required from the town that they would select as the permanent home of the College after it had spent its first 10 years in Elizabeth, and then Newark, New Jersey. The trustees required £1,000, 10 acres of cleared land for a campus, and 200 acres of woodland for fuel. FitzRandolph raised £1,700 and more than met the other requirements, far outpacing Princeton's sole competitor, New Brunswick. FitzRandolph himself donated £20 and the 4.5 acres that later came to be known as the front campus.

The FitzRandolph family owned several thousand acres of land in the surrounding area, and he was a determined fundraiser who rode among his family and neighbors to solicit donations. Research by the Princeton and Slavery Project has shown that most of the key donors were slaveholders, as were FitzRandolph and some of his relatives.

FitzRandolph took great interest in the construction of the principal college building, and he recorded its progress in his journal. He noted that on July 29, 1754, the digging of the cellar began and on September 17, 1754, he participated in the installation of the first cornerstone. On November 13, 1756, he wrote that "Aaron Burr, President, preached the first sermon and began the school in Princeton College."

FitzRandolph died in 1780 and was buried in the family burial ground, which was located where Holder Hall now stands. Workmen excavating for the foundations of that dormitory in 1909 discovered remains from 32 family graves. At President Woodrow Wilson's direction, the remains were reinterred under the eastern arch of Holder Hall and a memorial tablet was placed in the arch. The inscription says: "Near this spot lie the remains of Nathaniel FitzRandolph, the generous giver of the land upon which the original buildings of this university were erected. *In agro jacet nostro immo suo.* (In our ground he sleeps, nay, rather, in his own.)"

Until 1970 the FitzRandolph Gateway acted as a barrier between the University and the town. It was opened only to allow the 25th reunion class to enter the campus at the beginning of the annual alumni P-rade, for Commencement, and on other rare occasions. In 1970 the graduating senior class successfully called for the gates to be opened permanently "as a symbol of the University's openness to the local and worldwide community." Their class motto, "Together for Community," is inscribed in the east pillar of the main gate, with a peace symbol replacing the zero in 1970.

Since 1970 the gates have remained opened. At some point in the 1980s it became campus lore that if students exited through the gates before Commencement they would not graduate. Student tour guides backed up this assertion by claiming that John F. Kennedy 1939, who attended Princeton only for his freshman year, was among those who walked through the gates prematurely and that was why he failed to graduate—without noting that he had been on campus in 1935–36 and the gates were not opened until 1970.

FOOTBALL. The game now known as football was played at Princeton as early as the 1840s, when students organized impromptu games behind Nassau Hall. Opposing teams might be made up of residents of East College and West College, or of Whig and Clio halls. After the Civil War, increasing interest led to interclass matches and eventually to an epochal event—the first American intercollegiate football game, between Princeton and Rutgers, in New Brunswick on November 6, 1869.

Twenty-five players from each college played in their street clothes before several hundred spectators. The Rutgers *Targum*, on which we chiefly depend for the record of the game, tells us that Princeton's first goal was made "by a well-directed kick, from a gentleman whose name we don't know, but who did the best kicking on the Princeton side." By agreement, the home team's style of play was used, and Rutgers won, six goals to four. A week later, Princeton won the return match on its grounds, eight goals to zero.

The game that Princeton and Rutgers played was a form of association football, forerunner of modern soccer, as was the game that Princeton and Yale played in their first meeting in 1873. Harvard, meanwhile, had been playing the "Boston game," which was more like rugby, and in 1875 Harvard beat Yale,

4–0, in a rugby-type match, inaugurating that rivalry. Two Princeton spectators at that game, Jotham Potter 1877 and Earl Dodge 1879, were so taken with rugby that they pressed for its adoption at Princeton. Despite strong sentiment for retaining association football, Potter's and Dodge's views prevailed by a narrow margin. Subsequently, at Princeton's initiative, representatives from Columbia, Harvard, Yale, and Princeton met on November 23, 1876 to form the Intercollegiate Football Association, which adopted modified rugby rules.

Princeton's on-field success declined temporarily with the change in rules, but by 1878, when Woodrow Wilson 1879 and his classmate, Earl Dodge, were directors of the student-managed Princeton College Football Association, Princeton won all six of its games, defeating both Harvard and Yale in the same season for the first time.

American football, as it evolved from rugby, was a violent game. Princeton contributed to the brutality with its invention of the "V-formation wedge" in which players linked arms around the ball carrier and, with a running start, mowed down the opposition. Repeated calls for reform went unheeded until 1906, when, in response to public outcry, the game was opened up with legalization of the forward pass and other rule changes designed to reduce injuries.

Several Princeton players made significant contributions to the development of football as we know it. John T. Haxall 1883 place-kicked a 65-yard goal in an 1882 contest against Yale, setting an intercollegiate record that still stands. In the second half of the 1883 season, Alec Moffat 1884 is credited with inventing the spiral punt, further developed by Knowlton "Snake" Ames 1890, another superb kicker and a slippery open-field runner. His 62 career rushing touchdowns remain a Princeton record.

Throughout the 1880s and 1890s, the Princeton-Yale game was one of the most anticipated athletic events in the country. The games were played on Thanksgiving Day, often at New York's Manhattan Field, before thousands of spectators. Coverage filled the New York newspapers for days before and after.

Two moments from those games are among the most exciting in college football history. In 1898, Arthur Poe snatched the ball from a Yale player's arms and dashed the length of the field for a touchdown that gave Princeton a 7–0 victory. The next year he clinched an 11–10 victory over Yale by kicking a last-minute field goal, the only one he had ever attempted. Poe was one of six brothers who played for Princeton from 1882 to 1902.

The 1903 team, which posted a perfect record, was led by guard John DeWitt 1904, probably Princeton's most complete player in the pre-forward-pass era. He used his talents most strikingly in the last game of his career, when Princeton gave Yale its first defeat in two years. Toward the end of the first half, DeWitt scooped up a blocked Yale kick and returned the ball 75 yards for a touchdown. With only a minute left in the game, DeWitt kicked a 43-yard field goal (then worth five points) for the winning score. That Monday morning, placards all over the campus jubilantly announced: John DeWitt 11, Yale 6.

DeWitt made one other significant contribution to Princeton athletics. In the 1903 team photo, he wore a white sweater with a black P to replace the soiled and torn jersey he had brought with him to the photographer's studio. DeWitt's makeshift attire later became standard garb for captains of Princeton championship teams.

In 1911, Princeton won its first Big Three title in 15 years behind end Sanford White and tackle Eddie Hart, both of the Class of 1912. F. Scott Fitzgerald 1917, then a high school student, saw White return a blocked kick for a touchdown in the 1911 Harvard game and wrote on his ticket stub, "Sam White decides me for Princeton." In 1912, Hobey Baker 1914, better known as a hockey player, scored 92 points, an individual Princeton season record that stood for more than 60 years.

Bill Roper 1902, the team's head coach from 1919 through 1930, was known for his oratory, both in pregame pep talks and in politics. He served on the Philadelphia city council while coaching Princeton's football team. In 1922 Roper's "Team of Destiny," as it came to be known, completed Princeton's first perfect season since 1903. Its most thrilling victory was over the heavily favored University of Chicago. Trailing 18–7 in the fourth quarter, Princeton rallied for two touchdowns to take a 21–18 lead. With only seconds to play, Princeton held Chicago on fourth down, inches from the goal line, to preserve the victory. It was the first football game to be broadcast nationally on the radio.

Harland "Pink" Baker 1922, a tackle for the Team of Destiny, later became a fixture at Princeton football games. He attended every freshman and varsity contest for 60 years, except for his years in the military. An award named for him is given annually to the freshman defensive player who demonstrates good character, cooperative spirit, and the ability to motivate his teammates.

It took a few years to find a suitable replacement after Roper's retirement as coach, but Princeton found him in Herbert O. "Fritz" Crisler. His undefeated 1933 team shut out seven of its nine opponents and gave up only eight points to the other two. It overwhelmed Dartmouth in the last game of the season, played in a near blizzard and further made memorable when a spectator rushed out of the bleachers to join Dartmouth's line during a goal line stand. Crisler left Princeton in 1938 to become coach (and later athletic director) at the University of Michigan, where he introduced their signature winged helmets. He had first used the design at Princeton during the 1930s, and Princeton reinstated the design in 1998.

Charlie Caldwell 1925, another member of the Team of Destiny, coached at Williams before returning to Princeton in 1945. He coached the Tigers until his death in 1957. Caldwell perfected the single wing offense, which was Princeton's signature style of play for more than two decades. His teams won six successive Big Three championships, 1947 through 1952. During this run, the Tigers amassed a 24-game winning streak, going undefeated in 1950 and 1951, the only back-to-back perfect seasons in team history. Both teams were awarded the Lambert Trophy as Eastern champions. Their narrowest victory, 13–7 over Dartmouth in 1950, was ground out during a hurricane, in torrential rain, with an 80-mile gale blowing through the open end of the stadium; while the offensive team was in the huddle, an official had to hold the ball on the line of scrimmage to keep it from blowing away.

That team was led by Richard Kazmaier '52, the most storied player in Princeton's long football history. A single wing tailback, Kazmaier ran, passed, and punted equally well. Though he stood only 5′11″ and weighed 170 pounds, he possessed innate skill, perfected by concentration and practice, rather than power. In his senior year, Kazmaier gained 1,827 total yards, the best in the nation. He was a unanimous All-America selection twice, appeared on the cover of *Time* magazine, and won the Heisman Trophy in 1951. Two other Princetonians have also figured in the Heisman voting over the years: Pepper Constable '36, who finished fourth in the balloting in 1935, and Ron Landeck '66, who finished 12th in 1965.

In 2008, Princeton retired Kazmaier's number 42, which had also been worn by Bill Bradley '65, in basketball. It is the only number the University has ever retired.

Dick Colman, who had been an assistant at Williams and Princeton, took over the team during Caldwell's last illness. From 1957 through 1968, he taught single-wing football with the same conviction that Caldwell had, and with similar results: his teams won 75 games and lost 33. Princeton won the Ivy championship in 1957 and 1964 and shared it in 1963 and 1966. The Tigers also won the Big Three title in 1958, 1964, 1965, and 1966.

The mid-sixties were golden years, brightened by three future hall of famers: running back Cosmo Iacavazzi '65, linebacker Stas Maliszewski '66, and kicker Charlie Gogolak '66. Along with his brother, Peter, who starred at Cornell, Gogolak revolutionized football as the first soccer-style kickers. He ended his Princeton career holding six national collegiate kicking records. Both Gogolak brothers later kicked for professional teams; Charlie was a first round selection of the Washington Redskins in 1966, picked sixth overall.

Colman resigned at the end of the 1968 season to become director of athletics at Middlebury College. He was succeeded by Jake McCandless '51, who transformed the Princeton offense from single-wing to the more modern T-formation. His 1969 team tied for the Ivy League championship, but the era in which Princeton—or any Ivy team—could compete with national powerhouses was drawing to a close. The Tigers could, however, continue to produce winning teams and thrilling games. One highlight was Princeton's 1981 victory over Yale, behind quarterback Bob Holly's 501 passing yards, which snapped a 14-year losing streak against the Elis. The next year, Princeton and the rest of the Ivy League moved to what was then known as the NCAA's Division I-AA, now the Football Championship Subdivision (FCS). After a two-decade lull, the Tigers again won Ivy championships in 1989, 1992, and 1995 for head coach Steve Tosches. The 1992 champions were led by punishing tailback Keith Elias '94. In 1993, Elias was named the Ivy League's Player of the Year and was runner up for the Walter Payton Award as outstanding player in all of Division I-AA.

Princeton football teams continue to finish at or near the top of the Ivy League. Under coach Bob Surace '90, a former Tiger lineman, they won the title in 2013, 2016, and 2018, going undefeated in 2018 for the first time since 1964. On November 9, 2019, Princeton met Dartmouth at New York's Yankee

Stadium to commemorate the 150th anniversary of football, the game Princeton had helped invent.

From 1914 until 1996, Princeton played its home games in Palmer Stadium, which seated more than 42,000 fans and well into the late 1960s was usually packed. Princeton Stadium, which was built on the same site, opened on Sept. 19, 1998 with a 6–0 victory over Cornell.

In all, 12 Princeton players have won the Asa S. Bushnell Cup as Ivy League Player of the Year (the award was split beginning in 2011 to recognize offensive and defensive players of the year): Walt Snickenberger '75 (1974), Jason Garrett '89 (1989), Judd Garrett '90 (1989), Elias (1993), Dave Patterson '96 (1995), Jeff Terrell '07 (2006), Mike Catapano '12 (2012—defense), Quinn Epperly '15 (2013—offense), Mike Zeuli '15 (2014—defense), John Lovett '18 (2016—offense), Chad Kanoff '17 (2017—offense), and Lovett (2018—offense). The award is named for Asa Bushnell 1921, who served as commissioner of the Eastern College Athletic Conference and secretary of the US Olympic Committee.

Fifty Princetonians have been named first-team All-Americans (mostly in the late nineteenth and early twentieth century); the most recent were Iacavazzi in 1964 and Gogolak and Maliszewski in 1965.

Sixteen Princeton players have been inducted into the National Football Hall of Fame: Alexander Moffatt 1884, Hector Cowan 1888, Ames, Phillip King 1893, Langdon Lea 1896, Arthur Wheeler 1896, Garrett Cochran 1898, William Edwards 1900, Arthur Hillebrand 1900, Poe, DeWitt, James McCormick 1908, Hart, Hobey Baker 1914, Harold Ballin 1915, James Keck 1921, Donold Lourie 1922, Jac Weller '36, DeWitt, Hollie Donan '51, Kazmaier, and Iacavazzi. Four coaches have also been inducted: Roper, Tad Weiman, Crisler, and Caldwell.

A total of 41 players have played in the National Football League.

In football's early years, there was no official national champion, although the best team in the East could claim that honor. Later, several football historians devised systems to award championships retroactively. Several newspapers and magazines also declared champions in the decades before World War II. By those measures, Princeton can claim 28 national championships from 1869 to 1950, more than any other school in the country. The NCAA recognizes 15 of those titles, tying Princeton with Alabama for second all-time behind Yale.

FORRESTAL CAMPUS, THE PRINCETON, was established in 1951 on an 825-acre tract of land in Plainsboro Township, about three miles from the main campus along northbound US Route 1. It was named for the first Secretary of Defense, James Forrestal 1915, who, while secretary of the navy, established the office of Naval Research, and in doing so initiated government support for fundamental research in the sciences and engineering.

With help from Laurance Rockefeller '32, a member of the advisory council of the department of Aeronautical Engineering, and with determined advocacy by the department's enterprising chair, Daniel Sayre, the University purchased the land, along with its 16 laboratory buildings, for $1.5 million from the Rockefeller Institute for Medical Research, when the institute decided to relocate its Princeton activities to New York as part of what became Rockefeller University.

Sayre came to Princeton in 1941 and quickly elevated the Aeronautical Engineering department to a position of national leadership. With its faculty growing rapidly, the department was forced to build cinderblock laboratories under the stands of Palmer Stadium to support its research activities. In 1948 the Guggenheim Foundation selected Princeton as one of two sites (the other was Caltech) for new jet propulsion centers and the Air Force and Navy awarded the department a contract to produce a 12-volume series on high-speed aerodynamics and jet propulsion.

When Princeton was given the opportunity to acquire the Rockefeller Institute site, Rockefeller and Sayre raised the funds necessary to purchase it and renovate its facilities. In his 2002 book *Princeton's James Forrestal Campus: 50 Years of Sponsored Research*, J. I. Merritt '66 recalls that when the sale was announced, "a reporter for the *New York Herald Tribune*, noting that with a stroke of a pen the University had more than doubled the size of its land holdings, called it 'the second Louisiana Purchase.'" Shortly after Sayre died at the age of 53, one of the original buildings on the Forrestal Campus, now home of the Atmospheric and Oceanic Sciences (AOS) program, was named Sayre Hall in his honor.

At first, Forrestal was devoted principally to research activities in aerospace and mechanical sciences. Three major research facilities were subsequently added: Project Matterhorn, which later became the Princeton Plasma Physics Laboratory; the federal government's Geophysical Fluid Dynamics Laboratory (GFDL) for research in meteorology and oceanography, which moved to Princeton from Washington, DC, in 1968; and the $40 million Princeton-Pennsylvania Accelerator, which provided research facilities for the study of elementary particles from 1957 until 1972.

Today the Forrestal campus houses an expanded Princeton Plasma Physics Laboratory and continues to house GFDL (part of the National Oceanic and Atmospheric Administration) and AOS. It also houses the department of Mechanical and Aerospace Engineering's Gas Dynamics Laboratory, a chemical sciences building, a high-performance computing research center, the office of print and mail services, and overflow and storage space for the library and the art museum. For many years there were a wind tunnel, hangar, and landing strip on the Forrestal campus; the Frist Campus Center displays a photo of an experimental "air cushion" vehicle that was demonstrated at Forrestal in 1959.

The University's campus plan for development through 2026 and beyond supports retention of these kinds of uses and suggests modest incremental development along with enhancements that would improve this campus's landscape, circulation patterns, and connections to the rest of the University and the community. The Forrestal Campus is served by the University's Tiger Transit shuttle bus system.

Forrestal Center, Princeton. In 1951, Princeton University moved into neighboring Plainsboro Township when it purchased the 825-acre Forrestal campus for academic purposes. In the 1960s and 1970s, the University purchased an additional 774 adjacent acres—including more than 400 from the Walker Gordon dairy farm—and announced plans to develop the non-campus lands to achieve three goals: (1) set a high standard for commercial development along that section of Route 1, with respect to both the nature and the quality of development; (2) foster partnerships between the University and companies with research interests shared by faculty and students; and (3) generate long-term revenues to support its educational mission.

Forrestal Center began as a 1,600-acre planned development with office and research space, housing, hotels, retail establishments, and more than 600 acres of dedicated open space. Over time, the center expanded its land holdings to include a 108-acre tract from St. Joseph's Seminary and the 488-acre Princeton Nurseries property, which included land in South Brunswick Township as well as Plainsboro.

Today, Princeton Forrestal Center contains more than 2,200 contiguous acres. This includes some 840 acres within the center that have been sold over the years, including the headquarters site of the Robert Wood Johnson Foundation and Princeton Forrestal Village. The center houses more than 225 for-profit and not-for-profit businesses, ranging from prestigious multinational corporations to startups; among them they employ more than 15,000 people. It accounts for approximately 31,500 direct, indirect, or induced jobs and over $7.3 billion in direct, indirect, and induced economic output.

One recent addition to the center is the Princeton Innovation Center BioLabs incubator that opened with considerable fanfare, including an early visit from New Jersey's governor, in 2018. BioLabs offers co-working, lab, and office space for high-tech and science- and engineering-based startup companies formed by University faculty, students, and alumni as well as members of the wider New Jersey community.

Forrestal Center has six hotels and more than 1,300 residential units, including single family homes, condominiums, townhouses, apartments, age-restricted living, assisted living, and a nursing home. It has preserved more than 800 acres of open space with mature trees in both Plainsboro and South Brunswick. In addition to Forrestal Village, which offers retail, dining, and services, it has conference centers, day care centers, a fitness center, and a network of scenic trails, walkways, recreation fields, and bicycle paths.

The center worked with state and local officials to enable construction of overpasses at both Scudders Mill Road and College Road to facilitate access to the center by improving traffic flow along and across Route 1, and it has developed road networks within the center, while also supporting local mass transit bus and rail service.

Founding of Princeton, The, was one of the consequences of the First Great Awakening, a series of religious revivals that swept Britain and its colonies in America in the eighteenth century. The Great Awakening also brought an upsurge in missionary activity among Native populations and the first important movement against slavery. Of special importance for Princeton, it increased opposition to the Church of

England and the royal officials who supported it, and it created a democratic spirit in religion that was allied to an insistence on political home rule that eventually brought independence from Britain.

Early stirrings of an evangelical awakening in the Raritan Valley of New Jersey took the form of revival meetings in the 1720s led by a Dutch reformed pastor, Theodorus Jacobus Frelinghuysen. The spirit of evangelicalism spread through the middle colonies under the leadership of zealous graduates of the Log College, founded in Pennsylvania in 1726 by Presbyterian William Tennent. In 1734–35, the preaching of Congregationalist minister Jonathan Edwards at Northampton, Massachusetts, touched off waves of revivals throughout New England. These activities were stimulated in the years 1739 to 1741 by tours of the English evangelist George Whitefield, and they spread with the preaching of Presbyterian Samuel Davies in Virginia and later efforts by Baptists and Methodists in other parts of the south.*

In New England, the emotional excesses of some of the followers of the revivalists bitterly divided the churches between the "New Lights" and the "Old Lights." In the middle colonies a similar division between the "New Sides" and the "Old Sides" caused a split in the Presbyterian church from 1741 to 1758.

The four originators of the College of New Jersey were members of the moderate wing of the New Sides. Three of them were ministers in New Jersey and graduates of Yale: Jonathan Dickinson, pastor at Elizabethtown; Aaron Burr Sr., pastor at Newark; and John Pierson, pastor at Woodbridge. The fourth, Ebenezer Pemberton, a pastor in New York, was a graduate of Harvard. While they disapproved of the more contentious and intrusive methods of the New Sides graduates of Tennent's Log College, they defended them in their disputes with the Old Sides group that dominated the synod of Philadelphia. After the synod expelled the Presbytery of New Brunswick in 1741, Dickinson, Burr, and the others tried in vain to bring about a conciliation. They then withdrew from the synod of Philadelphia and joined with the Presbytery of New Brunswick to form the new synod of New York in 1745.

Disappointed by Yale and Harvard's opposition to revivalism and dissatisfied with the limited course of instruction available at the Log College, the four ministers devised a plan for the establishment of a new college. They persuaded three leading lay Presbyterians in New York to join them. These three, also graduates of Yale, were: William Smith, lawyer; Peter Van Brugh Livingston, merchant; and William Peartree Smith, a young man of independent means who was a generous supporter of the church and "an ardent patriot." Since there was no college between New Haven in Connecticut and Williamsburg in Virginia—a long distance by horseback or stagecoach—they felt that the need for an institution of higher education in the middle colonies was urgent.

Late in 1745 or early in 1746 these seven men applied for a charter to Governor Lewis Morris, an Anglican. He refused their petition because, he said, his instructions prevented him from granting such a charter to a group of dissenters. Following Morris' death, they applied anew to acting Governor John Hamilton. Although also an Anglican, Hamilton, with the consent of his Council, on which there were a number of friends of the proposed college, granted a charter on October 22, 1746. The Anglican clergy later complained that it was done "so suddenly and privately" that they "had no opportunity to enter a caveat against it."

John DeWitt 1861, in his 1896 sesquicentennial history of the College, wrote:

> The name of John Hamilton should be given a conspicuous place in any list of the founders of Princeton University. He granted the first charter; he granted it against the precedent made by the governor whom he succeeded in the executive chair; and he granted it with alacrity . . . What is more remarkable, at a time when Episcopalian governors were ill-disposed to grant to Presbyterians ecclesiastical or educational franchises, he—an Episcopalian—gave this charter to a board of trust composed wholly of members of the Presbyterian Church.

The College was not established under the auspices of the synod of New York. The seven persons who, in the words of their leader Jonathan Dickinson, "first concocted the plan and foundation of the College," were leading members of that body, but they acted independently as (in the words of the charter) "well disposed & publick spirited Persons." The new institution was not to be a seminary of the kind that had been planned earlier by the synod of Philadelphia, but a college of liberal arts and sciences.

"Though our great Intention was to erect a seminary for educating Ministers of the Gospel," one of

---

* Frelinghuysen received an honorary degree from Princeton in 1749, Davies in 1753, Whitefield in 1754. Two of Tennent's sons became trustees of the College, while Edwards became its third president and Davies its fourth.

the founders later wrote, "yet we hope it will be useful in other learned professions—Ornaments of the State as well as the Church. Therefore, we propose to make the plan of Education as extensive as our Circumstances will admit."

The College, furthermore, was not to be solely for Presbyterians: "The most effectual Care is taken in our Charter to secure the Rights of Conscience," the founder wrote. "Persons of all persuasions are to have free access to the Honours & Privileges of the College, while they behave themselves with Sobriety and Virtue." The charter assured that "those of every religious Denomination may have free and equal Liberty and Advantages of Education in the said College, notwithstanding any different Sentiments in Religion."

After they obtained the charter, the seven original trustees chose five ardent New Siders for the remaining places they were empowered to fill: Samuel Blair, Samuel Finley, Gilbert Tennent, William Tennent Jr., and Richard Treat, all graduates of the Log College except Treat, who was one of its close adherents. On April 27, 1747, the trustees announced the election of Jonathan Dickinson as president, and the College opened in his Elizabethtown parsonage during the last week of May. On President Dickinson's death the following October, the College moved to the Newark parsonage of Aaron Burr Sr., who was elected the second president. Burr played the principal role in developing the infant college's entrance requirements and course of study.

When the first charter was attacked—the Anglicans contended that Hamilton was superannuated when he granted it and threatened to test its validity in court—Hamilton's duly appointed successor, Governor Jonathan Belcher, a graduate of Harvard, a Congregationalist—and something of a contrarian—issued a second one on September 14, 1748. It left intact the essential features of the first charter, but developed further the founders' concern for "State as well as Church" by making the governor of New Jersey an ex officio trustee and including among those appointed to an enlarged board of 23 trustees four members of the Provincial Council and other prominent laymen, two of whom were members of the Society of Friends, two of the Episcopal church, and one of the Dutch Reformed church. Sixteen of these 23 early trustees were slaveholders.

Eight weeks later, at the College's first Commencement, the trustees conferred on Belcher Princeton's first honorary degree.

Belcher referred to the College as his "adopted daughter," and bestowed on it such gifts as his library of 474 volumes and 10 framed portraits of kings and queens of England, as well as a full-length portrait of himself. The trustees, in proposing to name the first college building in Princeton for him, said they viewed him as its "founder, patron, and benefactor." The governor, an active proponent of locating the College in Princeton, declined this honor, persuading them instead to name the building Nassau Hall in honor of King William the Third of the royal house of Nassau—a king regarded by dissenters as a champion of religious freedom and political liberty.

Unlike Harvard, William & Mary, and Yale, the three American colleges that preceded it, the College of New Jersey was located in a thinly populated province, and, as a result, drew its students from at least 12 of the 13 colonies, with barely a quarter of them from New Jersey. By drawing students from across the colonies, it was poised to be a national institution as soon as there was a nation.

Since it charged the lowest tuition in the colonies, the College attracted students from families who were farmers, artisans, merchants, lawyers, and members of the clergy, in addition to wealthier landowners. Although students enrolled as young as 13 and as old as 26, the average age of entering freshmen was about 16.

Fox, Frederic E. '39, beloved by generations of students and alumni as an iconic "Mr. Princeton," became recording secretary of the University in 1964, and then in 1976 was named "Keeper of Princetoniana," the only person ever to hold that title. In a tribute in the *Princeton Alumni Weekly*, Elyse Graham '07 described him as "a Princeton legend . . . custodian of school spirit, archivist of arcana, and occupant of an office in Nassau Hall that resembled an old curiosity shop, stuffed with Princeton rarities and a huge collection of tigers. He carried a squirt gun, wore a boater hat, and rode a jalopy bicycle with a tiger tail waggling behind."

As an undergraduate, Fox was a columnist for the *Alumni Weekly*, a featured performer in Triangle shows and one of its officers, active in Theatre Intime and the Glee Club, a program director of the Princeton Summer Camp, and an assistant manager of the University Band who dressed in a tiger suit for football games. He once earned five dollars by agreeing to have his head shaved as a walking advertisement for Jack Honore's barber shop. Upon graduation his class voted him "most original," "most entertaining," and "most likely bachelor."

Following graduation, he performed briefly in a community theater in Arizona, and then worked for NBC Radio in Hollywood.

After Pearl Harbor he joined the Army Signal Corps, attaining the rank of captain and earning the bronze star. He played a leading role in a "deception unit" (the Ghost Army) that used inflatable tanks, sound effects, and impersonation (on at least one occasion, Fox wore a mustache to impersonate an American general) to deceive the German army about the whereabouts of American troops. In its final deception in March 1945, it misled the Germans about where two American divisions would cross the Rhine.

After the war, Fox earned a bachelor of divinity degree from Union Theological Seminary in New York and a doctor of divinity degree from Defiance College of Ohio. He served as a minister in Congregational churches in Arizona, New York, Ohio, Massachusetts, and Washington, DC. During President Dwight Eisenhower's second term, he worked in the White House as a speechwriter and liaison to the nation's churches and volunteer agencies. On his final night on the staff, he slept at his desk so he could later say he had slept in the White House. In 1961 he left for Africa to work as a missionary and teacher.

As recording secretary, Fox's principal responsibility was to acknowledge gifts to the University and maintain an active correspondence with alumni and donors. As keeper of Princetoniana he had no real job description, which he demonstrated at one point when asked to place himself in the University's organization chart. While acknowledging some responsibility to the vice president for public affairs, to whom he nominally reported, he also depicted a reporting relationship to his class, his wife, Hannah, the University, and, ultimately, to himself. When someone suggested he was "dedicated" to Princeton, he said no, "I am obsessed by it."

In his job, he said, he dealt with "people, legends, myths, colors, artifacts, songs, and stories," but mostly he hoped to "continue working with things that are very much alive: orange and black things, both material and human, including primarily the people who give such a special spirit to this old place." He described tradition as a river with always-new water flowing through its banks, and he was an advocate for coeducation who encouraged his fellow alumni to welcome the change.

At the honor assembly each fall, Fox introduced the entering class to Princeton traditions and taught the new students the words to "Old Nassau." With Hannah's help, he sent a homemade Princeton banner to the moon with astronaut Pete Conrad '53 as a way, he said, "of putting Princeton 239,000 miles ahead of Harvard and Yale."

For his memorial service in 1981, he asked the band to play; the band still honors him with an annual Fred Fox Memorial Concert at reunions. At that service, President William Bowen said Fox was "unfailingly colorful, and two particular colors were, of course, his favorites." He quoted Fox as saying: "Obviously I can't touch everyone, every event, with my magic wand dipped in orange and black, but as long as I'm Keeper of Princetoniana, I'm sure going to try." As the long-time secretary of his class, Fox once traveled to Russia with his classmates and painted two cobblestones of Red Square orange and black.

After he died, Fox's classmates created a fund in his honor that provides grants to students for special projects, and the Alumni Council formed a committee on Princetoniana to carry on his spirit. His class also placed a stone in Fox's honor in the chapel; inscribed a stave for the band in his memory; refurbished a cabin at the Princeton-Blairstown camp that was named for him and his wife; and commissioned a portrait of him that initially hung in the library, but at the class's suggestion was later moved to Frist Campus Center.

FRANK, SALLY '80, a high-profile student activist as an undergraduate who was known for wearing multiple campaign-style buttons heralding the many progressive causes she championed, filed a lawsuit in 1979 against the University and the three eating clubs—Cottage, Ivy, and Tiger Inn—that 10 years after coeducation still did not admit women. Her lawsuit alleged discrimination in what she argued were places of public accommodation and sought damages for the pain and humiliation she suffered while attempting to participate in the clubs' selection process known as "bicker."

Frank pursued her case and related cases for 13 years through the New Jersey and federal courts. In February 1986 Cottage dropped its defense, paid $20,000 in damages and legal fees, and became coeducational. In September 1986 the University settled, paid $27,500 in attorney's fees, and dissociated itself from the all-male policies at Ivy and Tiger Inn. (Frank used the funds from the Cottage and University settlements to endow a fund at the Women*s Center that bears her name.) Court rulings required the remaining two clubs, Ivy and Tiger Inn, to begin admitting women in 1990 and 1991 respectively, and the last of the lawsuits was finally settled in 1992.

As activist and plaintiff, Frank provoked strong feelings, both from students and alumni who resented her activism and her use of the courts to challenge the right of clubs to remain all-male if they chose to do so, and from other students and alumni who acclaimed her as a "crusader for social justice" and a "catalyst for change." Her supporters admired her determination to ensure that women would have full access to the same opportunities that were available to men, and her courage in the face of the oftentimes mean-spirited opposition she endured.

After a series of conflicting rulings during the 1980s by the New Jersey Division on Civil Rights and the appellate division of the New Jersey Superior Court, in July 1990 the Supreme Court of New Jersey ruled that the remaining two all-male clubs had to admit women. The court upheld a 1987 ruling by the New Jersey Division on Civil Rights that the clubs, which drew all their members from Princeton's student body and served meals to a significant percentage, were not "distinctly private" associations, but places of "public accommodation;" as such, they were subject to state civil rights law and could not discriminate on the basis of gender.

Ivy Club accepted the ruling and began admitting women members that fall, although it also got permission from the federal district court in New Jersey to litigate questions related to its claim of a constitutional right to freedom of association that the state court had not addressed. Tiger Inn sought to appeal the 1990 ruling to the United States Supreme Court, but in January 1991 the justices refused to hear the case, and a month later Tiger Inn conducted its first coeducational selection process. Tiger Inn joined Ivy in the federal litigation, which continued until June 1992 when the two clubs and Frank reached a settlement under which the clubs dropped their federal lawsuit and agreed to contribute $43,000 each to the American Civil Liberties Union (ACLU), which had assisted Frank in her lawsuit.

After graduating from Princeton, Frank earned her law degree at New York University, taught at New York Law School, and in 1990 became a professor of law at Drake University. She returned often to Princeton for alumni gatherings and was increasingly appreciated for her unwavering commitment to inclusivity and women's rights. In 1990, when she received the Alumni Council Award for Service to Princeton, her citation referred to her as a "loving critic" of the University.

In 2020, when she was called upon to ask a question at the Alumni Day talk by Woodrow Wilson Award winner and ACLU executive director Anthony Romero '87, the audience erupted in applause when he described her as "a heroine of activism at the University" because of the changes her lawsuit engendered.

FRATERNITIES AND SORORITIES. Greek-letter fraternities arrived on campus during the middle of the nineteenth century. The first one, Beta Theta Pi, made its appearance in 1843, and, at one time or another, 11 other fraternities also were represented by Princeton chapters: Chi Phi, Chi Psi, Delta Kappa Epsilon, Delta Phi, Delta Psi, Kappa Alpha, Phi Kappa Sigma, Sigma Chi, Sigma Phi, Theta Delta Chi, and Zeta Psi.

Wary of their small size and cliquishness, concerned that they were dividing the student body along sectional lines in this pre-Civil War era, and fearing that they would undermine college discipline and prove injurious to the American Whig and Cliosophic societies, the trustees and faculty voted in 1853 to ban fraternities. President John Maclean Jr. launched a "Secret Society Crusade," notifying parents that the College would forbid students to join unsanctioned societies and asking for their cooperation. In 1854 the administration began requiring each entering student to pledge that he would not join such an organization while in college.

This pledge—which appeared in the catalogue through 1916–17 and officially remained in effect until just before World War II—was as follows:

> I pledge . . . that I will have no connection whatever with any secret society in this institution so long as I am a member of Princeton University; it being understood that this promise has no reference to the American Whig and Cliosophic Societies. I also declare that I regard myself bound to keep this promise and on no account whatever to violate it.

Some fraternities maintained an illicit existence until 1875 when a faculty committee obtained photographs of some 50 fraternity members, summarily suspended them, and readmitted them only on the condition that they forswear all future Greek-letter affiliations. The trustees and President James McCosh supported the faculty, despite opposition from some New York alumni who sought to persuade them to remove the prohibition. In 1876 the final five fraternities agreed to close their Princeton chapters, although Zeta Psi continued to operate surreptitiously into the 1880s.

When the pledge not to join fraternities was allowed to lapse in the late 1930s, it seemed entirely unnecessary to sustain it: the eating club system was firmly established, few students were arriving on campus expecting to find fraternities, and there had been no Greek-letter presence on campus for more than 60 years. The status quo held until the 1980s when the adoption of a residential college system for freshmen and sophomores reduced the opportunities for students in those classes to get to know juniors and seniors. (Previously, most dormitories housed students from all four classes, but now dorms in the residential colleges housed only freshmen and sophomores, along with a few resident advisers.)

With a more socioeconomically and geographically diverse student body, the University was enrolling more undergraduates from families that had a history of involvement in Greek-letter organizations at other colleges. And the increase in New Jersey's drinking age—first to 19 in 1980 and then to 21 in 1983—closed the on-campus pub, and with club membership restricted to juniors and seniors, first-year students and sophomores sought other access to of-age students.

Alumni advocates of fraternities campaigned for their return to campus and helped undergraduates form a Council of Fraternities, a group that included representatives from seven fraternities that had been present at Princeton in the nineteenth century. Initially, three organizations (Phi Kappa Sigma, Sigma Alpha Epsilon, and Zeta Psi) attracted 30 students, and soon two more fraternities and a sorority formed chapters. In 1983, in response, the trustees adopted a resolution denying them official recognition:

> RESOLVED that the longstanding tradition of Princeton opposing the formation of local chapters of national "Greek Letter" social fraternities and sororities has served the University well, and is reaffirmed as a sound policy for this Institution: accordingly such organizations will continue to be ineligible for University recognition.

In 1989 the faculty and student undergraduate life committees voted to reaffirm the trustee resolution, while also encouraging the University "to continue to explore alternative ways to address some of the needs met by Greek-letter organizations."

Lack of recognition notwithstanding, by 1993 18 unofficial Greek organizations enrolled about 15 percent of the student body, and it became clear that one of the largest groups of members were students who entered Princeton with a desire to join an eating club with which a particular fraternity or sorority was associated. In 2004 the University began sending letters to the parents of entering students strongly discouraging membership in Greek organizations and noting that fraternities and sororities were not officially recognized.

In 2010, a task force on relationships between the University and the eating clubs expressed concern that this feeder relationship was "forcing decisions and restricting social interactions very early in a student's Princeton career" as fraternities and sororities solicited newly admitted students when they first arrived on campus. The task force noted that since fraternity and sorority members were disproportionately white and from high-income families, the feeder relationships contributed to social and economic stratification of the clubs. The task force also noted concerns by students and alumni about "the association of fraternities, and, to a lesser degree, sororities, with excessive, and in some cases coerced, consumption of alcohol."

A student-faculty-staff working group on campus social and residential life issued a report in May 2011 that looked more closely at Greek life on campus. It described Princeton as having a "faux Greek" system with organizations that were not officially recognized, were not permitted to convene openly in campus space, and, unlike most Greek systems elsewhere, were not residential. It found that about 450 women were members of four sororities (including one small historically Black sorority) and about 330 men were in about a dozen fraternities.

The working group reported divided views among students about Greek organizations: some saw them as incongruous with Princeton's distinctive social paradigm that revolves around colleges and clubs and associated them with "social stratification, cliquishness, and high-risk drinking and hazing," while others saw them as meeting student needs not otherwise being met.

The working group recommended that the University prohibit students from affiliating with a fraternity or sorority or engaging in any form of rush during the freshman year and from conducting or having responsibility for any form of rush in which freshmen participate, with a minimum penalty of suspension for violating the prohibitions. It did not propose a prohibition on membership beyond freshman year and it proposed that the University should sustain its policy of not officially recognizing the organizations.

The working group said that its proposal grew out of a concern that "membership . . . in freshman year narrows students' social circles before they gain a full sense of the opportunities Princeton has to offer or experience the full diversity of backgrounds and interests among their fellow students . . . This concern is heightened by the pipeline relationship that exists between some of the Greek organizations and some of the eating clubs, which has the effect of tracking students very early in their Princeton careers."

The University adopted the committee's recommendations, and in August 2011 President Shirley Tilghman wrote to all returning students to inform them that the recommendations would take effect beginning in the fall of 2012. In her letter Tilghman said the decision to prohibit freshman year affiliation and recruitment "is driven primarily by a conviction that social and residential life at Princeton should continue to revolve around the residential colleges, the eating clubs, and the shared experience of essentially all undergraduates living and dining on campus."

FRENCH AND ITALIAN, THE DEPARTMENT OF. Although French and Italian, created in 2001, is one of Princeton's youngest departments, the French language has been taught from the University's earliest days. In 1769, President John Witherspoon offered extracurricular instruction in French, free of charge, and over time students also engaged outside instructors for a fee. In 1830 the College appointed its first regular instructor of French and Spanish, and in 1836 Benedict Jaeger arrived—an Austrian who, along with being curator of the zoological museum and lecturer in natural history, became a one-man language department, offering French, Italian, Spanish, and German, all as professor of modern languages.

Although the first instructors, and those who followed, had faculty standing, students did not receive academic credit for their offerings. It was a full century after Witherspoon's efforts that President James McCosh made instruction in language a regular part of the curriculum. In 1870 a gift from John Woodhull 1828 established the Woodhull Professorship of Modern Languages. The first incumbent of the chair was the larger-than-life swashbuckling General Joseph Kargé, a native of Prussia, twice jailed as a Polish freedom fighter, who had fled to the United States and served with distinction in the Second New Jersey Volunteer Cavalry during the Civil War. Not only did he teach French and German, he also accompanied students on summer field trips to explore the American West.

When President Woodrow Wilson organized the University into academic departments in 1904, the department of Modern Languages came into existence. For the first two decades, the faculty was primarily American. Then in 1923 the University began to recruit European faculty, including Augusto Centeno from Spain and Maurice Coindreau, a literary critic and translator from France, whose translations of Faulkner, Hemingway, and Dos Passos introduced major American writers to his country.

The creation in 1930 of the Pyne Professorship in French Literature furthered an international presence in the department. Endowed by the family of Meredith Howard Pyne Jr. 1921, the professorship was designed to strengthen ties between Princeton and France by bringing to campus for one-year appointments such illustrious French scholars and men of letters as André Maurois.

As happened in a number of programs, the Cold War era brought far-reaching changes to the study of foreign languages. Language learning by listening and speaking was instituted, and undergraduate programs evolved to integrate the teaching of language and literature into wider frameworks of history, politics, and cultural studies, with a goal to develop American students into world citizens. This was a central priority of Ira Wade, who chaired the department from 1946 to 1958, as was the Special Program in European Civilization he created to encourage students to explore topics other than those purely literary. The program subsequently evolved into the program in European Cultural Studies that is still vibrant today.

The Modern Languages department experienced an "amoeba-like fission" in 1958, resulting in two new departments: Germanic Languages and Literatures and Romance Languages and Literatures (including Russian). In the following two years, significant faculty appointments were made that shaped the study of European literature for decades, including André Maman for French, and for Italian, Robert Hollander '55, whose Dante courses, both on campus and abroad, were legendary—as were the seminars he offered alumni each year at reunions.

Ten years later, Slavic Languages and Literatures spun off into an independent department. And at the beginning of the twenty-first century, Romance Languages and Literatures experienced a further division, resulting in two new departments: French and Italian, and Spanish and Portuguese.

Today's department of French and Italian continues to draw strength from its roots in the past while being fully engaged in the global present. The Princeton Summer Work Abroad program, first established in 1954, is now known as Princeton in France. With the mission to introduce students to French culture in a professional environment, Princeton sends undergraduates to France in the summer to intern in a variety of businesses and other organizations. More than 2,000 students have participated.

In 2019 the department inaugurated Princeton in Pisa, a summer language immersion program during which students explore issues of contemporary culture in the city that is both the headquarters of Italian political parties and a community that works closely with immigrants who have come to Italy from Africa.

The department's courses not only ensure that students achieve linguistic proficiency in a foreign language but also give students a critical perspective on language and culture. Students encounter a wide range of authentic materials, including readings, videos, films, French and Italian television, news, and web-based activities. There are opportunities to be exposed to diverse areas to which French and Italian culture have uniquely contributed, such as the visual arts and cinema, music, popular culture, sociology, political science, and gastronomy.

Certain French language classes also take students beyond geographic boundaries to explore other countries in the Francophone world, from Africa to the Caribbean. The courses provide intensive language practice, with an emphasis on the acquisition of a rich transnational vocabulary. In a seminar setting, students engage with guest speakers from the regions studied and discuss topics that may include environmental, educational, health, social, cultural, and political issues as well as aesthetic considerations.

The department's graduate program trains students to become effective teachers and scholars of French language and literature. While it does not offer a graduate program in Italian, it does teach graduate-level courses in Italian literature.

The department's associated faculty members represent a number of other departments, including Comparative Literature, Music, and Politics. The department also coordinates with other departments and programs across campus, from Ecology and Evolutionary Biology to the Lewis Center for the Arts.

FRENEAU, PHILIP MORIN 1771 entered Princeton as a sophomore to prepare for the ministry. Though he was a serious student of theology, he found his true calling in literature. As his roommate, classmate, and close friend James Madison 1771 recognized early, Freneau's wit and verbal skills would make him a powerful wielder of the pen and a formidable adversary on the battlefields of print. Freneau soon became the unrivaled "poet of the Revolution."

Although Freneau produced several accomplished private poems before college, it was the intense experience of pre–Revolutionary War Princeton that turned his interest to public writing. Political concerns led Madison, Freneau, and their friends Hugh Henry Brackenridge 1771 and William Bradford Jr. 1772, to revive the defunct Plain Dealing Club as the American Whig Society. Their verbal skirmishes with the conservative Cliosophic Society provided ample opportunities to sharpen Freneau's skills in prose and poetic satire.

Freneau and Brackenridge collaborated on a rollicking, picaresque narrative, *Father Bombo's Pilgrimage to Mecca in Arabia*, which presented comic glimpses of life in 18th-century America. This piece, published by the Princeton University Library in 1975, may be the first work of prose fiction written in America.

During their senior year Freneau and Brackenridge labored long on another joint project to which Freneau contributed the greater share. Their composition was a patriotic poem of epic design, "The Rising Glory of America," a prophecy of a time when a united nation should rule the vast continent from the Atlantic to the Pacific. At the commencement exercises of September 1771, Brackenridge read this poem to a "vast concourse of the politest company," gathered at Nassau Hall. The poem articulated the vision and fervor of a young revolutionary generation.

After Princeton Freneau tried teaching, studied theology, sailed to the West Indies to write about nature and learn navigation, joined the militia, and sailed the Atlantic as a ship captain. By 1790, with two collections of poetry in print and a reputation as a fiery propagandist and skillful sea captain, Freneau tried to withdraw to a quiet job as an assistant editor in New York, but his friends Madison and Thomas Jefferson persuaded him to set up his own newspaper in Philadelphia to counter the powerful Hamiltonian paper of John Fenno.

Freneau's *National Gazette* upheld Jefferson's republican principles and condemned George Washington's foreign policy. Jefferson later praised Freneau for having "saved our Constitution which was galloping fast into monarchy," while Washington grumbled of "that rascal Freneau"—an epithet that became the title of Lewis Leary's authoritative biography in 1949.

FRESHMAN SCHOLARS INSTITUTE, or FSI, was established in 1995 by the office of the dean of the college to provide a designated group of entering undergraduates an early opportunity to enroll in Princeton courses, learn about campus resources, and build a network of peers, faculty members, and advisers before the start of their first year. It built on a tradition of pre-orientation programs dating back to the 1960s that were designed to promote access and inclusion. Participants in the eight-week residential summer program are students who are the first in their families to attend college or who attended high schools that typically do not send their graduates to highly selective colleges and universities.

The students take two credit-bearing courses taught by Princeton faculty that count toward graduation requirements and participate in a range of co-curricular and extracurricular programs that introduce them to campus life. One of the courses, "Ways of Knowing," is a seminar that introduces them to scholarly ways of thinking, reading, and writing in a range of disciplines. The second is quantitative; students may choose from courses on visualization of data (offered by the Politics department), laboratory research in the life sciences, or the foundations of engineering. The students work with peer tutors and fellows to draft and revise papers, lab reports, and presentations, and to tackle various problem-solving assignments.

Since FSI cannot accommodate all who would like to participate, the University offers an online summer pre-orientation option, FS Connect (FSC), which allows students to select one of two six-week, noncredit courses: a critical thinking, reading, and writing course called Connect & Critique, and a course called Connect & Solve that cultivates skills and habits of quantitative and scientific reasoning. FSC also introduces students to campus resources, mentors, and other entering students.

Because of the COVID-19 pandemic, in the summer of 2020 the FSI program itself was offered remotely. During that summer, only the Ways of Knowing course was offered for credit, but participants also could choose up to two two-week, non-credit-bearing mini courses in chemistry, physics, molecular biology, engineering, and statistics/data visualization.

A related academic-year program, the Scholars Institute Fellows Program (SIFP), was launched in 2015 to build on the goals of FSI. It provides peer and faculty mentorship, workshops on professional development and campus leadership, academic enrichment, and a support network of students, faculty, and staff during all four years on campus. It is open to all students who identify as first generation or low income, including students who have participated in FSI, and military veterans and transfer students; other students may participate as allies. About 400 undergraduates typically are members of SIFP.

The program also offers activities on campus and field trips off-campus during breaks in the academic year, particularly for students who cannot afford to go home.

In 2021, the University established the Emma Bloomberg ('01) Center for Access and Opportunity, which encompassed FSI and SIFP, along with a program for transfer, nontraditional, and veteran students, the Mellon Mays Undergraduate Fellowship Program, the Princeton University Preparatory Program, and the Princeton Summer Journalism Program. The center's founding director, Khristina Gonzalez, was responsible for programs and initiatives in the office of the dean of the college that supported and advanced Princeton's commitment to an inclusive undergraduate student body and for initiatives designed to enhance the experiences of students from lower socioeconomic backgrounds and other historically underrepresented groups.

FRESHMAN SEMINARS. The Program of Freshman Seminars in the Residential Colleges was launched in 1986 with nine seminars in the humanities that were especially designed to introduce entering students to scholarly inquiry in a setting that encourages independent thinking and active engagement with a member of the faculty and a small group of classmates. Over time, the number of seminars each year grew to about 75, spanning a wide range of disciplines, and frequently exploring topics that are interdisciplinary or fall outside the conventional curriculum. Many faculty members welcome the opportunity to pursue new, and sometimes off-beat, areas of interest, and many students describe their freshman seminar as one of their best academic experiences at Princeton. In some cases courses first presented as freshman seminars made their way into the permanent curriculum.

Each freshman seminar is a full-credit course, limited to 15 students. It is developed and taught by a faculty member and hosted by a residential college, which allows discussion to continue after class over meals or in other informal settings. Emphasis in the seminars is on discussion, papers, and in-class presentations, rather than on quizzes and exams. Occasionally, the seminars take students off-campus—a seminar on Active Geological Processes, for example, included a week-long trip to the Sierra Nevadas—and frequently take them into the library, the art museum, or the archives.

To illustrate the range of topics, a sampling of the 2019–20 freshman seminars is listed below:

The American Dream: Visions and Subversions in American Literature
The Architecturess: Women and Architecture
Art and Science of Motorcycle Design
Atomic-bombing and Firebombing Cities in World War II: Morality, Science, and Race
Before Hamilton: Histories of the Early American Republic
Behind the Scenes: Inside the Princeton University Art Museum
Connection and Communication in the Digital Bazaar
Consuming America: Five Critical Food Puzzles
Drug Discovery: From Snake Venoms to Medicines
The Evolution of Human Language
Excluded, Interned, Occupied: Asians in American History
Extraordinary Popular Delusions and the Wisdom of Crowds
How Not to Be a Leader
Imaging New York: The City in Fiction
Imprisoned Minds: Religion and Philosophy from Jail
Intellectual Foundations of Modern Conservatism
Life on Mars—Or Maybe Not
Once Upon a Time: Magic Tales and Their Meaning
Patagonia: From Landscape to Lifestyle Brand
Pathologies of Difference: Art, Medicine, and Race in the British Empire
Physics of Baseball and Softball
Race in Latin America
Sentencing and Punishment
What to Read and Believe in the Digital Age

Princeton's 18th, 19th, and 20th presidents all taught freshman seminars, some during their presidencies, and some before or after. Harold Shapiro *64 taught seminars on the history of American higher education, the purpose of college, bioethics, and science, technology, and public policy. Shirley Tilghman taught seminars on genetics and on "what makes a great experiment." Christopher Eisgruber '83's seminars were on the Supreme Court and constitutional democracy, and on "elite universities, public policy, and the common good." Nobel Laureate Eric Wieschaus of the department of Molecular Biology was teaching a freshman seminar in the term when his Nobel Prize was announced.

The freshman seminar program was introduced after alumni surveys showed that while Princeton graduates felt junior independent work and the senior thesis prepared them well for occasions in their careers when they worked on their own, many felt less well prepared for the more common occasions when they worked on teams or in groups, much as occurs in a seminar. Also, at a time when fewer preceptorials (small group discussions) in large lecture courses—common in the freshman year—were being taught by senior faculty, the program provided an opportunity for more undergraduates to work directly with, and get to know, senior faculty early in their years at Princeton.

FRICK CHEMISTRY LABORATORY, the home of Princeton's Chemistry department, opened in 2010. It provides laboratory space for research and teaching, a 260-seat auditorium named for Professor Edward C. Taylor, a sky-lit atrium (also named for Taylor), faculty and administrative offices, and a café whose name incorporates the symbols for the chemical elements calcium (Ca) and iron (Fe). When Chemistry moved into "new" Frick, it moved out of two buildings, Hoyt laboratory (built in 1979), and "old" Frick.

The original Frick was built in 1929 and named for Pittsburgh steelmaker Henry Clay Frick. His interest in the University had been cultivated originally by dean of the graduate school Andrew Fleming West 1874, who persuaded him to give the organ in the graduate college's Procter Hall. In 1916 Frick expressed interest in helping to start a law school at Princeton, but he agreed instead to give a chemical laboratory when President John Grier Hibben told him how urgently one was needed. Plans were drawn up, but Frick was appalled by the estimated cost of $1 million, which he thought due to inflated steel prices; the building was accordingly postponed.

Frick died in 1919, leaving almost $6 million to Princeton for its unrestricted use. All of his benefaction was used for the endowment of faculty salaries, then badly needed, and it was not until late in the 1920s that funds for the new laboratory became available. When the laboratory was completed, at a cost of $1,840,000, the trustees, mindful of Frick's earlier interest and his subsequent bequest, voted to name it for him.

Designed with a Collegiate Gothic façade by Charles Z. Klauder, and constructed with an interior that was state-of-the-art at the time, the three-story building at the southeast corner of Washington Road and William Street contained undergraduate laboratories, lecture rooms, faculty offices, and research laboratories. Beatrix Farrand's landscaping for the building included wisteria vines that seem to grow out of the stone. A new wing at the rear was completed in 1964 at a cost of $2 million, doubling the space available for research.

By the end of the twentieth century, Frick could no longer accommodate cutting-edge research. Professor Robert Cava was quoted as saying that while the building was "beautiful on the outside," it was hard to work in: "It is a labyrinth of renovation upon renovation, designed in a complex and inefficient way for a science building," he said.

After the new Frick was constructed, the former Frick was thoroughly renovated and expanded to become both the Julis Romo Rabinowitz Building (home to the department of Economics and a number of centers related to economics and finance) and the Louis A. Simpson International Building (home to the University's international initiatives, including the Princeton Institute for International and Regional Studies). The 200,000 square feet of space are divided into two complementary areas, each with its own architectural identity and its own entrance. There are two communal atria: the one on the south side of the building connects to Scudder Plaza and other social science buildings in the neighborhood.

The Julis Romo Rabinowitz Building was made possible by a gift from Mitchell R. Julis '77 and Joleen Romo Julis, and named in honor of their families, while the Louis A. Simpson building was made possible by a gift from Louis A. Simpson *60 and his wife, Kimberly K. Querry.

Construction of the four-story, 265,000 square foot new Frick was funded by Princeton's share of its royalties (in excess of $500 million) from an anti-cancer drug, Alimta, that was developed by the pharmaceutical company Eli Lilly in cooperation with, and based on decades-long research by, Professor Taylor. Suspended from the ceiling in the atrium (Taylor Commons) is a sculpture, "Resonance," consisting of multiple ovoid forms covered in semitransparent white cloth. The work is by Kendall Buster, who studied microbiology before pursuing art; it was commissioned specifically for the building and was inspired by models employed to represent molecular structures.

FRIST CAMPUS CENTER opened in 2000 in a location which, by then, had become the geographic center of a campus that over more than two centuries had expanded to the south, east, and west from its historic initial footprint in the immediate environs of Nassau Hall. The core of Frist was the former Palmer Hall, which was built in 1908 to house the University's burgeoning programs of teaching and research in physics and electrical engineering. A $48 million renovation and expansion of Palmer, designed by Robert Venturi '47 *50 and Denise Scott Brown and supported by a $25 million gift from the family of former US Senator and Princeton trustee William H. Frist '74, created a 185,000-square-foot facility that houses a wide range of programs and uses and meets needs of undergraduate students, graduate students, faculty, staff, alumni, and campus visitors.

Interest in creating a campus center of this kind dates back at least to the mid-1920s when candidates for student office included the idea in their campaign platforms and President John Grier Hibben engaged in serious discussion with the trustees about a possible location at the northeast corner of Prospect Avenue for what he called "a common ground for campus life."

By 1931, the proposed location had moved to the site of Reunion Hall, between Stanhope Hall and West College (now Morrison Hall). At their June meeting that year the trustees tentatively approved plans for a $400,000 building that would contain a variety of dining spaces; offices for student publications, the student government, and the Graduate Council (precursor of the Alumni Council); rehearsal space for musical groups; game rooms and lounges; spaces to host visiting athletic teams; and suites to provide overnight accommodations for visiting lecturers.

The Great Depression derailed the plans. In the 1940s, Murray-Dodge served as a gathering space for students and soldiers, and in 1954 sections of East Pyne and Chancellor Green were converted into a small social center and cafeteria, augmented between 1973 and 1983 by a pub in the rotunda of Chancellor Green that closed after New Jersey raised its drinking age to 21.

At the dedication of Frist in 2000, President Harold Shapiro called it "the absolute epicenter of campus life" and a "milestone for Princeton's history."

Frist offers a multi-station food gallery; an organic, sustainable, local food venue named Café Vivian in honor of President Shapiro's wife, Dr. Vivian Shapiro; a coffee, pastry, and ice cream stand named Witherspoon's; and a convenience store.

On its main level it supports mail and package delivery for students and offers a game room, a large screen television lounge, an office that sells tickets for campus performances, a large triangle sculpture placed by the Triangle Club, and an exhibit titled "Leaping Tiger and Saber Tooth" that was relocated from the natural history museum in neighboring Guyot Hall. There is also an 18-foot digital display wall between the coffee shop and the main stairwell. On its lowest level it has a reception area and a multipurpose space that can be configured as one large room (it is where the annual flu fest takes place) or as two or three smaller rooms.

On its second and third floors, Frist houses the Pace Center for Civic Engagement, the McGraw Center for Teaching and Learning, the Women*s Center, the Lesbian Gay Bisexual Transgender Center, the office of disability services, and the office of diversity and inclusion. It also houses the offices of the undergraduate student government and a 240-seat film/performance theater.

The East Asian library is located in Frist, as are offices for some of the faculty in East Asian and Near Eastern Studies, whose departments are based in the directly connected Jones Hall. Among the classrooms in Frist is the historic room 302, configured much as it was almost a century ago when Albert Einstein lectured there.

Frist frequently houses exhibits of various kinds. On permanent display are a plaque designed to look like orange ribbons that includes the name of every donor to the 1996–2000 anniversary campaign that raised $1.14 billion, and two quilts: the Class of 1935 reunions quilt that includes 50 years of reunion jackets, and the Class of 1965 reunion quilt that includes class jackets from 1932 to 1973 and the jacket of the Princeton band. Throughout the building, painted on its walls in the form of stylized graffiti, are 41 quotations by and about Princeton and Princetonians. The walls of Café Vivian include more than a hundred photographs, paintings, drawings, book and magazine covers, posters, postcards, and other representations of Princeton's history.

The north lawn of Frist is occasionally the venue for protest activities, just beyond the free-standing arcade whose top edge subtly spells out the name of the building. The more expansive south lawn hosts parties, reunions events, and gatherings of various kinds, including the annual Fristfest which celebrates the end of the academic year with games, entertainment, and food.

Looking back from the lawn, a careful observer can find the University shield imprinted on the building's glass south wall, and a viewer of the television series *House* may recognize Frist as the exterior of the fictitious Princeton-Plainsboro teaching hospital that is portrayed in that series' opening credits.

FUNDRAISING. Two years after the College of New Jersey was founded in 1746, a trustee remarked, "the principal thing we now want is a proper fund to enable us to go on with this expensive undertaking." A committee was formed, and Princeton's long history of fundraising began.

In the beginning, funds came from lotteries conducted on the College's behalf and subscriptions from colonists in New Jersey, New York, and Pennsylvania. (For one early lottery the trustees commissioned Benjamin Franklin to print 8,000 tickets, which were distributed in Philadelphia, New York, Boston, Virginia, and elsewhere—although not in New Jersey where the lottery was not allowed.)

Early nonmonetary gifts included the land on which the College was located and other nearby lands that provided it with fuel. Nathaniel FitzRandolph, who donated the 4.5 acres on which Nassau Hall was built, was a determined fundraiser who rode among his family and neighbors to solicit donations, eventually raising some £1,700, far more than the £1,000 the trustees required to bring the College to Princeton. (In the nineteenth and twentieth centuries there were several important—and sizeable—gifts of land, including the Potter, Springdale, and Olden farms, and Carnegie Lake in 1906.)

As Nassau Hall was being constructed, the trustees pursued the first "naming opportunity" associated with a major capital project when they asked "to dignify the edifice now erecting at Princeton" with the name of Jonathan Belcher, then the governor of New Jersey. Belcher declined the honor, suggesting instead that the building be named in honor of King William the Third of the House of Nassau. Belcher became an important early benefactor when he gave the young college his 474-volume library and other gifts, including the University's first donations of works of art.

Then as now fundraising required travel. In 1753 founding trustee Gilbert Tennent and Samuel Davies, later the College's fourth president, left on an expedition to Great Britain and Ireland seeking donations. They raised more than 10 times their goal of £300; the funds were used to build Nassau Hall and the president's house. They were away for 14 months, including a five-week sea voyage out and a 13-week voyage back; both trips were marked by storms and when they returned Davies was nearly dead from acute seasickness.

Early presidents traveled throughout the colonies seeking funds. On returning from one such arduous trip, Aaron Burr Sr. learned of the death of Governor Belcher and, despite exhaustion and a high fever, wrote the funeral sermon and rode to Elizabethtown on horseback to deliver it. He returned to Princeton grievously ill and died several weeks later. Shortly after John Witherspoon arrived at Princeton he traveled to New York and Boston, and then a year later he began a continuing practice of fundraising tours to Virginia and other parts of the south.

James Leslie 1759, a schoolteacher in New York City, received 13 British pounds from the College to help cover the cost of attendance when he was an undergraduate, and when he died in 1792 he left his carefully guarded savings as a perpetual fund "for the education of poor and pious youth." His was the University's first endowed scholarship.

Early fundraising was opportunistic. It largely aimed at keeping the college operating, although funds were also raised to meet specific purposes, such as rebuilding Nassau Hall after the fires of 1802 and 1855. Uneasy about the ad hoc nature of gifts, soon-to-be president John Maclean Jr. 1816 established a permanent endowment fund in 1853. But the endowment grew slowly, as Princeton continued to depend on annual gifts to meet its operating expenses and on the generosity of large donors to fund new buildings and other substantial capital improvements.

A number of these donors were women, including Susan Dod Brown, who funded Brown and Dod halls; Harriet Crocker Alexander, who provided the funds to build Alexander Hall; Margaret Olivia Slocum Sage, who funded the construction of Holder Hall and half of Madison Hall; and Josephine Ward Thomson Swann, who made the first gift to support construction of the graduate college.

Women continued to make transformative gifts throughout the twentieth century, including the $35 million donation of Marie Robertson and her husband, Charles Robertson 1926, to support the graduate program of the school of Public and International Affairs; Ethel Stockwell Jadwin's $27 million bequest that funded Jadwin Gym, Jadwin Hall, and Fine Hall; and the gift of Meg Whitman '77 that led to the construction of Whitman College. The tradition continued into the twenty-first century with, among other gifts, a donation from Mellody Hobson '91 and the Hobson/Lucas Family Foundation to replace First College, the former Wilson College, with Hobson College.

During Maclean's presidency the idea of class reunions caught on, and with them class gifts. At its 10th reunion the Class of 1859 endowed a senior prize in English, and a year later the Class of 1860 founded a graduate fellowship in experimental science. The Class of 1866 gave the clock in the cupola of Nassau Hall at its 10th reunion. In 1857 Silas Holmes gave Princeton its first endowed chair, in belles-lettres, and other endowed professorships soon followed. By 1900 there were 16.

The two donors who were most instrumental in the late nineteenth and early twentieth century in changing Princeton from a small college to a major university were John Cleve Green and Moses Taylor Pyne 1877. Green, the brother of the chancellor of New Jersey, Henry Woodhull Green 1829, gave the land at the northeast corner of the campus that now contains Firestone Library, the University Chapel, and McCosh Hall; the College's first classroom building, the original Dickinson Hall; its first library, Chancellor Green; and its first school of Science. When the John C. Green School of Science burned down in 1928, his name was moved across the street to what was then an engineering building and remains today as Green Hall. Green also gave professorships, and his estate helped pay for Edwards Hall and the College's first chemical laboratory, now Aaron Burr Hall. In 1889 his legatees purchased and donated the 155-acre Potter Farm that extended from the campus to the Delaware and Raritan Canal between Washington Road and the railroad.

Pyne and his family funded Upper and Lower Pyne halls, Pyne Library (now East Pyne), Pyne Tower at the graduate college, and the first residence for graduate students at Merwick; he also contributed to many other benefactions; built 23 faculty houses in the Broadmead area east of campus that he gave to the University; and annually made up any deficits that arose from introduction of the preceptorial system in 1905.

In the twentieth century four donors made individual gifts of $100 million or more: Gerhard Andlinger '52, who gave $100 million to create the Andlinger Center for Energy and the Environment and also funded the Andlinger Center for the Humanities; Peter Lewis '55, who gave $101 million to endow the Lewis Center for the Arts and also funded Lewis Library for the sciences and the Lewis-Sigler Institute for Integrative Genomics; William Scheide '36, who gave Princeton a library valued in the range of $300 million and provided funding to reconstruct and expand the Woolworth Center of Musical Studies and to construct the Scheide Caldwell House as part of the Andlinger Center for the Humanities; and Gordon Wu '58, who gave $100 million to support the school of Engineering and Applied Science and also funded the construction of Wu Hall in Butler College, Bowen Hall, and professorships in engineering and Chinese studies.

As transformative as these and many other major capital gifts have been, Princeton realized early that "her loyal, supportive alumni were her most important hope for continuing strength and sustenance." In 1904 the trustees established an alumni organization, the Committee of Fifty, to raise funds for "the immediate necessities and future development of the University."

Systematic annual appeals to the alumni body for unrestricted gifts began in 1940 with the establishment of Annual Giving under the leadership of founding chair Harold Helm 1920. During its first year it raised $80,000 from 18 percent of the alumni. Eighty years later it was raising more than $66 million, and over those 80 years almost 90 percent of undergraduate alumni participated at some time, with significant amounts also being contributed by graduate alumni and parents. Gifts through Annual Giving are unrestricted and immediately available; in recent years they have provided nearly 10 percent of the University's overall budget for educational expenses.

In 1956 the University established a development office to raise funds for endowment, construction, student aid, and other needs. In 1959, early in the presidency of Robert Goheen '40 *48, Princeton launched its first comprehensive capital campaign with a goal of $53 million. By its conclusion in 1962 it had raised almost $61 million from 17,925 donors, including the funding needed to construct what was then a state-of-the-art Engineering Quadrangle, the Woolworth music building, homes for the school of Architecture and the art museum, and the dormitories later known as the Old New Quad.

Between 1970 and 1974 the University conducted a development program among a select group of donors that brought in $127.2 million, $2.2 million over goal.

Recognizing that capital campaigns had become an integral part of planning for Princeton's future, President William Bowen initiated a study in 1977 to determine the University's needs over a 10- to 15-year period. This led to a five-year "Campaign for Princeton," launched on Alumni Day in 1982 with a goal of $275 million. Unlike many other universities, Princeton integrated Annual Giving into its capital campaign, with all alumni, including capital donors, encouraged to support Annual Giving.

In January 1984, the trustees increased the goal of the campaign to $330 million, and when it ended in 1986 more than $410 million had been raised. The campaign had many beneficiaries, including the new system of residential colleges and the creation of a new department of Molecular Biology and its new home in Lewis Thomas Laboratory.

In 1995, under the leadership of President Harold Shapiro, the University launched a five-year "Anniversary Campaign for Princeton" in conjunction with the celebration of its 250th anniversary. The campaign raised a total of $1.14 billion, far surpassing its original goal of $750 million, with participation by 78 percent of all undergraduate alumni. (A plaque naming all 58,358 donors hangs in the main stairwell of the Frist Campus Center.) The campaign results included a five-year total of $154 million in Annual Giving funds; Annual Giving set new records in each of the five years of the campaign.

The campaign's capital gifts included 60 percent for new endowment, 21 percent for construction, and 19 percent for term support. The campaign significantly strengthened Princeton's capacity to provide financial aid. New facilities included academic space at McDonnell Hall for physics, the Friend Center for Engineering Education, Wallace Hall for the social sciences, the Bendheim Center for Finance, and the Icahn Laboratory for genomics; dormitory space at Scully Hall; athletic space at Princeton Stadium, Weaver Stadium, the Class of 1952 Stadium, and the Shea Rowing Center; and such welcome additions to the campus as the Frist Campus Center, the Cotsen Children's Library, and Berlind Theater.

Under President Shirley Tilghman the University launched its fourth major fundraising campaign in 2007. The five-year "Aspire" campaign exceeded its $1.75 billion goal by raising $1.88 billion. More than 65,000 donors (undergraduate and graduate alumni, corporations and foundations, parents, and friends), including 77 percent of all undergraduate alumni, contributed more than 271,000 separate gifts, and among other purposes the gifts established 26 new professorships, 120 new undergraduate scholarships, and 25 new graduate fellowships. Over the five years of the campaign Annual Giving contributed more than $254.5 million in unrestricted support.

Notable achievements included the gifts from Peter Lewis and Gerhard Andlinger to support the Lewis Center for the Arts and the Andlinger Center for Energy and the Environment; a Grand Challenges initiative to allow faculty and students to work on developing sustainable energy, combating infectious diseases, and overcoming natural resource limitations in developing countries; the construction of Sherrerd Hall for the department of Operations Research and Financial Engineering and a new complex to house the Princeton Neuroscience Institute and the Psychology department; new dormitories for Butler College; and funding to enhance many other academic areas, financial aid, international programs, athletics, and community service.

In 2014 President Christopher Eisgruber and the trustees launched a comprehensive strategic planning process "to guide the University's ongoing efforts to enhance Princeton's core commitments to excellence in teaching and research and to such bedrock principles as affordability, diversity, inclusivity, and service." The 2016 plan identified three strategic priorities: supporting excellence in the University's core mission, meeting Princeton's responsibilities for leadership, and responding to technology's impact. It called for a 10 percent increase in the size of the undergraduate student body, which would require housing for an additional 500 students. An update to the plan in 2019 devoted added attention to the development of a Lake Campus and the future of the Princeton Plasma Physics Laboratory.

In 2018 the University announced gifts that would help fund construction of two new residential colleges just south of Poe Field to accommodate the 500 additional students and provide swing space to enable renovation of the University's existing housing stock and support future expansion. The new colleges are expected to open in academic year 2022–23. In 2020 the University announced Hobson's gift to replace First College, and a $20 million gift from Kwanza Jones '93 and José E. Feliciano '94 to name two adjoining dormitories in one of the new colleges then under construction.

In 2018 the University announced that Sir David Adjaye had been selected as design architect for a new Princeton University Art Museum, and in 2019 it announced a gift from Eric '76 and Wendy Schmidt to renovate and expand historic Guyot Hall as a new home for the department of Computer Science.

GARRETT, ROBERT 1897 became a trustee of Princeton in 1905 at the age of 29. He went on to serve the University for 40 years as charter trustee and for 16 more as trustee emeritus. He also served as president of his class for 64 years.

Garrett's father, Thomas Harrison Garrett 1868, died in 1888. While Robert Garrett and his two older brothers, Horatio W. Garrett 1895 and John W. Garrett 1895, were in college their mother, Alice, lived at 1 Bayard Lane in the house later occupied by the family of Edgar Palmer 1903, a house bequeathed to the University in 1968 by Palmer's widow, Zilph Palmer, to be used as a guest house. Alice Garrett's home was a center of hospitality for students in the 1890s; they later erected a tablet in her memory in Alexander Hall.

Robert Garrett excelled in track and field as an undergraduate, serving as captain of the team in both his junior and senior years. In 1896 he organized and personally financed an expedition for himself and three classmates to Athens for the modern revival of the ancient Olympic Games. Garrett stood out among the competitors from all nations, winning two first places and two seconds. One of his firsts was in the discus throw, in which he had never competed before.

Garrett also helped organize and finance an archaeological expedition to Syria, led by Howard Crosby Butler 1892 in 1899–1900. This expedition stimulated Garrett to start a collection of Near Eastern manuscripts that he gave to the University in 1942; at that time it consisted of 10,000 titles in Arabic, Persian, and Turkish, as well as several thousand European and American manuscripts. The Garrett Collection remains one of the principal scholarly resources of the department of Near Eastern Studies and is still without a peer in the United States.

GAUSS, CHRISTIAN, one of Woodrow Wilson's original preceptors and third dean of the college, had, in Edmund Wilson's phrase, "an imaginative gift of entering into other people's points of view." It was this quality that made him a great teacher of literature and an illuminating critic. It had much to do as well with his becoming, in his time, perhaps the best-known college dean in America.

Gauss was born and brought up in Ann Arbor, Michigan, and worked his way through the University of Michigan in three years. He began working after school early in life, and when he graduated from college at the age of 20, he could already look back on a versatile career as baker's boy, grocery clerk, farm hand, drug clerk, bill collector, bank clerk, tutor, and barkeeper at county fairs.

After college Gauss worked for a time as a newspaper correspondent in Paris, taught at Michigan and at Lehigh University, and was called to Princeton in 1905 as one of the youngest of its first preceptors. Two years later, at the age of 29, he was promoted to full professor. He became chair of the department of Modern Languages in 1912 and served until 1936. In 1925 he was appointed dean of the college, and in 1929 he was named first incumbent of a chair in modern languages endowed by the Class of 1900. He occupied both positions until his retirement in 1946.

Gauss also served as literary editor of the *Alumni Weekly*, reorganizer and adviser of the Press Club, guide and friend of the *Nassau Literary Magazine*, trustee and vice president of Princeton University Press, chair of the University Council on Athletics, and founder and first chair of the Creative Arts program.

Gauss' courses on Dante and on French writers of the Romantic Period profoundly influenced many Princeton students of literature in the first half of the 20th century. Edmund Wilson 1916, the literary critic, described the influence Gauss exerted on him, John Peale Bishop 1917, F. Scott Fitzgerald 1917, and other undergraduate writers for the *Nassau Literary Magazine*. "He made us all want to write something in which every word, every cadence, every detail, should perform a definite function in producing an intense effect."

Gauss served as dean of the college in an era plagued by Prohibition (which he publicly opposed), the Great Depression, and the Second World War. There were riots in the Prohibition era. One in the spring of 1926 involved a good deal of noise and jostling and some jeering of volunteer firemen, but no violence to any person or property; he downplayed its significance when called by the press. But in the fall of 1930 when students, after a football rally, tore down the statue of the Christian Student and rushed out onto Nassau Street, rocking an interurban bus with women and children in it, he publicly castigated them for their "Yahooism," and the ringleaders were subsequently suspended for a year.

As dean, Gauss came to be appreciated for his sympathy and human understanding. He showed his regard for those he had to discipline in the early years of his deanship by dedicating his book *Life in College* (1930) to them. In the latter years of his deanship, Gauss continued to command the same respect and admiration he had won at the beginning. "As a dean he was still in the best sense a teacher," recalled the writer John N. Brooks Jr. '42, who in college was chairman of the *Princetonian* and a member of the discipline committee.

GENERAL COUNSEL, THE OFFICE OF, was created in 1972 by incoming president William Bowen to provide in-house legal counsel on a broad range of topics and oversee the engagement of outside counsel when specialized expertise was needed. Today the office remains responsible for addressing all legal issues pertaining to or arising out of the activities of the University; it does not provide legal advice to individual faculty, staff, or students related to legal matters outside the scope of University business.

The first general counsel was Thomas H. Wright Jr. '62, who came to the University in 1972 from the Ford Foundation. Two years later he was also appointed secretary of the University. In 1990 Wright stepped down as general counsel and was promoted to the position of vice president and secretary. A year later Howard Ende was named general counsel, and in 2002 Ende was succeeded by Peter McDonough.

Ramona Romero succeeded McDonough in 2014, and in 2019 was also named a vice president of the University. Romero came to the University from the position of general counsel at the US Department of Agriculture. She was a former national president of the Hispanic National Bar Association and the founder of its Latina Commission; in 2020 the association honored her with its President's Award for her "instrumental work" helping to prevent termination by the federal government of the Deferred Action for Childhood Arrivals (DACA) program which protected immigrants who came to the United States as children from deportation. She played a leading role in preparing a lawsuit filed by the University, a member of the Class of 2018, and Microsoft that went all the way to the US Supreme Court.

Romero leads a staff of nine lawyers (including herself) whose areas of practice include advancement and gifts; endowment and restricted funds; antitrust; art museum and library; business transactions; contracting and procurement; transaction authority; export control and trade sanctions; facilities, real estate, development, and construction; finance and treasury; insurance and risk management; freedom of expression and freedom of association; health and safety; public safety; housing and leasing; intellectual property; international law; immigration; labor and employment; benefits; nondiscrimination (including Title IX and disability); the Princeton Plasma Physics Laboratory; privacy; information technology; information security; related organizations; alumni affairs; research and technology transfer; student affairs; athletics; and tax.

GEOSCIENCES, THE DEPARTMENT OF. Instruction in geology was first offered at Princeton from 1818 to 1822 with courses in paleontology. The discipline then languished for several decades until the arrival of Arnold Guyot in 1855, who laid the foundation for a focus on the study of geology and physical geography that would mark the department for over a century.

Until 1873 Guyot was the sole faculty member teaching geology. During the following 10 years four other faculty members came to Princeton to offer courses in mineralogy, physical geography, vertebrate paleontology, and biology. A department of Geology was formally created in 1904 with a faculty of six. A year later Charles H. Smyth arrived to teach petrology (the study of the structure and origins of rocks); he was the father of two other Princeton professors, the chemist Charles P. Smyth 1916 *1917 and the physicist Henry De W. Smyth 1918 *1921.

The department moved to Guyot Hall in 1909 under chair William "Geology Bill" Scott, a colorful figure and faculty stalwart for 50 years (from 1880 to 1930) who launched a series of bone-collecting expeditions in the Rocky Mountains early in his career. It was Scott who shaped Princeton's international reputation in the earth sciences in the early days of the department, and Smyth who attracted graduate students, especially in the relatively new fields of petrology and chemical geology in which he taught.

When it opened, Guyot Hall housed the department's famed museum of natural history, which grew out of a geological collection that had been installed in the Faculty Room of Nassau Hall in 1874 with what was then only the second-ever mounted dinosaur skeleton in the world. The collection was augmented through Scott's College Scientific Expeditions—nine in total—which made spectacular discoveries in the American West and established the department as a leader in fieldwork.

From 1920 to 1930, a new generation of geologists arrived, and in the years leading up to World War II the department experienced a large increase in undergraduate and graduate enrollment. During the war, the faculty introduced hundreds of armed forces trainees to the techniques of map and terrain interpretation as part of their officer training.

Beginning in 1950, Harry Hess *32 shaped the department into an entity that would be recognizable to modern graduates. A mineralogist, Hess served as chair for 16 years. He later developed into a remarkable generalist and was instrumental, for example, in arranging for Princeton to be among the institutions examining the first moon rocks brought back by Apollo astronauts. His most important achievement, and one of the department's great contributions to twentieth century science, was the formulation in the early 1960s of the concept of sea-floor spreading and the subsequent development of plate tectonics.

Geophysics became an important part of the departmental program of instruction and research in the early 1960s, and in 1968 the department changed its name to the department of Geological and Geophysical Sciences (which was later pared to the more succinct department of Geosciences). Its profile was magnified through the work of W. Jason Morgan *64 and Fred Vine, who expanded on Hess' ideas. Vine demonstrated the reality of the timing of sea-floor spreading through magnetic studies of the sea floor, and Morgan defined and described the plates that make up the jigsaw puzzle of the earth's crust.

During the 1970s the department maintained a cooperative program in Water Resources with Civil Engineering; another in Geophysical Fluid Dynamics with the National Oceanographic and Atmospheric Administration's laboratory on the Forrestal campus; and still another in Geological Engineering with the school of Engineering and Applied Science. The department remained relatively small, with a full-time faculty of 16.

In the late 1980s, the department shifted its focus toward environmental geosciences or biogeochemistry with the hiring of oceanographer Jorge Sarmiento, one of the first scientists nationally to underscore the importance of oceans in climate science and the global carbon cycle.

Another iconic figure of the modern department was Gerta Keller, a professor of paleontology and geology hired in 1984. Keller's research expanded the debate around mass extinction and drove the theory of Deccan volcanism as the primary cause for the disappearance of megafauna like the dinosaurs, using studies on single-celled marine organisms called foraminifera as undergirding for her work.

In 1990 the department hired Samuel Philander, who was born and raised in South Africa and later emigrated to the US with his family to escape apartheid. Philander's research focused on equatorial oceans and the fluid dynamics of tropical oceans and the El Nino phenomenon, subjects on which he became a world authority. He served as the department chair from 1994 to 2001, expanded its biogeochemistry focus, and established the prestigious Hess Postdoctoral Fellowship.

The 1990s saw the hiring of a series of remarkable biogeochemists, including Francois Morel and Michael Bender. When Morel joined the faculty in 1994, he was already a world leader in the chemistry of natural waters. Morel's research helped to establish the field of marine biogeochemistry. Bender, who joined the faculty in 1997, was a pioneer in environmental geochemistry; during his 17 years in the department he made fundamental discoveries on global-scale chemical cycles as they have occurred in the past and occur today among different climactic conditions.

Daniel Sigman joined the faculty in 1999, using nitrogen isotopes to investigate the history of biogeochemical cycles in order to understand the causes of past changes in the atmospheric concentration of carbon dioxide; the role of this greenhouse gas in the waxing and waning of ice ages; and the ocean's response to climate change.

Bess Ward, an authority on the marine and global nitrogen cycle, arrived in 1998, succeeding as chair the world-famous seismologist Anthony Dahlen. Ward was the main sea-going oceanographer on campus heading into 2020. One of her stated goals was increasing the number of women faculty in geosciences; under her leadership, the department added three women to the faculty. In the early 2010s, graduate students and postdocs started the Princeton Women in Geosciences, a peer mentoring and networking group.

In 2010 the department again expanded its focus, this time to encompass climate science. In collaboration with the Princeton Program in Atmospheric and Oceanic Sciences, an autonomous program within Geosciences, Princeton received a major, six-year National Science Foundation grant for the study of the southern ocean that sought to determine its influence on climate and biogeochemistry. The project, directed by Sarmiento, deployed an army of autonomous robotic observing floats to collect data on temperature, current, and salinity. The project was renewed in 2019 for another six years.

Despite the shifts in emphasis and expansion of scope, the department has never increased much in size; it operates today with fewer than 20 faculty members, at least half of them in biogeochemistry and climate. Department research ranges from earthquakes to molecular biology, with a broad and celebrated variety of approaches for the study and understanding of climate change.

Today, the department is a world leader in earth history, biogeochemistry, and climate science, and its scientific initiatives range from the measurement and modeling of biogeochemical cycles and global climate change, to high-pressure mineral physics, to seismic tomographic imaging of the earth's interior and the analysis of terrestrial and planetary tectonics.

GERMAN, THE DEPARTMENT OF. German was not established as a department until 1958, yet language study of German can be traced back more than 120 years. Prior to the 1830s, students who wanted to study any of the "modern languages" did so by hiring their own outside instructors. In 1830 the College appointed its first regular instructor of French and Spanish, and in 1836 Benedict Jaeger—an Austrian originally hired as curator of the zoological museum and lecturer in natural history—taught German as well as French, Spanish, and Italian, all as the College's sole professor of modern languages.

Jaeger discharged his diverse duties until 1843. Thereafter, German was taught by a succession of short-term instructors until the appointment in 1857 of the German-born Karl Langlotz (better known as the composer of the music to Princeton's anthem, "Old Nassau"), who served until 1869.

Although these early instructors had faculty standing, students did not receive academic credit for their offerings until 1868, when President James McCosh made instruction in languages a regular part of the curriculum. An 1870 gift from John Woodhull 1828 established the Woodhull Professorship of Modern Languages, and the first incumbent of the chair was the larger-than-life swashbuckling General Joseph Kargé, a native of Prussia. In addition to teaching French and German, he also accompanied students on summer field trips to explore the American West.

Kargé's arrival marked the beginning of a new era for the teaching of German. A number of additional faculty members were appointed over the next three decades, including two young Princeton alumni, J. Preston Hoskins 1891 and George Madison Priest 1894. When President Woodrow Wilson organized the University into academic departments in 1904, the department of Modern Languages came into existence. In 1905, when Wilson instituted the revolutionary system of precepts, Hoskins and Priest were among the first preceptors and remained in the department for the rest of their careers, teaching into the 1930s and remembered warmly by the first generations of students to experience the new pedagogy.

From the late 1930s into the 1950s, Princeton became a hub for many German writers and scholars who had chosen exile in response to the organized burning of books deemed "un-German" by the Nazi regime when it seized power in Germany in 1933. They were determined to rescue major voices in German literature and culture from extinction. Some, like Erwin Panofsky and Erich von Kahler, had been renowned professors at major German universities. They arrived in the late 1930s, taking joint appointments at the University and the Institute for Advanced Study, and passing the rest of their academic lives teaching in Princeton.

Ernst Hartwig Kantorowicz, who had left Frankfurt for Oxford and then the University of California at Berkeley, refused to take a loyalty oath required by that university in the early years of McCarthyism and left California to come to Princeton in 1949; he stayed until his death in 1963.

Others made shorter visits but left lasting legacies. Thomas Mann, the novelist and winner of the 1929 Nobel Prize in Literature, held the position of lecturer in humanities during the academic years 1938–40, financed principally by the Rockefeller Foundation. In 1939 the University bestowed on him an honorary doctorate.

Erich Auerbach, whose *Mimesis* is a seminal work in literary criticism, lived in Princeton for a year, and in 1949 gave the first series of lectures in the "Princeton Seminars in Literary Criticism," now called the "Gauss Seminars in Criticism." In 1953, Hannah Arendt gave six lectures as part of the Gauss Seminars. The first woman to be invited to give a Gauss Seminar, she returned to campus in 1959 as a visiting professor.

In 1957, the distinguished Germanist Victor Lange, who had been born in Leipzig, Germany, and had studied in Oxford, Munich, Leipzig, Toronto, and Paris, left Cornell University to join the department's faculty. The next year, the department of Modern Languages transitioned to two separate departments, Germanic Languages and Romance Languages, and Lange became the first chair of the department of Germanic Languages and Literatures and the Woodhull Professor of Modern Languages.

Lange enlarged the size and scope of the department with a number of significant faculty appointments in the 1960s, including the literary scholar (and later chair, and then dean of the graduate school) Theodore Ziolkowski, and Kafka translator and theorist Stanley Corngold. Lange, who retired from Princeton in 1977, was the president of the International Association of Germanists from 1965–70 and received two Guggenheim fellowships as well as international recognition. The department of German's senior thesis prize is named in his honor.

Over the course of the decades, Princeton's German department has continued Lange's tradition of expanding the scholarly scope of German studies to include strengths in related fields such as philosophy, critical theory, art history, media studies, and the visual arts. Besides covering the traditional curriculum of German literature and culture from the Middle Ages through the present, with particular emphasis on Romanticism, poetics, narrative structure, history and theory of the novel, and second-language acquisition, the department also offers five other tracks. A concentrator in the department might choose: study of two literatures, reading in German and another language; German philosophy and intellectual history; media and aesthetics, focusing on art, film, music, sound technology, and/or media theory; Germanic linguistics, including the history and structure of the German language; or the joint program in German culture and politics, combining a concentration in German literature and culture with a concentration in German/European politics and political theory that includes courses in the department of Politics.

Taking a rigorous interdisciplinary approach, faculty work with a variety of methods and objects that include critical theory, visual culture, history of science, systems theory, feminism, material culture, and psychoanalysis. Faculty members have directed other academic programs on campus, including the program in European Cultural Studies, the program in Media & Modernity in the school of Architecture, and the program in Medieval Studies. Many of the department's faculty are affiliated with other academic departments, such as Art and Archaeology, Comparative Literature, French and Italian, and the school of Architecture.

The department has an active program of visiting professors from German universities, and it benefits from the strategic partnership with Humboldt University in Berlin that Princeton established in 2012. The partnership supports departments, programs, and centers seeking resources to sustain ongoing transnational research and teaching collaborations. Based on the success of the institutional collaborations and flow of scholars, students, and ideas between the two institutions, the partnership agreement with Humboldt was renewed in spring 2017.

Princeton's graduate program in German offers students the opportunity to participate in a lively and engaged intellectual community composed of scholars working within an unusually wide range of interdisciplinary and theoretical approaches to German culture. In any given year, as many as 20 percent of graduate students in German study abroad. In addition, since the summer of 2011 the department has organized an international summer school for media studies in cooperation with Bauhaus Universität Weimar. The annual weeklong program alternates between Princeton and Weimar.

The department also offers undergraduates opportunities abroad with the Princeton-in-Munich summer language immersion program, begun in 2000 and taught by departmental faculty. The longstanding Summer Work Program, Princeton's oldest international undergraduate internship program, gives dozens of students each year the opportunity to live and work in Germany.

GILDERSLEEVE, BASIL LANNEAU 1849 was one of Princeton's most eminent graduates in the mid-nineteenth century. Andrew Fleming West 1874 called him "the most brilliant, richly furnished, and powerful master in Greek studies" the country had produced. Professor Paul Shorey of the University of Chicago, himself a distinguished Greek scholar, said that, during 50 years of American classical scholarship, "the figure of Gildersleeve had dominated throughout."

The son of a Presbyterian minister in Charleston, South Carolina, Gildersleeve read the Bible "from cover to cover" when he was five, and before he was 13 he had learned enough Latin to read Caesar, Sallust, Cicero, Virgil, and Horace, and enough Greek "to make out" the New Testament.

Such was his precocity that when he entered Princeton as a junior at the age of 16 he was able to devote most of his time to his own reading. "I gave a couple of hours to my classes each day," he recalled in a memoir about his student days, "and then ho! for the wide field of literature—English, French, German, Italian, Spanish." Besides his "multifarious, jubilant reading," he also indulged himself in "composition in prose and rhyme."

He admired the physicist Joseph Henry, "our one great man," and respected John Torrey, who taught chemistry and natural history, and Stephen Alexander, who taught mathematics. "Stevie" so inspired him, he recalled, that although he had always hated mathematics, he earned the best grade in his class.

After graduating from Princeton, Gildersleeve spent three years in Europe, chiefly at German universities. Shortly after his return, Princeton proposed that he join its faculty; but the position offered, he recalled years later, turned out to be so inferior to what he, "a conceited youngster," deemed his due—especially since he had received a PhD with high honors from the University of Göttingen—that negotiations broke off. For three years he pursued philological studies at home and nearly completed a novel. In 1856, just before his 25th birthday, he began a 20-year career as professor of Greek at the University of Virginia.

During the Civil War Gildersleeve became further disenchanted with Princeton "when the authorities thought it necessary to emphasize their loyalty to the Union in a way that exasperated all ardent Southerners like myself." Both of his Princeton roommates, who were Virginians, fell in the first major engagement of the war at Manassas. Gildersleeve himself was severely wounded while serving with the Confederate cavalry.

When the Johns Hopkins University was founded in 1876, Gildersleeve was the first of a small band of scholars invited to develop a school of graduate work and research. A year later Princeton "held out an olive branch," as Gildersleeve put it, by inviting him to make the annual address before the Whig and Cliosophic societies. But he "did not improve matters," he said, by the chief theme of his discourse: "an inquiry why Princeton, which had done so much for divinity, for medicine, for law, for legislation, for arms, had fallen so far short in letters."

Gildersleeve meantime was making his own mark as a man of letters as well as a scholar. In 1880 he founded the *American Journal of Philology*, and for 40 years his personality pervaded its pages. He became famous also for his *Latin Grammar*, his *Syntax of Classical Greek*, his editions of Greek poets, notably Pindar, and several books of critical essays and scholarly studies.

In 1899, at the 50th anniversary of his graduation, Princeton conferred on him an honorary degree—"the seal," he said, "of reconciliation." He took pride, also, in the fact that his son, Raleigh C. Gildersleeve, was the architect of McCosh Hall and Upper and Lower Pyne buildings.

Gildersleeve taught at Johns Hopkins until he was 84 and edited the *Journal of Philology* until he was 89. In his last years he spent most of his time in his book-lined study in his house in Baltimore, reading Greek and writing sonnets.

GLEE CLUB, THE PRINCETON UNIVERSITY, was founded in 1874 in response to an editorial in the February *Nassau Lit* by Andrew Fleming West 1874, later the first dean of the graduate school. The club was formed in March, and it gave its first concert that spring at commencement time. Initially it had only 13 members and a modest repertoire of college songs.

Early in its history, the Glee Club began touring the country; in the winter of 1893, for example, it traveled to 13 cities in the mid-Atlantic, south, and midwest with the Banjo and Mandolin clubs. The next year it ventured as far west as Denver. On campus in the early twentieth century, the club sang at football games until the founding of the University Band in 1920.

In 1907, Charles Burnham became the first professional musician to lead the club. Since that time it has established itself as the largest choral body on campus—it now has about a hundred members, including graduate students as well as undergraduates—and has distinguished itself both nationally and overseas.

The club first achieved national recognition when it performed the American premiere of Igor Stravinsky's *Oedipus Rex* with Leopold Stokowski and the Philadelphia Orchestra in 1931. Four years later, it performed at the Metropolitan Opera House in New York.

In the 1930s the club became a responsibility of the music faculty and in the 1950s, under the direction of long-serving director Walter Nollner, the club traveled outside the United States for the first time, establishing a pattern of international concert tours (now scheduled biennially) to Europe, Asia, South America, and the South Pacific. In 1974 the club celebrated its centennial with a concert in Carnegie Hall, after which a *New York Times* critic complimented the singers on their "flexible, transparent, even airy, massed tone."

The Glee Club presents several major performances on campus each year, and makes numerous special appearances at functions and gatherings. Its most celebrated performing tradition began in 1913 with annual concerts on the eves of the Harvard and Yale football games, presented jointly with their glee clubs. A more recent tradition is annual performances of choral masterworks with professional soloists and orchestra, supported by an endowment fund that honors Nollner.

The club's repertoire includes both sacred and secular music; it ranges from renaissance motets and madrigals, Romantic partsongs, and twenty-first century choral commissions to traditional spirituals, folk music, and college songs. During reunions each year, Glee Club alumni gather in Richardson Auditorium to sing Thomas Tallis' monumental 40-part motet, *Spem in Alium*, before joining in a multigenerational football medley.

Since 2010 the internationally recognized Gabriel Crouch, Princeton's director of choral activities and senior lecturer in music, has directed the Glee Club and a smaller Chamber Choir with 24–40 voices. The

Glee Club, he says, offers hard-working Princeton students "a special opportunity to just feel, to live and breathe music."

GOHEEN, ROBERT FRANCIS '40 *48, Princeton's 16th president, was born in Vengurla, India, where his parents were Presbyterian medical missionaries. When he was 15, he left India to complete his high school education at the Lawrenceville School, just down the road from Princeton. Two years later he graduated with honors and entered Princeton with the Class of 1940, following his grandfather, Joseph Goheen 1872 (also a Presbyterian missionary in India), his uncle Rhea Ewing 1924, and his older brother, Richard Goheen '36.

As an undergraduate, Goheen (known then and throughout his life as Bob) served as president of his eating club, Quadrangle, and as a reform-minded member of the Inter-Club Committee, which included the presidents of all the clubs. He was president of the Intramural Athletic Association; a Whig-Clio member known as a "strong persuader"; and an influential participant on the Undergraduate Council. In his junior year he was elected to Phi Beta Kappa. He graduated *magna cum laude* in Classics and *summa cum laude* from the Special Program in the Humanities; was Latin salutatorian at graduation; and was awarded the Pyne Prize, the highest general distinction conferred on an undergraduate.

An athlete all his life, Goheen won numerals as a freshman in soccer and baseball. For the next three years he was a high scorer as inside left on the varsity soccer team, and in his last two years his team won the league championship. After graduation, while enrolled as a first-year graduate student in the Classics department, he coached a freshman soccer team that lost only to Pennsylvania and defeated a previously unbeaten Yale team. Later he became an avid tennis player and golfer, and he was a life-long Princeton sports fan.

The 1940 senior class poll named him "biggest grind," "busiest," "most scholarly," and "most brilliant," but also "best all-around man."

In 1940 Goheen married Margaret Skelly of Wilmington, Delaware, and in November 1941 his graduate studies were interrupted when he entered the army, serving first in military intelligence and then in the Pacific, receiving decorations that included the Legion of Merit and the Bronze Star with two clusters. He left the army in 1945 with the rank of lieutenant colonel. Dean Rusk, who served with Goheen during the war and later went on to be president of the Rockefeller Foundation and US secretary of state, once told the Princeton trustees that if he were caught in the middle of a jungle anywhere with enemy soldiers all around and he had one man to choose to be at his side, it would be Goheen.

Following the war, Goheen returned to Princeton to continue his graduate studies. In 1945 he became one of the first four recipients of a Woodrow Wilson Fellowship under a program initiated at Princeton to encourage veterans to pursue careers in teaching and scholarship. He received his MA degree in 1947, and in 1948 he was awarded his PhD.

Goheen was immediately appointed an instructor in the Classics department, and in 1950 he was promoted to assistant professor. His colleagues considered him "a phenomenally good preceptor and an excellent lecturer." His major scholarly work, *The Imagery of Sophocles' Antigone*, was published by Princeton University Press in 1951. As a bicentennial preceptor from September 1951 to June 1954, he was entitled to a year's leave; he spent the year 1952–53 at the American Academy in Rome as a senior fellow.

After returning from Rome, Goheen became director of the national Woodrow Wilson Fellowship Program, a position to which he devoted half his time for the following three years. The program had been greatly expanded since 1945 and had become highly competitive; Goheen spent much of his time on the road, meeting with regional selection committees and becoming well known among educators across the country.

Goheen was highly regarded by the Princeton faculty and when the trustees sought a successor to President Harold Dodds, his colleagues recommended him despite the fact that he was just 37 years old and only an assistant professor. After inviting him to a meeting ostensibly to learn his views about the concerns of the younger faculty, the trustees elected him by unanimous vote on December 7, 1956, and at the same time promoted him to full professor.

For the next 15 years Goheen transformed the University in almost every dimension. He traveled the country on behalf of the University's first comprehensive capital campaign (a $53 million campaign that ended up raising $60.7 million), securing the substantial resources necessary to expand Princeton's capacity to support scholarship and graduate education across all its academic disciplines. In the words of his successor William Bowen *58, he transformed "a good college with pockets of excellence at the graduate level to one of the world's great universities."

Goheen cautiously introduced coeducation in the graduate school in 1961 with the admission of Sabra Meservey *66. The following year eight more women were admitted as graduate students. By 1968 this number had increased to 56, and a year later 200 graduate student women were enrolled.

With respect to undergraduate coeducation, Goheen was quoted in 1965 as saying that "Princeton doesn't have any social problems that coeducation would cure," and even two years later he was still leaning more toward a "co-ordinate education" model under which an all-male Princeton would be complemented by a women's college on the other side of Lake Carnegie.

Despite his own reservations, in June 1967 he persuaded the trustees to authorize a comprehensive study, led by professor of economics Gardner Patterson, of the desirability and feasibility of undergraduate coeducation. He found the Patterson Committee report's recommendation of full coeducation compelling, and after the trustees in January 1969 endorsed coeducation "in principle," he secured their approval three months later to begin enrolling undergraduate women that fall. Asked later about his shift in views between 1965 and 1969, he said "I was just plain wrong in 1965. It's no use pretending you're not wrong when you are."

Motivated both by the Civil Rights Movement and his own sense of fairness, Goheen sought to increase the ethnic and racial diversity of the University. In his 1962 commencement address he said, "The denial of human dignity and equal rights on the blind basis of color or creed is an abomination of our time and cancer in our society. Distinctions which unfairly curb the inherent potentials of individuals or groups are the direct antithesis of the aims of higher education." On October 13, 1963, he told an audience of 1,200 at a human rights gathering at the old Princeton Playhouse in Palmer Square that the University was seeking to enroll larger numbers of Black students; that year Princeton enrolled just 10 Black undergraduates, but by 1971 there were more than 300 Black undergraduates on campus.

When Black students called on him in 1968 to protest the University's initial tepid response to the assassination of Dr. Martin Luther King Jr., he agreed to their proposal to cancel classes for a full day of reflections and tributes that they would lead. When another group of Black students called on him two years later to press for creation of a designated space for students of color, he heard them out. Within a year the University had opened the Third World Center, now the Carl A. Fields Center for Equality and Cultural Understanding, named for the man Goheen brought to Princeton as the University's first Black administrator and later the first Black dean in the Ivy League. In 1967 he agreed to a faculty proposal to establish a research and teaching program in African American culture, and in 1969 a program in African American Studies was founded.

Goheen led the University through a period of intense and turbulent anti-Vietnam War protest with calmness, responsiveness, flexibility, and integrity that earned widespread respect, instituting significant changes in governance and institutional practice while steadfastly insuring that the core values of the University remained intact. In response to a May 1968 rally in front of Nassau Hall he appointed the student-faculty-staff Kelley Committee that proposed creation of the Council of the Princeton University Community (CPUC) and the election of graduating seniors to the Board of Trustees. In response to a May 4, 1970, mass meeting following the American bombing of Cambodia, he endorsed a fall-semester recess to allow undergraduates to engage in campaigning prior to that year's Congressional elections.

Other contentious issues included University investments in South Africa, where a faculty committee recommended divestment, but only from companies that did a primary amount of their business there; the University's role in the governance of the Defense Department-funded Institute for Defense Analyses that rented space in von Neumann Hall, where eventually the University removed itself from any institutional membership; and the role of ROTC on campus, where by 1972 the Navy and Air Force programs had left and the Army, after a year's hiatus, agreed to operate without academic credit for ROTC courses or academic standing for ROTC instructors.

Goheen disclaimed any ambition to be known as a "building president," but a building president he was, with some 25 new buildings constructed on the main campus during his presidency, and still others at the graduate college and the Forrestal campus. Measured in terms of square footage, the physical plant increased by 80 percent, and many older buildings were renovated. Among the additions were a new art museum; a building for the school of Architecture; the Woolworth Center of Musical Studies; Robertson Hall for the school of Public and International Affairs; the Engineering Quadrangle; a computer center at 87 Prospect Avenue; the mathematics and science complex of Peyton, Fine, and Jadwin halls; Jadwin Gymnasium; and new dormitories in the complexes known as the Old New Quad and the New New Quad.

The Old New Quad became the home of Princeton's first residential college, which Goheen created in response to student interest in having an alternative to the eating clubs. In 1970 the University converted two former eating club buildings on Prospect Avenue into a nonresidential alternative to the clubs, Stevenson Hall, and with the advent of coeducation the University renovated and expanded the former Princeton Inn hotel to become a residential college later named for Steve Forbes '70.

During Goheen's presidency, the faculty grew from just under 500 to more than 700, the number of graduate students more than doubled, and the University's annual budget quadrupled. The number of applicants for admission to the college in Goheen's last year was more than two and a half times the number who applied during his first year. With coeducation, the size of undergraduate classes increased from about 800 to about 1,100. A 1969 national survey of graduate programs sponsored by the American Council on Education rated 26 departments at Princeton and ranked 20 of them among the top 10 in the country.

The undergraduate program added flexibility by introducing student-initiated seminars and establishing a University Scholar Program that allowed selected students to craft their own areas of concentration. In addition to African American Studies, other new interdepartmental programs included the History and Philosophy of Science; Science in Human Affairs; Comparative Literature; and East Asian, Latin American, Russian, African, Urban, and Medieval Studies.

In 1966, a New Jersey commission chaired by Goheen urged the state to create a department of higher education and a system of county colleges, convert teacher colleges into multi-purpose institutions, found new state colleges, and establish medical schools—all of which happened. In 1969 Princeton University Press published a selection of Goheen's addresses and other papers under the title *The Human Nature of a University*.

After Goheen announced his intention to retire in June 1972, the *Daily Princetonian* devoted a special issue to the "Goheen Years," hailing him as "a superlative example of what a university president should be." The *Prince* concluded one of its articles by noting "that while other institutions were erupting in violence, Goheen's flexibility and leadership assured . . . a rational approach through even the fastest-changing times."

A year later, at Goheen's final faculty meeting as president, the faculty credited him with "the leadership we needed in a period of anxiety and confusion," and said, "It was not simply that we trusted your judgment, good as it has proved to be . . . We admired your dignity and calmness in times of stress, your open-mindedness and fairness in times of controversy, and your endless patience as we groped towards a solution of our problems. And it is because we trusted you and because you deserved our trust that Princeton still flourishes."

Following his retirement in 1972, Goheen became president of the Council on Foundations, and in 1977 he returned to the land of his birth when he was appointed United States ambassador to India—an ambassador heralded for his deep understanding of the country and his lifelong affection for it. He returned to Princeton in 1981 as a senior fellow in the school of Public and International Affairs and continued to be an active member of the University and the local community.

A fall 2006 Firestone Library exhibition titled "Student, Scholar, President: Robert F. Goheen at Princeton, 1936–2006" recounted his by then 70-year association with the University, and the Mudd Manuscript Library contains videotapes of four hours of interviews with University archivist Dan Linke in which Goheen reflects on his time at Princeton.

When Goheen died in 2008 at the age of 88, then-president Shirley Tilghman said,

> With the passage of time, it becomes more and more clear that Bob Goheen was one of the great presidents of Princeton history. He demonstrated remarkable courage in all he did, from introducing coeducation and increasing the diversity of the student body to strengthening the faculty and leading the University successfully through a time of societal upheaval . . . He was greatly admired and respected for his leadership and vision and attentiveness to the views of others, and widely beloved among Princetonians for the values and personal qualities that were evident from the day he arrived on campus as a freshman and throughout his life.

Bowen described him as "the architect of the modern Princeton" whose vision and character "shaped not only the visible contours of the University but even more its values and commitments," and Harold Shapiro *64, Princeton's eighteenth president, called Goheen "a man of enormous personal courage and integrity who could admit when he was wrong, who listened carefully to others, . . . who had a clear understanding of the University's core values and highest priorities," and who "started us on the path to what Princeton is today: a coeducational, diverse, research university of great international stature,"

Goheen is memorialized on campus by Goheen Walk, which crosses the campus from east to west just south of where Princeton's first residential college was established during his presidency.

GOLF. Princeton's history in competitive golf dates back to the country's first intercollegiate tournament in 1897 and includes an NCAA title in 1940 and dozens of Ivy League championships for the men's and women's teams.

Men's Golf

The start of men's golf closely followed the formation of Springdale Golf Club (originally known as the Princeton Golf Club), which was created by alumni, faculty, and students in 1895. The initial nine-hole course was laid out in a field near campus, and the modern version, situated along Alexander Road, was designed in 1915 by Gerard Lambert and revised by William Flynn in 1926.

In 1897 Princeton played in college golf's first event, finishing third in a four-team intercollegiate tournament with Columbia, Harvard, and Yale in Dobbs Ferry, New York. Princeton's Louis P. Bayard Jr., 1898 won the individual title. Four other Princeton players won the intercollegiate tournament in its early years: Percy Pyne II 1903 (1899), Francis Reinhart 1905 (1903), Albert Seckel 1912 (1909), and J. Simpson Dean 1921 (1921).

Princeton standouts made their mark in national amateur events as well. S. Davidson Herron 1918 won the US Amateur Championship in 1919, defeating 17-year-old Bobby Jones in the final. George T. Dunlap Jr., 1931, Princeton's lone two-time intercollegiate champion, won the 1933 US Amateur and tied for 34th in the inaugural Masters Tournament the following year.

Princeton's team success began in 1914 when the Tigers won the first of 11 intercollegiate championships, including four consecutive titles from 1927 through 1930. The team's first coach, Walter Bourne, arrived in 1928 and remained with the Tigers through 1942. When the NCAA golf championship began in 1939, Princeton and Northwestern tied for second place, two strokes behind champion Stanford. In 1940 Princeton and Louisiana State University shared the championship, the first NCAA team title in University history.

The Tigers' most accomplished amateur player, William Campbell '45, played for Princeton in the years immediately following World War II. Campbell, whose college years were interrupted by military service, won two Eastern Intercollegiate Golf Association (EIGA) individual titles and captained the 1947 Tigers to a 15–0 record and the EIGA team championship. Campbell went on to play in the US Amateur 37 times, winning the championship in 1964. He also represented the United States in the Walker Cup eight times and was a frequent competitor at the Masters, US Open, and British Amateur. In 1990 Campbell was inducted into the World Golf Hall of Fame.

Harry Kinnell, Princeton's coach from 1946 to 1965, led the Tigers to a school-record 161 wins and never had a losing season. Beginning in 1957, the Ivy League crowned as its champion the top Ivy finisher at the EIGA tournament—a designation that Princeton earned in 1961 and 1969, when it won the tournament, and 1972 and 1973, when it was runner-up to Penn State. Two Princetonians won the EIGA individual title in that era: Michael Porter '69 (1968) and Bud Zachary '70 (1969).

Since 1975, the Ivy League has held its own spring tournament to determine the conference champion, and the Princeton men have won the event a league-best 21 times, guided by a string of successful coaches that included Bill Quackenbush (1971–85), Gordon Jaehne (1986–88), Eric Stein (1989–97), and Will Green (2000-present).

In the Ivy Tournament era, 11 Princeton men have won the league's individual championship, including three two-time champions: Steve Loughran '82 (1981 and 1982); Jason Mraz '89 (1987 and 1989); and Steve Dana '94 (1993 and 1994).

Women's Golf

Princeton women's golf began as a club team in the late 1970s, coached by Betty Whelan, a 15-time women's club champion at Springdale. The Tigers split their first two matches against Rutgers in April 1979, winning in New Brunswick before losing at home. Whelan coached the team for nearly a decade, but in that time her effort to gain varsity status gained little traction.

That changed in 1990 when Lisa Olson '80, a member of one of Whelan's early teams and an attorney for the US Department of Justice, took up the cause, aided by the club's new part-time coach, Paget Berger *90, and the American Civil Liberties Union of New Jersey. The University, in its initial response to Olson, wrote that at least five Ivy institutions would have to sponsor women's golf before it could be considered a varsity sport (only Dartmouth and Yale had teams at the time). Olson and the ACLU countered that this amounted to a Catch-22.

After a year of behind-the-scenes discussions, Princeton announced the formation of a combined men's and women's varsity golf program, paving the way for the women to begin competing in the spring of 1992. Eric Stein coached the women from their first varsity campaign until the spring of 2005, overseeing a series of milestones: first tournament win (the Dartmouth Invitational in 1993); first individual Ivy champion (Mary Moan '97, at the inaugural league women's tournament in 1997); and first Ivy team championship (1999). Stein also guided Princeton to Ivy team titles in 2001, 2004, and 2005.

Moan was the program's first star player. She won 16 tournaments in her four years at Princeton and qualified for the NCAA tournament as a senior, finishing tied for 40th. Julia Allison '01 was the first woman to win two Ivy individual titles (1999 and 2001), and Avery Kiser '05 surpassed Allison's feat, winning three straight Ivy tournaments (2002, 2003, and 2004). Two-time champion Susannah Aboff '09 (2008 and 2009) set an Ivy tournament single-round record with her 7-under-par 65 in the opening round in 2008.

Kelly Shon '14 won the Ivy individual title in 2013 and later found success in professional golf as the first Ivy alumna to earn her LPGA tour card. In 2015, her rookie year on tour, Shon placed third at the ShopRite LPGA Classic. In 2017, she finished ninth at the Women's PGA Championship.

Amber Wang '19 became the sixth Princeton woman to win the Ivy individual championship in 2017, helping the Tigers to their first team championship under coach Erika DeSanty, who also led the team to a title in 2018.

Governors. Fifty-one governors of 21 states have been graduates of Princeton, ranging from eighteenth-century figures like "Light-Horse Harry" Lee 1773 of Virginia and William Richardson Davie 1776 of North Carolina, to prominent twentieth-century figures such as Woodrow Wilson 1879 of New Jersey and Adlai Stevenson 1922 of Illinois. Eleven Princetonians have served as governor of New Jersey and seven of North Carolina.*

The complete list follows:

COLORADO

Jared Polis '96 (2019–)

CONNECTICUT

Henry Edwards 1797 (1835–37)

DELAWARE

Pierre S. duPont IV '56 (1977–85)

GEORGIA

Peter Early 1792 (1814–15)
George Troup 1797 (1823–27)
John Forsyth 1799 (1827–29)
George Crawford 1820 (1843–47)
Alfred Colquitt 1844 (1876–82)

ILLINOIS

Adlai Stevenson 1922 (1949–52)

INDIANA

Mitchell E. Daniels Jr.'71 (2005–13)

MARYLAND

John Henry 1769 (1797–98)
Samuel Sprigg 1806 (1819–22)
Robert L. Ehrlich Jr. '79 (2003–07)

MICHIGAN

G. Mennen Williams '33 (1949–61)

MISSOURI

Christopher Bond '60 (1973–77, 1981–85)

NEW HAMPSHIRE

John Winant 1913 (1925–27, 1931–35)

NEW JERSEY

William Paterson 1763 (1790–92)
Aaron Ogden 1773 (1812–13)

---

* One Princeton graduate, Ingram Stainback 1907 (D), served as territorial governor of Hawaii from 1942–51. Thomas Riggs Jr. 1894 (D) served as territorial governor of Alaska from 1918–21.

Mahlon Dickerson 1789 (1815–17)
Samuel Southard 1804 (1832–33)
William Pennington 1813 (1837–43)
Daniel Haines 1820 (1843–44, 1848–51)
Joel Parker 1839 (1863–66, 1872–75)
Robert Stockton Green 1850 (1887–90)
Woodrow Wilson 1879 (1911–13)
Brendan Byrne '49 (1974–82)
Thomas Kean '57 (1982–90)

NEW YORK

Morgan Lewis 1773 (1804–07)
Eliot Spitzer '81 (2007–08)

NORTH CAROLINA

Alexander Martin 1756 (1782–85)
Nathaniel Alexander 1776 (1805–07)
William Richardson Davie 1776 (1798–99)
David Stone 1788 (1808–10)
James Iredell 1806 (1827–28)
Daniel Fowle 1851 (1888–91)
James Martin *60 (1985–93)

OHIO

George White 1895 (1931–35)
Robert A. Taft III *67 (1999–2007)

OKLAHOMA

Dewey Bartlett '42 (1967–71)

PENNSYLVANIA

James Pollock 1831 (1855–58)
James Duff 1904 (1947–51)

RHODE ISLAND

William Vanderbilt 1925 (1939–41)

SOUTH CAROLINA

John Taylor 1790 (1826–28)
Patrick Noble 1806 (1838–40)
Whitemarsh Seabrook 1812 (1848–50)

TENNESSEE

William P. Cooper Jr. 1917 (1939–45)

VERMONT

Isaac Tichenor 1775 (1797–1809)

VIRGINIA

Henry Lee Jr. 1773 (1792–95)
William Giles 1781 (1826–29)

John Rutherfoord 1810 (1841–42)
James McDowell 1817 (1843–46)

GRADUATE COLLEGE, THE, was dedicated on October 22, 1913. Designed by Ralph Adams Cram in close collaboration with the first dean of the graduate school, Andrew Fleming West 1874, this imposing group of connected Gothic buildings was the first residential college in the United States devoted solely to students pursuing postgraduate liberal studies. (In Princeton terminology, "graduate college" refers to this complex of residential and dining halls; "graduate school" refers to the program of instruction.)

Previously, beginning in 1905, graduate students lived in a three-story Victorian house known as Merwick on an 11-acre landscaped lot in the town of Princeton that had been purchased for this purpose by Moses Taylor Pyne 1877 at the request of West. (George Lansing Raymond, the original builder of the house, coined the name Merwick by combining the initials of his wife's name—Mary Elizabeth Raymond—with the Old English suffix "wick," which means "abode.")

The buildings of the graduate college are situated on a hill half a mile from the main campus. They house about 430 graduate students and serve as a center of graduate student life. The ensemble includes two towers; a great dining hall with hammerhead beams, an organ, and stained glass; a refectory; a common room; informal social, study, and dining spaces, including an underground, after-hours socializing and entertainment venue managed by the Graduate College House Committee and known as Debasement Bar; gardens; and a house for the dean. (Periodically the D-Bar is transformed into the Q-Bar, a safe and inclusive space for LGBTQ+ students and their allies.) The detailing of the graduate college includes humorous depictions of student life in the form of exterior gargoyles and grotesques, and caricatures of trustees carved on the dining hall hammerheads.

Thomson College, the central quadrangle of the college, is a memorial to United States Senator John Thomson 1817, funded by a bequest from his widow, Josephine Ward Thomson Swann, the graduate college's first benefactor.

Procter Hall, the college's formal dining hall, was given in memory of his parents by William Cooper Procter 1883, head of Procter and Gamble, the Cincinnati-based consumer products conglomerate. (One of the hall's carved caricatures depicts

Procter holding a bar of Ivory Soap.) Until the early 1970s, students were required to wear academic gowns to dinner in Procter Hall. That practice no longer exists, but once a month, in a tradition dating back to the graduate college's earliest days, students, faculty, deans, and guests convene at the hall's High Table for dinner and discussion.

The room includes portraits of all the deans of the graduate school, and inscribed on the mantel above the fireplace is the Latin motto *Bonus intra, melior extra* (Enter good, leave better). One of the stained glass windows, on the southern side of the entry room, was dedicated on June 6, 1923, as a memorial to the six Princeton graduate students who gave their lives in World War I.

Pyne Tower is named for Moses Taylor Pyne 1877, its donor and the chair of the trustee graduate school committee at the time the graduate college was built. It contains the living quarters of the college's resident administrator.

Wyman House, the residence of the dean of the graduate school, was named for Isaac Wyman 1848, who left the bulk of his estate to the graduate college.

Between Procter Hall and Wyman House, a gateway opens into the graduate college garden, from which can be seen the heraldic sculptures and elaborate grotesques that decorate the west facade of Procter Hall. This garden and the other landscaping of the graduate college were the first of many distinctive designs by Beatrix Farrand, who was hired as the University's first consulting landscape gardener in 1912 and who, over the next 31 years, established landscape design as a defining feature of the entire Princeton campus.

The 173-foot Cleveland Tower, which flanks the main entrance to the college, was erected through public subscription by "thousands of citizens of all parties in all walks and conditions of life from all parts of the United States," including schoolchildren who contributed their pennies, as a memorial to President Grover Cleveland. Following his retirement from public life, Cleveland was a trustee of the University and chaired the trustee graduate school committee until his death in 1908. The carillon in the belfry of the tower, originally containing 35 bells but now containing 67, was given in 1927 by the Class of 1892.

A quadrangle known as the North Court was added in 1927 following a gift from Procter. Two additional quadrangles built in 1963 northwest of the original group were named for Procter and three distinguished alumni of the graduate school, the Compton brothers; these buildings are commonly known as the new graduate college.

A bronze statue of Dean West on the upper terrace of the Thomson College court was also given by Procter and dedicated in the spring of 1928.

GRADUATE SCHOOL, THE, was formally established in 1900, but its antecedents reach back almost to Princeton's beginnings. In colonial times some graduates returned to prepare for the ministry with the College's president. James Madison 1771, who remained at Princeton for six months after graduation to study philosophy and Hebrew under President John Witherspoon, is thought to have been the first graduate to pursue nontheological postgraduate study, and is often referred to as Princeton's first graduate student. By 1823 there were 23 postgraduate students in residence, but their work was informal, and they were not candidates for degrees.

President James McCosh began to lay the groundwork for the development of a graduate school shortly after his inauguration in 1868. Under his leadership, graduate fellowships were established (beginning with three in 1869 in classics, mathematics, and philosophy), and systematized programs of study leading to master's and doctor's degrees were adopted. In 1879 Princeton conferred its first earned doctorates on James Williamson 1877 *1879 and William Libby 1877 *1879. When McCosh retired in 1888, 78 graduate students were enrolled in programs in Art and Archaeology, Astronomy, Biology, Classics, Geology, Mathematics, Philosophy, and Physics.

Although McCosh began the transformation of the College into a university, the change was not formalized until the sesquicentennial in 1896 when the trustees officially changed the name of the College of New Jersey to Princeton University. McCosh's successor, President Francis Patton, did little during his administration to develop the graduate program, but Latin professor Andrew Fleming West 1874, who played a leading role in overseeing the sesquicentennial, emerged as a determined and effective advocate for attaching higher priority to graduate studies and creating a structure to house graduate students.

On December 13, 1900, the trustees voted to establish a graduate school and appointed West its first dean. He took up his duties in the fall of 1901 as the graduate school became a reality.

West diligently pursued two primary goals: he insisted on high quality graduate work and he sought to create a residential setting that would produce broadly educated, well-rounded scholars. When Woodrow Wilson 1879 became president in 1902, he shared some of West's aspirations but not his passion for a graduate college. Wilson turned his efforts toward the preceptorial system he introduced and the quad plan he espoused, while West (who declined the presidency of MIT to pursue his Princeton ambitions) devoted most of his considerable energy to seeing the college built.

Beginning in 1905, West presided over an interim graduate student residence at a converted mansion in the town of Princeton called Merwick, even as he aggressively pursued funding for a more permanent college. Financial support first arrived when Josephine Thomson Swann died in 1906 and left the University $275,000 for the construction of a graduate college. In April 1908, after two years of debate about the site, the trustees voted to build the graduate college at Wilson's preferred location near Prospect Avenue where he hoped the graduate students would exert positive influence on the undergraduates who would live there under his proposed quad plan.

Since West wanted graduate students isolated from the distractions of undergraduate life, he campaigned against Wilson's plan. In May 1909 West's friend William Cooper Procter 1883 offered Princeton $500,000 for a graduate college, provided a site other than the one near Prospect was selected. For a year there was bitter controversy over the site and the character of the graduate college, a controversy fueled by the strong-willed personalities of Wilson and West.

Procter favored locating the graduate college near the golf course, and in October 1909 the trustees voted to accept his offer and choice of site. Thereafter, new proposals and counterproposals were developed—at one point, Wilson proposed two graduate colleges, one on the main campus (to satisfy what he contended were Mrs. Swann's wishes), and one near the golf course. In February 1910, noting the unfavorable reception it was receiving from the president and his associates, Procter withdrew his offer.

In May 1910, when West was on the verge of resigning as dean, Isaac Wyman 1848 died, leaving an estate estimated at over $2 million (but, it later developed, actually worth only $794,000) for a graduate college to be built as West desired. Procter renewed his offer, and the trustees accepted it. Wilson, turning toward state and national politics, resigned the presidency in October 1910. He was succeeded by John Grier Hibben 1882 *1883, the first president with a Princeton graduate degree; it would turn out that all his successors through the end of the twentieth century would similarly hold Princeton graduate degrees.

Construction of the graduate college at the edge of the golf course began in May 1911, and it was formally dedicated on October 22, 1913.

During West's 27 years as dean, the graduate school grew steadily. In addition to the fields covered in McCosh's day, graduate programs leading to master of arts and doctor of philosophy degrees were now offered also in Chemistry, Economics, English, German, History, Oriental Studies, Politics, Psychology, and Romance Languages, and after 1919 a master of fine arts degree was offered in Architecture.

West believed that excellence could best be attained with a small number of well-qualified graduate students, and during his tenure enrollment never exceeded 200—a limit set by the trustees in 1922. In his last report, in 1928, he spoke with pride of the achievements of the school's graduates. At that time, former members of what he called his "society of scholars" made up one-fourth of the Princeton faculty and were eagerly sought for academic posts elsewhere, while others held notable positions in the professions, diplomacy, research, and philanthropy.

In the next quarter-century, under physicist Augustus Trowbridge (1928–33) and mathematician Luther Eisenhart (1933–45), applications for admission rose, particularly in the sciences. In the Trowbridge years the trustees raised the enrollment limit to 250, and as demand increased under Eisenhart, almost all programs leading to terminal master's degrees were eliminated to make room for more PhD candidates.

During Hugh Stott Taylor's administration (1945–58) the trustees removed the limitation on enrollment; it eventually reached 660. The large number of married veterans needing accommodations led to what was supposed to be a temporary installation of military-style barracks on the former polo field known as the Butler Tract, the graduate school's first housing for married students. (The Butler Tract continued to house graduate students until 2015.) Fifth year programs in engineering, which had been in effect since 1922, were incorporated into the graduate school for the first time, and new doctoral programs were adopted in Aeronautical, Chemical, Civil, Electrical, and Mechanical Engineering, as well as in Architecture, Music, Religion, and Sociology.

Expansion continued in the 1960s under physicist Donald Hamilton (1958–65) and biologist Colin Pittendrigh (1965–69). A $35 million gift from the Robertson Foundation dramatically increased the scope of the graduate program in the school of Public and International Affairs and new PhD programs began in Anthropology, Astrophysics, Biochemical Sciences, Comparative Literature, East Asian Studies, Near Eastern Studies, and Statistics, as well as in an interdisciplinary program in the History and Philosophy of Science.

Applications for admission rose sharply, and after the successful launching of Sputnik, federal funding for graduate fellowships increased dramatically, particularly in the sciences and engineering but in other fields as well. Under a policy of controlled expansion, enrollment reached 1,440 by the time Pittendrigh stepped down in 1969. Increased housing needs for single students were met by the addition of two quadrangles at the graduate college in 1963, and housing for a growing number of married students was provided in 1966 by construction of the Lawrence Apartments just south of the golf course.

Rapid growth in the 1960s was followed in the 1970s by a period of consolidation made necessary by financial strains on the University, a significant decline in outside fellowship support, a declining applicant pool in the face of poor employment prospects, and a national shift of post-baccalaureate students to professional schools. Enrollment leveled off at about 1,400 under physicist Aaron Lemonick *54, who served as dean of the graduate school from 1969 until his appointment as dean of the faculty in 1973; literary scholar Alvin Kernan (1973–77); and the first woman to serve as dean, Armenian studies scholar Nina Garsoian (1977–79).

In 1961 Princeton's first woman graduate student, Sabra Follett Meservey *64 *66, was admitted to the department of Oriental Studies under a rule that limited admission to women for whom the Princeton graduate school offered a program not available to them elsewhere. (The rule remained in place until the end of the decade.) In 1962 the University admitted eight women as graduate students but, by 1968, with undergraduate coeducation imminent and a cap on the admission of women lifted, there were 56. A year later 200 women were enrolled, and by 1978 enrollment of women graduate students reached 432, or 30 percent of total enrollment.

In 1963, T'sai-Ying Cheng *63 *64, a student in Biochemical Sciences, became the first woman to receive a Princeton degree, and in 1964 she became the first woman to receive a Princeton PhD. In 1971, Ellen Chances *70 *72 became the first woman with a Princeton PhD (in Slavic Languages and Literatures) to be appointed to the Princeton faculty.

In the late 1960s conscious efforts began to increase the number of African Americans and other students of color in the graduate school. By 1973–74 the enrollment of African Americans had increased to 79 and the enrollment of all minority students to 119, 8.3 percent of total enrollment. But by the end of the 1970s these numbers had declined to the point where there were only 28 African American graduate students among only 72 minority students.

The 1980s were a decade of growth for the graduate school. During the administration of German and comparative literature professor Theodore Ziolkowski (1979–92), enrollment rose from 1,431 to 1,834, with increases in the representation of women (to 34 percent), foreign students (to 35 percent), and minority students (to 11 percent). Interdisciplinary programs were established in Late Antiquity, Medieval Studies, and Italian Studies; graduate-level initiatives were supported in Latin American Studies, Russian Studies, and Women's Studies; new PhD programs were established in Molecular Biology (replacing Biochemistry), Computer Science, and Atmospheric and Oceanic Sciences. The graduate program in Slavic Languages and Literatures, which had been suspended in 1971, was revived in 1990.

To accommodate the growth in enrollment, additional graduate student housing was constructed at the Butler Tract and the graduate college was renovated. In 2016 the Butler housing was finally demolished following the opening of new housing for more than 700 graduate students in the Lakeside apartments on the north shore of Lake Carnegie, where two of the courtyards are named for former graduate school deans Lemonick and Taylor. Additional housing for graduate students is planned in the 2020s as part of the initial development of the University's Lake Campus just south of the lake.

The energetic atmosphere of the 1980s helped to revitalize the Association of Princeton Graduate Alumni (APGA), which established annual teaching awards for graduate students, summer grants for travel and research, and career seminars. The APGA traces its roots to a committee called the Princeton Graduate College Pioneers that was founded in 1945 by three graduate alumni, including radio commentator Lowell Thomas *16. This committee evolved into the APGA four years later, and by the late 1950s it had changed from a dues-paying membership organization to one that includes all graduate alumni, who now account for 30 percent of the alumni body.

In 1973 the APGA established the James Madison Medal, which is presented each year on Alumni Day as the highest award the University can bestow on graduate alumni. In 1975 the APGA began participating in the P-rade at reunions, and graduate alumni now participate in a full range of reunions activities and have their own reunions headquarters, blazer, and beer jacket.

In 1989 a representative body of graduate students (known initially as the Graduate Student Union, but since 2000 as the Graduate Student Government) was formed to express graduate student perspectives and concerns and sponsor social and other events.

Ziolkowski was succeeded in 1992 by religion professor Albert Raboteau, the first African American dean of the graduate school, and he in turn was succeeded by religion professor John Wilson. During Wilson's tenure, the University expanded fellowship support for students in the sciences and engineering and gave students in the humanities and social sciences access to summer stipends. Wilson oversaw the graduate school's centennial celebration in 2000–01.

In 2002, Wilson was succeeded by chemical engineering professor William Russel. He oversaw further increases in support for graduate students; the addition of PhD programs in Quantitative and Computational Biology and Neuroscience and an interdisciplinary doctoral program in the humanities; creation of a new status of "dissertation completion enrollment (DCE)" for PhD students who do not complete their dissertations within their department's normal enrollment period; and planning for the University's first graduate alumni conference, *Many Minds, Many Stripes*, in 2013.

When Russel stepped down in 2014, he was succeeded by electrical engineering professor Sanjeev Kulkarni, who oversaw the work of a task force on the future of the graduate school as part of the University's overarching strategic planning process. Like his immediate predecessors, Kulkarni sought to expand support for graduate students, increase the diversity of the graduate school, enhance student life activities, increase the integration of graduate students into the life of the University, and expand the engagement of alumni.

All these goals continued to be pursued in earnest by philosophy professor Sarah-Jane Leslie *07, who was named dean of the graduate school in 2018 when Kulkarni was appointed dean of the faculty. Leslie was the second holder of a Princeton graduate degree, following Lemonick, to serve as dean of the graduate school. When appointed, she said her priorities would include "preserving and enhancing the excellence of graduate education at Princeton, diversifying the graduate student body, and supporting graduate students' professional development." She described the graduate school as "nurturing not only the faculty of the future, but also those creative intellects who will go on to make vibrant extra-academic contributions to our public intellectual, cultural and economic flourishing."

During her tenure, the University launched a one-year pre-doctoral fellowship program designed primarily for students from groups historically underrepresented in higher education who would benefit from additional training before formally entering a PhD program. In addition, the graduate school created a program for entering graduate students from diverse backgrounds to enhance and support the students' academic, social, and community development during their initial graduate student experience. It also launched a campus-wide initiative called GradFUTURES that was designed to develop students' professional competencies and help them prepare for a broad range of possible careers.

The roughly 650 graduate students who entered Princeton in the fall of 2019 came to the University after earning undergraduate degrees at 277 different colleges and universities all over the world. Forty-two percent of them were international citizens representing nearly 50 countries, and of the incoming students from the United States, 43 percent were minority students and 28 percent identified as low-income or first-generation college students.

Princeton is distinctive among graduate schools in its relatively small size and its emphasis on doctoral education, although it also offers highly selective final professional master's degree programs in Architecture, Engineering, Finance, Near Eastern Studies, Public and International Affairs, and Public Policy. Of a total enrollment in 2020–21 of 3,065 students, 90 percent were pursuing doctoral degrees. Some 41 percent of the students were women and 41 percent were international. Among the US citizens and permanent residents, 55 percent were white, 15 percent Asian, 12 percent Hispanic/Latino, 5 percent Black/

African American, 5 percent multi-racial, and 8 percent were listed as unknown. By division, 21 percent were in the humanities, 23 percent in engineering, 26 percent in the social sciences, and 29 percent in the natural sciences.

Doctoral students work toward a PhD in one of 42 degree-granting departments and programs; they must fulfill departmental requirements, pass a general departmental examination, prepare a doctoral dissertation, and present a public oral defense of the dissertation. Students may also participate in a broad range of graduate certificate programs. The graduate school offers joint degree programs in Interdisciplinary Humanities, Materials Science, Neuroscience, and Social Policy, and the University participates in two joint degree programs with other institutions: an MPA-JD program through the School of Public and International Affairs and an MD-PhD program through the department of Molecular Biology.

In its 2016 strategic planning framework, the University described graduate education as "indispensable to Princeton's core teaching and research mission." Graduate students, it said, "are essential collaborators in faculty research projects (especially in the natural sciences, engineering, and some social sciences); they teach undergraduates in precepts and laboratories; and they play an increasingly large role in the residential life of the University."

Princeton guarantees funding for all its regularly enrolled, degree-seeking PhD candidates for all years of regular program enrollment (generally five years). The funding, which covers full tuition and fees and a stipend for living expenses, may come from multiple sources, including, after a student's first year, an assistantship in instruction for teaching or an assistantship in research for engaging in research.

GREEN, ASHBEL 1783, eighth president of Princeton, was a native of Hanover, New Jersey. His father, Jacob Green, was an independent-minded Presbyterian minister and a trustee of the College. His mother, Elizabeth Pierson Green, was the daughter of another minister, John Pierson, one of the College's original trustees. Ashbel was educated at home by his father and at the age of 16 began a three-year stint as a local schoolmaster. He then entered Princeton as a junior and graduated as valedictorian of his class. His valedictory address was delivered before George Washington, other dignitaries, and members of the Continental Congress, then meeting in Princeton.

Green must have impressed President John Witherspoon favorably, for he spent the two years after his graduation as a tutor in the College, and another year and a half as professor of mathematics and natural philosophy. During this period Green married Elizabeth Stockton, daughter of a prominent Princeton family.

Undecided about his choice of career, Green sought advice from Samuel Stanhope Smith 1769, later his predecessor as president. Green decided to become a minister, studied with Witherspoon, and in 1787 began an association with Philadelphia's Second Presbyterian Church that would last until 1812.

Green soon rose to a position of prominence within his denomination. A long-term member of the Presbyterian general assembly, he was its stated clerk from 1790 to 1803. He also served as chaplain to the United States Congress from 1792 to 1800. He was a member of the committee that drew up plans for the Princeton Theological Seminary, and in 1812 he was elected president of its board. He maintained a close association with the seminary until his death in 1848.

Green served the College as a trustee beginning in 1790. By the early 1800s, the trustees were growing increasingly concerned that Princeton under President Smith was not producing enough Presbyterian ministers, was theologically suspect, and, worst of all, was beset with student unrest and dissipation. In 1812 Smith was eased out of the presidency, and the trustees unanimously elected Green as his successor.

Green was 50 years old when he took up his new position. He moved into the President's House, where he lived with his family and at least three slaves. His first wife had died in 1807, and he had remarried in 1809, but he retained an enslaved woman, Betsey Stockton, who had been given as a young child to his first wife by her father. Green's second wife, Christiana Anderson Green, died in 1814. A year later Green was married for the third and last time, to Mary McCullough Green, and she then died in 1817.

Meanwhile, in 1813, Green had sold three years of Betsey Stockton's time to his niece in Woodbury, New Jersey. Betsey returned to Green's household in 1816, and in 1817, after the death of Green's third wife, she was emancipated. She worked for wages in Green's home until he left the presidency in 1822, after which she traveled to Hawaii as a missionary. In 1828 she relocated to Philadelphia, and in 1833 she returned to Princeton, where she helped establish the sole public school for African American children and played a pivotal role in founding Witherspoon Street Presbyterian Church and leading its Sunday school.

Green approached the presidency as a stern but kindly pastor, rather than as an educator. Rigorous disciplinary rules were introduced, and a heavily religious tone soon pervaded the College. His efforts bore fruit in the form of religious revivals among the students, and, despite some serious student riots, enrollments rose. Academic standards were lax: "I fear it is an undeniable fact," he reported to the trustees in 1813, "that the majority of those who have received degrees with us, for a number of years past, could not possibly have translated their own diplomas into English."

Green's tenure as president ended in 1822. The immediate cause of his resignation appears to have been an effort by the trustees to ease his son, Jacob, out of the position of professor of natural philosophy. The larger cause may have been Green's involvement with the affairs of the seminary to the detriment of those of the College. Green went on to a long and influential career as a religious writer and journalist, and a major figure in the "Old School" wing of the Presbyterian Church.

In some ways, Green's administration augured changes to come throughout American higher education. The heavily authoritarian and evangelistic spirit that marked his regime would become characteristic of many American colleges in the mid-nineteenth century.

GREEN, JOHN CLEVE, was Princeton's greatest benefactor during the presidency of James McCosh. By the time McCosh retired in 1888, Green's generosity had contributed "to the good of the College upwards of a million and a half, perhaps two million dollars," as McCosh said in his farewell report.

Green was born in Lawrenceville, New Jersey, and was a member of the first class to enter what became the Lawrenceville School. Forgoing college, he went to work for New York merchants with extensive foreign trade. He spent 10 years as supercargo of ships visiting South America and China and by the time he was 40 had acquired a fortune in the China trade, derived from tea, textiles, and opium. He enhanced this fortune by investments in railroads. His three children having died young, Green made substantial gifts to various philanthropies, including Princeton.

In 1866 Green secured for the College the land that now forms the northeast corner of the main campus. In 1870 he gave the College its first classroom building, named for his great-great-grandfather, Jonathan Dickinson, first president of the College. This building, on the site of the current Firestone Plaza, burned down in 1920. In 1873 Green gave the College its first library building (present day Chancellor Green), named for his brother, Henry Woodhull Green 1820, chancellor of New Jersey and a Princeton trustee. The same year he donated funds for a school of Science, which was named for him.

Green endowed the Joseph Henry professorship, and his estate provided further funds for science and for civil engineering as well as for professorships in Latin and Greek. The benefactions from his estate also included the construction of one of the College's early dormitories, Edwards Hall, in 1880, and the College's first chemical laboratory building, in 1891, at the corner of Nassau Street and Washington Road (now Aaron Burr Hall).

After the John C. Green School of Science burned down in 1928, the engineering building that had just been completed on Washington Road was named for Green. In 1962, when the school of Engineering moved into the new Engineering Quadrangle, Green Hall was assigned to the departments of Psychology and Sociology; in 2013 it was re-designated for multiple uses; and in the 2026 campus plan it was identified as a prime location for the humanities.

GREEN HALL is named for John Cleve Green, the donor who provided funds in 1870 for Princeton's first classroom building (the original Dickinson Hall), and in 1873 for its first library (Chancellor Green) and its first school of Science, which was named for him. The John C. Green School of Science was located on the west side of Washington Road where Firestone Library is now located. When it burned down in 1928, a new engineering building that had just been opened on the east side of Washington Road was named for him.

When the school of Engineering moved to the Engineering Quadrangle in 1962, Green Hall was redesigned for the departments of Psychology and Sociology. When Psychology moved to Peretsman Scully Hall in 2013 after Sociology had previously moved to Wallace Hall, Green Hall was redesignated for multiple uses; the 2026 campus plan identifies it as a prime location for the humanities, thereby making it and Aaron Burr Hall the only buildings on campus that, over the course of their histories, have housed programs in each of the University's four academic divisions: humanities, social sciences, natural sciences, and engineering.

GUYOT, ARNOLD HENRI, began the first systematic instruction in geology at Princeton in 1855. He was born near Neuchatel, Switzerland, and obtained his doctoral degree from the University of Berlin. Between 1839 and 1848 he taught physical geography and history at the Academy of Neuchatel. In 1848 the academy closed, and at the suggestion of his friend Louis Agassiz, he came to the United States. He gave a series of lectures at the Lowell Institute in Boston entitled "The Earth and Man," which became the basis for a highly successful text of the same name. In 1854 he was appointed professor of geology and physical geography at Princeton, and the following year he began what is now the department of Geosciences.

Guyot's interests were in glaciology, physical geography, meteorology, and cartography. He was intimately involved in the formative years of weather forecasting in the United States and was responsible for selecting and equipping some 50 meteorological observation stations for a network developed through the efforts of Joseph Henry for the Smithsonian Institution. He spent many summers making barometric measurements to determine mountain elevations from Mt. Katahdin in Maine to Mt. Oglethorpe in Georgia along what is now the Appalachian Trail. He used these occasions as field exercises in which Princeton students could practice barometric techniques, an early example of Princeton geology including students in faculty field research as part of their educational experience.

In 1856 Guyot founded the Princeton museum of natural history and continued to contribute specimens to it until his death at the age of 78. He was the first incumbent of the Blair Professorship of Geology, the second oldest endowed chair at Princeton. Three Mt. Guyots—in the White Mountains of New Hampshire, on the North Carolina-Tennessee line in the Great Smoky Mountains, and in the Colorado Rockies—were named in his honor, as were the Guyot Glacier in southeastern Alaska and the Guyot Crater on the moon. The great flat-topped seamounts that characterize many parts of the ocean floor were named "guyots" in his honor by Harry Hess.

Guyot Hall was named for him at the request of Cleveland H. Dodge 1879 and his mother, who donated funds for its construction in 1909, and for more than a century the building supported Princeton's programs in Geology and Biology. In 2019 a gift from Eric Schmidt '76 and his wife Wendy Schmidt allowed for the building to be substantially rebuilt and expanded to become the home of the department of Computer Science and to be renamed Eric and Wendy Schmidt Hall, with Guyot's legacy to be commemorated in a new home for the environmental sciences programs to be constructed east of Washington Road, just north of Ivy Lane and Western Way.

GUYOT HALL, named for Princeton's first professor of geology and geography, Arnold Guyot, was given to the University by the mother of Cleveland H. Dodge 1879. In planning what was to become the home of the Biology and Geology departments, Professor William Berryman Scott 1877, chair of both departments, sent a faculty committee to study other American laboratory buildings. The floor plans for Guyot, worked out by the faculty of the departments concerned, were accepted by the architects with scarcely any change.

Guyot Hall was originally intended to be a large quadrangle, but when it opened in 1909 only the north wing (facing the year-old Palmer Physical Laboratory) was built; even so, it contained about two acres of floor space and some 100 rooms. A natural history museum occupied the ground floor.

In its exterior design Guyot followed the Tudor Gothic style inaugurated in Blair and Little Halls, but with the red brick and limestone trim first used in 1879 Hall. Added as an extra feature were some 200 living and extinct animals and plants in stone carvings on the molding around the building—living species to the east where Biology was housed, and extinct species to the west where Geology was located. These gargoyle-like ornaments were created in the South Dakota studio of Gutzon Borglum, sculptor of the Mount Rushmore presidential portraits.

Several additions were made to Guyot in the 1960s and later to accommodate the growth of the two departments. The George M. Moffett Biological Laboratory was built in 1960 and that same year a one-story addition was built for geology; in 1964 a larger three-story addition was built for geochemistry and geophysics; in 1981 a geology library wing was constructed; and in 1993 Schultz Laboratory was added to the south of Moffett.

The natural history museum, founded in 1856, was initially housed in the Faculty Room of Nassau Hall. After its move to Guyot Hall it expanded significantly, and at one time it possessed several hundred thousand geological, biological, and archaeological specimens. In its early days the museum featured the second mounted dinosaur skeleton in the world; in its later years it displayed a collection of fossil fishes that were recovered in 1946 from rocks exposed by the excavation for Firestone Library. After 2002 the museum's remaining holdings were no longer displayed, except for an Allosaurus skeleton that was too large to move and an exhibit, "Leaping Tiger and Saber Tooth," that was placed in Frist Campus Center.

In the 2020s Guyot Hall is to be renamed Eric and Wendy Schmidt Hall in honor of the Schmidt's 2019 gift that funded the renovations and expansion necessary for the building to become the home of the department of Computer Science.

HALL, WALTER PHELPS "BUZZER," was among the most popular teachers of Princeton undergraduates in the first half of the twentieth century. A graduate of Yale (1906) and Columbia (PhD 1912), he came to Princeton as a history instructor in 1913 at the age of 29. Soon his name began to appear among the favorite teachers selected in the annual senior poll; when he retired 39 years later, he had been first more often than any other member of the faculty in his time.

For most of his career Hall lectured to sophomores on modern European history. His course was a prerequisite for history majors, and his teaching made his department one of the largest in the University. His bulldog, "Eli," was a frequent guest in the preceptorials he conducted in 363 Cuyler Hall during his bachelor days. Sometimes, to make a new group of preceptees feel at home, he would grab a sword from the wall and fling it into the air, and Eli would catch it in his mouth.

A stocky man given to fancy vests, knickerbockers, and flowing ties, Hall usually carried a walking stick. Never without a pipe, he seemed to spend more time in preceptorials filling it than smoking it. Because he used a hearing aid, he was called "Buzzer."

His unorthodox methods of lecturing were legendary. He frequently sat on the desk and sometimes stood on it. Stories were handed down from class to class about celebrated examples of his uninhibited spontaneity. One recounted the time he lectured in his underwear. The explanation was simple enough: he had been drenched walking to McCosh Hall in a driving rain, and rather than call off the lecture or take the risk of catching cold, he peeled off his outer garments and held forth in his underwear. Another was about the dramatic way he roused a sleeping undergraduate in one of his 7:40 a.m. lectures. Suspecting that the student had been up all night in New York and had returned on the morning's first train, Hall quietly walked to the dozer's side, and with a broad grin shouted, as only Buzzer could shout, "Princeton Junction, change for Princeton!"

So many students and faculty wanted to attend his last lecture when he retired in 1952 that it had to be shifted from McCosh to Alexander Hall. A six-piece band led the audience in singing "For He's a Jolly Good Fellow," and he was given a seven-foot scroll with the signatures of undergraduate contributors to a fund in his honor, later enlarged by alumni gifts. This fund was to be used for a senior thesis prize in European history and for an annual lecture to be given by Buzzer "as long as he felt like it." He gave the lecture every year up to 1962 when he died, two days before his 78th birthday.

HEALTH SERVICES, UNIVERSITY. From its earliest days, health has been a central concern of the institution that began as the College of New Jersey. When the College was relocated in 1756, the trustees said that one of the advantages of the move from Newark was that "the little village of Princeton" was "not inferior in the salubrity of the air to any village on the continent."

Notwithstanding the favorable conditions, the health of the College's first five presidents was grievously poor; two died within months after taking office and only one remained alive for more than five years. Students, on the other hand, managed to keep well, despite substandard fare in the refectory, the dampness and chill of Nassau Hall's bedchambers, and the backwardness of medical practice. An epidemic of dysentery swept through the College in 1813, but there were no fatalities and President Ashbel Green informed the trustees that a "chemical fumigation" prepared by Professor Elijah Slack from a formula in a foreign scientific magazine had "a most wonderful, speedy, and happy effect in purifying the atmosphere."

For the better part of the nineteenth century, health care was in the hands of vice president and then president John Maclean Jr. 1816, whose father and both grandfathers had been physicians, and Isabella McCosh, daughter of an eminent Scottish physician, who nursed many students to health while her husband was president.

The need for a more substantial health service was evident when a malaria and typhoid fever epidemic in 1880 resulted in 10 deaths in a student body of 473. The epidemic brought about a thorough overhaul of the College's sewage system and the appointment of a faculty sanitary committee whose efforts led eventually to the construction in 1892 of an infirmary named for Isabella McCosh. In 1902 Josephine Perry Morgan founded a Ladies Auxiliary to the infirmary, and among other things the auxiliary raised funds for the appointment in 1908 of the first university physician, John Carnochan 1896.

Major developments in health care occurred in 1910 and 1911 with the beginning of a mental health program and the founding of a department of health and physical education.

Princeton was the first American college or university to provide mental health care for its students, a distinction it owed to Stewart Paton 1886. A pioneer in the teaching of psychiatry at Johns Hopkins and a man of independent means, Paton settled in Princeton in 1910 and for 16 years gave the University his services as a lecturer on neurobiology and a consultant on mental health for students.

In 1911 Joseph Raycroft, who had been medical director at the University of Chicago, was appointed founding chair of the health and physical education department. He held this position for 25 years and was widely recognized for the development of a comprehensive student health program and for broadening intramural competition to include some 90 percent of the undergraduate body.

In 1916 the University postponed its opening for three weeks because of an infantile paralysis epidemic, and two years later the worldwide Spanish influenza pandemic taxed the infirmary to its limit just as the University was opening for a new year.

The Raycroft administration oversaw the construction of the second Isabella McCosh Infirmary in 1925, and in 1928 began a program in athletic medicine that was directed for 36 years by Harry McPhee, a pioneer in the treatment and prevention of athletic injuries who also served as head team physician for American athletes at four Olympics and two Pan-American Games. (McPhee was the father of the author and long-time Princeton faculty member, John McPhee '53.)

In 1936 Raycroft was succeeded by Wilbur York, and in 1946 responsibility for physical education and intramural sport was transferred to the department of athletics. In 1957 an influenza epidemic affected one-quarter of the undergraduates and 10 percent of the graduate students, requiring that extra beds be placed in the hallways of the infirmary and that the student center in Chancellor Green be converted into an influenza ward.

Under Willard Dalrymple, who served as director from 1962 to 1977, the department of health was renamed University Health Services (UHS) to reflect its expanding scope. An occupational health and safety unit was created, a counseling center (now called counseling and psychological services) was established in 1971, and in 1972 a sexuality education, counseling, and health program (SECH) was introduced. The infirmary staff grew to include five full-time physicians, a physician's associate, and 11 nurses.

Louis Pyle Jr. '41, who had been a University physician since 1971, became the University's fourth medical director in 1977. In 1979 an area now called health promotion and prevention services was created to focus on education and prevention, and in 1980 a student health advisory board was established. Programs were inaugurated to address clinical, educational, and counseling needs related to abuse of alcohol and other drugs, sexual harassment and assault, and eating disorders. The professional staff increased to about 50 and an administrative division was established to address the growing complexities of health service operations and finances.

In 1982 UHS became the 13th college health service to be accredited by the Accreditation Association of Ambulatory Health Care. In 1983 an occupational medicine division (now occupational health) was formed to meet the needs of employees, and in 1988 the Sexual Harassment/Assault Advising, Resources, and Education (SHARE) office was created to provide consultation, crisis intervention, advocacy, community education, and prevention in the area of interpersonal violence and abuse.

In 1991 Pyle was succeeded by Pamela Bowen, who centralized and consolidated UHS services and brought information technology into the health center. In 2002 Daniel Silverman, a physician with experience in health systems management, academic administration, and medical education, succeeded Bowen. In 2004, after Marvin Geller retired following 35 years directing Princeton's counseling services, John Kolligian was named director of the counseling and psychological services unit, and in 2009 Kolligian was named executive director of UHS.

In 2003 President Shirley Tilghman appointed a student-faculty-staff task force to examine how the University should meet the needs of students for medical and mental health care and what programs, services, and facilities it should provide to promote their health and well-being; to what extent it should meet health care needs of faculty and staff and promote their health and well-being; and how the University could improve the balance between family and work by offering additional child care and other family support services.

In its 2004 report the task force recommended a substantial increase in UHS staff, with added strengths in education and nutrition; major enhancements of the facilities at McCosh Health Center and Dillon Gym; improvements in student and employee health plans (the student health plan is available to all enrolled undergraduate and graduate students and their eligible dependents); and a significant expansion of support for child care, including the construction of a new University-affiliated child care center (which opened in 2017).

The task force also recommended continuing attention to health and wellness issues, which led to the creation of a "Healthier Princeton" advisory board that included students, faculty, staff, alumni, and outside professionals which met twice a year to monitor progress and recommend additional measures to enhance the physical, psychological, and emotional health of all members of the campus community.

In 2006 UHS formed a mind-body team to develop new intervention in the areas of mindfulness therapies and the contemplative sciences. It coordinated the University's response to the H1N1 influenza outbreak in 2009, and from 2013 to 2015 it administered more than 13,000 doses of a vaccine against meningitis B to undergraduates and select graduate students and employees after eight undergraduates and a visiting high school student had been infected. In 2015 the occupational health division played a leading role in determining clearance for at-risk students and employees during a measles outbreak.

UHS opened a global and community health unit in 2017 that provides care and information regarding travel, immunization, and infectious disease-related issues. Two years later, when UHS launched a cross-campus health, well-being, and resilience initiative known as TigerWell, its outreach psychologists, working from satellite offices across campus, provided more than 500 individual "drop-in" counseling appointments and more than 60 outreach programs, events, and consultations.

In March 2020 UHS, like many offices of the University, shifted into overdrive in response to the COVID-19 pandemic, providing information, support, and guidance for members of the campus community.

UHS today is a fully accredited health care facility providing comprehensive health services to Princeton undergraduate and graduate students and their dependents, occupational health services, and a variety of wellness programs and services for members of the University community. Located in the McCosh Health Center with outposts at Caldwell Field House and Dillon Gym, UHS provides services to 84 percent of all undergraduate and graduate students in a given year; in 2019 this included almost a thousand admissions to its 15-bed infirmary.

UHS clinicians are available 24 hours a day, seven days a week during the academic year, and handle about 60,000 clinical encounters annually. The UHS staff of over 115 includes physicians, psychiatrists, nurse practitioners, physician assistants, psychologists, clinical social workers, health educators, registered nurses, nutritionists, athletics trainers, and other healthcare professionals, technicians, and administrators.

The medical services staff provides primary medical care as well as specialized services such as athletic medicine, sexual health and wellness, global and community health, nutrition counseling, occupational health services, physical therapy, and radiological and laboratory services. The counseling and psychological services staff of psychologists, psychiatric providers, clinical social workers, postdoctoral psychology fellows, and social work interns offers mental health services to Princeton graduate and undergraduate students and their dependents.

SHARE strives to foster a safe, respectful, inclusive, and supportive campus through interpersonal violence prevention efforts and by supporting survivors. The health promotion and prevention services team advocates for the creation and sustenance of conditions necessary for the well-being of the Princeton community and all its members. Student Peer Health Advisers, supervised by the health promotion and prevention staff, encourage students to make effective use of UHS and help implement health promotion programs.

Following the 2017 release of its 2026 campus plan, the University began designing a new 70,000-square-foot UHS facility that would double the space available in McCosh (which would be converted to other uses). The new facility is to be located on the north side of Goheen Walk, with construction expected to begin in 2022; the existing Eno Hall, which was constructed in 1924, initially to house the department of Psychology, is to be renovated and incorporated into the new facility.

HELM, HAROLD H. 1920 played a leading role in many of the decisions and developments of the mid-twentieth century that shaped the Princeton of the late twentieth century and beyond. He was the first chair of Annual Giving; chair of the Graduate Council (precursor of the Alumni Council); chair of the trustee executive committee (making him, de facto, chair of the board) during the University's first comprehensive capital campaign; chair of the committee that recommended the appointment of Robert F. Goheen '40 *48 as Princeton's 16th president; and chair of the trustee committee that recommended coeducation.

Helm was born in Auburn, Kentucky, in 1900. His family moved to Bowling Green, Kentucky, and he studied for two years at Ogden College (later part of Western Kentucky University) before enrolling at Princeton in 1917. His Commencement in 1920 was the first of 65 Princeton Commencements that he attended over the course of his life. After graduating he went to work for Chemical Bank, where he remained for 45 years, culminating in his appointment as chair and chief executive officer from 1956 to 1965.

An active Princeton volunteer, he served on the Graduate Council from 1937 until his election as a trustee in 1947. In 1940 he founded the Annual Giving program, which raised $80,000 from 18 per cent of the alumni in its inaugural year, and by 1945 was raising $187,000 from 38 percent. Helm believed that just as important as raising funds was the effect annual giving had on binding alumni to the University. "When you participate in giving to your church, to your university, to your community, or whatever it is, you feel much more a part of it than if you are a bystander," he said.

From 1945 to 1947, Helm chaired the Graduate Council, and then in 1947 he was elected a charter trustee, a position he held until 1971. In 1954 he was elected chair of the executive committee, a position he held for 12 years. While in that role he chaired the search committee that recommended the appointment of Goheen, then a 37-year-old assistant professor of classics, and in the early years of the new administration he traveled the country with Goheen on behalf of the $53 Million Campaign that ended in 1962 after having raised $60.7 million.

When Helm stepped down from chairing the executive committee, he became chair of the finance committee. When Goheen asked him also to chair a special trustee committee to examine coeducation, Helm told him he wasn't very keen about the idea: "It will take a lot of convincing for me to accept it," he said. "I think you better get somebody who has more enthusiasm for the idea." Goheen replied: "Hal, I didn't ask you to vote for it, I asked you to study it." Helm agreed, and in January 1969, Helm's committee recommended to the board that Princeton admit women undergraduates. The board approved coeducation, in principle, at that meeting, and then in April it voted to implement its decision beginning that fall.

Helm received an honorary degree from Princeton in 1980. In 1986 the University renamed the McCosh 50 lecture hall in his honor, and in 1995 an office building at 330 Alexander Street that housed the offices of development and annual giving was named the Harold Helm building. One of the most prestigious alumni awards, presented each year in connection with Alumni Day, is the Harold Helm Award, which recognizes exemplary and sustained service to Annual Giving.

Goheen called Helm the most helpful trustee during his time as president. When Helm died in 1985, President William Bowen said that Helm would "always be remembered for his vitality, his unfailing capacity to be constructive, and his infectious good spirit."

HENRY, BAYARD 1876, a life trustee for 30 years, represented the fifth generation of his family to serve in that office.

Descended from Nathaniel FitzRandolph, donor of the land on which Nassau Hall was built in 1756, Henry was one of a small group of alumni from the era of President James McCosh who helped secure almost a square mile of land for the University early in the twentieth century. He procured the plot on Nassau Street where Holder Hall now stands and the tract on University Place occupied by the dormitories south of Blair Hall, one of which was named for his son Howard Henry 1904, who died in France in World War I. He also played a pivotal role in the University's acquisition of the lands extending from Lake Carnegie to Route 1 between Washington Road and Alexander Road.

Henry practiced law in Philadelphia, served on the select council of that city and in the state senate of Pennsylvania, and was a director of many corporations.

Henry collaborated with Moses Taylor Pyne 1877 in collecting thousands of manuscripts relating to Princeton's history. The fruits of their labors are found in the Pyne-Henry Collection in the University Library.

Henry died in 1926. In their memorial minute, the trustees acknowledged that the University "owes much to his great foresight in securing lands adequate for our future needs."

HENRY, JOSEPH, the leading American scientist after Benjamin Franklin, was a professor at Princeton from 1832 to 1846. His chief scientific contributions were in the field of electromagnetism, where he discovered the phenomenon of self-inductance. The unit of inductance, called "the henry," immortalizes his name. Henry left Princeton to serve as the first secretary of the Smithsonian Institution, where he made extraordinary contributions to the organization and development of American science.

Henry was the son of a day laborer in Albany, New York. As a boy he was sent to live with his grandmother in a village about 40 miles away. There he worked in a general store after school, and at the age of 13 he was apprenticed to a watchmaker. In 1819 several well-positioned Albany friends persuaded him to attend the Albany Academy, where free tuition was provided. By 1823 his education was so far advanced that he was assisting in the teaching of science courses. By 1826, after a stint as a district schoolteacher and as a private tutor, he was appointed professor of mathematics and natural philosophy at the academy. Here, despite a teaching schedule that occupied him seven hours a day, he did his most important scientific experiments.

Henry became interested in terrestrial magnetism, which led him to experiment with electromagnetism. His apprenticeship as a watchmaker stood him in good stead in the construction of batteries and other apparatus. While others had observed magnetic effects from electric currents, Henry was the first to wind insulated wires around an iron core to obtain powerful electromagnets. Before he left Albany, he built one for Yale that would lift 2,300 pounds, the largest in the world at that time. In experimenting with such magnets, Henry observed the large spark that was generated when the circuit was broken, and he deduced the property known as self-inductance.

In 1832, when Henry was 35, Yale's distinguished geologist Benjamin Silliman was consulted regarding the possible appointment of Henry to Princeton. Silliman replied, "As a physical philosopher he has no superior in our country; certainly not among the young men." Henry, always modest, had responded to tentative inquiries, "Are you aware of the fact that I am not a graduate of any college and that I am principally self-educated?"

Henry's initial salary at Princeton was $1,000 per annum plus a house. The trustees also provided $100 "for the purchase of a new electrical machine &c." At that point the College was near bankruptcy and President John Maclean was trying to build up the faculty. Henry was a notable acquisition, and he found the lighter teaching schedule and the intellectual companionship at Princeton congenial, especially when his brother-in-law Stephen Alexander joined the faculty to teach astronomy. Henry continued his work on magnets, building for Princeton an even larger magnet than he had built for Yale, one that would lift 3,500 pounds. In his laboratory and his household, Henry was assisted for six years by a free Black man named Sam Parker, who played an indispensable role in his research and served as a test subject in some of his electrical experiments.

Henry rigged two long wires, one in front of Nassau Hall and one behind, so that he was able to send a signal by induction through the building. Another wire from his laboratory in Philosophical Hall was used to send signals to his home on the campus; he used it, among other purposes, to alert his wife when he was coming home for lunch. This signal system constituted, in effect, the invention of the magnetic relay. A similar arrangement was used by Samuel F.B. Morse in the invention of the telegraph; Morse had consulted Henry and had used one of his scientific papers. Later, Henry was called to testify in a patent suit involving the telegraph, *Morse* vs. *O'Reilly*. Although Henry had encouraged and helped Morse in his project, his testimony that the principle of the telegraph had been known to himself and others undermined Morse's claim to originality.

In addition to natural philosophy (physics), Henry taught chemistry, geology, mineralogy, astronomy, and architecture, and proposed a master plan for the development of the campus. The College gave Henry an opportunity, then unusual, to travel abroad on leave at full salary. In 1837 he went to England to meet with British scientists and returned home with a variety of scientific equipment purchased abroad.

During his remaining years in Princeton Henry continued his electrical investigations, but also branched out into the study of phosphorescence, sound, capillary action, and ballistics. In 1844 he was a member of a committee that investigated the explosion of a gun during a demonstration on the new USS *Princeton*; the secretaries of state and the navy and several members of Congress were among the spectators killed. His work for this committee included experiments on gun castings, which led him into study of the molecular cohesion of matter.

When the Smithsonian Institution was established in 1846, Henry was invited to head it. He was reluctant to leave Princeton, but he eventually accepted and threw his enormous energy, knowledge, and experience into its development. In 1853 the Princeton trustees invited him to return as the college's 10th president, but he declined.

Henry was one of the original members of the National Academy of Sciences and served as its second president. He was a trustee of Princeton and president of the American Association for the Advancement of Science. When he died in 1878 his funeral was attended by the president of the United States with his cabinet, the chief justice and associate justices of the Supreme Court, many members of both houses of Congress, and many scientists.

In 1872, John C. Green, Princeton's leading benefactor in the mid-nineteenth century, endowed a chair of physics in Henry's honor. Some of Henry's laboratory equipment is on display in the lobby of the physics building, Jadwin Hall. His home, built to his design, is called the Joseph Henry House; now in its fourth campus location, it houses the Humanities Council and other programs associated with the Andlinger Center for the Humanities. Henry is featured in murals painted in Green Hall, and his statue (by Daniel Chester French) stands at the entrance to Frist Campus Center (originally Palmer Physical Laboratory), across from the statue of another early experimenter with electricity, Benjamin Franklin. In Washington, a statue of Henry stands before the old Smithsonian Building.

HENRY, JOSEPH, HOUSE, THE, was built in 1837 for the eminent physicist of that name, and he occupied it until he left Princeton in 1846 to become the first secretary of the Smithsonian Institution in Washington, DC. At the time, it was one of three professors' houses on the front campus: one was occupied by vice president (later president) John Maclean Jr. 1816; another by mathematics professor Albert Dod 1822; and the third by Henry. It was to this house that Henry sent telegraphic messages (sometimes to signal that he was ready for lunch) from his laboratory in Philosophical Hall, which stood where Chancellor Green now stands.

The Joseph Henry House was made the official residence of the dean of the college soon after that office was created in 1909. In 1961 it became the home of William D'O. Lippincott '41, who served as dean of students from 1954 to 1968 and then executive director of the Alumni Council from 1968 to 1972. In 1973 it became the home of Aaron Lemonick *54, dean of the faculty and professor of physics. In 1988 it was converted to academic and administrative uses; it is currently part of the Andlinger Center for the Humanities, which also includes East Pyne, Chancellor Green, and the Scheide Caldwell House, and is home to, among others, the Humanities Council and the Society of Fellows in the Liberal Arts.

The Joseph Henry House, while solidly built of brick, has been well traveled. Three times since it was initially constructed on the south side of Stanhope Hall it moved to make way for other buildings: in 1879 for Reunion Hall (which was razed in 1966), in 1925 for the University Chapel, and in 1946 for Firestone Library. It now stands just north of Chancellor Green, across the front campus from the John Maclean House. It was designated a national historic landmark in 1965.

HIBBEN, JOHN GRIER 1882 *1893, 14th president of Princeton, was born on April 19, 1861, in Peoria, Illinois. His father, Samuel, was a Presbyterian minister who died while serving as a chaplain in the Union army when his son was just a year old. His mother, Elizabeth Grier Hibben, was a pioneer in the movement for woman's suffrage. John attended public schools in Peoria and entered Princeton in 1878, mid-way through the presidency of James McCosh. At graduation he was both class president and valedictorian.

Following a year of study in Berlin, Hibben attended Princeton Theological Seminary. In 1887, he married Jenny Davidson and was ordained. He served Presbyterian churches in St. Louis and Chambersburg, Pennsylvania, until a throat ailment cut short his career in the church and turned him toward graduate studies in philosophy at Princeton, where he became an instructor in logic in 1891 and received his PhD in 1893. Four years later, he was named Stuart Professor of Logic, a subject he continued to teach, along with psychology and the Bible, until his election to the presidency in January 1912.

The search for a successor to Woodrow Wilson lasted for 15 months, and Hibben's election was not unanimous. He was the candidate of the trustees who had most resisted Wilson's reforms, and this posed a challenge for the new president, whose friendship with Wilson had rapidly cooled after Hibben joined forces with Wilson's principal opponents in the graduate college controversy, Moses Taylor Pyne 1877 and Dean Andrew Fleming West 1874. The oldest newsreel in Princeton's archives records Hibben's 1912 inauguration, which US President William Howard Taft attended, but then-Governor Wilson, an ex officio trustee, did not.

The University had become sharply divided in Wilson's final years, and Hibben felt that his most urgent task was to overcome the divisiveness. At his first public appearance after his election, he set the tone for his entire administration. "If I am to prove myself worthy in some small way of the confidence reposed in me," he told the alumni of Orange, New Jersey, "my administration must make for peace. I wish to say to the alumni that which I said to the board of trustees on the day of election to this high office, and later to the faculty, that I represent no group or set of men, no party, no faction, no past allegiance or affiliation—but one united Princeton!"

Hibben's actions proved true to his words. One of his first acts as president was to seek out several faculty members of the Wilson faction and urge them to cooperate with him in continuing the work begun by Wilson. Many had feared that the election of Hibben "signified the triumph of Wilson's enemies on the board as well as in the faculty." But Hibben's "genial and kindly nature" soon healed the breach, and even Wilson's strongest supporter, Henry Fine 1880, who was stepping down as dean of the faculty but remaining dean of the departments of science, came to feel that Hibben was a "singularly happy choice." Hibben's style was more a conciliator, coordinator, and mediator than a dynamic, innovative leader—"temperate yet effective," "tolerant, candid, and fair," were the comments that recurred in the observations of colleagues, alumni, and trustees.

In the fall of 1913, Hibben presided over elaborate ceremonies formally opening the new graduate college. Former President Taft and Dean West gave the principal addresses. As dean during the presidencies of Francis Patton and Wilson, West had exercised nearly autonomous powers. Now, however, those powers were severely reduced by the trustees as they wrote new by-laws making the graduate school in every aspect of its administration subject to the president and the standing committees of the trustees and the faculty.

The outbreak of World War I in 1914 brought new challenges for the University. Hibben was a strong advocate of preparedness and of intervention on the side of the Allies. When the United States entered the war in 1917, he lost no time in placing the University's resources at the disposal of the government. Army, navy, and aviation training schools were soon functioning on campus, and many buildings, laboratories, and other facilities were made available to various research and operational programs. By September 1918, there were only 60 undergraduates who were not in the military. In all, more than 6,000 Princetonians—faculty, alumni, graduate students, and undergraduates—served in some branch of the armed forces, and of these 151 gave their lives.

After the war Hibben was distressed by the extent to which secular forces seemed to hold sway over undergraduate minds and habits. He thought these tendencies had been "largely affected by the hypocrisy attending the Eighteenth Amendment [prohibition], by false standards of living growing out of our period of fictitious prosperity and by a skepticism toward old concepts of morals and religion following the World War." The result, he said, was a greater emphasis on social activities; a more luxurious style of living, particularly in the eating clubs; and the development of "week-ending" as more undergraduates sought diversions away from Princeton—usually in the city.

Among Hibben's remedies was the building of eight new dormitories—Pyne, Henry, Foulke, Laughlin, 1901, Lockhart, 1903, and Walker halls—which permitted the housing of some 82 percent of the 2,200 undergraduates, a 28 percent increase over the situation immediately following the war. (Another dormitory, Cuyler Hall, had been built early in his presidency, and still another, Joline Hall, was built as it was coming to an end.) The eating clubs, viewed as a "vexing problem" by Hibben no less than by his predecessor, were brought under new regulations regarding membership eligibility and self-government. Another restriction, which involved what Hibben considered one of the "most serious enemies" of residential life at Princeton, came in 1927 when, with the president's approval, the trustees prohibited the operation of cars by undergraduates except in special cases.

Hibben's plans also included the establishment of a student center as a focal point for the meeting and interaction of all members of the community. These plans were well advanced when the onset of the Great Depression forced their postponement. They were not fully realized until the opening of the Frist Campus Center in 2000.

Hibben's practice was to look to the faculty for initiative in new programs, and he was rewarded with the cooperation of leading members, many of whom had been recruited during the Wilson years. The preceptorial system was further developed and extended to sophomore courses, but the most significant curriculum reform under Hibben's stewardship came in 1923 with the inauguration of the "four-course plan," or more formally, the "upperclass plan of study."

As Hibben reported to the trustees, this plan sought "to elevate the plane of endeavor and attainment of the whole undergraduate body" rather than of a few students as provided by the old honors program. The idea was to give students more freedom during the junior and senior years for independent reading in a particular subject in lieu of taking a fifth course, culminating in a senior thesis and a comprehensive examination in the field of concentration. As he told an alumni audience: "The emphasis would be changed from the absorption of those easily memorized facts to independent and original study of a subject, the very kind of mental process that the college graduates will be expected to carry on later in life."

Despite some initial doubts, the program quickly proved successful and was much emulated elsewhere. Professor Luther Eisenhart, as chair of the committee on the course of study, was responsible for conceiving and organizing the program, and in 1925 Hibben appointed him dean of the faculty.

One of Hibben's most enduring and consequential initiatives was the creation of a committee on appointments and advancements consisting of three members of the faculty chosen by that body and charged with advising the president regarding the faculty appointments and promotions that he would recommend to the trustees. The "committee of three" played a critical role in protecting the quality and distinction of the faculty—a role it still plays today, although it is now composed of six elected faculty members, along with the president, the provost, and three senior deans.

The years after the war brought a vast increase in the University's facilities for instruction and research. "Never in all her history," recalled one member of the faculty, "was Princeton the scene of such Aladdin magic as unfolded itself during the last twelve years of the Hibben administration." A number of departments were established or reconfigured, and three new schools were created: the school of Architecture (1919); the school of Engineering (1921); and the school of Public and International Affairs (1930). Significant support for research came with the establishment of the Industrial Relations Section in 1922, followed several years later by the International Finance Section in 1928 and a $3 million fund to support scientific discovery in 1929.

The endowment rose dramatically under Hibben and by the end of his administration topped more than $24 million, a 374 percent increase. The University benefited from the burgeoning national economy and the loyal support of the alumni. In addition to the dormitories constructed during his administration, the North Court quadrangle was added to the graduate college. Six new buildings were built for instruction and research: McCormick, Eno, Green, the first Frick, Dickinson, and Fine (later Jones) halls. Palmer Stadium, Baker Rink, the second McCosh Infirmary, McCarter Theater, faculty apartments on Prospect Avenue and College Road, and the new University Chapel, whose nave was named for Hibben, all date from this era. In all, some 30 buildings were constructed during Hibben's administration while the total area of the campus doubled in size.

The growth of the faculty was also impressive, in quality as well as quantity, as it expanded by some 73 percent. At the same time, the student body increased by nearly a thousand, even though a policy of limited enrollment and selective admission had been adopted in 1922. (There was some change in the composition of the student body; remembering his own matriculation from a public high school in Peoria, Hibben pressed for modified entrance requirements for applicants from public schools in the west that did not prepare their students for the College Board examinations.)

When Hibben retired in 1932, Professor Charles Osgood, a Wilson appointee, characterized Hibben's administration as the "flowering and harvest of Wilson's plantings." Hibben left office at the end of the school year, and a year later died in an automobile accident that also fatally injured his wife. "He had a profound sense of fairness and justice," the trustees observed in their memorial minute, "and the wounds of time were healed by it."

In addition to the nave in the Chapel, Hibben is remembered in a garden along the north side of the Chapel, by endowed scholarships that bear his name, by a street in town near the seminary, and by a roadway in the Lakeside graduate housing complex that was built on a site that previously housed two faculty/staff apartment buildings that were named for Hibben and William Magie 1879, who succeeded Fine and preceded Eisenhart as Hibben's first dean of the faculty.

HIGH MEADOWS ENVIRONMENTAL INSTITUTE (HMEI) was founded in 1994 as the Princeton Environmental Institute. As an interdisciplinary center for environmental research, education, and outreach, it seeks to inform solutions to local and global environmental challenges by conducting groundbreaking research across disciplines and preparing future leaders for a world increasingly shaped by climate change. In 2020 the institute was renamed to recognize a transformative gift from the High Meadows Foundation, a philanthropic organization co-founded by Judy and Carl Ferenbach III '64 to support environmental research and education at Princeton.

The institute brings together more than 120 faculty members from 29 academic departments, including more than 40 who serve as principal investigators on research projects that focus on climate science and modeling, carbon mitigation, biodiversity and conservation, water and biogeochemical cycles, the oceans and atmosphere, climate change and infectious disease, environmental policy and sustainable urban systems, environmental justice, and other topics. In 2012, HMEI was ranked the second-highest think tank on climate change in the world by the International Center for Climate Governance.

Central to HMEI's research activities are several long-term projects, including the Carbon Mitigation Initiative, a university-industry partnership launched in 2000 that seeks solutions to the carbon and climate problem; the Center for Biocomplexity, which examines the mechanisms that sustain the regional and global processes that underlie essential life-support systems; and the Integrated Ground Water Modeling Center that focuses on practical and applied areas of groundwater hydrology and modeling.

HMEI hosts several collaborative initiatives. The Climate Change and Infectious Disease initiative seeks to advance understanding of the impacts of climate on human health (it was particularly active in studying the environmental drivers of the COVID-19 pandemic); the Food and the Environment initiative seeks to develop practical solutions to the challenge of feeding a projected global population of 10 billion people by 2050; and the Climate Futures Initiative in Science, Values, and Policy (sponsored jointly with the University Center for Human Values) focuses on ethical issues related to climate change.

The Grand Challenges program, instituted in 2007, is an integrated research and teaching program that addresses urgent and complex global environmental issues with scientific, technical, public policy, and human dimensions. Through Grand Challenges, HMEI has seeded research projects focused on climate and energy, water and the environment, urban resilience and sustainability, global health and infectious disease, and sustainable development in Africa. A biodiversity challenge promoted innovative research and teaching related to biodiversity topics.

HMEI's Environmental Humanities program encourages the study of environmental subjects by faculty, researchers, and students in the humanities. A visitors' program brings scholars in the humanities from other campuses to spend a year examining environmental topics through the lenses of their disciplines, and seminars, lecture series, and conferences promote public dialogue on the ethical, visual, literal, and human dimensions of environmental topics.

The program in Environmental Studies, based in HMEI, is among the University's most popular undergraduate certificate programs. It prepares students in all disciplines to become leaders in addressing global environmental challenges. Courses in the program explore environmental topics from the perspectives of the natural sciences, engineering, the humanities, and the social sciences. PhD candidates may pursue a graduate certificate in environmental studies.

The Environmental Internship program offers undergraduates opportunities for research and project experience in the summer on field assignments around the globe and in the lab; each year more than 100 students participate in the program.

HMEI hosts or co-sponsors a broad range of public discussions on environmental topics. The HMEI Faculty Seminar Series features four faculty seminars each semester on topics ranging from sea-level rise, climate change, and carbon sequestration to green chemistry and ocean biogeochemistry. The Taplin Environmental Lecture Series brings scholars and environmental leaders from industry, government, nongovernmental organizations, and the private sector to campus to engage the public on environmental topics. These topics have ranged from the environmental humanities, climate science and policy, and economics and sustainability to environmental ethics, federal land-use policy, and the role of science, technology, and industry in environmental mitigation.

HISPANIC/LATINX STUDENTS AT PRINCETON. Students from Latin American backgrounds have been at Princeton since at least the 1880s. Until the 1960s, most of these were international students from Mexico and Central and South America, though an occasional student had grown up in Puerto Rico or the United States.

Born in Cuba, Pedro Rioseco 1888 was one of the first Latin American students at Princeton and the first to receive a degree. When he arrived, Spanish language courses were noticeably absent in the curriculum; in February 1885 the *Daily Princetonian* reported that a class for the study of Spanish finally had been started, and one week later it reported that Rioseco was in charge of the class. By 1892 Spanish was listed in the formal course catalogue, and by 1940, nearly 200 students registered for Spanish 101.

In the early decades of the twentieth century Spanish language courses and occasional extracurricular lectures and musical events were the only ways Latin American cultures appeared in Princeton's curriculum. The groundwork for a program in Latin American studies was laid in the 1930s by Professor Dana Munro, who taught courses in Latin American history, organized conferences at the school of Public and International Affairs, and found funding for students to conduct research in Latin America. In the spring of 1948, Munro introduced a program of study focusing on Latin American and Latino culture, history, economics, and politics.

Bolstered by a $1 million donation, the interdisciplinary program in Latin American Studies was established in 1967 with history professor Stanley Stein as chair.

A short-lived Hispanic Club, founded in 1951, hosted lectures in Spanish, served as a social space for students, and worked to increase the number of course offerings related to Latin America. A growing community beginning in the late 1960s led to the creation of multiple student groups reflecting the variety of Latino cultures represented on campus.

In the spring of 1969, Manuel del Valle '71 established a group that soon became known as Unión Latinoamericana. ULA members included Mexican Americans (who self-identified using the term Chicano), Puerto Ricans, and Cubans, as well as Latin American students from abroad, creating a comfortable environment of peers for both social and political purposes.

ULA's activism arm was strong. Provoked by low Latino enrollment, ULA members cultivated their networks to recruit more Latino students to Princeton. They joined forces with a coalition of African American and Asian American student leaders in a 1971 protest of the University's financial aid policies, which they felt limited the number of students from underrepresented backgrounds. In the protest's aftermath, the coalition successfully lobbied for the creation of the Third World Center (renamed the Carl A. Fields Center in 2002), which became a home for ULA and its successors, and a community center for students of color more broadly. ULA also participated in national movements, like the United Farm Workers' lettuce boycott.

Two student organizations replaced ULA as it lost momentum over the next couple years. Puerto Rican students founded Acción Puertorriqueña y Amigos (Acción) in 1972, with Margarita Rosa '74 as its first president. The next year, Mexican American students established Chicano Caucus, led by Frank Reed '76.

In an attempt to increase Latino representation in the student body, the admission office hired some Latino students as recruiters in the 1970s, but progress was limited. In 1974, Acción, led by Sonia Sotomayor '76 and Charles Hey '77, and Chicano Caucus, led by Reed, filed a complaint with the US Department of Health, Education, and Welfare (HEW) charging the University with discrimination as reflected in the limited representation of Latino culture in the curriculum and the relative lack of Latino students, faculty, and administrators. At that time, there were no Latino tenure-track professors and only about 60 Latino undergraduate students on campus.

The complaint to HEW prompted Princeton to draft an updated affirmative action plan. It also hired Frank Ayala Jr., a Mexican American graduate student at Columbia University, as assistant dean of student affairs in 1974. For the next five years, Ayala became a mentor and support system for many Latino students, serving as a liaison between them and the administration. His room became a gathering place for students. Ricardo Barragan, who worked in the financial aid office, was another mentor. Beginning in 1970, Barragan directed a summer orientation program aimed at providing additional academic support to students from underrepresented backgrounds, which included many Latinos.

Beyond recruitment efforts, Acción and Chicano Caucus worked together developing student-initiated seminars and hosting an annual Latino Cultural Festival. For a few years, the short-lived Cuban Student Association also co-hosted the festival, which featured workshops, talent shows, arts performances, food, and, occasionally, Catholic mass. The two clubs participated in the International Festival and Hispanic Heritage Month events, along with groups like Ballet Folklórico, which performed traditional Mexican dances. They also organized a small-scale graduation ceremony that eventually became Latinx Graduation, one of the culture-based graduation ceremonies organized annually through the Fields Center.

Acción and Chicano Caucus also operated independently. Chicano Caucus members participated in the annual Pachanga weekend, hosted at a different college each year. Initially a gathering of Mexican Americans from east coast schools who were unable to travel home over Thanksgiving break, Pachanga became a weekend-long celebration of speakers, food, and cultural solidarity. Princeton hosted Pachanga five times during the 1980s and 1990s. For a few years Chicano Caucus also published *El Chicanito*, which included poetry, essays, humor, and announcements.

Acción members consisted of both Puerto Ricans from the island and those raised on the mainland. At times, Acción struggled with catering to the different needs of these two groups, including striking a balance of social events and political activism. The group's magazine, *El Accionero*, included essays, stories, editorials, and interviews. For decades, Acción organized lecture series and hosted salsa parties throughout the year, including two large ones open to all featuring well-known bands.

In the broader campus community, Latino students rose to the highest levels of campus leadership and recognition. Sotomayor won the Pyne Prize her senior year, the top undergraduate award. In 1984, Manuel Gonzalez '85, a leader in Chicano Caucus, became the first Latino to serve as president of the Undergraduate Student Government. Six years later, Patricia García-Monet '92 became only the second woman to serve in that role, a position from which she initiated and oversaw the installation of a plaque in the University Chapel commemorating Dr. Martin Luther King Jr.'s sermons there in 1960 and 1962.

Student activism around the inclusion of Latino culture and experiences in the curriculum remained a focus for Latino students throughout the decades. This led to one-off courses on the histories of Puerto Rico and of Mexican Americans, offered as student-initiated seminars, the first of which were taught by history professor Peter Winn. When a 1985 Latino Task Force found that few changes had been made since the 1974 HEW complaint, the University responded by providing additional funding for Latino student groups, and the number of Latino students began to increase. Additional student-initiated courses were offered—in law, linguistics, literature, politics, and sociology—but they were all taught by visiting faculty members, not by the University's own faculty.

Still not seeing the permanent changes they had been pushing for since the 1970s, Latino students occupied Nassau Hall in 1989 in protest; in 1995, they staged a 35-hour sit-in in Nassau Hall with Asian American students similarly frustrated by the lack of courses and faculty in Latino and Asian American studies. After decades of activism, the interdisciplinary program in Latino Studies, a certificate program administered by the program in American Studies, was established in 2009.

Faculty appointed in the 1980s and 1990s made important contributions to the life of the campus and the development of the curriculum. Arcadio Diaz-Quinones, described by his colleagues as "one of the finest and most prominent Caribbean public intellectuals of his time, a talented writer and scholar whose essays already have become classics in the Latin American and Latino/a modern literary canon, and an extraordinary teacher," joined the faculty in 1983 as a professor of Spanish and directed the program in Latin American Studies for six years.

Sociology and international affairs professor Miguel Centeno arrived in 1990; in addition to chairing the Sociology department, he served as the head of Wilson College, founded the Princeton University Preparatory Program to prepare lower-income students in local high schools for college, and served as founding director of the Princeton Institute for International and Regional Studies. Sociology professor Patricia Fernandez Kelly arrived in 1997 and became an advocate for change both on campus and in the Princeton community.

Even so, by the first two decades of the 2000s, the number of Latino tenure-track faculty members—including scholars from abroad—had only reached the 30s, which meant that the issue of representation on the faculty continued to animate activism in the twenty-first century.

In 2013 Acción and Chicano Caucus formally merged into one group, Princeton Latinos y Amigos (PLA). For many of PLA's events, including the annual heritage month celebrations, PLA switched to using the gender-inclusive term Latinx, in line with changing ideas about gender and identity. Other student groups that celebrate Latin American life and promote conversations about Latinx experiences include the dance group Más Flow, the Latino Graduate Student Association, and Princeton University's Latinx Perspectives Organization (PULPO), an umbrella organization that includes groups focused on different aspects of Latinx identity.

While still an undergraduate, María Perales Sánchez '18 filed a lawsuit—along with the University and Microsoft Corporation—challenging termination by the federal government of the Deferred Action for Childhood Arrivals (DACA) program. Sánchez, an undocumented immigrant born in Mexico, attended the 2019 Supreme Court hearing with University president Christopher Eisgruber and Microsoft president Brad Smith '81. In June 2020 the court ruled that the government had acted improperly in terminating the program. The University's general counsel, Ramona Romero, a former national president of the Hispanic National Bar Association, played a leading role in preparing the lawsuit.

More than 750 alumni returned to campus in 2017 for ¡Adelante Tigres!, a conference for Latino alumni. Many were members of the Association of Latino Princeton Alumni (ALPA), first established in 1988. At the time of the conference, more than 500 undergraduates (10.6 percent) identified as Hispanic/Latino, as did 12 percent of graduate students. A year later, Eduardo Bhatia '86, minority leader and former president of the senate of Puerto Rico, delivered the baccalaureate address.

Two years after that, José E. Feliciano '94, along with his wife, Kwanza Jones '93, gave $20 million to name two adjoining dormitories in one of the new residential colleges then being constructed south of Poe Field—the first buildings at Princeton named after Latino and Black donors.

HISTORY, THE DEPARTMENT OF. President John Witherspoon was the first professor to lecture on history, and although he felt that it was "subservient to the interests of religion," he saw the utility of mapping social and intellectual change in relation to belief over time. History continued to serve this purpose for many decades, although in early years the focus in courses sometimes degenerated into mere chronology. In this guise, history education appears not to have made a favorable impression on undergraduates.

The first faculty member to have the title of professor of history, Charles Woodruff Shields 1844, preferred his position as professor of the harmony of science and revealed religion. After three years on the faculty, he wrote an anguished 18-page letter to the trustees begging to be relieved of his courses in history. They refused, but in 1883 they appointed a professionally trained historian, William Milligan Sloane, who was already professor of Latin, to a post as professor of history and political science.

Sloane was a significant scholar, publishing extensively on American government in the early national period and on European history in the late eighteenth and early nineteenth centuries. He remained at Princeton until 1896 when he accepted a position at Columbia. His ties to Princeton remained strong, however; he published a biographical study of James McCosh and was instrumental in the organization of the modern Olympic Games, in which Princetonians played a distinctive role.

The two most famous writers of history at Princeton in the late nineteenth and early twentieth century were not historians by training. John Bach McMaster, whose *History of the American People* revolutionized the writing of American history, taught civil engineering. When the trustees turned down a proposal to make him also a professor of history just as his monumental work appeared (1883), McMaster left to accept a chair at the University of Pennsylvania. (Princeton made token amends by awarding him an honorary degree in 1925.)

The other widely read Princeton writer of history, Woodrow Wilson 1879, was trained as a political scientist. When Wilson as president set up a departmental system in 1904, History, Politics, and Economics were combined. Preceptors in the department were expected to teach everything from medieval history to international law to money and banking. A few survived these challenges and became distinguished scholars—notably Edward Corwin, a scholar of constitutional interpretation, and Charles Howard McIlwain 1894, whose research specialty was medieval political theory. Economics became a separate department in 1913. In 1924, History and Politics achieved separate standing.

Three key appointments helped shape the future of the History department. One of Wilson's last acts was to name Thomas Jefferson Wertenbaker to the faculty. Wertenbaker became an eminent writer on early American history, and a revered mentor of many graduate students. In 1912 two unrelated Halls, Clifton ("Beppo") and Walter ("Buzzer"), joined the department. They were entirely different in temperament and interest; one student wrote of the "aristocratic Mr. Hall who believes in democracy" (Beppo) and the "democratic Mr. Hall who believes in aristocracy" (Buzzer). Yet they were both esteemed undergraduate teachers.

Dana Carleton Munro, a medievalist who joined the department in 1916, reinforced the combination of solid scholarship and excellent teaching. For 20 years (1916–36), first "old Dana" Munro (his son, Dana Gardner Munro, joined the department in 1932), and then Wertenbaker chaired the department. They recruited a remarkable group of young men who propelled the department to professional excellence while making it one of the most highly regarded teaching units in the University. These were the years (the 1920s and 1930s) of the famous freshman course called "Historical Introduction," taught first by Joseph Coy Green, later a high official in the US State Department, and then by John Pomfret, a future president of the College of William & Mary and director of the Huntington Library. Stimulated by this course, enrollment in the department began to grow.

These were also the years in which Raymond Sontag, Joseph Strayer 1925, E. Harris ("Jinks") Harbison 1928, Robert Palmer, Gordon Craig '36 *41, Cyril Black, and Eric Goldman began their Princeton careers. While Sontag departed for Berkeley in 1941, the others remained to form the nucleus of the postwar department.

Meanwhile, however, World War II put the department in a difficult position. Many of the regular members left for service in the armed forces or in Washington, while at the same time the government sent thousands of young soldiers, sailors, and marines to campus, all of whom needed education in American history. Professors of art, philosophy, political science, and music, who had relatively few students in their fields, were recruited to teach courses ranging from the American Revolution to the Civil War. To commemorate his service, the professor of music wrote a "Fanfare for History"; at the time, the dissonance of the piece was regarded as an unfavorable comment on his experience.

In 1945 the department confronted the fact that it needed to address the interests of a new generation of undergraduates who had an appetite for the history of many different cultures. This required the department to add new fields of study, recruit faculty to handle increased enrollment, and, in a rapidly expanding system of American higher education, provide incentives to keep new faculty at Princeton.

"Young Dana" Munro had begun teaching Latin American history before the war; his work was continued by Stanley Stein. The economic historian Jerome Blum, and the historian of scientific thought Charles Gillispie, joined the department immediately after the war; the colonial Americanist Frank Craven (as a replacement for Wertenbaker) joined four years later. Eric Goldman was instrumental in bringing contemporary American history into the curriculum. Cyril Black built up a strong program in Russian Studies, with James Billington '50, future Librarian of Congress, and S. Frederick Starr *68, future president of Oberlin.

Gillispie then assembled a remarkable group in history of science, while Marius Jansen '44, who studied Japanese while serving in the army and the occupation of Japan, played a pivotal role in building up a program in East Asian Studies. Joint appointments strengthened ties between History and the program in Near Eastern Studies. A little later Robert Tignor began giving courses in African history. These developments constituted a significant expansion of the old curriculum, which had been restricted to European and American history and was primarily political in emphasis.

With Strayer as chair (1941–1961), the department retained its reputation for teaching. Two scholars among many stand out: Harbison, valedictorian of his class, returned to his alma mater to teach Reformation history to rave reviews, and Scottish-born Craig, a Rhodes Scholar, was widely reputed to be a spellbinding lecturer on modern Germany. Courses in Russian history, medieval history, and modern American history, taught by Black, Strayer, and Richard Challener '44, the last ably assisted by Nancy Weiss Malkiel, the first female professor of history, attracted large numbers of students. Robert Palmer's book on the *Age of the Democratic Revolution* helped cement the department's international fame.

Meanwhile, Julian Boyd and Arthur Link commenced their major editing projects, the Thomas Jefferson Papers (still ongoing) and the Woodrow Wilson Papers (completed), under the auspices of the department.

European and American history have remained well represented in the curriculum, with significant course enrollment. Classes taught by Peter Brown on late antiquity and the early middle ages, by Pulitzer Prize winner James McPherson on the Civil War, and by Paul Miles on American diplomatic history were among those enrolling the largest numbers. Interest in new types of history and more thematic courses continued under chairs Jerome Blum, Lawrence Stone, Charles Gillispie, and Richard Challener in the 1960s and early 1970s.

Stone moved from Oxford to Princeton and injected social and quantitative—especially demographic—history into the curriculum. Robert Darnton was instrumental in teaching and training graduate students in cultural history, as were Carl Schorske and Natalie Zemon Davis, one of the earliest women appointed to the departmental faculty. Anthony Grafton's innovative research in intellectual history and widely admired undergraduate lectures also brought luster to the department.

Stone, Darnton, Davis, and Grafton all taught European history. They were exceptional scholars and teachers, but it was necessary to expand not only the methodological reach of the department but also its geographical reach. The Civil Rights Movement, the experience of the Vietnam War, and the Women's Movement all played a part in bringing about a reshaping of the curriculum and new appointments, like that of Nell Irvin Painter in African American history.

By the end of the century, the faculty included geographical specialists in Byzantine history, in South Asian and, soon thereafter, Southeast Asian history, as well as the history of the Ottoman Empire and the Balkans. Chairs like Tignor, Daniel Rodgers (an American intellectual historian), Philip Nord (a modern French specialist), Jeremy Adelman (a Latin Americanist) and William Jordan *73 (a medievalist) fostered additional appointments of specialists in subaltern, Latino, Asian American, global/transnational, urban, environmental, gender, and queer history.

Reflecting the diversity of its faculty, members of today's department are involved in a remarkable array of interdisciplinary programs, including African Studies, American Studies, the Ancient World, East Asian Studies, European Cultural Studies, Gender and Sexuality Studies, Hellenic Studies, Italian Studies, Judaic Studies, Latin American Studies, Latino Studies, Medieval Studies, Near Eastern Studies, Russian and Eurasian Studies, and South Asian Studies.

A graduate program in History and Philosophy of Science was established in 1960 under the leadership of Gillispie, who began offering undergraduate instruction in history of science in 1955–56 through a course sponsored jointly by History and the Council of the Humanities. Gillispie offered the first graduate seminar on the topic through the Council of the Humanities in 1959. The program was interdepartmental, with degrees awarded through the departments of History and Philosophy; the appointment of Thomas Kuhn in 1964 bridged the two units.

Over time the interests of the historians and philosophers of science diverged, and after Kuhn's departure for MIT in 1979, the program ceased being interdepartmental. The program in History of Science became fully administered through the department of History, while retaining its own director of graduate studies, admissions process, and graduate fellowships. Since 2010, Princeton graduate students outside the program can earn a graduate certificate in history of science through coursework and participation in the program seminar. Growing interest in history of science across the University has reignited the program's interdisciplinary reach, and a 2014 gift and a bequest of Gillispie created two named chairs in the history of science.

In 1964, Shelby Cullom Davis '30 gave $5.3 million to support the department of History. Under the leadership of Lawrence Stone, the gift was used to establish the Shelby Cullom Davis Center for Historical Studies. Since 1969, the center has hosted a renowned weekly seminar and a group of research fellows (faculty on leave from their home institutions). Both the seminars and the fellows focus on a particular theme, ranging from "History of Education" (1969–71) to "Law & Legalities" (2018–20).

Stone directed the Center for its first 21 years and established its format, a discussion with the author of an article-length research paper read ahead by all attendees. He encouraged vigorous interrogation of the paper's argument and evidence, giving the seminar a reputation in the profession for being gladiatorial. Since 1990, subsequent directors (Davis, Jordan, Gyan Prakash, Grafton, Rodgers, Nord, Angela Creager, and David Bell) have retained Stone's format and aim, if in a less confrontational spirit. The Davis Center seminars every Friday morning remain the major History department-wide event of the week, amidst a busy schedule of field-specific talks and papers on other days.

Many historians who taught at Princeton have served as president of the American Historical Association. Ten of them did so while active or emeritus members of the faculty: the elder Dana Munro (1926), Thomas Wertenbaker (1947), Julian Boyd (1964), Robert Palmer (1970), Joseph Strayer (1971), Arthur Link (1984), Natalie Zemon Davis (1987), Robert Darnton (1999), James McPherson (2003), and Anthony Grafton (2011).

By 2020, 14 members of the department had received Princeton's Howard T. Behrman awards for distinguished achievement in the humanities: Brown, Darnton, Davis, Gillispie, Grafton, Jan Gross, Jansen, Jordan, McPherson, Nord, Rodgers, Schorske, Stone, and Sean Wilentz.

HOAXES AND PRANKS. At Commencement each spring, a high-ranking senior delivers a salutatory address in Latin and parents and family members are amazed that so many members of the graduating class know when to laugh, groan, and hiss, until they realize that the class has been cued and they are witnessing a hoax, or a prank—admittedly a high-class one.

Princeton history is replete with many other hoaxes and pranks (none of them dependent on Latin). Some date to Princeton's earliest days: in 1812 a student climbed to the top of Nassau Hall at 3 a.m. to ring the bell and in 1864 a student climbed up to remove the clapper to prevent the bell from signaling the start of classes—beginning a tradition of clapper nabbing that lasted off and on until 1992. In 1814 students exploded a hollow log filled with two pounds of gunpowder inside Nassau Hall, cracking the interior walls and breaking windows throughout the building. In 1790 four students put a calf in the Nassau Hall pulpit, and one night during the presidency of John Maclean Jr. 1816, students led him to the third floor of the building where they had tethered two donkeys to greet him.

Some hoaxes and pranks are hardy perennials, such as the April 1 edition and the annual "joke issue" of the *Daily Princetonian*. Cane spree, an annual wrestling match between freshmen and sophomores, traces its roots to pranks and other skirmishes between the classes in the 1860s that over time evolved from prank to tradition.

Most hoaxes and pranks are more *sui generis*. A sampling of some of the more famous (or infamous) follows.

Joseph David Oznot '68 was one of the most celebrated applicants admitted to Princeton in the mid-1960s. His file showed that at high school in East Lansing, Michigan, he was a top student, a concert pianist, and class treasurer, with College Board scores in the 700s. He was notified of his admission on April 16, 1964, and two days later newspapers from coast to coast carried an Associated Press report that the University had been tricked into admitting a fictitious character by a clever, well-executed hoax, perpetrated by six sophomores: four at Princeton, one at Columbia, and one at Michigan State.

The Michigan State sophomore submitted Oznot's preliminary application for admission in October, giving his fraternity house as Oznot's address. During the Christmas recess the Columbia sophomore came to Princeton for Oznot's admission interview. In January two of the Princeton sophomores took Oznot's College Board exams. The final application papers, with space for grades and comment by the high school, were received by the Michigan State sophomore and carefully filled out by the six conspirators. They settled on April 1 for Oznot's birthday and private detective as the occupation of his father, William H. Oznot (W.H.O.).

Director of admission E. Alden Dunham III '53 found the hoax "ingenious" and said, "We would love to have had him." For many years Oznot made continuing appearances in 1968's class notes.

A similar personage, Ephriam Di Kahble '39, was invented by five classmates who rented a room at 36 University Place and decorated it to make it look like his. His name appeared on chapel attendance cards and the registrar received examination grades for him in several courses. He ran for class treasurer and placed an ad in the *New York Times* seeking information about an orange and black guinea pig, with the intent of proposing that it replace the tiger as Princeton's mascot.

His classmates recalled last seeing him at an intercollegiate cross-country race in Van Cortlandt Park one hazy afternoon. It was said that Di Kahble started out with the other runners but never returned. He resurfaced in the class's 25th reunion book and for many years he sent birthday cards to members of the class. The University's Graphic Arts Collection holds a collection of candy wrappers that he donated.

Another imaginary Princetonian, Bert Hormone 1917, was completely unknown in his student days, waiting to blossom after graduation. He was first mentioned in 1917's class notes in the *Alumni Weekly* in the spring of 1937, shortly before their 20th reunion. Although several members of the class said they vaguely remembered him, no one could place him with certainty. Under questioning, the class secretary, Harvey Smith 1917, admitted that Adelbert l'Homme-dieu X. Hormone—Bert's full name—was his invention, created to stimulate interest in the reunion. (Hormone appears in Smith's 1941 book, *The Gang's All Here*, published by Princeton University Press as a fictional account of a class's 25th reunion.)

In later years different members of the class reported chance encounters with him all over the world. He became a colonel in the French Foreign Legion, and Smith faithfully chronicled his global exploits. Shortly before the class's 50th reunion he reported that Bert had died and been buried in his beloved Tahiti, his grave covered with flowers kept fresh by the tears of several grieving widows.

An admission deception of a different kind took place in 1988 when James Hogue was admitted to the Class of 1992 as Alexi Indris-Santana. After briefly attending several universities, Hogue had enrolled at Palo Alto High School in California in 1985 when he was 25 years old, claiming he was a 16-year-old self-educated orphan who had been raised in a commune in Nevada. He told Princeton he was a self-educated ranch hand from rural Utah who had been tending sheep and reading philosophy in the Grand Canyon. Following admission to Princeton, he asked to defer a year to care for his dying mother in Switzerland, a subterfuge necessitated by his need to spend the year in a Utah prison for theft.

In his sophomore year at Princeton the fraud was discovered when a Yale student recognized him at a track meet as a former Palo Alto classmate. Hogue was arrested for violating his parole, pled guilty to defrauding Princeton of student aid, and served nine months in prison. After several other run-ins with the law, he secretly returned to Princeton in 1996 where he was discovered posing as a geology PhD student named James MacAuthor and eating his meals at the graduate college. He pled guilty to trespassing and was banned from the campus for life.

A very different kind of prank surfaced in 1975 when a local resident named Henry Fairfax sent valentines to every female freshman and sophomore. Fairfax supposedly had met a woman at a Princeton party, promised to send her a valentine, but forgot her name, so he sent cards to all who might be her. With a few exceptions, the practice continued until 1987 when it was discovered that members of Charter Club had been responsible for the valentines.

In the mid-1960s, a student called the Red Baron showed up at final exams dressed only in red accessories, such as a World War I flier's hat, ski mask, goggles, cape, socks, and tennis shoes, but otherwise unclothed. In February 1974, Charles Bell '76, later nicknamed "the Streak," ran naked through the student center and then ran for student government president on a platform of "if elected, I'll run."

In March 1936, several Princeton students formed a satirical organization called the Veterans of Future Wars, proposing that Congress pay $1,000 cash bonuses to all men between the ages of 18 and 36 so future veterans could receive their benefits while they were still alive to enjoy them. By June there were more than 500 chapters on other campuses and a membership of over 50,000 students. The organization received widespread media attention and was denounced in Congress and by legitimate veterans' groups. The Veterans of Future Wars suspended operation in the fall of 1936 and closed its doors the following April.

In 1967, when ABC televised a Princeton-Harvard football game, the network had not planned to broadcast the University Band's halftime show. But when the band formed "ABC" on the field, the cameras televised it—just as the band scrambled the "A" to form "NBC."

In 1979, a week prior to the Princeton-Yale football game, four supposed Yale cheerleaders picked up the bulldog Handsome Dan XII (Yale's first female mascot) from the professor who owned her; they said they needed her for a photo shoot. The Princeton undergraduates called the owner to reassure him that Dan was in good hands and then took her to Princeton where she visited the eating clubs and football practice wearing an orange and black t-shirt. On game day she appeared on the field at halftime when Princeton's mascot carried her, with an orange and black scarf around her neck, to the real Yale cheerleaders.

In 1969, a week before the 100th anniversary Princeton-Rutgers football game, a dozen Princeton students dug a hole next to the cannon buried face down between Whig and Clio Halls, piled dirt on top of the cannon, and left a note suggesting it had been carried away by Rutgers students. The next morning WPRB, the campus radio station, and Public Safety were notified that Rutgers students had stolen the cannon. The national press picked up the story, reporting that the students "apparently staged a predawn raid." When the Princeton students revealed the hoax, ABC television was on hand as the dirt was scraped away to show the cannon had been safely in place all along. The *Philadelphia Inquirer* headline: "Princeton 'Outguns' Rutgers."

Leading most all-time prank lists is the Great Dinky Train Robbery of May 3, 1963, when four Princeton students on horseback and wearing cowboy outfits and bandanas ambushed the 6:14 p.m. train as it arrived on campus just prior to Houseparties weekend. The students placed a convertible across the tracks to stop the train, approached it while firing blanks from six-shooters, abducted four women passengers, and carried them off on horseback to Prospect Avenue, home of the eating clubs.

[Accounts of two other pranks—the Nude Olympics and Poler's Recess—can be found in entries under those headings.]

Holder Hall forms a large quadrangle, with three sides containing dormitory rooms and the fourth a cloisters, and with 140-foot Holder Tower as its dominant feature. Noteworthy elements include heavy slate roofs and leaded casement windows in the dormitory buildings, the vaulted passages of the cloisters, and the unique finials atop the pinnacles on Holder Tower—four bronze tigers-rampant—which also function as weathervanes.

Holder Hall was given in 1909 by Margaret Olivia Slocum Sage, widow of the financier Russell Sage, and named at her request for her ancestor, Christopher Holder, "a member of the Society of Friends in America in the Seventeenth Century"; a tablet in the arch beneath the tower describes him as "devout, loving, loyal to duty, patient in suffering."

Holder Hall and the adjacent dining halls were erected on the site of the old University Hotel at the corner of Nassau Street and University Place. When the foundation for Holder was dug, the unmarked graveyard of the family of Nathanial FitzRandolph, one of the College's early benefactors and the donor of its original four and a half acres, was discovered. The University reinterred the graves and installed a commemorative plaque on the south wall of the new building's east arch.

Holder and the adjoining dining halls were designed by Day and Klauder. Supervising architect Ralph Adams Cram said in this project they reached "the highest point in their authoritative interpretation of Gothic as a living style." In addition to housing students (now as part of Rockefeller College), Holder also housed the student radio station, WPRB (earlier WPRU), from 1946 until it moved to Bloomberg Hall in 2004.

Honor System, The, had its origin in rampant cheating on exams in the late nineteenth century and student dissatisfaction with faculty proctoring. In 1893 the *Daily Princetonian* called for the establishment of a system whereby students would have "sole charge of examinations." Such a plan was in place at some southern schools, including William & Mary and the University of Virginia, where Professor Woodrow Wilson 1879 had become familiar with it. Princeton student leaders gained the support of the dean of the faculty, James Murray, who presented a proposal at a faculty meeting where Wilson's eloquent plea helped secure a favorable vote. The adoption of the honor system attracted wide attention in the press and on other campuses.

The faculty resolution said that "until due notice is given to the contrary," there would be no further faculty supervision of in-class examinations, which students would take on their honor. In 1895 the first constitution of the honor system established a student committee of six to administer it, and provided that if a student was found guilty of a violation of the honor code the committee would recommend to the faculty the student's permanent separation from the College. Initially only two of six committee votes were required to convict, but this was soon increased to five.

By unanimous vote of the student body at a mass meeting in 1921 the committee was enlarged to seven members and authorized to recommend leniency in exceptional cases. For a time in the 1920s the code was expanded to "cover the whole life of the students," but the idea was abandoned, and even today the honor system applies, as originally intended, only to written in-class exams. All other cases of academic misconduct, including those related to plagiarism on problem sets, papers, or take-home exams completed outside of class, go to the faculty-student committee on discipline.

In 1975 the constitution was amended to allow imposition of a lighter penalty (a one-year separation instead of expulsion) in certain cases, to enumerate the rights of the accused, and to place the power to amend the constitution with the undergraduate governing body rather than a mass meeting. Amendments since then have modified the composition of the honor committee, the process for selecting members, the procedures under which the committee operates, and the range of penalties.

The honor committee now has 15 members. The constitution may be amended upon the initiative of at least 13 of the 15 members followed by a three-fourths vote of the Undergraduate Student Government (USG), or by petition of at least 200 undergraduates followed by a three-fourths vote in a student referendum conducted by the USG.

In 2017–19, concerns arose about a lack of alignment between the penalties and procedures of the honor committee and those of the discipline committee for what in many cases were similar infractions, and several student referenda regarding the honor system were set aside for proposing changes that students were not empowered to make without faculty consent. A faculty-student Disciplinary Review Committee examined the standards and procedures of the discipline committee and a separate faculty-student Honor System Review Committee assessed the honor committee's processes, policies, and standards.

An Academic Integrity Report Reconciliation Committee was then asked to consider the findings of both reviews and make its own recommendations. The reconciliation committee expressed support for key aspects of the honor code: that in-class exams remain unproctored and that students continue to lead the honor committee. But it recommended changes in the composition of the honor committee and called for more collaboration between the discipline and honor committees, better training, changes in the penalty structure of both committees, and refinements of the honor committee's investigative processes and procedures.

Under the new penalty structure, a student found responsible for violating the honor code can be given a reprimand, placed on disciplinary probation for a set period of time, or suspended from the University for one semester or one, two, or three years. A second offense can result in expulsion. Censure may be added to all penalties to underscore the seriousness of the violation.

In 1928 some students complained that they were not aware they had to abide by the honor code or that they were expected to turn in cheating classmates. The University instituted an annual honor assembly at the beginning of freshman year to introduce students to the code and their obligations under it, and the honor committee began sending notice of the code to all entering students and requiring that they affirm their willingness to abide by it. This practice continues today: newly admitted students may not enroll until they have submitted a statement signifying that they understand and will abide by the conditions under which the honor system is conducted.

All students must acknowledge the obligation to report any suspected violation of the honor system that they observe. This requirement was implicit in the compact between faculty and students in 1893; today, the undergraduate announcement explicitly states, "an individual's obligation to the undergraduate student body as a whole" and to the academic integrity of the University "transcends any reluctance to report another student." This means that under the honor system students have a twofold obligation: individually, not to violate the code, and as a community, to see that suspected violations are reported.

Students are reminded of this obligation every time they take an in-class exam. On each examination paper students must write out and sign the following statement: "I pledge my honor that I have not violated the Honor Code during this examination."

Honorary Degrees have been awarded by Princeton since its earliest days. The degree of Master of Arts, *honoris causa*, was conferred on the governor of the province of New Jersey, Jonathan Belcher, at the College's first Commencement in 1748. But this was an exception; for the first century and a half, most degrees were conferred by the trustees at their stated meetings, and the recipients were then informed of the honor by a letter from the clerk.

In 1895 the trustees amended the bylaws to provide that thereafter all honorary degrees should be conferred in person. The sesquicentennial celebration the following year was the first occasion when honorary degree recipients assembled for the conferring of their degrees. There were 56, the largest number ever honored at one time. (During the year-long celebration of the bicentennial in 1946–47,

Among the honorary degree recipients in 1970 was later Nobel Laureate Bob Dylan who immortalized the "high whining trill" of the 17-year cicadas at that year's Commencement in his song, *Day of the Locusts*; he is shown here with then-dean of students Neil Rudenstine '56.

113 honorary degrees were conferred, but the largest number at any one convocation was 36.)

In 1905 Andrew Fleming West 1874 inaugurated the practice of reading a formal citation as each degree was presented. Most honorary degrees now are presented at Commencement; recipients must receive an affirmative vote from 80 percent of the board, upon the recommendation of its committee on honorary degrees, which includes members of the campus community in addition to trustees. The citations are read by an individual designated by the trustees as University Orator, who in recent years typically has been a retiring member of the board.

Occasionally degrees are conferred on other occasions, such as the degrees presented to Presidents Lyndon Johnson and George H. W. Bush when they visited Princeton to dedicate Robertson Hall in 1966 and Fisher-Bendheim halls in 1991.

In 2020 the requirement of in-person conferral was waived as five honorary degrees were conferred at a virtual commencement necessitated by that year's COVID-19 pandemic. In 2021 the University conducted an in-person Commencement in Princeton Stadium, but with the pandemic still a factor one of that year's six recipients (all of whom were from New Jersey) also was recognized *in absentia*.

John Gilbert Winant 1913 received two honorary degrees, one in 1925 while governor of New Hampshire and another in 1943 as ambassador to Great Britain. The first woman to receive an honorary doctorate was Willa Cather in 1931; Ralph Bunche, undersecretary of the United Nations, was the first Black recipient in 1951; the first woman of color to receive an honorary degree was Marian Anderson in 1959.

In 1996, Bill Clinton became the 18th US president to receive an honorary degree from Princeton. Seven received their degrees before becoming president: James Madison 1771 in 1787; Thomas Jefferson in 1791; John Quincy Adams in 1806; James Buchanan in 1850; Woodrow Wilson 1879 in 1910; Herbert Hoover in 1917; and Dwight Eisenhower in 1947. Sitting presidents who received degrees, in addition to Clinton, Johnson, and Bush, were James Monroe in 1822; Abraham Lincoln in 1864; Chester Arthur in 1884; Benjamin Harrison in 1889; William Howard Taft in 1912; Warren Harding in 1922; and Harry Truman in 1947. Grover Cleveland received a degree in 1897, a year after leaving office. The trustees authorized a degree for Calvin Coolidge, but it was never conferred.

Three presidents attended Princeton commencements without receiving honorary degrees: George Washington in 1783; Ulysses Grant in 1871 and 1875; and Rutherford Hayes in 1878.

Honorary degree recipients since 1970 are listed on pages 511–16.

HOODING CEREMONY. While graduate students formally receive their PhD or master's degrees at Commencement, since 1994 they have been recognized individually the day before Commencement during a ceremony at which they receive the hood appropriate to their rank and academic discipline so they can wear it the next day when they receive their diplomas. (In the late nineteenth century Princeton took the lead in establishing a code for US academic attire, and one of the first major displays of the code's academic dress occurred at Princeton's sesquicentennial in 1896.)

Masters' hoods are generally one foot shorter than doctors' hoods. Each hood is bordered by a velvet band in the color assigned to the discipline in which the degree is granted: blue for doctor of philosophy; peacock blue for public affairs; orange or yellow for engineering; white for arts and letters; brown for architecture; and light brown for finance. The hood lining is orange with a black chevron, indicating that the degree has been granted by Princeton.

In recent years, the Hooding Ceremony has taken place on Cannon Green (or Jadwin Gym in case of severe weather). PhD candidates may receive their hood from a faculty member (usually their adviser) or from the chief faculty marshal, and master's candidates are hooded by the chief marshal. For many participants, the ceremony symbolizes not only the culmination of graduate studies, but the recipient's transition from student to colleague.

The Hooding Ceremony also recognizes the recipients of each year's graduate mentoring awards, which are presented to faculty members for exceptional contributions as mentors to graduate students. Current and former students nominate faculty for the awards and the recipients are chosen by a committee of faculty and graduate students.

HOSACK, DAVID 1789, a leading physician of his day and an eminent botanist and mineralogist, was the son of a New York wine merchant who came to America to serve under Lord Jeffery Amherst in the French and Indian War. Hosack attended Columbia for two years and then transferred to Princeton, where he received his bachelor's degree.

He studied medicine, first in New York, then in Philadelphia, where he lived with the family of his favorite teacher, Benjamin Rush 1760. He later studied medicine and botany in Edinburgh and mineralogy in London, bringing back from Great Britain the beginnings of a mineralogical collection that he later gave to Princeton.

Hosack's circle of friends included Aaron Burr Jr. 1772 and Alexander Hamilton. As the surgeon in attendance at their duel in 1804, he treated Hamilton after he was mortally wounded, and he was one of the pallbearers at Hamilton's funeral. Three years later, after Burr was tried for treason and acquitted, Hosack lent him passage-money to go abroad to escape the notoriety resulting from the trial.

Princeton awarded Hosack an honorary degree in 1818. In 1830 he was elected a vice president of the Alumni Association of Nassau Hall, of which James Madison 1771 was president.

HOUSE OF REPRESENTATIVES, THE, of the United States has not been without a Princeton alum in any year since it first met in 1789. All told, more than 225 Princetonians have represented 29 states and territories in the lower house of Congress.

Eight members of the Class of 1805 served in the House, three of them from Georgia. The class of 1954 contributed three members: William Hudnut of Indiana, Donald Rumsfeld of Illinois, and Paul Sarbanes of Maryland. Since then, the classes of 1956, 1981, and 1996 have contributed two each: Pierre S. DuPont IV '56 (Delaware) and Michael Strang '56 (Colorado); Kenneth Buck '81 (Colorado) and Nan Hayworth '81 (New York); and Derek Kilmer '96 (Washington) and Jared Polis '96 (Colorado). Edward Livingston 1781 represented two states: New York from 1795 to 1801, and Louisiana from 1823 to 1829.

Following is a list of Princeton alumni representatives. The representative's party affiliation (in some cases, initial affiliation) is given in parenthesis, viz.: American (A), Anti-Administration (AA), Anti-Federalist (AF), Anti-Jacksonian (AJ), Democratic (D), Federalist (F), Free Soiler (FS), Independent (I), Jacksonian (J), Pro-Administration (PA), Republican (R), Unconditional Unionist War (UU), Whig (W).

ALABAMA

James Jones 1852 (D) 1877–79, 1883–89
Arthur Glenn Andrews '31 (R) 1965–67
Terri Sewell '86 (D) 2011–

TERRITORY OF ARKANSAS

James Bates 1807 (I) 1819–23

CALIFORNIA

Joseph McKibbin 1843 (D) 1857–59
John Hinshaw 1916 (R) 1939–56
Ed Zschau '61 (R) 1983–87
Mel Levine *66 (D) 1983–93
Walter R. Tucker III '78 (D) 1993–95

COLORADO

Robert Rockwell 1909 (R) 1941–49
Michael Strang '56 (R) 1985–87
Jared Polis '96 (D) 2009–19
Kenneth Buck '81 (R) 2015–

CONNECTICUT

Henry Edwards 1797 (D) 1819–23
Stewart McKinney '53 (R) 1971–87

DELAWARE

James Bayard 1784 (F) 1797–1803
James Broom 1794 (F) 1805–07
Nicholas Van Dyke Jr. 1788 (F) 1807–11
Kensey Johns Jr. 1810 (F) 1827–31
John Milligan 1814 (W) 1831–39
Thomas Robinson Jr. 1823 (D) 1839–41
George Rodney 1820 (W) 1841–45
Elisha Cullen 1819 (A) 1855–57
William Whiteley 1838 (D) 1857–61
Harry G. Haskell Jr. '44 (R) 1957–59
Pierre S. DuPont IV '56 (R) 1971–77

GEORGIA

Peter Early 1792 (R) 1803–07
George Troup 1797 (D) 1807–15
John Forsyth 1799 (D) 1813–18, 1823–27
Thomas Telfair 1805 (D) 1813–17
Alfred Cuthbert 1803 (D) 1813–16, 1821–27
John Cuthbert 1805 (D) 1819–21
James Wayne 1808 (D) 1829–35
Seaborn Jones 1807 (J) 1833–35, 1845–47
Walter Colquitt 1820 (W) 1839–40, 1842–43
Richard Habersham 1805 (D) 1839–42
George Crawford 1820 (W) 1843
Alfred Iverson 1820 (D) 1847–49
Alfred Colquitt 1844 (D) 1853–55
Tinsley W. Rucker Jr. (D) 1917
James Marshall '72 (D) 2003–11

ILLINOIS

Donald Rumsfeld '54 (R) 1963–69
Raja Krishnamoorthi '95 (D) 2017–

INDIANA

William Hudnut '54 (R) 1973–75

IOWA

James Leach '64 (R) 1977–2007

KENTUCKY

Addison White 1844 (W) 1851–53
Thomas Jones 1840 (D) 1867–71, 1875–77

LOUISIANA

Edward Livingston 1781 (D) 1823–29

MARYLAND

Samuel Smith 1795 (D) 1793–1803, 1816–22
John Archer 1760 (D) 1801–07

Stevenson Archer 1805 (D) 1811–17, 1819–21
Thomas Bayly 1797 (D) 1817–23
William H. Hayward Jr. 1808 (D) 1823–25
Ephraim Wilson 1789 (D) 1827–31
Benjamin Howard 1809 (D) 1829–33, 1835–39
John Stoddert 1810 (D) 1833–35
Richard Carmichael 1828 (D) 1833–35
James Pearce 1822 (W) 1835–39, 1841–43
John Mason 1836 (D) 1841–43
Joseph Cottman 1823 (W) 1851–53
Charles Phelps 1852 (UU) 1865–69
Stevenson Archer 1846 (D) 1867–75
John Findlay 1858 (D) 1883–87
Barnes Compton 1851 (D) 1885–89, 1891–94
John Cowen 1866 (D) 1895–97
George Pearre 1880 (R) 1899–1911
Daniel Brewster '46 (D) 1959–63
Clarence Long *38 (D) 1963–85
Paul. Sarbanes '54 (D) 1971–77
John Sarbanes '84 (D) 2007–

MASSACHUSETTS

John Bacon 1765 (D) 1801–03
Jonathan Mason Jr. 1774 (F) 1817–20
Abram P. Andrew Jr. 1893 (R) 1921–36
John Kennedy '39 (D) 1947–53

MISSOURI

John Scott 1805 (D) 1816–27
Francis P. Blair Jr. 1841 (FS) 1857–64
Roger Slaughter 1928 (D) 1943–47

NEW HAMPSHIRE

Samuel Livermore 1752 (F) 1789–93

NEW JERSEY

Jonathan Dayton 1776 (F) 1791–99
John Beatty 1769 (PA) 1793–95
Isaac Smith 1755 (F) 1795–97
Thomas Henderson 1761 (F) 1795–97
James Imlay 1786 (F) 1797–1801
James Linn 1769 (D) 1799–1801
John Scudder 1775 (D) 1810–11
George Maxwell 1792 (D) 1811–13
Richard Stockton 1779 (F) 1813–15
Thomas Ward 1803 (D) 1813–17
George Holcombe 1805 (D) 1821–28
Isaac Pierson 1789 (W) 1827–31
Silas Condit 1795 (D) 1831–33
William Chetwood 1792 (D) 1836–37

William Halsted 1812 (W) 1837–39, 1841–43
John Maxwell 1823 (W) 1837–39, 1841–43
Littleton Kirkpatrick 1815 (D) 1843–45
James Hampton 1835 (W) 1845–49
George Brown 1828 (W) 1851–53
Isaiah Clawson 1840 (W) 1855–59
William Pennington 1813 (W) 1859–61
John Stratton 1836 (R) 1859–63
John Nixon 1841 (R) 1859–63
Charles Haight 1857 (D) 1867–71
Frederick Teese 1843 (D) 1875–77
George Robeson 1847 (R) 1879–83
Henry Harris 1870 (D) 1881–83
Robert Green 1850 (D) 1885–87
Christopher Bergen 1863 (R) 1889–93
Samuel Fowler 1873 (D) 1889–93
Mahlon Pitney 1879 (R) 1895–99
Richard Parker 1867 (R) 1895–1911, 1911–19, 1921–23
Ira Wood 1877 (R) 1904–13
Walter McCoy 1881 (D) 1911–14
Charles Browne 1896 *1900 (D) 1923–25
Elmer Geran 1899 (D) 1923–25
Franklin Fort 1901 (R) 1925–31
Charles Howell 1927 (D) 1949–55
Alfred Sieminski '34 (D) 1951–59
Peter Frelinghuysen '38 (R) 1953–75
Leonard Lance *82 (R) 2009–19

NEW YORK

Jeremiah van Rensselaer 1758 (AA) 1789–91
Thomas Treadwell 1764 (AA) 1791–95
Edward Livingston 1781 (D) 1795–1801
L. Conrad Elmendorf 1782 (D) 1797–1803
William Kirkpatrick 1788 (D) 1807–09
Robert Livingston 1784 (F) 1809–12
William Smith 1774 (F) 1813–15
Nathaniel Howell 1788 (F) 1813–15
James Wilkin 1785 (D) 1815–19
Silas Wood 1789 (D) 1819–29
Stephen Van Rensselaer 1783 (F) 1822–29
Samuel Eager 1809 (R) 1830–31
Samuel Wilkin 1812 (D) 1831–33
William Seymour 1821 (D) 1835–37
Andrew Bruyn 1810 (D) 1837–38
Obadiah Bowne 1841 (W) 1851–53
Alexander Bailey 1837 (R) 1867–71
George McClellan 1886 (D) 1895–1903
Charles Talcott 1879 (D) 1911–15
Walter Andrews 1913 (R) 1931–49
Ralph Gamble 1909 (R) 1937–57
William Ryan '44 (D) 1961–72

Otis Pike '43 (D) 1961–79
Nan Hayworth '81 (R) 2011–13

NORTH CAROLINA

Nathaniel Macon 1777 (D) 1791–1815
David Stone 1788 (D) 1799–1801
Nathaniel Alexander 1776 (D) 1803–05
Evan Alexander 1787 (D) 1806–09
William Gaston 1796 (F) 1813–17
James Clark 1797 (D) 1815–17
Jesse Bynum 1821 (D) 1833–41
William Montgomery 1808 (D) 1835–41
Abraham Venable 1819 (D) 1847–53
Lawrence Branch 1838 (D) 1855–61
Richmond Pearson 1872 (R) 1895–1901
L. Richardson Preyer '41 (D) 1969–81
James Martin *60 (R) 1973–85
James Clarke '39 (D) 1983–85, 1987–91

OHIO

John Vanmeter 1821 (W) 1843–45
George White 1895 (D) 1911–15, 1917–19
Seward Williams 1897 (R) 1915–17
Michael Feighan 1927 (D) 1943–71

PENNSYLVANIA

John Kittera 1776 (F) 1791–1801
James Armstrong 1773 (PA) 1793–95
David Bard 1773 (R) 1795–99, 1803–15
John Hanna 1782 (AF) 1797–1805
William Crawford 1781 (D) 1809–17
John Sergeant 1795 (F) 1815–23, 1827–29, 1837–41
John Wurts 1813 (R) 1825–27
Thomas Crawford 1804 (D) 1829–33
Alem Marr 1807 (D) 1829–31
John Watmough 1811 (AJ) 1831–35
George Chambers 1804 (W) 1833–37
Joseph Ingersoll 1804 (W) 1835–37, 1841–49
Samuel Morris 1806 (D) 1837–41
George Toland 1816 (W) 1837–43
Henry Nes 1824 (I) 1843–45, 1847–50
James Pollock 1831 (W) 1844–49
Chester Butler 1817 (W) 1847–50
Thomas Ross 1825 (D) 1849–53
Henry Fuller 1839 (W) 1851–53, 1855–57
William Dewart 1841 (D) 1857–59
Robert McKnight 1839 (R) 1859–63
Charles Biddle 1837 (D) 1861–63
William Armstrong 1847 (R) 1869–71
James Strawbridge 1844 (R) 1873–75
Hiester Clymer 1847 (D) 1873–81

Edward Overton Jr. 1856 (R) 1877–81
Harry White 1854 (R) 1877–81
James Everhart 1842 (R) 1883–87
John Swope 1847 (D) 1884–87
Welty McCullogh 1870 (R) 1887–89
Thomas Crago 1893 (R) 1911–13, 1915–23
Lawrence Watres 1904 (R) 1923–31
William Richardson 1910 (D) 1933–37

SOUTH CAROLINA

Robert Harper 1785 (F) 1795–1801
John Taylor 1790 (D) 1807–10

TENNESSEE

George Campbell 1794 (D) 1803–09
John Rhea 1780 (D) 1803–15, 1817–23
Nathaniel Taylor 1840 (W) 1854–55, 1866–67
Hubert Fisher *1901 (D) 1917–31

TEXAS

David Kaufman 1833 (D) 1846–51
George Smyth 1831 (D) 1853–55
Dudley Wooten 1875 (D) 1901–03
Joseph W. Bailey Jr. 1915 (D) 1933–35
Bruce Alger 1940 (R) 1955–65

VERMONT

Nathaniel Niles 1766 (AA) 1791–95
Peter Smith '68 (R) 1989–91

VIRGINIA

James Madison 1771 (D) 1789–97
John Brown 1778 (AA) 1789–92
William Giles 1781 1790–98 (AF), 1801–03 (D)
Abraham Venable 1780 (D) 1791–99
Henry Lee Jr. 1773 (F) 1799–1801
John Randolph 1791 (D) 1799–1813, 1815–17, 1819–25, 1827–29, 1833
Thomas Bayly 1794 (D) 1813–15
Charles Mercer 1797 (F) 1817–39
Edward Colston 1806 (F) 1817–19
Alfred Powell 1799 (F) 1825–27
George Crump 1805 (D) 1826–27
John Patton 1816 (D) 1830–38
John Roane 1816 (J) 1831–33
James Gholson 1820 (D) 1833–35
James McDowell 1816 (D) 1846–51
Alexander Boteler 1835 (A) 1859–61

WASHINGTON

Derek Kilmer '96 (D) 2013–

WEST VIRGINIA

James Jackson 1845 (D) 1889–90
Joseph Gaines 1886 (R) 1901–11
Cleveland Benedict '57 (R) 1981–83

WISCONSIN

Michael Gallagher '06 (R) 2017–

ICE HOCKEY. The University's first ice hockey star may have been its brightest; the name of Hobey Baker 1914 remains synonymous with collegiate hockey excellence more than a century after he last wore a Princeton sweater. In recent years, the men's and women's teams have each earned trips to the NCAA tournament.

Men's Ice Hockey

Princetonians began playing hockey recreationally in the 1890s and took a more formal role in the sport when Princeton became a founding member of an intercollegiate hockey league that began in 1899, playing at rinks in Manhattan and Brooklyn. Harvard and Yale dominated the league in its early years, but Princeton managed to win the championship in 1907, when it was 4–0 against collegiate teams, and 1910, when it won three of four games against Yale.

The Tigers began a brief, dazzling era of dominance when Hobey Baker arrived, leading Princeton to championships in 1912 and 1914 (and narrowly missing another in 1913). Baker played rover, a position eliminated in 1921 when hockey teams were reduced from seven to six players. This position showcased his speed and creativity, attributes chronicled in John Davies '41's 1966 biography, *The Legend of Hobey Baker*. When defensemen crossed their sticks to block Baker, "he would push the puck ahead and vault the sticks to recover it," Davies wrote. As he looped his way down the ice, he would often dodge the same defender two or three times. The *Alumni Weekly*, in its summary of the 1914 season, wrote that Baker was "universally recognized as the most brilliant college hockey player of all time."

After graduation and a celebrated amateur career with Manhattan's St. Nicholas Hockey Club, Baker served with distinction as an American pilot and squadron commander in World War I. He was killed in an airplane crash soon after the armistice, just before his scheduled return to the United States. With funds contributed by his Princeton friends and admirers from many other colleges, Princeton built Baker Memorial Rink, dedicated in 1923, where the

Princeton teams continue to play beneath a banner that reads "Make Hobey Proud." Since 1981, the Hobey Baker Award has been presented to the nation's top men's collegiate hockey player.

Princeton had several winning seasons in the 1920s and 1930s, including 1928–29, when the Tigers were unbeaten in their first 13 games and finished 15-3-1. Coach Dick Vaughan joined the program in 1935 and guided the 1941 team to a championship. Led by top scorer Dan Stuckey '42, the Tigers took first place in the Quadrangular League over Dartmouth, Harvard, and Yale.

Hockey took a two-year hiatus during World War II and played limited schedules in 1945–46 and 1946–47 when Baker Rink was boarded over for use as a gym (and for other purposes) between the loss of the University Gymnasium to fire in 1944 and the completion of Dillon Gym in 1947. By 1953 Princeton had sufficiently recovered its momentum to win the Pentagonal League championship over Brown, Dartmouth, Harvard, and Yale. Captain and All-American center Hank Bothfeld '53 set a Princeton career record of 103 points (55 goals, 48 assists). That record was broken in 1960 by John McBride '60, and again in 1963 by John Cook '63, who totaled 132 points (67 goals, 65 assists). Cook's goals record would stand for nearly 56 years.

In 1961–62, men's hockey joined the Eastern College Athletic Conference (ECAC). In its first two decades in the league, Princeton managed just one winning season, 1967–68, the team's first year under coach Bill Quackenbush. The Tigers finished 13-10-1 overall and qualified for their first ECAC postseason tournament, losing to Cornell in the quarterfinals.

Coach Jim Higgins led Princeton to the ECAC postseason four times between 1985 and 1991, but the team never advanced beyond the quarterfinals. The Tigers' fortunes rapidly improved in the 1990s under coach Don Cahoon. In Cahoon's fourth season, 1994–95, Princeton won 18 games, then a program record, and finished as runner-up in the ECAC tournament. Two years later, the Tigers won 18 games again and lost in the league semifinals.

Princeton's 1997–98 team struggled in the regular season, finishing 7-9-6 in ECAC games, but hit its stride in the postseason, led by the high-scoring line of Casson Masters '98, Jeff Halpern '99, and Scott Bertoli '99. The Tigers won their first-round series at Brown, defeated Cornell in the next round, and edged Yale in the semifinals. In the final, a tightly contested game against Clarkson, Syl Apps III '99 scored in the second overtime period to break a 4–4 tie and send Princeton to the NCAA tournament for the first time. The 1998–99 team continued the championship season's momentum, winning a program-record 20 games and the Ivy League title on its way to the ECAC semifinals.

Cahoon left Princeton in 2000, and the program's next winning season didn't come until 2007–08, when coach Guy Gadowsky and captain Mike Moore '08 led the Tigers to 21 wins, including a 9–1 record against Ivy teams. Princeton won the Ivy title and the ECAC tournament, defeating Yale, Colgate, and Harvard in succession to earn an automatic bid to the NCAA tournament. The 2008–09 Tigers won 22 games, reached the ECAC semifinals, and returned to the NCAA tournament, receiving an at-large bid.

Coach Ron Fogarty led Princeton to its fourth NCAA tournament appearance in 2018, when the Tigers made a Cinderella run in the ECAC tournament that was reminiscent of the 1998 postseason. Princeton, the No. 7 seed, defeated No. 2 seed Union in the quarterfinals and No. 1 seed Cornell in the semifinals before prevailing in overtime against No. 3 seed Clarkson in the final, 2–1. Freshman goalie Ryan Ferland '21 was named the tournament's Most Valuable Player.

Two players from the 2017–18 team hold Princeton scoring records: Max Véronneau '19 set the single-season points record with 55 during the championship season; and Ryan Kuffner '19 finished his career with a program-best 75 goals.

Sixteen Princeton alumni have played in the National Hockey League, including Syl Apps Jr., '70, an all-star for the Pittsburgh Penguins; Halpern, whose career spanned 14 seasons; and George Parros '03, a hard-hitting winger who, in retirement, became the NHL's head of player safety.

Women's Ice Hockey

Princeton's first women's ice hockey team was organized in 1974 as a club run and coached by students. With a limited budget for travel and gear, the Tigers still managed promising results, finishing second to Cornell in the unofficial Ivy tournament in 1977 and 1978.

The program was promoted to varsity status in 1979–80, and its first full-time coach was Bill Quackenbush, an NHL hall of famer who had coached Princeton men's hockey for six seasons. Led by high-scoring center Kelly O'Dell '84, the Tiger women won three consecutive Ivy championships in 1982, 1983, and 1984. O'Dell set program bests for career goals, assists, and points. The championship teams also included all-Ivy defender Patty Kazmaier '86, a daughter of Princeton football's Heisman Trophy–winning tailback Dick Kazmaier '52. Patty Kazmaier died in 1990 of a rare blood disease, and in 1998 USA Hockey created the Patty Kazmaier Award, presented annually to the nation's most outstanding women's collegiate hockey player.

The 1990s brought a new wave of sharpshooters who led the Tigers on the ice and challenged O'Dell's team records. Mollie Marcoux '91 scored 30 or more goals in three of her four seasons and finished her career with 216 points (120 goals, 96 assists), beating O'Dell's record of 207. Kathy Issel '95 raised the bar with 218 points (96 goals, 122 assists) and won a pair of Ivy titles in 1992 and 1995 under coach Lisa Brown-Miller.

Princeton's longest-tenured women's hockey coach, Jeff Kampersal '92, led the program for 21 seasons (1996–2017) and won Ivy titles in 2006 and 2016. Those teams also made Princeton's first two appearances in the NCAA tournament. Kampersal's players included five Kazmaier Award finalists: Ali Coughlin '99, Andrea Kilbourne '03, Gretchen Anderson '04, Kim Pearce '07, and Kelsey Koelzer '17.

Kampersal was succeeded by assistant Cara Morey, who led Princeton to an Ivy title and its third NCAA bid in 2019. Freshman Sarah Fillier '22 led the nation in scoring and was named the NCAA Rookie of the Year as well as a finalist for the Kazmaier Award. In 2020 the Tigers won their first-ever ECAC tournament championship with a victory in overtime against top-ranked Cornell. The win earned the team an automatic bid to the NCAA tournament, which was canceled due to the COVID-19 pandemic. The Tigers finished the season with a program-best 26 wins.

Princeton women's hockey has sent three players to the Olympics: Kilbourne, who won a silver medal with the United States team in 2002; Nikola Holmes '03, who played for Germany in 2006; and Caroline Park '11, who represented the Korean unified team in 2018. Four Princeton women have played in the National Women's Hockey League (founded in 2015): Kelly Cooke '13, Gabie Figueroa '14, Denna Laing '14, and Kelsey Koelzer '17; and one, Stephanie Denino '10, has played in the Canadian Women's Hockey League.

INSTITUTE FOR ADVANCED STUDY, founded in 1930, is a private academic institution in Princeton that supports fundamental research in the sciences and humanities. From its earliest days, it has been one of the world's leading centers for theoretical research and intellectual inquiry. Located near the historic Princeton Battlefield, it has always enjoyed close academic connections to the University; during construction of the institute's original building, Fuld Hall, which opened in 1939, a number of institute scholars were temporarily housed on the University campus in Fine (now Jones) Hall.

The institute was funded initially with a $5 million gift from philanthropists Louis Bamberger and Caroline Bamberger Fuld, who used proceeds from the sale of their department store in Newark, New Jersey. It was founded on two principles: scholars should be selected on the basis of their abilities alone and with no regard to race, religion, or gender; and the institute should enable the curiosity-driven pursuit of knowledge with no view to its immediate utility or the expectation of meeting predetermined goals.

The institute has no degree programs or experimental facilities, and its faculty are not required to teach courses. Funding is entirely through endowment earnings, gifts, and grants.

The founding director of the institute was Abraham Flexner, and the first professor was the mathematician Oswald Veblen. Flexner and Veblen set out to recruit the best mathematicians and physicists in the world, and with the rise of fascism and anti-Semitism in Europe, the institute became a lifeline in the migration of European scholars to the United States. Among the first recruited to a professorship was Albert Einstein. Other early scholars included algebraist Emmy Noether and topologist Anna Stafford, both appointed at a time when women were not accepted by other leading scholarly institutions.

Work at the institute takes place in four schools: Historical Studies, Mathematics, Natural Sciences, and Social Science. A permanent faculty of approximately 30 guides the work of the schools, and each year some 250 visiting members from universities and institutions throughout the world pursue research residencies. About 60 percent of institute scholars come from outside the United States, typically from more than 30 countries.

Today the institute provides facilities for residence and study for its faculty and visiting members, and its dining facility is prized for the role it plays in encouraging intellectual exchange and a sense of community. The institute serves afternoon tea every weekday at 3 p.m. in the common room of Fuld Hall to further encourage interaction among scholars from different schools. Over time, some famous collaborations have started over tea.

Reflecting the close ties between the two institutions, the director of the institute is invited to march each year at the University's Commencement. Institute faculty are frequently appointed as visiting lecturers at the University and they teach classes and advise students on a voluntary basis. Harold Shapiro *64 and Shirley Tilghman joined the institute board after they stepped down from their Princeton presidencies.

In addition to Veblen and Einstein, past faculty at the institute have included J. Robert Oppenheimer (the institute's longest-serving director, from 1947 to 1966), Freeman Dyson, Clifford Geertz, Kurt Gödel, Hetty Goldman, George Kennan 1925, Robert Langlands, Eric Maskin, and Erwin Panofsky. More recent faculty have included such luminaries as Suzanne Akbari, Nima Arkani-Hamed, Camillo De Lellis, Juan Maldacena *96, Alondra Nelson, Avi Wigderson *83, Edward Witten *76, and Akshay Venkatesh *02. Karen Uhlenbeck, the first female mathematician to win the Abel Prize, was a scholar and visiting professor at the institute for many years, Over time, institute scholars have won 35 Nobel Prizes, 42 of the 60 Fields Medals, 21 of the 24 Abel Prizes, and many MacArthur fellowships and Wolf Prizes.

Over the course of its history, research at the institute has included:

- development of one of the first stored-program computers, whose structure (von Neumann architecture) formed the mathematical basis of computer software and influenced the development of modern computing;
- the foundations of game theory and much of the basis of modern theoretical meteorology;
- pioneering theories in the natural sciences, from string theory and astrophysics to systems biology, and their increasing interactions with mathematics;
- wide influence on the fields of global development, international relations, historical practice, and morality and ethics; and
- key texts in a range of historical disciplines, including essential contributions to the establishment of art history as a discipline in the United States.

Recent research has explored new ideas about space and time; the origins and long-term fate of the universe; the reconstruction of history using novel sources such as ancient DNA; the origins of modern democracy and human rights; and the development of an anthropology of morality.

INTERNATIONAL INITIATIVES. Princeton recruited its transformative presidents of the eighteenth and nineteenth centuries—John Witherspoon and James McCosh—from Scotland, and at various points in those two centuries it attracted important members of the faculty from Europe. In 1836, Benedict Jaeger came from Austria to teach French, Spanish, Italian, German, and natural history and to serve as curator of the zoological museum. In 1855, Arnold Guyot came from Switzerland to teach geology, lay the groundwork for what would become the department of Geosciences, and establish the natural history museum. The German musician Karl Langlotz came to Princeton in 1857 to teach German, taught fencing, and wrote the music to Princeton's anthem, "Old Nassau." Even the term "Nassau" is a reminder that Princeton's oldest and most historic building is named for an English king from a Dutch royal house.

In the late 1920s and 1930s, with fascism and anti-Semitism spreading across Europe, the University and the newly formed Institute for Advanced Study became the home of many prominent European scholars and intellectuals, especially physicists and mathematicians like Albert Einstein, John von Neumann, and Eugene Wigner, but also major figures in other fields, including the novelist Thomas Mann. Many were brought to Princeton at the initiative of mathematician Oswald Veblen.

While there were some international students on campus in the late nineteenth and early twentieth century, it was not until after World War II that Princeton became a truly international university, drawing not only more of its faculty, but more undergraduates and many of its graduate students from around the world—and not only from Europe. By 2020, some 11 percent of undergraduates were international students, as were some 45 percent of graduate students, with the largest number of students coming from China, Canada, India, the United Kingdom, and South Korea. In a 2017 *amicus* brief in a Supreme Court case regarding immigration policy, the University reported that at Princeton an "astonishing" 30 percent of its 1,152 faculty appointees were international, as were half of its academic professionals and visiting faculty and researchers.

The office of the associate provost for international affairs and operations provides support for internationalization efforts across campus. It seeks to encourage scholarly collaborations, identify research opportunities, create scholarly networks abroad for faculty members and graduate students, expand international programming for undergraduate and graduate students, and heighten emphasis on international and comparative perspectives in the curriculum.

The office oversees the Davis International Center, which assists international scholars and students with immigration advising and processing, cultural adjustment, and in many other ways. The International Center was founded by volunteers in 1974, with office space at 5 Ivy Lane; in 1978, the office moved to Murray-Dodge Hall and the University placed it under the auspices of the dean of undergraduate students, with the center's first director, Paula Chow, serving from 1978 until her retirement in 2010. In 1999 the center moved to Stevenson Hall, and then in 2001 to the new Frist Campus Center. In 2010 the office of visa services was integrated into the center, and after being temporarily located at 120 Alexander Road (2010–13) and 87 Prospect Avenue (2013–16), in 2016 the center moved into the newly renovated Louis A. Simpson International Building.

The office of the associate provost provides administrative oversight for the Mpala Research Centre in Kenya, which provides opportunities for field-based research on ecology, evolution, conservation, public health, sustainable development, and climate change, and hosts the department of Ecology and Evolutionary Biology's semesters in the field program. The office also manages the Princeton China Center, which was established in 2014 on the campus of Tsinghua University in Beijing to support faculty, students, and staff studying and conducting research in China, and the associate provost serves on the board of the Princeton University Athens Center for Research and Hellenic Studies, which provides opportunities for onsite research and learning in Greece. In 2020 the office established a Global Safety and Security unit with responsibility for global intelligence and risk management, traveler preparation and education, and incident and crisis response.

The Princeton Institute for International and Regional Studies (PIIRS) oversees regional studies programs, certificate programs, and translation studies; organizes and sponsors global and exploration seminars; manages the Fung global fellows and other visiting fellows programs; supports faculty, graduate student, and undergraduate research; sponsors conferences and other events on campus; and publishes the journal *World Politics*.

The Office of International Programs oversees undergraduate international programs, including semester and summer study abroad, the International Internship Program, the Novogratz Bridge Year program for newly admitted students who defer admission for a year to engage in international service, and post-graduate fellowship advising. In 2017–18, 61 percent of Princeton undergraduates spent significant time abroad (defined as four weeks or more); in 2018–19, 697 undergraduates studied abroad (the study abroad program offered more than 100 programs in 36 countries); and in the summer of 2019, 241 students participated in the International Internship Program, which placed the students in 146 organizations across 46 countries on six continents. (The most popular destinations were Argentina, India, Vietnam, Ecuador, and France.)

Princeton has many informal and some formal ties to universities around the world. Beginning in 1962, mechanical and aerospace engineering professor David Hazen '48 *49 served as Princeton's representative on a consortium of nine US universities that helped create the India Institute of Technology in Kanpur. For 10 years, University faculty and staff members were resident on the Kanpur campus in the fields of aeronautical, civil, and computer engineering. In a letter to the *Princeton Alumni Weekly* in 2016, Hazen recalled that the institute "not only has achieved a degree of independence from governmental interference unprecedented in Indian educational institutions, but has developed into the premier technological institution in the country."

In 1981 the University signed cooperative agreements with two universities in China, Beijing University and Fudan University in Shanghai, to assist those universities in re-establishing a degree of autonomy following the suppressions of that country's Cultural Revolution—agreements that grew out of the awarding of a Princeton honorary degree in 1980 to Beijing University president Zhou Peiyuan, a physicist who had lived in Princeton in 1936 while studying with Albert Einstein at the Institute for Advanced Study.

Over recent years, the University has developed strategic partnerships with three universities, on three continents, to encourage and support research and teaching collaborations. The partnerships were established at Humboldt University in Germany in 2012; the University of Sao Paulo in 2012; and the

University of Tokyo in 2013. The University created institutional research partnerships with the University of Geneva in 2013 and with Sciences Po in France in 2014.

Princeton has dozens of other research, teaching, and exchange agreements with universities on six continents.

IVY LEAGUE is the name generally applied to eight universities (Brown, Columbia, Cornell, Dartmouth, Harvard, Pennsylvania, Princeton, and Yale) that over the years have shared interests and aspirations in teaching and research as well as in athletics. Although these universities are among the oldest in the country, the Ivy League as an athletic conference, which is the only form in which it officially exists, is less than 70 years old.

The league originated in the imagination of eastern sportswriters two decades before its actual formation. As intercollegiate football became a national obsession following World War I, costs increased and the commitment to amateurism in other parts of the country declined, leading to speculation that Princeton, Harvard, and Yale, the dominant football powers before the war (known as the "Big Three"), would have to make some sort of alliance with like-minded schools. The ivy that adorned many of the college buildings provided an inspiring name.

On October 14, 1933, Stanley Woodward of the *New York Herald-Tribune* wrote an article that referred to "our eastern ivy colleges." This was the first time the "ivy" nickname was used in print. Alan Gould, sports editor of the *Associated Press*, appears to have been the first to use the exact term "Ivy League," in an article dated February 8, 1935.

The composition of the putative Ivy League varied: some writers included Army and Navy, others omitted Brown or Cornell. But in 1936, no doubt inspired by Woodward and Gould, the undergraduate newspapers of the eight current Ivy League universities simultaneously ran an editorial advocating the formation of an "Ivy League." The first formal move toward this end, however, was not taken until 1945, when the eight presidents entered into an agreement "for the purpose of reaffirming their intention of continuing intercollegiate football in such a way as to maintain the values of the game, while keeping it in fitting proportion to the main purposes of academic life."

In many respects the 1945 agreement built on a 1916 statement of principles by the presidents of Princeton, Harvard, and Yale that set common standards for athletic eligibility both as to scholastic standing and financial aid, and a 1922 agreement that reduced the length of football schedules and outlawed spring practice and postseason games.

To achieve the objectives of the 1945 agreement, two interuniversity committees were appointed: one, made up primarily of the college deans, was to administer rules of eligibility; the other, composed of the athletic directors, was to establish policies on the length of the playing season and of preseason practice, operating budgets, and related matters. Two other interuniversity committees, on admission and financial aid, were added later.

The first step toward organizing full league competition came in 1952 with the announcement that, beginning with the fall of 1953, each college would play every other college in the group at least once every five years. This plan was superseded in 1954 when the presidents announced the adoption of a yearly round-robin schedule in football, starting in 1956, and approved the principle of similar schedules in "as many sports as practicable." Brown defeated Columbia, 20–0, on September 29, 1956, in the first-ever official Ivy League football game.

Thereafter, the Ivy Group (as the league was called in the Presidents' Agreement of 1954) established schedules in other sports, including some in existing leagues with non-Ivy members. As the previously all-male Ivy League schools began to admit women, women's sports were added beginning in the early 1970s and continuing thereafter.

As of 2020, the Ivy League schools, or some group of them, competed in 16 men's sports: baseball, basketball, cross country, fencing, football, golf, ice hockey, lacrosse, rowing, soccer, squash, swimming and diving, tennis, indoor and outdoor track and field, and wrestling. They also competed in 16 women's sports: basketball, cross country, fencing, field hockey, golf, ice hockey, lacrosse, rowing, soccer, softball, squash, swimming and diving, tennis, indoor and outdoor track and field, and volleyball.

Since its inception, hallmarks of the Ivy League have been opportunity and amateurism. The Ivy League offers more intercollegiate sports than any other athletic conference and all eight schools rank in the top 20 NCAA Division I schools in terms of number of sports offered. The Ivy League also insists that all of its student-athletes be students first and athletes second. It prohibits athletic scholarships.

Since 1985 the Ivy League has applied an Academic Index, which uses test scores and grade point average, to ensure that admitted athletes are academically comparable with nonathletes at the same school. Academically, the Ivy League has consistently led the nation in NCAA graduation success rate and academic progress rate rankings.

The Ivy League also has been a national leader in ensuring the safety of its athletes. In 2011, on the recommendation of a committee chaired by the presidents of Cornell and Dartmouth, both medical doctors, it established new rules to lower the risk of concussions in football, such as cutting the number of full-contact practices. Five years later, the league banned full-contact drills completely during the season, the first athletic conference in the country to do so.

In 1973, the post of executive director of the Council of Ivy League Presidents—the Ivy League's official name—was created, with an office just off the Princeton campus. Ricardo Mestres '31, Princeton's former financial vice president and treasurer, served in that post until 1976, when he was succeeded by James Litvack, a visiting lecturer in economics and public affairs at the University. Jeff Orleans, who succeeded Litvack in 1984, served in the post for 25 years. In 2009, Robin Harris became the first woman to head the Ivy League.

Occasionally the director assists member schools in pursuing shared interests unrelated to athletics. For example, in response to student activism regarding sweatshop labor practices in factories producing collegiate merchandise, Orleans provided guidance as all eight of the schools chose in March 1999 to be among the first 17 college and university members of the newly formed Fair Labor Association, a Washington, DC-based organization that assists schools in holding their licensees accountable for their treatment of workers and conditions in their factories.

The eight Ivy League schools share commitments to such core values as academic excellence, need-based financial aid, and diversity and inclusion. In 2017 the league adopted the following statement:

> When the Ivy League was formally established in 1954, one of its defining principles was a commitment to access and opportunity exemplified by need-based financial aid. Another was that its recruited athletes be academically representative of each institution's overall student body. More than 60 years later, the League continues to adhere to these principles, and the student bodies of its members—along with their faculties and staffs—have become increasingly diverse in multiple ways. An expanded commitment to diversity and inclusion today stands as a core value of all eight Ivy schools. This commitment applies to all of their activities, including all aspects of their athletic programs, ranging from the recruitment of students to the hiring of staff, and it plays a central role in enabling the Ivy schools to achieve their missions of educational excellence, research, and service to others.

JACOBUS FELLOWS. The Porter Ogden Jacobus fellowship was established in 1905 by Clara Cooley Jacobus and is awarded to doctoral students who, in the judgment of the faculty committee on the graduate school, demonstrate the highest scholarly excellence. It is considered the highest honor the University can bestow on a graduate student. Each year's fellows are recognized on Alumni Day.

Current practice is to name four fellows each year, one from each division of the University: humanities, social sciences, natural sciences, and engineering and applied science. The fellowship provides full tuition and a stipend for the student's final year of study.

At least seven former Jacobus fellows became members of the Princeton faculty: Richard Jeffrey *57 (Philosophy), David Bell *91 (History), Yueh-Lin Loo *01 (Chemical and Biological Engineering), Sarah Milne Pourciau '98 *07 (German), Egemen Kolemen *08 (Mechanical and Aerospace Engineering), Marcus Hultmark *11 (Mechanical and Aerospace Engineering), and Silviu Pufu '07 *11 (Physics).

Previous winners of the Jacobus fellowship are listed on page 518.

JADWIN GYMNASIUM was built as a memorial to Leander Stockwell Jadwin 1928, a hurdler who captained the track team his senior year and died of injuries suffered in an automobile accident eight months after his graduation. When his mother, Ethel Stockwell Jadwin, died in 1964, she left the University an unrestricted bequest of $27 million—virtually the entire family estate. Because the Jadwin family had earlier expressed an interest in a fieldhouse for indoor track, the trustees decided to use part of the Jadwin gift to help fund a $6.5 million multipurpose athletic building and name it for Stockwell Jadwin.

They also used some of the gift to construct Jadwin Hall (named for Mrs. Jadwin's late husband, Stanley Palmer Jadwin) and Fine Hall, home of the Mathematics department. Jadwin Hall opened in 1970 when the Physics department relocated to it from the 60-year-old Palmer Physical Laboratory, which it had outgrown.

Construction of Jadwin Gymnasium began in 1964 and, following significant delays, was completed in 1969. Situated just below the football stadium and (later) Weaver Track on a hillside overlooking Lake Carnegie, the gym is one of the University's largest structures, with more than enough floor space to enclose eight football fields. It serves as the home venue for Princeton's basketball, fencing, squash, tennis, track and field, and wrestling teams, but it also hosts the Senior Prom, Alumni Day, and the annual staff Service Recognition Lunch; it is the rain-site for Commencement; and over its history it has accommodated campus-wide meetings (including a pivotal meeting at the height of the anti–Vietnam War protests in 1970), conferences, receptions, concerts, and presentations by prominent speakers ranging from then-Secretary of State Condoleeza Rice and the Dalai Lama to Supreme Court justices Elena Kagan '81 and Sonia Sotomayor '76.

In 1971 the Beach Boys performed in the first concert ever held at Jadwin, and a 1978 concert featured New Jersey native Bruce Springsteen. In 1987 Jadwin hosted a circus, during which the weight of the elephants damaged its floor and the beams underneath.

Jadwin has two primary levels beneath a roof formed by three interlocking shells. On the upper level the first shell covers the entrance lobby, which was thoroughly renovated in 2017. The area beneath the middle shell contains the main basketball court (named in 2009 for legendary coach Pete Carril) and four practice courts. The area beneath the third shell to the south contains a 200-meter indoor track with an infield straightaway for sprints.

The lowest (E) level has a baseball/softball artificial surface practice area, a throwing area for the track and field teams, a wrestling room, and six indoor tennis courts. Intermediate levels beneath the entrance lobby contain one of the world's largest fencing rooms and 11 international-sized squash courts with spectator galleries.

The Jadwin lobby highlights Princeton's decision in 2008 to retire the number 42 across all sports in honor of football's Dick Kazmaier '52, who won the 1951 Heisman Trophy as the nation's top college football player, and Bill Bradley '65, who received the Sullivan Award as the outstanding US amateur athlete in his senior year. Statues of Bradley and Kazmaier are located outside the lobby.

JEFFERSON, THOMAS, THE PAPERS OF, had its genesis at the time of Jefferson's 200th birthday in 1943. President Harold Dodds said it was "truly the child of the creative imagination" of Julian P. Boyd, University Librarian from 1940 to 1952 and later professor of history at Princeton, who was then serving as historian to the Thomas Jefferson Bicentennial Commission.

Encouraged by the commission's endorsement and a gift of $200,000 from the New York Times Company, the University assumed editorial responsibility for the project, and Princeton University Press agreed to publish what was initially projected as a 42-volume series to be completed in about a decade. The first volume was published to considerable fanfare in 1950, with Boyd serving as editor, a position he held until his death in 1980.

In 2019 the Papers published the 44th volume of a now-projected 62-volume series.

The Papers provide the authoritative edition of the correspondence and other writings of the nation's third president and the author of, among other documents, the Declaration of Independence. They comprise more than 70,000 items, including approximately 18,000 letters Jefferson wrote and more than 25,000 he received, with each document transcribed, annotated, and edited to exacting standards. They cover Jefferson's life from his youth in the early 1760s through the end of his presidency on March 3, 1809.

In 1999 the Thomas Jefferson Foundation at Monticello began a projected 23-volume Jefferson Retirement Series, also published by Princeton University Press, that picks up where the Princeton project will leave off, encompassing Jefferson's papers from his retirement from the presidency through his death in 1826. The first volume in that series was published in 2004. The Princeton project has also commissioned four topically arranged volumes; the first, published in 1983, focused on Jefferson's extracts from the Christian gospels.

In 2009, in partnership with Princeton University Press, the Papers launched a digital edition which makes all the documents available in digital form 18 months after their print publication.

The Jefferson Papers served as a prototype for such projects as the Hamilton Papers at Columbia, the Franklin Papers at Yale, the Adams Papers at the Massachusetts Historical Society, the Madison Papers at Chicago and Virginia, and the Wilson Papers at Princeton.

Jefferson visited Princeton in 1783 as a member of the Continental Congress, which met that year in Nassau Hall. In 1791, Princeton awarded both Jefferson and his political rival Alexander Hamilton honorary degrees. Jefferson gave Princeton $100 toward rebuilding Nassau Hall after the fire of 1802.

JEWISH STUDENTS AT PRINCETON. The story of Jewish life at Princeton is one of recurring student initiative. Early generations of Jews at Princeton—few in number, socially isolated, and reticent to identify publicly as such—had to seek out their Jewish classmates. Every few years, they had to reconsider what kind of Jewish life, if any, should be available on campus. Still, each generation of Jewish students had more success than the last integrating into Princeton's social fabric and garnering institutional support for their needs.

The history goes back at least as far as Mordecai Myers 1812, a great-grandson of the first rabbi of Charleston, South Carolina, who entered Princeton at age 14 in 1809. Like 48 percent of his classmates, Myers was a southerner, who likely owned 30 to 40 slaves during his adult life.

Only a few other Jewish students enrolled at Princeton over the next century. Among them was Philip King 1893, who captained the football and baseball teams and stayed on as Princeton's first paid athletic coach (football) for a year after graduating.

By the fall of 1915 approximately 50 of Princeton's 1,400 undergraduates were Jewish. This proved large enough to compel monthly visits to campus by a rabbi from Trenton, likely the first instance of an intentional gathering of Princeton's Jewish students. Jewish students at Princeton have gathered to observe and celebrate Jewish traditions ever since.

Early gatherings were small and often furtive; new Jewish students did not always find out about them. Unaware of the Trenton rabbi's visits, Marcus Lester Aaron 1920 began to organize Princeton's Jewish students during his junior year, with two goals in mind: he believed in the importance of maintaining a connection to Judaism, and he wanted to provide an alternative way for Jewish students to fulfil Princeton's weekly chapel attendance requirement, which existed in some form until 1964.

Aaron encountered significant opposition from students who feared being publicly identified as Jews and who worried that a congregation would call attention to the growing Jewish population on campus. Nonetheless, weekly Shabbat services began in 1919, and two years later the University recognized the Jewish Student Congregation as an official student group, granting chapel credit to those who attended. By 1923, about 40 men attended each service. Over time, the gatherings grew to include social, educational, and intellectual components.

No records exist to prove that Princeton maintained official quotas limiting the number of Jewish students. However, behind closed doors, administrators worried that using academic merit as the sole admission criterion would lead to an increase in Jewish students. Indeed, the percentage of Jewish students in the freshman class had a positive upward trend for the first 20 years of the twentieth century, topping out at just over four percent in the fall of 1920.

New admission policies implemented in the 1920s intentionally sought to prevent Jewish students from enrolling. These policies, which introduced subjective assessments of an applicant's overall "character"—including leadership qualities, athletic abilities, and social status—weeded out Jewish applicants, who, according to the bigoted stereotypes under which these policies operated, were considered deficient in these areas. With only one exception, Jewish enrollment remained under three percent from then until the years following World War II.

Those who did enroll often experienced anti-Semitism and social isolation. In contrast to the significant majority of juniors and seniors who joined eating clubs—up to 90 percent by the 1930s—only a few Jewish students were club members, and they were concentrated in clubs considered part of the "lower tier." In contrast, in the twenty-first century, some Jewish students organize holiday celebrations like Passover seders at their eating clubs.

This social shunning came to a head most publicly in 1958, in an episode that became known as "dirty bicker." In that year's eating club selection process (bicker), despite a policy guaranteeing club admission to any student who wanted it, 23 sophomores were rejected by all the eating clubs; about half were Jewish. The story made national news.

Aided by the provisions of the GI Bill, Princeton's class size, including its Jewish members, grew after World War II. By 1948, 6.5 percent of the freshman class was Jewish, the highest percentage in any class to that time.

As in previous generations, Jewish students organized themselves. The Student Hebrew Association (SHA) was founded in 1946 with help from the national B'nai B'rith Hillel Foundation. Albert Einstein, who had spoken at formal gatherings of Jewish students in previous years and attended services occasionally, spoke at SHA's first official service on January 10, 1947, and the assistant dean of the chapel attended. The next fall, the group at Princeton became one of more than 150 Hillel chapters on campuses across the country. Rabbi Dr. Irving Levey was its professional director for the next 20 years.

While Shabbat services continued to provide the most consistent and visible demonstration of Jewish life on campus in the 1950s, through Hillel students could also enroll in noncredit courses and attend lectures, intercollegiate colloquia, and mixers with Jewish students, including women, from other schools. Among the longest lasting of these were the annual Harvard-Yale-Princeton Colloquia, which brought together Jewish students from those institutions and others between 1948 and 1972. During that time, Jewish life expanded into all realms of the student experience. Jewish students published a monthly newsletter, formed an intramural basketball team, organized faculty discussions, launched fundraising campaigns, and put on theatrical performances.

Expanding programming beyond religious services helped maintain attendance at Hillel events after Princeton eliminated chapel attendance requirements in 1964. Off campus, a group of Orthodox undergraduate and graduate students established Yavneh House in 1961, where they hosted Orthodox services and hired a cook to provide kosher food. Yavneh's existence enabled religiously observant students to live a comfortable life at Princeton. An *eruv*—a symbolic boundary that permits activities normally prohibited on Shabbat and holidays—proposed by the University and completed in the town of Princeton in 2015 further enabled the growth of the religiously observant community.

Princeton's Jewish population grew with the arrival of undergraduate coeducation. The number of Jewish first-year students nearly doubled between 1968 and 1970, when almost a quarter of all Jewish first-year students were women, and almost 20 percent of women in the first-year class were Jewish. With that growth came an outpouring of new programming and a push for kosher dining on campus. In 1971, Princeton became only the third college in the country to provide a kosher dining hall. It opened in Stevenson Hall (composed of two former eating clubs) and became a de facto center for Jewish life on campus for students and faculty alike for 20 years.

Under the guidance of Rabbi Edward Feld, who served as Hillel director from 1973 to 1992, Jewish life and programming gained a more visible presence on campus. Feld aimed to reach students from all backgrounds of Jewish observance, and he also worked to create a centralized home for Jewish life, publicize Jewish programming broadly on campus, and engage alumni.

Jewish representation on the faculty and in other academic settings increased during this period as well. Through the middle of the twentieth century, Jews were sparsely represented on Princeton's faculty. But thanks to Hillel programming in the 1950s, a few Jewish faculty members made notable connections to Jewish students, and the number and eminence of Jewish faculty members grew in the following decades.

By the 1970s Jews were serving in a number of senior administrative positions. Even with this increased representation in leadership roles, Princeton's selection of a Jewish man (Harold Shapiro *64) as its president in 1988 astonished many Jewish alumni who had attended Princeton in the days of covert anti-Semitism. The Ronald O. Perelman Institute for Jewish Studies, established in 1995, for the first time offered students an academic certificate in Judaic Studies.

Princeton's commitment to building a physical home for Hillel on campus solidified under President William Bowen. After years of planning, the Center for Jewish Life (CJL) opened in 1993. It is unique among Hillels in that both the building and its continued upkeep are financed by the University, which also contributes to the CJL's administrative costs.

The CJL is built on the former location of two eating clubs (first Gateway Club, then Prospect Club) that accepted disproportionately large numbers of Jewish men prior to the 1960s. It houses a kosher dining hall and administrative offices for its full-time professional staff; hosts many of the religious, spiritual, educational, and social programs that take place each day of the week; and is the umbrella organization for many special interest and affinity groups of Jewish students. Students also take part in Jewish programming through Chabad on Campus, a national organization whose Princeton chapter became a recognized student organization in 2006.

Rabbi Julie Roth, who became the CJL's executive director in 2005, was the first person designated by Princeton as a Jewish chaplain; Rabbi Eitan Webb, the founding co-director of Chabad at Princeton, was the second.

In 2015, nearly 1,000 Jewish alumni returned to campus for the *L'Chaim* conference, celebrating 100 years of organized Jewish life on campus.

JOHNSON, JAMES COLLINS, was a fugitive slave from Maryland who arrived on campus in 1839 and worked as a janitor until 1843. A student recognized Collins and alerted the man who still claimed ownership. Collins was tried and convicted as a runaway under the Fugitive Slave Act of 1793. Following his trial a local woman, Theodosia Prevost (a great-granddaughter of John Witherspoon), lent him approximately $500 to purchase his freedom, and students at the College took up a collection that raised $100 to help him start a business. He opened a used clothing and furniture store on Witherspoon Street and obtained the right to sell snacks on campus. He ended up working on campus for more than 60 years, mostly as a vendor who sold fruits, candies, and other snacks from a wheelbarrow.

While Johnson was the victim of taunts and mistreatment by some students, especially in his earlier Princeton years, by the 1870s he had become a popular figure on campus. For many African Americans in the community, he was a role model for developing a business and achieving economic success. When he died in 1902, alumni and students purchased a headstone for him in Princeton Cemetery, with an epitaph that described him as a friend.

In 2018 the University named the easternmost arch in East Pyne Hall in his honor. The arch looks out on Firestone Plaza and the Chapel; it is the first arch students pass through after leaving Opening Exercises and Baccalaureate.

A plaque on the south wall of the arch includes a photo of Johnson and the following text:

> James Collins Johnson (1816–1902) arrived on campus in 1839 and worked as a janitor until 1843 when a student identified him as a fugitive slave from Maryland. After a trial in which he was ordered to be returned to his master, a local citizen loaned Johnson approximately $500 to buy his freedom. Johnson returned to work on campus and repaid the debt. He sold used clothing and furniture to students, and for almost 60 years was also the only licensed campus vendor, selling fruits, candies, lemonade and other snacks from a wheelbarrow near this site. After he died in 1902, students inscribed an epitaph on his gravestone in the Princeton cemetery that described him as "the students friend."

JONES HALL was built in 1931 as an addition to Palmer Hall to serve as the first home of the Mathematics department. It was originally named in memory of the department's founding chairman, Henry Burchard Fine 1880. When a new Fine Hall was dedicated in 1970, the old one was renamed in honor of its donors, Thomas D. Jones 1876 and his niece Gwethalyn Jones, and became the home of the departments of East Asian and Near Eastern Studies.

Thomas Jones and his older brother David shared first honors at graduation from Princeton in 1876. Both became wealthy lawyers in Chicago, and both were trustees of the University. In 1907, when the cornerstone of Palmer Hall was laid, the Jones brothers gave a $200,000 endowment for the Physics and Electrical Engineering departments. In the late 1920s, after David Jones had passed away, Thomas and David's daughter Gwethalyn were the University's most generous benefactors as it sought to raise $2 million for scientific research; Thomas gave professorships in mathematics and in physics, and Gwethalyn endowed chairs in chemistry and mathematical physics.

In 1929, shortly after Fine's death, Thomas and Gwethalyn Jones provided funds for the construction of a mathematics building named in his memory and an endowment for its upkeep. The building had a spacious wood-paneled library, common rooms, offices, and a locker room with a shower/bath for faculty wishing to use the then-nearby tennis courts.

When the Mathematics department moved into the new Fine Hall, it left its marks behind on the old one, including mathematical formulas and figures in the leaded design of the windows and Einstein's famous remark over the fireplace in the lounge: *Raffiniert ist der Herr Gott, aber Boshaft ist Er nicht* (God is subtle, but He is not malicious). The departments of East Asian and Near Eastern Studies moved in, along with the world-famous Gest Library (now part of the University's East Asian library), whose rare holdings attract visitors from many parts of the world.

KELLER, SUZANNE, a sociologist who conducted pioneering research on elite life and community in America, was the first woman faculty member to receive tenure at Princeton.

A native of Vienna, Austria, Keller moved to New York City and became an American citizen as a child. After graduating from Hunter College in New York City and earning a PhD from Columbia University in 1953, she held research and teaching positions at several colleges and universities before joining the Princeton faculty in 1966 as a visiting lecturer in sociology. Two years later she became the first woman to receive tenure at Princeton when she was named a professor of sociology.

Her scholarly interests included social stratification, social architecture, the family, the design of communities, and elites and leadership. A dedicated teacher and mentor, she was the author of several books, including two path-breaking works: *Beyond the Ruling Class: Strategic Elites in Modern Society* (1963), an examination of the elite power structure in America; and *Community: Pursuing the Dream, Living the Reality* (2003), an account of three decades of change in New Jersey's Twin Rivers housing complex. Her other books included a widely taught textbook, *Sociology* (1983).

Keller's colleague Viviana Zelizer described her as "brilliant, charismatic, generous," and noted her gift for forging "enduring connections with colleagues, students, and friends." As a teacher, Zelizer said, "she did not just instruct, but inspire."

In addition to teaching in sociology, Keller played a major role in promoting women's studies at Princeton; she taught the University's first course on gender and society in the early 1970s. She also taught in the school of Architecture for 10 years and served as a consultant to industry and government agencies in areas such as housing, new communities, and family and gender issues.

In a 1986 booklet, *Conversations on the Character of Princeton*, she noted that the letter she received advising her of her promotion to tenure began with the salutation, "Dear Mr. Keller." She said undergraduate coeducation, beginning the year after she received tenure, brought welcome changes to the "ethos" of the University: "Now there is a freer spirit," she said. "It's more ecumenical. There is more wit, humor, less pretentiousness. It's more improvisational. I wouldn't have stayed at the old Princeton."

In 1994 Keller earned a master of social work degree from Rutgers University. At its 30th reunion in 1998, the Class of 1968 welcomed her as an honorary classmate. She retired from the Princeton faculty and transferred to emeritus status in 2004.

KELLEY, STANLEY, JR., a professor of politics at Princeton from 1957 until his retirement in 1995, played a central role in developing new governance practices and structures at the University, most of which remain in place 50 years later, and in shaping the University's responses to activism on campus and throughout the country in the late 1960s.

From 1968 to 1970, Kelley chaired a faculty-student Special Committee on the Structure of the University, known as the Kelley Committee, which was appointed by President Robert Goheen following demonstrations on campus that called for "restructuring the decision-making apparatus of the University." The committee's 99-page report transformed governance at Princeton by increasing transparency and expanding participation by students and nontenured faculty members.

In 1969 the committee proposed the creation of a Council of the Princeton University Community (CPUC) composed of senior officers of the University, faculty, undergraduates, graduate students, members of the staff, and alumni. Known at the time as "Kelley's Republic," the Council was designed as "a permanent conference of all major groups of the University" where all "could raise problems that concern them and . . . be exposed to each other's views." The committees of the Council enabled students and faculty to participate actively in the development of each year's operating budget (priorities committee), develop policies related to campus conduct (rights and rules), advise on matters related to divestment (resources), and help select each year's honorary degree recipients (governance).

The committee also recommended adding students to faculty committees and creating four new positions on the Board of Trustees (young alumni trustees), with one elected each year from the graduating class for a four-year term. (In 2019 the board designated one of its other alumni-elected positions to be filled by a member of one of the five most recent graduate alumni classes, also to serve for a four-year term.)

President William Bowen, who served as provost and thus chaired the priorities committee when the CPUC was established (he would later chair the full Council as president), said the final report of the Kelley Committee had profound and lasting effects on Princeton and was "the best commentary I have ever seen on how universities should be run." He described Kelley as "the consummate university citizen . . . one of a kind."

One of his faculty colleagues described him as "a force for principled reconciliation that helped to sustain civility amid a welter of tensions." This was evident on April 30, 1970, at a meeting of more than 2,500 students in the chapel following President Richard Nixon's announcement of American bombing in Cambodia, when Kelley urged students to express their opposition to national policy by engaging in elective political reform. Several days later a Princeton-based organization known as the Movement for a New Congress was created to motivate and prepare students nationwide to participate in that fall's Congressional campaigns.

Kelley was an accomplished scholar and teacher on topics such as the American political party system, elections, and voting and mass communications. His *Professional Public Relations and Political Power* (1956) was a pioneering study of the role of professional consultants in politics. His other two books focused on "creating an informed electorate" and "interpreting elections."

Described by one of his graduate students as the "consummate teacher," he won the President's Distinguished Teaching Award in 1995; the teaching award in the Politics department is named for him.

One of his undergraduate students called him a "uniquely wise, caring, thoughtful, and decent human being" who, in commenting on drafts, was a "master of both microscope and telescope," making suggestions that ranged from central themes to methodology and word choice.

A native of Detroit, Kansas, Kelley served in the army during World War II. He earned his bachelor's and master's degrees from the University of Kansas, and his PhD from Johns Hopkins in 1955.

Kennedy, John Fitzgerald 1939, 35th president of the United States, was admitted to Princeton in 1935 as a member of the Class of 1939. He fell ill with jaundice in London that summer and did not matriculate until October 26, 1935, a month after college opened; he withdrew on December 12, 1935, because of a recurrence of the illness. He later entered Harvard, from which he graduated *cum laude* in 1940. While at Princeton he roomed in 9 South Reunion Hall, a building later condemned as a fire hazard and torn down in 1965.

Bricks from the fireplace in his dorm room, rescued by Kennedy's classmates, frame a bronze plaque honoring him in the south entry of 1939 Hall, one of the dormitories of the "Old New Quad" that became part of Wilson (later First) College.

In his application for admission Kennedy said his intended career was in banking, and he wrote: "To be a Princeton Man is indeed an enviable distinction." After graduating from Harvard, he told one of his former Princeton classmates "I will always have a tender spot in my heart for old Nassau," and he told another, "at Princeton-Harvard football games, I cheer for Harvard, but I pray for Princeton."

Kopp, Wendy '89 converted an idea she explored in her 177-page senior thesis, "An Argument and Plan for the Creation of the Teacher Corps," into an organization, Teach For America, through which college graduates teach for at least two years in some of the nation's most under-resourced urban and rural public primary and secondary schools. She was a "social entrepreneur" at a time when that term was just gaining currency. Her idea was that school systems would get an infusion of energy and talent, and even teachers in the program who did not remain in public education would carry insights from their experiences with them as they pursued careers in other fields and served their communities in other ways.

Kopp came to Princeton from Dallas, Texas, and majored in the school of Public and International Affairs. She became involved with the Press Club and with *Business Today*, where she organized a conference on improving American public education, especially in poorly served urban and rural areas.

The national service organization she proposed in her thesis was modeled after the Peace Corps. Even before graduation she began lining up financial support and over the summer she visited school systems, recruited a board of directors, and hired a small staff. She contacted campuses, attracted media attention, and received some 2,500 applications from students at over 100 colleges. After a summer of intensive training, 489 teachers were sent out in the fall of 1990, the program's first year, to schools in New York, Los Angeles, eastern North Carolina. southern Louisiana, and rural Georgia.

By the end of its third year, the number of teachers and the number of regions had doubled. By the end of its third decade, Teach For America was in more than 50 regions and the number of teachers it had trained and placed since its inception had passed 60,000. Almost 15,000 of them were still classroom teachers; more than 1,300 were principals; and some 80 percent reported that they were working in fields that impacted public education in lower-income communities.

In 2007, Kopp founded Teach For All, a global network of enterprises similarly committed to expanding educational excellence and equity around the world. She is the author of *One Day, All Children: The*

Unlikely Triumph of Teach for America and What I Learned Along the Way (2000) and *A Chance to Make History: What Works and What Doesn't in Providing an Excellent Education for All* (2011).

In 1993, just four years out of college, she became the first woman to receive the Woodrow Wilson Award, the highest honor the University can confer on undergraduate alumni, and in 2000 she received an honorary degree from Princeton; her citation commended her for creating a corps of recent college graduates who, "as they teach for America . . . lead us closer to her goal of quality and equality in education for all."

In 2008 she was awarded the Presidential Citizens Medal by President George W. Bush, and that same year the *Princeton Alumni Weekly* ranked her 13th on its list of the 25 all-time most influential Princeton alumni—the only woman to make the list. Ten years later, the *PAW* compiled a list of the 25 most influential living alumni, and she again made the list.

In her 2011 commencement remarks, President Shirley Tilghman described Kopp as "the stuff of Princeton legend" for her success in developing her thesis into a movement with national and international impact, and noted that "this year, 16 percent of the members of the Class of 2011 applied to join Teach For America and spend at least two years in some of the poorest performing schools in the nation—making teaching one of the most competitive things to do after graduation. Wendy," she said, "started a revolution!"

LACROSSE. Princeton's men's and women's lacrosse teams have both distinguished themselves in national and Ivy League competition.

Men's Lacrosse

Although Native American tribes played lacrosse as far back as the seventeenth century, the modern sport was introduced to the United States by two Canadian teams in a series of exhibition matches in 1877. Columbia, Harvard, and New York University took up lacrosse in 1880; Princeton followed in 1881. The Tigers finished 1–3 in their first season of play and lost to Harvard 3–0 in the first intercollegiate lacrosse tournament, held that year. An intercollegiate lacrosse association was organized by the four schools in 1882.

Princeton was recognized as national champion three times during its first decade of play, in 1884, 1888, and 1889. After its opening game of the 1891 season competition was suspended. Princeton dropped its lacrosse program the following year because of a lack of space for practice (in competition with baseball and track), and the feeling that lacrosse's training value for other sports—its chief appeal at the beginning—had been overestimated.

The sport did not return to Princeton for nearly three decades. In 1921 freshman Harland Meistrell 1925, a star lacrosse player from Erasmus Hall High School in Brooklyn, reintroduced lacrosse, as he had previously done at Rutgers before transferring to Princeton. A trophy bearing his name is awarded to the winner of the annual Rutgers-Princeton game.

Under the leadership of coach Al Nies, who also coached the soccer team, the Tigers enjoyed three successive undefeated seasons in 1933, 1934, and 1935. Bill Logan, who succeeded Nies, led Princeton to their first national championship in 1937, which they shared with Maryland. In 1942, the Tigers finished 7-1-1 and were voted national champion again, this time outright. From 1936 until the creation of the first NCAA lacrosse tournament in the early 1970s, the national championship was awarded by the United States Intercollegiate Lacrosse Association (USILA) based on regular season record. The winning team received the Wingate Trophy.

Two Princeton players from this period died in World War II: John Higginbotham '39, captain his senior year, and Tyler Campbell '43, All-American defenseman in 1941 and 1942. Higginbotham is memorialized by a lacrosse trophy for sportsmanship, play, and influence; Campbell by a campus playing field.

Princeton excelled in the 1950s and 1960s under coach Ferris Thomsen, who was later inducted into the National Lacrosse Hall of Fame. The 1951 team shared the Wingate Trophy with Army, and Princeton won the national championship outright in 1953. After the formal organization of the Ivy League in 1956, Princeton was either champion or co-champion for nine consecutive years, 1957 through 1965, and boasted a 35-game unbeaten streak in Ivy play during that period. Cornell toppled Princeton in 1966, but Princeton regained first place the next year with a perfect 6–0 Ivy League record.

National title hopes were revived two decades later with the hiring of Bill Tierney as head coach. Tierney, who had coached Rochester Institute of Technology and been an assistant at Johns Hopkins University, led the Tigers for 21 seasons, from 1988 to 2009. After a slow start and a 2–13 record in Tierney's first season, Princeton appeared in the NCAA tournament for 14 consecutive years between 1990 and 2003. During that period, they won the national championship six times (1992, 1994, 1996, 1997, 1998, and 2001) and finished second twice. Four of Princeton's national titles were won in overtime. Tierney, who compiled an overall record of 238–86 at Princeton, was inducted into the Hall of Fame in 2002.

Over the decades, the program has produced more than 50 All-Americans, nine Ivy League Players of the Year, and 11 Ivy League Rookies of the Year. Two players have been awarded the Lt. Raymond Enners Award as national Player of the Year: defenseman David Morrow '93 in 1993 and goaltender Scott Bacigalupo '94 in 1994.

As a freshman, Morrow, a Detroit native, nearly gave up lacrosse to play ice hockey. Starting at lacrosse as a sophomore, he broke or bent 25 aluminum lacrosse sticks before he developed a titanium stick in his father's machine shop, which he introduced at the 1992 NCAA tournament. Morrow scored two goals with the stick in the Tigers' victory over North Carolina in the semifinals, on their way to the national championship. Morrow patented the technology and founded his own company, Warrior Lacrosse, to produce it. Today, nearly all lacrosse sticks are made of titanium. Morrow also co-founded Major League Lacrosse, a professional lacrosse league. He is one of 17 Princeton men's lacrosse players who have been inducted into the Hall of Fame.

The 17 players are Conrad Sutherland 1924, Meistrell, Charles Murphy '34, Campbell, Frederick Allner '46, Henry Fish '48, L.M. Gaines '49, Donald Hahn '51, Ralph Willis '53, Alvin Krongard '58, Howard Krongard '61, Morrow, Scott Bacigalupo '94, Kevin Lowe '97, Hubbard, Matthew Striebel '01, and Boyle. Numerous Tigers have gone on to play lacrosse professionally, several with great success. Jesse Hubbard '98 retired as the Major League Lacrosse all-time leader in goals scored while Ryan Boyle '04 retired as the MLL leader in points and assists.

Women's Lacrosse

The Princeton women's lacrosse team also has an illustrious history, winning 15 Ivy League titles (more than any other school), reaching the NCAA tournament 26 times, and winning the national championship three times (1994, 2002, and 2003). The team began play in 1973, finishing 0–2 in its first season under coach Penny Hinckley while competing in the Association for Intercollegiate Athletics for Women.

In 1979 they reached the AIAW quarterfinals, falling to Rutgers in overtime.

Women's lacrosse became an Ivy League sport in 1980. The first NCAA women's lacrosse tournament was held in 1982 and Princeton reached the national quarterfinals a year later under coach Betty Logan.

Perhaps the most important moment in program history came with the hiring of Chris Sailer as head coach in 1987. Sailer, who had been an assistant coach for both field hockey and lacrosse at Penn, has been named national Coach of the Year three times, and has coached more NCAA playoff games than any other coach. She was the first lacrosse coach, male or female, to win 400 games at one Division I school. She was inducted into the Hall of Fame in 2008, and in 2020 she became the first head coach of a women's team at Princeton to have her position endowed.

In 1992, the Princeton women reached the NCAA semifinals, the beginning of a streak that saw them appear in the NCAA tournament 25 times in 28 years. They won three national titles during that period, defeating Maryland, 10–7, in 1994; Georgetown, 12–7, in 2002; and then repeating as champions by defeating Virginia, 8–7 in overtime, in 2003. The Tigers have been runners-up four times, in 1993, 1995, 2000, and 2004.

Nine Princeton women's players were named Ivy League Player of the Year between 1981 and 2012, when the award was split among positions. Since then, two players have been named offensive player of the year, two best midfielder, and one best defender. In 2003, Rachel Becker '03 won the Tewaarton Award as the outstanding player in the country; in 2019 she became the first Princeton women's lacrosse player to be inducted into the Hall of Fame. Attacker Olivia Hompe '17 ended her career as Princeton's all-time leader in goals (195) and points (282). She also graduated *summa cum laude* from the school of Public and International Affairs with a certificate in Near Eastern Studies.

Both the men's and women's lacrosse teams played their home games on Finney Field (with an occasional game at Palmer Stadium) until the opening of Class of 1952 Stadium in 1996. The lacrosse teams shared the stadium with the field hockey team until 2011, when field hockey moved to Bedford Field. A revamped and upgraded playing surface, Sherrerd Field, was dedicated in Class of 1952 Stadium in 2012.

LAKE CAMPUS. In December 2017, the University released a campus planning document subtitled, "A

Framework for Development through 2026 and Beyond." The plan recommended that for the first time the University begin significant development of a "Lake Campus" on its lands in West Windsor Township between Lake Carnegie and Route 1.

In a 2019 update to the University's strategic planning framework, the trustees endorsed two principles to guide planning for the Lake Campus: that the campus "will feel like a lively, attractive, and yet distinctive part of Princeton University," and "will advance the University's educational and research mission, and contribute to the regional innovation ecosystem by providing co-working spaces for projects that will bring together Princeton faculty, postdocs, or students with industry, government, non-profits, or other research institutions."

The University began obtaining these lands almost a hundred years earlier when Bayard Henry 1876 proposed to his fellow trustees in 1922 that he and several other alumni would donate one farm extending south from the lake along Washington Road if the University would purchase the farm adjoining it to the west. The trustees agreed, and the combination of the donation and the purchase gave the University ownership of 216 acres between Washington Road and Alexander Road. In 1945 and 1948 the University purchased two farms east of Washington Road, giving it a total of almost 400 acres bounded by Lake Carnegie, Alexander Road, Route 1, and Harrison Street.

The trustees had no immediate plan for these lands, but they expected the properties would be "needed by the University in the next fifty years." Over time the University improved some of these lands for recreational athletic use (including summer softball), for the men's and women's rugby teams, for a cross-country course, and for the installation of solar panels, a plant nursery, and a support complex for the facilities department. For many years, thousands of visitors flocked to the fields each June for the Princeton Hospital's annual fundraising Fete which offered food, frolic, a flea market, and a 10-K race.

The 2017 campus plan anticipated that the evolution of the Lake Campus would occur over many decades (through 2026 and well beyond). It proposed that initial steps to realize the century-old trustee expectation begin in the 2020s on the lands just south of the lake between Washington Road and Harrison Street. The plan predicted that as other parts of the campus were developed over time, eventually the lake would "evolve from a feature that defines the southern edge of the campus to a feature that is central to the campus, connecting campus lands to its north and its south."

The initial development was envisioned as a "vibrant, mixed-used community with space for academic partnerships and innovation initiatives; administrative offices; athletics and recreation [including new and improved space for facilities displaced by the construction of two new residential colleges just south of Poe and Pardee fields on the existing campus], graduate student and possibly post-doc housing; retail, convening, amenities, and potentially a hotel; and campus and visitor parking" with a "transit hub offering shuttle, pedestrian, and bicycle connections to other parts of the campus and the community." The plan also suggested a possible pedestrian bridge across the lake to connect the Lake Campus to the University lands north of the lake.

Early planning for the campus focused on constructing 379 housing units for graduate students and postdocs, a new racquet center for squash and for indoor and outdoor tennis that also would include a fitness center, a parking garage, and a new home for the softball team. Cynthia Paul '94, a member of the team that won the 1991 Ivy softball championship, and her husband, Scott Levy, gave a gift to help build and name the softball stadium, making it the first athletic field at Princeton to be named by an alumna. The initial development would include relocation of the rugby fields, and over time it was anticipated that other sports might be located on the Lake Campus, including potentially a hockey arena to replace the aging Baker Rink.

In a January 2020 presentation to the West Windsor Planning Board, the University identified the following as the goals for the Lake Campus:

- Develop a state-of-the-art campus that Princeton University and West Windsor Township can take pride in.
- Create an attractive "gateway" to both West Windsor Township and Princeton University.
- Respect and enhance the Washington Road elm allée.
- Use best practices in sustainable development.
- Make walkable and bikeable connections to and through the Lake Campus for both the campus community and the community at large.
- Advance opportunities that encourage alternative transportation: walking, biking, mass transit.

- Incorporate open space in the campus to encourage recreation and reflection.

LAW SCHOOL, A, had a brief existence at Princeton in the middle of the nineteenth century. In 1824 the trustees appointed a committee to hire a law professor, but the first two choices died before they could begin classes. In 1835 and 1839, other offers were made but declined. A school was finally established in 1846 with three prominent professors: former chief justice of New Jersey Joseph Hornblower, of Newark, and two local lawyers, US attorney James Green and Richard Stockton Field 1821, the New Jersey attorney general.

Classes were held in a brownstone building on Mercer Street, which Field built at his own expense on a piece of his family's land. The school was formally opened at the College's centennial celebration in 1847, with an extended discourse by Chief Justice (later Chancellor) Henry Woodhull Green 1820 on the need for a well-educated bar.

Despite its auspicious beginnings, the law school failed to become viable. The school was largely independent from the College; lacking any endowment, it depended solely on tuition for its expenses, and enrollment was insufficient to provide adequate salaries for the lecturers. Only seven men qualified for the degree of Bachelor of Laws: four in 1849, two in 1850, one in 1852. The school was dropped from the catalogue in 1852, the names of the three professors were removed in 1854, and the school formally closed in 1855.

The law school building became a railroad and canal office before Josephine Ward Thomson (later Swann) purchased it and renamed it Ivy Hall in 1871. For eight years it was the home of a women's library and hosted lectures for women. Then, from 1879 to 1883, it was the first home of Princeton's first eating club, Ivy Club, which took its name from the building. The building was later acquired by its neighbor, Trinity Episcopal Church,

In 1871 the trustees looked into reviving the law school, but nothing came of the idea. In 1890 President Francis Patton raised the subject at an alumni gathering: "We have Princeton philosophy, Princeton theology, but we have to go to Harvard and Columbia for our law. Gentlemen: that is a shame. Just as soon as I find a man with half a million, I am going to found a law school."

No such donor came forward, much to the disappointment of Princeton's professor of jurisprudence, Woodrow Wilson 1879. Shortly after his election as president in 1902, Wilson proposed a school of jurisprudence in which law would be taught "only to university graduates and by men who could give it full scholarly scope and meaning without rendering it merely theoretical or in any sense unpractical—men who could, rather, render it more luminously practical by making it a thing built upon principle, not a thing constructed by rote out of miscellaneous precedents." But other priorities—including funds for faculty salaries, preceptorships, the library, a recitation hall, science laboratories, and a graduate school—took precedence; when Wilson resigned in 1910, the school of jurisprudence had not been realized.

A proposal to create a law school was seriously considered from 1923 to 1925 but abandoned in 1926. Another proposal in 1929 received little attention.

In 1973 a four-year joint Master of Public Affairs-Doctor of Jurisprudence program was established by the school of Public and International Affairs in collaboration with the law schools at Columbia University and New York University (and later Stanford University); students in the program have also obtained joint degrees with law schools at the University of California at Berkeley and at Georgetown, Harvard, Pennsylvania, Virginia, and Yale.

In 1974, President William Bowen appointed a committee to consider whether Princeton should develop a program in law. Following a year-long study, this committee, which was chaired by the dean of the school of Public and International Affairs, Donald Stokes '51, and included New York lawyer Robert Owen '52 and politics professor Dennis Thompson, submitted an extensive report that identified a number of concerns about the impact a law school could have on Princeton's distinctive identity. The committee ultimately concluded that while a law program with qualities adapted both to Princeton's special characteristics and the special needs of legal education "could bring new strength to Princeton and could make a genuine contribution to the nation," very substantial gifts would be needed to endow such a program and to meet its initial plant and library costs. Bowen and the trustees accepted the committee's recommendation that in view of the "serious financial constraints" facing Princeton, active consideration of a law program should be postponed.

In 1999 the University created a program in Law and Public Affairs (LAPA), jointly sponsored by the school of Public and International Affairs and the

University Center for Human Values, to "explore the role of law in politics, society, the economy, and culture in the United States, countries around the world, and across national borders." By combining the multidisciplinary expertise of the Princeton faculty with experts on American, international, and comparative law in the academy, legal practice, the government, and policy-making institutions, LAPA provides a forum for teaching and research about the role of law and the legal technologies and institutions needed to address the complex challenges of the twenty-first century.

LEE, HENRY 1773, an American Revolutionary cavalry officer known as "Light-Horse Harry" Lee and father of Robert E. Lee, entered Princeton with his younger brother Charles when they were 14 and 12, after a 10-day journey from Virginia by stagecoach and horseback alongside their friend James Madison 1771.

The Lee brothers roomed together in Nassau Hall. Charles, who graduated two years after Henry, later became attorney general of the United States. Henry joined the Cliosophic Society but later transferred to its rival, Whig, of which Madison was a founder.

After the war Lee was elected governor of Virginia and, later, a member of Congress. A close friend of George Washington all his adult life, Lee was the author of the historic tribute, "first in war, first in peace, and first in the hearts of his countrymen." He used these words in a eulogy he prepared for Congress on the death of Washington, and in one he delivered at a funeral service for the first president in Philadelphia.

LEFSCHETZ, SOLOMON, came to the United States in 1907 as an engineer but turned to mathematics when he lost both hands in an accident while working for the Westinghouse Company. He became world renowned for his contributions to the topological study of algebraic geometry and the algebraic study of topology. At Princeton, as professor and department chair, he carried on where Henry Fine 1880, Luther Eisenhart, and Oswald Veblen left off in making Fine Hall an internationally acclaimed center for mathematics.

Lefschetz was born in Moscow and grew up in Paris, where he graduated from the École Centrale in 1905 with a degree in mechanical engineering. Following the accident, in 1910 he won a fellowship in mathematics at Clark University and earned his PhD there after only one year. He came to Princeton in 1924 from the University of Kansas, was named Fine Professor in 1933, and was appointed department chair in 1945; he continued in both offices until his retirement in 1953.

After the newly founded Institute for Advanced Study recruited Veblen, James W. Alexander II 1910 *1915, and John von Neumann from the University in the early 1930s, Lefschetz supplied the creative drive that maintained the Mathematics department's research strength and led it to new heights. Under his guidance the *Annals of Mathematics*, which he edited for 25 years, became one of the world's foremost mathematical journals.

In his early research in algebraic geometry Lefschetz made innovative use of topological methods, winning the Bordin Prize of the Paris Academy of Sciences in 1919 and the Bôcher Prize of the American Mathematical Society in 1924. In the 1920s he began to concentrate on topology itself. "Topology" is a word he coined in 1930 as the title for a monograph that brought this subject to the forefront of pure mathematics. On his retirement from the University in 1953, he helped build a school of pure mathematics at the National University of Mexico, and in recognition of this achievement received Mexico's Order of the Aztec Eagle. In 1965, when he was 81, he was awarded the National Medal of Science "for indomitable leadership in developing mathematics and training mathematicians."

LEWIS, SIR ARTHUR, was the first Black student and the first Black teacher at the London School of Economics, the first Black faculty member at the University of Manchester, the first Black full professor at Princeton, and well into the twenty-first century the only person of African descent to have won a Nobel Prize in any field other than literature and peace. He won the prize for economics in 1979 for his pioneering research into economic development, with particular consideration of the problems of developing countries.

Lewis joined the Princeton faculty in 1963 as a professor of economics and international affairs, and later was appointed the James Madison Professor of Political Economy. He taught undergraduate and graduate courses in economic development and economic history. The *New York Times* reported that students praised his courses "for focusing on ideas rather than numbers." He retired from the faculty in 1983 but remained associated with the University in an emeritus status until his death in 1991.

Lewis' office was in Robertson Hall, the home of the school of Public and International Affairs, and in 2017 the University named the hall's most prominent teaching and public lecture space the Arthur Lewis Auditorium in recognition of "his scholarly distinction, his commitment to teaching, his pioneering research into the economies of developing nations, and his lifetime commitment to public service." On display in the auditorium is a portrait of Lewis and a photograph from the 1970s, provided to the University by one of Lewis' daughters, showing Lewis lecturing in the auditorium with a number of distinguished guests in attendance, including his wife Gladys.

Lewis was born on the Caribbean island of St. Lucia in 1915. He earned his bachelor's degree and his PhD (in 1940) from the London School of Economics, and in 1948 was appointed to the faculty at Manchester. He became internationally prominent for his research into the economics of the developing world and into political and social change in emerging nations. Over the course of his career he published over 80 professional articles and wrote 12 books. He was knighted in 1963, the year he came to Princeton.

Outside of his academic career, Lewis epitomized Princeton's commitment to public service. He served as economic adviser to the government of Ghana when it gained independence in 1957, and as a consultant to such other nations as Trinidad and Tobago, Jamaica, Nigeria, and Barbados. He served as the first West Indian-born principal and then vice chancellor of the University of the West Indies, and was chancellor of the University of Guyana and first president of the Caribbean Development Bank.

Arthur Lewis Community College on his home island of St. Lucia is named in his honor, as is the Arthur Lewis Building at the University of Manchester where he taught for a decade. Princeton awarded him an honorary degree in 1988, and his papers are housed in Princeton's library.

Prior to being named in honor of Arthur Lewis, the Robertson Hall auditorium was named for Princeton's 15th president, Harold Dodds *14. In renaming the auditorium for Lewis, the trustees named the building's atrium for Dodds, in recognition of the critical roles he played in the development of the school of Public and International Affairs, first as chair of the faculty committee that initially directed it, and then, as president, in raising the funds necessary to provide an endowment for the school, create its graduate program, and construct its first home—then known as Woodrow Wilson Hall and now as Corwin Hall.

LEWIS CENTER FOR THE ARTS. In January 2006 President Shirley Tilghman announced a gift of $101 million from Peter B. Lewis '55, one of the largest gifts in the history of the University, to support a major new initiative in the creative and performing arts. Two months later she announced that Paul Muldoon, a Pulitzer Prize–winning poet and a Princeton faculty member since 1990, would serve as founding chair of the center, and in November 2007 she announced that the center would be named the Peter B. Lewis Center for the Arts in honor of its principal donor. The goal of the center, Tilghman said, "is to ensure that the arts become a part of every Princeton student's experience and that they play a greater and more central role in the life of our campus and our community."

In 2012, Muldoon was succeeded as chair by theater scholar Michael Cadden, and in 2019 Cadden was succeeded by another Pulitzer Prize–winning poet, US Poet Laureate Tracy K. Smith.

Today the Lewis Center is the academic home for Princeton's certificate programs in Creative Writing, Dance, Music Theater, Theater, and Visual Arts, and an interdisciplinary Atelier founded in 1994 by Princeton faculty member and Nobel Laureate Toni Morrison. Students in the certificate programs meet the requirements of their program and complete a creative thesis in their home department, and students from all backgrounds—nearly 2,000 a year—enroll in Lewis Center courses. Each year the center presents more than 120 performances, exhibitions, readings, film screenings, concerts, and lectures, including many that are open to the public.

The programs in Dance, Music Theater, and Theater, the Atelier, and the center's administrative offices are located in the three-building, 145,000-square-foot Lewis Arts complex that is located just east of Forbes College and just south of McCarter Theatre Center, which houses the Berlind and Matthews theaters. Designed by Steven Holl Architects and opened in 2017, the complex includes the Effron Music Building, which includes the acoustically isolated 3,500-square-foot Lee Music Performance and Rehearsal room; the Wallace Dance Building and Theater (which includes a 3,600-square-foot dance theater and a 3,600-square-foot black box theater); and a six-story arts tower that includes exhibition space for the visual arts.

An 8,000-square-foot ground-level "forum" connects all three buildings, serving as a lobby and gathering space and containing entrances to the Hearst Dance Theater, the black box Wallace Theater, and the Lee Music room. The buildings are part of a 22-acre development that also includes two restaurants (in former train station buildings), a Wawa convenience store, a new train station, and two outdoor sculptures by Maya Lin: a granite water structure called *Einstein's Table*, and a sculpted line of molded earth called *The Princeton Line* in honor of the site's historic connection to the train known as the Dinky.

The program in Visual Arts is housed in a former Princeton elementary school building at 185 Nassau Street where it has been based since 1966, and the Creative Writing program is headquartered in New South.

The initial precursor to the Lewis Center was a program in Creative Arts that was organized in 1939 by a faculty committee led by Christian Gauss, one of President Woodrow Wilson's original preceptors and Princeton's third dean of the college. It was supported by a five-year grant from the Carnegie Corporation to pay the salaries of "practitioners of the arts," and its aim was "to allow the talented undergraduate to work in the creative arts under professional supervision while pursuing a regular liberal arts course of study, as well as to offer all interested undergraduates an opportunity to develop their creative faculties in connection with the general program of humanistic education."

The Creative Arts program focused on music, painting, sculpture, and writing. Student composers of music met weekly with Professor Roger Sessions, while students interested in drawing and painting worked with James Davis 1923 and Alden Wicks '37. The boxing coach, Joseph Brown, conducted classes in sculpture in the cellar of Dean Gauss' residence, the Joseph Henry House. Students with talent in writing worked with the poet and critic Allen Tate who came to Princeton in 1939 as Princeton's first resident fellow in creative writing. A year later Richard P. Blackmur arrived to assist Tate; Blackmur was named director of the creative writing component of the program and in 1948 he became a professor of English.

In 1971 Edmund Keeley '48 became director of the Creative Writing program. Keeley changed the format of creative writing courses from precepts to workshops. For Keeley, the goal of the program "was primarily to teach students how to read as a writer might read and to begin writing with knowledge of the creative process. For many students, taking creative writing courses at Princeton was also how they first discovered literature, or at least a passion for literature."

In 1966 the Creative Arts program moved into the Nassau Street school, which had just been acquired by the University. Joseph Brown fell heir to the school's old gymnasium for his sculpture classes, and there was space for additional sculpture studios and five painting studios. Enrollment doubled in courses in creative writing, musical composition, and painting; a playwriting workshop was added; and extracurricular woodcarving with economics professor William Baumol supplemented the regular courses in sculpture. In 1971 Visual Arts assumed separate status with the architect Michael Graves as director. Dance officially came to Princeton in 1969 along with the arrival of undergraduate coeducation, and in 1975 Theater and Dance was granted separate status with Daniel Seltzer '54 as director.

Creative Writing

In 1981 Keeley was succeeded as director of the Creative Writing program by the poet James Richardson '71, who in turn was succeeded by English professor A. Walton Litz '51, Paul Muldoon, Edmund White, Chang-rae Lee, Susan Wheeler, Tracy K. Smith, and Jhumpa Lahiri. Toni Morrison taught in the program, and other long-time faculty included Joyce Carol Oates, Jeffrey Eugenides, and John McPhee '53. In 2010 the program moved to New South, where it occupies an entire floor.

In the decade following creation of the Lewis Center, the number of creative writing courses grew by almost 70 percent; annual enrollment in its courses doubled to almost 500; and each year some 25 to 30 seniors work with a member of the faculty on a creative thesis—a novel, a screenplay, or a collection of short stories, poems, or translations. Distinguished writers visit the campus each year to participate in the Althea Ward Clark reading series and discuss their work; the center draws poets from around the world to a biennial Princeton Poetry Festival; and the C.K. Williams reading series connects thesis students with established guest writers.

Dance

Formal instruction in dance began with the arrival of dancer and choreographer Ze'eva Cohen, who oversaw the development of dance at Princeton for

40 years. She was hired initially in response to anticipated interest on the part of newly admitted women students, but of the 60 students in her first class, 50 were men. She later wrote: "Clearly, both female and male students had a hunger for physical expression in an artistic context and a desire to develop self-awareness through movement."

In April 1970, the first out-of-doors dance demonstration, "To Dance is to Live, #1," took place on Poe Field. Cohen said: "A group of long-haired, bare-chested, body-painted men and a few women performed to the accompaniment of conga drums and a rock 'n roll band before a large crowd. They presented a 20-minute assemblage of work prepared in class throughout the year—a bold, proud performance that gave expression to their youthful exuberance and their . . . feelings of anger and fear about the Vietnam War."

In 1975 Dance became part of the program in Theater and Dance, and in 1986 it moved into a fully equipped dance studio at 185 Nassau Street. In 2009 Dance became a separate program with Susan Marshall as its founding director. With a faculty of professional dance artists, the program aims to nurture and develop beginners as well as dancers at the pre-professional level, always within the context of a broad liberal arts education. Each year it enrolls more than 400 students and between 10 and 15 of them earn certificates. The first purpose-built dance spaces, including the Hearst Dance Theater and three other dance studios, opened in the Lewis Arts complex in 2017.

Music Theater

The certificate program in Music Theater was approved in 2015 with Stacy Wolf, one of the country's foremost scholars on musical theater, as its founding director. The program brings together students, faculty, and guest artists to create, study, and perform music theater, including Broadway musicals, musical comedy, cabaret, music hall, operetta, singspiel, comic opera, grand opera, chamber opera, and experimental music theater. Students can create new music theater, participate in music theater production, and produce new scholarship in music theater history, theory, and criticism; their studies (like those of students in the Theater program) are augmented by collaborations with McCarter Theatre and travel to New York and Philadelphia to see performances, observe rehearsals, explore archives, and meet artists and scholars.

Theater

Following the death of Daniel Seltzer in 1980, directors of the program in Theater (until 2009, the program of Theater and Dance) were Alan Mokler, Melissa Smith, and for 19 years beginning in 1993, Michael Cadden. When Cadden was named director of the Lewis Center in 2012, he was succeeded as director of the Theater program by Tim Vasen, and then in 2016 by the award-winning lighting designer Jane Cox.

The program in Theater seeks to engage students in the making of theater through practical studio classes and a student-driven theater season, and to familiarize students with the role theater has played, and continues to play, in different cultures. The program teaches acting, directing, design, playwriting, community engagement, dramaturgy, performance history, and criticism. In addition to its faculty, the program staff includes theatrical craftspeople working in scenery, costumes, lighting, and stage management.

The program's productions offer students hands-on opportunities to write, direct, act, design, stage manage, and crew shows under the guidance of visiting artists and the program's faculty and staff. The program presents its productions in the Roger S. Berlind '52 Theatre at the McCarter Theatre Center and in the Wallace Theater, the Donald G. Drapkin Studio, and other studios, including a theatrical design studio, in the Lewis Arts complex, as well as in other traditional and nontraditional venues elsewhere on campus.

The programs in Theater and Music Theater together enroll more than 300 students a year in their courses, including about 30 pursuing certificates.

Visual Arts

After Michael Graves led the program in Visual Arts for two years and art historian Rosalind Krauss for a year, the sculptor James Seawright was appointed acting director and, in 1975, director, a position he held until 2001. He was succeeded by the film historian P. Adams Sitney, the painter Eve Aschheim, the sculptor Joe Scanlon, and, in 2017, the sculptor Martha Friedman.

The program in Visual Arts offers courses in painting, drawing, graphic design, photography/digital photography, film/video, and sculpture. It provides extensive contact with a faculty of practicing visual arts professionals as well as access to technical, analog, and digital labs including darkrooms, ceramics facilities, welding and mold-making areas, a letterpress studio, film editing bays, and a renovated theater for 35 mm and 16 mm film projections. The program occupies the entire building at 185 Nassau Street. It attracts more than 500 students a year to its courses, with about 15 concentrators.

Employing an interdisciplinary and multi-media approach, the program encourages non-concentrators to enrich their educations with art-making experience and urges concentrators to weave different art-making modalities and media into their overall practice. Students interested in pursuing a thesis in studio arts or film production can earn their degree through a Visual Arts certificate or through the Practice of Art concentration offered by the department of Art and Archaeology and administered by the program in Visual Arts. In either case students have round-the-clock access to shared studio loft spaces as juniors and semi-private studios as seniors. Throughout the year, student work is exhibited in the Hagan Studio, the Lucas Gallery, and the James Stewart Film Theater at 185 Nassau Street and the Hurley Gallery in the Lewis Arts complex.

Princeton Atelier

The Princeton Atelier is a unique academic program that brings together professional artists from different disciplines and students (about 75 a year) to create new work in a workshop environment during a semester-long course. Through this program, "a painter might team with a composer, a choreographer might join with an electrical engineer, a company of theater artists might engage with environmental scientists, or a poet might connect with a videographer."

Toni Morrison founded the program after realizing in her own work with musicians and composers that "there is a powerful impetus to stretch and freshen one's work by collaborating with artists in genres other than one's own." One of her first collaborations through the Atelier was with the cellist Yo-Yo Ma, the composer Richard Danielpour, and the bassist Edgar Meyer; another collaboration was with the novelist Gabriel García Márquez.

After directing the program for 10 years she was joined in 2004 by Paul Muldoon as co-director. When Morrison transferred to emeritus status in 2006, Muldoon became the director. Muldoon says of the Atelier that it "is not a place for the tried and tested—it's a place where some of our most adventurous student artists rise to the challenge of working with some of the most adventurous artists from beyond the university. As with all our courses in the Lewis Center for the Arts, we're committed to the idea that the eighteen-year-old stands at least as good a chance of making significant art as the eighty-year-old. This is not about limbering up for something. This is for real."

LEWIS LIBRARY. After almost four years of construction, an 87,000-square-foot science library named for its donor, Peter B. Lewis '55, and designed by acclaimed architect Frank Gehry, opened in the fall of 2008. It brought together science libraries from across campus into a research and study space that also included lecture halls, classrooms, and seminar rooms; the University's map collection; the digital map and geospatial information center; the office of information technology's education technologies center and media center; a broadcast center; and the Princeton Institute for Computational Science and Engineering.

One of its most distinctive features, popular with students and event planners, is a large second-floor reading room with lights hanging from a 34-foot-high ceiling that is called the "tree house" because its glass walls look out into neighboring tree tops.

The library is located at the southeast corner of Ivy Lane and Washington Road, adjacent to Fine (math), Jadwin (physics), and Peyton (astrophysics) halls; it is also near the homes of chemistry, molecular biology, psychology, neuroscience, and genomics, and new spaces for geosciences and engineering are planned for construction nearby. Its collections came from astrophysics, biology, chemistry, geosciences, mathematics, physics, psychology, and neuroscience, and a 2020 renovation of the library's Fine Hall wing created space to accommodate the engineering library as well.

Constructed of stainless steel, clay brick, steel, glass, and stucco in a soaring design that blends curves and colors and resembles sculpture as much as architecture, the building quickly became a campus icon, drawing visitors both because of its distinctive appearance and the celebrity of its designer.

Lewis, a Princeton trustee and chair of the board of the Progressive Corporation, gave $60 million to support the construction and the programs of the library. He said the library "brings together two things that are very close to my heart—Princeton University and the architecture of Frank Gehry. The building represents the kind of inspired risk-taking that is necessary for education and progress, and I am thrilled that Princeton has embraced Gehry's unique architecture on its campus."

Lewis also contributed $35 million to endow the Lewis-Sigler Institute for Integrative Genomics in honor of his classmate and roommate, Paul Sigler '55, and $101 million to endow the Lewis Center for the Arts. Over the course of his lifetime, his total giving to Princeton in capital gifts and annual giving exceeded $220 million.

LEWIS-SIGLER INSTITUTE FOR INTEGRATIVE GENOMICS, THE, was founded in 1998 through a gift of $35 million from Peter B. Lewis '55 to create innovative research and teaching programs at the interface of modern biology and the more quantitative sciences. Lewis made his gift in honor of his classmate, roommate, and lifelong friend, Paul Sigler '55, a structural biologist at Yale. The founding director of the institute was molecular biology professor Shirley Tilghman, who three years later would become Princeton's 19th president.

In 2001, construction began on a 90,000-square-foot home for the institute, the Carl Icahn Laboratory, with funding from Carl Icahn '57. The building was designed for maximum flexibility and collaboration by Rafael Vinoly, who also designed Princeton's football stadium. Its two-story atrium houses a large undulating metal sculpture designed by Frank Gehry and donated by Lewis that serves as a conference room. Known as the Horse-Head Conference Room, it looks more like a giant whale that has swallowed those who have come together inside. The south-facing glass curtain wall of the atrium is shaded by louvers that move with the sun to regulate light and shade and cast shadows in the double-helix shape of DNA.

In 2003 the building opened and David Botstein, one of the world's leading geneticists and a pioneer of the Human Genome Project, was appointed director. He served in that role until he transferred to emeritus status in 2015. In 2004, a graduate program in quantitative and computational biology was formed; it was approved as a PhD-granting program in 2008. The program includes 70 faculty from 12 departments and covers the fields of genomics, computational biology, systems biology, biophysics, quantitative genetics, and molecular evolution.

Also in 2004 the institute was selected to house one of five federally-funded centers of excellence in quantitative biology, with Botstein as principal investigator, and it introduced a revolutionary new integrated science curriculum that prepares undergraduates for majors in any of several disciplines, including physics, chemistry, computer science, and molecular biology. The integrated curriculum also leads to a certificate program in quantitative and computational biology.

According to its website, one impetus for the institute "came from the need to deal with the explosion of information based on the genomic sequences of the human and all major experimental organisms." The other major impetus "came from the realization that the most interesting and difficult problems in the quantitative disciplines, especially physics, chemistry, and computer science, frequently lie in biological phenomena and applications."

The institute brings together scientists from the departments of Chemistry, Chemical and Biological Engineering, Computer Science, Ecology and Evolutionary Biology, Molecular Biology, and Physics, and provides cutting-edge research infrastructure to encourage and support their interdisciplinary research, including research in such areas as experimental and computational development of genome-scale technologies, mathematical and physical modeling, and innovative molecular imaging.

The institute's endowment supports exceptional early career experimental scientists and theorists as Lewis-Sigler fellows, funding their independent research at the institute for five years while they also participate in the design and execution of the institute's teaching programs.

LGBTQIA STUDENTS AT PRINCETON. The existence of LGBTQIA Princetonians was unacknowledged for generations. Until relatively recently, even those who recognized their sexual orientation privately hid their identities on campus and in public. (LGBTQIA is an acronym that stands for lesbian, gay, bisexual, transgender, queer and/or questioning, intersex, and asexual.)

Many of the gay students at Princeton in the 1950s and 1960s did not have the vocabulary to describe their sexual orientation or relationships until well after they graduated. Most were not out, and most knew few people, if any, who were out, even in the outside world, let alone at Princeton. Despite the challenges, some students developed deep friendships with their classmates that took romantic turns—but only in private, kept secret even from roommates and close friends.

Although some students, faculty, and staff participated in informal, underground gatherings with other gay men in town and on campus, many gay students found Princeton a difficult place socially. They endured homophobic jokes and stereotyping comments that made them anxious about being outed, and sometimes they were teased in eating clubs and elsewhere by classmates who suspected their sexuality. In the years after graduating, some gay alumni were surprised to learn just how many of their classmates also were gay.

Gay students at Princeton began to organize publicly in 1972, three years after the Stonewall uprising in New York's Greenwich Village that marked a turning point in the gay rights movement. That spring, Arthur Eisenbach '74 placed an ad in the *Daily Princetonian* reading: "Closet Queens Unite!" In the fall, the Gay Alliance of Princeton (GAP) held its first meeting. For some students, GAP events—like its first annual dance, attended by more than 300 people (including many local community members)—were the first time they interacted on campus with other students who were out.

The names of the clubs, student organizations, and support groups at Princeton since the 1970s reflect terminology changes over the decades. In response to what they saw as male domination in GAP, a group of women started Gay Women of Princeton (GWOP) in the early 1980s. A few years later, GAP rebranded as the Gay and Lesbian Alliance at Princeton (GALAP) to assert itself as attuned to the needs of lesbian women. In 1999 the group adopted the name Pride Alliance as a more complete representation of the spectrum of queer communities.

Working with student leaders on campus (like GAP president Shawn Cowls '87), Dick Limoges '60 and other gay alumni created the Fund for Reunion (FFR) in 1986 as a way to provide support to LGBTQIA groups on campus and to influence Princeton's position toward the community; the group later used the name FFR/Princeton BTGALA (Bisexual, Transgender, Gay and Lesbian Alumni Association). In 2003 graduate students formed the Queer Graduate Caucus for lesbian, gay, bisexual, transgender, queer, and questioning graduate students and their allies.

Even as gay students built a community at Princeton, homophobia on campus often made LGBTQIA students feel unsafe or uncomfortable in their identities. For example, when two students hung a GAP banner outside their dorm window in 1976, a group of eight students broke into the room, ransacked it, stole the banner, and then mailed the vandalized banner to the *Princetonian* with an anti-gay note. Three years later, the campus pub was closed after a group of gay students was verbally and physically attacked by other students. On multiple occasions in the 1990s, students removed and burned posters advertising events for the LGBTQIA community. These incidents and other harassment pressured many LGTBQIA students into hiding their identities and relationships, for fear of being subject to similar attacks.

At the same time, some of the events that began in the 1980s and 1990s continued well into the twenty-first century. In 1989 graduate student Daniel Mendelsohn *94 brought Gay Jeans Day to Princeton; this annual event, which had originated at Rutgers University, offered an opportunity for allies to show support and empathy for gay students. Gay Jeans Day took place at Princeton for nearly 20 years, prompting decades of conversations on campus about what it means to be out. In 2018, Mendelsohn, an acclaimed author, critic, and translator, received the James Madison Medal, the University's highest award for graduate alumni.

Pride Week has happened on an annual basis since the late 1980s. An annual Drag Ball, intended to encourage attendees to subvert gender norms, has been held annually at Terrace Club since 1994. Pride Alliance continued to sponsor dances like those first organized by GAP in the 1970s.

Members of the Princeton LGBTQIA community have met in a variety of spaces over the years, including 185 Nassau Street, Burr Hall, and the basement of Murray-Dodge Hall, where the office of religious life (ORL) is housed. In the late 1980s students acquired a computer and a small office space there, which they called "the closet." The space enabled GALAP to have a home base and to begin building a library of books on LGBTQIA history, theory, and culture.

Institutional support for the community grew during the 1980s and 1990s, in many ways stemming from the advocacy of the ORL, and especially of Sue-Ann Steffey Morrow, an assistant dean of the chapel. Morrow arranged for the first part-time LGBTQIA program coordinator, Princeton Theological Seminary student Paul Davis, half of whose salary was paid by the ORL. In addition to Morrow, a number of out LGBTQIA staff members supported the campus community, notably Susan Packer, a mental health clinician at University Health Services, who supported a coming-out group run by students.

In response to student activism and protests, Princeton amended its nondiscrimination policy to prohibit discrimination based on sexual orientation. This change led to a 1991 decision permitting gay couples—legally unable to marry in the United States at the time—to live in student family housing, after a graduate student petitioned for his partner to live with him. As the result of a 1994 task force, Princeton updated its domestic benefit policy for employees to include those in same-sex partnerships. There was still backlash from alumni, as when Morrow officiated at a same-sex marriage in the chapel in 1997, but by the early 2010s Princeton offered among the most comprehensive transgender-inclusive healthcare policies in the country, including things like voice lessons in addition to gender-affirmation surgery.

The push toward creating an LGBT center began in earnest in the early 2000s. When Debbie Bazarsky became the full-time LGBT coordinator in 2001—by then in the domain of the office of the dean of undergraduate students rather than the ORL—she began to lay the foundations for many sub-groups within the community. For example, she advertised a transgender support group, hoping it would demonstrate to transgender members of the Princeton community that they were welcome on campus; although there had been alumni who came out as transgender and transitioned after Princeton, like Susan Faye Cannon '46 and Alice Miller '66, a transgender community at Princeton was nonexistent at the beginning of the twenty-first century.

By co-sponsoring events with numerous departments across the university, and with additional financial support from ORL and alumni in FFR/BTGALA, LGBTQIA programming was able to far exceed Bazarsky's budget. Knowing that the LGBT community had support from top administrators, in particular dean of undergraduate students Kathleen Deignan and President Shirley Tilghman, students submitted a proposal for an LGBT center in 2003. The LGBT center, which serves the needs of LGBTQIA students, staff, and faculty, held its grand opening in the Frist Campus Center in 2006. Bazarsky was its first director, running the center for 10 years.

The LGBT center oversees events and programming associated with more than 20 student organizations and discussion and support groups, including for students of color and other identity groups, employees, and scholars of LGBT studies. Some events, like Lavender Graduation, an annual celebration of LGBTQIA graduates first held in 2001, are primarily attended by members of the LGBTQIA community. Throughout the year, the LGBT center also hosts events attended by the campus community more broadly, including the Welcome Back BBQ, which helps create a sense of community for LGBTQIA staff and students. Still other events, like Hack the Drag—an annual hackathon in which teams create drag costumes that incorporate wearable technology—integrate elements of LGBTQIA culture into students' broader academic and extracurricular interests.

Students also initiated efforts and informal groups outside the realm of the LGBT center, many of them putting additional focus on LGBTQIA students of color. More than 350 LGTBQIA students from all eight Ivy League schools and other colleges attended the IvyQ conference, hosted at Princeton in 2014, which featured speakers who identified as queer and transgender people of color.

The LGBT Center was endowed with a $50,000 donation from FFR/BTGALA in 2015 in memory of the organization's longtime treasurer Gordon Harrison '68 *70. FFR/BTGALA has also supported independent research in LGBT studies and it sponsors a postdoctoral fellowship which has helped build the ranks of tenured faculty focusing on sexuality.

In 2013 more than 600 alumni, faculty, and staff returned to campus for *Every Voice*, a conference for LGBTQIA and ally alumni, many of whom had never before returned to Princeton. To continue the storytelling and story-gathering begun at the conference, then-LGBT center director Judy Jarvis created the LGBTQIA oral history project in 2017 in partnership with FFR/BTGALA, the program in Gender and Sexuality Studies, and the University archives. Student research assistants recorded more than 140 interviews with alumni and with current and former faculty and staff as part of the project, which is stored in the archives and available through its website.

LIBRARY, THE PRINCETON UNIVERSITY, has evolved in step with the University's educational mission. Initially little more than an ornament to the early College, the library grew and matured along with the institution's research and teaching capacities and ambitions. When Firestone Library opened in 1948, it was widely hailed as a "laboratory of the humanities" and "the intellectual heart of the university."

The library's first inception consisted of two large boxes of books moved from Newark in 1756 to the newly constructed Nassau Hall, supplemented by 474 books that were donated by provincial governor Jonathan Belcher, making Princeton's library the sixth largest in the colonies. Although only six of Belcher's books have survived, he is still recognized as the library's oldest benefactor: when Firestone Library was built, the governor's arms were carved in stone over the main entrance. Even with this substantial addition, as well as other gifts, a 1760 catalogue compiled by President Samuel Davies listed a total of only 1,281 volumes, significantly fewer than Yale's 3,000 or Harvard's 5,000.

In his catalogue, Davies solicited additional donations, saying: "A large and well-sorted Collection of Books on the various Branches of Literature is the most proper and valuable Fund with which [the College] can be endowed. It is one of the best Helps to enrich the Minds both of the Officers and Students with Knowledge . . . and to lead them beyond the narrow Limits of the Books to which they are confined in their stated Studies and Recitations."

The library was initially located in what is now the upper part of Nassau Hall's memorial atrium. In the devastating Nassau Hall fire of 1802, all but 100 of the library's volumes were destroyed. With the construction of what is now Stanhope Hall in 1803, the library relocated to a room there, but for the next half century it was a neglected resource, with acquisitions scant and access limited to one hour per week. The Whig and Clio societies' libraries filled the gap, providing students with newer books than those of the library, including novels and poetry.

In 1855 another Nassau Hall fire led to its renovation, with the library moving back to what is now the faculty room. Still, as the library counted only about 10,000 volumes and was open only a few hours per week, it was more of a warehouse than a library.

Under President James McCosh the library began its trajectory to its current eminence. In 1868 John Cleve Green, Princeton's greatest benefactor during the McCosh presidency, gave an endowed fund, the Elizabeth Foundation, for "the purchase of rare and valuable books needed for the purposes of research and study by literary and learned men." Today the library draws on more than 400 endowments in building its collections.

Green also funded the University's first dedicated library building, Chancellor Green (named for his brother), which was constructed in 1873. Under the first full-time librarian, Frederic Vinton, who had been hired away from the Library of Congress, the library increased both its hours and its holdings. The popularity of its beautiful reading room combined with a doubling of the student body over the next 25 years meant that the striking octagonal structure, ideal for a small library, was soon stretched beyond its capacity for books, students, and staff.

Pyne Library was constructed adjacent to Chancellor Green in 1897 and connected via "The Carfax" (later the hyphen)—a reference to a busy Oxford intersection. It was a sesquicentennial gift of Albertina Shelton Taylor Pyne, mother of Moses Taylor Pyne 1877. Some believed that with the addition of Pyne, the combined library was well set for a hundred years, but less than a quarter century would pass before the need for a new, larger structure became apparent.

Princeton's library paled in comparison to many of its Ivy peers, and unlike institutions located in urban areas, Princeton's library users could not avail themselves of a great municipal library. These shortcomings were exacerbated with the 1924 implementation of the undergraduate four-course plan, which emphasized independent reading within one's discipline as well as original research and scholarship in preparing a senior thesis. By the 1920s the faculty was beginning to discuss a new library.

The establishment of specialized libraries ameliorated some of Pyne's shortcomings. In addition to adding shelf space for the library system's nearly half million books, the creation of departmental libraries augmented Pyne's meager 100 student study spaces.

The Marquand Library of Art and Archaeology, established in 1908 (most recently renovated in 2002), was the first of what would be more than 10 branch libraries by midcentury. Other branch libraries were created within other academic departments, particularly the natural sciences, in the schools of Public and International Affairs and Engineering and Applied Science, and at the office of Population Research and the plasma physics laboratory (Furth Library). The Gest (now East Asian) library attracted scholars from around the world. (In 2008 eight departmental science libraries were consolidated in the Frank Gehry-designed Lewis Science Library.)

In 1930 a small group of Friends of the Princeton University Library began helping to support the acquisitions and operations of the library, and in 1939 it began publishing the *Princeton University Library Chronicle*. Today the group includes more than 800 members, and it continues to publish the *Chronicle*.

The Great Depression and World War II delayed construction of a new library, but in 1944 Librarian

Julian Boyd brought together a dozen other universities planning to construct new libraries after the war. The resulting Cooperative Committee on Library Building Plans led to a revolution in academic library architecture as it incorporated emerging educational, research, and technological trends, as well as physical features such as open stacks, floor layouts, lighting, seminar and reserve reading rooms, air conditioning, and special collections.

This planning culminated in the Harvey S. Firestone Memorial Library, financed by gifts from 1,250 individuals and groups (21 alumni classes from 1890 to 1943 contributed $1.5 million), with the largest gifts coming from the Firestone family (his five sons all graduated from Princeton). The Institute for Advanced Study contributed $500,000, in recognition of the University's early support of that institution and appreciation for the University granting library privileges to the institute's faculty—including a dedicated study room—in perpetuity.

The last of the Gothic-themed buildings constructed on campus until Whitman College in 2007, Firestone incorporated many of the Cooperative Committee's recommendations, with a functional interior that sought to connect books with readers. The design included two-person study carrels for thesis-writing seniors, scattered in clusters around the library.

Among the largest buildings on the campus, Firestone houses many of the administrative functions that support the entire multi-building library system. The University looks upon this system as a singular Princeton University Library, with one budget and one administration, but with its holdings dispersed for the convenience of users. The building is deceptively large, with most of its usable space on the three floors beneath the ground floor; because it is built on a downward slope, the lower levels enjoy natural light on at least one side.

With available space and a modern building, the library's special collections expanded significantly after Firestone's opening. The first special collections, kept in the "art room" in Chancellor Green, were joined later by Civil War materials donated by John Pierson 1840 and the Junius Morgan 1888 collection of Virgil. The gifts of Robert Garrett 1897 in the 1930s laid the foundation for superb collections of medieval, renaissance, and Islamic manuscripts. In 1937 the Institute for Advanced Study transferred the Gest collection of Chinese rare books, and several donations by alumni of rare books of English literature, particularly from the latter half of the nineteenth century, collectively created a distinguished collection of rare books and manuscripts.

Librarians actively sought new literary collections, particularly from alumni, securing donations from the Scribner family and the estates of F. Scott Fitzgerald 1917 and Sylvia Beach, as well the papers of many who embraced the University's informal motto of "Princeton in the Nation's Service," including three secretaries of state, a Supreme Court justice, and many noted diplomats, including George Kennan 1925.

The availability of space and staffing that allowed for conservation, cataloguing, and access also was the catalyst for the acquisition of the records of the American Civil Liberties Union, even though the organization had no strong association with the University. Several significant donations of early and Western Americana, graphic arts, historic maps, and numismatics, along with the establishment of the Princeton University Archives in 1959, rounded out the library's special collections at the time. The construction of the Seeley G. Mudd Manuscript Library in 1976 (renovated in 2020) to house the archives and the public policy papers created two locations for the special collections department.

Several extremely noteworthy additions would come years later. In 1996, Lloyd Cotsen '50 donated his premier collection of children's rare books, manuscripts, and games; they are now housed in the Cotsen Children's Library, located just off Firestone's main lobby and open to the public. William Scheide '36 moved his world-renowned library of extremely rare books and manuscripts into Firestone in 1959, and his collection, valued in the range of $300 million, was formally given to the University in 2015 following his death at age 100.

In 2014 the University announced that the papers of emerita professor and Nobel Laureate Toni Morrison would be part of the library's permanent collection, along with the papers of another Nobel Laureate who taught at Princeton, Mario Vargas Llosa, strengthening an already strong group of modern literary collections. (Vargas Llosa's papers joined a collection of almost 100 Latin American authors.)

Other notable library holdings include Ethiopic manuscripts; papyri and cuneiform; thousands of Greek, Roman, and Byzantine coins; death masks; early illustrated books, including a first edition of John J. Audubon's *Birds of America*, as well as some of that book's copper printing plates; early photography;

. and, within Marquand Library, five centuries of rare art books from five continents.

Firestone Library underwent major expansions in 1971 and 1988 that increased the size of the subterranean B and C floors, and there were many smaller changes, including the addition of the John Foster Dulles 1908 reading room in the mid-1960s.

Although the construction of an annex on the Forrestal Campus in the 1970s provided storage for less-circulated books, Firestone struggled to keep pace with growing acquisitions. By the turn of the century, as the building became an increasingly confusing warren of shelves, offices, and study spaces with little natural light, talk of a major renovation began. As these discussions took place, construction was completed for the Friend Center for Engineering Education, which housed a new engineering library relocated from the Engineering Quadrangle. (In 2020 the engineering library moved to the Lewis library, and plans were being made to include library-related services in new engineering space to be constructed along Ivy Lane and Western Way.)

In 2000, Princeton, Columbia University, and the New York Public Library (Harvard joined in 2016) collaborated to create ReCAP (Research Collections and Preservation Consortium), a state-of-the-art library storage facility run collectively but operated by Princeton. Its first storage module, on the University's James Forrestal Campus, opened in 2002, and by 2020 there were nine modules storing over 16 million items and circulating over 200,000 items among the four institutions per year, using integrated software that seamlessly represented ReCAP's combined holdings in each institution's catalog.

ReCAP is one of many endeavors that illustrate the growing emphasis in academic libraries on sharing, collaboration, and technology in support of universities' teaching and research missions. As of 2020 the Princeton University Library has over 160,000 items and 5 million images from its collections digitally available online, and half of its annual acquisitions budget goes toward electronic books, databases, serials, datasets, and other digital resources.

The Center for Digital Humanities, physically located within the renovated Firestone Library, promotes the application of "digital tools to humanistic questions," and Princeton participated in a project coordinated by Google (as part of their Google Books service) in which participating academic libraries incorporated their digitized holdings into the HathiTrust, a 17 million digital book collection that proved especially crucial during the 2020-21 COVID-19 pandemic.

The 10-year Firestone renovation that began in 2008 touched every corner of the building but did not physically expand it; with creative and meticulous planning, the renovation was accomplished without ever having to close. The renovation renewed and repurposed space to create more seating for students while also maintaining the number of volumes in the building. This was accomplished, in part, by relocating cataloging staff off-campus (more than 60 employees, or about one-quarter of the total who worked in Firestone), as they no longer needed proximity to the card catalog. (Additions to the physical card catalogue stopped in 1981 and it was removed from the first-floor lobby in 2011, with its drawer fronts becoming part of an exhibit in the renovated library lobby.)

The installation of compact shelving throughout much of the lowest floor permitted a much greater number of volumes within the same floor space, and removal of all but three of the original almost 500 metal two-person study carrels, both beloved and detested by generations of seniors, provided space for new study room configurations. The renovation returned much natural light to the building, consolidated special collections onto one floor, organized the physical location of the collections by call number, and introduced a café ("Tiger Tea Room") to the first floor.

Firestone today is one of the largest open-stack libraries in the world and it has more books per student than any other university in the United States. The library's overall holdings include 10 million printed volumes, 2 million of them in Firestone, as well as 5 million manuscripts, 400,000 rare or significant printed works, thousands of journals, 2 million non-print items in over 200 languages, and extensive collections of digital text, data, images, audio, video, and online resources

As of 2020 the Princeton University Library employed over 300 professional and support staff in the library system (in addition to Firestone, its nine other libraries were Architecture, East Asian, Engineering, Lewis Science, Marquand Art, Mendel Music, Mudd Manuscript, Plasma Physics, and Stokes in the school of Public and International Affairs). The size of the staff had remained relatively constant over five decades as technology eliminated some positions but created many newer demands, including digital camera operators and electronic resource coordinators. Especially as traditional academic fields evolve and new academic fields emerge, the library continues to need specialists in dozens of areas, as students and faculty continue to depend on the library in all of its many dimensions to continue to serve as "the intellectual heart of the university."

As Princeton's first full-time librarian, Vinton published the first subject guide to the collections. His successor in 1890, Ernest Richardson, introduced a classification system long used at Princeton. Richardson was succeeded in 1920 by James Gerould and then in 1940 by Boyd, who resigned in 1952 to edit the papers of Thomas Jefferson, a project still housed at Firestone. Boyd's successors have been William Dix (1953–75), Richard Boss (1975–78), Donald Koepp (1978–95), Karin Trainer (1996–2016), and Anne Jarvis (2016–).

LINCOLN, ABRAHAM, was awarded an honorary degree *in absentia* in 1864 shortly after his reelection to a second term as president. It was the third and last honorary degree Lincoln would receive. With the Civil War still being fought, the degree was conferred at a meeting of the trustees on December 20th of that year, and President John Maclean Jr. wrote to Lincoln the same day to inform him of their action. The reply, in Lincoln's own handwriting, is one of the University's treasured possessions. The letter is as follows:

Executive Mansion

Washington, December 27, 1864.

My Dear Sir:

I have the honour to acknowledge the reception of your note of the 20th of December, conveying the announcement that the Trustees of the College of New Jersey have conferred upon me the Degree of Doctor of Laws.

The assurance conveyed by this high compliment, that the course of the government which I represent has received the approval of a body of gentlemen of such character and intelligence in this time of public trial, is most grateful to me.

Thoughtful men must feel that the fate of civilization upon this continent is involved in the issue of our contest. Among the most gratifying proofs of this conviction is the hearty devotion everywhere exhibited by our schools and colleges to the national cause.

I am most thankful if my labors have seemed to conduce to the preservation of those institutions under which alone we can expect good government and in its train sound learning and the progress of the liberal arts.

I am, sir, very truly
Your obedient servant

A. LINCOLN

Dr. John Maclean.

LITTLE, STAFFORD, HALL, which F. Scott Fitzgerald 1917 likened to a "black gothic snake" winding its way from Blair Hall to the gymnasium, was built in two halves: one in 1899 and one in 1901. It was Princeton's second Collegiate Gothic building, following Blair Hall. Little was the first dormitory in the country with indoor bathrooms.

When constructed, Little Hall followed what was then the western property line of the campus, prior to the railroad tracks being moved from the foot of Blair Arch to the south. It ran parallel to University Place for 196 feet, then made a right angle turn to the east for another 154 feet; it originally extended another 40 feet to the south, although later more entries were added to connect it to University Gymnasium and subsequently to Dillon Gym.

A window on the east façade of Little's four-story northern tower has the University's coat-of-arms (which was adopted at the sesquicentennial of 1896) held up by a pair of tigers; tigers are also displayed in a gateway between the southern end of Blair Hall and the northern end of Little that marks the western end of McCosh Walk.

The donor of Little Hall, Stafford Little 1844, was a founder and first president of the New York and Long Branch Railroad, and for several years was president of the New Jersey Senate. He was a trustee of Princeton from 1901 to 1904.

LOWRIE, WALTER, HOUSE at 83 Stockton Street was given to the University in 1960 by Barbara Armour Lowrie in memory of her husband, Walter Lowrie 1890. It was used as a University guest house until 1968, when it replaced Prospect House as the official residence of the president. The first president to live in Lowrie House was Robert Goheen '40 *48.

The house was designed in an Italianate revival style by Philadelphia architect John Notman (architect also of Prospect and of the 1855 restoration of Nassau Hall). It was built in 1845 by Commodore Robert F. Stockton for his son, John P. Stockton

1843, attorney general of New Jersey and United States senator. The Stocktons were members of one of New Jersey's most powerful and well-connected slaveholding families.

In 1860 the house was purchased from John Stockton by Paul Tulane, Princeton-born founder and benefactor of the university that bears his name.

In 1895 the house was acquired by George Allison Armour 1877, and it became the childhood home of Barbara Armour and her four brothers. Barbara and Walter Lowrie took up residence there in 1930, following their return from Rome, where he had been for many years rector of the Episcopal congregation at St. Paul's-within-the-Walls.

At the age of 62, Lowrie began teaching himself Danish, and for the next 27 years he devoted himself to the translation of all the works of the Danish philosopher, Søren Kierkegaard, and to writing a biography that one authority at the time called "the greatest one-volume work on Kierkegaard in any language." Lowrie wrote other books as well; all told, he published 27 volumes in those 27 years.

MACLEAN, JOHN, JR. 1816 was a member of the faculty for 50 years, serving successively as tutor, professor, vice president, and Princeton's 10th president; after his retirement in 1868, he served for the remaining 18 years of his life as president of the alumni association that he had founded in 1826. His life-long devotion to Princeton was notable not only for its remarkable longevity, but for the multiple roles he played.

As the son of America's first professor of chemistry, John Maclean Sr., John junior was born in Princeton and raised there. He matriculated at the College in 1813 and graduated three years later, at age 16 the youngest member of his class. After two years earning a divinity degree at Princeton Theological Seminary, he joined the college faculty as a tutor in Greek. He became a full professor of mathematics and natural philosophy at 23, vice president at 29, and president at 54.

Maclean was the mainstay of the 31-year administration of his predecessor, James Carnahan 1800. When Carnahan, dismayed by the state of affairs he found on his arrival in 1823, thought of resigning, Maclean persuaded him to remain. A few years later, when Carnahan thought of closing the College because a drop in enrollment necessitated cuts in faculty salaries and led to a lowering of morale, Maclean proposed a plan to reverse the decline by enlarging and improving the faculty.

The trustees accepted his plan and made him vice president. Maclean established the alumni association, secured a few gifts, discovered some funds due the College that had not previously been collected, shifted his own field from mathematics back to classics in order to make way for an able young mathematician, and secured the half-time services of several older men as an inexpensive means of broadening the curriculum. Making the most of the College's limited means, he was able to add to the faculty such outstanding figures as Joseph Henry (physics), John Torrey (chemistry), Stephen Alexander (astronomy), Albert B. Dod 1822 (mathematics), and James Alexander 1820 (belles-lettres). He made funds available for scholarships and financial aid. Enrollment rose from 87 in 1829 to 228 a decade later.

Maclean never married, but he was aided in his duties by two sisters who lived with him. He was said to be vigilant in detecting wrongdoing but sympathetic to the culprit once caught; frequently, the penalty was rustication at a nearby farm. Students recalled seeing him, armed with a lamp, a teakettle, and food, on his way to visit a sick student. In cases of serious illness, the student was brought to his house. One student, who broke his leg in a fall from a second-floor window of West College after the senior ball of 1847, was cared for at Maclean's house for six weeks.

Maclean was not without a sense of humor. One night two donkeys from a nearby farm were found on the top floor of Nassau Hall. A student on hand at the discovery asked Maclean, with an innocent air, how he thought they had gotten there. "Through their great anxiety to visit some of their brethren," Maclean replied.

Maclean showed the same concern for his fellow townspeople. He was Princeton's first non-slaveholding president, and he took particular interest in the welfare of African Americans in the community, working with them as one of the organizers and supporters of the Witherspoon Street Presbyterian Church. However, he was also a leading member of New Jersey's chapter of the American Colonization Society, which advocated for the resettlement of both formerly enslaved and free Black people in Liberia in West Africa.

A member of the Prison Association, he sometimes walked 10 miles to Trenton on Sundays to conduct services in the state prison. He was one of the earliest advocates of public education in New Jersey and an architect of the state's public school system; though a staunch Presbyterian, he insisted that the public schools should be completely nonsectarian.

Maclean's election in 1854 as President Carnahan's successor was as much a reward for previous service as it was an expectation of future achievement. There was a strong feeling among the trustees that the College needed a leader of greater distinction, and many favored Joseph Henry for the post. But Henry declined to be a candidate and urged the election of Maclean, stressing particularly his "untiring devotion to the interest of the college."

As it turned out, Maclean's "untiring devotion" was just what the College needed for the two extraordinary challenges it had to face during his presidency: the destruction of Nassau Hall by fire in 1855, and the division of the campus and a drop in enrollment during the Civil War.

Maclean rallied alumni and friends to contribute funds toward the rebuilding of Nassau Hall, augmented these funds by operating the College on an austerity budget for five years, and then helped liquidate the debt that remained by giving up part of his own salary. Since about 40 percent of Princeton's students came from the south, the College suffered a significant drop in enrollment during the Civil War—from 314 in 1861 to 221 a year later—but he managed to keep his faculty together and maintain a full program for the students who remained.

He supported the Union cause—more strongly than some of his student friends from the south thought necessary, but less quickly or urgently than some from the north would have preferred. In 1864 he conveyed to President Abraham Lincoln the honorary degree (Lincoln's third and last) that had been awarded to him by the trustees.

During his presidency, Maclean made a number of significant appointments to the faculty, including the Swiss geographer Arnold Guyot, but as a whole the appointments during his presidency lacked the luster of those he had secured earlier, in part because as he looked for good scholars he was also looking for good Presbyterians. He outlawed Greek fraternities, saw the beginning of baseball at Princeton and the first use of orange and black as Princeton's colors, and heard the earliest version of what became Princeton's alma mater, "Old Nassau."

On his retirement in 1868, friends bought him a house at 25 Alexander Street, where he lived out his years with one of his brothers. In 1877 he completed a two-volume history of the College, assigning the royalties to a fund "for the aid of indigent and worthy students engaged in seeking a liberal education."

Although he stayed away from the campus during term time, except when he was asked to preach in the chapel, he made brief appearances at Commencement, and whenever alumni caught sight of him a cheer went up for "Johnny." His last appearance—six weeks before he died—was at the commencement meeting of the alumni association in 1886. As president of the association (which he had founded as its first secretary 60 years earlier), he was given an ovation which, by contemporary accounts, was loud, long, and tearful.

"Some of us old fellows . . . who cheered first and cried afterward," one of them said later, "put a meaning into our action which nobody but Doctor Maclean and ourselves knew. There were secrets between us which he was too good ever to tell, and which, perhaps, we were ashamed to. His full biography will never be written. Its materials would have to be gathered from too many hearts."

In 1968, the house on the front campus in which he had lived as president was named Maclean House in his honor. Earlier that decade, as the University developed faculty housing on the former Gray Farm along the north shore of Lake Carnegie east of Harrison Street, it named one of the streets Maclean Circle, adjacent to the McCosh Circle that is named for Maclean's successor as president, James McCosh. Maclean Street, in the town of Princeton's historically African American Witherspoon-Jackson neighborhood, is also named for him.

MACLEAN, JOHN, SR., was Princeton's first professor of chemistry, and his lectures constituted the first American undergraduate course in chemistry.

Maclean entered the University of Glasgow in his native Scotland at the age of 13, determined to become a surgeon like his father. Under the influence of his friend Charles Macintosh (who later invented waterproof cloth), he joined the Chemical Society, before which he read several papers. In 1791, when he was only 20, he was licensed to practice medicine and admitted to the faculty of physicians and surgeons at the University of Glasgow.

He moved to the United States in the spring of 1795 and, on the advice of Benjamin Rush 1760, established himself in Princeton in the practice of "physic" and surgery. That summer, at President Samuel Stanhope Smith's invitation, he delivered a short course of chemistry lectures, which made so favorable an impression that the trustees in October appointed him professor of chemistry with the understanding that he could continue his medical practice. Two years later, Maclean assumed responsibility for instruction in mathematics and natural philosophy as well as in chemistry; at that point he gave up his medical practice and from then on devoted himself wholly to the College.

Maclean died at the age of 43 in 1814, two years after his resignation had been requested by trustees more concerned with training ministers than scientists, and two years before the graduation of his eldest son, John Maclean Jr. 1816, who was to become the 10th president of the College. His son's papers in the University's archives reveal that his father owned several slaves during his life, and still owned two of them when he died.

MACLEAN, JOHN, HOUSE, originally the President's House, shares with Nassau Hall the place of seniority among University buildings; both are accorded the same date of construction (1756) in official records, although it is probable that the President's House was not ready for occupancy until several months after Nassau Hall. Designed and built by Robert Smith, co-architect and builder of Nassau Hall, it was occupied by 10 presidents of the College—Burr, Edwards, Davies, Finley, Witherspoon, Smith, Green, Carnahan, Maclean, and McCosh—until McCosh moved into Prospect House when it was acquired as the president's residence in 1878.

After McCosh moved into Prospect, English professor James Ormsbee Murray occupied the old President's House and continued to live there after his appointment to the new office of dean of the faculty in 1883. From then until 1967, the house was the residence of the first seven deans of the faculty—Murray, Winans, Fine, Magie, Eisenhart, Root, and Brown—and it was called the Dean's House. In 1968, when it became the home of the Alumni Council, it was renamed in honor of John Maclean Jr. 1816, founder of the Alumni Association and the last president to occupy the house for the duration of his administration.

In addition to housing presidents, between 1756 and 1822 the building also housed enslaved people. Princeton's first nine presidents were all slave owners at some point in their lives, and five of them brought slaves to Maclean House. (Maclean was the first president to live in the house who never owned slaves.) In 2019 a plaque was installed in front of the house to commemorate 16 enslaved men, women, and children known to have lived and worked there. The plaque is near the site where an estate sale took place in 1766 for six slaves who had been owned by President Samuel Finley at the time of his death; it is also near the two oldest trees on campus, known as the Stamp Act sycamores, which by order of the trustees were planted in 1765. (Legend says the trustees had them planted to commemorate repeal of the Stamp Act that Britain had imposed on its colonies, but the act was not repealed until 1766, months after the sycamores were already in the ground.).

Maclean House was designated a National Historic Landmark in 1971. Georgian in style, it originally had flat walls to the east and west that attracted ball-playing, which led the trustees in 1761 to "ban playing at Ball against the President's House, under the Penalty of Five Shillings for every Offence."

Over time, the Maclean House roof was raised, a front porch was constructed, bays were added on the east and west sides, the originally detached kitchen to the rear was attached, and the brick was painted yellow. To the west of the house is a garden that was given by the Class of 1946, and to the south a garden given by the Class of 1936 that was thoroughly redesigned and replanted in 2005. The interior of the building was renovated in 2014 to better accommodate the staff of the Alumni Association and alumni visitors to the campus.

MADISON, JAMES, JR. 1771 was a statesman and political philosopher who, by tradition, should have attended the College of William & Mary. Most aspiring young Virginia men of his family's station did so. Three influences, however, diverted him. One was his tutor, Thomas Martin 1762, who persuaded him of the merits of the young institution in New Jersey. Another was President John Witherspoon's fame, which had begun to spread through the colonies. The third was Madison's family, which had differences with the administration of William & Mary. So in the summer of 1769 Madison, the eldest of 12 children, set out for Princeton.

Entering as a sophomore, Madison joined a group of students who remained his close and lifelong friends: William Bradford Jr. 1772, later US attorney general; Hugh Henry Brackenridge 1771, jurist and novelist; and Philip Freneau 1771, the "poet of the Revolution." Other future leaders whom he came to know at the College—which, more than any other, drew its students from throughout the colonies—

included Gunning Bedford Jr. 1771, signer of the Constitution from Delaware; Samuel Spring 1771, Massachusetts cleric and founder in 1808 of Andover Theological Seminary; and Aaron Burr Jr. 1772, future senator from New York and vice president of the United States, who was responsible for introducing Madison to his future wife, the widow Dolley Payne Todd.

Samuel Stanhope Smith 1769, Witherspoon's successor as president of the College of New Jersey, became Madison's college tutor and lasting friend. And Witherspoon himself served as Madison's moral preceptor and faithful champion. These were, as Madison called them in 1774, his "old Nassovian friends."

The College had begun to feel the winds of revolutionary politics by 1770, but Madison's two years of study were spent in reasonable tranquility. He worked hard to master the classics and the great works of the Scottish Enlightenment, often sleeping, despite his sickly disposition, fewer than five hours a night. He was one of the earliest members of the Whig Society, and spent much of his time debating with its members the affairs of government and society. He also wrote lusty, ribald doggerel.

After completing his junior and senior work in one year, Madison took his degree in the fall of 1771. However, he remained at the College until the spring of the next year to study philosophy and Hebrew under Witherspoon's tutelage, making him, in effect, Princeton's first graduate student.

Returning in 1772 to the pre-Revolutionary War calm of the Virginia piedmont and his family's tobacco plantation, Montpelier, he buckled down to a regimen of reading and tutoring his younger siblings. He felt isolated, directionless, and beset with depression and doubt. He was not interested in entering the pulpit or practicing law, but soon the Revolution gave his life a focus, released his energies, and dispelled his gloom.

At five feet four inches tall and weighing fewer than 100 pounds, Madison was not hardy enough to join the army. He instead helped govern Orange County, Virginia, as a member of its pro-Revolution Committee of Safety, and then helped draft the state's first constitution as a member of the Virginia general convention in 1776. These opportunities marked the beginning of one of the most distinguished public careers in the nation's history.

During these early years of national service, Madison continued to harbor doubts about his own capacities. Even after he had served in the Continental Congress as its youngest member and won election to the Virginia House of Delegates, where with Thomas Jefferson he played a major role in the passage of the historic Virginia Bill for Establishing Religious Freedom, his continued self-doubting elicited from Samuel Stanhope Smith the exasperated wish that "you had the same high opinion of yourself that others have."

Madison steadily accumulated the respect of others with whom he served in Virginia and the Continental Congress. (He returned to Princeton at least once during this period when the Congress fled Philadelphia in 1783 to escape the mutiny of American troops.) He attended the Annapolis convention of 1786 and the constitutional convention in Philadelphia in 1787. Without his careful note taking during the convention debates, little would be known of the proceedings of that historic meeting. His presence and intelligence during the convention, acknowledged by almost everyone, won him enduring renown as "Father of the Constitution."

His work in Philadelphia done, Madison turned to securing the Constitution's acceptance. His arguments on behalf of the Constitution at the Virginia ratifying convention carried that state, without which the ratification of New York might have been lost and the federal union with it. Moreover, his co-authorship, with Alexander Hamilton and John Jay, of the *Federalist Papers*, written in 1787 and 1788 to win over doubters and opponents of the new Constitution and embodying ideas and learning that Madison traced to his days in Nassau Hall some 20 years earlier, produced one of the nation's greatest contributions to Western political science.

Madison's *10th Federalist*, which overturned conventional arguments about the dangers of an extended republic and provided an analysis of the social bases of political factions and a plan to check their worst effects, alone worked a revolution in political theory and is rightly considered a classic expression of American thought. For his service during this period, Princeton awarded Madison an honorary degree in 1787. Witherspoon wrote Madison at the time to say that Princetonians were proud to recognize in this way "one of their own sons who had done them so much honor by his public service."

In the 1790s, Madison served in the US House of Representatives, where he sponsored the Bill of Rights and, with Jefferson's encouragement, created a legislative opposition to Treasury Secretary Alexander Hamilton that helped lay the basis for the

Democratic-Republican party, the first modern political party in the world. In 1798, in protest against the Federalist-backed Alien and Sedition Acts (which criminalized speech deemed to be antigovernment), he wrote the controversial Virginia Resolution, which put forward for the first time the doctrine of state interposition, a doctrine that would deeply influence the later theories of nullification and secession.

Upon the inauguration of his close friend Jefferson as president in 1801, Madison became secretary of state. After eight years of demanding service during the era of the Napoleonic Wars and the Louisiana Purchase, he succeeded Jefferson in 1809 as the fourth president of the United States. His two terms in the White House were fraught with difficulties born of war and bitter partisan struggles. Yet Madison and his administration were able to see the nation through the War of 1812, the country's "second war for independence," which finally ended Britain's threat to the growing republic.

He left the presidency in 1817 after over 40 years of public service, but continued to work for the public good by helping Jefferson found the University of Virginia, serving as its rector after Jefferson's death, and participating in the Virginia constitutional convention of 1829.

Madison always maintained a lively interest in his alma mater. In 1796 he contributed toward the purchase of materials for instruction in chemistry. In 1826 he accepted election as first president of the newly formed Alumni Association of Nassau Hall, a post he held until his death 10 years later. He contributed regularly to the alumni fund in his last years and, upon his death at age 85 as the last surviving signer of the Constitution, he bequeathed $1,000 to the College library from the proceeds of his posthumously published "Notes" on the debates at Philadelphia, the largest gift to the library until after the Civil War.

Madison's greatest contribution to the nation's history was his ability to translate theory into institutions and norms. Jefferson said of him in 1812, "I do not know in the world a man of purer integrity, more dispassionate, disinterested, and devoted to genuine republicanism; nor could I in the whole scope of America and Europe point out an abler head."

At the same time, while Madison spoke out against slavery and seemed to believe it was morally wrong, he owned more than 100 slaves who worked for him at Montpelier, and several served him during his time in the White House. Early in his life he emancipated one of his slaves, but it was the only time he did so. After his presidency he sold some of his land and many of his slaves to cover his debts; when he died, he willed his remaining slaves to his wife. In 1816 Madison joined the American Colonization Society, which generally held the view that free African Americans could not be integrated into white society, and therefore sought to remove them from the United States by repatriating them to Liberia. In 1833 Madison became its president.

In its January 23, 2008, issue, the *Princeton Alumni Weekly* published a list of the 25 most influential Princeton alumni of all time. Madison ranked first. In 1973 the Association of Princeton Graduate Alumni established the James Madison Medal as the highest honor the University can confer on its graduate alumni; the medal is presented each year on Alumni Day.

MADISON, JAMES, MEDAL, is the highest honor the University can bestow on alumni of its graduate school. First awarded in 1973, it is formally presented each year at Alumni Day. It recognizes alumni who have attained distinction in their professional careers, in the advancement of higher education, or in public service.

The medal is named for James Madison, the fourth president of the United States who, after receiving his bachelor's degree in 1771, remained at Princeton for another year to continue his studies under President John Witherspoon, effectively becoming Princeton's first graduate student. Madison left the White House in 1817 and in 1826 was elected the first president of the newly formed Alumni Association of Nassau Hall, a position he held until his death in 1836.

Previous Madison Medal winners are listed on page 519.

MADISON HALL originally was the collective designation for freshmen and sophomore dining halls (Commons) erected in 1916 at the corner of Nassau Street and University Place and named for James Madison 1771. Five great Collegiate Gothic dining halls were grouped around a central kitchen: Upper and Lower Cloister (next to the cloister that forms the west side of Holder Court), Upper and Sub Eagle (named for the carvings at the ends of the ceiling beams) on University Place, and the area still referred to as Madison Hall on Nassau Street. During both world wars these spaces served as mess halls for military units stationed on campus. In the late 1950s Madison Hall served as the home of Woodrow Wilson Lodge, an alternative to the eating clubs for juniors and seniors and precursor to Princeton's first residential college. Now all these spaces are integral components of Mathey and Rockefeller colleges.

Designed by Day and Klauder, this imposing group of buildings was the gift of Margaret Olivia Slocum Sage (the donor of adjacent Holder Hall), the Classes of 1916, 1917, and 1918, and others. They occupied a site where a hotel of more than 100 rooms and a student dining hall (University Hotel) had been constructed in 1875. After eight unprofitable years, the hotel was obtained by the College in 1883, renamed University Hall, and used as a dormitory and dining hall until it was demolished in 1916 to make way for Madison Hall.

MAGIE, WILLIAM FRANCIS 1879, a founder of the American Physical Society and its president from 1910 to 1912, taught physics at Princeton for almost half a century and was chair of the department during 20 of its formative years. He was one of the able group of alumni from the McCosh era who nurtured Princeton's development from a college to a university.

Magie was an editor of the *Princetonian*, as were his classmate Woodrow Wilson and Henry Fine 1880. At graduation he was valedictorian. He thought about following his father into the practice of law but, stirred by news of the first Princeton expedition to the West in 1877 and the subsequent paleontological researches of William Berryman Scott 1877 and Henry Fairfield Osborn 1877, Magie "could not help wishing" that he too "might have a chance to work in some scientific field."

His chance came toward the end of his senior year when Professor Cyrus Fogg Brackett, who was doing all physics instruction single-handedly, suffered a breakdown and his friends insisted he should have an assistant. Brackett offered Magie the job on commencement day, and he accepted. "I did not then know it," Magie told his classmates 50 years later, "but I now know that the subject of physics, into which I was inducted in this somewhat casual way, was the one subject which was best suited to my habits of thought. I never had enough originality or mathematical skill to do great original work, but I always loved the fundamental and philosophical aspects of the subject, and loved to teach it."

Magie did not neglect the scholarly side of his career. He and Fine were given leave in 1884 and went to Germany, where Magie studied at the University of Berlin and earned his PhD with a thesis on the measurement of surface tensions. A decade later he collaborated with two physicians in publishing the first paper in this country on the possible use of Roentgen's newly discovered X-rays in surgery. He later published occasional papers on the properties of solutions and was the author of a highly regarded account of the rise and content of physical theories, *Principles of Physics*.

His greatest contribution, however, was in teaching and administration. After 1889, when Brackett began a graduate program in Electrical Engineering, Magie took over the undergraduate courses in physics. He shared increasingly in the administration of the department, and in 1908 became its chair. Magie and Brackett worked closely with Fine to build up a strong Physics department as part of Fine's efforts, as dean of the faculty, to strengthen all the science departments. In the controversy between President Wilson and Dean Andrew Fleming West 1974, Fine supported Wilson, but Magie sided with West.

When John Grier Hibben 1882 *1893 became president in 1912, he appointed Magie as Fine's successor as dean of the faculty; Magie held this office until 1925 and continued to serve as chair of the Physics department until his retirement in 1929.

In 1965 apartments for junior faculty, on the north side of Lake Carnegie next to the Hibben apartments, were named for Magie. When those apartments were later replaced by the Lakeside apartments for graduate students, one of the roadways through the Lakeside complex was named for Hibben and Magie.

MALKIEL, NANCY WEISS, a scholar of twentieth-century American history, was one of only three women on the Princeton faculty, and the first in the History department, when she arrived on campus as an assistant professor in 1969 just as undergraduate coeducation was beginning. In 1975 she was promoted to associate professor, and in 1982 to full professor. From 1982 to 1986, as Princeton instituted a program of residential colleges for all freshmen and sophomores, she was the founding head of Mathey College, one of five such colleges at the time. From 1987 to 2011, she oversaw Princeton's undergraduate academic program as the University's longest-serving dean of the college. In 2016 she transferred to emeritus status, and her landmark study, "*Keep the Damned Women Out": The Struggle for Coeducation*, was published by Princeton University Press.

Malkiel earned her bachelor's degree *summa cum laude* from Smith College, where she was a student government leader and newspaper editor, and her master's and doctoral degrees from Harvard. At Princeton, she taught in both the History department and the program in American Studies; her signature history course, "The United States since 1940," enrolled more than 300 students on six different occasions. As one of the few women on the faculty, she had many opportunities to participate on campus-wide committees; an ad hoc committee of senior faculty that she chaired made recommendations on the place of women's studies in the Princeton curriculum.

As dean of the college, Malkiel described Princeton as "a world-class research university with the heart and soul of a liberal arts college. There aren't any others like us." When she stepped down after 24 years as dean, President Shirley Tilghman said she "leaves behind a remarkable legacy that arises from her deep and abiding commitment to ensuring that each student receives the finest possible liberal arts education."

Tilghman recalled that when Malkiel had been in office for only a year, she identified six ways in which the undergraduate curriculum could be strengthened: expanding small group learning experiences for first-year students, bringing greater coherence to the senior year, improving the teaching of science and technology to humanists and social scientists, teaching writing more effectively, invigorating introductory courses, and encouraging a wider distribution of academic majors.

As dean she advanced all these goals, and others. She expanded the freshman seminar program (and taught in it several times), introduced a writing program for all first-year students, established a writing center where all students could sharpen their writing skills, created the McGraw Center for Teaching and Learning, encouraged innovation through a 250th anniversary teaching fund, and launched a four-year college system in which all students remained affiliated with their college for all four years, and in which three of the then-six residential colleges (including Mathey) housed juniors and seniors as well as first-year students and sophomores.

Malkiel oversaw a thorough revamping of the University's general education requirements, categorizing courses by "modes of thinking" and instituting new requirements in areas such as quantitative reasoning, ethical thought and moral values, and epistemology and cognition. She expanded opportunities for Princeton students to study abroad, and she championed a grading policy, adopted in 2004, that provided guidelines aimed to rein in "grade inflation" and achieve greater consistency across disciplines. The policy was revised in 2014 to call upon each department and program to articulate its own well-defined and meaningful grading standards, and to call upon faculty members to use grades and substantive feedback to give students clear and detailed information about their work.

As dean, Malkiel had oversight responsibility for the offices of admission and financial aid, and it was during her tenure that the University implemented its groundbreaking no-loan financial aid policy.

Malkiel's book on coeducation examines the processes by which elite colleges and universities in the United States and the United Kingdom, including Princeton, made decisions about becoming coeducational in the late 1960s and early 1970s. The book takes its title from a letter a Dartmouth alumnus wrote to that institution's board of trustees. In conjunction with her research for the book, Malkiel taught undergraduate seminars on coeducation and on women in higher education.

Outside of Princeton, Malkiel served as assembly chair of the Consortium on Financing Higher Education (COFHE), chair of the editorial board of Princeton University Press, chair of the board of the Woodrow Wilson National Fellowship Foundation, a commissioner and member of accrediting teams for the Middle States Commission on Higher Education, and a trustee of Smith College, Princeton Day School, and McCarter Theatre.

In 1988, she married economics professor Burton Malkiel *64. Their miniature schnauzer, Skipper, became a regular inhabitant of the dean's office and a visitor to other campus venues, beginning in 2001 when she was 12 weeks old. Dubbed "dog of the college," Skipper was befriended by many. In 2008 Skipper had her "life goals" published as a Top 10 list in the humor issue of the *Daily Princetonian*, one of which was to doggie paddle in what was then called "the Woody Woo fountain."

MARQUAND, ALLAN 1874 founded the department of Art and Archaeology, and for more than 40 years devoted his talents and his means to making it one of the best in the country. He shared with Charles Eliot

Norton of Harvard the distinction of being the first to introduce the serious study of art into the curriculum of an American college.

Marquand's father, Henry Gurdon Marquand, was a New York banker and one of the founders and chief benefactors of the Metropolitan Museum of Art. Allan was educated at St. Paul's School and Princeton. In college he was an excellent student, an accomplished gymnast, first-place winner in three track events, and president of the boating club, which sponsored the crew. He graduated second in his class and was Latin salutatorian and class president.

After graduation he studied theology at Princeton Theological Seminary and at Union Theological Seminary in New York, and then, after a year of study at the University of Berlin, went to Johns Hopkins University, where he received his PhD in philosophy. At Johns Hopkins he invented an ingenious "logic machine"—a forerunner of the computer—which is preserved in Firestone Library. He was called back to Princeton as a lecturer in logic and a tutor in Latin in 1881. President James McCosh encouraged him to teach the history of art and he became an instructor in this subject in 1882. A year later, he was appointed the first incumbent of a professorship of art and archaeology, endowed by his uncle, Frederick Marquand.

He held this chair until 1910 when he relinquished it to provide funds for an additional professor in the department; thereafter he served the University without salary. He made important gifts to the art museum, of which he was the first director, and supplied the department's library with books and photographs from his own collection and paid for other departmental purchases out of his own pocket. He also founded and financed the *Princeton Monographs in Art and Archaeology*.

In 1882 Marquand was the lone instructor of a few students. Forty years later he presided over an art faculty of 13 members who gave 16 courses elected by 800 undergraduates. In all the colleges east of the Mississippi, half of the teachers of art had been trained in the graduate curriculum he developed.

A chief ornament of the *Princeton Monographs in Art and Archaeology* was Marquand's own life-work—his eight-volume *catalogue raisonné* detailing the works of the ateliers of the Della Robbia family, fifteenth- and sixteenth-century Florentine sculptors and ceramists. The first Della Robbia volume, which inaugurated the *Princeton Monographs*, appeared in 1912 and a second followed in 1914. After five more years of research, five additional volumes appeared in rapid succession between 1919 and 1922. Failing health interrupted completion of the eighth and last volume, but the manuscript he left was so advanced that it was readily completed by his colleagues after his death. All eight volumes were republished in 1972.

Outside of Princeton, Marquand was one of the founders of the Archaeological Institute of America and of the *American Journal of Archaeology*. For some 30 years he anonymously financed traveling fellowships of the institute, and as chair of the committee on medieval and renaissance studies—his own creation—he helped initiate the careers of a long line of students and teachers of the fine arts. He also supported the American School of Classical Studies in Rome, at which he served a year as professor of archaeology.

Marquand began to build an outstanding art library for his own use early in his career. He transferred it from his house to the campus in 1900, formally deeded it to the University in 1908, and continued to add to it during his lifetime. It provides the nucleus of the library that was developed as a memorial to him and is now considered one of the finest art libraries in the world.

In 1887 Marquand acquired an estate in the western section of town, which he renamed Guernsey Hall after the island home of his Huguenot ancestors. There he and his wife, Eleanor Cross Marquand, a recognized authority on flowers and trees in old paintings and manuscripts and recipient of an honorary Master of Arts degree from the University, frequently entertained faculty and students. In 1953 their children gave 17 acres of the estate to Princeton Borough for use as a park. It provides open playing fields and walks among handsome, venerable trees, many of them rare species.

MATHEMATICS, THE DEPARTMENT OF. Mathematics has been prominent in the Princeton curriculum since the founding of the College. By 1760 entering students were required to have an understanding of the rules of arithmetic, and freshmen and sophomores learned algebra, trigonometry, geometry, and conic sections. The first trained mathematician on the faculty was Walter Minto, who came to Princeton in 1787. In 1853 a Boston newspaper reported that at Princeton the study of mathematics was carried on "to an extent not excelled by any other college in the country."

Mathematics at Princeton changed dramatically early in the twentieth century as Princeton moved well beyond these earlier levels of accomplishment to become one of the world's great centers of mathematical teaching and research. In 1904, a year after Henry Fine 1880 was appointed dean of the faculty, he was also appointed chair of the newly established department of Mathematics. He brought in a generation of talented young mathematicians including Luther Eisenhart, a differential geometer; Oswald Veblen, a geometer and later a distinguished statesman of mathematics; J.H.M. Wedderburn, a noted algebraist; James Alexander II 1910 *1915, a topologist; and Solomon Lefschetz, a major figure in algebraic geometry and topology. In addition to producing a mathematics faculty of the first rank, these appointments attracted many of the ablest young mathematicians to postgraduate study at Princeton

In 1911, Princeton took over from Harvard the publication of the *Annals of Mathematics*. Under Wedderburn and Lefschetz, successively chief editors for over 40 years, the *Annals* became one of the principal journals of research mathematics in the world and it remains so today, published in collaboration with the Institute for Advanced Study.

A commodious new home for the department—named Fine Hall in honor of Dean Fine—was opened in 1931. It was a gift from Thomas Jones 1876 and his niece Gwethalyn Jones; an additional gift from Thomas Jones endowed the Henry Burchard Fine Professorship, the first research professorship in mathematics in the United States.

Mathematical research in the United States was enhanced in 1930 with the founding in Princeton of the Institute for Advanced Study. The first five professors appointed by the institute were provided with temporary office space in Fine Hall until 1939. Three of them were Princeton mathematics professors: Alexander, Veblen, and John von Neumann, and one, Hermann Weyl, had been on the faculty. The fifth was Albert Einstein.

Fine's successor as chair, Luther Eisenhart, continued to appoint outstanding young mathematicians, including Eugene Wigner, who won the Nobel Prize in Physics in 1963, and the noted logician Alonzo Church 1924 *1927. Church and his graduate student, Alan Turing *38, catalyzed the founding stages in the modern development of computing with their Church-Turing thesis. With its permanent faculty and visiting members of the University and the Institute for Advanced Study, Princeton became an immensely active center for mathematical research in the 1930s.

During the 1920s and 1930s Princeton's graduate program developed, and for two decades after 1935 Princeton produced more PhDs in mathematics than any other American university.

Political developments and virulent anti-Semitism in Europe in the 1930s increased the flow of talented mathematicians to the United States. The first postwar international gathering of mathematicians took place in Fine Hall in 1946 as part of Princeton's bicentennial celebration.

The size of the faculty increased after the war, and a program in mathematical statistics, led by Samuel Wilks and John Tukey *39, was created for students interested in a variety of statistical applications. A program in game theory, led by Albert Tucker and Harold Kuhn *50, trained graduate students who went on to have a significant impact on the field. The doctoral thesis of John Nash *50 was a major contribution to game theory, for which he won a Nobel Prize in Economics in 1994. Nash joined the department as a senior research mathematician in 1995 and, until his untimely death 20 years later, was a regular presence on campus. A program in Mathematical Physics, led by Wigner and Arthur Wightman and run jointly with the Physics department, developed into a long-term strength of the department.

In the 1960s, the discovery of exotic spheres by John Milnor '51 *54 opened the door to the field of differential topology. Robert Langland's research connecting representation theory to number theory led him in the mid-1960s to a series of conjectures that form what is known today as the Langlands Program. In 1969, Charles Fefferman *69 earned his Princeton PhD; two years later he became a full professor of mathematics at the University of Chicago, and in 1972, at age 23, he was appointed to a professorship at Princeton, equaling a record for Princeton's youngest full professor set a century and a half earlier by another professor of mathematics, John Maclean Jr. 1816—later president of the College.

These and other appointments during this period gave Princeton a strong faculty in topology, in algebraic number theory and algebraic geometry, in various branches of analysis, and in mathematical physics.

A program in Applied and Computational Mathematics was founded by Martin Kruskal in 1968. The program began with a focus on applied mathematics, but in 1984, in response to widespread use of computers, the faculty approved an expansion to include computational math. Today, the program provides an interdisciplinary and interdepartmental home for people from many fields and directions who share a passion for mathematics and its applications.

The considerable expansion of the department in the 1960s led to its move to a new and larger building in 1969, adjacent to a new building for Physics. (The new building also housed the department of Statistics, which had separated from the Mathematics department in 1965; the Statistics department was discontinued in 1985.) The name Fine Hall was transferred to the new building, while the former Fine Hall was renamed Jones Hall in honor of its donors.

Princeton first admitted women graduate students in the early 1960s, and it began admitting women undergraduates in 1969. As the University became increasingly coeducational, the Mathematics department began appointing women to the faculty. Over the succeeding years tenured appointments included Ingrid Daubechies, Alice Chang, Maryam Mirzakhani, Sophie Morel, and Maria Chudnovsky; Chang chaired the department from 2009 until 2012. The Noetherian Ring, named after the famous mathematician Emmy Noether, is an informal group in the department to provide advice and support for women undergraduate and graduate students in mathematics.

Since 1962, seven Princeton alumni (four of whom served on the faculty) plus an additional seven Princeton faculty members, for a combined total of 14 alumni and faculty members, have won the Fields Medal, one of the most prestigious international awards honoring the mathematical achievements of younger mathematicians. In addition, eight alumni and Princeton faculty members, plus a visiting senior research scholar, have won the Abel Prize for overall mathematical achievements.

In 1994 Andrew Wiles was able at long last to prove Fermat's Last Theorem by demonstrating the modularity of some elliptic curves, thereby opening a new area of research in number theory. Wiles had joined the Princeton faculty in 1982.

In 2020 the department's graduate and undergraduate programs were among the strongest in the world, with some 70 graduate students in residence and more than 70 undergraduate majors. The tradition of the mathematics afternoon tea, established by Veblen, continues to this day, sustaining a sense of community, continuity, and stability that stretches back for almost a century.

MATHER SUN DIAL, THE, in the courtyard of McCosh/Dickinson Hall, is a replica of the historic Turnbull Sun Dial constructed in 1551 at Corpus Christi College, Oxford. It was given by Sir William Mather, governor of Victoria University in Manchester, England, to "symbolize the connection between Oxford and Princeton [and] . . . Great Britain and America," and was unveiled on his behalf by the British ambassador to the United States in 1907. The monumental shaft, rising from a broad base to a height of more than 20 feet, is topped by a pelican, religious symbol of Corpus Christi. Inscribed around the base are these words from Samuel Butler's *Hudibras*:

Loyalty is e'er the same
Whether it win or lose the game
True as the dial to the sun
Although it be not shined upon.

MATHEY, DEAN 1912, who served as a trustee under Presidents John Grier Hibben, Harold Dodds, and Robert Goheen, was one of the most devoted, energetic, and generous supporters of the University in the twentieth century. His association with Princeton covered a period of 65 years.

Mathey first came to Princeton in 1907 to play in an interscholastic tennis tournament, which he won. In his book of Princeton reminiscences, *Men and Gothic Towers*, he recalled the "lovely starlit early May evening" when, as an overnight guest of a student in Blair Hall, he heard the seniors singing on the steps of Nassau Hall and was inspired by the beauty of "Blair Arch with its spectacular steps, the clock in the tower."

The next summer he won the national interscholastic tennis championship at Newport, Rhode Island, and that fall he entered Princeton. He twice won the national intercollegiate doubles championship and was captain of the tennis team in his senior year. He was elected to Phi Beta Kappa and graduated with honors.

After graduation, Mathey began working as a bond salesman in New York, at $15 a week, for William A. Read & Co. He eventually became a partner of its successor, Dillon, Read & Co., and built up a sizable fortune. He later chaired the board of the Empire Trust Company and served as honorary chair of the Bank of New York. (Mathey also continued to play tennis after graduation, and in 1923 he defeated Bill Tilden, the world's number one player, in straight sets at Wimbledon.)

Mathey came to live in Princeton in 1927 in a farmhouse on property he bought from the estate of Moses Taylor Pyne 1877 near the Drumthwacket residence that had been Pyne's home. Mathey was an alumni trustee from 1927 to 1931, a charter trustee from 1931 to 1960, and an emeritus trustee from 1960 until his death in 1972. At one time or another he served on every board committee.

Prior to the stock market crash of 1929, as chair of the University's investment committee, he moved much of Princeton's endowment from stocks into bonds, and just before the market collapsed in late October he sold much of its remaining stock just as the Dow hit its then all-time high. Under his leadership, Princeton's endowment lost value in only one year during the Great Depression. In the early 1940s he anticipated the market recovery and moved much of the endowment back into equities in what a *Fortune Magazine* writer described as "an exquisitely timed maneuver." In 1938 he gave the University some 360 acres of land in northwest Princeton Township, which it held for almost 50 years before selling it in the 1980s.

Mathey's 12 years as chair of the finance committee, from 1949 to 1960, were marked by a six-fold increase in the University's budget and a doubling in the value of its investment pool. His greatest love as a trustee, however, was the committee on grounds and buildings, which he served for 34 years and chaired from 1942 to 1949.

Mathey's generosity took many forms, including some that remain anonymous to this day. He conceived of the Henry B. Thompson Memorial Court at East Pyne, and with Margaret Dodds he planned the garden in memory of President Hibben and the bench in memory of Beatrix Farrand on the north side of the chapel. He gave the wall enclosing the rear garden of Maclean House in memory of his father-in-law, former dean of the faculty Samuel Winans, and faculty housing near the graduate college in memory of his first wife, Gertrude Winans Mathey. (His second wife, Helen Newsom Mathey, was a survivor of the Titanic when it sank in 1912.) With another Princeton tennis captain, Joseph Werner 1921, he donated the tennis pavilion that was originally constructed for the courts on the former Brokaw Field; he also contributed the Class of 1912 pavilion that looks out to the north over Poe and Pardee fields.

In the Princeton community, Mathey was a generous donor to Princeton Day School and contributed the Great Road property on which it is located.

During Hibben's presidency, Mathey set up a fund to be used at the discretion of the president to meet special and emergency needs of faculty and staff. Knowing of Mathey's strong interest in affordable faculty and staff housing, in 1962 President Goheen proposed using half of what by then was a substantially larger fund to construct the first of two high-rise faculty apartment buildings (to be named for Hibben) along Carnegie Lake. When the University later constructed a complex of 15 townhouses and 12 single-level apartments on Harrison Street near the lake, it named the complex Dean Mathey Court.

In 1983, when the University created a system of five residential colleges to house all freshmen and sophomores, a foundation Mathey had established to manage his philanthropic interests provided funding for one of the colleges, which was named for him. (In 2007, Mathey became a four-year college, paired with the adjacent two-year Rockefeller College.)

Fittingly, one of the dormitories of Mathey College is the same Blair Hall where the high-school-age Mathey spent his first night on campus.

McCarter Theatre Center. Over more than 125 years, the Princeton Triangle Club has made many contributions to the cultural life of the University, but none more majestic than the edifice at the corner of College Road and University Place that was constructed to house Triangle; the building became the home of what is now the McCarter Theatre Center, one of the country's leading nonprofit regional theaters, which seeks "to create world-class theater and present the finest performing artists for the engagement, education, and entertainment of our community."

For almost a century, in close affiliation with the University, McCarter has hosted a broad range of dramatic, musical, dance, and other events; in 1994 it won a Tony Award for outstanding regional theater, and in 2013 the Tony for best play was won by Christopher Durang's *Vanya and Sonia and Masha and Spike*, which McCarter had commissioned and premiered.

The student dramatic organization that named itself the Triangle Club in 1893 quickly became famous for musical extravaganzas written and performed by undergraduates. Triangle performed in temporary quarters until 1895 when it built a wood-framed building called the "Casino" on the site of today's Dillon Gymnasium. The building was moved twice, and after it was leveled by fire in 1924 serious fundraising began for a new theater that would serve as the club's permanent home. In June 1927, between acts of Triangle's *Samarkand*, Professor Donald Clive Stuart came on stage, introduced Thomas McCarter 1888, and accepted his check for $250,000 toward a new theater.

Under the stewardship of its graduate treasurer B. Franklin Bunn 1907, Triangle accumulated substantial reserves. With funding from McCarter's gift, Triangle's reserves, and other small gifts, construction began on land donated by the University in June 1928. In 1929 the University entered into an agreement to lease the building to the Triangle Club, with the club agreeing to manage, operate, and maintain the theater, and with the understanding that the building also would be used by other student organizations and for drama-related teaching.

The building was designed by former Triangle Club member D. K. Este Fisher Jr. 1913 and built of native shale relieved by red brick in a style described at the time as Georgian with Gothic accents. On February 21, 1930, McCarter Theatre opened its doors to its first audience, for Triangle's *The Golden Dog*, and the next night the 1,100-seat theater was formally dedicated.

The Triangle Club now had a grand performance space made to order for its annual large-cast shows, but it also had the makings of an equally imposing financial headache. While the theater had been conceived during the boom years of the 1920s, it opened at the beginning of the Great Depression, in a world in which talking pictures and radio were beginning to give spirited competition to live performances of all kinds.

For some years McCarter was a popular house for pre-Broadway tryouts of new plays and post-Broadway tours of both new plays and established hits. Among its world premieres were *Our Town* by Thornton Wilder *1926; *Bus Stop* by William Inge; *You Can't Take It With You* by George S. Kaufman and Moss Hart; *Without Love* by Philip Barry; *The Wisteria Trees*, adapted from Chekhov's *The Cherry Orchard* by Triangle stalwart Joshua Logan '31; and *Separate Tables* by Terence Rattigan. It would be difficult to name an American stage star of the 1930s, 1940s, and 1950s who did not play McCarter: John Barrymore, Ethel Barrymore, George M. Cohan, Helen Hayes, Katharine Hepburn, Paul Robeson (as Othello), Cornelia Otis Skinner, and many others.

While not explicitly designed for music or dance, McCarter presented its first major classical music performance, by the Philadelphia Orchestra, in 1932, and for decades it was the home of Princeton University Concerts. In 1963 McCarter began its own Music-at-McCarter series; in 1965 and again in 1967 it brought pianists Arthur Rubinstein and Van Cliburn to Princeton. The first dance performance took place in 1930; in 1935 McCarter hosted a company assembled by George Balanchine and touring as "American Ballet" that later evolved into the New York City Ballet. A Dance-at-McCarter series began in 1965; over time it maintained continuing relationships with several prominent dance companies and scheduled frequent visits by the Alvin Ailey American Dance Theatre and Pilobolus.

After World War II the number of touring Broadway shows declined and New York producers began substituting in-town previews for out-of-town tryouts. As McCarter's income shrank, the Triangle Club was increasingly in debt to the University for insurance, utilities, repairs, and the like. In 1953 the University and the Triangle Club agreed that the University would assume responsibility for the theater's management, operation, and maintenance. The University canceled most of Triangle's debt—"in recognition of Triangle's services to the University and significant contributions to McCarter Theatre"—while Triangle retained access to the theater for rehearsals and productions and to the club's office and workroom.

In the late 1950s the University appointed two faculty committees to determine the best use of the theater and engaged the noted director Milton Lyon as a consultant. He proposed a theater which would "reflect the outlook of the University, and thus become an educational asset to the University and the community, as well as a place of entertainment." He also proposed that the theater house a resident professional theater (the first on a university campus in the United States), and that McCarter be a "producing" theater that performed its own plays, not solely a "booking" theater that hosted plays produced by visiting companies.

The faculty committees endorsed these recommendations and recommended forming a permanent committee advisory to the University president to operate the theater. In 1959 the University approved the recommendations and in 1960 the McCarter Theatre Advisory Committee formally established a board to run the theater as a center for the performing arts. The key faculty leader was English professor Alan Downer, a specialist in theater, but the final decisions were made by President Robert Goheen, who said, "I'd like to see the climate of Princeton changed... to make it more natural about the arts and more hospitable to them... Living theater is just as important to the humanities as a cyclotron is to the sciences, and anything we can do within reason to make this a culturally more sophisticated community—by providing music and drama and dance—will make it more attractive to faculty members and students."

The trustees of the center were members of the faculty and staff, and Lyon was named McCarter's first executive producer. For the 1960-61 season he formed a company by hiring the Association of Performing Artists under artistic director Ellis Rabb. During the 1960s future stars such as Dustin Hoffman, John Lithgow, and Princeton resident Christopher Reeve appeared on McCarter's stage.

Meanwhile, in his senior year William Lockwood Jr. '59 began booking performing artists and groups into McCarter, and in 1963 he was hired by the theater to oversee its presentations of music, dance, and other special events, a role he continues to play almost six decades later as McCarter's special programming director. With a remarkable eye for identifying artists early in their careers, he introduced Princeton audiences to jazz musician Wynton Marsalis, pianist Lang Lang, dancer/choreographer Twyla Tharp, and singer/songwriter Rhiannon Giddens, among many others.

The theater program under Lyon and his successor Arthur Lithgow incurred steadily mounting deficits. In 1971 English professor Daniel Seltzer '54 was named chair of the McCarter board and at his recommendation the theater suspended its drama season in 1971-72. Drama resumed the following year under artistic director Louis Criss, and in 1974 Criss was succeeded by Michael Kahn, who had the title of producing director. In 1975 Seltzer stepped down as chair of the board and was replaced by Thomas Wright Jr. '62, the University's secretary and general counsel.

In the mid-1970s the University began exploring whether the theater would benefit from greater community engagement in the programming, leadership, and financial support of the company. In 1973 operation of the theater was transferred to the McCarter Theatre Company, which was separately incorporated as a nonprofit organization, and in 1978 the University and the company signed a lease that granted responsibility to the company for management, day-to-day maintenance, and use of the theater.

The lease made the building available to McCarter without charge (in 1985 this was changed to charge rent of $1 a year) and the University assumed responsibility for major maintenance, utilities, property taxes, and insurance. McCarter was required to accommodate the Triangle Club and permit use of the theater by other University groups (in later years, as the size of the undergraduate student body increased, McCarter began hosting the welcoming assembly for each year's entering class). McCarter's initial certificate of incorporation and bylaws provided that its board of trustees should consist of between 20 and 50 trustees, and that among them should be no fewer than five nor more than eight appointed by the president of the University. (The practice of including University-appointed trustees was discontinued in 2020.)

The lease called upon McCarter to operate a program of performing arts "designed to complement the educational and cultural programs and objectives of the University and designed to provide cultural and artistic offerings for the community, state, and region. The program will include... a professional drama season, as well as performances of dance, music, children's theater, movies, lectures, and any other kinds of programs related to the performing arts."

In 1979 Nagle Jackson succeeded Kahn. In his 11 years as artistic director, he sustained the intellectual and literary caliber of McCarter's productions. During his tenure the theater was designated a "regional center of excellence" by the New Jersey Council on the Arts; it identified itself as a "center for the performing arts;" and it established an exchange program with the Gorky Theatre in Leningrad. Jackson's adaptation of Charles Dickens' *A Christmas Carol* launched what remains today, following several iterations, a beloved annual McCarter tradition.

In 1990 Jackson was succeeded as artistic director by Emily Mann, who served in that role to international acclaim for 30 years. Mann brought a broad range of voices to the McCarter stage by incubating, producing, and presenting new plays by emerging as well as established artists, with particular emphasis on women and people of color, and by reexamining the classical repertoire through a contemporary lens.

As artistic director, Mann directed almost 50 plays. She also served as McCarter's resident playwright; her plays included: *Execution of Justice; Still Life; Annulla, an Autobiography; Greenboro (A Requiem); Meshugah; Mrs. Packard; Hoodwinked (a Primer on Radical*

Islamism); *Gloria: A Life* (about feminist icon Gloria Steinem); and the Tony-nominated *Having Our Say.*

Noteworthy productions during her tenure included new plays by Edward Albee, Nilo Cruz, Christopher Durang, Athol Fugard, Danai Gurira, Beth Henley, Ken Ludwig, Tarell Alvin McCraney, Dael Orlandersmith, Regina Taylor, and Sarah Treem. World premieres included *Having Our Say*; *The Brother/Sister Plays*; *Vanya and Sonia and Masha and Spike*; and *The Convert*. Gurira's play, *Eclipsed*, which originated at McCarter in 2009, premiered on Broadway in 2016 and received a Tony nomination for best play. McCarter's production of Cruz's *Anna in the Tropics* won the 2013 Pulitzer Prize for drama.

In 2002 Mann received an honorary degree from the University and in 2019 she was inducted into the Theater Hall of Fame. McCarter's incubator space is named the Emily Mann LAB for the Development of New Works in her honor.

In August 2020 Sarah Rasmussen was appointed Mann's successor as artistic director. She came to McCarter from the Jungle Theater in Minneapolis, where she gained national attention for bringing inclusive and bold stories, diverse talent, and gender parity to the stage. Her resourcefulness and ingenuity were evident from her first day as COVID-19 required McCarter to cancel its entire 2020–21 live season and develop virtual ways to reach and engage its audiences.

In 1991, new east and west lobbies were added to the McCarter building (the east lobby is named for Lockwood), and in 2003 McCarter expanded into a second performance space, the 360-seat Berlind Theatre, designed by the acclaimed theater architect Hugh Hardy '54 *56. The Berlind was a joint venture between McCarter and the University, and was named for its principal donor, Broadway producer Roger Berlind '52. The Berlind Theater opened with Mann's production of Cruz's *Anna in the Tropics*, which went on to Broadway where Berlind was one of its producers.

With the opening of the Berlind, McCarter officially became the McCarter Theatre Center and named its historic 1,100-seat auditorium for former McCarter trustee Marie Matthews and her husband, former McCarter board president Edward Matthews '53. The Matthews Theater is the setting for each year's Triangle Club performances, as well as dozens of other performances and concerts of many genres and the University's entering-students assembly.

In addition to providing McCarter with a more intimate setting well suited for many of its dramas and other performances, the Berlind provides rehearsal and performance space for the University's programs in Theater, Dance, and Music Theater. Shared use of the Berlind is only one of many examples of collaborations between McCarter and the University, whose Lewis Arts complex directly across the street opened in 2017. For example, McCarter has partnered with the Lewis Center for the Arts on new play commissions and other projects through the Roger S. Berlind Playwright-in-Residence program and in 2017 it commissioned and presented a series of 10-minute plays in connection with the Princeton and Slavery project.

McCarter sponsors a robust array of educational and outreach activities that include after-school, in-school, and creative aging programs, student matinees, summer camps, internships, and audience engagement opportunities. These programs take place in Princeton, Trenton, and throughout central New Jersey.

McClenahan, Howard 1895 *1897, second dean of the college, completed the undergraduate electrical engineering course at Princeton in 1895, earned a master's degree in science and became an instructor in physics in 1897, and was appointed a professor in 1906.

As an instructor he was principal assistant to Cyrus Fogg Brackett, professor of physics and founder of the department of Electrical Engineering. As a professor he was largely responsible for the design and construction of Palmer Physical Laboratory in 1908 and for the choice and organization of its equipment. After serving as dean of the college from 1912 to 1925, he resigned to accept appointment as secretary of the Franklin Institute in Philadelphia.

McCormick Hall was built in 1922–23 with funds given to the University by Cyrus H. McCormick 1879 and his family. While considered a separate building, in large measure it was an extensive western addition to a three-story Romanesque Revival building known as the museum of historic art that had been constructed in 1890 to house the art museum, the department of Art and Archaeology, a fine arts library, and the newly created school of Architecture. The new structure was designed by Ralph Adams Cram in a medieval Italian style to harmonize with the varied architecture of its neighbors (Whig and Clio, Murray-Dodge, Dod, and Brown halls). The construction of McCormick permitted the original space to be devoted solely to museum uses.

Additions to McCormick were built in 1927 and 1935, but they and the museum of historic art were demolished in 1964, shortly after the school of Architecture moved into a separate building of its own in 1963. In 1966 McCormick was enlarged and its interior modernized while a new adjoining art museum was constructed.

In addition to the department of Art and Archaeology, McCormick housed Marquand Library of Art and Archaeology, which was established in 1908 and is one of the oldest and most extensive art libraries in the country. Marquand Library was renovated and expanded in 2003. In 2021 the University began constructing a new, significantly larger art museum that would provide a home for the department of Art and Archaeology and incorporate Marquand Library, with its three-story glass wall that looks north onto McCosh Walk, but would require the demolition of the rest of McCormick.

McCosh, James, 11th president of Princeton, took office in 1868, precisely a century after another renowned Scottish minister, John Witherspoon.

McCosh was born in 1811 on a farm in Ayrshire. He matriculated at the University of Glasgow in 1825 and moved to the University of Edinburgh in 1829 to study religion, philosophy, and psychology. In the spring of 1834 he was licensed to preach by the presbytery of Ayr. "I preached all around," he later wrote, "both in town and country, but chiefly in the country. I had a good horse, and set out on the Saturday with my sermons in a saddlebag behind me, preached twice on the Sabbath, and returned home on the Monday."

His first ministerial charge was in Arbroath and his second in Brechin, where he was soon involved in the reformation movement within the Church of Scotland. This movement, known as "The Disruption," resulted in the organization of the evangelical Free Church, to which he devoted his considerable powers as thinker, propagandist, and orator. During his pastorate at Brechin he met Isabella (daughter of the eminent physician Alexander Guthrie), and they married in September 1845.

McCosh went on to make his mark as a professor of philosophy, and his 1850 volume, *The Method of Divine Government, Physical and Moral,* was instrumental in leading to his appointment to the chair of logic and metaphysics at Queen's College, Belfast, which had been founded that year by the British government "for the promotion of nonsectarian education."

During his 16 years in Ireland, he enhanced his reputation in a series of books, so he was well known throughout the English-speaking world when, two years after his first triumphal visit to the United States in 1866 as a representative of the Evangelical Alliance, the trustees of the College invited him to succeed John Maclean Jr., 1816 when he stepped down as president in 1868.

Just as the Revolutionary War had attenuated the student body and impoverished the College's finances in Witherspoon's time, so had the Civil War severely stunted the development of the College in the decade prior to McCosh's presidency. When he arrived, the College had 20 faculty members (only 10 full-time) and fewer than 300 students. When he retired almost 20 years later, the number of students had more than doubled and the size of the faculty had more than tripled. Tellingly, when he arrived almost none of the faculty had PhDs, but when he left a quarter of them did, as compared to just 10 percent of the faculty at Harvard.

Andrew Fleming West 1874, who entered as a freshman in 1870, compared the new president's influence to "an electric shock, instantaneous, paralyzing to the opposition, and stimulating to all who were not paralyzed."

McCosh raised Princeton's sights and broadened its ambitions, recruited a distinguished faculty in fields ranging from physics, mathematics, and art to history and the classics, revised and greatly modernized the undergraduate plan of study, developed elective course options, instituted graduate work leading to master's and doctoral degrees (Princeton awarded its first PhD in 1879), created fellowships for graduate students, brought in an expensive array of scientific equipment, dedicated the new Bonner-Marquand gymnasium ("every college should have a gymnasium for the body as well as for the mind," he said), founded a school of Science, introduced the teaching of art and instruction in languages as regular parts of the curriculum, and oversaw an ambitious program of building and landscaping that greatly enhanced and beautified the hitherto austere campus.

Woodrow Wilson 1879, an undergraduate while McCosh was president, wrote that "he found Princeton a quiet country college and lifted it to a conspicuous place among the most notable institutions of the country . . . He laid the foundations of a genuine university, and his own enthusiasm for learning vivified the whole spirit of the place."

McCosh was a teaching president, with regular classes in the history of philosophy and in psychology. In 1878 he moved into Prospect, which had been given to the College to be the home of the president, and he enjoyed inviting students to seminars in its library where guest lecturers presented papers and led discussions on a wide range of philosophical and ethical topics. When Darwin's *Origin of Species* threatened to overturn age-old religious beliefs, McCosh "stood out almost alone" among American clergymen in defending evolutionary doctrine, insisting that the Darwinian hypothesis, far from denying the existence of God, only served "to increase the wonder and mystery of the process of creation."

A staunch believer in books, McCosh strongly supported building up Princeton's collections. Under his aegis the octagonal 70,000-volume Chancellor Green library was dedicated in 1873 with a stirring address by the poet William Cullen Bryant. "I remember," wrote McCosh, "that some critics found fault with me for laying out too much money on stone and lime; but I . . . knew what I was doing. I viewed the edifices as means to an end, at best as outward expressions and symbols of an internal life." McCosh insisted that the building face Nassau Street to reinforce his view that a college should engage with the world, not retreat from it.

At the time Chancellor Green ranked among the leading college libraries in the United States, although demand quickly outpaced its capacities.

With respect to the curriculum, McCosh believed students should take a large number of required courses from the start; no one, he said, "should be a graduate of a college who does not know mathematics and classics, the one to solidify the reasoning powers, and the other to refine the taste." At the same time, he recognized the enormous advances that were being made in the physical sciences, as well as in philology, history, and psychology. From these branches of knowledge, Princeton students were encouraged to choose a wide range of electives to be taken "side by side with obligatory and disciplinary courses."

In his inaugural address, he proposed that students "first be taken . . . to an eminence, whence he may behold the whole country . . . lying below him, and then be encouraged to dive down into some special place, seen and selected from the height, that he may linger in it and explore it minutely and thoroughly." In that same address he said that Princeton's "doors should be open to all nationalities," and on a number of occasions he admitted African American graduate students into his classes and lectures—an action that led some of his southern students to withdraw.

In the winter of 1885 President Charles Eliot of Harvard came to New York—a sufficiently neutral territory—to debate McCosh on the ideal college curriculum. Princeton's president was highly critical of Eliot's scheme, which gave students essentially free rein to choose from among some 200 courses. This, said McCosh, encouraged dilettantism. Even worse, Harvard students were not obliged to attend classes, with the result that professors often found themselves lecturing to a roomful of empty seats. At Princeton, regular attendance was required, and a curriculum composed of obligatory core courses and a reasonable variety of solid electives, in which one subject led to another, allowed students to develop their powers in an orderly fashion. Not surprisingly, most Princetonians believed that McCosh won the debate handily.

McCosh was highly supportive of athletic competition and extracurricular life; during his presidency the Glee Club, the precursor of the Triangle Club, the *Princetonian*, and other student organizations were formed, and Princeton played in the first intercollegiate football game. He was adamantly opposed to Greek letter fraternities and secret societies, and after a long struggle he succeeded in removing them, although given the lack of sufficient dining facilities on campus, he was tolerant of the eating groups that were forming in town and, starting with Ivy Club, beginning to construct buildings on the country road later named Prospect Avenue.

He was eager to have more students living on campus in dormitories, which led to the construction of Reunion, Witherspoon, and Edwards halls. To support the academic program, he raised funds to construct the original school of Science building, the original Dickinson Hall, and a chemical laboratory (now Aaron Burr Hall), in addition to Chancellor Green.

As these projects attest, McCosh was an effective fundraiser. He believed strongly in the value to the College of lifelong engagement by its alumni, and beginning early in his presidency he traveled around the country to encourage the development of local and regional associations; by the time he left office there were 17 of them.

Even more popular than Jimmy McCosh was his wife Isabella, who, McCosh said, "advised and assisted me in all my work." As Princeton's unofficial nurse, she cared for students who were ill and wrote reassuring notes to their families. Following her husband's retirement, the trustees raised funds for an infirmary building and named it for her; a successor building, erected in 1925, continues to bear her name.

McCosh was 77 when he retired from the presidency in 1888, moving out of Prospect to a new house that had been planned and built under his supervision approximately on the site later occupied by Quadrangle Club. His parting words to the College reflected the simplicity of his nature:

> It is not without feeling that I take the step which I now take . . . But I take the step firmly and decidedly. The shadows are lengthening, the day is declining. My age, seven years above the threescore and ten, compels it, Providence points to it, conscience enjoins it, the good of the college demands it . . . I leave the college in a healthy state . . . with . . . the prospect of its having greater usefulness in the future than even that which it has had in the past.

In 1885 McCosh had proposed to change the institution's name to Princeton University, but the trustees had turned him down. In his farewell message, he said: "The college has been brought to the very borders [of a university], and I leave it to another to carry it over to the land of promise."

During Princeton's sesquicentennial in 1896, McCosh's successor, Francis Patton, announced the change in the institution's name. Patton observed admiringly that McCosh was "more than a model president: he was a model ex-president," although as the torch was being passed, the Class of 1889 unanimously requested that their diplomas should carry McCosh's signature along with Patton's.

While McCosh lived, he was often seen strolling along the pathway on campus that in 1889 was named McCosh Walk in his honor, admiring the shrubs and trees he had planted and the buildings he had caused to be constructed. As he passed students on the walk, he typically was unable to remember their names. His greeting was nearly always, "I know ye, whooo air ye, whatsyourname?"

McCosh died on November 16, 1894, 100 years and one day after Witherspoon's death. These stalwart Scots, in their respective centuries, each contributed mightily to the growth and stature of Princeton, and the modern university is indebted to both of them.

In addition to McCosh Hall (built in 1907), McCosh Walk, and McCosh Circle in the faculty/staff housing complex known as Gray Farm, McCosh is commemorated (along with Witherspoon) in a stone statue on the clock tower of East Pyne Hall and a bronze sculpture in the north transept of the chapel.

McCosh Hall, built in 1907, was "the gift of a small group of friends of the University" who were "devoted to the memory of James McCosh." When constructed it was the largest building on the campus, extending 400 feet along McCosh Walk and 100 feet along Washington Road. It contained four large lecture rooms paneled in oak, including two of the largest on campus: 445-seat McCosh 50, named in 1987 in honor of Harold Helm '20, and 350-seat McCosh 10, named in 1984 for Arthur Wood '34. The building also contained 14 recitation rooms and 26 smaller rooms especially planned for the preceptorials that had been introduced the year before.

McCosh Hall was designed by Raleigh C. Gildersleeve in the Tudor Gothic style of architecture then dominant at Princeton, with exterior walls of gray Indiana limestone, with nine separate entrances, and with the campus's first flying buttresses.

McCosh Hall serves as home for the department of English and the program in American Studies. Situated at the crossroads of university life, it has often been the site for public lectures, open forums, class meetings, concerts, celebrations, demonstrations, and protests.

Dickinson Hall, home of the department of History and named for the first president of the College, Jonathan Dickinson, was built in 1930 as an extension of the wing of McCosh Hall along Washington Road. Dickinson is connected to the chapel by the Rothschild Arch, with the chapel, Dickinson, and McCosh forming a major courtyard anchored by Mather Sundial. Dickinson replaced an earlier classroom and lecture hall of the same name that stood for 50 years at the southwest corner of the site now occupied by Firestone Library; the earlier Dickinson was lost in 1920 in a fire that also destroyed Marquand Chapel.

McCosh Infirmary was erected in 1925, replacing an infirmary built on the same site in 1892. Both were named for Isabella McCosh, the daughter of eminent Scottish physician Alexander Guthrie and wife of Princeton President James McCosh. During the 20 years of McCosh's presidency, Isabella visited and cared for sick students in their rooms. One of them,

Alexander J. Kerr 1879, left this portrait of one of her missions:

> She had given strict orders to the Scottish college proctor, Matt Goldie, that any student who was ill should be immediately reported to her. Her orders were faithfully obeyed and when any boy was sick . . . she would take her large basket, place in it one of her own bed sheets, a pillow case, a towel, a wash cloth, some of her own jams and jellies, homemade cookies and tempting cakes and a jug of tea, over which she would place a tea caddy to keep it hot. She would then carry the basket to the sickroom, no matter though she had to climb four flights of iron stairs to do so. . . .
>
> She would tap on the door and say, "May I come in?" But without waiting for a reply she would enter and, after expressing a mother's sympathy, immediately proceed to wash the face, chest and hands of the young man, put the clean sheet on his bed, the pillow case on his pillow, brush his hair and make him as comfortable as possible and encourage him to eat the good things she had brought and to drink a cup of her good tea. Then, sitting down at his desk, she would write a note to his mother, telling her she need not worry about her boy, as "we are looking after him here."

President McCosh repeatedly pressed the trustees for an infirmary, but not until after he retired was a campaign begun to build one. The decision to name it for Isabella McCosh was made at a trustee meeting in 1891.

The cornerstone of the first infirmary was laid at Commencement in 1892 and the building was ready for use the following April. Two years later Isabella contributed a $1,000 bond and asked that the income be used for the support and care of students confined in the infirmary. In 1902 Josephine Perry Morgan, the wife of Junius Morgan 1888, organized a group of 15 women and founded a Ladies Auxiliary to furnish designated rooms for women in the gymnasium; soon thereafter the group's membership grew to 100 and it began committing funds to the infirmary. In 1904 the group changed its name to the Ladies Auxiliary of the Isabella McCosh Infirmary.

Annual dues were used to purchase supplies and equipment, and gifts were obtained for the initial salary of the first university physician (appointed by the trustees in 1908 on the recommendation of the auxiliary), for a fund to help needy students, and for an endowment. By 1910 funds had also been raised to pay for additional nursing and maintenance personnel, new patient rooms, solaria, and bedrooms for nurses and housekeepers.

With steadily increasing enrollment, the original infirmary soon became inadequate. In 1919 the auxiliary hired an architect to design a new building and began to raise funds to construct it. A committee of women raised $345,000 from 1,500 donors (1,300 of whom were women). The building's cornerstone was laid at Commencement in 1924, and it was dedicated a year later.

This building was designed by Charles Z. Klauder, who used rough-textured red brick and limestone trim to tie it in with its neighbors, Palmer and Guyot halls. A portrait of Isabella McCosh, painted a few years before she died in her 92nd year, hangs in the oak-paneled waiting room. Jenny Davidson Hibben, the wife of President John Grier Hibben, was president of the Ladies Auxiliary for many years and presided at the building's dedication. After her death a tribute to "her unfailing devotion in guarding and guiding the spirit of this Infirmary" was carved on an oak panel in the entrance hall.

The first doctor attached to the infirmary was John Carnochan 1896, who was appointed university physician in 1908 and served in that capacity part-time while carrying on his private practice in town until his death in 1929. Employment of full-time university physicians began in 1911.

For many years, the infirmary was graced by the presence of three members of the Hillian family, African Americans who first came to Princeton from South Carolina in 1917. For half a century they contributed to the infirmary's healing ways: Mabel and Bessie as cooks and Tom as head orderly. Mabel retired after 47 years of service. At her golden anniversary retirement party Bessie spoke of meeting sons of students she had known in earlier years and, recently, their grandchildren. When Tom died, the auxiliary hung a framed tribute to him in the entrance hall which said that for 45 years he had always fulfilled the infirmary motto: "*Non ministrari, sed ministrare*"—not to be ministered unto, but to minister.

The Isabella McCosh building today houses University Health Services (UHS) and includes an increasingly rare commodity on college campuses: a 15-bed infirmary that provides 24-hour-a-day care. There is also a parents' suite where parents or guardians of ill or injured students can stay free of charge.

In 2001 the Ladies Auxiliary changed its name to The Auxiliary to the Isabella McCosh Infirmary. The auxiliary maintains the parents' suite and supports UHS in many other ways: through earnings on endowments and its annual fundraising the auxiliary helps fund laboratory expenses, repairs and improvements, specialized medical equipment and software, professional journal subscriptions, staff training, and students with special needs. It also helps to increase awareness of health services available on campus and its members serve as volunteers on projects and at events.

The presence of the auxiliary is marked in the infirmary by rooms such as the Frantz Cottier Parents' Suite, the Margaret S. Goheen Medical Library (dedicated in 1989), and the Janet C. Morgan Health and Wellness Library (dedicated in 2004).

Growth in enrollment and in use of McCosh required a number of renovations over the years, most recently in 2016 when the outpatient clinic was upgraded. In 2017 the University issued a campus plan that recognized a need to expand the capacity of UHS, most likely by constructing "a purpose-built facility on the current site of Eno Hall," which in turn would make the existing McCosh building available for other uses. Construction of the new building—twice the size of McCosh, attached to Eno, and east of Wilcox Hall along Goheen Walk—is expected to begin in 2022; it is intended to accommodate the growth of the student body as well as changing needs of students and evolving models for wellness services.

MCGRAW CENTER FOR TEACHING AND LEARNING, THE, was established in 1999–2000 to help teachers become better teachers and students become better learners. It is principally located in the Frist Campus Center.

The McGraw Center provides support for new teaching initiatives, educational and classroom technologies, learning programs and instructional design for both classroom and online environments, and graduate student teaching. It offers undergraduate tutoring, study halls, academic skills and time management workshops, study groups, one-on-one consultations, and online resources for first-year students, including Principedia, an "encyclopedia" containing articles about learning effectively in specific Princeton courses. In a typical year, the center has more than 9,000 undergraduate visits for tutoring, workshops, and learning consultations.

The center helps faculty reflect on what they want students to learn and how best to assess that learning. It offers guidance on how to teach inclusively and equitably by incorporating diverse course content and creating an inclusive learning environment. It helps faculty design course assignments, write syllabi, and make pedagogical use of technology.

The center's groups on educational and classroom technologies and online learning environments foster the application of new technologies to enhance teaching and learning, and its digital learning lab in Lewis Library supports the use of digital tools and resources, including interactive maps, animations, digital media annotation, and interactive video streaming platforms. When the COVID-19 pandemic prevented in-person instruction in the spring of 2020, the center quickly provided guidance and support to faculty in adapting courses to virtual formats.

Graduate students develop their teaching skills in the center's pedagogy and professional development workshops and teaching seminars, and all new assistants in instruction must participate in the center's orientation program before teaching for the first time. The center supports the Princeton University/Community College Teaching Partnership Program that enables graduate students to teach courses at participating New Jersey community colleges.

The center also serves as the administrative home of the Prison Teaching Initiative, which enables graduate students, postdocs, faculty, and staff to teach accredited college courses to people incarcerated in New Jersey prisons. The center's English Language Program enables all graduate students who are not native English speakers to satisfy the graduate school's requirement for English language proficiency.

The center sponsors an annual program of graduate mentoring awards; faculty nominated by graduate students are recognized at the graduate school Hooding Ceremony just before Commencement for exceptional achievement in nurturing the intellectual, professional, and personal growth of graduate students. A faculty member in each of the four divisions (humanities, social sciences, natural sciences, and engineering) is recognized each year.

MCMILLAN, CHARLES, was the College of New Jersey's first engineering professor. A graduate of Rensselaer Polytechnic Institute, he had been a draftsman and engineer for various New York water works and a professor at Rensselaer and Lehigh University before being called to Princeton in 1875 to organize a department of Civil Engineering.

As Borough Engineer, McMillan designed Princeton's first sewage system and planned the town's modern streets. He was often consulted by the College, the Princeton Water Company, and the state of New Jersey about sanitation and water problems.

MCPHEE, JOHN '53, a revered author, teacher, and Princeton icon, published his first book in 1965, began teaching at Princeton in 1975, and continued to publish creative nonfiction and help students become better writers well into his 80s. Many of his students achieved their own literary distinction, including the Pulitzer Prize–winner David Remnick '81, who became McPhee's editor at the *New Yorker*.

McPhee grew up in the town of Princeton and on the Princeton campus where his father worked in McCosh Infirmary as the physician for the athletics department. His elementary school was the building at 185 Nassau Street that now houses the program in Visual Arts. He attended Princeton High School and then spent a postgraduate year at Deerfield Academy before enrolling at Princeton and graduating in 1953 after writing the University's first creative thesis, a novel titled *Skimmer Burns*. While an undergraduate he served as the On-the-Campus columnist for the *Princeton Alumni Weekly*, traveled regularly to New York to appear as a panelist on the radio and television quiz program *Twenty Questions*, and, during his junior year, roomed with Heisman Trophy-winner Dick Kazmaier '52.

After a year at Cambridge University, McPhee wrote for television between 1955 and 1956, and then joined *Time* magazine to write about show business. In 1963 he began writing for the *New Yorker*; two years later he became a staff writer there and never left. Many of his more than 30 books include material originally written for the magazine. One of his early pieces was a profile of Princeton basketball legend Bill Bradley '65, which in 1965 became his first book, *A Sense of Where You Are*.

As an author he is known for his eclectic interests, painstaking and intensive research, meticulously constructed narratives (he says he is "obsessed with the structure of pieces of writing," and he structures his writing with the help of diagrams), and captivating prose. He wrote about a prep school headmaster, tennis players, the decline of the United States Merchant Marine, cattle rustling, farmers' markets, family doctors, Russian art, and the building of birch-bark canoes. His 1971 book, *Encounters with the Archdruid*, a discussion of three wildernesses with the conservationist David Brower, was nominated for a National Book Award.

He also wrote about the central New Jersey Pine Barrens, the Scottish Highlands, the Swiss army, and Alaska. (His 1977 book about the Alaskan wilderness, *Coming into the Country*, also was nominated for a National Book Award.) Four books about the geology of the western United States were collected and updated in a volume titled *Annals of the Former World*, which won the Pulitzer Prize for general nonfiction in 1999; it tells the story of how North America came to exist. Other books examined the citrus industry (*Oranges*), aeronautical engineering, nuclear terrorism (*The Curve of Binding Energy*—a National Book Award finalist), American shad, and freight transportation. One of his later works was a book on writing long-form nonfiction. He also published more than a half dozen collections of essays.

McPhee received the Award in Literature from the Academy of Arts and Letters in 1977, and in 2008 he received the George Polk Career Award for his "indelible mark on American journalism during his nearly half-century career." In 2018 he received the Sandrof Award for Lifetime Achievement from the National Book Critics Circle, which cited his "pioneering work in the fields of journalism and creative nonfiction; his explorations of widely varying topics, including science, sports, and the environment; and his mentorship of countless young writers and journalists."

In 1982, he received Princeton's Woodrow Wilson Award, the highest honor the University can bestow on undergraduate alumni, and in 1999 he received the President's Award for Distinguished Teaching.

McPhee was named the Ferris Professor of Journalism in 1974 and began teaching at Princeton in the spring of 1975. He has taught more than 500 students, including at least three parent-child pairs: Eric Lander '78 and his daughter Jessica '10; Alex Gansa '84 and his son, Will '17; and Bart Gellman '82 and his daughter Lily '17. He describes teaching and writing as "symbiotic"—he teaches in the spring and then writes through the summer, fall, and January. "I have no way to prove this," he says, "but I think I've written and published more, over the years, than I would have had I not spent those semesters teaching."

His course, Creative Nonfiction (originally called Literature of Fact), is offered each spring, open to sophomores by application, and limited to 16 students. It is taught in seminar format, with weekly one-on-one conferences where he and the student go over each essay "with a fine-toothed comb." Students marvel at the attention he gives them. One student said, "I found that he knew my papers almost better than I knew them—down to the last semicolon—and we'd dissect these papers down to the semicolons."

A longtime Princeton sports fan, dating back to childhood Saturday afternoons on the sidelines of Princeton football games, McPhee played lacrosse at Deerfield—a game he has described as "football, basketball, and ice hockey in an advanced state of evolution." He began attending Princeton games in 1992, and 15 years later agreed to become an academic-athletic fellow for the men's team. He gets to know the players, attends games and practices, and watches game films; not surprisingly, on more than one occasion, he has written about the sport for the *New Yorker*.

MECHANICAL AND AEROSPACE ENGINEERING, THE DEPARTMENT OF, traces its roots to the 1920s when Arthur Greene Jr. came to Princeton to establish a department of Mechanical Engineering and serve as dean of the newly created school of Engineering. The modern department was formed in 1963 by a merger of the departments of Mechanical Engineering and Aeronautical Engineering.

Starting with only two young assistants, Greene taught over half the courses in the original Mechanical Engineering department in addition to performing his administrative duties. Classes were held in the old school of Science building, with a makeshift laboratory in a boiler house across Washington Road, until the John C. Green Engineering Building (now Green Hall) was constructed in 1928. Louis Rahm and Alfred Sorenson joined the department in 1926; Lewis Moody arrived in 1930 as a professor of fluid mechanics and machine design.

During the Great Depression, graduating seniors unable to obtain employment returned for graduate study, spurring the development of both the engine and hydraulics laboratories. By 1941, when Greene retired and was succeeded as dean and chair by Kenneth Condit 1913, the department was both well-staffed and well-equipped, and it remained so during the hectic war years when year-round teaching of military and civilian students was required.

In the summer of 1941 Condit invited Daniel Sayre to conduct a three-month study of the "possibility and desirability" of introducing courses relating to aeronautical engineering into the curriculum of the Mechanical Engineering department. Sayre, energetic and irrepressible, made a compelling case for the creation of a separate department of Aeronautical Engineering; in early 1942 he became Princeton's first professor of aeronautical engineering and the new department's entire faculty.

Sayre recruited Alexander Nikolsky, who had helped Igor Sikorsky develop the helicopter, and Harry Ashworth, a machinist and instrument expert. These three, aided by a few graduate assistants and equipped with a small wind tunnel on a balcony of what is now Aaron Burr Hall, constituted the entire department until the end of the war. In the immediate postwar years, the department began a steady increase in the number of faculty members—and a meteoric rise in achievement—that culminated in its recognition as a leader in the field by the mid-1950s.

The first of the new faculty to arrive was Courtland Perkins, who had pioneered in-flight test analysis of aircraft stability and control at Wright-Patterson Air Force Base. His research interests led to the creation of the Flight Dynamics Laboratory, a unique facility for an academic institution, in which theory was tested in actual flight.

The department grew in the following years, moving to new facilities near Lake Carnegie and to installations behind Palmer Stadium that had housed wartime research in physics. A master's program was begun in 1942, and a doctoral program in 1949.

Recognition of the stature of the department came in 1948 when the Guggenheim Foundation selected Princeton as the site for one of two jet propulsion research centers. (The other was at the California Institute of Technology.) In 1951 Sayre spearheaded the effort that led to the acquisition of the Rockefeller Institute for Medical Research site just north of Princeton on Route 1 that was developed as the James Forrestal Campus. Princeton at last had a place to house research that, in Sayre's words, "makes loud noises or bad smells," and the department soon moved into these new quarters. It was here that Charles "Pete" Conrad '53, the third man to walk on the moon, completed his undergraduate studies.

Forrestal housed numerous aircraft and sported wind tunnels, rocket pits, a one-of-a-kind helicopter research facility, and a long runway. Eventually the entire Aeronautical Engineering department moved there, and five different laboratories occupied the space: the Flight Research Laboratory; the Gas Dynamics Laboratory; the Guggenheim Propulsion Laboratory; the Low Speed Aerodynamics Laboratory; and the Rotor Dynamics Laboratory. At the height of its activity, research funding at Forrestal made up a quarter of the entire University budget, and the department was called the "second best aeronautical department in the world."

In 1951 Sayre relinquished his position to Perkins, who expanded research activities into fields ranging from low speed flight to hypersonic reentry. In 1954 Luigi Crocco of the University of Rome was appointed the first Goddard Professor of Jet Propulsion at Princeton. He was a world-renowned expert on jet propulsion and supersonic aerodynamics, who made seminal contributions to rocket engine development.

In 1963, the two departments merged to form a department of Aerospace and Mechanical Sciences under Perkins' leadership. Activities of the new department reached a then all-time high in 1967 with a research budget of almost $3.25 million and an enrollment of 140 graduate students and 125 undergraduates.

The late 1960s and early 1970s were years of considerable campus unrest in opposition to the war in Vietnam. Since the department was deeply involved in a technology closely linked in the public mind with weaponry, it suffered decreasing enrollments and faced critical questions related to the appropriateness of some of its research. The department responded by expanding the scope of its endeavors, shifting from narrowly focused research on aircraft systems to larger societal challenges such as air pollution and noise pollution. The department pioneered early "green" technologies, such as high efficiency windmills for power generation.

Perkins retired as chair in 1974. By then, enrollments were recovering, budgets were expanding, and, under the leadership of Seymour Bogdonoff from 1975 to 1983 and his successor Harvey (Sau-Hai) Lam, the department ushered in new fields of research while continuing its interests in alternative energy sources and efficiency. During these years, the Gas Dynamics Laboratory, which had been created in 1950, became a national leader in aeronautical research.

The Center for Energy and Environmental Studies (CEES) was founded in 1971; it was initially directed by Irvin Glassman, a leading authority on combustion and propulsion, who later chaired the department. Later directed by Robert Socolow, the CEES spearheaded efforts to achieve energy efficiency and improve air quality in buildings, investigated energy challenges in the developing world, and led research into proliferation-resistant nuclear energy. The CEES became part of the Princeton Environmental Institute (now High Meadows Environmental Institute) in 2001; in 2015 it moved to the Andlinger Center for Energy and the Environment, then directed by MAE professor and later Engineering school dean Emily Carter.

During the late 1970s and 1980s, as federal funding for aerospace research declined and hands-on research was increasingly replaced by computer simulation, many of the Forrestal Campus facilities fell into disuse. Most of the aeronautical labs moved back to the main campus and the name of the department changed to Mechanical and Aerospace Engineering (MAE). Spearheading the return to campus and a headquarters for the department in the Engineering Quadrangle was MAE professor and dean of the Engineering school Robert Jahn '51 *55, a pioneer in the use of electrically-charged particles instead of chemical fuels to propel rocket engines. Jahn also led efforts to recruit women to the faculty.

When Glassman's successor, Garry Brown, chaired the department from 1990 to 1998, he played a key role in developing collaborative research agreements between the University and private industry, including many leading aerospace corporations. He was instrumental in helping to understand the root cause of design flaws in the solid rocket motor for the Titan IV, a class of rockets plagued by four catastrophic launch failures.

Alexander (Lex) Smits succeeded Brown and chaired MAE for 13 years; he also chaired the Gas Dynamics Laboratory at the Forrestal campus for 33 years. Although he is acclaimed primarily for his contributions to fluid mechanics, especially an understanding of fundamental turbulence, he remained dedicated to pursuing research into green and alternative technologies and was influential in moving the department toward materials science.

Howard Stone, an acclaimed teacher and a member of the National Academy of Engineering, the American Academy of Arts and Sciences, and the National Academy of Sciences, was named chair in 2014. Under his leadership the department ranked among the nation's top mechanical and aeronautical engineering schools, and its research interests ranged from space propulsion for interplanetary missions and the use of robotics in complex and dangerous environments, to oil-spill mitigation strategies and the development of policies for transitioning to net-zero emissions energy systems. Stone's interests are in fluid dynamics, especially as they arise in research and applications at the interface of engineering, chemistry, physics, and biology.

Another faculty member interested in the intersection between engineering and biology, as well as the intersection between engineering and art, is MacArthur Fellow Naomi Leonard '85, who also serves as director of the Council on Science and Technology.

MAE's core research areas are applied physics; biomechanics and biomaterials; control, robotics, and dynamical systems; fluid mechanics; materials science; and propulsion and energy sciences. Cross-disciplinary strengths include astronautics, bio-inspired design, bioengineering, medical applications, combustion and energy conversion, computational engineering, the environment and energy technologies, laser-matter interactions, security, and vehicle sciences and applications. Areas of interest include satellite technology, pollution and alternative fuels, energy usage, battery technology, novel optical systems, propulsion systems, mechanics of fluids and solids, stability and control of vehicles, aircraft performance, and instrumentation.

At the undergraduate level, the department offers interdepartmental and topical programs in such fields as engineering physics, engineering management, applied and computational mathematics, engineering biology, robotics and intelligent systems, materials science and engineering, and applications of computing. At the graduate level, the department offers a PhD and a Master of Science in Engineering and offers graduate certificate programs in Computational and Information Science, and in Statistics and Machine Learning.

MEDIEVAL ART, THE INDEX OF, was founded in 1917 as the Index of Christian Art by Professor Charles Rufus Morey, later chair of the department of Art and Archaeology from 1924 to 1945. The Index changed its name in the summer of 2017 to reflect its expanded scope and mission.

The Index of Christian Art initially took the form of a thematic and iconographic index of early Christian and medieval art objects from early apostolic times up to the year 700 CE housed on file cards in two shoeboxes. Alison Smith MacDonald did the first formal cataloguing from 1918 to 1920, and then Phila Calder Nye, director from 1920 to 1933, kept the project going with voluntary assistance from nine women (known as the nine muses). Under her successor, Helen Woodruff, the format still used today for recording descriptive and bibliographic information was developed.

A century later the index has expanded to encompass both religious and secular imagery, including Jewish and Islamic works, and it extends up to the sixteenth century. It is the largest and most important archive of medieval iconography in the world, and while its emphasis is on the art of Western Europe and Byzantium, in recent years it has added documentation of art from Coptic Egypt, Lebanon, Ethiopia, Syria, Armenia, and other locations in the Near East.

Works of art in 17 media are represented in the archive, including manuscripts, metalwork, sculpture, painting, glass, and ivory. Until 1991, the index was only a print resource, housed in McCormick Hall, with satellite copies in four locations: Dumbarton Oaks in Washington, DC, the Vatican, the University of Utrecht in the Netherlands, and the University of California, Los Angeles (later moved to the Getty Research Center in Los Angeles).

Since 1991 the index has been available in both manual and electronic formats; it has approximately 200,000 images in its physical archive, with about half of them in the digital database. About 2,000 works of art are added to the archive every year.

MOLECULAR BIOLOGY, THE DEPARTMENT OF. Even though the department of Molecular Biology was not established until 1984, its ancestry dates back to 1830 when the American botanist John Torrey accepted a part-time faculty appointment as a professor of chemistry and natural history and began giving courses in botany. In the 1870s, Princeton formed a school of Science and for the first time named a full-time biologist to the faculty. The trustees turned down President James McCosh's first choice for that position, the zoologist Theodore Gill, because he subscribed to Charles Darwin's then-new theory of evolution. The position instead went to George Macloskie, an amateur naturalist from Ireland with degrees in divinity and law, who wrote a well-regarded textbook of elementary botany in 1883 and contributed to the highly respected *Reports of the Princeton Expedition to Patagonia, 1896–1899.*

The geologist Arnold Guyot had three brilliant students in the Class of 1877 who straddled biology, geology, and paleontology, and then became assistant professors at Princeton in 1881. In 1904, at a time when most universities had separate botany (plants) and zoology (animals) departments, Princeton formed a department of Biology that combined both fields; one of Guyot's former students, William Berryman Scott 1877, chaired both that department and the department of Geology. Four years later, as Guyot Hall was being constructed as a home for both departments, President Woodrow Wilson persuaded Edwin Grant Conklin to become the first full-time chair of what Wilson hoped would become "a great school of biology." Conklin held the position until he retired in 1933.

By the time Guyot Hall opened in 1910, Biology had a faculty of five. To accommodate growth, part of Guyot's natural history museum was later converted to laboratory space, and in 1960 the Moffett Laboratory was added to the south end of Guyot, almost doubling the department's space. When Eno Hall was vacated by the Psychology department in 1963, Biology expanded into that space as well. The department also used the 99-acre Stony Ford Field Station, northwest of Princeton, for experimental work in ecology and animal behavior; the field station remains in use, now under the auspices of the department of Ecology and Evolutionary Biology.

In 1920, E. Newton Harvey started what may have been the first undergraduate course in biochemistry in the country. In the early 1960s, Arthur Pardee launched a program in biochemical sciences, composed of professors in biology and chemistry; the program became a separate department in 1970. The 1960s and 1970s also saw the introduction of new areas of teaching and research, including neurophysiology and behavior, and ecology and evolution, along with growing interest in molecular, cellular, and developmental biology and genetics.

In his book *Lessons Learned*, President William Bowen recalls that "by the early 1970s, it was evident . . . that the intellectual breakthroughs in the life sciences were profound and that no university with high aspirations could be anything but very good in these fields." Princeton needed to be better, and with the field rapidly evolving and the University losing some of its most promising younger faculty members in the increasingly important field of biochemistry, Bowen sought first to build strengths incrementally. Eventually he concluded that "halfway measures . . . would not work," and he set out, simultaneously, to create a new department of Molecular Biology, build a new state-of-the-art laboratory (designed by Robert Venturi '47 *50 and Denise Scott Brown, funded by Laurance S. Rockefeller '32, and named at his request for the noted cell biologist and science writer Lewis Thomas '33), add faculty positions, and attract two transformative faculty leaders to Princeton: Arnold Levine and Thomas Shenk.

The new department came into existence in 1984 with Levine, an authority on the molecular basis of cancer, as its founding chair. Levine had become an assistant professor of biochemistry at Princeton in 1968 and had been promoted to associate professor in 1973, but he left Princeton in 1979 for the State University of New York at Stony Brook. After his return, Levine remained as chair until 1998 when he accepted the presidency of Rockefeller University; he later returned to the Princeton area as a professor at the Institute for Advanced Study.

Shenk, a colleague of Levine's at Stony Brook and later a chair of the department at Princeton, studies the functions and origins of viruses that cause tumors and birth defects. A past president of the American Society for Virology and the American Society for Microbiology, his research has contributed to the fields of biochemistry, cell biology, genetics, microbiology, and virology.

Levine and Shenk recruited James Broach, a pioneer in the use of budding yeast as a simple model system to understand fundamental biological processes common to all organisms. As the new department took shape, several faculty members in the department of Biochemical Sciences joined it. By 1990 biochemistry had been completely absorbed into Molecular Biology, and the department of Biochemical Sciences was closed.

For a few years, the departments of Biology and Molecular Biology coexisted, but then in 1988–89 they fused into what three-time chair of the Biology department John Bonner called a "mega-department." After a year, the mega-department subdivided into the department of Molecular Biology and a new department of Ecology and Evolutionary Biology composed of faculty working in those fields.

The Molecular Biology department achieved the level of international distinction that Bowen had sought, attracting many faculty members who made major contributions to the field. Arriving in 1986 was Shirley Tilghman, whose work in molecular genetics focused on the regulation of genes during development, particularly in the field of genomic imprinting. In 1998, with the support of President Harold Shapiro, Tilghman was instrumental in founding the multi-disciplinary Lewis-Sigler Institute for Integrative Genomics, with which the department enjoys deep connections. Tilghman went on to serve as the 19th president of Princeton University.

Eric Wieschaus arrived at Princeton in 1981 as a member of the Biology department, later moving to Molecular Biology. Much of his research focused on embryogenesis in the fruit fly *Drosophila melanogaster*, specifically in the patterning that occurs in the early *Drosophila* embryo. The genes Wieschaus found to control patterning and organ development in the fruit fly have since been shown to be the same genes that control similar processes in humans. Wieschaus won the 1995 Nobel Prize in Physiology or Medicine.

Bonnie Bassler arrived in 1994. Her work focused on the chemical communication between bacteria known as quorum sensing and contributed to the idea that disruption of chemical signaling can be used as an antimicrobial therapy. For that work, she was named a MacArthur Fellow in 2002. In the late 2010s, at a time when an increasing number of bacteria were resistant to traditional antibiotics, Bassler's work offered a promising approach for treating bacterial disease. A former president of the American Society for Microbiology, former board chair of the American Academy of Microbiology, and a leader in shaping American science policy, Bassler took office as chair of the department in 2013.

The research interests in the department of Molecular Biology span molecular, cell, and systems biology; its faculty study organisms ranging from viruses, bacteria, and yeast to worms, flies, fish, mice, and humans. Members of the department have expertise in genomics, proteomics, cancer biology, developmental biology, neurobiology, and microbiology, and many of them have joint appointments in Chemistry, Ecology and Evolutionary Biology, Engineering, Physics, the Lewis Sigler Institute, and the Princeton Neuroscience Institute. The department has programs in Molecular Biology, Neuroscience, Quantitative Biology, and Global Health.

Morrison, Toni (aka Chloe Anthony Wofford Morrison), was a highly esteemed novelist, editor, essayist, playwright, librettist, children's book author, and educator who left an indelible imprint on Princeton and the world.

She joined the Princeton faculty in 1989 as the Robert F. Goheen Professor in the Humanities and remained a member of the Creative Writing program until she transferred to emeritus status in 2006. In 1993 she became the first African American to be awarded the Nobel Prize in Literature. She also won the Pulitzer Prize in 1988 for her novel, *Beloved*; the National Humanities Medal in 2000; and the Presidential Medal of Freedom in 2012.

In 2017 one of the University's oldest and most prominent buildings, previously known as West College, was named Morrison Hall in tribute to her "transformative role in expanding Princeton's commitments to the creative and performing arts and to American Studies and African American Studies." Her portrait is displayed inside the building's north entrance.

Morrison's arrival at Princeton helped to attract other faculty and students of color, and to invigorate interest in the arts. In 1994 she founded the Princeton Atelier, which brings acclaimed artists and performers to campus for interdisciplinary collaborations with students on original projects in a workshop environment. (One of her first guest artists was the cellist, and later Princeton honorary degree recipient, Yo-Yo Ma.). She taught courses in the humanities and African American studies; one of her courses led to her 1992 book of literary criticism: *Playing in the Dark: Whiteness and the Literary Imagination*.

In 1996 she gave the keynote address—"The Place of the Idea, the Idea of the Place"—as Princeton celebrated its 250th anniversary. "The place of the idea represents the value of tradition, of independence; the idea of the place is its insightful grasp of the future," she said. "Negotiating these two ideas, conservation and change, is no small matter . . . they're not necessarily adversarial ideas, and even when they appear so that irreconcilability is the clash that stirs inquiry and fosters knowledge."

Morrison spoke at the community gathering in 2001 following the attacks of September 11. She was the baccalaureate speaker in 2005, when she told the graduating class: "I'm a believer in the power of knowledge and the ferocity of beauty, so from my point of view your life is already artful—waiting, just waiting, for you to make it art."

In 2013, she received an honorary degree from the University, with a citation that said:

> She ranks among the most versatile, gifted, acclaimed and beloved artists and intellectuals this nation has produced. In prose that is elegant, spare, deeply learned and redolent with the cadences of colloquial speech, she reanimates and reframes the past through stories of the aspirations and losses, desires and despair of those who have been written out of history. A global ambassador for the arts and humanities, she reminds us all of the power of the creative and performing arts to heal traumatic suf-

fering, traverse our differences and attune the moral imagination.

In 2016, the Princeton University Library announced that the major portion of her papers—part of the permanent library collections since 2014—were open for research to students, faculty, and scholars worldwide. The papers were gathered from multiple locations over more than two decades, beginning with files recovered by the library's preservation office after a tragic fire that destroyed Morrison's home in 1993.

In addition to the Nobel and Pulitzer prizes, Morrison won a National Book Critics Circle Award for *Song of Solomon* in 1978. In 2019 she received the gold medal from the American Academy of Arts and Letters. She was awarded the American Academy of Arts and Sciences Emerson-Thoreau Medal in 2016, and two major awards from France: the Commandeur de l'Ordre des Arts des Lettres in 1993, and the Ordre National de la Legion d'honneur in 2010.

She was the author of 11 novels, beginning with *The Bluest Eye* in 1970; her final book, *The Source of Self-Regard: Selected Essays, Speeches, and Meditations*, was published in early 2019, only months before she died. That summer, a documentary about her life, "Toni Morrison: The Pieces I Am," was released in theaters.

The fall 2017 dedication ceremony for the naming of Morrison Hall followed her keynote address for the Princeton and Slavery Project symposium. Before a packed house in Richardson Auditorium, she talked about her family's connections to slavery and her 1930s childhood in Lorain, Ohio, a steel-mill town west of Cleveland. She described it as a mixed neighborhood where "everybody was dirt poor."

While her older sister remembered racial slurs, she did not. She said she learned about race when she went to the historically Black Howard University in Washington, DC, where she received a bachelor's degree in English in 1953. After earning a master's degree in American literature at Cornell University in 1955, she taught at Texas Southern University and Howard before spending 20 years as a senior editor at Random House in New York. From 1984 to 1989 she held the Albert Schweitzer Chair in the Humanities at the State University of New York, Albany. She also held teaching posts at Yale University, Bard College, and Rutgers University.

The annual Toni Morrison lectures, sponsored by the department of African American studies and Princeton University Press and first delivered in 2006, spotlight new and exciting work of scholars and writers and celebrate "the expansive literary imagination, intellectual adventurousness, and political insightfulness that characterize" her writing.

In 2019 the Lewis Center for the Arts awarded the inaugural Toni Morrison Prize, which is presented to one or more graduating seniors "whose individual or collaborative artistic practice has pushed the boundaries and enlarged the scope of our understanding of issues of race." The prize honors work in any form that, in the spirit of Morrison's, is "characterized by visionary force and poetic import."

In 2020 Morrison was inducted posthumously into the National Women's Hall of Fame along with five other Black women, including singer and activist Aretha Franklin, who received an honorary degree from Princeton in 2012.

MORRISON HALL, a building previously known as West College, was named in 2017 in honor of eminent Princeton faculty member and 1993 Nobel Laureate in Literature Toni Morrison. In the words of the plaque displayed with her portrait in the north entrance of the building, "as writer, teacher, and inspiration to others," she "played a transformative role in expanding Princeton's commitments to the creative and performing arts and to American Studies and African American Studies." She was the first African American to be awarded the Nobel Prize in Literature; at the time of the naming she held the title of Robert F. Goheen Professor in the Humanities, Emerita, at Princeton.

The naming of Morrison Hall was one of the first two recommendations from a Council of the Princeton University Community committee on naming—a committee composed of faculty, students, staff, and alumni—that was established in 2016 to advise the trustees on the naming of "buildings or other spaces . . . to recognize individuals who would bring a more diverse presence to the campus." (The committee's other recommendation in its first year was the naming of Arthur Lewis Auditorium in Robertson Hall.)

The committee recommended that the University preserve Toni Morrison's legacy "by inscribing her name on the building that stands at the heart of the undergraduate academic and co-curricular experience at Princeton, housing as it does, among other offices, the dean of the college [and] the dean of undergraduate students . . ." For many years, the building also housed the offices of admission, financial aid, and the registrar, but in the early 2020s these offices were relocated to the Helm building, allowing the department of African American Studies to move into a Morrison Hall space that accommodated its needs more fully than the smaller space it had been occupying in neighboring Stanhope Hall.

Morrison Hall, then West College, was constructed in 1836 as Princeton's second dormitory, across Cannon Green from its twin, East College, which had been built in 1833. The buildings were not named for individuals, but for their placement to the east and west of the green.

East College was razed in 1896 to make way for Pyne Library (now East Pyne), but West College remained a dormitory until 1964, except for space on its first floor which was occupied by the Princeton University Store from its founding in 1896 until it relocated to a new building on University Place in 1958. In 1964, West College was converted for use by deans and other officers responsible for the administration of the undergraduate college.

A remodeling in 1925–26 added a second-floor balcony along the front of the building and an addition to the rear and redesigned the two main east-facing entrances. A 1996 renovation provided improved workspaces inside the building and added a terrace at the front of the building facing Cannon Green. A limestone engraving on the north-facing side of the building informs passersby that from 1871 to 1965 the dormitory Reunion Hall stood between Morrison Hall and Stanhope Hall, and that the bronze stars circling the engraving had been relocated from Reunion Hall, where they had marked the rooms of students who gave their lives in military service during the world wars.

Carl A. Fields, the University's first Black administrator and the first African American dean in the Ivy League, had his offices in Morrison Hall, and his portrait hangs in the building's south entrance.

MOVEMENT FOR A NEW CONGRESS, THE, was, in the words of its mission statement, "a campus-based movement operating within the American political tradition to mobilize massive grass-roots volunteer efforts" as part of "a national coalition of students and faculty members dedicated to reversing American war policy and reordering American priorities" by electing candidates committed to these goals in the fall 1970 Congressional elections.

By the summer of 1970 MNC had local chapters on about 350 campuses, 30 regional centers, more than 10,000 volunteers across the country, and a national headquarters located in Princeton's Palmer Hall that was conducting research, distributing instructional materials, providing expertise, handling national publicity, encouraging voter registration drives, and supplying names of volunteers to local and regional offices, especially in the 50–70 Congressional districts where success seemed most achievable.

The roots of MNC trace back to a meeting of more than 2,500 students in the chapel following President Richard Nixon's announcement on April 30, 1970 that American troops had invaded Cambodia. At that meeting, politics professor Stanley Kelley Jr., widely respected as the principal architect of dramatic changes in university governance that had recently been enacted, urged those assembled to channel their energies into elective political reform. Shortly thereafter, *Daily Princetonian* chair Luther Munford '70 published an article proposing a two-week recess in November to allow students to return home to work for Congressional candidates.

At a University-wide assembly on May 4 of more than 4,000 students, faculty, and staff in Jadwin Gym, politics professor Gary Orfield proposed the creation of an organization through which students could alter the composition of Congress by volunteering in Senate and House races in competitive states and districts. A resolution calling for the creation of MNC passed overwhelmingly, and by later that day 400 students had signed up. Within a week, the movement's research staff had printouts on each member of Congress, the margin of victory in the 1968 elections, and the member's position on 24 litmus-test issues.

On May 5 the faculty endorsed a resolution proposed by the Council of the Princeton University Community calling for a two-week recess immediately prior to the November 3 Congressional elections to "guarantee all members of the University community full freedom to exercise their responsibilities as concerned individuals"; the recess was created by beginning the academic year a week early, eliminating Thanksgiving recess, and delaying the start of the Christmas holiday by three days.

In a statement a week later, President Robert Goheen described the recess, which continues today at a length of one week, as "a positive response to grave national problems, a response which facilitates constructive efforts by individuals working within the democratic system, while neither committing the University to any particular political position nor interfering with its prime educational responsibility."

About two dozen other colleges and universities similarly adjusted their calendars for that fall.

On May 9, a meeting of 29 colleges in New York created a national organization and designated Princeton as its national headquarters. With the Physics department having moved into its new Jadwin Hall home, a vacated basement storeroom in Palmer Hall became the MNC national office, with a full-time staff of about 20. The office operated under coordinators Henry Bienen (a politics professor who later served as dean of the school of Public and International Affairs and then president of Northwestern University) and graduate student William Murphy *74, the son of a six-term member of Congress from Chicago and a Navy veteran.

MNC attracted extensive and highly favorable media attention, with most coverage focusing on the constructive nature of the initiative and the respectful behavior of the canvassers. In one early article, Orfield was quoted as saying that students were ready to move beyond demonstrations and moratoria: "The idea of working for a new antiwar Congress appealed both to the intelligence and the idealism of the students," he said. Articles appeared throughout the country in many major newspapers and magazines, including several lengthy articles in the *New York Times*, and there were a number of regional and national television appearances, including a segment on the August 25 broadcast of the *Today* show.

MNC had an impact in a number of Congressional primaries. For example, the campaign manager for the upset victory of Paul Sarbanes '54 in Maryland's fourth Congressional district attributed much of the credit to the 200 volunteers from MNC, saying "they did everything humanly possible to help in the campaign."

By November the momentum of the movement had diminished, and after the election MNC closed up shop.

Mpala Research Centre, in central Kenya's Laikipia County, is one of the world's leading field-based centers for research on ecology, evolution, conservation, public health, sustainable development, and climate change. The 48,000-acre center is administered as a trust, with the University serving as the managing partner in a consortium with the Smithsonian Institution and two government agencies mandated to conserve biodiversity in Kenya, the National Museums of Kenya and the Kenya Wildlife Service. As a Kenyan nongovernmental organization, the center receives financial support from the University and the Mpala Wildlife Foundation, which owns the land leases on which the center is located.

In 1989 George Small '43 approached the University about establishing a research center on a large ranch he inherited from his brother, Samuel Small '40. With leadership from Princeton ecology and evolutionary biology professor Daniel Rubenstein and longtime Mpala Wildlife Foundation trustee (as well as longtime Princeton trustee) Dennis Keller '63, the center opened in 1994 to long-term researchers and short-term workshops and began providing unparalleled opportunities for students to conduct field research for undergraduate independent work and doctoral dissertations.

The department of Ecology and Evolutionary Biology's semesters in the field program in Kenya began in 2006. The four-course program on tropical biology and sustainability is taught in three-week segments, with hands-on opportunities to study the ecology of savannas, conservation in Africa, the natural history of mammals, tropical agriculture, engineering and field hydrology, and paleoecology. Other undergraduates and graduate students from various disciplines participate in internships at the center, and conduct independent research on conservation, ecology, biology, and anthropology alongside overseas faculty and Kenyan scientists.

Located on the savanna north of Mount Kenya, Mpala offers a dynamic ecosystem with arid grasslands as well as lush riverside woodlands, and an array of wildlife that includes black rhinos, elephants, giraffes, lions, leopards, Grevy's zebras, and hundreds of bird species. Its research facilities include the first field-based genomics and stable isotope lab in Africa. Scholars from around the world conduct research at the center, and over time the center aims to expand its reach by further engaging scholars in the humanities, social sciences, and engineering.

The Mpala Wildlife Foundation is an active ranch with a herd of cattle as well as camels and goats. At times, the reserve is used by neighboring ranchers for grazing animals. The center connects with its surrounding communities through education programs, as well as such efforts as a rabies vaccination program for dogs to help prevent attacks on livestock, wildlife, and people.

Murray, James Ormsbee, a graduate of Brown University and Andover Theological Seminary, was Holmes Professor of Belles-Lettres from 1875 to 1899 and dean of the faculty from 1883 to 1899. He was Princeton's first dean.

"The office was at first a difficult one," Professor George McLean Harper later noted in a biographical sketch, "for it included discipline and the enforcement of standards of scholarship, but Dean Murray soon obtained general good will without sacrificing just severity." When President James McCosh retired in 1888, he said that "for sixteen years I had the somewhat invidious task of looking after the morals and discipline of the College. Since that time this important work has been committed to Dean Murray, who has shown more patience than I did in the discharge of his duties."

On January 18, 1893, in response to a request from students, Murray presented a resolution to a faculty meeting that called for an honor system for exams. The resolution passed and the honor system it created has remained a defining characteristic of Princeton ever since.

MURRAY-DODGE HALL consists of two buildings, joined by a 52-foot-long cloister, each a memorial to a Princetonian who died young. Murray Hall was built in 1879 with a bequest left by Hamilton Murray 1872, who died when the SS *Ville de Havre* sank in mid-ocean in 1873; he had written his will the night before he sailed. Dodge Hall was built in 1900 in memory of Earl Dodge 1879 (a former president of the student religious organization, the Philadelphian Society) who died five years after graduation. The funds were given by his father, William Earl Dodge Jr. and his brother Cleveland H. Dodge 1879.

Murray Hall was built of Trenton brownstone in a Victorian Gothic style. Dodge was built in Collegiate Gothic style, with a 51-foot tower in its northeast corner. Both buildings were originally used by the Philadelphian Society. Dodge Hall continues to be a center for religious activities; it is described as an "interfaith haven," housing the offices of the dean of religious life and of the chapel, a number of University chaplains of various faiths, and a number of campus ministries.

Murray Hall, once used for weekday chapel services, has since the 1920s been the home of Theatre Intime. Since 1968 its Hamilton Murray Theater has served as the home of Princeton Summer Theater as well.

Between the two buildings on the south is a garden given by the Class of 1969. It includes a polished marble tablet inscribed with lyrics from Joni Mitchell's song "Woodstock," which concludes with the words "we've got to get ourselves back to the garden."

In the basement of Murray-Dodge is a café that, according to its entry sign, is "dedicated to the fine art of being open." The café is open from 3 p.m. to midnight every day during the academic year; it offers students freshly baked cookies, coffee, and tea, and occasionally hosts musical performances and poetry readings.

MUSIC, THE DEPARTMENT OF. Students sang odes at Commencement in 1760, and a student orchestra played from Nassau Hall's belfry for President John Witherspoon's wedding in 1791. The Glee Club was founded in 1874, and step songs were introduced in the 1880s. Yet music remained only an extracurricular pastime until the early twentieth century when the first incremental steps were taken toward a formal program in music.

In 1917 an endowment funded the acquisition of both the great organ in the graduate college's Procter Hall and the appointment of a part-time organist/director of music who gave weekly recitals and public lectures on music. When the University Chapel was dedicated in 1928, the University engaged Ralph Downes, the English organist and organ designer who went on to become professor of organ at the Royal College of Music, as the chapel's first organist and choirmaster. He also taught several courses on music history and theory for undergraduates.

On the recommendation of a faculty committee, in 1934 the University invited Roy Dickinson Welch, professor of music at Smith College, to give two undergraduate courses in music and to design a future plan of study. Students responded to his course with such enthusiasm that Welch was persuaded to stay and build the music program himself. The program was lodged in the department of Art and Archaeology as the "Section of Music." Within three years, the number of music courses had grown to seven, and 10 percent of the student body was taking at least one music course sometime during their college career.

The expanded curriculum allowed students to begin concentrating in music theory and the history of music. Welch made several key faculty appointments, beginning in 1937 when he hired Roger Sessions, already creating major compositions himself, for theory and composition, and Oliver Strunk, the influential musicologist, for music history. The following year, he added Milton Babbitt *42 *92, Edward Cone '39 *42, and Merrill Knapp as instructors. In 1940 a one-year Master of Fine Arts program was begun, and Babbitt and Cone enrolled, becoming the first graduates of the program. All three early instructors spent the rest of their academic careers at Princeton and achieved international reputations as composers and musicologists.

In addition to being "a founding father of music as an academic discipline," Babbitt was a brilliant composer and a pioneer of electronic music. (He also was enough of a mathematician to teach math at Princeton during World War II.) He taught off-campus as well, and one of his private students was the songwriter Stephen Sondheim. In 1991 Princeton awarded Babbitt an honorary degree, and a year later his department awarded him his PhD, accepting a dissertation it had rejected in 1946.

The "music section" attained departmental status in 1946. The department was given a home in the basement of Clio Hall, after having made do with spare spaces all over campus, including Alexander Hall, Murray-Dodge, McCormick, and the crypt in the chapel. The department continued to flourish and the graduate program was extended to include PhDs, the first one being awarded in 1950.

Following the death of Welch, the Bach scholar Arthur Mendel joined the department as chair in 1952 and presided over a 15-year period of evolution. Initially the department separated composition and musicology: composition was considered a craft, but musicology (including theory and history) was thought of as an extension of the liberal arts. For just over a decade the graduate program awarded PhDs in music history only.

With composers such as Babbitt and Cone gaining seniority in the department and new faculty members—including composers Earl Kim (vocal and theater works), James Randall (electronic music), and Peter Westergaard *56 (opera and chamber music)—coming aboard, composition's intellectual credentials and its relationship to mathematics and science soon put it on par with musicology. In 1961 Princeton joined Brandeis in being one of only two universities at the time to offer a PhD in composition.

During the same years, Mendel was overseeing plans for the construction of the Woolworth Center of Musical Studies. The department moved into Woolworth from Clio, where there had been no practice or performance facilities, in 1963. Within 10 years Woolworth was filled to overflowing, with the department's faculty and students vying for space with student concerts and vocal and instrumental practice rooms.

The abundance and frequency of musical notices across campus in the late 1970s and early 1980s spoke to how pervasive musical performance had become in campus life. It was time to consider student performance as a discipline comparable to composition and musicology.

During his two terms as chair (1974–78 and 1983–86), Westergaard was an ardent advocate for raising the profile of performance. Carl Weinrich, organist and choirmaster in the chapel for 30 years, brought renown to Princeton through his organ recitals and provided professional leadership for the Glee Club and the Chapel Choir. He was succeeded by Walter Nollner, who took over the Glee Club when he joined the music faculty in 1958 and became choirmaster in 1973. After Westergaard himself conducted the Princeton University Orchestra for several years, he brought Michael Pratt to the faculty as the orchestra's professional conductor in 1977.

From the beginning of his tenure, Pratt was committed to opera performance for students. He established Princeton University Opera Theater and was the music director, with Westergaard as stage director. In 1991 the department established the program in Musical Performance, with Pratt as director. The program has come to serve as a model platform from which students can deepen their musical skills and insights from within a liberal arts curriculum. The program provides studio instruction with top professionals in New York, master classes by international artists, and numerous performance classes by department faculty.

Today graduate students can earn PhDs in composition or musicology. Undergraduates can major in music, in a program with emphasis on writing music or writing about music, and they can earn certificates in music performance, as music majors or as majors of other departments. In addition to enrolling in courses, they can take instrumental or voice lessons, and audition to perform with jazz groups, choruses, orchestras, a wind ensemble, the opera theater, a musical comedy troupe, at least a dozen chamber music ensembles, a laptop orchestra, or a cappella singing groups. They also can volunteer with the Trenton Youth Orchestra or Trenton Youth Singers to provide coaching and private instruction to young musicians from Trenton.

The department emphasizes collaboration with other departments and programs across campus, and frequent interdisciplinary collaborators include students and faculty from Architecture, African American Studies, Computer Science, Irish Studies, and the programs in Theater, Dance, Visual Arts, Music Theater, and Creative Writing, all housed within the Lewis Center for the Arts.

The most serious undergraduates have opportunities for study abroad. In 2009 the department began a partnership with the Royal College of Music in London that allows qualified students to spend the fall semester of junior year studying voice, instrument, or composition in London. In March 2019 department chair Wendy Heller traveled to Imola, Italy, as part of the inaugural Imola Piano Academy Exchange. The cultural exchange immerses piano students from Princeton in the rich and intense environment of the Imola Academy, while introducing pianists from the Imola Academy to the highest levels of composition and musicology at Princeton.

As for performance space, the mid-1980s renovation of Richardson Auditorium provided the University with an appropriate concert hall, and Taplin Auditorium in Fine Hall provides a recital hall. The renovation of Woolworth in 1997 added rehearsal space for choral groups and small instrumental ensembles.

In 2006 President Shirley Tilghman launched an "Arts Initiative" to expand Princeton's programs in the creative and performing arts, and to establish Princeton "as a global leader in the quality of its offerings and in their integration into a broader liberal arts education." The initiative led to the Lewis Arts complex, including the Effron music building that opened in 2017; the building includes space devoted to rehearsal and practicing, teaching studios, jazz practice rooms, and a studio for the Princeton Laptop Orchestra. The building's two-story, 3,500-square-foot Lee Rehearsal Room is acoustically isolated and large enough so the orchestra can rehearse there, rather than on the stage at Richardson.

NADER, RALPH '55 came to national attention in 1965 with the publication of his bestselling book, *Unsafe at Any Speed*, which criticized the safety of American automobiles (especially Chevrolet's Corvair and Ford's Pinto); the book led to the enactment of legislation that empowered the government to establish safety standards for all automobiles sold in the United States.

Nader became a full-time activist for consumer protection, environmental issues, and government reform; he helped establish a number of advocacy organizations and watchdog groups; and with a group of volunteer law students known as "Nader's Raiders" he pursued issues related to nuclear safety, international trade, meat processing, pension reform, land use, banking, and the regulation of insecticides. He was named to lists of the 100 most influential Americans in the twentieth century by *Time*, *Life*, and the *Atlantic Monthly*. In 2008 the *Princeton Alumni Weekly* ranked him in a tie for 25th in its list of the most influential Princeton alumni of all time. In 1972 he received the Woodrow Wilson Award, the highest distinction the University can bestow on undergraduate alumni.

While a number of Princeton alumni sought their party's nominations to run for president of the United States in the twentieth and early twenty-first centuries, including Bill Bradley '65, Ted Cruz '92, Mitch Daniels '71, and Steve Forbes '70, Nader was one of only four alumni who competed in the general election. (The others were Adlai Stevenson 1922, Norman Thomas 1905, and Woodrow Wilson 1879.) Nader ran for president four times: in 1996 and 2000 as the Green Party candidate, and in 2004 and 2008 as an independent. He received nearly three million votes in 2000 in a tightly contested race between George W. Bush and Al Gore that was ultimately decided by the Supreme Court.

Nader is the author or co-author of more than two dozen books, and was the subject of a documentary film, *An Unreasonable Man*, which debuted at the 2006 Sundance Film Festival. In 2015, capping a 17-year effort, he opened the only American museum devoted to tort law in his hometown of Winsted, Connecticut; among the displays are a 1963 Chevy Corvair, a Fisher-Price toy school bus with removable figures that were found to be choking hazards, and an explanation of a 1994 New Mexico lawsuit that held McDonald's accountable for serving scalding hot coffee.

In 1989, the Class of 1955 held a gathering in Washington, DC, in anticipation of its 35th reunion the following year. Nader challenged his classmates to take advantage of the influential positions they held and the increased time they had as they approached retirement to make a more concerted commitment to the betterment of society. The class responded by creating an independent, nonprofit organization, Project 55, to place Princeton undergraduates and recent graduates in paid summer internships or year-long fellowships with public service organizations and provide them with alumni mentors.

The program began in 1990 with 14 summer interns and eight year-long fellows, and by 2020 it had placed almost 2,000 Princetonians in intern and fellowship positions. In 2010 the program changed its name to Princeton AlumniCorps and focused its attention on its Project 55 fellowship program. AlumniCorps also sponsors a mid-career leadership training program for emerging leaders in the nonprofit or public interest sector.

Project 55 inspired similar alumni initiatives, including ReachOut 56 (later renamed ReachOut 56-81-06), which was founded by the Class of 1956 in 1991 and began a fellowship program for graduating seniors in 2001, and the Princeton Internships in Civic Service (PICS), which was established by the Class of 1969 in 1996 and formally affiliated with the University's Pace Center for Civic Engagement in 2020.

NASH, JOHN FORBES JR., *50, an enigmatic campus figure for many years and the subject of the Academy Award-winning movie *A Beautiful Mind*, was a brilliant mathematician, renowned for breakthrough work in several areas, including game theory, who struggled for much of his life with mental illness. He was awarded the 1994 Nobel Prize in Economics for work on the mathematics of game theory that was the subject of his 1950 doctoral dissertation at Princeton. In 2015 he won the Abel Prize, the equivalent of a Nobel Prize for mathematics, for his "striking and seminal contributions to the theory of nonlinear partial differential equations and its applications to geometric analysis." His is the only person to have won both prizes.

Born in 1928 in Bluefield, West Virginia, Nash studied chemistry and mathematics at what is now Carnegie Mellon University in Pittsburgh. He received both his bachelor's and master's degrees in 1948 and, two years later, completed his doctorate at Princeton at the age of 22. (When he was applying to Princeton, his Carnegie adviser wrote a letter of recommendation describing him as "a mathematical genius.")

In April 1950 he published his first paper, "The Bargaining Problem," in the journal *Econometrica*, and in 1951 his 27-page doctoral dissertation, "Non-Cooperative Games," appeared in the *Annals of Mathematics*. These works established the mathematical principles of game theory, which examines the dynamics of rivalries between competitors. His concepts of "Nash equilibrium" and "Nash bargaining" today pervade not only economics, but psychology, evolutionary biology, war and nuclear strategy, politics, contract negotiations, and business decision-making.

Nash's Princeton colleagues described him as a devoted mathematician whose ability to see old problems from a new perspective resulted in some of his most influential work. "He had a profound originality as if he somehow had insights into developing problems that no one had even thought about," one said. His influential work included the Nash-Moser inverse function theorem, the Nash-De Giorgi theorem, and the Nash embedding theorems, which the Norwegian Academy of Science and Letters, conferrer of the Abel Prize, described as "among the most original results in geometric analysis of the 20th century." His other honors included the 1978 John von Neumann Theory Prize and the 1999 American Mathematical Society's Leroy P. Steele Prize for a Seminal Contribution to Research.

In 1951 Nash joined the faculty at MIT, but he resigned in the late 1950s after bouts of paranoid schizophrenia. He spent years being treated for his mental illness and, over that time, began an informal association with Princeton; in 1995, he officially became a senior research mathematician. In the years following his return to campus and prior to his Nobel Prize, he was an almost ghostly presence on campus, known to generations of students as the phantom of Fine Hall.

In 1957 Nash married Alicia Larde Lopez-Harrison, a naturalized US citizen from El Salvador and a graduate of MIT with a degree in physics. They divorced in 1963, but after years of sharing a household, they remarried in 2001. In 2015 they were together in a taxi on the New Jersey Turnpike, returning from his visit to Norway to accept the Abel Prize, when they both died tragically in a fatal car crash.

Sylvia Nasser's 1998 biography of Nash, *A Beautiful Mind*, served as the basis for the movie of that name that was released in 2001 and won four Academy Awards, including best picture. The actor Russell Crowe played Nash; portions of the filming took place on the Princeton campus, some of it with Nash watching and critiquing.

NASSAU HALL, the metaphorical heart of the University and since 1960 a national historic landmark, was the largest stone building and the largest academic structure in the colonies when it opened in 1756. It provided inspiration for other college buildings, notably Hollis Hall at Harvard, University Hall at Brown, Dartmouth Hall at Dartmouth, and Queens Hall at Rutgers.

According to Aaron Burr Sr., then the president of the College, the guiding principle of its design was to "do everything in the plainest and cheapest manner, as far as is consistent with Decency and Convenience, having no superfluous Ornaments." Robert Smith, a carpenter-architect from Philadelphia, designed the building based on sketches by another Philadelphia architect, William Shippen, whose brother was a trustee of the College. The trustees originally voted that "the College be built of Brick if good Brick can be made at Princeton and if sand can be got reasonably cheap," but the plans were changed, and the building, with walls 26 inches think, was built of light brown sandstone from a quarry most likely on the south bank of what is now Lake Carnegie.

That it was good stone and that it was well and truly laid by the mason William Worth is substantiated by the fact that its walls have withstood the extraordinary shocks and strains of military occupation in the American Revolution; devastating fires in 1802 and 1855; and rebellious students who on one occasion exploded a hollow log charged with two pounds of gunpowder inside the main entrance, cracking the adjacent interior walls from top to bottom.

It took two years to erect the building and even before it was completed the trustees voted to name it for the governor of the province, Jonathan Belcher. "Let BELCHER HALL proclaim your beneficent acts . . . to the latest ages," they wrote the governor. With what President John Maclean Jr. later called "a rare modesty," the governor declined the honor, and at his suggestion the building was named Nassau Hall in memory of King William the Third, of the "Illustrious House of Nassau."

Smith's Nassau Hall had three stories and a basement. It was about 176 feet long and 54 feet wide at the ends, with a central element projecting about four feet in front and about 12 feet in back. Over the center of the hip roof was a modest cupola. There were three entrances at the front of the building and two at the back.

The building was designed to house the entire college. On each of the three floors, a central corridor ran the whole length of the building east to west and all the rooms opened on these corridors. There was a two-story prayer hall, 32 by 40 feet, at the rear of the central projection, and a library on the second floor above the main entrance hall. There were rooms for classes and for tutors, and for 147 students on all three floors. In the basement were the kitchen dining room, steward's quarters, and, after 1762, additional rooms for students.

The first state legislature of New Jersey held its inaugural meeting in Nassau Hall in 1776, and at that meeting it approved the first state constitution, inaugurated the first governor of the state, and adopted the state seal.

Later that year, the building suffered severely as the Revolutionary War engulfed it and its surroundings. The British and American troops quartered there at different times plundered the library, ruined the organ in the prayer hall, and used furniture and woodwork for fuel. During the battle of Princeton, a turning point in the American Revolution in January 1777, Nassau Hall changed hands three times and once, when the British were in possession, felt the effects of the Continental Army's artillery. One American cannonball came through a window of the prayer hall, destroying a portrait of King George II, and another hit the south wall of the west wing and left a scar that is visible today.

Funds being in short supply, recovery from the Revolution was slow, yet by 1783 Nassau Hall was ready to serve as the national capitol. For four months that summer, July through October, the Continental Congress met in the library on the second floor, using the prayer hall for state occasions. Here Congress thanked George Washington for his leadership during the war, received news of the signing of the definitive treaty of peace with Great Britain, and welcomed the first foreign minister—from the Netherlands—accredited to the United States

While in Princeton, Washington agreed to a request from the trustees to sit for a portrait by Charles Willson Peale, which, at their direction, was placed in the prayer hall in the frame that had been occupied previously by the portrait of George II.

The fire of 1802 left only the outside walls of Nassau Hall standing. To restore the building the trustees called on Benjamin Latrobe of Philadelphia, the country's first professional architect, who later worked on the restoration of the national capitol after it was burned in 1814.

The changes Latrobe made in Smith's original design were chiefly practical ones to lessen the hazards of fire. Instead of wood, the floors were laid with brick and the stairs rebuilt of stone with iron railings. The building was given a sheet-iron roof—a new idea in this country and an experiment on the part of Latrobe.

The roof was raised about two feet from its former position to allow space for transom lights over the doors; this improved the whole exterior appearance of the building. The horizontal lintels over the three entrances at the front of the building were replaced by triangular pediments, and the circular window in the central pediment rising from the eaves line was replaced by a fanlight. The belfry was raised on a large square base to accommodate a clock and to give the cupola added height. Latrobe's changes gave Nassau Hall a Federal rather than a Colonial style, adding grace without marring the original simplicity.

The fire of 1855 was just as disastrous as the fire of 1802, and once more only the walls were left standing. This time the trustees called on another Philadelphia architect, John Notman, who had designed three residences in the village, including Prospect House and the building later named Lowrie House.

Notman's interior changes were chiefly concerned with fireproofing. Iron beams and brick arches were used to support the floors. The roof was made of slate, laid upon and fastened to iron-laths. Most important of all, since the 1855 fire was believed to have been caused by a spark from a stove in a student's room, nine furnaces were installed to provide central heating. The old prayer hall, no longer needed for that purpose following the construction of a separate chapel in 1847, was extended farther southward to more than twice its previous size for use as the college library.

Notman made more extensive changes to the exterior of the building. Two of the three entrances at the front of the building were removed and towers were built on either end to house the stairways which were removed from the interior halls. The doorway at the center of the building was replaced by a larger, arched doorway of Florentine style with more massive steps below and a similarly arched window, with a balcony, above. This heightened vertical emphasis culminated in a cupola even loftier than Latrobe's. (The tops of the Italianate towers housing the staircases on either end of the building, which rose high above the roof line, were removed in 1905.)

As the University built new dormitories toward the end of the nineteenth century, fewer and fewer students lived in Nassau Hall; by 1903 the last students had moved out. And as students moved out, museums, laboratories, and classrooms moved in. In the east wing, part of the third floor was removed to create a two-story well for a natural history museum and a skylight was cut in the roof to provide light. With construction of Palmer Laboratory and Guyot Hall these facilities were no longer needed, and by 1924, when Eno Hall was completed and the department of Psychology had departed, Nassau Hall was devoted entirely to offices of the central administration.

In 1967 additional space was obtained by flooring over the two-story well in the east wing, and the exterior appearance was improved by the removal of the skylight above it.

From its early days, a bell rang from Nassau Hall. Made in England, the bell had to be recast after the fire of 1802, and it was completely melted in the fire of 1855. A second bell, cast in West Troy, New York, was hung in the cupola in 1858. It struck the hour and called students to classes and chapel for 97 years. In time it developed a slight crack and by 11:30 a.m. on February 18, 1955, its peal was reduced to what the *Princeton Alumni Weekly* called "a plaintive croak." A new bell was waiting in the wings and hoisted into place on February 22. On the following day at 9:00 p.m. it rang out the hour in a D tone, a half note lower than that sounded by the earlier bell. With the electrification of bell ringing in 1962, regular visits to the third floor to ring the bell with a rope came to an end.

As recounted by Elizabeth Greenberg '02 in her senior thesis, in 1812 a "mischievous student forced the door of the belfry" at 3 a.m. to ring the bell and "faculty members tumbled out of bed to hold a meeting on the spot and dismiss him." On a winter's night in 1864, an undergraduate disrupted the College's schedule by removing the clapper from the bell, requiring a member of the maintenance staff to strike the bell with a hammer until a new clapper was installed.

Stealing the clapper became a tradition, and the University kept a barrel of clappers on hand for rapid replacement. In 1991, one student sprained an ankle while scaling Nassau Hall to steal the clapper and another narrowly missed students on the ground when dropping the clapper from the roof. In 1992, after another student was injured falling from the building, the clapper was removed. Recordings of the bell are now broadcast over speakers, and the bell rings live only for a few special occasions each year when technicians reinstall the clapper temporarily and remain in the bell tower while it is in use.

A tower clock was first installed sometime after Latrobe's restoration of 1802 when the cupola was raised; it was probably destroyed in the fire of 1855. The clock with the four faces one sees today on the cupola was donated by the Class of 1866 at the 10th anniversary of their graduation. The clocks were modernized in the 1950s and the clock mechanism was changed from analog to digital in the 1980s. In 2018, the four clocks, each five feet in diameter and weighing 150 pounds, were removed from the cupola to be rebuilt, rehabilitated, and repainted. During that restoration, the weathervane was also restored, a new roof (with 21,000 new slate tiles) was installed, copper gutters were replaced, snow guards were added, and safety features were enhanced.

In Notman's rebuilding after the fire of 1855, the former prayer hall was more than doubled in size for use as the college library and portrait gallery. After the completion of Chancellor Green Library in 1873, this room was used for the college museum until 1906 when President Woodrow Wilson had it remodeled to look like the House of Commons in England.

Today the Faculty Room is used for meetings of the faculty and the Board of Trustees, which makes it the room where most major decisions charting the course of the University are made. On its walls are portraits of two English kings, George II (the king when Princeton's charter was granted) and William the Third (of the house of Orange-Nassau); Governor Belcher; Washington at the Battle of Princeton; James Madison 1771 (with Wilson, one of Princeton's two US presidents, and its first graduate student); Benjamin Rush 1760, and the 19 former presidents of the University. By custom, the portrait of the current president hangs in the Princeton Club of New York until it moves into the Faculty Room when the president leaves office.

The bronze tigers on either side of the front steps were presented in 1911 by Wilson's classmates to replace the lions they had given on their graduation in 1879. By then the tiger had become established as the symbol of Princeton. For more than a century, the tigers have invited generations of Princetonians and visitors to the campus to climb on their increasingly polished backs. In recent years Princeton seniors frequently celebrate the completion of their theses by posing with the tigers and their thesis for a celebratory photo.

The entrance hall to Nassau Hall was remodeled in 1919 as a memorial to Princetonians who died in the country's wars. Carved into the marble walls are the names of 10 who died in the American Revolution, one in the War of 1812, 70 thought to have died in the Civil War, five in the Spanish-American War, 152 in World War I, 353 in World War II, 29 in the Korean War, and 24 in the war in Southeast Asia. (The total number of alumni now known to have died in the Civil War is 86, including 62 of the 70 whose names are listed in the atrium.) At the dedication of the memorial on Alumni Day 1920, President John Grier Hibben 1882 *1893 said, "Their work is finished, ours is hardly begun. The vision of the new world, that better order of things for which they died, is yet unrealized."

In the early nineteenth century, some graduating classes installed class stones on Nassau Hall and later classes began a tradition of planting class ivy around the foundations of various campus buildings, including Nassau Hall. With the building reaching capacity, a new tradition of installing a class stone for each year's graduating class on the walkways of the front campus leading to Nassau Hall began in 2018 with installation of the stone for that year's senior class, along with stones for the 17 other classes from the previous 100 years that did not have stones on Nassau Hall.

NATIVE AMERICAN AND INDIGENOUS STUDENTS AT PRINCETON. Princeton's earliest history is linked with Indigenous people. The University's lands are part of the Lenapehoking, the historical homeland of the Lenape people. In 1758, just two years after the College of New Jersey moved to Princeton, English colonists forced the remaining Lenape of New Jersey westward to Pennsylvania and Ohio. The following year, Jacob Woolley, a Lenape, enrolled as Princeton's first Native student. Thus, Native people represented the first ethnic minority to attend Princeton, but none graduated until the middle of the nineteenth century. It was not until the 1970s that more than a handful attended Princeton simultaneously.

Each of the three Native students who matriculated at Princeton in the eighteenth century—all of whom were Lenape—left Princeton without a degree. The first two, Woolley and Shawuskukhkung (Wilted Grass), had attended Moor's Charity School, established by Puritan ministers to train Native Americans as missionaries, prior to matriculating at Princeton.

Woolley, a member of the class of 1762, fell prey to alcohol, and reportedly was distracted by his relationship with a woman in town; he was expelled for failing his courses. The Scottish missionary society provided financial support for Shawuskukhkung (known as Bartholomew Scott Calvin) to attend Princeton as a member of the class of 1776; he left Princeton to join the army during the Revolutionary War.

The third Lenape student was George Morgan White Eyes 1789, son of a Lenape sachem in the Ohio Valley, whose Princeton education, funded by Congress, was the young country's first instance of federal aid for education. It became clear only later that Congress expected the Lenape to repay the costs of education with a grant of Lenape land.

George Morgan White Eyes was named by his father in honor of his friend, Colonel George Morgan, a trusted agent of Indian Affairs for the US government. When Morgan learned that the sachem had been murdered by a white soldier, he resigned his position in protest, and as a result of Morgan's lobbying, Congress invited the sachem's children east for schooling. When a delegation of Ohio Lenape traveled to Philadelphia in 1779, the delegation included George Morgan White Eyes and two of his cousins. On their way to Philadelphia, the Lenape set up an encampment on Morgan's newly purchased Princeton property, Prospect Farm, which then abutted the College's campus.

All three boys enrolled in the Princeton grammar school, but only George Morgan White Eyes excelled, mastering Greek and Latin in addition to learning English. Of the three, he was the only one to matriculate at the College, becoming a member of the class of 1789. Despite his initial successes, just before his senior year he learned that his mother had been murdered by a band of white men. Far from home and now an orphan, he fell in with a crowd of students who had been expelled and began to neglect his studies. He wrote to President George Washington begging for permission to return home to Ohio; by the end of 1789, financial support from Congress stopped.

More than half a century passed before John McDonald Ross 1841 became the first Native student known to graduate from Princeton. Ross was one of three members of his family to receive Princeton degrees in the 1840s. All three were nephews of the principal chief of the Cherokee Nation, who led the Cherokee through removal to Oklahoma. A brother, Robert Daniel Ross 1843 *1846, became one of the first Native physicians in the country. A cousin, William Potter Ross 1842, served as a lieutenant colonel in the Confederate army and succeeded his uncle as principal chief in 1861.

The Rosses also had Scottish heritage and, like many Cherokees in the nineteenth century, grew up bicultural. While there is no evidence of George Morgan White Eyes and his Lenape predecessors being treated poorly by their classmates, it is clear that the bicultural upbringing of the Rosses contributed to their success at Princeton. The Rosses spoke English as a native language and attended prep school at Lawrenceville along with other future Princeton students prior to college, giving them the same level of preparation as their white classmates.

Mainstream white schooling proved essential for the two Native students who graduated in the early decades of the twentieth century. Both Howard Edward Gansworth (Rho-whas-ne-uh, or "News Carrier") 1901 *1906 and Joseph Paul Baldeagle 1923 were alumni of the Carlisle Indian School, a federally funded assimilationist boarding school established in 1879.

While at Princeton, Gansworth—a member of the Seneca tribe born on a reservation in western New York—was cast in the Triangle Club's 1898 red-face spoof of the story of Pocahontas. Gansworth's academic interests centered on Native Americans, and as Princeton's first Native American graduate student he wrote his master's thesis about the Iroquois Confederacy; he was an activist in preserving Native heritage and culture for the rest of his life. Following graduation, Gansworth became an active member of the Princeton Club of Buffalo and in 1915 was elected its president.

Baldeagle, a member of the Sioux tribe, advocated for Native rights throughout his life and donated his collection of artifacts to the New Jersey State Museum. Upon his retirement as a teacher, he volunteered as a guard at Firestone Library.

At least two dozen self-identified Native students enrolled during the 1970s. The increase was due in part to the recruitment efforts of anthropology professor Alfonso Ortiz (Pueblo) and longtime curator at Firestone Library Alfred Bush. At the time, Ortiz was the only Native faculty member at Princeton. In 1970 he joined with Native American scholars from across the country to host, at Princeton, the First Convocation of American Indian Scholars, which sought to establish Native American Studies as a discipline. Ortiz's personal and professional papers, as well as a collection of oral literature he recorded with the Tewa-speaking Pueblo, are in the Princeton University Library.

Bush spent four decades as the curator of western Americana at Princeton, significantly increasing

Princeton's collections related to Native Americans and Indigenous people; he also taught related courses in several departments. On some occasions, he provided financial support for Native American applicants to visit campus.

The Native students of the 1970s represented a stark contrast to those of the past. For the most part, a majority had grown up on reservations, coming to Princeton after having been educated in their own communities; at least five of them had been raised by parents who were monolingual speakers of their native languages. For many Native students, the transition to Princeton was difficult culturally; several took time off before completing their degrees.

Students representing a variety of Native American tribes established the Organization of Native American Students at Princeton (ONASP), which worked on recruitment efforts, organized conferences, hosted fundraisers, and provided a social framework. They and their successors in the 1980s, who created Natives at Princeton (NAP), put in significant effort toward educating the rest of the Princeton community not only about Native histories and cultures, but also about the continued existence and reality of Native communities, about which many white Americans knew little. Many Native students found a home at the Third World Center, which was established in 1971 as a place of community for students of color.

Many ONASP and NAP alumni pursued careers and leadership roles in their home communities after graduation. Among those who have served in senior positions in Native governments are: Regis Pecos '77, former governor of Cochiti Pueblo, who in 1997 became Princeton's first Native American trustee; Helen Blue-Redner '85, former chair of the Upper Sioux tribe; Rex Lee Jim '86, former vice president of the Navajo Nation; and Doreen Hobson McPaul '95, appointed attorney general of the Navajo Nation in 2019.

Others have made important contributions to Native communities at the tribal, state, national, and international levels, impacting policies and programs in fields such as education, health care, law, and language preservation. On a national stage, Kevin Gover '78 (Pawnee) became the director of the National Museum of the American Indian after a career working with Native communities in legal affairs, academia, and the US government, including as Secretary of Indian Affairs, the highest ranking Native American in the nation. In 2001, Gover became the first Native person to receive an honorary degree from Princeton.

The 2010s saw an increased commitment to ensuring the representation of Native American histories and cultures in campus life and in the curriculum. The Princeton American Indian and Indigenous Studies Working Group, first founded by graduate students in 2011, organized conferences, reading groups, and speakers for scholars working on Indigenous studies topics, and the program in American Studies served as the academic home for Native American/Indigenous studies.

In 2017 the admission office began establishing partnerships with programs such as College Horizons and the Santa Fe Indian School Leadership Institute as part of an expanded effort to identify and attract more Native American and Indigenous students to Princeton.

An Indigeneity at Princeton task force established by the Undergraduate Student Government in 2019 renewed calls for more course offerings in Native American and Indigenous studies, a formal land acknowledgement by Princeton of its location on Lenapehoking, and an increase in the number of Native faculty members and students. The Indigenous Princeton Advocacy Coalition was a student group that sought to bolster Indigenous life on campus through increased representation in academic offerings, the faculty, social life, service opportunities, and space on campus.

Students also revived NAP, with a modified mission of representing all students who come from Indigenous backgrounds, not just those in North America. NAP hosts events throughout the year, particularly during November, which is American Indian and Alaska Native Heritage Month. These events have included raising a tipi on Prospect lawn and collaborating with the dining halls to feature Native cuisines. In 2017 the University hosted an Ivy Native Council conference that brought together Native and Indigenous students from all Ivy League schools, and a 2018 symposium on Indigenous communities and climate change examined the impact of climate change on these communities.

By 2020 Indigenous scholarship at the University was drawing faculty from more than 20 academic disciplines and courses ranged from introductions to Native American and Indigenous studies to classes on Indigenous literatures and languages. That year a group of students, faculty, and staff launched an Indigenous studies website for Indigenous scholarship, teaching, and research, and Wendy Schmidt, her husband Eric Schmidt '76, and the Schmidt Family Foundation endowed a professorship of Indigenous studies to allow the University to expand its faculty expertise in this area of study.

A Native American Alumni of Princeton (NAAP) group supports and fosters discussion among alumni and students, welcoming all individuals from Native American, Alaskan Natives, and Native Hawai'ian nations.

NEAR EASTERN STUDIES, THE DEPARTMENT OF. The department of Near Eastern Studies was founded in 1927 as a department of Oriental Languages and Literatures (later known as Oriental Studies). Its first chair, Henry Bender, built on groundwork laid by three Princeton alumni of the late nineteenth-century: David Paton 1874, Howard Crosby Butler 1892, and Robert Garrett 1897.

Paton was a self-taught Egyptologist who spent his career at Princeton studying and translating material from Egypt, Assyria, and West Asia. In 1919, the William and Annie S. Paton Foundation Professorship in Ancient and Modern Literature was established in his honor by his mother. On his death in 1925, he bequeathed his library to the University as well as an endowment to maintain a fellowship for "research work in the languages, literature, history, geography, and religions of West Asia and Northeastern Africa."

While Paton was working in a tower of Pyne Library, Howard Crosby Butler, a professor in the department of Art and Archaeology and a specialist in Near Eastern archaeology and architecture, was mounting expeditions in Syria and Anatolia and heading excavations at Antioch and Sardis as early as 1899. A charter trustee of the Jerusalem School for Oriental Research, Butler brought to Princeton the first of two German scholars who taught Semitic philology during the early 1900s.

Only two years after his graduation, Robert Garrett helped to organize and finance Butler's first expedition to Syria. From this expedition, Garrett collected Arabic manuscripts, which he deposited in the University Library in 1900. A Princeton trustee for more than 40 years, Garrett continued to acquire and lend to the University valuable Near Eastern collections, donating them all in 1942. In 1943 he further donated over 5,000 medieval Arabic items. With these gifts, added to earlier gifts such as Paton's, Princeton possessed one of the world's finest collections of Near Eastern books and manuscripts.

Bender joined the Princeton faculty in 1909 and taught a wide variety of languages, including German, Gothic, Old Norse, Lithuanian, and Sanskrit. He was a renowned scholar of linguistics, who served as chief etymologist for Webster's New International Dictionary. He founded the Linguistic Society of America and was president of the American Oriental Society. During his years as chair of the department, he focused on coordinating graduate work in comparative Indo-European and Semitic studies with Professor Philip Khuri Hitti, who was the second incumbent of the Paton chair.

When Bender stepped down as chair in 1944, Hitti succeeded him. Largely through Hitti's vision and fundraising abilities, the department was able to establish the country's first program in Near Eastern Studies, concentrating on the post–World War II modern Near East. The program began with the three major Islamic languages: Arabic, Turkish, and Persian. With language and literature study as the core, the program integrated courses in history, politics, and sociology. In 1951, the program was reorganized with separate interdisciplinary status, emphasizing the social sciences and administered by a committee of representatives from the departments of Economics, History, and Politics, along with Oriental Languages and Literatures.

The department of Oriental Languages and Literatures continued to grow from the mid-1950s through the 1960s, with an emphasis on Arabic and Islam, including modern history and contemporary affairs. Key appointments brought to Princeton specialists in Turkish and Persian fields, ancient Near Eastern history and West Semitic languages, and medieval Islam and modern Arab and North African studies. The department also made its first appointments in the study of Chinese and Japanese literature, language, and culture. Those fields of study developed rapidly, and in 1969 the department of Oriental Studies was divided into two departments, Near Eastern Studies and East Asian Studies.

In the early 1970s, the family of Cleveland and Bayard Dodge (both Class of 1909) endowed two chairs in Near Eastern studies in their honor. These chairs made it possible to add faculty of unusual distinction to the department. Bernard Lewis, the leading historian of the Near East in the English-speaking world, came to Princeton in 1974 from the University of London, with a joint appointment at the Institute for Advanced Study. In 1975, Charles Issawi, the most renowned economist and economic historian of the

Middle East, came to Princeton from Columbia University.

Over the years, the department continued to make exceptional appointments to its faculty. In 2020 Michael Cook was awarded the Middle East Medievalists Lifetime Achievement Award for his contributions to the fields of Islamic and Middle East studies, having previously won the Balzan Prize for Islamic Studies in 2019, the Holberg Prize in 2014, and, at Princeton, a Behrman Award for Distinguished Achievement in the Humanities in 2006 and a President's Award for Distinguished Teaching in 2016. In 2015 Marina Rustow was awarded a MacArthur Fellowship in recognition of her "extraordinary originality and dedication" in her study of the medieval Middle East.

From its earliest days, Princeton has contributed much to the national development of Near Eastern studies. Not only has it sent its graduate students out to teach and head up programs elsewhere, it also provided leadership in cooperative ventures such as the national Critical Languages Program, the Center for Arabic Study Abroad in Cairo, and the founding of the Middle East Studies Association.

Over the decades the department has maintained its traditional strength in medieval and pre-modern studies of the geographical area that includes the Arab lands, Iran, Israel, and Turkey, while it has also expanded its definition of the "Near East" to give greater emphasis to the modern Muslim world, including countries in South Asia (India, Pakistan, and Bangladesh), the Caucasus, and Central Asia.

The department's approach is multi-faceted, embracing a range of disciplinary approaches from the humanities and the social sciences. Students in the department gain solid grounding in the region's pre-modern and modern histories, societies, politics, languages, literatures, and religions through departmental courses as well as cognate courses in history, literature, religion, law, anthropology, politics, economics, and public policy.

The population in the heart of the region numbers more than 400 million, and millions more around the world use its languages, thanks to the influence of its religions and cultures on the wider world. The department offers instruction in four major languages: Arabic (including colloquial dialects such as Egyptian or Levantine), Hebrew, Persian (classical and modern), and Turkish (Ottoman and modern). Students in the department acquire competence in at least one of them.

While called "Near Eastern," these languages also open doors in Morocco, Azerbaijan, Tajikistan, or Xinjiang. The department encourages and helps to facilitate participation in intensive summer language programs in the United States and, when geo-political conditions allow, in countries where the languages are spoken.

The department remains the hub of the interdisciplinary program in Near Eastern Studies. Although most students in the program come from the departments of Anthropology, History, Politics, Religion, Sociology, or the school of Public and International Affairs, the program provides students in any department of the University an opportunity to study the region's languages, modern history, contemporary institutions, and challenges. In recent years, the department has offered global summer seminars in Istanbul, Turkey, and Baku, Azerbaijan.

NEW SOUTH was built in 1965 to provide office space for the expanding administration, and to release for faculty and student use some of the offices near the library that were being used by business departments of the University. Named New South as a counterpoint to Old North, as Nassau Hall was once called, it was a step toward developing more of the southern part of the campus; it was also a step toward moving administrative space away from the historic campus—a practice later extended by moving some administrative offices to locations in West Windsor Township.

Built of glass and concrete, New South was one of the University's first high-rise buildings, with two stories below ground as you approach from the north, and seven above. The building was originally open on the first floor except for its main entrance; a 1981 alteration filled in the first-floor space that had been left open in the original design. Long derided as one of the campus's least attractive buildings from the outside, it was renowned for the views of the campus and the countryside from the inside, and especially from its seventh floor.

In 1969 the building received national attention when members of the Association of Black Collegians occupied it for 11 hours to protest University investments in companies doing business in South Africa.

As a result of subsequent developments nearby, New South is now strategically located between Whitman College and the Lewis Arts complex. In 2010 the double-height first floor was renovated to accommodate dance and theater rehearsal studios, and the sixth floor was modified to provide offices and seminar rooms for creative writing. Originally built to free up other locations for academic uses, New South has now become the home of academic spaces itself.

NOBEL AND OTHER MAJOR PRIZES. Forty-six Nobel prizes have been awarded to Princeton graduates and members of the faculty and research staff, including 36 since 1970. Of those 36, 21 have been awarded since 2000. No other university can claim as many twenty-first century winners. Two of the Nobel laureates, Woodrow Wilson 1879 (Peace 1919) and James Peebles *62 (Physics 2019), were alumni and members of the faculty; another alumni laureate, John Nash Jr. *50, worked at the University as a senior research mathematician. John Bardeen *36 won the Physics Nobel twice (in 1956 and 1972). In 1993 Princetonians won three Nobels, two in Physics and one in Literature.*

Princeton faculty and alumni have also received other prestigious awards, including the National Humanities Medal, the National Medal of Science, the John Bates Clark Medal, the Abel Prize, the Fields Medal, the Nevanlinna Prize, and the Turing Award.

Guggenheim Fellowships, established in 1926, are awarded to individuals who have "demonstrated exceptional capacity for productive scholarship or exceptional creative ability in the arts." The fellowships further the development of the scholars and artists by assisting them in engaging in "research in any field of knowledge" and "creation in any of the arts." Faculty awarded Guggenheim Fellowships since 1970 are listed on pages 508–10.

Nobel Prizes

Princeton's Nobel Laureates are listed below; alumni are in *italics*.

Chemistry
1951: *Edwin McMillan *33*
1996: *Richard Smalley *74*
2008: Osamu Shimomura, research chemist
2015: Tomas Lindahl, research chemist
2018: *Frances Arnold '79*

Economics
1979: Sir Arthur Lewis, professor of political economy
1992: *Gary Becker '51*
1994: *John Nash Jr. *50*, research mathematician
2000: *James Heckman '68 *71*

---

* Princeton won five Nobels in 2021 (not included here): faculty members David MacMillan (Chemistry) and Syukuro Manabe (Physics), former faculty member David Card *83 (Economics), Joshua Angrist *89 (Economics), and Maria Ressa '86 (Peace).

2001: *A. Michael Spence '66*
2002: Daniel Kahneman, professor of psychology and public affairs
2007: Eric Maskin, visiting lecturer with rank of professor in economics
2008: Paul Krugman, professor of economics and international affairs
2011: Thomas Sargent, visiting professor of economics
2011: Christopher Sims, professor of economics
2012: *Lloyd Shapley *53*
2015: Sir Angus Deaton, professor of economics and international affairs
2016: *Oliver Hart *74*

Literature
1936: *Eugene O'Neill 1910*
1993: Toni Morrison, professor in the humanities
2010: Mario Vargas Llosa, visitor in Latin American studies and visiting lecturer in creative writing and at the Lewis Center

Peace
1919: *Woodrow Wilson 1879*, professor of jurisprudence and president emeritus

Physics
1927: *Arthur Compton *1916*
1928: Owen Richardson, professor of physics
1937: *Clinton Davisson *1911*
1956: *John Bardeen *36*
1961: *Robert Hofstadter *38*
1963: Eugene Wigner, professor of mathematical physics
1965: *Richard Feynman *42*
1972: *John Bardeen *36*
1977: Philip Anderson, professor of physics
1978: Arno Penzias, visiting lecturer with rank of professor
1979: *Steven Weinberg *57*
1980: Val Fitch, professor of physics
1980: James Cronin, professor of physics
1993: Russell Hulse, research physicist
1993: Joseph Taylor, professor of physics
1998: Daniel Tsui, professor of electrical engineering
2004: David Gross, professor of physics
2004: *Frank Wilczek *75*
2015: Arthur McDonald, professor of physics
2016: F. Duncan Haldane, professor of physics
2017: *Kip Thorne *65*
2019: *James Peebles *62*, professor of physics

Physiology or Medicine
1995: Eric Wieschaus, professor of molecular biology
2013: James Rothman, professor of molecular biology

National Humanities Medal

The National Humanities Medal, inaugurated in 1997, is sponsored by the National Endowment for the Humanities. It recognizes individuals or groups for work that has "deepened the nation's understanding of the humanities and broadened our citizens' engagement with history, literature, languages, philosophy, and other humanities subjects." The medals are conferred by the president of the United States.

Princeton faculty members and alumni who have received the medal are listed below, with alumni in *italics*.

1999: *Taylor Branch *70*
1999: *John Rawls '43 *50*
2000: Toni Morrison, professor in the humanities
2005: *Alan Kors '64*
2006: Robert Fagles, professor of comparative literature
2006: Bernard Lewis, professor of Near Eastern studies
2009: *Robert Caro '57*
2010: Stanley Katz, lecturer with the rank of professor in public and international affairs
2010: Joyce Carol Oates, professor in the humanities
2011: Kwame Anthony Appiah, professor of philosophy
2011: Robert Darnton, professor of history
2011: *Charles Rosen '48, *51*
2011: *Teofilo Ruiz *74*
2012: *William Bowen *58*, professor of economics and president emeritus
2012: Natalie Zemon Davis, professor of history
2012: *Frank Deford '61*
2014: *Rebecca Goldstein *77*
2014: Jhumpa Lahiri, professor of creative writing
2015: Elaine Pagels, professor of religion

National Medal of Science

The National Medal of Science was established in 1959. It is bestowed by the president of the United States on individuals in the sciences and engineering who have made important contributions to the advancement of knowledge in the fields of behavioral and social sciences, biology, chemistry, engineering, mathematics, and physics. It is administered by the National Science Foundation.

Princeton faculty members who have received the medal include:

1964: Solomon Lefschetz, professor of mathematics
1966: John Milnor '51 *54, professor of mathematics
1968: Eugene Wigner, professor of physics
1969: William Feller, professor of mathematics
1970: Robert Dicke '39, professor of physics
1970: John Wheeler, professor of physics
1973: John Tukey *39, professor of statistics
1976: Hassler Whitney, professor of mathematics
1979: Lyman Spitzer Jr. *38, professor of astrophysical sciences
1982: Philip Anderson, professor of physics
1989: Donald Spencer, professor of mathematics
1991: George Miller, professor of psychology
1993: Val Fitch, professor of physics
1993: Martin Kruskal, professor of physics and mathematics
1997: Martin Schwarzschild, professor of astrophysical sciences
1998: John Bahcall, visiting lecturer in astrophysical sciences
2000: Jeremiah Ostriker, professor of astrophysical sciences
2001: Elias Stein, professor of mathematics
2002: W. Jason Morgan *64, professor of geosciences
2008: James Gunn, professor of astrophysical sciences
2011: Anne Treisman, professor of psychology
2014: Simon Levin, professor of ecology and evolutionary biology

John Bates Clark Medal

The American Economic Association awards the John Bates Clark Medal to an American economist under the age of 40 who has "made the most significant contribution to economic thought and knowledge." Presented biennially from 1947 until 2009, it has subsequently been awarded annually.

Princeton faculty and alumni who have won the medal are listed below, with alumni who were not faculty members in *italics*. With the one noted exception, all faculty members were in the department of Economics.

1967: *Gary Becker '51*
1979: Joseph Stiglitz
1981: *A. Michael Spence '66*
1983: *James Heckman *71*
1987: Sanford Grossman
1991: Paul Krugman
1995: *David Card *83*
1999: Andrei Shleifer
2010: Esther Duflo (visiting scholar at the center for Health and Wellbeing)
2016: *Yuliy Sannikov '00*
2019: *Emi Nakamura '01*

Abel Prize

The Abel Prize, named after the Norwegian mathematician Niels Henrik Abel, is awarded by the Norwegian Academy of Science and Letters, and is recognized as the equivalent of a Nobel Prize for mathematics. It was first awarded in 2003.

Princeton faculty and alumni (in *italics*) who have won the prize include the following:

2010: *John Tate *50*
2011: *John Milnor '51 *54*
2014: Yakov Sinai, professor of mathematics
2015: *John Nash *50*
2016: Sir Andrew Wiles, professor of mathematics
2018: Robert Langlands, professor of mathematics
2019: Karen Uhlenbeck, visiting senior research scholar in mathematics
2020: *Hillel Furstenberg *58*
2021: Avi Wigderson *83

Fields Medal

The Fields Medal, named after Canadian mathematician John Charles Fields, is presented every four years to mathematicians under the age of 40 based on the influence of their existing work and their "promise of future achievement." The medal was first awarded in 1936 but was then suspended until 1950. Since then the medals have been awarded every four years.

Princeton faculty and alumni who have won the medal are listed below, with alumni who were not faculty members in *italics*.

1954: Kunihiko Kodaira
1962: John Milnor '51 *54
1978: Charles Fefferman *69
1982: William Thurston
1986: Gerd Faltings
1986: *Michael Freedman *73*
1990: Edward Whitten *76
1998: Curtis McMullen
2006: Andrei Okounkov
2006: *Terence Tao *96*
2010: Elon Lindenstrauss
2014: *Manjul Bhargava *01*
Maryam Mirzakhani (first woman to win the medal)
2018: *Akshay Venkatesh *02*

Nevanlinna Prize

The Rolf Nevanlinna Prize, named after a Finnish mathematician, was established in 1981 to recognize outstanding contributions to the mathematical aspects of information science. It is awarded every four years to a computer scientist under the age of 40.

Princeton faculty and alumni who have won the prize are listed below, with alumni who were not faculty members in *italics*.

1982: Robert Tarjan
1994: *Avi Wigderson *83*
2014: Subhash Khot *03

A. M. Turing Award

The Turing Award is named for Alan M. Turing *38, who is widely recognized as the father of computer science. It was established in 1966 and is considered to be the equivalent of the Nobel Prize for computer science.

Princeton faculty and alumni (in *italics*) who have won the prize are listed below.

1969: *Marvin Minsky *54*
1971: *John McCarthy *51*
1976: *Michael Rabin *57*
1976: *Dana Scott *58*
1986: Robert Tarjan
1993: *Richard Sterns *61*
2000: Andrew Yao
2004: *Robert Kahn *64*
2014: *Michael Stonebreaker '65*
2021: Alfred Aho *67
Jeffrey Ullman *66

NUDE OLYMPICS. The nude olympics were a campus phenomenon of the last quarter of the twentieth century that attracted national attention. They came to an end following trustee action in April 1999 to ban them because of the serious risks they had come to pose for students' health, safety, and well-being.

There are differing recollections about when and how the nude olympics began. In her senior thesis titled "Barely Remembered: A History of Princeton University Prank Traditions," Elizabeth Greenberg '02 recalls "one of the most legendary characters in Princeton's history," the so-called Red Baron, who, beginning in the mid-1960s, "would show up at several large final exams dressed only in red accessories (such as a World War I fliers hat, ski mask, goggles, cape, socks, and tennis shoes), thrilling the otherwise captive and stressed audiences . . . The Red Baron even occasionally shocked prospective students and tourists by running past an Orange Key tour."

In that same era, the rugby team staged an annual "jock run" with members wearing "either jockstraps or nothing at all." In 1966, Cannon Club members and their dates staged a nude volleyball game. As early as 1968–69, nude or semi-nude athletic contests and events took place in Holder Courtyard, fueled by alcohol, and catalyzed by the year's first snowfall. Following a surprise snowstorm on December 14, 1970, a naked student skied around the courtyard and others joined in nude relays, and the *Daily Princetonian* reported that more than 250 students "led by half-naked pranksters" romped across campus between 1 and 3 in the morning.

While these early events in Holder where "permissible attire was limited to scarves, hats, and ski masks" received minimal off-campus attention, "streaking" on campus became national news. On February 3, 1974, Charles Bell '76, later nicknamed "the Streak," ran naked through the student center and then ran for student government president on a platform of "if elected, I'll run." He lost the election but gained a *New York Times* headline: "The Streak Strikes Out in Race for Princeton Student President."

Streaking spread to other campuses and quickly developed into a competition. On the evening of March 9, 1974, with the Princeton band playing "Old Nassau," 75 streakers left Cuyler courtyard and ran to Holder and Nassau Hall; through Firestone Library, McCosh 10, the Chancellor Green pub, and Whig Hall; and then to Dillon pool which was crowded with spectators at a swim meet that was being taped for television. They returned to Cuyler and claimed an Ivy League record of 112,500 "nude person yards," more than 60,000 more than the previous record held by Yale.

While streaking turned out to be a fad, the nude olympics became a tradition. By 1974 it was well-established that they would begin in Holder courtyard on the evening of the first snowfall, and by the early 1980s the start time was set at or around midnight. Events included jogging, calisthenics, snowball throwing, pushups, jumping jacks, wheelbarrow races, and crew racing in imaginary boats. Most of the participants were sophomores. By 1981, the event had become an entry in the *Prince* dictionary: "Nude Olympics, n. An annual festival held in Holder courtyard the night of the first snowfall of the school year." By the late 1980s women began to participate in increasing numbers; in 1990–91, 60 of the 200 participants were women.

With the passage of time, the number of participants increased: by the mid-1980s, it had grown from a few dozen students to over a hundred. By 1987 it had become a spectator sport: that year there were not only 125 participants, but 500 spectators. In 1992 there were more than 400 participants and 1,000 spectators, and when more than 150 naked students crowded into J. B. Winberie's, a local restaurant, a $1,500 stained glass window was broken. When 31 students were arrested and charged with lewdness and disorderly conduct, the incident received national attention in the *Philadelphia Inquirer*, the *New York Times*, and the *Miami Herald*. (The previous year the nude olympics had been the subject of a nationally syndicated Ann Landers column.)

As the local and regional press became aware that the event occurred each year at the first snowfall, they sent reporters and cameras to the campus in anticipation, while spectators filmed the event hoping to make sales to media outlets. (In 1992 the tabloid television show *Hard Copy* solicited amateur footage through ads in the *Prince*.) Students who in the past could count on some degree of anonymity by running in packs with other students found that anonymity disappeared when they ended up in newspaper photos and television coverage.

While alcohol had always played a role in reducing inhibitions, as the olympics grew in scope and visibility heavy drinking became the norm, and there were increasing reports of students being sexually assaulted and harassed. After a snowless winter in 1998, there was greater than usual anticipation when snow fell on January 9, 1999. In that year's olympics, six students were taken to the hospital with alcohol poisoning and one with head lacerations; four other students were taken to McCosh infirmary. There were multiple reports of serious sexual misconduct. There also was extensive building damage and members of the staff were assaulted when they tried to intervene.

Two days later, President Harold Shapiro submitted a letter to the *Prince* announcing a thorough review of the olympics by a committee of students, faculty, and staff, to be chaired by dean of student life Janina Montero. In March, the committee recommended banning the nude olympics and comparable activities and imposing a penalty of suspension for at least one year for any student who failed to respect the prohibition.

In their statement endorsing the committee's recommendations, the trustees said they understood that there were students and alumni "who value what they have found to be positive aspects of the 'nude olympics,'" but that it was "not possible to reduce the risks of serious injury or death or of sexual abuse and assault to an acceptable level."

While some lamented the passing of the tradition, others welcomed it, or at least acknowledged that the time had come to bring it to an end. In her thesis, Greenberg says her research found that "many students . . . were relieved to be rid of the . . . pressures of deciding whether to run and whether to drink before doing so," and suggests that "the relative lack of protest over its termination demonstrates the degree of student discomfort with the ritual."

OATES, WHITNEY JENNINGS 1925 *1931, successively Ewing Professor of Greek, West Professor of Classics, and Avalon Professor of the Humanities, was a prime mover in the founding and development of a number of important University programs. Mike, as he was known to his colleagues and students, first came to Princeton from Evanston Township High School in Illinois. He graduated *summa cum laude* in classics, and then earned his master's degree in 1927 and his PhD in 1931. As student and teacher, he was associated with Princeton for 49 years.

Chair of the Classics department for 16 years, Oates published extensively in his special fields of interest, Greek drama and philosophy, and played a leading role in the teaching of the classics in translation. He was frequently voted a favorite preceptor and lecturer in senior class polls.

In the 1930s he was a principal organizer, and from 1945 to 1959 was chair, of the Special Program in the Humanities, an interdisciplinary plan of study that exerted lasting influence on the form and spirit of education at Princeton.

During World War II, Oates served with the Marines in the southwest Pacific. Soon after he came back to Princeton in 1945, he conceived and found the money for a plan to attract returning veterans into college teaching; under his guidance this project eventually became the National Woodrow Wilson Fellowship Program.

In 1953 he was largely responsible for the establishment of the Council of the Humanities as a means of fostering significant teaching and research throughout these fields, and he was its chair until his retirement from the faculty in 1970.

Outside of Princeton, he showed similar leadership as a founding member of the National Commission on the Humanities, whose 1963 report did much to secure the establishment by Congress of the National Foundation for the Arts and the Humanities.

OBAMA, MICHELLE LAVAUGHN ROBINSON '85 arrived in Princeton in the late summer of 1981 from the south side of Chicago to participate in a three-week summer orientation program prior to beginning her freshman year. She was following in the footsteps of her brother Craig '83, a star player on the basketball team, who had arrived two years earlier and was living that year as a caretaker in an upstairs bedroom at the Third World Center. (Craig Robinson, a two-time Ivy League basketball player of the year, was elected a Princeton trustee in 2018.)

In her book *Becoming,* Obama writes that the Third World Center (TWC) became a kind of "home base" for her, and that she "was happy with the community of Black and Latino students I'd found through the TWC." Being the only Black person in a lecture or one of the few nonwhite people trying out for a play or joining an intramural team, Obama wrote, required exceptional effort and an "an extra level of confidence, to speak in those settings and own your presence in the room." This was why, she said, "when my friends and I found one another at dinner each night, it was with some degree of relief."

During her freshman year, Obama had two white roommates in a one-room triple in Pyne Hall. Midway through the year, one of them moved out into a single room. In her book she says that at the time she had no idea why, but during her husband's 2008 presidential campaign her former roommate revealed that her mother, "a schoolteacher from New Orleans, had been so appalled that her daughter had been assigned a Black roommate that she'd badgered the university to separate us."

For her work-study job Obama was hired as an assistant to the director of the TWC; she later became a member of its governing board and founded and ran its after-school program, which provided tutoring and child care for elementary school-age students. She majored in sociology (and later became a member of the department's advisory council); wrote a thesis on "Princeton Educated Blacks and the Black Community" that earned an award from what was then the program in African American Studies; graduated with honors; and after graduation headed to Harvard Law School.

When her thesis began to attract partisan political attention during the 2008 presidential campaign, she told the *Princeton Alumni Weekly* that "one of the points I was making, which is a reality for Black folks in majority-white environments, is [that] it is a very isolating experience—period. The question is, how do people deal with that isolation? Does it make you cling more to your own community or does it make you try to assimilate more?"

After law school, Obama joined the Chicago-based law firm of Sidley Austin and met and mentored another young lawyer named Barack Obama. She left the firm to become assistant commissioner of planning and development for the city of Chicago and then founding executive director of the Chicago chapter of Public Allies, an AmeriCorps program that prepares young people for public service. She worked for the University of Chicago, developing its first community service program as associate dean of student services, and later became vice president of community and external affairs for the University of Chicago Medical Center.

In 1992 she married Barack Obama and they had two daughters, Malia and Sasha. She campaigned actively for him during his presidential campaigns, and upon his inauguration in January 2009 became the country's first African American first lady. During their eight years in the White House, she championed issues ranging from equal pay for women and helping military families, to increasing awareness about poverty; fighting obesity by promoting health, physical activity, and nutrition; empowering young women around the world; and encouraging students to continue their educations.

In his address at Princeton's virtual 2020 Commencement, Nicholas Johnson '20, the University's first Black valedictorian, quoted the following sentence from Obama's book: "It was possible, I knew, to live on two planets at once, to have one's feet planted in reality but pointed in the direction of progress."

In a video message to the October 2019 Black alumni conference titled "Thrive: Empowering and Celebrating Princeton's Black Alumni," Obama said, "if there's one thing I've learned since I left Princeton, it's this: No matter what direction you're headed, nobody gets there alone. We all need to help each other to sharpen our skills and soften our landings or jump-start a change for the better. That's how we can not only make progress for ourselves, but continue along the journey of discovering who we are, and that, to me, is what it means to thrive."

"OLD NASSAU" has been Princeton's anthem since 1859. Its words were written that year by a freshman, Harlan Page Peck 1862, who sent them to the *Nassau Literary Magazine* and won its prize for best college song. The magazine published the song in its March issue. When an effort to sing it to the tune of "Auld Lang Syne" proved unsuccessful, Karl Langlotz, who taught German, coached fencing, and directed a choral group, was persuaded to write music for it. Langlotz had studied with Franz Liszt and had once played violin in an orchestra conducted by Richard Wagner. He wrote the music for "Old Nassau" on the porch of his house at 160 Mercer Street, where a plaque commemorates his composition. The piano Langlotz used is now in Prospect House and his violin is in the University's archives.

The words and music appeared together for the first time in *Songs of Old Nassau*, published in April 1859. A few days after this collection appeared, a group of students gathered in the evening near the Bulletin Elm at the northeast corner of Nassau Hall to try some of the songs. When the group finished their singing of "Old Nassau," the listeners responded with an enthusiastic "skyrocket" cheer.

There have been changes in the words over the years. The opening line, originally "Tune every *harp* and every voice," became "Tune every *heart* and every voice" early in the 1890s. Peck wrote seven verses, but three dropped out of use by 1914.

In 1987, almost 20 years after women first arrived as undergraduates, Janet Sarbanes '89, daughter of US Senator Paul Sarbanes '54, led a successful effort, endorsed by the Undergraduate Student Government and the executive committee of the Alumni Council and formally approved by the Board of Trustees, to make the words of the song gender neutral by changing *my boys* to *we sing* in the third line of the chorus, and *Her sons will give while they shall live*, to *Our hearts will give while we shall live* in the final line.

The song's phrase "with one accord" was the theme of the 250th Anniversary Campaign for Princeton that ended in 2000 after having raised $1.14 billion.

While the song has four verses, typically only the first is sung, along with the chorus, which is accompanied by a "from the heart" salute that can sometimes be disconcerting to first-time observers. The first verse of the song and the chorus follow:

Tune every heart and every voice,
Bid every care withdraw;
Let all with one accord rejoice,
In praise of Old Nassau.

In praise of Old Nassau, we sing
Hurrah! Hurrah! Hurrah
Our hearts will give while we shall live,
Three cheers for Old Nassau.

The words of the other three verses are as follows:

Let music rule the fleeting hour,
Her mantle round us draw;
And thrill each heart with all her power,
In praise of Old Nassau.

And when these walls in dust are laid,
With reverence and awe,
Another throng shall breathe our song,
In praise of Old Nassau.

Till then with joy our songs we'll bring,
And while a breath we draw,
We'll all unite to shout and sing,
Long life to Old Nassau.

OLYMPIANS. Princeton played a leading role in the 1896 revival of the ancient Olympic games in Athens, Greece. Professor William Sloane, a professor of Latin and then history at Princeton, was a member of the International Olympics Committee that organized the games (he served from 1894 to 1924 and also founded and served as first chair of the American Olympic Committee), and Robert Garrett 1897 organized and personally financed an expedition to Athens for himself and three classmates to compete in the games.

Garrett stood out among all the competitors, winning two first places (discus, shot put) and two seconds (high jump, long jump). His classmates Herbert Jamison, Albert Tyler, and Francis Lane, among them won two silvers and a bronze. At the 1900 Olympics in Paris, Garrett added bronzes in the shot put and standing triple jump.

The University's archives include the laurel branch presented to Tyler at the 1896 Olympics and the discus that Garret threw in an event in which he had never competed before.

In the summer and winter Olympics from 1896 through 2021, a total of 130 Princetonians have participated a total of 184 times and have won 20 gold, 24 silver, and 27 bronze medals. Only one Princetonian has won three golds: Karl Frederick 1903 in 1920, for 50-meter individual pistol shooting, and both 30-meter and 50-meter team shooting. Five alumni, including Garrett, have won two golds, including, most recently, women's water polo goalie Ashleigh Johnson '17 in 2016 and 2021.

A list of Princeton Olympians appears on pages 520–22.

OPERATIONS RESEARCH AND FINANCIAL ENGINEERING, THE DEPARTMENT OF. In 1986, Princeton's department of Civil Engineering added Operations Research to its name in recognition of the increasing role in engineering of financial analysis and statistics. In 1999 the University created a new department, Operations Research and Financial Engineering (ORFE), and the Civil Engineering department became the department of Civil and Environmental Engineering.

Princeton was the first major university to appreciate the importance of ORFE and create a department devoted to its study and teaching. Combining expertise in probability, statistics, optimization, and finance, the department uses mathematical and computational tools to solve problems associated with uncertainty and risk—classic problems that extend into many different applications. It has faculty who are experts in "big data" analysis, machine learning, and financial technology.

ORFE is an outgrowth of groundbreaking scholarly work at Princeton between 1930 and 1960. Princeton faculty made major contributions to the development of the theory of convex optimization, as it relates to both individuals and groups. Harold Kuhn *50 and Albert Tucker in the 1950s, as well as Tyrrell Rockafellar in the following decade, played important roles in the development of much of convex analysis.

John Nash Jr. *50 (the mathematician on whom the movie *A Beautiful Mind* is based), John von Neumann, and Oskar Morgenstern did seminal work in multi-agent, non-cooperative optimization (game theory).

Modern probability and statistics have also been significantly influenced by members of the Princeton faculty. Samuel Wilks in the 1930s and William Feller and John Tukey *39 in the 1950s played major roles, and Gilbert Hunt developed the potential theory of Markov processes in the early 1960s. The use of digital computers in operations research owes much to von Neumann, Alan Turing *38, and Alonzo Church 1924 *1927, who made enormous contributions in such areas as the theory of cellular automata, computer memory, and computer reliability.

Erhan Cinlar was ORFE's founding chair from 1999 to 2005. While the department began small, with seven faculty and approximately 30 undergraduates, it quickly became one of the University's most popular undergraduate majors.

Robert Vanderbei, an expert in optimization techniques, was chair from 2005 to 2012. He oversaw further growth and expansion, along with the construction of a new building to house the department. In 2008 ORFE moved into Sherrerd Hall, a three-story, 45,000-square-foot building along the southeast end of Shapiro Walk, near the other engineering departments and the Bendheim Center for Finance, with which it shares scholarly interests.

Jianqing Fan, chair from 2012 to 2015, played a role in recruiting younger faculty, especially experts in optimization and machine learning, which was fast becoming a major field of study. At the same time, the University created a center for Statistics and Machine Learning, of which Fan became an executive committee member. Today, ORFE faculty continue to be an integral part of the center's executive committee and participating faculty.

In addition to this center and the Bendheim center, ORFE faculty are also affiliated with the program in Applied and Computational Mathematics, the Andlinger Center for Energy and the Environment, and the High Meadows Environmental Institute.

Rene Carmona served as chair from 2015 to 2018. He is recognized as a leading expert in applied mathematics, and in probability and its applications. During his tenure, he undertook a program of hiring senior faculty, including Matias Cattaneo, who has worked in the areas of applied economics, machine learning, empirical finance, and decision theory, and Mete Soner, a mathematician who has made significant contributions to stochastic control, financial mathematics, and mathematical economics.

Ronnie Sircar, an expert in financial mathematics and engineering, became chair in 2018 of a department that had 17 faculty, 62 PhD candidates, and 217 undergraduate majors.

During Sircar's tenure, the department made a significant commitment to hiring a diverse faculty. The department had two Black professors and one Hispanic professor along with faculty from Argentina, Hungary, Turkey, Ukraine, Germany, China, and Italy. One member of its faculty, William Massey '77, came to the department in 2001 from Bell Labs as the first African American Princeton undergraduate to become a full professor at the University and the first Black mathematician to receive tenure at any Ivy League university. In 2020 ORFE major Nicholas Johnson '20 was Princeton's first Black valedictorian.

The department's research and teaching focus on the foundations of data science, probabilistic modeling, and optimal decision-making under uncertainty, with applications in communications, economics and finance, energy and the environment, healthcare management, physical and biological sciences, social networks, and transportation. The core graduate and undergraduate programs provide strong technical grounding in statistics, stochastics, and optimization.

Expertise in these areas has produced important breakthroughs; for example, insights into large-scale optimization and high-dimensional random structures play a crucial role in the statistical analysis of massive datasets in areas as diverse as the human genome and financial data, and ideas from statistics and machine learning are central to the development of new algorithms for making online decisions and for other complex optimization problems with applications ranging from clinical trials to internet advertising.

Since its inception, ORFE has undertaken several significant collaborations with private industry and government. One of the first was a joint venture between ORFE and SAP, a German software company. More recently, the department has been collaborating with the US Department of Energy on a risk-management assessment of the national electric grid. Other recent collaborations include a multidisciplinary University Research Initiative award from the US Department of Defense for a project on verifiable, control-oriented learning directed by faculty from ORFE, Mathematics, and Mechanical and Aerospace Engineering.

ORFE's courses appeal to students from many other departments, and graduate students from other departments routinely take ORFE's courses in probability and statistics. ORFE students acquire the quantitative skills, including mathematical modeling, required to solve complex problems. Sircar sums up the department's broad-based appeal by stating, "Our students, both undergraduates and graduate students, learn fundamental skills in probability, statistics, and optimization, including computational implementation and utilization of data. These are taught without focus on any specific application, but with many applications as examples. As such, our students are able to apply these fundamental tools to a wide variety of applications, informed by their broad exposure and depth of understanding."

Orange Key Guide Service was organized in 1935 on the model of Dartmouth's Green Key Society, which won the admiration of President Harold Dodds when he visited Hanover to speak at a conference. Due at midnight, he missed a train connection and, arriving at two in the morning, was surprised and pleased to find a Green Key undergraduate waiting for him with a car, a thermos of hot coffee, and a friendly greeting.

Originally the Orange Key's primary mission was to welcome visitors to the University and shepherd athletic teams from other colleges around Princeton. Gradually it assumed other functions: the campus guide service, the Red Cross blood drive, the sponsorship of student-faculty get-togethers, the organization of dances and other social events, and a Freshman Keycept program that was a forerunner of the residential adviser program in the residential colleges. The name of the Keycept program evoked the small-group "precept" discussions that were an integral part of the University's teaching program; the purpose of the keycepts was to introduce entering students to life at Princeton through periodic meetings in small groups with "keyceptors" from the junior class.

In the summer of 1939, President Dodds anticipated a busy tourist season in Princeton with the opening of the New York World's Fair, so he hired three students who escorted some 2,700 campus visitors. In 1953, Orange Key began offering campus tours year round, and in the 1960s it began compiling its extensive "Guide for Guides," a training manual filled with facts, figures, and other background information that the guides are expected to master. In 1962 Orange Key made a film, "An Undergraduate View of Princeton University," which was staged as an instructional meeting for Orange Key guides in the Faculty Room of Nassau Hall.

By the 1970s, with the number of applicants for admission and, consequently, the number of campus visitors growing dramatically, Orange Key became primarily a campus guide service, offering tours of the campus throughout the academic year and over the summer. It gained a part-time administrator based in the communications office, and then became part of the Frist Campus Center when it opened in 2000.

In 2006, administrative responsibility for the service was transferred to the admission office, in recognition of the fact that the majority of tours include prospective students and their families. The organization remained student-run, with students responsible for selecting, training, and supervising the guides.

The guides worked on a volunteer basis, except for those hired to work in the summer and during fall and spring breaks, until 2011 when the admission office began paying all the guides. According to then-Orange Key chair Sarah Van Cleve '12, "I thought a paid model would help improve tour attendance and quality." Paying the guides also made it possible to diversify the roster of guides by allowing students to participate who otherwise might need to work for pay at campus jobs.

Several years before the pandemic of 2020 forced the cancellation of on-site campus tours, Orange Key developed a 23-stop virtual tour of the campus led by undergraduates. The virtual tour was designed for potential applicants who are not able to visit in person, and was made available in four languages: Chinese, English, Korean, and Spanish.

Orchestra, The University, can lay claim to rudimentary antecedents as far back as June 1791, when a number of student musicians, seated in the belfry of Nassau Hall above the glow of 600 candles illuminating its facade, entertained the crowd that had gathered to celebrate President John Witherspoon's second marriage with, the *United States Gazette* reported, "a most agreeable and delightful concert from different kinds of instruments."

Almost a century later, a small "Instrumental Club" occasionally appeared in concerts with the newly formed Glee Club. Among its early members was flutist Henry Fine 1882, later dean of the faculty and of the departments of science. There were also banjo and mandolin clubs that played and traveled with the Glee Club.

In 1891 the name "Princeton University Orchestra" appeared for the first time in the *New York Times*. To this day the orchestra recognizes its founding date as February 13, 1896, when a group of students performed in Alexander Hall with professional musicians from New York.

Initially the orchestra was small and largely student-led, but after World War I it acquired professional leadership when Richard Weaver was named its first director. Since 1935, the music faculty has been responsible for naming the director.

The modern history of the orchestra dates from 1977 when Michael Pratt was brought to Princeton as conductor by his predecessor, mentor, and music department professor and chair, Peter Westergaard *56. When Pratt arrived, student interest in the orchestra was relatively low—there were only about 50 members at the time—and its rehearsal and performance spaces on campus were barely adequate. In 1984 the interior of the orchestra's home, Alexander Hall, was renovated into a first-rate concert hall and renamed Richardson Auditorium, and student interest in music performance began to increase dramatically, as did overall campus interest in the arts.

In 1991 Pratt was the founding director of the Music department's certificate program in music performance. He helped create a partnership with one of the world's leading conservatories, the Royal College of Music in London, which, beginning in 2009, permitted qualified Princeton students to spend the fall semester of their junior year at the college; the students can return to the college after graduation to complete performance-oriented master's degrees. Pratt also co-founded the Richardson Chamber Players, an ensemble that provides opportunities for exceptionally talented students to perform alongside members of the faculty and guest artists.

In 2017 the orchestra moved its rehearsals into the new 3,500-square-foot Lee rehearsal room in the Effron music building that is part of the University's Lewis Arts complex. The rehearsal room is acoustically isolated, and the building also features sound-isolated practice rooms and rehearsal studios.

Today the orchestra has more than 110 students, including graduate students as well as undergraduates. Its repertoire includes a remarkable variety of orchestral and operatic works, from early Baroque Italian operas through symphonies of Mahler to the latest compositions by students and faculty. The orchestra collaborates with other theater and dance programs on campus, and every other year it performs in Europe. There is also a second student orchestra, the Princeton University Sinfonia, which features a less-demanding rehearsal and concert schedule.

Pratt is credited with being the architect of one of the finest university orchestras and music performance programs in the country. He says if students have "an ability on an instrument, you want to allow them to give voice to that experience and play this great music every bit as much as you want them to read the works of Shakespeare. It's a part of what forms our human soul."

PACE CENTER FOR CIVIC ENGAGEMENT. At the Charter Day ceremony in 1996 celebrating its 250th anniversary, the University announced plans to expand and bring together campus community service activities through what would become the John H. Pace Jr. '39 Center for Civic Engagement. The anniversary planning committee chair, economics professor Burton Malkiel *64, said the center would "show that community service is not simply a useful add-on, a discretionary extracurricular activity, but rather an essential part of a liberal education. Experiences in service to communities will not then be peripheral to the academy but rather directly connected to learning and to the full possibilities and promises of education."

The Pace Center for Community Service opened in the Frist Campus Center in 2001 and was renamed four years later. It aims to make service and civic engagement central elements of the Princeton experience for undergraduates and graduate students, building on a tradition of volunteerism and service that is articulated in the University's informal motto, "in the nation's service and the service of humanity."

In 2007 two long-established programs, Community House and the Student Volunteers Council, joined the center. Community House began in 1969 as a student-initiated program at 164 Witherspoon Street in downtown Princeton where undergraduates worked with underrepresented area youth and their families to help close the achievement gap in the community. The program moved on campus in 1982 and into the Third World Center in 1995. In 2007 it became part of the Pace Center, and in 2009 it moved into specially designed space in the new Carl A. Fields Center for Equality and Cultural Understanding. Community House continues to engage with community families to support students in preschool through high school.

The roots of the Student Volunteers Council (SVC) date back to the establishment of the Philadelphian Society in 1825. Long associated with the dean of the chapel and the office of religious life, the SVC adopted its current organizational structure in 1967 and joined the Pace Center in 2007. The SVC sponsors volunteering opportunities in fields ranging from health, education, and mentorship to the arts, special needs, and hunger and homelessness.

In 1987 students established a Community Action program to give first-year students an opportunity during orientation to participate in small group community service experiences, much as Outdoor Action had been offering small-group outdoor adventures since 1974. In 2016 both programs were integrated into a comprehensive orientation program for all entering undergraduates, with Community Action continuing to focus on community building, fostering connections with community organizations, and challenging new students to think about the role service will play in their lives at and after Princeton.

In 2008 undergraduates created a Breakout Princeton program to offer off-campus service-learning trips during fall and spring break and established the Pace Council for Civic Values as a corps of service ambassadors on campus.

The Pace Center leads Service Focus, a program the University launched in 2018 to bridge service and learning across the first two undergraduate years. Students participate from the spring of their first year to the spring of their sophomore year. The program includes a summer service internship following the first year, a service-related course in the second year, faculty mentorship, and a peer group with which the students can reflect on their experiences and engage with community partners.

The center offers a range of summer internship and fellowship programs, including the Guggenheim Internships in Criminal Justice, which provide opportunities to intern with criminal justice nonprofit organizations; the John C. Bogle '51 Fellows in Civic Service, which offer first-year students an opportunity to design their own summer service internship experience; Projects for Peace, which enables undergraduates to design grassroots summer projects that promote peace and address the root causes of conflict; and the High Meadows Fellowship Program, which offers graduating seniors opportunities to work with nonprofit environmental organizations.

In the summer of 2020, the center added Princeton Internships in Civic Service (PICS), which was founded in 1996 by the Class of 1969 as an independent nonprofit organization and which over its history had already provided more than 1,500 undergraduates with internships and alumni mentoring.

In 2019 the Pace Center joined with the Music department and the Lewis Center for the Arts to form Trenton Arts at Princeton, an arts outreach program for the greater Trenton area. During the COVID-19 pandemic in 2020 the center collaborated with campus dining and the office of community and regional affairs to create a summer food and nutrition program that provided meals for people in neighboring communities, and it established an online tutoring network with the department of Computer Science to provide academic assistance to K-12 students.

In response to calls on campus and nationally for racial justice, in 2020 Pace launched an anti-racist grant initiative called Princeton RISE (Recognizing Inequalities and Standing for Equality), through which Princeton RISE fellows had opportunities to work with a broad range of organizations to advocate for racial justice and learn about societal inequities in areas such as health, criminal justice, and education.

PALMER HALL, originally Palmer Physical Laboratory, was given by and named for Stephen S. Palmer, a trustee of the University from 1908 to 1913. At its dedication in 1909 Palmer said he had made this gift in recognition of the "absolute necessity of extending Princeton's usefulness in the field of science and of placing her in a position where she can respond to the demands that will be made upon her."

Initially the building housed both Physics and Electrical Engineering. Its three floors provided a total area of about two acres, and when it opened it was considered the best university physical laboratory in the world. It provided space for both instruction and research, and possessed many specialized features such as machine shops, darkrooms, a liquid air plant, constant temperature capability, advanced pressure systems, and a large Foucault pendulum to demonstrate the rotation of the earth.

During World War II the atom-smashing cyclotron in its basement was partially dismantled so its power unit could be moved to Los Alamos in connection with the Manhattan Project, a government-sponsored research program that produced the first atomic bombs. Rebuilt after the war, the cyclotron was nearly destroyed by fire in 1950 but was repaired and used for another two decades.

In 1962 Electrical Engineering moved into the new Engineering Quadrangle. By 1969 the Physics department had seriously outgrown Palmer. It moved into a facility three times larger, the newly constructed Jadwin Hall, although some classrooms for underclass instruction in physics remained in the east side of Palmer, while the western portion was given over to East Asian Studies and the program in the History and Philosophy of Science. The building was officially renamed Palmer Hall in 1970. In 1998, McDonnell Hall was constructed next to Jadwin to accommodate physics classrooms, and over the next two years Palmer was closed for the renovation and expansion necessary to convert it into the Frist Campus Center, which opened in September 2000.

Statues of Benjamin Franklin and Joseph Henry, by Daniel Chester French, flank the front entrance of the building, and high up on the rear wall of the west wing—as a reminder that Palmer was built during the presidency of Theodore Roosevelt—is a mustached figure in pince-nez glasses energetically shaking a big stick.

Palmer House, named for charter trustee Edgar Palmer 1903, was bequeathed to the University by his widow, Zilph Palmer, in 1968 on condition that it be used exclusively for "college purposes" for at least 25 years. Mrs. Palmer also left $250,000 for the development of the house and grounds and a $200,000 trust fund to provide for maintenance. Since its acquisition, Palmer House has been used to provide accommodations for trustees and guests of the University, and as a venue for University meetings and events.

Situated at the northeast corner of Bayard Lane and Nassau Street, it was designed and built circa 1823–24 by Charles Steadman for the daughter of John Potter, a wealthy merchant of Charleston, South Carolina, who in 1824 purchased Prospect farm just south of the then-existing Princeton campus. Potter's daughter, Maria, was married to the naval hero, Commodore Robert F. Stockton 1813. In 1840, Stockton sold the house to his brother-in-law, James Potter.

The Potter family subsequently sold the house to the Garretts of Baltimore. While three Garrett sons, two in the Class of 1895 and one in the Class of 1897, were students at Princeton, their mother, Alice, lived in the house, and it was renowned as a center of hospitality for students.

In 1923 the house became the home of Edgar Palmer, a charter trustee from 1936 to 1949, who gave Palmer Stadium in memory of his father, Stephen S. Palmer, also a trustee and the donor of Palmer Physical Laboratory. The Palmer family owned the house until 1968 when Zilph Palmer bequeathed it to the University.

The house contains nine guest rooms and several meeting, dining, and event spaces, including a south-facing solarium/breakfast room. An innkeeper resides on the property.

Paterson, William 1763, one of the principal founders of the governments of New Jersey and the United States, was brought up in the village of Princeton, where his father, an immigrant tinsmith and shopkeeper, settled when William was five years old. As a boy of 10 he watched the local mason, William Worth, erect Nassau Hall, and when he was 14 he went there to live as a student in the College.

For four years he followed the classical curriculum of that day, excelling in the monthly orations then required of every student, and he graduated near the top of his class. While reading law with Richard Stockton 1748, the leading attorney in Princeton, he kept in touch with the College and helped found the Well-Meaning Club, forerunner of the Cliosophic Society. At Commencement in 1766 he received a Master of Arts degree and delivered an eloquent and widely admired oration on "Patriotism."

In 1769, shortly after he had begun the practice of law (supplementing his meagre income by keeping a general store), he wrote a college friend that "to live at ease and pass through life without much noise and bustle" was all he wished for. Six years later, however, when he was 30, he embarked on one of the most active public careers of his generation, serving successively as secretary of the New Jersey Provincial Congress, member of the convention that drafted the state constitution, first attorney general of New Jersey, head of the New Jersey delegation to the federal Constitutional Convention, one of the first two United States senators from New Jersey, governor of New Jersey, and finally, for the last 13 years of his life, associate justice of the United States Supreme Court. From 1787 to 1802, he was also a trustee of the College.

At the federal Constitutional Convention, Paterson offered the New Jersey "small states" plan in opposition to the Virginia "large states" plan drafted by James Madison 1771, but then accepted the Connecticut compromise supported by Oliver Ellsworth 1766, which was adopted.

While senator, Paterson helped Ellsworth draft the Judiciary Act of 1789. While governor, he undertook the codification of all existing New Jersey laws—the English statutes which by state constitution remained in force, as well as acts adopted by the legislature since the Revolution. He continued this monumental task after his elevation to the Supreme Court, and the results of his labors, the first published Laws of the State of New Jersey, appeared in 1800.

Patton, Francis Landey, 12th president of Princeton, was born in Warwick, Bermuda, in 1843. His early schooling was at Warwick Academy; later he attended Knox College of the University of Toronto and studied for two years at Princeton Theological Seminary. After ordination in June 1865, he held pastorates in New York City; Nyack, New York; Brooklyn, New York; and Chicago. His teaching career began in 1872 with his appointment to the faculty of the Presbyterian Theological Seminary of the Northwest (now McCormick Seminary).

As part of his faculty duties, Patton was expected to defend conservative Presbyterianism against new liberal currents of thought that had all but taken over the Chicago presbytery. He plunged into the task with zeal, as editor of the *Interior*, a Presbyterian weekly, and as professor and public speaker. The culmination of his crusade came in April 1874 with a much-publicized heresy trial of the Rev. David Swing, whom Patton charged with serious departures from the faith. Patton lost the case before the presbytery but gained a reputation as an eloquent champion of orthodoxy, leading to his election as moderator of the general assembly in 1878.

Three years later, Princeton Theological Seminary appointed him to a new chair in the relations of philosophy and science to the Christian religion, which had been endowed especially for him.

Patton arrived in Princeton in the spring of 1881. His reputation as a teacher and theologian grew rapidly, and his services as an after-dinner speaker were much in demand. Even those who disagreed with his orthodox beliefs admired his platform performances, embellished as they were with literary allusions and laced with incisive wit. In 1884 he ventured beyond his seminary teaching to offer a course at Princeton College in ethics and the philosophy of religion.

In 1888 he was elected by the trustees of the College to succeed the much-revered James McCosh as president, but his election did not meet with universal approval. Alumni had hoped for an experienced administrator who would bring efficiency to the expanding business needs of the College, and some noted that Patton was not an American citizen. Undergraduates feared that they were to be "admonished, sermonized, disciplined" after the fashion of John Knox.

Patton managed to allay many doubts in his first speaking engagement, a self-effacing talk before the New York alumni in March 1888. The classes of the 1890s—the "golden nineties" to their members—evinced respect and affection for him, and his course in ethics was popular. His kindly wisdom and ready wit became legendary, and students frequently sought him out for guidance and counsel.

During Patton's administration, the student body increased from slightly over 600 to more than 1,300, while the faculty, too, more than doubled. Patton appointed a number of promising and accomplished scholars and teachers, including his two immediate successors, Woodrow Wilson 1879 and John Grier Hibben 1882 *1893. More than a dozen major buildings were completed, including Princeton's first two Collegiate Gothic dormitories, Blair and Little halls. Campus life changed as eating clubs proliferated and there was a surging interest in athletics, particularly football.

In 1896 Patton presided at the sesquicentennial celebration and proclaimed that the College would "in all future time be known as Princeton University." This change in title, hailed as signaling the beginning of a new era in the institution's history, also marked the beginning of the end for the Patton administration, for it brought sharply into focus the president's failures as an administrator.

Even by the standards of the day, the administrative structure of Princeton was spare to the extreme. Patton conducted college affairs from his study in Prospect. He had no personal secretary until 1895 when he assigned the position to his son, George Stevenson Patton 1991. There was no college or university secretary until the election of Charles Williston McAlpin 1888 in December 1900. He turned aside the faculty's urgent appeals to inaugurate a system of deans (beyond the one position that had been created in the McCosh administration). Faculty accounts indicate that Patton lacked initiative in important policy matters, resisted meaningful curriculum reform, was lax in matters of discipline and in scholarly standards—in short, as one faculty member put it, he was "a wonderfully poor administrator."

To many of the faculty, enthused by the promise of the sesquicentennial, the time had come to take concrete measures toward making Princeton in fact what she now claimed to be in name. The faculty did manage an important step forward when the trustees established the graduate school in 1900; its dean, Andrew Fleming West 1874, was appointed directly by the trustees and given nearly autonomous powers.

The efforts of the faculty reformers gained the sympathetic attention of many influential trustees who, although they continued to admire Patton as a teacher, preacher, and public speaker, were becoming deeply concerned about his administrative inadequacies. The profile of the board had changed during the 1890s as the traditional clerical majority was reduced by the election of more business and professional men, and most of the 16 new trustees elected in the last five years of the century were business leaders and lawyers, products of a burgeoning industrial America who were not patient with Patton for long.

During the spring of 1902, several trustees and faculty members proposed that an executive committee of two trustees and three faculty members be formed to assume many of the president's administrative powers. Patton protested, but even his friends on the board gave him little encouragement. Finally, after some negotiation, he resigned at the trustee meeting on June 9, 1902, and the board, with Patton's endorsement, immediately chose Wilson to succeed him.

To compensate Patton for retiring six years earlier than he had intended, a group of trustees, alumni, and friends gave him a sum in cash that, together with his yearly salary of $4,000 as professor of ethics for one term a year, would equal his salary as president for six years. He continued to teach at the seminary as well as the University, and in the fall of 1902, he was elected as the first president of the seminary.

Patton retained his sense of humor. Once, when asked by a seminary visitor if he had any connection with the University, he wryly replied, "Yes, indeed, I am president of Princeton University—once removed."

Patton retired from the seminary in 1913 and returned to Bermuda to write and preach. He died on November 25, 1932, and was buried there, making him one of only four presidents—along with Jonathan Dickinson (Elizabeth), Samuel Finley (Philadelphia), and Woodrow Wilson (Washington, DC)—not to be interred in the Presidents' Lot in Princeton Cemetery.

In 1906, the Collegiate Gothic Patton Hall (now Patton-Wright Hall) was constructed; it was funded by gifts from the classes of 1880 and 1892–1901. Known for its large bay windows and tower, it is watched over by monkey clown gargoyles in pointed hats, ruffs, and pantaloons.

PELL, CLAIBORNE DE BORDA '40 was a six-term Democratic senator from Rhode Island whose name is known to college students around the country because of the grant program for lower-income students that he sponsored in 1972 and that was named for him in 1980. He also was the main sponsor of the 1965 act that created the National Endowment for the Arts and the National Endowment for the Humanities, and legislation in 1980 that established a fellowship program to support graduate students in the arts, humanities, and social sciences.

At Princeton, Pell majored in history and in public and international affairs, was on the rugby and cross-country teams, and was active in Whig-Clio. After graduating, he worked at an oil field in Oklahoma and then briefly for his father, a former member of Congress, US Ambassador to Portugal, and, as of February 1941, US Ambassador to Hungary. In August 1941, Pell enlisted in the Coast Guard and during World War II served on patrol duty in the North Atlantic and the Mediterranean. After being discharged from active duty in 1945, he worked for the State Department and then in investment banking before being elected to the Senate in 1960. His 36 years in the Senate is the longest tenure ever for a graduate of Princeton.

Pell's legislation creating the national endowments for the arts and humanities established two independent agencies of the US government, one to support the creation, dissemination, and performance of the arts, broadly defined, and one to support research, education, preservation, and public programs in the humanities, also broadly defined. Both have provided significant financial support for programs in these fields at Princeton.

His 1972 amendments to the Higher Education Act of 1965 created what were initially called Basic Educational Opportunity Grants (BEOGs) to provide need-based financial aid for lower-income college students. They played a transformative role in expanding educational opportunity for lower-income students at a broad range of American colleges and universities. BEOGs were renamed Pell Grants in 1980.

That same year, with the co-sponsorship of New York Republican Senator Jacob Javits, Pell successfully introduced legislation to create a national graduate fellowship program that had been proposed to him by Princeton. (The initial draft of the authorizing legislation was composed in Nassau Hall.) While there were a number of federal programs supporting graduate study in the sciences and engineering, this was the first to provide support in the arts, humanities, and social sciences. While authorized in 1980, the program was not funded until 1984, when at Pell's suggestion it was named for Javits. The program remained in place for almost three decades, basing its awards on demonstrated achievement, financial need, and exceptional promise.

Pell received Princeton's Woodrow Wilson Award, the highest distinction the University can confer on undergraduate alumni, in 1974, and an honorary degree in 1981. In a *Princeton Alumni Weekly* article recalling highlights of previous Alumni Days, Mary Hui '17 noted that after Pell accepted the Wilson Award, "he changed from his brown double-breasted suit to white gym shorts and a purple sweater" to jog a four-mile course that he ran three times a week as an undergraduate—"he started at Colonial Club, cruising to the graduate college, down to Lake Carnegie, and finally sprinted the last 20 yards to the tennis courts."

PHILOSOPHY, THE DEPARTMENT OF. Long before 1904, when President Woodrow Wilson instituted a departmental structure and created a department of Philosophy, students at Princeton would routinely engage in the study of philosophy or, perhaps more accurately in most cases, would sit in a classroom or lecture hall amidst philosophical discourse. Some of the College's earliest presidents were recognized as leading philosophers and regularly gave lectures on ethics and political theory.

Although Jonathan Edwards died only two months after taking office in January 1758, his presence at Princeton was considered a coup as he was widely regarded as one of the greatest philosophers America had produced. John Witherspoon, who became president just 10 years later, was famous for his lectures on moral philosophy. Before arriving in Princeton from Scotland, Witherspoon had been a disciple of Thomas Reid, one of the progenitors of the Scottish Enlightenment, in Glasgow. He brought to Princeton a philosophy of common sense realism which posited that human beings had the innate ability to perceive ideas "take[n] for granted in the common concerns of life," and that common sense was the foundation of philosophical inquiry. This school of thought still prevailed 100 years later when another renowned Scottish theologian-philosopher, James McCosh, was elected president in 1868.

By the time the department came into existence in the early 1900s, a new school of thought, the German Kantian-Hegelian viewpoint, with its premise of "absolute idealism," made inroads in philosophical academia, and Princeton's department shifted—slightly. Several scholars who joined the new department lectured and wrote on Kant and Hegel, including Alexander Ormond, the first chair of the department (1904 to 1913), and John Grier Hibben 1882 *1893, who would become president of the University in 1912 following Wilson's departure two years earlier.

It was not long before there were rumblings among American scholars of a return to realism. In fact, one of the authors of *The New Realism* (published in 1912), Edward Spaulding, was among the original preceptors appointed in 1905; he continued to teach at Princeton until his death in 1940. Another original preceptor who wrote about the new realism was Roger B. C. Johnson 1888, who chaired the department from 1926 to 1934.

By the time Robert Scoon followed Johnson as chair, from 1934 to 1952, philosophy departments across the country were wrestling with the various schools of thought that had arisen in contrast to Hegelianism, including not only the new realism but also pragmatism and positivism. Rising young scholars attracted to more than one strand of philosophy were often not hired by departments who were entrenched in one school or another.

Princeton took a middle course under Scoon, who believed in balance. Established members of the department continued to teach Aristotle, Aquinas, the history of modern philosophy, and the importance of philosophy's contact with the natural sciences and the arts and humanities, while new faculty members specialized in a variety of fields.

Three appointments during that time brought international eminence to the department. Walter Stace had been writing books on philosophy as an avocation while in the British civil service. On his retirement, and at the suggestion of Hibben, he came to Princeton as a visiting professor in 1932, and in 1935 he was named Stuart Professor of Philosophy, a chair he held until his retirement in 1955. He was noted for his work in the philosophy of mysticism and was described by the *New York Times* as "one of the pre-eminent philosophers of the English-speaking world."

In 1947 Walter Kaufman came to Princeton after receiving his PhD at Harvard. Appointed as an instructor, he was promoted to full professor in 1962 and appointed to the Stuart chair in 1979. Kaufmann was a philosopher, teacher, translator, poet, and photographer. His first book, a critical study of Nietzsche published in 1950, immediately established his philosophical reputation. Although Princeton was home base for him throughout his teaching career, he held visiting appointments at numerous universities, both in the United States and abroad.

Also appointed in 1947 was Arthur Szathmary, who was wooed away from two other schools when the department needed a faculty member to be the backbone of its offerings in aesthetics.

The mid-1950s through the 1960s saw other key appointments that solidified the department's ranking among the world's best. In 1955 Carl Hempel, a major figure in the philosophy of science and the theory of knowledge, joined the department from Yale. That same year Gregory Vlastos, a leading scholar of classical philosophy, came to Princeton from Cornell. Vlastos chaired the department twice in that era, and the "Three Lectures Series," when the department hosts a leading figure in the field, was inaugurated. In 1989 the department renamed the "Three Lectures Series" the "Carl G. Hempel Lectures," and they still take place today.

By 1969 the department was ranked first in the nation in both quality of faculty and effectiveness of doctoral program. In 1970, the department appointed its first woman faculty member, Margaret Dauler Wilson, who joined as associate professor and was promoted to full professor in 1975. Wilson had interests in the history of early modern philosophy, but also worked in the philosophy of religion, the philosophy of mind, and the theory of perception. She taught for 28 years, earning accolades in her field inside and outside the University. The department created a lecture series in her honor in 2016.

By the 1990s the department was primed for several major developments. One was the construction of new space adjoining its headquarters in 1879 Hall. Graduate seminars no longer had to take place in Firestone Library, and members of the department were no longer scattered over several buildings.

Another development was a series of significant faculty appointments, including Alexander Nehamas *71 in 1990, and two more senior women, Sarah Brodie in 1993 and Béatrice Longeusse in 1994. Nehamas took up the Edmund N. Carpenter II Class of 1943 Professorship in the Humanities, the first person to hold the position. Now known for his work in aesthetics, Nehamas had received his doctorate under the direction of Vlastos.

The third major development in the 1990s was the establishment of the University Center for Human Values, with political philosopher Amy Gutmann as its founding director. UCHV had a significant effect on philosophy at Princeton; it had an active visiting fellowship program that brought several philosophers from elsewhere to Princeton each year, and it made joint appointments with Philosophy as well as other departments. UCHV also was authorized to make its own faculty appointments, including the internationally prominent bioethicist Peter Singer.

The end of the first decade in the 2000s saw the retirement of Paul Benacerraf '52, *60, described as "one of the most penetrating minds in contemporary philosophy," whose unbroken 60-year association with the University began when he came to Princeton as an undergraduate in 1948.

Today's department of Philosophy continues to welcome a diversity of views, methods, and questions, and to connect with other disciplines. The department covers the full range of areas studied in an analytic philosophy department: logic and philosophy of science, philosophy of mind and language, metaphysics and epistemology, value theory, and the history of philosophy, including both early modern and ancient.

The department actively supports various initiatives aimed at helping philosophers from a wide range of backgrounds join the profession. It partially funds *Athena in Action*, a mentoring workshop that addresses problems faced by women studying philosophy at the graduate level. It also helps fund Minorities and Philosophy (MAP), which sponsors talks and seminars and facilitates a mentorship program for minority graduate students and undergraduates in philosophy.

PHYSICS, THE DEPARTMENT OF. In 1832 the trustees appointed Joseph Henry to a professorship of natural philosophy. A one-time watchmaker's apprentice who exemplified the ideal of the teacher-scholar, Henry was perhaps the greatest American natural philosopher—what today would be called a research physicist—of his time. He performed a series of experiments in electromagnetic induction that put him at the forefront of the first golden age of science in America and assured a strong start for physics at Princeton.

After Henry's departure in 1848 to become the founding secretary of the Smithsonian Institution, physics at Princeton went through an arid period until the appointment of Cyrus Fogg Brackett in 1873 and William Francis Magie 1879 in 1882. Along with their colleague in mathematics, Henry Fine 1880, they began, under President Woodrow Wilson, to build up the Physics and Mathematics departments by appointing promising young scholars, laying a solid academic foundation from which would rise one of the world's great centers of theoretical physics.

In 1906 the trustees brought the brilliant English physicist Owen Richardson to Princeton. He took a particular interest in upgrading the woefully inadequate facilities for physics lectures and, when he returned to England in 1914, he left behind an enthusiasm for research that would animate the developing department for decades.

During Magie's term as chair, from 1908 to 1929, the department appointed the theoretical physicists Eugene Wigner and John von Neumann, the first of a remarkable group of Hungarians who had a transformative impact on physics in the United States. With their appointments, the field of theory became more important at the University, and collaborations with the neighboring Institute for Advanced Study soon made the town of Princeton the greatest center for theoretical physics in the world.

In the 1930s Princeton provided temporary office space to several professors from the institute—including Albert Einstein, who shaped modern concepts of space, time, and gravity with his general theory of relativity.

Princeton entered the nuclear age when Milton White joined the department in 1935 and oversaw the construction of a cyclotron in Palmer Laboratory. During World War II the cyclotron's power unit was moved temporarily to Los Alamos. It was reinstated after the war, but then nearly destroyed by fire in 1950. It was repaired and used for another two decades until it moved with the Physics department in 1969 to Jadwin Hall, where it is still used for teaching purposes.

During the war, the physics faculty engaged in war-related research either in Princeton or at national laboratories. A considerable number went to a new radiation laboratory at MIT. Others were involved in the highly secret development of the atomic bomb. While this dispersal resulted in a reduced faculty, teaching demands increased to include all the military recruits being trained at Princeton. To help meet these demands, in 1942 the department hired its first female faculty member, Chien-Shiung Wu, who later became the first woman to receive a Princeton honorary doctorate in science; that year it also appointed Elda Emma Anderson as its first female visiting research associate.

The period between 1945 and the 1970s was one of continuous expansion. By 1970, the faculty's size and increased space demands for research compelled its move into Jadwin Hall.

The department's reputation during this period was burnished by giants in the field like David Gross, whose work with his graduate student Frank Wilczek eventually resulted in both being named 2004 Nobel Laureates for revealing fundamental insights into the force that holds the parts of an atomic nucleus together.

David Wilkinson, who led pioneering studies of experimental cosmology, joined the department as a postdoc in 1963 under Robert Dicke '39, one of the pioneers in the study of the experimental foundation for the study of relativity. Wilkinson later pursued Dicke's early measurements of the cosmic microwave background—the thermal afterglow of the Big Bang. He was a main driver behind the Cosmic Background Explorer (COBE) satellite, which later informed the design of the Microwave Anisotropy Probe. That probe was eventually renamed the Wilkinson Microwave Anisotropy Probe (WMAP) satellite, and it is largely from that mission that the standard model of cosmology is derived.

Another founding member of WMAP, Lyman Page, came to Princeton as a postdoc in 1990 and joined the faculty in 1991. He had a leading role in half a dozen experiments that mapped the cosmic microwave background (CMB) anisotropy and polarization. He was also the founding director of the Atacama Cosmology Telescope.

In 1967, particle physicist A.J. Stewart Smith *66 joined the faculty. He was the department's longest-serving chair in the modern era, from 1990 to 1998, and oversaw the building of James S. McDonnell Hall, one of the facilities in which physics classes are taught today.

One of the great theoretical physicists of the post-war era, Philip Anderson, joined the faculty part-time in 1975, and then served full-time from 1984 until he reached emeritus status in 1996. He won the 1977 Nobel Prize for earlier research on the electronic structure of magnetic and disordered systems. His resonating valence bond theory of high-temperature superconductivity led to the field of "spin liquids," which is at the root of the still-flourishing field of topological matter. He also advised condensed matter physicist F. Duncan Haldane, winner of the 2016 Nobel Prize.

Theoretical physicist Igor Klebanov joined the department in 1989, focusing on the exact relations between quantum field theories in four and three space-time dimensions and higher dimensional theories. The last few decades of the twentieth century also saw several exceptional graduate students like Edward Witten *76, who went on to become a leader in the field of string theory, and Juan Maldacena *96, later a visiting faculty member, who published a theory on the precise holographic correspondence between gravity and the theory that describes particles, now known as the Maldacena Correspondence.

More recently, a strong group of experimentalists working in concert with the department's theoretical cosmologists took up a battery of CMB experiments; among them were the department's first tenured woman faculty member, Suzanne Staggs, and Jo Dunkley, who joined the faculty in 2016 and is a co-leader with Staggs on the Atacama Cosmology Telescope project.

Other recent initiatives for the department include the Princeton Center for Theoretical Science, led by Curtis Callan, to further theoretical research through postdoc and faculty fellowships, and the Princeton Gravity Initiative, launched in 2018 with the departments of Astrophysical Sciences and Mathematics to explore the fundamental nature of gravity.

Today's department is world-renowned in both theoretical and experimental physics, and has an equal emphasis on theoretical and experimental studies. In addition to its traditional strengths in elementary particle physics, gravity and cosmology, nuclear and atomic physics, mathematical physics, and condensed matter physics, it has growing groups in biophysics and condensed matter physics.

Princeton faculty and graduates have won 23 Nobel Prizes in physics. They include Arthur Compton *1916 (1927), Owen Richardson (1928), Clinton Davisson *1911 (1937), John Bardeen *36 twice (1956 and 1972), Robert Hofstadter *38 (1961), Eugene Wigner (1963), Richard Feynman *42 (1965), Philip Anderson (1977), Arno Penzias (1978), Steven Weinberg *57 (1979), Val Fitch and James Cronin (1980), Russell Hulse and Joseph Taylor (1993), Daniel Tsui (1998), David Gross and Frank Wilczek *75 (2004), Arthur McDonald (2015), F. Duncan Haldane (2016), Kip Thorne *65 (2017), James Peebles *62 (2019), and Syukuro Manabe (2021).

Peebles taught in the department his entire career and was a true founding father of theoretical cosmology. One of a handful of scientists doing original research in the field when he began his research in the early 1960s, he won his Nobel for developing a theoretical framework over a 50-year career that serves as the basis for contemporary understanding of and ideas about the universe. He is best known for his theory of cold dark matter, proposed in 1982, as well as his contributions in identifying cosmic background radiation as a remnant of the Big Bang.

POE BROTHERS, THE, contributed to many Princeton football victories in the 20 years beginning in 1882 and were the special nemeses of Harvard and Yale. There were six of them, sons of John Prentiss Poe 1854, attorney general of Maryland and a cousin of the writer Edgar Allan Poe.

(1) Samuel Johnson Poe 1884, the eldest, played halfback in 1882 and 1883, and was also a lacrosse All-American.

(2) Edgar Allan Poe 1891 was quarterback and captain in his junior and senior years. In 1889, the year he was named All-American, he played a leading part in the 41–15 defeat of Harvard at Cambridge. During the excitement, a Harvard fan asked a Princeton alumnus whether Poe was related to the great Edgar Allan Poe; the alumnus looked at him in astonishment and replied, "He *is* the great Edgar Allan Poe." He graduated Phi Beta Kappa and became, like his father, attorney general of Maryland.

(3) John Prentiss Poe Jr. 1895 was a star halfback on the varsity and class president during his freshman year. That spring he was required to withdraw for scholastic reasons, but he was readmitted in the fall and played even more brilliantly. Later that year, again in academic arrears, he was obliged to leave, this time for good. For a time, he coached football at other colleges, and then embarked on an adventurous career as cowpuncher, gold prospector, surveyor, and soldier of fortune. When World War I broke out he went to England to fight and was killed in action in France. Poe Field was provided in his memory by

classmates and friends, and the John Prentiss Poe Football Cup, given by his mother, is awarded annually to the member of the varsity football team who has best exemplified courage, modesty, perseverance, and good sportsmanship. It is Princeton's highest football award.

(4) Neilson (Net) Poe 1897 played in the backfield in 1895 and 1896 and returned to coach in later years.

(5) Arthur Poe 1900, another All-American, made the decisive score that beat Yale in two successive years. In 1898 he ran 90 yards for a touchdown and the only score of the game. In the 1899 game, with less than a minute to play and with the score 10–6 in Yale's favor, Princeton recovered a fumble on Yale's 30-yard line. The only feasible strategy was to try for a field goal, then worth five points, but Princeton's two drop-kickers were out with injuries. Arthur Poe volunteered to try a drop-kick even though he had never kicked in a college game before. The others agreed, Poe dropped back to the 35-yard line, and the ball cleared the uprights for a Princeton victory.

(6) Gresham Poe 1902 spent most of his time on the bench as a substitute quarterback, but he did get into the Yale game his senior year. He entered in the fourth quarter when Yale was leading 12–0. The Princeton fans had practically conceded victory to Yale, but when Gresham appeared on the field they rose to their feet with a rousing cheer—such was the magic of the name Poe. "Poe's presence seemed to rejuvenate the Tigers," *Harper's Weekly* reported, "and for the last ten minutes of the contest they fairly outplayed the weary Elis. The ball was twice carried half the length of the field, but the whistle blew before Princeton could score."

POLER'S RECESS, a 10-minute break while cramming for exams, was a Princeton custom noisily observed from the late nineteenth century almost up to World War II. Derived from a mid-nineteenth century prank known as the "horn spree," it occurred every night during the final examination period. As soon as the nine o'clock bell began to ring, all windows on campus were opened and all means employed to produce a din that would divert the most diligent poler from his work. ("Poler" was a Princeton synonym for "grind," apparently derived from the laborious poling of a boat.)

Firecrackers were exploded, pistols, revolvers, and shotguns fired with blank cartridges, horns blown, drums and tin pans beaten. As an undergraduate writer observed in 1918, it was "probably the most juvenile" of all campus customs, but it brought "a welcome break for everyone in a long night's hard work."

Poler's Recess was revived after World War II in response to the urging of a young alumnus in a letter to the *Princetonian*. He proposed that beginning at 11 p.m. (rather than at 9, so as not to disturb those taking evening exams), 10 minutes be given over to total pandemonium, and thereafter absolute silence should prevail.

In the same issue of the *Prince*, "Examinitus" quoted "a prominent psychologist" as saying: "The break will be of incalculable aid to all those suffering from mental blocks, hallucinations, paranoia, schizophrenia, psychosis, neurosis, and blocking of the digestive tract."

That night undergraduates responded enthusiastically, and the next morning the *Prince* pronounced the revival an unqualified success, awarding championship honors to Holder Court, where students staged a mock battle with blank cartridges and flaming tennis balls. But the revival was short-lived; observance of the "11 p.m. catharsis" was sporadic the next year or two, and then it faded away. Recent offspring of the recess include the Holder Howl and the Whitman Wail, minute-long outbursts which occur at midnight in Holder Courtyard and Whitman College before every Dean's Date when all written work for the semester is due.

POLITICS, THE DEPARTMENT OF. Although Politics did not become a separate department until 1924, the teaching of this subject at Princeton goes back to the early days of the College. When James Madison 1771 chose Princeton rather than his home state's College of William & Mary, it was in part because John Witherspoon extended his course in moral philosophy to include the general principles of public law and politics.

The first course labeled political science was introduced in 1871 and was taught by Lyman Atwater. William Sloane took over Atwater's work in 1883 and offered upper-class courses in the philosophy of history and political science. The next year Alexander Johnson gave courses in jurisprudence, political economy, and public and international law. English common law was taught as a graduate-level course.

When Woodrow Wilson 1879 joined the faculty in 1890 to fill the vacancy caused by Johnson's death, the curriculum in political studies was extensive. By 1896, the study of philosophy included history and political science under Sloane, jurisprudence under

Wilson, and political economy under Winthrop More Daniels, who had come to assist Wilson in 1892.

In 1898, history and political science became simply history, and political economy became political economy and sociology. In 1904, when Wilson, as president, reorganized the curriculum into 11 departments, History, Politics, and Economics were reassembled as a single department. At Wilson's insistence, the term "politics" replaced political science, as it remains today.

When Wilson's "preceptor guys" began to arrive in 1905, notable additions in politics were Edward Corwin, Charles McIlwain, and William Starr Myers, all of whom had been trained as historians. In 1913, when the centrifugal forces of specialization again asserted themselves, History and Politics, and Economics and Social Institutions, became two separate departments. Politics broke off in 1924, with Corwin, McCormick Professor of Jurisprudence, as chair. Corwin stands among the giants of American constitutional scholars and, from 1925 until the end of World War II, graduate study in politics at Princeton primarily meant work with Corwin. During this period, graduate students were few but highly accomplished.

At the undergraduate level, Corwin's course Constitutional Interpretation ("Con Interp") featured source material and required students to write opinions in cases currently pending in the Supreme Court. It enjoyed a reputation of being the toughest course in the University; in succeeding generations, and to this day, it has consistently been voted most valuable by seniors.

Princeton's response to Wilson's call in his sesquicentennial address to be "in the nation's service" took a practical turn in 1930 with the establishment of the school of Public and International Affairs, initially headed by politics professor Harold Dodds *14 (later president of the University), and the Princeton Survey in State and Local Government under the direction of John Sly. In 1932 a team of 21 Princeton faculty members, including seven from politics, worked under the direction of Dodds to compile a comprehensive survey of the government of New Jersey with a view to recommending economies without impairing essential services.

Also in 1932 Harwood Childs came to Princeton to teach and research public opinion, then an uncharted academic field. Childs founded and edited the *Public Opinion Quarterly*, which in a relatively short time became one of the most prestigious journals in the field of politics. Childs and his colleague, international law specialist John Whitton, authored propaganda that was distributed abroad by short wave programs during World War II.

George Graham joined the department as part of a drive in the 1930s to expand the curriculum to include public affairs, domestic and international. A specialist in public administration, Graham was in Washington throughout World War II with the US Bureau of the Budget. To this day, the Politics department's connection with the school of Public and International Affairs has meant that many faculty members are engaged in public service. Faculty such as Aaron Friedberg and Anne-Marie Slaughter '80 have taken public service leaves to fill high-ranking positions in presidential administrations.

After 1950, politics at Princeton moved increasingly toward a scientific approach that included quantitative analysis, comparative study of foreign systems, and international relations. Even "Con Interp," under the direction of Walter Murphy and later Robert George, broke new ground by taking a quantitative and comparative approach. In the mid-1990s the department took a major step toward more methodological breadth when it appointed three of the country's most prominent scholars in the quantitative areas of the field: Larry Bartels, Thomas Romer, and Howard Rosenthal.

From the 1960s through the present, the intellectual diversity of the department has broadened. Offerings have encompassed the whole range of politics: domestic and international, normative and positivist, as well as theoretical and empirical. In the first decade of the 2000s, the department made major strides, providing better support for junior faculty to increase the rate at which they were promoted to tenure, and in one year alone, 2004, making 10 new appointments to the faculty.

Today the department is one of the largest and most intellectually diverse political science programs in the world, and one of Princeton's largest departments with nearly 60 faculty, 150 undergraduate concentrators, and 140 graduate students.

The department currently has six main subfields for graduate study: American politics, comparative politics, international relations, political theory, formal and quantitative methods, and public law. At the undergraduate level, popular courses now include not only the classic Constitutional Interpretation, but also Introduction to Quantitative Social Science, the international relations course Grand Strategy, and Political Theory.

The department's intellectual breadth is matched by the strength and depth of its faculty. Since 1966, 41 members of the department have been elected to the American Academy of Arts and Sciences. Consistent with this faculty strength, the graduate program is one of the top-ranked in the country, and every year graduates go on to top positions at leading universities in the United States and around the world.

Before Princeton became coeducational at the undergraduate level in 1969, the Politics department enrolled women in its graduate program. Politics was also among the first departments to admit Black students for graduate study. In 2020 the department's tenured ranks included 11 women, representing more than 28 percent of its total tenured faculty. The department also had four Black faculty members, two of them tenured.

The department's early chairs served lengthy terms but beginning in the 1970s the position of chair has rotated and been held by faculty from the range of its subfields. Its most recent chairs, for example, include Helen Milner from international relations, Nolan McCarty from American politics, and Alan Patten from political theory.

From the beginning of its history, Princeton has appreciated the educational requirements of a free society. Reflected in the offerings of its Politics department is recognition that citizens need to understand not only the organization, operation, and functions of government, but also the intersections between government and industry, commerce, finance, law, and international relations. Students should learn about people as well as things, and moral philosophy is as basic now to the study of politics as it was in Witherspoon's time.

Through the diversity of its instructors and program, as well as its ecumenical approach, the Politics department continues to conduct ground-breaking research with both practical and theoretical applications, and to prepare students for lives of service to their communities, their nations, and humanity.

PORTRAIT COLLECTION. The University's portrait collection, maintained by the University Art Museum, contains more than 600 paintings and sculptures. The portraits span centuries and encompass varying styles and subjects, with one of the earliest being Charles Willson Peale's landmark portrait of George Washington at the Battle of Princeton which the trustees commissioned in 1783 with funds given by Washington himself.

John Maclean Jr. 1816 established the collection when he was vice president in the mid-nineteenth century. From then until 2017, the only regular additions were portraits of the presidents of the University and of the deans of the graduate school and the school of Engineering and Applied Science. The portraits of the presidents are displayed in Nassau Hall; the graduate school deans in Procter Hall at the graduate college; and the engineering deans in the Friend Center for Engineering Education.

Beginning in 2017, the University launched a concerted effort to diversify the portrait collection and, in doing so, to represent a much broader range of individuals who have made exceptional contributions to Princeton. Special efforts also were to be made to diversify the portraitists, as well as the visual language of the portraits themselves. In the fall of that year the University installed a portrait of emeritus faculty member and Nobel Laureate Toni Morrison in the newly renamed Morrison Hall, and in the following spring one of former faculty member and Nobel Laureate Sir Arthur Lewis in the newly renamed Arthur Lewis Auditorium in Robertson Hall.

Morrison, a professor in the humanities and creative writing, played a transformative role in attracting students and faculty of color to Princeton and in expanding the University's commitment to the creative and performing arts, American Studies, and African American Studies. She was the first Black woman to be awarded the Nobel Prize in Literature. Lewis, a professor of economics and international affairs, was the first Black full professor at Princeton; he was awarded the Nobel Prize in Economics, and to this day remains the only person of African descent ever to have won a Nobel Prize in any field other than literature or peace.

In 2018 the University commissioned eight additional portraits of alumni and former faculty members and administrators to reflect the diversity of the University community.

William W. "Bill" Bradley '65 was a United States senator from New Jersey, a star basketball player for the New York Knicks and for Princeton, Princeton's all-time leading scorer, winner of an Olympic gold medal in 1964, and the 1987 winner of the Woodrow Wilson Award, the highest honor the University can bestow on undergraduate alumni.

Denny Chin '75, a first generation Chinese American and the first in his family to attend college, was named a federal district judge in 1994 and later

Nobel Laureate Toni Morrison

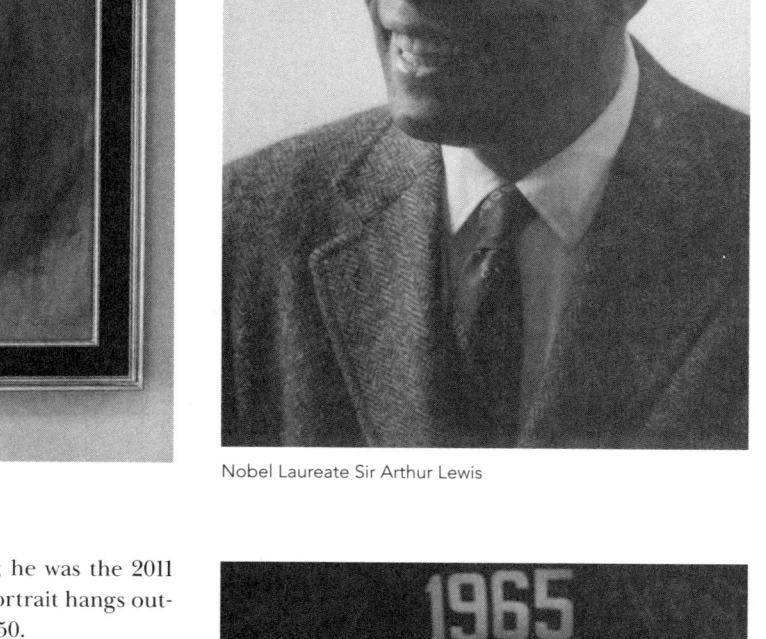
Nobel Laureate Sir Arthur Lewis

promoted to federal circuit judge; he was the 2011 winner of the Wilson Award. His portrait hangs outside the main entrance to McCosh 50.

Carl A. Fields was appointed in 1964 as Princeton's first African American administrator and he became the first Black dean in the Ivy League when he was promoted to assistant dean of the college in 1968. He implemented policies and programs that increased enrollment and retention of students of color, and was instrumental in establishing the Third World Center, later named the Carl A. Fields Center for Equality and Cultural Understanding in his honor. His office was in Morrison Hall, and his portrait hangs in the south entry to that building.

Elaine Fuchs *77, a world-renowned leader in cell biology and molecular genetics, was awarded the 2009 National Medal of Science and the 2011 James Madison Medal, the highest honor the University can bestow on graduate alumni.

Robert J. Rivers Jr. '53 was among the first Black students admitted to Princeton and was the first African American elected by the trustees to serve on the board. He grew up in the town of Princeton, and after

Bill Bradley '65

a distinguished career as a vascular surgeon and professor and dean at the University of Rochester School of Medicine and Dentistry, he returned to the Princeton house where he grew up. Rivers Way, the road-

Denny Chin '75 with his portrait and the artist, Ying-He Liu.

Carl A. Fields

Elaine Fuchs *77

Ruth Simmons served in a number of pioneering roles at Princeton. She was the first director of studies at Butler College, vice provost, and acting director of the program in African American Studies before leaving Princeton to become president of Smith College. She then served as president of Brown University (the first Black president of an Ivy League institution) and of Prairie View A&M University.

Sonia Sotomayor '76 was the first justice of Hispanic heritage to be named to the Supreme Court and the third woman justice in Supreme Court history. As a student she won the highest undergraduate award, the Moses Taylor Pyne Honor Prize, and

way onto campus from Nassau Street just west of Firestone Library, is named for him; his portrait hangs in McCosh Infirmary, home of University Health Services.

Robert J. Rivers Jr. '53 receiving an honorary degree in 2016

Ruth Simmons with Toni Morrison and Mackenzie Scott '92 at the 2017 dedication ceremony for Morrison Hall

Sonia Sotomayor '76

in 2014 she won the Woodrow Wilson Award. Her remarks on that occasion inspired the 2016 modification of the University's informal motto from "Princeton in the Nation's Service and in the Service of All Nations" to "Princeton in the Nation's Service and the Service of Humanity." Like Bradley, Chin, Rivers, and Simmons, Sotomayor also served Princeton as a trustee.

Alan M. Turing *38, widely recognized as the father of computer science and an icon in the history of lesbian, gay, bisexual, and transgender rights, played a central role in the British government's cryptographic success in breaking codes produced by the German Enigma machine during World War II. A *Princeton Alumni Weekly* article ranked him second (to James Madison) among the University's most influential alumni of all time. His portrait is in the Lewis Science Library.

In 2018–19, while the visual artist Mario Moore was spending a year at Princeton as a Hodder Fellow in the Lewis Center for the Arts, he created 10 paintings and a number of prints and drawings of staff members at the University, mostly African Americans, which were exhibited for three months in the fall of 2019 at the Lewis Arts complex. The subjects

Alan M. Turing *38

Art Museum security officer Michael Moore with Mario Moore's portrait of him at work

included two security guards at the art museum, cooks in the Rockefeller-Mathey dining hall, and two members of the athletics department staff. The exhibition attracted widespread national attention, and the University and the art museum purchased seven of the paintings and related drawings to become part of the museum's collections or to hang permanently on campus.

At its graduation a year later, the Class of 2020 made Moore an honorary member.

POSTAGE STAMPS. Twice the United States Postal Service has recognized Princeton University anniversaries by issuing commemorative postage stamps. On September 22, 1956, the service issued its first-ever commemorative stamp printed on colored paper (orange, of course) to honor the bicentennial of Nassau Hall. The three-cent stamp depicted a front view of the historic building (the capitol of the United States in 1783) and its text said: 200th Anniversary of Nassau Hall, 1756–1956.

On September 20, 1996, the Postal Service issued a 20-cent postcard to honor the University's 250th anniversary. The card was part of the service's "historic preservation" series and featured a rendering of Alexander Hall as viewed from the south. (The rendering was painted by stamp designer Howard Koslow of Toms River, New Jersey.) The postcard identifies the building as Alexander Hall and its text says, "Princeton University 250th Anniversary."

A program for the first day of issue ceremony describes Alexander Hall as "one of the University's most distinctive structures, steeped in history and beautifully embellished with stained glass, mosaics, and sculpture. Commissioned in 1892 and designed by architect William A. Potter, the building was a gift of Mrs. Harriett Crocker Alexander, who named it for three generations of Alexanders who served as Princeton trustees." Fittingly, the first day of issue ceremony took place on the stage of Alexander Hall.

In a March 5, 2008, article, *Princeton Alumni Weekly* writer Brett Tomlinson reported that, over time, more than a dozen Princeton alumni had been featured on postal issues, beginning with an 1869 stamp commemorating the signing of the Declaration of Independence that included Benjamin Rush 1760 and Richard Stockton 1748, along with President John Witherspoon.

Other stamps featured James Madison 1771, Woodrow Wilson 1879, John Foster Dulles 1908, Eugene O'Neill 1910, F. Scott Fitzgerald 1917, Adlai Stevenson 1922, Thornton Wilder *1926, John Bardeen *36, and Richard Feynman *42. The American Scientists series that included Bardeen and Feynman also included Princeton University and Institute for Advanced Study mathematician John von Neumann.

Pre-rade, The, began in 2004 as a festive opportunity for older students and alumni to welcome the entering class to the Princeton experience. Originated by the Undergraduate Student Government with the encouragement of alumni, it is modeled on, and bookends, the P-rade at reunions in which the entering class will march four years later as seniors.

The Pre-rade begins at the end of Opening Exercises. Wearing the t-shirts of their residential colleges, the class leaves the chapel behind the president, trustees, faculty, and senior officers of the University. It follows the banners of the colleges and the band through the Collins and East Pyne arches, past the east side of Nassau Hall toward Nassau Street, and then through the FitzRandolph Gateway—according to recent tradition, a passage through the gateway they will not make again until they graduate.

The class makes its way slowly and loudly across the front campus past student and alumni well-wishers (including alumni in reunion garb), passes Morrison Hall and Alexander Hall, and finally arrives at Blair Arch. There they are introduced to Princeton songs and cheers, including the alma mater "Old Nassau" and the locomotive cheer, both of which date back to the mid-nineteenth century.

The Pre-rade ends with a picnic dinner on the lawn known as Alexander Beach between Alexander and Witherspoon halls.

President of the University is Princeton's chief executive officer. The president is charged with the general supervision of the interests of the University, and with special oversight of the various departments of instruction. The president presides at all meetings of the Board of Trustees, at meetings of the faculty and of the Council of the Princeton University Community (CPUC), at all University convocations, and represents the University before the public.

Princeton's presidents have been:

1.	Jonathan Dickinson	1747
2.	Aaron Burr Sr.	1748–57*
3.	Jonathan Edwards	1758
4.	Samuel Davies	1759–61
5.	Samuel Finley	1761–66
6.	John Witherspoon	1768–94
7.	Samuel Stanhope Smith 1769	1795–1812
8.	Ashbel Green 1783	1812–22
9.	James Carnahan 1800	1823–54
10.	John Maclean Jr. 1816	1854–68
11.	James McCosh	1868–88
12.	Francis Landey Patton	1888–1902
13.	Woodrow Wilson 1879	1902–10
14.	John Grier Hibben 1882 *1893	1912–32
15.	Harold W. Dodds *1914	1933–57
16.	Robert F. Goheen '40 *48	1957–72
17.	William G. Bowen *58	1972–88
18.	Harold T. Shapiro *64	1988–2004
19.	Shirley M. Tilghman	2004–13
20.	Christopher L. Eisgruber '83	2013–

Acting presidents during interregnums were David Cowell, 1757–58; Jacob Green, 1758–59; John Blair, 1767–68; Philip Lindsly 1803, 1822–23; John Aikman Stewart, 1910–12; and Edward Dickinson Duffield 1892, 1932–33.

The first five presidents together served fewer than 20 years. Their tenures were cut short by untimely deaths owing in part to overwork and in part to the backward state of the art of medicine at the time: Edwards died at 55 of a fever after an inoculation for smallpox; Davies, who was tubercular, died at 38 after being bled for a bad cold.

In the early years there were two instances of succession by in-laws: Aaron Burr Sr., second president, was succeeded by his father-in-law, Jonathan Edwards. John Witherspoon, sixth president, was succeeded by his son-in-law, Samuel Stanhope Smith.

The first nine presidents were slaveholders at some point in their lives; at least five held slaves while living in the president's house (now Maclean House).

Two presidents came from Scotland, John Witherspoon in 1768 and James McCosh, a hundred years later, in 1868; both left lasting marks on Princeton and on the nation. They died in Princeton: Witherspoon on November 15, 1794 and McCosh on November 16, 1894—a century and a day apart.

Aaron Burr Sr., at 32, was the youngest to be elected president; Jonathan Dickinson, at 59, the oldest. James Carnahan's administration has been the longest (31 years), Jonathan Edwards' the shortest (five weeks).

The royal charter of 1746, which gave the trustees power to "elect . . . such qualified persons as they . . . shall think fit to be the President," also empowered them "at any time [to] Displace and discharge such President." Three presidents were induced to resign: Smith in 1812, Green in 1822, and Patton in 1902.

The first three presidents—Dickinson, Burr, and Edwards—were graduates of Yale. The next two lacked college degrees; they were trained in classics and divinity, both in Pennsylvania (Davies in Samuel

---

* Although Burr was formally elected president in November 1748, he had been in charge of the College since Dickinson's death in October 1747.

Gathered in the Nassau Hall Faculty Room prior to the 2013 installation of Christopher Eisgruber '83 as Princeton's 20th president and wearing the distinctive Princeton presidential robe are (from left) Harold Shapiro *64, Eisgruber, Shirley Tilghman, and William Bowen *58.

Blair's school at Faggs Manor, Finley in William Tennent's "log college" at Neshaminy). Witherspoon was a graduate of Edinburgh, McCosh of Glasgow and Edinburgh, Patton of Knox College in Toronto, and Tilghman of Queen's University in Kingston, Ontario, with a PhD from Temple University. Eight earned undergraduate degrees at Princeton—Smith, Green, Carnahan, Maclean, Wilson, Hibben, Goheen, Eisgruber—and five earned graduate degrees from the University: Hibben, Dodds, Goheen, Bowen, and Shapiro.

The President's Lot in the Princeton Cemetery on Witherspoon Street contains the graves of all the deceased presidents of Princeton, except four: Dickinson, who died and was buried in Elizabethtown before the college was moved to Princeton; Finley, who died and was buried in Philadelphia (there is a cenotaph for him in the President's Lot); Patton, who died and was buried in Bermuda; and Wilson, who died in Washington, DC, and was interred in the Washington National Cathedral.

PRESIDENTS OF THE UNITED STATES who graduated from Princeton are:

James Madison 1771 (1809–17)
Woodrow Wilson 1879 (1913–21)

John F. Kennedy attended Princeton as a member of the Class of 1939 but withdrew after several months because of illness and later graduated from Harvard in the Class of 1940.

Aaron Burr Jr. 1772 was an unsuccessful candidate for the presidency in 1800. In the twentieth century, three Princeton graduates gained their party's nomination but fell short in the general election: Norman Thomas 1905, the Socialist party candidate in six successive campaigns from 1928 through 1948; Adlai Stevenson 1922, the Democratic party candidate against Dwight Eisenhower in 1952 and 1956; and Ralph Nader '55, Green Party candidate in 1996 and 2000, and then an independent candidate in 2004 and 2008.

Michelle Obama '85 served two terms in the White House as First Lady of the United States, 2009–17.

In 2015, University Archivist Dan Linke posted a list of at least 26 and possibly as many as 30 US presidents who had visited the campus at some point, with 11 of them visiting while in office. The list, indicating the year of their first Princeton visit, follows [those lacking definite verification are bracketed]:

George Washington 1773
[John Adams 1772]
Thomas Jefferson 1783

James Madison 1766
[John Quincy Adams 1806]
Martin Van Buren 1841
William Henry Harrison 1836
John Tyler 1843
[Franklin Pierce 1848]
[James Buchanan 1850]
Abraham Lincoln 1865 (funeral train)
Ulysses S. Grant 1871
Rutherford B. Hayes 1878
James A. Garfield 1881 (funeral train)
Chester A. Arthur 1884
Grover Cleveland 1896
Benjamin Harrison 1889
Theodore Roosevelt 1917
William Howard Taft 1912
Woodrow Wilson 1875
Warren G. Harding 1922
Herbert Hoover 1917
Harry S. Truman 1947
Dwight D. Eisenhower 1947
John F. Kennedy 1935
Lyndon B. Johnson 1966
Jimmy Carter 1981
George H.W. Bush 1948 (Yale baseball player)
Bill Clinton 1996
George W. Bush 1967 (attended a football game)

The 11 who visited while in office were Tyler, Grant, Hayes, Arthur, Cleveland, Taft, Wilson, Truman, Johnson, Bush, and Clinton.

PRESS CLUB, THE UNIVERSITY, is composed of students who write (and are remunerated) as professional freelance journalists for local, regional, and national newspapers, magazines, and wire services; they cover breaking news, feature stories, and sporting events at the University and in the surrounding community. As undergraduates they have unique access to campus stories and venues and are able to cover important events quickly; when students led by the Black Justice League occupied the president's office in the fall of 2015, a member of the Press Club live blogged the protest for 36 hours from inside Nassau Hall.

The Press Club was first organized in 1900, although it seems probable that campus correspondents were functioning long before that. President James McCosh may have had them in mind 20 years earlier when, in an effort to ward off threatened misbehavior, he warned students that "tomorrow it will be in all the New York papers and the next day in the Philadelphia papers."

Former president Grover Cleveland, who lived in Princeton after completing his second term in the White House, was a good source of stories in the club's early days. He disliked being interviewed but he granted exceptions for students. "It may mean five or ten dollars for the boy," he told a faculty friend, "and that would pay his board for a week." Once, however, he felt obliged to rebuff an undergraduate reporter who pressed him for his opinion on President William McKinley's Philippine policy. "That, sir," Cleveland said, "is a matter of too great importance to discuss in so brief an interview, now rapidly drawing to a close."

In the early years, Press Club members usually worked independently and came together only for social occasions. Seniors approaching graduation sold their positions as correspondents for particular newspapers to the highest bidders—a process that gave more weight to the new reporter's financial capacity than to his nose for news or his ear for a good sentence.

All this changed in 1915 when, following a study he made at the request of the Graduate Council (precursor to the Alumni Council), Professor Christian Gauss reorganized the club along the lines it has followed ever since. He persuaded the Graduate Council to purchase all the correspondents' rights from club members (the Council was later repaid) and replaced the old auction system with freshman and sophomore competitions for membership. He also introduced the practice of having club members pool their efforts.

Gauss accepted appointment as faculty adviser, a position he held until 1924, when he left Princeton for a year's leave of absence before becoming dean of the college. This role is played today by the club's alumni advisory board which meets with the students twice a year.

Sometimes when news was scarce, Press Club stringers created stories. In the 1920s, at the suggestion of Gauss, they asked a number of professors what 10 books they would want to have with them if they had to spend the rest of their lives on a desert island. The composite results were unsensational (Shakespeare and Homer led, followed by the Bible, Plato, Dante, and Virgil), but the story got lots of attention, nonetheless. Several years later, the club asked another group of professors to list the six most important words ("loyalty" was mentioned most frequently), and once more the story ran widely.

There were other occasions when Press Club members had more than enough real news to keep them busy. Off-campus stories included the kidnapping of Charles Lindbergh's infant son in nearby Hopewell in 1932 and the frenzy following Orson Welles' 1938 radio broadcast of "an invasion from Mars" which "landed" four miles from Princeton.

The Press Club office was first located in the back room of the Western Union office at the corner of Nassau and Witherspoon Streets. It later moved on to campus, and eventually into its current location, 48 University Place, a building that also houses the *Daily Princetonian* and other student publications and agencies.

In addition to freelancing, Press Club members also run a blog called *The Ink* which covers campus activities. The club regularly sponsors lectures and events on campus, including the annual Louis Rukeyser '54 memorial lecture series which brings prominent journalists to the University.

In 1979 a group of Press Club members founded the campus weekly student newspaper, the *Nassau Weekly*.

PRINCETON, THE MUNICIPALITY OF. It is estimated that 10 million Native Americans lived in what is now the United States before the arrival of European settlers. Many thousands lived in Lenapehoking, the historic homeland of the Lenni Lenape, which encompassed Princeton. Europeans first settled there in the late 1600s, with the first house and tavern built in 1683. After originally being considered part of the nearby settlement of Stony Brook, by the 1720s the village was known variously as Princetowne, Prince's Town, and finally Princeton. A Lenni Lenape trail connecting the Raritan and Delaware rivers was already established as the King's Highway (later Nassau Street), and the royal nomenclature along the highway included villages of Queenston and Kingston to the north and Princessville to the south.

Because it was located roughly halfway between New York and Philadelphia, the agrarian village became prosperous as a convenient overnight stop for travelers. In 1756 the 10-year-old College of New Jersey moved to Princeton. The trustees were attracted by its remoteness from and yet easy access to the larger cities of the region and the generosity of local landowners in providing grounds for a campus, a fund of some £1,700, and more than 200 acres of woodlands north of the village for fuel. The principal donors, led by Nathaniel FitzRandolph, were all slaveholders.

Princeton played several pivotal roles in the American Revolution. Two of its residents—Richard Stockton 1748, the town's leading attorney, and the College president, John Witherspoon—signed the Declaration of Independence. In 1776 Princeton was the first capital of New Jersey, and in 1777 it was the site of the Battle of Princeton, an early turning point in the war. For four months in the summer of 1783 the Continental Congress met in Princeton, making it the capital of the country.

In 1813 the Borough of Princeton (essentially today's downtown) was created within what were then the perimeters of West Windsor and Montgomery townships. When Mercer County was formed in 1838, Princeton Township was incorporated, with the quasi-independent Borough encompassed within its borders. The Borough became fully independent in 1894. There were two minor boundary adjustments in 1928 and 1951 so Princeton hospital and then Princeton high school could be located entirely within the Borough.

The first mayor of the Borough was Samuel Bayard 1784. Many other University alumni played leading roles in governing both municipalities. B. Franklin Bunn 1907, longtime manager of the Princeton University Store, was the only person to serve as mayor in both the Borough (1928–30) and the Township (1940–50), although years later Richard Woodbridge '65 served as Borough Council president and afterwards as Township mayor.

In time, the campus expanded beyond the Borough's borders into the Township. When the former Princeton Inn was converted to a residential college in 1970, the boundary bisected it, requiring some students each year to re-register to vote when their change in dorm room moved them from one municipality to the other. The boundary also bisected the site that was proposed in 2006 for the Lewis Arts complex; as part of that project the University relocated the Princeton train station 460 feet to the south, which had the controversial effect of moving it from the Borough to the Township.

By the time the arts complex opened in 2017, the Borough and Township had consolidated into a single municipality. While three previous merger initiatives had failed (in 1953, 1979, and 1996), in 2011 voters in

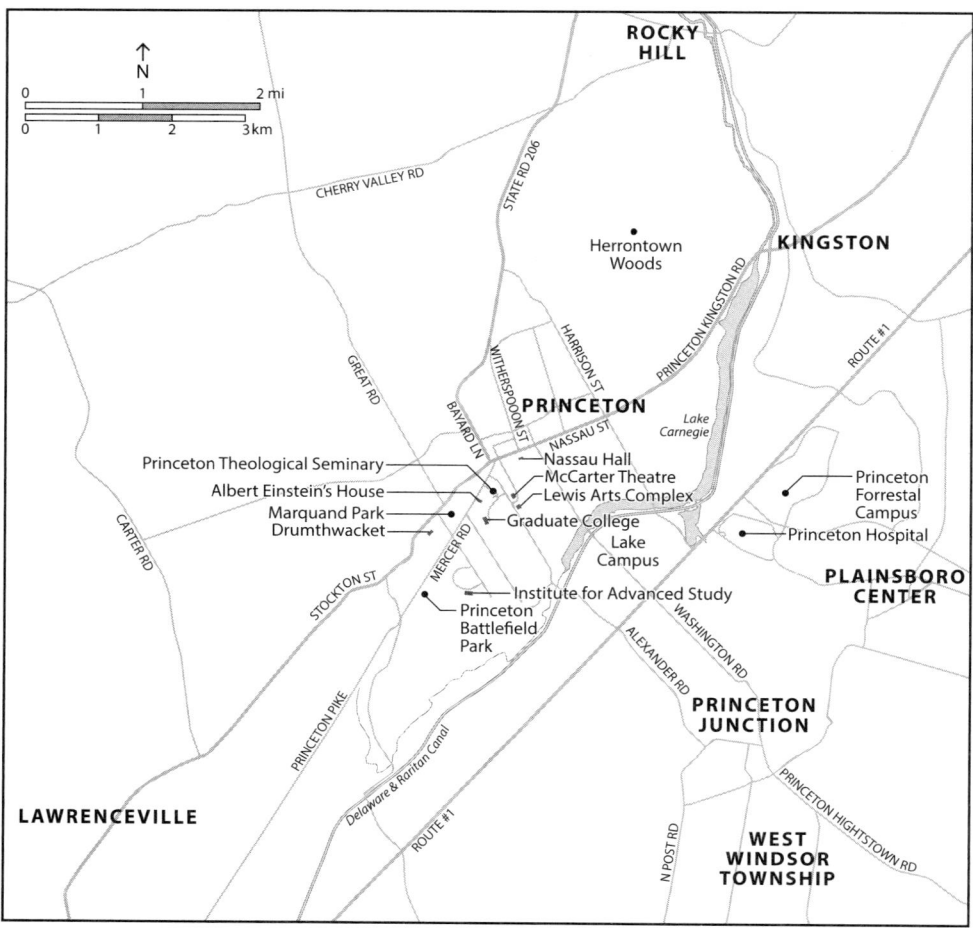

both municipalities approved consolidation, effective January 1, 2013.

Princeton today has a population of roughly 32,000. While clearly a college town, with about a third of its residents working in education, there is also a sizeable commuting population (the train station connects Princeton to the New Jersey Transit and Amtrak northeast corridor) and there is regular bus service to New York, New Brunswick, and Trenton. The New Jersey capital is only about a dozen miles away, making Princeton a convenient home for state workers; since 1945 the official home of the governor has been in Princeton, first at Morven (built in the 1750s as the Stockton family home), and then at Drumthwacket (built in 1835 and then expanded in 1893 by Moses Taylor Pyne 1877).

The community prides itself on its diversity. About a quarter of its population is foreign born. Approximately 6 percent of its residents are Black, 8 percent are Latino, and 17 percent are Asian. There is a sizeable Italian American population descended from the craftsmen who came to Princeton at the turn of the twentieth century to help build the University's Collegiate Gothic structures.

Princeton's Black community was first established following the end of the American Revolution, settling initially along Witherspoon Street, and by the early nineteenth century expanding to include other nearby streets in what is now known as the Witherspoon-Jackson neighborhood. (In 2016 the town designated the neighborhood a historic district.) By the 1830s as many as 20 percent of Princeton's 3,000 residents were free African Americans. In 1832 the first African American church in Princeton, Mt. Pisgah AME Church, was built at the corner of Witherspoon and Maclean Streets.

In 1837 Betsey Stockton, a formerly enslaved person, established a school for Black children, and in

Princeton, Municipality of 367

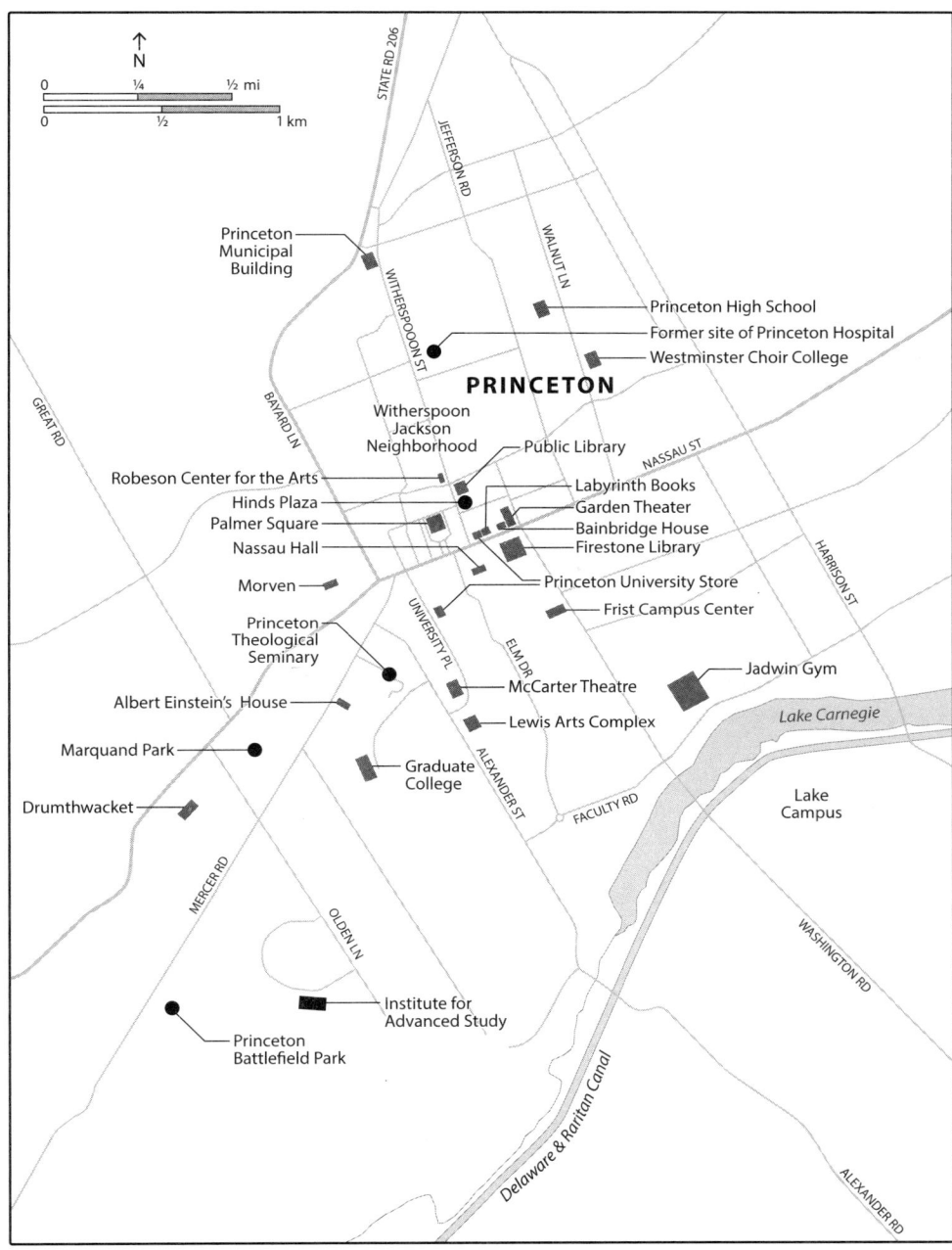

1840 she played a leading role in founding what today is the Witherspoon Street Presbyterian Church, where she led its Sunday School. From 1880 to 1901 the church's pastor was William Drew Robeson, whose son, Paul, unwelcome at Princeton University because of his race, became valedictorian and an All-American football player at Rutgers University and earned a law degree at Columbia before earning international acclaim as a singer, actor, activist, and humanitarian.

Betsey Stockton is commemorated today by a garden named for her between the University's Firestone Library and Nassau Street, immediately adjacent to a roadway that is named for Robert Rivers Jr. '53, a native of Princeton who was one of the first Black students admitted to the University and the first

African American elected by the Board of Trustees to serve as a trustee. The Paul Robeson Center for the Arts, home of the Princeton Arts Council, is named for Robeson, and in 1976 Jackson Street was renamed Paul Robeson Place in his honor.

In addition to the University, Princeton is home to the Institute for Advanced Study and the Princeton Theological Seminary. Between 1932 and 2020 it also was home to Westminster Choir College, before it was relocated to the Lawrenceville campus of its parent Rider University. The town's highly rated public school system is complemented by a charter school and several private schools, including Princeton Day School, the Hun School of Princeton, and Stuart Country Day School.

Historic sites in Princeton include the homes of Albert Einstein and of US presidents Grover Cleveland and Woodrow Wilson 1879, and Bainbridge House (1766), which was built by Job Stockton, named for the commander of the USS *Constitution*—"Old Ironsides"—in the War of 1812, and used later as a boarding house, the town's public library, the home of the town's historical society, and an exhibition gallery for the Princeton University Art Museum. Other sites include one of Princeton's oldest surviving homes, the Barracks, which is thought to have quartered troops during the French and Indian War and then in 1783 housed both James Madison and Alexander Hamilton when the Continental Congress was meeting in Princeton; the Thomas Clarke House (1772), a field hospital for the Battle of Princeton, which was fought on its surrounding 200-acre farm; Paul Robeson's birthplace at 110 Witherspoon Street; and a monument commemorating the Battle of Princeton that was dedicated in 1922 at the junction of Nassau Street, Bayard Lane, and Stockton Street.

The town's many spaces for outdoor recreation, in addition to the University campus and Lake Carnegie, include Marquand Park, which was given to the Borough by the children of Allan Marquand 1874, founder of the University's department of Art and Archaeology, and his wife, Eleanor Cross Marquand, and Herrontown Woods, which was donated to Mercer County by the distinguished mathematician Oswald Veblen and his wife, Elizabeth Richardson Veblen.

In the 1930s Baker's Alley, a historic African American neighborhood, was demolished and many of its residents were relocated to Birch Avenue to make way for Edgar Palmer 1903's Colonial Revival-style Palmer Square, a mixed-use development of shops, restaurants, offices, residences, and a hotel, the Nassau Inn, that traces its lineage to a predecessor hotel that opened in 1769 at 52 Nassau Street (now the site of Tiger Park). The square also originally included a 1,200-seat movie theater, the Princeton Playhouse.

A second downtown square, Hinds Plaza, borders the town's public library and is named for Albert Hinds, a beloved member of Princeton's African American community who was born in the Witherspoon-Jackson neighborhood in 1902 and remained an active member of the community until his death 104 years later in 2006.

The fates of town and gown have been closely intertwined since 1756. In 1956, on the 200th anniversary of the opening of Nassau Hall, the town gave the University a ceremonial mace as a symbol of their mutually beneficial relationship. The mace is carried by a faculty "mace bearer" each year at Opening Exercises, Baccalaureate, and Commencement, and the mayor is invited each year to march at Commencement.

The University brings economic, intellectual, and cultural vitality to the town, and the town offers an exceptional quality of life, excellent schools, and homes for many University faculty and staff. The University and the town work together on issues related to land use, traffic, transportation, biking, and sustainability.

Over time the University has made many direct contributions to the community. The earliest recorded cash contribution was in 1891. In the 1960s it began making regular contributions and adopted a policy of leaving properties that qualified for tax exemption on the tax rolls if they potentially could add children to the public schools (for example, faculty, staff, and graduate student nondormitory housing).

By the early 1970s an annual voluntary unrestricted financial contribution to the Borough was institutionalized, and every few years the amount was increased, reaching $100,000 in 1999. Periodically the University also made capital contributions to the Borough, as well as to the public library, the public schools, and other community organizations, and it made annual contributions to support the fire department, the First Aid and Rescue Squad, and affordable housing. The University also contributed land south of Springdale golf course for the community to construct affordable housing, and itself developed some 65 units of affordable housing for the community in connection with its development of faculty/staff housing at a site known as Merwick Stanworth that is adjacent to the Witherspoon-Jackson neighborhood.

In 2006 a six-year agreement was reached to consolidate many of the University's financial contributions into a $1 million unrestricted annual payment that would increase annually at the rate that the Borough's tax rate increased. In 2011 and 2012, the University extended its agreement with the Borough and made one-time contributions to the Township prior to negotiating a 2013 agreement with the newly consolidated municipality. Under a seven-year accord reached in 2014, the University agreed to make a $2.75 million unrestricted contribution that year and escalate it by four percent each year, while also making one-time capital contributions valued at $2.59 million.

In 2020 the agreement was extended for two years, and the University agreed also to provide $850,000 to support hiring for the Princeton fire department, which had begun to add paid staff, and $250,00 toward the construction of a new public works storage facility. (The University also continued to sponsor a program, first established in 2009, under which it allows University staff members who are trained as volunteer fire fighters to leave campus when needed to assist the municipal fire department; in 2020 34 University employees were enrolled in this program.)

The University's voluntary contributions are in addition to its tax payments to the municipality. As the town's largest taxpayer, the University in 2020 paid $9.5 million in property taxes, including about $6.4 million in voluntary tax payments for properties eligible for exemption from such taxes. The University owns, maintains, and pays taxes on five miles of roads in the municipality that are open to the public, including Faculty Road and College Road.

The University owns and subsidizes the town's two-screen movie theater, the Garden, and partners with the Arts Council in organizing each year's town-gown Communiversity festival that typically attracts more than 20,000 people to downtown Princeton and the front campus. In 2007 it helped insure there would continue to be an independent bookseller, Labyrinth Books, in downtown Princeton, and in 2015 the town approved a plan developed by the University to install an eruv in the community—a symbolic enclosure that allows observant Jews to carry objects outdoors on the Sabbath.

Princeton students serve the community through many community service projects and provide critical staffing for the Princeton First Aid and Rescue Squad. Since 1971 students have partnered with the recreation department to offer a youth basketball league in Dillon Gym on Saturday mornings from January through March for fourth-through-ninth graders from the community. Students patronize local shops and restaurants, with some of their favorites being Hoagie Haven, Thomas Sweet Ice Cream, Olives Deli and Bakery, and Small World Coffee.

Community members attend performances at McCarter Theatre, Theater Intime, Princeton Summer Theater, and the Lewis Center for the Arts; lectures and concerts; the art museum; the chapel; the Cotsen Children's Library in Firestone; athletic events; and a breathtaking fireworks display each year at reunions. Approximately 700 area residents participate in the Community Auditing Program each semester. Community residents are free to board the University's Tiger Transit shuttle buses to get around town and even to the Princeton Medical Center in Plainsboro.

In 2020, during the COVID-19 pandemic, the University committed $1 million to a relief fund to help area nonprofits combat the impact of the pandemic, provide grants for small businesses in town affected by it, and aid families and individuals in economic distress. The University directly supported organizations providing meals for at-risk families, children, and individuals; donated personal protective equipment to state and local agencies; hosted blood drives; provided perishable food items to local food kitchens; and even gave dormitory refrigerators to local organizations and families who needed them.

PRINCETON IN ASIA, AFRICA, AND LATIN AMERICA. The oldest of these three "Princeton Ins," Princeton in Asia, dates to 1898, when a group of undergraduates raised $500 to support the YMCA in Tianjin, China. Robert "Pop" Gailey *1896 went to China with the funds and started the program now known as Princeton in Asia (PiA). Eight years later he was joined by Dwight Edwards 1904, and together they established the first YMCA in Beijing.

Over the next 30 years, other Princetonians joined them and, under the auspices of a program they called Princeton-in-Peking, worked on famine relief programs, organized China's first athletic associations, and opened a school of commerce and finance. In 1923, when Princeton-in-Peking established the Princeton School of Public Affairs at Yenching University, the program changed its name to the Princeton-Yenching Foundation.

In 1949 the establishment of the People's Republic of China under Communist Party rule forced the foundation to cease work in China. Shortly thereafter, the new Chinese government closed Yenching University. Some of its arts and science faculties were absorbed into Beijing University, which moved from downtown Beijing to the former Yenching campus, and its engineering section was merged into Tsinghua University.

In 1952, Princeton-Yenching began to work with Tungai University in Taiwan and Yonsei and Chosun universities in Korea, providing scholarships, helping to support faculty salaries, and funding libraries. Princeton-Yenching also awarded scholarships for students from Hong Kong to attend Princeton.

In 1955 the organization changed its name again, this time to Princeton in Asia. In the early 1950s, Princeton graduates were not sent abroad under the auspices of the program, but in the summer of 1958 two undergraduates went to Japan to teach English, and in 1959 a graduating senior crossed the Pacific to teach in Taiwan. By 1969, PiA had sent some 30 Princetonians to teach in Hong Kong, Japan, Korea, and Taiwan. It also continued to support the education of Asian students and provided scholarships for government officials in Singapore to attend Princeton's school of Public and International Affairs.

In 1970 PiA hired its first full-time executive director, Robert Atmore. He increased participation in the program by opening it to graduates from other universities and extended its reach into South East and South Asia, while expanding the definition of "Asia" on occasion by sending interns to Egypt, Lebanon, Iran, Afghanistan, Turkey, Yemen, and Greece. PiA sent recent graduates as year-long teaching fellows, and it helped alumni and undergraduates obtain summer jobs in teaching, business, journalism, or at nongovernmental organizations (NGOs).

Over PiA's first century, it provided opportunities for more than 1,200 men and women to serve as teachers and in other capacities in 24 countries. Today, at any one time more than 150 recent college graduates (a minority of them from Princeton) are serving as year-long fellows or as summer interns at some 80 partner institutions in 45 cities in 22 Asian countries and regions. Princeton in Asia fellows teach in kindergartens, secondary schools, polytechnics, and universities; they work with international and local nonprofits, businesses, and social enterprises; and they write for newspapers and create content for news platforms with an international reach.

Princeton in Africa (PiAf) was founded in 1999 to provide year-long fellowships to recent Princeton graduates in locations across the African continent, and in 2010 it expanded to include graduates of other universities. In 2019–20 it placed 48 fellows from 29 colleges and universities at 31 organizations across 18 different countries. Over its first 20 years it placed over 600 fellows at more than 100 organizations in 36 countries.

Princeton in Africa fellows work in advocacy, research, and civil society; agricultural development; business and economic development; education and youth capacity building; environment and conservation; income generation; international humanitarian aid and development; and public and community development.

Princeton in Latin America (PiLA) is the youngest of the Princeton Ins. It was founded in 2002, and in its first year it placed two Class of 2003 graduates in year-long service fellowships; in 2008–09, PiLA opened applications to graduates of all North American colleges and universities. Since its founding it has placed almost 400 fellows with partners in 20 countries throughout Latin America and the Caribbean.

PiLA partners with NGOs and multinational organizations to place its fellows with nonprofit, public service, humanitarian, and government organizations in the following areas: education and youth development, entrepreneurships and microfinance, environmental conservation, food security, public health, and social development and human rights.

All three Princeton Ins are independent, not-for-profit organizations affiliated with the University and housed in the Louis A. Simpson International Building.

There are also several summer language programs known as "Princeton Ins." Princeton in Beijing and Princeton in Ishikawa are independent, not-for-profit organizations under the aegis of the department of East Asian Studies, while the others (such as Princeton in Argentina, Princeton in Cuba, and Princeton in Spain) are departmentally-sponsored programs.

PRINCETON-BLAIRSTOWN CENTER is the latest incarnation of the Princeton Summer Camp, which was founded in 1908 near Bay Head on the New Jersey shore by a student evangelical group, the Philadelphian Society, and was moved in 1930 to a site that eventually grew to 264 acres on Bass Lake near Blairstown in the northwestern part of the state.

The original camp program involved two-week summer sessions for low-income boys from New York and Philadelphia. In 1946, when former *Daily Princetonian* chair Frank Broderick '43 was serving as director, he arranged for eight African American boys from Princeton to attend the camp; one of them, Robert Rivers Jr. '53 became one of the first Black students admitted to Princeton and the first African American elected by the Board of Trustees to serve on the board.

The camp remained student-run and staffed by student volunteers until the 1970s. In 1971 it became coeducational, and shortly thereafter it launched a rebuilding program that winterized its facilities and used natural power—sun, wind, and flowing water—to give campers firsthand lessons in ecology. With professional staff it evolved into a more extensive and eventually year-round outdoor education program, although the facilities also continued to host retreats and workshops for student, faculty, and staff groups as well as for community organizations.

Blairstown had always been an independent non-profit entity with a largely alumni board. In 1995 it became a supporting organization of the University under federal tax law and, as required by that status, the University began appointing a majority of its board members. The University assigned the center to administer Outdoor Action, its experiential education program; provided the center's staff with office space on campus; and through the Princeton University Investment Company assumed responsibility for managing its endowment.

By 2009, however, Outdoor Action had grown too large to be administered outside the University, and in 2013 the center's status as a supporting organization came to an end. By then student engagement with the center had been minimal for many years, and the center was expanding its programming not only at Blairstown, but in urban schools in New Jersey and East Harlem. A year later the center moved off-campus, where it continues to operate year-round adventure-based, experiential education programs that serve nearly 8,000 young people each year. Its signature Summer Bridge Program is a free one-week leadership and enrichment experience for approximately 550–600 low-income students from Trenton, Newark, and Camden, New Jersey.

PRINCETON CLUB OF NEW YORK, THE, was founded in 1866 as the Princeton Alumni Association of New York. It was the first such association, and others quickly followed in Philadelphia in 1868 and Washington, DC, in 1872. By 1888 there were 17 associations.

The New York association reorganized in 1886 as the Princeton Club of New York and was incorporated in 1899 with Moses Taylor Pyne 1877 as its first president. Its first home was a house at the corner of 34th Street and Park Avenue, and eight years later it moved to the former residence of the architect Stanford White on Gramercy Park North at Lexington Avenue. During World War I, when many of its younger members and members of other similar clubs were serving in the military, it moved in with the Yale Club on Vanderbilt Avenue at 44th Street, and in gratitude the Yale Club endowed a Princeton Club of New York scholarship at Yale.

In 1922 the Princeton Club moved into its third home, a mansion with a 10-story annex at 39th Street and Park Avenue. At different times Princeton shared these facilities with the Brown and Dartmouth clubs. It occupied this home for almost 40 years until the early 1960s when it built a nine- (now 10-) story limestone clubhouse at 15 West 43rd Street, between Fifth and Sixth Avenues and two blocks west of Grand Central Station.

Ground was broken on June 15, 1961, and while awaiting completion of the building, rooms were leased in the Columbia University Club across the street. The new clubhouse opened in March 1963, and in the mid-1970s, when many university clubs were consolidating, the membership of the Columbia Club moved across the street to the Princeton Club.

Membership in the Princeton Club is open to alumni, students, faculty, administrators, and parents of current students. It is a private club, although it often hosts activities open to nonmembers as well as University meetings and events. There is a separate Princeton Association of New York City (PANYC, pronounced "panic") that includes all alumni in the city and frequently participates in gatherings at the club.

In 1990 the club completed a renovation designed by Robert Venturi '47 *50 that, among other things, added women's locker rooms and removed a controversial stone engraving in the floor that described the club as a place "where women cease from troubling and the wicked are at rest." The club was again extensively renovated between 2008 and 2010, and now offers an interior of almost 64,000 square feet.

The club offers two dining areas, a lounge, a business center, a library, a squash and fitness center, two floors of meeting and conference rooms, an outdoor terrace on the fourth floor, and 34 rooms for overnight accommodations. It hosts more than 200 events each year, and in 1999 it launched an annual

Princeton Night in New York to bring representatives from the campus to join with alumni for a program that typically featured prominent alumni speakers and the presentation of awards.

The club's members include alumni from affiliated schools, including Georgetown, Williams, NYU, the London School of Economics, and about a dozen others. From 1998 through 2017 Columbia was affiliated, and some of its alumni retain individual memberships.

By tradition, the portrait of the University's president hangs at the Princeton Club of New York until it is moved to the Faculty Room in Nassau Hall after the president leaves office. Also by tradition, the president of the Princeton Club of New York is an ex officio member of the Alumni Council, along with the presidents of all the regional associations, and is invited to attend meetings of the Alumni Council Executive Committee.

PRINCETON INSTITUTE FOR INTERNATIONAL AND REGIONAL STUDIES (PIIRS) promotes collaborative and interdisciplinary research and teaching on issues of global importance and sponsors a variety of programs and activities aimed at advancing knowledge of world regions and global issues. It was formed in 2003 through a merger of the Center for International Studies, a research center that had existed since 1951, and the Council on Regional Studies which supported the University's regional studies programs. The founding director of the institute was sociology professor Miguel Centeno, whose scholarly work was in Latin American society and politics, political sociology, historical-comparative sociology, and societies in transition.

The predecessor Center for International Studies encouraged research in international relations (studies of world order, foreign policy, military affairs) and national development (studies of comparative politics and of modernization in countries at various levels of development). The center's members included economists, historians, and sociologists as well as political scientists, and many of its group research projects involved multidisciplinary, comparative, and cross-cultural approaches.

PIIRS supports research, teaching, and scholarly dialogue that cuts across disciplines and world regions, and it provides funding for innovative research aimed at improving the understanding of world cultures and promoting knowledge about issues of global concern. It supports regional studies undergraduate certificate programs in African Studies, South Asian Studies, Contemporary European Politics and Society, and Russian, East European, and Eurasian Studies. It also sponsors a program in Translation and Intercultural Communication.

Through its undergraduate fellows program, PIIRS provides funding for senior thesis research abroad in the summer. It coordinates the global seminars program, which offers six-week courses open to 12 to 15 students that are taught by University faculty who create programs of study that can only be fully experienced by traveling to the international location at the heart of the course's subject matter. The seminars include lectures by seminar faculty and guests, daily language classes, weekend excursions to sites relevant to the course, and community service. Since the seminars were launched in 2007, more than 800 undergraduates have participated in locations in Africa, East Asia, South Asia, Europe, the Near East, and South America.

The institute's exploration seminars provide seven to nine days of international travel, usually during fall or spring break, in association with a course taught on the campus. PIIRS also provides funding for graduate student summer language study and dissertation field research abroad.

The institute co-sponsors conferences and seminars, and, through the Fung Global Fellows program, each year brings six exceptional early-career scholars from around the world to Princeton for a year of research, writing, and collaboration around a common topic.

PIIRS is home to the Paul and Marcia Wythes Center on Contemporary China, the M. S. Chadha Center for Global India, and the Brazil LAB (Luso-Afro-Brazilian Studies), each of which serves as a hub for an extensive network of scholars focused on these countries and their places in the world, as well as a Migration Lab that focuses research on contemporary migration issues.

PIIRS is also the home of *World Politics*, an internationally renowned quarterly journal of comparative politics and international relations published by Cambridge University Press that was founded in 1948 and has been based at Princeton since 1951.

In addition to PIIRS, other institutes and centers provide opportunities for international study and research. For example, the Institute for the Transregional Study of the Contemporary Middle East, North Africa, and Central Asia was established in 1994 and then integrated into the department of

Near Eastern Studies in 2008. The Sharmin and Bijan Mossavar-Rahmani Center for Iran and Persian Gulf Studies was established in 2012 to support teaching and research in all aspects of Iran and Persian Gulf studies at Princeton.

PRINCETON INVESTMENT COMPANY (PRINCO) is responsible for managing the University's endowment, which by 2020 had reached $26.6 billion—the fifth largest in the country and the largest on a per student basis. Its 12-member board of directors includes eight members elected by the University's trustees and four members who serve ex officio: the University's president, its vice president and treasurer, the chair of the trustee finance committee, and Princo's president. The office (located just off campus at 22 Chambers Street) is organizationally distinct from the University, but its staff members are University employees and its president reports both to the president of the University and the chair of the Princo board.

Princo operates largely as a "manager of managers," overseeing a global network of over 60 carefully selected investment firms in diverse asset categories who ultimately make the decisions about where to invest. Princo attributes much of its success to its ability to select and gain access to top-tier managers and actively engage with them. It describes its other advantages as the endowment's size (neither too large nor too small), its long-term time horizon (allowing above-average volatility and investments in assets that take time to mature), its relatively low annual spending requirements as a percentage of its value (allowing for below-average liquidity), and the fabled loyalty and desire to be helpful of the University's alumni.

Princo uses an aggressive "equity-biased" strategy to achieve long-term returns sufficient to meet the University's current and future operating needs, support its strategic priorities and capital requirements, and preserve real value for future generations. Its nontraditional asset allocation aims to balance equities versus fixed income, domestic versus foreign investments, and publicly traded versus nonmarketable assets (with a heavy investment in nonmarketable assets). Following this strategy, Princeton achieved an annual return of 9.2 percent in the 20 years prior to 2020, which ranked in the top 1 percent among all institutional investors.

Until the early twentieth century, Princeton had little endowment to manage and devoted little attention to managing it. In the 1920s, as the endowment passed $20 million, the legendary Dean Mathey 1912 began managing the University's investments, first as an outside volunteer and then as a trustee. By the time he left the board in 1960, responsibility for the endowment was vested in a three-member trustee subcommittee of the finance committee that approved the purchase and sale of all securities. In 1977 the subcommittee delegated responsibility for day-to-day management of the University's investments to four outside advisers, and then in 1987, when endowment assets were at $2.2 billion, the trustees decided to create Princo.

The founding chair of the Princo board was John Beck '53, president of the investment-counseling firm of Beck, Mack & Oliver, who had been chairing the investment subcommittee. He was succeeded in 1990 by Richard Fisher '57, who in turn was succeeded by Edward Matthews '53 (1998–2002), Peter Wendell '72 (2002–08), Kathryn Hall '80 (2008–11), Philip Hammarskjold '87 (2011–19), and Bob Peck '88 (2019–). The founding president was Dennis Sullivan '70. Randall Hack '69 succeeded him in 1990, followed by Andrew Golden, who came to Princo in 1995 after working in the investment offices at Yale and Duke. (From 1995 to 2000 Hack continued to manage the University's venture capital and other private equity investments through a company called Nassau Capital.)

In recent years Princo has sought to increase diversity within its staff and among its roster of external managers. Golden says "studies and experience show that diverse teams have an advantage in solving complex problems like those common in investing." In a 2020 letter to members of Congress, he noted that women and minorities made up a majority of the board's outside directors and that five of the seven outside firms Princo had hired in the previous two years were diverse, including three that were led and substantially owned by African Americans.

Because of his responsibility for managing the endowment, Golden has played an active role in campus discussions about investment-driven social responsibility issues, including proposals for divestment, and he and his senior colleagues frequently meet with the CPUC resources committee to contribute their expertise to its discussions.

PRINCETON IN THE MOVIES AND ON TELEVISION. Princeton and Princetonians have a long history of appearing in and producing movies and television shows.

A movie commissioned by the University, *Princeton: A Search for Answers*, won the 1973 Academy Award for best documentary short subject. Designed primarily for potential applicants and alumni audiences, the film described the core purpose of the University as a search for answers and depicted both the vibrancy and the increased diversity of a campus that only recently had become coeducational. It was released in enough theaters to qualify for an Oscar, and when it caught the attention of film producer and director Joshua Logan '31 he wrote to his fellow academy members, urging them to see it and expressing his hope that they "will vote the way I will vote when the time comes."

A movie partially filmed on campus, *A Beautiful Mind*, won four 2001 Academy Awards, including best picture. It recounts the struggles with mental illness of John Nash Jr. *50, a brilliant mathematician and enigmatic campus figure who was awarded the 1994 Nobel Prize in Economics for his groundbreaking work on game theory. Russell Crowe played Nash in the movie, with Nash occasionally watching the filming.

Another enigmatic campus figure, Albert Einstein, as portrayed by Walter Matthau, was featured in the movie *I.Q.*, which was filmed on campus and in neighboring communities in 1994. It is a romantic comedy in which Einstein plays cupid for his fictional niece. In 2008, movie cameras were on campus to film scenes for *Transformers: Revenge of the Fallen*, and in the 2012 movie *Admission*, starring Tina Fey as a Princeton University admission officer, campus footage includes Clio Hall and the Holder Hall cloisters; then-dean of admission Janet Rapelye makes a cameo appearance.

The oldest movie about Princeton is an 1899 silent film called *A Football Tackle*, which showed "Capt. Edwards of the Princeton varsity team making a tackle in a football scrimmage on the Princeton field." The 1928 silent film *Varsity* was partly filmed on campus; its negative depiction of campus life led President John Grier Hibben to demand it be withdrawn, and as of February 1, 1929, it was.

Other movies with scenes filmed on campus include the biopic *Wilson* (1944), which dramatized the life of Woodrow Wilson 1879 and won five Academy Awards; *People Will Talk* (1951), starring Cary Grant; *Class of '44* (1973), a sequel to *Summer of '42*; *Hoop Dreams* (1994), which includes a scene filmed in Jadwin Gym; *Scent of a Woman* (1992), by Robert "Bo" Goldman '53, which uses Holder Hall as a stand-in for a prep school; and *One True Thing* (1998). On television, the series *House* used the south-facing wall of Frist Campus Center in its opening credits to depict the program's fictitious Princeton-Plainsboro teaching hospital.

Dramatizations of the lives of Princetonians, in addition to *A Beautiful Mind* and *Wilson*, include *Infinity* (1996), with Matthew Broderick as Nobel Laureate Richard Feynman *42. Two movies, *Breaking the Code* (1996) and *The Imitation Game* (2014)—an Academy Award winner for best adapted screenplay—introduced audiences to the life and achievements of Alan Turing *38, and especially his central role in hastening the Allied victory in World War II by cracking Nazi Germany's Enigma code. In *Too Big to Fail* (2011), Paul Giamatti plays former Princeton professor Ben Bernanke.

Fermat's Last Theorem, a documentary about mathematics professor Andrew Wiles, was produced for the BBC in 1996. A 2008 documentary, *Examined Life*, featured Princeton philosophers Kwame Anthony Appiah, Peter Singer, and Cornel West *80. West's movie credits include his role as Councilor West in the 2003 science fiction movies *The Matrix Reloaded* and *The Matrix Revolutions*. Josue Lajeunesse, a custodial worker at the University, was featured in the 2009 documentary, *The Philosopher Kings*.

Fictitious Princetonians abound in the movies and on television. In *She Loves Me Not* (1934), a woman who witnesses a murder disguises herself as a male student to hide out at Princeton; in *Meet Me in St. Louis* (1944), Princeton is the college destination for the oldest child in the Smith family; the ambitious lawyer played by Paul Newman in *The Young Philadelphians* (1959) attended Princeton; the main character in *Risky Business* (1983) interviews with a Princeton admission officer, is told "Princeton can use a man like you," and gets accepted; the movie *Spanglish* (2004) begins with a first-generation Mexican American high school student applying to Princeton; *A Cinderella Story* (2004) ends with the protagonist and her prince attending Princeton; lawyer Rose Feller of *In Her Shoes* (2005), based on a novel by Jennifer Weiner '91, attended Princeton; as did a CIA analyst in the 2008 movie *Burn After Reading* by Ethan Coen '79 and his brother, Joel.

On television, the eldest daughter, Sondra, on *The Cosby Show*, and her boyfriend and later husband Elvin, graduated from Princeton; the main character in the series *Doogie Howser, MD*, graduated from Princeton at the age of 10; Will Smith, the *Fresh Prince* of *Bel Air*, is admitted to Princeton; White House staffer Sam Seaborn in *West Wing* is a Princeton alum, as are President Charles Logan in *24*, television executive Jack Donaghy in *30 Rock*, physicist Leonard Hofstadter in *The Big Bang Theory*, and OB/GYN Mindy Lahiri on *The Mindy Project*.

For almost a century, Princetonians have been playing leading roles on movie and television screens. In a career of more than 50 years, Jimmy Stewart '32 made some 80 films, including *The Philadelphia Story*, *Mr. Smith Goes to Washington*, *It's a Wonderful Life*, *Vertigo*, and *Rear Window*. In 1947 the University presented him with an honorary degree; from 1959 to 1963 he served as a trustee; and in 1990 he received the Woodrow Wilson Award, the University's highest honor for undergraduate alumni. More recently, Ellie Kemper '02, whose breakout television role was in *The Office* and who earned critical acclaim as the star of *Unbreakable Kimmy Schmidt*, was the 2019 Class Day speaker, after having delivered the closing address at the previous year's *She Roars* conference.

The University archives report that among the most frequently requested senior theses have been those of Wentworth Miller III '95 (*Prison Break*), Dean Cain '88 (*Lois & Clark: The New Adventures of Superman*), Brooke Shields '87 (*Pretty Baby*, *Blue Lagoon*, *Endless Love*), and David Duchovny '82 (*The X-Files* and *Californication*). *The X-Files* have another Princeton connection; the series was developed by Rose Catherine Pinkney '86 when she was director of programming at Twentieth Century Fox Television.

A "leading role" of a different kind was played by Charles Gibson '65, who, during a career of more than 40 years in broadcast journalism, joined Americans at their breakfast tables for almost two decades as host of ABC's *Good Morning America* from 1987 to 2006, and then served as anchor of *ABC's World News with Charles Gibson* from 2006 to 2009. Gibson received the Woodrow Wilson Award in 2018 and was the Class Day speaker in 2010.

Acclaimed writers, producers, and directors include Coen (*Fargo*, *O Brother, Where Art Thou?*, *No Country for Old Men*, and *Bridge of Spies*), David E. Kelley '79 (creator of such TV series as *Picket Fences*, *Chicago Hope*, *Ally McBeal*, *Boston Public*, *Boston Legal*, and *Harry's Law*); and Douglas McGrath '80 (*Bullets Over Broadway*). Jeff Moss '63, the founding head writer of *Sesame Street*, created the Cookie Monster and Oscar the Grouch and won 14 Emmy and four Grammy awards.

Craig Mazin '92 won Golden Globe and Emmy awards for a 2019 television miniseries he created, produced, and wrote about the 1986 explosion at the Chernobyl nuclear power plant. That same year Elizabeth Chai Vasarhelyi '00 won an Academy Award for best documentary feature for *Free Solo*, which she directed with her husband; the film follows a climb without ropes of Yosemite's famous 900-meter rock face, El Capitan. In 2020 Cathy Yan '08 was profiled in the *Washington Post* as "the first woman of Asian descent to steer a major Hollywood superhero movie" for her role as director of *Birds of Prey*.

Groundbreaking television executives include Ward Chamberlin '43, one of the visionaries who helped create public television and National Public Radio; he served as executive vice president at WNET in New York, president of WETA in Washington, DC, and senior vice president for Public Broadcasting Service (PBS). In 1979 Robert L. Johnson *72 founded the television network Black Entertainment Television (BET) and served as its CEO and chair; in 1991 BET became the first Black-controlled company to be listed on the New York Stock Exchange. Garth Ancier '79, who produced and hosted a national radio program *American Focus*, as an undergraduate, is one of only two people to have programmed three of the five US broadcast television networks: NBC, Fox, and The WB (later The CW). He also served as the first president of BBC Worldwide America.

PRINCETON NEUROSCIENCE INSTITUTE (PNI) traces its origins to the spring of 2004 when Jonathan Cohen, a professor of neuroscience in the department of Psychology, and David Tank, a professor in the department of Molecular Biology, began developing a proposal to create an institute whose overarching goal was to understand behavior at all levels of function, from systems to cells. Their proposal was approved by the trustees in the spring of 2006.

Cohen and Tank remain the co-directors of the institute, which they view as a stimulus for teaching and research in neuroscience and related fields, and an impetus for collaboration and education in disciplines as wide-ranging as economics and philosophy. Collaborators come from mathematics, physics, engineering, chemistry, computer science, molecular biology, ecology and evolutionary biology, philosophy, psychology, and economics.

Cohen, who has an MD as well as a PhD, specializes in cognitive neuroscience; his research focuses on the neurobiological mechanisms underlying cognitive control; their role in higher cognitive functions such as reasoning, problem solving, and planning; and their disturbance in psychiatric disorders such as schizophrenia and depression. He uses behavioral and brain imaging methods together with computational modeling in his work.

Cohen was named the director of the Center for the Study of Brain, Mind, and Behavior when it was created in 2000, and he was responsible for acquiring its functional magnetic resonance imaging (fMRI) scanner. (Princeton was the first institution outside a medical setting to have a human brain imaging facility.) Cohen also has directed the certificate program in Neuroscience since it was established in 2001.

Tank joined the molecular biology and physics faculties in 2001. He develops and applies physics-based measurement techniques to study dynamic aspects of the nervous system, from the level of single neurons to the whole brain. From 1983 to 2001 he conducted research at Bell Laboratories and directed its biological computation research department.

In describing PNI's mission, Tank says, "in some sense, a main emphasis of neuroscience over the last century has been characterizing the elements, such as neurons and synapses, that make up the brain. One of the goals of the institute is to understand how the whole system works together as one unit from all of the very complex interactions and underlying parts."

The institute emphasizes close connections among theory, modeling, and experimentation using the most advanced technologies. "It's all about a balance between quantitative theory and experimentation," Cohen says. "Much of existing theory has not been very precise or very mathematical, and there hadn't been an extensive use of computer simulations to understand the dynamics of brain function."

The institute's PhD program trains researchers to develop new techniques and approaches to answer two fundamental questions: How do millions of individual neurons work together to give rise to behavior at the level of a whole organism, and how do our brains work?

Undergraduates concentrating in neuroscience study molecular, cellular, developmental, and systems neuroscience as it interfaces with cognitive, behavioral, and computational research. Since modern neuroscience increasingly relies on quantitatively sophisticated methods and theory, concentrators are expected to gain competencies in physics, mathematics, and computation. A certificate program is available for students who have a strong interest in the brain but whose primary studies are in other fields; students earning the certificate have majored in molecular biology, psychology, engineering, chemistry, applied mathematics, economics, politics, history, and music.

PNI is home to three centers: the Bezos Center for Neural Circuit Dynamics, the McDonnell Center for Systems Neuroscience, and the Scully Center for the Neuroscience of Mind and Behavior.

In the fall of 2006, Rafael Moneo was chosen to design a two-building complex to house PNI and the department of Psychology. The building was completed in 2013.

PRINCETON PLASMA PHYSICS LABORATORY (PPPL), THE, can trace its origins to a ski slope in Colorado. It was there in 1951 that Lyman Spitzer Jr. *38 had the idea of meeting the world's ever-growing demand for safe, reliable, and abundant energy by replicating on earth the process of nuclear fusion that powers the sun.

As an astrophysicist, Spitzer had studied the behavior of electrically charged (ionized) gases, or plasmas, in interstellar space. He conceived the idea of confining a plasma in a figure-8 shaped tube using magnetic forces generated by coils wrapped around the outside; at sufficiently high temperatures, hydrogen nuclei would fuse into helium atoms and release tremendous amounts of energy to generate electricity. Because only very low-density plasma could be contained in this way, there would be no possibility of explosion.

Spitzer called his concept a "stellarator." In March 1951 he proposed to the United States Atomic Energy Commission (AEC) the construction of such a device and later that spring the AEC approved funding.

The first home for what was to become the world's leading center for both theoretical and experimental research on nuclear fusion was a former rabbit hutch on the University's recently acquired Forrestal campus. The site, code named Project Matterhorn, initially was classified because it conducted research on hydrogen bombs as well as fusion energy. The government declassified the site in 1958; in 1961 Project Matterhorn became the Princeton Plasma Physics Laboratory and Melvin Gottlieb succeeded Spitzer as director. Gottlieb led the lab until 1981 when he was succeeded by Harold Furth (1981–90).

With declassification, graduate study was introduced, and over the years more than 260 students have received doctorates through the program in Plasma Physics in the department of Astrophysical Sciences. Many went on to leading roles in the field, including PPPL directors Ronald Davidson *66 (1991–96), who succeeded Furth; Robert Goldston *77 (1997–2008), who succeeded Davidson and in turn was succeeded by Stewart Prager (2008–16); and Steven Cowley *85 (2018–). Princeton has been the top-ranked university for graduate study in plasma science since rankings began.

Magnetic confinement proved to be subject to an array of instabilities, which were attacked by theoreticians, experimentalists, and engineers. Late in the 1950s the figure-8 geometry was abandoned in favor of a "racetrack" design, and in 1970 this gave way to the "tokamak," a Russian donut-shaped design. In 1971 the first tokamak experiments in the US began at PPPL, and in 1975 Congress approved construction of the TFTR (Tokamak Fusion Test Reactor), which would become the first magnetic fusion device in the world to conduct experiments with a 50/50 mixture of the two hydrogen isotopes, deuterium and tritium, most likely to be used as fuels in fusion power plants. By 1976 PPPL had 800 employees and an annual operating budget of approximately $28 million, fully one-third of the University's overall budget.

The University manages the laboratory for the US Department of Energy. The lab today has more than 500 employees and its current budget of $120 million, while now only about five percent of the University's budget, accounts for about a third of the funding the University receives for sponsored research. The lab now encompasses 30 buildings over 90 acres.

Three conditions must be met to achieve fusion in a laboratory: very high temperatures (roughly 150 million degrees Celsius), enough plasma particle density so collisions occur, and sufficient length of confinement. In 1982 TFTR produced its first plasma, and over the next 15 years it set increasing records for ion temperatures and fusion power. In the 1990s, plasma in TFTR reached temperatures up to 510 million degrees Celsius, more than 30 times hotter than the core of the sun. In 1990 TFTR set a world record of 60,000 watts of fusion power, and by 1994 it was producing 10.7 million watts. This was the first demonstration that significant fusion could be obtained in a controlled environment.

As the worldwide fusion community began designing an international fusion research tokamak in France called ITER (Latin for "the way"), PPPL shifted its research focus to the development phase beyond ITER. The NSTX (National Spherical Torus Experiment) was built to explore a more compact configuration; in 1999 it created its first plasma and it then operated very successfully for a decade. In 2016 an upgrade known as NSTX-U was dedicated; it, too, was designed to investigate smaller and less expensive concepts so that fusion energy will be not only achievable but affordable throughout the world.

The worldwide quest to harness fusion energy is attracting growing interest from the private sector. At Princeton, the quest continues into its eighth decade, gaining new knowledge each year and passing a succession of milestones. Cowley says one of his goals as PPPL's seventh director is "to drive the science and technology innovations necessary for commercial fusion power—in a sense, to complete the job Spitzer started. While we know how to do fusion, we cannot yet make electricity from fusion at a reasonable cost."

Cowley's other goal is to diversify PPPL's research by leveraging the lab's connection to the University, and especially to the department of Astrophysical Sciences, thus making PPPL a multi-purpose national laboratory. PPPL scientists and engineers have developed capabilities in such fields as computational simulations, vacuum technology, mechanics, materials science, electronics, computer technology, and high-voltage power systems, and have applied their knowledge in areas ranging from the development of plasma thrusters and the propagation of intense beams of ions, to forecasts of the impact of solar storms and the manufacture of semiconductor chips.

PPPL scientists seek to advance the science of nanoscale fabrication and further the scientific understanding of plasmas from nano- to astrophysical-scales. The lab's spinoffs have included a highly sensitive radiation detector called MINDS (Miniature Integrated and Nuclear Detection System), a lightweight, portable unit that can be used to detect radionuclides for anti-terrorism purposes.

While the scientific and engineering challenges of producing affordable fusion energy are formidable, the potential benefits are manifold. There are no dangerous byproducts or byproducts suitable for nuclear weapons and there is little radioactive waste. Fusion's fuels are readily available, plentiful, safe, not dependent on weather, and they produce no carbon emissions.

In a June 2019 update to the University's strategic planning framework, the trustees reaffirmed both of Cowley's goals. The board "agreed that the laboratory's ambitious research program is consistent with the University's aspiration to make a difference to the world through teaching and research of unsurpassed quality," and it "encouraged the administration to explore possibilities for increasing the connections between the University and the laboratory in ways that advance the missions of both organizations."

To insure that the laboratory would be fully represented in the president's cabinet, in 2013 former dean for research and professor of physics A. J. Stewart Smith *66 was named the University's first vice president for PPPL; he was succeeded in 2016 by astrophysical sciences professor David McComas.

PRINCETON PRIZE IN RACE RELATIONS, THE, was founded in the fall of 2003 by Henry Von Kohorn '66, a former chair of the Alumni Council's Princeton Schools Committee and future chair of the council, who thought it was important for Princeton to play a role in recognizing and encouraging high school students who were fostering positive race relations within their schools or communities.

With financial support from alumni and the University and the active engagement of alumni volunteers, the program began as a pilot program in two cities, Washington and Boston. Over the next decade and a half, it grew to 28 regions nationally plus an at-large region for students from areas that did not have a regional committee. More than 400 alumni participated in the program each year through the regional committees that solicited applications, selected a prize winner and certificate of accomplishment awardees, and planned local ceremonies to recognize the recipients, frequently in conjunction with the local alumni association. When possible, honorees were also recognized by Princeton Prize committee members at school awards assemblies.

Each prize winner receives a $1,000 award and an all-expenses-paid trip to a symposium on the campus where they meet and share ideas with the other winners and with Princeton students, faculty, staff, and alumni. (In 2020 the symposium was held virtually because of the COVID-19 pandemic, and a virtual symposium was also held in 2021.)

The mission of the prize is "to identify and recognize high school-age students who significantly engage and challenge their schools and communities to advance racial equity in order to promote respect and understanding among all people." Over its first 17 years (through 2020) it recognized a total of 1,587 students across the country

The program is overseen by a national board of alumni volunteers of which Von Kohorn was the founding chair. The chair and vice chair of the board serve on the executive committee of the Alumni Council, and the prize receives staff support from the University. In 2020–21 representatives from the board and the University began discussing ways to enhance the program and increase its impact.

While there is no connection between the prize program and the Princeton admission process, a number of prize winners have attended Princeton (for example, there were four in the Class of 2019); all prize winners who attend Princeton automatically become members of the national board while they are undergraduates.

In addition to supporting the symposium, members of the Class of 1966 also endowed a Princeton Prize in Race Relations Senior Thesis Prize, awarded annually beginning in 2018 to a senior whose thesis significantly adds to an understanding of race and race relations in the United States, and a Princeton Prize in Race Relations Research Fund to support research related to understanding and improving race relations.

PRINCETON AND SLAVERY PROJECT. The Princeton and Slavery project began in an undergraduate seminar first offered in the spring of 2013 by history professor Martha Sandweiss. She taught the seminar in the University Archives with the assistance of university archivist Dan Linke and his staff. One goal was to investigate how the University had benefited from slave labor or money derived from slave labor; whether early college presidents, trustees, faculty, and staff owned slaves; whether students brought slaves to campus; and how the culture of slavery in America shaped campus life. Another goal was to introduce students to the methods of archival research: students examined letters, diaries, wills, sermons, speeches, newspaper advertisements, census data, genealogy records, student directories, business and court records, and minutes of trustee and faculty meetings.

With initial support from the Humanities Council and later support from other departments, programs, and groups (including the Friends of the Princeton University Library, the Center for Digital Humanities, and the Princeton Histories Fund, which provides funding to explore "aspects of Princeton's history that have been forgotten, overlooked, subordinated, or suppressed"), the investigation into Princeton and slavery soon expanded in scope, eventually becoming the largest study of its kind. When the project released its initial findings in November 2017, its website featured more than 80 articles, video documentaries, and interactive maps, and some 360 primary source documents.

The project hosted discussions and other events, including a symposium whose keynote speaker was Nobel Laureate and emerita Princeton professor Toni Morrison, and McCarter Theatre presented performances of seven newly commissioned one-act plays derived from materials discovered by the project. The art museum commissioned a sculpture by Titus Kaphar that was displayed in front of Maclean House, site of a 1766 estate sale that included six enslaved people who had been owned by President Samuel Finley; the sculpture is now part of the museum's collection. The project partnered with the Princeton public schools, the public library, and the historical society to develop lesson plans and produce exhibitions.

The project did not find evidence that the University as an institution held slaves or that student's slaves lived with them on campus (in 1794 the College formally prohibited students from bringing their servants to campus). But it did find that all of the first nine Princeton presidents were slaveholders at some point in their lives; that five of them brought slaves to the President's House (now Maclean House); and that 16 enslaved African Americans, including children, lived and worked in Maclean House between 1756 and 1822—all of whom are now commemorated on a plaque in front of the house.

One of the enslaved young women, Betsey Stockton, is memorialized in a garden in front of Firestone Library that the University named for her in 2018, the same year it named an arch in East Pyne Hall for James Collins Johnson, a fugitive slave who was betrayed by a student, tried in town, freed with the assistance of a local citizen (President John Witherspoon's great-granddaughter), and ended up working on campus for more than 60 years before he died in 1902.

The project found that 16 of the University's 23 founding trustees "bought, sold, traded, or inherited" slaves, and that most of the key donors who brought the fledgling college to Princeton were slave owners, including Nathaniel FitzRandolph, who gave the land on which Nassau Hall and the President's House were built, and the other residents of the town who donated lands to house the college and meet its needs for fuel.

Princeton faculty who owned slaves included John Maclean Sr., the father of Princeton's 10th president (Maclean Jr. was the first president not to own slaves), and Albert Dod 1822, a professor of mathematics, who in 1840 was the last Princeton faculty member recorded as owning a slave. Prospect House, which became the home of the president in 1868, was built in 1849 with funds derived from slave labor on the Potter family's southern rice plantations.

"Yet, within this landscape of slavery," the project reported, "Princeton during its first 75 years produced a staggering number of leaders of the American clergy, military, and government, many of whom were 'antislavery' in the sense that they disapproved of slavery and sought to abolish the institution. The venerated Dr. Benjamin Rush (Class of 1760) and the theologian Jonathan Edwards Jr. (Class of 1765) provided crucial moral leadership during the north's transition into 'free states.' John Witherspoon provided the intellectual underpinnings for this antislavery sentiment at Princeton. Although Witherspoon owned slaves, his teachings gave a generation of students 'a language for challenging slavery.'"

At the same time, largely as a result of Witherspoon's annual expeditions, early nineteenth-century Princeton attracted not only funding but students from the south, and even into the twentieth century it received substantial financial support from donors whose wealth derived from human bondage. One of the most generous benefactors in Princeton history, Moses Taylor Pyne 1877, inherited his fortune from his grandfather, whose shipping business transported sugar grown by slaves on Cuban plantations.

With respect to students, the project found that before John Witherspoon's presidency began in 1768, about 20 percent of Princeton's students came from the south, but by 1790 the percentage was 67 percent. Between 1746 and 1863 the proportion of southern students averaged 40 percent, as compared to roughly 10 percent at Harvard and Yale. From 1820 to 1860, 12 Princeton classes enrolled more southern than northern students, with southern enrollment in the Class of 1851 reaching 63 percent.

Not surprisingly, this had a significant impact on campus culture in the years leading to the Civil War, as did the fact that the state of New Jersey did not fully abolish slavery until 1865. There were periodic eruptions of violence on campus and in town, and there were discussions about slavery in the dormitories and at Whig and Clio, but students made concerted efforts to sustain their friendships notwithstanding their political differences and the administration did all it could to accommodate the sensibilities of southern students and their families.

The project noted that while the antislavery movement in Princeton was relatively weak, Princeton alumni and faculty played leading roles in the 1816 founding of the American Colonization Society, which sought to send freed slaves to Africa. The project described Princeton as "ground zero" for the movement, whose founders included Charles Fenton Mercer 1797, a slaveholder from Virginia; Elias Caldwell 1796, clerk of the US Supreme Court; and Robert Finley 1787, a trustee of the Princeton Theological Seminary. James Madison 1771 became the colonization society's president in 1833, and both President James Carnahan and President Maclean served as directors of the society in New Jersey.

PRINCETON IN SPACE. In 1969, Keeper of Princetoniana Frederic Fox '39 prevailed upon his wife, Hannah, to make five homemade Princeton flags that he could send to the moon with astronaut Charles "Pete" Conrad Jr. '53, as a way, he said, "of putting Princeton 239,000 miles ahead of Harvard and Yale." Conrad had already carried a Fox-provided Princeton banner into space in 1965 when he traveled on an eight-day Gemini V mission that set a new endurance record at the time, and he had been in space a second time in 1966, commanding the Gemini XI mission.

On November 19, 1969, as commander of the Apollo 12 mission, Conrad spent seven hours on the moon, becoming the third human to step foot on its surface. Referring to the landing four months earlier by the taller Neil Armstrong, he famously quipped "that may have been a small step for Neil, but that's a long one for me." He took the flags with him, and following his return to earth he presented one to Princeton. That flag was consumed by fire in 1977 at the local shop where it had been sent to be framed. In 1996, Conrad presented a replacement flag to the University, which can be found in the archives.

In 1973 Conrad commanded the first manned Skylab mission, Skylab 2, and set a record of 28 days in space, repairing damage to the Skylab Orbital Workshop. The mission prevented him from attending his 20th reunion, but he did send regrets to his class reunion chair that he could not be present because "he was out of town on business."

Other alumni who followed Conrad into space include Gerald Carr *62, who in November 1973 commanded Skylab 4, the third and final manned mission to the Skylab space station, and set a new record of 84 days in space; James Adamson *77, who flew on the space shuttles Columbia in 1989 and Atlantis in 1991; Gregory Linteris '79 *90, who flew two missions on Columbia in 1997; and Daniel Barry *80, who traveled to space three times between 1996 and 2001, and on those missions participated in four spacewalks totaling 25 hours and 53 minutes. On his first mission he carried a banner commemorating the centennial of Princeton's graduate school, which he presented to the University at the ceremony that officially opened its 250th anniversary celebration.

Brian Binnie *78 was not an astronaut, but in 2004 he set world records as a test pilot for the privately funded SpaceShipOne, reaching altitudes a winged aircraft had never achieved before. Gregory Olsen, appointed in 2007 as Princeton's first entrepreneur-in-residence, was the third private citizen to become a space tourist when he made a self-funded 10-day trip to the International Space Station in 2005 on Russian shuttles, taking a Princeton flag with him.

Part of the story of Princeton in space is told through its astronauts and other space travelers, but another, and quite extraordinary, part is told through the scientific explorations of its astrophysicists and physicists. To cite just a few examples: Professor Lyman Spitzer Jr. *38 inspired the development of the National Aeronautics and Space Administration's orbiting astronomical observatory program, which led to the launching of the 32-inch Copernicus ultraviolet satellite in 1972 and the Hubble Space Telescope in 1990. A satellite created by Professor David Wilkinson was launched in 1989 to study cosmic background radiation, and the eponymous Wilkinson Microwave Anisotropy Probe, a successor satellite 45 times more sensitive, was launched in 2001. The Sloan Digital Sky Survey, the brainchild of Professor James Gunn, revolutionized the nature of ground-based astronomy when it began making observations in 2000.

PRINCETON THEOLOGICAL SEMINARY. In 1811 the Presbyterian General Assembly decided that the College of New Jersey was becoming too secular in its curriculum and general climate, and that ministers required professional training beyond the scope of a liberal arts college. The College, for its part, had come to feel that the influence of the church was too restrictive. The founding of the seminary deprived the College of the financial support of the Presbyterian establishment, thereby requiring it to turn to its graduates to help meet its financial needs. In time, as its alumni began to acquire both wealth and increased devotion to its well-being, they played a central role in transforming the college into a leading liberal arts university.

The Princeton Theological Seminary is the country's second oldest seminary. Founded in 1812, it became the dominant influence in Presbyterianism in the United States for more than a century. It opened with a handful of students and one professor, Archibald Alexander, who previously had served for nine years as president of Hampden-Sydney College in Virginia, and who then served on the faculty of the seminary for 39 years. For 90 years the seminary was administered by its faculty with a rotation of leadership (beginning with Alexander); in 1902 it appointed its first president, Francis Landey Patton, who recently had stepped down as president of the University.

Initially the seminary operated out of Nassau Hall. Its first building, later named Alexander Hall, opened in 1817, and in 1834 a chapel was constructed that was later named for the seminary's second faculty member, Samuel Miller. In 1843 the seminary opened Lenox Library as one of the first free-standing academic library buildings in the United States; in 1957 an expanded Lenox Library was replaced by the Robert Speer Library, and that library, in turn, was replaced by the Princeton Theological Seminary Library (the "new" library) in 2013. The new library holds the bulk of the seminary's collection of over 1.2 million bound volumes, pamphlets, and microfilms.

In 1943 the seminary acquired the adjacent campus of the Hun Preparatory School, which relocated elsewhere in Princeton, and the former Hun lands and buildings became the seminary's Tennent campus.

The seminary today describes itself as "a denominational school with an ecumenical, interdenominational, and worldwide constituency." It enrolls about 400 students in six degree programs, about a third of its students are Presbyterian, and there are over 60 Christian traditions and denominations represented in the student body. Roughly half of its graduates enter ordained pastoral ministry, while others pursue careers in chaplaincy, social work, nonprofit management, and teaching and research. The seminary's 11,000 living alumni work in 77 countries. The eminence and impact of the seminary are sustained by an endowment of roughly $1.1 billion, more than four times larger than any other seminary.

Reflecting the two institution's historical ties, the president of the seminary is invited each year to march in the processional for the University's Commencement.

In 2019 the seminary launched an extensive review of its historical connections to slavery. While the seminary did not own slaves or use slave labor to construct its buildings, like many institutions it benefited from the slave economy through investments and gifts from donors who profited from slavery, and its founding faculty members and some of its other early leaders owned slaves at some points in their lives. In addition, several early professors and board members were deeply involved in the American Colonization Society, which advocated sending free Blacks to Liberia.

In 2019 the seminary announced a $27 million multi-year plan to repent for its ties to slavery. The commitments included new scholarships, changes in curriculum, and other initiatives.

PRINCETON UNIVERSITY PREPARATORY PROGRAM, or PUPP, is an intensive, multi-year, tuition-free academic and cultural enrichment program supported by and based at Princeton University that seeks to prepare high-achieving, low-income students from nearby school districts for admission to and then success at selective colleges and universities. The program is located in the office of the dean of the college, along with other initiatives designed to support college opportunity and success for first generation and low-income students.

The program traces its origins to discussions in the summer of 2000 led by sociology professor Miguel Centeno and Teacher Preparation Program director John Webb with University faculty and educators from three central New Jersey school districts. A year later, PUPP welcomed its first class of high school sophomores from Ewing High School, Princeton High School, and Trenton Central High School. When they completed high school in 2004, the students enrolled in a number of selective institutions, including Princeton.

In 2008 the program expanded to include two other central New Jersey schools, Lawrence High School and Nottingham High School in Hamilton.

PUPP students participate in six-and-a-half-week summer institutes on campus for three summers, beginning after their freshman year in high school. They take courses in art, writing, science, literature, and math; prepare for the college admission process and standardized tests; engage in yoga, mindfulness, community-building, and leadership development; and visit local colleges, universities, and cultural institutions.

During the school year, sophomores and juniors participate in enrichment sessions to develop their critical communications skills and in cultural excursions. During senior year PUPP provides guidance and support to students and their parents during the college admission and financial aid application processes. Juniors and seniors take a three-to-four day college tour; PUPP students typically visit close to 30 colleges and universities over the course of the program.

After high school graduation, PUPP offers continued college counseling with a "transition to college" workshop and provides guidance and support to the students throughout, and even after, their college careers.

A 2018 study of the program by the Educational Testing Service called PUPP a national leader, finding that its "record of success . . . is unassailable." "Few college access programs . . . have succeeded as well as PUPP," it said. The study attributed PUPP's success to its comprehensive and multi-year approach and noted that PUPP serves as a role model for similar programs at other universities.

More than 90 percent of PUPP students complete the program; nearly 100 percent of them enroll in college; and nearly two-thirds enroll in highly competitive schools. PUPP alumni at selective colleges and universities have a nearly 70 percent graduation rate, which is above average for students overall, and significantly above average for students from low-income, first-generation backgrounds. A third of PUPP alumni enroll in graduate or professional degree programs after college.

PRINCETON UNIVERSITY PRESS was founded in 1905 as Princeton Alumni Press when Whitney Darrow 1903, manager of the *Princeton Alumni Weekly*, obtained $1,000 from University trustee Charles Scribner II 1875 (of the publishing house Charles Scribner's Sons) and raised other funds to purchase Zapf Press, a small local printer, to publish the magazine. The Press operated out of rented space above Marsh's drugstore on Nassau Street in downtown Princeton.

Scribner was interested in creating a company that would more broadly serve the University and publish scholarly books not feasible for a commercial firm. In 1906 the Alumni Press was renamed Princeton University Press, and in 1910 it was reincorporated as a nonprofit corporation "to establish, maintain, and operate a printing and publishing plant, for the promotion of education and scholarship, and to serve the University by manufacturing and distributing its publications."

In 1911 Scribner gave the Press land, an endowment, and a Collegiate Gothic building on William Street, then a half-block from the campus and now surrounded on three sides by University academic structures. The building was designed by Scribner's brother-in-law, the architect Ernest Flagg, and modeled on the Plantin-Moretus Museum in Antwerp, Belgium. At first the Scribner building was mainly a printing plant, but in 1967 it was completely renovated as a publishing house (an addition facing Shapiro Walk opened in 2001), and a separate printing plant with warehouse space was constructed in nearby Lawrenceville.

While the Press is privately owned and controlled, it has always had a close relationship with the University. Its six-member editorial board, which makes decisions about which books to publish, is appointed from the faculty by the president of the University and 10 of the 15 members of the Press board of trustees must be University faculty, staff, or alumni; the president and the director of the Press are ex officio members of the board.

From 1905 to 1917, Darrow served as the Press's first director. In 1912 the Press published its first book, a new edition of *Lectures on Moral Philosophy*, by the University's sixth president, John Witherspoon. In 1914, with Darwinism still controversial, it published its first best seller, *Heredity and Environment in the Development of Men*, by biology professor E. G. Conklin.

Darrow was succeeded by Paul Tomlinson 1909, who built up the printing plant and published many notable books during his 21-year tenure. In 1918 the Press published *Wasp Studies Afield*, by Nellie Rau—its first female author—and her husband Phil Rau. In 1920 it published Edward Corwin's *The Constitution and What It Means Today*, which subsequently was reprinted in 13 revised editions and numerous translations. In 1922 it published *The Meaning of Relativity*, Albert Einstein's first book published in the United States, which remains in print today, and in 1931 it published Frank Lloyd Wright's *Modern Architecture*. Over its first 25 years, the Press published nearly 400 books

The brief tenure of Joseph Brandt, 1938–41, marked a turning point in the development of the Press, with an increasing emphasis on publishing rather than printing. The publication of Angie Debo's *And Still the Waters Run: The Betrayal of the Five Civilized Tribes* in 1940 became a catalyst for the scholarly exploration of Native American history. In 1941 the Press published its first novel, *The Gang's All Here*, by Harvey Smith 1917, a fictional account of a class's 25th reunion.

The Press's emphasis on scholarly publication accelerated under Datus Smith Jr. 1929. During his 10 years as director (1942–52), the Press published 450 books and developed international relations as a major field. The most significant military book of this period was *Atomic Energy for Military Purposes*, by Henry D. Smyth 1918 *1921—the "Smyth Report" of Manhattan Project fame. Herbert Bailey '42, then the Press's science editor, described the book as "the literary beginning of the atomic age." Another groundbreaking book of the 1940s was *Theory of Games and Economic Behavior*, by John von Neumann and Oskar Morgenstern, which revolutionized economics and spawned new fields of scientific inquiry.

In 1950, in a ceremony at the Library of Congress, the Press presented the first volume of the Papers of Thomas Jefferson; in 2019 it published the 44th volume of a now projected 62-volume series.

In 1954, at the age of 32, Bailey became the director of the Press and served in that capacity for 32 years. (He received a Princeton honorary degree in 1977.) The Press began publishing the Papers of Woodrow Wilson (a 69-volume series which was completed in 1994), the writings of Henry David Thoreau, and the collected papers of Albert Einstein. In 1963 it published *A Monetary History of the United States, 1867–1960* by Milton Friedman and Anna Jacobson Schwartz, which had a transformative impact on economic policy. In 1965 the Press built its new printing plant in Lawrenceville and launched a paperback publication program.

In 1969 the Press acquired the world-renowned Bollingen Series, first established in 1941, with responsibility for carrying on its work in the fields of aesthetics, archaeology, cultural history, ethnology, literary criticism, mythology, philosophy, psychology, religion, and symbolism. The series includes such projects as *The Collected Works of C. G. Jung*, *The Collected Works of Samuel Taylor Coleridge*, and *The Collected Works of Paul Valéry*. The *New York Times Book Review* called the series "undoubtedly one of the most distinguished and ambitious series of books ever issued by an American publisher."

The series also includes Aleksandr Pushkin's *Eugene Onegin*, translated and with commentary by Vladimir Nabokov; *The Hero with a Thousand Faces* by Joseph Campbell, which sold more than 750,000 copies; and the *I Ching, or Book of Changes*, which is the Press's single best-selling book with more than 900,000 copies in print. One part of the series, the A. W. Mellon Lectures in the Fine Arts, co-sponsored by the National Gallery of Art, continues to produce new volumes; the *New York Times* has called it "a great contribution to civilized discourse."

In 1986 Walter Lippincott '60 succeeded Bailey. In 1993 the Press sold its printing plant to focus exclusively on acquiring and publishing scholarly books. (In 1996 it sold the entire Lawrenceville building.) In 1990, after being housed at the Press for 85 years, the *Princeton Alumni Weekly* became an independent entity and 10 years later it became an office of the University. Notable books during this time included Joseph Frank's multivolume biography of Dostoevsky, and *The Nature of Space and Time* by Stephen Hawking and Roger Penrose. In 1999 the Press launched a European and United Kingdom initiative with the opening of an office in Woodstock, England, and in 2000 it published Robert Shiller's *Irrational Exuberance*, which became an international best seller.

Irrational Exuberance was among the many influential books developed by the Press's economics editor, Peter Dougherty, who was named director in 2005—the first director who was not a graduate of the University. Other titles on his economics list included William Bowen *58 and Derek Bok's *The Shape of the River: Long-Term Consequences of Considering Race in College and University Admissions*; Linda Babcock and Sara Laschever '79's *Women Don't Ask: Negotiation and the Gender Divide*; and Harold Kuhn *50 and Sylvia Nasar's *The Essential John Nash*.

As director, Dougherty set out to publish what was described as "a healthy variety of content: textbooks that likely become required reading in survey courses, highly specialized monographs, and serious scholarly books that might also find an audience outside their own fields."

By "textbook" he meant books like 2016's *Welcome to the Universe: An Astrophysical Tour*, by Neil deGrasse Tyson, Michael Strauss, and J. Richard Gott *73, which was based on an introductory astrophysics course they taught at Princeton. It became a bestseller, as did a scholarly work the Press published in 2005, *On Bullshit*, by a Princeton emeritus philosophy professor, Harry Frankfurt. *On Bullshit* became the Press's most translated title, available in 29 languages. (In second place is Martha Nussbaum's *Not for Profit*, in 24 languages.)

Electronic publishing evolved rapidly, and in 2011 the Press published its first app, *Mammals of North America*. In 2014 it partnered with the Einstein Papers Project to launch the first complete online collection of Einstein's writings, the Digital Einstein Papers, which makes his work freely available, with translations and scholarly annotations. The Press has actively engaged its intellectual property in two ambitious digitization projects, the Princeton Legacy Library in 2014 and Princeton Global Discovery in 2020.

In 2017 the Press opened an office in Beijing, China, and Christie Henry succeeded Dougherty as director. The first woman to lead the Press, Henry came from the University of Chicago Press, where she had been the editorial director responsible for the sciences, social sciences, and reference publishing. Among her priorities have been furthering the Press's digital presence, expanding its global reach and partnerships, and launching the Press's first equity and inclusion strategic initiative, which includes diversity publishing fellowships and global equity grants.

To expand its science and nature publishing, the Press formed a publishing partnership with the Cornell Laboratory in Ornithology in 2019 and that year also acquired Wild Nature Press in the UK. In 2020 it commenced a distribution partnership with the nonprofit publisher Zone Books. These developments were featured on the Press's new website, press.princeton.edu, which it launched in 2019 to amplify its digital outreach; further amplification came with the creation of PUPAudio, the first audio imprint of a university press, one of the initiatives recognized when the 2020 Digital Book World Awards named the Press a winner in its category of university press of the year.

In 2020 the Press also was awarded the London Bookfair Excellence Award for an Academic and Professional Publisher, recognizing innovation in global publishing, adding this award to the many honors it has received over the years, including six Pulitzer Prizes, three National Book Awards, five Bancroft Prizes, a National Book Critics Circle Award, three R. R. Hawkins Awards, and many awards from professional scholarly associations. Multiple Princeton University Press authors have been recognized with Nobel Prizes, mostly in economics and physics, but also in literature.

The Press has received numerous awards for excellence in design and printing, including honors from the American Institute of Graphic Arts for books designed by P. J. Conkwright, the Press's chief designer and typographer from 1939 to 1970 and a Princeton honorary degree recipient in 1986.

Today the Press publishes approximately 250 new books each year in print, digital, and audio, and licenses its intellectual property throughout the world in translation, audio, dramatization, and more. Its peer reviewed book publication program is known for its strengths and impact across disciplines, its creativity and excellence of form, its diversity of audiences, and its global resonance.

PRINCETON UNIVERSITY STORE, THE, known colloquially as the U-Store, was incorporated in 1905. It is an independent not-for-profit cooperative governed by a board of trustees made up of four undergraduates, two graduate students, five alumni, two members of the University staff, and the president of the store. (Two of the most influential early trustees were dean of the faculty Henry Fine 1880 and university secretary Charles McAlpin 1888.)

Membership in the co-op was for many years open to students, alumni, faculty, and staff, as well as members of the Princeton Theological Seminary and the Institute for Advanced Study, but since the early 2000s it has been open to anyone for an annual fee of $10 or a lifetime fee of $25; as of 2020, total co-op membership was over 75,000. For much of its history, the store shared its profits with its members by providing annual rebates that were handed out shortly before Christmas, but over recent decades it has provided members with discounts instead.

The U-Store was an outgrowth of a student-managed bookstore that began operation in a corner room of West College (now Morrison Hall) in 1896. Robert C. McNamara 1903, the store's first nonstudent manager from 1905 to 1908, added athletic supplies and expanded into two additional rooms. In

1908 B. Franklin Bunn 1907 became manager of the store and served in that role until 1947. He further expanded the scope of the store and extended its quarters to include the entire first floor of West College, with a separate music shop located in town.

In 1958 the U-store and the music shop relocated together to a new building at 36 University Place. The U-store originally operated on two floors, but in 1968 the basement was opened for sales and the store expanded into office space that was being vacated by the *Daily Princetonian* and the *Bric-a-Brac* as they moved down the street to 48 University Place. In 1989 the store added a third floor especially for textbooks. In 2000 a major renovation refurbished all three floors and added a second elevator.

In November 2007, two major changes took place. Responsibility for meeting the University's bookstore needs was transferred from the U-Store to a University-subsidized independent bookseller, Labyrinth Books, and the U-store opened a second location on Nassau Street adjacent to Labyrinth, in a space known to earlier generations of Princetonians as Woolworth's.

The Nassau Street store specializes in insignia items, apparel, gifts, and accessories, serving largely a public clientele, while the on-campus store, which was consolidated onto the ground floor and basement of the building with access from the campus as well as from University Place, primarily serves a student clientele with groceries and prepared foods, convenience store items, dormitory and school supplies, printing services, sportswear, and small electronics. It stays open well into the wee hours of the morning to accommodate late night student needs and cravings.

The rest of the University Place building houses University offices associated with the office of the dean of the college, including the office of career development, and provides a first-floor space where the admission office and the Orange Key Guide Service can accommodate visits by potential applicants and others interested in learning about Princeton and touring the campus.

PRINCETONIAN, THE DAILY, came into existence on June 14, 1876. In its formative years, it was closer in form and style to an eighteenth-century coffeehouse journal than to a modern newspaper. Brief essays explored topics such as American education, life on the Nile, and the college loafer. Editorials condemned the faculty's disciplinary action following a classroom disorder and curtly dismissed the "visionary schemes" of "puerile graduates" for the improvement of college discipline. One of the first issues contained a plea for unproctored examinations, a cause the *Prince* continued to advocate until the faculty adopted the honor system in 1893.

The original "fortnightly" became a weekly in 1883, a tri-weekly in 1885, and began appearing as the *Daily Princetonian*, four pages five afternoons a week, in 1892. (It was the second college newspaper, following Yale's, to publish daily.) For a time, beginning in 1895, it was published six days a week. One of its early managing editors, James Williamson 1877 *1879 was one of the first recipients of a Princeton PhD. Other early editors included Woodrow Wilson 1879, who became Princeton's 13th president, and Henry Fine 1880, who became dean of the faculty and, later, of the departments of science.

Two events in the 1890s inspired special coverage: the paper devoted an entire issue to a tribute to President James McCosh when he died in 1894, and its extensive coverage of the sesquicentennial ceremonies in 1896 included the full text of all the addresses, among them Wilson's famous "Princeton in the Nation's Service."

In 1893 the *Prince* published its first photograph, from the football team's 6–0 victory over Yale. In 1894 the editors launched a weekly *Alumni Princetonian* that was made available to alumni by subscription, but fewer than 500 of Princeton's 6,000 alumni subscribed, and six years later it was replaced by the *Princeton Alumni Weekly*. In 1895 the *Prince* published an extra with a telegraphic report of a Princeton-Yale baseball game in New Haven—one of the first, if not the first, uses of the telegraph by a college newspaper

After Wilson became president in 1902, he was a frequent subject of editorials and news. The editors were enthusiastic about his preceptorial system, skeptical of his quad plan, and regretful when he resigned to enter political life. On his election as president of the United States in 1912, front-page stories captured the spirit of jubilation that swept the campus and culminated in a midnight student procession to Wilson's house on Cleveland Lane.

The pre-World War I years saw further advances in news coverage and editorial policy as the *Prince* became an indispensable staple of campus life, reporting campus news, shaping campus opinion, and conveying official information to the campus community. In 1910 the paper enlarged its page size and was the first college newspaper to become a member of the Associated Press and publish its dispatches. That year the paper also incorporated as an independent entity. In 1939 it became a nonprofit.

In 1911 a letter to the editor touched off an extended argument about compulsory chapel attendance, a perennial source of comment in the *Prince* until 1964 when the last vestige of the requirement was removed. In 1915, when women's suffrage was being voted on in New Jersey, the *Prince* conducted a well-articulated campaign on its behalf, calling it "the greatest social question of the day—the enfranchisement of the other half of the people." Two years later, the paper came out in favor of a revolt against the eating clubs, an early stance on an issue destined to attract more editorial commentary than even compulsory chapel.

In the 1920s, the *Prince*, true to the times, was enterprising, prosperous, lighthearted, and, on occasion, irreverent and boisterous. It added a weekly photographic supplement and a monthly "Literary Observer" (both of which succumbed to the Great Depression); introduced a number of popular humorous columns such as "Diogene's Lamp," "The Ivory Tower," and "The Crow's Nest;" and initiated two diversions that were carried on for many years, the *Gaily Printsanything* and the April Fool's Day story.

The *Gaily Printsanything* (in later years called "the joke issue") was the title retiring boards gave their satirical last issue, in which they abandoned journalist constraints, let their imaginations run amok, and frequently published lurid tales (accompanied by doctored photographs) depicting the president, deans, and faculty as dissolute rogues and scoundrels.

The April Fool's Day story that caused the greatest stir was the announcement on April 1, 1927, that the trustees had accepted a gift of $20 million from the executors of the estate of "Nettie Green" to establish coeducation at Princeton. At the end of the article attention was called to the date of the issue, but not everybody read that far, and Nassau Hall was besieged with protesting telephone calls, telegrams, and letters. In the electronic age, when articles circulate on the internet detached from the issue in which they appeared, the *Prince* has become more scrupulous about building disclaimers into its April Fool's Day stories. ("Don't believe everything you read on the internet!")

Not surprisingly, President John Grier Hibben once confided to his staff that he made it a rule never to read the *Princetonian* until *after* breakfast.

In the decade before World War II, the *Princetonian* collaborated with the Harvard *Crimson* in marshaling student opposition to Prohibition. It issued emergency scrip for student use during the 1933 bank holiday. It gave increased attention in news and editorials to the developing world crisis, and as time for decision drew nearer, it opened its columns to opposing views on American intervention. With President Franklin Roosevelt's declaration of a national emergency in May 1941, the paper headlined a front-page editorial "The Debate is Over," and the day after Pearl Harbor it proclaimed in a banner headline: PRINCETON PRESENTS UNITED FRONT AS UNITED STATES FACES TOTAL WAR.

In 1942 the *Prince* editorialized in favor of admitting African American students in a three-part series entitled "White Supremacy at Princeton." In February 1943 it suspended publication for the duration of the war, resuming publication on January 5, 1946—the first college paper to do so at war's end. That same year it ran articles by Doris Pike and Ruth Donnelly, the wives of returning veterans, making them the first women to write for the *Prince*. (In 1968 C. Holly Hofmeister would become the first undergraduate woman to write for the paper when she was on campus as a Critical Languages student.)

In 1955 the *Prince* published an extra edition on the morning of Albert Einstein's death and devoted most of the next day's regular issue to tributes from friends and colleagues. An extra in 1956 reported President Robert Goheen's election a little more than three hours after it had been announced at a faculty meeting. The following year there were special editions on the retirement of President Harold Dodds and the death of football coach Charlie Caldwell. Eating club elections continued to be an important focus of news and editorials through the 1950s and 1960s, with emphasis first on the ideal of "100 percent bicker," guaranteeing admission to at least one club for every sophomore who participated in the selection process, and later on the importance of developing alternatives to the club system.

In 1957, when Dodds retired from the presidency, the trustees of the *Princetonian* established one of the University's most prestigious undergraduate awards, the Harold Willis Dodds Achievement Prize, which is presented each year at Class Day.

In 1963 an extra edition covered the assassination of President John F. Kennedy '39 and the cancellation of University events that weekend, and for a week following Dr. Martin Luther King Jr.'s assassination in

1968, the paper featured editorials, letters, and accounts of various meetings on how best to advance the cause he embodied. In 1968 a feature on "A New Era for the Negro at Princeton" won an award as the best college newspaper story of the previous year.

In the spring of 1967 the *Prince* broke the story that, in the words of President Goheen, undergraduate coeducation was "inevitable," and in the spring of 1968 it was the only newspaper with a reporter inside Columbia University's Low Library when it was occupied by students opposing the war in Vietnam. For the next several years the *Prince* news pages were filled with articles about campus protest, coeducation, and changes in the governance structures of the University. Editorials sharply criticized the war in Vietnam, pressed for a larger role for students in campus affairs, urged adoption and then expansion of coeducation, and supported the administration's efforts to increase the enrollment of minority students.

In the spring of 1969 banner headlines announced trustee approval of coeducation beginning that fall; the same issue reported trustee adoption of a proposal to elect a member of each graduating class to a four-year term on the board, and added a word of congratulation to the trustees for their "courage" and "foresight" in an editorial captioned "Victory for the Student Voice." At Commencement, the paper distributed a two-page reunion extra headlining the fact that the newly constituted electorate—juniors, seniors, and members of the two youngest alumni classes—had chosen Princeton's first Black alumni trustee, Brent Henry '69.

These and other innovations were summed up in the annual June issue for incoming freshmen in a lead editorial whose headline, "The times, they are a changin'," unwittingly quoted one of the following year's honorary degree recipients, Bob Dylan.

During the spring of 1970, the *Prince* took an active part in covering the growing campus anti-war protest, which culminated in an unprecedented student strike following the extension of the war into Cambodia. Besides providing up-to-the-minute schedules of strike activities, the *Prince* staff hand-set and distributed a special Sunday 2 a.m. strike extra; gave detailed coverage of student rallies, faculty meetings, and a community-wide Jadwin Gym assembly; and in the place traditionally used for University condolences, extended its sympathy to the families and friends of the four Kent State University students killed while protesting the war.

The editors also promoted adoption of a two-week recess for student campaigning before the November congressional elections, which, they later wrote, allowed the University "to channel the energy of the strike into constructive action." The fall recess remains today as a one-week break following fall midterms.

In 1975 the *Prince* elected its first woman business manager, Judy Piper '76, and in 1979 it elected Anne Mackay-Smith '80 its first woman editor-in-chief. Five years later it elected its first Black editor-in-chief, Crystal Nix Hines '85. (Both Mackay-Smith and Nix Hines would later serve as University trustees.)

In addition to news and opinion, the *Prince* covers the arts and culture (for many years the editor-in-chief wrote the opening night review of each year's Triangle Show) and sports. Probably the most famous headline on its sports pages, "David 43, Goliath 41," was published in 1996 when the men's basketball team upset defending national champion UCLA in the first round of the NCAA tournament.

The *Prince* celebrated its 100th anniversary in 1976 with a two-day symposium on "The Press and Social Change." A hundred years earlier, the original fortnightly had an office in the original Dickinson Hall and a staff of eight or nine, and it took five days to print the paper by hand press in Trenton. In 1976, as a five-day-a-week tabloid headquartered at 48 University Place, it required more than a hundred editors, reporters, photographers, and business staffers, but printing took only hours by the photo-offset process it converted to in 1972, with the printing itself being done in Philadelphia. This ended the days when each night's editors went to the *Princeton Herald* building then on Chambers Street and were up until the wee hours of the morning reading galleys from a hot-lead linotype machine before the pages were fed into an aging letterpress.

In 1998 the *Prince* supplemented its printed edition with a website that increasingly became the medium by which members of the campus community, alumni, and other readers gained access to the paper's news, features, editorials, sports, and opinion columns; later on, most of the website's readership would come through social media, including Facebook and Twitter.

In 2002 four members of the Class of 2001 who had been editors of the *Prince,* including its editor-in-chief Richard Just '01, founded the Princeton Summer Journalism Program. Their goal was to diversify college and professional newsrooms where women, people of color, and individuals from lower-income and middle-class backgrounds and rural communities had been historically underrepresented. Staffed by volunteers and undergraduate interns, the program brought 25 high school students to campus each year for a 10-day immersion in journalism that also provided advice and mentorship on admission to selective colleges and universities. Many of these students worked on their college papers and a number became professional journalists. In 2017 the program expanded to 40 students a year and hired its first full-time employee.

In 2012 the *Prince* digital archives were launched. They were named in honor of Larry Dupraz, the paper's gruff, demanding, but much beloved production supervisor (an honorary member of the Classes of 1971 and 2000) who from 1946 to 1987 chided and guided the editors of the *Prince* through their many trials and tribulations, and for almost 20 years after his retirement remained a fixture in the *Prince* offices, mentoring successive generations of editors and keeping tabs on developments in town on his police radio.

In 2016, former editor-in-chief Marcelo Rochabrun '15 won an award for best investigative journalism from the nonprofit organization Investigative Reporters and Editors for an article his senior year examining the use of charitable gifts by eating clubs to support their social facilities.

With the onset of the COVID-19 pandemic in 2020, the *Prince* announced that it was becoming "digital-first," with a frequently updated website that would feature more stories than could be accommodated in a print medium, and with interactive content, including videos, podcasts, and graphics. The *Prince* also published a daily newsletter and sent three print issues to students at home during the fall 2020 semester to complement its online efforts. In August 2021 it announced it was remaining "digital first," but with a print edition every Friday.

By then the staff had grown to nearly 200 writers, editors, reporters, photographers, podcasters, and others. While the medium was evolving, the paper's mission remained much as it had been throughout its history. The editors pledged to "serve Princetonians past, present, and future through transparent, accurate, and empathetic reporting," and to "drive campus conversation, uphold high journalistic standards, and innovate in how we tell stories." They also committed to enhanced diversity on the *Prince* staff and in its coverage and "to elevate voices that have historically been underrepresented."

The *Prince* continues to be student-run, not-for-profit, and financially independent of the University. In addition to selling ads and subscriptions and drawing from endowed funds, the paper occasionally has generated revenues through other ventures. Perhaps the most lucrative was *Where the Girls Are*, a paperback it first published in 1965 when the undergraduate colleges at Princeton, Yale, and a number of other schools were still all-male. Initially a guide to about two dozen east coast women's colleges, the book was expanded two years later to include about 125 colleges and universities around the country, including many that were coeducational.

PROSPECT, once the home of the president and now a dining-social-meeting space for faculty and staff, was acquired by the College in 1878. At that time, it occupied a 30-acre estate that extended as far east as the present site of the school of Public and International Affairs.

The land on which Prospect stands was part of a large tract owned by Richard Stockton, one of the first settlers of Princeton and grandfather of Richard Stockton 1748. It was later acquired by Benjamin Fitz-Randolph, who conveyed it to his son, Nathaniel FitzRandolph, donor of the land on which Nassau Hall was built. Colonel George Morgan, a farmer as well as United States agent for Indian Affairs, purchased it in 1779. Morgan lived in a stone farmhouse on the crest of the hill and, observing the superb view of the landscape to the east, called it "Prospect."

Colonel Morgan's estate became famous in revolutionary times as "Prospect near Princeton." A delegation of Delaware Indian chiefs spent a few days on its lawns as guests of Colonel Morgan in 1779 before going to Philadelphia to confer with the Continental Congress. Some 2,000 mutinous soldiers pitched camp there in 1781, en route to Philadelphia to demand a redress of their grievances. The Continental Congress held some of its sessions at Prospect in 1783 before establishing itself in Nassau Hall.

Both free and unfree Black laborers worked the farm in the eighteenth and nineteenth centuries. In 1824 John Potter, a wealthy merchant from Charleston, South Carolina, acquired Prospect, and in 1849 his son, Thomas F. Potter, replaced Colonel Morgan's stone farmhouse with the present mansion, which was designed by John Notman in the Italianate style.

The house was built with funds derived from slave labor on the family's southern rice plantations. An Englishman named Petrey laid out the grounds, planning the flower garden and importing a beautiful cedar of Lebanon, a large hawthorn, and a fine English yew to plant west of the house. The cedar was one of the highlights of the grounds until it was toppled by a snowstorm in April 2003.

In 1878, Alexander and Robert Stuart, wealthy Scottish American merchants and Presbyterian-minded philanthropists, bought Prospect and presented it to the College for use as the residence of President James McCosh and his successors. In the 1890s President Francis Patton pastured a cow where Frist Campus Center now stands.

In 1904, with students increasingly taking shortcuts through the garden, President Woodrow Wilson had an iron fence built, to the annoyance of the undergraduates who tore part of it down. Wilson's wife, Ellen, redesigned the garden approximately in its present form and planted the background of hemlock trees.

One spring night in 1925, a caravan of student cars drove through the Prospect grounds to protest an edict of the trustees banning automobiles from the campus, and during a spring riot in the early 1960s undergraduates again tore down a section of the fence at the back of the garden.

After the official residence of the president was changed to the Walter Lowrie House when President Robert Goheen moved there with his family in 1968, Prospect was converted for use by the faculty, administration, staff, and trustees, who hold many of their committee meetings and dinners there. A large concrete and glass addition to the southeast corner of the house provides a dining space for approximately 135 people upstairs and a less formal "tap room" downstairs. The upstairs bedrooms became meeting rooms of varying sizes; all told, the house offers three main dining rooms, four reception rooms, and seven meeting rooms.

Prospect is operated by an outside company which also manages several other University venues, including Palmer House. A Prospect House Association Board composed of faculty and staff, founded in 1969, provides advocacy, assistance, and advice.

In front of Prospect House is a manicured lawn (Sherrerd Green), punctuated by a large sculpture titled *Moses*. The formal garden behind the house, as designed by Ellen Wilson, is laid out in a semicircular plan with two radiating paths centered on a fountain. Looked at from above, the garden's pathways resemble the outline of the University's shield. The fountain sculpture of a pipe-playing centaur was commissioned by Goheen when Prospect was still his home; it was completed in 1971.

The flowers in the garden are changed at regular intervals with the re-plantings supported by the gift of an anonymous donor. Eight thousand flowers are planted each May after the tulip bulbs that bloomed that year are removed. The seven-foot wide flower beds contain geraniums, begonias, ageratum, impatiens, four kinds of marigolds, and a dozen other types of flowers; the garden's permanent collection of perennials includes day lilies, hibiscus, iris, and other plants.

The entrance to Prospect from McCosh Walk is defined by the original stone gateposts; more modern ones designed by Machado and Silvetti are at the east and west entrances of Garden Walk, which separates the garden to the south from a stepped embankment to the north which, at its upper level, has a rose garden bordered by a yew hedge.

PROTEST ACTIVITY. The founding of Princeton University was an act of protest. As Don Oberdorfer '52 wrote in *Princeton University: The First 250 Years*, the founders were considered "radicals if not heretics" by the elders of the Presbyterian church; their expulsion from the synod of Philadelphia led them to form not a seminary, but a college providing instruction in the liberal arts and sciences. They hoped to educate "ornaments of the state as well as the church," and, protesting the orthodoxies of the time, their charter welcomed students "of every religious denomination" and assured them "free and equal liberty . . . notwithstanding any different sentiments in religion."

The fledgling college attracted students whose revolutionary fervor was fueled with the establishment in 1765 of debating societies that soon evolved into Whig and Clio. During the presidency of John Witherspoon, the College of New Jersey became known as a "seedbed" of the revolution. As the colonies fought for independence, many alumni played leading roles on the battlefields, in the civic arenas, and through the printing presses and pulpits. The campus itself was caught in the crossfires of the Battle of Princeton; Witherspoon was a delegate to the Continental Congress, as were many alumni. Nassau Hall served briefly in 1783 as the capitol of the country, and in 1787 more Princeton alumni attended the Constitutional Convention than graduates of any other college or university.

In time, revolutionary fervor gave way to protests that focused mainly on unpopular regulations governing student behavior. In 1817 a riot broke out over reading assignments that students said were too long. Rioters nailed all Nassau Hall entrances shut, locked the tutors in their rooms, covered the walls in graffiti, burned down the outhouse, and threw firewood and ice at anyone trying to enter the building. After order was restored, more than a dozen students were expelled, an action protested by students and parents who felt some were being punished without proof.

In the 1840s, when students were required to take their meals on campus, protests of the poor quality of the food became so intense that students were given permission to board with families in town, a practice that eventually led to the creation of the private eating clubs, which remain a distinctive feature of Princeton today. Required attendance at daily prayers and Sunday chapel services was another frequent target of protest. On one occasion the seats of the original chapel were tarred; another time its benches were buried in hay; and once a cow was discovered near the pulpit before the morning service began.

The pre–Civil War era brought political protest to a deeply divided campus. As early as 1835 southern students attacked a visiting abolitionist, and in 1859 they led a march on Nassau Street protesting John Brown's raid and other abolitionist activities. On the morning of April 13, 1861, following the Confederacy's first attack on Fort Sumter, southern students protested on the front lawn after northern students raised the stars and stripes over Nassau Hall.

In 1868 and 1876, students protested the presence of African American seminary students in lectures on campus, but President James McCosh affirmed their right to attend. In the 1870s students protested McCosh's decision to ban fraternities, but he held firm and fraternities largely disappeared from campus until the 1980s.

During the presidency of Woodrow Wilson 1879, alumni successfully protested his attempts to diminish the influence of the eating clubs through his proposed quad plan. When the four-course plan was introduced in the 1920s, students and alumni protested that it was asking too much of undergraduates. The University again held firm, and the plan, with its emphasis on independent work and a senior thesis, became a defining characteristic of Princeton.

In March 1936, a group of students from Terrace Club protesting the accelerated payment of bonuses to veterans of World War I created a satirical organization called the Veterans of Future Wars and proposed immediate payment of cash bonuses of $1,000 to all men between the ages of 18 and 36 so future veterans could receive their benefits while they were still alive to enjoy them.

In 1950, in a protest aimed at the eating club selection process known as "bicker," sophomores in the Class of 1952 vowed not to join clubs unless every sophomore who bickered received at least one bid. That year all students did receive bids, but protests resumed after the "dirty bicker" of 1958 when 23 students, more than half of whom were Jewish, were not chosen for any club. In the late 1960s some students chose to pursue alternative dining arrangements rather than join the clubs, and some clubs chose to admit students on a sign-in basis.

In 1979 Sally Frank '80 filed a lawsuit protesting the admission policies of the three clubs that still did not admit women. She pursued her case for more than a decade through state and federal courts before the last of the clubs, Tiger Inn, became coeducational in 1991. Frank was later described as "a heroine of activism at the University" because of the changes that resulted from her initiative and persistence.

Sparked by the Civil Rights Movement and growing opposition to the war in Vietnam, students in the late 1960s launched an extended era of activism and protest on and off campus. In 1965 students participated in a Washington anti-war march, carrying a 10-foot banner that read "Even Princeton." The banner reappeared at many other protests, including a pivotal event on the front lawn of Nassau Hall on May 2, 1968, when more than 1,000 students rallied to demand a greater role for students in University governance; the severance of University ties to the Institute for Defense Analyses (IDA), which conducted confidential military research in von Neumann Hall; removal of academic credit from ROTC courses; and University-provided draft counseling. The rally also pressed the University to become coeducational and more diverse, and to prohibit any investment of the endowment in companies doing business in South Africa.

At the rally, President Robert Goheen announced his support for "a fresh and searching review of the decision-making processes of the University." Shortly thereafter a committee chaired by politics professor Stanley Kelley Jr. proposed creation of a broadly representative Council of the Princeton University Community (CPUC), with committees through which members of the campus community could participate in developing the University's annual operating budget, rules of campus conduct, and policies related to the procurement and management of the University's resources. The council's judicial committee got its first test in 1970 when nine students were placed on disciplinary probation and three were suspended after disrupting a speech by US Interior Secretary Walter Hickel (an incident known as the "Hickel Heckle").

The Kelley Committee proposed the election each year of a member of the graduating senior class to a four-year position on the Board of Trustees. The board, meanwhile, adopted a statement clarifying its roles and responsibilities and the various ways in which it delegated responsibilities to the president of the University, the faculty, and others. The Kelley Committee also recommended changes in the procedures for making tenure decisions to put greater emphasis on teaching, proposed opening faculty meetings to members of the CPUC and the campus press, and called for the creation of an ombuds office.

A separate committee proposed divestment from South African companies (although not from multinational companies doing business there), and another committee recommended that Princeton become coeducational. The University eventually withdrew from IDA, eliminated academic credit for ROTC courses, hired staff to provide draft counseling, and expanded efforts to diversify the student body and faculty.

On April 30, 1970, following President Richard Nixon's announcement of American bombing in Cambodia, more than 2,500 students gathered in the chapel to protest this escalation of the war in southeast Asia, and on May 4 more than 4,000 students, faculty, and staff met in Jadwin Gym to consider actions the University and the campus community might take. By a vote of 2,066 to 1,522, the meeting endorsed a resolution calling for a "strike against the war" and committing the University to work against its expansion, rather than a competing resolution that called for a "strike against the University." Most students elected not to take exams and most seniors chose not to participate in reunions and or wear academic regalia for Commencement.

The May 4 meeting also voted to create an organization, the Movement for a New Congress (MNC), to encourage students nationwide to register, vote, and campaign for candidates who would change the composition of Congress. The next day the faculty endorsed a CPUC resolution creating a two-week fall break so students who wished to do so could return home prior to election day to campaign and vote. Located in Palmer Hall with MNC was an organization called UNDO (Union for Draft Opposition) that served as a national clearinghouse for information on draft resistance.

While anti-war protest attracted by far the most attention, campus activism targeted many other issues as well. In 1966 African American students organized the Association of Black Collegians (ABC), and the following year ABC led a walkout from a speech by the segregationist former Alabama governor George Wallace. In 1968 leaders of ABC called on Goheen at home to protest the University's minimal response to the assassination of Martin Luther King Jr.; he agreed to their proposal that classes be canceled for a full day of reflections and tributes that they would lead. In 1969 ABC captured national news coverage when its members occupied New South for 11 hours to protest Princeton's continuing investment in companies doing business in South Africa.

In 1970 a group of Black students again called on Goheen at home, this time to propose what in the fall of 1971 became the Third World Center (now the Carl A. Fields Center for Equality and Cultural Understanding). In March 1971, ABC and other members of a Third World Coalition staged a sit-in in Firestone Library to demonstrate support for the creation of such a center and to call for admission of more minority students and increased financial aid.

Campus activism in opposition to the University's policies regarding investment in South Africa continued through the 1970s and into the 1980s. On April 14, 1978, following weeks of picketing outside Nassau Hall and several large rallies organized by the People's Front for the Liberation of Southern Africa, 210 students began a 27-hour Nassau Hall sit-in. They left the next morning and marched with 300 other students to Corwin Hall where the trustees were meeting. In March 1980 more than 70 students staged a "study-in" in Firestone Library, and on May 23, 1985, 88 demonstrators were arrested for blocking access to Nassau Hall. In November 1985, the faculty adopted a resolution calling for divestment from companies doing business in South Africa; by

January 1987, the University had dissociated from three companies, and it eventually would dissociate from one more.

In 1969, Mexican American, Puerto Rican, Cuban, and other Latin American students established Unión Latino Americana. ULA members joined with African American and Asian American students in the 1971 protest on behalf of increased recruitment of students of color, enhanced financial aid, and a third world center.

ULA was succeeded by two organizations, Acción Puertorriqueña y Amigos (Acción), founded in 1972 by Puerto Rican students, and the Chicano Caucus, founded the next year by Mexican American students. In 1974, Acción and the Chicano Caucus filed a complaint with the US Department of Health, Education, and Welfare charging the University with discrimination. The complaint prompted the University to draft an updated affirmative action plan and hire Frank Ayala Jr., a Mexican American graduate student at Columbia University, as an assistant dean of student affairs.

Shortly after Harold Shapiro *64 became president in 1988, Asian American students met with him to request that Princeton create an Asian American studies program. In 1989 nearly 50 protestors occupied the Faculty Room of Nassau Hall for 17 hours in support of creating a program in Latino studies. In 1995, 17 Asian American and Latino students joined together in a 35-hour sit-in at Nassau Hall to call for additional courses and faculty in Latino and Asian American studies. After decades of activism, a program in Latino Studies was established in 2009 and a program in Asian American Studies in 2018.

In the late 1990s, in response to student activism regarding sweatshop labor practices in factories producing collegiate merchandise, the University helped form the Fair Labor Association, a Washington, DC–based organization that assists schools in holding their licensees accountable for their treatment of workers and conditions in their factories.

In 2015, the Black Justice League coordinated a 32-hour sit-in at Nassau Hall protesting racial injustices on campus. The protest was a catalyst for establishing a trustee committee to assess Woodrow Wilson's legacy at Princeton. The trustees issued a report in the spring of 2016 that affirmed the University's commitment to diversity and inclusivity, endorsed several initiatives to enhance and express that commitment, and modified the University's informal motto to "Princeton in the Nation's Service and the Service of Humanity." At the time the trustees decided not to remove Wilson's name from the school of Public and International Affairs or the residential college that was named for him, but in 2020 they reconsidered, removing Wilson's name from the school and changing the name of Wilson College to First College.

On the evening of April 27, 1987, 300 students participated in Princeton's first "Take Back the Night" march. Organized by the Women*s Center, the march was intended to raise awareness of sexual harassment and provide support to its survivors. After winding through campus, the march turned onto Prospect Avenue where some men students shouted obscenities and threats.

In the aftermath of the march, the University expanded its sexual harassment education program, hired counselors trained in aiding survivors, revised its disciplinary system for handling cases of sexual harassment or assault, and created the SHARE office (Sexual Harassment/Assault Advising, Resources, and Education). Over the years the nature of the march evolved although its purposes remained the same; today it is organized by SHARE every April as part of Sexual Assault Awareness Month.

The University's policies and practices for handling matters related to sexual misconduct also have evolved over time, through campus-initiated reforms and in response to changing federal guidelines. In May 2019 students conducted a nine-day protest in front of Nassau Hall to call for further reform. That summer the University conducted an external review of its processes and took steps to strengthen its policies, resources, and communications in consultation with faculty, students, and staff.

Provost, The, serves as general deputy of the president in the supervision of the University, and holds the only position that, under the bylaws, is both an officer of the corporation and an academic officer. In the absence or disability of the president, if no acting president has been appointed, the provost exercises the powers and duties of the president.

The provost is both the chief academic officer and the chief budgetary officer of the University, with administrative oversight of the offices of the vice president for computing and information technology, the dean of the graduate school, the dean of the college, the dean for research, the dean of the School of Engineering and Applied Science, the dean of the school of Public and International Affairs, the dean of the school of Architecture, the librarian, and the vice president for the Princeton Plasma Physics Laboratory.

The provost's office has primary responsibility for academic planning and budgeting, space planning, international initiatives, institutional equity, and institutional research. The provost chairs the priorities committee of the Council of the Princeton University Community, which since 1970 has made annual recommendations to the president and the trustees regarding the University's operating budget.

Provosts have been:

J. Douglas Brown 1919 *1928 (Economics) 1966–67
William Bowen *58 (Economics) 1967–72
F. Sheldon Hackney (History) 1972–75
Albert Rees (Economics) 1975–77
Neil Rudenstine '56 (English) 1977–88
Paul Benacerraf '52 (Philosophy) 1988–91
Hugo Sonnenschein (Economics) 1991–93
Stephen Goldfeld (Economics) 1993–95
Jeremiah Ostriker (Astrophysical Sciences) 1995–2001
Amy Gutmann (Politics) 2001–04
Christopher Eisgruber '83 (Public and International Affairs) 2004–13
David Lee *99 (Economics) 2013–17
Deborah Prentice (Psychology) 2017–

Psychology, The Department of. In Princeton's 1868 catalog, psychology was listed as a required course for the junior class, and for the next two decades it was taught by President James McCosh. In 1893 a laboratory for experimental psychology was established under J. Mark Baldwin. Housed in Nassau Hall, it thrived as a center for research and scholarship in the then-fledgling science. The *Psychological Review*, co-founded by Baldwin in 1894, soon became the leading publication in American psychology.

Following a pattern that developed throughout the western world, psychology was initially treated as a subfield of philosophy. It was not until 1920 that a department of Psychology was established, largely through the efforts of Howard Warren, its first chair. In 1924 the department moved into newly constructed Eno Hall, designed by Day and Klauder and named for its principal donor, Henry Lane Eno. In Warren's words, Eno was "the first laboratory in this country, if not in the world, dedicated solely to the teaching and investigation of scientific psychology." The department remained there until 1963, when it moved to the former engineering building, Green Hall.

From the beginning, psychology at Princeton has been among the foremost programs in the country. McCosh was one of the first to bring the "new" experimental psychology of the German psychologists Wundt and Fechner to the attention of scholars in this country, and Baldwin became one of the country's most distinguished psychologists.

Herbert Langfeld, another early chair, co-authored a textbook considered the first modern survey of psychology. The department's program was further strengthened by the appointment of Ernest Wever, a pioneer in the study of hearing; Hadley Cantril, noted for his work in public opinion and his study of reactions to Orson Welles' Martian invasion broadcast; and Harold Gulliksen, one of the country's foremost authorities on mental testing.

This blend of theoretical and practical interests continued in the decades following World War II. When the department moved to Green Hall, its faculty enjoyed laboratories equipped to house new branches in experimental psychology. In 1968 Leon Kamin became chair as the department focused on four major areas: physiological psychology and the neurosciences, social psychology, cognitive processes and perception, and the psychology of learning and motivation. Within each area, the department emphasized the study of behavioral development.

In the early 1970s, Kamin's introductory psychology lectures averaged over 300 students, while John Darley and Joel Cooper attracted as many to their courses in social psychology and personality.

Following the Vietnam War and into the 1980s, there was growing interest in understanding the social environment and what motivated individuals to behave the way they did—in short, the business of thinking. Social psychology was a big movement, as was the new science of cognitive psychology, which, as it grew and flourished, engendered the so-called "cognitive revolution."

The department seized on these new directions with pioneers in the field like George Miller, who joined the faculty in 1979 to focus on language and cognition; Philip Johnson-Laird, a renowned expert on the psychology of thinking and language; and Edward Jones, whose research focused on the way people perceive themselves and others.

There was an infusion of accomplished women faculty. Ziva Kunda, a faculty member from 1978 until her early death in 2004, was known for her work in social cognition, stereotyping, and motivated reasoning; Deborah Prentice, who arrived in 1988 and later would serve as department chair, dean of the faculty, and provost, studied the way individuals are shaped by social interactions and relationships.

In the 1990s social psychology moved into the study of issues like prejudice and the factors that drive it. One of the most significant developments was the installation in 2000 of an fMRI (functional magnetic resonance imaging) machine. Under the leadership of chair and former dean of the college Joan Girgus and neuroscience professor Jonathan Cohen, Princeton was the first nonmedical school to take this step. This development catapulted Princeton to the head of the field and paved the way for the creation of the world-renowned Princeton Neuroscience Institute.

Daniel Kahneman was a cognitive psychologist whose research into behavioral economics laid the foundations of a new field of research on what motivates human decision-making. Arriving at Princeton in 1993, Kahneman taught the immensely popular course, "Introduction to Psychology." For "having integrated insights from psychological research into economic science," he was awarded the 2002 Nobel Prize in Economics.

The 2000s saw faculty hired whose research interests were linked with the Princeton Neuroscience Institute, and who began using the tools of computational psychology in their work. Other faculty explored the social application of theory, including J. Nicole Shelton, who joined the faculty in 2000, and whose work explores how prejudice and interpersonal concerns about issues of prejudice influence the dynamics of group interactions, and Stacey Sinclair, who came to Princeton in 2008 and whose research looks at how interpersonal interactions translate culturally held prejudices into individual thoughts and actions.

Susan Fiske, who joined the faculty in 2000, addressed stereotyping, prejudice, and discrimination, and how these are encouraged or discouraged by social relationships. Fiske was part of a cadre of psychologists who sought to inform public policy through the study of behavioral science, along with Betsy Levy Paluck and Eldar Shafir.

In the 2010s, the department began encouraging the study of developmental psychology, and in 2016 it opened the Baby Lab under Casey Lew-Williams and Lauren Emberson. The Baby Lab studies children and their thinking and social behaviors.

Moving into the 2020s, interdisciplinary and collaborative work remain the hallmark of the department, which reaches out to sociologists, economists, linguists, philosophers, biologists, and chemists as it seeks to expand understanding of human behavior.

Its undergraduate program offers courses on sensation, perception, movement, language, reasoning, decision making, and social interaction, and because psychological science involves working with large and complex data sets, students learn basic statistical methods. Students also gain a grounding in neuroscience since mental processes and behavior arise from the brain.

The department's graduate program offers specialization in such areas as behavioral economics, cognitive neuroscience, developmental psychology, language, learning and memory, perception and cognition, the psychology of inequality, social neuroscience, social psychology, and systems neuroscience; it also offers interdisciplinary programs in psychology and neuroscience and in psychology and social policy.

PUBLIC AND INTERNATIONAL AFFAIRS, THE PRINCETON SCHOOL OF, was founded in 1930 as a unique cooperative undergraduate initiative of the departments of History, Politics, and Economics. Today its teaching and research span the fields of economics, politics, sociology, psychology, the natural sciences, history, and other disciplines. It offers a multidisciplinary undergraduate major for students who are passionate about public policy and graduate programs that emphasize policy-oriented research and teaching for students preparing for careers in public service.

In 1948 the trustees named the school for Princeton's 13th and the country's 28th president, Woodrow Wilson 1879, and established a graduate program which was considerably expanded after the University received a $35 million gift in 1961 for this purpose. In 2020 the trustees removed Wilson's name from the school because of his racist views and policies at Princeton and in the White House.

The prime movers in the founding of the school were trustees William Church Osborn 1883 and Albert Milbank 1896, who obtained its early financing and were key members of its original advisory board. Initially the school was administered by a faculty committee chaired by politics professor and later Princeton president Harold Dodds *14. A leading authority on municipal government, Dodds guided the school's first faculty research project, a survey of state expenditures in New Jersey undertaken at the request of the governor.

The school's first director was Dewitt Clinton Poole, previously counselor at the United States embassy in Berlin, who served from 1933 until 1939. Poole was chiefly responsible for the early development of a conference course in which undergraduates were trained to apply the analytical methods of their academic studies to the world's practical problems—a contribution which, Dodds said, made the school at that time "the most significant experiment in the teaching of the social studies . . . in any American university."

In 1935 a state and local government research program was created which continued until 1961, and in 1936 an Office of Population Research (OPR) was founded; it was the first university-based program in the country to combine research and teaching in the field of population studies.

History professor Dana Munro, who came to Princeton in 1932 after serving as chief of the State Department's Division of Latin American Affairs and as minister to Haiti, succeeded Poole as director in 1939. That year the school became a separate department, which allowed juniors and seniors to do their independent work and take their final examination in the fields of public or international affairs rather than in a participating department. Under Munro the conference course continued to be the school's most distinctive feature, but its program was further enriched by senior seminars and, in later years, by policy task forces that were smaller versions of the conference.

The Munro years saw the beginning of a Master in Public Affairs (MPA) graduate program, the strengthening of the faculty, and the creation of the school's first purpose-built home, Woodrow Wilson Hall, now Corwin Hall. Originally constructed at the corner of Prospect Avenue and Washington Road, Wilson Hall was dedicated in 1952, replacing temporary quarters the school had occupied in Dickinson and Whig halls and the former Arbor Inn eating club on Ivy Lane. These developments followed the naming of the school for Wilson, which Dodds described as "natural and fitting:" Wilson, he said, "expressed in one sentence . . . the central truth to which instruction in this school is dedicated: 'We are not put into this world to sit still and know; we are put here to act.'"

The school's work in international affairs was strengthened in 1951 when Frederick Dunn 1914 was appointed the first director of its Center of International Studies. In 1952 trustee John D. Rockefeller III 1929 instituted a program of annual awards for outstanding public service that were administered by the school. Originally restricted to federal career officials, the program was broadened in 1976 to honor individuals from both within and outside government for outstanding, and frequently unsung, contributions to the public welfare at local, state, and national levels.

In 1961, Marie and Charles Robertson 1926 made their $35 million gift to support the school's graduate program. For a dozen years the donors remained anonymous, but in the face of continuing speculation about the source of the funds, in 1973 the Robertsons agreed to be identified. The Robertson gift permitted a marked increase in enrollment of graduate students, enlargement of the faculty, and the construction of a new home for the school (later named Robertson Hall), designed by Minoru Yamasaki on the site of the school's previous home after Wilson/Corwin was moved to its current location.

Robertson Hall is ringed by 58 elegantly tapered white, quartz-surfaced pillars; the atrium of the building, named for Dodds, provides access to the building's main auditorium, named in 2017 for Princeton's first Black full professor, Nobel Laureate Sir Arthur Lewis. The new building was dedicated in May 1966 with addresses by President Robert Goheen, New Jersey Governor Richard Hughes, and President Lyndon Johnson.

At the dedication, Goheen paid particular tribute to three faculty members who had "directed the school so ably in this great new phase of its development": Gardner Patterson, director from 1958 to 1963; Lester Chandler, acting director for 1963–64; and Marver Bernstein, the school's first dean from 1964 to 1969. (Bernstein was the first director of the graduate program after the Robertson gift; he was succeeded in that post by William Bowen *58, later president of the University, and Richard Lester, later dean of the faculty.)

New faculty of the school included Lewis, an authority on the economies of developing nations, and Richard Falk, an authority on the international legal order and comparative world order systems. Two other new faculty members came to Princeton as deans: John Lewis, who had previously served on the President's Council on Economic Advisers and as minister-director of the AID mission to India, was dean from 1969 to 1974; his successor, Donald Stokes

'51, an authority on American and British voting behavior, served for 18 years, from 1974 to 1992.

In 1966 the school launched a PhD program. As the faculty expanded, new specialized research resources were added, including a program founded in 1967 under the direction of Arthur Lewis, and later John Lewis, on the economic development of less developed nations. A research program on criminal justice, under the direction of Jameson Doig, began in 1973. To facilitate student and faculty involvement in public affairs within the state, a Center for New Jersey Affairs, under the direction of Michael Danielson, was established in 1975.

The school's work in mid-career education, begun on a small scale in 1948, was considerably expanded in the early 1960s by the development of two new, one-year, nondegree programs. One program brought to the school annually a group of some 20 officials of federal, state, and local governments, and another brought six to eight fellows from developing countries. In 1975 a third program was established that brought eight journalists each year for training in the application of modern economic analysis to questions of public policy.

In a 1976 *Princeton Alumni Weekly* interview, Stokes said that Princeton's program of public and international affairs was unusual in admitting both undergraduates and graduate students, and that while most other schools were devoted mainly to the study of either domestic or foreign affairs, Princeton's school was equally committed to both, and the career interests of its students reflected a similar balance. "Those whose interests are international," Stokes said, "need to know more about the way things work in Washington and, indeed, in Trenton, NJ. . . . And many jobs in the domestic field require knowledge of how foreign countries handle similar problems. Much can be learned, for example, about the problems of our own cities by studying urban problems overseas, and this thrust toward comparative study is far more likely to be real in a school with a strong international dimension."

During Stokes' tenure, the Center of International Studies was revitalized and a center of Domestic and Comparative Policy Studies was established. The school's faculty nearly doubled in size and its graduate program developed an interdisciplinary core curriculum and an expanded public affairs program. At the undergraduate level, the school increased the number of majors, created interdisciplinary courses, and offered opportunities to study public policy questions raised by advances in science, engineering, and the humanities. In 1981 and 1991, Stokes served the state of New Jersey as the tie-breaking "public" member of the legislative apportionment commission, which adjusts the boundaries of voting districts to reflect shifts in population following each decennial census.

Stokes was succeeded by the economist Michael Rothschild, who served from 1995 to February 2002. During his tenure the school began its one-year Master in Public Policy (MPP) program for mid-career professionals; a program in Science, Technology, and Environmental Policy; a center for the Study of Democratic Politics; and a center for Health and Well-being. The school added graduate policy workshops, expanded course offerings, and made multi-year appointments of practitioners to the faculty.

Anne-Marie Slaughter '80, who had majored in the school as an undergraduate, became dean in September 2002 and served until January 2009 when she resigned and took a public service leave from the faculty to become director of the policy planning staff at the US State Department. Slaughter rebuilt the international relations faculty of the school, expanded the size of the faculty, and increased the school's connections to disciplines such as history and the natural sciences.

She expanded the MPP program to include specialized concentrations for medical doctors, lawyers, and PhD scientists; helped create a joint PhD program in social policy; and played a leading role in creating and launching in 2006 the school's Scholars in the Nation's Service Initiative. SINSI is a four-year graduate fellowship program in which students study for a year in the school's MPA program, work for two years at a federal executive branch department or agency, and then complete the MPA program; SINSI also supports a summer internship program for Princeton undergraduates.

Slaughter oversaw the creation of several new research centers and programs; expanded the undergraduate curriculum to include two new required courses and the graduate curriculum to include certificate programs in health and health policy and in urban policy and planning; and convened and co-chaired a multi-year Princeton Project on National Security aimed at developing a bipartisan national security strategy for the United States.

During Slaughter's tenure, in 2002, the University was sued by some of the descendants of Marie and Charles Robertson, principally William Robertson

'72, who challenged the ways the University was investing and using the Robertson gift and sought to gain control of the funds. The University vigorously defended its stewardship of the gift—both in terms of how it had been invested and how it had been used—and insisted that the funds should continue to be deployed by the University as Marie and Charles Robertson had intended.

With the Robertson plaintiffs funding their lawsuit through a family foundation whose assets were being depleted and with both parties facing steep legal costs, the lawsuit was settled in 2008, by which time the value of the gift had grown to more than $900 million. Under the terms of the settlement the University agreed to reimburse the Robertson family foundation for legal fees connected to the litigation and to transfer $50 million over seven years to a new foundation that had been established to prepare students for careers in public service. All other assets were retained by the University for use at its sole discretion in continuing to support the graduate program of the school of Public and International Affairs.

In 2009 Slaughter was succeeded by Christina Paxson, a Princeton faculty member since 1986, founding director of the school's Center for Health and Wellbeing, and chair of the department of Economics. After serving as dean for three years, Paxson was named to succeed Ruth Simmons as president of Brown University.

By longstanding practice, the school of Public and International Affairs was the only department at Princeton that conducted a competitive admission process to select its incoming undergraduate majors. During Paxson's tenure as dean, the school ended its selective admission process for the undergraduate major (effective with the Class of 2015), while also establishing new prerequisites, expanding the core curriculum, and increasing training in research methods. Paxson also initiated a review of the MPA curriculum and established the Julis-Rabinowitz Center for Public Policy and Finance.

In 2012, Cecilia Rouse, a professor in the economics of education and a former member of President Barack Obama's Council of Economic Advisers, was selected as dean. Rouse had been the founding director of the Princeton Education Research Section, an interdisciplinary unit within the Industrial Relations Section and the school of Public and International Affairs that promotes the use of research in education decision-making. In 2021 she stepped down as dean to become chair of President Joe Biden's Council of Economic Advisers (CEA) and a member of his cabinet, the first African American and the fourth woman to lead the CEA in the 74 years of its existence.

Rouse was dean in 2016 when the trustees conducted a thorough review of Wilson's legacy at Princeton and chose to retain his name on the school. She led efforts within the school to develop an exhibit, "In the Nation's Service? Woodrow Wilson Revisited," to provide a more complete and multifaceted understanding of Wilson, and when the trustees called for a "permanent marker" to be installed at the school to educate the campus community and others about Wilson, she co-chaired a committee that recommended a 39-foot-high installation, *Double Sights*, by the artist Walter Hood, on Scudder Plaza near Washington Road. The sculpture was dedicated in October 2019; it consists of two columns, one white and one black, leaning on each other, and etched with quotations representing both positive and negative aspects of Wilson's legacy.

Rouse supported the trustees' June 2020 decision to remove Wilson's name from the school and endorsed naming the school simply the Princeton School of Public and International Affairs. She said at the time that "retiring the name does not take the place of systemic change, but it does signal that we are prepared to do the hard work of confronting racism and other injustices." As a first step, in July 2020 the school's faculty voted to require MPA students to take at least one half-term course exploring diversity, equity, and inclusion. The faculty also agreed to conduct a thorough review of the MPA core curriculum and the undergraduate concentration in 2020–21.

Students in the school are taught to think about policy questions from multiple perspectives and to strike a balance between theory and practice. The school's faculty largely comes from the fields of history, politics, economics, and psychology, but it also includes engineers, legal scholars, sociologists, and natural scientists, as well as practitioners such as former government officials and diplomats who bring real-world experience to the classroom.

In addition to a core curriculum and electives, undergraduate concentrators enroll in a policy task force and a policy research seminar during their junior year. Policy task forces examine timely questions of public policy, and can involve travel in the United States and abroad. Students often interact with government officials and other decision-makers in developing their findings and recommendations, which they frequently present to policymakers directly involved with the topic they address.

The school's graduate programs include a two-year curriculum leading to the MPA degree, a one-year MPP degree for mid-career professionals, and a PhD program in which students focus either on security studies or on science, technology, and environmental policy. MPA candidates follow a core curriculum and then concentrate in one of four fields: international relations, international development, domestic policy, or economics and public policy. They gain professional experience during a summer internship between their two years of study.

Graduate students can earn a dual degree in public affairs and law or a dual degree in public affairs and business, and the school offers a joint degree program in social policy in collaboration with the departments of Politics, Psychology, and Sociology and the program in Population Studies. Through the school, Princeton doctoral students in other departments can earn graduate certificates in health and health policy; science, technology, and environmental policy; or urban policy.

Since 1985 the school has sponsored a Junior Summer Institute (JSI) that serves as a pipeline to the policy world for students from underrepresented communities. JSI is open to rising college seniors at accredited colleges or universities who demonstrate academic aptitude and a passion for policy.

Consistent with the interdisciplinary nature of its origins, the school houses 20 centers and programs, including the following:

Bendheim-Thoman Center for Research on Child Wellbeing
Center for Health and Wellbeing
Center for Information Technology Policy
Center for International Security Studies
Center for Policy Research on Energy and the Environment
Center for the Study of Democratic Politics
Education Research Section
Empirical Studies of Conflict Project
Initiative for Data Exploration and Analytics
Innovations for Successful Societies
Julis-Rabinowitz Center for Public Policy and Finance
Kahneman-Treisman Center for Behavioral Science and Public Policy
Liechtenstein Institute on Self-Determination
Niehaus Center for Globalization and Governance
Office of Population Research
Princeton Survey Research Center
Program in Law and Public Affairs
Program on Science and Global Security
Research Program in Development Studies
Research Program in Political Economy

In 2015, when Angus Deaton, a professor of economics and international affairs, won the Nobel Prize in Economics, he said, "Nobel Laureates don't normally come from public policy schools." Noting that his was the fourth Nobel Prize awarded to a faculty member in the school, he suggested that, in a sense, "this is like a Nobel Prize for the school." The other members of the school's faculty who won Nobel Prizes in Economics were economics professor Sir Arthur Lewis in 1979, psychology professor Daniel Kahneman in 2002, and economics professor Paul Krugman in 2008.

PULITZER PRIZES, established in 1917, have been awarded to the following Princeton alumni and faculty:

Letters, Drama, Music

Biography
1934 Tyler Dennett (professor of politics), *John Hay*
1936 Ralph Barton Perry 1896, *The Thought and Character of William James*
1961 David Donald (professor of history), *Charles Sumner and the Coming of the Civil War*
1968 George Kennan 1925, *Memoirs (1925–1950)*
1971 Lawrance Thompson (professor of belles-lettres), *Robert Frost: The Years of Triumph*
1999 A. Scott Berg '71, *Lindbergh*
2003 Robert Caro '57, *The Years of Lyndon Johnson, Master of the Senate*
2005 Mark Stevens '73, Annalyn Swann '73, *de Kooning: An American Master*
2008 John Matteson '83, *Eden's Outcasts: The Story of Louisa May Alcott and Her Father*

Drama
1918 Jesse Lynch Williams 1892, *Why Marry?*
1920 Eugene O'Neill 1910, *Beyond the Horizon*
1922 Eugene O'Neill 1910, *Anna Christie*
1928 Eugene O'Neill 1910, *Strange Interlude*
1938 Thornton Wilder *1926, *Our Town*
1943 Thornton Wilder *1926, *The Skin of Our Teeth*
1950 Joshua Logan '31, *South Pacific*
1957 Eugene O'Neill 1910, *Long Day's Journey into Night*

2004 Doug Wright (Hodder Fellow), *I Am My Own Wife*
2009 Lynn Nottage (visiting professor, theatre), *Ruined*
2017 Lynn Nottage (visiting professor, theatre), *Sweat*
2018 Martyna Majok (Hodder Fellow), *Cost of Living*

Fiction
1918 Ernest Poole 1902, *His Family*
1919 Booth Tarkington 1893, *The Magnificent Ambersons*
1922 Booth Tarkington 1893, *Alice Adams*
1928 Thornton Wilder *1926, *The Bridge of San Luis Rey*
1988 Toni Morrison (professor in the humanities), *Beloved*
2000 Jhumpa Lahiri (professor of creative writing), *Interpreter of Maladies*
2003 Jeffrey Eugenidies (professor of creative writing), *Middlesex*
2015 Anthony Doerr (Hodder Fellow), *All the Light We Cannot See*
2017 Colson Whitehead (visiting professor, creative writing), *The Underground Railroad*
2020 Colson Whitehead (visiting professor, creative writing), *The Nickel Boys*

General Nonfiction
1977 William Warner '43 *Beautiful Swimmers: Watermen, Crabs, and the Chesapeake Bay*
1984 Paul Starr (professor of sociology), *The Social Transformation of American Medicine*
1994 David Remnick '81, *Lenin's Tomb: The Last Days of the Soviet Empire*
1997 Richard Kluger '56, *Ashes to Ashes: America's Hundred-Year Cigarette War, the Public Health, and the Unabashed Triumph of Philip Morris*
1999 John McPhee '53 (professor of journalism), *Annals of the Former World*
2006 Caroline Elkins '91, *Imperial Reckoning: The Untold Story of Britain's Gulag in Kenya*
2017 Matthew Desmond (professor of sociology), *Evicted: Poverty and Profit in the American City*
2019 Eliza Griswold '95 (visiting professor, journalism), *Amity and Prosperity: One Family and the Fracturing of America*

History
1924 Charles McIlwain 1894 *1898, *The American Revolution: A Constitutional Interpretation*
1934 Herbert Sebastian Agar 1919 *1922, *The People's Choice*
1957 George Kennan 1925, *Russia Leaves the War*
1989 James McPherson (professor of history), *Battle Cry of Freedom*
2002 Louis Menand (visiting professor, humanities), *The Metaphysical Club: A Story of Ideas in America*
2005 David Hackett Fischer '57, *Washington's Crossing*
2017 Heather Ann Thompson *95, *Blood in the Water: The Attica Prison Uprising of 1971 and its Legacy*

Music
1974 Donald Martino *54, *Notturno*
1980 David Del Tredici *64, *In Memory of a Summer Day*
1987 John Harbison *63, *The Flight into Egypt*
2013 Caroline Shaw (graduate student), *Partita for 8 Voices*
2015 Julia Wolfe *12, *Anthracite Fields*

Poetry
1936 Robert Tristram Coffin *1916, *Strange Holiness*
1971 William Merwin '48, *The Carrier of Ladders*
1983 Galway Kinnell '48, *Selected Poems*
1988 William Meredith '40, *Partial Accounts: New and Selected Poems*
1994 Yusef Komunyakaa (professor of humanities and creative writing), *Neon Vernacular: New and Selected Poems*
2000 C. K. Williams (professor of creative writing), *Repair*
2003 Paul Muldoon (professor of humanities and creative writing), *Moy Sand and Gravel*
2009 W. S. Merwin '48, *The Shadow of Sirius*
2012 Tracy K. Smith (professor of humanities and creative writing), *Life on Mars*

Journalism

Breaking News Reporting
2005 Jim Willse (visiting professor, journalism), included in award to staff of the *Newark Star Ledger*
2008 Ian Shapira '00, included in award to staff of the *Washington Post*
2009 Nicholas Confessore '98, Deborah Sontag (visiting professor, journalism), included in award to staff of the *New York Times*
2010 Ken Armstrong (professor of writing), included in award to staff of the *Seattle Times*

2015   Ken Armstrong (professor of writing), included in award to staff of the *Seattle Times*

Commentary
1977   George Will *68, *Washington Post*
2004   Leonard Pitts (visiting professor, journalism), *Miami Herald*

Correspondence
1935   Arthur Krock 1908, *New York Times*
1938   Arthur Krock 1908, *New York Times*

Criticism
2006   Robin Givhan '86, *Washington Post*
2008   Mark Feeney (visiting professor, journalism), *Boston Globe*
2010   Sarah Kaufman (visiting professor, journalism), *Washington Post*
2017   Hilton Als (visiting professor, creative writing), the *New Yorker*
2019   Carlos Lozada *97, *Washington Post*

Editorial Writing
2014   Eric Lukens *95, *Oregonian*

Explanatory Reporting
2002   Chris Hedges (visiting professor, journalism), Judith Miller *72, included in award to staff of the *New York Times*
2003   David Wessel (visiting professor, journalism), included in award to staff of the *Wall Street Journal*
2012   David Kocieniewski (visiting professor, journalism), *New York Times*
2013   Keith Bradsher *89, David Kocieniewski (visiting professor, journalism), included in award to staff of the *New York Times*
2016   Ken Armstrong (professor of writing), the Marshall Project
2020   Juliet Eilperin '92 (visiting professor, creative writing), included in award to staff of the *Washington Post*

Feature Writing
2005   Julia Keller (visiting professor, journalism), *Chicago Tribune*
2011   Amy Ellis Nutt (visiting professor, journalism), *Newark Star Ledger*
2020   Ben Taub '14, the *New Yorker*

International Reporting
1949   Price Day 1929, *Baltimore Sun*
1990   Sheryl Wu Dunn *88, *New York Times*
2001   Paul Salopek (visiting professor, journalism), *Chicago Tribune*
2011   Clifford Levy '89, *New York Times*
2015   Pam Belluck '85 (visiting professor, journalism), Norimitsu Onishi '92, included in award to staff of the *New York Times*
2017   Jo Becker (visiting professor, journalism), included in award to staff of the *New York Times*
2020   David Kirkpatrick '92, included in award to staff of the *New York Times*

Investigative Reporting
1992   Lorraine Adams '81, *Dallas Morning News*
2000   Martha Mendoza (visiting professor, journalism), Associated Press
2003   Clifford Levy '89, *New York Times*
2006   James Grimaldi (visiting professor, journalism), included in award to staff of the *Washington Post*
2008   Walt Bogdanich (visiting professor, journalism), *New York Times*
2012   Ken Armstrong (professor of writing), *Seattle Times*

Local Reporting
2014   Michael LaForgia (visiting professor, journalism), included in award to staff of the *Tampa Bay Times*
2016   Michael LaForgia (visiting professor, journalism), *Tampa Bay Times*

National Reporting
2002   Barton Gellman '82 (visiting professor, journalism and information technology policy), included in award to staff of the *Washington Post*
2005   Walt Bogdanich (visiting professor, journalism), *New York Times*
2008   Jo Becker (visiting professor, journalism), Barton Gellman '82 (visiting professor, journalism and information technology policy), *Washington Post*
2016   Marc Fisher '80 (visiting professor, journalism), Kimbriell Kelly (visiting professor, journalism), included in award to staff of the *Washington Post*
2018   Jo Becker (visiting professor, journalism), included in award to staff of the *New York Times*

Public Service
1924   *The World*, New York, for articles written by Samuel Duff McCoy 1905
2008   Anne Hull (visiting professor, journalism), included in award to staff of the *Washington Post*

2014 Marc Fisher '80 (visiting professor, journalism), Barton Gellman '82 (visiting professor, journalism and information technology policy), included in award to staff of the *Washington Post*

2016 Martha Mendoza (visiting professor, journalism), included in award to staff of the Associated Press

PYNE, MOSES TAYLOR 1877 inherited great wealth that was accumulated by his maternal grandfather, Moses Taylor. (Moses Taylor founded a shipping company whose business included shipping sugar to North America from slave-labor plantations in Cuba; he also served as the first president of the National City Bank of New York and was the principal stockholder in the Delaware, Lackawanna and Western Railroad Company.) For most of his adult life, Pyne devoted his time and much of his fortune to helping Princeton grow from a college into a university. During 36 years on the Board of Trustees he did not miss a single meeting.

As a Princeton student Pyne acquired a lasting taste for Latin and Greek. A year after receiving his LLB at Columbia Law School in 1879, he married Margaretta Stockton, a great-great-granddaughter of Richard Stockton 1748, and became general counsel for the Delaware, Lackawanna and Western Railroad Company. In 1891 he resigned from this position to give more time to his other interests, especially Princeton.

In his history of Pyne's Princeton estate, Drumthwacket, William Selden '34 notes that Pyne was a director of four banks, four steel and metal manufacturing companies, a gas company, an insurance company, eight railroads, two hospitals, two secondary schools, two YMCAs, and a vestryman of four Episcopal churches. He was president of the Princeton Township governing board and president of the board of the first Princeton Inn, which he helped to finance and build in 1891 on part of the original Morven property. In 1907 he was made an honorary member of 12 of the then-14 eating clubs at Princeton, more than half of which he had helped establish.

Pyne was 28 when he was elected to the Board of Trustees in 1884. His election was engineered by President James McCosh, who told Pyne's classmate, Henry Fairfield Osborn 1877, that the board was "full of old dotards" and that it badly needed "a fine young man" like Pyne.

Pyne's first major initiative was to organize the alumni in support of the College. He collected and stimulated others to collect information about alumni, which resulted in rich archival material and comprehensive address lists. With his classmate, Professor William Libbey Jr. 1877, he prepared and published an alumni directory in 1888. He was one of the founders and first president of the Princeton Club of New York, and he helped establish other alumni associations throughout the country.

In 1900 Pyne played a leading role in the adoption of a plan for electing alumni trustees and in the founding of the *Alumni Weekly*, serving as first chair of its executive committee. In 1905 he was one of the organizers of the Committee of Fifty, a forerunner of the Alumni Council. His classmate Osborn said Pyne "virtually created the modern alumni spirit" at Princeton.

As chair of the trustee committee on grounds and buildings, Pyne exerted a strong influence in favor of the use of Collegiate Gothic for the buildings that were erected at the time of the sesquicentennial in 1896. He himself had two Tudor Revival buildings constructed on the north side of Nassau Street, which he gave to the University; they were named Upper and Lower Pyne in his honor. He persuaded his mother to give the Tudor Gothic Pyne Library (now East Pyne), which opened as the University's main library in 1897 and continued to serve in that capacity until the opening of Firestone Library in 1948.

Later, as chair of the trustee committee on finance, Pyne sought the funds necessary to support President Woodrow Wilson's preceptorial system, and he dipped into his own pocket yearly to meet any deficit. To provide housing for the original preceptors and other new faculty members, he acquired land and built 23 houses in the Broadmead section of town. He rented them at modest charges during his lifetime and bequeathed them to the University upon his death.

Pyne also took a deep interest in furthering Dean Andrew Fleming West 1874's plans for the development of a residential graduate college. In 1905 he acquired Merwick, a mansion on Bayard Lane, which he made available to the University rent-free as a residence hall for graduate students, pending the construction of the graduate college.

After Grover Cleveland's death in 1908, Pyne gave up the finance committee chair to take Cleveland's place as chair of the committee on the graduate school. In this capacity he sided with West's proposal to locate the graduate college at a distance from the main campus—in opposition to Wilson's wish to have it integrated with the undergraduate college.

After Wilson's resignation in the fall of 1910, Pyne was urged by his friends to accept the presidency of the University, but he refused because he felt he could be more useful as a trustee. He continued his efforts on behalf of the graduate school, contributing funds for the construction of Pyne Tower at the graduate college and for the endowment of a professorship. After World War I he took a leading part as contributor and canvasser in the 1919 endowment campaign.

Pyne's generosity to the University was matched by many acts of kindness, frequently anonymous, on behalf of faculty, students, alumni, and townspeople. A *New York Evening Post* editor, reflecting on Pyne's benefactions, wrote: "He went around doing good as Pater said of Leonardo, like a man on a secret errand."

Pyne's Drumthwacket estate was for many years the focus for much of the social life of the University and the town. The grounds were always open to visitors, and many a Princetonian strolled along the path that led from a rustic gate on Lover's Lane past a deer park and through the woods to a series of small lakes amid flower gardens. The black squirrels that scamper about a campus much adorned in orange and black were first brought to Princeton when Pyne introduced them at Drumthwacket. Following Pyne's death in 1921, his granddaughter, Agnes, owned the estate until 1941; in 1966 it was purchased by the state of New Jersey to succeed Morven as the official residence of the governor, a role it officially assumed in 1981.

During Pyne's last illness, the trustees voted to name the first of the new post-World War I dormitories, then under construction, in his honor.

The day Pyne was buried, university activities were suspended and all business stopped on Nassau Street. After the services at Drumthwacket, the funeral cortege drove slowly through the grounds of the graduate college, past the site of Pyne dormitory and Upper and Lower Pyne, to the FitzRandolph Gateway where it entered the campus. To the tolling of the Nassau Hall bell, the procession passed through a student guard of honor to the steps of Nassau Hall, then westward around the rear of the building, and through the arches of Pyne Library, and then back to Nassau Street. After the procession left the campus, the students walked with it down Witherspoon Street to the cemetery.

In addition to the buildings and the professorship that bear his name, Pyne is remembered by the Pyne Honor Prize, founded in 1921, the highest honor that can be bestowed on an undergraduate. His portrait hangs in Procter Hall of the graduate college.

PYNE HALL, one of the largest undergraduate dormitories, enjoys the distinction of having been the first to house female candidates for bachelor's degrees (in 1969). During that first year of undergraduate coeducation, all women undergraduates lived there after the administration outfitted it with lounges, a kitchen, a laundry room, additional toilet facilities, electronic locks, and $70,000 worth of new furniture.

Pyne Hall was built in 1922 with funds given by alumni; its entries are designated as gifts of the Classes of 1902, 1906, 1908, 1912, 1920, 1921, 1922, and 1923. The intent of the donors was to honor longtime trustee and generous benefactor Moses Taylor Pyne 1877, who had died in April 1921.

In 1918 the railroad station at the foot of Blair Arch moved to a site a quarter mile to the south, thereby making land available for the construction of what became Pyne, Foulke, Henry, Laughlin, 1901, and Lockhart Halls—an area often referred to as the "junior slums"; since these dorms are not attached to any of the residential colleges, a large number of juniors, along with some seniors, live in them.

Pyne anchors the southern end of this collection of Collegiate Gothic dorms. Its four-story U-shaped design creates a small elevated courtyard that features two large saucer magnolias. Shortly after Pyne was constructed, the University planted six elm trees in the courtyard to honor the Princeton Naval Unit of World War I.

In 1940 Princeton's student radio station WPRU (later WPRB) broadcast for the first time from 441 Pyne Hall; five years later it moved to Holder Hall, and in 2004 to Bloomberg Hall.

PYNE HONOR PRIZE, THE, was established in 1921 by May Taylor Moulton Hanrahan and named for her cousin, longtime Princeton trustee and benefactor Moses Taylor Pyne 1877. It is awarded annually on Alumni Day to the member or members of the senior class who have most clearly manifested excellent scholarship, character, and effective support of the best interests of the University. It is the highest general distinction the University can confer on an undergraduate. The prize is equivalent to the prevailing undergraduate comprehensive fee for one academic year.

Among those awarded the prize have been former Princeton President Robert Goheen '40 *48; former US Senator Paul Sarbanes '54 and his son, Michael Sarbanes '86; and Supreme Court Justice Sonia Sotomayor '76. In addition to Goheen, 19 other Pyne Prize winners have gone on to serve as Princeton trustees: Ralph Hills 1925, H. Chapman Rose 1928, F. Tremaine Billings Jr. '33, Arthur Lane '34, Daniel Toll '49, Paul Sarbanes '54, Michael Kelly '59, John McCarter '60, Robert Rawson Jr. '66, Stephen Oxman '67, Jerome Davis '71, Marsha Levy '73, Thomas Barron '74, Sonia Sotomayor '76, Eric Lander '78, Nancy Newman '78, Kirsten Bibbins '87, Robert Peck '88, and Derek Kilmer '96. Rawson and Oxman served successively as chairs of the trustee executive committee, making them functionally chairs of the board.

Previous winners of the Pyne Prize are listed on page 523.

REEVE, TAPPING 1763 was the founder of one of America's earliest law schools. After teaching for a number of years following graduation, Reeve moved to Connecticut to read law. In 1773 he married Sally Burr, the daughter of Princeton's second president, and settled in Litchfield. He began giving law instruction in his office (his brother-in-law, Aaron Burr Jr. 1772, was one of his first students) and in 1784, to accommodate a growing number of students, built a cottage next to his house, which became known as the Litchfield Law School.

Although not the first institution for instruction in the law—the first American chair of law was established at the College of William & Mary in 1779—Reeve's school represented a major advance in the development of legal education in this country.

Reeve operated the school single-handedly until 1798, when he was appointed to the Connecticut Supreme Court (of which he was later chief justice). He invited James Gould, who had just graduated from the school, to join him in its management. They delivered carefully prepared lectures and held moot courts for practical instruction. They attracted students from almost every state in the union, who came by horseback, steamboat, and stage to study in the unheated, one-room school.

The school trained some of the most eminent men in public life in the early nineteenth century, including, in addition to Burr, John C. Calhoun, Horace Mann, Samuel Morse, and Noah Webster. Its graduates included 16 United States senators, 50 members of Congress, 40 justices of higher state courts, two justices of the United States Supreme Court, 10 governors, and five cabinet officers.

Reeve retired from active connection with the Litchfield School in 1820 when he was 76, while Gould continued to lecture until he closed the school in 1833. By then other law schools had been founded at Harvard (1817), and Yale (1824).

RELIGION, THE DEPARTMENT OF. In 1935 a faculty committee determined that "the study of religion is an intellectual discipline, and as such has a proper place in the curriculum of instruction of a university." This was a breakthrough moment in American higher education, where religion had not been taught since the nineteenth century, when it was considered part of other disciplines such as philosophy, literature, or history.

In 1940 President Harold Dodds acted on the committee's recommendation and George Thomas was appointed the University's first professor of religious thought. In 1945 the University created a department of Religion and 10 years later added a graduate program. In 1953, Religion became one of the founding departments of what is now the Council of the Humanities.

By the early 1950s, the study of religion at Princeton was thriving and many other colleges and universities were following Princeton's lead. During Thomas' first year, 21 undergraduates elected courses in religion. By the mid-1950s, more than 700 students were taking at least one course in religion, and 28 juniors and seniors were concentrating in the department; these numbers grew in the 1960s and 1970s to as high as 1,300 enrollments and as many as 69 concentrators.

The strength of the faculty quickly established the department's international reputation for excellent instruction and scholarship. In 1955, R.B.Y. Scott was appointed the first Danforth Professor of Religion, and that same year Philip Ashby, later chair of the department, published *The Conflict of Religions*. Malcolm Diamond, who taught psychology, religion, and philosophy of religion and became a leading figure for his work on Jewish studies, was hired as an instructor in 1953 and spent his entire academic life at Princeton, holding the Danforth chair from 1978 until his retirement in 1992. K.K.S. Ch'en, a renowned scholar on Buddhism, came to Princeton as the Stewart lecturer on the history of religion in 1961 and stayed until 1971.

Early members of the department knew they were engaged in a pioneering endeavor, developing the study of religion as an academic subject outside the context of theological seminaries and without formal ties to particular religious traditions. They frequently fielded inquiries from other universities eager to learn from their experience, and by the end of the 1960s, the department's PhD graduates were teaching in colleges and universities across the United States and Canada, as well as in Australia, Japan, and South Africa.

In 1970 Professors Paul Ramsey and John F. Wilson published *The Study of Religion in Colleges and Universities.* In 1971 a comparative study of graduate education in religion sponsored by the American Council of Learned Societies reported: "Princeton is clearly established in the front rank . . . and has been the most rigorously disciplined."

Scholars who joined the department since the 1970s have explored such diverse fields as religions of the Roman Empire, ethics of belief, ancient Judaism, religion in the Americas, Buddhist approaches to language and the ethics of personal cultivation, institutions and traditions of learning in Islam, liberation theology, social criticism, political thought, modern theology, film and theories of religion, and the role of religion in public life.

The impact of some members of the department extended beyond the halls of academia into popular culture. For example, Elaine Pagels, who came to Princeton in 1982 after receiving a MacArthur Fellowship, had books become *New York Times* bestsellers: an academic work on the gospel of Thomas (2003) and *Why Religion? A Personal Story* (2018). Cornel West *80, who received his PhD in philosophy at Princeton and taught in the department of Religion and in African American Studies from 1988 to 1994 and again from 2002 until he was awarded emeritus status in 2012, is a prominent public intellectual, as is associated Religion department faculty member Eddie Glaude Jr. *97.

The department's courses engage a wide range of religious traditions, geographic regions, time periods, and critical methods to explore how religions shape and are shaped by cultures and societies. Faculty approach the teaching of religions through the study of ethics and philosophy, texts and contexts, arts and culture, and history, politics, and social formations.

During their junior and senior years concentrators must take at least one course in each of the department's subfields: Islam; religion and critical thought; religion in the Americas; religions of Asia; and religions of the ancient Mediterranean. The graduate program has two additional subfields: religion and philosophy; and religion, ethics, and politics.

The department welcomes study abroad for undergraduates in their junior year, and students are encouraged to explore interdisciplinary programs. Because of the close connection between the department of Religion and the department of African American Studies, since 2010 the two departments have offered students an opportunity to complete the requirements for the major in Religion and the certificate in African American Studies in a coordinated manner.

Beginning in 2019, the University Center for Human Values launched the Princeton Project in Philosophy and Religion in cooperation with the departments of Philosophy and Religion. The project brings together an interdisciplinary group of students and scholars who share a research interest in the philosophy of religion as it is typically practiced by analytic philosophers. The project also explores the history of philosophical thinking about religious issues, the psychology and cognitive science of religion, theories and methods in the study of religion, the philosophical study of non-western religious traditions, and religious ethics.

RELIGIOUS LIFE. The founding of Princeton University as the College of New Jersey grew out of the religious ferment of the First Great Awakening. The founders were supporters of the religious revivals occasioned by the Awakening: so-called "New Side" Presbyterians who set out to create in New Jersey a liberal arts college rather than a seminary and wrote a guarantee of religious freedom into the institution's charter.

At the same time, the founders expected that religious practice would be integral to student life, and it was from the College's earliest days when daily services were conducted in the studies of the first two presidents. After the College moved to Princeton, services were held in the prayer hall in Nassau Hall until 1847 when the first purpose-built chapel was constructed. This chapel was replaced by Marquand Chapel in 1882, which in turn was replaced by the current University Chapel in 1928, the year in which the position of dean of the chapel was created.

For 136 years, students were required to attend morning and evening prayers daily and morning and afternoon services on Sunday. By 1882 required daily attendance at evening prayers was abolished and in 1902 the required Sunday afternoon service was discontinued. By 1905 attendance at morning prayers was required only twice a week and this requirement was abolished 10 years later. Required attendance at Sunday chapel ended for juniors and seniors in 1935; for sophomores in 1960; and for first-year students in 1964.

Student engagement in religious service (as opposed to religious "services") dates back at least to the establishment of the Philadelphian Society in 1825. In the words of former dean Thomas Breidenthal, the aim of the society was to "promote personal holiness lived out in service to others," and was "decidedly ecumenical in its approach." Over its century of existence, the group established and nurtured the Princeton YMCA, the Princeton-Blairstown Camp, the Student Volunteer Society, Princeton-in-Asia, and Murray-Dodge Hall.

The Philadelphian Society's commitment to service lives on today through the Student Volunteers Council, which after many years under the auspices of the office of Religious Life became part of the Pace Center for Civic Engagement in 2007. Its commitment to Christian fellowship evolved in 1931 into the Princeton Evangelical Fellowship, now named the Princeton Christian Fellowship.

While most student religious engagement through the mid-twentieth century was Protestant, there were Catholic students on campus, and they became more active and visible with the creation of the Aquinas Institute in the 1950s. The number of Jewish students was very small and kept so intentionally until after World War II; in 1915 only approximately 50 of Princeton's 1,400 undergraduates were Jewish. In 1921 the University recognized the Jewish Student Congregation as an official student group, granting chapel credit to those who participated, and in 1946 the Student Hebrew Association was founded. It held its first service in January 1947, with Albert Einstein and the assistant dean of the chapel in attendance. A year later the group became a Hillel chapter, and in 1993 the University built it a physical home on campus as the Center for Jewish Life. Students also take part in Jewish programming through Chabad on Campus, which became formally recognized in 2008.

When Frederick Borsch '57 was named dean in 1981, his title was expanded to include dean of religious life as well as dean of the chapel. Today the office of religious life includes the dean, two associate deans, the coordinator of a Hindu Life program, the coordinator of a Muslim Life program, the building administrator of the Center for Jewish Life, the director of the University Chapel Choir, and the University organist. (The Hindu Life program was established in 2008 and its coordinator, Vineet Chander, was the first person in the country to serve as a full-time university Hindu chaplain; that same year the Muslim Life program, led by Sohaib Nazeer Sultan until his untimely death in 2021 from a rare form of cancer, was established as the country's second university-supported Muslim chaplaincy.)

Based in Murray-Dodge Hall (home also of the Murray-Dodge Café, which it oversees), the office of religious life offers interfaith programming and councils, worship services, choirs and concerts, meditation, study of sacred texts, and trips to explore how religion is practiced in other cultures. It supports a Religious Life Council—undergraduates committed to fostering conversation between people of all faiths and beliefs at Princeton. In the chapel it oversees weekly ecumenical services; major University convocations such as Opening Exercises, the Service of Remembrance, and Baccalaureate; and memorial services and other special events such as what since 2008 has become an annual celebration of the Hindu festival of Diwali.

The office also coordinates the work of chaplaincies and student groups of various kinds. The faiths represented by these chaplaincies and groups include Baha'i, Buddhism, Christianity, Hinduism, Judaism, Islam, Sikhism, and Unitarian Universalism. The Christian chaplaincies include the following denominations: Baptist, Catholic, Episcopal, Latter Day Saints, Lutheran, Methodist, Orthodox Christian, and Presbyterian. Other Christian chaplaincies include the Christian Fellowship, the Manna Christian Fellowship, the Faculty Commons, the Graduate Christian Fellowship, Athletes in Action, and the Hallelujah Church at Princeton.

In their senior surveys, some 33 percent of undergraduates indicate that they have participated in religious life while at Princeton.

RESERVE OFFICER TRAINING CORPS (ROTC) at Princeton officially began in the fall of 1919 with the establishment of an army field artillery unit, one of the first permanent peacetime ROTC units in the country. As prescribed by a 1916 War Department directive, the purpose of ROTC on college campuses was to prepare undergraduates to serve as military officers.

The origins of the Princeton unit date back to February 3, 1917, the day Germany and the United States severed diplomatic relations and just months before the US officially entered World War I, when a Princeton Provisional Battalion was organized and over 500 students signed up. Eleven days later the battalion would include almost 900 students—some 60 percent of all undergraduates. The program combined theoretical classes, practical training, and off-campus military exercises during the summer and received support from both the army and the navy. Princeton also created naval training and aviation training programs. As early as March 1917, the faculty voted to ask the War Department to turn the provisional battalion into an official ROTC unit.

While the naval and aviation training units ultimately dissolved, in 1919 Princeton's wartime army program was formally reconstituted as the Princeton Field Artillery ROTC battalion (later, the "Tiger Battalion"), dedicated to producing field artillery officer candidates.

Princeton was "an ideal location" for such a unit, according to Major John McMahon Jr., who served as professor of military science and tactics. "It is out in the country where there is plenty of available land for riding," he wrote. The military training unit under his command included 90 horses, and in the early 1920s ponies furnished to the ROTC by the War Department played a pivotal role when polo was established as an intercollegiate sport at Princeton.

With World War I proclaimed to be the "war to end all wars," early enrollment in ROTC lagged, but an unlikely combination—the *Daily Princetonian* and President John Grier Hibben—urged students to participate. By late fall 1919, 127 students had enrolled, and by 1925 the number had grown to 600. By the time of Pearl Harbor, more than 2,000 Princetonians had been commissioned in the field artillery.

The Army ROTC unit was suspended during World War II, but extensive naval training took place on campus. By late 1942 the navy had several training programs under way, and in 1943 it brought its V-12 program to campus. In 1945 this program enrolled four African American students, three of whom would go on to earn Princeton degrees, and one of whom, John Howard '47, would become Princeton's first African American alumnus.

In the summer of 1942, engineering professor Philip Kissam introduced a tuition-free course on photogrammetry, and of the 45 students selected, 23 were women—making them the first women to enroll in a Princeton course.

In 1946 the Army ROTC unit was reactivated, and a Naval ROTC unit replaced the V-12 program. In 1951 an Air Force ROTC unit was established. With students preparing to serve as officers in the army, navy, and air force, ROTC became a significant presence on campus, with annual reviews, military balls, and commissioning by the president as part of Class Day ceremonies. The Cold War, the draft exemption for ROTC students, and the scholarships offered by all three services pushed enrollments to an all-time high of 1,107 undergraduates in 1951, about one-third of the entire student body. In 1957 Army ROTC officially converted from a field artillery unit to a general military science program.

As early as 1927, an article in the *Princeton Alumni Weekly* argued that ROTC courses were "not . . . properly . . . a part of a University curriculum," and in the 1950s, faculty grew hesitant about granting academic credit for ROTC courses. At the same time, students were increasingly reluctant to give up one course a semester for ROTC, and some professional associations, most notably in engineering, threatened not to accredit programs that gave course credit for ROTC.

Under the leadership of dean of the faculty J. Douglas Brown 1919 *1928, the University sought to add academic substance to ROTC by creating a series of special University-taught courses for ROTC students in psychology, politics, economics, and military history. The army and air force responded favorably, but the navy did not. The "Princeton Plan" for reforming ROTC found little support outside the University, and even locally it proved only a partial interim solution to a growing problem.

In the 1960s, as the war in Vietnam became a galvanizing issue on campus, enrollments in ROTC dwindled and tensions mounted. By 1964 there were only 334 students in all three units and by 1970 there were only 113. Student groups and members of the faculty began to insist on an end to course credit for ROTC, as well as to departmental standing for ROTC programs and faculty status for on-campus military officers. President Robert Goheen appointed a faculty committee, which recommended these changes, and in the spring of 1969, the faculty overwhelmingly approved proposals that converted ROTC into a noncredit program with the status of an extracurricular activity.

On May 2, 1970, following the American invasion of Cambodia, four students (two from Princeton) were arrested for firebombing the ROTC offices in the Armory. Soon thereafter the Council of the Princeton University Community called for removal of ROTC from the campus, and a month later the trustees voted to terminate all three ROTC programs no later than June 1972.

Within a year, students in a 1971 Undergraduate Assembly referendum voted in favor of retaining ROTC under the conditions set by the faculty in 1969. The air force and the navy were unwilling to accept these conditions, and closed their programs in 1971 and 1972, respectively. But the army, which had left campus in 1971, accepted the conditions, signed a contract offered by the University in June 1972, and returned to campus that fall as a noncredit elective program with no faculty status for its instructors.

In 1973, the trustees voted 26–7 to retain ROTC "as presently constituted" and "endorsed the non-compulsory nature of the current program and the fact that decisions as to whether or not academic credit will be given rest with the faculty." By 1976, 74 students (including 13 women) were enrolled.

In the 1980s, Princeton Army ROTC was led by Lieutenant Colonel Douglas Lovejoy *68, the only time in the battalion's history when it was commanded by a Princeton graduate. Lovejoy later served for 16 years on the staff of the University's development office. Another army instructor who transitioned to a career at the University was Richard Williams *72, who held increasingly responsible positions in the dean of the college office from 1974 until 2010. Stanley Adelson came to Princeton in 1962 to command the Air Force ROTC unit, and then held senior positions in the personnel (later human resources) office from 1968 to 1988. Another Air Force ROTC instructor, H. Dennis Gray, served as an assistant dean of the college.

In 1980, one of the seniors commissioned from the Army ROTC's Tiger Battalion was Mark Milley '80, who in 2015 became the US Army chief of staff. He received the University's Woodrow Wilson Award, the highest honor it can bestow on undergraduate alumni, in 2016, and in 2019 was confirmed as chair of the Joint Chiefs of Staff, making him the country's highest-ranking military officer.

In the 1990s, students and faculty members called for the removal of ROTC from campus because of the military's ban on members of the LGBTQIA community serving in the armed forces. In 1993 the faculty voted 42–33 to recommend termination of the ROTC program unless the army repealed all regulations restricting the speech of gay men, lesbians, and bisexuals. The trustees elected to retain the program because they continued to believe "that it is in the national interest to provide opportunities for Princeton students to participate in ROTC." But the University noted in its publications that ROTC was operated and controlled by the army, not by the University, and that the military's policy of discrimination was inconsistent with the policy of the University. President Harold Shapiro issued a statement pledging to continue his efforts to urge that federal policy be overturned (which it finally was in 2011).

In 2014 a Princeton Navy ROTC unit was reestablished as a cross-town affiliate of the NROTC program at Rutgers. While the University does not house its own air force unit, Princeton students have been able to participate in an Air Force ROTC program at Rutgers since the 1980s.

In 2019, on the 100th anniversary of the founding of Army ROTC at Princeton, General Milley played a leading role in the University's first tri-service commissioning ceremony since 1972, commissioning nine officers into the army, navy, and air force. In 2020, 12 students were commissioned in the army, navy, and marines in a virtual ceremony occasioned by the COVID-19 pandemic.

In 2019–20, 67 Princeton students were in ROTC: 47 in the army, 13 in the navy, and seven in the air force. Army cadets were spending 10–14 hours a week in ROTC classes, outdoor training, physical fitness training, and homework, and they also devoted several weekends to off-campus field exercises and marksmanship training. Princeton's Army ROTC program is also open to students from the College of New Jersey, Rider University, Rowan University, and Rutgers University-Camden.

RESIDENTIAL COLLEGES serve as a nexus of intellectual and social life at Princeton and provide environments where undergraduates, graduate students, faculty, staff, and even some town residents can interact formally and informally. In addition to housing and dining options, the colleges provide academic advising, structured peer advice, co-curricular support, and programming that enhances the intellectual, cultural, social, and recreational life of the campus.

All first- and second-year students are required to live in one of the residential colleges; juniors and seniors may choose to remain in their college, but even if they live elsewhere they retain an affiliation with it and are encouraged to remain engaged with it. Following Commencement, all seniors receive their degrees at the residential college with which they are affiliated.

Each college houses approximately 500 undergraduates, along with about 10 graduate students who assist with programming and mentoring, and sometimes a resident faculty fellow who lives and eats in the college. Except for Forbes, each residential college consists of a cluster of dormitories, a dining hall, lounges, recreational facilities, seminar classrooms, and study rooms. Other features may include college libraries, computer facilities, and spaces for the practice, performance, and viewing of music, theater, dance, and film. Elected college councils work with the college staff to plan a broad range of programs and activities.

A senior faculty member heads each residential college, providing vision and direction for its social and academic activities. Each college also has a dean and a director of studies to oversee students' academic progress, coordinate faculty and peer academic advising, provide individual academic advising and support to all students in or affiliated with the college, and coordinate academic programming in the college. A director of student life supervises the residential college advisers, juniors and seniors resident in the college who are assigned to first-year-student "zee-groups" (advisee groups). The director of student life is also responsible for nonacademic advising, adjudicating disciplinary matters, and supporting students' well-being.

Faculty engage with the colleges in several ways: as fellows who meet with students in informal settings, as academic advisers who help first-year students and sophomores select courses and make other decisions about their academic work, and as teachers of freshman seminars in classrooms within the colleges. Students also have access to academic advice from upperclass students in the colleges who serve as peer academic advisers.

Beyond academic programming, the colleges work with students to develop speakers' programs, language and current events tables, film series, art exhibits, and other intellectual and cultural activities. The colleges provide opportunities to participate in intramural athletic contests and sponsor trips to museums, musical performances, and theatrical productions in New York and Philadelphia.

While the colleges share many common elements, each has some facilities or programs that are unique to it, and each has a distinctive identity that has evolved over time. This identity is expressed in each college's shield, which is proudly on display at events like Opening Exercises, competitions among the colleges, and graduation.

The residential college system dates to 1982–83, but it has deeper roots. In some sense, these roots go back to Princeton's earliest days when all students lived, ate, and learned under one roof in Nassau Hall. The seeds of the current colleges were first sown in 1907 when President Woodrow Wilson proposed dividing the University into groups of dormitories with resident faculty (Wilson called them "quadrangles") to bring faculty and students together in a "truly organic way which will ensure vital intellectual and academic contacts, the comradeships of a common life with common ends." The faculty and trustees rejected the plan, handing Wilson the first of the political defeats that would mark his final years at Princeton.

Wilson's concept was revived a half century later with the creation of the Woodrow Wilson Lodge, which grew, in turn, into the Woodrow Wilson Society and, ultimately, Woodrow Wilson College (renamed First College in 2020). Woodrow Wilson Lodge was founded in 1957 by a small group of students in the Class of 1959 as an alternative to the eating clubs. From the outset, it sought to combine intellectual and social activities, and it incorporated a group of faculty fellows, who took meals with the undergraduates.

Initially, the Lodge organized its dining and social activities in an existing dining facility, Madison Hall. With the construction of a new dormitory quadrangle toward the southern part of the campus (the "New Quad," later the "Old New Quad") and the opening of an adjacent dining and social facility, Wilcox Hall, the Lodge relocated in 1961, changing its name to the Woodrow Wilson Society, and broadening its membership to include sophomores.

The society sought, in the words of President Robert Goheen, to realize the Wilsonian vision "of closely interweaving the intellectual and social life on campus." Led by a faculty member, with a corps of affiliated faculty fellows, the society offered a wide variety of intellectual, cultural, social, and recreational activities. In 1967, Professor Julian Jaynes, the resident head of the society, proposed that it become a truly residential entity, and in 1968 it became a four-year residential college, still carrying Wilson's name, with members of the college required to live in the dormitories of the Old New Quad.

Two years later, the former Princeton Inn hotel, having been converted into a student residential facility to accommodate the increased undergraduate enrollment that came with coeducation, opened as the University's second four-year residential college.

The plan for a full-fledged residential college system emerged from the work of the Committee on Undergraduate Residential Life (CURL), appointed in February 1978 by President William Bowen "to study and make recommendations concerning the development of social and dining facilities that would have a direct bearing on the quality of undergraduate life." The CURL committee, as it came to be known, issued its final report in June 1979.

The most important of its recommendations was the creation of a residential college system, with five colleges that would house all freshmen and sophomores and a limited number of juniors and seniors. The proposed college system would provide entering students with a ready-made community within the larger university. It would give freshmen and sophomores the opportunity to get to know each other more easily and effectively than was the case when underclass students were scattered in dormitories across the campus and eating in the cavernous dining halls known as Commons. It would improve academic advising for freshmen and sophomores and provide them with greater access to programming of various kinds through their colleges.

In October 1979 the trustees endorsed the general direction of the proposals and authorized further discussions to develop specific plans for implementation. The ability to establish the new residential college system depended critically on raising funds to create three new colleges. One new dining and social facility was needed, which, in conjunction with the dormitories of the "New New Quad" would form a new college down-campus. It was also necessary to renovate the five dining rooms of Commons to become the college offices and the dining and social spaces for two up-campus colleges.

The project advanced quickly with strong support from key donors, including, among others, Lee D. Butler 1922 and his wife, Margaret; Gordon Wu '58; Laurance Rockefeller '32, the John D. Rockefeller 3rd Foundation, and other members of the Rockefeller family. As a result, three new colleges—Lee D. Butler College, Dean Mathey College, and John D. Rockefeller 3rd College—opened in 1982 and in 1983, joining with Woodrow Wilson College and Princeton Inn College to form a college system for all freshmen and sophomores. (By 1982 sufficient renovation had been completed to accommodate all first-year students, and by 1983, with the completion of Wu Hall, the system could accommodate all sophomores as well.) A subsequent gift from Malcolm S. Forbes '41 made possible the renovation of Princeton Inn College, which was rededicated in 1984 as Malcolm S. Forbes Jr. '70 College.

Prior to the opening of Whitman College in 2007 to accommodate a 10 percent increase in the size of the undergraduate student body, all the residential colleges were two-year colleges for freshmen and sophomores, with only a small number of juniors and seniors in roles like residential college advisers. With the opening of Whitman, three of the colleges were designated as four-year colleges and each of them was paired with a two-year college (Mathey with Rockefeller, Butler with Wilson, and Whitman with Forbes).

The goal was to encourage more interaction across all four classes by providing opportunities for students to remain in their college or their paired college during junior and senior years. Juniors and seniors who moved out of the colleges could still take some meals in their college and they retained their academic advisers. A "shared meal program" was introduced to allow some juniors and seniors to join eating clubs and remain college residents, with the goal of reducing the degree of separation during junior and senior years between students in eating clubs and students in colleges.

In 2016 the trustees approved a further 10 percent increase in the size of the student body, creating a need for at least one additional residential college. The University decided to construct two colleges and hired a team led by Deborah Berke, dean of architecture at Yale, and Maitland Jones '87 to design them. The construction of two colleges provided swing space that enabled the University to undertake substantial renovation of its existing housing stock, and eventually could support additional expansion of the student body. The two colleges are adjacent to each other along the southern boundary of Poe Field, on a site previously occupied by the varsity softball field, the varsity tennis courts, and Roberts soccer stadium; they are scheduled to open for academic year 2022–23.

Each college will accommodate 510 beds and have its own dining hall, but with shared food preparation and service space. Residences for the heads of the colleges are included as part of each college. In September 2020, the University announced that two adjoining dormitories in one of the new colleges would be named for their donors, the married couple Kwanza Jones '93 and José E. Feliciano '94, making them the first two buildings on campus named for Black and Latino benefactors.

Butler College

Butler College was established in the fall of 1983 and named in honor of former trustee Lee D. Butler 1922. In 2007 it became one of the four-year colleges, paired with Wilson College. It houses approximately 550 residents, mostly in dormitories that were completed in 2009 on the site of the former "New New Quad." Its social and dining space is Gordon Wu Hall, constructed in 1983. The college includes an amphitheater, an art gallery, and innovation space for entrepreneurial students.

In addition to Wu Hall (which also contains the Matthew Mellon 1922 Library), Butler's buildings include 1915 Hall, 1967 Hall, Bloomberg Hall (which houses the broadcast studio of the student radio station, WPRB), Yoseloff Hall and Bogle Hall (both of which have green roofs), 1976 Hall, and Wilf Hall.

Forbes College

The original Princeton Inn hotel was located near the intersection of Nassau Street and Route 206 (later the site of Borough Hall) between 1893 and 1918. In 1924–25, a new Princeton Inn was constructed overlooking Springdale Golf Course. In 1970 the University, which held a majority interest in the hotel, converted the main building of the Inn into a residential college with hotel-style dormitory rooms, a hotel-size dining room, and activity spaces of various kinds. The University expanded the college's housing capacity by converting the former employees' quarters (the Annex) into dormitory spaces, and then constructing a new building (the Addition—later known as the New Wing) in 1971.

In its earliest years Princeton Inn College had a bohemian air, and in 1975 it named its college library for six-time Socialist candidate for president of the United States, Norman Thomas 1905. The college was remodeled and renamed Forbes College in 1984, and in 2007 it was paired with four-year Whitman College.

Forbes is home to about 500 freshmen and sophomores. It has long been renowned for the strong sense of community that results from being located just off the main campus and from being largely encompassed within a single building ("students can go from their rooms to breakfast in their slippers"). It has always had the distinction of being the college closest to the train station and the ever-popular 24-hour convenience store, the Wawa. The construction of the Lewis Arts complex immediately across the street in 2017 brought the campus closer to the college and enlivened the surrounding area; Forbes itself has supported student interest in the arts with a dance studio and a music practice room.

Forbes students operate a demonstration garden on site that provides student-grown produce to the Forbes dining hall. An adjacent building at 99 Alexander Street, affectionately known as the Pink House, served until 2020 as the home of about 10 students each year with a particular interest in sustainability and the environment; beginning in 2020 the house was made available to members of Forbes who wished to remain as juniors and seniors.

Mathey College

Mathey College (pronounced "matty") was established in 1983. In 2007 it became a four-year college paired with Rockefeller College, housing about 400 freshmen and sophomores, along with about 140 juniors and seniors. It is named for Dean Mathey 1912, a legendary Princeton donor and long-time (33-year) trustee.

Mathey students live in some of the most historic buildings on campus, including Hamilton, Joline, Blair, Edwards, and parts of Campbell and Little Halls. Its facilities include a theater, a library and a servery that it shares with Rockefeller College; a recording studio and dark room; and kitchens in four of its dorms.

The kitchen in Edwards Hall is home to a student-run "Real Food Co-op" whose members prepare eight meals a week for each other. Edwards is also home to the Edwards Collective, a group of about 35 students who live in a designated area and share a deep interest in the humanities and creative arts.

Rockefeller College

Rockefeller College, the 500-student, two-year complement to Mathey College, is universally known as "Rocky." It opened in 1982 and was named for philanthropist and former trustee John D. Rockefeller 3rd 1929. Its gothic dormitories include Holder Hall, Witherspoon Hall, Buyers Hall (formerly part of Blair), and a portion of Campbell Hall; its social, dining, and academic facilities occupy spaces that previously served as the Commons dining halls for all freshmen and sophomores.

The college shares a theater, library, and servery with Mathey College; it also has a digital arts room (Holder Center), rehearsal spaces and music practice rooms, and a kitchen in Witherspoon Hall. It is home to the Cyclab, a bicycle cooperative where students can repair their bikes, and along with Mathey College it hosts the Peter S. Firestone '62 Society, which offers students opportunities to engage in book discussions and meet authors.

Many scenes in the 2001 Academy Award-winning movie, "A Beautiful Mind," were filmed in Rockefeller College.

Whitman College

Whitman College is named after its lead donor, trailblazing business leader and former trustee Meg Whitman '77. It opened in 2007 as a four-year college of about 500 students, paired with Forbes. Collegiate Gothic in design, it includes a theater, an art gallery, a dance studio, and a spacious dining hall known as Community Hall.

Its residence halls include Fisher Hall, Wendell Hall, Murley-Pivirotto Family Tower, Hargadon Hall, Lauritzen Hall, Baker Hall, and 1981 Hall.

Wilson College/First College/Hobson College

Princeton's first residential college dates back to 1968. While initially open to students in all four years, in 1982 it became a two-year college, later paired with adjacent four-year Butler College, with which it shares a servery. Its social and dining space continues to be Wilcox Hall, and it continues to incorporate the dormitories of the Old New Quad (1937, 1938, 1939, Dodge-Osborn, Gauss), supplemented by Feinberg Hall, 1927-Clapp Hall, and Walker Hall.

In 2020 the University announced that plans were in place to close the college in a few years when the two new colleges south of Poe Field were completed, but that while it remained open its name would be changed from Wilson College to First College to remove its association with Wilson's racist views and recognize its status as Princeton's first residential college. Later that year the University announced that former trustee Mellody Hobson '91 (a business leader, philanthropist, and national voice for financial literacy and investor education) had donated funds to establish a new residential college, Hobson College, on the site then occupied by First College, with an opening tentatively scheduled for the fall of 2026.

Wilson/First College included a dance studio, music room, ceramics studio, black-box theater, a kitchen in Dodge-Osborn Hall, and the Julian Street Library and Media Center. The Julian Street Library was given in 1961 by Graham Mattison 1926 in memory of the writer Julian Street, who lived in Princeton in the 1920s and befriended many undergraduates; Mattison's gift built the library, purchased an initial selection of books, and provided an endowment for the addition of new books each year. Street's son, Julian Street Jr., graduated from Princeton in 1925.

In 2009 Wilcox Hall was renovated by the firm of long-time Princeton faculty member (then emeritus) Michael Graves, and as part of the renovation a large photograph was added to its dining hall showing Wilson as president of the United States throwing out the first pitch at a 1915 Washington Senators baseball game. The photograph became a point of contention in 2015-16 when, in response to student protests, the University conducted a thorough review of Wilson's legacy at Princeton and in the course of that review asked the head of the college to consider removal of the photograph.

Upon the advice of an ad hoc student committee, the head of the college decided to remove the photograph, citing the students' observation that "the name of the college was chosen in honor not of Wilson but of his vision for the residential college system," and concluding that the photo was "unduly celebratory" of Wilson the man, and not in keeping with the college's "founding wish to have Princeton be a place that is truly diverse and inclusive, and one that embraces, respects and values all its members."

RESIDENTIAL LIFE for students revolved around Nassau Hall after the 10-year-old College of New Jersey moved to Princeton in 1756. All undergraduates lived there (or had lodgings in town) until 1833, when the first dormitory, East College, was built. As other dormitories were erected, Nassau Hall was increasingly taken over for administrative and faculty use, although one or two students continued to live there as late as 1903.

By 1973, when Spelman Halls, the first campus buildings to offer apartment living, were completed, Princeton had built 40 dormitories, all but six of which were still being used for their original purpose, and it had two residential colleges: Wilson, which encompassed the dormitories known as the "Old New Quad," and Princeton Inn (later Forbes). Three former dormitories had been razed: East College in 1896, Upper Pyne in 1963, and Reunion Hall in 1965, and three had been converted to other uses: Lower Pyne in 1950 for commercial offices, and 1879 Hall and West College (now Morrison Hall) in the early 1960s for academic and administrative uses.

Over the next 50 years the University added Feinberg and 1927-Clapp halls to Wilson (later renamed First) College; replaced the "New New Quad" dormitories of Butler College with five new dormitories (Bogle, Wilf, Yoseloff, 1967, and 1976); and later added Bloomberg Hall, originally opened as an upperclass dorm, to Butler. It constructed an entirely new residential college, Whitman, with seven dorms (Baker, Fisher, Hargadon, Lauritzen, Murley-Pivirotto, Wendell, and 1981); built Scully Hall as a new upperclass dorm; and incorporated 2 Dickinson Street as a residential co-op. A small house at 99 Alexander Street was added to Forbes. Patton Hall was renamed Patton-Wright and a portion of Blair Hall was renamed Buyers.

In 2020 construction began on two new residential colleges south of Poe Field, each with 510 beds, and it was announced that First College would be replaced by a new college named for its donor, Mellody Hobson '91.

In addition to housing students, Nassau Hall contained the College's dining room and kitchen (originally in the basement, later in a connecting wing) until 1804, when a refectory opened on the first floor of Philosophical Hall, built where Chancellor Green now stands. For a dozen years, starting in 1834, a second refectory, on William Street, supplied board at a cheaper rate ($1.50 a week rather than the regular $2.00). Students called it the "poor house."

Meals in those early days were spartan. Breakfast usually consisted of bread and butter with coffee, supper of bread and butter with milk and occasionally chocolate. Students sometimes filled out their meagre evening fare by stealing chickens or turkeys in town and roasting them over their chamber fires—a common college custom at the time. Mid-day dinner was more ample, usually offering meat, fish, or poultry, potatoes, fresh vegetables in season, "small beer and cyder," and sometimes for dessert "pye" or cake.

In diaries and letters home, students complained about the poor quality and monotony of their meals. In the 1840s their protests began taking a forceful turn: at a given signal, up would go the windows and out would fly the tablecloths and all that was on them. Beginning in 1843 students were permitted to take their meals with families in town, where the cost was somewhat higher than in the college refectory, although in some cases, the catalogue said, "select associations of students have been formed, whose expenses do not exceed $1.25 a week."

The college refectory gradually lost out in competition with the local boardinghouses and associations and was finally closed in 1856. The associations grew in number and evolved into a system of eating clubs. Attempts to revive a Commons in 1877 and 1891 failed, and it was not until 1906 and 1908 that first freshman, and then sophomore, Commons were instituted in the old University Hall. Their place in campus life was solidified in 1916 by the construction of Madison Hall.

In 1943 the University turned over food preparation in Commons to Howard Johnson's, but in 1960 it ended the contract and established its own food services department. Commons (in halls called Upper and Lower Cloister, Upper and Sub Eagle, and Madison) remained a fixture of campus life into the 1980s and became a prime source of campus jobs for students on financial aid, but Commons was closed when the University adopted a system of residential colleges for all freshmen and sophomores.

After a brief flirtation with Greek-letter fraternities between 1843 and the official banning of them in 1853 (and despite lingering affiliations with some of them until 1875, notwithstanding a University-required pledge not to join them), student life in the mid-nineteenth century increasingly revolved around the "select associations" that evolved into eating clubs, as well as the literary and debating societies of Whig and Clio, interclass rivalries and pranks, and, increasingly, athletic competitions. As early as 1844 students were dividing themselves into teams and engaging in spirited football games on the green behind Nassau Hall. In 1857 a cricket club and two baseball clubs were formed, and in 1864 Princeton played its first intercollegiate contest, winning a baseball game against Williams. In 1869 Princeton played in the first intercollegiate football game against Rutgers.

The mid-to-late nineteenth century also saw the emergence of other extracurricular activities. The *Nassau Lit*, the country's second oldest literary magazine, first appeared in 1842, and the Glee Club was founded in 1874. In 1887 students founded an orchestra, but before that there was an "Instrumental Club," along with banjo and mandolin clubs that played and later traveled with the Glee Club. The *Princetonian* published its first edition in 1876 and became a daily in 1892. The *Princeton Tiger*, after a false start in 1882, began regular publication in 1890. The Princeton College Dramatic Association was founded in 1883 and 10 years later became the Triangle Club.

Today Princeton is home to more than 300 student organizations catering to almost every conceivable interest or activity, in categories that range from music, dance, and theater to media, religion, politics, and service. If students arrive on campus with an interest that is not being met, they are welcome to seek out others with a similar interest and create an organization to meet it.

As part of their residential experience, students have access to the resources of the residential colleges and such offices as health services, campus recreation, and religious life, as well as to such centers as the Carl A. Fields Center for Equality and Cultural Understanding, the Center for Career Development, the Davis International Center, the Lesbian, Gay, Bisexual, Transgender Center, the Women*s Center, and, as of fall 2021, a center for gender and sexuality.

More than 98 percent of undergraduates live on campus, and most take full advantage of the extracurricular and co-curricular experiences that Princeton offers and the opportunities it provides to develop life-long friendships and learn from others while living together on a campus designed to encourage interaction and reflection. Many believe that the extraordinary alumni attachment to Princeton owes much to the powerful and lasting impact of the shared residential experience and the strong sense of community that it fosters.

Undergraduate life in the twenty-first century revolves around the residential colleges and, for many juniors and seniors, the eating clubs. Many applaud the fact that the clubs are not residential, which means that most students have at least two "friend groups," one where they live and one where they eat, and many students develop strong affiliations with other groups as well through their athletic teams, extracurricular pursuits, and community service activities.

The concept of residential colleges can be traced to the Quad Plan that President Woodrow Wilson proposed to the trustees in 1907. He said he was trying to rectify what he feared was "the almost imperceptible and yet increasingly certain decline of the old democratic spirit of the place." His plan called for the establishment of residential quadrangles or colleges, each with its own dining hall, common room, and resident faculty, with every undergraduate required to live in a college. The trustees initially approved the plan in principle, but they later withdrew their support in response to opposition from alumni and students and concerns about its cost.

Wilson's successor, President John Grier Hibben, pursued a different approach to improving student life. Plans for a million-dollar complex containing dining spaces, a theater, and quarters for undergraduate activities were announced in the mid-1920s but suspended during the Great Depression. A campus center for soldiers on campus was established in Murray-Dodge during World War II and remained in use by undergraduates until 1954 when the University created a student center in Chancellor Green by renovating the north wing of Pyne Library for a cafeteria and the reading room in Chancellor Green library for a lounge. When the legal age for drinking in New Jersey was lowered to 18 in 1973, a pub was installed in the lounge and student bartenders began serving beer, wine, and soft drinks, while student cooks started to bake "the best pizza in town."

In the first half of the twentieth century there were sporadic efforts to develop alternatives to the eating clubs, and these efforts accelerated in the 1950s as the GI Bill and expanded access to student aid began to shift the composition of the student body to include more students from public high schools and lower-income families. These efforts were galvanized by the "dirty bicker" of 1958 when 23 students, more than half of whom were Jewish, were not chosen for any club despite an earlier commitment to guarantee that every student who sought a bid to a club (in other words, every student who "bickered") would receive one.

In 1957 students seeking an alternative to the clubs formed Woodrow Wilson Lodge, which in 1961 moved into Wilcox Hall as the Woodrow Wilson Society and then in 1968 became Princeton's first residential college by combining the dining, social, and library space of Wilcox with the dormitories of the Old New

Quad. In 1968 the University converted two former eating club buildings into a University-operated dining and social facility called Stevenson Hall (adding a kosher kitchen in 1972 which remained until the Center for Jewish Life opened in 1993), and in 1969 it created Madison Society, a low-cost alternative that provided up to 200 members with opportunities to eat breakfast at Wilcox Hall, lunch at Commons or the Student Center, and "candlelight and beer" dinners atop New South. In 1970 Princeton Inn College opened as the University's second residential college.

Some students chose not to have dining contracts with the University or the clubs. Known as "independents," they could select rooms in Spelman Halls with apartment-style kitchens, eat meals in their rooms or in town, or, beginning in 1977–78, join a co-op at 2 Dickinson Street (and later other co-ops).

When the residential college system was introduced in the early 1980s, the colleges housed, fed, and provided social facilities and a support infrastructure for all freshmen and sophomores. When Whitman College opened in 2007, the system was modified so three of the then-six colleges would also offer spaces to interested juniors and seniors, and a shared meal program was developed to allow some juniors and seniors to join clubs, live in the colleges, and take meals in both.

Hibben's quest for a "common ground for campus life" was finally realized in 2000 with the opening of the Frist Campus Center, a facility that brings together undergraduates, graduate students, faculty, staff, alumni, and visitors to the campus, and offers dining options, meeting and gathering spaces, opportunities for recreation and refreshment, and a variety of centers and services. In 2009 a reconstituted Campus Club opened as a University-operated and largely student-programmed gathering place for undergraduates and graduate students.

Princeton began providing housing for graduate students in 1905 in a three-story Victorian house just north of campus known as Merwick. In 1913 it opened an imposing group of Gothic buildings just west of campus as the first residential college in the United States devoted solely to graduate students. The graduate college houses about 430 graduate students and serves as a center of graduate student life; in addition to housing, it provides a dining hall, a common room, informal study spaces, and an underground socializing and entertainment venue known as Debasement Bar.

Beginning just after World War II the University installed military-style barracks on a field known as the Butler Tract to house graduate students with spouses and families. Designed to be temporary, these increasingly deteriorating but highly affordable barracks remained in place until 2016 following the completion of new Lakeside apartments and townhouses for graduate students on the north shore of Lake Carnegie. Graduate student housing is also provided in the Lawrence apartments and in apartments on Edwards Place. Princeton houses more than 70 percent of its graduate students, far more than most universities, and its initial development plans for the Lake Campus just south of Lake Carnegie included 379 additional units of housing for graduate students and post-docs.

While most graduate student life revolves around the students' departments, their housing units, and the graduate college, graduate students engage in graduate student government and participate actively in the work of the Council of the Princeton University Community (CPUC). Graduate students play on intramural athletic teams, and there are more than 100 graduate student organizations; many undergraduate organizations welcome the participation of graduate students, as do groups such as the University Orchestra, the Glee Club, and the Chapel Choir.

Resident graduate students live in each residential college, taking meals in the dining hall, advising undergraduates, developing programming in their areas of interest, and generally engaging in the intellectual, social, and communal life of the college.

REUNION HALL, a five-story dormitory, was built in 1870 to commemorate the reunion of the Old and New Schools of the Presbyterian Church. It was razed in 1965 after it had been condemned as a fire hazard. During his short stay on campus as a freshman in 1935, John F. Kennedy '39 lived in Reunion Hall.

The space Reunion Hall occupied between Stanhope Hall and Morrison Hall was filled in 1971 with what became one of the most photographed features of the campus: an 11-foot tall, two-and-a-half-ton bronze sculpture titled *Oval With Points*, by the British sculptor Henry Moore. The sculpture bears a relationship to one of Moore's favorite objects, an elephant skull from East Africa given to him by the distinguished biologist Sir Julian Huxley and his wife Juliette (although generations of Princeton students also noted its resemblance to President Richard Nixon's nose).

Within a few months of the sculpture's installation on campus, the interior curves of the oval had been burnished through contact with bodies sitting on or sliding through it, much to Moore's delight.

REUNIONS. In the College of New Jersey's early years, alumni regularly returned to campus around Commencement. The centennial Commencement of 1847 drew 700 alumni for a formal dinner. Until 1859 all alumni gathered together, but that year the Class of 1856, in celebration of its third reunion, organized the first such gathering for a single class. The reunion came with an extra bonus: in that era anyone who returned for Commencement three years after graduation qualified automatically for a master's degree, a practice that lasted until 1892.

The idea of class reunions caught on, and with them the idea of class gifts. At its 10th reunion the Class of 1859 endowed a senior prize in English, and a year later, at its 10th, the Class of 1860 founded a graduate fellowship in experimental science. When the Class of 1866 observed its decennial, it gave the clock in the cupola of Nassau Hall.

In 1861, when a regiment bound for battle in the Civil War passed through Princeton, it captivated students with its "skyrocket" cheer, which imitated the sound of fireworks: sis, boom, and ahh. This evolved into Princeton's locomotive cheer, later adding the word tiger and becoming "rah, rah, rah, tiger, tiger, tiger, sis, sis, sis, boom, boom, boom, ahh" and then ending with the name of the person or entity being celebrated. The locomotive cheer is an integral—and frequently expressed—feature of Princeton reunions.

By the 1890s many classes were holding reunions at commencement time. They were modest affairs at first: meetings held in classrooms or in Nassau Hall, followed by a dinner in University Hall or the old Princeton Inn. Over time, attendance at reunions grew and programs became more elaborate, sometimes lasting two or three days. Houses were rented to accommodate class members, bands were engaged for their entertainment (and to welcome classmates arriving by train), and various means of identification were gradually adopted, such as class banners, hatbands, blazers, and costumes.

It became the custom for each class to have a major reunion at five-year intervals following graduation. For these occasions, alumni made a determined effort to return to Princeton even if they lived in distant places, and even if they had to walk. William Vail 1865 is reported to have walked 50 miles from his home in Newark to attend his 50th reunion, reaching campus just in time to join his classmates for "the last mile," the alumni parade, or P-rade.

It was also the case that sometimes even the most determined alumni simply could not make the trip. In 1973, for example, astronaut Charles "Pete" Conrad Jr. '53 sent word to his reunion chair that he could not be present for his class's 20th because "he was out of town on business." He sent his message from the space station Skylab 2 to the Johnson Space Center at Houston, which relayed it to Princeton.

The 25th reunion came to be regarded as the most important, and for many years the 25th reunion class led the P-rade. In 2018, however, the 25th reunion class of 1993 ceded the lead-off position to the Old Guard—alumni more than 65 years past graduation. The 50th is another milestone reunion, and over recent decades alumni in the first five reunion classes have returned in staggering numbers—with the first reunion typically attracting well over half the class.

Reunions were canceled in 1917 and 1918 during World War I. The "victory commencement" in 1919 coincided with Flag Day, and a parade of 5,000 alumni marched across University Field, waving their flags with each step—"a moving sight," the *Alumni Weekly* reported, which "brought the 10,000 spectators to their feet." An even larger "victory reunion" in 1946 (following the canceled reunions of 1943–45) brought back 7,300 alumni, with each class carrying flags showing the number in each class who had served in the war and the number who had given their lives

In 1947 the Class of 1922 held its 25th reunion in Holder Hall courtyard, making it the first on-campus reunion site. Now all major reunions have sites on campus, and they invite four off-year "satellite" classes (the two immediately before them and the two immediately after them) to share their sites with them. The University provides the headquarter sites across campus and other services, including in recent years an elaborate shuttle system and child care, but the classes pay for their own meals, refreshments, entertainment, costumes, and, to the extent they are available, on-campus rooms.

Princeton reunions are unusual in many respects. Every class is welcomed back every year—not just during major reunions—and reunions take place prior to Commencement so alumni can meet with seniors and other students who remain on campus to work or perform, and so that seniors can participate in the festivities, including the P-rade. This puts enormous pressure on the University's housing, dining, public safety, and other staffs, who not only need to accommodate the roughly 25,000 alumni and other guests for three days of reunions, but then need to make a rapid transition between Saturday night and Sunday morning to accommodate parents and other family members for three days of graduation.

In 1951 the Class of 1926 introduced the idea of Alumni-Faculty Forums to add academic content to its 25th reunion. The idea caught on, and typically there are about two dozen such panels each year, usually composed of alumni experts and faculty moderators, discussing pressing issues in many fields. During reunions, many classes, alumni groups, and student organizations conduct meetings and events, and special efforts are made to provide opportunities for community service.

In 1996, in connection with its 250th anniversary, the University began sponsoring a fireworks display following the annual lawn concert on the Saturday night of reunions; the thousands of shells, a custom-made sound track honoring many of that year's major reunion classes (cleverly conceived by 250th anniversary executive director and former Alumni Association president Dorothy Bedford '78), and intricately tailored choreography between the soundtrack and the shells quickly became an annual highlight not only for alumni, but for members of the local community as well. The fireworks proved so popular that during the economic downturn of 2008–2009, when University budgets were under stress, a donor stepped forward to make sure the fireworks could go on as planned.

The P-rade is held on the Saturday before Commencement. It originated in the 1890s but is related to an earlier alumni event: beginning soon after the Civil War, alumni classes began taking part, on commencement day, in an ordered procession to the place of their class dinner. A more lighthearted migration grew out of the baseball rivalry between Yale and Princeton. The teams first met in 1868, and 20 years later they began playing at Princeton on the Saturday before Commencement. Alumni attendance grew, and now and then a class back for a reunion would march to the game behind a band. In 1897, stimulated by a torchlight procession of some 2,000 alumni and 800 undergraduates at the sesquicentennial celebration the previous fall, all of the "reuning" classes joined in a parade to the game, thus beginning what has evolved into the most colorful event of reunions.

A written description from 1906 of the now annual event said, "The Alumni Pee-rade on Saturday afternoon was quite as spectacular as usual; the bands, banners, transparencies, uniforms, and vaudeville features encircling University Field with color and noise."

At first the sole decoration worn by returning alumni was a badge with class numerals on it. Gradually classes began to distinguish themselves by using class hats, balloons, parasols, large palm leaf fans, and before long younger classes were wearing colorful costumes, carrying humorous signs, and sometimes performing comic stunts. In 1912 some of the seniors dressed in denim overalls and jackets, and the following year the Class of 1913 adopted white "beer jackets" as their costume. By 1920 the jackets had become a "tradition" with each class developing its own design; the practice, now known as senior jackets or class jackets, continues today, with classes wearing their jackets as seniors and through their fourth reunion, and then typically designing new costumes for their 5th, 10th, 15th, and 20th reunions before designing a class blazer for their 25th that will last them for the rest of their lives.

Graduate alumni introduced a polo shirt decorated with Cleveland tower in 1975, t-shirts with various designs in 1991, and a diagonally striped orange and black polo in 2000. In 2003, the Association of Princeton Graduate Alumni introduced a reunions blazer for graduate alumni, and in 2018 it introduced jackets similar to the undergraduate class jackets.

From the early to mid-twentieth century, the P-rade formed in front of Nassau Hall, moved across campus to 1879 Arch, and then proceeded down Prospect Avenue, through the Thompson Gateway, and around University Field, passing in review before the president's box behind first base. Beginning in 1961, following construction of the Engineering Quadrangle on University Field, the end of the route was switched to Clarke Field. In 1966 a further change was required when Yale could no longer keep its team together for the post-season Princeton game. A game between the varsity and a team of alumni provided a temporary focus for the P-rade in 1967, but in 1968 the P-rade's terminating event was changed to an Alumni Association meeting, where seniors are formally welcomed into the alumni ranks.

In 1991 the route was modified again to keep the P-rade entirely on campus, winding around Cannon Green and then down Elm Drive to a terminus on Poe Field. When Bloomberg Hall was constructed in 2004, the classes began passing through its echoing arch before making their way to the reviewing stand and offering a locomotive to the University's president.

The P-rade begins at 2 p.m. with the tolling of the Nassau Hall bell. Just behind the grand marshal and other dignitaries is the Old Guard—many in golf carts, but also many who walk. It is led by the oldest member of the oldest class at that year's reunion, who carries the Class of 1923 cane, a black wooden staff topped by a leaping silver tiger. Joseph Schein '37 was 104 when he walked the route and carried the cane for the fourth time in 2019, and 105 and 106 when he led the virtual P-rades of 2020 and 2021 that were necessitated by the COVID-19 pandemic.

The P-rade was initially restricted to alumni, but over time it increasingly became a family affair. Watching the P-rade is like watching a march of history, as women graduates begin to appear in the classes of the 1970s, and the growing diversity of the student body becomes evident in the classes of that decade and later. Beginning in 1975, graduate alumni were invited to march between the 24th and 26th reunion classes, in the space vacated by the 25th reunion class that now marches right after the Old Guard. Alumni marshals in distinctive Da Vinci hats attempt to keep the P-rade moving apace, albeit with only limited success, and the P-rade ends when the senior class "marches" onto Poe Field and passes the reviewing stand.

Bands play an important role in the P-rade. Classes celebrating major reunions usually have one, and occasionally classes celebrating "off-year" reunions have them, too. At times there have been as many as 30 bands punctuating the long procession—brass bands, bagpipers, fife and drum corps, high school marching bands—and the University Band appears twice, once leading the P-rade and again heralding the arrival of the senior class.

Rain puts an occasional damper on the P-rade, but only once, in 1953, did it force a cancellation. In 2018 the P-rade was suspended because of the risk of lightning, and in 2020 and 2021 in-person reunions had to be canceled because of the coronavirus pandemic, but there were virtual P-rades; a number of Alumni-Faculty Forums took place online; and many classes held virtual meetings and other gatherings.

RHODES AND OTHER SCHOLARSHIPS. For many years following its American inception in 1904, the Rhodes Scholarship was considered the most prestigious recognition a Princeton undergraduate could earn for postgraduate study. Competition was intense (although until 1976 the competition was restricted to men), and many Rhodes Scholars went on to positions of eminence and distinction. In recent decades, and especially in the last decade, the number of competitive academic scholarships and fellowships has grown and Princeton undergraduates and alumni can now apply for over 100 of them, providing a broad range of opportunities. As with the Rhodes, leadership skills as well as academic performance are often critical to the selection process.

The Rhodes remains the most visible program, with each year's list of increasingly diverse winners receiving national press coverage. Between 1904 and 2020, 215 Princeton students and recent alumni (a number exceeded only by Harvard and Yale) were awarded Rhodes Scholarships to pursue postgraduate study at Oxford University. Princetonians from other countries, including Canada, Zimbabwe, and India, have also been awarded Rhodes Scholarships.

In 1953 the British government established the highly coveted Marshall Scholarship program (open to women as well as men from the beginning), and since then 136 Princeton seniors and recent alumni have been named Marshall Scholars, allowing them to obtain graduate degrees at universities throughout the United Kingdom.

Princeton is the all-time national leader in the number of Churchill Scholarships, with 43 recipients since the award was first offered in 1963. Under this program, a small number of top science and engineering students are selected each year to pursue master's degrees at Churchill College, University of Cambridge.

The Gates Cambridge Scholarship, established in 2000, enables students from around the globe to pursue graduate degrees in a wide range of fields at Cambridge. From 2000 to 2020, 57 Princeton seniors and alumni were named Gates Scholars.

Princeton alumni have established and contributed to several postgraduate scholarships for talented Princeton seniors. The Sachs Scholarship, established by his classmates in honor of Daniel Sachs '60, marked its 50th year in 2020. Sachs, a distinguished student and athlete and himself a Rhodes Scholar, died of cancer at age 28. Sachs Scholars receive support for two years of study at Oxford

University, and most have pursued graduate degrees while affiliating with Worcester College. In recent years, the Sachs committee has funded a second annual scholarship that enables a Princeton senior to pursue an independent academic project or a graduate degree in other locations abroad, and a third Sachs Scholarship makes it possible for a Worcester College student each year to pursue graduate study at Princeton.

ReachOut Scholarships, established and administered by alumni from the classes of 1956, 1983, and 2006, fund two or more Princeton seniors each year to undertake innovative community-based projects in the United States and abroad. The family of Henry Labouisse 1926 created a scholarship in his honor that allows several students each year to undertake a project focused on addressing specific challenges in the developing world. The Martin Dale '53 Fellowship provides funding to permit a senior to undertake an independent creative project immediately following graduation.

The Fulbright US Student Program, administered by the US Department of State, has funded large numbers of Princeton undergraduates, alumni, and graduate students to undertake academic research or a creative project, pursue a master's degree, or teach, in one of approximately 140 countries. In 2018–19 Princeton ranked second in Fulbright's annual list of top producing universities, garnering over 30 awards.

Other popular international awards among Princeton undergraduates and alumni include the recently established Schwarzman Scholarship Program that funds a master's degree at the Stephen A. Schwarzman College at Tsinghua University in Beijing, and the Yenching Academy Program at Peking University, also in Beijing.

The Harry S. Truman Scholarship for college juniors planning a public service career; the National Science Foundation's Graduate Research Fellowship for students pursuing PhDs in science, engineering, and other fields; and the Barry S. Goldwater Scholarship for promising science and engineering students in their sophomore or junior years, are among the domestic awards that Princetonians regularly attain.

The Mellon Mays Undergraduate Fellowship Program, established in 1988–89 to address underrepresentation on college and university faculties, provides support and mentorship during the junior and senior years, and support for graduate study, for highly qualified underrepresented students and others who have demonstrated a commitment to diversity and inclusion as they prepare for doctoral programs and careers in the professoriate.

In 2018–19, a total of 197 Princeton students and recent alumni received major fellowships and scholarships.

RITTENHOUSE ORRERY, THE, one of Princeton's oldest instruments for the teaching of science, is on display in the lobby of Peyton Hall. Devised to represent the motions of the planets about the sun, orreries were regarded in the eighteenth century as essential equipment for teaching science, or "natural philosophy," as it was then known. They derived their name from the Earl of Orrery, for whom one of the most famous was named around 1713.

Princeton's Rittenhouse Orrery was the first of two remarkably accurate orreries made by David Rittenhouse, a Pennsylvania clockmaker, self-educated astronomer, and later first director of the US Mint. He made the second one for the College of Philadelphia, now the University of Pennsylvania.

Princeton's orrery was purchased by President John Witherspoon and installed in Nassau Hall in 1771. It was damaged during the American Revolution and later repaired. When travelers passed through Princeton in the late century and stopped to see the sights, at the top of their lists were Nassau Hall and the orrery. It remained in active use for about a half-century, but thereafter it became merely a curiosity and did not come to attention again until it was included as part of Princeton's exhibit at the World's Fair in Chicago in 1893.

After that it disappeared and was thought lost until it was discovered in 1948, still crated, in the basement of McCosh Hall. Through the generosity of Bernard Peyton 1917, it was once again restored and given a place of honor in Firestone Library until Peyton Hall was built in 1966. To this day it remains on display in the Peyton Hall lobby.

In this restoration one concession was made to the twentieth century: electric motors were added to provide smooth motive power, thus eliminating the damage to the intricate wheelwork which in earlier days resulted from hasty and irregular turning of the crank that set the orrery in motion.

RIVERS, ROBERT J., JR., '53 was among the first African American students admitted to Princeton, and in 1969 was the first African American elected by the Board of Trustees to serve as a trustee; four years later he was reelected to serve a second term. In 2016 he was awarded a Princeton honorary degree; in 2019 his portrait was added to the University's portrait collection; and also in 2019 the roadway onto campus from Nassau Street just west of Firestone Library was named Rivers Way in his honor.

Rivers and his family have had deep ties to the town of Princeton and the University. His grandfather planted the first elms along Washington Road; his father worked for 43 years as a servant at the eating club Tiger Inn and as a dormitory janitor; his mother was a live-in maid for engineering professor Lewis Moody; and his aunts and an uncle began working at the original McCosh Infirmary in 1918.

As a child, Rivers attended the segregated Witherspoon Elementary School in Princeton and then the integrated Princeton High School. In 1946, he was one of eight African American boys from the Witherspoon YMCA in Princeton invited to attend the Princeton Summer Camp at Blairstown, whose new director, Frank Broderick '43, had served as chair of the *Daily Princetonian*, and in 1942 had editorialized in favor of admitting Black students to the University. (Following publication of the editorials, the Undergraduate Council voted against admitting Black students; letters to the *Princetonian* opposed African American students on campus by a margin of three to one.)

Between 1946 and 1949, three African American students who had come to Princeton with the Navy's V-12 program graduated from Princeton, and three Black applicants were admitted, including Joseph Ralph Moss '51, who had graduated from Princeton High School.

Rivers decided to apply and was admitted. While a student and for a few summers afterward, he volunteered at the Princeton Summer Camp. The chef at the camp, George Reeves, was a highly respected member of the Princeton community. His son-in-law, James Floyd, Sr., later became the first Black mayor of Princeton Township, and his grandson, James Floyd '69, was among the still-small number of African American students to have received Princeton degrees by the late 1960s.

After graduation, Rivers attended Harvard Medical School and trained in surgery at the University of Rochester. He then launched a distinguished career as a vascular surgeon and educator, including service as associate dean for minority affairs at the University of Rochester School of Medicine and Dentistry. When he retired, he returned to Princeton and moved back into the same house in which he had grown up.

The family's connections to the University expanded over the years as three of Rivers' sons graduated from Princeton, and his brother coached several Princeton baseball and football teams.

In 2008, Rivers spoke to African American seniors and their families at a Pan-African pre-graduation ceremony in Richardson Auditorium. In closing his remarks he cited former president Robert Goheen, former dean Carl Fields, and Frank Broderick, saying, "On the day I was born, no African American or woman had ever received a baccalaureate degree from Princeton University, and we were not included in thoughts about 'Princeton in the nation's service.' The courage and human understanding of these three giants affected my life—and your lives. And the quality of a Princeton education has been enriched for all students."

At the dedication ceremony for Rivers Way in October 2019, trustee vice-chair Brent Henry '69, who was elected one of the first young alumni trustees and initially joined the board along with Rivers in 1969, described Rivers "as a true Princeton trailblazer" who "helped prepare a path for thousands of African American men and women to follow in your footsteps at this University."

The plaque marking Rivers Way says the following:

> Rivers Way is named in honor of Robert J. Rivers, Jr. '53, a Princeton native with deep family ties to the town and the University, who was one of Princeton's first black undergraduates and the first African American elected by the Board to serve as a Princeton trustee. His 2016 Princeton honorary degree called him a "true Princeton pioneer" and a "role model" who "paved the way toward a University increasingly committed to diversity and inclusion . . . with dignity, grace, integrity, and a lifelong devotion to this University's highest values."

ROOT, ROBERT KILBURN, Chaucer scholar and fourth dean of the faculty, first came to Princeton in the spring of 1905. President Woodrow Wilson had written him about the University's plan to institute a preceptorial system and asked him to come down from New Haven for an interview.

Root later recalled that he had misgivings "as to this newfangled method of teaching and more personally as to whether a Yale man could be happy in Princeton," but as Wilson spoke "with winning eloquence" about his plans for Princeton, he knew "before the talk was over my loyalties were entirely committed to him."

This loyalty and devotion, Root said, were shared by the other teacher-scholars who made up the original group of preceptors; they felt "they were embarked upon a great educational adventure under the immediate guidance of a great and wise innovator."

Root proved to be an adept preceptor and a popular lecturer. He wrote books on Chaucer, Shakespeare, and Pope. His most important work was a definitive edition of Chaucer's *Troilus and Criseyde* (1928). In his study of the poem, Root performed a notable piece of literary detective work. Scholars had long puzzled over the date of the writing of *Troilus*, which they placed sometime between 1373 and 1386. Root thought he had found a clue in the lines of the poem beginning "The bent moone with hire hornes pale, / Saturne and Jove, in Cancro joyned were." He wondered if the astronomical phenomenon thus described—the conjunction of Saturn, Jupiter, and the crescent moon (her horns pale from the lingering twilight) in the sign of Cancer—was possible.

He consulted his colleague, Henry Norris Russell 1897 *1900, the astrophysicist, who said that the conjunction of the three heavenly bodies within a single segment of the heavens was possible, but extremely infrequent. After complicated calculations, Russell informed Root that the configuration described by Chaucer had in fact occurred in May or early June of 1385, for the first time in 600 years.

In the poem the unusual heavenly configuration was followed by a violent thunderstorm, which prevented Criseyde from leaving her uncle's home after having supper with him and thus resulted in her first encounter with Troilus. Root wondered if he could find evidence of such a storm. By consulting the chronicles of the medieval historian Thomas Walsingham, he discovered that a powerful thunderstorm had in fact flooded England in July 1385.

From these findings Root and Russell concluded, in a joint paper in the *Publications of the Modern Language Association of America* (1924), that *Troilus and Criseyde* was not finished earlier than the spring or summer of 1385, thus establishing that it was a product of Chaucer's mature years, written shortly before he began the *Canterbury Tales*.

Root became dean of the faculty when Harold Dodds *14 assumed the presidency in 1933. As dean he achieved economies that permitted the University to avoid salary cuts during the depression of the 1930s, and during World War II he adjusted the curriculum to accommodate the shifts and strains brought on by the war. At the end of the war, he played a leading role in developing the University's program for returning veterans.

ROPER LANE, which extends between Cap and Gown Club and Cottage Club from Prospect Avenue to the main entrance of Princeton Stadium, is named for William W. Roper 1902, varsity football coach during the years 1906–1908, 1910–1911, and 1919–1930.

Roper's style was eclectic and opportunistic; among other things, he borrowed plays from teams that did well against Princeton. For example, in 1919 West Virginia overwhelmed Princeton with its spread formation, 25–0. On the next two weekends, Princeton employed the same formation to good advantage, tying Harvard 10–10 and beating Yale 13–6.

For many years Roper was the principal speaker at the annual meeting to acquaint freshmen with the history and principles of the honor system. "No one," Dean Christian Gauss said, "ever had a more withering scorn for the dishonest, the hypocritical, and the unsportsmanlike. No one ever had a higher faith in the human spirit and in its possibilities."

In addition to Roper Lane, Roper is remembered by a trophy, established in 1939 by his widow and the Class of 1902, which is considered the highest award that can be conferred on a male student-athlete at Princeton; it is presented annually to a male senior of "high scholastic rank and outstanding qualities of sportsmanship and general proficiency in athletics." The comparable annual recognition for Princeton's top female student-athlete is the C. Otto Von Kienbusch Award, named for a member of the Class of 1906 who was an early supporter and benefactor of women's athletics at Princeton.

ROWING. Princeton's Lake Carnegie is home to a rowing tradition that has produced national championship crews in all four varsity programs—men's heavyweight, men's lightweight, women's open, and women's lightweight—as well as more Olympians than any other sport at the University.

Men's Heavyweight Crew

Rowing is the oldest of the American intercollegiate sports, beginning with Harvard and Yale's boat races in the 1850s. Princeton was a relative latecomer, in part because of its lack of a natural venue for training. In 1870 a group of undergraduates formed the first crew and bought two old six-oared gigs from

Yale. One immediately sank to the bottom of the Delaware and Raritan Canal; the other proved serviceable enough to keep the team afloat for a few years. In 1872, Princeton raced at the National Amateur Regatta in Philadelphia, finishing last in its race. After a decade and a half of middling results, varsity crew was suspended from 1885 to 1910.

The team's fortunes rebounded, thanks to serendipity; artist Howard Russell Butler 1876, a member of one of the early crews, was commissioned to paint a portrait of philanthropist Andrew Carnegie, and during sittings for the portrait, Carnegie talked about lochs he had built in Scotland. Butler raised the idea of building a lake in Princeton, alongside the canal, by creating a dam at the confluence of the Millstone River and Stony Brook—an idea Butler and his friends had talked about as undergraduates. Carnegie warmed to the proposal and funded the lake, which was completed in 1906. Interclass racing began the following spring. (Shortly afterward, the Class of 1877 gave funds for a boathouse, which in 1972 was refurbished to include an enclosed rowing tank for year-round training, and in 2000 was expanded and renamed the Shea Rowing Center.)

Princeton rejoined the varsity ranks in 1911 with J. Duncan Spaeth, an English instructor who had rowed at Penn, serving as the coach. The Tigers earned their first major victory in 1913, beating Harvard and Penn at Cambridge. In 1921, the varsity was 6-1, with its only loss coming to Columbia in the Childs Cup. Under coach Gordon Sikes, Princeton had a string of successful crews in the 1930s as well. Other notable coaches included Delos "Dutch" Schoch (1946-65) and Peter Sparhawk (1966-80).

It would take several decades for Princeton to reach the head of the pack at the Intercollegiate Rowing Association (IRA) championships, but once it did, the heavyweight men became perennial contenders. The Tigers earned their first IRA gold in 1985, stroked by Harold Backer '85 and coached by Larry Gluckman. In 1996, under coach Curtis Jordan, Princeton swept the IRA varsity, second varsity, and third varsity eights. The 1997 team finished with a perfect 9-0 regular-season record, and in 1998 the Tigers won IRA gold again. Jordan's heavyweights won medals at the Eastern Sprints in eight straight years, from 1995 through 2002; the coach's final Eastern gold came in 2006. Jordan was succeeded in 2010 by Greg Hughes '96, who won two national championships as an undergraduate rower for the men's lightweight crew.

Men's Lightweight Crew

Varsity lightweight crew was introduced at Princeton in 1920 and added to the Eastern Sprints championships in 1938. The Tigers won their first Eastern title in 1942, right before competition was suspended for World War II, and they picked up where they left off after the war, winning another championship in 1948. Since then, the men's lightweights have won 14 Eastern titles—three in the 1950s, one in the 1970s, four in the 1980s, three in the 1990s, and three since 2000—under coaches Arthur Sueltz (1952-53), Donald Rose (1956-57), Gary Kilpatrick (1973-1988), Joe Murtaugh (1989-2005), Greg Hughes '96 (2005-09), and Marty Crotty '98 (2010-present).

A national championship for men's lightweight crew was a late addition, in part because relatively few schools supported a varsity lightweight team. Kirkpatrick led Princeton to the sport's first national title in 1986 and repeated the feat in 1988. Murtaugh, Kilpatrick's successor, won four national championships (1989, 1994, 1996, and 1998), and two of his rowers returned to coach the Tigers to IRA gold as well—Hughes in 2009 and Crotty in 2010.

Women's Open Crew

When women's rowing started in the spring of 1972, the team did not receive a warm welcome. Merrily Dean Baker, then an associate director of athletics, recalled the situation in her keynote address at a 1999 Ivy League celebration of women in sports: "I remember starting the program without [the men's coach's] help, buying used equipment from a nearby prep school, hiring a coach, and going out in the launch with him at six o'clock in the morning, which was the only time the women were allowed to row on the lake."

Captained by Amy Richlin '73, Princeton won the Women's Eastern Intercollegiate Regatta in 1972, shaving nine seconds off the national record for a 1,000-meter race, and placed third in the National Regatta in 1973. After the crew's early success, the women's practice time was bumped up to 1 p.m., Baker said. Access to locker rooms would come later.

Carol Brown '75, a standout on Princeton's early crews, recalled leaving practice and heading straight to the dining hall, since the boathouse had no facilities for women. "We'd come up from the boathouse wet and dripping cold and sweaty in our sweats and sit in a corner," Brown told the *Alumni Weekly* in 2015. "People knew, 'That's the rowers.'" Brown later rowed for the US national team and became the first Princeton woman to win an Olympic medal in 1976 when she earned bronze in the women's eight.

The women's open crew won its first Eastern Sprints championship in 1982 and won the title again in 1985 and 1990 under coach Curtis Jordan. Jordan's successor, Dan Roock, led the team to three straight Eastern titles (1993–95).

When the NCAA championships for women's rowing began in 1997, first-year coach Lori Dauphiny led her team to a victory in the second-varsity eight. Princeton qualified for the NCAA regatta in every year since, and Dauphiny has become the program's most successful coach. A two-time national Coach of the Year, in 2019 Dauphiny was named to the Collegiate Rowing Coaches Association Hall of Fame.

Two of Dauphiny's crews have won the NCAA varsity eight, capping undefeated seasons both times. The 2006 Tigers were stroked by future two-time Olympic gold medalist Caroline Lind '06 and included three other future Olympians: Kate Bertko '06, Andreanne Morin '06, and Gevvie Stone '06. They won the NCAA grand final by more than six seconds. In 2011, the NCAA-champion boat was stroked by another future Olympian, Canadian silver medalist Lauren Wilkinson '11.

Since 2012, the Ivy League has hosted a championship for women's open rowing. Princeton won the varsity eight title four times in its first seven years.

Women's Lightweight Crew

Women's lightweight crew is the newest addition to Princeton's boathouse. A varsity sport since 1998, the crew won the Eastern Sprints in its first season and placed third in the first women's lightweight IRA national championships that spring.

Heather Smith, the Tigers' first coach, led the crew to five consecutive national championships from 1999 to 2003, and four Eastern Sprints titles in that span. In 2004, Smith was succeeded by Paul Rassam, whose crews have finished in the top three at the IRA regatta six times and won the Eastern Sprints in 2011.

Rowing Olympians

Princeton rowing alumni have qualified for every Summer Olympics since 1964. (Rowers on the 1980 US team did not compete due to the American boycott of the Moscow Olympics.) The following Princeton rowers have won Olympic medals: Seymour Cromwell II '56 (silver, US men's double sculls, 1964); Peter Raymond '68 (silver, US men's eight, 1972); Carol Brown '75 (bronze, US women's eight, 1976); Mike Evans '80 (gold, Canada men's eight, 1984); Anne Marden '81 (silver, US women's four, 1984; silver, US women's single sculls, 1988); Christopher Penny '85 (silver, US men's eight, 1984); W. Douglas Burden '88 (bronze, US men's eight, 1988; silver, US men's four, 1992); Christian Ahrens '98 (gold, US men's eight, 2004); Tom Herschmiller '01 (silver, US men's four, 2004); Lianne Bennion Nelson '95 (silver, US women's eight, 2004); Steve Coppola '06 (bronze, US men's eight, 2008); Caroline Lind '06 (gold, US women's eight, 2008 and 2012); Andreanne Morin '06 (silver, Canada women's eight, 2012); Glenn Ochal '08 (bronze, US men's four, 2012); Lauren Wilkinson '11 (silver, Canada women's eight, 2012); Gevvie Stone '07 (silver, US women's single sculls, 2016) Tom George '18 (bronze, Great Britain men's eight, 2021); and Fred Vystavel '16 (bronze, Denmark men's pair, 2021).

RUDENSTINE, NEIL L. '56. Modern Princeton has, of course, been shaped by its presidents, but also by a number of deans, and later provosts, who had lasting impact on the nature of the University and helped steer it through challenging times. Neil Rudenstine, who served Princeton as dean of students, dean of the college, provost, and trustee, is one of them.

Andrew Fleming West 1874, the founding dean of the graduate school who continued in that role for 27 years, played a central role in defining the nature of graduate education at Princeton. He staked out a position in opposition to his president, Woodrow Wilson 1879, on the question of where to locate the graduate school and prevailed with the support of influential trustees.

Most, however, exercised their influence in concert with the presidents they served. In the early twentieth century, transformative deans included Luther Eisenhart, progenitor of the four-course plan that gave rise to Princeton's distinctive required senior thesis, who served as both dean of the faculty and dean of the graduate school, and Henry Fine 1880, who made Princeton a world leader in mathematics and the sciences and served both as dean of the faculty and dean of the departments of science.

In the mid-twentieth century, J. Douglas Brown 1919 *1928, Princeton's longest-serving dean of the faculty and its first provost, helped transform Princeton into a major international research university while retaining its distinctive commitment to undergraduate education. William Bowen *58 and Christopher Eisgruber '83 played central roles in the presidencies of Robert Goheen '40 *48 and Shirley Tilghman before themselves succeeding to the Princeton presidency.

Rudenstine was an administrator of principled and compassionate decision-making, and gentle but persistent persuasion. His father, a prison guard, emigrated to the United States from Ukraine and his mother was the daughter of immigrants from Italy. At Princeton he majored in the Special Program in the Humanities and wrote his thesis for the English department on the poetry of John Keats, Matthew Arnold, and T. S. Eliot. He also participated in Army ROTC.

After graduation he spent three years at Oxford as a Rhodes Scholar and six months fulfilling his ROTC obligations as an artillery lieutenant at Ford Sill, Oklahoma, before earning his PhD in English literature at Harvard with a specialty in Renaissance literature. He then taught at Harvard before being persuaded by Goheen to return to Princeton in 1968 as dean of students and associate professor of English.

Years later, Rudenstine told the *Harvard Gazette* that while he was reluctant to interrupt his scholarly work, "I started thinking about the whole issue of working one's way through this very difficult period of universities in turbulence. And while I didn't have much experience in that area, I did care deeply about universities. I didn't want to see them broken up and traumatized and destroyed."

Rudenstine served as dean of students during four tumultuous years that included frequent, widespread, and occasionally highly confrontational anti-war protests (Rudenstine was punched by a frustrated employee of the Institute for Defense Analyses during a protest over the classified research it conducted for the government in rented campus space); unrest related to issues of race, including an occupation of New South by Black students protesting University ties to apartheid in South Africa and an occupation of Firestone Library by students advocating greater support for students of color and creation of a third world center; and challenges to free speech, including interruptions of a speech by Interior Secretary Walter Hickel that led to disciplinary action in the first test of the new judicial committee of the Council of the Princeton University Community. Rudenstine played a central role in all these issues, in discussions about the place of ROTC on the campus, and in the University's initial adjustment to undergraduate coeducation, which began in the fall of 1969.

When Bowen became president in 1972, he appointed Rudenstine to the position of dean of the college, and then in 1977 to the position of provost. Much as Bowen and Goheen had led the University in tandem during Bowen's years in the provost's office, so did Rudenstine and Bowen for the last 11 years of the Bowen presidency. Bowen said he particularly valued Rudenstine's ability to work with people (he was renowned for his personalized hand-written notes) and his talent for "seeing the potential complications of anything we did or didn't do. He saw around corners that I didn't even know were corners."

In 1980, while Bowen was on leave, Rudenstine gave the address at Princeton's Opening Exercises, where he told the entering students, "Education . . . comes from those moments when we are drawn by something and feel compelled to understand as much as we possibly can about it—whether it is some part of nature, or a work of art, or a mathematical problem, or an historical event, which we simply cannot leave alone until we have done all we can to explain or master it, and in some sense take advantage of it."

When Bowen left office and became president of the Andrew W. Mellon Foundation, Rudenstine joined him as the foundation's executive vice president where he oversaw the awarding of grants in the arts and humanities. In 1991 he was named Harvard's president, a position he held for 10 years. That same year he was awarded a Princeton honorary degree, and in 1997 he received the Woodrow Wilson Award, the University's highest distinction for undergraduate alumni.

While serving as Harvard's president he spoke at Princeton's 250th anniversary celebration in 1996, describing Princeton as "the quintessence of institutions devoted to the liberal arts and sciences, as a place where undergraduates and graduate students are equally cherished, and where an unwavering clarity of purpose and an unrivaled spirit of unity have inspired generation upon generation of students and colleagues and graduates and friends."

After leaving the Harvard presidency, Rudenstine became chair of the advisory board for Artstor, a nonprofit organization that develops, maintains, and distributes digital images and related materials for the study of art, architecture, and other fields in the humanities. In 2002 he was elected to a four-year term on the Princeton Board of Trustees. He chaired the grounds and buildings committee, and after leaving the board served on the steering committee for the development of a campus plan that looked ahead 10 years to 2016. He also taught freshman seminars at Princeton. In 2011 he was named chair of the New York Public Library's board of trustees.

Rudenstine and his wife, Angelica, are commemorated at Harvard by the Neil L. and Angelica Zander Rudenstine Gallery at the W.E.B. Du Bois Institute for African and African American Research, the only exhibition space at Harvard devoted to works by and about people of African descent.

RUGBY. One of Princeton's longest-running club sport programs, rugby has a winning tradition that dates back to the 1930s for the men's team and the late 1970s for the women, who won back-to-back national titles in 1995 and 1996.

Men's Rugby

British graduate students Montefiore Barak *31 and Harold Cooper *31 taught the game to Princeton's first rugby players, and politics professor John Whitton served as the coach when the team first took the field in 1931. Early players included Harry Langenberg '31, who later fostered the sport in his native St. Louis, and Ed Lee '34, captain of a championship team in his senior year who became an ambassador for American rugby over more than five decades. Both were posthumously enshrined in the US Rugby Hall of Fame.

Suspended during World War II, the rugby team reorganized in the spring of 1946 and won its first postwar championship in 1948, capturing the Bermuda Cup by defeating Harvard and Yale. When the Ivy Rugby Conference created its tournament in 1969, Princeton won the inaugural championship, led by captain Terry Larrimer '69. Princeton won three more Ivy titles in 1971, 1973, and 1979.

One the team's most accomplished alumni, Rob Bordley '70, played only briefly in college after starring on Princeton's football and lacrosse teams. Bordley captained the US Eagles in 1976 and was elected to the US Rugby Hall of Fame in 2013.

Ivy tournament success eluded the men's team in the 1980s and 1990s. From 1998 through 2001, Princeton had a run of four consecutive runner-up finishes. The team finally ended a 25-year Ivy title drought in 2004, edging defending-champion Harvard in the Ivy semifinals and dominating Cornell in the final.

Since 2007, the men's team has hosted the Rickerson Cup, a state championship tournament for New Jersey's collegiate squads. In 2013, Princeton opened a rugby-specific field house, Haaga House, on its West Windsor/Lake Campus fields, where the men's and women's teams train and compete.

Women's Rugby

The first Princeton women's rugby team was organized in 1979 by Cathy Chute '81, Cathy Mueller '81, and Caroline Harcourt '82. With relatively few teams nearby, early schedules included a mix of collegiate and club teams. Princeton upset top-ranked Dartmouth to win its first Ivy tournament title in 1989.

In 1991, women's collegiate rugby held its inaugural national championship tournament, and within a few years Princeton emerged as a perennial contender. Led by Kim Henderson '95's three tries, the Princeton women defeated Penn State 20-0 to win the 1995 national championship. Alex Curtis *95, a graduate student, coached the team until receiving his PhD in art history. The team then turned to captains Ashley Kline '96 and Erin Kennedy '96 to serve as player-coaches and continued its dominance. Princeton won all but one game in its fall and spring seasons in 1995-96 and repeated as national champion with another title-game win over Penn State. Six Princeton players were named All-Americans.

Princeton reached the national semifinals six more times between 1997 and 2005, including runner-up finishes in 1999, 2000, and 2004. More recently, the women's team has excelled in sevens rugby (7-on-7, the version played in the Olympics), reaching the USA Rugby College Sevens Championships several times and finishing third in the Division I tournament in 2019. Princeton women's coach Emil Signes, who also coached the US men's and women's national sevens teams, was inducted into the US Rugby Hall of Fame in 2015.

In 2021, the University announced that women's rugby would become a varsity sport in 2022-23.

RUSH, BENJAMIN 1760 was a physician and teacher who played a dramatic role in the early history of the country and his college. More than any other person he was responsible for bringing John Witherspoon to Princeton as its sixth president.

Rush lost his father when he was six. He was brought up by his mother, Susanna Hall, who kept a grocery shop in Philadelphia to help support and educate her seven children. When he was eight, he entered an academy conducted by his uncle, Samuel Finley (later president of Princeton), at Nottingham, Maryland, where he made such progress that on entering Princeton five years later he was admitted to the junior class; he graduated in 1760 when he was not quite 15.

President Samuel Davies thought he should take up the law, but his uncle persuaded him to study medicine. He served an apprenticeship for almost six years and attended the first lectures in the newly formed medical department of the College of Philadelphia (later the University of Pennsylvania). In the summer of 1766, when he was 20, he sat up every night for several weeks with Finley, then president of Princeton, during his last illness. That fall he went to Edinburgh, Scotland, then the medical center of the world, where after two years of study he received his MD degree.

While in Scotland, in cooperation with trustee Richard Stockton 1748, Rush invited John Witherspoon to come to Princeton as the College's president. Stockton's authority and dignity were indispensable to the mission, but it was Rush's confident, audacious, and engaging youth that won the day. When Witherspoon felt obliged to decline because of his wife's fear of leaving home (the very mention of going to America made her physically ill), Rush persisted. On Witherspoon's invitation, he spent several days with the Witherspoons at their home in Paisley. Shortly afterward a friend of Witherspoon wrote to Stockton in Princeton that "to Mr. Witherspoon's great satisfaction, his wife has at last given a calm hearing to Mr. Rush, argued the Matter with him, and received a satisfying Answer to all her objections; so that now she is willing if the Doctor is rechosen . . . to go with him without Grudge." Witherspoon was reelected, and he and his wife came to America in August 1768.

Rush spent the following year in London and Paris. Soon after his return home, he was appointed to a chair of chemistry in the College of Philadelphia's medical department, thus becoming at the age of 23 the first professor of chemistry in America.

He built up a large private practice, but he also found time to further other interests. He published a pamphlet on the iniquity of the slave trade and helped organize the first antislavery society in America, the Pennsylvania Society for Promoting the Abolition of Slavery and the Relief of Free Negroes Unlawfully Held in Bondage, and later became its president. (Despite his views on slavery, Rush owned a slave, and came to believe that dark skin color was caused by a disease that could be cured.) In the growing quarrel between the colonies and the mother country, Rush associated with such leaders as Thomas Paine. It was on his urging that Paine wrote a pamphlet arguing passionately and eloquently for American independence, which he titled *Common Sense*—as suggested by Rush.

In the summer of 1775, Rush met Richard Stockton's 16-year-old daughter, Julia. The following January, a few days after his 30th birthday, he and Julia were married. Less than seven months later, having been elected a delegate to the Continental Congress from Pennsylvania, he joined his father-in-law and President Witherspoon, both delegates from New Jersey, in signing the Declaration of Independence.

Rush served the army as a doctor (and for a time as the army's surgeon general) during the early months of the Revolutionary War (he was present at the Battle of Princeton), but in 1778 he returned to Philadelphia and resumed his medical practice, teaching, and humanitarian endeavors. He became the most admired teacher of medicine in Philadelphia; all told, he taught more than 3,000 medical students, who carried his influence to every corner of the growing nation.

Rush founded the Philadelphia Dispensary for the relief of the poor, the first of its kind in the United States, and for many years gave it hours of service without pay. He also founded Dickinson College, was one of the charter trustees of Franklin College (later Franklin and Marshall), and, being persuaded of the importance of removing "the present disparity which subsists between the sexes in the degrees of their education and knowledge," became an ardent incorporator of the Young Ladies Academy in Philadelphia.

His greatest contributions to medical science were the reforms he instituted in the care of the mentally ill during his 30 years of service as a senior physician at the Pennsylvania Hospital. The year before he died, he published *Medical Inquiries and Observations upon the Diseases of the Mind*, the first textbook on psychiatry in America.

In 1837 some of Rush's former students founded a medical college in Chicago, which they named for him. The American Psychiatric Association, whose official seal bears Rush's portrait, placed a bronze plaque at his grave in Philadelphia in 1965, designating him the "Father of American Psychiatry."

On the Princeton campus, his portrait hangs in Nassau Hall; he and James Madison 1771 are the only two Princeton alumni so honored who did not serve as Princeton's president.

RUSSELL, HENRY NORRIS 1897 *1900, for many years the leading theoretical astronomer in America, graduated from Princeton at the age of 19 *insigni cum laude* (with extraordinary honor), a designation never used before or since.

Russell's father was a Presbyterian minister; his mother, Eliza Hoxie Norris, and his maternal grandmother had both won prizes in mathematics. His favorite study in college was mathematics; his interest in astronomy was stimulated by Professor Charles Young, with whom he continued to study after graduation, earning his PhD *summa cum laude* in 1900. Following postdoctoral study at Cambridge University, he was appointed instructor in astronomy at Princeton in 1905; he became a full professor in 1911; and director of Princeton's Halstead Observatory in 1912.

Russell was a pioneer in the use of atomic physics for the analysis of the stars and thus played a principal role in laying the foundations of present-day astrophysics. His name is perpetuated by the Hertzsprung-Russell color magnitude diagram (stellar evolution), Russell-Saunders coupling (atomic spectroscopy), and the Henry Norris Russell Lectureship of the American Astronomical Society, endowed at his retirement by gifts from fellow astronomers and Princeton classmates, which is awarded each year in recognition of a lifetime of excellence in astronomical research. The first such lecture was given by Russell himself in 1946.

Russell's position as America's leading astronomer was recognized by his presidency of the American Astronomical Society, the American Association for the Advancement of Science, and the American Philosophical Society. He was awarded the gold medal of the Royal Astronomical Society of England, two medals of the French Academy, five other medals of American scientific societies, and numerous honorary degrees. Mexico conferred on him its Order of the Aztec Eagle and issued a postage stamp in his honor—printed in orange and black.

Russell attracted to Princeton an outstanding group of graduate students who went on to occupy positions of leadership in observatories throughout the country. Notable among his students was Lyman Spitzer Jr. *38, who succeeded Russell as director of Princeton's observatory in 1947 and delivered the Russell Lecture in 1953.

Among Russell's 241 published papers were articles written jointly with Princeton colleagues in both astronomy and physics, and a joint paper with Robert Root, professor of English, on "A Planetary Date for Chaucer's *Troilus;*" they also included a paper "On the Navigation of Airplanes," for which Russell made observations in airplanes flying at 105 miles per hour, at heights up to 16,000 feet, as a consultant to the federal government in World War I. To reach a more general audience, between 1900 and 1943 he wrote a total of 500 monthly columns in *Scientific American* discussing all aspects of astronomy.

SALUTATORY ORATION. The salutatory oration, which dates back to the first Commencement in 1748, is Princeton's oldest student honor. Originally the salutatory, rather than the valedictory, which came later, was delivered by the highest-ranking member of the senior class. In recent years, the faculty has chosen both speakers for their special qualifications as well as for their high scholastic standing.

The first salutatorian, Daniel Thane 1748, delivered his address "in a modest and decent manner," according to an account in *Parker's Gazette and Post Boy* of New York. As was customary, he apologized "for his Insufficiency," and then enumerated "the Numberless Benefits the liberal Arts and Sciences yield to Mankind in private and social life," and addressed "becoming Salutations to his Excellency [the governor] and the Trustees, the President and whole Assembly." All of this was "performed in good Latin from his Memory in a handsome oratorical Manner in the Space of about half an Hour." Thane later employed his oratorical talents as a preacher.

Two salutatorians became Princeton presidents: Samuel Stanhope Smith 1769 and Robert Goheen '40 *48. Others became professors in the University: Allan Marquand 1874 (Art and Archaeology), Samuel Winans 1874 (Classics), William Berryman Scott 1877 (Paleontology), Henry Burchard Fine 1880 (Mathematics), Henry Norris Russell 1897 (Astrophysics), Edward Cone '39 (Music), D. Graham Burnett '93 (History), and Dan-el Padilla Peralta '06 (Classics).

When Marquand and Winans tied for first place in 1874, Marquand gave a salutatory in Latin, Winans in Greek.

When two brothers, David B. Jones 1876 and Thomas D. Jones 1876, tied for first place, they gave the salutatories in Latin and English, respectively. Two other brothers were salutatorians in the 1930s:

Lewis Van Dusen Jr. '32, later a lawyer in Philadelphia, and Francis Van Dusen '34, later a federal appeals court judge in the same city.

Over time the salutatory oration came to provide a kind of comic relief at Commencement. It is delivered in Latin to a largely uncomprehending audience, with parents and family members initially astounded by how many seniors know when to cheer, groan, laugh, and applaud. The seniors are cued by footnotes in programs made available only to them, and eventually the rest of the audience catches on, but for a few moments at least there is widespread amazement that so many members of the class seem to know Latin.

The first woman salutatorian, Lisa Siegman '75, introduced a variation on the usual footnotes, calling for shouts from the boys ("Pueri, hic vociferate") when she observed that for 229 years the greeting of commencement audiences in Latin had been the duty of a male student ("discipuli"), and calling for shouts from the girls ("Puellae, hic vociferate") when she added with spirit that at last it was the duty of a female student ("discipulae").

In 1999, salutatorian Thomas Wickham Schmidt stunned his audience by including a marriage proposal—in English—in the closing lines of his address. His intended, Anastacia Rohrman '99, was favorably inclined, and when Schmidt's classmate Timothy Webster offered her a sign reading "YES" in big block letters, she held it aloft, eliciting a roaring cheer from the crowd and headlines in the next day's newspapers.

Salutatorians since 1970 are listed on page 524.

SAYRE, DANIEL CLEMENS, first chair of the then-department of Aeronautical Engineering and first director of the James Forrestal Research Center, was born in Columbus, Ohio, the same year that two other Ohioans, Orville and Wilbur Wright, made the first controlled and sustained flights in a power-driven airplane. Sixteen years later Sayre began the study of civil engineering at Massachusetts Institute of Technology, but after taking a year off to earn money working on dams in Ohio and Alabama, he changed his course to aeronautical engineering, earning his BS in 1924 and his MS in 1929.

While still a student he earned his pilot's license and then organized the Boston Airport Corporation, which played a leading role in establishing this country's first commercial airline run, between New York and Boston. He served as instructor and assistant professor at MIT from 1927 to 1933. During the last two years, he conducted an extensive investigation of American air masses. The data he and his associates gathered during almost daily flights, at altitudes from 16,000 to 18,000 feet in an instrument-laden plane, proved of great value in the development of commercial and military aviation.

Sayre served on the editorial staff of the magazine *Aviation*, then as aviation editor of *Newsweek*, director of statistics and information for the Civil Aeronautics Authority, and chief of the Safety Division of the Civil Aeronautics Board. In 1941 he was called to Princeton, where he organized an Aeronautical Engineering department. He recruited some of the ablest aeronautical scientists in the country and secured the necessary support for their work from outside sources as well as from the University. As a result, the department rose in a very few years to a position of national leadership, as evidenced in 1948 when the Guggenheim Foundation selected Princeton and the California Institute of Technology as the places for the two Guggenheim Jet Propulsion Centers.

In 1951, when Princeton was given the opportunity to acquire new laboratory facilities for the natural and engineering sciences from the Rockefeller Institute for Medical Research on land just a few miles from the campus, Sayre played a leading role in the establishment of the James Forrestal Research Center, later renamed the Forrestal Campus. Shortly after he died at the age of 53, one of the original buildings on the Forrestal Campus, now home of the Atmospheric and Oceanic Sciences program, was named Sayre Hall in his honor.

SCHEIDE, WILLIAM H. '36 was a musician, musicologist, bibliophile, and philanthropist who made many transformative gifts to Princeton, including the Scheide library, an extraordinary collection of some 2,500 rare books and manuscripts valued in the range of $300 million, making it the largest gift in the University's history.

The library was given to the University in 2015 following Scheide's death at the age of 100. It had been housed at Firestone Library since 1959, when Scheide moved the collection there from his boyhood hometown of Titusville, Pennsylvania. It holds the first six printed editions of the Bible, starting with the 1455 Gutenberg Bible; the original printing of the Declaration of Independence; Beethoven's autograph (in his own handwriting) music sketchbook for 1815–16, the only one outside Europe; Shakespeare's first, second, third, and fourth folios; significant autograph music manuscripts of Bach, Mozart, Beethoven, Schubert, and Wagner; a lengthy 1856 autograph speech by Abraham Lincoln on slavery; and General Ulysses S. Grant's original letter and telegram copy books from the last weeks of the Civil War.

History professor Anthony Grafton, a specialist in the cultural history of Renaissance Europe, called the library "the richest collection anywhere of the first documents printed in fifteenth-century Europe. But its magnificent books and manuscripts illuminate many areas, from the printing of the Bible to the ways in which the greatest composers created their music."

The library also contains important documents on American history, including early travel accounts of voyages to the New World; the rare 1754 "Journal" of Major George Washington; and the earliest newsletter report of the Battle of Lexington from April 1775.

In addition to the library, Scheide's gifts to Princeton included an endowed scholarship fund, the Scheide Scholars program; an endowed professorship in music history; primary funding for the 1997 reconstruction and expansion of the Woolworth Center of Musical Studies, including the Arthur Mendel music library; funding for the construction of the Scheide Caldwell House to provide offices and classrooms for several initiatives and programs associated with the Andlinger Center for the Humanities; donations to Firestone's department of rare books and special collections; and support for the Princeton University Art Museum.

Scheide was born in 1914, the only son of John H. Scheide 1896 and Harriet Hurd. His grandfather made a fortune in oil in the late nineteenth century and retired at age 42. In 1865, when he was 18 years old, he bought *The Chemical History of a Candle*, which launched the collection that grew into the Scheide library. Scheide's grandfather, and then his father, expanded the collection, and in 1954 William Scheide started acquiring books and manuscripts for the library when he was living in Princeton.

Scheide started playing piano at age 6 and later learned the organ and oboe. He became an avid musician, but since there was no music department at Princeton when he attended, he majored instead in history. He earned a master's degree in music at Columbia University in 1940 and then taught musicology at Cornell University. As a renowned Bach scholar, in 1946 he founded the Bach Aria Group, an ensemble that performed and recorded under his direction for 34 years.

In the early 1950s, he was a leading funder of the lawsuit brought by the National Association for the Advancement of Colored People's Legal Defense Fund (LDF) that resulted in the Supreme Court's landmark *Brown v. Board of Education* decision in 1954 that desegregated public schools. He served on the LDF board for 38 years.

The University awarded Scheide an honorary degree in 1994, recognizing him as an "advocate, scholar, student, benefactor, and friend."

SEAL OF PRINCETON UNIVERSITY, THE, which is in the custody of the secretary of the University, is the corporate signature of the trustees. It is embossed on diplomas and printed on certain other official documents, and is affixed by the secretary to legal instruments requiring its use.

The seal of the College of New Jersey was used for almost a century and a half. In the upper part of a circle was an open Bible with Latin characters VET NOV TESTAMENTUM signifying the Old and New Testaments. Over the Bible was the motto VITAM MORTUIS REDDO [*I restore life to the dead*]. Underneath, on the right, was a table with books, and on the left, a diploma. On the outside of the circle were the words SIGILLUM COLLEGII NEO-CAESARIENSIS IN AMERICA [seal of the College of New Jersey in America].

In 1896, when the College of New Jersey became Princeton University, the seal was simplified. As described in the trustee minutes of February 13, 1896, it is ". . . a shield resting upon a circle. In the upper part of the shield an open Bible with Latin characters VET NOV TESTAMENTUM signifying the Old and New Testaments . . . In the lower part a chevron, denoting the rafters of a building. In the spaces between the sides of the shield and the circle the motto DEI SUB NUMINE VIGET [*Under God's power she flourishes*]. On the outside of the circle SIGILLUM UNIVERSITATIS PRINCETONIENSIS [seal of Princeton University]."

The seal is reserved for the purpose described in the college's original charter, namely as "a Common Seal under which they [the trustees] may pass all Diplomas, or Certificates of Degrees, and all Other the Affairs & Business of and Concerning the said Corporation . . ."

The shield portion of the seal, removed from the circle and with the motto in a ribbon beneath the

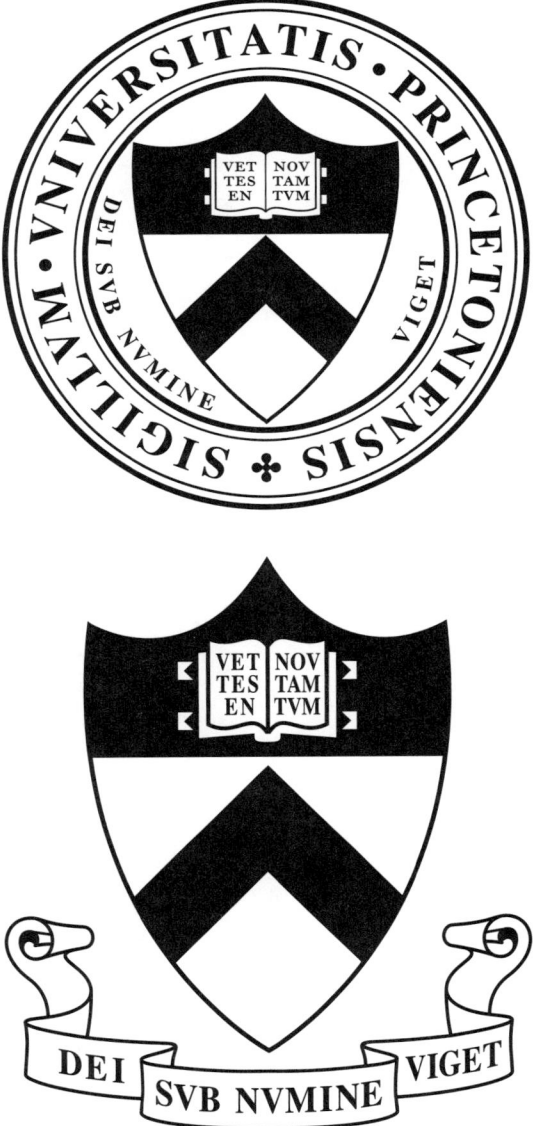

The University's official seal (top) and the shield that has been adapted from it for more informal use

shield, serves as the University's insignia and may be employed by organizations or individuals connected with the University where its use is appropriate. Its use is overseen by the University's office of communications and its office of trademark licensing. In practice, the shield is almost always used without the motto.

SECRETARY OF THE UNIVERSITY, THE, has administrative responsibility for the Board of Trustees, which includes making all necessary arrangements for meetings of the board and its executive committee, preparing the minutes of these meetings, and serving as secretary of the committees on honorary degrees and board development.

The secretary has charge of the general correspondence of the University, and in that capacity formally notifies all members of the faculty or administration who are elected or appointed to office by the board. The secretary also oversees the official convocations of the University, including Commencement.

The secretary is one of four officers specifically required by the University's charter, along with the president, the treasurer, and the clerk of the Board of Trustees. The secretary has custody of the University seal and is responsible for ensuring its appropriate use; on occasion the secretary attests to its use by signature, such as by signing all University diplomas. With the assistance of the archivist, the secretary has custody of the charter of the University and of the minute books and papers related to the records of the University.

The University's first full-time secretary was Charles McAlpin 1888, who served from 1901 to 1917. His successors have been:

V. Lansing Collins 1892 (1917–36)
Alexander Leitch 1924 (1936–66)
Jeremiah Finch (1966–74)
Thomas H. Wright Jr. '62 (1974–2004)
Robert Durkee '69 (2004–19)
Hilary Parker '01 (2019–)

SENATE OF THE UNITED STATES, THE, has numbered among its members 86 Princeton alumni from 26 states. Since its establishment in 1789 there have been only 20 years when it has been without a Princetonian.

Following is a list of Princeton senators. The party affiliation is given in parentheses, viz., Democrat (D), Republican (R), Federalist (F), Whig (W).

ALABAMA

John Walker 1806 (D) 1819–22

ARKANSAS

Kaneaster Hodges Jr. '60 (D) 1977–79

CALIFORNIA

John Hager 1836 (D) 1873–75

CONNECTICUT

Oliver Ellsworth 1766 (F) 1789–96
Henry Edwards 1797 (D) 1823–27

DELAWARE

James Bayard 1784 (F) 1804–13
Nicholas Van Dyke Jr. 1788 (F) 1817–26
Arnold Naudain 1806 (R) 1830–36
Richard Bayard 1814 (W) 1836–39, 1841–45
George Gray 1859 (D) 1885–99

GEORGIA

George Troup 1797 (D) 1816–18, 1829–33
John Forsyth 1799 (D) 1818–19, 1829–34
John Berrien 1796 (D) 1825–29, (W) 1841–52
Alfred Cuthbert 1803 (D) 1835–43
Walter Colquitt 1820 (D) 1843–48
Alfred Iverson 1820 (D) 1855–61
Alfred Colquitt 1844 (D) 1883–94

KENTUCKY

John Brown 1778 (D) 1792–1805
George Bibb 1792 (W) 1811–14, 1829–35

LOUISIANA

Edward Livingston 1781 (D) 1829–31
Edward Gay 1901 (D) 1918–21

MARYLAND

John Henry 1769 (D) 1789–97
Samuel Smith 1795 (D) 1803–15, 1822–33
Robert Harper 1785 (F) 1816
James Pearce 1822 (W) 1843–62
Blair Lee 1880 (D) 1914–17
Daniel Brewster '46 (D) 1963–69
Paul Sarbanes '54 (D) 1977–2007

MASSACHUSETTS

Jonathan Mason Jr. 1774 (F) 1800–03
John Kennedy '39 (D) 1953–60

MISSISSIPPI

Thomas Reed 1807 (D) 1826–27, 1829
John Henderson 1812 (W) 1839–45

MISSOURI

Francis P. Blair Jr. 1841 (D) 1871–73
George Williams 1894 (R) 1925–26
John Danforth '58 (R) 1977–95
Christopher "Kit" Bond '60 (R) 1987–2011

NEW HAMPSHIRE

Samuel Livermore 1752 (F) 1793–1801

NEW JERSEY

William Paterson 1763 (F) 1789–90
John Rutherford 1776 (F) 1791–98
Frederick Frelinghuysen 1770 (F) 1793–96
Richard Stockton 1779 (F) 1796–99
Jonathan Dayton 1776 (F) 1799–1805
Aaron Odgen 1773 (F) 1801–03
Mahlon Dickerson 1789 (D) 1817–33
Samuel Southard 1804 (D) 1821–23, (W) 1833–42
Theodore Frelinghuysen 1804 (D) 1829–35
William Dayton 1825 (W) 1842–51
Robert Stockton 1813 (D) 1851–53
John Thomson 1817 (D) 1853–62
Richard Field 1821 (R) 1862–63
James Wall 1838 (D) 1863
John Stockton 1843 (D) 1865–66, 1869–75
David Baird Jr. 1903 (R) 1929–30
H. Alexander Smith 1901 (R) 1944–59
William Bradley '65 (D) 1979–97

NEW YORK

Aaron Burr Jr. 1772 (D) 1791–97
John Armstrong Jr. (D) 1800–02, 1803–04
John Foster Dulles 1908 (R) 1949

NORTH CAROLINA

Benjamin Hawkins 1777 (F) 1789–95
Alexander Martin 1756 (F) 1793–99
David Stone 1788 (D) 1801–07, 1813–14
Nathaniel Macon 1778 (D) 1815–28
James Iredell 1806 (D) 1828–31

OHIO

Jacob Burnet 1791 (F) 1828–31
Atlee Pomerene 1884 (D) 1911–23

OKLAHOMA

Dewey Bartlett '42 (R) 1973–79

OREGON

James Kelly 1839 (D) 1871–77
Jeffrey Merkley *82 (D) 2009–

PENNSYLVANIA

George Dallas 1810 (D) 1831–33
J. Donald Cameron 1852 (R) 1877–97
David Reed 1900 (R) 1922–35

Joseph Guffey 1894 (D) 1935–47
James Duff 1904 (R) 1951–57

RHODE ISLAND

Claiborne Pell '40 (D) 1961–97

SOUTH CAROLINA

John Colhoun 1774 (D) 1801–02
John Taylor 1790 (D) 1810–16
Daniel Huger 1798 (D) 1843–45
James Chesnut Jr. 1835 (D) 1858–60
John Irby 1874 (D) 1891–97

TENNESSEE

George Campbell 1794 (D) 1811–14, 1815–18
William Frist '74 (R) 1995–2007

TEXAS

Rafael Edward "Ted" Cruz '92 (R) 2013–

VERMONT

Isaac Tichenor 1775 (F) 1796–97, 1815–21

VIRGINIA

Abraham Venable 1780 (D) 1803–04
William Giles 1781 (D) 1804–15
John Randolph 1751 (R) 1825–27

SENIOR THESIS. Widely regarded as the capstone of the undergraduate academic experience, the senior thesis embodies the defining characteristics of undergraduate education at Princeton. The thesis presumes that through the foundational work of general education and the focused study of departmental concentration, undergraduates develop the capacity to engage in independent study, on a topic of their own devising, with the guidance and supervision of a faculty adviser, and then to compile and present their findings in a thoughtfully considered, carefully researched, and well-reasoned way.

Every Princeton senior is required to write a thesis or, in some engineering departments, undertake a substantial independent project. This universality sets Princeton apart from other colleges and universities, where the thesis may be an elective option (or perhaps a requirement for seniors in an honors program), and it means that no matter how their undergraduate experiences may differ in other respects, all seniors have shared the sense of accomplishment that comes from successfully completing something as formidable as a thesis.

The origin of the thesis requirement cannot be traced directly to a specific decision taken by the faculty. Two short-lived initiatives in the early years of the twentieth century provided limited experience with optional independent work. The first of these, dating to 1904, allowed high-ranking seniors in some departments to substitute a "pro-seminary" for one of their departmental courses; members of the "pro-seminary" prepared independent papers that were read and discussed at weekly class meetings. The second initiative was the Special Honors Program (1913–17), which allowed high-ranking students to substitute departmental independent work for a fifth course.

The principal foundation for the senior thesis requirement was the New Plan of Study (often referred to as the four-course plan) that was adopted by the faculty in 1923. The plan required all juniors and seniors to do concentrated work in a single department. The program of study included two departmental courses and two electives each term, junior and senior independent work, and departmental comprehensive examinations.

While the plan made no mention of a senior thesis, several of the departments—first Biology and English in 1927, then Art and Archaeology and Politics—soon identified the thesis as the best vehicle for the independent thinking, investigation, and writing they expected of their seniors. One department after another followed suit, such that by 1930 a senior thesis had come to be required of practically all Princeton undergraduates.

Today, the Princeton University archives are the central repository for senior theses. They contain theses written by undergraduates from 1924 to the present, and since 2013 all senior theses have been collected in digital format. In a 2015 blog, the archives noted that the longest thesis then on record, 756 pages, had been submitted in 1976 by a student majoring in English, while the shortest, by an Electrical Engineering major in the Class of 1989, was three pages.

The basic work done by seniors writing theses in the twenty-first century matches closely the work done by their counterparts almost a century ago. Most departments assign thesis advisers early in the fall of the senior year. The adviser ideally works with the student through the year, although in practice the advising becomes more intense during the spring term. Patterns vary, with some students managing their time carefully throughout the year and others trying to complete the thesis in a big push very close to the due date. The norm lies somewhere between these two extremes. In some cases, students begin their research over the previous summer.

The topic of the thesis is chosen in consultation between the adviser and the student. Some students have specific topics in mind and are sufficiently self-directed to organize and carry out the necessary research on their own; others need considerable direction at every stage of the process.

The experience of doing junior independent work provides most students with a preview of the research strategies and writing skills needed for the senior thesis, and some departments have informal senior thesis workshops which allow students to discuss their work and benefit from the constructive criticism of their peers.

Funding to support some of the expenses that may be involved in senior thesis research (travel, supplies, specialized research materials) is available from several departments, from endowments administered by the office of the dean of the college, and from other funds.

Typically, undergraduates approach the thesis with a mixture of fear and anticipation. Describing "The Thesis Syndrome" in the *Princeton Alumni Weekly*, senior Jill Smolowe '77 wrote,

> The bane of every Princeton student's existence, it starts as a distant and incomprehensible word your freshman year, creeping up silently through the middle-class years, only to pounce with a fierce vengeance in the autumn of your senior year. Until then, the dimensions of that massive undertaking elude you, easily reconciled as something everyone else manages to live through, so when your time comes, so will you.

While the typical thesis is based on scholarly investigation or scientific experimentation, some students produce creative theses, including novels, plays, collections of poetry or short stories, films, photography exhibits, and dance performances. To mention only three examples: John McPhee '53 wrote the first creative thesis, a novel, *Skimmer Burns*; Maria Katzenbach '76 produced a novel, *The Grab*, which later became a best-seller under the same title; and Michael Rosenfeld '84 wrote a musical murder mystery, *Dead Give-Away*, that was presented at Theater Intime and later broadcast on cable television.

Often senior thesis topics prefigure their authors' subsequent pursuits. Notable examples include A. Scott Berg '71's thesis, later published as *Max Perkins: Editor of Genius*; Federal Reserve Board chair Paul Volcker '49's study, "The Problems of Federal Reserve Policy since World War II"; United States Senator Bill Bradley '65's thesis, "'On That Record I Stand:' Harry S. Truman's Fight for the Senatorship in 1940"; Congresswoman Terry Sewell '86's "Black Women in Politics: Our Time Has Come"; and business leader Meg Whitman '77's "The Marketing of American Consumer Products in Western Europe."

In "The Economic Role of the Investment Company," John Bogle '51 laid out the principles on which the $400 billion Vanguard Group came to be established; Wendy Kopp '89's "An Argument and Plan for the Creation of the Teachers Corporation" served as the blueprint for Teach For America.

In other cases, the relationship between theses and subsequent pursuits is more distant: consider actor Jose Ferrer '34's study, "The Comparative Sensitivity of the Etching Test for Fluorides with Different Types of Apparatus"; financier Carl Icahn '57's "The Problem of Formulating an Adequate Explication of the Empiricist Criterion of Meaning"; corporate executive Andrea Jung '79's "The Fiction of Katherine Mansfield: Reconciliation of Duality" and Queen Noor (Lisa Halaby) '74's "96th Street and Second Avenue." Actor Ellie Kemper '02 wrote a thesis that captured life after Princeton for many Princetonians; her title was "Isn't It Ironic?"

What is most important, thesis-writers and faculty members agree, is less the subject matter itself than the contribution of the thesis in developing traits that augur well for future success, no matter what one's professional and civic commitments. These include mental discipline; independence of mind and judgment; the capacity to focus and pursue a subject in depth; the ability to design and execute a large, complex project; the skills of analysis, synthesis, and clear, economical writing; and the self-confidence that grows from mastering a difficult challenge.

In the words of President Harold Dodds, "The real purpose of the thesis . . . is . . . to provide a means for the self-development of the student."

SERVICE OF REMEMBRANCE, THE, conducted annually in the chapel on the afternoon of Alumni Day, honors alumni, students, and members of the faculty and staff whose deaths were recorded by the University during the previous calendar year. The first Service of Remembrance was held in 1919, and it became an annual event beginning in 1946.

The address at the service is traditionally given by a member of the 25th reunion class. The service includes a procession composed of representatives from every alumni class, the graduate school, the student body, and the faculty and staff, each of whom carries a symbolic white carnation that is placed inside a memorial wreath.

When the wreath is completed, the president pronounces the following dedication, after which the organist plays "Old Nassau":

> By the dedication of this wreath, we, the living members of the Princeton family, join together to honor those of our company who are now numbered with the great communion of the eternal. May this wreath be the symbol of our continuing unity so that we may uphold their allegiance to the mission of this University, their dedication to the service of all people, and their devotion to the ideals of their faith.

Before the service begins, colorful processional kites are "flown" in the chapel by students from the Chapel Choir. The kites, which represent fire, earth, water, and air, are also incorporated in each year's Opening Exercises and Baccalaureate ceremonies.

SEVENTY-NINE HALL was presented to Princeton in 1904 by Woodrow Wilson's classmates and named for their Class of 1879. They said it was a small gift that came from great love or, in the Latin inscribed above the fireplace in the oak-paneled tower room, *ex amore magno donum parvum*. The names of the 170 classmates are recorded in bronze in the vaulted passageway beneath the tower.

Seventy-Nine's architect followed the Tudor Gothic style previously employed in Blair and Little halls, but instead of stone he used red brick with limestone trim, materials later chosen for neighboring buildings. Gutzon Borglum, later the sculptor of Mount Rushmore, carved the monkey and tiger grotesques that peer out from the moldings on the tower arches. The vaulted passageway beneath the tower provides a favorite spot for a cappella singing groups. The tower room, with fine mullioned windows at either end, was used by Wilson as an office when he was president of the University.

Seventy-Nine was originally a dormitory much coveted by juniors and seniors because of its proximity to the eating clubs. In 1960, when new dormitories were being erected elsewhere on the campus and increased academic space was needed in this area, Seventy-Nine Hall was converted for use by the Philosophy and Sociology departments. When Sociology moved to Green Hall in 1964, the Religion department took its place.

For many years two gilded lions guarded the Washington Road steps to the passageway beneath the tower. The lions were given to the University by the Class of 1879 at their graduation and flanked the front door of Nassau Hall until 1911, when the class presented the bronze tigers that have taken their place ever since. The lions were moved to Seventy-Nine Hall, where they remained for more than 60 years. After being retrieved from storage and restored, in 1998 they were installed in front of 1927-Clapp Hall, along Goheen Walk, between Wilson and Butler colleges.

In 1993 the University constructed an addition to the north end of 1879 Hall which houses the University Center for Human Values, seminar rooms, and academic offices.

SHAPIRO, HAROLD TAFLER *64 became Princeton's 18th president in January 1988 after eight years as president of the University of Michigan and led the University into the twenty-first century before stepping down in June 2001. During much of his presidency, his twin brother Bernard served as principal and vice chancellor of McGill University, a position he held from 1994 to 2004.

Born in Montreal, Canada, on June 8, 1935, with dual American and Canadian citizenship, Shapiro received his bachelor's degree from McGill in 1956, winning the highest academic honor in its faculty of commerce. He married Vivian Rapoport of Montreal in 1957 and spent five years working in his family's restaurant business before enrolling at Princeton in 1961 as a graduate student in economics. After receiving his doctorate in 1964, he joined the faculty of the University Michigan as an assistant professor of economics. He was promoted to associate professor in 1967 and full professor in 1970; was named vice president for academic affairs in 1977; and was elected president in 1980.

Shapiro's fields of special interest include econometrics, mathematical economics, science policy, the evolution of higher education, and money and banking. Because of his expertise in economic forecasting, colleagues at Michigan recalled that when he appeared before the Michigan legislature to make budget requests, the chamber turned into a classroom as the legislators questioned Shapiro about his economic predictions for the state.

In his inaugural address at Princeton, Shapiro reflected on the "evolutionary interplay of tradition and change—the process of selective adaptation—that has characterized Princeton's history." In 1996, under his leadership, the University celebrated its 250th anniversary, during which it announced plans to expand and bring together campus community service activities through what would become the Pace Center for Civic Engagement. Following the anniversary, he and his predecessor, William Bowen *58, edited a volume of essays, *Universities and Their Leadership*, that had been presented at an anniversary symposium and were published in 1998 by Princeton University Press.

At the official Charter Day convocation on October 22, 1996, Shapiro unveiled an engraved stone on the front campus that expressed the University's appreciation to its alumni for "their devotion to the University and its mission of education, scholarship, and service" and incorporated a revised version of the University's informal motto that expanded on "Princeton in the Nation's Service" to add "and in the Service of All Nations." (In 2016 the motto was changed to "Princeton in the Nation's Service and the Service of Humanity.")

In conjunction with the 250th, the University launched a five-year "Anniversary Campaign for Princeton" that raised a total of $1.14 billion, far surpassing its original goal of $750 million; the campaign's largest single gift was $100 million from Gordon Wu '58 to strengthen the school of Engineering and Applied Science.

The campaign significantly expanded Princeton's capacity to provide undergraduate financial aid and to increase graduate fellowship support. For undergraduates, the University reduced loan requirements for middle income students and eliminated them entirely for lower income students in 1998, and then in 2001 it adopted a groundbreaking policy of not requiring loans for any financial aid recipients, excluding home equity from its calculation of need, and extending its policy of "need-blind" admission to include all international students. "We want to ensure that no student admitted to Princeton feels that he or she cannot attend because it would present a financial hardship," Shapiro said.

During Shapiro's presidency, the percentage of international students in the undergraduate student body nearly doubled, to 10 percent.

In addition to increasing financial aid dollars, the Anniversary Campaign raised funds for the endowment, which grew from $2 billion to $8 billion while Shapiro was president. Gifts also supported the construction and renovation of such buildings as McDonnell Hall for physics, the Friend Center for Engineering Education, Wallace Hall for the social sciences, the Bendheim Center for Finance, the Scully Hall dormitory, the Berlind Theater as an addition to the McCarter Theatre Center, and athletic spaces such as Weaver Stadium, the Class of 1952 stadium, the Shea rowing center, and a new Rafael Viñoly–designed football stadium, named Princeton Stadium.

When the stadium opened in 1997, Shapiro described it as "a work of art, of science, of intellect, of imagination, and of athletic grace." Three years earlier, when the University Band celebrated its 75th anniversary, Shapiro had appeared on the turf of the stadium's predecessor, Palmer Stadium, wearing the band's signature orange and black plaid jacket and playing a washboard during a halftime show.

Under Shapiro's leadership, the University opened its Center for Jewish Life in 1993 on the site of two former eating clubs (Gateway and Prospect), and in 2000 it realized an 80-year-old ambition with the opening of Frist Campus Center in an expanded and renovated Palmer Hall. Shapiro described Frist as "the absolute epicenter of campus life" and a "milestone for Princeton's history." The center includes an organic, sustainable, local food venue named Café Vivian in honor of Vivian Shapiro, who had been an associate professor at the University of Michigan School of Social Work before coming to Princeton and while at Princeton had earned her doctorate from the Smith College School of Social Work in 1994.

Several undergraduate teaching initiatives were implemented during Shapiro's presidency, including a fund for innovation in undergraduate education and a program to bring exceptional teachers to Princeton as visiting faculty. Awards for teaching excellence were established, to be presented each year at Commencement, and the McGraw Center for Teaching and Learning was created. Shapiro oversaw major expansions in opportunities for students to study abroad and in the freshman seminar program—a program in which during and after his presidency he taught seminars on the history of American higher education, the aims of education, bioethics, and science, technology, and public policy.

In 1998 the University created a President's Award for Academic Excellence to recognize outstanding achievement on the part of first- and second-year students, and in 2001 he and Vivian Shapiro endowed the award, which was renamed the Shapiro Prize for Academic Excellence.

Shapiro presided over the development of such new academic programs as the Lewis-Sigler Institute for Integrative Genomics; an interdisciplinary center for the Study of Religion; the Society of Fellows in the Liberal Arts (anchored by the Cotsen Fellows in the Humanities); the University Center for Human Values; new master's programs in Finance, Engineering, and Public Policy; and new initiatives in alumni education.

In 1997 the trustees appointed a committee to consider long-term strategic issues facing the University, and in 2000 the "Wythes Report," named for committee chair Paul Wythes '55, recommended that the University increase the number of undergraduates by 10 percent, from 4,600 to 5,100 and construct a sixth residential college.

Shapiro was the only person to be listed by *Change* magazine among the country's most influential university presidents in both the 1980s and the 1990s. Outside the academy, he served President George H. W. Bush as a member and vice chair of the President's Council of Advisors on Science and Technology and President Bill Clinton as chair of the National Bioethics Advisory Commission, which in 1997 issued a report on *Cloning Human Beings*. He chaired an Institute of Medicine committee that issued a report in 1993 on employer-based health benefits, and 10 years later he chaired a National Academy of Sciences committee on the organization of the National Institutes of Health. In 2000 the Council of Scientific Society Presidents awarded him its leadership citation for "stellar leadership toward resolution of the most complex ethical issues created by frontier life sciences research."

At the state level, Shapiro served on a gubernatorially-appointed panel that restructured the system of higher education in New Jersey and co-chaired the state's Edison Partnership, which sought to encourage public investment and public-private partnerships to strengthen New Jersey's high-tech economy.

During and after his presidency, Shapiro served on many other federal and state panels and on boards in the public and private sectors. He chaired the boards of the Association of American Universities, the Consortium on Financing Higher Education, and the Alfred P. Sloan Foundation. He received more than a dozen honorary degrees, including one from Princeton in 2001, and in 2004 he received Princeton's James Madison Medal, the highest distinction the University can confer on alumni of its graduate school.

His numerous other awards include the Clark Kerr Medal for Distinguished Leadership in Higher Education from the University of California-Berkeley, the William D. Carey Award for Leadership in Science Policy from the American Association for the Advancement of Science, and the Public Welfare Medal from the National Academy of Sciences.

In 2003 he delivered a series of lectures at the University of California on "The Transformation of the Antebellum College: From Right Thinking to Liberal Learning," "Liberal Education, Liberal Democracy, and the Soul of the University," and "The University and the Ethical Dimensions of Scientific Progress." In 2005 Princeton University Press published the lectures in a book titled *A Larger Sense of Purpose: Higher Education and Society*.

When Shapiro announced his decision to step down in 2001, the trustees said "thanks to his vision, his sensitivity to the concerns of everyone in the Princeton family, and his unlimited energy, Harold Shapiro has provided extraordinary leadership for Princeton over these past 12 years—strengthening its faculty, enhancing its programs of teaching and research, revitalizing its campus, and dramatically increasing its endowment. He also has served with great distinction in a number of major leadership roles outside of Princeton, while also finding time to teach both undergraduate and graduate students. We will be sorry to see his presidency come to an end."

After retiring from the presidency, Shapiro returned to teaching and research in the department of Economics and the school of Public and International Affairs. He had an office in Wallace Hall, which opens onto Shapiro Walk, a landscaped continuation of McCosh Walk that extends from Washington Road to Olden Street and links the school of Public and International Affairs with the school of Engineering and Applied Science. The walk honors him for leading "Princeton into the 21st century with wisdom, integrity, courage, and grace, in service to the nation and all nations."

A plaque honoring both Harold and Vivian Shapiro is embedded in the pavement near two granite benches, one dedicated to him and one to her, and both of them engraved with an inscription that reads, in part, "a place to pause and reflect in the company of friends, ideas, and dreams."

SHERRERD HALL opened in 2008 as the home for the department of Operations Research and Financial Engineering and the center for Information Technology Policy. The 45,000-square-foot cubist building, along the southeast end of Shapiro Walk, was named for its donor, John J. F. Sherrerd '52, one of Princeton's most active and supportive alumni.

As a trustee for 20 years, Sherrerd twice chaired the board's resources (fundraising) committee and served as vice chair of the executive committee. From 1995 to 2000 he co-chaired the Anniversary Campaign for Princeton that raised a then-record $1.14 billion. He also played a leadership role in two other capital campaigns, and was a 34-year member of the national annual giving committee, president and treasurer of his class, a director of the Princeton University Investment Company (Princo) from 1987 to 1990 and 1991–98, and a trustee and founding chair of the investment committee of the Robertson Foundation, which at the time provided support for the school of Public and International Affairs.

Sherrerd Hall is located at the intersection of buildings for engineering and the social sciences, reflecting the interdisciplinary interests of its occupants. It was designed by Frederick Fisher with a glass façade that provides transparency and reflects the facades of the neighboring Friend Center for Engineering Education and Mudd Manuscript Library. The building was the first at Princeton constructed with a green roof. Its main entrance opens to a three-story atrium, with a 30-foot-high sculpture of light and mirrors suspended in the stairwell.

Sherrerd's many contributions to Princeton are also commemorated through Sherrerd Field at the stadium named for his class. The Class of 1952 Stadium opened in 1996 as a home for both lacrosse and field hockey, but when field hockey moved to Bedford Field after the 2011 season, the installation of Sherrerd Field transformed the stadium into one of the top lacrosse-only venues in the country.

SIMMONS, RUTH, played several key roles in diversifying the faculty, the academic program, and campus life at Princeton before, in 1995, becoming the first African American president of Smith College, and then in 2001 becoming the president of Brown University; she was Brown's first woman president and the first African American president in the Ivy League. She returned to Princeton in 2012 as a member of the Board of Trustees, and in 2017 she became the first woman president of Prairie View A&M University in her native Texas.

Simmons was born in Grapeland, Texas, the youngest of 12 children of a sharecropper and a domestic worker. In the world in which she grew up, "the boundary between black and white was absolute; the possibility of crossing it was not in my comprehension," she later wrote. When her family moved to Houston and her father began working in a factory, she was able to attend public school, and at a time when it was almost impossible for an African American child to even think about attending college, she earned a bachelor's degree from Dillard University, a historically Black institution in New Orleans, graduating *summa cum laude.*

After earning her master's and doctoral degrees in Romance languages and literatures at Harvard, Simmons taught and held administrative positions at the University of New Orleans, California State University, Northridge, and the University of Southern California before moving to Princeton in 1983 to serve as director of studies at Butler College, one of the newly established residential colleges. She became acting director of the African American Studies program in 1985; assistant dean of the faculty in 1986; and associate dean of the faculty in 1987.

In 1990 Simmons left to become provost of Spelman College, a prominent historically Black institution. A year later she was appointed vice provost at Princeton, and for a semester she shared her time between Princeton and Spelman before returning full-time to Princeton in 1992. As vice provost, she assisted academic and administrative units with planning and helped to integrate department plans with larger university-wide planning efforts.

In 1993 she prepared a comprehensive report on campus race relations which resulted in the appointment of an ombuds officer, the establishment of a Race Relations Working Group to foster and monitor continuing efforts to improve race relations, and increased coordination of campus race-relations activities.

In a number of her positions, Simmons led efforts to bring African American faculty to Princeton, including future Nobel Laureate Toni Morrison in 1989. In a spring 1993 conversation among Simmons, Morrison, religion professor Albert Raboteau, and English professor Wahneema Lubiano, when Morrison was asked why she had decided to come to Princeton, she said she was impressed by Princeton's highly motivated students and its faculty, "and I was very impressed with Ruth Simmons. There was something about her manner, her constructive negotiation, that set her apart." When told that Morrison needed a *curriculum vitae* to be appointed, Simmons prepared it.

At Smith, Simmons started the first engineering program at an American women's college. At Brown, where she also held the position of professor of comparative literature and Africana studies, she was widely recognized as one of the country's leading university presidents. She received national attention for her leadership of Brown's response to an inquiry she initiated into its historical connections to slavery when she appointed a steering committee on slavery and justice in 2003.

After stepping down as Brown's president in 2012, Simmons was elected to a four-year term as a Princeton trustee, where she served, among other assignments, on the special trustee committee that examined the Princeton legacy of Woodrow Wilson 1879. In 2017, she was a featured speaker and panelist at the symposium of the Princeton and Slavery Project, which explored Princeton's historical connections to slavery.

Earlier in 2017 she agreed to serve as interim president of Prairie View A&M, a historically Black university in Texas, and later that year she was officially named its eighth (and first woman) president.

In 1996, Princeton awarded Simmons an honorary degree. She is one of at least nine members of the provost's office to have gone on to college or university presidencies, including William Bowen *58 (Princeton), Sheldon Hackney (Tulane and the University of Pennsylvania), Neil Rudenstine '56 (Harvard), Janet Holmgren *74 (Mills), Hugo Sonnenschein (Chicago), Georgia Nugent '73 (Kenyon), Amy Gutmann (University of Pennsylvania), and Christopher Eisgruber '83 (Princeton).

SLAVIC LANGUAGES AND LITERATURES, THE DEPARTMENT OF. On the heels of World War II, Princeton students petitioned then-president Harold Dodds for courses in Russian language and literature. Chemistry professor John Turkevich, a strong advocate for introducing Russian studies, taught a course himself, and pulled together a small group of instructors, including his wife Ludmilla, who became one of Princeton's first Russian language teachers and received the United States Information Agency award "for distinguished service in recognition of outstanding assistance to the USIA in advancing understanding and goodwill between the peoples of the US and the peoples of other countries." Another early instructor was Valentine Bill, who continued until her retirement in 1974.

Russian offerings were incorporated into the then-department of Modern Languages, and when that department was divided, Russian became a subsidiary of French in the department of Romance Languages. The number of faculty and students remained modest until the Soviet Union's launch of Sputnik in 1957, which gave an immense boost to interest in the Russian language, and in all Russian studies. Enrollments increased substantially, and the United States government, concerned about being overtaken by Soviet science, began allocating significant funding to Russian and Slavic programs.

In 1959, several new assistant professors arrived, including Herman Ermolaev, a survivor of both the Soviet system of education and the Nazi invasion of the USSR. Ermolaev spent his entire academic career at Princeton, transferring to emeritus status in 2007. His world-renowned scholarship on the Soviet Union was informed by his early life experiences at the hands of the Nazis and the Soviets. As a teacher, he was known for his survey course on Soviet literature, which he brought to life through his vivid personal memories and history. As many as 350 students a semester enrolled in this course.

With the further influx of noted scholars such as Clarence Brown (later affiliated with Comparative Literature) and increasing lecture sizes, Slavic Languages and Literatures became an independent program in 1961. Shortly thereafter a graduate program in Russian literature and Slavic languages was initiated, and an interdisciplinary program in Russian Studies was established. In 1967, the program in Slavic Languages and Literatures became a full-fledged department.

During the 1960s, faculty numbers grew. Additions included Veronica Dolenko, who directed the rigorous Russian language program until her retirement in 1992; Nina Berberova, who was instrumental in furthering graduate studies; and Charles Townsend, who oversaw the linguistics part of the graduate program and served as chair of the department from 1970 until his retirement in 2002.

The graduate program produced scholars who went on to teach across the Ivy League and beyond, including Ellen Chances *72, who became a tenured faculty member at Princeton, taught for five decades, and served as clerk of the faculty from 1999 to 2011. Despite its academic success, the program ran into hard times financially as the government curtailed its support. In 1971 the graduate program was suspended, but undergraduate students continued to take language and literature courses, and Princeton continued to attract Russian visitors, from composers to religious thinkers. Svetlana Alliluyeva, daughter of Joseph Stalin, spent some years in Princeton, where she enjoyed a warm friendship with Richard Burgi, Townsend's predecessor as chair of the department.

If Sputnik and the Cold War helped create the first graduate program, "perestroika" was the catalyst for its reconstitution. In 1987, Caryl Emerson joined the faculty. An exceptional scholar and teacher, Emerson won both the President's Award for Distinguished Teaching and a Behrman Award for outstanding achievement in the humanities. With her advocacy (coupled with the persistent efforts of Townsend), the graduate program was reinstated in 1990. Its PhD degree is in Russian Literature and Culture.

In the following years, the department continued to expand as new and returning faculty members brought expertise in a broad array of fields to complement the existing Russian language and literature curriculum on both the graduate and undergraduate levels.

Today, the department aspires to develop in its majors a critically informed appreciation for the literature and culture of Russia and the Slavic world, welcoming students with interests not only in literature, but in politics, cultural anthropology, and film and visual arts. In addition to the traditional Russian language classes, other Slavic language courses are taught "on demand," including Czech, Polish, Bosnian-Croatian-Serbian, and Bulgarian. A course on Russian for heritage speakers, intended for students who were raised in a home where Russian was spoken, is taught through authentic cultural materials, e.g., historical documents and literary texts by classical and contemporary Russian authors.

Courses in Russian literature, art, music, and cinema, as well as courses that focus on Eastern Europe, offer a wide cultural range. The certificate program in Russian language and culture attracts students from other departments, from concentrators in Comparative Literature to pre-med students in the sciences. The program in Russian, East European, and Eurasian Studies, an affiliate of the Princeton Institute for International and Regional Studies (PIIRS), draws on a core faculty in the humanities, history, and social sciences to support and maintain a diverse undergraduate curriculum and an outstanding library collection in Slavic and other languages, as well as a range of on-campus and off-campus activities.

The academic program is supplemented each year by numerous lectures, concerts, and other activities. In addition, the department regularly hosts leading Russian writers and scholars for semester-long appointments.

With financial support from PIIRS, the department established the Princeton in St. Petersburg program in 2004. This program offers Princeton undergraduates a chance to improve their knowledge of Russian language and culture during a two-month summer course in St. Petersburg, the cultural capital of Russia.

SMITH, SAMUEL STANHOPE 1769 was Princeton's seventh president and the first graduate of the College to hold the office. He was born in 1751, the year in which his father, Robert Smith, was installed as pastor of the Presbyterian church in Pequea, Pennsylvania. His father was a trustee of the College from 1772 to 1793; his mother, Elizabeth, was a daughter of Samuel Blair, one of the founding trustees. Two younger brothers, John Blair and William Richmond Smith, graduated with the Class of 1773, and his personal ties to Princeton were augmented in 1775 when he married Ann, the oldest daughter of President John Witherspoon, whom he would succeed in 1795.

Smith attended his father's school in Pequea and was admitted to the College in 1767 as a member of the junior class. He excelled in mathematics and joined what would become the American Whig Society. He graduated two years later with the highest honor of delivering the Latin salutatory address at Commencement. He returned to Pequea to assist his father in the school and begin the study of theology. In 1770 he returned to Princeton as a tutor, where he continued his preparation for the ministry. Licensed to preach in 1773, he then went as a missionary to Virginia.

There Smith became an advocate, in his sermons and writings, for the separation of church and state (a radical idea at the time), and he played a leading role in founding two academies. One of them, located first in Augusta County, later became Washington College, and still later Washington and Lee University. Prince Edward Academy, of which Smith was appointed first rector in 1775 at the age of 24, became

Hampden-Sydney College in 1783. In 1779 he was called back to Princeton as professor of moral philosophy.

Smith and his family took up residence in the President's House as Witherspoon moved to Tusculum, the house and farm he owned outside the village. Smith would occupy the President's House (now Maclean House) for almost 33 years. He owned at least one slave in the house, and in 1784 he placed an advertisement seeking to exchange an enslaved man accustomed to farm work for a servant "accustomed to cooking."

Witherspoon remained active in the affairs of state and church, but he turned over a large part of his administrative duties to Smith, who was named vice president in 1786. On Witherspoon's death in 1794 there was no question as to who should succeed him.

Smith was highly regarded as a scholar and was elected to the American Philosophical Society in 1785. In 1787 he delivered "An Essay on the Causes of Variety of Complexion and Figure in the Human Species," in which he argued that all people belong to the same family and that diversity within the species should be attributed to environmental influences. After initial publication in Philadelphia, his paper was reprinted in Edinburgh and London and became one of the most influential studies prior to Darwin's *Origin of Species* in 1859.

One of Smith's ideas was to resettle freed slaves in the west and encourage whites to marry them as a way to eliminate both slavery and race. He hoped that interracial marriages would "bring the two races nearer together, and, in a course of time . . . obliterate those wide distinctions which are now created by diversity of complexion."

Two of Smith's students later transformed his concept of resettlement into a plan to relocate freed American slaves to a colony in West Africa. This led in 1816 to the founding of the American Colonization Society, which proposed just such a resettlement; its adherents included many graduates of the College, including a then-graduating student and later College president John Maclean Jr. 1816.*

As president, Smith upheld the fundamental place of classical languages and literature, but he also focused increased attention on the study of science and modern languages. He strengthened requirements for admission so that further classical instruction could be limited to the first year. Another proposal, which the trustees adopted in 1799 but then withdrew in 1809, was to allow students to pursue a special program leading to a certificate of achievement, a significant step toward the later Bachelor of Science degree.

When Smith took office, the College was still struggling to recover from the disastrous effects of the war years. His success in 1796 in obtaining a grant from the state legislature of £600 per year for three years provided partial relief. But the grant was not renewed, and the College remained primarily dependent upon tuition for its income.

An enrollment of just over 75 students in 1794 had grown to 182 in 1805, and the 54 degrees awarded in 1806 was the largest number since the founding of the College. A faculty of two professors, including the president, had grown to four professors in addition to the president, along with the usual two or three tutors and an instructor in French. Among the professors was John Maclean Sr., a graduate of Edinburgh, whose special interest was chemistry.

Smith himself continued to carry a heavy teaching schedule, even as he worked to expand the reach of the College. He was fond of describing Princeton as a mecca for students drawn from the region extending southward from the Hudson River to Georgia. In January 1805 the College enrolled 32 students from New Jersey, 31 from Pennsylvania, 28 from Maryland, 22 from Virginia, 13 from South Carolina, and nine from Georgia. Of the other states, only New York had as many as Georgia.

The high point in Smith's presidency came after the fire in 1802 that destroyed Nassau Hall. The constituency of the College rallied to its support so well that funds were raised not only for the reconstruction of that building, but for the addition of two new buildings to flank it on the front campus: Geological (later Stanhope) Hall and Philosophical Hall.

The low point of Smith's presidency occurred when a student riot in 1807, resulting from his mishandling of a disciplinary matter, led to the suspension of 125 students and a growing distrust of the president by the trustees. For some, his educational reforms had gone too far, and there was discontent over the declining number of students preparing for the clergy. Enrollments declined and four professors left the faculty, including Maclean, whose resignation

---

* In an essay about Smith, the Princeton and Slavery Project noted that "the ACS quickly became the most popular solution to the problem of slavery among 'moderate' whites across the nation. Colonization struggled to win support from free Blacks, however, who suspected its motives and its white managers, and the ACS eventually drew fire from William Lloyd Garrison and other radical white abolitionists."

was requested in 1812 by trustees more concerned with training ministers than scientists. That was the year when Smith also was given no choice but to resign. He was provided a pension and a house, and he died on August 21, 1819.

SMITH, TRACY K., a member of the Princeton faculty from 2006 to 2021 and a 2012 winner of the Pulitzer Prize for Poetry for her book *Life on Mars*, was named director of the Creative Writing program in 2015; the Roger S. Berlind '52 Professor of the Humanities (succeeding the first incumbent in that professorship, Joyce Carol Oates) in 2016; and chair of the Lewis Center for the Arts in 2019. From 2017 to 2019 she served two terms as the 22nd Poet Laureate of the United States. In 2021 she joined Oates and several other current and former Princeton faculty members, including the founding chair of the Lewis Center, Paul Muldoon, as a member of the prestigious American Academy of Arts and Letters.

The position of poet laureate, officially the poet laureate consultant in poetry to the Library of Congress, was first filled in 1937. The second poet laureate, in 1943–44, was Allen Tate, who helped found Princeton's Creative Writing program when he was hired in 1939 as the first "resident fellow" in creative writing. Two alumni have served as poet laureate: William Meredith '40 from 1978–80, and W. S. Merwin '48 in 2010–11.

Smith was appointed by Librarian of Congress Carla Hayden, who received a Princeton honorary degree in 2018. In announcing the appointment, Hayden described Smith as "a poet of searching. Her work travels the world and takes on its voices; brings history and memory to life; calls on the power of literature as well as science, religion, and pop culture. With directness and deftness, she contends with the heavens or plumbs our inner depths—all to better understand what makes us most human."

The role of the poet laureate is to foster a more widespread appreciation of the reading and writing of poetry. Smith hosted poetry readings in small towns across the country as part of a series called "American Conversations: Celebrating Poems in Rural Communities." She visited libraries, prisons, rehabilitation centers, retirement facilities, and youth detention centers. In 2018 she began a podcast and public radio show, "The Slowdown," billed as five minutes of poetry every weekday, during which she read and discussed poems of her choosing.

Smith was born in Massachusetts and grew up in northern California, the youngest of five children. Her mother was a teacher and her father an engineer who worked on the Hubble Space Telescope. Her memoir, *Ordinary Light*, was a finalist for the 2015 National Book Award for nonfiction. As chair of the Lewis Center, she succeeded theater scholar Michael Cadden, who served from 2012 to 2019; he, in turn, had succeeded Muldoon, the founding chair of the center and also a Pulitzer Prize–winning poet.

SOCCER. The Princeton men's and women's soccer teams have each reached the NCAA Final Four, a feat unmatched by any other Ivy League school. The programs have produced All-Americans, professional players, a two-time Olympic bronze medalist (Canada's Diana Matheson '08), and a US men's national team coach (Bob Bradley '80).

Men's Soccer

Princeton's early football games, played with a round ball kicked into a rectangular goal, may have borne some resemblance to "association football," or soccer, but the University did not field a soccer team until 1905, three and a half decades after the first intercollegiate football game. The 1905 team won its first game, defeating a Merion Cricket Club team, 3–0.

In the early years the team had to seek out its own coaches, including Jack Taylor, a former all-England soccer player who was working as a bartender at the old Princeton Inn. Princeton played in a succession of eastern leagues—the Intercollegiate Association Football League (IAFL), the Intercollegiate Soccer Football Association, and the Middle Atlantic League—until Ivy League soccer began in 1955.

Princeton's best season in the early years came in 1916 when it tied for first place in the IAFL but lost a postseason playoff to Penn, whose All-American forward William Nassau scored two goals. "Just how we let this man get away from us," the *Princeton Alumni Weekly* commented, "is a matter worthy of consideration."

Under Al Nies, the Tigers' first full-time coach, Princeton won or tied for five league championships in the 1920s. Standouts of that era included Jack Packard 1928, a left-footed forward who tallied 53 goals in the championship seasons of 1925, 1926, and 1927. Nies' successor, Bill Logan, won two championships as well, in 1936 and 1937.

Coach Jimmie Reed, who led the Tigers from 1938 through 1966, won 136 games and six league titles, including Princeton's first two Ivy championships in 1957 and 1960. The 1942 team went 8-0-1 with eight shutouts, outscoring opponents 42–2. Several of

Reed's players went on notable careers after college: Ward Chamberlin '43, captain of the 1942 team and an All-American who became a leading figure in public television; Butch van Breda Kolff '45, another All-American, better known as the coach of Princeton's 1965 Final Four men's basketball team; David Billington '50, a star goalie who returned to join the faculty as a professor of civil engineering; and Robert Goheen '40 *48, a spirited forward who became a Princeton classics professor and eventually served as the University's 16th president.

After Jack Volz coached the Tigers from 1967 through 1972, Bill Muse coached them from 1973 through 1983, and although he never won the Ivy championship, he led the program to its first two NCAA tournament appearances, in 1977 and 1979. The 1977 team, paced by All-American Paul Milone '78's 13 goals, lost its first-round game, while the 1979 team, captained by Charlie Stillitano '81, won in the first round against Philadelphia Textile before bowing out to Penn State.

Bob Bradley '80, who played for Muse, followed him as coach in the 1984 season and oversaw a successful stretch that saw the Tigers win the Ivy crown twice, in 1988 and 1993, and reach the NCAA tournament three times. Princeton's 1993 team made a remarkable postseason run, defeating Columbia, the only team that had beaten it in the Ivy season; Penn State, the Big Ten champion; and Hartwick, in front of 2,400 fans at Lourie-Love field.

The Hartwick game was scoreless well into the second half when John Talbot '94, in the game as a substitute for injured All-American midfielder Joe Thieman '94, poked in a rebound to break the stalemate and send "the crowd and the Tiger bench, including Thieman, into hysterics," as Grant Wahl '96 wrote in the *Daily Princetonian*. Two more goals followed, both assisted by a rejuvenated Thieman.

The Tigers were finally halted by Virginia, the eventual national champion, 3–1, in the national semifinals. Virginia's coach, Bruce Arena, had been Bradley's boss in one of his first coaching jobs, when he was a young assistant for the Cavaliers. The two would be reunited in 1996 when Bradley left Princeton to become Arena's assistant with DC United of Major League Soccer (MLS). Bradley made a career in pro soccer, in the United States and abroad, and he served six years as coach of the US men's national team, leading the Americans to the knockout round of the 2010 World Cup.

Bradley, like Muse, was succeeded by one of his former players: former Ivy League Rookie of the Year, Player of the Year, and later Coach of the Year Jim Barlow '91, who would become Princeton's winningest coach. As of 2019, Barlow's teams had won or shared the Ivy title five times, including the Tigers' first 7–0 Ivy season in 2010, and reached the NCAA tournament five times as well. In 2020 an anonymous donor endowed the head coach position for men's soccer in honor of Barlow's leadership.

Since the beginning of MLS, Princeton has sent several alumni to the pro league, including Thieman, Jesse Marsch '96, Andrew Lewis '98, Matt Behncke '02, Antoine Hoppenot '12, and Cameron Porter '16. Marsch, who played 14 seasons as a pro, later coached in MLS and in Europe.

Women's Soccer

Women's soccer was a relatively late arrival to Princeton athletics, beginning as a club team in 1977 and ascending to varsity status in 1980. Bob Malekoff, the program's first coach, helped the Tigers to a strong start, with four straight winning seasons, a share of the Ivy championship in 1982, and NCAA tournament appearances in 1982 (the tournament's first year) and 1983. It would take another 16 years for Princeton to earn its way back to the NCAA postseason, in 1999, under coach Julie Shackford.

Shackford, an All-American player at William & Mary, came to Princeton in 1995 and built the struggling program into a consistent winner. Her Tigers earned NCAA tournament bids in six consecutive years, from 1999 to 2004, and made a run in 2004 that was reminiscent of the men's team's 1993 postseason.

The 2004 team, with a 15–2 regular-season record, earned the No. 7 seed in the tournament and validated that lofty position with shutout wins over Central Connecticut State, Villanova (in double-overtime), and Boston College in the first three rounds. The Tigers hosted Washington in the national quarterfinals in front of 2,500 fans at Lourie-Love field and surged ahead early in the second half to win 3–1. Esmeralda Negron '05 scored the tie-breaking second goal, her school-record 20th of the season. The following week UCLA, coached by Shackford's friend and college teammate Jill Ellis, would end Princeton's magical season in the semifinals, 2–0. Reflecting on the season, Shackford told the *Princeton Alumni Weekly*, "I don't think there was a day when this group wasn't excited to get out on the field and train. And they had an answer for everything."

Shackford left Princeton after the 2014 season, having led Princeton to six Ivy titles and eight NCAA tournaments. Her successor, Sean Driscoll, emulated her Ivy and postseason success. In his first five seasons, Driscoll's teams won the league and advanced to the NCAA tournament three times. Princeton's 2017 team won a pair of memorable games in the second and third rounds of the NCAA tournament, defeating North Carolina State in a penalty shootout and edging North Carolina, 2–1, in overtime. The Tigers traveled to UCLA for the national quarterfinals, where the Bruins prevailed, 3–1.

Notable players in the women's program include Diana Matheson '08, an All-American as a freshman on the 2004 team who played more than 200 games for the Canadian national team, including three World Cups and three Olympic tournaments; Negron, who also was named an All-American in 2004 and finished her career with 47 goals and 18 assists; Jen Hoy '12, who played seven seasons in the National Women's Soccer League (NWSL); Tyler Lussi '17, another NWSL player, who holds Princeton's career record for goals with 53; and Natalie Grossi '20, a goalkeeper who set an Ivy record with 31 career shutouts.

SOCIOLOGY, THE DEPARTMENT OF. Sociology became an independent department at Princeton only in the 1960s, but as early as 1895 the catalogue listed a course on "Sociology: A historical review of the evolution of modern industrialism ... The genesis and development of a science of sociology." The instructor, Walter Wyckoff 1888, a lecturer in sociology and later assistant professor of political economy known to his students as "Weary Willie," spent 1891 to 1893 working his way from Connecticut to California as a day laborer, mostly on foot, to learn firsthand about the lives of unskilled workers. A plaque commemorating Wyckoff is affixed to a wall of East Pyne Hall in Collins arch.

In 1912, the economist Frank Fetter began teaching a course on "social economics." A year later it was offered by the department of Economics and Social Institutions, which had just split off from the department of History, Politics, and Economics.

The Office of Population Research (OPR) was founded in 1936 with the demographer Frank Notestein as its first director. Princeton's program in population studies was the first university-based program in the country to combine research and teaching in the field. Its staff included Irene Barnes Taeuber, who served as editor of the journal *Population Index* from 1936 to 1954 and whose scholarly work helped found the science of demography.

The creation of OPR provided impetus for the field of sociology to take a more scientific direction that would complement its earlier and continuing interest in social problems and reform. Soon after World War II, specialists in social statistics, East Asia, social class, race relations, and urban studies joined Princeton's faculty, among them two noted scholars, Melvin Tumin and Marion Levy. A doctoral program in sociology was established in 1948, and the first PhD was granted in 1951.

In 1954 the department of Economics and Social Institutions became Economics and Sociology; in 1960 Sociology merged with Anthropology to form a department of Sociology and Anthropology. Anthropology assumed separate departmental status in 1965, making way for a new stand-alone department of Sociology.

During the 1950s, 1960s, and 1970s, Charles Westoff, Marvin Bressler, Norman Ryder, Gilbert Rozman, Jane Mencken, and Robert Wuthnow joined the faculty, and under their leadership the department became one of the most diverse departments of sociology in the country and among the most diverse departments at Princeton. In 1968 sociologist Suzanne Keller became Princeton's first female full professor and, in 1971 and 1975, Walter Wallace and Howard Taylor, both African American, joined the department's tenured faculty. Taylor would become an early director of the program in African American Studies and serve in that role for 14 years.

With growing student and societal interest in the Vietnam War, race relations, and issues related to sex, gender, and the environment, the department expanded rapidly. The number of undergraduate concentrators rose from 20 in 1965 to about 150 in 1969 and 1970, making it the University's largest department at the time.

Marvin Bressler became chair in 1973 and led the department for two decades. By the mid-1980s the department's prestige was in decline and the most extraordinary of its younger faculty members, sociologist of religion Robert Wuthnow, began seriously considering outside offers. Bressler was able to retain him by securing a commitment from the administration to rebuild the department.

As a first step, Princeton appointed Paul Starr, a recipient of the Bancroft Prize for History and the Pulitzer Prize, who was widely regarded as the most capable young scholar in the profession. With Starr and Wuthnow on board, Bressler formed a committee to assess the department's goals and develop a plan for shaping its future. The committee recommended the appointment of Viviana Zelizer, who had made a name for herself with two major historical books, and Sara McLanahan, a pioneer in the demography of single parent families, poverty, and inequality.

Realizing it was too small to cover the entire discipline or compete with departments two or three times its size, the department organized around four clusters—culture, comparative and regional studies, demography, and social differentiation and inequality. A fifth cluster in economic sociology was added later. These clusters made it possible for a relatively small department to construct a distinctive identity and attract outstanding faculty.

Bressler's eye for young talent was matched by his unwavering commitment to diversity. In 1989 he hired Miguel Centeno, a graduate student at Yale who had already made a name for himself as one of the best young sociologists working on Latin America and one of the most dynamic teachers on the Yale campus. Bressler also began courting Marta Tienda, a distinguished demographer at the University of Chicago, knowing that her appointment would further raise the department's eminence. In 1997 the courtship came to fruition when Tienda accepted Princeton's offer.

In 1991 Paul DiMaggio, a sociologist of culture and organizations who had already shown unusual aptitude for working with graduate students, joined the department as Bressler was being succeeded as chair by Zelizer, the first woman to serve in that capacity. The faculty hired under Bressler achieved his goal of creating a strong nucleus of younger tenured faculty who would hire junior scholars capable of continuing the department's rise in the national rankings.

From 1992 to 1996 Zelizer led the department to new milestones; the department tenured junior faculty Michele Lamont, Frank Dobbin, Bruce Western, and Centeno, all of whom became renowned scholars. Centeno was also appointed the founding director of the Princeton Institute for International and Regional Studies. When Zelizer hired Patricia Fernandez-Kelly and Alejandro Portes she solidified the department's status as one of the most prominent and diverse of any sociology department in the country. In 1998 Portes launched the department's Center for Migration and Development, and in 2009 he became the founding director of the University's program in Latino Studies.

During this period, enrollment grew and applications to the graduate program multiplied. In 2003, with Thomas Espenshade as chair, the department hired urban ethnographer Mitchell Duneier and the demographer Douglas Massey *78. During their terms as chairs, Wuthnow and Centeno made additional crucial hires with Devah Pager, Matthew Salganik, Dalton Conley, and Yu Xie.

In 2016, when Duneier became chair, the department faced the imminent retirement of much of its senior faculty and no longer had a senior Black professor. (No senior Black scholar had been hired for three decades.) The department eliminated its traditional subfields and focused more on fields in which minority scholars were well represented. Duneier pursued collaborations with others, most notably the school of Public and International Affairs, who would share faculty with Sociology and thus allow it to grow.

The 2016 appointment of Fred Wherry *04, an African American, as well as Matthew Desmond and Kathryn Edin, became crucial to building new momentum. Over the next three years the department hired or tenured a group of young stars who could maintain the department's excellence and diversity for decades to come: Filiz Garip, Tod Hamilton, Jennifer Jennings, Shamus Khan, James Raymo, Patrick Sharkey, Janet Vertesi, and Sanyu Mojola, the department's first Black female professor. Mojola would become the youngest scholar ever to lead a population center when she succeeded Massey as OPR director in 2020.

With 28 professors appointed to fill 13.5 full time equivalent positions, the department was the largest in its history. It included two Pulitzer Prize winners, five members of the National Academy of Sciences, four recipients of the C. Wright Mills Award, and four recipients of the American Sociological Association's Distinguished Scholarly Publication Award.

Softball. In 1977, Cathy Azar '77 and her sister Leila '81 formed a club softball program at Princeton. The team was coached by Claire "C. B." Tomasiewicz '79, a star of the women's basketball team and a standout softball player in Connecticut summer leagues. The team's uniforms were matching t-shirts from the Princeton University Store, and they practiced at a nearby Little League field.

Princeton began playing an Ivy League schedule in 1980 and gained varsity status in 1982. After an inauspicious start, dropping a doubleheader to Temple in Philadelphia, the team rallied to finish 12–7 overall and place second in the Ivy League for coach Diane Schumacher, who pulled double duty by coaching the women's basketball team at the same time. Schumacher was a member of the 1978 and 1983 US softball teams that won silver and gold medals, respectively, at the Pan-Am games, and she played the sport professionally.

Schumacher positioned Princeton for consistent success. Cindy Cohen, who succeeded her in 1983, led the team for 18 seasons and remains the program's all-time winningest coach with a career record of 560-277-3. Her teams won the Ivy League title in each of her first seven seasons (1983–1989), a streak that has not been equaled in league play. She was named northeast region Coach of the Year four times.

Princeton players were named Ivy League Player of the Year nearly as regularly as their teams were winning championships. Second baseman Margaret Niemann '85, a religion major who played both basketball and softball before deciding to concentrate on softball, was the first to win the honor, in 1985. Pitcher Angela Tucci '88 won the award twice, in 1986 and 1988, bracketing teammates Suzanne Fiske '87 (1987) and Linda Smolka '89 (1989). From March 22-April 17, 1988, shortstop Chris Stuppi '90 hit safely in 27 consecutive games, an Ivy League record.

After a brief respite, the team won five more Ivy championships during the 1990s. In 1995, the Tigers became the first Ivy team to post 12 league victories (in a seven-team league). In 2008, with all eight Ivy schools participating, Princeton became the first team to win 18 league games in a season. The 1996 team set a then-NCAA Division I record by winning 37 consecutive games against both Ivy and non-Ivy opponents, before finally falling to Brown, 3–1, in the second game of a doubleheader. Both the 1995 and 1996 teams finished the year ranked No. 1 in the northeast region.

Four more Tigers earned Ivy League Player of the Year awards during the decade of the 90s: third baseman Leslie Silverman '92 (1992), pitcher Karen Drill '94 (1993), outfielder Stacy Thurber '96 (1994), and outfielder Mandy Pfeiffer '97 (1995, 1997).

Both the 1995 and 1996 teams advanced to the Women's College World Series, losing to University of Nevada, Las Vegas (UNLV) in 1995 and defeating Washington in 1996 before falling to Northeast Louisiana. Princeton remains the only Ivy softball program to play in the College World Series. In all, Princeton has advanced to the NCAA tournament 10 times and has played in the National Invitational Championship three times, in 1987, 1992, and 1993. The Tigers finished second in 1992, losing the final game to Northeast Louisiana, and third the following year.

As a player, pitcher Maureen Davies '97 won 83 games during her career (1984–87), an Ivy League record. She also holds the team's season and career records for games started, innings pitched, complete games, and shutouts. In 2001, she succeeded Cohen as coach and led Princeton to four more Ivy titles during her seven years at the helm (2002, 2003, 2005, 2006).

In 2001, Brianne Galicinao '02 became the first player in Ivy League history to be named the Ivy League Player of the Year and Pitcher of the Year in the same season. She repeated as Pitcher of the Year the following season. A few years later, Erin Snyder '06 was also named Ivy League Pitcher of the Year in back-to-back seasons (2005 and 2006). Outfielder Melissa Finley '05, who was named Ivy Player of the Year in 2003 with a .414 batting average, ended her career as Princeton's all-time leader in home runs, with 37, but also won 22 games as a pitcher.

Princeton again won the Ivy championship in 2008 for coach Trina Salcido, as Jamie Lettire '10 was named Ivy League Player of the Year and Kristen Schaus '08 Pitcher of the Year for a squad that went 18–2 in Ivy League play. The program's most recent Ivy titles have come in 2016 and 2017 for coach Lisa Van Ackeren, who was named Ivy Coach of the Year both times. Claire Klausner '17 was Ivy League Pitcher of the Year for the 2017 champions.

Through the 2018 season, Princeton had won nearly half of all Ivy League softball championships (19 of 41) and nearly three times as many as any other school. Princeton has also won more Ivy League Player of the Year and Pitcher of the Year awards than any of its rivals. One hundred and ten Princeton players have received first team All-Ivy honors; from 1981 to 2011, the team had at least one first-team All-Ivy selection in 29 of 30 seasons.

The team played its first three seasons on Broadmead Field, before moving to Class of 1895 Field in 1985. In the 2020s it will become one of the first teams to move to a new home field on the Lake Campus in that venue's early years of development. The field will be partially funded by a gift from Cynthia Paul '94, a member of the 1991 Ivy championship team, and her husband, Scott Levy, making it the first athletic field at Princeton to be named by an alumna.

SOTOMAYOR, SONIA '76 graduated from Princeton with highest honors in history; was elected to Phi Beta Kappa; won the Pyne Prize, which is awarded to a senior who has most clearly manifested excellence in scholarship, character, and leadership; received an honorary degree in 2001 for her "wisdom and judgment that cross cultural boundaries"; served four years as a Princeton trustee; and in 2014 received the Woodrow Wilson Award, the highest honor the University can bestow on undergraduate alumni. In 2009 she became the first Latina and third female justice to serve on the US Supreme Court.

Upon receiving the Wilson Award, Sotomayor credited the University with instilling in her and other alumni a commitment to service and suggested broadening Princeton's informal motto to encompass not just service to the nation, as Wilson had proposed, but also the "service of humanity, one person and one act at a time." She told how her mother had served as a nurse and caretaker to neighbors while working and raising a family. In 2016 the trustees added her words to Wilson's and engraved the University's new informal motto, "In the Nation's Service and the Service of Humanity" in a stone medallion on the front lawn of Nassau Hall.

Sotomayor grew up in a Bronx housing project as the daughter of Puerto Rican parents. When she arrived at Princeton in 1972, she felt like "a visitor landing in an alien country." She dedicated herself to academics and service, becoming a leader of the Latino Student organization and sitting on the governing board of the Third World Center (now the Carl A. Fields Center for Equality and Cultural Understanding). She organized Latino students to provide Spanish-speaking translation for patients at the Trenton Psychiatric Hospital, and she co-chaired a student group called Acción Puertorriqueña that in 1974 filed a complaint with the US Department of Health, Education, and Welfare charging the University with discrimination as reflected in the limited representation of Latino culture in the curriculum and the relative lack of Latino students, faculty, and administrators.

In a 2013 interview with the *Princeton Alumni Weekly*, Sotomayor said that two of the most fascinating courses she took during freshman year were an introductory economics course and a sociology course. She said, "learning about supply and demand, the theories of the marketplace—these were concepts that were completely alien to me, coming from a family that didn't even have a checking account."

Sotomayor wrote her thesis on "La Historia Ciclica de Puerto Rico: The Impact of the Life of Luis Muñoz Marín on the Political and Economic History of Puerto Rico, 1930–1975." In an interview in 2009, her thesis adviser, Peter Winn, described her thesis as "extremely ambitious ... clearly conceptualized, solidly researched, incisively analyzed, persuasively argued, and very well written, with pithy summaries of her arguments that she could still be proud of today—whether in a published article or a judicial opinion."

After Princeton, Sotomayor attended Yale Law School and was an editor of the Yale Law Journal. She began her legal career as an assistant district attorney in New York City, and then in 1984 joined the law firm of Pavia & Harcourt and became a partner with a focus on intellectual property, copyright, and international trade.

In 1992 she was appointed a US District Court judge for the southern district of New York, and in 1998 she was confirmed to the US Court of Appeals for the 2nd Circuit. Her decisions included an injunction that ended an impasse between baseball owners and players, halting an eight-month strike just in time to allow the 1995 season to begin (she is known to be a lifelong New York Yankees fan). Other decisions involved a reinterpretation of copyright law in the context of new media, and rulings in favor of public access to private information and in defense of religious freedom.

She played active roles on the boards of the Puerto Rican Legal Defense and Education Fund, the State of New York Mortgage Agency, and the New York City Campaign Finance Board, and she taught at Columbia and New York University law schools.

In 2009 Sotomayor was nominated by President Barack Obama to replace retiring justice David Souter on the US Supreme Court. Asked about the nomination, President Shirley Tilghman noted that Sotomayor had brought to her role as a trustee "the same kind of insight, discernment, wisdom, and good judgment that we are confident she will bring to the deliberations of the highest court in the land."

When Sotomayor was sworn in on August 8 she joined fellow Princetonian Samuel Alito Jr. '72, and a year later they were joined by Elena Kagan '81, the first time since 1842 that three sitting justices had attended Princeton, and the first time ever that three Princeton graduates had served on the court.

An approachable and charismatic public figure with a compelling life story, Sotomayor is frequently cited as a source of inspiration, especially by young women and people of color seeking to follow her example of overcoming disadvantage through education. In her 2014 Alumni Day talk, Sotomayor left the Alexander Hall stage to answer questions while mingling with the audience. She said her "personal key to happiness" was asking herself two questions each night: Have I helped someone today and what have I learned today? She said she had started volunteering at a local charity in Washington, DC, to help needy members of the community. "It is so important to squeeze out time from our overwhelming professional commitments to remember we need to serve people, not just institutions," she said.

Sotomayor returned to campus for both *She Roars* conferences for Princeton alumnae, in 2011 and 2018, and for the *Adelante Tigres! Celebrating Latino Alumni at Princeton University* conference in 2017. At the 2011 conference she described her judicial philosophy as follows: "I am very precedent bound and practical, fact bound . . . but there's something about judging that requires a certain type of vision, not seeing beyond the case or policy, but to see the entire relationship of those cases to the law. . . . you're not deciding that individual case in the abstract."

In 2013, Sotomayor published a memoir, *My Beloved World*, that includes reflections on her undergraduate years at Princeton. That year she administered the oath of office to Joe Biden as he began his second term as vice president of the United States. Eight years later, during Biden's inauguration as president, she administered the oath to his vice president Kamala Harris, the first woman, first Black American, and first South Asian American to hold the country's second-highest office.

In 2019 the University announced the establishment of the Sonia Sotomayor 1976 Scholarship Fund to support Princeton students from first-generation backgrounds who have demonstrated a commitment to service.

SPANISH AND PORTUGUESE, THE DEPARTMENT OF. Students and faculty in the department of Spanish and Portuguese explore the importance and influence of the Spanish, Latin American, and Luso-Brazilian histories, cultures, and languages in the Americas, Europe, Africa, and Asia, from the Middle Ages and the Renaissance to the globalized present.

While today's department was not formally established until 2001, Princeton students were studying Spanish, as well as Italian, French, and German, as early as the 1830s, although not for academic credit. In the late 1880s, President James McCosh made the study of these "modern" languages a regular, credited part of the curriculum, and in 1904 President Woodrow Wilson organized the University into academic departments, including a department of Modern Languages.

For the next 25 years, most of the Spanish instructors were American. By the 1930s the University had begun to appoint scholars from European countries as tenured professors and to attract others as visiting professors, including Salvador de Madariaga, the Spanish diplomat, historian, and pacifist noted for having been nominated for both the Nobel Prize in Literature and the Nobel Peace Prize.

With the post–World War II advent of new pedagogy in the teaching of languages, the number of students and faculty interested in language learning grew. At the same time, more courses were developed to integrate the study of both language and literature within a broader context of history, politics, and cultural studies. As course offerings expanded throughout the 1950s, the University realized that a single department for all modern languages had become unsustainable. In 1958 two new departments Germanic Languages and Literatures and Romance Languages and Literatures, replaced the department of Modern Languages and Literatures.

Through the 1960s the new Romance Languages and Literatures department made a number of exceptional faculty appointments, creating a roster of scholars who brought distinction to the department for decades. Two in the Spanish language program were James Irby and the Argentine writer and critic Sylvia Molloy.

Irby created and taught the first Latin American literature courses ever to be given at Princeton on both the undergraduate and graduate levels and was the first translator into English of Jorge Luis Borges. He was also the first to introduce Portuguese and Brazilian studies into the curriculum. In 1973, Molloy was the first woman at Princeton to be promoted to tenure from the assistant professor ranks. She was a pioneer in exploring LGBT culture issues, and in tribute to her work the Sexualities Section of the Latin American Studies Association, the largest scholarly association of Latin Americanists, created the annual Sylvia Molloy award, which recognizes the best peer-reviewed article in the humanities.

By the end of the twentieth century it was time for the Romance languages to be divided into two departments, as had been done with Modern Languages 40 years earlier. A department of Spanish and Portuguese and a department of French and Italian were created in 2001.

The department of Spanish and Portuguese contributes to the academic community at a time when more than half a billion people across five continents speak Spanish or Portuguese as their first language. At the same time, with more than 38 million Spanish speakers in the United States, the Hispanic legacy is embedded in myriad aspects of American politics, arts, and culture. Interest in Latin American studies, both nationally and internationally, has seen ever-increasing growth.

In this environment, the department has a dual role: to introduce the rich cultural worlds of Spanish- and Portuguese-speaking countries to the campus community, and to send out into those worlds students with a high degree of linguistic proficiency in those languages, whether they choose to join international corporations, government agencies in foreign countries, or professional fields, such as medicine, that work with underserved populations. Its mission is to help Princeton students flourish as global citizens, facing the challenges posed by an increasingly cosmopolitan and multilingual professional world.

Students are able to study not only the Spanish and Portuguese languages, but also literatures, visual arts, music, and urban cultures, as well as the complex political and social histories of the Hispanic and Luso-Brazilian worlds. Students become familiar with renowned writers, influential artists, contemporary musicians, and international filmmakers. One of the most renowned writers, the Peruvian novelist Mario Vargas Llosa, first came to teach at Princeton in 1992. He was teaching at Princeton in 2010 when he was awarded the Nobel Prize in Literature, and he returned three years later to teach again. Firestone Library houses his literary papers.

At the undergraduate level, the department encourages interdisciplinary work. To experience cultural and linguistic immersion, students have opportunities to study abroad with summer programs in Argentina, Portugal, and Spain. At the graduate level, the department offers innovative and comprehensive training in Iberian, Latin American, and Luso-Brazilian literatures and cultures, as well as in other languages, combining rigorous training in these fields with an emphasis on interdisciplinary work. It seeks graduate students working in all time periods, within and across traditional fields, and at interstices of literary history, aesthetics, cultural studies, history, philosophy, and new media.

The department's associated faculty members include representatives from the departments of History and Anthropology and the school of Public and International Affairs, among others. Its own faculty members are active in other departments and programs across campus, including Latin American Studies, International and Regional Studies, Brazil LAB (Luso-Afro-Brazilian studies), Latino Studies, Global Health, Media and Modernity, Architecture, Comparative Literature, Renaissance Studies, History, Art and Archaeology, the art museum, and the High Meadows Environmental Institute.

SPELMAN HALLS, completed in 1973, provided the first on-campus apartment living for undergraduates. They were named for Laura Spelman Rockefeller, who, with her husband, John D. Rockefeller Sr., founded Spelman College in Atlanta, Georgia, the first American college for Black women. A former public schoolteacher, Laura Spelman Rockefeller maintained a life-long interest in education, particularly for women. Her grandson, Laurance S. Rockefeller '32, gave the University $4 million in 1969 to help institute undergraduate coeducation; most of that gift was used to construct Spelman Halls to help meet the housing needs of an expanding and increasingly diverse student body.

The eight-building complex, which was designed in a modernist style by I. M. Pei and Partners, contains 58 apartments for 220 students. Each unit includes a living and dining area, outside balcony, kitchen, bath, and, typically, four study-bedrooms. Six of the apartments, with single large bedrooms, were designed to accommodate married students.

Set in a naturally wooded landscape on the western edge of the main campus, the halls are arranged as linked triangles along a diagonal axis extending south from Pyne Hall and Dillon Gymnasium in such a way as to provide vistas between Spelman and its neighbors. An innovative use of pre-cast concrete slabs, glass, and light enabled the architects to integrate the eight buildings into an architecturally varied campus, according to one observer, "in an elegant, respectful, and restrained manner." The exterior concrete walls are white, but the inside walls of each entry are painted a bright color and identified by a large numeral in that same color.

In 2002, the concrete sculpture *Head of a Woman* was moved from a location near the entrance to the art museum to a site just south of Spelman; the sculpture had been fashioned on campus by a Norwegian artist in 1971 from a 12-inch maquette that Pablo Picasso had completed in 1962.

SPITZER, LYMAN, JR. *38, a towering figure in the fields of theoretical astrophysics and plasma physics, joined the Princeton faculty in 1947 as chair of the department of Astrophysical Sciences and director of the Princeton Observatory, positions he held until 1979. In 1967 he was named to a five-year term as chair of the University Research Board, which oversees policies related to sponsored research at Princeton. He retired in 1982 but continued to work in his Peyton Hall office until the day of his death in 1997, analyzing data from the Hubble Space Telescope, an instrument he conceived in 1946. He died just 10 days before his closest colleague and long-time friend, Martin Schwarzschild, who also joined the faculty in 1947.

Astrophysics professor and former provost Jeremiah Ostriker described Spitzer as one of "the two giants of twentieth century theoretical astrophysics," and said he "ranks with Joseph Henry and a very few others among the major contributors to world science over Princeton's 250 years. He was also an exemplary citizen of the University and the nation, an outstanding teacher, an avid mountain climber, and one of the finest and most decent individuals I have ever known."

In 1965, as a mountain climber, Spitzer, along with his former student and colleague Donald Morton *59, became the first to climb Mount Thor on Baffin Island, Canada. Spitzer was also an accomplished skier, and while skiing in Aspen, Colorado, in 1951 he had an insight that led to the creation later that year of what was initially called Project Matterhorn S, but later became the Princeton Plasma Physics Laboratory (PPPL): a federally funded research facility on Princeton's Forrestal Campus which continues today its decades-long effort to harness the thermonuclear fusion process that powers the sun to create an unlimited, safe, clean, and affordable source of energy on earth. Spitzer obtained funding to develop a figure eight-shaped device to confine hot charged plasma gas inside magnetic fields that was known as a "stellarator." (This concept was later superseded by a different design, a "tokamak," but in recent years the stellarator design has attracted renewed interest.)

Spitzer remained at PPPL until the late 1960s; today, the principal administrative building at the lab is named for him.

Spitzer's contributions included seminal and fundamental advances in the interstellar medium stellar dynamics, and space astronomy, in addition to plasma physics. He was known for clear exposition and an ability to identify critical questions for research. In his introduction to *Dreams, Stars and Electrons: Selected Writings of Lyman Spitzer Jr.*, published by the Princeton University Press in 1997, Ostriker said that, for Spitzer, "complexities unravel and the fundamental simplicities become apparent."

During World War II, Spitzer worked on underwater sound and its relation to undersea warfare, research which ultimately led to the development of sonar technology.

In 1946, more than a decade before the launch of the first artificial satellite, he proposed the development of large space-based telescopes which could view the cosmos without interference from Earth's atmosphere. His paper, "Astronomical Advantages of an Extra-Terrestrial Observatory," described the advantages in detail. Later, under his direction, Princeton scientists developed the 32-inch Copernicus ultraviolet satellite which made important discoveries in the 10 years following its launch in 1972. Spitzer later steered the development of the Hubble Space Telescope, which was hailed as the most significant advance in astronomy since Galileo's telescope when it was launched in 1990.

In 2003, the National Aeronautics and Space Administration (NASA) launched an infrared space telescope, the Space Infrared Telescope Facility, on a mission to orbit the sun. This observatory became the first to spot light directly from planets outside the solar system. NASA sponsored a contest to name the telescope, and after receiving more than 7,000 entries, named it for Spitzer. The Spitzer Space Telescope far exceeded all initial expectations before it was retired in January 2020.

In theoretical physics, Spitzer is credited with founding the discipline of "interstellar matter," which concerns the gas and dust between stars from which new stars form. His numerous contributions were codified in a 1968 monograph, "Diffuse Matter in Space," which became the standard text in the field. Spitzer also made major advances in stellar dynamics, with his contributions to this field summarized in a 1987 volume, "Dynamical Evolution of Globular Clusters."

From 1960 to 1962, Spitzer served as president of the American Astronomical Society, and in 1979 he received the National Medal of Science. His various international honors culminated with the 1985 Crafoord Prize of the Royal Swedish Academy, the equivalent of the Nobel Prize for his field. He received a Princeton honorary degree in 1984, and the James Madison Medal, Princeton's highest award for graduate alumni, in 1989. His papers are in Firestone Library.

SPRINT (LIGHTWEIGHT) FOOTBALL. In March 1928, an editorial in the *Daily Princetonian* under the headline "Football For All" promoted the idea of fielding a 150-pound football team, in addition to the varsity and freshman squads, to give playing opportunities for students who weren't among the "especially qualified few" who represented the University on Saturday afternoons. A lightweight team on which all players had to tip the scales under a prescribed maximum weight, the *Prince* continued, "would be real proof of football's attractions solely as a sport."

Backed by a student petition, the idea eventually gained support from the athletics department and Princeton fielded its first 150-pound team in 1931, beginning a program that would continue for nearly 85 years. The University discontinued the sport in 2016 after a string of winless seasons, citing safety concerns and the difficulty of fielding a competitive team.

The Princeton 150-pound team's early years showed promise on a campus well-acquainted with winning football. From 1933 to 1935, under the guidance of three different coaches, the Tigers posted a combined record of 13–3. In 1934 Princeton became one of seven founding members of the Eastern Intercollegiate 150-Pound Football League. Coach Harry Mahnken took over the program in 1936, and from 1937 to 1942, he guided Princeton to six consecutive league championships, including five undefeated seasons. After playing an abbreviated schedule in 1942, 150-pound football was suspended for the remainder of World War II.

Winning seasons were harder to come by in the postwar years. Navy and Army emerged as the league's dominant teams, but Princeton remained a consistent contender under the guidance of coach Dick Vaughan. His 1953 team was captained by Donald Rumsfeld '54, the future US Secretary of Defense. The following year, Princeton won the league championship, completing a 6–0 season with a win at Navy in the final game.

As the sport raised its weight limit from 150 to 172 pounds, its name shifted to "lightweight" football in 1967, and later to "sprint" football in 1998. Vaughan left Princeton in 1968 after compiling a program-best 56 wins in 22 seasons. He was succeeded by Dan White '65, who fielded a string of winning teams in the mid-1970s. Quarterback Lawrence Pupa '76 set the team record for passing touchdowns in a season with 12 in 1973, and tied that mark as a senior in 1975 when he helped the Tigers defeat both Army and Navy to share the league title with Cornell.

The lightweights' final championship came in 1989 when the 4-2-1 Tigers shared the title with Army. That would also be Princeton's last winning season. Longtime coach Tom Murray left the program in 1997, after 20 seasons. From 1999 through the team's final season in the fall of 2015, the Tigers won just one league game (the 1999 opener against Cornell) and one nonleague game (a 19–7 victory at Virginia Military Institute in 2005).

During Princeton's winless string, the underdog Tigers became a source of fascination. *Sports Illustrated*'s Phil Taylor wrote a 2012 column about the team titled "Losing Isn't Everything." The week after it was published, Princeton pushed Post University to overtime but lost by a field goal, 32–29.

As the losses mounted and the team struggled to maintain a healthy roster, Princeton was forced to forfeit games in 2011, 2013, and 2014. A university committee and a group of advisors reviewed the program and concluded that it created a high risk of injury and could not be competitive without taking positions for recruited athletes from other varsity teams and transferring them to sprint football. It noted that Princeton was by then one of only three Ivy League schools offering the program, and that sprint football was the only Princeton varsity team that did not play in either the Ivy League or the National Collegiate Athletic Association (NCAA).

In April 2016, the University announced that the team would be discontinued because, in the words of President Christopher Eisgruber, "we do not believe we can sustain the program at a level that is safe for our students and meets the high standards we achieve in the rest of our varsity athletics program."

SQUASH. Princeton has made a lasting mark in men's and women's collegiate squash, winning team or individual national championships in every decade since the 1930s. Notable alumni include Yasser El Halaby '06, collegiate squash's first four-time men's national individual champion, and Demer Holleran '89, who won three national championships in college and a record nine US women's open titles.

Men's Squash

The men's varsity program began in 1929, playing on courts that were constructed in a repurposed power plant near the University Gymnasium. In 1933 Princeton produced both the individual national champion and the runner-up, William G. Foulke II '34 and Sheldon Stephens '34. Nine years later, in 1942, the Tigers won their first national team championship under the direction of coach John Conroy. After the 1942 season, the sport went on hiatus for the remainder of World War II, but Conroy would return to lead the Tigers to four more national titles, compiling a 184–69 record in 30 seasons at Princeton.

Conroy, who also coached tennis, joked that his first challenge was explaining to students that squash was something other than a "vegetable that they don't like." Many of his varsity players were introduced to the game as undergraduates, but his most accomplished star, Stephen Vehslage '61, picked up the sport much earlier, at age 6.

Vehslage, the first three-time national individual champion, was praised by the *New York Times* for his "low drives down the side walls and clever corner shots." A versatile athlete who also earned All-Ivy honors as a soccer player, he excelled in spite of a medical condition that occasionally caused him to pass out when bumped in the head or shoulders—a not insignificant risk on the soccer field or within the tight quarters of a squash court. *Sports Illustrated* chronicled the problem in 1968, when Vehslage was the reigning national amateur champion. At the time, he estimated that he had been knocked out 25 times in his collegiate and amateur squash career, usually returning to action about five minutes after passing out.

After Conroy left the squash program in 1969, the winning tradition he had established continued on the new courts of Jadwin Gymnasium. From 1973–74 to 1978–79, the Tiger men lost just two dual meets in six seasons and won five national titles under three different coaches (Bill Summers, David Benjamin, and Norm Peck). Peter Thompson would guide the Tigers to another national title in 1981, his lone season as coach. The following year, Bob Callahan '77, the captain of the 1977 national championship squad, returned to campus and began a coaching career that would surpass Conroy's in both longevity and success.

Callahan's teams won national titles in 1982 and 1993, when American colleges were still playing "hardball" squash. After colleges made the switch to the international "softball" game, Princeton hosted the boys' world junior championships in 1999, the first world softball squash tournament in the United States. The event has been credited for accelerating the internationalization of the American collegiate game.

Callahan's first major overseas recruit, Egyptian Yasser El Halaby '06, was arguably the most dominant player in collegiate squash history. He won the national individual title in each of his four seasons at Princeton—a feat unmatched before or since—and helped his team to two Ivy League titles. El Halaby also "set a new level of sportsmanship for the sport," Callahan told the *New York Times*, by using his exceptional quickness to get out of the way and give opponents a clear path to the ball.

The arrival of international players raised the level of competition in intercollegiate squash and aided the rise of a new powerhouse program, Trinity (Conn.) College. Harvard, Yale, or Princeton had won every national title in the three decades preceding Trinity's first championship in 1999.

The Trinity Bantams proceeded to win 13 consecutive titles, but that streak was brought to a dramatic close at Jadwin in 2012. Callahan's Tigers trailed the Bantams midway through the championship meet, four matches to two, with Trinity needing just one more win to extend its title run. But Princeton stormed back to even the tally, and Kelly Shannon '12, the No. 4 player, won his match in straight sets to score the decisive fifth point. It was the eighth time Callahan's team had faced Trinity in a national final, and the first time it had come out on top.

Weeks after his team won the national championship, Callahan was diagnosed with a malignant brain tumor. He coached one more season, his 32nd, before stepping down with a career record of 316–68, three national championships, and 11 Ivy titles. Coach Sean Wilkinson succeeded Callahan, who died in 2015.

In addition to Princeton's success in team competition, the men's program has produced 11 national individual champions: Foulke (1933), Stanley Pearson '41 (1939), Charles Brinton '42 (1941, 1942), Roger Campbell '55 (1954, 1955), Vehslage (1959, 1960, 1961), John Nimick '81 (1981), Jeff Stanley '89 (1987, 1988), Peter Yik '00 (1999, 2000), David Yik '03 (2001) El Halaby (2003, 2004, 2005, 2006), and Todd Harrity '13 (2011).

Women's Squash

One of six varsity sports for women introduced in the 1971–72 academic year, Princeton women's squash was an immediate national-title contender under the guidance of Betty Howe Constable, a five-time US women's champion in the 1950s. Constable would become "the queen of women's intercollegiate squash," according to James Zug's 2003 book *Squash: A History of the Game*. Her family's name graces the women's collegiate team championship tournament, the Howe Cup, which Princeton has won 17 times, including 12 during Constable's 20 years at the helm. Her Tigers lost just 16 dual matches in those two decades and posted undefeated seasons 12 times.

Constable's early teams had stars who had grown up playing squash, like Wendy Zaharko '75, a three-time national individual champion. But they also included women like Sally Fields '73, who picked up the sport in a physical-education class, developed her skills under Constable, and finished as runner-up to Zaharko in the 1972 national tournament.

Near the end of Constable's career, Demer Holleran '89 matched Zaharko's feat of three national individual championships, winning the title in her freshman, sophomore, and senior years. Holleran also won the United States Squash Racquets Association women's national championship in her senior year, a feat she would repeat eight times in the decade after graduation—more national championships than any woman in the sport's history.

Emily Goodfellow '76, a team captain and three-sport star as an undergraduate, succeeded Constable as the Princeton coach for three seasons, winning 20 of the 25 dual matches in that span before handing off the program to Gail Ramsay.

Ramsay, a four-time women's national individual champion at Penn State, guided Princeton's return to national-championship form, winning five national titles between 1998 and 2009, including three undefeated seasons. She also mentored Princeton's third three-time national individual champion, Julia Beaver '01. In a *Princeton Alumni Weekly* feature written in Beaver's senior year, Ramsay described her as "modest but quietly confident. You'd never imagine how accomplished she is."

Only Harvard has won more national team championships than Princeton. In addition to the Tigers' team success, five women have won the national individual title: Zaharko (1972, 1974, 1975), Nancy Gengler '80 (1976), Holleran (1986, 1987, 1989), Katherine Johnson '97 (1997), and Beaver (1999, 2000, 2001).

STANHOPE HALL, the University's third oldest building, was erected in 1803. It originally housed the college library, study halls, and the two literary societies, Whig and Clio, and was called the Library. Later it contained the "geological cabinet" and lecture rooms and was known as Geological Hall. Still later it contained the offices of the treasurer, the superintendent of grounds and buildings, the registrar, other administrative offices, and, for a time, the meeting room of the faculty; it was called the college offices and then the university offices.

In 1915 the trustees named the building in honor of Samuel Stanhope Smith, who was president when it was built. In later years Stanhope housed the University's communications and public safety offices, and then it was thoroughly renovated to become, in 2007, the home of first the center, and then the department, of African American Studies. In the early 2020s it was renovated again for administrative uses after African American Studies moved into Morrison Hall.

Another building, an exact duplicate of the present Stanhope, was also built in 1803 on the other side of Nassau Hall facing the "Library." In its basement were the college kitchen and refectory; on its upper floors were rooms for the college's "philosophical apparatus" and for classes in mathematics and natural philosophy. Known at first as the Refectory, it was later called Philosophical Hall. It was here that Joseph Henry conducted his experiments in electromagnetism and telegraphy. Philosophical Hall was razed in 1873 to make room for Chancellor Green library.

STEVENSON HALL was formed in 1968 as a nonselective University-managed dining facility at the initiative of students in the classes of 1968 and 1969 who did not wish to join any of the traditional eating clubs, all of which participated in a selective admission process known as "bicker." Stevenson opened with approximately 130 members in adjacent buildings at 91 and 83 Prospect Avenue that previously housed two eating clubs: Court Club and Key and Seal Club.

Religion professor Malcolm Diamond served as Stevenson's first faculty "master" (1969–71). He was succeeded by politics professor Gerald Garvey (1971–74), and then by chemistry professor Maitland Jones and his wife, Susan Hockaday, who served from 1974 to 1977. Four decades later, in 2018, their son Maitland Jones '87, who had first-hand experience with Stevenson as a young boy and with residential colleges as an undergraduate, was one of the architects selected to design the two new residential colleges that were then being planned along the southern edge of Poe Field.

In Stevenson Hall's early years, its members earned a reputation for a strong commitment to political activism. In the spring of 1970, the suggestion of a fall break to permit students to participate in campaigning just prior to election day originated at a Stevenson Hall meeting, and Stevenson became the initial focal point for the newly-established Movement for a New Congress that sought to encourage and prepare students nationwide to mobilize on behalf of candidates who advocated changes in American policy, especially with regard to the war in Vietnam.

Stevenson Hall sought to provide its members with good food, a sense of community, and an appealing alternative to the traditional eating clubs, even as a number of the clubs chose to discontinue bicker and admit students on a sign-in basis. Like Wilson College, which opened in the fall of 1968, Stevenson offered opportunities to engage with faculty fellows, as well as with graduate students, especially from the nearby engineering and science departments.

In the early 1970s sophomores were permitted to become full members and a kosher dining facility was installed at 83 Prospect, with even observant first-year students eligible to eat there. The kosher facility was the first of its kind in the Ivy League, and it remained at Stevenson until the Center for Jewish Life opened in 1993. Stevenson membership grew to more than 300 students, with more than 100 dining in the kosher facility and the rest in the dining hall in 91 Prospect.

In the late 1990s the International Center and the Women*s Center moved into Stevenson, only to move again into Frist Campus Center when it opened in 2000. The opening of Frist, with its multiple opportunities for dining and socializing, led to the closing down of Stevenson, whose membership in its last years had dropped to about 35 students, although some 200 students were still eating in the 91 Prospect dining hall each night. The Stevenson buildings were converted to academic and administrative uses, with 91 Prospect housing the office of the dean for research, and 83 Prospect housing the Mamdouha S. Bobst Center for Peace and Justice and the James Madison Program in American Ideals and Institutions.

Stevenson Hall was named for Adlai Stevenson 1922, who served as governor of Illinois, ran twice (in 1952 and 1956) against Dwight Eisenhower as the Democratic candidate for president, and in 1961 was appointed US ambassador to the United Nations by President John F. Kennedy '39.

Stevenson's maternal great-grandfather, Jesse Fell, a founder of the Republican Party, was the first to propose Abraham Lincoln for the presidency. His paternal grandfather, Adlai Stevenson, was vice president during Grover Cleveland's second term. His father, Lewis Stevenson, was once secretary of state for Illinois.

As a boy of 12, Stevenson accompanied his father when he called on Governor Woodrow Wilson 1879 at his summer home in Sea Girt, New Jersey, to discuss the presidential campaign of 1912. Stevenson later said it was that visit that "decided me on going to Princeton, right then, and there." At Princeton he studied history and literature; took a course in public speaking; became managing editor of the *Daily Princetonian;* and was elected one of the 15 members of the student government. In the senior class vote at his graduation in 1922, he received eight votes for "biggest politician," but 28 for "*thinks* he is . . ."

As a young lawyer, he served as president of the Chicago Council on Foreign Affairs. In the early 1930s he spent a year in Washington with the New Deal, and during World War II he was special assistant first to the secretary of the navy and later to the secretary of state. He was an active participant in the formulation of the charter of the United Nations in San Francisco in 1945, chief of the United States delegation at the meeting of the UN Preparatory Commission in London, and a member of the United States delegation at the first three sessions of the General Assembly.

Stevenson won the governorship of Illinois over a Republican incumbent in 1948 by the largest majority ever received in Illinois up to that time. His achievements during his four-year term as governor were impressive, and he attracted attention for messages that were remarkable for both substance and style. He courageously vetoed a bill, overwhelmingly passed by both houses, which would have set up elaborate procedures for detecting subversives and require loyalty oaths of teachers and state officials: "Basically, the effect of this legislation," he wrote, "will be less the detection of subversives and more the intimidation of honest citizens."

In a lighter vein, he explained his refusal to approve a bill that sought to protect birds by restricting the movement of cats: "If we attempt to resolve [this problem] by legislation, who knows but what we may be called upon to take sides as well in the age-old problems of dog versus cat, bird versus bird, even bird versus worm. In my opinion, the state of Illinois and its local governing bodies already have enough to do without trying to control feline delinquency."

As a presidential candidate Stevenson elevated American political discourse, beginning with his acceptance speech in 1952: "Let's talk sense to the American people. Let's tell them the truth, that there are no gains without pains, that we are now on the eve of great decisions, not easy decisions . . . but a long patient, costly struggle which alone can assure triumph over the great enemies of man—war, poverty and tyranny—and the assaults upon human dignity which are the most grievous consequences of each."

In 1952, when it was considered politically imprudent to tangle with Senator Joseph McCarthy, Republican of Wisconsin, Stevenson publicly denounced McCarthyism in the senator's own state. In 1956 he urged a treaty to ban nuclear testing even though public opinion polls supported the view of some of his associates that he would lose votes thereby. "There are worse things than losing an election," he said. "The worst thing is to lose one's convictions and not tell the people the truth."

Stevenson served as ambassador to the United Nations from 1961 until his death four and a half years later and captured worldwide attention for his confrontations with the ambassador from the Soviet Union during the Cuban Missile Crisis in 1962. Early in his tenure he visited the representatives of all 116 governments then represented in the UN. He was especially appreciated by representatives of the developing nations. "He had that quality," said Barbara Ward, the British economist, "for which the Africans . . . have found a special term . . . 'Nommo,' . . . the Bantu word for the gift of making life rather larger and more vivid for everyone else."

He was admired for his eloquence, moderation, and reason. Speaking to the United Nations Economic and Social Council in Geneva in 1965, Stevenson said:

> We travel together, passengers on a little space ship, dependent on its vulnerable reserves of air and soil; all committed for our safety to its security and peace; preserved from annihilation only by the care, the work, and I will say, the love we give our fragile craft. We cannot maintain it half fortunate, half miserable, half confident, half despairing, half slave—to the ancient enemies of man—half free in a liberation of resources undreamed of until this day. No craft, no crew can travel with such vast contradictions. On their resolution depends the survival of us all.

Five days later, while visiting England on his return from Geneva, Stevenson died of a heart attack on a London sidewalk. "To the public dialogue of his time he brought intelligence, civility and grace," the *New York Times* said in tribute, "We who have been his contemporaries have been companions of greatness."

Stevenson returned to campus for reunions and on other occasions, most memorably to address the Class of 1954 at its banquet in the spring of its senior year. The function of a university, he told them, is "the search for truth and its communication to succeeding generations. Only as that function is performed steadfastly, conscientiously, and without interference, does the university realize its underlying purpose."

In closing, he delivered the following frequently quoted reminder:

> Your days are short here; this is the last of your springs. And now, in the serenity and quiet of this lovely place, touch the depths of truth, feel the hem of Heaven. You will go away with old, good friends. And don't forget when you leave why you came.

Princeton awarded Stevenson an honorary degree in 1954 and the highest honor it can confer on undergraduate alumni, the Woodrow Wilson Award, in 1963. He is memorialized on campus by a bronze bust in Robertson Hall and a stained-glass window in the chapel, both of which were given by his Class of 1922. Except for materials related to his governorship of Illinois, all his other papers are housed in Firestone Library.

STOCKTON, BETSEY, was born into slavery around 1798 in Princeton and given by Robert Stockton to his daughter Elizabeth, who was married to the Reverend Ashbel Green 1783, then a Presbyterian minister in Philadelphia. When Green became president of the College in 1812, Betsey Stockton moved with him into his Maclean House home. In 1813 Green sold three years of her time to a niece in Woodbury, New Jersey. In 1817, a year after her return, Green freed her, although she remained in his household for five more years working for wages. In 1822 she traveled to Hawaii as a missionary, where she established a school for native Hawaiian children. In 1828 she relocated to Philadelphia and established a school for African American children.

In 1833 she returned to Princeton where she helped found, and for almost 30 years taught in, the sole Princeton public school for African American children. In 1840 she played a leading role in founding what is now Witherspoon Street Presbyterian Church and led its Sunday school. She is commemorated in a stained-glass window in the church that was presented by her former students.

An essay prepared in connection with the Princeton and Slavery Project reported that when she died in 1865, "her funeral brought together a considerable crowd of both races" and that then-President John Maclean Jr. conducted the service.

In 2018 the University named a garden between Firestone Library and Nassau Street in her honor. The plaque at the entrance to the garden includes her photo and says the following:

> This garden celebrates the life and legacy of Betsey Stockton (c. 1798–1865). As a young girl she was enslaved on campus in the household of college President Ashbel Green. She gained her freedom in 1817. In 1822 she traveled as a missionary to Hawaii, where she established a school for native Hawaiian children. In 1833 she returned to Princeton, and in 1837 she helped establish the sole Princeton public school for African American children. She taught there for almost 30 years. In 1840 she helped found the Witherspoon Street Presbyterian Church, where she led the Sunday school. With courage and vision, Betsey Stockton nurtured many lives; it is fitting that she be remembered in a place of beauty and reflection for both town and gown.

STOCKTON, RICHARD 1748, a member of the first graduating class and the first alumnus elected a trustee, was born in Princeton to a family that was among the community's earliest settlers and slaveholders. His grandfather came to the colonies in 1696 and a few years later acquired from William Penn a large tract of land that embraced what later became the borough of Princeton. His father inherited the portion of the property that included the dwelling later named "Morven," where Richard was born.

Richard attended future Princeton president Samuel Finley's academy in Nottingham, Maryland, and graduated from the College in 1748 when it was still located in Newark. While all five of his classmates went into the ministry, Stockton read law in Newark and was admitted to the bar in 1754. He opened an office in Princeton and acquired a reputation for being the most eloquent and persuasive advocate in New Jersey.

In 1757, when he was 27, Stockton was elected a trustee of the College. Ten years later, while on an extended visit in Great Britain, he was asked to go to Scotland to extend to John Witherspoon the trustees' invitation to succeed the recently deceased Finley as president. Stockton was "successful in removing all the objections which originated in Witherspoon's mind," but not those in his wife's. Eventually, with the help of Benjamin Rush 1760, then a medical student at the University of Edinburgh, Mrs. Witherspoon gave her consent and her husband accepted the call.

After his return, Stockton took an increasingly active role in the political life of the province of New Jersey. In 1768 he was made a member of its council, and in 1774 a judge of its supreme court. Elected a delegate to the Continental Congress on June 22, 1776, he took his seat in Philadelphia in time to hear the closing debate on the Declaration of Independence and to sign it along with Witherspoon and Rush. Two months later, in a vote by the state legislature, he was narrowly defeated for the governorship of New Jersey by William Livingston.

The following November, as British troops approached Princeton, Stockton evacuated his family to the home of a friend in Monmouth County. While there, he was betrayed to the British. Taken to New York and put in the notorious Provost Jail, he suffered brutal treatment until January 3, 1777.

Upon Stockton's return to Princeton, it became known (according to a letter from President Witherspoon to his son, David) that during his imprisonment he had signed General Howe's Declaration, which required an oath of allegiance to the king—an act Stockton revoked later that year by signing an oath of allegiance prescribed by the New Jersey legislature. He died four years later, in 1781.

Stockton's wife, Annis Boudinot, was the daughter of a merchant and silversmith who was for a time postmaster of Princeton; she became one of America's first published female poets. As the British army approached Princeton in December 1776, she famously hid the papers of the student Whig Society while burying her family silver at Morven; she was later posthumously elected Whig's first female member.

The Stockton's eldest daughter Julia married Benjamin Rush. Their family home, Morven, served as New Jersey's first governor's mansion from 1945 to 1981; a national historic landmark, it then became the site of a public garden and museum. New Jersey's Richard Stockton State College was dedicated in Stockton's honor in 1971.

STUDENT GOVERNMENT did not begin at Princeton until the twentieth century, but its essential spirit was evident as early as the eighteenth century when the literary and debating societies Whig and Clio were governed entirely by undergraduates. In the nineteenth century athletic, literary, and musical activities were all student-governed, and the end of the century saw the arrival of another form of undergraduate self-government with the adoption of a student-controlled honor system for examinations.

Princeton's first formal agency of student government, the Senior Council, was founded in June 1905 at the initiative of the Class of 1906. It was welcomed by President Woodrow Wilson as a means of calling leaders of undergraduate opinion into consultation with trustees and faculty "upon matters of moment in which it was not only proper but desirable that authority should wait upon opinion."

The Senior Council had its strengths, but its weakness was a lack of continuity. Since it was composed only of seniors, its membership each year was entirely new, which militated against both developing institutional memory and taking the longer view. One year, after the Council failed to produce acceptable regulations for the safe use of automobiles by undergraduates, the trustees issued an edict forbidding student use after July 1, 1927. The 1927 Senior Council thereupon resigned, and although the reason given was that they had not been properly consulted, the underlying difficulty was the Council's reluctance to make decisions "which would not affect their own liberty but would affect only their successors."

The following fall, an Undergraduate Council representing all four classes was formed to replace the Senior Council. Among the products of its 40-year existence were a marriage course for seniors, chartered flights to Europe, an extension of Firestone Library hours, an increase in carrel space for seniors, and the end of required chapel attendance. The Council also agitated successfully for the repeal of the edict prohibiting student use of automobiles, the improvement of club elections, the development of alternative social facilities, and the extension of curfew hours for women visitors in dormitories.

In 1967 the Undergraduate Council gave way to a larger Undergraduate Assembly designed to provide wider student participation through the campus-wide election of representatives from dormitory areas and the scheduling of frequent meetings open to any undergraduate who wanted to attend. According to one observer, the Assembly was "more constructively vocal" than the old Council, but the operation of the larger organization proved unwieldy, attendance fell off, and in time, the Assembly, like its predecessor, was being criticized for its failure to represent student opinion effectively.

Beginning in the fall of 1969 the Assembly also had to figure out how to work with a new governance structure, the Council of the Princeton University Community (CPUC), which had 12 undergraduate members and seven graduate student members, held open meetings at regular intervals throughout the academic year, included undergraduates and graduate students on all of its committees, and was designed to provide venues for student engagement in discussions about a broad range of University policies, practices, and priorities.

In 1975 the Assembly was superseded by a body known as the Undergraduate Student Government (USG). The new organization vested significant responsibility in committees on academic matters and undergraduate life, and in a projects board which served as the main source of funding for student groups, activities, and events on campus. The USG included a "caucus" composed of student government officers, committee chairs, class presidents, class delegates, and the undergraduate members of the CPUC.

In 1995 a new constitution was adopted that reorganized the USG around a student senate, an executive committee, class governments, core committees, and the projects board. The core committees addressed matters related to academics, undergraduate life, campus and community affairs, and social events.

The USG describes its mission as supporting "the undergraduate experience by collaborating with students, administrators, faculty, and other campus life stakeholders to address student concerns." It collaborates with the administration "to revise and propose policies that improve campus life, provide high-quality services to students, and organize innovative events to foster a sense of community."

The senate's 24 voting members include the USG president and vice president; the 10 other undergraduates who, with the president and vice president, serve on the CPUC; the USG treasurer; five core committee chairs (the chairs of academics, campus and community affairs, and undergraduate student life, along with the social chair and the sustainability chair); and six class senators (two each from the sophomore, junior, and senior classes). The nonvoting members include the USG executive secretary, chief elections manager, historian, parliamentarian, website manager, TigerApps chair, director of communications, and chairs for the projects board, a student groups recognition committee, movies, alumni affairs, diversity and equity, the USG's mental health initiative, and its Princeton perspective project.

The student groups recognition committee works with the office of the dean of undergraduate students to oversee the creation of new student groups and help them achieve the approval they need to attain official recognition and apply for projects board funding.

Each undergraduate class has its own elected government that focuses on class-specific programs and seeks to establish class identity, unity, and spirit. The first-year class council is elected in the fall; the other three classes have a president, vice president, treasurer, secretary, and social chair who are all elected the previous spring to serve during the following year. The senior class government helps plan many commencement-related activities.

In 1989 Princeton's first graduate student government was created through a referendum among all graduate students; its mission is to express graduate student perspectives and concerns and to sponsor or support social and other events geared toward graduate students. In October 2000, the graduate student body ratified a new Graduate Student Government (GSG) constitution and bylaws, later amended in 2014 and 2019.

The GSG officers include a president, vice president, vice president for internal affairs, secretary, treasurer, communications director, special events officer, academic affairs chair, facilities and transportation chair, health and life chair, and social chair. The GSG assembly includes representatives from every graduate academic department and program; the graduate student housing units (the graduate college, Lakeside apartments, Lawrence apartments, and off-campus housing); and delegates representing such interest groups as the Black graduate caucus, the joint degree program, the Latino graduate students association, the African graduate student network, and "tigers with cubs."

STUDENT PUBLICATIONS. When Harold Shapiro *64 was nearing the end of his first year as Princeton's president he was asked how his experience differed from his previous presidency at the University of Michigan. He said there were two main differences. One was that Princetonians expect their president to be involved in everything that happens on campus. The other was that Princetonians loved to write, which they did often, at great length, and frequently to him.

This passion for writing serves students well in their junior papers and senior theses, but it also has found expression for close to two centuries in an array of student publications.

In the 1830s, the Class of 1835 briefly published the *Chameleon*, which was followed by the *Princeton Whig*, the *Tattler*, the *Rattler*, and the *Princeton Standard*. Princeton's longest-running undergraduate publication is the *Nassau Lit*, which dates to 1842 as the country's second oldest college literary magazine (Yale's began in 1836). [The history of another early student publication, the *Princetonian*, can be found in a separate entry on that topic.]

Nassau Lit

When the *Nassau Lit* first appeared, it was called the *Nassau Monthly*. In 1847 it changed its name to the *Nassau Literary Magazine*, and in 1930 it became known more simply as the *Nassau Lit*. (Its official name now is the *Nassau Literary Review*.) Over time it has been published bi-monthly and quarterly, but it now comes out semi-annually in print and online. It publishes fiction, poetry, essays, and art, and hosts events with other arts groups on campus.

In the beginning, its first editor said, its objective was "to afford a medium through which young writers might publish incognito their first lucubrations to the world." Since manuscripts were submitted under assumed names or initials, they were not returned, and rejections were often publicly announced in "Notices to Correspondents"—sometimes scornfully. As the editors said about one poem, "The 'Parting,' by D.L.D., is between the writer and common sense."

During its first few years, the *Lit* was largely the work of three students: Theodore Cuyler 1841, George Boker 1842, and Charles Leland 1845. Cuyler wrote "A Chapter on College Writing" in which he gave students advice that remains apt today: "to produce the highest effect," a writer "must use short, simple, pointed words . . . Nor let him be content to write a composition once, but rewrite, and rewrite it again, until he is well assured that there is not a word in it which is not *the very word*, in *the very place*." Leland was the *Lit's* most prolific contributor, but one article that did not appear was a ballad about Satan's admission to Princeton, his involvement in student escapades, and his suspension by the faculty. His allusions to members of the faculty were less complimentary than his references to the devil, which probably explained why the *Lit* chose not to publish the piece.

In its March 1859 issue, the *Lit* published for the first time the words written by a freshman, Harlan Page Peck 1862, that would become the University's anthem, "Old Nassau."

In the early 1890s an informal literary club called the Coffee House provided a focal point for *Lit* writers such as Jesse Lynch Williams 1892 (later the founding editor of the *Princeton Alumni Weekly*), Booth Tarkington 1893, and McCready Sykes 1894. Tarkington and Williams won Pulitzer Prizes and Sykes won the affection of his Princeton contemporaries with his accounts of Princeton football exploits in *Poe's Run and Other Poems* (1904). Contributors between 1912 and 1917 included Edmund Wilson 1916 and F. Scott Fitzgerald 1917.

In February 1942 the *Lit* published a 196-page centennial issue, and in 1976 it published another retrospective featuring submissions from past notables like Tarkington and Fitzgerald, as well as from more recent contributors, including poets William Meredith '40, Galway Kinnell '48, and W. S. Merwin '48, John McPhee '53, and artist Frank Stella '58.

Nassau Herald/Bric-a-Brac

The *Nassau Herald* first appeared in 1864 as a four-page newspaper. It took the form of a paperback book in 1869 and added a hard cover in 1892. At first its contents were limited to the texts of senior orations and lists of participants in student activities, but gradually it added vital statistics; facts about the habits and opinions of the seniors, as gathered in an annual class poll; and class histories. The Class of 1915 was the first to publish photographs of its members and biographies that enumerated their successes at college and what they intended to do next.

The *Bric-a-Brac* first appeared in 1876 as a yearbook documenting student activities, clubs, teams, and other aspects of undergraduate life. It too began as a paperback, but within a decade of its founding switched to hard cover. In 1899 it began to include photographs, typically consisting of a group photo for each club and game photos for athletic teams.

After 2013 the two publications merged to become a *Nassau Herald* that combines senior portraits with the reflections and reminiscences of a yearbook.

Tiger Magazine

Founded as the *Princeton Tiger*, the nation's third-oldest humor magazine, *Tiger Magazine* first appeared in March 1882 but ceased publication that December after only nine issues. In 1890 it was reborn, struggling to survive against an unsympathetic faculty and advertisers who were "far from warm-hearted." Booth Tarkington said it was easy to get students to accept membership on the *Tiger* board, but harder to get them to write, draw, or edit.

In the 1920s the *Tiger* prospered; circulation reached 10,000; average issues numbered 60 pages; and a fund was started to finance a building like the *Harvard Lampoon's* (a hope never realized). In 1924 the magazine's board felt flush enough to contribute $1,000 to the new chapel.

In 1932 the *Tiger* celebrated its golden jubilee by issuing "A Compendium of Half a Century of Princeton Wit and Humor, if any, in Prose, Picture, and Poesy." In May 1942, several months after Pearl Harbor, the *Tiger* suspended operations for the duration of the war (publication resumed in 1947). In 1952 the columns of managing editor John McPhee '53 foreshadowed the style that would later distinguish his writing for the *New Yorker*.

Tiger Magazine today describes itself as a quarterly satire magazine which is "funny, marginally literate, free, and distributed to every undergraduate room, common area, eating club, and elite social circle in Princeton, even the equestrian team (when they get off their high horses)." In 2011 it began hosting an annual national intercollegiate humor conference.

Business Today

The magazine *Business Today* was founded in 1968 by Steve Forbes '70, Michael Mims '71, and Jonathan Perel '71. (Forbes, the namesake of Forbes College, later served as editor-in-chief of Forbes Magazine and twice sought the Republican nomination for president of the United States; his father, Malcolm Forbes '41, founded a publication called the *Nassau Sovereign* when he was an undergraduate.) *Business Today* became the most widely distributed undergraduate publication in the country; today it publishes twice a year and is circulated nationwide to more than 200,000 students and business executives.

The magazine's parent entity, also called Business Today, is a nonprofit foundation that, in addition to the magazine, publishes an online journal and podcasts, sponsors seminars and visits to corporate headquarters, and hosts two annual conferences for students and business leaders: an international conference on business issues and a conference focused on issues related to design. Wendy Kopp '89 organized the 1988 international conference on improving American public education and credited it with helping to develop the concepts she incorporated in founding Teach For America.

Nassau Weekly

The *Nassau Weekly* was founded in 1979 by Press Club members Robert Faggen '82, Marc Fisher '80, and David Remnick '81, who became editor of the *New Yorker* in 1998. Published every Sunday and distributed free on campus, it contains news, reviews, essays, humor, original art, fiction, and poetry, and a popular "overheard-on-campus" column called Verbatim. The Princeton Broadcasting Service, the tax-exempt entity that operates the student radio station WPRB, acquired the *Nassau Weekly* in 2009.

Princeton Tory

Yoram Hazony '86 founded the *Princeton Tory*, a journal of conservative political thought delivered free to all Princeton students and faculty, in 1984. It aims to provide its readers with investigative journalism and analysis of events on the Princeton campus from a right-of-center perspective.

Princeton Progressive

The *Princeton Progressive* (the *Prog*) is Princeton's left-of-center political publication. In the early 1980s a group of students formed the *Princeton Progressive Review*, and in 2001 a competing publication, the *Idealistic Nation*, was formed. In 2005 they merged to form the *Princeton Progressive Nation*, which ceased publication in 2011. After two years of refinancing and re-energizing, the first issue of its successor, the *Princeton Progressive*, was published in 2014.

Princeton's history is replete with many other publications, some short-lived, but others less so. One of the longer lasting publications, *The Princeton Engineer*, began in 1941 and lasted into the 1970s, while the *Nassau Sovereign*, founded by Malcolm Forbes, was published from 1938 to 1950.

Today many publications exist on campus—some in print, others only online—and they encompass a wide variety of interests and perspectives. *Stripe Magazine*, for example, was Princeton's first student-run fashion publication, and there are other publications that focus on fashion, as well as on food, travel, health, and other lifestyle issues.

Other publications focus on academic, political, and societal issues. *The Stripes*, for example, is one of several publications that provide a platform for traditionally underrepresented groups to discuss matters pertaining to culture and identity on Princeton's campus and beyond.

SUPREME COURT OF THE UNITED STATES. Since its establishment in 1789, the court has numbered among its justices 11 Princeton graduates. With the presidents who appointed them, they are:

GEORGE WASHINGTON

William Paterson 1763: 1793–1806
Oliver Ellsworth 1766: 1796–1800—Princeton's only chief justice

THOMAS JEFFERSON

William Johnson Jr. 1790: 1804–1834
(Henry) Brockholst Livingston 1774: 1806–1823

JAMES MONROE

Smith Thompson 1788: 1823–1843

ANDREW JACKSON

James Moore Wayne 1808: 1835–1867

WILLIAM HOWARD TAFT

Mahlon Pitney 1879: 1912–1922

DWIGHT D. EISENHOWER

John Marshall Harlan 1920: 1955–1971

GEORGE W. BUSH

Samuel Alito '72: 2006–

BARACK OBAMA

Sonia Sotomayor '76: 2009–
Elena Kagan '81: 2010–

Sonia Sotomayor was the first Hispanic/Latina justice appointed to the court. When Elena Kagan joined the court in 2010 it marked the first time since 1842 that three sitting justices had attended Princeton, although one of the earlier three, Peter V. Daniel 1805 (an appointee of Martin Van Buren) had attended Princeton for only one year and had not graduated.

SUSTAINABILITY. In 2008 the University published a campus plan that devoted an entire chapter to sustainability; it cited the United Nations in defining sustainability as "meeting the needs of the present without compromising the ability of future generations to meet their own needs," and it noted that sustainability had "long been a priority at Princeton, from research and education to university planning and operations."

That year the University also issued a comprehensive sustainability plan that set ambitious goals in the areas of greenhouse gas emission reduction, natural resource conservation, and research, education, and civic engagement. The plan included a commitment to reduce carbon dioxide emissions to 1990 levels by 2020 without the purchase of off-campus "offsets," even as the University was planning to add as much as two million square feet of new space over the next 10 years.

Development of the sustainability plan began in 2002 when President Shirley Tilghman established an environmental oversight committee (later the Princeton Sustainability Committee) to identify means to improve the University's environmental footprint. In 2006 the University created an office of sustainability and hired Shana Weber as its founding director.

To reduce emissions, the plan called for improving the efficiency of the central co-generation plant (which had been in place since 1996), installing ground-source heat pump (geo-exchange) systems, investing in energy efficiency measures in buildings, and creating a photovoltaic array (27 acres of solar panels that meet nearly six percent of the campus's energy needs) on University lands south of Lake Carnegie.* The plan also sought to decrease the number of cars commuting to campus and reduce emissions related to campus vehicles.

Princeton had already adopted a policy of relying entirely on recycled paper for all basic uses and an aggressive sustainable food purchasing policy; new goals included reduced water usage, increased recycling rates, expanded use of green cleaning products, decreased use of disposable paper products, and increased purchasing of sustainably produced food items. The plan called for using the campus as a laboratory to test and develop sustainability solutions and it sought to encourage increased engagement by faculty and students in teaching, research, and the development of new ideas and strategies.

In 2017 the University published a new campus plan which outlined a sustainability framework to make further progress in several areas. The plan set a new target of reaching net zero campus greenhouse emissions by 2046 and reaffirmed the University's "overarching goal of developing even more of a 'sustainability ethos' on campus."

In 2019, the University adopted an action plan to achieve the 2046 target of net zero greenhouse gas emissions by reducing direct emissions from on-site energy production and fleet fuel uses and indirect emissions from purchased electricity. This was part of a broader set of initiatives that built on "the University's significant progress during the past 10 years in reducing greenhouse gas emissions, designing efficient buildings, encouraging alternatives to single-occupancy vehicles, and adopting award-winning practices in sustainable dining, construction, and other University operations."

By this point the University was close to achieving its goal of reducing carbon dioxide emissions to 1990 levels without the purchase of offsets; had achieved energy cost savings even as it opened new buildings across campus; had reduced single-occupancy cars driving to campus, with 44 percent more commuters using sustainable transportation options such as buses, trains, bikes, and carpools; had achieved an eight percent decline in overall campus waste volume and a 23 percent recycling rate across campus; and had increased emphasis on sustainable and local purchasing and products, with 44 percent of food purchased by campus dining coming from local sources, up from 27 percent in 2008.

The new plan proposed further steps in the areas of energy, waste and water reduction, alternative modes of transportation, healthy water and habitats, responsible development, and sustainable purchasing. It continued to emphasize the role of the campus as laboratory and classroom, with increasingly active engagement by faculty and students in helping to achieve the goals of the plan, and it recognized the leverage University purchasing and contracting

---

* In 2020 the University announced it was installing eight new solar projects, mostly above parking decks and fields, that would increase its photovoltaic generating capacity to 19 percent of current electric energy use.

can apply to encourage greener supply chains and manufacturing.

"The plan is ambitious," Weber said, "with an intent to inform three decades of institutional decision-making and individual-scale action. At the same time, the plan strives to be honest about clear progress as well as intractable challenges as we grapple and tinker with solutions."

SWIMMING AND DIVING. Princeton's men's swimming program started in 1906 with a victory over Yale in its only meet. The following year, their first full season, the Tigers won the championship of the newly founded Intercollegiate Swimming Association, composed of City College of New York, Columbia, Pennsylvania, Yale, and Princeton. Princeton's women's team achieved varsity status in 1971–72 as one of Princeton first six women's varsity teams, and in its first year had a perfect 8–0 dual meet record.

Men's Swimming and Diving

Princeton's 1924 men's team, coached by Frank Sullivan, beat Yale twice in close contests while going undefeated in dual meet competition. The first of those victories broke the Elis' seven-year string of 44 straight intercollegiate victories. Both meets were decided in the final event by Princeton's 200-yard relay team, whose anchor, John Hawkins 1926, won the national collegiate championship in the 440-yard freestyle the following year.

When Sullivan suddenly resigned in 1928, Princeton accepted Yale's offer to lend its assistant coach, Howard Stepp, for the rest of the season—and then kept him as swimming coach for 25 years and as registrar from 1947 until his retirement in 1969. Stepp's teams won 162 of their 228 meets for an overall percentage of .711. His 1938 team was the first to beat Yale, the perennial Eastern champions, since 1924.

In 1936, shortly after the Intercollegiate Swimming Association went out of existence, the Eastern Intercollegiate Swimming League (EISL) was formed, composed of the future Ivy League schools plus Army, Navy, and other eastern colleges.

Stepp's swimmers included seven national collegiate champions: Edwin Moles Jr. '31, Richard Hough '39, and Robert Brawner '52 in the 200-yard breaststroke; Albert Vande Weghe '40 and James Shand '48 in the 100-yard backstroke, Edward Sherer '32 in the 50-yard freestyle; Brawner in the 100-yard butterfly; Vande Weghe, Hough, and Hendrik Van Oss '39 in the 300-yard medley relay. In 1939 Hough was named the NCAA's outstanding swimmer of the year. Another of Stepp's swimmers, Howard Canoune '37, followed his mentor as varsity coach for five years from 1953 to 1958.

Robert Clotworthy, 1956 Olympic gold medalist in the three-meter dive, was coach from 1958 to 1970. "A bubbly little man who treats swimming with . . . an enthusiastic reverence" (in the words of Frank Deford '61), Clotworthy guided his 1962 swimmers to Princeton's first Eastern Seaboard team championship. He trained three national champions: G. Gardiner Green '63 (100-yard breaststroke), Jed Graef '64 (200-yard backstroke), and Ross Wales '69 (100-yard butterfly).

Clotworthy's successor, William Farley, led the team to a number of dramatic finishes during the 1970s. His 1972 team went undefeated. In 1973 Princeton trounced North Carolina to win its first Eastern Seaboard title in 11 years. Farley's 1974 team won a second straight Eastern Seaboard championship with a breathtaking 419 to 411 victory over Harvard, accomplished in the final event when Princeton's 400-yard freestyle relay anchor, Mal Howard '75, nipped his Crimson opponent by less than half a second. Entering the last day of the 1975 Eastern Seaboard championships, Princeton trailed North Carolina by 13 points, but a sweep by Joe Loughran '77, Curtis Hayden '75, and Rob Maass '78 in the 1650-yard freestyle, and winning scores for diver Bill Heinz '75 on the three-meter board, helped Princeton win its third successive title. From 1972 to 1977, Princeton won six consecutive Eastern Seaboard championships.

When Farley left for Michigan in 1979, Princeton hired Rob Orr, an assistant at the highly successful University of Southern California swimming program. Over the next four decades, Orr's teams won 330 dual meets—third most in NCAA Division I history—and 23 Ivy League titles, while producing 38 individual All-Americans and 24 All-America relay teams. Princeton finished either first or second in the EISL for 24 consecutive seasons, from 1982–83 until 2016–17. In four NCAA championships between 1986 and 1990, Princeton finished in the top 20, including 13th-place showings in 1987, 1988, and 1990. The 1989 and 1990 teams won back-to-back NCAA championships in the 200 medley relay, setting an American record in 1990.

Several of Orr's teams won in thrilling fashion. In 2011, Princeton lost to Harvard in their annual double dual meet but held on to defeat the Crimson in the Ivy League championships by a razor-thin score of 1,400–1,394.5. Five years later, in 2016, Princeton trailed for most of the Ivy meet but closed the gap throughout the final day to edge Harvard for the title by just 21.5 points. In all, Princeton's men have won 26 EISL and Ivy League championships. The team has placed among the NCAA's top 25 teams 33 times.

Ten Princeton male swimmers have competed in the Olympics and four have won medals: Al Vande Weghe (silver) in the 100-meter backstroke in 1936, Jed Graef (gold) in the 200-meter backstroke in 1964, Ross Wales (bronze) in the 100-meter butterfly in 1968, and Nelson Diebel '95, who won two gold medals in 1992, in the 100-meter breaststroke (setting a new world record) and as a member of the 4×100 medley relay, which also set a world record.

Women's Swimming and Diving

Women's swimming competed for the first time as a varsity sport in 1971–72. But even before the women's swimming and diving team achieved varsity status, Jane Fremon '75 and Cece Herron '74 entered the 1971 EISL women's championships and together scored enough points to help Princeton to a fifth-place finish. Fremon set new Eastern records in the 100-yard butterfly and the 100- and 200-yard freestyle and Herron finished second among the divers. From 1972 through 1975, Princeton women placed third, second, and then first twice in succession in the EISL.

At the 1973 finals of the Association for Intercollegiate Athletics for Women (the governing body for women's athletics until 1982), Princeton's team of six women finished third behind Arizona State and Florida as Cathy Corcione '74 set national records in the 100-yard freestyle and 100-yard butterfly, while joining Carol Brown '75, Barbara Franks '76, and Fremon to set a national record in the 200-yard freestyle relay. Herron was both the 1-meter and 3-meter diving champion at the 1973 EISL meet. At the 1974 meet, Corcione set another national record—in the 100-yard individual medley—and EISL records in four other events.

Led by Captain Liz Osborne '76, who took first in the 50-, 100-, and 200-yard breaststroke, Princeton placed second at the EISL in 1976. The following year, paced by Mary Sykes '79 and Beth Mauer '80, the Princeton team decisively outpointed Yale, 657 to 520, to win the first official women's Ivy championship.

Princeton women won four consecutive Ivy championships from 1979 to 1982. At the 1982 AIAW meet (in the last year of the AIAW's existence), the 800-yard free relay team of Diana Caskey '85, Ann Heusner '83, Liz Richardson '84, and Betsy Lind '85 won a national championship.

Coach Susan Teeter, who took over in 1984, led the team for 33 seasons, during which they achieved some of their greatest success. Teeter's teams won 17 Ivy League championships. They also won 47 straight meets between 1998 and 2004, a University record in any sport, and ran off another 42-meet winning streak between 2007 and 2012.

Alicia Aemisegger '10 can lay claim to being Princeton's greatest female swimmer. She was an All-American honoree 13 times, won 12 Ivy League individual championships (in as many attempts), and was a member of numerous championship relay teams. By the time she graduated, Aemisegger held nine Princeton swimming records and four Ivy League championship records. During her freshman and sophomore seasons, she also commuted to her family's home outside Philadelphia for extra workouts in preparation for the 2008 Olympic trials. She qualified in six events in the Olympic trials and reached the finals of the 400 individual medley, finishing seventh. In 2009, she was voted Princeton's female athlete of the decade.

Through 2018, the Princeton women had won 22 Ivy League championships, more than any other school.

Diving has been part of Princeton's swimming program since its beginning—even before that, in fact. In the late nineteenth century, members of the gymnastics team engaged in "fancy diving" for campus exhibitions. Princeton's greatest diving coach was Greg Gunn, who spent 30 years with the program (1987–2016), coached 36 Ivy League team champions (19 men, 17 women), 30 Ivy League individual champions, and nine All-Americans: Beth Bridgewater '87, Andrea Suess '88, Lyle Suess '91, Kenny Iams '91, Erin Lutz '01, Danielle Stramandi '01, Kent DeMond '07, Michelle DeMond '07, and Kathrine Giarra '11.

Princeton's swimming and diving teams first competed in the Brokaw Tank, which adjoined University Gymnasium. It was named for Frederick Brokaw 1892, a catcher on the baseball team, who drowned trying to save a young girl. Though Brokaw Tank survived the fire that destroyed University Gym in 1944, it was demolished two years later to make way for Dillon Gymnasium. Teams competed in Dillon Pool until the opening of DeNunzio Pool, named for Ralph DeNunzio '53, in 1990.

Taylor, Hugh Stott, came to Princeton in 1914. Hired as a chemistry instructor, he rose quickly to full professor at age 32 and became the first David B. Jones Professor in 1927. He served as chair of the department of Chemistry for 25 years and was dean of the graduate school from 1945 until his retirement in 1958.

While chair of the Chemistry department from 1926 to 1951, he was influential in securing the original Frick Chemical Laboratory. The graduate school trebled its enrollment while he was dean, added nine PhD programs (in five engineering departments and in Architecture, Music, Religion, and Sociology), and strengthened its ties with former students through the creation of the Association of Princeton Graduate Alumni in 1949.

His achievements brought him many honors. In 1953 he was knighted twice, first by Pope Pius XII in the Order of St. Gregory the Great, and five days later by Queen Elizabeth in the Order of the British Empire. After his retirement, he served as president of the Woodrow Wilson National Fellowship Foundation and as editor-in-chief of *American Scientist*, the periodical publication of the Society of Sigma Xi, of which he had been president.

His role in strengthening Princeton's graduate school is commemorated through Taylor Court, one of the roadways in the Lakeside graduate student apartments.

Teacher Preparation traces its origins to 1965 when President Robert Goheen appointed a faculty committee to develop a program based on the belief that a broad undergraduate curriculum with concentration in one subject, combined with experience as a student teacher under competent supervision, would prepare a student to teach that subject at the secondary school level.

The Teacher Preparation program was approved by the faculty in 1967 and began that year under the direction of Henry Callard, former headmaster of the Gilman School in Baltimore. He was joined in 1968 by Henry Drewry, former chair of social studies at Princeton High School, who became director for 20 years following Callard's retirement. Drewry was one of Princeton's first Black administrators, and he taught its first courses in Black history and culture.

In 1969 the program was approved by the New Jersey Department of Education, and for the first time a graduating Princeton senior received a permanent certificate for secondary school teaching. For many years Princeton students had entered the teaching profession, but mostly in independent schools; lack of certification was an impediment for those who wished to become public school teachers. This program made certification possible upon graduation.

Participants in the program can become certified in art, English, mathematics, music, biology, earth science, chemistry, physics, the physical sciences, social studies, world languages, and psychology. The program regularly partners with 14 area schools for student teaching and observing.

By the program's 50th anniversary in 2019, more than 1,100 students had received its certificate and many had gone on to careers in teaching, administration, and other positions related to education. The program is nationally accredited; its graduates are eligible to teach at the middle and high school levels in New Jersey and may transfer the New Jersey certificate to other states through reciprocity agreements.

Teacher Preparation also manages a program that allows exceptional high school students to enroll in University courses at no cost.

Tennis. Princeton produced a string of men's national champions in tennis at the turn of the twentieth century, and the women's team had a similarly strong start in the early years of coeducation, winning every dual match in its first five seasons.

Men's Tennis

Princeton's participation in intercollegiate tennis began in 1882, though the first official team match would come nearly two decades later, in 1901. The Tigers regularly sent representatives to the Intercollegiate Lawn Tennis Association tournament, and three of the early entrants won the national individual title: Samuel Thomson 1898 (1897), Raymond Little 1901 (1900), and Fred Alexander 1902 (1901).

George Church 1915 was the first Princetonian to win the intercollegiate title twice (1912 and 1914). He also won a national doubles title, with Wynn Mace 1915 (1912). Four other Princeton pairs won doubles championships in the early years of collegiate tennis: Alexander and Little (1900); Dean Mathey 1912 and Burnham Dell 1912 (1910); Mathey and Charles Butler 1912 (1911); and John Van Ryn 1928 and Ken Appel 1929 (1927).

Van Ryn was Princeton's most accomplished player after graduation, teaming with two different partners, Wilmer Allison and George Lott, to win six

Grand Slam doubles championships (including three at Wimbledon). He also reached the singles quarterfinals of Wimbledon and the French Open in 1931. Van Ryn and Allison were inducted as a team in the Tennis Hall of Fame in 1963.

Mercer Beasley, who became coach in 1933, led Princeton to undefeated seasons in 1933 and 1934, an Eastern championship in 1933, and the Tigers' first Eastern Intercollegiate Tennis Association (EITA) titles in 1941 and 1942. John McDiarmid, an instructor in the Politics department, coached the team for one season, 1938, in which the Tigers won 10 matches and the Eastern title.

John Conroy took over as head coach in 1946, beginning a 26-year tenure that included eight undefeated teams and 14 EITA championships. From 1960 to 1965, his teams compiled a program-record 54 consecutive victories. Bob Goeltz '70 was twice named All-American in the Conroy years, in 1969 and 1970. In the latter, the Princeton team elected to forfeit its final three matches in observance of the student strike that followed the American invasion of Cambodia. Princeton lost its chance at the EITA title as a result.

Bill Summers coached the Tigers to an undefeated season and an EITA title in 1974. The following year David Benjamin arrived as Princeton's new coach, and the Tigers won or shared the EITA championship in six consecutive seasons from 1975 through 1980.

Two All-American players and future pros, Jay Lapidus '81 and Leif Shiras '81, headlined those talented squads. Lapidus and Shiras reached the quarterfinals of the 1978 NCAA doubles championship, where they lost to Stanford's John McEnroe and Bill Maze. Lapidus would go on to a successful coaching career at Duke. Both Lapidus and Shiras were inducted into the Collegiate Tennis Hall of Fame in 2010.

In 1983, Ted Farnsworth '84 won the Rolex National Intercollegiate indoor singles championship, making him the first Princeton player since Church to win a national collegiate singles title. Farnsworth, a Navy lieutenant and fighter pilot in the years after his graduation, died in an accident on a training flight in 1993. The men's team's fall invitational was renamed in his honor.

Benjamin's Tigers won a seventh EITA title in 1988, and in 1996 Princeton had its first EITA Player of the Year, Reed Cordish '96. Benjamin left the program after the 2000 season but continued to work in tennis as executive director of the Intercollegiate Tennis Association (ITA).

Glenn Michibata (2001–12) and Billy Pate (2012–present) succeeded Benjamin. The most accomplished player in recent years, Matija Pecotic '13, played for both of them. Pecotic, raised in Malta, won the Ivy League Player of the Year award three times, reached the top 10 of the national singles rankings, and was an All-American in his senior year.

Women's Tennis

Women's tennis was one of Princeton's first women's teams. It was organized in the fall of 1970 and played its first match in 1971. The Tigers won their first 39 dual matches, playing against other teams in the northeast and the handful of Ivies that had varsity teams. Their first loss came on the road at the University of North Carolina to open its season in 1976. After a second loss at Duke, Princeton won its remaining matches that year.

Singles star Marjory Gengler '73 never lost a set while playing for Princeton and was the first woman to be awarded the white sweater with black "P," traditionally given to captains of Ivy championship teams. A May 1973 *Alumni Weekly* cover dubbed her "Princeton's best athlete." By senior year, she had competed at Wimbledon and the US Open and stood at the top of the Eastern singles and doubles rankings (with sister Louise '75 as her partner); another sister, Nancy '80, would star for the team as well.

Princeton won the year-end Middle States tournament in 10 consecutive years (1971–80), and in 1977 freshman Susan Replogle '80 became the program's first All-American. The early success came despite persistent turnover in the coaching staff. Of the first four coaches—Eve Kraft, Ann Marie Hicks, Carla Gaiser, and Maree McCallum—none stayed more than three seasons.

That changed after the 1979 season with the hiring of Louise Gengler as head coach. She would spend 25 years at the helm, winning seven Ivy titles and 259 team matches. Her 1982 team had a program-best eighth-place finish at the Association for Intercollegiate Athletics for Women (AIWA) nationals; entering as an 11-seed, Princeton beat both six-seed Mississippi and five-seed Southern Methodist.

Notable players in Gengler's tenure included Joy Cummings '84, an All-American in 1984 and a four-time All-Ivy singles player; Diana Gardner '90, Princeton's only other four-time All-Ivy singles player; and Kavitha Krishnamurthy '03, the Ivy Player of the Year as a freshman in 2000 and the ITA Senior of the Year in 2003.

Gengler's two immediate successors each led Princeton to an Ivy title: Kathy Sell in 2009 and Megan Bradley in 2010. The 2010 team, led by Ivy Player of the Year Hilary Bartlett '12, was the first to win 20 matches in a season.

Coach Laura Granville came to Princeton in the 2012–13 school year, and her 2014 team, paced by Ivy Player of the Year Lindsay Graff '15, had a perfect 7–0 mark in league play. That year the Tigers won the program's first-round NCAA tournament match against Arizona State, and in 2019 it again won a first round match, this time against Northwestern. Granville's teams won five Ivy titles in her first seven years at Princeton. She was the second coach to win more than 100 matches with the Tigers.

THEATRE INTIME, an on-campus theater company run entirely by students, provides undergraduates with experience in every aspect of running a theater: selecting, producing, directing, and casting plays; performing in them; creating sets and costumes; fundraising, advertising, and selling tickets; and preparing each successive student generation to take over management responsibility. Intime, pronounced "AHN-teem," comes from the French word for "intimate," an apt description for the company's 200-seat theater.

Theatre Intime was founded by three juniors on the third floor of Witherspoon Hall in 1919. Its first production, in February 1920, was in a dormitory room; the curtain was a blanket hung over a string. The intrepid audience of four watched a cast of five perform a parody of *Nijinski and the Ballet Ruse*. In 1921 the theater moved into Hamilton Murray Hall, then a chapel being used for religious services by the Philadelphian Society.

Intime has long taken a special interest in lesser-known or less-frequently-performed works and student-written plays, the latter exemplified in recent years by its festival of student playwrights, held each spring. Originally run like a private club with admittance by invitation only, Intime quickly developed into a more open company, and as it did its focus expanded to encompass a more conventional repertoire. In 1932 the Academy Award-winning actress Mary Pickford and representatives from several Hollywood studios came to campus to see its production of *Nerissa*, with senior Jimmy Stewart '32 appearing in the supporting role of McNulty.

When a fire in June 1933 gutted the interior of Murray Theatre, it was remodeled into roughly its current configuration. Its 1936 production of *The Great God Brown* earned a telegram of congratulations from its playwright, Eugene O'Neill 1910. For three years during World War II, Murray was given over to the Navy for use as a lecture hall, but after the war a group of former Triangle and Intime members reestablished the organization, reaching new dramatic heights in 1948 with a memorable production of *Richard II*.

Over the years several plays had their world or American premiers at Intime, beginning with John Milton's *Samson Agonistes* in 1921, followed by Tolstoy's *Tsar Fyodor Ivanovitch* (1929), Jules Romains' *Give the Earth a Little Longer* (1942), Jean Cocteau's *The Typewriter* (1949), John O'Hara's *The Searching Sun* (1952), and Lawrence Durrell's *An Irish Faustus* (1969).

In the late 1960s and early 1970s, with growing student interest in the arts and the advent of coeducation, Intime increased membership, expanded the number of productions each year, and further diversified its repertoire to include experimental and avant-garde performances—endeavoring always to find a sustainable financial balance between box office appeal and artistic experimentation. (The story of Intime's first half century inspired a senior thesis by John Kendall '74 entitled *I Also Swept the Floor: Theatre Intime from 1920 to 1974*.)

In 2000 the University and the Friends of Theatre Intime provided funding for an extensive renovation of Murray Theatre, substantially improving its lighting and sound systems, seating, lobby, and backstage and basement areas. In addition to presenting its ambitious regular seasons and playwright festivals, Intime provides facilities for other campus performance and dance groups.

In the late 1920s, students from Theatre Intime formed a summer company called University Players, which performed in the early 1930s, the late 1940s, and the mid to late 1950s. In 1968 three members of Intime who wanted to continue acting during the summer founded Summer Intime, which was incorporated as a separate nonprofit organization governed by a board composed of alumni, faculty, and staff. It was renamed Princeton Summer Theater (PST) in 1980 and continues under that name today, although in 1982 and 1983 it was known as Newstage at Intime.

Each summer a new company of Princeton students is formed to present a season of four plays in nine weeks, along with a children's show. The company typically includes Princeton students and recent alumni, along with students from other schools and guest artists. PST draws appreciative audiences from the campus and the surrounding communities, who welcome the opportunity to attend live theater during the summer.

THOMAS, NORMAN MATTOON 1905, six times Socialist candidate for president of the United States from 1928 through 1948, began what he called a lifelong "love affair with Old Nassau" when, as a child in Marion, Ohio, a family friend gave him a copy of Jesse Lynch Williams' *Princeton Stories*.

After a year at Bucknell University, Thomas was admitted to Princeton in the fall of 1902 as a sophomore. He excelled in debate, ranked first in his class, and was valedictorian at Commencement. He regarded himself as a Presbyterian and a Republican, was called "Tommy" by his classmates, and intended to become a minister like his father and his grandfather.

For two years after graduation, Thomas worked at Spring Street Church and Neighborhood House in New York City. He told his class secretary that he had come to see that "as a nation we face a social problem of tremendous gravity, whose solution will take the best that we have in us of thought and service."

For 1905's five-year record, Thomas reported that he and his wife were living in an apartment in a crowded tenement district where he was doing social work for Christ Church while attending Union Theological Seminary. In the class's 20-year record, he reported that he was executive director of the League for Industrial Democracy. He had been a parish minister in East Harlem, an editor of three publications, and an "advocate of unpopular causes." "My path has led me away from the road travelled by many old friends," he wrote. "That I regret, but nothing else."

Thomas later recalled that he had been barred as a speaker from the Princeton campus from 1917 to 1924 but that to his "pleased surprise" he was given an honorary degree in 1932. His citation called him "a brilliant and successful clergyman . . . who for conscience's sake gave up a conventional form of ministry . . . to become the fearless and upright advocate of change in the social order."

Thomas ran for president as a candidate of the Socialist Party of America, where his platform called for minimum wage laws, low-cost housing for the poor, a five-day work-week, unemployment insurance, health insurance for the aged, civil rights, and old-age pensions. He was also a founder of the American Civil Liberties Union. Ralph Nader '55 once told the *Princeton Alumni Weekly* that when he was an undergraduate, he walked Thomas back to his hotel after a speech on campus and asked him what had been his biggest success. "My biggest success was having the Democratic Party inherit my platform," Thomas said.

In 1955 the editors of 1905's half-century record said Thomas was beloved by all his classmates, and no 1905 gathering was complete without his presence and some utterance from his "silver tongue." Thomas wrote his classmates:

> I've failed—doubtless to your general satisfaction!—in the chief purpose of my career. That was to bring about, or help bring about, in our country a more realistic political alignment which might give us two major responsible parties, one of them democratic socialist in principle whatever its name.
>
> None of us at Princeton in 1905 could possibly have dreamed what this half-century has brought forth. But I suspect that in years of war and turmoil, among our comforts has been satisfaction that Princeton and the things it stands for has endured. Often we have warmed our hearts at the flame of our Princeton loyalties.

Thomas enjoyed Princeton reunions, and marched in the P-rade with political leaders from across the political spectrum, including Adlai Stevenson 1922 and John Foster Dulles 1908. A photo of Thomas in his class jacket at his 60th reunion hangs in Frist Campus Center; Thomas is also commemorated on campus through the library named in his honor in Forbes College.

In a speech to students from 30 countries just before his 83rd birthday, Thomas castigated the United States for its policies in Vietnam and its inadequate antipoverty efforts, but insisted nevertheless that he had affection for his country. He did not like the sight of young people burning the American flag. "A symbol?" he asked, "if they want an appropriate symbol, they should be washing the flag, not burning it."

Thomas died in his sleep soon after his 84th birthday. In the *Alumni Weekly*, the secretary of 1905 reminded his 45 surviving classmates that in senior year they had voted Tommy the brightest man in the class. "If we could have foreseen the future," the secretary added, "we must also have acclaimed him the most courageous."

THOMPSON, HENRY BURLING 1877 played a central role in the development of the Princeton campus during the presidencies of Woodrow Wilson 1879 and John Grier Hibben 1882 *1893. A textile manufacturer in Wilmington, Delaware, he was a Princeton trustee for almost 30 years.

Thompson was chair of the trustee committee on grounds and buildings from 1909 to 1928. Seeing a need to formulate a master plan for the development of the campus, he proposed the creation of the offices of supervising architect and consulting landscape gardener, and he was influential in bringing Ralph Adams Cram and Beatrix Farrand to Princeton to fill these positions. During his time as chair, 25 campus buildings were erected, beginning with Holder Hall and ending with the University Chapel.

Thompson headed the 1919 drive that raised $10 million in new endowment, and he helped found the school of Engineering in 1921. He was chair of a trustee committee that drew up the University's basic plan of physical education and encouraged the development of a greatly expanded number of tennis courts and playing fields near the dormitories. He spoke against undue emphasis on gate receipts in intercollegiate athletics and pushed the idea of "athletics for all."

Thompson is commemorated by a memorial court created in 1956 with a gift from his family. The court is situated at the center of the walk that passes through the arches of East Pyne Hall on the former site of East College, where Thompson roomed as an undergraduate.

THOMPSON GATEWAY and the adjacent brick wall on Prospect Avenue near Olden Street were given in 1911 by Ferris Thompson 1888. Until the early 1960s, when the Engineering Quadrangle was built, the wall marked the southern boundary of the athletic grounds known as University Field, and the gate was opened annually to admit the alumni parade to the baseball game with Yale on reunion Saturday. The wall and the ornamental iron gateway with marble tigers poised atop pillars were designed by McKim, Mead, and White, who also designed the FitzRandolph Gateway in front of Nassau Hall.

As an undergraduate, Thompson held the Princeton record for the mile walk and was president of the Princeton Athletic Association in his senior year. On his death in 1913, he left the University $3 million, a third by immediate bequest, and the balance in his estate which came to the University in 1948. His gifts were used for general endowment, for bicentennial preceptorships, and for the Ferris Thompson faculty/staff housing on Western Way.

TILGHMAN, SHIRLEY MARIE, was elected Princeton's 19th president on May 5, 2001, and assumed office on June 15. An exceptional teacher and a world-renowned scholar and leader in the field of molecular biology, she served on the faculty for 15 years and as founding director of the Lewis-Sigler Institute for Integrative Genomics before being named president. When her predecessor, Harold Shapiro *64, announced his intention to step down, Tilghman was elected as one of five faculty representatives on an 18-member presidential search committee. On a day when she left a meeting early to teach, the rest of the committee decided to ask her to become a candidate. She did, and not long after she was elected by the Board of Trustees upon the committee's "unanimous and more than enthusiastic" recommendation.

Like Shapiro, Tilghman was a native of Canada. She was born in Toronto but attended high school in Winnipeg, Manitoba. A top student, she also served as treasurer of the student council, edited the yearbook, played three sports, and sang and played guitar in an all-girl band called the Ladybugs. She received an honors bachelor's degree in chemistry from Queen's University in Kingston, Ontario, and after two years teaching secondary school in Sierra Leone, West Africa, she earned her PhD in biochemistry from Temple University in Philadelphia.

During postdoctoral studies at the National Institutes of Health (NIH), Tilghman made groundbreaking discoveries while participating in cloning the first mammalian gene. She continued to make scientific breakthroughs at the Institute for Cancer Research in Philadelphia and as an adjunct associate professor of human genetics and biochemistry and biophysics at the University of Pennsylvania. She was a founding member of the national advisory council of the Human Genome Project for the NIH and served on the National Research Council's committee that created the blueprint for US participation in the project. When the first draft of the human genome was published in 2000, it provided an invaluable resource for biologists working in fields ranging from evolution to development to cancer.

Tilghman came to Princeton in 1986 as a professor in the newly formed department of Molecular Biology. She continued her research into the control of gene expression in developing mouse embryos and launched what has been described as her "now textbook analysis of parental imprinting in mice." Two years later she was named a Howard Hughes investigator and in 1998 she took on the responsibility of helping to create the Lewis-Sigler Institute. She was nationally recognized for her leadership on behalf of women in science and for promoting efforts to make the early careers of young scientists as meaningful and productive as possible.

In 1993 Tilghman taught one of Princeton's first science-based freshman seminars and later began teaching a science course for freshmen and sophomores who were not planning to major in the sciences. She chaired the Council on Science and Technology, which encourages the teaching of STEM subjects to students outside the sciences, and she initiated a fellowship program in the sciences and engineering to bring postdoctoral students to Princeton to gain experience in both research and teaching. In 1996 she received the President's Award for Distinguished Teaching.

When she realized that many members of the men's lacrosse team were taking her course, she began attending their games at their invitation and became a knowledgeable fan. Herself a high school athlete—basketball, volleyball, and track—and throughout life an avid tennis player and skier, she regularly attended Princeton athletic events—especially men's and women's basketball games—before, during, and after her presidency.

Less than three months into Tilghman's presidency her leadership was tested by the terrorist attacks of September 11, 2001, that claimed the lives of more alumni of Princeton (14) than any but one other university (John Jay College of Criminal Justice in New York, which educates many first responders). Freshmen were just arriving on campus and many students and family members were understandably anxious. Tilghman quickly communicated with the campus community and began planning a series of public events and memorials that brought comfort and reassurance to the campus and the town.

She authorized a major initiative called Arts Alive that sent more than 10,000 New York City schoolchildren in communities especially hard hit by the attacks to cultural events in the city, accompanied by some 200 Princeton students who conducted workshops for them beforehand. Two years later a memorial garden in honor of those who died in the attacks was dedicated just outside the west door of Chancellor Green.

A few years later, when Hurricane Katrina devastated New Orleans, Tilghman became personally engaged in finding ways for Princeton to help some of the schools and students most affected, including those at Tulane and Dillard universities.

During her presidency, the undergraduate student body grew by 10 percent. The University built a new Collegiate Gothic-style residential college (named for its donor, Meg Whitman '77) and constructed new dormitories for Butler College. The residential college system was reconfigured to pair three colleges for first-year students and sophomores with three others that housed students from all four classes.

The University greatly increased the number of undergraduates on financial aid (from just under 40 percent to nearly 60 percent); significantly increased the aid they received; adopted a provision that increased the meal allowance in junior and senior years to allow students to afford an eating club if they wished to join one; and launched a major effort to increase the number of undergraduates in each class who would qualify for the Pell Grants that the federal government provides to lower income students.

In 2007 the University launched the public phase of the five-year "Aspire" campaign that exceeded its $1.75 billion goal by raising $1.88 billion. Prior to the formal announcement of the campaign, Tilghman secured a gift of $101 million from Peter Lewis '55 to support a major new initiative in the creative and performing arts. The goal of the Lewis Center for the Arts, Tilghman said, was "to ensure that the arts become a part of every Princeton student's experience and that they play a greater and more central role in the life of our campus and community."

When the Lewis Arts complex opened in 2017, it included a music building, a building for theater and dance, a six-story arts tower that included exhibition space for the visual arts, an 8,000-square-foot "forum" gathering space, outdoor sculptures, a new train station and Wawa convenience store (once, when asked whether a Wawa would be included in the plans for the complex, Tilghman characterized the Wawa as "eternal"), and a restaurant and a café in the converted former train station buildings.

The campaign also raised funds to bring visiting artists to campus, create new faculty positions, endow the directorship of the art museum, and establish new curator positions.

In 2008, a $100 million gift from Gerhard Andlinger '52 established a center for Energy and the

Environment in the school of Engineering and Applied Science. A center for innovation in engineering education, later endowed by Dennis Keller '63 and his wife Constance, was established, as was a Grand Challenges initiative to address issues related to developing sustainable energy, combatting infectious diseases, and overcoming natural resource limitations in developing countries.

Other major academic accomplishments of the Tilghman administration included constructing a new Frick laboratory and attracting a new generation of world-class faculty as part of a renewal of the department of Chemistry; creating a Princeton Neuroscience Institute and the Princeton Institute for the Science and Technology of Materials; and elevating the program in African American Studies to the status of a center and locating it prominently on the front campus in historic Stanhope Hall. African American Studies would become a department in 2015.

In addition to new and renovated buildings for the arts, the Andlinger Center, chemistry, and neuroscience, Tilghman oversaw the construction of Sherrerd Hall for the department of Operations Research and Financial Engineering and the center for Information Technology Policy; Peretsman Scully Hall for the department of Psychology; and the Frank Gehry-designed Lewis Science Library. Development of the campus was guided by a campus plan, initiated in 2005 and published in 2008, that proposed a campus of "neighborhoods," including an arts and transit neighborhood that would house the Lewis Arts complex, and a natural sciences neighborhood that would link departments on both sides of Washington Road with a pedestrian (Streicker) bridge and the shared resources of the Lewis library.

Tilghman encouraged a growing global perspective, forming the Princeton Institute for International and Regional Studies, introducing global summer seminars, and in 2009 launching a groundbreaking Bridge Year program through which a number of admitted students each year can defer admission to engage in a nine-month tuition-free international service program before beginning their freshman year.

In 2003 Tilghman appointed a task force to examine issues related to the health and well-being of students, faculty, and staff and the need for additional child-care and other family support services. The task force recommended a substantial increase in health services staffing, with added strengths in education and nutrition; enhancements to McCosh Health Center and Dillon Gym; and improvements in student and employee health plans. It also called for expanded support for child-care, including construction of a new University-affiliated child-care center, which eventually opened in 2017.

In 2009 she asked a task force to develop recommendations to strengthen relationships between the University and the eating clubs, and she subsequently asked a different group to examine Greek life on campus. In August 2011 she announced the adoption of that group's recommendations that students be prohibited from affiliating with a fraternity or sorority during freshman year and from conducting any form of rush in which freshmen participate. That same year she asked Princeton professor and former Duke University president Nannerl Keohane to chair a committee that made recommendations to reverse what was then a declining number of women undergraduates serving in campus leadership positions.

One of Tilghman's major accomplishments was leading the University through a severe economic downturn in 2008–09 when the endowment lost 23 percent of its value and the University had to reduce its operating budget by $170 million. The University was able to sustain its core programs and preserve its full-need, no-loan financial aid program, while making adjustments that Tilghman said made the University "stronger financially than we were before the recession—not because we have more money, but because we are much more disciplined about how we allocate our resources and prioritize them."

Tilghman stepped down in June 2013. Her last weeks in office were filled with tributes, including a "Shirleypalooza" on Cannon Green during which student dance and musical groups took the stage and Triangle Club members serenaded her with a musical number in which they begged her not to leave. At Commencement she was presented with an honorary degree citation that read:

> For 12 transformative years, she has led this University with exceptional integrity, humanity, and courage. Passionate scientist, teacher, and champion of the arts, she has blazed new paths of discovery, learning, expression, and service; she has widened the doors of opportunity in the name of equity and excellence; and she has strengthened Princeton's presence throughout the world. Greatly admired and much beloved, she has been the personification of Tiger spirit, aiming always, with determination and grace, to live up to her own admonition to aim high and be bold.

After retiring from the presidency, she returned to the faculty in the department of Molecular Biology and the school of Public and International Affairs, where she continued to teach, even after she transferred to emerita status in 2020.

Throughout her career, Tilghman served the larger scientific community in many ways, including as chair of the molecular biology study section at the NIH; on scientific advisory boards and committees of the Jackson Lab, the Whitehead Institute, and Genentech; as a trustee of the Cold Spring Harbor Laboratory, Rockefeller University, and King Abdullah University of Science and Technology in Saudi Arabia; and on the selection committees of the Pew Charitable Trusts Scholars Program in the Biomedical Sciences and the Lucille P. Markey Charitable Trust.

She served as a member of the Harvard Corporation; a trustee of Amherst College, the Carnegie Endowment for International Peace, and Leadership Enterprise for a Diverse America; and as a director of Google Inc. In 2010–11 she chaired the board of the Association of American Universities, which represents the leading US and Canadian research universities, providing national leadership on issues ranging from college affordability and the federal investment in basic research to immigration policy and accountability.

Among her many honors were the L'Oréal-UNESCO Award for Women in Science (2002) and the Lifetime Achievement Award from the Society for Developmental Biology (2003). In 2007 she was awarded the Genetics Society of America Medal for outstanding contributions to her field.

In 2013 a major east-west campus walkway linking the Lewis Center for the Arts to the buildings that house genomics, neuroscience, and psychology was named in her honor. In addition to connecting two of her signature achievements, the walkway passes by both Whitman College and Butler College. In their announcement, the trustees said they were naming the walkway "so that forevermore Tilghman Walk will remind future generations of the many ways her legacy shaped and strengthened Princeton."

TRACK AND FIELD. Princeton's national and international success in track and field spans more than a century, from Robert Garrett 1897's two gold medals at the first modern Olympics in the last decade of the nineteenth century to the NCAA championships won by Donn Cabral '12 and Julia Ratcliffe '17 in the second decade of the twenty-first.

Men's Track and Field

On June 21, 1873, George Goldie, then director of the Princeton gymnasium, organized an intramural meet called the Caledonian Games, the first track and field contest on campus. Three years later Princeton won the team championship at the first meet hosted by the Intercollegiate Association of Amateur Athletes of America (IC4A), and the Tigers' track and field story was off to a running start.

At the first Caledonian Games Allan Marquand 1874, later founder of the department of Art and Archaeology, won three first places and one second, and at the fourth games Andrew McCosh 1877, son of President James McCosh, won four first places and one second. In the 1878 and 1879 IC4A's, Francis Larkin Jr. 1879 won intercollegiate championships in the shotput, hammer throw, standing high jump, and standing broad jump, making him the first four-event winner in the country and the only one in Princeton history.

Princeton sent four track athletes from the Class of 1897—Robert Garrett, Herbert Jamison, Francis Lane, and Albert Tyler—to the first modern Olympics in Athens in 1896. Garrett was the US team's breakout star, winning first place in two throwing events, the shotput and discus, and second place in the long jump and high jump. Garrett would win bronze in the shotput and the standing triple jump at the 1900 Olympics, and more than a century later he remains the University's most decorated Olympian.

Princeton's outstanding runner in its early years was John Cregan 1899, a three-time intercollegiate champion in the mile. He won both the mile and half-mile in the 1898 IC4A meet, the first runner in the country to accomplish this feat, and anchored Princeton's record-setting intercollegiate two-mile relay team at the 1900 Penn Relays. Cregan also won a silver medal in the 800-meter run at the 1900 Olympics.

John DeWitt 1904, captain of Princeton's undefeated football team in 1903, was a track and field star as well. He won the intercollegiate hammer throw for four straight years—a feat unmatched by any Princetonian in any event—and claimed the silver medal in that event at the 1904 Olympics.

Coach Keene Fitzpatrick arrived at Princeton in 1911 and guided the team for 22 seasons. With Fitzpatrick at the helm, the Tigers placed second at the IC4A meet four times and won national titles in individual events 15 times. Fitzpatrick also oversaw the start of the Oxford-Cambridge meets, a series of exhibitions featuring Princeton, Cornell, Oxford, and Cambridge, between 1921 and 1949. In a memorable mile run at Palmer Stadium in the 1933 meet, New Zealander Jack Lovelock, a Rhodes Scholar at Oxford, outdueled Bill Bonthron '34 and broke the world record in the process. Another notable miler ran at Palmer in the 1949 meet: Oxford captain Roger Bannister won a race that included Tiger Ron Wittreich '50, who had finished third at that spring's NCAAs. Five years later, Bannister would make history as the first miler to break the 4-minute barrier.

Bonthron was Princeton's most decorated track athlete of the 1930s. His style was to run in the middle of the pack until late in the race, when he was "a bundle of dynamite in the homestretch," as one *Associated Press* reporter put it. His 4:08.7 mile in 1933 set a school record that survived until 1968, and he won the NCAA mile run in his senior year, becoming Princeton's first individual champion at an NCAA meet. In 1934, Bonthron set a world record in the 1,500-meter run. At the end of that year, he received the Amateur Athletic Union's Sullivan Award.

The 1930s also brought success under Fitzpatrick's successor, Matty Geis, who led Princeton to its first victory at the Heptagonal championships in 1938. "Heps" began in 1935 with seven schools (Columbia, Cornell, Dartmouth, Harvard, Penn, Princeton, and Yale). The meet later added Army, Navy, and Brown. Since 2004 only the eight Ivy schools have participated, but the Greek prefix for seven endures.

After a second-place finish in 1941, Princeton had limited team success at the Heptagonal meet until the arrival of two prominent coaches in the 1970s. Larry Ellis, who was hired as the track and cross-country coach in 1970, was the first African American head coach in the Ivy League. His assistant and eventual successor, Fred Samara, joined the program in 1979. Under Ellis and Samara, Princeton became an Ivy juggernaut, winning 22 indoor championships and 19 outdoor championships between 1980 and 2019.

Ellis, who had been an All-American distance runner at NYU, led the Princeton teams to their first "triple crown"—league championships in cross-country, indoor track and field, and outdoor track and field in the same academic year—in 1981–82. In 1984 he was selected as head coach of the US Olympic track and field team. After his retirement in 1991, he served as president of USA Track and Field for five years.

Samara, a 1976 Olympian in the decathlon, made the triple crown a more common occurrence at Princeton, repeating the feat eight times between 1997–98 and 2018–19. Samara also coached US Olympians, serving as an assistant in charge of field events and the decathlon at the 1992 Summer Games.

In the Ellis and Samara years, 11 Princetonians won NCAA titles: Charles Norelli '77, Richard Aneser '77, Charles Hedrick '76, and Craig Masback '77 in the indoor two-mile relay (1975); Dave Pellegrini '80, in the indoor weight throw (1980); Tora Harris '02, in both the indoor and outdoor high jump (2002); Donn Cabral '12, in the 3,000-meter steeplechase (2012); and Peter Callahan '13, Russell Dinkins '13, Austin Hollimon '13, and Michael Williams '14 in the indoor distance-medley relay (2013).

Other notable athletes include August Wolf '83, who set school records in the shotput and discus, won shotput titles at the US national indoor and outdoor meets in the year after his graduation, and competed at the 1984 Olympics; and Bill Burke '91, the first Tiger to break the 4-minute mark in the mile as an undergraduate (3:58.70 at the 1991 Millrose Games).

Women's Track and Field

The history of women's track and field at Princeton falls largely under the purview of Peter Farrell, the program's coach from its first varsity meet in 1978 until the end of the 2016 season. His successor, Michelle Eisenreich, has coached the Tigers since 2016.

Before the varsity team was formed an ambitious first-year student, Nancy Kraemer '79, organized a club team, coached by student Bill Farrell '77 (no relation to Peter). Kraemer captained the first varsity team and was named the most valuable performer at the Ivy League meet when Princeton won the team championship in 1979. Two years later, Princeton would be the first women's program to win the triple-crown of cross-country, indoor track and field, and outdoor track and field championships in one academic year.

Lynn Jennings '83, one of the greatest distance runners in Ivy history, was the first Tiger woman to compete at the NCAA championships. She placed fourth in the 3,000-meter run in 1983. Jennings would become a three-time Olympian and won a bronze medal in the 10,000-meter run at the 1992 Olympics. Princeton also produced an Olympian in the field events: shotput star Deborah Saint Phard '87, who represented Haiti in 1988.

Other standouts in Farrell's tenure include Kristin Beaney '94, an All-American during her senior year in cross-country, indoor track and field (5,000-

meter run), and outdoor track and field (also the 5,000-meter run); and Lauren Simmons '02, who finished second in the 800-meter run at the 2002 NCAA outdoor meet, the final run of her Princeton career. Other strong competitors in the 2000s included Emily Kroshus '04, who placed fourth in the 10,000-meter run at the NCAA outdoor meet in 2004; Cack Ferrell '06, who finished fourth in the 3,000-meter run at the NCAA indoor meet in 2006; and Ashley Higginson '11, a three-time NCAA finalist in the 3,000-meter steeplechase, who finished third in the event in 2010.

Farrell won 18 Ivy track and field titles and sent dozens of athletes to the NCAA meets, but it wasn't until relatively late in his remarkable career that the first Tiger woman reached the top of the NCAA podium: Julia Ratcliffe '17, who won the hammer throw as a sophomore at the 2014 NCAA outdoor meet with a heave of 219 feet, 5 inches, nearly seven feet farther than the second-place mark. Ratcliffe nearly repeated the feat as a junior, placing second, and after taking a year off to try for a spot in the 2016 Olympics, she returned to the NCAA meet in 2017, finishing sixth and earning All-America honors for the third time. She threw the hammer for New Zealand in the 2021 Olympics.

TRIANGLE CLUB, THE PRINCETON, is an undergraduate musical comedy club that has written, produced, and performed a full-scale musical comedy each year since the late nineteenth century, except for brief interruptions during the two world wars and in 2020–21 when, because of the COVID-19 pandemic, the club presented its first-ever virtual show in January 2021 during the University's first-ever Wintersession. Each year 12 undergraduate writers come together to write an original musical comedy in about 10 months—some years writing "book" shows with a storyline and fixed characters, and other years writing revues with thematically connected or unconnected skits and songs. The show debuts in McCarter Theatre's 1,100-seat Mathews Theater each fall, goes on the road over the winter, and returns for encore performances during reunions.

Triangle's Frosh Week Show welcomes entering students each fall with a selection of well-loved songs and sketches, many centering on campus life, and its Spring Showcase in one of the campus's black box theaters debuts material that may be trying out for (or in other cases is not suitable for) the mainstage show. Some students in Triangle participate in the Lewis Center for the Arts Musical Theater program, while for others Triangle is their only theater activity. Club members serve in the cast, in the pit orchestra, as writers, on the tech crew, or on the business staff; they are supported by a team of outside professionals who coach the writers, direct and choreograph the show, and design costumes, sets, sound, and lighting.

Triangle evolved from the Princeton College Dramatic Association, which changed its name to Triangle Club in 1893, 10 years after its founding. According to Booth Tarkington 1893, the club's name, which fittingly referred to a "somewhat musical instrument," was inspired by a favorite walk on which students would sing Henry Van Dyke 1894's Triangle Song: "Well the old Triangle knew the music of our tread / How the gates were left unhinged, the lamps without a head / While we were marching through Princeton." The sides of the triangle walk were Stockton and Mercer streets, which join at the top of University Place; a base at Lover's Lane forms a "little triangle," while a base at Quaker Road forms a "big triangle."

In 1891 the association gave up formal drama for musical comedy, joining forces with the Glee Club to present *Po-Ca-Hon-Tas*; since this show launched the Triangle tradition of musicals written and performed by students, 1891 is the year Triangle considers its official starting date. The 1907 show, *The Mummy Monarch*, included a "pony ballet" which originated another Triangle tradition—including a kickline in each year's production. With some exceptions, particularly in the early years of coeducation in the 1970s, Triangle kicklines have featured men dressed as women, but the 2018–19 show, *Night of the Laughing Dead*, featured an all-female kickline, and the following year the kickline included both male and female cast members dressed as Benjamin Franklin in *Once Uponzi Time*.

In his senior year, Tarkington wrote and performed in *The Honorable Julius Caesar*, a musical parody of Shakespeare's play that was the first performed under the Triangle name. To provide a home for the Triangle Club—its early performances were staged in University Hall's dining room—Tarkington initiated a campaign to raise funds for a small building that was erected in 1895 on what is now the site of Dillon Gymnasium. For more than a quarter of a century until it was destroyed by fire in 1924, this modest structure, which was called the Casino, served as a home for club rehearsals and performances; as a location for dances, tennis, and bowling; and as an armory for a local company of the National Guard.

By 1930 the club had raised sufficient funds to build McCarter Theatre as its permanent home. Thomas McCarter 1888 provided $250,000; the Triangle Club committed reserves of over $100,000; and other gifts included the proceeds of a benefit performance by the Hasty Pudding Club of Harvard. The opening night performance at the new theater, on February 21, 1930, was Triangle's *The Golden Dog*.

In the face of financial challenges, in 1953 the University and Triangle Club agreed that the University would assume responsibility for the theater and cancel most of Triangle's debt, while Triangle would retain office space and performance dates for its shows. In the mid-1980s, Triangle moved its rehearsals to a similarly sized space in a former school building on Broadmead Street on the eastern end of campus. The experience of executing a show in the grand setting of McCarter Theatre remains a key differentiator of Triangle from other theater organizations on campus.

From the very beginning, Triangle took its shows on the road. The 1900 show, *A Woodland Wedding*, was the first to tour past Trenton and New Brunswick. In 1901 *The King of Pomeru* was the first show to travel to New York; the following year the club reprised the show and took it to Pittsburgh. By 1910 Triangle was touring as far west as Chicago and St. Louis. Following a Washington performance of the 1913–14 show, *The Pursuit of Priscilla*, the club was invited to the White House. In 1917–18, a four-man Triangle troupe toured Europe to entertain soldiers. In 1948 *All in Favor* became the first college show on television when it was broadcast on WNBC in New York. Triangle productions appeared on the *Ed Sullivan Show* from 1950 to 1957.

In 1955 Milton Lyon began a decades-long relationship with Triangle as director, writing coach, and tour chaperone, shepherding Triangle through one of its several golden ages. Two of his productions, *Breakfast in Bedlam* (1959–60) and *Tour de Farce* (1961–62), made summer tours of United States army bases in Europe. Two other shows from the 1960s, *Grape Expectations* (1964–65) and *A Different Kick* (1968–69), won prizes as the best college shows in the country.

In 1970 Triangle changed its schedule from a December show followed by a Christmas tour and then a reprise at reunions, to a spring opening on campus to be followed by a reunion show and a winter tour the following year. *Cracked Ice* opened in April 1971, was repeated at reunions, and toured in December. Spring/reunion show cast sizes frequently reached 40 or 50; with seniors graduating, the shows needed to be recast in the fall with cast size reduced to 25 to fit the whole company on a tour bus. After 1998 Triangle reverted to its former schedule, opening on campus in the fall, touring in the winter, and coming back for an encore at reunions in the spring.

In 1991 the club celebrated its centennial with a show entitled *The Older, the Better*, and an exhibition at Firestone Library of more than 850 items from the Triangle archives. It celebrated its 125th anniversary in 2016 with an exhibit at the University archives, performances of that year's show *Greece'd Lightning* (one of which was attended by the University's Board of Trustees), and a show featuring the best of Triangle performed by seven decades of Triangle alumni.

Greece'd Lightning was the eighth and last in a remarkable string of shows with Glen Pannell '87 as director, Hans Kriefall '87 as choreographer, and Pete Mills '95 as music director and writer's workshop co-director. Kriefall went on to choreograph two more shows, and Mills played his dual roles several more times.

Triangle's long history can be a burden as well as a blessing. Some material considered funny in its time is shameful now, as are the club's use of blackface, redface, and racist or otherwise offensive lyrics and storylines. Today's Triangle is committed to being an equitable, diverse, and inclusive organization where every Princeton student interested in musical comedy wants to write, perform, and produce.

Triangle welcomed women even before the University did. Sue Jean Lee '70 appeared in the 1968–69 show, *A Different Kick*, while enrolled as a Critical Languages student. When undergraduate coeducation began in the fall of 1969, the show included six women in a 17-member cast, including Lee and Vera Marcus '72. Marcus was Triangle's first female writer, first woman of color, and the first woman to graduate from Princeton after entering as a freshman, having entered with the Class of 1973 and completed her degree in three years. Triangle's other first women were stage manager Claire Townsend '74; board member Carey Davis '73, club president Mary Stewart '83; and board chair Kendall Crolius '76. In 1982 the club hired the first of many women directors, Miriam Ford.

Favorite songs and sketches from Triangle's history include "Ships That Pass in the Night" (from the 1923–24 show *Drake's Drum*), "Vagabond Heart" (1955–56 *Spree de Corps*), "Where There's a Song" (1950–51 *Too Hot for Toddy*), "Ivy League Look" (1957–

58 *After A Fashion*), "Elevator" (1972–73 *Future Schlock*), "What A Morning," "Examination," and "Sewn in a Pocket of Gloom" (all from 1974–75 *American Zucchini*), "Carpool" (1981–82 *Stocks and Bondage*), "Yale/The Slammer" (1986–87 *Business Unusual*), "Yes! I Got In" (1996–97 *It's a Wonderful Laugh*), and "So Much to See (In New Jersey)" (2007–08 *A Turnpike Runs Through It*).

Princeton exam takers may find themselves silently singing Mills' Honor Code song (1991–92 *Do-Re Media*) when they sign the pledge. "East of the Sun (and West of the Moon)," by Brooks Bowman '36, one of three memorable songs from the 1935–36 show *Stags at Bay*, remains the most popular and longest-lasting national hit ever to come out of the Triangle Club. It was recorded by Louis Armstrong, Tony Bennett, Ella Fitzgerald, Billie Holiday, Diana Krall, Charlie Parker, Frank Sinatra, and Sarah Vaughan, among others, and still provides the club with royalties.

Many of Triangle's alumni have gone on to make their marks professionally in the performing arts. Between 1914 and 1917 three shows were written by F. Scott Fitzgerald 1917. One, *Fie! Fie! Fi-Fi!*, became *Ha-Ha Hortense!* in *This Side of Paradise*, where Fitzgerald says: "How a Triangle show ever got off was a mystery, but it was a riotous mystery anyway, whether or not one did enough service to wear a little gold triangle on his watch-chain."

Other notable alumni include writer-director Joshua Logan '31; actors James Stewart '32, José Ferrer '33, Brooke Shields '87, Ellie Kemper '02, and Jarod Spector '03; author of the much-performed musical *You're a Good Man, Charlie Brown*, Clark Gesner '60; head writer for TV's *Sesame Street*, Jeffrey Moss '63; playwright-screenwriter-director Doug McGrath '80; television writer-producers David E. Kelley '79 and Lesley Wake Webster '96; and playwright-television writer Winnie Holzman '76.

TRUSTEES OF PRINCETON UNIVERSITY is the legal title of a corporation "organized for educational purposes in the state of New Jersey." These purposes include "the conduct of a university not for profit, including colleges and schools . . . both graduate and undergraduate" and "the promotion, advancement, evaluation, and dissemination of learning by instruction, study, and research in the humanities, religion, social sciences, natural sciences, engineering, and applied sciences." The charter vests in the trustees all powers "necessary, convenient, or incident to its purposes."

The charter requires that the board consist of not fewer than 23 nor more than 40 trustees, of whom two (the governor of the state and the president of the University) serve ex officio. The board includes nine trustees elected by alumni to serve four-year terms (three of whom must be graduate alumni, with one of them a recent degree recipient) and four "young alumni trustees" who are elected to four-year terms, one each year from the graduating undergraduate class, by an electorate that includes the two most recently graduated classes plus juniors and seniors.

The remaining trustees are chosen by the board itself. The board may elect between four and 10 term trustees, who serve four-year terms; the rest are charter trustees who serve six-year terms that are renewable for two additional years. Upon retirement from the board, charter trustees are designated emeritus trustees.

The charter originally required that 12 trustees be inhabitants of the state of New Jersey. This number was reduced over time and the requirement was eliminated in 1991.

Of the original 12 trustees named in the College's first charter in 1746, nine were clergymen, one was a merchant, one—the person who drafted the charter—a lawyer, and the 12th was described as "a man of leisure and wealth and given to good works."

The 23 trustees named in a second charter, granted in 1748, represented a broader spectrum of society and reflected the founders' avowed purpose of educating men who would be "ornaments of the State as well as the Church." The governor of the province, Jonathan Belcher, was added, as were four members of the provincial council of New Jersey, two judges and a merchant from Philadelphia, and three more members of the clergy. This meant that 12 of the 23 were members of the clergy—a clerical majority of one. At least 16 of the 23 had bought, sold, traded, or inherited slaves.

The clergy maintained a majority for more than a century. They lost their majority when the number of trustees was increased after the Civil War, but as late as 1905 the by-laws stipulated that at least 12 trustees should be from the clergy. The following year the number was reduced to eight, and in 1913 this requirement was removed completely.

Most of the original trustees were graduates of Yale, Harvard, or William Tennent's "Log College" in Neshaminy, Pennsylvania. The first graduate of the College to join the board, in 1757, was Richard

Stockton 1748, who practiced law in Princeton. Four years later he was joined by his classmate, Israel Read 1748, a minister in Bound Brook, New Jersey. By 1768, when John Witherspoon became president, there were five graduates of the College on the board; a century later, under McCosh, there were 17.

John A. Stewart was an active member of the board longer than any other trustee in Princeton's history. An 1840 graduate of Columbia College and a trusted financial adviser to President Abraham Lincoln and later to President Grover Cleveland, Stewart was elected a Princeton trustee in 1868 and served for 58 years until his death in 1926 at the age of 104. He was acting president of the University in the interregnum between the Woodrow Wilson and John Grier Hibben administrations.

In 1900, in recognition of the increasing role that alumni were playing in Princeton's growth, the board amended the charter and by-laws to permit adding to its membership five trustees, one to be elected each year by the alumni to a five-year term. This number became eight in 1917. The method of election was subsequently modified several times, resulting in a plan adopted in 1934 which provided that two alumni trustees be elected annually for four-year terms—one each year would be elected from one of four geographical regions and the other would be chosen at large. In both instances the candidates would be nominated by a committee of the Alumni Council. (The Committee to Nominate Alumni Trustees, known as CTNAT, reaches out widely for suggestions and conducts extensive review before nominating three candidates for each open position.)

The range of alumni trusteeships was further extended by two developments in the 1960s. The first came in 1964 when the board added a ninth alumni-elected trustee position and designated it to be filled by a graduate of the graduate school.

In 1969 the board added four more alumni trustees, one elected each year from the graduating class by vote of the members of the junior and senior classes and the two most recently graduated classes. (In these elections, the slate of three candidates is determined in a primary election in which only members of the senior class may vote.)

To avoid beginning this practice with only one such trustee on the board, a special election was conducted in May 1969 in which Richard Cass '68 was elected for a three-year term, while in the regular election Brent Henry '69 was elected for a four-year term. Henry and Robert Rivers Jr. '53, who was elected a term trustee in 1969, were the first African American members of the board. Rivers would be elected to a second term four years later. Henry would return to the board in 1999 as a charter trustee, and then be elected to a second term as a charter trustee in 2010, making him the only trustee who served on the board during the Goheen, Bowen, Shapiro, Tilghman, and Eisgruber presidencies. (In 2011 Henry was elected vice chair of the board.)

In 2004 the board reduced the number of regional trustee positions from four to three, freeing a position to be designated solely for graduate alumni and thereby guaranteeing that there would always be at least two graduate alumni among the nine alumni-elected trustees. In 2019 the board reduced the number of at-large positions from four to three to create an alumni-elected trustee position for a recent graduate of the graduate school, defined as an individual who received a Princeton graduate degree within the five years prior to the year of the election.

In 1942 the board renounced the life tenure that board-elected trustees had enjoyed for almost two centuries, converting "life trustees" to "charter trustees." In 1956 the board reduced the number of charter trustees by four, replacing them with term trustees. The bylaws now permit up to 10 term trustees.

The board added women to its membership for the first time in 1971 when it elected as charter trustees Mary St. John Douglas and Susan Savage Speers (daughters of alumni in the classes of 1905 and 1920 and wives of alumni in the classes of 1943 and 1950). Other early female trustees included the mathematician Cathleen Synge Morawetz, whose daughter Nancy was a member of the Class of 1976, and the economist Marina von Neumann Whitman, whose father, John von Neumann, had been one of the first professors at the Institute for Advanced Study.

The governor of New Jersey was the presiding officer of the board until 1939. Since then, the president of the University has presided. Until 2011, the ranking trustee was the chair of the executive committee, who spoke for the board and presided in the president's absence. That year the title of the position was changed to chair of the board. The other officers of the board are the vice chair and the clerk, who has formal responsibility for the minutes of the board.

Starting with the McCosh administration, most of the work of the board has been done by standing committees, of which there are now 12: executive, academic affairs, advancement, audit and compliance, board development, compensation, diversity and inclusion, finance, grounds and buildings, honorary degrees, public affairs, and student life, health, and athletics. Between board meetings, the executive committee has all the powers and duties of the board except removing or electing a trustee or the president.

The executive committee was first established in 1919. Its chairs were Edward Duffield 1892, Walter Hope 1901, Fordyce St. John 1905, Harold Helm 1920, James Oates Jr. 1921, John Irwin II '37, R. Manning Brown '36, John Kenefick '43, James Henderson '56, Robert Rawson Jr. '66, and Stephen Oxman '67. In 2011, Kathryn Hall '80 was named chair of the board and in that capacity chaired the executive committee, as did her successor, Louise Sams '79.

In 1969 the board adopted a resolution to clarify the duties and responsibilities of the trustees, especially as they relate to delegations of authority to administrative officers, faculty, or students. The resolution was reaffirmed, with amendments, revisions, and interpretations, in 1992, 2005, 2011, and 2019. It describes the three modes by which trustees delegate, share, or directly exercise their powers and responsibilities: through broad delegation subject to oversight and general review; through delegated responsibility subject to prior review and approval; and through authority directly exercised, primarily in matters concerning the financial health, resource allocation, and physical properties of the University.

The board has control of the finances and funds of the University. It sets the operating and capital budgets and supervises the investment of the University's endowment, which is managed by the Princeton University Investment Company. All campus real estate and long-range physical planning, the determination of architectural styling and landscaping, and the general condition of the physical plant are directly overseen by the board.

The trustees exercise prior review and approval of substantial new claims on funds, any significant allocation of resources, the setting of priorities for development, changes in instructional method with broad implications for the University, the determination of tuition and fees, changes in admission policies affecting sizeable categories of potential students, and changes in relations with outside educational and social institutions and government agencies.

Except for alumni-elected trustees, there is no requirement that trustees be alumni, although most trustees in the modern era have been, reflecting in part the significant time commitment to serve on a board that typically meets for two days five times a year, with extensive preparation required for each meeting. (One recent trustee who did not attend Princeton was former vice provost Ruth Simmons, who joined the board after leaving the presidency of Brown.)

Frequently alumni who first join the board as alumni trustees, as well as alumni who compete unsuccessfully in the alumni trustee election, are later invited by the board to serve as term or charter trustees. (Hall, who chaired the board from 2011 to 2019, lost an alumni trustee election before serving as both a term and a charter trustee.) The name of every person who has ever served as a trustee is engraved on a glass wall of the trustee reading room in Firestone Library; among alumni classes, the one most represented is the Class of 1952, with 12 members who served on the board.

Turing, Alan M. *38 is widely recognized as the father of computer science and a central figure in the history of lesbian, gay, bisexual, transgender, and queer (LGBTQ) rights. In 2008, when the *Princeton Alumni Weekly* published a list of the 25 most influential alumni of all time, he ranked second, behind only James Madison 1771. In 2019, his portrait was one of the first to be added to the University's collection as part of an ongoing commitment to diversification.

At the unveiling of the portrait, Professor Jennifer Rexford '91, chair of the department of Computer Science, noted that Turing had "long been a household name in computer science circles" because of the Turing machine, "a universal computing device that lay the theoretical foundation for the computers of today"; the Turing Test, "a simple, intuitive way to tell if a machine is intelligent, a harbinger for the field of artificial intelligence that is transforming our world"; and the Turing Award, "our field's Nobel Prize named in his honor."

She expressed her department's "tremendous intellectual debt" to Turing for "our historical strength in theoretical computer science . . . but also research in artificial intelligence and machine learning, and even working at the intersection of computing and biology, a topic Turing pursued in the last few years of his short life."

She noted his much deserved broader recognition as a result of the 2014 movie, *The Imitation Game*, which introduced a worldwide audience to his central role in developing machines and algorithms to crack Nazi Germany's seemingly impenetrable Enigma code, a major step toward hastening the end of the war with an Allied victory.

Finally, she said that for the LGBTQ community, "Turing is an enduring icon, and the growing appreciation of his life and his great contributions to the world is a cause for hope and celebration."

In its 2008 article, the *PAW* noted that Turing, born in England in 1912, "as a child was cheeky and tantrum prone.... [His] independent character was a source of endless exasperation for his teachers." He studied mathematics at King's College, Cambridge, where, in 1936 at age 23, he wrote "On Computable Numbers," which conceived of abstract machines, now called Turing machines, which would function much like modern computers. That year he arrived at Princeton to work with Professor Alonzo Church 1924 *1927, make final revisions to his paper, and write his dissertation. In 1938, a PhD in mathematics in hand, he turned down an offer from John von Neumann to continue his research at the Institute for Advanced Study and returned to England.

After World War II, Turing turned his interest to artificial intelligence, imagining a machine that would simulate human thought. He invented the Turing test, which says that a computer can be said to be intelligent if it can fool a questioner into thinking it is human.

An openly gay man when homosexual acts were still criminal offenses in the United Kingdom, Turing was convicted of "gross indecency" in 1952, and to avoid prison he had to agree to a series of estrogen injections. In June 1954, at age 41, he was found dead in his home from what was ruled to be suicide. In 2013 the British government granted Turing a posthumous pardon, after apologizing four years earlier for "the appalling way he was treated."

In 2019 the Bank of England announced that Turing would appear on its 50-pound note, the highest denomination English bank note, beginning in 2021. The note will also include a table and mathematical formulas from his 1936 paper and the following quote from a 1949 interview with him about one of the computers he helped develop: "This is only a foretaste of what is to come, and only the shadow of what it is going to be."

A biography of Turing, *Alan Turing: The Enigma*, was published in 1983 by Princeton University Press, and an updated edition was published in 2015. Turing's Princeton portrait hangs in the Lewis Science Library.

UNIVERSITY CENTER FOR HUMAN VALUES (UCHV) was established in 1990 to foster inquiry into important ethical issues in private and public life and to support teaching, research, and discussion of ethics and human values throughout the curriculum and across the disciplines of the University.

A series of gifts from Laurance Rockefeller '32 enabled the University to create the center and support its signature activities. Rockefeller, who wrote his senior thesis on "The Concept of Value and its Relation to Ethics," also provided major funding to Princeton in support of undergraduate coeducation, the development of the residential colleges, and the construction of Lewis Thomas Laboratory to house the department of Molecular Biology.

The founding director of UCHV was politics professor Amy Gutmann, who later became dean of the faculty and provost at Princeton, and then president of the University of Pennsylvania. On the occasion of the center's 25th anniversary, she said, "The University Center has provoked not one or two, but thousands of students ... to tackle important ethical questions, central to living a more examined life and creating a better society ... [It is] nothing less, to my mind, than the ideal collegial environment for doing this important work, unsurpassed anywhere in the world."

UCHV sponsors a program of visiting faculty fellowships, nominates and hosts visiting professors for distinguished teaching, and nominates and hosts preceptorships for untenured Princeton faculty. It hosts several seminar and lecture series, including an interdisciplinary colloquium on ethics and public affairs, the DeCamp bioethics seminars, and the Moffett lectures about moral issues in public life.

The center supports a number of faculty positions, including joint appointments with such departments as Politics, Philosophy, Religion, History, and the school of Public and International Affairs. It sponsors an interdepartmental PhD program in Political Philosophy for students in Classics, History, Philosophy, Politics, and Religion, as well as a graduate prize fellowship program for graduate students in any field. Since 2010 UCHV has offered an undergraduate certificate program in Values and Public Life, and each year it sponsors a series of freshman seminars. It also periodically advertises postdoctoral research associate positions, including one in bioethics that is endowed in honor of Princeton's 18th president, Harold Shapiro *64.

The center's Human Values Forum provides opportunities for informal discussion among undergraduates and faculty members of questions concerning ethics and human values; the adviser to the student leaders of the forum is the prominent bioethicist Peter Singer, who has served on the UCHV faculty since 1999. Its Film Forum does the same for members of the campus community and the town who watch films and discuss them together.

The Tanner Lectures on Human Values are a multi-university lecture series that was founded in 1978; it is established at nine institutions, including Princeton. UCHV hosts these lectures at Princeton, in which an eminent scholar from philosophy, religion, the humanities, sciences, creative arts, or learned professions, or a person eminent in political or social life, is invited to present a series of lectures reflecting on scholarly and scientific learning relating to "the entire range of values pertinent to the human condition."

University League/UNow. On April 13, 1920, "women of the Faculty, Library and Administration" were invited by the faculty tea committee to meet at Prospect, the home of the president. At this meeting, the University League was founded "to promote a friendly spirit among wives and families of men connected with the University" and to help integrate new faculty families into the community. Membership in the league was later broadened to include all "women who are, or whose husbands are, members of the University faculty, administration or staff," and in 1973 membership was opened to men. In the 1990s there were some 650 members.

In the early days, weekly teas often honored different departments in the University. League-sponsored parties at Prospect on Christmas night, when the entire faculty could fit comfortably into the president's home, were gala occasions with dancing, mahjong, bridge, music, and refreshments.

Over time, special interest groups were formed on foreign languages, English conversation, piano, art exhibitions, travel, child-care, literature, the performing arts, sports, and cooking. A business registry was started in 1927 to match members' skills with faculty needs and in 1967 the league began a job roster for professional women seeking employment. The league created an exchange that offered reconditioned furniture to members of the University community. In 1929 the league's Ladies Musical Committee provided an endowment to Princeton University Concerts that continues to underwrite its presentations of classical music.

The league's Committee for Overseas Wives merged with the Princeton Friends of Foreign Students in 1974 and evolved into the University's International Center.

In 1949 the University League Nursery School (ULNS) was established as a cooperative in which parents assisted the teachers, volunteered in the classroom, and repaired equipment to keep tuition costs low. In time the nursery school became independent, while continuing to rely on the league for fundraising. In 1967 the league played a leading role in establishing a docent program at the art museum that provided guided tours, presented slide shows to schoolchildren, and staffed the museum store.

Over time, the league received memorial gifts that were used to assist University families with medical emergencies and provide scholarships for the nursery school.

After operating for many years in a University-owned building at 171 Broadmead and expanding to include children from non-University families, in 2015 ULNS relocated to an early childhood center at the Jewish Center of Princeton on Nassau Street east of the campus. Five years later the school closed. Before closing it transferred funds to an even older preschool in the community, the Princeton Nursery School, to establish a University League scholarship to be awarded annually to a child in need.

From its inception, the University League focused on service to the University community, reinventing itself over the years as needs changed. In 2020 the league became independent of the University but remained a social group that continued to promote fellowship through a variety of cultural and social activities.

University Now (UNOW)

In May 1969, Betty Friedan, founder of the National Organization for Women, came to Princeton to urge NOW's recently formed Central New Jersey Chapter to take an interest in childcare. Without full-day care, she argued, mothers could not exercise their right to work. By the end of the year the chapter had secured premises from a local church and by January it had recruited qualified teachers. In February the chapter advertised that NOW Day Nursery would welcome its first children in September 1970 for $28 a week with priority access for the children of students and working mothers.

Meanwhile, as the University was adapting to coeducation and groups on campus were pressing for daycare for faculty and staff, Mary Procter, an analyst working for Provost William Bowen *58, was asked to explore options.

Just weeks before the nursery was slated to open, the church withdrew its offer to house it; upon reflection, they said, mothers should stay home with their children. After three days of trying to save its school, Central New Jersey proposed that the University rent them space at 171 Broadmead, which already housed the University League cooperative nursery school.

The proposal landed on Procter's desk. As a NOW member herself, she recommended that the University accept the proposal, suggesting it would gauge campus demand for childcare. Bowen approved a one-year trial, and the school was named the University-NOW Day Nursery. It opened in September 1970 with the University covering the costs of rent, utilities, and certification, and providing half-scholarships for University-affiliated children.

Over the years the school's name changed simply to UNOW. In 2017 the University built a purpose-designed facility at 185 Broadmead and asked UNOW to operate it as a full-day, full-year program for children from three months to five years. On September 5, 2017, more than 150 children and teachers began their first day at the new childcare center that had space for up to 180 infants, toddlers, and preschoolers, from University and non-University families, with University families given preference in admission.

UNIVERSITY RESEARCH BOARD (URB), THE, advises the dean for research and the president on matters pertaining to research administration and policy. It establishes policies for the solicitation, acceptance, and administration of research grants and contracts and monitors the implementation of these policies. The dean for research, who chairs the board, oversees organized research activities throughout the University, adjudicates questions of policy regarding the acceptance and administration of research funds, and has general supervision over the application of policy in this area.

The URB consists of six tenured or tenure-track members of the faculty, two elected by the faculty and four appointed by the president. The director of the office of research and project administration serves as its administrative officer, and the vice president for finance and treasurer and the dean of the graduate school are ex officio members of the board.

The URB was formed in 1959 to replace a more narrowly focused committee on project research and invention that had been established in 1946. Physics department chair Henry De.W Smyth 1918 *1921, who had chaired the earlier committee for several years, became the board's first chair, serving with the rank of dean. After Smyth stepped down in June 1966, his successors were Lyman Spitzer Jr. *38 (astrophysical sciences), 1966–1972; Sheldon Judson '40 (geosciences), 1972–1977; Robert May (biology), 1977–1988; Sam Treiman (physics), 1988–1995; Will Happer *64 (physics), 1995–2005; and A. J. Stewart Smith *66 (physics).

A year after Smith was appointed URB chair in 2005 he was named the University's first dean for research, with responsibilities that included chairing the URB. In 2013, Smith moved to the newly created position of vice president for the Princeton Plasma Physics Laboratory and was succeeded as dean for research by former vice dean of the engineering school Pablo Debenedetti (chemical and biological engineering).

In 2020 sponsored research expenditures at the University amounted to $364 million, including $120 million at the Princeton Plasma Physics Laboratory (PPPL). While the natural sciences and engineering accounted for more than 90 percent of the non-PPPL expenditures, there was also significant outside support for the humanities and social sciences. Federal agencies provided more than 80 percent of the non-PPPL funding, led by the National Science Foundation and the National Institutes of Health. These funds came to the University through more than 1,500 separate awards.

Under long-established University policy, contracts or grants for research that are expected to generate classified information are accepted only under unusual conditions and with specific approval by the URB, and the University does not administer funds whose purpose and the character of whose sponsorship cannot be publicly disclosed.

The office of the dean for research helps faculty and others connect with external and internal resources to support their research. The offices that report to the dean include corporate engagement and foundation relations, laboratory animal resources, research and project administration, research integrity and assurance, and technology licensing.

An animal research advisory group advises the dean regarding the University's program of animal care and a conflict of interest in research panel oversees the University's processes for disclosing and addressing conflicts of interest in research. Also advising the dean are:

- An Institutional Animal Care and Use Committee that ensures the appropriate care and use of animals involved in the University's research, educational, and training activities.
- An Institutional Biosafety Committee that is responsible for the review and approval of research that involves biological materials.
- An Institutional Review Board for Human Subjects that reviews research projects involving human subjects to ensure protection of the subjects' rights, privacy, and welfare.
- A Radiation Safety Committee that ensures that radioactive research materials are used in a safe and responsible manner.

In February 2020 the University created a new position of vice dean for innovation, reporting to the dean for research, and in May 2020 the Princeton Entrepreneurship Council became part of the office, reporting to the vice dean, to emphasize the role of entrepreneurship in enhancing the societal impact of innovations that emerge from research.

UPPER AND LOWER PYNE, gifts of Moses Taylor Pyne 1877, were built in 1896 on the model of half-timbered sixteenth-century Tudor Revival houses in Chester, England. They were designed to provide space for shops at the street level and dormitory rooms for undergraduates on the floors above. In 1950 the dormitory rooms were converted to offices.

In 1963 Upper Pyne was razed as part of an expansion of Palmer Square to make way for the Princeton Bank and Trust Company (now PNC Bank) building at 76 Nassau Street. Lower Pyne still stands at the northeast corner of Nassau and Witherspoon streets. For a time, it housed the Suburban Transit bus station, but since 1986 its ground-floor space has been the flagship location of the retail store, Hamilton Jewelers.

VALEDICTORY ORATION. The valedictory oration was first given by a graduating senior in 1760. Originally, a high-ranking student particularly suited for the role delivered the valedictory, and the highest-ranking senior gave the salutatory address. In recent years, the faculty has chosen both speakers for their special qualifications, as well as for high scholastic standing.

In 1783 the valedictorian was Ashbel Green, later Princeton's eighth president. The Continental Congress was meeting in Princeton that summer, and it adjourned its sessions to attend Commencement. Green concluded his remarks with an address of some length to George Washington, who was present. "The next day," Green later recorded, "General Washington met me in the entry of the College . . . took me by the hand, walked with me a short time, flattered me a little, and desired me to present his best respects to my classmates . . . There has never been such an audience at a commencement before and perhaps there never will be again."

One of the other early valedictorians was James Roosevelt 1780, great-grandfather of Franklin D. Roosevelt. George Mifflin Dallas, valedictorian in 1810, became the 11th vice president of the United States. William Jay Magie, valedictorian in 1852, became chancellor of New Jersey; his son, William Francis Magie, was valedictorian in 1879 and later dean of the faculty, while John Grier Hibben, 14th president of the University, delivered the address in 1882. Other notable valedictorians include future six-time presidential candidate Norman Thomas in 1905 and future secretary of state John Foster Dulles in 1908.

Several valedictorians became members of the faculty: Donald Stauffer 1923 (English), E. Harris Harbison 1928 (History), Gordon Craig '36 (History), James Billington '50 (History), Steven Gubser '94 (Physics), Andrew Addison Houck '00 (Electrical Engineering), and John Vincent Pardon (Mathematics) '11.

In 2001, when the faculty was unable to choose between two candidates, it selected two valedictorians, Jared Kramer '01 and Christine McLeavey '01. The valedictory orations in 1993 and 2002 were given by a brother and sister, Niles Pierce '93 and Lillian Beatrix Pierce '02.

Valedictorians since 1970 are listed on page 525.

VEBLEN, OSWALD, the son of a professor of mathematics and physics and the nephew of the economist and social theorist Thorstein Veblen, played a major role in the development of mathematics at Princeton and in the United States. He earned an AB at the University of Iowa in 1898, a second AB at Harvard in 1900, and a PhD at the University of Chicago in 1903. When dean of the faculty Henry Fine 1880 was building up the Mathematics department, he heard of Veblen's work at Chicago and, at his suggestion, President Woodrow Wilson brought

Veblen to Princeton as one of the original preceptors in 1905.

Fine had a remarkable knack for picking promising young mathematicians, and none of his choices was more successful. Veblen attracted many able graduate students, some of whom were added to the faculty, and he helped Fine recruit other distinguished members for the growing department. His research and that of his students covered many fields, including the foundations of geometry, differential geometry and its connection with relativity theory, symbolic logic, and analysis situs (later known as topology). Under his leadership, Princeton became one of the world's great centers in topology.

Veblen's influence on his profession extended beyond Princeton. As president of the American Mathematical Society in 1923–24, he led a successful effort to obtain support from foundations, corporations, and individuals for mathematical research and publication. It was on his urging that the National Research Council began granting postdoctoral fellowships in mathematics in 1924.

When the Fine Professorship, the first American research chair in mathematics, was founded in 1926, Veblen was named its first incumbent. When the Jones family provided funds for the original Fine Hall in 1929, Veblen supplied most of the ideas that went into its design.

He conceived of Fine Hall as a center in which mathematicians could (in his words) "group themselves for mutual encouragement and support," and where "the young recruit and the old campaigner" could have "those informal and easy contacts that are so important to each of them." The common room, which he hoped would increase colleginality among the mathematics faculty and students and encourage their closer relation to the physics group from the adjacent Palmer Laboratory, was placed so that everyone had to pass it to get to the library on the top floor. There was another room reserved solely for professors on the principle that "in all forms of social intercourse the provisions for privacy are as important as those for proximity."

In 1932 Veblen resigned the Fine Professorship to accept appointment as the first professor at the Institute for Advanced Study, which had just been established. He was largely responsible for selecting the other members of its original mathematics faculty (James Alexander II 1910 *1915, Albert Einstein, John von Neumann, and Herman Weyl), and for establishing the institute's policy of concentrating on postdoctoral research. In its early years, the institute was housed in Fine (now Jones) Hall along with the University's mathematics faculty.

Veblen played a critical and heroic role in rescuing Jewish scholars from persecution in Europe as he helped to bring many distinguished mathematicians, as well as scholars in physics, economics, and art history, to the United States after Hitler's rise to power. In his later years (as the institute's director J. Robert Oppenheimer observed), he "provided a real clearing house at the institute for mathematicians from all over the world."

Veblen was influential in the purchase of a large tract of land for the institute, whose woods continue to attract its members and the Princeton community to its walks. In 1957, he and his wife deeded to Mercer Country 81 acres of wooded land in the northeast quadrant of Princeton known as Herrontown Woods, where they lived in their later years, to provide a place where, in their words, "you can get away from cars and just walk and sit."

VETERANS OF FUTURE WARS was a satirical organization created in March 1936 by Lewis Jefferson Gorin Jr.'36, a politics major then writing a senior thesis on Niccolo Machiavelli. He and other members of Terrace Club were disturbed by an act of Congress that advanced by 10 years—from 1946 to 1936—the date at which veterans of World War I would receive their soldiers' bonuses. This legislation, the consequence of intensive lobbying by the American Legion and the Veterans of Foreign Wars, struck the Princetonians as an intolerable raid upon the United States Treasury during the Great Depression for the benefit of an organized special interest group.

The first manifesto of the Veterans of Future Wars appeared in the *Daily Princetonian*. It argued that sooner or later there would be another war, and thus it would be appropriate for Congress to grant a $1,000 cash bonus to all men between the ages of 18 and 36. Legally the bonus would be payable in 1965, but since Congress was bent on paying bonuses before they were due, the actual payment date should be June 1936—with, of course, an additional three percent annual interest compounded back from 1965 to 1936 (bringing the total to $2,400).

In this way the future veterans would receive their benefits while they were still alive to enjoy them. The manifesto also called for immediate payment of $50 per month for the rest of their lives to "all mothers and future mothers of male children."

The Press Club sent out stories, the wire services took an interest, and all across the country newspapers ran articles on the Future Veterans. Overnight, local chapters mushroomed on college campuses; by June 1936 there were more than 500 chapters and a paid-up membership of over 50,000 students. Gorin rented an office in Princeton and hired a secretary to deal with the correspondence generated by news about his organization.

The Future Veterans were denounced in Congress and vigorously criticized and condemned by the organized veterans' movement. The commander of the Veterans of Foreign Wars called them "insolent puppies" who ought to be spanked. "They'll never be veterans of a future war," he predicted.

Part of what gave the Future Veterans such rapid visibility was their rare appeal both to conservatives and to liberals. Conservatives saw the founders as allies who would help them keep the country from spending itself into bankruptcy. Liberals who were pacifist, anti-war, and anti-military saw in the movement an opportunity to satirize war. At Princeton the emphasis was largely on the joke, although an anti-war note was evident when the national headquarters adopted a resolution calling upon Congress to declare that the United States would not enter a foreign war except by majority vote of the residents of three-fourths of the states of the union. In spirit and language this resolution paralleled the then-pending Ludlow Amendment, which in 1937 barely failed of passage in the House of Representatives.

Future Veteran activity peaked by the close of the academic year. After summer vacation Lorin was in law school, the joke was stale, and national attention was focused on the Roosevelt-Landon presidential campaign. The Princetonians gamely issued a few proclamations and sent questionnaires to the presidential candidates about the bonus—and about conscription and wartime controls over capital. But operations were suspended in the fall, and in April 1937, with the organization's treasury showing a deficit of 44 cents, the Veterans of Future Wars closed their books forever.

Except for one student who was paralyzed in an automobile accident, every one of the Princetonians who founded the Veterans of Future Wars served in the armed forces of the United States in World War II.

VICE PRESIDENT was the title accorded to several persons who served as acting president during brief periods in the early years of the college, but the first vice president in the conventional sense was Samuel Stanhope Smith 1769, son-in-law of President John Witherspoon, who was appointed in 1786 to act for the president when he was away from Princeton, as he frequently was, on affairs of state. After Smith, the title was held by Elijah Slack 1805 *1811 and Philip Lindsly 1804 during the Ashbel Green 1783 and early James Carnahan 1800 presidencies, and then for 25 years until Carnahan's retirement by John Maclean Jr. 1816. Smith and Maclean became Princeton's seventh and 10th presidents, respectively.

Later, the duties that had been discharged by these vice presidents were more likely to be performed by deans (beginning in 1883) and, since 1966, by provosts. Since 1939 the title vice president has been associated primarily with administrative, rather than academic, responsibilities.

Over most of the past century, the financial vice president, a position first instituted in 1939, typically (but not always) also served as treasurer. The position of treasurer is one of the University's oldest offices; the treasurer is one of only four officers, along with the president, the secretary, and the clerk of the board, specified in the charter. The first treasurer was appointed in 1748, a year after the election of the first president. In the eighteenth century, and during most of the nineteenth, it was a part-time office, usually held by a trustee, and occasionally by a member of the faculty.

Beginning in 1885, the following served as treasurer full time, with some also serving as financial vice president:

Edwin Osborn (1885–1901)
Henry Duffield 1881 (1901–30)
George Wintringer 1894 (1930–41)
George Brakeley 1907 (1941–53)
Ricardo Mestres '31 (1953–72)
Carl Schafer (1972–87)
Raymond Clark (1987–2001)
Christopher McCrudden (2001–08)
Carolyn Ainslie (2008–18)
Jim Matteo (2019–)

The financial vice presidents have been:

George Brakeley 1907 (1939–53)
Ricardo Mestres '31 (1959–72)
Paul Firstenberg '55 (1972–76)
Carl Schafer (1976–87)
Richard Spies *72 (1988–2001)*
Christopher McCrudden (2005–08)
Carolyn Ainslie (2008–18)
Jim Matteo (2019–)

---

* Official title was vice president for finance and administration.

Other vice presidencies and their incumbents have been:

Administrative Vice President/Senior VP for Administration/Executive Vice President

Edgar Gemmell '34 (1959–65)
Charles Kalmbach Jr. '68 *72 (2002–04)
Mark Burstein (2004–13)
Treby Williams '84 (2013–)

Vice President and Secretary

Thomas Wright Jr. '62 (1990–2004)
Robert Durkee '69 (2004–19)
Hilary Parker '01 (2019–)

Vice President for Development

Henry Bessire '57 (1969–80)
Van Zandt Williams Jr. '65 (1980–2002)
Brian McDonald '83 (2002–10)
Elizabeth Boluch Wood (2010–16)

Vice President for Advancement

Kevin Heaney (2016–)

Vice President for Public Affairs

William Weathersby (1970–78)
Robert Durkee '69 (1978–2018)
Brent Colburn (2018–21)*

Vice President for Administrative Affairs

Anthony Maruca '54 (1972–88)

Vice President for Human Resources

Audrey Smith (1989–95)
Joan Doig (1996–2002)
Maureen Nash (2003–05)
Lianne Sullivan-Crowley (2005–)

Vice President for Facilities

John Moran '51 (1973–78)
Eugene McPartland (1983–99)
Kathleen Mulligan (1999–2003)
Michael McKay (2003–17)
KyuJung Whang (2017–)

Vice President for Computing/Information Technology

Ira Fuchs (1985–2000)
Betty Leydon (2001–12)
Jay Dominick (2012–)

Vice President for Campus Life

Janet Smith Dickerson (2000–10)
Cynthia Cherrey (2010–15)
W. Rochelle Calhoun (2015–)

Vice President for University Services

Chad Klaus (2012–)

Vice President for the Princeton Plasma Physics Laboratory

A.J. Stewart Smith *66 (2013–16)
David McComas (2016–)

Vice President and General Counsel

Ramona Romero (2019–)

Vice President and Chief Audit and Compliance Officer

Nilufer Shroff (2019–)

VICE PRESIDENTS OF THE UNITED STATES who graduated from Princeton are:

Aaron Burr Jr. 1772 1801–1805 (Jefferson)
George Mifflin Dallas 1810 1845–1849 (Polk)

VOLLEYBALL. After three years as a club sport, Princeton's women's volleyball team played its first varsity match on September 28, 1977, defeating Kean University, 3–0. The team split its six Ivy matches and finished its inaugural season with a respectable overall record of 18–19. (The Ivy League championship was determined in an end-of-the-season tournament until 2000; round robin play within the Ivy League did not begin until 1987.)

Success built quickly. In its second season, the team improved to 22–17 and tied for first place in the Ivy tournament before losing in a tie breaker. Three Princeton players—captain Katherine Reeves '79, Patricia Hannigan '82, and Kathryn Wilson '81—were named first team All-Ivy, the first year an All-Ivy volleyball team was named. Princeton then won the Ivy League tournament for the next four consecutive years and seven of the next nine. The 1984 team won 33 matches, which was a University record for most team wins in a season at that time. Princeton advanced to the tournament finals every year from 1978 to 1987.

The team's first coach, Susana Occhi, was born in Argentina and coached the University of Delaware's first volleyball team before moving to Princeton. In 1982, Occhi was succeeded by Glenn Nelson, who was already coaching the men's club volleyball team.

---

* Official title was vice president for communications and public affairs.

Nelson coached the Princeton women for 27 seasons (1982–2008) and the men for 30 (1979–2009), winning 1,086 games in his career. In 1997–98, Nelson became the only coach in the history of intercollegiate volleyball to lead both a men's and women's team to the NCAA Final Four in the same academic year. On November 9, 2007, he became Princeton's all-time winningest coach in any sport with a 3–0 victory over Brown. Princeton also clinched its 14th Ivy League title that night and would go on to become the first Ivy team to win the league with a 14–0 record.

Nelson-led teams were in the hunt for the Ivy title almost annually, winning the championship in 1994, 1995, 1997, 1999, 2000, 2004, and 2007. To date, Princeton has won 18 Ivy League titles and advanced to the NCAA tournament seven times, in both cases more than any other school.

Six Tigers have been named Ivy League Player of the Year: Kristi Hakman '92 (1990), Kristin Spataro '96 (1995), Sabrina King '01 (1999), Parker Henritze '09 (2007), Cara Mattaliano '17 (2015 & 2016), and Maggie O'Connell '20 (2017). Hakman and Ayesha Attoh '98 are two of only five players to achieve first-team All-Ivy honors four times.

King won three Ivy titles as a player and ranked in the top five all-time in kills, digs, and aces. She returned to Princeton as an assistant coach for seven seasons before assuming head coaching responsibilities in 2011. Her 2015 team won the league title after losing its first three starts, something no other Ivy team has done. It was the first of three straight Ivy titles and NCAA tournament appearances. King won back-to-back Ivy Coach of the Year awards in 2015 and 2016.

Although men's volleyball had been a club sport since 1979 and played against varsity teams from other schools, it was not made a varsity sport until 1997. Princeton is one of only 22 NCAA Division I schools to field a men's volleyball team, and one of only two Ivy League teams to do so, along with Harvard. Princeton competes in the Eastern Intercollegiate Volleyball Association (EIVA), the champion of which receives an automatic berth in the NCAA Division I men's volleyball championships. Men's volleyball is not an official Ivy League sport.

The men reached the EIVA championship game in both of their first two seasons as a varsity sport and won the title in 1998. In 1997, after leading the nation in hitting percentage, Derek Devens '98 became just the second player in school history to earn All-America honors (Marin Gjaja '91 was the first). The 1998 champions defeated two Top 15 teams during the regular season. In the EIVA semi-final round, they defeated Penn State, 15–7, 15–13, and 16–14. It proved to be the only time in the 20-year period from 1997–2016 that Penn State did not win the EIVA championship. Princeton then defeated Rutgers-Newark to earn an NCAA tournament berth, before losing to top-ranked Pepperdine.

Under coach Sam Shweisky, who succeeded Nelson after the 2009 season, the Tigers advanced to the EIVA championship game in 2010 and 2014, losing both times to Penn State. In 2019, however, Princeton defeated Penn State for its second EIVA title. In the NCAA tournament, the Tigers defeated Barton College before losing to Pepperdine.

VON NEUMANN, JOHN, often described as a polymath, was one of the greatest mathematicians of the twentieth century. He was a professor of mathematical physics at the University and one of the first professors at the Institute for Advanced Study.

Von Neumann was born in Budapest, Hungary, and was recognized early as a child prodigy. Even before he began formal schooling, he could divide eight-digit numbers in his head, memorize pages in phone books, and converse in ancient Greek. By age eight he was familiar with differential and integral calculus and was an avid reader of history. His interest in mathematics was fostered by his teachers at the Lutheran High School of Budapest, where Princeton's Nobel Laureate physicist Eugene Wigner was also a student, and by age 15 he was studying advanced calculus. By age 19 he had published two major mathematical papers.

After graduation from high school, von Neumann studied chemistry for two years in Berlin and chemical engineering for two years in Zurich, but he spent much of his time with mathematicians, taking a PhD in mathematics at the University of Budapest at age 22, not long after receiving his chemical engineering diploma at Zurich.

In 1929 von Neumann accepted an invitation to come to Princeton as a lecturer in quantum statistics. By then he had already published five papers: three that set out a mathematical framework for quantum theory; one that was a pioneering work in game theory; and one exploring the link between formal logic systems and the limits of mathematics. Appointed a full professor and given a continuing half-time appointment the following year, he spent one term each year in Princeton and one in Germany until 1933 when, at the age of 30, he accepted appointment as the youngest and one of the first professors in the newly founded Institute for Advanced Study.

In 1932 von Neumann published his book, *The Mathematical Foundations of Quantum Mechanics*, which established a strong mathematical framework for quantum physics. His work in this field gave him profound knowledge regarding the application of nuclear energy to military and peacetime uses, and during World War II he played a major role among the scientists who developed the atomic bomb. After the war he served on the advisory committee of the Atomic Energy Commission and on the commission itself from 1954 until his death.

In collaboration with the economist Oskar Morgenstern, he developed further the interest in game theory he had first evidenced in a paper published in 1928. Modern game theory is based on their classic work, *Theory of Games and Economic Behavior* (published by Princeton University Press in 1944), which developed a mathematical theory of economic and social organization based on a theory of games of strategy.

As a mathematician, von Neumann produced papers in logic, set theory, ergodic theory, and operator theory; his work influenced quantum theory, automata theory, economics, and defense planning. Wigner and others noted that, of all the principal branches of mathematics, he failed to make important contributions only in topology and number theory.

Along with Alan Turing *38, he was a founding figure in computing. He envisioned applications for computers that went well beyond being high-speed calculating devices, and in 1945 he persuaded the Institute for Advanced Study to build an electronic computing device in the basement of Fuld Hall that introduced the basic architecture, known as von Neumann architecture, used by modern stored-program digital computers.

Von Neumann published over 150 papers, including about 60 in pure mathematics, 60 in applied mathematics, and 20 in physics. His final work, *The Computer and the Brain*, published posthumously in 1958, explored analogies between computers and the human brain.

Von Neumann received many honors for his contributions to science and the nation. In 1937 he won the American Mathematical Society's highest award, the Bocher Prize. In 1947 he was awarded the Presidential Medal for Merit and the Navy Distinguished Civilian Service Award for his work during World War II. From 1951 to 1953 he was president of the American Mathematical Society, and in 1956 he received three top honors: the Albert Einstein Commemorative Award, the $50,000 Enrico Fermi Award for his contributions to the design and construction of computing machines used in nuclear research and development, and the Medal of Freedom.

In the summer of 1955, only a few months after his appointment to the Atomic Energy Commission, von Neumann became ill with what was soon diagnosed as cancer. His last public appearance came early in 1956 when he received the Medal of Freedom from President Dwight Eisenhower.

Analyzing the qualities of mind that made possible von Neumann's extraordinary contributions, Wigner, von Neumann's friend since high school days in Budapest, emphasized the accuracy of his logic, his brilliance, and his exceptional memory. He said that he had learned more mathematics from von Neumann than anyone else and much more about the "essence of creative thinking in mathematics" than he could have learned in a lifetime of study without him. In a memoir written for the American Philosophical Society, Wigner declared: "His was a great mind—perhaps one of the greatest of the first half of this century."

WASHINGTON, GEORGE, made two memorable visits to Princeton. The first took place in 1777 when, 10 days after crossing the Delaware on Christmas night and defeating the British at Trenton, he made an early-morning surprise attack that drove the British from Nassau Hall and sent them in retreat from Princeton. The second visit occurred in 1783, in the closing days of the war, when he came at the request of the Continental Congress, which had fled from Philadelphia to avoid mutinous troops and was meeting in Nassau Hall.

Since no suitable house could be found for Washington in the village of Princeton, "Rockingham" was rented for him in Rocky Hill, four miles away. He arrived late in August and stayed until November. He became a familiar figure in Princeton and was a frequent visitor to Nassau Hall, where at a formal ceremony in August he received the thanks of the Congress for his conduct of the war.

In September he attended the College's Commencement in the First Presbyterian Church along with the members of Congress who had adjourned their meetings so they could attend. Ashbel Green 1783 (later president of the College) delivered the valedictory oration and paid tribute to Washington, observing later that "there had never been such an audience at a Commencement before, and perhaps, there never will be again."

The trustees met immediately after the commencement exercises. Their only business was the adoption of the following resolution:

> The Board being desirous to give some testimony of their high respect for the character of his Excellency General Washington, who has so auspiciously conducted the armies of America,
> Resolved, That the Rev. Drs. Witherspoon, Rodgers, and Johnes be a committee to wait upon his Excellency to request him to sit for a picture, to be taken by Mr. Charles Wilson Peale, of Philadelphia. And that this portrait be placed in the Hall of the College, in the room of the picture of the late King of Great Britain [George the Second], which was torn away by a ball from the American artillery in the battle of Princeton.

At a meeting on the following day President John Witherspoon reported to the board that "his Excellency General Washington had delivered to him fifty guineas . . . as a testimony of his respect for the College." The board directed that the committee it had appointed to solicit his portrait also present to him "the thanks of the Board for . . . his politeness and generosity."

Washington consented to the portrait, which was completed in time for presentation at Commencement the following year. It depicts Washington with uplifted sword at the battle of Princeton; at his side is the mortally wounded General Hugh Mercer, a surgeon for whom Mercer County is named, and another officer bearing an American flag, with Nassau Hall in the distance. For more than two centuries the portrait hung in Nassau Hall, where it escaped two fires; since 2005 it has been on display in the art museum, still in its original frame, which survived a cannonball during the Battle of Princeton that destroyed the portrait of King George II that it was holding at the time. A replica of Peale's portrait of Washington hangs in the Faculty Room.

Washington demonstrated his high regard for the College when he sent his step-grandson, George Washington Parke Custis, to study there in 1796. In a letter to Custis in 1797, Washington wrote: "no college has turned out better scholars or more estimable characters than Nassau."

WATER POLO. Water polo is both one of Princeton's older sports and one of its newest.

The sport was first played from 1907 to 1930 before packed galleries in the Brokaw Tank adjacent to University Gymnasium. Ably coached by Frank Sullivan, Princeton teams won championships in the water polo league of the Intercollegiate Swimming Association in 10 of the 23 seasons in which they participated: 1912 through 1917; 1919; and 1921 through 1923. Princeton did not lose a single game in any of these years. The 1916 team was exceptionally strong defensively: it permitted its opponents only 12 points—against its own 335—during the entire season. The 1917 team was outstanding on offense, scoring a record total of 370 points. Herbert W. Warden Jr. 1918 led in scoring with 230 points in 1916, and 210 in 1917.

Water polo has always been a rough sport, but its initial demise was due as much to hygiene as to violence. In February 1930, the faculty committee on athletics announced that 19 of the 23 members of the varsity squad and 14 of the 17 members of the freshman squad were suffering from ear injuries or nose and throat infections and that water polo would be discontinued for the rest of the season. Later, on recommendation of the medical staff, the committee announced the abolition of the sport at Princeton.

In the ensuing decades, a few informal efforts were made to revive water polo, but not until the mid-1990s did it again become a varsity sport. A men's team began play in 1996 (with a loss to Slippery Rock) and a women's team began the following year (with a victory over George Washington). The women finished with a winning record in their first season and earned a national ranking.

Both squads were coached in their inaugural seasons by Paul Nelson, who had coached the men for several years previously when water polo was a club sport. Notwithstanding its lack of varsity status, the men made their first appearance in the NCAA tournament in 1992, and Chad Elliot '94 became Princeton's first All-American. Nelson was succeeded by Luis Nicolao, who had himself been an All-American water polo player at the Naval Academy. Nicolao coached the men's and women's squads for 18 seasons, until 2017.

Competing in several conferences, Princeton's teams have compiled strong records. The women have won two Ivy League championships (1999, 2015), seven Eastern Collegiate Athletic Conference (ECAC) championships (1999, 2000, 2001, 2003, 2005, 2006, 2007), and numerous titles in the Collegiate Water Polo Association (CWPA). They have appeared in the NCAA tournament three times (2012, 2013, 2015). In

2017, goalie Ashleigh Johnson '17 was named a first-team All-American, only the second Princeton water polo player to achieve that honor. A Miami native, Johnson won gold medals at the 2015 world championships and the 2016 and 2021 summer Olympics.

The men's teams have appeared in the NCAA tournament six times (1992, 2004, 2009, 2011, 2015, 2019), finishing third twice. They won the ECAC title in 2003 and have recorded numerous CWPA and other conference championships. The 2004 squad set a program record with 25 wins, finishing ninth in the final CWPA Division I poll. In 2017, goaltender Vojislav Mitrovic '18 was voted the Northeast Water Polo Conference Player of the Year.

WEST, ANDREW FLEMING 1874, first dean of the graduate school, was born in Allegheny, Pennsylvania. He entered Princeton in 1870, but soon withdrew because of poor health and for two years attended Centre College in Danville, Kentucky, where his father was a professor at the Danville Theological Seminary. He returned to Princeton in 1872, graduating in 1874. After college, he taught high school Latin in Cincinnati for six years and, following a period of study in Europe, served for two years as principal of the Morris Academy in Morristown, New Jersey.

In 1883 West was called to Princeton by President James McCosh to fill the newly founded Giger chair in Latin. Organizing and fundraising talents he used on behalf of the classics led to his appointment as secretary of the committee in charge of the University's highly successful sesquicentennial celebration in 1896. The three-day affair included a program of public lectures by visiting scholars from abroad and a spectacular torchlight procession of 2,000 gaily costumed alumni that stimulated the development of the most colorful event of the annual commencement season—the alumni parade (P-rade).

West helped to obtain President Grover Cleveland's participation in the celebration and, after his second term as president, Cleveland moved to Princeton, naming the house and grounds that West found for him "Westland." Upon his election as a Princeton trustee, Cleveland became chair of the committee on the graduate school and West's strong supporter.

As secretary of the committee that sought gifts in connection with the sesquicentennial celebration, West played a significant role in raising funds for the endowment and for a library and three dormitories. He also played a major role in introducing Collegiate Gothic architecture at Princeton, communicating his enthusiasm for the Gothic of Oxford and Cambridge to Moses Taylor Pyne 1877 and other donors and—through Pyne's influence as chair of the grounds and buildings committee—to other members of the Board of Trustees.

Following his appointment in December 1900 as first dean of the graduate school, West devoted his energy and talents to its development and particularly to the creation of a residential graduate college. In the spring of 1903, after visiting Oxford, Cambridge, and other universities in Britain and on the European continent, he outlined his proposal for a residential college in a handsomely illustrated book, which he proceeded to use, with great effectiveness, in raising funds for this project. One of the first results of his effort was a $275,000 bequest in the spring of 1906 by Josephine Thomson Swann for a graduate college in memory of her first husband, United States Senator Robert Thomson 1817.

The Swann bequest brought to light a disagreement between West and President Woodrow Wilson regarding the location of the graduate college. From the beginning, Wilson had wanted the graduate college "at the heart" of the University as "a means of vitalizing the whole intellectual life" of the place. In his book, West spoke of the influence the proposed graduate college would have on "every undergraduate who passes it in his daily walks," but as his plans developed, he settled on a location geographically separate from the main campus, where, as he put it, the graduate college would be free from the distractions of undergraduates, and thus able to develop "its own true life."

West's position was greatly strengthened in the fall of 1906 when he received an invitation to serve as president of Massachusetts Institute of Technology. What his loss would mean to Princeton was widely discussed in the nation's press as well as in the *Princetonian* and the *Alumni Weekly*. After the adoption of a trustee resolution (drafted by Wilson) declaring that the board would consider his loss "quite irreparable" because it had "particularly counted upon him to put into operation the graduate college which he conceived and for which it has planned," West declined the invitation, and the *New York Sun* headlined its announcement "WEST WON'T GO."

West suffered a setback in the spring of 1908 when the trustees voted to locate the graduate college between Prospect House and 1879 Hall. A year later, however, West's continuing efforts were rewarded when he received a letter from William Cooper Procter 1883, president of Procter and Gamble, whose wife had been a high school student of West's in Cincinnati. Procter offered the University $500,000 for the graduate college, provided the trustees raised an equal amount from other sources and selected a site other than the Prospect one.

The stalemate that followed the Procter offer ended abruptly in May 1910 with the death in Salem, Massachusetts, of Isaac Wyman 1848, a wealthy bachelor. West had visited him a number of years before, seeking to persuade him to leave his money to the University for a graduate college to be built near where his father had fought in the Revolutionary War battle of Princeton. From Salem, where he had gone for the funeral and probate of the will, West telegraphed Wilson and Pyne (by then chair of the graduate school committee) that Wyman had left his residuary estate (estimated originally at upwards of $2 million but eventually realized at a little less than $800,000) for the purpose of constructing the graduate college, and had named West as one of two executors and trustees.

Wilson acknowledged defeat in the matter of location; he told his wife, "we've beaten the living, but we can't fight the dead."

The trustees unanimously authorized acceptance of the Procter gift, and the graduate college was built on the north edge of the golf course, half a mile from the main campus; it was dedicated on October 22, 1913, with speeches by, among others, West and former US President William Howard Taft. Its chief supporters are remembered on the site by Thomson College, Procter Hall, Pyne Tower, Cleveland Tower, and Wyman House, the residence of the dean of the graduate school. (The long-barreled flintlock musket and powder horn which Wyman's grandfather used in the French and Indian Wars and which his father carried in the battle of Princeton hang over the fireplace in the Wyman House library.)

Although his main ambition was now fulfilled, West continued to exercise his money-raising talent. When Henry Clay Frick, on being shown Procter Hall, observed that it "looked too damn much like a church—all it needs is an organ," West quickly persuaded him to give one.

A wit and a satirist, West delighted in epigrams and limericks. He also took special pleasure in writing honorary degree citations, and he was always ready to respond to a request for an elegant inscription for a new building.

West retired in 1928 after 45 years as Giger professor of Latin and 27 as dean of the graduate school. A few months earlier, a bronze statue of him, given by Procter, had been erected in the main quadrangle of the graduate college and a small house was completed next to Wyman House for his use the rest of his life.

WEST, CORNEL R. *80—Princeton faculty member, acclaimed teacher and scholar, public intellectual, and prominent activist—was born in Tulsa, Oklahoma, in 1953, the grandson of a Baptist minister and the son of a civilian Air Force administrator and an elementary school teacher and later principal. From his parents, siblings, and community, he said, he derived "ideals and images of dignity, integrity, majesty, and humility." He completed his undergraduate work at Harvard in three years, graduating *magna cum laude* in 1973 with a BA in Near Eastern languages and civilization. He then began doctoral study at Princeton, earning a PhD in philosophy in 1980. A year before completing his graduate education he published his first book, *Black Theology and Marxist Thought*. His doctoral dissertation on "Ethics, Historicism, and the Marxist Tradition" was revised and published in 1991 as his sixth book, *The Ethical Dimensions of Marxist Thought*.

After receiving his doctorate, West returned to Harvard as a W.E.B. Du Bois Fellow; taught at Union Theological Seminary, Yale Divinity School, and the University of Paris; and in 1988 joined the Princeton faculty as a professor of religion and director of its program in African American Studies. He remained at Princeton until 1994, returned to Harvard as a professor in African American studies and the Harvard Divinity School, and then in 2002 returned to Princeton, saying that in doing so he was "turning towards something that is positive, something that is visionary, something that is appreciative." He later became the first faculty member with a full appointment in the center for African American Studies.

In 2012 West retired from Princeton as the Class of 1943 University Professor, emeritus, and returned to teaching at Union Theological Seminary. In 2016 Harvard appointed him a professor of the practice of public philosophy and in 2021 he announced he was returning to Union. But his ties to Princeton remained strong, and he frequently returned to campus to teach, lecture, and engage in public dialogue, frequently with politics professor Robert George, director of the James Madison Program in American

Ideals and Institutions. His dialogues with George brought together prominent public intellectuals from both ends of the political spectrum in highly civil and mutually respectful discourse. (West describes himself as a radical democrat and George is one of the country's leading conservative intellectuals. Both are habitually attired in three-piece suits—in West's case, invariably black with white shirt and black tie.)

West was a popular teacher. When he taught the introductory African American studies course, he attracted an enrollment of more than 400 students, and more than 100 students typically applied for the 15 spaces in his freshman seminars. In 1996 the University awarded him the James Madison Medal, the highest distinction it can bestow on its graduate alumni, and in 2010 the Fields Center for Equality and Cultural Understanding presented West with the first Fields Memorial Award for Social Justice. The award recognizes innovators, scholars, activists, and educators whose work and example have fundamentally shaped campus conversation at Princeton and have had transformative effects on the collective life of the University. West was honored for his work as a scholar, activist, public intellectual, and leader on issues of social justice, race, equality, and cultural understanding.

In his scholarly work, West focuses on the area where religious thought, social theory, and pragmatic philosophy meet. A best-selling author, he has written 20 books and edited 13. He is best known for his groundbreaking book on race and America, *Race Matters* (1993); its sequel, *Democracy Matters* (2004); his memoir, *Brother West: Living and Loving Out Loud* (2009); and his influential *The American Evasion of Philosophy: A Genealogy of Pragmatism* (1989)—a history of pragmatism from Emerson to the present. His *Beyond Eurocentrism and Multiculturalism: Volume I: Prophetic Thought in Post-Modern Times* and *Volume II: Prophetic Reflections: Notes on Race and Power in America* were collectively granted the American Book Award in 1993.

West has recorded two spoken-word albums, *Sketches of My Culture* (2001) and *Street Knowledge* (2004), and a collection of spoken-word and music, *Never Forget: A Journey of Revelations* (2007). He frequently appears as a commentator on television and in other media, and from 2010 to 2013, he and talk show host Tavis Smiley co-hosted a popular radio show, Smiley & West, on National Public Radio. In 2003 he appeared as the character Councillor West in the movies *The Matrix Reloaded* and *The Matrix Revolutions*.

WHIG-CLIOSOPHIC SOCIETY, THE AMERICAN, is the oldest college literary and debating club in the United States. Originally two separate groups, Whig and Clio (as they have been known for most of their history) grew out of two earlier student societies, the Plain Dealing Club (Whig) and the Well-Meaning Club (Clio), that were founded around 1765. Similar groups appeared in other American colleges during the eighteenth century but most of them were short-lived. Such was also the fate of the Plain Dealing and Well-Meaning clubs; conflicts between the two groups led to their demise in March 1769.

Undergraduate interest in literary and debating activities did not end with the dissolution of the clubs. The prime agent in their revival appears to have been William Paterson 1763, later governor of New Jersey. After graduation, Paterson remained in Princeton to study law. During these years he maintained close contact with students, encouraging their more constructive activities. It seems to have been Paterson, along with a few other alumni, who persuaded the new president, John Witherspoon, to permit the formation of successors to the Plain Dealing and Well-Meaning clubs.

The American Whig Society was born on June 24, 1769, and the Cliosophic Society on June 7, 1770. The name "American Whig" derived from a series of essays by a new trustee of the College, William Livingston, shortly to become first governor of the state of New Jersey. It signified adherence to ancient principles of British political and religious dissent, principles that later found concrete form in the founding of the American republic. The adjective "Cliosophic" seems to have been invented by Paterson. Signifying "in praise of wisdom," it bears no relation to the muse of history.

The years immediately preceding the American Revolution were active ones for the societies. They afforded an arena in which many future leaders of the republic, such as James Madison 1771 (Whig) and Aaron Burr Jr. 1772 (Clio), developed and sharpened the skills of persuasion, exposition, and cooperation (and conflict) with peers.

The disruptions caused by the war brought a hiatus in the societies' activities. Revived in 1781, they then entered their period of greatest influence, one that extended to the 1880s. Housed at first in two small chambers in Nassau Hall, in 1805 Whig and Clio moved into more spacious quarters on the second floor of newly constructed Stanhope (then Geological) Hall. By the 1830s the societies had outgrown these rooms. They then constructed handsome wooden neo-classical halls for their own exclusive use, which were completed in 1838. The present marble halls, opened in 1893, are enlarged copies of the buildings of the 1830s.

Whig and Clio, like similar literary societies at other American colleges, were the principal focus of undergraduate life for much of the nineteenth century. Elaborately organized, self-governing youth groups (though often receiving advice from alumni and faculty), they were, in effect, colleges within colleges. They constructed and taught their own curricula, selected and bought their own books, operated their own libraries (often larger and more accessible than those of the college itself), and developed and enforced elaborate codes of conduct among their members. They competed intensely for members and college honors. Their debates trained generations to consider the great public issues of the day, from slavery to American expansion, from women's rights to the dismemberment of the union.

The societies reached their apogee in the 1880s. Almost every undergraduate belonged to one or the other of them, and diplomas were decorated with ribbons in the colors of the graduate's hall: blue for Whig, pink for Clio. As an undergraduate, Woodrow Wilson 1879 was elected speaker of the Whig society in recognition of his skills in debate.

As Princeton moved toward becoming a university and, in the process, significantly increased enrollment, a new network of social clubs and student organizations, expanded library facilities, and a widened curriculum replaced many of the functions once performed by the societies. By World War I, Whig and Clio were only two among the scores of student groups that appealed to a wide range of undergraduate interests.

After being dormant during World War I, the societies revived in the early 1920s, but they faced a student generation largely indifferent to their traditional concerns. In an effort to attract interest, in 1925 the Polity, Law, and Fine Arts clubs, along with the Speaker's Association, were absorbed into the halls. As interest continued to decline, in 1928 the two societies merged and moved into Whig Hall, with university offices moving into Clio Hall.

In 1941, Whig Hall and the assets of the society were transferred to the University, with the understanding that the building and funds were to be "used for purposes associated with undergraduate activities in the fields of public speaking, debate, conferences on public affairs, literature and journalism." These remain the principal pursuits of the society today. A variety of subsidiary organizations have been established, such as the Princeton Debate Panel, the Princeton Mock Trial, the International Relations Council, the Model United Nations, the Model Congress, the Woodrow Wilson Honorary Debating Panel, and others.

Whig-Clio continues to bring influential, and sometimes controversial, public figures to speak on the campus, and it continues to provide a venue for students to discuss pressing concerns of the day, ranging from contentious campus issues to some of the most challenging questions facing the outside world. Since 1960 it has bestowed its highest honor, the James Madison Award for Distinguished Public Service, on individuals who have devoted their lives to the betterment of society. The 2020 honoree, Terri Sewell '86, a member of Congress from Alabama, was the first African American woman to receive the award.

WHIG HALL has been the home of the American Whig-Cliosophic Society, commonly known as Whig-Clio since the merger of the American Whig and Cliosophic Societies in 1928. Whig Hall was built in 1893 for the American Whig Society, at the same time as its twin, Clio Hall, was built for the Cliosophic Society. Both current buildings were designed in marble in the Ionic style of a Greek temple, the style that also had been used for their stucco and wood predecessors, built in approximately the same locations in 1838. Both buildings had libraries, reading rooms, gathering spaces, and third floor senate chambers. The Whig senate chamber remains a popular location for student debates and invited speakers, as well as for other campus gatherings.

After Whig was gutted by fire in November 1969, extensive renovations, including a modern treatment of the destroyed east wall, were made. The renovations were completed in 1972. Twenty-five years later a semi-attached circular elevator tower was added to the building's south side.

WILSON, THOMAS WOODROW 1879 was Princeton's 13th president. Along with John Witherspoon, James McCosh, and Robert Goheen, he ranks among the presidents who played the most profound and pivotal roles in transforming a small colonial college into the esteemed and distinctive university it is today. Of the four, his tenure was the briefest—only eight years.

While many of Wilson's accomplishments and ideas have had lasting beneficial impact, he was a divisive figure both during and after his Princeton presidency and his record of racist views and actions has deeply tarnished his legacy. In 2020 the Board of Trustees voted to remove Wilson's name from Princeton's school of Public and International Affairs, which had been publicly named for him in 1948, because his "racist thinking and policies make him an inappropriate namesake for a school whose scholars, students, and alumni must be firmly committed to combatting the scourge of racism in all its forms." The trustees also removed his name from the residential college that was named for him.

Wilson significantly elevated the scholarly distinction of the faculty, created academic departments, raised academic standards, revised the undergraduate curriculum, introduced a new model of teaching with his appointment of "preceptors," pressed for the development of a graduate college (although not in its eventual location), promoted the library and art museum as teaching instruments, hired the first Jewish and the first Catholic faculty members, and called upon Princeton and Princetonians to be "in the nation's service." In the words of a 2016 trustee report, he "transformed an intellectually lethargic campus into a renowned institution of higher learning."

That same trustee report also made it clear that Wilson "held racist views and took or permitted racist actions." During his Princeton presidency he prevented the enrollment of Black students, and policies he instituted during his two terms as the country's 28th president resulted in the re-segregation of the federal civil service, especially in the two departments (the Treasury and the Post Office) that had significant numbers of Black employees. One historian said these actions "devastated not only careers but also the very foundation of full citizenship for African Americans."

Wilson was born in 1856 in Staunton, Virginia, the son of Joseph Ruggles Wilson, a Presbyterian minister, and Jessie Janet Woodrow. His father was one of the founders of the Southern Presbyterian Church in the United States after it split from the northern church in 1861. Tommy, as he was known until after his graduation from college, grew up in Augusta, Georgia, and Columbia, South Carolina. After a year at Davidson College, he matriculated as a freshman at Princeton in 1875.

During his undergraduate years he was a voracious reader and kept a commonplace book of passages from his readings. He organized a student club for discussion of public affairs, and his peers elected him speaker of the American Whig Society, secretary of the Football Association, president of the Baseball Association, and managing editor of the student newspaper, the *Princetonian*.

From 1879 to 1883, Wilson studied law at the University of Virginia and practiced in Atlanta. He then went to Johns Hopkins University for graduate work in political science and history. His doctoral dissertation, *Congressional Government* (1885), brought immediate recognition and academic appointments at Bryn Mawr College and then Wesleyan University. In 1885 he married Ellen Louise Axson and they had three daughters. Ellen died in 1914, and Wilson married Edith Bolling Galt in 1915.

In 1890 Wilson joined the Princeton faculty as the first incumbent of the McCormick Professorship of Jurisprudence. When his efforts to prod President Francis Patton to raise money for a law school failed, Wilson set about preparing what was considered the best pre-law curriculum in the country. Year in and year out he was voted the most popular teacher on the faculty. He played an active role in encouraging faculty approval of a student-initiated honor system for in-class exams. He spoke widely, contributed to popular magazines, and wrote best-selling books. In 1896 he delivered his eloquent oration, "Princeton in the Nation's Service," at the College's sesquicentennial celebration: "When all is said and done," he said, "it is not learning but the spirit of service that will give a college place in the public annals of the nation."

Wilson helped persuade the trustees that Patton should be replaced, and when arrangements were made for Patton to retire in June 1902, the trustees immediately and unanimously elected Wilson—Princeton's first lay president—to succeed him.

Wilson tightened academic standards so severely that enrollment declined sharply until 1907. (When asked early in his presidency how many students there were at Princeton, he answered, "about 10 percent.") He created departments of instruction with heads directly responsible to him. He later arranged for new deanships of the departments of science and of the college. He took the power of faculty appointments out of the control of the trustees and lodged it with the president and the academic departments.

These innovations were a prelude to more far-reaching changes. In 1904, the same year in which he created the departments, Wilson led the faculty in instituting a curricular reform that replaced the free elective system then in place with a unified curriculum of general studies with distribution requirements during the first two years, followed by concentrated study in one discipline and related fields during the junior and senior years. He also made provision for an honors program requiring independent work for ambitious students.

The following year Wilson revolutionized teaching at Princeton. Supported by alumni fund-raising, Wilson increased the size of the faculty by almost 50 percent by appointing 49 assistant professors called preceptors. They were to engage with undergraduates through guided reading and small-group discussion, serving as "companions and coaches and guides." With a remarkable eye for quality, Wilson assembled what was probably the finest young faculty anywhere, many of whom came to play leadership roles as scholars, teachers, and administrators over the course of their careers. Despite Wilson's initial intention that preceptors stay for about five years, almost half of them remained on the faculty until their retirement.

In the words of one newspaper, by making the changes he had made in the curriculum and the faculty, Wilson had "ruined what was universally agreed to be the most agreeable and aristocratic country club in America by transforming it into an institution of learning."

Over the course of his presidency, Wilson added three buildings for instruction (McCosh Hall, Palmer Laboratory, and Guyot Hall), four dormitories (Seventy-Nine, Patton, Campbell, and Holder halls), and a gymnasium.

Wilson sought unsuccessfully to replace the socially exclusive eating clubs with a system of residential quadrangles, or colleges, in which undergraduate students of all four classes would live, with their own recreational facilities and resident faculty. Membership would be by assignment or lot, and the clubs would either be absorbed into the quads or abolished. Early in 1906 he resolved to act, knowing that it might take years to effect significant change. After a severe stroke in May 1906 threatened his life, he decided to move more quickly. With little attempt to build broad support for his idea, he presented a tentative plan to the trustees in December 1906, and a refined plan six months later.

The trustees approved the quad plan in principle and Wilson announced it at Commencement in June 1907. Alumni, particularly in New York (led by trustee Moses Taylor Pyne 1877) and Philadelphia, were soon up in arms against the plan; as opposition grew, alumni giving declined, and in October 1907 the trustees withdrew their approval.

Meanwhile, Andrew Fleming West 1874, dean of the graduate school since its creation in 1900, was pursuing his dream of erecting a handsome graduate college where he could preside in Gothic splendor. At first, he said he wanted the college located in the center of the campus. Wilson heartily concurred, for he believed that graduate students living among undergraduates would elevate the intellectual life of the entire university.

Relations between Wilson and West deteriorated after 1906 when West changed course, now preferring a graduate college sequestered away from the distractions of undergraduate life and overlooking the recently acquired golf course. Josephine Ward Thomson Swann, a Princeton resident, died in 1906, leaving $275,000 for a graduate college, and in support of Wilson the trustees in 1908 voted that it should be built between Prospect House and 1879 Hall. While the plans were being drawn, in May 1909 William Cooper Procter 1883, of Cincinnati, announced that he would give $500,000 for the graduate college, provided that the trustees raised an equal amount and agreed to an off-campus location for the college.

Wilson fought desperately against the Procter offer. The New York and Philadelphia alumni again joined the fray, with Pyne leading the anti-Wilson forces. Procter withdrew his offer in February 1910 before a special trustee committee could recommend against it. However, Isaac Wyman 1848, of Salem, Massachusetts, died on May 18, 1910, leaving his entire estate, estimated to be worth well in excess of $2 million, for a graduate college at the Springdale site and naming West as one of his two executors. Wilson surrendered at once. "We've beaten the living," he said to his wife, "but we can't fight the dead." Ironically, the Wyman estate turned out to be worth only $794,000.

With West and Pyne triumphant and Pyne maneuvering for Wilson's removal, Wilson turned a receptive ear to those who were urging him to accept the Democratic nomination for governor of New Jersey, as a stepping-stone to the White House. Wilson accepted the nomination in September and went on to win the governorship in 1910 and the presidency in 1912. He was re-elected in 1916. In 1919 he was awarded the Nobel Prize for Peace as the leading architect of the League of Nations. After he died at his home in Washington on February 3, 1924, he was interred in the Washington Cathedral.

Wilson's divisiveness as Princeton president is reflected in the trustees' decision to wait until 1948 to announce the formal action they took in 1935 to name the school of Public and International Affairs for him. In 1956 the trustees accepted an endowment to establish the Woodrow Wilson Award as the highest distinction the University can confer on undergraduate alumni. In the 1960s they also approved a recommendation from students that Princeton's first residential college be named for Wilson in recognition of his efforts as president to create such a residential arrangement on campus.

By the last half of the twentieth century Wilson had become a revered figure on campus for many. While some members of the campus community and some alumni were aware of Wilson's racist views and actions at Princeton and as president of the United States, it was not until the mid-2010s that there was sufficient awareness, and sufficient concern about the largely unquestioning veneration of Wilson on campus, to generate sustained campus discussion.

Following a Nassau Hall sit-in in 2015 led by the Black Justice League, the University launched a thorough review of Wilson's legacy, conducted by a 10-member trustee committee with vice chair of the board Brent Henry '69 as its head. The committee created a website to collect observations and opinions about Wilson; conducted open forums and small-group discussions on campus for anyone who wanted to participate; and invited nine scholars and biographers to submit essays that were posted on the website.

Two specific questions posed to the committee were whether the school of Public and International Affairs and the residential college that bore Wilson's name should continue to do so. In its 2016 report, the committee recommended that the school and the college should retain their names, but that the University should be "honest and forthcoming about its history" and transparent "in recognizing Wilson's failings and shortcomings as well as the visions and achievements that led to the naming of the school and the college in the first place."

In adopting the committee's report, the trustees reaffirmed the University's determination "to be a university where people of all backgrounds and perspectives are welcomed, valued, and respected; where they learn with and from each other; and where all feel that the Princeton they attend is their Princeton."

The board established a continuing trustee committee to monitor progress toward achieving these goals. It called for greater efforts to encourage students from underrepresented groups to pursue graduate degrees; modified the University's informal motto to connect Wilson's phrase "Princeton in the Nation's Service" with the phrase "In the Service of Humanity" that had been suggested by 2014 Woodrow Wilson Award recipient and Supreme Court justice Sonia Sotomayor '76; encouraged diversification of campus art and iconography; and pledged support for educational and transparency initiatives to create a more multi-faceted understanding and representation of Wilson on campus and focus attention on "aspects of Princeton's history that have been forgotten, overlooked, subordinated, or suppressed."

One specific recommendation was to install a permanent marker on the site of the school of Public and International Affairs to educate the campus community and others about "both the positive and negative dimensions of Wilson's legacy." In the fall of 2019, a 39-foot-tall structure, *Double Sights*, by the sculptor Walter Hood, was installed on the plaza adjacent to Robertson Hall. The installation featured a slanted white column resting on a straight black column, with both columns etched with quotes from Wilson as well as images and quotes from contemporaries—including W. E. B. Du Bois, Ida B. Wells-Barnett, and David Lloyd George—who were critical of his views and policies, particularly as they related to race and gender.*

The trustees' 2020 statement recognized that "during his time on the faculty and as a transformative president, Wilson improved Princeton as much as or more than any other individual in the University's long history." But in asking whether "it is acceptable for this University's school of public affairs to bear the name of a racist who segregated the na-

---

* A 2021 trustee report on "principles to govern questions about when and under what circumstances it might be appropriate for the University to remove or contextualize the names and representations of individuals present on the Princeton campus" described the *Double Sights* sculpture as a "cautionary tale," noting that some objected to it as "another glorification of Wilson" and that the University had to create signage to explain the sculpture's purpose, "thereby contextualizing the contextualization of Wilson's name and history."

tion's civil service after it had been integrated for decades," the trustees concluded that the continued use of Wilson's name on the school impeded the school's and the University's capacity to pursue their missions. The trustees also announced that plans were already in place to close Wilson College when two new colleges under construction south of Poe Field were completed, but that while the college remained open it would be renamed "First College" to remove its association with Wilson's racist views and recognize its status as Princeton's first residential college.

Trustee and Wilson biographer A. Scott Berg '71, in a *Princeton Alumni Weekly* interview posted in July 2020, supported the decision, saying that while Wilson "accomplished great things," he also "inflicted great harm."

The trustees decided not to change the name of the Woodrow Wilson Award, which is presented each year on Alumni Day; the board noted that unlike the naming of the school and the college, in both cases done at the discretion of the board, the name of the award was established as the result of a gift, and that it "explicitly honors specific and positive aspects of Wilson's career."

Firestone Library houses the records of the Papers of Woodrow Wilson project, which in 1994 completed publication of a 69-volume annotated compilation of his papers.

WILSON, WOODROW, AWARD, THE, presented annually on Alumni Day, is the highest distinction the University can confer on an undergraduate alumnus or alumna. The award, named for Princeton's 13th president, was established in 1956 when the trustees accepted an endowment gift from an anonymous donor, resolving that they intended it to be an "ever-living recognition of Woodrow Wilson's conviction that education is for 'use' and as a continuing confirmation by Princeton University of the high aims expressed in his memorable phrase, 'Princeton in the Nation's Service,'" a phrase preserved today as part of Princeton's informal motto, Princeton in the Nation's Service and the Service of Humanity.

Previous Wilson Award winners are listed on page 526.

WILSON, WOODROW, NATIONAL FELLOWSHIP FOUNDATION, headquartered in Princeton, New Jersey, changed its name in June 2020, noting that Woodrow Wilson's "racist policies and beliefs" were "fundamentally incompatible with the foundation's values and work." It renamed itself the Institute for Citizens and Scholars, with an overarching goal of shaping "an informed, productively engaged, and hopeful citizenry."

The organization had its roots in a fellowship program that began on the Princeton campus at the end of World War II. The idea, as conceived by Professor Whitney Oates 1925 *1931 in collaboration with the dean of the graduate school, Hugh Stott Taylor, was to create a program of fellowships, funded by individual donors, to attract returning veterans to PhD programs in the humanities and prepare them for careers in college teaching. In 1945 these separate fellowships were combined into one program, which was named for Wilson. One of the first four participants in the program was classicist Robert Goheen '40 *48, who later became president of the University.

In 1949 the Carnegie Corporation granted Princeton $100,000 to extend the fellowship program nationwide. The program broadened beyond veterans and into fields other than the humanities. Beginning in 1951 administration of the program was transferred to the Association of Graduate Schools (under the auspices of the Association of American Universities). For three years, beginning in 1953, Goheen served as national director of the program. The number of fellowships grew to 200 nationally, with support from the 37 universities then comprising the AAU and grants from the Carnegie Corporation, the Rockefeller Foundation, and others.

In 1957 the Ford Foundation committed $24.5 million to support 1,000 fellowships a year for five years, and the program became a new independent nonprofit, the Woodrow Wilson National Fellowship Foundation, with Taylor as president. With two renewal grants in 1962 and 1966, Ford contributed a total of $52 million to support the fellows and the graduate schools that hosted them.

The fellows became intellectual leaders within the academy, but also in other fields such as government, the corporate world, and the nonprofit sector. One Wilson fellow, Ralph Nader '55, went on to become a prominent crusader for consumer interests.

In the early 1970s funding for the program diminished and the number and amounts of the awards were reduced. By 1974, when the original program ended, it had supported more than 20,000 fellows.

Beginning in the late 1960s and early 1970s and continuing today, the foundation developed other programs to meet pressing and emerging needs. Among them were programs to improve graduate education and teaching, including teaching at the elementary and secondary levels; develop leaders and institutions; promote more gender and racial diversity in American higher education; increase understanding of American history and civics; encourage work in fields such as women's studies and women's health; and prepare students with doctoral training for nonacademic careers, both within and outside of higher education.

In 2020 the foundation expanded its mission to broaden civic engagement, support civil discourse, and re-emphasize excellence, opportunity, and diversity in higher education.

WILSON, WOODROW, THE PAPERS OF, is a 69-volume annotated compilation published over 35 years by Princeton University Press and edited by Princeton history professor Arthur S. Link. It is the first comprehensive edition of the documentary record of the life and times of Woodrow Wilson (1856–1924), and the first full-scale edition of the papers of any modern American president. The series won critical acclaim as one of the twentieth century's "distinguished historical enterprises" whose "scholarship, format, and scrupulous editing meet the highest standards of the craft."

The Papers were an outgrowth of the Wilson centennial year of 1956. The Woodrow Wilson Foundation of New York, which had been founded in 1922, secured contributions to start the project and then suspended all its other activities to devote its own capital resources to their completion. Princeton University became co-sponsor in 1959, assuming responsibility for housing the project.

Link was appointed chief editor in 1958, the same year he was called back to Princeton from a faculty position at Northwestern University. (He previously taught at Princeton from 1945 to 1949.) The first volume of the Papers appeared in the fall of 1966, and the final volume, the 69th, was published in 1994. Volume 1 and Volumes 7 through 20 cover Wilson's years as Princeton student, professor, and president.

The Papers include transcripts of many of the shorthand notes Wilson made throughout his life, using what was known as the Graham method. The editors found several Graham experts to prepare the transcripts and thus secure for posterity much material that Wilson wrote in shorthand, including a diary he kept while an undergraduate at Princeton, which opens with the maxim: "To save time is to lengthen life."

WITHERSPOON, JOHN arrived from Scotland in 1768 to serve as Princeton's sixth president. He was the only member of the clergy and the only college president to sign the Declaration of Independence and, from 1776 to 1782, was a leading member of the Continental Congress.

In his book *Princeton University: The First 250 Years*, commissioned during the celebration of Princeton's 250th anniversary, Don Oberdorfer '52 refers to the presidential "Princeton Jinx": over its first 20 years, the College had five different presidents, all of whom died in office, including one within a year of taking office and another after only six weeks. Witherspoon broke the jinx; his presidency of 26 years was longer than all his predecessors combined. He served until 1794, when he became the last Princeton president to die in office. In the more than 250 years since Witherspoon's presidency, Princeton has had just 14 presidents, but only one of them, James Carnahan 1800, served longer than Witherspoon (31 years).

A graduate of the University of Edinburgh and an ordained minister, Witherspoon was widely known as a leader of the evangelical or "Popular Party" in the Church of Scotland. The trustees of the College first elected him president in 1766, after Samuel Finley's death, but his wife, Elizabeth Montgomery, was reluctant to leave Scotland, and he declined. Thanks largely to the efforts of Benjamin Rush 1760, then a medical student at Edinburgh, they reconsidered. Informed that Witherspoon would now accept the call, the trustees again elected him to the presidency in December 1767.

With their five surviving children (five others had died in early childhood), and 300 books for the college library, the Witherspoons left their home in Paisley and reached Philadelphia early in August 1768. When they moved to Princeton a few days later, they were greeted a mile out of town by the College's vice president, three tutors, and all 63 students, who escorted them to Morven, home of Richard Stockton 1748. That evening the students celebrated the occasion by "illuminating" Nassau Hall with a lighted tallow dip in each window.

Witherspoon arrived in time to participate in Commencement, which in those days was held in September. He later wrote Rush that he had delivered "an inaugural Oration in Latin" before "a vast Concourse of People." He was heartened by the warmth of his reception, but he also reported a number of disturbing conditions. He found far too many of the students inadequately prepared for college work, and he was seriously concerned about the low state of the College's finances and its enrollment.

With characteristic vigor, Witherspoon moved immediately to find remedies. Between Commencement and the beginning of a new term in November, he went first to New York and then to Boston for consultation with friends of the College. During the next fall's vacation he visited Williamsburg, where, the *Virginia Gazette* reported, he "preached to a crowded audience in the Capital yard (there being no house in town capable of holding such a multitude) and gave universal satisfaction." A collection taken at the end of the sermon amounted "to upwards of fifty-six pounds." The following February he returned to Virginia, part of what became a continuing practice of fundraising tours in the south.

His itinerant preaching also led to an increased enrollment of students, whose tuition continued to be the major source of revenue, and to a change in the regions from which they were drawn. While most still came from the middle colonies, the representation from New England declined markedly, and enrollment from the southern colonies increased significantly. One of the southern students, James Madison 1771, stayed on after graduation to study with Witherspoon, making him Princeton's first graduate student.

Not all of Witherspoon's preaching was done on the road. When in Princeton he usually preached twice each Sunday to a mixed congregation of towns-people and students, in a church that had been constructed where Nassau Presbyterian Church stands today. Rush described Witherspoon's manner in the pulpit as "solemn and graceful," and made particular note of the fact that he carried no notes into the pulpit, in sharp contrast with the "too common practice of reading sermons in America."

Witherspoon was struck by the unconventional layout of the campus, with its principal building, Nassau Hall, set back from the main street of the town, unlike European universities and the other colleges of the colonies whose buildings abutted the street. He is credited with first applying the word *campus*, Latin for field, to the college setting, referring to the expanse of green between the College and the town.

Throughout his life, Witherspoon's speech retained his Scottish burr. A man of medium height, tending toward stoutness, with bushy eyebrows, a prominent nose, and large ears, he had a quality his contemporaries described as "presence." One of his students said Witherspoon had more presence than any other man he had known, except for George Washington.

Witherspoon lived in the President's House (now Maclean House) until 1779, when he moved to a country home and farm, "Tusculum," about a mile north of the village; the house still exists on Cherry Hill Road. His route to and from the College was along what is now the street that bears his name. He purchased two enslaved people to help him farm the 500-acre estate.

Like other early Princeton presidents, Witherspoon had a complex relationship to slavery. As a minister in Scotland he baptized an enslaved man, and in the early 1770s, while serving as president, he privately tutored two free African men, Bristol Yamma and John Quamine. In 1792, John Chavis, a free Black man from Virginia, began private lessons with Witherspoon at Tusculum. Just before that, in 1790, Witherspoon chaired a committee to consider the abolition of slavery in New Jersey that recommended the state take no action on the issue. The Princeton and Slavery Project noted that although Witherspoon owned slaves, he provided intellectual underpinnings for antislavery sentiment; his teachings gave a generation of students "a language for challenging slavery."

In addition to managing the College's affairs and preaching twice on Sundays, Witherspoon devoted many hours to teaching students. His "faculty" normally included two or three tutors (recent graduates who may have been pursuing advanced studies in divinity) and one, later two, professors. Considering himself less than an accomplished scholar in mathematics and astronomy, he secured the appointment of a professor of mathematics and natural philosophy in 1771. This left to him the main responsibility for instruction in moral philosophy, divinity, rhetoric, history, and French, for students who might elect to study the language.

Witherspoon's administration marked an important turning point in the life of the College, but the changes he made were mainly of method and emphasis within the broad objectives that the founders had originally set. He brought to Princeton a fresh emphasis upon the need for a well-educated clergy, and his influence in overcoming divisions to bring about a reunion of all Presbyterians in support of the College was one of his major accomplishments.

The founders had hoped that the College might produce men who would be "ornaments of the State as well as the Church," and Witherspoon realized this hope in full measure. In addition to a president and vice president of the United States, he taught nine cabinet officers, 21 senators, 39 members of Congress, three justices of the Supreme Court, and 12 governors. Five of the nine Princeton graduates among the 55 members of the Constitutional Convention of 1787 had been his students.

Witherspoon broadened and enriched the curriculum of the College. He introduced instruction in English grammar and composition, and added substantially to the equipment of the College, especially books for the library and "philosophical apparatus" for demonstration in the sciences, including the famous Rittenhouse Orrery acquired in 1771.

Witherspoon introduced to Princeton, and through it to other institutions, some of the more advanced ideas of the Scottish enlightenment. He subscribed to the scientific method of testing theory by experience; he saw no conflict between faith and reason; and in assessing propositions, he was inclined to apply the test of common sense and reduce them to their simplest terms. In lecturing on rhetoric he advised his students of the multiple components into which a discourse traditionally had been divided, but then suggested that it was enough to say that every discourse or composition "must have a beginning, a middle, and an end."

Though a man of strong convictions, he made no effort to protect his students from exposure to ideas with which he disagreed. The many books he added to the library gave the undergraduates access to a wide range of contemporary literature, including authors with whom he had publicly disputed. In his famous lectures on moral philosophy, not published until after his death, he laid out contending points of view and relied upon persuasive reasoning to guide students toward conclusions of their own.

Witherspoon subscribed wholeheartedly to John Locke's political philosophy and brought from Scotland a strong sense of "British liberty," which he came to see as greatly endangered by British policy. When John Adams stopped in Princeton on his way to the first meeting of the Continental Congress in 1774, he met Witherspoon and pronounced him "as high a Son of Liberty as any Man in America." Largely because of Witherspoon, Princeton became known as the "seedbed" of the revolution.

Through the years he served in Congress, Witherspoon's patriotism and judgment won the respect of his colleagues, as evidenced by his assignment to many committees, including some of the most important, such as the committee responsible for military affairs and the one responsible for diplomacy. He struggled through these years—not always successfully—to keep the College in session, and he became a frequent commuter between Princeton and Philadelphia. He resigned from Congress in November 1782, when a war that had cost him the life of his son James 1770 was ended, and peace, with American independence, seemed assured.

Witherspoon's later years were filled with difficulty. The College had suffered extensive damage to its building and instructional equipment during the war, and its finances were in disarray. His wife died in 1789 and two years before his death in 1794 he became totally blind. His second marriage, in 1791 to a young widow of 24, occasioned a celebration by students that illuminated Nassau Hall even brighter than upon his initial arrival. Through these years his son-in-law, Samuel Stanhope Smith 1769, increasingly took on responsibility for conducting the College's affairs.

Even in these later years, Witherspoon remained active and influential. He was a member of the convention that led to New Jersey becoming the third state to ratify the Constitution. He contributed greatly to the organization of a newly independent and national Presbyterian Church, and in 1789 he opened its first general assembly with a sermon and presided until the election of the first moderator. Above all, his reputation as a preacher, patriot, and president help restore the strength of the College.

A stone sculpture of Witherspoon faces west from the clock tower on East Pyne Hall, and in 2001 a 10-foot-tall bronze statue of Witherspoon, by the Scottish sculptor Sandy Stoddard, was installed on the east side of East Pyne, looking toward the chapel. (The statue's twin stands in front of the University of Paisley in Scotland.)

The John Witherspoon preceptorship is one of the 10 bicentennial preceptorships that were established in 1949 in honor of the University's bicentennial, and a John Witherspoon scholarship was created in 2015 by Witherspoon's alma mater, the University of Edinburgh, to be awarded annually to allow a graduating Princeton senior to study there. The dormitory Witherspoon Hall is named for him; when it opened in 1877, one of its first occupants was another of

Princeton's transformative presidents, Woodrow Wilson 1879.

WITHERSPOON HALL was named in honor of Princeton's sixth president, John Witherspoon. When it was completed in 1877, it was considered the most beautiful and luxurious college dormitory in the country. *Harper's Weekly* called it "one of the most commanding college buildings in the world." One of its first occupants was Woodrow Wilson 1879, who moved into room no. 7 in the west entry at the beginning of the second term of his sophomore year and lived there until his graduation.

Witherspoon was designed with more well-to-do students in mind; at a time when dorm rooms were variably priced, it provided commodious rooms at relatively steep prices. When built, its five stories overlooked the train station, as did a great tower on the west side facing the tracks that was removed in the 1940s. For some 20 years, it was the first building passengers saw when arriving on campus by train.

Originally intended to house 140 students in 80 rooms, Witherspoon included such amenities as indoor plumbing, dumbwaiters, fireplaces, stained-glass windows, and special corridors and rooms for servants.

The style of the building was high Victorian Gothic, with a ground floor constructed of dark blocks of Newark brownstone, and upper floors of blue-gray Pennsylvania marble set off by bands of the dark brownstone. Each floor had a different style of windows and the southwest corner featured a turret with a conical cap.

By 1969 the top three floors had been condemned as a fire hazard. In 1974, following a "Save our 'Spoon" campaign among students and alumni, the University installed a sprinkler system, replaced bathrooms, improved fire egress, and otherwise modernized the building. A major renewal in 2003 added new common rooms on the first and ground floors and an elevator, and Witherspoon became the first building on campus to incorporate trash chutes instead of trash pickup on each floor.

Today Witherspoon Hall is part of Rockefeller College.

WOMEN. For more than two centuries, the story of Princeton was largely a story told of and by men. Women played supportive—and frequently important—roles, but they rarely had opportunities to make contributions in their own right, much less be recognized for them. In the College's earliest years, some women on campus were enslaved; through 1840 there were at least 10 girls and women who were enslaved by members of the faculty and presidents, and at least six of them lived in the President's House (now Maclean House) between 1756 and 1822, including Betsey Stockton, for whom a garden in front of Firestone Library is now named.

Women who did receive recognition included Annis Stockton, wife of Richard Stockton 1748, who was one of America's first published female poets and was posthumously elected an honorary member of the American Whig Society for safeguarding society treasures during the American Revolution. Isabella McCosh, wife of Princeton's 11th president, ministered to the health of students and is memorialized in the infirmary that bears her name. Josephine Perry Morgan, wife of Junius Morgan 1888, founded a Ladies Auxiliary (now The Auxiliary to the Isabella McCosh Infirmary) that for more than a century has provided indispensable support to the infirmary. In 1920, Jenny Davidson Hibben, wife of Princeton's 14th president, help found the University League, which provided services of many kinds to members of the University community and their families; among other things, it created a nursery school and helped establish the docent program at the art museum.

In 1931 the writer Willa Cather was the first woman to receive an honorary degree from the University, and in 1959 the singer Marian Anderson was the first woman of color to achieve that distinction. The first female recipient of a Princeton honorary doctorate in science was a former Princeton faculty member, the physicist Chien-Shiung Wu, in 1958.

One of the first women to be employed by the University other than as a domestic worker was Anne Shaw, who was hired in 1877 as an assistant to the College librarian; three years later Charlotte Martins began a 40-year career in the library, including more than two decades heading the purchasing department. (In 1996, Karin Trainer would become the first woman to be the University's head librarian.) In the early 1900s, when Dean Andrew Fleming West 1874 was presiding in regal splendor over the graduate college, the graduate school office in Nassau Hall was managed by Anna B. H. Creasey, who was nicknamed Dean East by graduate students.

In 1912 Beatrix Farrand was hired as the University's first consulting landscape gardener (working initially at the graduate college), and over the next 31 years she established landscape design as a defining feature of the entire Princeton campus; the wisteria vines on buildings and the magnolia and cherry blossoms that herald the arrival of spring are part of her legacy. In 2019 the University named a courtyard in her honor.

In 1917 Mable and Bessie Hillian joined the staff of McCosh Infirmary as dishwashers and five years later their brother Tom joined them, as did two nieces in later years. Mabel and Bessie became cooks and Tom became head orderly. During World War II they created a "victory garden" on campus that they used to feed patients in the infirmary. In total, the family contributed nearly 200 years of service to the University. Today, women comprise half the members of the staff.

From 1918 to 1920, Alison Smith MacDonald did the first formal cataloguing for the Index of Christian Art (now the Index of Medieval Art), and Phila Calder Nye kept the project going as director from 1920 to 1933, with voluntary assistance from nine women known as the nine muses. Her successor, Helen Woodruff, developed the format still used to record descriptive and bibliographic information.

When the Office of Population Research was founded in 1936 one of its researchers, Irene Barnes Taeuber, edited the journal *Population Index*; she continued in this role until 1954 and her scholarly work helped found the science of demography. In 1942 the Physics department appointed Elda Emma Anderson a visiting research associate and hired later honorary degree recipient Chien-Shiung Wu as a member of the faculty. That same year, 23 women enrolled in a government-sponsored course in photogrammetry (making maps from aerial photographs).

In 1943 five women were hired as instructors in Turkish and other European and Slavic languages. A year later, Ludmilla Buketoff Turkevich began 17 years of teaching Russian language and literature as a lecturer, and from 1945 to 1974 Valentine Tschebotarioff Bill taught modern languages, including Russian. In 1947 three women on the library staff enrolled in a Russian language course.

After the war, wives of returning veterans often sat in on courses informally, and two wives of members of the Class of 1943, Doris Pike and Ruth Donnelly, became the first female reporters for the *Daily Princetonian*. In 1948 Helen Baker, associate director of the Industrial Relations Sector, became the first woman at Princeton granted "faculty status with the rank of associate professor." Hannah Arendt gave six lectures as part of the Gauss Seminars on Criticism in 1953, and in 1959 as a visiting professor she became the first woman to lecture to Princeton undergraduates.

The first woman graduate student, Sabra Follett Meservey *64 *66, was admitted in 1961, and the first woman to earn a Princeton degree, T'sai-Ying Cheng *63 *64, received her master's degree in 1963 and her PhD in 1964. In 1963, five women arrived to take a full year of undergraduate courses as part of a Critical Languages program that allowed students from other colleges to become visiting students at Princeton to study such languages as Chinese, Japanese, Russian, and Arabic. In 1969, Princeton admitted its first undergraduate women students—70 transfer students, including nine who had spent the previous year as Critical Language students, and 101 first-year students in the Class of 1973.

By 2020, there were just over 5,200 undergraduates, and 50 percent of them were women; there were just under 3,000 graduate students, and 40 percent of them were women. (For a more complete account of coeducation, please see the entry on that topic.)

In 1968, Suzanne Keller (Sociology) became the first tenured woman faculty member. She was directly appointed (as opposed to promoted) to a tenured position, as were Evelyn Harrison (Art and Archaeology) and Margaret Wilson (Philosophy) in 1970, and Hildred Geertz (Anthropology) in 1971. In 1973, Sylvia Molloy in Romance Languages and Literatures became the first woman promoted to tenure from the assistant professor ranks; she was followed in 1975 by Nancy Weiss Malkiel (History) and in 1976 by Janet Martin (Classics).

In 1977, four women were appointed to tenure: Natalie Davis (History), Nina Garsoian (Near Eastern Studies), Joan Girgus (Psychology), and Froma Zeitlin (Classics). A year later they were followed by Ellen Chances *70 *72 (Slavic Languages and Literatures). In 1971, Chances had been the first woman with a Princeton graduate degree to be appointed to the faculty. In 1979, S. Georgia Nugent '73 became the first Princeton undergraduate alumna to return to the University as a member of the faculty when she was appointed an assistant professor of Classics.

By 2020, 42 percent of the assistant professors, 40 percent of the associate professors, 27 percent of the full professors, and 50 percent of the non-tenure-track faculty were women.

In 1972 Adele Simmons was appointed dean of student affairs, becoming Princeton's first woman dean. In 1977 she was joined by Garsoian as dean of the graduate school and Girgus as dean of the college.

In 2020, seven of the nine academic officers of the University were women: the provost, Deborah Prentice; the dean of the graduate school, Sarah-Jane Leslie *07; the dean of the college, Jill Dolan; the dean of the school of Engineering and Applied Science, Andrea Goldsmith; the dean of the School of Public and International Affairs, Cecilia Rouse; the dean of the school of Architecture, Monica Ponce de Leon; and the university librarian, Anne Jarvis.

Women also were serving in other senior officer positions at that time, including executive vice president Charlotte Treby Williams '84; vice president and secretary Hilary Parker '01; vice president for campus life W. Rochelle Calhoun; vice president for human resources Lianne Sullivan-Crowley; and both the University's general counsel (Ramona Romero) and its chief audit and compliance officer (Nilufer Shroff).

In 1971 Mary St. John Douglas and Susan Savage Speers became the first women trustees (both were elected to 10-year charter terms), and in 1973 Marsha Levy-Warren '73 became the first woman elected a young alumni trustee. In 2011 the trustees changed the title of its most senior officer from chair of the executive committee to chair of the board and elected Kathryn Hall '80 to serve in that position. She served for eight years and then was succeeded by Louise Sams '79.

In 2001 molecular biology professor Shirley Tilghman was elected Princeton's 19th, and first woman, president.

In 2011 the first "She Roars: Celebrating Women at Princeton" conference brought more than 1,300 alumnae to the campus; the second conference, in 2018, drew more than 3,000. From the beginning of coeducation, women have been active alumnae, serving in multiple roles; Dorothy Bedford '78 was elected the first woman president of the Alumni Association in 1991, and since 2001, half of the association's presidents have been women.

Long before coeducation, however, women shaped Princeton in significant ways with their gifts. In the 1890s, Susan Dod Brown donated funds to construct Dod Hall in honor of her brother, Professor Albert Dod 1822, and Brown Hall in honor of her husband. In 1892, Harriet Crocker Alexander donated $350,000 to build Alexander Hall in honor of three generations of trustees in her husband's family; her name is engraved in the south-facing wall of the building.

Between 1908 and 1912, Margaret Olivia Slocum Sage funded the construction of Holder Hall (including its dormitories, towers, cloisters, and courtyard) and half of the cost of Madison Hall which served as the "commons" dining hall. She also left a bequest to the University upon her death in 1918, bringing her total giving to more than $500,000. The first benefactor of the graduate college, Josephine Ward Thomson Swann, bequeathed $275,000 to the University in 1906 in honor of her first husband, former US Senator John R. Thomson 1817.

East Pyne was originally built in 1897 as Pyne Library, a gift from Albertina Shelton Pyne, the mother of Moses Taylor Pyne 1877. The original Fine Hall was built in 1931 with a gift from Thomas D. Jones 1876 and his niece Gwethalyn Jones and was named for its donors when a new Fine Hall was dedicated in 1970; Gwethalyn Jones also endowed chairs in chemistry and mathematical physics. Lowrie House was given to the University in 1960 by Barbara Armour Lowrie in memory of her husband, Walter Lowrie 1890, and was used as the University's guest house until 1968 when it became the official residence of the University president. Palmer House, which replaced Lowrie House as the guest house, was bequeathed to the University in 1968 by Zilph Palmer, the widow of Edgar Palmer 1903, along with $250,000 for the development of the house and grounds and a $200,000 fund to provide for maintenance.

A $35 million gift in 1961 from Marie Robertson, wife of Charles Robertson 1926, created a fund to support the graduate program of the school of Public and International Affairs. When Ethel Stockwell Jadwin died in 1964, she left the University an unrestricted bequest of $27 million which was used to construct Jadwin Gymnasium as a memorial to her son, Leander Stockwell Jadwin 1928; Jadwin Hall, the home of the Physics department, which was named for her husband, Stanley Palmer Jadwin; and the new Fine Hall, home of the Mathematics department.

When Laurance Rockefeller '32 gave the University $4 million in 1969 to help institute undergraduate coeducation, most of the gift was used to construct Spelman Halls, the first on-campus apartment living for undergraduates. They were named for his grandmother, Laura Spelman Rockefeller, who with her husband had founded Spelman College in Atlanta, Georgia, as the first American college for Black women. When the University expanded the size of its undergraduate student body by 10 percent in the mid-2000s, a gift from Meg Whitman '77 enabled the construction of Whitman College to provide housing, dining, and social space for the 500 additional undergraduates.

In 2012 a gift from Nancy Peretsman '76 and Robert Scully '72 funded the construction of Peretsman Scully Hall, home of the Psychology department; the hall is named for them and their daughter, Emma Scully '12.

Across Poe-Pardee fields from Peretsman Scully Hall is Bloomberg Hall, a dormitory in Butler College that is named for Emma Bloomberg '01. In 2020, Kwanza Jones '93 and her husband José E. Feliciano '94 gave $20 million to name two adjoining dormitories in one of two new residential colleges being constructed just south of Poe Field to accommodate a second 10 percent increase in the size of the undergraduate student body.

Also in 2020, Mellody Hobson '91 donated funds to establish a new residential college on the site then occupied by First College (the former Wilson College). It was expected that construction of Hobson College would begin in 2023 following completion of the two new colleges then under construction, with opening tentatively scheduled for the fall of 2026 to welcome the Class of 2030.

WPRB, the undergraduate radio station first known as WPRU, was founded in 1940, just 20 years after public broadcasting was introduced in the United States by station KDKA in Pittsburgh. Henry Theis '42 operated WPRU from his room in 441 Pyne Hall, using the University's electric wiring system to transmit recorded music, news of sports events, and local advertising to campus listeners three hours a day. After a hiatus during World War II, the station moved into the basement of Holder Hall in 1945.

In 1955 WPRU obtained a license to build an FM transmitter and became the first student-owned and operated FM station in the country. From an antenna on top of Holder Tower it beamed a 250-watt signal to listeners within a radius of 20 miles, while continuing to broadcast to the campus on the AM dial.

Its new status as a licensed station required a change in name when it was discovered that a ship at sea was using the same call letters. The station changed from its Princeton University-derived WPRU to a Princeton Broadcasting Service-derived WPRB.

In 1960 WPRB asked the Federal Communications Commission for authority to increase its power from 250 to 1,000 watts on the frequency it was using. Its application was denied, but it was informed that another frequency at 103.5, carrying 17,000 watts, was available. WPRB applied, and when the application was granted, it borrowed $10,000 for equipment and became one of the most powerful FM stations in New Jersey.

At first WPRB had trouble controlling its newfound power. Nearby radio users complained that it was blocking half the FM dial. A freshman claimed that he was picking up its music on his electric shoe polisher; an older citizen of the borough said he was hearing it on his false teeth. These difficulties were eventually ameliorated.

One profitable consequence of WPRB's new 17,000-watt signal was its interference with the programs of station WTFM in Lake Success, Long Island. WTFM offered WPRB $5,000 and technical assistance if it would change its frequency from 103.5 to 103.3. WPRB replied that it would make the change, without any technical assistance, for $10,000, and WTFM agreed. In 1962, with the approval of the FCC, the change was made and the proceeds were used a year later to purchase equipment that enabled WPRB to become the first college station in the United States to broadcast in stereo.

By the mid-1970s, WPRB was utilizing the energies of about a hundred undergraduates in its program, business, technical, and public relations departments to provide an estimated audience of 45,000, in a five-state area, with the same basic ingredients it had given its campus listeners in 1940—music, sports, advertising—along with more diverse elements added over the years, including national news, public affairs programs, University public lectures, chapel services, and live concerts.

In 2004 the station moved to the newly constructed Bloomberg Hall. It remains an independently financed, not-for-profit commercial station, managed by students and overseen by a board of alumni trustees. Its signal covers approximately 15,000 square miles through central New Jersey, Philadelphia and eastern Pennsylvania, Wilmington, Delaware, and parts of the Jersey shore. Its live internet stream carries its programs around the world.

WPRB's DJs are students and community members. It offers a blend of new, classical, little known, and unfamiliar music—music it describes as "weird, engaging, quirky, off-beat, and lovely"—as well as coverage of Princeton football and men's basketball games and a weekly news and culture show. Part of its mission is aptly captured in the name of its oldest and one of its most popular programs, *Music You Can't Hear on the Radio*, which John Weingart *75 has been hosting since his graduate student days. The show features folk and blues that, according to its tag line, are heard on the radio "very seldom."

In 2009, WPRB acquired the *Nassau Weekly*, a weekly news, humor, and literary publication that was founded by students in 1979 and is distributed free to members of the campus community.

WRESTLING. Wrestling became an intercollegiate sport at Princeton in 1905, with back-to-back victories over Penn. Before that time, freshmen and sophomores participated in a Princeton variant, the cane spree, which originated after the Civil War as a series of rough-and-tumble bouts between freshmen sporting forbidden canes and sophomores trying to wrest them away. Later, three specially trained representatives of the freshman and sophomore classes—light, middle, and heavyweight—wrestled for possession of a cane. In the early 1900s, the cane spree inspired freshmen-sophomore wrestling matches, which in turn led to the formation of the first varsity wrestling team.

In the second year of organized competition, Donald "Heff" Herring 1907 won the intercollegiate heavyweight championship in record time, throwing one opponent in 16 seconds and another in 13. Herring, an All-American football player in 1906 and later a Rhodes Scholar, was known for sometimes attending professional wrestling matches in Newark dressed in white tie, tails, and top hat.

In 1911 Princeton won the team championship of what is now the Eastern Intercollegiate Wrestling Association (EIWA) when its wrestlers took four of the six individual titles. One of them, welterweight champion Jacob Frantz 1913, successfully defended his title in 1912 and 1913 to become Princeton's first three-time champion. Frantz had only one hold—the front chancery and bar lock—but he was very proficient at it and lost no time in applying it to his opponent after the customary opening handshake. In three years of varsity competition he was never thrown; the only match he did not win was lost by a close decision, and all the others he won by falls.

In the 1920s, four Princetonians won EIWA individual championships: Charles Carpenter 1921, Robert Morrison 1923, Theodore Buttrey 1926, and William Graham 1929. Heavyweight champion Carpenter, later Protestant Episcopal Bishop of Georgia, further distinguished himself by scoring a technical victory in a handicap match with the professional wrestler "Strangler" Lewis.

Buttrey and Graham won their titles under Clarence Foster, who coached from 1924 through 1934. Other EIWA champions coached by Foster were William Barfield '30, Russell Hooker '34, and Thomas Snelham '35, as well as Julian Gregory Jr. '35 and George Treide '36, who both went on to win second championships under Foster's successor, Jimmie Reed.

A former two-time EIWA champion at Lehigh, Reed was varsity coach for 30 years, through 1964. His 1936 and 1937 teams were undefeated, and his 1938 team won seven successive meets before losing their final bout with Lehigh, thus extending Princeton's unbroken string of victories to 21. The 1937 and 1938 teams took second place in the EIWA tournament, and the 1941 team tied Yale for first place. Reed's wrestlers won the Big Three title in the years from 1936 through 1939, from 1941 through 1943, and in 1947, 1949, 1950, 1953, and 1957. In 1942, Warren Taylor '43 became Princeton's first wrestling All-American. He also won the EIWA championship at 136 pounds and placed fourth in NCAA competition.

Reed's roster of EIWA champions was impressive. Bradley Glass '53 also won the 1951 NCAA heavyweight championship, Princeton's only individual national title. Richard Harding '40 and Robert Eberle '41 won EIWA championships in each of their three years of varsity competition. Charles Powers '38, who won twice, was awarded the coaches' cup as the most accomplished wrestler in the 1937 EIWA meet. W. Eugene Taylor '43 and Glass were also double winners.

Glass, who had starred at New Trier High School in Illinois, played an important role in persuading another New Trier wrestler, Donald Rumsfeld '54, to attend Princeton. Rumsfeld reached the EIWA finals in the 157-pound class his junior year and the semifinals as captain in his undefeated senior year. He later became congressman from Illinois, ambassador to NATO, White House chief of staff, and two-time secretary of defense.

John Johnston, a former national champion at Penn State, succeeded Jimmie Reed as coach in 1965, and Princeton soon became a formidable power in Ivy competition, winning sole possession of the League crown in 1967, 1970, and 1971, sharing it with Penn in 1972 and with Cornell in 1973, and winning it outright again in 1975, 1977 and, with a 19–0 season record, in 1978, when it also won the EIWA tournament.

In 1972, Emil Deliere '72 won the EIWA championship in the 190-pound class and reached the finals of the NCAA championship tournament, where the recurrence of a back injury compelled him to default. Captain John Sefter '78 won the EIWA championship in the heavyweight class in 1977 and 1978 and reached the finals of the NCAA championship tournament in 1978. Steve Grubman '78 won the EIWA championship in the 142-pound class in 1978, and the same year, along with Keith Ely '79 in the 177-pound class, reached the quarterfinals of the NCAA championship tournament. Johnston's teams won their final Ivy team championships in 1985 and 1986.

After conducting a review of gender equity in its athletics programs and facing constraints on its athletics budget, the University announced in 1993 that it was dropping wrestling as a varsity sport. It became a "transitional non-varsity sport," and then a "club varsity" sport permitted to compete at the varsity level but without the admission or financial support available to varsity teams. From 1993 to 1996, Princeton did not compete in the Ivy League, and upon resuming Ivy competition it did not defeat an Ivy opponent until 2000. Strong alumni support and funding led to wrestling's reinstatement as a varsity sport in 1997, although the team remained funded solely through donations until an endowment was completed in 2004.

A slow rebuilding process followed reinstatement, but the program took a giant step forward in 2006 with the hiring of Lehigh assistant Chris Ayres as head coach. Ayres' debut could not have been rockier—in his first three seasons, the team posted a combined record of 2–53—but by 2010 it achieved its first winning record in Ivy competition since 1987.

In 2012, Princeton sent three wrestlers to the NCAA tournament (Daniel Kolodzik '12, Garrett Frey '14, and Adam Krop '16) for the first time since 2001. Ayres was named Ivy League Coach of the Year three times (2016, 2017, 2019). As the second decade of the twenty-first century ended, Princeton wrestling had returned to prominence, defeating top national teams and beginning the 2019–20 season ranked 15th in the country by the National Wrestling Coaches Association. The 2019–20 team lived up to its promise, winning its first Ivy League championship in 34 years, and in doing so making Princeton the first Ivy League school to win 500 team championships.

Overall, Princeton has won 12 Ivy League team championships (1956, 1967, 1970, 1971, 1972, 1973, 1975, 1977, 1978, 1985, 1986, 2020) and three Tigers have been named Ivy League Wrestler of the Year (John Orr '85 in 1984 and 1985, Dave Cristiani '86 in 1986, and Pat Glory '22 in 2020). Princeton has earned 77 first-team All-Ivy League honors. Seventy-five Princeton wrestlers have also been EIWA champions, and five have been inducted into the EIWA Hall of Fame (Eberle, Frantz, Glass, Harding, and Clay McEldowney '69), along with three Princeton coaches (Johnston, Eric Pearson, and Reed). In addition, 12 wrestlers have combined to earn 19 All-America honors.

Wu Hall played a catalytic role in the creation of the residential college system at Princeton. In 1979, when the trustees endorsed the recommendation of the Committee on Residential Life that all freshmen and sophomores and a limited number of juniors and seniors be housed in five residential colleges, three new colleges needed to be created in addition to the existing Woodrow Wilson and Princeton Inn. The five dining rooms of Commons at the northwest corner of campus could be used to create two of them using adjacent dorms, but the third required construction of a new dining and social facility to permit development of a south-campus college in conjunction with the dormitories of the so-called "New New Quad."

Gordon Y.S. Wu '58, a Hong Kong structural engineer, entrepreneur, and businessman, stepped forward with a gift of nearly $4.3 million to construct such a facility, which was designed by another Princeton graduate, Robert Venturi '47 *50 and his partner Denise Scott Brown. Wu Hall provides dining facilities and social space for Butler College; it also houses the Matthew Mellon 1922 library.

Prior to this gift, Wu donated a professorship in Chinese studies, and later he contributed a professorship in engineering and supported the construction of Bowen Hall, which houses research in materials science. In 1995, Wu pledged an additional $100 million to support the school of Engineering and Applied Science, making him one of four donors in the modern era to provide donations at that level, along with Gerhard R. Andlinger '52, Peter B. Lewis '55, and William Scheide '36.

As an undergraduate engineering student at Princeton, Wu became enamored with the name of the nearby town of Hopewell and was fascinated by the toll-generating New Jersey Turnpike. When he returned to Hong Kong, he named his company Hopewell Holdings, and the highways, hotels, bridges, and power plants he constructed throughout Asia included a highway in China modeled after the turnpike. In 1997 he was knighted by England's Queen Elizabeth II.

The architectural challenge in constructing Wu Hall was to relate both to the neighboring neo-Jacobean 1915 Hall and the New New Quad buildings that had been designed in the "New Brutalism" style of the 1960s when speed of construction and lowering costs were priorities. Venturi described Wu Hall as a "hyphen," connecting two kinds of buildings in the way a hyphen connects two words. In 2007 the New New Quad dorms were demolished to make way for a new red brick and limestone complex designed by Pei Cobb Freed and Partners that opened two years later to rave reviews from the students who lived in them.

Wu Hall was constructed of the kind of brick walls, limestone trim, and strip windows that characterize traditional Gothic architecture at Princeton, but with modern and even whimsical elements. The entrance to the building faces west where it is set off-center and marked by a bold gray granite and white marble panel composed of circles, triangles, and rectangles. Wu was proud of the fact that he had been an international student at Princeton, and at his suggestion his name is affixed to the building in Chinese characters as well as in English.

For Venturi and Scott Brown, Wu Hall was the first of several major commissions at Princeton. They also designed Lewis Thomas Laboratory (1986), Fisher and Bendheim halls (1990), Schultz Laboratory (1993), and Frist Campus Center (2000).

This Day in Princeton History Calendar

JANUARY

1 — 1915 The Triangle Club completes a 10-day tour of *Fie! Fie! Fi-Fi!*, visiting New York, Baltimore, Cincinnati, Louisville, St. Louis, Chicago, Detroit, Cleveland, and Pittsburgh. Spanning a total of 3,500 miles, it is the longest trip to date by any college organization.

2 — 1879 James Williamson 1877 *1879 finishes his thesis, written in longhand; with it he and William Libbey 1877 *1879 will receive Princeton's first earned PhD's.

3 — 1777 The victory of the Continental Army, led by George Washington, at the Battle of Princeton changes the course of the American Revolution.

7 — 1926 World-famous explorer and naturalist Roy Chapman Andrews, one of the inspirations for fictional archeologist Indiana Jones, lectures at McCosh 10 about his recent trip into the Gobi Desert heading an American Museum of Natural History expedition. He illustrates his lecture with slides, maps, and motion pictures.

8 — 1988 Harold Shapiro *64, former president of the University of Michigan, is inaugurated as Princeton's 18th president.

9 — 1951 The *Prince* reports on the purchase of buildings and land along Route 1 in Plainsboro to establish a research center named for James Forrestal 1915.

13 — 1933 The *Prince* reports on a new plan of admission, approved by the trustees, to admit students of exceptional achievement and promise without examination, including in regions where school programs do not prepare them for College Board examinations. The new policy substantially broadens the geographical distribution of Princeton's student population.

14 — 1926 Princeton trustees announce a $150,000 pledge toward the establishment of a professorship in mathematics in honor of Henry Burchard Fine 1880, who made Princeton a leading center of mathematics as first chair of the department, third dean of the faculty, and first dean of the departments of science.

15 — 1974 Brendan Byrne '49 is sworn in as New Jersey's 47th governor. Eight years later Thomas Kean '57 will be inaugurated as Byrne's successor.

19 — 1887 The *Prince* announces that a new college for young women in Princeton will be named Evelyn College. The college, where a number of Princeton faculty teach, operates until 1897.

20 — 2009 Michelle Obama '85 becomes First Lady of the United States upon the inauguration of her husband.

21 — 1974 Reading period starts after a two-week delay due to the energy crisis.

25 — 1780 British soldiers burn down the building in Elizabeth where the first classes of the College of New Jersey were held before the College moved to Newark and ultimately to Princeton.

26 — 1901 The just-formed Princeton basketball team, in its first game, defeats New Jersey States Schools (later Trenton State, now the College of New Jersey) by a score of 23-5.

27 — 2001 Princeton announces that students on financial aid will receive all their aid as grants and will not be required to take out loans.

31 — 1917 Poet Robert Frost gives a reading to the University's newly organized literary society, the Freneau Club.

Evelyn College's 1891–92 catalogue cover

Michelle Obama '85 as a Princeton undergraduate

4 1960 — The British Broadcasting Company airs an episode of *Panorama* featuring interviews with Princeton students on America's role in foreign affairs. Princeton is the only college on the program; the interviewer, David Webster, explains, "This is the place which produces the leadership" in the United States.	**5** 1923 — The $250,000 Baker Rink opens as a collective gift of 1,537 donors in honor of Hobey Baker 1914, the dominant hockey player of his time and perhaps the best amateur hockey player ever. It remains the oldest continuously used collegiate rink in the country.	**6** 1911 — The *Daily Princetonian* reports that the Nassau Hall lions have been replaced with tigers, a gift from the Class of 1879 after learning that the tiger was to be Princeton's mascot.
10 1947 — The Student Hebrew Association holds its first official service on campus; speakers include Albert Einstein and the assistant dean of the chapel.	**11** 1969 — By a vote of 24 to 8, the trustees approve undergraduate coeducation "in principle."	**12** 1942 — The faculty approves a new program in American Civilization (later renamed American Studies).
16 1813 — Students successfully petition the faculty "to be allowed this day as a holy day [sic], for the purpose of spending it in the amusement of sleighing."	**17** 1952 — Six faculty members begin teaching classes at the Princeton Adult School about "Communism as it exists today and what may be done to fight it."	**18** 1893 — The faculty approves a resolution ending supervision of exams; students will be required to pledge, on their honor, that they have "neither given nor received aid" during the test.
22 1938 — *Our Town*, by Thornton Wilder *1926—destined to become a classic—premieres at McCarter Theatre. Student reviewer says it is "not great," but calls it "brave and honest." While calling it "the most exciting play of the season," he predicts it will not have a long Broadway run.	**23** 1871 — President James McCosh asserts in a lecture that Darwin's theory of evolution is consistent with Christianity.	**24** 1753 — The trustees vote to move the College of New Jersey from Newark to Princeton.
28 1987 — In the eighth year of the lawsuit of Sally Frank '80 against the two remaining all-male eating clubs, Judge Robert Miller rules that Ivy and Tiger do not have to admit women, provided they sever all remaining ties with the University. This ruling is reversed on May 26, and a 1990 ruling requires both clubs to admit women.	**29** 1760 — The first *Catalogue of Books in the Library of the College of New Jersey* (enumerating 1,281 volumes) is published to show the need for more books, "especially modern authors."	**30** 1922 — President John Grier Hibben writes parents a letter expressing the wish that students abandon the use of cars on campus.

Sally Frank '80

Albert Einstein on Lake Carnegie with University librarian Johanna Fantova

The Class of 1879 bronze tigers guarding Nassau Hall wore appropriate face coverings during the COVID-19 pandemic

FEBRUARY

1 | 1950 — University officials deny a report in the *New York Journal-American* that Princeton scientists working with Albert Einstein are getting ready to fly to the moon, with testing beginning in the summer.

2 | 1916 — The *Prince* reports that the historic Nassau Inn at 52 Nassau Street, which has been operated continuously since 1769 and entertained six US presidents, is under new management. It will eventually be relocated when Palmer Square is developed in the 1930s.

3 | 1980 — Alison Carlson '77 carries the Olympic torch around the Garrett track in Jadwin Gymnasium on its way to the winter games in Lake Placid, New York. Robert Garrett 1897 led a Princeton delegation to the first modern Olympics in Athens in 1896, winning two events and placing second in two others.

7 | 1956 — In a full-page advertisement in the *Prince*, Roman Catholic chaplain Hugh Halton attacks the Religion department for putting the book *Morals and Medicine* on its reading list. His outspoken views of the University as a center of "moral and political subversion" lead to his dismissal in 1957.

8 | 1991 — Tiger Inn admits 27 women, making all eating clubs coeducational.

9 | 1893 — The trustees appoint Therese B. Hill, widow of the museum curator, as matron of the new Isabella McCosh Infirmary. The infirmary, which will have gas lighting and trained nurses for "severe or special cases," can accommodate 16 students and will open by May 1.

13 | 1896 — The trustees agree to change the name of the College of New Jersey to Princeton University.

14 | 1960 — WPRB, the first undergraduate-operated commercial radio station in the United States, roars up to 17,000 watts, making it the most powerful student-run station in the world.

15 | 1960 — The *New York Times* reports that the Orange Key's fund-raising dance with women from Centenary College in Hackettstown, NJ, advertised as "one hundred dates to be sold," is cancelled due to protests from the girls' mothers; the $5 tickets are refunded.

19 | 1982 — The $275 million Campaign for Princeton is formally launched. It eventually raises $410.5 million.

20 | 1953 — Following the unanimous recommendation of the faculty to establish the Council of the Humanities, the executive committee of the Board of Trustees recommends approval.

21 | 1930 — McCarter Theatre formally opens with the Triangle Club's production of *The Golden Dog*.

25 | 1985 — The National Science Foundation announces that it has selected Princeton as one of four sites for national supercomputer facilities. Princeton's facility, known as the John von Neumann Center, will operate for five years.

26 | 1987 — The University announces that the lyrics to the alma mater, "Old Nassau," will be officially changed, eliminating the phrases "my boys" and "her sons."

27 | 1993 — Wendy Kopp '89, creator of Teach For America (the subject of her senior thesis), is the first woman to receive the Woodrow Wilson Award.

The first McCosh Infirmary, 1892

Sabra Follett Meservey *64 *66

Wendy Kopp '89 with her advisor, sociology professor Marvin Bressler

4 **2002** — The University announces there will be three four-year residential colleges, including Whitman College, which opens in 2007.

5 **2014** — The University announces that the Naval Reserve Officers Training Corps (NROTC) program will return to Princeton later in the year.

6 **1962** — The *Prince* reports that a special advisory committee on nuclear fall-out shelters has suggested shelter areas for 5,050 persons on campus and at the graduate college, and for 1,000 persons at Forrestal.

10 **1966** — Sabra Meservey *66 gives a "spirited, successful defense of her dissertation" to earn her PhD; in 1961 she enrolled as Princeton's first female graduate student.

11 **1788** — Town citizens establish a voluntary hook and ladder company in response to growing concerns that the fire protection provided by the College's students and faculty was becoming inadequate.

12 **1915** — The first Alumni Day is observed on Lincoln's birthday; the following year it is moved to Washington's birthday.

16 **1758** — A rule requiring students to wear caps and gowns is repealed (but is reinstated in 1768).

17 **1962** — The University formally closes the $53 Million Campaign, Princeton's first comprehensive capital campaign, which ended up raising $60.7 million.

18 **1934** — Two local children report seeing a "sea serpent" in Lake Carnegie. The "Carnegie Monster" will become campus lore for a few decades.

22 **1794** — Students celebrate George Washington's birthday for the first time. During the late 1800s and early 1900s, it becomes one of the most important campus events.

23 **1941** — Members of the Class of 1943 organize Prospect Cooperative Club for students who cannot afford or are not admitted to Princeton's traditional eating clubs.

24 **1991** — In the final game of coach Betty Constable's legendary 20-year career, the women's squash team defeats Brown 9-0 for its eighth undefeated season.

28 **1946** — The University announces that women will live in student housing on campus for the first time as it opens Brown Hall to married veterans after providing only single-gender accommodations for 200 years.

29 **2020** — Several attendees at a private party in Princeton, including two University staff members, are infected with the COVID-19 virus. On March 9 the University announces that mandatory virtual instruction will begin on March 23 and continue for the remainder of the spring semester.

Princeton's shield, adapted from its official seal

Whitman College

Alumni Day lunch in Jadwin Gym

Alumni Day audience in Richardson Auditorium

MARCH

1 | 1969 — Jadwin Gym is dedicated at the Harvard-Yale-Princeton track meet; Ethel Stockwell Jadwin P1928 attends.

2 | 1927 — Angered by a campus-wide ban on automobiles effective the following year, many juniors take up roller-skating, often while bearing protest signs.

3 | 1969 — The faculty approves a program in Afro-American Studies. After becoming a center in 2006, it becomes the department of African American Studies in 2015.

7 | 1882 — The first issue of the *Princeton Tiger* appears with a tiger cub on the cover and 6 drawings, 5 essays, and 2 jokes inside.

8 | 1900 — The trustees accept a proposal to let authorized assessors appraise furniture in college rooms at a fair value to prevent the practice of selling it to new occupants at excessive rates.

9 | 1950 — The Class of 1952 insists on "100 percent bicker"; all eligible sophomores receive eating club bids.

13 | 1960 — Dr. Martin Luther King Jr. preaches for the first of two times in the chapel.

14 | 1996 — The men's basketball team defeats defending champion UCLA in the first round of the NCAA tournament; the *Prince* headline reads "David 43, Goliath 41."

15 | 1933 — Nine days after President Franklin Roosevelt's emergency measure temporarily closes all banks, Princeton banks reopen. During the closure students used scrip issued by the *Daily Princetonian* which was accepted by local businesses.

19 | 1900 — The *Prince* reports the organization of the University Band, consisting of 4 cornets, 2 clarinets, 1 trombone, and 1 baritone horn.

20 | 1965 — The Bill Bradley-led basketball team scores Princeton's most points ever in trouncing Wichita State, 118–82, to finish third in the NCAA tournament—Princeton's only appearance in the final four.

21 | 1952 — After a trustee decision to stop janitors making students' beds and cleaning their rooms, the *Prince* asks students to sign alternative petitions to endorse or reject the decision. More than 80% favor paying more rent to keep the practice, but the trustees turn down a proposal to permit optional services.

25 | 1745 — Princeton obtains its first endowment when 10 pledges specifying use of the income on a fund of £185 to establish a college in New Jersey are received by the college's organizers.

26 | 1920 — F. Scott Fitzgerald 1917's debut novel, *This Side of Paradise*, is published. All 3,000 copies sell out in three days.

27 | 2001 — Filming begins on campus for the movie *A Beautiful Mind*, starring Russell Crowe as John Nash Jr. *50. The film wins four Academy Awards, including Best Picture.

31 | 1957 — A new window depicting scenes from the book of Genesis is dedicated in the chapel. It was executed by Henry Lee Willet 1922, one of the nation's leading stained-glass artists.

Bella Allarie '20, all-time leading scorer for Princeton women's basketball

Future basketball coach Mitch Henderson '98 celebrates Princeton's 1996 first-round upset of defending champion UCLA; future coach Sydney Johnson '97 watches.

4 1809 — James Madison 1771 is inaugurated as the fourth US president.	**5** 1970 — 75 hecklers interrupt a speech by Secretary of the Interior Walter Hickel to protest the Vietnam War. The "Hickel-heckle" is the first case brought before the new CPUC judiciary committee; after five days of contentious public hearings, disciplinary measures are imposed.	**6** 1802 — A fire guts Nassau Hall. When it is repaired, two other buildings are also constructed – Geological (now Stanhope) Hall and its twin, Philosophical Hall, where Chancellor Green now stands.
10 2015 — The women's basketball team defeats Pennsylvania 55-42, ending a historic 30-0 season, and heads to its first NCAA tournament win.	**11** 1936 — Some 200 Princeton undergraduates form the satirical organization Veterans of Future Wars, which enjoys widespread media attention.	**12** 1971 — Led by the Third World Coalition, 170 students stage a three-hour sit-in after Firestone Library closes at 11:45 p.m. to advocate for admission of more minority students, increased financial aid, and creation of a Third World Center.
16 1751 — James Madison 1771 is born; he will become Princeton's first graduate student, the fourth president of the United States, and the first president of the alumni association.	**17** 1973 — With just six athletes, the women's swimming team finishes third at the national championships, setting one collegiate and two national records.	**18** 1907 — On the 70th birthday of former US president Grover Cleveland, students decide to give him a loving cup, which they present to him on the 26th after marching to his Princeton home.
22 1758 — Jonathan Edwards, elected president of the College five days after the death of his son-in-law Aaron Burr Sr., dies from a smallpox inoculation only two months after taking office.	**23** 1975 — Princeton's men's basketball team defeats Providence to win the National Invitational Tournament in Madison Square Garden.	**24** 1900 — Scribner's publishes Henry Van Dyke 1873's first book of poems since his appointment as Murray Professor of English Literature in 1899. Van Dyke had delivered his lauded ode "The Builders" at Princeton's sesquicentennial in 1896.
28 1921 — The faculty approves the organization of a school of Engineering.	**29** 1933 — The *Prince* circulates a petition at the request of Brown's student newspaper in which signers pledge "not to bear arms, except in case of invasion of the mainland of the United States." Only 26 Princeton students sign.	**30** 1868 — John C. and Sarah H. Green endow a building and library fund. Later gifts include the first Dickinson Hall, Chancellor Green Library, and a School of Science building, and benefactions from his estate include Edwards Hall and Aaron Burr Hall.

This plaque commemorates the 1960 and 1962 visits to the chapel by the Rev. Dr. Martin Luther King Jr.

King on the chapel steps in 1960

APRIL

1 | 1927 — The *Prince* celebrates April Fool's Day with a banner headline that reads: "Princeton Gets $20,000,000 to Become Co-Educational."

2 | 1974 — Princeton's recruitment film, *Princeton: A Search for Answers*, wins an Academy Award for "Best Documentary Short Subject."

3 | 1987 — Vice President George H.W. Bush speaks on "Leadership in the Modern Presidency" during a conference sponsored by the school of Public and International Affairs.

7 | 1900 — The *Princeton Alumni Weekly* is founded, with Jesse Lynch Williams 1892, a former *Nassau Lit* editor and future Pulitzer Prize winner, as editor.

8 | 1960 — The trustees select the official "Princeton orange." Prior to their decision, a variety of shades were used.

9 | 1968 — As urged by the Association of Black Collegians, the University suspends normal operations to memorialize Dr. Martin Luther King Jr. following his assassination on April 4.

13 | 1922 — At their spring meeting, the trustees agree to proceed with a plan to obtain 216 acres of farmland between Lake Carnegie and Route 1 for future use.

14 | 2002 — The trustees approve a recommendation to change the name of the Third World Center to the Carl A. Fields Center for Equality and Cultural Understanding.

15 | 1896 — The first modern Olympic Games end; Princeton men record two first place finishes, three seconds, and one third. They receive laurel branches.

19 | 1969 — The trustees vote to implement undergraduate coeducation in the fall and to add four "young alumni trustees" to the board, with one elected each year from the graduating senior class. In 2019 they designate a position on the board for a recent graduate of the graduate school.

20 | 1939 — The trustees approve a plan for a new program in the Creative Arts, with Allen Tate as first poet-in-residence.

21 | 1689 — William, Prince of Orange (House of Nassau), ascends to England's throne as William III. Nassau Hall will be named after him.

25 | 1924 — For the first time, Princeton's debate team goes up against a women's college when Vassar's team visits. Vassar wins 2-1.

26 | 1875 — Students from Rutgers College take the small cannon from the Princeton campus, but will be forced to return it a few weeks later.

27 | 1987 — A "Communiversity" festival is held to bring together town and gown. Over 7,000 attend, inspiring organizers to make it an annual event that in later years attracts as many as 40,000 people to downtown Princeton and the front campus.

Betsey Stockton

Princeton's first coeducational a cappella group, the Katzenjammers, in East Pyne Arch

4 **2016** — The trustees announce that Princeton's informal motto will become "Princeton in the Nation's Service and the Service of Humanity," combining phrases from Woodrow Wilson 1879 and Sonia Sotomayor '76.

5 **1943** — The University shifts its schedule forward 10 minutes to allow Army trainees enough time after breakfast to re-form in sections at the barracks and march to their classes.

6 **1771** — The Rittenhouse Orrery, the most-noted scientific instrument of its time, arrives at Nassau Hall.

10 **1931** — The Glee Club presents the premiere of Stravinsky's *Oedipus Rex* in Philadelphia alongside the Philadelphia Orchestra directed by Leopold Stokowski.

11 **1935** — Compulsory chapel is abolished for juniors and seniors. In 1960, it is abolished for sophomores, then in 1964 for freshmen.

12 **1923** — The trustees approve the "four-course plan" (proposed by professor, later dean, Luther Eisenhart) which paves the way for departmental concentration and the senior thesis.

16 **1936** — The *Prince* reports on the trustees' adoption of a "Roving Student Policy" (officially "A Divisional Program of Humanistic Studies"). Capable juniors and seniors are permitted to pursue interests which cut across various humanities departments.

17 **2018** — The University announces the naming of the Betsey Stockton Garden and the James Collins Johnson Arch as part of a commitment to diversify the naming of campus spaces.

18 **1813** — The first recorded meeting to elect town of Princeton officials under a new charter dated February 11 takes place at Follet's Tavern.

22 **1977** — The Association of Black Princeton Alumni and Princeton University sponsor the first conference for Black alumni: "Princeton Blacks: From the '60s into the '80s."

23 **2018** — The faculty votes to revise the University's academic calendar. Beginning in 2020-21, fall semester final exams will be conducted in December and an optional two-week "Wintersession" will be offered in January.

24 **1865** — Students assemble at the station as Abraham Lincoln's funeral train passes Princeton at 6:40 a.m. Four months earlier the University awarded Lincoln his third and final honorary degree.

28 **1905** — President Woodrow Wilson outlines his preceptorial teaching plan, whereby faculty members meet with small groups of students; the program requires a 50 percent increase in the size of the faculty.

29 **1868** — The trustees elect Scottish author, philosopher, and Free Churchman James McCosh from Queen's College, Belfast, as the College of New Jersey's 11th president.

30 **1970** — More than 2,500 students gather in the chapel following President Richard Nixon's announcement of American bombing in Cambodia to protest this escalation of the war in Southeast Asia.

The Rittenhouse Orrery

Professor Stanley Kelley Jr. in the chapel, April 30, 1970

MAY

1 / 1970 — Roughly 80 percent of students skip class to protest the escalation of the Vietnam War. Three days later more than 4,000 members of the campus community vote in Jadwin Gym to strike against the war; most students elect not to take final exams and most seniors choose not to participate in reunions.

2 / 1968 — More than 1,000 students and other members of the campus community rally in front of Nassau Hall to oppose the war in Vietnam, apartheid in South Africa, and the nature of University governance. President Robert Goheen pledges a "searching review of the decision-making processes of the University"; one outcome of the review is the creation of the Council of the Princeton University Community (CPUC).

3 / 1894 — The group formerly known as the Princeton College Dramatic Association puts on its first show *The Honorable Julius Caesar*, under its new name, the Triangle Club.

7 / 1937 — Forced by police to abandon their car, *Prince* reporters walk and run eight miles to report on the Hindenburg disaster near the Lakehurst, NJ, Naval Air Station.

8 / 1755 — Provincial governor Jonathan Belcher wills his personal collection of 474 books to the College library, instantly making it one of the largest in the colonies.

9 / 1921 — Albert Einstein gives his first lecture in a series of five in McCosh 50 on the theory of relativity and receives an honorary degree in Alexander Hall.

13 / 1915 — With the last of six weekly addresses, a Philadelphian Society program to help students find a vocation comes to an end. Speakers described opportunities in the ministry, the medical profession, teaching, missionary work, law, and business.

14 / 1920 — Marquand Chapel and Dickinson Hall are destroyed by fire. A new chapel will be dedicated in 1928.

15 / 1963 — The University mails letters to the first students admitted to the Critical Languages program—17 students from eight colleges—including five women who arrive in the fall as the University's first enrolled female undergraduates.

19 / 1970 — The Princeton chapter of the Union for National Draft Opposition (UNDO) begins a two-day national convocation with speeches and workshops.

20 / 1963 — The renamed Corwin Hall is moved 100 yards east to make way for a new home for the school of Public and International Affairs; the new building is later named for donors Marie and Charles Robertson 1926. A neighbor sells viewing space for the 12-hour move to benefit charity.

21 / 1995 — The Alumni Council introduces a searchable electronic alumni directory, TigerNet.

25 / 1992 — The men's lacrosse team wins the NCAA national championship in a double-overtime upset.

26 / 1828 — A giant firecracker explodes in a classroom in Nassau Hall. The investigation is dropped after the faculty receives an apology and $150 to replace the windows and stoves.

27 / 1747 — The first class of the College of New Jersey meets at Jonathan Dickinson's parsonage in Elizabeth, NJ.

31 / 1938 — At the 17th annual exhibition of books owned by Princeton undergraduates, 70 student book collectors compete for cash prizes. Each student's collection of 10 volumes is judged by three faculty members based on the significance of the contents, the quality of the bookmaking, and the importance of the editions.

President Goheen at the May 2, 1968, rally in front of Nassau Hall

4 1960	The *Princeton Herald* reports that the University has started constructing an eight-story junior faculty building overlooking Lake Carnegie, the first of three multiple housing units for faculty financed by the $53 Million Campaign. The building is named for former President John Grier Hibben.
5 2001	Shirley Tilghman is elected the University's 19th, and first female, president.
6 1977	Joan Stern Girgus is named dean of the college. She is the first woman to serve as an academic officer of the University.
10 1905	The *Prince* reports that 70 percent of students have subscribed to a co-operative society being established to provide student supplies. Named the University Store, it opens in September.
11 1912	John Grier Hibben 1882 *1893 is inaugurated as the University's 14th president; participants include US President William Howard Taft, but not Hibben's predecessor, Woodrow Wilson 1879.
12 1893	Princeton wins the first intercollegiate relay race, defeating the University of Pennsylvania. After the success of this and the following year's event, the Penn Relays are born.
16 2021	A year after the COVID-19 pandemic necessitated an entirely virtual ceremony, the University conducted an in-person Commencement in Princeton Stadium, while still requiring masks and social distancing and limiting degree recipients to two guests.
17 1939	The second game of a Princeton-Columbia baseball doubleheader is the first live televised sporting event in the United States, broadcast by NBC to about 400 TV sets. Princeton wins 2–1 in 10 innings at Baker Field, New York. The success of the broadcast leads to the first televised major league baseball game three months later from Brooklyn's Ebbets Field.
18 1939	Thomas Mann, winner of the Nobel Prize in literature and a lecturer at Princeton since 1938, receives an honorary degree at Nassau Hall.
22 1950	Vermeer's *The Art of Painting*, rescued at the end of World War II by the "Monuments Men," including Princeton University Art Museum director Ernest DeWald *1916, arrives at the museum from Austria by way of the Metropolitan Museum of Art under armed guard for an eight-day exhibition.
23 1952	At 8:30 a.m. 700 students and faculty pack Alexander Hall for professor of history Walter "Buzzer" Hall's final lecture after 39 years of teaching; enrollment of 500 in his course sets a record.
24 1777	At a meeting at Cooper's Ferry on the banks of the Delaware, the trustees vote that the 27 students who were not able to receive their diplomas in 1776 due to the absence of a quorum should receive their diplomas "as soon as the confusions of the war will admit of it."
28 1900	Non-stop train service between Princeton and New York is instituted, obviating a need to change trains in Princeton Junction; each day one train runs to New York and one returns, except on Sunday.
29 1875	Joseph Mann 1876, the first collegiate pitcher to master the curve ball, shuts out Yale 3–0 in what is believed to be the first no-hitter in baseball history.
30 1928	The majestic University Chapel is dedicated. It replaces Marquand Chapel, destroyed by fire in the spring of 1920.

Sue Jean Lee Suettinger '70, the first woman to appear in a Triangle Show

In 1963 Woodrow Wilson Hall was moved on railroad ties and became Corwin Hall.

At a May 4, 1970 meeting in Jadwin Gym, the campus community voted to strike against the war in Vietnam.

JUNE

1 | 1925 — The Observatory of Instruction (constructed in 1887 on the current site of Robertson Hall) is open to the public from 8:30-10:30 p.m. to observe the moon and Saturn. This observatory is demolished in 1963 and the research-intensive FitzRandolph Observatory (successor to the Halstead Observatory) is razed in 2020. An observatory remains on the roof of Peyton Hall.

2 | 2015 — Graduate students are moving into the new Lakeside apartments and townhomes.

3 | 1989 — One day before the Tiananmen Square massacre, East Asian studies professor Perry Link escorts a prominent Chinese dissident to safety in the American Embassy in Beijing.

7 | 1770 — The Cliosophic Society is founded, less than a year after the American Whig Society, following the disbanding of predecessor organizations in March 1769. Whig-Clio remains the oldest college literary and debating society in the United States.

8 | 1911 — To enable western alumni to attend Commencement, a special train is arranged for a $30 round-trip fare. The "Commencement Special" leaves Chicago at 10:30 a.m. and reaches Princeton at 7:30 the next morning. The train offers compartment cars, open sleepers, a buffet, a dining car, and special accommodations for women.

9 | 1970 — Bob Dylan receives an honorary degree; his song "Day of the Locusts" memorializes the 17-year cicadas that infested that year's Commencement. In connection with its graduation, the Class of 1970 permanently opens FitzRandolph Gate, inscribing its class motto, "Together for Community," in the gate's east pillar.

13 | 1894 — Four days after its dedication, Alexander Hall hosts it first Commencement.

14 | 1876 — Students issue the first copies of the *Princetonian*; in 1892 it becomes the country's second daily college newspaper.

15 | 1971 — The University announces the election of the first women to the Board of Trustees: charter trustees Mary St. John Douglas and Susan Savage Speers.

19 | 2010 — Streicker Bridge, connecting campus lands on both sides of Washington Road, is dedicated.

20 | 1888 — Cuban-born Pedro Rioseco 1888 becomes Princeton's first Hispanic graduate.

21 | 1938 — Alan Turing *38 receives his PhD in mathematics.

25 | 1917 — The Princeton Military Camp begins; in eight weeks it will train more than 300 soldiers between the ages of 16 and 41 for service in World War I.

26 | 2020 — The trustees remove the name of Woodrow Wilson from the school of Public and International Affairs and change the name of the University's first residential college, which had been named for Wilson, to "First College."

27 | 1876 — Hikoichi Orita 1876 from Japan graduates—the first Asian student to receives a degree from Princeton.

Cynthia Chase '75 (l) and Lisa Siegman '75

The Class of 1970 permanently opening FitzRandolph Gate

4 / 1996 — President Bill Clinton speaks at Commencement and receives an honorary degree during Princeton's 250th anniversary festivities, following the precedent of Grover Cleveland speaking at the 150th and Harry Truman speaking at the 200th.

5 / 1772 — The last of five lotteries to benefit the College is announced; it is drawn in Delaware to circumvent anti-lottery laws in New Jersey. The fourth lottery, in 1763, was drawn in New Jersey, but the earlier three were in Philadelphia and Connecticut.

6 / 1944 — After receiving news of the allied invasion of France on D-Day, Princeton holds a prayer service in the chapel at 5:00 p.m.

10 / 1975 — Seniors Cynthia Chase '75 and Lisa Siegman '75 are Princeton's first female valedictorian and salutatorian, respectively.

11 / 1901 — The first alumni trustee election taps five winners as 1,200 alumni vote.

12 / 1900 — The annual meetings of the Cliosophic and Whig societies are informed that the Board of Trustees has agreed to add a two-hour elective course in debating to the curriculum.

16 / 1931 — Novelist Willa Cather becomes the first woman to receive an honorary degree from Princeton.

17 / 1947 — Bicentennial celebrations end with a convocation featuring President Harry Truman and an academic procession of 1,000.

18 / 1963 — T'sai-Ying Cheng *63 *64 receives her master's degree in Biochemical Sciences, making her the first woman to earn a degree from Princeton. The following year she receives her PhD.

22 / 1887 — The *Prince* reports on yesterday's groundbreaking for a new museum of historic art which also will house the department of Art and Archaeology, the school of Architecture, and an art library. When the building formally opens, the *Prince* predicts that "the Art Building with its tasty collection is destined to become one of the most popular possessions of the campus."

23 / 1857 — Silas Holmes provides the University's first endowed chair, in belles-lettres.

24 / 1783 — Elias Boudinot, College trustee and president of the Continental Congress, proclaims that the Congress will move to Princeton; for four months the seat of government is housed in Nassau Hall.

28 / 1978 — Justice Lewis Powell's majority opinion in the Supreme Court's *Bakke* case, upholding affirmative action in college admissions, includes a footnote citing an article by President William Bowen about the use of affirmative action at Princeton.

29 / 1847 — Princeton celebrates its centennial at Commencement; the oldest alumnus present is from the Class of 1787.

30 / 1972 — William Bowen *58, economics professor and provost, is installed as Princeton's 17th president.

Joe Schein '37 carries the Class of 1923 cane while leading the 2018 P-rade at age 103.

Alumni Association president Jennifer Daniels '93 gets the 2018 P-rade off to a rousing start.

JULY

1 / 1957 — At age 37, professor of classics Robert Goheen '40, *48 assumes office as the 16th president of the University.

2 / 1776 — New Jersey becomes the fourth American colony to adopt a constitution declaring independence from Great Britain. The main drafter of the constitution, written in five days and ratified two days later, is Jonathan Dickinson Sergeant 1762.

3 / 1835 — Sixteen members of the Princeton Blues, a local volunteer militia, return the "big cannon" to the outskirts of Princeton from New Brunswick, where it had been taken during the War of 1812. Three years later students led by Winston Churchill's grandfather, Leonard Jerome 1839, return it to campus and in 1840 it is buried face-down on what becomes known as Cannon Green.

7 / 1894 — The Peary Auxiliary Expedition, including geography professor William Libbey 1877 *1879, sails to Greenland; it is led by Henry Bryant 1883, who participated in an earlier search for explorer Robert Peary and his party, which had left for Greenland in 1891.

8 / 2016 — The trustees adopt a policy to achieve greater diversity in the honorific naming of programs, positions, and spaces on campus.

9 / 1880 — The *Prince* resumes publication after an epidemic of typhoid costs the lives of 10 students.

13 / 1942 — The International Relations Club holds its inaugural meeting as part of Whig-Clio's first summer program in its 175-year history.

14 / 1970 — Larry Ellis is named head coach of track, the first African American head coach in the Ivy League; he later coaches in the Olympic Games of 1984.

15 / 1874 — During an intercollegiate regatta in Saratoga, New York, hundreds of yards of orange and black ribbon are sold at the Grand Union Hotel as "Princeton's colors." By the end of the first race, they are sold out.

19 / 1943 — The interval between classes is increased from five to 10 minutes; the Nassau Hall bell will ring for 90 seconds at the beginning and end of each interval.

20 / 1865 — Poet and a founder of *The Nassau Monthly* (later *Nassau Lit*) George Henry Boker 1842 reads his poem, *Our Heroic Themes*, before the Phi Beta Kappa Society of Harvard, one of the earliest tributes to Abraham Lincoln following his assassination.

21 / 1865 — A public meeting in Mercer Hall leads to the formation of a new hook, ladder, and bucket company in Princeton and the reorganization of the two existing engine companies.

25 / 1956 — *The Princeton Herald* reports that the University purchased a 154-unit garden apartment complex, Stanworth, on Bayard Lane to address acute housing shortages created by growing teaching, research, and administrative staffs.

26 / 1952 — Adlai Stevenson 1922 is nominated by the Democratic Party to run for president. He is nominated again in 1956.

27 / 1764 — Oliver Ellsworth 1766, a future chief justice of the US Supreme Court, transfers from Yale to the College of New Jersey.

31 / 1766 — An auction of six enslaved people is held in front of the President's House (now Maclean House) after the death of their owner, President Samuel Finley.

Robert Goheen '40, *48

This plaque in front of Maclean House commemorates 16 enslaved men, women, and children who lived and worked there.

4 / 1783 — Rain and the non-arrival of fireworks disrupt one of the first official celebrations of the Fourth of July in Princeton, where the Continental Congress is housed in Nassau Hall from June to November.

5 / 2005 — David Madden '03 begins a 19-day winning streak on *Jeopardy* that will earn him $430,400, one of the highest totals in the history of the game show.

6 / 2020 — The University announces that because of the COVID-19 pandemic, first-year students and juniors will be the only undergraduates on campus for the fall semester. On August 7 it announces a revised plan under which only a handful of undergraduates may return in the fall and the undergraduate program will be fully remote. (Graduate students are permitted to be on campus.)

10 / 1936 — New Jersey experiences its hottest day in history, 110 degrees Fahrenheit.

11 / 1804 — Aaron Burr Jr. 1772 fatally wounds Alexander Hamilton during a duel in Weehawken, New Jersey.

12 / 1968 — The Committee on the Education of Women at Princeton gives its final report to the Board of Trustees, urging that the University "move as quickly as possible to implement coeducation."

16 / 1979 — Firestone Library announces a federal grant to help make its rare collections more accessible to the public. Today, records from the American Civil Liberties Union archives are the largest and most frequently accessed collection at the Seeley G. Mudd Manuscript Library.

17 / 1898 — Spain's surrender in Santiago, Cuba, leads to the end of the Spanish American War. According to the *Prince* about 130 Princeton men enlisted, and nine served in Theodore Roosevelt's "Rough Riders."

18 / 1997 — Some 250 alumni, friends, and others climb Mt. Princeton in Colorado as the final event of the 250th anniversary celebration.

22 / 1955 — The University announces the appointment of its first African American faculty member, assistant professor of English Charles Davis.

23 / 1797 — In a letter to his step-grandson George Washington Parke Custis 1799, George Washington observes that "no college has turned out better scholars or more estimable characters than Nassau."

24 / 1961 — In its special issue for the incoming Class of 1965, the *Prince* announces that this year's sophomores will have to find a new way of "leaving their mark" on freshmen after head shaving was banned in 1959, and spraying class years on newcomers' heads with orange paint turned out to be a failure.

28 / 1938 — *Princeton News* reports that a circus at Williams and Olden Field, a Works Progress Administration project aiming to put theater professionals to work, attracted more than 800 visitors of all ages.

29 / 1754 — Ground is broken for Nassau Hall; two years later the College of New Jersey moves to Princeton and occupies two buildings: Nassau Hall and the President's House (now Maclean House).

30 / 2008 — President Shirley Tilghman informs the trustees that a pioneering "bridge year" program offering admitted students opportunities to engage in year-long international service projects prior to freshman year will begin as a pilot program in 2009.

Track and field coach Larry Ellis

Cannon Green

AUGUST

1 / 1877 — Princeton's first faculty-student geological expedition leaves Colorado for Wyoming, where it finds a Palaeosyops, a herbivorous dinosaur.

2 / 1865 — Princeton's first gymnasium is burned to the ground by an unknown person, perhaps to prevent the spread of smallpox after someone found sleeping there died of it.

3 / 1984 — The summer Olympics in Los Angeles complete the last of five days of competition in rowing, during which seven Princetonians participated, with one woman and two men winning medals.

7 / 1783 — Meeting in Nassau Hall, Congress votes unanimously that an equestrian statue of George Washington shall be erected where the seat of government is established.

8 / 1843 — The start of the first term is changed from November to August and the start of the second term is moved from May to February.

9 / 1946 — The *Princeton Herald* reports that more than 2,000 scholars and figures of world prominence will participate in Princeton University's bicentennial celebration in a nine-month program throughout the academic year 1946-47.

13 / 1747 — An advertisement in the *Pennsylvania Gazette* announces that the first seven trustees of the College of New Jersey will be "Messrs. William Smith, Peter Vanbrugh Livingston, William Peartree Smith, gent, and Messrs. Jonathan Dickenson, John Pierson, Ebenezer Pemberton and Aaron Burr, ministers of the gospel."

14 / 1969 — *Town Topics* reports on a six-week summer program at the school of Engineering and Applied Science on aircraft, electricity, structural design, and computers for 18 African American Princeton boys aged 11–15.

15 / 1919 — Future Princeton president Robert Goheen '40 *48 is born in Vengurla, India, to missionary parents.

19 / 1942 — Princeton native Paul Robeson plays "Othello" at McCarter Theatre.

20 / 1945 — The *Princeton Bulletin* reports that a number of Princeton faculty were engaged in radar research during the war and 896 Navy radar officer-specialists were trained in the Navy pre-radar school, which was quartered on the campus for two years.

21 / 1972 — NASA's Copernicus satellite is launched, carrying an ultraviolet telescope developed by Princeton scientists under the direction of Lyman Spitzer *38—as of then, the largest and most complex telescope ever sent into space.

25 / 1970 — Robert Durkee '69 and James Miller '70 appear on NBC's *Today* show to discuss the Movement for a New Congress, headquartered in Palmer Hall, and its mission to encourage and prepare college students to engage in that fall's congressional elections. To facilitate this engagement, Princeton schedules a fall break that year for the first time.

26 / 1933 — Nassau Hall is fully illuminated to mark the 150th anniversary of the Continental Congress formally thanking George Washington for his conduct in the Revolutionary War.

27 / 1776 — The first legislature of New Jersey meets in Nassau Hall.

31 / 1981 — Five freshmen in a group of Outdoor Action students remove the clapper in the Nassau Hall bell tower. Since purloining the clapper prior to freshman week may not meet the rules of this century-old tradition, the group returns on September 5 to repeat the theft.

Oval with Points sculpture by Henry Moore

4 / 2015 Former ice hockey and soccer star Mollie Marcoux '91 becomes the first female director of athletics.

5 / 2016 The opening ceremony of the Olympic Games takes place in Rio de Janeiro; four women among the 15 Princeton students and alumni competing will win medals.

6 / 2009 The Senate confirms Sonia Sotomayor '76 as the nation's first Hispanic Supreme Court justice.

10 / 1839 James Collins Johnson, who escaped slavery in Maryland, settles in Princeton as a janitor in Nassau Hall. When he is claimed by his former owner in 1843, his freedom is bought by Theodosia Prevost, a great-granddaughter of John Witherspoon.

11 / 1944 A play about Navy life called "Lower North" that is scheduled to open on Broadway in late August premieres at McCarter Theatre.

12 / 1812 Archibald Alexander is inaugurated as the first professor at the newly established Princeton Theological Seminary.

16 / 1884 Professor Charles Augustus Young describes an earthquake felt in Princeton, New York, and Philadelphia: "Taking it altogether it was certainly an excellent earthquake, vigorous enough to be instructive and interesting."

17 / 1768 John Witherspoon is installed as the sixth president of the College of New Jersey; students welcome him by illuminating Nassau Hall with a tallow dip in each window.

18 / 1997 Princeton announces that Regis Pecos '77, a former lieutenant governor of the Pueblo de Cochiti in New Mexico, has joined the Board of Trustees. He is believed to be the first Native American trustee in the Ivy League.

22 / 1867 The College converts to three terms per year. All freshmen study algebra, geometry, geography, declamation and composition, Latin, Greek, and biblical history.

23 / 1944 The *Prince* reports that President Harold Dodds will present a plan to the faculty in the fall to prepare for the post-war departure of Army and Navy training programs and the return to campus of large numbers of veterans.

24 / 1783 George Washington arrives in Princeton to be "near at hand" as the Congress meets in Nassau Hall. He stays in a Rocky Hill residence, "Rockingham," until November 10; while there he arranges the evacuation of British troops from New York and writes his farewell speech to the Army.

28 / 1950 President Harry Truman signs a law enabling employees of educational institutions to qualify for social security benefits; one of the principal architects of the social security program was Princeton economist and long-time dean of the faculty J. Douglas Brown 1919 *1928.

29 / 1962 The *Prince* reports that the school of Public and International Affairs has thoroughly revised its curriculum, preparing students for careers "in the nation's and the world's public service."

30 / 1911 The seventh annual conference of the Chinese Students' Alliance of the Eastern States, hosted by Princeton, enters its final day. The conference is attended by 150 students (135 men and 15 women) sent by China to be educated in the West.

Director of Athletics Mollie Marcoux Samaan '91

James Collins Johnson behind Nassau Hall, circa 1890

McCarter Theatre

SEPTEMBER

1 | 1947 — B. Franklin Bunn 1907 hands over management of the University Store to his successor, ending a 39-year tenure that began the year after he graduated.

2 | 1756 — President Aaron Burr Sr. purchases an enslaved man named Caesar for 80 pounds from the brother of a trustee.

3 | 1947 — In a new program, freshman interested in engineering are required to arrive prior to the start of the semester to participate in studies designed to acquaint them with engineering techniques before they begin the highly concentrated engineering curriculum.

7 | 1898 — The Princeton chapter of the Phi Beta Kappa Society is granted a charter. Formally established on June 7, 1899, it is known as the "Beta Chapter of New Jersey," the second established in the state. The state's Alpha Chapter was established at Rutgers College in 1869.

8 | 1958 — Princeton announces it will increase tuition from $1,200 to $1,400 in a move coordinated with Yale, making their rates the highest in the country. This will allow an increase in faculty salaries of $1,000 for full professors and $500 for assistant and associate professors.

9 | 1973 — University phones in the dormitories are connected to the New Jersey Bell Centrix system, permitting their use for more than just outgoing emergency calls. Under the previous system, messages to students were delivered by proctors and university police.

13 | 2003 — Princeton dedicates a memorial garden just to the west of Chancellor Green to alumni who died in the terrorist attacks of September 11, 2001.

14 | 1964 — Thomas R. Reid III '66 appears on the game show *To Tell the Truth* with the story of how he and his friends created a fake student named Joseph David Oznot '68, who was admitted to the University.

15 | 1954 — Orientation for first-year students begins in the new student center in the former Chancellor Green library. The center contains a dining space, a small auditorium, a game room, lounging alcoves, and meeting places for the Undergraduate Council and other campus organizations. From 1975 to 1983 the student center also includes a pub.

19 | 1998 — Princeton Stadium, designed by world-famous architect Rafael Viñoly, opens with a football game against Cornell that the Tigers win, 6-0.

20 | 1948 — Students herald the first day of the new academic year by swimming in Dillon Gym's newly completed pool, deemed "one of the best equipped in the world." (Completion had been delayed by more than a year by drainage problems.) The pool includes submarine windows and a movable wall, enabling various lengths necessary for college and national competitions.

21 | 1970 — The op-ed (opposite editorial) page, pioneered by editorial page editor John Oakes '34, makes its debut in the *New York Times*. Its intense popularity will lead to its adoption by many other newspapers.

25 | 1760 — Trustees add knowledge of "vulgar arithmetick" to the existing admission requirements.

26 | 1826 — The Alumni Association of Nassau Hall is organized with James Madison 1771, the University's first graduate student, as president.

27 | 1869 — After a proclamation by sophomores forbidding freshmen to carry canes, the entering Class of 1873 brings canes to campus, resulting in a battle that begins the annual cane spree.

The football upper right is about to become the first three points scored in Princeton Stadium.

The Pre-rade

4 1949 — *Town Topics* reports that the Class of 1953 will be the first not required to wear the black skullcaps ("dinks") that have visibly marked freshmen on campus since the 1920s.	**5** 2004 — The first annual Pre-rade for entering undergraduates takes place after Opening Exercises to welcome them to the campus.	**6** 1969 — The first women enrolled as undergraduate degree candidates arrive on campus. On September 8, the school year begins with 171 women, including 70 sophomores, juniors, and seniors.
10 1873 — The school of Science opens to candidates for the Bachelor of Science degree. Seven students are admitted.	**11** 2001 — In the wake of terrorist attacks on the United States, students and community members gather for a candlelight vigil at the end of the day. Fourteen alumni die in the attacks.	**12** 1958 — The University Store, incorporated in 1905, officially opens in its new home at 36 University Place.
16 1939 — Under a revamped academic calendar, Princeton begins the year nine days earlier and expands reading periods to include first-year students and sophomores.	**17** 1947 — Student registration takes place in the new Dillon Gym, which had been dedicated on June 14 during the bicentennial celebrations.	**18** 1968 — The *Prince* reports on plans to install an IBM system 360/91 in May 1969. One of the largest, fastest computers of its era, it can be used by up to 150 people simultaneously.
22 1876 — In its third issue the *Daily Princetonian* questions the practice of hazing. To make a freshman "understand his position in College," the *Prince* prefers the Princeton tradition of cane wrestling, or "cane spree."	**23** 1956 — A public celebration of the 200th anniversary of Nassau Hall is attended by the assistant postmaster general, who issues a commemorative orange three-cent stamp depicting the building. In 1996 a stamp featuring Alexander Hall is issued to commemorate the University's 250th anniversary.	**24** 1783 — Members of the Continental Congress attend Commencement; the next day George Washington gives the College 50 guineas, which the trustees use to commission an iconic portrait of Washington by Charles Willson Peale which hung for many years in Nassau Hall and is now in the art museum.
28 1841 — John McDonald Ross 1841 of the Cherokee nation is the first Native American student to be granted a Princeton degree.	**29** 1915 — US President Woodrow Wilson 1879 visits Princeton and refuses to answer reporters' questions about whether he supports female suffrage. Later in the day, Beatrice Forbes-Robertson Hale, author of *What Women Want: An Interpretation of the Feminist Movement*, gives an address in Alexander Hall calling for American women to be given the right to vote.	**30** 1959 — The *Daily Princetonian* reports that an "air scooter," similar to a flying saucer, is being tested at the Forrestal Research Center by the department of Aeronautical Engineering.

September 11, 2001, memorial garden

250th anniversary Alexander Hall postcard

1959 experimental air cushion vehicle at Princeton Forrestal campus

OCTOBER

1 | 1970 More than 200 alumni leaders visit Princeton for a three-day conference called by President Robert Goheen to discuss recent developments on campus. Trustees, administrators, faculty, and 12 students participate with alumni in panel discussions and workshops.

2 | 1931 The *Princeton Alumni Weekly* and the *Prince* report that the trustees have approved plans for a proposed $400,000 University Center between Stanhope and West College (now Morrison Hall). The onset of the Great Depression forces postponement of the plans, which are not fully realized until the Frist Campus Center opens in 2000.

3 | 1964 Preliminary plans for a new three-building science complex to house the Astrophysics, Physics, and Math departments are discussed by the Board of Trustees. Peyton Hall opens in 1966; Jadwin Hall and Fine Hall in 1970.

7 | 1993 Professor Toni Morrison is named a Nobel Laureate in Literature, the first Black American woman so honored.

8 | 1966 The world premiere of Igor Stravinsky's latest composition, *Requiem Canticles*, takes place in McCarter Theatre, with the composer conducting. The composition was commissioned by Princeton University.

9 | 1920 The University Band debuts as a permanent student organization when 20 students in black sweaters and white flannels play at halftime during the Maryland football game in Palmer Stadium. Princeton wins the game, 35–0.

13 | 1962 The new $8 million state-of-the-art Engineering Quadrangle is dedicated at the conclusion of symposia on engineering education.

14 | 1971 Native American student Victor Masayesva '74 submits a letter to the *Prince* to protest the removal of a poster that designated Columbus Day as a "day of mourning for American Indians."

15 | 1936 Princeton's "social season" opens with the first meeting of the Orange Key Society, formed the previous year to entertain official visitors to the Princeton campus.

19 | 1979 The trustees endorse a residential college system for first- and second-year students.

20 | 2000 The Frist Campus Center, designed by Robert Venturi '47 *50 and Denise Scott Brown, is dedicated with Senator William Frist '74 and other members of his family in attendance.

21 | 1896 As part of the sesquicentennial celebration, Professor Woodrow Wilson 1879 delivers his speech, "Princeton in the Nation's Service." That evening 3,000 people march by torchlight to Nassau Hall, where they are greeted by fireworks.

25 | 1902 Woodrow Wilson 1879 is inaugurated as the 13th president of Princeton University.

26 | 1963 100 people from Princeton, including students, join an estimated 4,000 participants from all over New Jersey in a "March on Trenton for Jobs and Freedom." Patterned after the August 28 March on Washington, it is the first statewide civil rights demonstration in the nation.

27 | 1868 In his inaugural address President James McCosh states that Princeton's "doors should be open to all nationalities." He allows African American students to attend his lectures, despite protests from some southern students.

31 | 1917 The *Prince* publishes the election results of representatives to the Undergraduate Council, established during a student mass meeting on October 18. The council, which acts as a student government body, supersedes the former Senior Council.

Frist Campus Center from the south

4 1910 — Princeton University Press, initially founded in 1905 as a private corporation above a drug store on Nassau Street, is reincorporated as a nonprofit company. In 1911 Charles Scribner 1875 gives the Press the Collegiate Gothic William Street building which has housed it ever since.	**5** 2017 — With a four-day festival, Princeton celebrates the opening of the Lewis Center for the Arts and the Lewis Arts complex.	**6** 1942 — About 800 naval reserve officers arrive for training and move into Brown, Cuyler, and Patton halls as rooms that previously accommodated two students are refitted to house six to eight.
10 1916 — Classes finally begin after being delayed several weeks due to a severe polio epidemic. Students are still prohibited from going to the movies, eating off-campus, or leaving town until the epidemic passes.	**11** 1989 — Princeton's first "gay jeans day" encourages students to show support for gay rights.	**12** 1868 — The faculty passes a resolution permitting students to adopt and wear orange ribbons imprinted with "PRINCETON."
16 1971 — The Third World Center (later the Carl A. Fields Center for Equality and Cultural Understanding) opens with a "housewarming" a month after receiving trustee approval.	**17** 1957 — The University annexes the student center to the infirmary to help care for 600 students who fall victim to a flu epidemic. It is partially staffed by student volunteers and nurses from the Red Cross.	**18** 2000 — Maurice Sendak, author of the 1963 children's book *Where the Wild Things Are* and a 1984 Princeton honorary degree recipient, tells an audience in McCosh 50: "Adults were critical of the book, but children loved it."
22 1746 — The first charter is issued; its guarantee of equal access to any person regardless of religion distinguishes the College of New Jersey from other colonial colleges.	**23** 1967 — Police arrest 31 student protesters at a sit-in on the steps of the Institute for Defense Analyses (IDA), which is renting space in von Neumann Hall adjacent to the Engineering Quadrangle.	**24** 1914 — Princeton plays its first football game in the newly constructed Palmer Stadium, defeating Dartmouth 16–12.
28 1969 — Following the previous evening's first-ever meeting of the Council of the Princeton University Community, the CPUC presses ahead to complete its membership and plan meetings for the rest of the year.	**29** 1966 — The Princeton University Art Museum reopens in a new building it will occupy for more than five decades; in 2020 plans are announced for the construction of a much larger new space.	**30** 1938 — Orson Welles' live radio broadcast *War of the Worlds* leads some listeners to believe there has been a Martian invasion four miles from Nassau Hall.

The original Third World Center

The Lewis Arts complex

NOVEMBER

1 | 1982 — Coretta Scott King kicks off Black Solidarity Day at a rally on Cannon Green that is attended by over 500 people. In 1970 she received an honorary degree.

2 | 1920 — On the evening of election day a special wire is run to Alexander Hall by the Western Union Telegraph Company to announce results as fast as they are received. In between, moving pictures are shown and the University Band plays.

3 | 1785 — On the day of her wedding, Robert Stockton gives his daughter Elizabeth the enslaved girl Betsey Stockton as a gift. In 1817, Elizabeth's husband, Princeton President Ashbel Green, manumits Betsey Stockton and recommends her as a missionary to the American Board of Commissioners for Foreign Missions, making her the first unmarried female overseas missionary.

7 | 1955 — *Life Magazine* features a photo of Princeton mascot Michael Briggs '57 lounging in his tiger suit on the lawn of Colonial Club.

8 | 1907 — After a lapse of 23 years, an interclass regatta is held on the newly created Carnegie Lake. The race is won by the Class of 1910 crew, and the Carnegie Cup is presented in person by Andrew Carnegie, who financed the building of the lake.

9 | 1748 — At its first Commencement the College of New Jersey admits "six young scholars" to the degree of "Batchelor of the Arts" and awards its first honorary degree to provincial governor Jonathan Belcher.

13 | 1998 — Princeton begins offering its first free non-credit online course, open to alumni, students, parents, and the campus community.

14 | 1989 — The Graduate Student Union, precursor to Princeton's Graduate Student Government, holds its first meeting.

15 | 1873 — During Princeton's first football game against Yale, two players kick the ball at the same time, causing it to burst. A collection is taken among the spectators to buy a new ball in town. The injured ball is returned to Princeton in 1926 and remains in the trophy room of University Gymnasium until the gym is destroyed by fire in 1944.

19 | 1969 — Astronaut Charles "Pete" Conrad Jr. '53 becomes the third man to walk on the moon; he takes five Princeton flags to the moon with him.

20 | 1936 — Nineteen-year-old Ella Fitzgerald is the featured vocalist at a dance in the old gymnasium; 54 years later she receives an honorary degree.

21 | 1879 — The *Prince* defends the freshman class against charges that they should not be allowed to wear orange and black; the allegation was that only football players should be permitted to wear the colors.

25 | 1950 — Princeton beats Dartmouth 13–7 despite 108-mile-per-hour wind gusts and drenching rain, with only 5,000 ticket holders braving the storm at Palmer Stadium. With an undefeated season, Princeton wins the Lambert Trophy as the best team in the east; it will go undefeated and win the trophy again the following year.

26 | 1896 — The *Prince* reports that the student honor committee, which has already been successful in stopping "cribbing in examinations," adjudicated a hazing incident and suspended six sophomores. The *Prince* believed this precedent "will no doubt prevent any such misconduct" in the future.

27 | 1965 — A 10-foot-long "Even Princeton" banner makes its first appearance at a march on Washington to end the war in Vietnam; the banner was unfurled often in anti–Vietnam War protests on and off campus.

A rendering of the first intercollegiate football game (Rutgers/Princeton) in 1869

One of the flags carried to the moon by Pete Conrad '53

The "Even Princeton" banner first carried in 1965 at an anti–Vietnam War protest in DC

4 1933	Princeton defeats Brown in football, 33–0, en route to a perfect season; some fans traveled to the game the previous evening on a chartered steamer on which the University Band played 10 songs, including *The Orange and the Black* and *Old Nassau*, which were broadcast over two radio stations.	**5** 1925	The *Prince* announces that the Class of 1892, in honor of its 35th reunion, will order a set of 35 bells from Croydon, England. Intended initially for the chapel and then for Holder Tower, they end up in the carillon in Cleveland Tower, which now has 67 bells.	**6** 1869	Rutgers defeats Princeton 6–4 in the first intercollegiate football game.
10 1920	Following pressure on the administration, a grill room under student management opens on the ground floor of the University dining halls as a place where students can "drop in and get a bite to eat during the evening."	**11** 1922	After the football team beats Harvard, the father of team member Albert "Red" Howard 1925 donates a tiger cub to Princeton as a mascot. Following that year's graduation, the cub is donated to the Philadelphia zoo.	**12** 1941	The *Prince* suggests that students make their own beds on Sundays so that underpaid janitors have one day off a week.
16 2017	The Princeton and Slavery Symposium begins a four-day event featuring panels, performances, guided tours, exhibitions, film screenings, and a keynote speech by Nobel Laureate and Princeton professor emerita Toni Morrison.	**17** 2014	A new Dinky train station opens as part of the development of the Lewis Arts complex, about 460 feet south of the previous station, where it had been located since 1918. The first station opened in 1865 on a site farther north, which placed the train at the foot of Blair Arch when Blair Hall opened in 1897.	**18** 1929	The National Academy of Sciences holds its annual autumn meeting in the auditorium of the brand-new Frick Chemical Laboratory, now the Julis-Romo-Rabinowitz building.
22 1864	In its first-ever intercollegiate baseball game, Princeton defeats Williams, 27–16.	**23** 1939	When a train wreck blocks all traffic on the main line of the Pennsylvania Railroad near Princeton Junction station, 300 stranded undergraduates returning from Thanksgiving hold an impromptu "songfest" in the Trenton station.	**24** 1919	The first Princeton hospital opens on Witherspoon Street in a converted farmhouse with a staff of five doctors.
28 1756	With carpenters and others still at work on the building, students and tutors move into Nassau Hall.	**29** 1994	The *Prince* announces that an Asian American Studies course will be offered for the first time in the fall after petitioning by the Asian-American Students Association.	**30** 1834	On Princeton's first astronomical expedition, Professor Stephen Alexander observes a total solar eclipse in Georgia; his Fraunhofer telescope is one of the best refractors of its time.

The Dinky

The Graduate College overlooks the golf course.

DECEMBER

1 | 1960 — The Undergraduate Council votes to recommend to the faculty that the hours women are permitted in dormitories be extended from 9 p.m. to midnight on Friday and Saturday. The initial trustee response extends just the Saturday deadline, and only to 11 p.m.

2 | 1956 — The Triangle Club's annual appearance on the Ed Sullivan TV show is a full-length performance of a ballet satire, "Goose Lagoon," based on Tchaikovsky's "Swan Lake." Sullivan's producer says the number was "about the best thing I've seen in a college show in a long, long time."

3 | 1846 — Joseph Henry, Princeton professor since 1832 and one of the leading American scientists of his time, becomes secretary of the newly created Smithsonian Institution.

7 | 1776 — As the British Army reaches Princeton to begin "20 days of tyranny," Annis Boudinot Stockton hides Whig Society treasures; later she is posthumously elected Whig's first female member.

8 | 1979 — Sir Arthur Lewis, winner of the Nobel Prize in Economics for his pioneering research into economic development, primarily in developing countries, delivers his Nobel lecture; in 2017 the main auditorium in Robertson Hall is named for Lewis.

9 | 2008 — Settlement of a six-year lawsuit transfers all assets of the Robertson Foundation to the University for continuing support of the graduate program in the school of Public and International Affairs.

13 | 1900 — The trustees vote to establish a graduate school and appoint professor of Latin Andrew Fleming West 1874 as its first dean.

14 | 1961 — On the last day of the annual College Brand Round-Up contest, sponsored by Philip Morris Tobacco Co., students submit empty packs of Marlboro, Parliament, Alpine, and Philip Morris cigarettes. First prize is a stereo hi-fi phonograph.

15 | 1940 — WPRB's predecessor, WPRU, hits the air with daily broadcasts from 7:15 to 9:15 a.m. and from 5:00 to 6:00 p.m.

19 | 1907 — The Glee, Banjo, and Mandolin clubs depart to present "An Evening on the Princeton Campus" during their annual Christmas tour through five cities. In Scranton, Buffalo, and Cleveland they use their new drop curtain, an innovation that is "welcomed heartily."

20 | 1864 — The trustees award Abraham Lincoln an honorary degree, the third and last one he receives; he accepts *in absentia*.

21 | 1918 — With orders home in his pocket celebrated athlete Hobey Baker 1914 is killed in France while testing a repaired plane.

25 | 1752 — Four months after deciding that the college "be fixed at Princeton," the trustees of the College of New Jersey in Elizabeth decide to hold their next meeting in Princeton on January 24, 1753.

26 | 1943 — President Harold Dodds announces that Princeton University will sponsor publication of the writings and correspondence of Thomas Jefferson. Originally thought to take 15 years, the project is now expected to be finished by 2037, when the 62nd volume is published.

27 | 1892 — The first annual intercollegiate chess tournament starts in New York with teams from Princeton, Columbia, Harvard, and Yale. It will last until January 2.

31 | 1948 — The newly opened Firestone Library grants special passes to 36 students who want to ring in the new year by studying until midnight.

Firestone Library following early twenty-first-century renovations

Heisman Trophy winner Dick Kazmaier '52

4 | 1951 Triple-threat tailback Richard Kazmaier '52 is awarded the Heisman Trophy as the best college football player of the year.

5 | 1906 Enthusiastic undergraduates give Andrew Carnegie a "hearty reception" at a ceremony in Alexander Hall where he formally presents Lake Carnegie to the University.

6 | 1919 Word spreads that the will of Henry Clay Frick, made public the previous day, includes a bequest to Princeton calculated at $15 million. Princeton eventually receives almost $6 million, all of which it uses to endow faculty salaries.

10 | 1972 John Bardeen *36 accepts his second Nobel Prize in Physics, the only two-time laureate in the field.

11 | 1978 The Committee on Undergraduate Residential Life proposes that all freshmen and sophomores live and eat in residential colleges, and juniors and seniors be assigned to Prospect Avenue eating clubs operating under contract with the University. Only the first part of the plan comes to fruition.

12 | 1935 Afflicted with a recurring case of jaundice, freshman John Fitzgerald Kennedy '39 withdraws from the University.

16 | 1941 The *Prince* publishes President Harold Dodd's address during yesterday night's mass meeting about accelerated programs and emergency war training courses that will enable undergraduates to be of "maximum service to the nation while getting their Princeton degrees."

17 | 1873 President James McCosh reports that Chancellor Green Library is complete, save for the furnace, and that 26 people per day are borrowing books.

18 | 1936 Pennsylvania Railroad trains to Chicago, Cincinnati, Detroit, and St. Louis make special stops at Princeton Junction for students leaving for the holidays.

22 | 1869 The *New York Tribune* reports that the College of New Jersey's new gymnasium has been completed. It features the first bathtubs on campus.

23 | 1944 The first of three classes of a Navy School of Military Government completes its course. After studying the challenges of governing liberated lands, they are preparing to go to the South Pacific in the wake of Allied victories there.

24 | 1982 The Princeton Plasma Physics Laboratory's Tokamak Fusion Test Reactor produces its first plasma, a significant step forward in its decades-long effort to realize fusion as a safe, abundant, and environmentally attractive energy source for the world.

28 | 1799 A eulogy for George Washington, prepared by Henry Lee 1773, known during the American Revolution as "Light-Horse Harry" and father of Robert E. Lee, is presented to Congress. He describes Washington as "first in war, first in peace, and first in the hearts of his countrymen."

29 | 1958 The *Indianapolis Star* reports in an editorial that "some 15-odd students at Princeton, led along by one Professor Eric F. Goldman, are rewriting the American Constitution as an 'intellectual exercise,'" as it was written "in an agrarian society." The editorial says "the Princetonians have been... admonished to exhibit their powers as practical statesmen, not Utopians."

30 | 1949 The Association of Princeton Graduate Alumni (APGA) is founded.

PPPL's Tokamak Fusion Test Reactor (TFTR)

Rowing on Lake Carnegie

REFERENCE LISTS

Baccalaureate Speakers: 1973-2021

1973 The Rev. Dr. John Coburn '36, Bishop, Episcopal Diocese of Massachusetts
1974 The Rev. Thomas Stewart '51, Pastor, Westminster Presbyterian Church, Buffalo, New York
1975 Professor Gregory Vlastos, Stuart Professor of Philosophy, Princeton University
1976 James McCord, President, Princeton Theological Seminary
1977 The Rev. Theodore Hesburgh, President, Notre Dame University
1978 Gerson Cohen, Chancellor, The Jewish Theological Seminary of America
1979 Redmond Finney '51, Headmaster, The Gilman School
1980 Michael Stewart '57, MD, Associate Professor of Medicine, Columbia University
1981 Sisela Bok, Lecturer on Medical Ethics, Harvard Medical School
1982 Charles Renfrew '52, Partner, Pillsbury, Madison and Sutro
1983 The Rev. Dr. Homer U. Ashby Jr. '68, Professor, McCormick Theological Seminary
1984 Paul Sarbanes '54, US Senator from Maryland
1985 Ira Silverman, President, Reconstructionist Rabbinical College
1986 Thomas Kean '57, Governor of New Jersey
1987 George Rupp '64, President, Rice University
1988 Patricia Schroeder, US Representative from Colorado
1989 Andrew Young, Mayor of Atlanta, Georgia
1990 Johnnetta Cole, President, Spelman College
1991 William Crowe Jr. *65, USN Ret., former Chairman of the Joint Chiefs of Staff
1992 Cokie Roberts, Congressional Correspondent for National Public Radio and ABC
1993 Garry Trudeau, Cartoonist
1994 Wynton Marsalis, Artistic Director of Jazz at Lincoln Center
1995 Jane Alexander, Chair, National Endowment for the Arts
1996 Bill Bradley '65, US Senator from New Jersey
1997 William Frist '74, US Senator from Tennessee
1998 Thomas Harkin, US Senator from Iowa, and Ruth Harkin, Senior Vice President, United Technologies
1999 Marian Wright Edelman, President, Children's Defense Fund
2000 Queen Noor of Jordan (Lisa Halaby '73)
2001 Garrison Keillor, humorist, writer, creator of Prairie Home Companion
2002 Meg Whitman '77, President and CEO, eBay Inc.
2003 Fred Hargadon, Dean of Admission, Princeton University
2004 James McPherson, George Henry Davis '86 Professor of American History, Princeton University
2005 Toni Morrison, Robert F. Goheen Professor in the Humanities, Princeton University
2006 David Sedaris, National Public Radio humorist and bestselling author
2007 John Fleming *63, Louis W. Fairchild '24 Professor of English and Comparative Literature, Emeritus, Princeton University
2008 Paul Farmer, physician, medical anthropologist, and a founding director of Partners In Health
2009 General David Petraeus *87, Commander of the US Central Command
2010 Jeff Bezos '86, CEO and founder, Amazon
2011 Michael Bloomberg P01, Mayor, New York City
2012 Michael Lewis '82, Author
2013 Ben Bernanke, Chair of the US Federal Reserve
2014 Christopher Lu '88, Deputy Secretary, US Department of Labor; former White House assistant to President Obama
2015 Lisa Jackson *86, Vice President, Environmental Initiatives, Apple; former administrator of the US Environmental Protection Agency
2016 Randall Kennedy '70, Michael R. Klein Professor of Law at Harvard Law School and Princeton Trustee
2017 Anne Holton '80, Former First Lady and former Secretary of Education of Virginia
2018 Eduardo Bhatia '86, Minority Leader and former President of the Senate of Puerto Rico
2019 George Will *68, Pulitzer-prize-winning columnist
2020 Maria Ressa '86, journalist, CEO and executive editor of the Philippines-based news organization Rappler.com. (Because the COVID-19 pandemic required cancellation of the Baccalaureate service, her address was delivered as part of that year's virtual Commencement.)
2021 Ruth Simmons, President of Prairie View A&M University, former President of Smith College and Brown University, and former Princeton administrator and trustee

Behrman Award Winners

1976
Carlos Baker *40, English
Lawrence Stone, History
Gregory Vlastos, Philosophy

1977
Milton Babbitt *42 *92, Music
Thomas Kuhn, History of Science

1978
Durant W. Robertson Jr., English
Theodore Ziolkowski, Germanic Languages and Literatures and Comparative Literature

1979
Victor Brombert, Romance Languages and Literatures and Comparative Literature
Marius Jansen '44, History and East Asian Studies

1980
Edward Cone '39, Music
Carl Schorske, History

1981
Charles Gillispie, History
A. Walton Litz '51, English

1982
David Coffin '40, *54, Art and Archaeology
Edmund Keeley, English and Creative Writing

1983
Natalie Zemon Davis, History
Kenneth Levy *49, Music

1984
David Furley, Classics
Alvin Kernan, English

1986
W. Robert Connor *61, Classics
Robert Hollander '55, Comparative Literature and Romance Languages and Literatures

1987
Robert Darnton, History
John Fleming *63, English

1988
Peter Brown, History
Saul Kripke, Philosophy

1989
Robert Fagles, Comparative Literature
Elaine Showalter, English

1990
Lionel Gossman, Romance Languages and Literatures
Samuel Hynes, English

1991
David Lewis, Philosophy
James McPherson, History

1992
Toshiko Takaezu, Humanities and Visual Arts
John Wilson, Religion

1993
Earl Miner, English
François Rigolot, Romance Languages and Literatures

1994
Hans Aarsleff, English
Margaret Wilson, Philosophy

1995
Bas van Fraassen, Philosophy
Froma Zeitlin, Classics

1996
Anthony Grafton, History
Arnold Rampersad, English

1997
Caryl Emerson, Slavic Languages and Literatures
Harold Powers, Music

1998
George Kateb, Politics
Albert Raboteau, Religion

1999
Maria DiBattista, English
Alexander Nehamas *71, Philosophy and Comparative Literature

2000
Paul Benacerraf '52 *60, Philosophy

2001
Thomas Roche Jr. *58, English

_2002_
Michael Wood, English

_2003_
William Jordan, History

_2004_
Joel Cooper, Philosophy
James Seawright, Humanities and Visual Arts

_2005_
John G. Gager Jr., Religion
Paul Lansky *73, Music

_2006_
Michael Cook, Near Eastern Studies
Emmet Gowin, Humanities and Visual Arts

_2007_
Robert Kaster, Classics
Ulrich Knoepflmacher, English

_2008_
Paul Muldoon, Lewis Center for the Arts and Creative Writing
Daniel Rodgers, History

_2009_
Stanley Corngold, German and Comparative Literature
Gilbert Harman, Philosophy

_2010_
K. Anthony Appiah, Philosophy and University Center for Human Values
Leonard Barkin, Comparative Literature

_2011_
V. Kofi Agawu, Music
Denis Feeney, Classics

_2012_
Elaine Pagels, Religion
Joyce Carol Oates, Lewis Center for the Arts and Creative Writing

_2013_
Scott Burnham, Music
Peter Schafer, Religion

_2014_
Jan Gross, History
Susan Stewart, English

_2015_
Claudia Johnson, English
Brent Shaw, Classics

_2016_
Steven Mackey, Music
Michael Wachtel, Slavic Languages and Literatures

_2017_
Simon Gikandi, English
Philip Nord, History

_2018_
Harriet Flower, Classics
Mark Johnston *83, Philosophy

_2019_
David Bellos, French and Italian and Comparative Literature
Sean Wilentz, History

_2020_
Hal Foster '77, Art and Archaeology
Esther Schor, English

Guggenheim Fellowships Since 1970

1970
James M. Banner Jr., History
James Cronin, Physics
Michael Curshmann, German
Robert Darnton, History
Robert B. Hollander Jr., '55 French and Italian
Goro Shimura, Mathematics
Abraham Udovich, Near Eastern Studies

1971
John Bonner, Biology
Jerome Blum, History
Sam Hunter, Art and Archaeology
Robert Martin, English
Noboru Sueoka, Biology

1972
David Coffin '40 *54, Art and Archaeology
Vincent Dethier, Biology
Edmund Keeley '48, English
Suzanne Keller, Sociology
Donald McClure, Chemistry
Stuart Schwartz, Electrical Engineering
Stanley Stein, History

1973
L. Carl Brown, Near Eastern Studies
Alan Gelperin, Biology
Walter Murphy, Politics
Richard Rorty, Philosophy

1974
William Browder '58, Mathematics
Emmet Gowin, Humanities Council

1975
Nicholas Katz *66, Mathematics
Peter Kenen, Economics
Wu-chung Hsiang *62, Mathematics

1976
Steven Cohen, Politics
Fred Greenstein, Politics
Joseph Kohn *56, Mathematics
Robert Socolow, Mechanical and Aerospace Engineering
Elias Stein, Mathematics

1977
Stanley Corngold, German and Comparative Literature
Michael Goldman *62, English

1978
Gilbert Harman, Philosophy
Martin Semmelhack, Chemistry
John Suppe, Geosciences

1979
Peter Bunnell, Art and Archaeology
Marius Jansen '44, East Asian Studies
Gilbert Rozman *71, Sociology
Edward Taylor, Chemistry

1980
Ralph Freedman, Comparative Literature
Zoltan Soos, Chemistry
John Wilson, Religion

1981
Richard Lipton, Computer Science
Lawrence Rosen, Anthropology

1982
Harold Kuhn *50, Mathematics
Robert Mark, Architecture and Civil Engineering
Francois Rigolot, French and Italian

1984
Michael Aizeman, Physics
Froma Zeitlin, Classics and Comparative Literature

1985
Natalie Zemon Davis, History
Richard Falk, Politics
Nathaniel Fisch, Astrophysical Sciences
Peter Grant, Ecology and Evolutionary Biology
Steven Mackey, Music
Andrew Wiles, Mathematics

1986
David Bromwich, English
Joan DeJean, French and Italian
Alban Forcione '60*68, Spanish and Portuguese
George Miller, Psychology
Sylvia Molloy, Spanish and Portuguese
Suzanne Nash *72, French and Italian
David Quint, Comparative Literature
Theodore Weiss, English

1987
R. Douglas Arnold, Politics
John Cooper, Philosophy
James Gould, Ecology and Evolutionary Biology
Nicholas Katz *66, Mathematics
William Schowalter, Chemical and Biological Engineering
Julian Wolpert, Public and International Affairs

1988
David Dobkin, Computer Science
Anthony Grafton, History
John Mather *67, Mathematics

Harold Powers *59, Music
Thomas Spiro, Chemistry

1989

Patricia Fortini Brown, Art and Archaeology
Peter Brown, History
Michael Cook, Near Eastern Studies
Victoria Kahn, English
Susan Sugarman, Psychology

1990

John Darley, Psychology
Paul Lansky '69 *73, Music
Paul Muldoon, Humanities Council
Albert Raboteau, Religion
Sean Wilentz, History

1991

Pablo Debenedetti, Chemical and Biological
    Engineering
Avinash Dixit, Economics
Stanley Kelley, Politics
Edward Tenner '65, Humanities Council
Andrew Yao, Computer Science

1992

Sally Price, Art and Archaeology

1993

Francis Dahlen, Geosciences
Harry Frankfurt, Philosophy
Gene Grossman, Economics
Thomas Kauffman, Art and Archaeology

1994

Bernard Chazelle, Computer Science
Christine Stansell '71, History

1996

Larry Bartels, Politics
Mark Cohen, Near Eastern Studies
Josiah Ober, Classics
Kay Warren *74, Anthropology
Viviana Zelizer, Sociology

1997

Paul Chalkin, Physics
Laura Engelstein, History
Sergiu Klainerman, Mathematics

1998

Scott Burnham, Music
Sun-Yung Alice Chang, Mathematics
Hal Foster '77, Art and Archaeology
Abdellah Hammoudi, Anthropology
Salvatore Torquato, Chemistry

1999

Ben Bernanke, Economics
Paul Koonce, Music
Emily Martin, Anthropology

2000

April Alliston, English
Jennifer Hochschild, Politics
Peter Jeffery *80, Music
Claudia Johnson *81, English

2001

Jeremy Adelman, History
Elizabeth Lunbeck, History
Francois Morel, Geosciences

2002

Peter Lake, History
H. Vincent Poor *77, Electrical Engineering
Yu Xie, Sociology

2003

Charles Beitz *78, Politics
Roland Benabou, Economics
Perry Cook, Computer Science and Music
Sean Kelly, Philosophy
Howard Rosenthal, Politics
Barbara White, Music
Robert Wuthnow, Sociology

2004

Charles Boix, Politics
Jeffrey Herbst '83, Politics
Stephen Kotkin, History

2005

Leonard Barkan, Comparative Literature
Yannis Kevrekidis, Chemical and Biological Engineering
Stephen Morris, Economics
Philip Nord, History
John Pinto, Art and Archaeology
D. Vance Smith, English
Valerie Smith, English
Bruce Western, Sociology

2006

Diana Fuss, English
Daniel Trueman *99, Music

2007

Daniel Rogers, History
Jose Scheinkman, Economics
Nigel Smith, Engliish
Dimitri Tymoczko, Music
Michael Wachtel, Slavic Languages and Literatures
Tommy White, Art and Archaeology

2008
Yacine Ait-Sahalia, Economics
Joao Biehl, Anthropology
Martha Himmelfarb, Religion
Sean Keilen, English
Alan Stahl, Curator of the University Numismatic Collection
Christian Tomaszewski, Visual Arts

2009
Caryl Emerson, Slavic Languages and Literatures
Jianqing Fan, Electrical Engineering
Denis Feeney, Classics
Susan Fiske, Psychology
Steve Gubser '94 *98, Physics
Muhammad Zaman, Religion

2010
Markus Brunnermeier, Economics
Ingrid Daubechies, Mathematics
Bernard Haykel, Near Eastern Studies
Daniel Heyman, Visual Arts
Joshua Katz, Classics
Igor Klebanov *86, Physics
Pinelopi Koujianou Goldberg, Economics
Philip Pettit, Politics
Alexander Todorov, Psychology

2011
Michael Gordin, History
Simon Morrison *97, Music

2012
Eve Aschheim, Visual Arts
Timothy Donnelly, Creative Writing
Laura Landweber '89, Molecular Biology
Melissa Lane, Politics
Eldar Shafir, Psychology

2013
D. Graham Burnett '93, History
Deana Lawson, Visual Arts
Colson Whitehead, Creative Writing

2014
Mung Chiang, Electrical Engineering
Andrew Cole, English
Devin Fore, Comparative Literature and Slavic Languages and Literatures

Meghan O'Rourke, Creative Writing,
Serguei Oushakine, Anthropology
Emily Thompson *92, History
Claire Watkins, Creative Writing

2015
Jeff Dolven, English
Rowan Ricardo Phillips, Creative Writing

2016
Daniel Garber, Philosophy
Juri Seo, Music
Raphael Xavier, Dance

2017
Mark Beissinger, Politics
B. Andrei Bernevig, Physics
Linda Colley, History
Phil Klay, Creative Writing
Aaron Landsman, Theatre
Fiona Maazel, Creative Writing
Claudia Rankine, Creative Writing
Stacy Wolf, Theatre

2018
John Heginbotham, Dance
Brooke Holmes *05, Classics
Martin Kern, East Asian Studies
Ekaterina Pravilova, History
Monica Youn '93, Creative Writing

2019
Kevin Kruse, History
Lena Salaymeh, History
Ilya Vinitsky, Slavic Languages and Literatures

2020
Michael Dickman, Creative Writing
Yaacob Dweck, History
Yiyun Li, Creative Writing

2021
William Bialek, Physics
Donnacha Dennehy, Music
Atif Mian *97, Economics
Imani Perry, African American Studies
Laurence Ralph, Anthropology
Keeanga-Yamahtta Taylor, African American Studies

Princeton University Honorary Degree Recipients 1970–2021

Last Name	First Name	Degree	Year Awarded
Aaron	Henry	HHD	2011
Abdul-Jabbar	Kareem	HHD	2017
Abed	Fazle Hasan	LLD	2014
Ailey	Alvin	DFA	1972
Alberts	Bruce	DSc	1997
Albright	Madeleine	LLD	2014
Ali	Muhammad	HHD	2007
Annan	Kofi	LLD	1999
Arendt	Hannah	LittD	1972
Arnold '79	Francis	DSc	2020
Ashe	Arthur	HHD	1982
Augustine '57 *59	Norman	LLD	2007
Babbitt *42 *92	Milton B.	DMus	1991
Bailey Jr. '42	Herbert Smith	LLD	1986
Baker *39	William O.	LLD	1993
Baker III '52	James A.	LLD	1991
Ball	George W.	LLD	1984
Baumol	William J.	LHD	1999
Beam	Jacob Dyneley	LLD	1970
Beardslee	Bethany	DMus	1977
Becker '51	Gary S.	LHD	1991
Belafonte	Harry	LLD	2015
Bergen Jr. '51	Stanley S.	LLD	1995
Bernanke	Ben S.	LLD	2016
Billington '50	David	DSc	2015
Bishop	Elizabeth	LittD	1979
Blackburn	Elizabeth	DSc	2007
Bogle '51	John	LLD	2005
Bok	Derek Curtis	LLD	1971
Bon Jovi	Jon	DMus	2021
Bonner	John	DSc	2006
Bowen *58	William	LLD	1987
Boyle	Gregory	L.H.D.	2018
Bradley	Tom	LLD	1979
Bradley '65	William W.	LLD	1983
Brennan Jr.	William Joseph	LLD	1986
Brody	Jane E.	HHD	1987
Brown	Charles L.	LLD	1983
Brown 1919 *1928	J. Douglas	LLD	1973
Bunch	Lonnie	LHD	2018
Burke	James Edward	LLD	1997
Bush	George H. W.	LLD	1991
Calabresi	Guido	LLD	1992
Canada	Geoffrey	LLD	2011
Carril	Peter	HHD	2012
Carter	Bennett Lester	HHD	1974
Chambers	Ray	LHD	2020
Chavez-Thompson	Linda	LLD	1998
Church 1924 *1927	Alonzo	DSc	1985
Clark	Kenneth Bancroft	DSc	1971
Clinton	William Jefferson	LLD	1996
Coale '39 *47	Ansley J.	LHD	1994
Coburn	Kathleen	LHD	1983
Cohen	Gerson D.	DD	1976
Cole	Johnnetta Betsch	LLD	1988
Collins	Francis	DSc	2013

Honorary Degree Recipients Since 1970

Last Name	First Name	Degree	Year Awarded
Comer	James P.	HHD	1991
Cone '39 *42	Edward T.	LHD	2004
Conkwright	Pleasant Jefferson	DFA	1977
Cooney	Joan Ganz	LHD	1973
Cortès Jr.	Ernesto	LLD	2009
Craig '36 *41	Gordon Alexander	LittD	1970
Crim	Alonzo A.	LLD	1984
Cutler	Lloyd N.	LLD	1994
d'Harnoncourt	Anne	LLD	2005
Daston	Lorraine	LHD	2013
Davis	Natalie Z.	LHD	2003
Dee Davis	Ruby	DFA	2009
Desmond-Hellmann	Susan	DSc	2011
Dicke '39	Robert Henry	DSc	1989
Doby	Larry	HHD	1997
Drake	Michael	LLD	2019
Dresselhaus	Mildred S.	DSc	1992
Dunwoody	Ann	LLD	2015
Dylan	Bob	DMus	1970
Dyson	Freeman J.	DSc	1974
Edelman	Marian Wright	LLD	1993
Eisenberg	Pablo S.	LLD	2004
Epps	Linda Caldwell	HHD	2021
Fagles	Robert	LHD	2007
Farmer	Paul	DSc	2006
Fauci	Anthony S.	LLD	2002
Faust	Drew	LLD	2013
Fenwick	Millicent	LLD	1985
Fitch	Val Logsdon	DSc	2000
Fitzgerald	Ella	DMus	1990
Fleming *63	John V.	LHD	2021
Florovsky	Georges	DD	1974
Foner	Eric	LHD	2015
Forbes Jr.	James A.	LLD	2002
Franklin	Aretha	DMus	2012
Franklin	John Hope	LLD	1972
Frelinghuysen	Rodney	LLD	2019
Fugard	Athol	LittD	1993
Galvan	Enrique Tierno	LHD	1980
Gardner	Howard E.	LHD	1998
Geddes	Robert	DFA	2018
Geertz	Clifford James	LHD	1995
Gehry	Frank	DFA	2013
Geisel	Theodore Seuss	DFA	1985
Giamatti	A. Bartlett	LLD	1978
Gillispie	Charles	LHD	2011
Ginsburg	Ruth Bader	LLD	2010
Gittenstein	R. Barbara	LLD	2018
Glassman	Irvin	DSc	2009
Godel	Kurt	DSc	1975
Goheen '40 *48	Robert Francis	LLD	1972
Goldstone	Richard J.	LLD	2005
Goodpaster *50	Andrew Jackson	LLD	1979
Gossman	J. Lionel	LHD	2005
Gover '78	Kevin	LLD	2001
Grant	Peter and B. Rosemary	DSc	2019
Gray	Hanna Holborn	LLD	1982
Gray III	William H.	LLD	1992
Greenfield	Meg	LLD	1990

Last Name	First Name	Degree	Year Awarded
Gross	Terry	HHD	2002
Grossman	Edith	LittD	2019
Hamm	Mia	HHD	2006
Hanks	Nancy	LHD	1971
Hawking	Stephen	DSc	1982
Hayden	Carla Diane	LHD	2018
Heaney	Seamus	LittD	2006
Height	Dorothy I.	LLD	1990
Helm 1920	Harold	LLD	1980
Hempel	Carl G.	LHD	1979
Higginbotham Jr.	A. Leon	LLD	1983
Holt	Rush	LLD	2021
Hrabowski	Freeman	LLD	2006
Hu	Shuli	LLD	2016
Hudson	Roy D.	LLD	1975
Huerta	Dolores	LLD	2006
Hughes	Phillip Samuel	LLD	1985
Jamison	Judith	DFA	2011
Jemison	Mae	HHD	2000
Johnson Jr.	Frank M.	LLD	1974
Jones	James Earl	DFA	1980
Jones Jr.	Quincy D.	DFA	2008
Jordan	Barbara	LLD	1977
Jordan Jr.	Vernon Eulion	LLD	1978
Kahn *64	Robert E.	DSc	1998
Kao	Charles K.	DSc	2004
Kateb	George	LHD	2008
Kelleher Jr.	Herbert Smith	LLD	2014
Kemeny '46 *49	John George	LLD	1971
Keohane	Nannerl O.	LLD	2004
Khama	Seretse	LLD	1976
King	Coretta Scott	HHD	1970
King	Mary-Claire	DSc	2008
Kirkland	Lane	LLD	1977
Koop	C. Everett	LLD	1989
Kopp '89	Wendy S.	HHD	2000
Kornberg	Arthur	DSc	1970
Kurtz	Stephen	LLD	1981
Kwapong	Alex A.	LLD	1974
Labatut	Jean	HHD	1975
Lambert	Phyllis	DFA	1999
Lavizzo-Mourey	Risa Juanita	DSc	2021
Lee 1920 *1926	Rensselaer W.	LHD	1982
Lee	Shelton Jackson "Spike"	DFA	2001
Leffall Jr.	LaSalle	DSc	2007
Lemonick *54	Aaron	DSc	2001
Lessing	Doris	LittD	1989
Levin	Richard Charles	LLD	1993
Lewis	Bernard	DD	2002
Lewis	Flora	LLD	1981
Lewis	John	LLD	1987
Lewis	W. Arthur	LHD	1988
Lichtenstein	Harvey	DFA	1999
Lippmann	Walter	LLD	1970
Lubchenco	Jane	DSc	2001
Lucas	Colin	LLD	2002
Lyon	Mary F.	DSc	2000
Ma	Yo-Yo	DMus	2005
MacNeil	Robert B. W.	LLD	1995

Last Name	First Name	Degree	Year Awarded
Mann	Emily	LittD	2002
Marceau	Marcel	DFA	1981
Marsalis	Wynton	DFA	1995
Maruyama	Masao	LittD	1973
Mason	Alpheus Thomas	LLD	1974
Matson	Pamela	DSc	2017
May	Robert McCredie	DSc	1996
McCormack	Elizabeth Jane	LLD	1974
McDermott '30	Walsh	DSc	1974
McGraw Jr. '40	Harold W.	LLD	1982
McHenry	Donald F.	LLD	1981
McPherson	James	LHD	2014
McPherson	Mary Patterson	LLD	1984
Meiss 1926	Millard	LLD	1973
Merwin '48	William S.	LittD	1993
Meselson	Mathew Stanley	DSc	1983
Miller	George A.	DSc	1995
Mitchell	Arthur	DFA	1985
Mobley	Sybil Collins	LLD	1993
Moore	Elizabeth Luce	LLD	1972
Moore	Gordon E.	LLD	2000
Morawetz	Cathleen Synge	DSc	1986
Morrison	Toni	LittD	2013
Moses	Robert	LLD	2004
Motley	Constance Baker	LLD	1989
Murakami	Haruki	LLD	2008
Myers	Constance Mercer	LHD	2021
Norton	Eleanor Holmes	LLD	1973
Nusslein-Volhard	Christiane	DSc	1991
Ochoa	Ellen	DSc	2019
Ogata	Sadako	LLD	1995
Okita	Saburo	LLD	1985
Olopade	Olufunmilayo Falusi	DSc	2010
Ostriker	Jeremiah P.	DSc	2017
Padron	Eduardo	LLD	2012
Palkhivala	Nani Ardeshir	LLD	1978
Panofsky '38	Wolfgang K. H.	DSc	1985
Papp	Joseph	DFA	1979
Parks	Gordon	DFA	1999
Paton	David R.	DSc	1985
Patrick	Ruth	DSc	1980
Pei-Yuan	Chou	LLD	1980
Pell '40	Claiborne	LLD	1981
Perkins	Courtland D.	DSc	2001
Perry Jr.	Matthew J.	LLD	1998
Pirrotta	Nino	LHD	1988
Polier	Justine Wise	LLD	1976
Poritz	Deborah	LLD	2015
Prausnitz	John M.	DSc	1995
Press	Frank	LLD	1991
Ramphele	Mamphela Aletta	LLD	1997
Rawls '43 *50	John	LHD	1987
Rawson '66	Robert	LLD	2011
Reagon	Bernice Johnson	DFA	1992
Richards	Lloyd G.	DFA	1985
Ripken Jr.	Cal	LHD	2002
Rivers '53	Robert J.	HHD	2016
Roberts	Robin	DFA	2020
Robertson Jr.	Durant W.	LHD	1987

Last Name	First Name	Degree	Year Awarded
Rockefeller '32	Laurance S.	HHD	1987
Rodino Jr.	Peter W.	LLD	1975
Rostropovitch	Mstislav	DMus	1976
Rouse	James W.	LLD	1993
Rowland	F. Sherwood	DSc	1990
Roy	Bunker	LLD	2017
Rubin	Vera	DSc	2005
Rudenstine '56	Neil L.	LLD	1991
Russell	William Felton	HHD	2001
Sachs	Albie	LLD	2010
Sanchez	Oscar Arias	LLD	1999
Saunders	Stuart J.	LLD	1997
Scheide '36	William	HHD	1994
Schmidt	Adolph	LLD	1977
Schmidt Jr.	Benno C.	LLD	1986
Schorske	Carl E.	LHD	1997
Schwarzschild	Martin	DSc	1992
Schowalter	William R.	DSc	2020
Scorsese	Martin	DFA	1991
Scott	Joan Wallach	LHD	2012
Sendak	Maurice	DFA	1984
Sessions	Roger Huntington	DMus	1972
Shalala	Donna E.	LLD	1991
Shapiro *64	Harold T.	LLD	2001
Shriver	Eunice Kennedy	LHD	1979
Shultz '42	George Pratt	LLD	1973
Simmons	Ruth J.	LLD	1996
Singleton	Charles S.	LHD	1981
Smyth 1918 *1921	Henry D.	DSc	1977
Soares	Mario	LLD	1988
Sotomayor '76	Sonia	LLD	2001
Soyinka	Wole	LittD	2005
Spitzer Jr. *38	Lyman	DSc	1984
Steele	Claude M.	LHD	2003
Steitz	Joan Argetsinger	DSc	2003
Stella '58	Frank P.	DFA	1984
Stern	Fritz	LHD	2007
Stevens	John Paul	LLD	2015
Stevenson	Bryan A.	LLD	2016
Stewart	Ellen	DFA	1982
Stone	Lawrence	LHD	1995
Strayer 1925	Joseph R.	LHD	1980
Streep	Meryl	DFA	2009
Sullivan	Richard J.	LLD	1973
Summers	Lawrence H.	LLD	2003
Swearer '54	Howard R.	LLD	1977
Takaezu	Toshiko	DFA	1996
Taylor	Edward Curtis	DSc	2010
Taylor	Joseph	DSc	2012
Tharp	Twyla	DFA	2007
Thomas '33	Lewis	DSc	1976
Thompson	Homer A.	LHD	1997
Thorp *1926	Willard	LLD	1978
Tilghman	Shirley	LLD	2013
Train '41	Russell Errol	LLD	1970
Tucker	Robert Charles	LHD	1990
Tukey *39	John Wilder	DSc	1998
Uhlenbeck	Karen Keskulla	DSc	2012
Vagelos	P. Roy	LLD	1990

Last Name	First Name	Degree	Year Awarded
Vargas Llosa	Mario	LittD	2015
Varmus	Harold	DSc	1999
Veil	Simone	LLD	1975
Venturi '47 *50	Robert	DFA	1983
Vermeule	Emily Townsend	LHD	1989
Villarreal Garcia	Juliet	LLD	2017
Vlastos	Gregory	LHD	1983
Volcker '49	Paul A.	LLD	1982
Walker	John Thomas	DD	1989
Walker	LeRoy T.	LLD	1996
Warner Jr. '44	Rawleigh	LLD	1984
Washington	Walter Edward	LLD	1970
Waterbury '61	John	LLD	2008
Waters	Alice L.	HHD	2009
Weitzmann	Kurt	HHD	1993
Welty	Eudora	LittD	1988
West	James	DSc	2014
Wheeler	John Archibald	DSc	1986
Widnall	Sheila	DSc	1994
Wigginton	Eliot	HHD	1992
Wilson	August	DFA	1993
Wilson	E. Bright	DSc	1981
Wilson	William Julius	LHD	1994
Winfrey	Oprah Gail	DFA	2002
Wiseman	Frederick	DFA	1994
Wood '34	Arthur	LLD	1976
Woodward	C. Vann	LHD	1971
Yacoobi	Sakena	LLD	2013
Yalow	Rosalyn Sussman	DSc	1978
Yang	Linda Tsao	LHD	2020
Ylvisaker	Paul Norman	LLD	1970
Zeitlin	Froma I.	LHD	2016

Interdisciplinary/Interdepartmental Certificate Programs, Undergraduate and Graduate

Undergraduates may supplement their areas of concentration by participating in any of the following interdisciplinary certificate programs. Most undergraduates earn at least one certificate, and many earn more than one.

African American Studies
African Studies
American Studies
Applications of Computing
Applied and Computational Mathematics
Archaeology
Architecture and Engineering
Asian American Studies
Biophysics
Cognitive Science
Contemporary European Politics and Society
Creative Writing
Dance
East Asian Studies
Engineering and Management Systems
Engineering Biology
Engineering Physics
Entrepreneurship
Environmental Studies
Ethnographic Studies
European Cultural Studies
Finance
Gender and Sexuality Studies
Geological Engineering
Global Health and Health Policy
Hellenic Studies
History and the Practice of Diplomacy
Humanistic Studies
Jazz Studies
Journalism
Judaic Studies
Language and Culture
Latin American Studies
Latino Studies
Linguistics
Materials Science and Engineering
Medieval Studies
Music Performance
Music Theater
Near Eastern Studies
Neuroscience
Planets and Life
Quantitative and Computational Biology
Robotics and Intelligent Systems
Russian, East European, and Eurasian Studies
South Asian Studies
Statistics and Machine Learning
Sustainable Energy
Teacher Preparation
Technology and Society
Theater
Translation and Intercultural Communication
Urban Studies
Values and Public Life
Visual Arts

PhD candidates may concentrate in or receive certificates in the following interdisciplinary/interdepartmental programs:

African American Studies
American Studies
Ancient World
Bioengineering
Classical Philosophy
Computational Science and Engineering
Environmental Studies
Gender and Sexuality Studies
Health and Health Policy
Hellenic Studies
History of Science
Italian Studies
Latin American Studies
Media and Modernity
Medieval Studies
Political Economy
Political Philosophy
Population Studies
Renaissance and Early Modern Studies
Science, Technology, and Environmental Policy
Statistics and Machine Learning
Urban Policy

Jacobus Fellows

1950–1959
James Snyder, Art and Archaeology
Richard C. Jeffrey, Philosophy
James B. Meriwether, English
Hugh J. Greenwood, Geology

1960–1969
Jaegwon Kim, Philosophy
Robert Nozick, Philosophy
Henry M. Gladney, Chemistry
Ian I. Weinberg, Sociology
Peter C. Saccio, English
John S. Earman III, Philosophy
Graham Smith, Art and Archaeology
Anthony Ephremides, Electrical Engineering

1970–1979
David Lenson, Comparative Literature
Georgia Fisanick Englot, Chemistry
Robert B. Israel, Mathematics
Robert B. Brandom, Philosophy
Russell H. Fazio, Psychology
Susan Cotts Watkins, Sociology
James S. Amelang, History

1980–1989
George Sugihara, Biology
Norma Moore Field, Near Eastern Studies
Kenneth G. Libbrecht, Physics
Daniel T. Gilbert, Psychology
Timothy E. Hampton, Comparative Literature
Barbara S. Ryden, Astrophysical Sciences
Marisa Carrasco, Psychology
David H. Weinberg, Astrophysical Sciences
David A. Bell, History

1990–1999
Pamela B. Beluh, Molecular Biology
Allan Roy Hajek, Philosophy
Mark R. Convery, Physics
Nickolay Y. Gnedin, Astrophysical Sciences
Ue-Li Pen, Astrophysical Sciences
Nikita Alex Nekrasov, Physics
Harindran Manoharan, Electrical Engineering
Claire S. J. Adjiman, Chemical Engineering
Stanislav Boldyrev, Plasma Physics
Xiaohui Fan, Astrophysical Sciences
Joy Landin, English

2000–2009
Kristine Louise Haugen, English
Yueh Loo, Chemical Engineering
Joshua Benjamin Plotkin, Applied and Computational Mathematics
Kathleen Sarah-Jane Murray, French and Italian
Paul Florencio Copp, Religion
Holly Vincele Sanders, History
Michael Shell, Chemical Engineering
Lior Siberman, Mathematics
Liang Feng, Molecular Biology
Guy Geltner, History
Gerard Paul Passannante, English
David Chen-yu Shih, Physics
Carmen Drahl, Chemistry
Egemen Kolemen, Mechanical and Aerospace Engineering
Sarah Milne Pourciau, German
William Trent Slauter, History
Thomas Samuel Clark, Politics
Kellam M. Conover, Classics
Vasily Pestun, Physics
Ning Wu, Chemical and Biological Engineering
Hannah Jane Crawforth, English
Peter A. DiMaggio, Chemical and Biological Engineering
Jianfeng Lu, Applied and Computational Mathematics
Vaneet Aggarwal, Electrical Engineering
Melinda Clare Baldwin, History of Science
Charles Conroy, Astrophysical Sciences
Joseph Moshenska, English

2010–2019
Giada Damen, Art and Archaeology
Marcus Hultmark, Mechanical and Aerospace Engineering
Noam Lupu, Politics
Silviu Pufu, Physics
Richard C. Baliban, Chemical and Biological Engineering
William Palmer Cavendish, Mathematics
William P. Deringer, History of Science
Andrew C. Huddleston, Philosophy
Angele Christin, Sociology
Laura Gandolfi, Spanish and Portuguese
George F. Young, Mechanical and Aerospace Engineering
Jiaying Zhao, Psychology
Cristina Domnisoru, Neuroscience
Sonika Johri, Electrical Engineering
James Pickett, History
Emily Vasiliauskas, English
Yu Deng, Mathematics
Evan Hepler-Smith, History of Science
Catherine Reilly, Comparative Literature
Kimberly Shepard, Chemical and Biological Engineering
Kellen Funk, History
Carlee Joe-Wong, Applied and Computational Mathematics
Joshua Bennet, English
Rajesh Ranganath, Computer Science
Cole Bunzel, Near Eastern Studies
Mate Bezdek, Chemistry
Sarah Carson, History
Daniel Floryan, Mechanical and Aerospace Engineering
Matthew Ritger, English

2020–
Vinicius de Aguiar Furuie, Anthropology
Talmo Pereira, Neuroscience
Karan Singh, Computer Science
Raissa von Doetinchem de Rande, Religion

James Madison Medal Recipients

1973	John Bardeen *36 (Physics)
1974	Thornton Wilder *1926 (Modern Languages and Literature)
1975	William O. Baker *39 (Chemistry)
1976	Andrew J. Goodpaster *49 *50 (Politics, Civil Engineering)
1977	John W. Milnor '51 *54 (Mathematics)
1978	Frederick Seitz *34 (Physics)
1979	W. Michael Blumenthal *53 *56 (Woodrow Wilson School, Economics and Sociology)
1980	Lowell Thomas *1916 (History and Politics)
1981	Ira O. Wade *1924 (Modern Languages and Literature)
1982	Jack W. Peltason *47 (Politics)
1983	Lewis H. Sarett *42 (Chemistry)
1984	John W. Tukey *39 (Mathematics)
1985	Robert Venturi '47 *50 (Architecture)
1986	Milton B. Babbitt *42 *92 (Music)
1987	J. Hugh MacLennan *35 (Classics)
1988	Robert F. Goheen '40 *48 (Classics)
1989	Lyman Spitzer Jr. *38 (Physics)
1990	William J. Crowe Jr. *65 (Politics)
1991	Steven Weinberg *57 (Physics)
1992	George F. Will *68 (Politics)
1993	Edward Witten *76 (Physics)
1994	William G. Bowen *58 (Economics and Sociology)
1995	Norman R. Augustine '57 *59 (Aeronautical Engineering)
1996	Cornel R. West *80 (Philosophy)
1997	W. Anthony Lake *74 (Woodrow Wilson School)
1998	Charles Rosen '48 *51 (Modern Languages and Literature)
1999	Ralph E. Gomory *54 (Mathematics)
2000	Chang-Lin Tien *59 (Mechanical Engineering)
2001	N. Lloyd Axworthy *72 (Politics)
2002	George B. Rathmann *51 (Chemistry)
2003	Peter D. Bell *64 (Woodrow Wilson School)
2004	Harold T. Shapiro *64 (Economics)
2005	Nathan P. Myhrvold *83 (Applied Mathematics)
2006	Arthur D. Levinson *77 (Biochemical Sciences)
2007	Julius E. Coles *66 (Woodrow Wilson School)
2008	Lawrence P. Goldman *69 *76 (Woodrow Wilson School)
2009	Claire Max *72 (Astrophysical Sciences)
2010	David H. Petraeus *85 *87 (Woodrow Wilson School)
2011	Elaine Fuchs *77 (Biochemistry)
2012	Lisa Jackson *86 (Chemical Engineering)
2013	Arminio Fraga *85 (Economics)
2014	Hunter R, Rawlings III *70 (Classics)
2015	Martin Eakes *80 (Woodrow Wilson School)
2016	James Heckman *71 (Economics)
2017	Pedro Pablo Kuczynski *61 (Woodrow Wilson School)
2018	Daniel Mendelson *94 (Classics)
2019	Carol Quillen *91 (History)
2020	Kip Thorne *65 (Physics)

Princeton All-Time Olympians

Name	Class	Olympics	Sport	Medals
Robert Garrett Jr.	1897	1896 (Athens), 1900 (Paris)	Track & Field	Gold (discus, shot put) 1896, Silver (high jump, long jump) 1896, Bronze (shot put, standing triple) 1906
Herbert Jamison	1897	1896 (Athens)	Track & Field	Silver (400m)
Francis Lane	1987	1896 (Athens)	Track & Field	Bronze (100m)
Albert Tyler	1987	1896 (Athens)	Track & Field	Silver (pole vault)
John Cregan	1900	1900 (Paris)	Track & Field	Silver (800m)
Frank W. Jarvis	1900	1900 (Paris)	Track & Field	Gold (100m)
John DeWitt	1904	1904 (St Louis)	Track & Field	Silver (hammer throw)
J. L. Eisele	1906	1908 (London)	Track & Field	Silver (3-mile relay), Bronze (steeplechase)
Rupert Thomas	1913	1912 (Stockholm)	Track & Field	
Henry Breckenridge	1907	1920 (Antwerp), 1924 (Paris), 1928 (Amsterdam)	Fencing	Bronze (team foil) 1920
Karl T. Frederick	1903	1920 (Antwerp)	Shooting	Gold (50m free pistol, 50m team free pistol, 30m team military pistol) 1920
Ralph Hills	1925	1920 (Antwerp), 1924 (Paris)	Track & Field	Bronze (shot put) 1924
Leon M. Schoonmaker	1904	1920 (Antwerp)	Fencing	
William E. Stevenson	1922	1924 (Paris)	Track & Field	Gold (4×400)
J. Coard Taylor	1923	1924 (Paris)	Track & Field	
B. V. D Hedges	1930	1928 (Amsterdam)	Track & Field	Silver (high jump)
Herman Whilton	1926	1928 (Amsterdam), 1948 (London), 1952 (Helsinki)	Sailing	Gold (6m) 1948 & 1952
Gerald Hallock, III	1926	1932 (Lake Placid)	Ice Hockey	Silver
Robert C. Livingston	1931	1932 (Lake Placid)	Ice Hockey	Silver
Horace C. Disston	1928	1932 (Los Angeles), 1936 (Berlin)	Field Hockey	Bronze 1932
Samuel E. Ewing	1927	1932 (Los Angeles), 1936 (Berlin)	Field Hockey	Bronze 1932
Warren Ingersoll	1931	1932 (Los Angeles)	Field Hockey	Bronze
Tracy Jaeckel	1928	1932 (Los Angeles), 1936 (Berlin)	Fencing	Bronze (team epee) 1932
David McMullin III	1930	1932 (Los Angeles), 1936 (Berlin)	Field Hockey	Bronze 1932
E. J. Moles	1931	1932 (Los Angeles)	Swimming	
Frederick A. Kammer	1934	1936 (Garmisch Partenkirchen)	Ice Hockey	Bronze
Malcolm E. McAlpin	1932	1936 (Garmisch Partenkirchen)	Ice Hockey	Bronze
Paul L. Fentress	1936	1936 (Berlin)	Field Hockey	
Ellwood W. Godfrey	1933	1936 (Berlin)	Field Hockey	
Al Van de Weghe	1940	1936 (Berlin)	Swimming	Silver (100 backstroke)
C. R. P. Rodgers	1942	1948 (St. Moritz)	Ice Hockey	
James R. Sloane	1943	1948 (St. Moritz)	Ice Hockey	
G. L. Schoonmaker	1953	1952 (Helsinki), 1964 (Tokyo)	Sailing	
Kinmott T. Hoitsma	1956	1956 (Melbourne)	Fencing	
Robert Stinson Jr.	1955	1956 (Melbourne)	Sailing	
John Allis	1965	1964 (Tokyo), 1968 (Mexico City), 1972 (Munich)	Cycling	
Frank Anger	1961	1964 (Tokyo)	Fencing	
William Bradley	1965	1964 (Tokyo)	Basketball	Gold
Seymore Cromwell	1965	1964 (Tokyo)	Rowing	Silver (double scull)
Jed Graef	1964	1964 (Tokyo)	Swimming	Gold (200 backstroke)
F. Gardner Cox	1941	1968 (Mexico City)	Sailing	
Doug Foy	1969	1968 (Mexico City)	Rowing	

Name	Year	Olympics	Sport	Medal
Peter Raymond	1968	1968 (Mexico City), 1972 (Munich)	Rowing	Silver (8) 1972
Carl Van Duyne	1968	1968 (Mexico City)	Sailing	
Ross Wales	1969	1968 (Mexico City)	Swimming	Bronze (100 butterfly)
Gary Wright	1970	1968 (Mexico City)	Rowing	
Cathy Corcione	1974	1968 (Mexico City)	Swimming	
Thorsteinn Thorstensson Gislason	1969	1972 (Munich)	Track & Field	
Carol Brown	1975	1976 (Montreal), 1980 (Moscow), 1984 (Los Angeles)	Rowing	Bronze (8) 1976
Mimi Kellogg	1976	1976 (Montreal)	Rowing	
Anne Marden	1981	1980 (Moscow), 1984 (Los Angeles), 1988 (Seoul), 1992 (Barcelona)	Rowing	Silver (4 plus cox scull) 1984, (single scull) 1988
Harold Backer	1985	1984 (Los Angeles), 1988 (Seoul), 1992 (Barcelona)	Rowing	
Tina Clark	1976	1984 (Los Angeles)	Rowing	
Mike Evans	1980	1984 (Los Angeles)	Rowing	Gold (8)
Ridgely Johnson	1980	1984 (Los Angeles)	Rowing	
Christopher Penney	1985	1984 (Los Angeles)	Rowing	Silver (8)
Lee Shelley	1978	1984 (Los Angeles), 1988 (Seoul)	Fencing	
August Wolf	1983	1984 (Los Angeles)	Track & Field	
Doug Burden	1988	1988 (Seoul), 1992 (Barcelona), 1996 (Atlanta)	Rowing	Silver (4 without cox) 1992, Bronze (8) 1988
Lynn Jennings	1983	1988 (Seoul), 1992 (Barcelona), 1996 (Atlanta)	Track & Field	Bronze (10k) 1992
Deborah St. Phard	1987	1988 (Seoul)	Track & Field	
Dan Veatch	1987	1988 (Seoul)	Swimming	
Nelson Diebel	1987	1992 (Barcelona)	Swimming	Gold (100 breaststroke, 4×100 relay)
Dan Nowosielski	1991	1992 (Barcelona), 1996 (Atlanta)	Fencing	
John Parker	1989	1992 (Barcelona)	Rowing	
Nathalie Wunderlich	1993	1992 (Barcelona)	Swimming	
Lianna Bennion	1995	1996 (Atlanta), 2000 (Sydney), 2004 (Athens)	Rowing	Silver (8) 2004
Kevin Cotter	1996	1996 (Atlanta), 2000 (Sydney)	Rowing	
Chris Ahrens	1998	2000 (Sydney), 2004 (Athens)	Rowing	Gold (8) 2004
Morgan Crooks	1998	2000 (Sydney)	Rowing	
Tom Herschmiller	2001	2000 (Sydney), 2004 (Athens)	Rowing	Silver (4-) 2004
Sean Kamman	1998	2000 (Sydney)	Rowing	
Paul Teti	2001	2000 (Sydney), 2004 (Athens), 2008 (Beijing)	Rowing	
Juan Pablo Valdivieso	2004	2000 (Sydney), 2004 (Athens)	Swimming	
Tom Welsh	1999	2000 (Sydney)	Rowing	
Andrea Kilbourne	2002	2002 (Salt Lake)	Ice Hockey	Silver
Soren Thompson	2005	2004 (Athens), 2012 (London)	Fencing	
Kamara James	2008	2004 (Athens)	Fencing	
Danika Holbrook	1995	2004 (Athens)	Rowing	
Simon Carcagno	1998	2004 (Athens)	Rowing	
Andreanna Morin	2006	2004 (Athens), 2008 (Beijing), 2012 (London)	Rowing	Silver (8) 2012
Tanya Kalivas	2001	2004 (Athens)	Soccer	
Tora Harris	2002	2004 (Athens)	Track & Field	

Name	Class	Olympics	Sport	Medals
Nikola Holmes	2003	2006 (Turin)	Ice Hockey	
Steve Coppola	2006	2008 (Beijing)	Rowing	Bronze (8)
Sandra Fong	2013	2008 (Beijing)	Shooting	
Doug Lennox	2009	2008 (Beijing)	Swimming	
Caroline Lind	2006	2008 (Beijing), 2012 (London)	Rowing	Gold (8) 2008, 2012
Samuel Loch	2006	2008 (Beijing), 2012 (London)	Rowing	
Diana Matheson	2008	2008 (Beijing), 2012 (London), 2016 (Rio)	Soccer	Bronze 2012, 2016
Meredith Michaels-Beerbaum	1992	2008 (Beijing), 2016 (Rio)	Equestrian	Bronze (team) 2016
Lia Pernell	2003	2008 (Beijing)	Rowing	
Bryan Tay	2012	2008 (Beijing)	Swimming	
Konrad Wysocki	2004	2008 (Beijing)	Basketball	
Donn Cabral	2012	2012 (London), 2016 (Rio)	Track & Field	
Sara Hendershot	2012	2012 (London)	Rowing	
Maya Lawrence	2002	2012 (London)	Fencing	Bronze (team epee)
Glenn Ochal	2008	2012 (London), 2016 (Rio)	Rowing	Bronze (4 without cox) 2012
Robin Prendes	2011	2012 (London), 2016 (Rio)	Rowing	
Julia Reinprecht	2014	2012 (London), 2016 (Rio)	Field Hockey	
Katie Reinprecht	2013	2012 (London), 2016 (Rio)	Field Hockey	
Susannah Scanlan	2014	2012 (London)	Fencing	Bronze (team epee)
Gevvie Stone	2007	2012 (London), 2016 (Rio), 2021 (Tokyo)	Rowing	Silver (singles) 2016
Lauren Wilkinson	2011	2012 (London), 2016 (Rio)	Rowing	Silver (8) 2012
Derek Bouchard-Hall	1992	2000 (Sydney)	Cycling	
Ariel Hsing	2017	2012 (London)	Table Tennis	
Erica Wu	2018	2012 (London)	Table Tennis	
Joey Cheek	2011	2006 (Turin)	Speed Skating	Gold (500m), Silver (1000m) 2006; Bronze (1000m) 2002
Katherine Holmes	2017	2016 (Rio), 2021 (Tokyo)	Fencing	
Mohamed Hamza	2023	2016 (Rio), 2021 (Tokyo)	Fencing	
Kathleen Sharkey	2013	2016 (Rio)	Field Hockey	
Ashleigh Johnson	2017	2016 (Rio), 2021 (Tokyo)	Water Polo	Gold 2016, 2021
Tyler Nase	2013	2016 (Rio)	Rowing	
Kate Bertko	2006	2016 (Rio)	Rowing	
Caroline Park	2011	2018 (PyeongChang)	Women's Hockey	
Lizzie Bird	2017	2021 (Tokyo)	Track & Field	
Claire Collins	2019	2021 (Tokyo)	Rowing	
Nathan Crumpton	2008	2021 (Tokyo)	Track & Field	
Tom George	2018	2021 (Tokyo)	Rowing	Bronze (8)
Sondre Guttormsen	2024	2021 (Tokyo)	Track & Field	
Tim Masters	2015	2021 (Tokyo)	Rowing	
Nick Mead	2017	2021 (Tokyo)	Rowing	
Kathleen Noble	2018	2021 (Tokyo)	Rowing	
Julia Ratcliffe	2017	2021 (Tokyo)	Track & Field	
Hannah Scott	2021	2021 (Tokyo)	Rowing	
Eliza Stone	2013	2021 (Tokyo)	Fencing	
Ed Trippas	2022	2021 (Tokyo)	Track & Field	
Anna Van Brummen	2017	2021 (Tokyo)	Fencing	
Fred Vystavel	2016	2021 (Tokyo)	Rowing	Bronze (2-)

Total Athletes
130

Total Appearances
184

Total Medals
Gold: 20
Silver: 24
Bronze: 27

Pyne Prize Recipients

Year	Recipient(s)
1922	Charles Denby Jr.
1923	John S. Martin
1924	W. Winslow Dulles
1925	Ralph G. Hills
1926	Richard R. Quay Jr.
1927	Ernest C. Bartell
1928	H. Chapman Rose
1929	Joseph V. Quarles Jr.
1930	William D. Barfield
1931	Nelson P. Rose
1932	John H. Rice
1933	F. Tremaine Billings Jr.
1934	Arthur S. Lane
1935	Henry Allison Page III
1936	Pepper Constable
1937	Thomas Gucker III
1938	Frank Wendell Rounds Jr.
1939	John Williams Pitney
1940	Robert Francis Goheen, James H. Worth
1941	Charles Leslie Rice Jr.
1942	Laurence Bedwell Holland
1943	John Woolman Douglas
1944	Karl Gotlieb Harr Jr.
1945	Richard T. West, awarded in 1948
1948	Donald J. Sterling Jr., awarded in 1948
1949	Daniel R. Toll, awarded in 1948
1950	Bernard S. Adams
1951	Jack T. Davison
1952	James H. Leslie
1953	William M. Ruddick
1954	Paul S. Sarbanes
1955	James B. Hurlock
1956	Coleman B. Brown
1957	Michael M. Stewart
1958	Steven C. Rockefeller
1959	Michael J. Kelly
1960	John W. McCarter, Edward Pell
1961	Jeremiah M. Sullivan
1962	Joseph Raymond Lundy
1963	Walter B. Slocombe
1964	Hugh MacMillan Jr.
1965	Michael E. Smith
1966	Robert H. Rawson Jr.
1967	Stephen A. Oxman
1968	Marc E. Lackritz
1969	Mark W. Janis, Stephen B. Thacker
1970	Howard W. Bell Jr., Raymond J. Gibbons
1971	Jerome Davis
1972	Peter P. Cole, David A. Jones
1973	Marsha H. Levy
1974	Thomas A. Barron
1975	Jo R. Backer, Henry B. Handler, Alexander M. Ward
1976	James David Germany, Sonia Sotomayor
1977	Joshua M. Rafner
1978	Eric S. Lander, Nancy J. Newman
1979	Philip Barnett
1980	Debra Ann Firstenberg, Ronald Derek Lee
1981	Harmon Grossman
1982	Michele Susan Warman
1983	Mark A. Goldsmith, Brent V. Woods
1984	Stephen A. Vavasis, Lynn A. Weston
1985	Steven Dunne, Craig Leon
1986	Michael Sarbanes
1987	Kirsten Bibbins
1988	Robert Peck, Jan Rivkin
1989	Suzanne Hagedorn, Harold Fernandez
1990	Loren Walensky
1991	Erica Fox, Jennifer Rexford
1992	Caroline Levine
1993	Graham Burnett, Miriam Ticktin
1994	Larisa Heimert, James Iannone
1995	Jennifer Babbitt, Benjamin Jones
1996	Derek Kilmer, Daniel Walter
1997	Davis McCallum, Andrea Rolla
1998	Shalani Alisharan, Julia Lee
1999	Renee Hsia, Alexander Sierk
2000	Michael Bosworth, Benjamin Sommers
2001	Adam Friedman
2002	Abbie Liel, Lillian Pierce
2003	Daniel Hantman, Christopher Wendell
2004	Katherine Linder, Steven Porter
2005	Amy Saltzman
2006	Jeremy Golubcow-Teglasi, James Williams
2007	Alisha Holland, Lester Mackey
2008	Sarah Vander Ploeg, Landis Stankievech
2009	Alexander Barnard, Andy Chen
2010	Connon Diemand-Yauman
2011	Alex Rosen, Amelia Thomson-DeVeaux
2012	Ann-Marie Elvin, James Valcourt
2013	Caroline Hanamirian, Jake Nebel
2014	Joe Barrett, Izzy Kasdin
2015	Yessica Martinez, Jake Robertson
2016	James Agolia, Andrew Nelson
2017	Solveig Gold, Marisa Salazar
2018	John "Newby" Parton, Maggie Pecsok
2019	Annabel Barry, Sydney Jordan
2020	Emma Coley, Ben Press
2021	Paige Allen, Amy Jeon, James Packman

Salutatorians Since 1970

1970	James Harvey Maguire	1996	Charles Parker Stowell
1971	Donald John Mathison	1997	Jessica Marie Davis
1972	James Joseph O'Donnell Jr.	1998	Jacob Andrew Rasmussen
1973	John Joseph Schier	1999	Thomas Wickham Schmidt
1974	James Francis Donlan	2000	Kenneth Lee Shaitelman
1975	Lisa Delger Siegman	2001	Christopher Gibson Bradley
1976	Susan Lynn Hurley	2002	Josephine K. H. Dru
1977	Bruce Allan Thompson	2003	Jesse Isaac Liebman
1978	Frank Ermanno Ferruggia	2004	Brian Joseph Tsang
1979	Joshua Keith Scodel	2005	Graham E. Phillips
1980	Robert James Levy	2006	Dan-el Padilla Peralta
1981	Seth J. Masters	2007	Maya Maskarinec
1982	Stephen H. Behnke	2008	James W. Morrison
1983	Simina Farcasiu	2009	Stephen J. Hammer
1984	Shara L. Aranoff	2010	Marguerite B. Colson
1985	Rayner Cheung	2011	Veronica Shue-Ron Shi
1986	Gwendolyn Brown Gwathmey	2012	Elizabeth W. Butterworth
1987	Shadi Bartsch	2013	Amelia Bensch-Schaus
1988	Shinichi Mochizuki	2014	Alexander Daniel Iriza
1989	Michael J. Anderson	2015	Neil John Hannan
1990	Jorge Bravo	2016	Esther H. Kim
1991	Harold S. Reeves	2017	Grant J. Storey
1992	Peter Viechnicki	2018	Katherine Marie Lim
1993	D. Graham Burnett	2019	Rafail Zoulis
1994	William Stull	2020	Grace Sommers
1995	John Van De Weert	2021	Lucy Wang

Valedictorians Since 1970

1970	Raymond John Gibbons	1997	David Jerome Katz
1971	Alan Mark Weinstein	1998	Andrew M. Neitzke
1972	Halbert Lynn White Jr.	1999	Chan Vee Chong
1973	Robert Dennis Comfort	2000	Andrew Addison Houck
1974	Orlando Alvarez	2001	Jared George Kramer
1975	Cynthia Chase	2001	Christine Adrienne McLeavey
1976	James David Germany	2002	Lillian Beatrix Pierce
1977	John Garret Loeser	2003	Peggy Ping Hsu
1978	Eric Steven Lander	2004	Ruth Ilana Tennen
1979	Anthony Michael Szpilka	2005	Varun Kishor Phadke
1980	David Hibbard Romer	2006	Christopher Leake Douthitt
1981	David D. Chambliss	2007	Eric Glen Weyl
1982	Andrew R. Golding	2008	Zachary A. Squire
1983	Tobe Mann	2009	Holger J. Staude
1984	Gabriel I. Goodman	2010	David Eric Karp
1985	Andrew Feldherr	2011	John Vincent Pardon
1986	Lisa Jeffrey	2012	Nathaniel Hamilton Fleming
1987	Kenneth L. Shepard	2013	Aman Sinha
1988	Jan Rivkin	2014	Katherine Pogrebniak
1989	Raj Gupta	2015	Misha Semenov
1990	Loren David Walensky	2016	Cameron M. Platt
1991	Timothy Chow	2017	Jin Yun Chow
1992	Daniel Eisenstein	2018	Kyle Michael Berlin
1993	Niles A. Pierce	2019	Katharine Reed
1994	Steven S. Gubser	2020	Nicholas Johnson
1995	Allison Kalben	2021	Taishi Nakase
1996	Bryan Patrick Duff		

Woodrow Wilson Award Recipients

1957	Norman Armour 1909		1989	T. Berry Brazelton Jr. '40
1958	Allen O. Whipple 1904		1990	James M. Stewart '32
1959	Charles L. House 1909		1991	Laurance S. Rockefeller '32
1960	Bayard Dodge 1909		1992	James H. Billington '50
1961	Raymond B. Fosdick 1905		1993	Wendy S. Kopp '89
1962	Clinton T. Wood 1921		1994	Sidney D. Drell '47
1963	Adlai E. Stevenson 1922		1995	Douglas I. Foy '69
1964	Henry D. Smyth 1918		1996	Don Oberdorfer '52
1965	Nicholas deB. Katzenbach '43		1997	Neil L. Rudenstine '56
1966	William F. Ballard 1927		1998	Eric Lander '78
1967	Eugene C. Blake 1927		1999	John C. Bogle '51
1968	Harlan Cleveland '38		2000	Forrest C. Eggleston '42
1969	Walsh McDermott '30		2001	J. Stapleton Roy '56
1970	John B. Oakes '34		2002	David J. Remnick '81
1971	George P. Shultz '42		2003	William H. Frist '74
1972	Ralph Nader '55		2004	Joseph S. Nye Jr. '58
1973	John D. Rockefeller III 1929		2005	Thomas H. Kean '57
1974	Claiborne de B. Pell '40		2006	George E. Rupp '64
1975	John M. Doar '44		2007	Paul S. Sarbanes '54
1976	George F. Kennan 1925		2008	John Rogers '80
1977	Thomas P. F. Hoving '53		2009	Rajiv Vinnakota '93
1978	Henry R. Labouisse Jr. 1926		2010	James A. Leach '64
1979	Robert F. Goheen '40 *48		2011	Denny Chin '75
1980	Paul A. Volcker Jr. '49		2012	Robert S. Mueller III '66
1981	Lewis Thomas '33		2013	Mitchell E. Daniels Jr. '71
1982	John A. McPhee '53		2014	Sonia Sotomayor '76
1983	James A. Baker III '52		2015	Queen Noor of Jordan (the former Lisa Halaby) '73
1984	William D. Ruckelshaus '55		2016	Mark Milley '80
1985	Donald H. Rumsfeld '54		2017	Eric Schmidt '76
1986	William H. Hudnut III '54		2018	Charles Gibson '65
1987	William W. Bradley '65		2019	Mellody Hobson '91
1988	Frank C. Carlucci '52		2020	Anthony D. Romero '87

ILLUSTRATION CREDITS

Pages 18–25: drawings by Jon Hlafter '61.
Page 26: front-campus medallion, photo by Danielle Alio, Office of Communications, Princeton University.
Page 48: Black alumni conference, photo by Sameer A. Khan/Fotobuddy, Office of Alumni Affairs, Princeton University.
Page 48: Latino alumni conference, photo by Denise Applewhite, Office of Communications, Princeton University.
Page 48: Asian and Asian American alumni conference, photo by Sameer A. Khan/Fotobuddy, Office of Alumni Affairs, Princeton University
Page 49: Jewish alumni conference, photo courtesy of Alumni Association, Princeton University
Page 49: graduate alumni conference, photo courtesy of Alumni Association, Princeton University.
Page 49: LGBT+ conference, photo by Denise Applewhite, Office of Communications, Princeton University
Page 49: She Roars conference, photo courtesy of Alumni Association, Princeton University.
Page 95: four Princeton farms, drawing by Jon Hlafter '61; courtesy of Office of the University Architect, Princeton University.
Page 96: West Windsor land acquisitions, image courtesy of Office of Communications, Princeton University.
Page 97: Beatrix Farrand, courtesy of Environmental Design Archives, University of California, Berkeley.
Page 98–99: campus map, courtesy of Office of Communications, Princeton University.
Page 100: new residential colleges, photo by Daniel Day, Office of Communications, Princeton University.
Page 101: east campus development, courtesy of Office of the University Architect, Princeton University.
Page 102: Lake Campus development, courtesy of Office of the University Architect, Princeton University.
Page 265: photo by Robert Matthews, Office of Communications, Princeton University.
Page 358: Toni Morrison portrait, photo by Nick Donnoli, Office of Communications, Princeton University.
Page 358: Arthur Lewis, photo by Robert Matthews, Office of Communications, Princeton University.
Page 358: Bill Bradley '65, photo by John W. H. Simpson '66.
Page 359: Denny Chin, photo by Denise Applewhite, Office of Communications, Princeton University.
Page 359: Carl Fields portrait, photo courtesy of the Princeton University Art Museum

Page 359: Elaine Fuchs, photo by Denise Applewhite, Office of Communications, Princeton University.
Page 360: Robert J. Rivers Jr. '53, photo by Denise Applewhite, Office of Communications, Princeton University.
Page 360: Ruth Simmons, photo by Nick Donnoli, Office of Communications, Princeton University.
Page 360: Sonia Sotomayor '76, photo by Denise Applewhite, Office of Communications, Princeton University.
Page 361: Alan Turing *38 portrait, photo courtesy of the Princeton University Art Museum.
Page 361: portrait by Mario Moore, photo by Hope VanCleaf for Lewis Center for the Arts, Princeton University.
Page 363: photo by Denise Applewhite, Office of Communications, Princeton University.
Pages 366–367: maps prepared by Dimitri Karetnikov, Princeton University Press.
Page 429: courtesy of Princeton University.

Calendar

January

Evelyn College catalogue cover 1891–92, photo courtesy of University Archives, Princeton University Library.
Michelle Obama '85, courtesy of Michelle Obama '85.
Sally Frank '80, photo by Ira Starr '81, *Daily Princetonian*.
Einstein photo courtesy of University Archives, Princeton University Library
Nassau Hall tiger, photo by Danielle Alio, Office of Communications, Princeton University.

February

University shield, courtesy of Princeton University.
McCosh Infirmary 1892, photo courtesy of University Archives, Princeton University Library.
Sabra Meservey *64 *66, photo courtesy of *Princeton Alumni Weekly*.
Wendy Kopp '89, photo courtesy of University Archives, Princeton University Library.
Whitman College, photo by Denise Applewhite, Office of Communications, Princeton University.
Alumni Day lunch and audience, photos by Denise Applewhite, Office of Communications, Princeton University.

527

March

Bella Allarie '20 and men's basketball vs. UCLA, photos courtesy of Princeton University's Office of Athletic Communications, with special thanks to assistant director Chas Dorman.

Chapel plaque, photo by Denise Applewhite, Office of Communications, Princeton University.

King on chapel steps, photo courtesy of University Archives, Princeton University Library.

April

Betsey Stockton, photo courtesy of Hawaiian Mission Children's Society Library.

Katzenjammers, photo by Denise Applewhite, Office of Communications, Princeton University.

Rittenhouse Orrery, © Ricardo Barros .com 2013, all other rights reserved.

Professor Kelley in the chapel, photo courtesy of University Archives, Princeton University Library.

May

May 2, 1968, rally, photo courtesy of University Archives, Princeton University Library.

Sue Jean Lee Suettinger '70, photo courtesy of University Archives, Princeton University Library.

Corwin Hall, photo courtesy of University Archives, Princeton University Library.

Jadwin Gym meeting, photo courtesy of University Archives, Princeton University Library.

June

Cynthia Chase '75 and Lisa Siegman '75, photo by Marie Bellis.

FitzRandolph Gate, photo by Robert Matthews, Office of Communications, Princeton University.

Joe Schein '37 and Jennifer Daniels '93 leading the P-rade, photos by Maddy Pryor, Office of Communications, Princeton University.

July

Robert Goheen '40, *48 at reunions 1965, photo by Fred Maroon.

Maclean House plaque, photo by Joey Scelza, Office of Communications, Princeton University.

Larry Ellis, photo courtesy of Princeton University's Office of Athletic Communications.

Cannon Green, photo by Denise Applewhite, Office of Communications, Princeton University.

August

Oval with Points, photo by Daniel Day, Office of Communications, Princeton University.

Mollie Marcoux Samaan '91, photo by Amaris Hardy, Office of Communications, Princeton University.

James Collins Johnson, photo courtesy of University Archives, Princeton University Library.

McCarter Theatre, photo by Robert Matthews, Office of Communications, Princeton University.

September

Princeton Stadium first points, photo by Robert Durkee '69, Princeton University.

Pre-rade, photo by Daniel Day, Office of Communications, Princeton University.

September 11, 2001, memorial garden, photo by Maddy Pryor, Office of Communications, Princeton University.

Alexander Hall postcard, photo courtesy of University Archives, Princeton University Library.

Air scooter, photo courtesy of University Archives, Princeton University Library.

October

Frist Campus Center, photo by Christopher Lillja, Facilities Communications, Princeton University.

Third World Center, photo courtesy of University Archives, Princeton University Library.

Lewis Arts complex, photo by Jaclyn Sweet, Lewis Center for the Arts, Princeton University.

November

Depiction of first football game, Princeton v. Rutgers, painted by William Boyd, Rutgers Class of 1932; photo courtesy of Special Collections and University Archives, Rutgers University Libraries.

Moon flag, photo courtesy of University Archives, Princeton University Library.

"Even Princeton" photo courtesy of University Archives, Princeton University Library.

Dinky, photo by Denise Applewhite, Office of Communications, Princeton University.

Graduate College, photo by Daniel Day, Office of Communications, Princeton University.

December

Firestone Library, photo by Shelley Szwast, Princeton University Library.

Dick Kazmaier '52, photo courtesy of Princeton University's Office of Athletic Communications.

TFTR, photo courtesy of Princeton Plasma Physics Laboratory.

Lake Carnegie, photo by Denise Applewhite, Office of Communications, Princeton University.

INDEX

Page numbers in italics refer to illustrations.

ABC's World News with Charles Gibson, 375
Abel Prize, 339
academics and research, 33–37; African American Studies, 44–46, 182; Anthropology, 60–61; Architecture, 61–63, 147; Art and Archaeology, 63–65; Astrophysical Sciences, 70–72; auditing program, 74; certificate programs, 37, 517; changes under Woodrow Wilson, 34, 36, 122, 131, 180, 187, 219; Chemical and Biological Engineering, 113–115; Chemistry, 115–117; Civil and Environmental Engineering, 118–119; Classics, 121–123; Comparative Literature, 131–133; Computer Science, 133–135; current Bachelor's degree options, 36; current doctoral degree options, 36–37; current Master's degree options, 37; dean of the college, 145–146; development of Bachelor's level, 35; development of departments and, 36; East Asian Studies, 156–158; Ecology and Evolutionary Biology, 162–164; Economics, 164–166; Electrical and Computer Engineering, 172–174; Engineering and Applied Science, 176–179; English, 180–182; four-course plan, 8, 34, 80, 168–169, 254, 390, 422, 431; French and Italian, 219–220; Freshman Scholars Institute, 221; Freshman Seminars, 221–222; Geosciences, 229–230; German, 230–232; graduate level, 6–7, 15–16, 34, 35–36; graduate school, 6–7, 15–16, 34, 35–36, 240–244; History, 258–261; honors, 34–35; joint degrees, 37; law school, 285–286; Mathematics, 305–307; Mechanical and Aerospace Engineering, 318–320; Molecular Biology, 320–322; Music, 326–328; Near Eastern Studies, 335–336; Office of the Dean and, 145; Operations Research and Financial Engineering (ORFE), 178, 342–345; Philosophy, 351–352; Physics, 352–354; Politics, 355–357; preceptors and, 6–7, 34, 122, 139, 168, 180, 187, 228; "Princeton Ins," 369–370; Princeton University Preparatory Program (PUPP), 381–382; principles of liberal education in, 35; Psychology, 393–394; Public and International Affairs, 147–148, 394–398; reading periods, 37; Religion, 403–404; residential colleges and, 407–411; Science, 146; semester calendars, 37; senior thesis and, 431–432; Slavic Languages and Literatures, 437–438; Sociology, 442–443; Spanish and Portuguese, 446–447; Teacher Preparation program, 462; University Research Board (URB) and, 147, 478–479; writing and foreign language requirements, 35
a cappella singing groups, 33
Acción, 256–257, 392
activism, campus: 1960s/70s, 12–13; Frank, Sally, and, 216–217; Movement for a New Congress, 12, 324–325, 391; protest activity and, 389–392
Adams, John Quincy, 265
Adelante Tigres! conference, 48, *48*, 258, 446
Adjaye, David, 25, 67–68, 227
administration. *See also* trustees, Princeton: deans (*See* dean(s)); General Counsel, Office of, 228–229; provost, 392–393; secretary of the University, 429; student government and, 455–456; University president, 362–363; vice presidents, 481–482
admission, 37–40; COVID-19 pandemic and, 39; Dean of Admission and, 145; discrimination in, 38–39; first African American and female, 6, 39; standardized testing and, 39–40; transfer, 40
Admission (the movie), 374
advisory councils, 40–41
Aerial Arts Club, 33
affinity conferences, alumni, 47–48
African American students at Princeton, 8, 15–16, 41–44; 1960s commitment to recruit and enroll, 11; activism at Princeton, 42; in administration at Princeton, 42; Association of Black Collegians (ABC), 42; Association of Black Princeton Alumni (ABPA), 43, 47; Black culture on campus and, 43; Black Justice League and, 14, 43–44; Civil Rights Movement and, 235; discrimination against, 38; first enrollments of, 6, 9–10, 39, 41–42, 125; first full professor at Princeton, 15; graduate students, 43; Johnson, James Collins, 279; Lewis, Sir Arthur, 15, 30, 43, 164, 165, 286–287; Navy V-12 program and, 9–10, 39; recruitment of, 42–43; Rivers, Robert J., Jr., 10, 15, 39, 42, 358–359, *360*, 418–419; Simmons, Ruth, and, 436–437; Stockton, Betsey, and, 366–368, 453–454; *Thrive* conference, 48; West, Cornel R., 42–44, 487–488
African American Studies Department, 44–46, 182
Alan Turing: The Enigma, 476
Alexander, Harriet Crocker, 46, 47, 225
Alexander, Stephen, 4, 46, 70; National Academy of Sciences and, 196
Alexander Hall, 46–47, 130
Alito, Samuel, 28, 137
Allen, Stanley T., 62, 146
All the Sad Young Men, 208
Alphabet, Inc., 183
alumni, Princeton: affinity conferences, 47–48, *48*; Alumni Association of Nassau Hall established for, 5; Alumni Council, 48–51; Alumni Day, 51–52; as ambassadors, 28, 453; Black Princeton Alumni, 43–44; as college and university founders, 127–128; Concerned Alumni of Princeton (CAP), 85, 136–137; at the Constitutional

529

alumni, Princeton (*continued*)
  Convention of 1787, 137–138;
  education programs, 52–53; in
  federal government, 7, 28, 88,
  92–93, 266–269, 350–351, 363–364,
  429–431; as international leaders,
  28; in the military, 28–29, 51; as
  "ornaments of the state," 27;
  as president of United States,
  363–364; Pulitzer Prizes won by,
  398–401; reunions of, 415–417;
  Service of Remembrance for,
  432–433; in state government,
  28, 238–239; as Supreme Court
  justices, 15, 26, 28, *48*, 80, 125,
  137, 171, 202, 359–360, 458–459
alumni affinity conferences, 47–48, *48*
Alumni Association of Nassau Hall, 5
Alumni College, 52
Alumni Committee to Involve
  Ourselves Now (ACTION), 137
Alumni Council, 48–51
Alumni Day, 51–52
Alumni Princetonian, 53
Alumni Weekly, The Princeton (PAW),
  6, 51, 53–54
Amazon, 183
ambassadors, Princeton alumni as,
  28, 453
Amboseli Baboon Project, 163
American Academy of Arts and
  Letters, 189–190, 212
American Academy of Arts and
  Sciences, 190–193
American Association for the
  Advancement of Science, 46
American Colonization Society (ACS),
  4, 106, 298, 302, 380, 381, 439
American Economic Association (AEA),
  165–166
*American Evasion of Philosophy: A
  Genealogy of Pragmatism, The*, 488
American Focus, 375
American Historical Association, 145
American Institute of Architects, 62
American Journal of Archaeology, 305
American Philosophical Society,
  193–195
*American Philosophy on Social Security:
  Evolution and Issues, The*, 88
American Physical Society, 87
American Psychiatric Association, 27
American Society of Landscape
  Architects, 198
American Studies, program in, 109
American Whig Society, 3, 86, 90,
  220; merger with the Cliosophic
  Society, 124, 488–489; Smith,
  Samuel Stanhope, and, 438; Whig
  Hall and, 489; Wilson, Woodrow,
  and, 490; women and, 497

A. M. Turing Award, 339
Anderson, Marian, 42
Andlinger, Gerhard R., 54, 226, 227
Andlinger Center for Energy and the
  Environment, 54–55, 135, 226
Andlinger Center for the Humanities,
  55
*And Still the Waters Run: The Betrayal
  of the Five Civilized Tribe*, 383
Annals of Mathematics, 306, 329
anniversary celebrations, 55–59;
  bicenquinquagenary, 57–59;
  bicentennial, 57, 155; centennial,
  55–56; sesquicentennial, 56–57
annual giving, 59–60, 156; fundraising, 224–227; Helm, Harold, and,
  250; by women, 499–500
anthem, "Old Nassau," 342–343;
  gender neutral wording changes
  to, 342–343; Langlotz, Karl, and,
  72, 231, 272, 342; original
  composition of, 5, 72, 231, 342;
  revisions of, 342
Anthropology Department, 60–61
anti-Semitism, 9, 187
Appiah, Kwame Anthony, 43, 45, 170
Aquinas Institute, 405
Arbor Inn, 162
Arch Club, 162
Architecture, School of, 61–63, 147
Arden, Bruce, 133, 173
art, campus, 102–104; portrait
  collection, 357–361
Art and Archaeology, Department of,
  63–65
Arthur, Chester, 265
Articles of Confederation, 130
Art Museum, Princeton University,
  65–68
Art of Painting, The, 66
Arts Alive program, 31
Ashe, Arthur, 181
Asian American Alumni Association
  of Princeton, 50, 68–70
Asian American and Asian students at
  Princeton, 6, 15–16; female, 124,
  125; We Flourish conference, 48, 70
Asian American Students Association
  (AASA), 69
Associated Press, 274
Association of Black Collegians
  (ABC), 42, 201, 202
Association of Black Princeton
  Alumni (ABPA), 43, 47, 50, 201
Association of Collegiate Schools of
  Architecture, 62
Association of Latino Princeton
  Alumni, 50
Association of Princeton Graduate
  Alumni (APGA), *49*, 50, 54, 58–59,
  81, 242–243, 462

Astrophysical Sciences, Department
  of, 70–72
athletics, 5, 6, 72–74; baseball, 76–77;
  basketball, 77–80; Carril, Peter J.
  "Pete" and, 78–79, 107–108;
  cross-country, 142–143; development of women's, 126; fencing,
  199–200; field hockey, 200–201;
  football, 209–212; future plans
  for physical facilities, 25; golf,
  237–238; ice hockey, 269–271;
  Jadwin Gymnasium and, 22, 73,
  130–131, 275–276; lacrosse,
  282–283; Princeton Olympians, 342,
  422, 520–523; rowing, 420–422;
  rugby, 424; soccer, 440–442;
  softball, 443–444; sprint (lightweight) football, 449; squash,
  449–451; swimming and diving,
  460–461; tennis, 462–464; track
  and field, 469–471; volleyball,
  482–483; water polo, 485–486;
  wrestling, 501–502
Atlantic Monthly, 180, 328
Atomic Energy for Military Purposes, 383
auditing program, 74
Austin College, 127
Aviation, 427

Baccalaureate address, 74; speakers,
  1973–2021, 505
Bainbridge House, 67
Baker, Hobart Amory Hare, 74–75,
  210, 212, 269
Baker Memorial Rink, 74–75
Baldeagle, Joseph Paul, 333
Band, University, 75–76
Barry S. Goldwater Scholarship,
  418
baseball, 76–77
basketball, 77–80
Battle of Princeton, 3
Baumol, William, 83, 166
Bayard, Samuel, 80, 365
Beautiful and the Damned, The, 208
Beautiful Mind, A, 329, 374
Becoming, 341
Bedford, Dorothy, 51, 58, 126
beer/class/senior jackets, 80–81
Behrman Awards, 81, 506–507
Belcher, Jonathan, 2, 3, 65, 81–82,
  215; commencement ceremonies
  and, 129; fundraising and, 225
Bendheim Center for Finance, 81
Bernanke, Ben, 28, 81
*Best of PAW: 100 Years of the Princeton
  Alumni Weekly, The*, 54
*Beyond Eurocentrism and Multicultur-
  alism*, 488

Beyond the Ruling Class: Strategic Elites in Modern Society, 280
Bezos, Jeff, 183
bicenquinquagenary celebration, 57–59
bicentennial celebration, 57, 155
Biden, Joe, 137, 164
Big Bang Theory, The, 375
Birds of America, 295
Birds of Prey, 375
Black Arts Company, 33, 43
Black Graduate Caucus, 43
Black in Two Worlds: A Personal Perspective on Higher Education, 201
Black Justice League, 14, 43–44, 171, 392
Black Student Union, 43
Black Theology and Marxist Thought, 487
Blair Arch, 19
Blair Hall, 6, 21, 81–82, 150
Bluest Eye, The, 323
BodyHype Dance Company, 33
Born, Max, 167
Bowen, William Gordon, 35, 58–59, 83–86, 169, 216, 321, *363*; fundraising and, 226; on scholarships, 204
Brackenridge, Hugh Henry, 86–87, 220; commencement ceremonies and, 129
Brackett, Cyrus Fogg, 87, 172, 176, 179
Bradley, Bill, 15, 77–78, 79, 150, 211, 357, *358*
Brave Voices Project, 202–203
Brazelton, T. Berry, Jr., 29
BrazilLab, 61
Breaking the Code, 374
Bridge Year Program, Novogratz, 30, 87–88
Brother West: Living and Loving Out Loud, 488
Brown, J. Douglas, 28, 57, 83, 88–89, 146, 165
Brown, Susan Dod, 89, 153, 225
Brown Food Cooperative, 139
Brown Hall, 89
Brown v. Board of Education, 428
Buchanan, James, 265
Bunn, Benjamin Franklin, 89–90
Bureau of Urban Research, 62
Burn After Reading, 374
Burr, Aaron, Jr., 3, 28, 90
Burr, Aaron, Sr., 33–34, 90–91, 149, 166; commencement ceremonies and, 129; at the Constitutional Convention of 1787, 137; founding of Princeton and, 2, 18, 214, 215; fundraising and, 225
Burr Hall, Aaron, 91–92
Bush, George H. W., 265
Bush, George W., 283
Bushnell, Asa, 54, 137, 212
Business Today, 281, 457–458

Butler, Howard Crosby, 61, 63–64, 92; archaeological expedition by, 228
Butler, Samuel, 307
Butler College, 22–24, 409–410
Buyers Hall, 82
By Scholarship, Vision, and Generosity, They Made Possible a Community of Students and Works of Art, 66

cabinet officers, 92–93
Caldwell, Charles W., Jr., 77, 211, 212
Caldwell Field House, 73, 93
Campbell Hall, 93
camp program, Princeton-Blairstown Center, 370–371
campus, 17; 1756, 18; 1866, 19; 1896, 20; 1936, 21; 1976, 22; 1996, 23; 2016, 24; 2026, 25; Alexander Hall, 46–47, 130; art, 102–104; Burr Hall, 91–92; Caldwell Field House, 73, 93; Campbell Hall, 93; cannons, 105; Carnegie Lake, 106–107; Chancellor Green, 4–6, 13, 19–20, 46–47, 109–110; Clio Hall, 97, 99, 101, 104, 105, 106, 124, 154, 158, 209, 263, 327, 374, 489; Corwin Hall, 139–140, 152, 391, 395; Dillon Gymnasium, 22, 30, 57, 149–150; Dod Hall, 153–154; early land acquisitions for, 93–95; East College, 158; East Pyne, 158; Edwards Hall, 166–167; Engineering Quadrangle, 179–180; expansion of, 95–96; Fine Hall, 205–206; fires on, 206–207; FitzRandolph Gateway, 208–209; Forrestal Campus, 212–213; Forrestal Center, 213; Frick Chemistry Laboratory, 24, 63, 116, 117, 222–223; Frist Campus Center, 24, 110, 223–224; graduate college, 239–240; Green Hall, 245–246; Guyot Hall, 246–247; Henry House, 252; Holder Hall, 263; Jones Hall, 279; Lake Campus, 283–285; Lewis Library, 290–291; Little Hall, 6, 21, 82, 297; Lowrie, Walter, House, 297–298; Maclean House, 3, 67, 300; Madison Hall, 10, 302–303; Mather Sun Dial, 307; McCarter Theatre Center, 308–311; McCormick Hall, 311–312; McCosh Hall, 314; McCosh Infirmary, 41, 314–316; Morrison Hall, 323–324; municipality of Princeton and, 365–369; Murray-Dodge Hall, 326; Nassau Hall (*See* Nassau Hall); New South, 336–337; Palmer Hall, 347–348; Palmer House, 348; phases in development of, 96–102; Philosophical Hall, 4, 19, 99–100, 159, 251–252, 412, 439, 451; portrait collection, 357–361; Prospect House, 51, 98, 104, 297, 300, 331, 342, 379, 388–389; Pyne Hall, 402; residential colleges, 407–411; residential life, 411–414; Reunion Hall, 414–415; Roper Lane, 420; Seventy-Nine Hall, 433; Sherrerd Hall, 436; Spelman Halls, 22, 24, 412, 447–448; Stanhope Hall, 4, 19, 45, 46, 451; Stevenson Hall, 451–453; Thompson Gateway, 466; University Chapel, 21, 110–112, 147; Upper and Lower Pyne, 479; Whig Hall, 489; Wilcox Hall, 10, 160, 316, 408, 411, 413–414; Witherspoon Hall, 20, 46, 47, 497; Wu Hall, 23, 502–503

campus art, 102–104; portrait collection, 357–361
Campus Club, 104–105, 162
Cannon Club, 162
Cannon Green, 5
cannons, 105
Cap and Gown Club, 162
Carnahan, James, 4, 56, 90, 105–106; cholera epidemic of 1832 and, 185; enrollment under, 182
Carnegie, Andrew, 124
Carnegie Lake, 106–107
Carril, Peter J. "Pete," 78–79, 107–108
Catcher Was a Spy, The, 77
Catholic students at Princeton, 405
centennial celebration, 55–56
Center for Complex Materials, 108–109
Center for Digital Humanities, 108, 182, 296
Center for Energy and Environmental Studies (CEES), 54
Center for Hellenic Studies, 109, 123
Center for Information Technology Policy, 108
Center for Jewish Life (CJL), 10, 23, 33, 85
Center for Statistics and Machine Learning, 108
Center for the Study of Religion, 108
Center for Transnational Policing (CTP), 61
centers and institutes, 108–109; Andlinger Center for Energy and the Environment, 54–55, 135, 226; Andlinger Center for the Humanities, 55; Bendheim Center for Finance, 81; Center for Complex Materials, 108–109; Center for Digital Humanities, 108, 182, 296; Center for Energy

centers and institutes (*continued*)
and Environmental Studies (CEES), 54; Center for Information Technology Policy, 108; Center for Jewish Life (CJL), 10, 23, 33, 85; Center for Statistics and Machine Learning, 108; Center for the Study of Religion, 108; Center for Transnational Policing (CTP), 61; Davis International Center, 273; Fields Center for Equality and Cultural Understanding, 30, 42, 44, 201, 202–203; Forrestal Center, 213; Freshman Scholars Institute, 221; Frist Campus Center, 24, 110, 223–224; High Meadows Environmental Institute (HMEI), 14, 54, 182, 255–256; High Performance Computing Research Center (HPCRC), 135; Institute for Advanced Study (IAS), 133, 134, 271–272; Keller Center for Innovation in Engineering Education, 31, 183–184; Lewis Center for the Arts, 14, 16, 131, 140, 141, 150, 182, 188, 226, 287–290; Lewis-Sigler Institute for Integrative Genomics, 16, 134, 188, 226, 291; McCarter Theatre Center, 308–311; McGraw Center for Teaching and Learning, 186, 316; Mpala Research Centre, 13, 61, 163, 273, 325; M.S. Chadna Center for Global India, 70; Pace Center for Civic Engagement, 13, 30, 31, 32, 58, 346–347; Paul and Marcia Wythes Center for Contemporary China, 70; Princeton Center for Complex Materials, 108–109; Princeton Innovation Center BioLabs, 171, 184; Princeton-in-Peking, 30; Princeton Institute for Computational Science and Engineering (PICSciE), 109; Princeton Institute for International and Regional Studies (PIIRS), 13, 157, 273, 372–373; Princeton Institute for the Science and Technology of Materials (PRISM), 109, 173; Princeton Neuroscience Institute (PNI), 14, 16, 188, 375–376; Princeton Plasma Physics Laboratory (PPPL), 70, 135, 212–213, 376–378; Smithsonian Tropical Research Institute, 163; Stanley J. Seeger Center for Hellenic Studies, 109, 123; Third World Center, 11, 42, 43, 202; University Center for Human Values (UCHV), 16, 476–477; Women*s Center, 30
ceremonies, commencement, 129–131
certificate programs, 37, 517
Chancellor Green, 4–6, 13, 19–20, 46–47, 109–110, 294
Chance to Make History: What Works and What Doesn't in Providing an Excellent Education for All, A, 282
Chapel, University, 21, 110–112; dean of religious life and, 147
Charter, The, 112–113, 128
Charter Club, 162
Charter Day, 58
Chaucer, Geoffrey, 419–420
Chavis, John, 41
Chemical and Biological Engineering, Department of, 113–115
Chemical History of a Candle, The, 428
Chemistry, Department of, 115–117
Chicano Caucus, 256–257
Chin, Denny, 357–358, *359*
Chinese Students' Monthly, 68
cholera epidemic, 1832, 185
Christian Art, Index of, 320, 498
Christian music, 33
Christian Student, The, 117–118
Churchill Scholarship, 15, 417
Cinderella Story, A, 374
Civil and Environmental Engineering, Department of, 118–119
Civil Rights Movement, 235, 260, 390
Civil War, 5, 20, 120–121; enrollment during, 182
Clark, Margaret, *49*
Classics, Department of, 121–123
class jackets, 80–81
Class of '44, 374
class reunions, 415–417
Cleveland, Grover, 46, 56–57, 123–124, 131, 265; University Press Club and, 364
Cleveland, Richard Folsom, 123, 160
Cleveland Tower, 240
Clinton, Bill, 58, 131, 164, 265
Clio Hall, 101, 104, 124, 158, 209, 489; basement of, 327; cannon between Whig and, 105, 263; Carnahan, James, and, 106; in movies, 374; site of, 97; style of, 99; terrace at, 154
Cliosophic Society, 3, 86, 124, 174
Cloister Inn, 162
coeducation, 124–127
Cohen, Jonathan, 375–376
Cold War era, 10–11; annual giving in, 59; enrollment in, 183; Slavic Languages and Literatures, Department of, and, 438
Collected Works of C. G. Jung, The, 383
Collected Works of Paul Valéry, The, 383
Collected Works of Samuel Taylor Coleridge, The, 383
college and university founders, Princeton alumni as, 127–128
College Entrance Examination Board, 38
College of New Jersey, 1–3, 33; charter in creation of, 128; enrollment in, 182; original site of, 18; renamed Princeton University in 1896, 21
College of New Jersey (current), 200, 407
Colonial Club, 162
colors, Princeton's, 128–129
Coming Back and Looking Forward, 44, 47
Coming Back conference, 48
Coming into the Country, 317
commencement, 129–131; hoaxes and pranks at, 261; honorary degree recipients, 215, 264–265, 511–516; Hooding Ceremony, 265–266; salutatorians, 426–427, 524; salutatory oration, 426–427; valedictorians, 525; valedictory oration, 479
Committee of Fifty, 50
Committee on Residential Life (CURL), 23
Community: Pursuing the Dream, Living the Reality, 280
Comparative Literature, Department of, 131–133
Compton, Arthur H., 133, 354
Compton, Karl T., 133
Compton, Wilson M., 133
Compton Brothers, the, 133, 240
Computer and the Brain, The, 484
Computer Science, Department of, 133–135
computing, 135–136
Concerned Alumni of Princeton (CAP), 85, 136–137
Condit, Kenneth, 147, 176–177
Conflict of Religions, The, 403
Congressional Government, 490
Conrad, Charles "Pete," Jr., 89, 216, 318, 380, 415
Constitutional Convention of 1787, 27, 137–138
Constitutional Self-Government, 170
Constitution and What It Means Today, The, 139, 382
Continental Congress, 27, 130, 138, 144, 301
Conversations on the Character of Princeton, 280
Coolidge, Calvin, 265
co-ops, 138–139; Princeton University Store, 384–385
Corwin, Edward S., 139, 258–259, 356, 382

Corwin Hall, 139–140, 152, 391, 395
Cosby Show, The, 374
Cosmic Background Explorer (COBE) project, 71
Council of the Humanities, 140–141
Council of the Princeton University Community (CPUC, U-Council), 141, 152, 280
Council on Science and Technology (CST), 141–142
council(s): advisory, 40–41; alumni, 48–51; Council of the Humanities, 140–141; Council of the Princeton University Community (CPUC, U-Council), 141, 280; Council on Science and Technology (CST), 141–142; faculty committees and, 188–189
Court Club, 162
COVID-19 pandemic, 15, 16, 31–32, 45, 172, 185–186; Alumni Council annual meeting and, 50; annual giving during, 60; Bridge Year Program canceled due to, 87; commencement ceremonies canceled due to, 131; endowment and, 176; Freshman Scholars Institute (FSI) and, 221; honorary degrees during, 265; Princeton University libraries and, 296; *Prince* transition to digital-first and, 388; relief fund and, 369; sports canceled due to, 79, 80; standardized admissions tests and, 39
Cowell, David, 142
Cram, Ralph Adams, 21, 154
Creative Arts program, 288
Creative Writing program, 288
cross-country, 142–143
Cryo Electron Microscope (CryoEM), 135
Curve of Binding Energy, The, 317

Daily Princetonian, 236, 385; on admission of women, 125; advocacy for admitting African American students, 9, 41; on Alumni Day, 51; annual "joke issue," 261; on Bill Bonthron, 142; Bunn, Benjamin Franklin, and, 89; on the Concerned Alumni of Princeton (CAP), 137; on eating clubs, 159, 160; on Einstein, 168; first female reporters for, 498; Fleming, John, and, 181; founding of, 6, 53; on the Harold WIllis Dodds Achievement Prize, 156; on the honor system, 263; Kwong,

Hsu Kun, as president of, 68; Mackay Smith, Anne, as chair of, 126; on the nude olympics, 340; on Pedro Rioseco, 256; on the Philadelphian Society, 30; on political activism, 324; sports and, 76, 79; Veterans of Future Wars and, 480
Dallas, George Mifflin, 28, 55, 56
dance groups, 33, 258
Dance program, 288–289
Darrow, Whitney, 382
Darwin, Charles, 439
Davie, William Richardson, 127–128, 138
Davies, Samuel, 27, 74, 129, 142, 143–144, 206, 214, 225
Davis, Charles, 10, 43, 44, 187
Davis International Center, 273
Days of Grace: A Memoir, 181
Dead Give Away, 432
dean(s): of admission, 145; of the college, 145–146; of the departments of science, 146; for diversity and inclusion, 146; of the faculty, 146; of freshmen, 146; of the graduate school, 146–147, 486–487; Office of the, 145; of religious life and of the Chapel, 147; for research, 147; of the School of Architecture, 147; of the School of Engineering and Applied Science, 147; of the School of Public and International Affairs, 147–148; of student life, 148; of undergraduate students, 148
dean's date, 148
Declaration of Independence, 4, 27, 130, 144
Deferred Action for Childhood Arrivals (DACA) program, 258
Defining Moments, 58
Democracy Matters, 488
Denny, Abraham Parker, 41
Dial Lodge, 162
Dickinson, Jonathan, 127, 148–149, 182; founding of Princeton and, 2–3, 214–215
Dickinson College, 27, 127
Dickinson Hall, 45, 207
Dillon Gymnasium, 22, 30, 57, 149–150, 155, 207
dining cooperatives, 138–139. *See also* eating clubs
Dinky, the, 150–151
discrimination, 7–10, 38–39, 277
diSiac Dance Company, 33
diversity and inclusion, dean for, 146
divestment, 151–153, 391
Dodds, Harold Willis, 9–10, 57, 59, 130, 154–156, 168; endowed

professorships under, 174; on financial aid, 204
Dodge, W. Earl, 117–118
Dod Hall, 153–154
Don Quixote, 87
Doogie Howser, MD, 374
Double Sights, 492
Dreams, Stars and Electrons: Selected Writings of Lyman Spitzer Jr., 448
Dylan, Bob, 131, *265*

East Asian Studies, department of, 156–158
East College, 158
East Pyne, 158
eating clubs, 158–162
eBay, 183
Ecology and Evolutionary Biology, department of, 162–164
Econometrica, 329
Economics, department of, 164–166
Economics of Labor Force Participation, The, 83
Economics of the Major Private Universities, 83
Edison, Thomas, 172
Edwards, Jonathan, 3, 144, 166, 214
Edwards Hall, 166–167
Einstein, Albert, 8, 10, 156, 167–168, 224, 374
Eisenhart, Luther Pfahler, 8, 139, 146, 147, 168–169
Eisenhower, Dwight, 7, 57, 155, 216, 265
Eisgruber, Christopher Ludwig, 86, 169–172, 183–184, *363*; Freshman Seminars, 222; fundraising and, 227
Electrical and Computer Engineering, department of, 172–174
Elgin, Joseph, 113–114, 147, 177–178
Eliot, T. S., 57, 181
"Ellipse, The," 24
Ellsworth, Oliver, 27, 28, 137, 138, 174, 206; East Pyne statue of, 158
Elm Club, 42, 162
Embodied Computation Lab, 63
Encounters with the Archdruid, 317
Encyclopedia of Biodiversity, 163
endowed professorships, 174–175
endowment, Princeton, 16, 175–176; Leslie Fund as part of, 203; Princeton Investment Company (Princo) management of, 175–176, 373
Engage, 184
Engineering and Applied Science, School of, 176–179; dean of, 147
Engineering Quadrangle, 179–180
English, department of, 180–182
Enjoyment of One's Older Years, The, 88

enrollment, 182–183. *See also* racial diversity at Princeton
entrepreneurship/innovation, 183–185
environmental initiatives: carbon mitigation efforts, 13–14, 54; sustainability, 459–460
epidemics, 185–186
Equity and Excellence in American Higher Education, 86
Essays on Social Security, 88
Essential John Nash, The, 383
Ethical Dimensions of Marxist Thought, The, 487
Ethnographic Data Visualization Lab (VizE Lab), 61
Eugene Onegin, 383
Evelyn College for Women, 187
Ever the Teacher, 85
Every Voice conference, 48, *49*
Examined Life, 374
exclusionary policies, 7–9
eXpressions Dance Company, 33

faculty, 187–189; dean of the, 146; endowed professorships, 174–175; honor societies, 189–198
Faculty Advisory Committee on Appointments and Advancements, 188
Familiar Letters to a Gentleman, upon a Variety of Seasonable and Important Subjects in Religion, 149
Farrand, Beatrix, 15, 21, 150, 198–199, 497–498
Father Bombo's Pilgrimage to Mecca in Arabia, 86, 220
federal government, Princeton alumni in, 7, 28, 88. *See also* presidents, US; cabinet members, 92–93; House of Representatives, 266–269, 301–302; senators, 350–351, 429–431; vice presidents, 482
Federal Government and Princeton University; Economic Aspects of Education, The, 83
Federalist Papers, 138, 301
Feld, Edward, *49*
Feliciano, José E., 44, 171; fundraising and, 227
fellowships: Guggenheim Fellowships, 508–510; Jacobus, 52, 275, 518; Mellon Mays Undergraduate Fellows Program, 418; National Science Foundation's Graduate Research Fellowship, 418; Scholars Institute Fellows Program (SIFP), 221; Wilson, Woodrow, National Fellowship Foundation, 493–494

Feminization of American Culture, The, 181
fencing, 199–200
Fermat's Last Theorem, 374
Fiction in the Archives: Pardon Tales and Their Tellers in 16th-Century France, 144–145
field hockey, 200–201
Fields, Carl A., 11, 42, 201–202, 358, *359*
Fields Center for Equality and Cultural Understanding, 30, 42, 44, 201, 202–203
Fields Medal, 339
financial aid, 13, 40, 176, 203–204; GI Bill, 10, 122, 155, 182, 204
Fine, Henry Burchard, 8, 146, 168, 204–205
Fine Hall, 205–206
Finley, Samuel, 3, 137, 144, 206, 215
Fire Hazards, 33
fires, 206–207, 294
Firestone Library, 3, 9, 22, 29, 66, 81, 155, 295–296
First Aid and Rescue Squad, 31
First College, 10, 22, 44, 171, 225, 227, 281, 392, 408, 411–412, 493, 500
Fitzgerald, Francis Scott Key, 207–208, 210, 228
FitzRandolph, Nathaniel, 3, 18, 209; fundraising by, 224–225
FitzRandolph Gateway, 208–209
FitzRandolph Observatory, 71
football, 209–212
Football Tackle, A, 374
Footnotes, the, 33
Forbes College, 43, 410
foreign government leaders, Princeton alumni as, 28
Forrestal Campus, 212–213
Forrestal Center, 213
founding of Princeton, 1–3, 127–128, 174, 213–215
four-course plan, 8, 34, 80, 168–169, 254, 390, 422, 431
Fox, Frederic E., 215–216
Frank, Sally, 12, 126, 216–217
Franklin, Benjamin, 138, 193
Franklin College, 27
fraternities and sororities, 5, 217–219
Frederick Douglass Service Award, 42, 201
Freedom of the Will, The, 166
Free Solo, 375
French and Italian, department of, 219–220
Freneau, Philip Morin, 86, 129, 220–221
Freshman Scholars Institute (FSI), 221
Freshman Seminars, 221–222
freshmen, dean of, 146
Fresh Prince of Bel Air, 374–375

Frick Chemistry Laboratory, 24, 63, 222–223
Frist Campus Center, 24, 110, 223–224
Fuchs, Elaine, 358, *359*
Fullbright US Student Program, 418
Fuller, Buckminster, 62
Fund for Reunion/Princeton Bisexual, Transgender, Gay and Lesbian Alumni, 50
fundraising, 59–60, 156, 224–227; by women, 499–500
future of Princeton, 16, 25

Game of Life: College Sports and Educational Value, The, 86
Gang's All Here, The, 262, 383
Gansworth, Howard Edward, 335
Garrett, Robert, 227–228
Garsoian, Nina, 12, 126, 147
Gates Cambridge Scholarship, 417
Gateway Club, 162
Gauss, Christian, 139, 146, 228; University Press Club and, 364
Gauss Seminars, 140
Geddes, Robert, 62, 146
Geertz, Clifford, 61
Gehry, Frank, 14, 24
General Counsel, Office of, 228–229
Geological Hall, 4, 19
Geophysical Fluid Dynamics Laboratory (GFDL), 213
George II, King, 65
Geosciences, Department of, 229–230
German, Department of, 230–232
GI Bill, 10, 122, 155, 182, 204
Gibson, Charles, 375
Gift in 16th-Century France, The, 145
Gildersleeve, Basil Lanneau, 232–233
Glee Club, 33, 233–234
Global Health Program (GHP), 61
Global Justice and the Bulwarks of Localism: Human Rights in Context, 170
Goheen, Robert Francis, 11–12, 83, 89, 155, 234–237; on admission of women, 125; African American students and, 39, 42, 44; annual giving under, 59; bicensquinquagenary celebration and, 58; on Carl Fields, 201–202; Classics department and, 122; on eating clubs, 160; endowed professorships under, 174; fundraising and, 226; New Jersey community college system and, 29
Goldsmith, Andrea, 147, 178, 185
golf, 237–238
Good Morning America, 375
Google, 183, 296

government service by Princeton alumni. *See* federal government, Princeton alumni in; state government, Princeton alumni in
governors, US, 4, 238–239
Grab, The, 432
graduate college, 239–240
Graduate Council of Princeton University, 50
graduate school, 240–244; creation of, 6–7, 34, 35–36; current degree offerings in, 36–37; dean of, 146–147, 486–487; enrollment in, 183; first women student, 498; Hooding Ceremony, 265–266; joint degrees, 37; *Many Minds* conference, 48; present day enrollment in, 15–16
Grant, Ulysses, 265
Great Awakening, 149, 166, 206, 213–214
Great Depression, 38, 294–295; endowment during, 175; Frist Campus Center and, 224
Great Gatsby, The, 208
Greek organizations, 5, 217–219
Green, Ashbel, 4, 6, 56, 244–245
Green, Henry W., 55–56; fundraising and, 225–226
Green, John Cleve, 245
Greene, Arthur M., Jr., 147, 176–177
Green Hall, 245–246
Guggenheim Fellowships, 508–510
Guyot, Arnold Henri, 4, 56, 81, 196, 229, 246
Guyot Hall, 246–247

Hall, Walter Phelps "Buzzer," 247
Hallelujah Chorus, 125
Halsted Observatory, 46, 70, 71
Hamilton, Alexander, 127
Hamilton, John, 81, 149, 214
Hamilton College, 127
Harper's Weekly, 355, 497
Harrison, Benjamin, 265
Harry S. Truman Scholarship, 418
Harvard Gazette, 423
Hayes, Rutherford, 265
Health Services, University, 247–250
Heermance, Radcliffe, 8, 38, 40; as dean of freshmen, 146
Helm, Harold H., 59, 125, 226, 250
Henry, Bayard, 250–251
Henry, Joseph, 4, 19, 28, 43, 46, 174, 251–252; lectures on architecture, 61, 63; National Academy of Sciences and, 196; school of Engineering and Applied Science and, 176; sesquicentennial celebration and, 56

Henry, Patrick, 144
Henry House, Joseph, 252
Heredity and Environment in the Development of Man, 382
Hero with a Thousand Faces, The, 383
Hewlett-Packard, 183
Hibben, John Grier, 7–8, 34, 51, 121, 123, 252–255; Einstein, Albert, and, 167; Eisenhart, Luther, and, 168–169; endowed professorships under, 174; endowment under, 175; on "Engineering Plus," 177; enrollment under, 182; epidemics and, 185; Faculty Advisory Committee on Appointments and Advancements created under, 188; Fine, Henry B., and, 205; Frick Chemistry Laboratory and, 223; Frist Campus Center and, 223; polio outbreak and, 171
Higher Education in a Digital Age, 86
High Meadows Environmental Institute (HMEI), 14, 54, 182, 255–256
High Performance Computing Research Center (HPCRC), 135
Highsteppers, 33
Hispanic/Latinx students at Princeton, 15–16, 256–258; *Adelante Tigres!* conference, 48; first, 6
Hiss, Alger, 156
History, Department of, 258–261
history of Princeton: activism of the 1960s/70s and changes at, 12–13; in aftermath of World War I, 7–9; The Charter in, 112–113, 128; as College of New Jersey, 1–3; discrimination in, 7–10; Dodds era in, 9–10; era of decline, 1794–1868, 4–5; Goheen era in, 11–12; graduate school and preceptors introduced in, 1896–1910, 6–7; hoaxes and pranks in, 261–263; Lake Campus in, 283–284; looking ahead to 2046 and, 16; Maclean, John, Jr., in, 298–299; Maclean, John, Sr., in, 299–300; McCosh, James, and early, 5–6; mission statement in, 1; original founding, 1; Paterson, William, in, 348–349; post-World War II, 10–11; Princeton today and, 15–16; Rush, Benjamin, and, 3–4, 27, 127, 129, 206, 424–426; as "seedbed" of the Revolution, 3–4; in the twenty-first century, 13–15; Witherspoon, John, and, 3–4, 27, 34, 41, 129–130, 137, 138, 158, 182, 206, 219, 225, 494–497
History of the American People, 258
hoaxes and pranks, 261–263
Hobart College, 127

Hobson, Mellody, 10, 29, 44, 171, 225, 500
Hobson College, 10, 44
Holder Hall, 263
honorary degrees, 264–265; recipients of, 215, 297, 375, 497, 511–516
Honor Code: How Moral Revolutions Happen, The, 170
honor societies, faculty, 189–198; American Academy of Arts and Letters, 189–190; American Academy of Arts and Sciences, 190–193; American Philosophical Society, 193–195; National Academy of Engineering, 195–196; National Academy of Medicine, 196; National Academy of Sciences, 46, 196–198
honors program, 34–35
honor system, 263–264
Hooding Ceremony, 265–266
Hoop Dreams, 374
Hoover, Herbert, 57, 88, 155, 265
Hosack, David, 266
House, 374
House of Representatives, US, 4, 266–269, 301–302
Howard, John L., 9, 39, 41–42, 154
Hubble Space Telescope, 70
Hudibras, 307
Human Nature of Organizations, The, 88
Hurricane Katrina, 31, 467

ice hockey, 269–271
I Ching, or Book of Changes, 383
Ikeda, Kentaro, 68, 154–155
Imitation Game, The, 374, 475
Index of Christian Art, 320, 498
Index of Medieval Art, 320, 498
India Institute of Technology, 30
Infinity, 374
influenza epidemic, 1918, 185
In Her Shoes, 374
Ink, The, 365
Institute for Advanced Study (IAS), 133, 134, 271–272
institutes and centers. *See* centers and institutes
Intelispark Consulting, 185
Intellectual Property Accelerator Fund, 184
International Food Cooperative, 139
international initiatives, 272–274
internship programs, 347
I.Q., 168, 374
Irish Dance Company, 33
Irrational Exuberance, 383
Isles, Inc., 29
ITHAKA, 85

It's a Wonderful Life, 375
Ivy Club, 162
Ivy League, 39, 274–275

Jacobus fellows, 52, 275, 518
Jadwin Gymnasium, 22, 73, 130–131, 275–276
Jaeger, Benedict, 230–231
James Madison Medal, 29, 42, 52, 69, 86, 302, 519
Javits, Jacob, 351
J. Douglas Brown Dean's Fund, 89
Jefferson, Thomas, 4, 301–302; Constitutional Convention of 1787 and, 138; Freneau, Philip, and, 221; honorary degree awarded to, 265; Papers of, 276–277, 383
Jewish students at Princeton, 8–9, 277–279, 405; Center for Jewish Life (CJL) and, 10, 23, 33, 85; discrimination against, 9, 38–39; *L'Chaim! To Life* conference, 48, 49; music groups, 33; Student Hebrew Association and, 10
John Bates Clark Medal, 338–339
Johns Hopkins University, 233, 305
Johnson, James Collins, 279
Johnson, Lyndon, 265
Jones, Kwanza, 44, 171, 227
Jones Hall, 279
Joseph Henry House, 55; fire at, 207
Joyce, James, 181
JSTOR (Journal Storage), 85
Julis Romo Rabinowitz Building, 81, 165, 223
Junior Summer Institute (JSI), 398

Kagan, Elena, 28, 80, 458–459
Kahneman, Daniel, 165
Kaleidoscope: An Alumni Conference on Race on Community, 47
"*Keep the Damned Women Out*": *The Struggle for Coeducation*, 303
Keller, Suzanne, 279–280
Keller Center for Innovation in Engineering Education, 31, 183–184
Keller School of Management, 127
Kelley, Stanley, Jr., 12, 141, 280–281, 324, 391
Kennedy, John Fitzgerald, 281
Key, Francis Scott, 207
Key and Seal Club, 162
Kindred Spirit, 33
King, Martin Luther, Jr., 47, 235
Klagsbrun, Sarah, 49
Kobayashi, Hisashi, 69, 147, 178

KoKo Pops, 33
Koleinu, 33
Kopp, Wendy, 29, 126, 183, 281–282
Kwong, Stanley, 69, 202

lacrosse, 282–283
Lake Campus, 283–285
Lanahan, Frances Scott Fitzgerald, 208
Langlotz, Karl, 5, 72, 199, 231
Lapidus, Leon, 114
Large Hadron Collider (LHC), 135
Last Tycoon, The, 208
law school, 285–286
L'Chaim! To Life conference, 48, 49
Le Corbusier, 62
Lectures on Moral Philosophy, 382
Lee, Henry, 286
Lee, Robert E., 286
Lefschetz, Solomon, 286
Lemonick, Aaron, 16, 146, 147
Lenni Lenape Native Americans, 3, 6, 332–333
Leslie, James, 8, 175, 203, 225
Leslie Fund, 203
Lesson Plan: An Agenda for Change in American Higher Education, 86
Lessons Learned: Reflections of a University President, 84, 321
Lewis, Sir Arthur, 15, 30, 43, 164, 165, 286–287, 358
Lewis Center for the Arts, 14, 16, 131, 140–141, 150, 182, 287–290; creative writing program, 288; dance program, 288–289; faculty of, 188; fundraising for, 226; music theater program, 289; Princeton Atelier, 290; theater program, 289; visual arts program, 289–290
Lewis Science Library, 24, 290–291
Lewis-Sigler Institute for Integrative Genomics, 16, 134, 188, 226, 291
Lewis Thomas Laboratory, 23
LGBTQIA students at Princeton, 291–293; Black students, 43; *Every Voice* conference, 48, 49; in singing groups, 33; Turing, Alan, and, 475–476
Li, Rose, 49
Liberal University: An Institutional Analysis, The, 88
libraries: Firestone Library, 3, 9, 22, 29, 66, 81, 155, 295–296; Lewis Science Library, 24, 290–291; Marquand Library of Art and Archaeology, 294; Princeton University Library, 293–297; Pyne Library, 294; Scheide Library, 14, 427–428

Library, Princeton University, 293–297
Library of Congress, 28, 294, 383
Life, 328
Life on Mars, 440
Lincoln, Abraham, 120, 265, 297
Lincoln University, 29, 41
Link, Arthur S., 494
Litchfield Law School, 403
Little, Stafford, Hall, 6, 21, 82, 297
Liu, Yin-He, 359
Lowe, Eugene Y., Jr., 42, 148
Lower Pyne, 479
Lowrie, Walter, House, 297–298
Luminaries: Princeton Faculty Remembered, 58

Maclean, John, House, 3, 67, 300
Maclean, John, Jr., 3, 4, 5, 29, 50, 298–299; Civil War and, 120; enrollment under, 182; fire at Nassau Hall and, 207; fundraising and, 225; Lincoln, Abraham, and, 297; scholarships given under, 204; on secret societies, 217
Maclean, John, Sr., 4, 299–300; Engineering Quadrangle hall named after, 179
Madison, James, Jr., 3–5, 7, 27–28, 50, 86, 174, 300–302; commencement ceremonies and, 129; at the Constitutional Convention of 1787, 138; East Pyne statue of, 158; as first president of the alumni association, 5, 50; Freneau, Philip, and, 220, 221; as Hampden-Sydney College trustee, 127; honorary degree awarded to, 265; Virginia Plan and, 138
Madison, James, Medal, 29, 42, 52, 69, 86, 302, 519
Madison Hall, 10, 302–303
Mad Woman in the Attic, The, 181
Magic Project, 141
Magie, William Francis, 303
Malkiel, Burton, 57–58, 151, 165
Malkiel, Nancy Weiss, 146, 259, 303–304, 498
Mammals of North America, 384
Many Minds, Many Stripes conference, 48, 49
Marquand, Allan, 61, 63, 65, 187, 304–305; Classics Department and, 122; Princeton's colors and, 129; Princeton University Art Museum and, 65–66
Marquand Chapel, 46; fire at, 207
Marquand Library of Art and Archaeology, 294
Marshall Scholarship, 126, 417

Mas Flow, 33
Mathematical Foundations of Quantum Mechanics, The, 484
Mathematics, Department of, 305–307
Mather Sun Dial, 307
Mathey, Dean, 307–308
Mathey College, 409–410
Matrix Reloaded, The, 374, 488
Matrix Revolutions, The, 374, 488
Max Perkins: Editor of Genius, 432
McCarter Theatre Center, 308–311
McClenahan, Howard, 311
McCormick Hall, 311–312
McCosh, Isabella, 247–248, 314–315
McCosh, James, 5–7, 20, 34, 58, 312–314; African American students admitted under, 41; alumni associations and, 50; Classics Department and, 122; dean of the faculty and, 146; East Pyne statue of, 158; Edwards Hall and, 166–167; enrollment under, 182; epidemics on campus and, 185; fraternities under, 217–218; language instruction requirement under, 219; Princeton University Art Museum and, 65–66; Princeton University Library and, 294
McCosh Hall, 314
McCosh Infirmary, 41, 314–316, 498
McCosh Walk, 3
McGraw Center for Teaching and Learning, 186, 316
McMillan, Charles, 118, 316–317
McPhee, John, 317–318
Meaning of Relativity, The, 167, 383
Mechanical and Aerospace Engineering, Department of, 318–320
media and publishing: *Business Today*, 281, 457–458; *Nassau Herald/Bric-a-Brac*, 5, 457; *Nassau Lit*, 5, 54, 74, 208, 228, 233, 342, 413, 456–457; *Nassau Weekly*, 365, 458; *Princeton Alumni Weekly*, 85, 137, 186, 198, 200, 208, 215–216, 228, 283, 302, 328, 351, 361, 382, 383; *Princeton Engineer*, 177, 458; *Princetonian, Daily*, 52, 160, 204, 303, 341, 385–388, 413; *Princeton Progressive*, 365; *Princeton Tory*, 365; Princeton University Press, 6, 53, 86, 139, 167, 382–384; Pulitzer Prizes, 398–401; student publications, 5, 456–458; *Tiger Magazine*, 89, 413, 457; Veterans of Future Wars, 480–481; WPRB radio, 500–501
Medieval Art, Index of, 320, 498
Meet Me in St. Louis, 374
Mellon Foundation, 132

Mellon Mays Undergraduate Fellows Program, 418
Men and Gothic Towers, 307
Merwick House, 239
Meservey, Sabra Follett, 498
military service by Princeton alumni, 28–29, 51. *See also* Reserve Officer Training Corps (ROTC)
Mimesis, 231
Mindy Project, The, 375
mission statement, Princeton University, 1, 26–27; alumni as ornaments of the state/servants of all, 27; "in the service of all nations" added to, 27–28
Modern Architecture, 62, 383
Modern Chivalry, 87
Molecular Biology, Department of, 320–322
Monroe, James, 265
Moore, Michael, 360–361, *361*
Morey, Charles Rufus, 320
Morgan White Eyes, George, 333
Morrison, Toni, 14, 15, 43, 44, 58, 181, 290, 322–323, 357, *358*, 360
Morrison Hall, 323–324
Movement for a New Congress (MNC), 12, 324–325, 391
movies and television, Princeton in, 373–375
Mpala Research Centre, 13, 61, 163, 273, 325
Mr. Smith Goes to Washington, 375
M.S. Chadna Center for Global India, 70
municipality of Princeton, 365–369
Munro, Dana, 256
Murray, James Ormsbee, 325–326
Murray-Dodge Hall, 326
Music, Department of, 326–328
music and singing groups: a cappella, 33; Glee Club, 33, 233–234; Tiger Band, 75–76; University Orchestra, 345–346
Music Theater program, 289
Music You Can't Hear on the Radio, 501

Naacho, 33
Nader, Ralph, 328–329
Nash, John Forbes, Jr., 329, 374
Nassau Hall, 3–5, 12, 14, 18, 41, 46, 47, 329–332, 411–412; 1802 fire at, 19; commencement ceremonies and, 130–131; fire at, 207; Princeton motto etched at, 26; Princeton University Library, 294
Nassau Herald/Bric-a-Brac, 5, 457
Nassau Lit, 5, 54, 74, 208, 228, 233, 342, 413, 456–457

Nassau Sovereign, 458
Nassau Weekly, 365, 458
Nassoons, the, 33
National Academy of Engineering, 195–196
National Academy of Medicine, 196
National Academy of Sciences, 46, 196–198
National Aeronautics and Space Administration (NASA), 70–71, 448
National Gazette, 221
National Humanities Medal, 86, 338
National Medal of Science, 338
National Museum of African American History and Culture, 25, 67–68
National Science Foundation's Graduate Research Fellowship, 418
Native American and Indigenous students at Princeton, 166, 332–335; Princeton alumni serving in senior government positions of, 28; as students at Princeton, 6
Nature of Space and Time, The, 383
Navy V-12 program, 9–10, 39, 130
Near Eastern Studies, Department of, 335–336
Nevanlinna Prize, 339
Never Forget: A Journey of Revelations, 488
New New Quad, 22, 236
New South, 336–337
Newsweek, 427
New Yorker, 78, 317
New York Evening Post, 402
New York Herald Tribune, 55, 212, 274
New York Times, 64, 75, 86, 286, 340, 383, 404
New York Times Book Review, 383
New York Weekly Post Boy, The, 149
Next Justice: Repairing the Supreme Court Appointments Process, The, 170
Nimitz, Chester, 57
Nixon, Richard, 324
Nobel and other major prizes, 15, 337–339; Abel Prize, 339; A. M. Turing Award, 339; Fields Medal, 339; John Bates Clark Medal, 338–339; National Humanities Medal, 86, 338; National Medal of Science, 338; Nevanlinna Prize, 339; Nobel Prizes, 71, 133, 165, 337–338
North Court, 240
North Garage, 23
Not for Profit, 384
Novogratz Bridge Year Program, 30, 87–88
nude olympics, 339–341

Oates, Whitney Jennings, 57, 122, 140, 341
Obama, Barack, 69, 80, 164, 342
Obama, Michelle LaVaughn Robinson, 7, 28, 43, 202, 341–342
Office, The, 375
Ohio University, 128
"Old Nassau," 342–343
Old New Quad, 22, 236
Olympians, Princeton, 342, 422, 520–523; in fencing, 199–200
On Bullshit, 384
One Day, All Children: The Unlikely Triumph of Teach for America and What I Learned Along the Way, 281–282
One True Thing, 374
Operations Research and Financial Engineering (ORFE), 178, 342–345
Oral History of African Americans at Princeton, 58–59
"Orange and the Black, The," 129
Orange Key Guide Service, 345
Orchestra, University, 345–346
Ordinary Light, 440
Origin of Species, 439
Oval With Points, 414
Oznot, Joseph David, 261

Pace Center for Civic Engagement, 13, 30, 31, 32, 58, 346–347
Palmer Hall, 347–348
Palmer House, 348
Palmer Physical Laboratory, 87
Palmer Stadium, 24, 73, 212
Parker's Gazette and Post Boy, 426
Paterson, William, 348–349
Patton, Francis Landey, 6–7, 56, 128, 182, 349–350
Paul and Marcia Wythes Center for Contemporary China, 70
PAW Online, 54
Pell, Claiborne de Borda, 350–351
Pennsylvania Society for Promoting the Abolition of Slavery and the Relief of Free Negroes Unlawfully Held in Bondage, 27
People Will Talk, 374
Performing Arts Council, 33
Performing Arts: The Economic Dilemma, 83
Peyton Hall, 4, 71
Philadelphia Inquirer, 263
Philadelphian Society, 30, 405
Philadelphia Story, The, 375
Philosopher Kings, The, 374
Philosophical Hall, 4, 19, 99–100, 159, 251–252, 412, 439, 451
Philosophy, Department of, 351–352

physical campus. *See* campus
Physics, Department of, 352–354
Pittsburgh Gazette, The, 87
PJ&B, 150
Place of the Idea, The Idea of the Place, The, 58
Plain Dealing Club, 3
PlanetLab, 134
Plasma Physics Laboratory, 3
Playing in the Dark: Whiteness and the Literary Imagination, 322
Poe, Arthur, 355
Poe, Edgar Allan, 354
Poe, John Prentiss, 354–355
Poe, Neilson, 355
Poe brothers, 354–355
Poe Field, 25
Poe's Run and Other Poems, 457
Poler's Recess, 355
Politics, Department of, 355–357
Population Index, 498
portrait collection, University, 357–361
postage stamps, 361
P-rade, 243, 362, 415–417, 465, 486
Pratt, Michael, 346
preceptors, 6–7, 34, 122, 139, 168, 180, 187, 228
preceptorships, 174–175
Preface to Chaucer, A, 181
Pre-rade, 362
presidents, US, 363–364; Adams, John Quincy, 265; Arthur, Chester, 265; Buchanan, James, 265; Bush, George H. W., 265; Bush, George W., 283; Cleveland, Grover, 46, 56–57, 123–124, 131, 265; Clinton, Bill, 58, 131, 164, 265; Coolidge, Calvin, 265; Eisenhower, Dwight, 7, 57, 155, 216, 265; Grant, Ulysses, 265; Harrison, Benjamin, 265; Hayes, Rutherford, 265; Hoover, Herbert, 57, 88, 155, 265; Jefferson, Thomas, 4, 138, 221, 265, 276–277, 302; Johnson, Lyndon, 265; Kennedy, John Fitzgerald, 281; Lincoln, Abraham, 120, 265, 297; Madison, James, Jr., 3–5, 7, 27–28, 50, 86, 127, 129, 138, 158, 174, 220, 221, 265, 300–302; Monroe, James, 265; Nixon, Richard, 324; Obama, Barack, 69, 80, 164; Taft, William Howard, 124, 265; Truman, Harry, 57, 58, 131, 155; Washington, George, 128, 130, 138, 165, 174, 221, 265, 484–485; Wilson, Thomas Woodrow, 6–8, 13, 14–15, 21, 26–28, 34, 36, 44, 46, 56, 122, 123, 131, 139, 164, 171, 180, 187, 204, 205, 209, 210, 219, 265, 489–493, 494
presidents of Princeton, 362–363; Bowen, William Gordon, 12, 35,

58–59, 83–86, 169, 204, 216, 226, 321; Burr, Aaron, Sr., 2, 18, 33–34, 129, 166, 225; Carnahan, James, 4, 56, 90, 105–106, 182, 185; Davies, Samuel, 27, 143–144; Dickinson, Jonathan, 2, 3, 148–149, 182; Dodds, Harold Willis, 9–10, 57, 59, 130, 154–156, 168, 174, 204; Edwards, Jonathan, 3, 166; Eisgruber, Christopher Ludwig, 14, 86, 169–172, 183–184, 222, 227; Finley, Samuel, 3, 137, 144, 206, 215; Goheen, Robert Francis, 11–12, 29, 39, 42, 44, 58, 59, 83, 89, 122, 125, 155, 160, 174, 201–202, 226, 234–237; Green, Ashbel, 4, 5, 56, 244–245; Hibben, John Grier, 7–8, 34, 51, 121, 123, 167, 168–169, 171, 174, 175, 177, 182, 185, 188, 205, 223, 252–255; Maclean, John, Jr., 3, 4, 5, 29, 50, 120, 182, 204, 207, 217, 225, 297, 298–299; McCosh, James, 5–7, 20, 21, 34, 41, 50, 58, 65–66, 122, 146, 158, 166–167, 182, 185, 217–218, 219, 294, 312–314; Patton, Francis Landey, 6–7, 56, 128, 182, 349–350; Prospect home of, 136, 137, 388–389; Shapiro, Harold, 13, 27, 58, 73, 75, 86, 224, 226, 433–435; Smith, Samuel Stanhope, 4, 6, 106, 127, 207, 438–440; Tilghman, Shirley, 12, 13, 14, 24, 44–45, 84, 126–127, 170, 227, 236, 466–469; Wilson, Woodrow, 7, 8, 14, 21, 26–27, 34, 36, 46, 56, 122, 171, 204, 210; Witherspoon, John, 3–4, 27, 34, 41, 129–130, 137, 138, 158, 182, 206, 219, 225, 494–497
Press Club, University, 364–365
Princeton, municipality of, 365–369
Princeton Acapellago, 33
Princeton Alumni Association, 48–51
Princeton AlumniCorps, 30
Princeton Alumni Weekly, 85, 137, 186, 382, 383; Farrand, Beatrix, in, 198; on field hockey, 200; Fitzgerald, F. Scott, and, 208; Fox, Frederic E., and, 215–216; Gauss, Christian, and, 228; Kopp, Wendy, and, 283; Nader, Ralph, and, 328; Pell, Clairborne de Borda, 351; on postage stamps featuring alumni, 361; ranking of most influential Princeton alumni of all time, 302; on the senior thesis, 432; Thomas, Norman Mattoon, and, 465; Turing, Alan, and, 475; on women's squash, 451
Princeton and Slavery Project, 2, 41, 121, 154, 166, 209, 378–380 454

Princeton Architecture Laboratory, 63
Princeton: A Search for Answers, 16, 374
Princeton Atelier, 290
Princeton Belly Dance Company, 33
Princeton Bhangra, 33
Princeton-Blairstown Center, 370–371
Princeton Book, The, 148
Princeton Center for Complex Materials, 108–109
Princeton Club of New York, 50, 371–372
Princeton Eating Clubs, The, 162
Princeton Engineer, The, 177, 458
Princeton Entrepreneurship Council (PEC), 14, 184
Princetonian, Daily, 52, 160, 204, 303, 341, 385–388, 413
Princeton: Images of a University, 58
Princeton in Africa, 30, 369–370
Princeton in Asia, 30, 369–370
Princeton in Latin America, 30, 369–370
Princeton Inn, 43
Princeton Innovation Center BioLabs, 171, 184
Princeton-in-Peking, 30
Princeton in space, 380
Princeton Institute for Computational Science and Engineering (PICSciE), 109
Princeton Institute for International and Regional Studies (PIIRS), 13, 157, 273, 372–373
Princeton Institute for the Science and Technology of Materials (PRISM), 109, 173
Princeton Internships in Civic Service, 30
Princeton in the movies and television, 373–375
Princeton Investment Company (Princo), 175–176, 373
Princeton Latinos y Amigos (PLA), 258
Princeton-Mellon Initiative in Architecture, Urbanism, and the Humanities, 182
Princeton Monographs in Art and Archaeology, 305
Princeton Neuroscience Institute (PNI), 14, 16, 188, 375–376
Princeton Plasma Physics Laboratory (PPPL), 70, 135, 212–213, 376–378
Princeton Prize in Race Relations, 31, 50, 378
Princeton Progressive, 365
Princeton's James Forrestal Campus: 50 Years of Sponsored Research, 212
Princeton Stadium, 24
Princeton Stories, 465
Princeton TapCats, 33

Princeton Theological Seminary, 6–7, 41, 380–381
Princeton Tiger, 89, 413, 457
Princeton Tory, 365
Princeton University and Neighboring Institutions, 167, 198
Princeton University Ballet, 33
Princeton University Library, 293–297
Princeton University Library Chronicle, 294
Princeton University Mentoring Program (PUMP), 202
Princeton University Preparatory Program (PUPP), 381–382
Princeton University Press, 6, 53, 86, 139, 167, 382–384
Princeton University Store, 384–385
Princeton University: The First 250 Years, 58, 389, 494
Princeton Veterans Alumni Association, 51
Principles of Physics, 303
Procter Hall, 239–240
Professional Public Relations and Political Power, 281
Program for Community-Engaged Scholarship, 30–31
Prospect, 136, 137, 388–389
Prospect Club, 162
Prospect House, 51, 98, 104, 297, 300, 331, 342, 379, 388–389
protest activity, 389–392
provost, the, 392–393
Psychological Review, The, 393
Psychology, Department of, 393–394
Public and International Affairs, School of, 147–148, 394–398
Pulitzer Prizes, 398–401
Pyle, Louis, Jr., 248
Pyne, Moses Taylor, 21, 158, 401–402; fundraising and, 225–226
Pyne, Percy, 158
Pyne Hall, 402
Pyne Honor Prize, 42, 43, 52, 125, 402–403, 523
Pyne Library, 294
Pyne Tower, 240

Quadrangle Club, 162
Quamine, John, 41
Quibi, 183

Race Matters, 488
racial diversity at Princeton. *See also* African American students at Princeton; Asian American and Asian students at Princeton; Hispanic/Latinx students at Princeton; Native American and Indigenous students at Princeton: faculty, 187–188; student, 15–16, 38, 39, 182–183
radio station, WPRB, 500–501
Rapid Switch, 55
Raqs, 33
Raycroft, Joseph, 248
R&B and soul music groups, 33
ReachOut Scholarships, 30, 418
reading periods, 37
Rear Window, 375
ReCAP (Research Collections and Preservation Consortium), 296
Reeve, Tapping, 403
Religion, Department of, 403–404
Religious Freedom and the Constitution, 170
religious life, 404–405; Davies, Samuel, and, 143–144; dean of, 147; founding of Princeton and, 213–215; Great Awakening and, 149, 166, 206, 213–214; Princeton Theological Seminary, 6–7, 41, 380–381; University Chapel and, 21, 110–112
Reports of the Princeton Expedition to Patagonia, 1896–1899, 320
research, dean for, 147
Reserve Officer Training Corps (ROTC), 186, 406–407; commencement ceremonies and, 131; Eisgruber, Christopher, and, 171
residential colleges, 407–411; Butler College, 22–24, 409–410; Forbes College, 43, 410; Hobson College, 10, 44; Mathey College, 409–410; Rockefeller College, 411; Whitman College, 411; Wilson/First College, 10, 22, 44, 171, 225, 227, 281, 392, 408, 411–412, 493, 500
residential life, 411–414
Return of Martin Guerre, The, 144
Reunion Hall, 414–415
reunions, 415–417
Revolutionary War era, 3, 4, 27, 86–87, 174, 220, 286, 301; commencement ceremonies during, 129–130; Constitutional Convention of 1787, 27, 137–138; Continental Congress, 27, 130, 138; Princeton as "seedbed" of, 3–4
Rhodes and other scholarships, 15, 42, 126, 169, 417–418
Rioseco, Pedro, 256
Risky Business, 374
Rittenhouse Orrery, 4, 34, 70, 418
Rivers, Robert J., Jr., 10, 15, 39, 42, 358–359, *360*, 418–419

Roaring 20, 33
Robertson Hall, 71
Rockefeller, John D., III, 165
Rockefeller, John D., Jr., 165
Rockefeller, Laurance, 125, 212
Rockefeller College, 409, 411
Romero, Ramona, 229
Root, Robert Kilburn, 419–420
Roper Lane, 420
Rosa, Margarita, *48*
Ross, John McDonald, 333
Ross, Robert Daniel, 333
Ross, William Potter, 333
Roundtree, Irwin William Langston, 41
Rouse, Cecilia, 28, 137, 148, 164, 165
rowing, 420–422
Rudenstine, Neil L., 58, 83, 146, 148, 422–424
rugby, 424
Rules and Procedures of the Faculty, 188
Rush, Benjamin, 3–4, 27, 127, 129, 206, 424–426
Russell, Henry Norris, 426
Rutgers University, 209–210, 263

Sachs Scholarship, 417–418
salutatorians, 426–427, 524
Sarbanes, Paul, 266, 325, 342, 403
Sayre, Daniel Clemens, 427
Scent of a Woman, 374
Scheide, William H., 14, 55, 427–428; fundraising and, 226
Scheide Library, 14, 427–428
Schmidt, Eric, 134, 171, 183; fundraising and, 227
Schmidt, Wendy, 134, 171; fundraising and, 227
Scholars Institute Fellows Program (SIFP), 221
Schwarzman Scholarship Program, 418
Scott, Mackenzie, *360*
Scribner, Charles, II, 382
sculptures, campus, 103–104; portrait collection, 357–361
Seal of Princeton University, 428–429
secretary of the University, 429
senators, US, 4, 429–431; Bradley, Bill, 15, 77–78, 79, 150, 211, 357, *358*; Burr, Aaron, Jr., 90, 301; Frist, William H., 223; Javits, Jacob, 351; Paterson, William, 348–349; Pell, Claiborne de Borda, 350–351; Sarbanes, Paul, 342; Stockton, John P., 298; Thomson, John, 239
senior jackets, 80–81
senior thesis, 431–432
Sense of Where You Are, A, 317
September 11, 2001, terrorist attacks, 31

service, alumni in, 26–32; government, 7, 28; international, 28; many forms of, 29–30; meeting special needs, 31–32; military, 28–29; student service, 30–31; Wilson Award winners and, 29
Service Focus program, 31, 347
Service of Remembrance, 432–433
Sesame Street, 375
sesquicentennial celebration, 56–57
Seventy-Nine Hall, 433
Shakespeare, William, 181, 420
Shape of the River: Long-Term Consequences on Considering Race in College and University Admissions, The, 86, 383
Shapiro, Harold Tafler, 13, 27, 58, 73, 75, 86, *363*, 433–435; Frist Campus Center and, 224; fundraising and, 226
SHARE office, 392
Shawuskukhkung (Wilted Grass), 332
She Loves Me Not, 374
Shere Khan, 33
She Roars conference, 48, *49*, 446
Sherrerd, Anne, *49*
Sherrerd Hall, 436
Simmons, Ruth, 359, *360*, 436–437
Six14Christian Dance Company, 33
Sketches of My Culture, 488
Skimmer Burns, 317, 432
slavery, 2–4, 41, 279; American Colonization Society (ACS) and, 4; antislavery organizations and, 27, 120; debates over, 5; Princeton and Slavery Project and, 2, 41, 121, 154, 166, 209, 378–380
Slaves on Screen: Film and Historical Vision, 145
Slavic Languages and Literatures, Department of, 437–438
Sloan Digital Sky Survey (SDSS), 71
Smith, Harvey, 262
Smith, Samuel Stanhope, 4, 6, 127, 207, 438–440
Smith, Tracy K., 43, 131, 182, 440
Smith, Valerie, 45, 146, 181
Smithsonian Institution, 4, 28
Smithsonian Tropical Research Institute, 163
soccer, 440–442
Socialist Party of America, 465
Society and Culture in Early Modern France, 144
Sociology, Department of, 442–443
Socolow, Robert, 54
softball, 443–444
Songs of Old Nassau, 342
Sotomayor, Sonia, 80, 359–360, *360*, 444–446, 458–459; at *Adelante Tigres!* conference, *48*; Liberation Hall and, 202; portrait in University collection, 15; as recipient of Pyne Prize, 125; as recipient of Woodrow Wilson Award, 26, 171; as Supreme Court justice, 28, 137
Source of Self-Regard: Selected Essays, Speeches, and Meditations, The, 323
South Africa, divestment from, 151–153
Spanglish, 374
Spanish and Portuguese, Department of, 446–447
Spelman Halls, 22, 24, 412, 447–448
Spingdale Golf Course, 25
Spitzer, Lyman, Jr., 448–449
Spitzer Space Telescope, 135
Sports Illustrated, 75, 143, 450
Springdale golf course, 25, 237, 368, 410
sprint (lightweight) football, 449
squash, 449–451
Squash: A History of the Game, 451
Stanhope Hall, 4, 19, 45, 46, 451
Stanley J. Seeger Center for Hellenic Studies, 109, 123
state government, Princeton alumni in, 28; as governors, 238–239
statues, campus, 103–104; Christian Student, The, 117–118
Steerage, The, 66
Stevenson, Adlai, 7, 28, 452–453
Stevenson Hall, 451–453
Stewart, Jimmy, 375
Stockton, Betsey, 366–368, 453–454
Stockton, Richard, 454–455
Street Knowledge, 488
Stripe Magazine, 458
student government, 455–456
Student Hebrew Association, 10
student life, dean of, 148
student publications, 5, 456–458
Student Volunteers Council (SVC), 346–347
StudioLab, 142
Subaru Telescope, 71–72
Suettinger, Sue-Jean Lee, 69, 125
Summer of '42, 374
Supreme Court justices, 4, 15, 26, 28, 458–459; Alito, Samuel, 28, 137; Kagan, Elena, 28, 80, 458–459; Sotomayor, Sonia, 15, 26, 28, *48*, 80, 125, 137, 171, 202, 359–360, 444–446, 458–459
sustainability, 459–460
swimming and diving, 460–461

Taft, William Howard, 124, 265
Tank, David, 375–376
Taps at Reveille, 208
Tarana, 33

Taylor, Hugh Stott, 116, 462
teacher preparation, 462
Teach for America, 29, 183, 281–282
Techstars, 185
Tender Is the Night, 208
Tennent, Gilbert, 144, 215, 225
Tennent, William, 206, 214, 215
tennis, 462–464
Terrace Club, 162
TFTR (Tokamak Fusion Test Reactor), 377
Thane, Daniel, 426
Theater program, 289
Theatre Intime, 464–465
Theory of Games and Economic Behavior, 383, 484
Third World Center, 11, 42, 43, 202. *See also* Fields Center for Equality and Cultural Understanding
This Side of Paradise, 208
Thomas, Norman Mattoon, 465
Thompson, Henry Burling, 465–466
Thompson Gateway, 466
Thomson College, 239
Thrive conference, 48, *48*
Tiger Band, 75–76
Tiger Challenge program, 31
Tiger Inn, 162
Tiger Magazine, 457
Tigertones, the, 33
Tilghman, Shirley Marie, 12, 13, 14, 24, 44–45, 84, *363*, 466–469; committee on undergraduate women's leadership under, 126–127; Eisgruber, Christopher, and, 170; fundraising and, 227; on Robert Goheen, 236
Time, 317, 328
Tom Jones, 87
Too Big to Fail, 374
Tower Club, 162
track and field, 469–471
traditions. *See also* anniversary celebrations: Alumni Day, 51–52; anthem, "Old Nassau," 342–343; beer/class/senior jackets, 80–81; colors, Princeton's, 128–129; dean's date, 148; nude olympics, 339–341; Poler's Recess, 355; Pre-rade, 362; reunions, 415–417; Seal of Princeton University, 428–429; Service of Remembrance, 432–433
train, the Dinky, 150–151
Transformers: Revenge of the Fallen, 374
Transylvania College, 128
Treaty of Paris, 138
Triangle Club, 308–309, 471–473
Trickster Travels: A 16th-Century Muslim Between Worlds, 145
Triple 8, 33
Troilus and Criseyde, 420

Trowbridge, Alexander, 147
Truman, Harry, 57, 58, 131, 155
trustees, Princeton, 6–7, 9, 11–16, 50, 473–475. *See also* administration; Belcher, Johnathan, and, 81; Blair, John Insley, 82; Carnahan, James, 106; charter, 112–113; Cleveland, Grover, 240; Concerned Alumni of Princeton (CAP) and, 136–137; Cowell, David, 142; Davies, Samuel, 143–144; divestment and, 151–153; endowment and, 175–176; Finley, Samuel, 206; first African American, 42; on fraternities and sororities, 217–218; fundraising and, 224–227; Garrett, Robert, 227–228; Green, Ashbel, 244–245; Guyot, Arnold, 82; Helm, Harold H., 250; Henry, Joseph, 252; Hibben, John Grier, 253–254; Mathey, Dean, 307–308; mission statement adopted by, 2015, 1, 26; original, 2–3, 96–97; Paterson, William, 348; Pyne, Moses Taylor, 93, 99, 401–402; Revolutionary War era, 27; Stockton, Richard, 454–455; vote to admit Black and women students, 39
Turing, Alan M., 15, 133, 135, 360, *361*, 475–476
Turing Award, 339
Tusculum College, 128
Twenty Questions, 317
2D co-op, 139

Umqombothi, 33
Unbreakable Kimmy Schmidt, 375
Undergraduate Student Government (USG), 455–456
undergraduate students, dean of, 148
Union College, 128
Unión Latinoamericana (ULA), 256
United Nations University, Tokyo, 29, 128
United States Magazine, 86–87
Universities and Their Leadership, 86, 434
University Center for Human Values (UCHV), 16, 476–477
University College Club, 162
University Gymnasium, 21; fire at, 207
University League/UNow, 477–478
University Magazine, 53
University of Medicine and Dentistry of New Jersey, 127
University of North Carolina, 127–128
University of the West Indies, 30
University Research Board (URB), 147, 478–479
Unsafe at Any Speed, 328

Upper Pyne, 479
Upstart II, 180
URODA, 55
U-Store, 384–385

valedictorians, 479, 525
Varsity, 374
Veblen, Oswald, 8, 204, 205, 479–480
Vegetable: or From President to Postman, The, 208
Venturi, Robert, 23, 24, 84, 223
Vertigo, 375
Veterans of Future Wars, 480–481
vice presidents of Princeton, 481–482
vice presidents of the US, 482
Vietnam War, 12, 390
Vinton, Frederic, 294
Virginia Plan, 138
Visual Arts program, 289–290
volleyball, 482–483
von Neumann, John, 483–484
VTone, 33

Washington, George, 128, 130, 138, 174, 221, 265, 484–485
Washington and Jefferson College, 128
Washington and Lee University, 128
Wasp Studies Afield, 382
water polo, 485–486
Watkins, Alexander Dumas, 43
We Flourish conference, 48, 70
Wei, James, 69, 147, 178
Welcome to the Universe: An Astrophysical Tour, 384
Well-Meaning Club, 3
West, Andrew Fleming, 5–6, 56, 123, 486–487; Classics Department and, 122; as dean of the graduate school, 147, 240–241
West, Cornel R., 42–44, 487–488
West Wing, 375
Wharton, Edith, 198
Whig-Cliosophic Society, American, 3, 5, 120, 124, 488–489
Whig Hall, 489
Whitman, Meg, 183, 225
Whitman College, 411
Why Religion? A Personal Story, 404
Wilcox Hall, 10, 160, 316, 408, 411, 413–414
Wilkinson Microwave Anisotropy Probe (WMAP), 71
William III, King, 3, 128, 215, 225
Williams, Paul C., 42
Wilson, 374

Wilson, Arthur Jewell, 9–10, 39, 42
Wilson, Thomas Woodrow, 6–8, 13, 21, 123, 489–493; academic program changes under, 34, 36, 122, 131, 180, 187, 219; Corwin, Edward S., and, 139; as director of Princeton College Football Association, 210; Fine, Henry B., and, 204, 205; honorary degree awarded to, 265; interment of Nathaniel FitzRandolph and, 209; legacy of, 14–15, 44, 171; Papers of, 494; Princeton "in the nation's service" and, 26–28, 46, 56; as professor of jurisprudence and political economy, 164; scholarships given under, 204
Wilson, Woodrow, Award, 28, 29, 42, 69, 283, 493, 526
Wilson, Woodrow, National Fellowship Foundation, 493–494
Wilson College, 22
wintersession program, 14
Witherspoon, John, 3–4, 27, 34, 41, 206, 494–497; commencement ceremonies and, 129–130; at the Constitutional Convention of 1787, 137; at the Continental Congress, 138; East Pyne statue of, 158; enrollment under, 182; French instruction by, 219; fundraising and, 225
Witherspoon Hall, 20, 46, 47, 497
Witherspoon School for Colored Children, 41

women at Princeton, 11–12, 13, 497–500; in administration, 126–127; in basketball, 79–80; in classics, 122; coeducation development and, 124–127; in computer science, 134; in cross-country, 143; current enrollment of, 40; in ecology and evolutionary biology, 163; in economics, 164–165; Evelyn College for Women, 187; first African American, 42; first enrollments of, 11–12, 39, 124; first faculty, 187; Frank, Sally, 216–217; in golf, 237–238; honorary degree awarded to, 265; in ice hockey, 270–271; Keller, Suzanne, 279–280; Kopp, Wendy, 281–282; in lacrosse, 283; Malkiel, Nancy Weiss, 303–304; milestone achievements of, 125–126; Morrison, Toni, 14, 15, 43, 44, 58, 181, 290, 322–323; in rowing, 421–422; in rugby, 424; *She Roars* conference, 48, 49; Simmons, Ruth, 436–437; singing groups, 33; Smith, Tracy K., 440; in soccer, 441–442; in squash, 451; Stockton, Betsey, 366–368, 453–454; in swimming and diving, 461; in tennis, 463–464; Tilghman, Shirley (*see* Tilghman, Shirley); in track and field, 470–471; in volleyball, 482–483; in water polo, 485–486
Women Don't Ask: Negotiation and the Gender Divide, 383

Women on the Margins: Three 16th-Century Lives, 145
Women's Center, 30
Woodrow Wilson Lodge, 10
Woodrow Wilson Society, 10
Woolley, Jacob, 332–333
World Economic Forum, 55
World Politics, 273
World War I, 7–9, 29, 121; annual giving during, 59–60; commencement ceremonies and, 130; enrollment during, 182
World War II, 9–10, 38, 88, 294–295; annual giving during, 59; Classics Department and, 122; enrollment during, 182; German exiles during, 231; Japanese students during, 68–69, 154–155
WPRB radio station, 500–501
wrestling, 501–502
Wright, Bruce, 8–9, 38, 41
Wright, Frank Lloyd, 62
Wright, Thomas H., Jr., 228
Wu, Gordon, 48
WuDunn, Sheryl, 48
Wu Hall, 23, 502–503
Wyman House, 240

Yamma, Bristol, 41
Yenching University, 30
Young, Charles, 56, 70, 87, 172
Young Ladies Academy, 27
Young Philadelphians, The, 374